Almanack 1869: Facsimile Edition first published in Great Britain 2014

© 2014 Bloomsbury Publishing Plc

shed 1868 by J. Whitaker

ry Publishing Plc. 50 Bedford Square, London WC1B 3DP
msbury.com

ry Publishing, London, New Delhi, New York and Sydney

1-4729-0708-0

LLUSTRATION

spiece which has appeared in each edition of *Whitaker's Almanack* since 1868.

s is a registered trade mark of J. Whitaker and Sons Ltd, Registered Trade Mark Nos.
125/09; 13422126/16 and 1322127/41; (EU) 19960401/09, 16, 41, licensed for use by
ck (Publishers) Ltd, a subsidiary of Bloomsbury Publishing Plc.

hers make no representation, express or implied, with regard to the accuracy of the
n contained in this book and cannot accept legal responsibility for any errors or
that take place.

logue record for this book is available from the British Library.

AL STAFF
tors: Ruth Northey; Oli Lurie

d bound in Great Britain by CPI Group (UK) Ltd, Croydon, CR0 4YY

WHITAKE
ALMANACK

Whitake

Copyrigh

First Pu

Bloomst
www.blo

Bloomst

ISBN 97

COVER
The fror

All righ
or trans
or other

Whitak
(UK) 13
A & C F

The pub
informa
omissio

A CIP c

EDITO
Project

Printed

B L O O M S B
LONDON • NEW DELHI • NEW YC

PREFACE TO THE FACSIMILE EDITION

The first edition of *Whitaker's Almanack* was published on 10 December 1868. Queen Victoria had been on the throne for 31 years and Gladstone had been Prime Minister for just seven days.

The compilation of that very first edition must have been a task of the utmost enormity. Even now, with all our modern-day innovations, the phone, the internet and email, the task of updating *Whitaker's* annually remains one of giant proportions. It is nearly impossible to conceive in this day and age how Joseph Whitaker even began such an extensive undertaking. Where did he find the thousands of facts, figures and statistics relating not just to Great Britain, but to all the colonies and countries of the world as well? The fact that he would have done all this by post, makes the existence of this book truly remarkable.

Joseph Whitaker was born in 1820 the son of a silversmith, and began his career in books at an early age as an apprentice at Parker's, a scholarly bookshop in Oxford. He moved to London when the company sent him there to open a branch on the Strand, and it was in the capital that Whitaker became involved in publishing, founding the *Penny Post*, a monthly church magazine, in 1849.

During the 1850s, he was an editor at *The Gentleman's Magazine* in charge of the correspondence pages. This required him to answer a selection of readers' questions that were notoriously broad in their scope, and it was here that Joseph consequently accumulated a substantial collection of invaluable newspaper cuttings, government statistics, and questions and answers from a variety of sources.

In addition to his work at *The Gentleman's Magazine*, he founded and edited *The Bookseller*, the magazine for the book trade that continues to this day. It is thought that it was his growing number of financial dependants – he married twice and fathered 13 children – that prompted his decision to publish his collection of facts as an almanack. Joseph Whitaker edited his Almanack up to his death in 1895, and was succeeded by his son Cuthbert, later Lt.-Col. Sir Cuthbert Whitaker.

Despite the immediacy of the Almanack's 'establishment' status – just ten years later it was considered worthy of a space in the 'time capsule' buried beneath Cleopatra's Needle on London's Embankment – it is unlikely that Joseph Whitaker could have imagined that 146 years later, *Whitaker's* would still be published annually.

Ruth Northey
Executive Editor, Whitaker's
E: whitakersalmanackteam@bloomsbury.com

W: www.whitakersalmanack.com
T: @WhitakersAlmnck

ADVERTISEMENT.

THE Editor does not put forward this Almanack as perfect: yet he ventures to think that he has succeeded in preparing a work which will commend itself to those who desire to see improvement in this direction.

The Almanack is essentially a Household Book. From it is derived the knowledge ordinarily possessed of the Course of the Seasons, and other Astronomical phenomena, the nature of our Constitution, and the statistics of our Ecclesiastical, Legal, Naval, and Military systems. In addition to all such information, herein given in an unusually full and complete manner, the reader will discover other and important features not hitherto easily obtainable. He is referred, for instance, to the summaries of the Public Income and Expenditure, the proceedings of Parliaments during the last Session; to the Scientific Discoveries and Inventions of the Year; to the Trade, Commerce, and Finance of the Kingdom; and to the particulars of our Municipal and Social Institutions.

A popular writer has remarked that wars and other dreadful calamities were intended by Providence as a means of teaching geography to Englishmen; for, until attention is thus drawn to a foreign country, its existence is almost unknown. Without attempting to combat the "Providential theory," the Editor suggests that the pervading ignorance is due rather to the absence of such information in a Manual "familiar as a household word"; and that the present work, containing a clear and concise account of India, Australia, Canada, and our other possessions, together with a similar description of Foreign Countries, will enable our children to gather this knowledge for themselves; and that, should another earthquake happen at Ecuador, or a tornado at Tobago, they, better than their elders, will know where those places are.

It is not intended that the work shall take a stereotyped form, and thus become, as it were, fossilized. On the contrary, many improvements have suggested themselves while the sheets were passing through the press, and many more will doubtless be suggested by friendly correspondents and by unfriendly critics. Both classes of criticism are useful, and all suggestions will be adopted as far as they may be deemed judicious.

No attempt has here been made to peep into futurity. Predictions respecting the Weather, the fate of Kingdoms, and the fortune and death of Eminent Persons, are made only by those who rely upon the superstition, the gullibility, and the ignorance of that imperfectly educated class which, happily, is every year decreasing in number.

December 10, 1868.

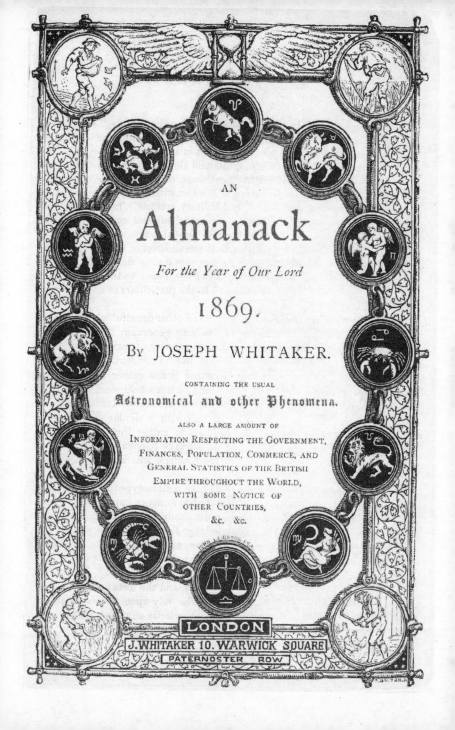

AN

Almanack

For the Year of Our Lord

1869.

By JOSEPH WHITAKER.

CONTAINING THE USUAL

Astronomical and other Phenomena.

ALSO A LARGE AMOUNT OF

INFORMATION RESPECTING THE GOVERNMENT,
FINANCES, POPULATION, COMMERCE, AND
GENERAL STATISTICS OF THE BRITISH
EMPIRE THROUGHOUT THE WORLD,
WITH SOME NOTICE OF
OTHER COUNTRIES,
&c. &c.

LONDON

J. WHITAKER 10. WARWICK SQUARE

PATERNOSTER ROW

WHITAKER'S ALMANACK FOR 1869.

Common Notes for the Year.

Golden Number	...	...	...	...	8	*Low Sunday* ... ... April 4
Epact	...	...	...	...	XVII	St. George ... ... ,, 23
Solar Cycle	...	...	...	...	2	*Rogation Sunday* ... ... May 2
Roman Indiction	...	...	...	12	*Ascension Day—Holy Thursday* ... ,, 6
Dominical Letter	...	...	...	C	*Pentecost—Whit Sunday* ... ... ,, 16
Sundays after Trinity	...	...	26	*Trinity Sunday* ... ... ,, 23
Epiphany	...	...	...	Jan. 6	Birth of Queen Victoria ... ... ,, 24
Septuagesima Sunday	...	...	,, 24	*Corpus Christi* ... ... ,, 27
Quinquagesima—Shrove Sunday	...	Feb. 7	Accession of Queen Victoria ... June 28
Ash Wednesday	...	...	,, 10	*St. John Baptist*—Midsummer Day ... ,, 24
Quadragesima Sunday	...	...	,, 14	Queen's Coronation ... ... ,, 28
St. David	...	...	...	March 1	*St. Michael*—Michaelmas Day ... Sept. 29
St. Patrick	...	...	...	,, 17	Birth of Prince of Wales ... ... Nov. 9
Palm Sunday	...	...	...	,, 21	*First Sunday in Advent* ... ... ,, 28
Annunciation—Lady Day	...	,, 25	*St. Andrew* ... ... ,, 30
Good Friday	...	...	...	,, 26	*St. Thomas* ... ... Dec. 21
Easter Sunday	...	...	...	,, 28	CHRISTMAS DAY ... ... ,, 25

Beginnings of the Seasons.

Spring...Sun enters Aries........March 20 1 32A | Autumn, Sun enters Libra ....Sept. 23 0 28M
Summer   ,,   ,,   Cancer.....June 21 10 4M | Winter   ,,   ,,   Capricornus Dec. 21 6 23A

Law Terms.

Hilary Term	...	...	Begins January 11 and ends February 1
Easter Term	...	...	,, April 15 ,, May 8
Trinity Term	...	...	,, May 22 ,, June 12
Michaelmas Term		...	,, November 2 ,, November 25

University Terms.

OXFORD.	Begins.	Ends.	CAMBRIDGE.	Begins.	Divides.	Ends.
Lent	January 14	March 20	Lent	Jan. 13 ... Feb. 14M ... Mar. 19
Easter	March 31	May 14	Easter	April 2 ... May 14N ... June 25
Trinity	May 15	July 10	Michaelmas... Oct. 1 ... Nov. 8N ... Dec. 16
Michaelmas	October 11	December 17		
The Act, July 6.			The Commencement, June 22.

Jewish Calendar.

(Those days printed in Italics are strictly observed.)

THE YEAR 5629.   COMMENCED Sept. 17, 1868. | Ab 10 *Fast. Destruct. of Temple* July 18
| Elul 1 New Moon ... ... Aug. 8

Sebat	1	New Moon	...	...	...	Jan. 13
Adar	1	New Moon	...	...	...	Feb. 12
,,	13	Fast of Esther	...	...	,, 24
,,	14	Purim	...	...	...	,, 25
,,	15	Schuschan Purim	...	...	,, 26
Nisan	1	New Moon	...	...	March 13
,,	15	*Passover commences*	...	,, 27
,,	16	*Second Feast*	...	...	,, 28
,,	21	*Seventh Feast*	...	...	April 2
,,	22	*Eighth Feast*	...	...	,, 3
Yiar	1	New Moon	...	...	,, 12
,,	18	Lag-B'omer	...	...	,, 29
Sivan	1	New Moon	...	...	May 11
,,	6	*Feast of Weeks*	...	...	,, 16
,,	7	*Second Feast*	...	...	,, 17
Tamuz	1	New Moon	...	...	June 10
,,	18	Fast of Tamuz	...	...	,, 27
Ab	1	New Moon	...	...	...	July 9

COMMENCEMENT OF THE YEAR 5630.

Tisri	1	*New Year's Feast*	...	...	Sept. 6
,,	2	*Second Feast*	...	...	,, 7
,,	3	*Fast. Day of Guedaliah*	...	,, 8
,,	10	*Fast. Day of Atonement*	...	,, 15
,,	15	*Feast of Tabernacles*	...	,, 20
,,	16	*Second Feast*	...	...	,, 21
,,	21	Feast of Branches	...	,, 26
,,	22	Feast of the Eighth Day	...	,, 27
,,	23	*Feast of the Law*	...	...	,, 28
Hesvan	1	New Moon	...	...	Oct. 6
Kislev	1	New Moon	...	...	Nov. 5
,,	25	Feast of Dedication	...	,, 25
Tebeth	1	New Moon	...	...	Dec. 5
,,	10	Fast. Siege of Jerusalem	,, 14
Sebat	1	New Moon	...	...	Jan. 3, 1870.

Mohammedan Calendar.

Year.	Name of Months.				Month begins.	Year.	Name of Months.				Month begins.
1285.	Shawal	...	...	...	Jan. 15	1286.	Latter Rabia	...	...	July 11
,,	Dulkaadah	...	...	...	Feb. 13	,,	Gomada	...	...	...	Aug. 9
,,	Dulhagee	...	...	...	Mar. 15	,,	Latter Gomada	...	...	Sept. 8
1286.	Mulharram	...	...	April 13	,,	Rajab	...	...	...	Oct. 7
,,	Saphar	...	...	...	May 13	,,	Schabân	...	...	...	Nov. 6
,,	Rabia	...	...	...	June 11	,,	Ramadán	...	...	Dec.

Time of High Water at the undermentioned Ports—

Day of Month	Week	Average daily Temperature*	LOND. BDGE. Morn.	After.	LIVERPOOL Morn.	After.	S'HAMPTON Morn.	After.	NEWCASTLE Morn.	After.	HULL Morn.	After.	DOVER Morn.	After.	BRISTOL Morn.	After.	Day of the Year
		Deg.	H. M.	H. M.	H. M.	H. M.	H. M.	H. M.	H. M.	H. M.	H. M.	H. M.	H. M.	H. M.	H. M.	H. M.	
1	F	37	3 46	4 10	0 57	1 21	0 3	0 27	6 11	6 36	8 13	8 37	0 37	1 4	9 13	9 34	1
2	S	37	4 32	4 56	1 44	2 8	0 51	1 15	7 1	7 26	9 1	9 26	1 30	1 55	9 56	10 18	2
3	S	37	5 20	5 46	2 32	2 57	1 40	2 5	7 52	8 18	9 51	10 16	2 21	2 46	10 41	11 3	3
4	M	36	6 11	6 36	3 22	3 47	2 30	2 55	8 45	9 14	10 42	11 11	3 11	3 36	11 25	11 48	4
5	Tu	36	7 2	7 31	4 13	4 43	3 20	3 47	9 44	10 17	11 42	..	4 1	4 26	..	0 13	5
6	W	36	8 1	8 34	5 10	5 53	4 16	4 48	10 53	11 30	0 16	0 50	4 53	5 22	0 39	1 9	6
7	Th	36	9 9	9 44	6 32	7 10	5 22	5 58	..	0 4	1 23	1 55	5 52	6 25	1 45	2 25	7
8	F	36	10 20	10 56	7 46	8 21	6 35	7 12	0 38	1 12	2 28	3 1	7 1	7 38	3 7	3 47	8
9	S	36	11 31	..	8 52	9 20	7 47	8 18	1 45	2 14	3 34	4 7	8 12	8 41	4 24	4 56	9
10	S	36	0 4	0 32	9 44	10 6	8 45	9 9	2 41	3 4	4 36	5 0	9 8	9 32	5 24	5 49	10
11	M	36	0 59	1 23	10 27	10 49	9 31	9 54	3 25	3 46	5 21	5 43	9 56	10 20	6 14	6 39	11
12	Tu	36	1 47	2 8	11 11	11 32	10 16	10 37	4 7	4 28	6 5	6 28	10 44	11 6	7 4	7 26	12
13	W	36	2 29	2 48	11 52	..	10 56	11 14	4 48	5 6	6 50	7 9	11 27	11 47	7 46	8 5	13
14	Th	36	3 7	3 24	0 11	0 29	11 33	11 51	5 24	5 43	7 27	7 46	..	0 7	8 24	8 40	14
15	F	36	3 42	3 58	0 45	1 2	..	0 8	6 0	6 17	8 3	8 19	0 25	0 44	8 56	9 12	15
16	S	37	4 14	4 31	1 19	1 36	0 25	0 43	6 35	6 52	8 36	8 53	1 3	1 21	9 27	9 41	16
17	S	37	4 48	5 6	1 52	2 9	0 59	1 16	7 9	7 27	9 10	9 27	1 38	1 56	9 56	10 12	17
18	M	37	5 23	5 39	2 26	2 44	1 34	1 52	7 45	8 4	9 45	10 3	2 14	2 33	10 29	10 45	18
19	Tu	37	5 56	6 14	3 2	3 20	2 10	2 28	8 23	8 44	10 21	10 41	2 52	3 10	11 1	11 18	19
20	W	37	6 33	6 53	3 39	4 0	2 47	3 7	9 7	9 31	11 3	11 28	3 28	3 48	11 36	11 55	20
21	Th	37	7 15	7 40	4 23	4 52	3 29	3 54	9 57	10 27	11 55	..	4 9	4 33	..	0 19	21
22	F	37	8 9	8 42	5 24	5 59	4 22	4 54	11 1	11 36	0 26	0 58	4 59	5 28	0 45	1 15	22
23	S	38	9 17	9 53	6 39	7 19	5 29	6 6	..	0 11	1 30	2 2	5 59	6 33	1 52	2 34	23
24	S	38	10 29	11 5	7 55	8 30	6 43	7 21	0 47	1 21	2 35	3 9	7 9	7 47	3 16	3 57	24
25	M	38	11 40	..	9 1	9 28	7 56	8 27	1 54	2 23	3 44	4 16	8 21	8 50	4 34	5 5	25
26	Tu	38	0 13	0 43	9 54	10 19	8 56	9 24	2 49	3 15	4 44	5 10	9 19	9 47	5 35	6 4	26
27	W	38	1 9	1 34	10 42	11 6	9 47	10 11	3 40	4 2	5 35	5 59	10 13	10 39	6 31	6 59	27
28	Th	38	1 59	2 23	11 31	11 57	10 36	11 0	4 24	4 48	6 24	6 50	11 6	11 33	7 26	7 51	28
29	F	38	2 48	3 12	..	0 21	11 25	11 50	5 11	5 35	7 15	7 39	11 59	..	8 16	8 39	29
30	S	38	3 34	3 56	0 44	1 8	..	0 14	5 58	6 22	8 2	8 24	0 24	0 49	9 1	9 23	30
31	S	38	4 19	4 43	1 31	1 53	0 37	1 0	6 46	7 10	8 47	9 10	1 14	1 38	9 43	10 4	31

Rising and Setting of Seven Principal Planets on the 5th, 15th, and 25th.

	MERCURY ☿ Rises	Sets	VENUS ♀ Rises	Sets	MARS ♂ Rises	Sets	JUPITER ♃ Rises	Sets	SATURN ♄ Rises	Sets	URANUS ♅ Rises	Sets	NEPTUNE ♆ Rises	Sets
D.	h. m.	h. m.	h. m.	h. m.	h. m.	h. m.	h. m.	h. m.	h. m.	h. m.	h. m.	h. m.	h. m.	h. m.
5	8 28M	3 56A	5 50M	2 0A	8 20A	10 42M	11 6M	11 34A	5 34M	1 54A	3 55A	8 19M	11 32M	0 22A
15	8 40M	4 48A	6 16M	2 5A	7 34A	10 3M	10 38M	11 2A	5 2M	1 16A	3 13A	7 39M	10 52M	11 40A
25	8 36M	5 50A	6 30M	2 18A	6 41A	9 24M	10 2M	10 32A	4 27M	0 41A	2 32A	6 58M	10 13M	11 1A

ECLIPSES, OCCULTATIONS, AND OTHER CELESTIAL PHENOMENA.

January 1. There will be an occultation of a Leonis (Regulus), the disappearance taking place at 9h. 28m. aft., distant from the vertex 46°. The reappearance at 10h. 25m. aft., distant from the vertex 211°.

Jan. 1. Apparent obliquity of the Ecliptic 23° 27′ 15″ 34.

Jan. 1. Day breaks at 6h. 2m. morn., and Twilight ends at 6h 6m. aft., the length of Day being 7h. 51m.

Jan. 3. Mercury in superior conjunction with the Sun at 8h. 45m. morn.

Jan. 19. The Sun enters Aquarius 11h. 1m. aft.

Jan. 23. There will be an occultation of a Tauri (Aldebaran), the disappearance taking place

at 8h. 49m. aft., distant from the vertex 106°. The reappearance at 10h. 5m. aft., distant from the vertex 314°.

Jan. 28. Partial Eclipse of the Moon visible at Greenwich. The first contact with the Earth's shadow takes place at 0h. 29m. morn., the obscuration is at its greatest phase at 1h. 38m. morn., and the shadow leaves the Moon at 2h. 47m. morn. At the greatest phase nearly one half of the Moon will be eclipsed.

In this month the mornings increase 26m., and the afternoons 45m.

* The Temperature column gives the daily average of the Thermometer for 50 years.

Days of M.	Days of W.	Fasts and Festivals. Remarkable Days—Events.	The Sun. Rises H. M.	The Sun. Sets. H. M.	The Sun. After Clock. M. S.	The Moon. Rises. after. H. M.	The Moon. Souths morn. H. M.	The Moon. Sets morn. H. M.	Days to end of the year.
1	F	**Circumcision.**	8 9	4 0	3 58	8 2	2 28	10 1	364
2	S	⊙ Semidiameter 16′ 18″	8 8	4 1	4 26	9 20	3 25	10 35	363
3	S	**2nd Sunday after Christmas.**	8 8	4 2	4 54	10 39	4 19	11 4	362
4	M	Arrest of five Members, 1641.	8 8	4 3	5 21	11 55	5 12	11 31	361
5	Tu	Dividends due at Bank.	8 8	4 4	5 48	Morn.	6 2	11 57	360
6	W	**Epiphany.** Old Christmas Day.	8 7	4 6	6 14	1 10	6 52	Aftn.	359
7	Th	☿ rises *8h. 26m. morn.*	8 7	4 7	6 40	2 23	7 41	0 48	358
8	F	*Lucian.* Pr. Albert Victor, b. 1864	8 6	4 8	7 6	3 36	8 31	1 19	357
9	S	Fire Insurance expires.	8 6	4 9	7 31	4 44	9 21	1 54	356
10	S	**1st Sunday after Epiphany.**	8 5	4 10	7 55	5 47	10 12	2 34	355
11	M	HILARY LAW TERM. Plough M.	8 5	4 12	8 19	6 45	11 3	3 21	354
12	Tu	☾'s Ascending Node 18° 5′ ☊	8 4	4 14	8 43	7 35	11 53	4 14	353
13	W	Cambridge Lent Term.	8 3	4 15	9 5	8 18	Aftn.	5 11	352
14	Th	Oxford Lent Term.	8 3	4 17	9 27	8 54	1 30	6 13	351
15	F	British Museum opened, 1759.	8 1	4 18	9 48	9 22	2 15	7 14	350
16	S	Battle of Corunna, 1809.	8 0	4 20	10 9	9 48	2 59	8 18	349
17	S	**2nd Sunday after Epiphany.**	7 59	4 21	10 29	10 12	3 42	9 21	348
18	M	*Prisca.*	7 58	4 23	10 48	10 34	4 24	10 25	347
19	Tu	♀ sets *2h. 10m. aft.* [1838.	7 57	4 24	11 7	10 53	5 6	11 29	346
20	W	*Fabian.* Murphy's cold day.	7 56	4 26	11 24	11 15	5 49	Morn.	345
21	Th	*Agnes.* Henry Hallam d. 1859.	7 55	4 28	11 41	11 39	6 35	0 35	344
22	F	*Vincent.* [1820.	7 54	4 30	11 57	Aftn.	7 22	1 42	343
23	S	W. Pitt d. 1806. D. of Kent d.	7 53	4 32	12 12	0 36	8 14	2 51	342
24	S	**Septuagesima.**	7 52	4 33	12 27	1 15	9 9	4 1	341
25	M	**Conversion of St. Paul.**	7 51	4 34	12 41	2 3	10 7	5 8	340
26	Tu	Length of day *8h. 46m.*	7 50	4 36	12 53	3 4	11 8	6 10	339
27	W	N. South Wales founded, 1788.	7 49	4 38	13 5	4 15	Morn.	7 6	338
28	Th	Charlemagne died, 814.	7 48	4 40	13 17	5 32	0 9	7 53	337
29	F	George III. died, 1820.	7 46	4 42	13 27	6 55	1 9	8 33	336
30	S	Charles I. beheaded, 1649.	7 45	4 44	13 37	8 18	2 7	9 4	335
31	S	**Sexagesima.**	7 43	4 45	13 45	9 38	3 3	9 33	334

PHASES OF THE MOON.

☾ Last Quarter	5*d.*	6*h.*	22m.	Morn.
○ New Moon	12	6	53	After.
☽ First Quarter	21	0	26	Morn.
● Full Moon	28	1	30	Morn.

In Apogee 16*d.* 7*h* A. | In Perigee 29*d.* 1*h.* M.

RAINFALL IN JANUARY, 1868.

In this month rain fell during 19 days. The total fall for the month was 3·89 inches; an amount *in excess* of the average, since 1860, of 1·94 inch.

MORNING AND EVENING STARS.

♀ VENUS will be a morning star throughout this month.

♂ MARS will be visible this month throughout the night, not far from Regulus: near to the Moon on the *2nd.*

♃ JUPITER will be seen in the north-west quarter of the heavens, and near the Moon on the morning of the *19th.*

♄ SATURN is a morning star, but not well situated for observation this month, owing to its large southern declination.

Day of Month	Week	Average daily Temperature	Time of High Water at the undermentioned Ports—														Day of the Year
			LOND. BDGE.		LIVERPOOL.		S'HAMPTON.		NEWCASTLE.		HULL.		DOVER.		BRISTOL.		
			Morn.	After.	Morn.	After.	Morn.	After.	Morn.	After.	Morn.	After.	Morn.	After.	Morn.	After.	
		Deg.	H. M.	H. M.	H. M.	H. M.	H. M.	H. M.	H. M.	H. M.	H. M.	H. M.	H. M.	H. M.	H. M.	H. M.	
1	M	38	5 6	5 30	2 16	2 40	1 23	1 48	7 34	7 59	9 34	9 59	2 3	2 28	10 26	10 47	32
2	Tu	38	5 52	6 15	3 3	3 24	2 11	2 33	8 23	8 48	10 22	10 46	2 51	3 14	11 6	11 25	33
3	W	38	6 39	7 4	3 47	4 11	2 55	3 18	9 14	9 42	11 10	11 39	3 36	4 0	11 47	..	34
4	Th	38	7 29	7 56	4 40	5 11	3 44	4 12	10 14	10 47	..	0 13	4 25	4 50	0 11	0 35	35
5	F	38	8 27	9 4	5 46	6 26	4 43	5 18	11 23	12 0	0 46	1 19	5 18	5 49	1 4	1 40	36
6	S	39	9 43	10 22	7 9	7 49	5 57	6 37	..	0 38	1 53	2 29	6 25	7 3	2 23	3 9	37
7	S	39	11 2	11 40	8 27	9 1	7 18	7 55	1 16	1 52	3 5	3 41	7 44	8 20	3 53	4 32	38
8	M	39	..	0 15	9 31	9 57	8 25	8 55	2 23	2 52	4 16	4 46	8 52	9 19	5 6	5 35	39
9	Tu	39	0 45	1 10	10 18	10 38	9 21	9 43	3 17	3 38	5 13	5 34	9 44	10 7	6 1	6 24	40
10	W	38	1 34	1 56	10 57	11 16	10 2	10 20	3 58	4 16	5 54	6 14	10 28	10 48	6 47	7 8	41
11	Th	39	2 16	2 35	11 34	11 52	10 38	10 55	4 33	4 50	6 33	6 51	11 7	11 27	7 27	7 46	42
12	F	38	2 52	3 8	..	0 9	11 12	11 29	5 6	5 23	7 9	7 26	11 45	..	8 3	8 20	43
13	S	38	3 24	3 40	0 25	0 42	11 47	..	5 39	5 56	7 43	8 0	0 3	0 21	8 37	8 52	44
14	S	38	3 55	4 10	0 58	1 13	0 4	0 20	6 12	6 28	8 15	8 30	0 38	0 55	9 7	9 20	45
15	M	38	4 25	4 41	1 28	1 43	0 35	0 50	6 43	6 59	8 45	8 59	1 12	1 28	9 33	9 47	46
16	Tu	38	4 55	5 11	1 58	2 14	1 5	1 21	7 15	7 32	9 15	9 32	1 44	2 1	10 1	10 16	47
17	W	38	5 27	5 43	2 30	2 47	1 38	1 55	7 49	8 7	9 49	10 6	2 18	2 36	10 32	10 47	48
18	Th	39	6 0	6 19	3 5	3 23	2 13	2 31	8 26	8 47	10 24	10 44	2 55	3 13	11 3	11 20	49
19	F	39	6 37	6 57	3 43	4 5	2 50	3 12	9 11	9 37	11 7	11 34	3 32	3 53	11 41	..	50
20	S	39	7 21	7 48	4 31	5 5	3 36	4 6	10 6	10 41	..	0 4	4 16	4 43	0 3	0 29	51
21	S	39	8 22	9 0	5 45	6 27	4 41	5 19	11 23	..	0 40	1 17	5 16	5 50	1 2	1 42	52
22	M	39	9 41	10 24	7 13	7 54	6 1	6 43	0 2	0 41	1 54	2 31	6 27	7 9	2 27	3 15	53
23	Tu	39	11 8	11 48	8 34	9 8	7 25	8 4	1 21	1 58	3 9	3 48	7 51	8 29	4 1	4 41	54
24	W	39	..	0 22	9 32	10 4	8 37	9 6	2 30	3 0	4 23	4 54	9 0	9 29	5 15	5 45	55
25	Th	39	0 51	1 18	10 28	10 52	9 33	9 57	3 24	3 47	5 19	5 44	9 57	10 23	7.14	6 42	56
26	F	40	1 44	2 7	11 16	11 40	10 20	10 44	4 10	4 32	6 8	6 33	10 49	11 15	7 9	7 34	57
27	S	40	2 30	2 54	..	0 3	11 7	11 31	4 55	5 18	6 57	7 21	11 40	..	7 58	8 22	58
28	S	40	3 18	3 40	0 26	0 49	11 54	..	5 40	6 3	7 44	8 6	0 5	0 29	8 43	9 4	59

RISING and SETTING of SEVEN PRINCIPAL PLANETS on the 5th, 15th and 25th.

D.	MERCURY ☿		VENUS ♀		MARS ♂		JUPITER ♃		SATURN ♄		URANUS ♅		NEPTUNE ♆	
	Rises	Sets	Rises	Sets	Rises	Sets	Rises	Sets	Rises	Sets	Rises	Sets	Rises	Sets
	h. m.	h. m.	h. m.	h. m.	h. m.	h. m.	h. m.	h. m.	h. m.	h. m.	h. m.	h. m.	h. m.	h. m.
5	8 7M	6 39A	6 36M	2 42A	5 34A	8 37M	9 21M	10 1A	3 48M	0 2A	1 46A	6 12M	9 30M	9 20A
15	7 11M	6 9A	6 37M	3 7A	4 32A	7 50M	8 46M	9 32A	3 12M	11 24M	1 5A	5 33M	8 51M	9 41A
25	6 13M	4 33A	6 29M	3 37A	3 31A	7 2M	8 10M	9 4A	2 35M	10 47M	0 24A	4 52M	8 12M	9 4A

ECLIPSES OCCULTATIONS, AND OTHER CELESTIAL PHENOMENA.

February 1. Day breaks at 5h. 43m. morn., and twilight ends at 6h. 45m. aft., the length of the day being 9h. 4m.

Feb. 4 (0h. 22m. morn.) Mercury at its greatest elongation East = 18°.

Feb. 6. Mercury in Perihelion, 10h. 20m. morn.

Feb. 9. Mercury stationary 1h. 0m. aft.

Feb. 10—11. An Annular Eclipse of the Sun: invisible at Greenwich; begins on the Earth generally at 11d. 10h. 55m. morn., in longitude 80° 15' W. and latitude 35° 43' S.; ends on the Earth generally at 11d. 4h. 38m. aft. in longitude 26° 34' E., and latitude 9° 51' S. A Partial Eclipse is visible at the Cape of Good Hope, beginning 11d. 2h. 42m. aft., and ending 11d. 5h. 29m. aft. mean time at the Cape.

Feb. 13. Mars in opposition with the Sun, 4h. 39m. aft.

Feb. 18. Sun enters Pisces, 1h. 30m. aft.

Feb. 19. Mercury in inferior conjunction with the Sun, 0h. 57m. aft.

Feb. 19. Occultation of *f* Tauri. The disappearance takes place at 0h. 24m. morn., 110° from the vertex ; star below the horizon at the time of reappearance.

Feb. 19. Occultation of γ Tauri. The disappearance takes place at 11h. 14m. aft., 103° from the vertex ; the reappearance on the 20th at 0h. 3m. morn., 352° from the vertex.

Feb. 25. Occultation of α Leonis (Regulus). The disappearance takes place at 6h. 38m. aft., 33° from the vertex ; the reappearance at 7h. 37m. aft., 223° from the vertex.

Feb. 27. Occultation of σ Leonis. The disappearance takes place at 1h. 32m. morn., 28° from the vertex ; the reappearance at 2h. 19m. morn., 311° from the vertex.

Feb. 28. Mercury and Venus in conjunction, 6h. 35m. morn.

In this month the mornings increase 52m., and the afternoons 49m.

Days of M.	Days of W.	Fasts and Festivals. Remarkable Days—Events.	THE SUN. Rises. H. M.	THE SUN. Sets. H. M.	THE SUN. After Clock. M. S.	THE MOON. Rises after. H. M.	THE MOON. Souths morn. H. M.	THE MOON. Sets morn. H. M.	Days to end of the year.
1	M	Hilary Term Ends. [mas Day.	7 41	4 46	13 53	10 55	3 56	9 59	333
2	Tu	**Purification B. V. M.** Candle-	7 39	4 48	14 1	Morn.	4 47	10 27	332
3	W	*Blasius.*	7 39	4 50	14 7	0 13	5 38	10 58	331
4	Th	John Rogers burnt, 1555.	7 37	4 52	14 13	1 26	6 28	11 22	330
5	F	*Agatha.* Galvani died, 1799.	7 35	4 54	14 17	2 37	7 19	11 56	329
6	S	Dr. Priestley died, 1804.	7 33	4 55	14 21	3 41	8 9	Aftn.	328
7	**S**	**Quinquagesima.**	7 31	4 57	14 25	4 41	9 0	1 19	327
8	M	Half Quarter Day.	7 29	4 59	14 27	5 33	9 50	2 8	326
9	Tu	Shrove Tuesday. [1840.	7 27	5 2	14 29	6 17	10 39	3 4	325
10	W	**Ash Wednesday.** Q. Vict. m.	7 25	5 4	14 29	6 53	11 26	4 3	324
11	Th	London University founded, 1826	7 24	5 6	14 30	7 25	Aftn.	5 5	323
12	F	Immanuel Kant died, 1804.	7 22	5 7	14 29	7 54	0 57	6 9	322
13	S	Insurrection at Vienna, 1848.	7 21	5 9	14 27	8 17	1 40	7 13	321
14	**S**	**1st Sunday in Lent.** *St. Valen-*	7 18	5 11	14 25	8 38	2 22	8 16	320
15	M	[*tine.*	7 16	5 13	14 22	9 0	3 4	9 20	319
16	Tu	Lindley Murray died, 1826.	7 14	5 15	14 19	9 20	3 46	10 23	318
17	W	Ember Week.	7 12	5 17	14 14	9 42	4 30	11 29	317
18	Th	Capture of Trinidad, 1797.	7 10	5 18	14 9	10 8	5 15	Morn.	316
19	F	Ember Day.	7 8	5 19	14 3	10 36	6 4	0 34	315
20	S	Ember Day.	7 6	5 21	13 57	11 10	6 55	1 43	314
21	**S**	**2nd Sunday in Lent.**	7 4	5 24	13 50	11 52	7 50	2 49	313
22	M	George Washington born, 1732.	7 2	5 26	13 42	Aftn.	8 48	3 53	312
23	Tu	French Revolution began, 1848.	7 0	5 28	13 33	1 47	9 48	4 50	311
24	W	**St. Matthias.**	6 58	5 30	13 24	3 1	10 48	5 41	310
25	Th	Sir C. Wren died, 1723.	6 57	5 31	13 14	4 20	11 47	6 24	309
26	F	Bank suspend. Cash Paym. 1797	6 55	5 33	13 4	5 45	Morn.	7 0	308
27	S	Hare Hunting ends.	6 53	5 34	12 53	7 9	0 45	7 30	307
28	**S**	**3rd Sunday in Lent.**	6 50	5 35	12 42	8 32	1 41	7 59	306

PHASES OF THE MOON.

		d.	h.	m.	
☾	Last Quarter	3*d.*	4*h.*	56*m.*	After.
●	New Moon	11	1	54	After.
☽	First Quarter	19	5	6	After.
○	Full Moon	26	0	5	After.

In Apogee 13*d.* 3*h.* M. | In Perigee 26*d.* 1*h.* A.

RAINFALL IN FEBRUARY, 1868.

In this month rain fell during 10 days. The total fall for the month was 1·21 inch; an amount *less* than the average, since 1860, of 0·01 inch.

MORNING AND EVENING STARS.

♀ Venus is a morning star during this month; in conjunction with the Moon on the 9*th*, at 1*h.* 48*m. aft.*

♂ Mars is well situated for observation; it may be seen rising soon after sunset, continuing visible throughout the night: in conjunction with the Moon on the 25*th*, at 10*h.* 46*m. morn.*

♃ Jupiter is an evening star, and well situated for observation, after sunset, in the north-western quarter of the heavens; in conjunction with the Moon on the 15*th*, at 5*h.* 34*m. aft.*

♄ Saturn is not favourably situated for observation this month; in conjunction with the Moon on the 5*th*, at 11*h.* 51*m. aft.*

Time of High Water at the undermentioned Ports—

Day of Month	Week	Average daily Temperature* (Deg.)	Lond. Bdge. Morn.	Lond. Bdge. After.	Liverpool Morn.	Liverpool After.	S'hampton Morn.	S'hampton After.	Newcastle Morn.	Newcastle After.	Hull Morn.	Hull After.	Dover Morn.	Dover After.	Bristol Morn.	Bristol After.	Day of the Year
1	M	40	4 1	4 24	1 11	1 33	0 17	0 39	6 25	6 48	8 27	8 49	0 52	1 16	9 25	9 44	60
2	Tu	41	4 46	5 6	1 54	2 15	1 1	1 23	7 10	7 33	9 11	9 33	1 39	2 2	10 3	10 23	61
3	W	40	5 27	5 49	2 37	2 57	1 45	2 6	7 56	8 18	9 55	10 16	2 25	2 47	10 41	11 0	62
4	Th	40	6 9	6 31	3 19	3 42	2 28	2 50	8 42	9 9	10 40	11 6	3 9	3 31	11 20	11 42	63
5	F	40	6 56	7 22	4 6	4 33	3 13	3 38	9 37	10 7	11 34	··	3 54	4 19	··	0 5	64
6	S	40	7 50	8 23	5 7	5 48	4 7	4 43	10 43	11 25	0 6	0 42	4 46	5 18	0 31	1 4	65
7	S	40	9 2	9 44	6 32	7 16	5 23	6 4	··	0 5	1 19	1 57	5 54	6 31	1 46	2 31	66
8	M	41	10 25	11 7	7 58	8 36	6 47	7 27	0 45	1 25	2 35	3 13	7 13	7 53	3 19	4 2	67
9	Tu	41	11 47	··	9 9	9 37	8 4	8 35	2 0	2 31	3 49	4 24	8 29	8 58	4 41	5 13	68
10	W	41	0 23	0 51	9 59	10 19	9 0	9 22	2 58	3 19	4 52	5 14	9 22	9 45	5 38	6 2	69
11	Th	41	1 12	1 34	10 36	10 53	9 40	9 58	3 38	3 56	5 34	5 52	10 5	10 24	6 25	6 44	70
12	F	41	1 54	2 13	11 10	11 27	10 15	10 31	4 12	4 28	6 10	6 28	10 43	11 0	7 3	7 21	71
13	S	41	2 29	2 43	11 43	11 59	10 47	11 3	4 44	4 59	6 45	7 1	11 18	11 35	7 38	7 53	72
14	S	41	3 0	3 15	··	0 15	11 19	11 35	5 14	5 29	7 16	7 32	11 52	··	8 9	8 25	73
15	M	41	3 0	3 44	0 31	0 46	11 51	··	5 45	6 0	7 48	8 3	0 9	0 25	8 40	8 55	74
16	Tu	42	3 58	4 14	1 2	1 17	0 8	0 23	6 16	6 32	8 18	8 33	0 42	0 59	9 10	9 23	75
17	W	42	4 29	4 44	1 31	1 46	0 39	0 54	6 48	7 4	8 48	9 4	1 16	1 33	9 37	9 51	76
18	Th	42	5 0	5 16	2 2	2 19	1 10	1 27	7 21	7 38	9 20	9 37	1 50	2 7	10 6	10 22	77
19	F	43	5 33	5 49	2 36	2 54	1 44	2 2	7 56	8 16	9 55	10 14	2 25	2 44	10 38	10 56	78
20	S	43	6 9	6 29	3 15	3 37	2 23	2 44	8 39	9 5	10 36	11 2	3 4	3 25	11 15	11 38	79
21	S	43	6 53	7 19	4 2	4 33	3 9	3 37	9 34	10 8	11 32	··	3 50	4 16	··	0 3	80
22	M	43	7 50	8 27	5 10	5 55	4 10	4 49	10 47	11 31	0 7	0 45	4 46	5 22	0 33	1 11	81
23	Tu	43	9 11	9 57	6 46	7 33	5 34	6 21	··	0 16	1 24	2 7	6 4	6 47	1 58	2 51	82
24	W	42	10 41	11 24	8 13	8 49	7 4	7 43	1 1	1 39	2 49	3 28	7 30	8 8	3 39	4 20	83
25	Th	42	··	0 32	9 20	9 46	8 18	8 47	2 11	2 41	4 4	4 35	8 41	9 10	4 56	5 26	84
26	F	42	0 32	1 0	10 9	10 31	9 13	9 36	3 6	3 29	5 2	5 25	9 36	10 1	5 54	6 20	85
27	S	43	1 26	1 48	10 54	11 17	9 58	10 21	3 50	4 11	5 47	6 10	10 26	10 50	6 45	7 10	86
28	S	43	2 11	2 33	11 40	··	10 43	11 6	4 33	4 54	6 34	6 57	11 15	11 39	7 34	7 57	87
29	M	44	2 55	3 17	0 2	0 24	11 29	11 52	5 16	5 38	7 19	7 41	··	0 3	8 20	8 40	88
30	Tu	44	3 39	3 59	0 46	1 8	··	0 14	6 0	6 23	8 3	8 24	0 26	0 50	9 0	9 20	89
31	W	45	4 20	4 42	1 29	1 50	0 36	0 57	6 45	7 7	8 46	9 7	1 13	1 36	9 40	9 59	90

Rising and Setting of Seven Principal Planets on the 5th, 15th, and 25th.

D.	Mercury ☿ Rises	Mercury ☿ Sets	Venus ♀ Rises	Venus ♀ Sets	Mars ♂ Rises	Mars ♂ Sets	Jupiter ♃ Rises	Jupiter ♃ Sets	Saturn ♄ Rises	Saturn ♄ Sets	Uranus ♅ Rises	Uranus ♅ Sets	Neptune ♆ Rises	Neptune ♆ Sets
	h. m.	h. m.	h. m.	h. m.	h. m.	h. m.	h. m.	h. m.	h. m.	h. m.	h. m.	h. m.	h. m.	h. m.
5	5 47M	3 41A	6 19M	4 3A	2 45A	6 24M	7 41M	8 43A	2 5M	10 17M	11 52M	4 20M	7 41M	8 35A
15	5 32M	3 22A	6 6M	4 32A	1 55A	5 38M	7 5M	8 17A	1 27M	9 39M	11 13M	3 41M	7 2M	7 56A
25	5 5M	3 38A	5 47M	5 5A	1 14A	4 54M	6 29M	7 51A	0 48M	9 0M	10 33M	3 1M	6 24M	7 18A

ECLIPSES, OCCULTATIONS AND OTHER CELESTIAL PHENOMENA.

March 1. Day breaks at 4h. 53m. morn., and Twilight ends at 7h. 31m. aft., the length of the day being 10h. 50m.

Mar. 3. Mercury stationary in the heavens 6h. 25m. aft.

Mar. 5. Mars in Aphelion 4h. 36m. morn.

Mar. 8. Venus in Aphelion 6h. 16m. morn.

Mar. 18. (5h. 52m. morn.) Mercury at greatest elongation west = 28°.

Mar. 19. Occultation of α Tauri (Aldebaran). The disappearance takes place at 10h. 54m. morn., 84° from the vertex; the reappearance at 11h. 50m. morn., 229° from the vertex.

Mar. 20. Sun enters Aries, Spring commences, 1h. 30m. morn.

Mar. 22. Mercury in Aphelion 9h. 54m. morn.

Mar. 26. Saturn stationary in the heavens 4h. 0m. aft.

Mar. 27. Mars stationary in the heavens 11h. 12m. morn.

* The temperature column gives the daily average of the Thermometer for 50 years.

Days of		Fasts and Festivals. Remarkable Days—Events.	THE SUN.			THE MOON.			Days to end of the year.
M.	W.		Rises.	Sets.	After Clock.	Rises aftr.	Souths morn.	Sets morn.	
			H. M.	H. M.	M. S.	H. M.	H. M.	H. M.	
1	M	*St. David's Day.*	6 47	5 37	12 30	9 51	2 35	8 26	305
2	Tu	*Chad.* Boileau died, 1711.	6 45	5 39	12 18	11 10	3 28	8 53	304
3	W	John Wesley died, 1791.	6 44	5 41	12 5	Morn.	4 21	9 23	303
4	Th		6 42	5 42	11 52	0 24	5 13	9 55	302
5	F	War with Burmah com. 1824.	6 39	5 45	11 38	1 34	6 5	10 33	301
6	S	Battle of Malavelly, 1799.	6 37	5 47	11 24	2 35	6 56	11 15	300
7	☉	4th **Sunday in Lent.** *Perpetua.*	6 35	5 48	11 9	3 30	7 46	Aftn.	299
8	M	Attack on Donabew, 1825.	6 33	5 50	10 54	4 17	8 36	0 58	298
9	Tu	Dr. E. D. Clarke died, 1822.	6 32	5 52	10 39	4 56	9 24	1 56	297
10	W	Prince of Wales married, 1863.	6 29	5 54	10 24	5 29	10 10	2 57	296
11	Th	Benjamin West died, 1820.	6 27	5 55	10 8	5 57	10 55	4 0	295
12	F	*Gregory.* Vauxhll.Bdge.opd.1816	6 24	5 56	9 51	6 21	11 38	5 3	294
13	S	Battle off Lissa, 1811.	6 22	5 59	9 35	6 44	Aftn.	6 8	293
14	☉	5th **Sunday in Lent.** *Passion.*	6 19	6 0	9 18	7 6	1 3	7 11	292
15	M		6 17	6 1	9 1	7 26	1 45	8 16	291
16	Tu	Duchess of Kent died, 1861.	6 14	6 3	8 44	7 47	2 28	9 20	290
17	W	*St. Patrick's Day.* [b. 1848.	6 12	6 5	8 26	8 11	3 13	10 27	289
18	Th	*Edward K. W. Saxons.* Ps. Louisa	6 10	6 7	8 9	8 38	4 0	11 34	288
19	F	Cambridge Term ends.	6 8	6 9	7 51	9 8	4 49	Morn.	287
20	S	Oxford Term ends.	6 6	6 11	7 33	9 46	5 41	0 38	286
21	☉	**Palm Sunday.** *Benedict.*	6 3	6 13	7 15	10 33	6 36	1 41	285
22	M	Goethe died, 1832.	6 1	6 14	6 56	11 30	7 33	2 40	284
23	Tu	Kotzebue assassinated, 1819.	5 58	6 16	6 38	Aftn.	8 31	3 31	283
24	W	Saladin d. 1193. [dy *Thursday.*	5 56	6 17	6 20	1 52	9 29	4 16	282
25	Th	**Annunciation.** Lady Day. *Maun-*	5 54	6 19	6 1	3 11	10 26	4 53	281
26	F	**Good Friday.** D. Camb. b. 1819	5 51	6 20	5 43	4 35	11 22	5 25	280
27	S		5 49	6 22	5 24	5 58	Morn.	5 55	279
28	☉	**Easter Sunday.** [b. 1799.	5 46	6 23	5 5	7 20	0 18	6 22	278
29	M	**Easter Monday.** Earl of Derby	5 44	6 25	4 47	8 44	1 12	6 50	277
30	Tu	**Easter Tuesday.**	5 42	6 26	4 28	10 3	2 7	7 20	276
31	W	Oxford Term begins.	5 39	6 28	4 10	11 16	3 1	7 51	275

PHASES OF THE MOON.

(Last Quarter   5d. 5h. 43m. Morn.
● New Moon   13   8 47 Morn.
) First Quarter 21   5 54 Morn.
O Full Moon   27   9 33 After.
In Apogee 11d. 5h. M. | In Perigee 27d. 1h. M.

MORNING AND EVENING STARS.

♀ VENUS is a morning star; rises with the Sun at the end of the month, in conjunction with the Moon on the 11th, at 11h. 7m. aft.

♂ MARS visible through the night; in conjunction with the Moon on the 24th, at 0h. 14m.; aft.

♃ JUPITER is an evening star; in conjunction with the Moon on the 15th, at 11h. 28m. morn.

♄ SATURN in conjunction with the Moon on the 5th, at 9h. 1m. morn.

In this month the mornings increase 1h. 10m., and the afternoons 52 minutes.

RAINFALL IN MARCH, 1868.

In this month rain fell during 16 days. The total fall for the month was 1·29 inch; an amount *less* than the average, since 1860, of 0·79 inch.

Time of High Water at the undermentioned Ports—

Day of Month	Week	Average daily Temperature.*	LOND. BDGE. Morn.	After.	LIVERPOOL. Morn.	After.	S'HAMPTON. Morn.	After.	NEWCASTLE. Morn.	After.	HULL. Morn.	After.	DOVER. Morn.	After.	BRISTOL. Morn.	After.	Day of the Year
		Deg.	H. M.	H. M.	H. M.	H. M.	H. M.	H. M.	H. M.	H. M.	H. M.	H. M.	H. M.	H. M.	H. M.	H. M.	
1	Th	45	5 3	5 23	2 10	2 31	1 17	1 39	7 29	7 51	9 29	9 50	1 58	2 20	10 17	10 35	91
2	F	45	5 44	6 6	2 51	3 13	2 0	2 22	8 13	8 38	10 12	10 35	2 42	3 3	10 54	11 14	92
3	S	45	6 30	6 53	3 36	4 3	2 45	3 10	9 5	9 36	11 1	11 33	3 26	3 51	11 38	..	93
4	S	45	7 20	7 50	4 34	5 11	3 37	4 10	10 9	10 49	..	0 8	4 17	4 46	0 3	0 32	94
5	M	45	8 26	9 8	5 54	6 40	4 48	5 29	11 30	..	0 45	1 23	5 21	5 58	1 10	1 53	95
6	Tu	45	9 51	10 34	7 23	8 11	6 11	6 50	0 11	0 51	2 2	2 40	6 37	7 16	2 40	3 24	96
7	W	46	11 13	11 49	8 36	9 4	7 28	8 0	1 27	2 0	3 16	3 50	7 54	8 25	4 4	4 37	97
8	Th	45	..	0 19	9 28	9 48	8 27	8 49	2 26	2 49	4 19	4 44	8 50	9 12	5 5	5 28	98
9	F	45	0 42	1 3	10 7	10 24	9 10	9 28	3 8	3 27	5 4	5 22	9 33	9 52	5 50	6 10	99
10	S	45	1 23	1 41	10 40	10 56	9 45	10 1	3 43	3 59	5 39	5 56	10 10	10 28	6 29	6 47	100
11	S	45	1 57	2 13	11 12	11 28	10 16	10 32	4 14	4 28	6 13	6 29	10 45	11 2	7 5	7 22	101
12	M	45	2 27	2 43	11 44	11 59	10 47	11 3	4 43	4 58	6 45	7 1	11 19	11 36	7 38	7 54	102
13	Tu	45	2 59	3 14	..	0 15	11 20	11 37	5 13	5 28	7 16	7 32	11 53	..	8 10	8 26	103
14	W	45	3 30	3 45	0 32	0 48	11 54	..	5 45	6 2	7 49	8 4	0 11	0 28	8 41	8 57	104
15	Th	45	4 1	4 17	1 4	1 20	0 10	0 27	6 19	6 36	8 20	8 37	0 46	1 5	9 12	9 27	105
16	F	45	4 34	4 50	1 37	1 54	0 44	1 2	6 54	7 13	8 54	9 13	1 23	1 42	9 43	10 0	106
17	S	46	5 9	5 27	2 13	2 33	1 21	1 41	7 32	7 53	9 32	9 52	2 1	2 22	10 18	10 37	107
18	S	46	5 48	6 10	2 55	3 19	2 3	2 27	8 17	8 45	10 15	10 42	2 45	3 9	10 58	11 22	108
19	M	46	6 35	7 3	3 45	4 18	2 53	3 23	9 16	9 52	11 14	11 51	3 35	4 3	11 49	..	109
20	Tu	46	7 35	8 13	4 56	5 40	3 56	4 35	10 32	11 17	..	0 31	4 34	5 9	0 20	0 56	110
21	W	47	8 56	9 39	6 27	7 12	5 17	6 0	11 59	..	1 11	1 50	5 47	6 26	1 41	2 20	111
22	Th	47	10 21	11 3	7 51	8 26	6 40	7 19	0 40	1 17	2 29	3 6	7 6	7 44	3 14	3 55	112
23	F	47	11 39	..	8 55	9 22	7 52	8 21	1 49	2 17	3 40	4 10	8 16	8 44	4 30	5 0	113
24	S	48	0 9	0 37	9 45	10 8	8 48	9 13	2 42	3 5	4 38	5 1	9 11	9 37	5 28	5 55	114
25	S	48	1 2	1 26	10 31	10 54	9 36	9 58	3 28	3 50	5 24	5 48	10 2	10 26	6 21	6 46	115
26	M	48	1 48	2 8	11 17	11 40	10 21	10 43	4 11	4 32	6 11	6 34	10 51	11 16	7 10	7 34	116
27	Tu	48	2 31	2 54	..	0 2	11 6	11 29	4 54	5 16	6 57	7 19	11 39	..	7 56	8 18	117
28	W	48	3 14	3 37	0 24	0 46	11 51	..	5 38	6 0	7 41	8 2	0 0	0 26	8 39	8 59	118
29	Th	49	3 57	4 18	1 6	1 26	0 12	0 33	6 21	6 42	8 22	8 42	0 49	1 11	9 16	9 34	119
30	F	50	4 38	4 59	1 46	2 6	0 53	1 14	7 3	7 25	9 3	9 24	1 32	1 54	9 53	10 13	120

RISING and SETTING of SEVEN PRINCIPAL PLANETS on the 5th, 15th, and 25th.

D.	MERCURY ☿ Rises h. m.	Sets h. m.	VENUS ♀ Rises h. m.	Sets h. m.	MARS ♂ Rises h. m.	Sets h. m.	JUPITER ♃ Rises h. m.	Sets h. m.	SATURN ♄ Rises h. m.	Sets h. m.	URANUS ♅ Rises h. m.	Sets h. m.	NEPTUNE ♆ Rises h. m.	Sets h. m.
5	5 11M	4 21A	5 26M	5 38A	0 38A	4 7M	5 52M	7 22A	0 5M	8 17M	9 50M	2 38A	6 37A	6 1A
15	4 58M	5 20A	5 6M	6 10A	0 6A	3 32M	5 16M	6 56A	11 19A	7 37M	9 12M	1 40M	5 3M	6 1A
25	4 48M	6 34A	4 48M	6 42A	11 47M	2 52M	4 42M	6 30A	10 38A	6 56M	8 35M	1 1M	4 22M	5 22A

ECLIPSES OCCULTATIONS, AND OTHER CELESTIAL PHENOMENA.

April 1. Day breaks at 3h. 37m. morn., and Twilight ends at 8h. 31m. aft., the length of the day being 12h. 53m.

Apr. 6. Occultation of θ Capricorni. The disappearance takes place at 2h. 54m. morn., 57° from the vertex; the reappearance at 4h. 3m. morn., 247° from the vertex. The disappearance will not be visible at London, the star being below the horizon.

Apr. 17. Jupiter in conjunction with the Sun 6h. 12m. morn.

Apr. 20. Sun enters Taurus 1h. 39m. morn.

Apr. 21. Occultation of α Leonis (Regulus). The disappearance takes place at 1h. 56m. aft., 335° from the vertex; the reappearance at 2h. 19m. aft., 283° from the vertex.

Apr. 29. Mercury in superior conjunction with the Sun 1h. 23m. aft.

In this month the mornings increase 1h., and the afternoons 48m.

* The Temperature column gives the daily average of the Thermometer for 50 years.

APRIL XXX DAYS.

Days of M.	Days of W.	Fasts and Festivals. Remarkable Days—Events.	THE SUN. Rises. H. M.	THE SUN. Sets. H. M.	THE SUN. After Clock. M. S.	THE MOON. Rises morn. H. M.	THE MOON. Souths morn. H. M.	THE MOON. Sets morn. H. M.	Days to end of the year.
1	Th	All Fools' Day.	5 37	6 30	3 52	...	3 54	8 26	274
2	F	Coalition Ministry formed, 1782.	5 36	6 33	3 34	0 24	4 48	9 9	273
3	S	*Richard.*	5 34	6 34	3 16	1 25	5 40	9 56	272
4	S	**Low Sunday.** *St. Ambrose.*	5 30	6 36	2 58	2 15	6 31	10 49	271
5	M	Robert Raikes died, 1811.	5 29	6 38	2 40	2 57	7 20	11 47	270
6	Tu	Battle of Jellalabad, 1842.	5 27	6 40	2 23	3 31	8 7	Aftn.	269
7	W	Prince Leopold born, 1853.	5 25	6 41	2 6	4 2	8 53	1 51	268
8	Th	Dividends due.	5 23	6 42	1 49	4 26	9 36	2 53	267
9	F	Fire Insurance expires.	5 20	6 44	1 32	4 49	10 19	3 57	266
10	S	Battle of Toulouse, 1814.	5 17	6 46	1 16	5 10	11 1	5 0	265
11	S	**2nd Sunday after Easter.**	5 15	6 47	0 59	5 30	11 43	6 5	264
12	M	Rodney's Victory, 1782.	5 13	6 49	0 44	5 53	Aftn.	7 13	263
13	Tu	Mohammedan Era c. 1286.	5 10	6 50	0 28	6 16	1 11	8 19	262
14	W	Princess Beatrice born, 1857.	5 8	6 52	0 13	6 41	1 57	9 27	261
15	Th	EASTER LAW TERM.	5 6	6 53	Befor.	7 10	2 46	10 33	260
16	F	Battle of Culloden, 1746.	5 5	6 55	0 17	7 46	3 37	11 36	259
17	S	Benjamin Franklin died, 1790.	5 3	6 57	0 31	8 29	4 31	Morn.	258
18	S	**3rd Sunday after Easter.**	5 1	6 58	0 45	9 20	5 26	0 37	257
19	M	*Alphege.* Lord Byron died, 1824	4 59	7 0	0 58	10 22	6 22	1 29	256
20	Tu	Long Parliament dismiss. 1653	5 37	7 2	1 11	11 32	7 18	2 14	255
21	W	Abelard died, 1142.	4 53	7 3	1 24	Aftn.	8 14	2 53	254
22	Th		4 51	7 5	1 36	2 8	9 9	3 25	253
23	F	*S. George.* Shakespeare d. 1616.	4 49	7 6	1 48	3 30	10 3	3 55	252
24	S	Daniel Defoe died, 1731.	4 47	7 8	1 59	4 52	10 56	4 22	251
25	S	**4th Sunday aft. Easter. S. Mark**	4 45	7 10	2 10	6 13	11 50	4 48	250
26	M	Magellan, Navigator, killed, 1522	4 43	7 11	2 20	7 35	Morn.	5 15	249
27	T	☾'s Ascending Node, 12° 32′ ☊	4 41	7 13	2 30	8 52	0 45	5 45	248
28	W	Chaucer died, 1400.	4 39	7 14	2 39	10 4	1 39	6 19	247
29	Th		4 37	7 16	2 48	11 11	2 34	6 59	246
30	F	Battle of Fontenoy, 1745.	4 36	7 18	2 57	...	3	7 45	245

PHASES OF THE MOON.

☾ Last Quarter	3*d.*	8*h.*	48*m.*	After.
● New Moon	12	1	48	Morn.
☽ First Quarter	19	3	6	After.
○ Full Moon	26	6	21	Morn.

In Apogee 8*d.* 1*h.* A. | In Perigee 24*d.* 7*h.* M.

RAINFALL IN APRIL, 1868.

In this month rain fell during 12 days. The total fall for the month was 1·49 inch; an amount *more* than the average, since 1860, of 0·36 inch.

MORNING AND EVENING STARS.

♀ VENUS not well situated for observation this month, being too near the Sun; in conjunction with the Moon on the *11th*, at *7h. 18m. morn.*

♂ MARS visible in the evenings in the north-west quarter of the sky; in conjunction with the Moon on the *21st*, at *1h. 10m. morn.*

♃ JUPITER may be seen as an evening star, but towards the end of the month approaches too near to the Sun for observation; in conjunction with the Moon on the *12th*, at *6h. 34m. morn.*

♄ SATURN in conjunction with the Moon on the *29th*, at *1h. 53m. morn.*

Time of High Water at the undermentioned Ports—

Day of Month	Week	Average daily Temperature.*	LOND. BDGE. Morn.	LOND. BDGE. After.	LIVERPOOL. Morn.	LIVERPOOL. After.	S'HAMPTON. Morn.	S'HAMPTON. After.	NEWCASTLE. Morn.	NEWCASTLE. After.	HULL. Morn.	HULL. After.	DOVER. Morn.	DOVER. After.	BRISTOL. Morn.	BRISTOL. After.	Day of the Year.
		Deg.	H. M.	H. M.	H. M.	H. M.	H. M	H. M	H. M.	H. M.	H. M.	H. M.	H. M.	H. M.	H. M.	H. M.	
1	S	50	5 18	5 40	2 27	2 49	1 36	1 58	7 47	8 11	9 46	10 9	2 16	2 39	10 32	10 52	121
2	S	51	6 4	6 28	3 12	3 36	2 21	2 45	8 38	9 7	10 34	11 3	3 2	3 26	11 14	11 38	122
3	M	51	6 53	7 20	4 5	4 37	3 11	3 39	9 38	10 12	11 36	..	3 52	4 19	..	0 4	123
4	Tu	51	7 50	8 28	5 14	5 53	4 11	4 47	10 52	11 29	0 11	0 47	4 47	5 19	0 33	1 9	124
5	W	51	9 8	9 45	6 34	7 12	5 23	6 0	..	0 5	1 22	1 56	5 52	6 26	1 47	2 29	125
6	Th	52	10 22	10 59	7 47	8 17	6 36	7 8	0 40	1 13	2 29	3 2	7 2	7 34	3 9	3 44	126
7	F	51	11 31	11 59	8 44	9 7	7 39	8 4	1 41	2 7	3 32	4 0	8 4	8 28	4 16	4 42	127
8	S	52	..	0 23	9 27	9 45	8 26	8 47	2 28	2 47	4 22	4 43	8 49	9 10	5 5	5 26	128
9	S	51	0 43	1 2	10 2	10 20	9 6	9 25	3 5	3 22	5 1	5 18	9 30	9 50	5 47	6 8	129
10	M	51	1 21	1 38	10 37	10 55	9 42	10 0	3 39	3 56	5 36	5 54	10 9	10 27	6 27	6 46	130
11	Tu	51	1 54	2 10	11 13	11 31	10 18	10 35	4 12	4 29	6 12	6 31	10 46	11 6	7 6	7 25	131
12	W	52	2 28	2 47	11 47	..	10 52	11 10	4 46	5 3	6 49	7 6	11 25	11 44	7 43	8 1	132
13	Th	52	3 3	3 20	0 7	0 24	11 29	11 48	5 20	5 38	7 24	7 42	..	0 3	8 19	8 36	133
14	F	52	3 36	3 53	0 42	1 0	..	0 6	5 56	6 15	7 59	8 17	0 23	0 43	8 53	9 10	134
15	S	52	4 12	4 31	1 19	1 39	0 26	0 46	6 35	6 56	8 36	8 57	1 4	1 25	9 28	9 47	135
16	S	52	4 51	5 13	2 0	2 22	1 9	1 30	7 18	7 41	9 19	9 41	1 47	2 10	10 7	10 29	136
17	M	52	5 34	5 58	2 46	3 12	1 54	2 21	8 7	8 37	10 5	10 34	2 36	3 3	10 53	11 18	137
18	Tu	53	6 26	6 56	3 40	4 12	2 48	3 18	9 9	9 45	11 6	11 43	3 30	3 59	11 45	..	138
19	W	54	7 28	8 5	4 47	5 28	3 50	4 24	10 23	11 0	..	0 22	4 28	5 0	0 14	0 47	139
20	Th	53	8 45	9 24	6 10	6 50	5 2	5 38	11 44	..	1 0	1 36	5 33	6 6	1 25	2 4	140
21	F	55	10 0	10 35	7 25	7 59	6 14	6 50	0 19	0 52	2 9	2 41	6 40	7 16	2 45	3 25	141
22	S	54	11 9	11 40	8 28	8 55	7 22	7 53	1 23	1 49	3 12	3 42	7 47	8 17	3 59	4 31	142
23	S	54	..	0 8	9 21	9 46	8 23	8 49	2 16	2 42	4 10	4 37	8 46	9 12	5 2	5 30	143
24	M	55	0 35	1 2	10 8	10 31	9 13	9 36	3 6	3 28	5 1	5 24	9 38	10 3	5 56	6 22	144
25	Tu	55	1 27	1 50	10 56	11 20	10 0	10 23	3 50	4 12	5 48	6 13	10 28	10 53	6 48	7 13	145
26	W	55	2 13	2 35	11 42	..	10 46	11 9	4 34	4 56	6 37	7 0	11 18	11 42	7 36	7 59	146
27	Th	56	2 57	3 17	0 4	0 26	11 31	11 53	5 18	5 40	7 22	7 44	..	0 5	8 21	8 40	147
28	F	56	3 39	3 58	0 47	1 7	..	0 13	6 1	6 22	8 3	8 23	0 27	0 50	8 59	9 18	148
29	S	56	4 19	4 39	1 28	1 48	0 34	0 54	6 44	7 5	8 44	9 6	1 13	1 35	9 37	9 56	149
30	S	57	4 59	5 20	2 9	2 30	1 16	1 38	7 27	7 49	9 28	9 49	1 57	2 19	10 15	10 34	150
31	M	56	5 41	6 3	2 51	3 13	2 0	2 22	8 12	8 38	10 11	10 35	2 41	3 3	10 54	11 14	151

RISING and SETTING of SEVEN PRINCIPAL PLANETS on the 5th, 15th, and 25th.

D.	MERCURY ☿ Rises h. m.	MERCURY ☿ Sets h. m.	VENUS ♀ Rises h. m.	VENUS ♀ Sets h. m.	MARS ♂ Rises h. m.	MARS ♂ Sets h. m.	JUPITER ♃ Rises h. m.	JUPITER ♃ Sets h. m.	SATURN ♄ Rises h. m.	SATURN ♄ Sets h. m.	URANUS ♅ Rises h. m.	URANUS ♅ Sets h. m.	NEPTUNE ♆ Rises h. m.	NEPTUNE ♆ Sets h. m.
5	4 39M	8 9A	4 32M	7 13A	11 26M	2 18M	7 7M	6 5A	9 57A	6 15M	7 57M	0 23M	3 45M	4 47A
15	4 47M	9 27A	4 19M	7 47A	11 10M	1 44M	3 33M	5 39A	9 14A	5 34X	7 19M	11 41A	3 7M	4 9A
25	5 5M	10 3A	4 14M	8 16A	10 56M	1 11M	2 58M	5 12A	8 31A	4 52M	6 42M	11 4A	2 28M	3 32A

ECLIPSES, OCCULTATIONS, AND OTHER CELESTIAL PHENOMENA.

May 1. Day breaks at 2h. 3m. morn., and twilight ends at 9h. 51m. aft., the length of the day being 14h. 44m.

May 5. Mercury in Perihelion, 9h. 34m. morn.

May 9. Venus in superior conjunction with the Sun, 8h. 23m. morn.

May 18. Occultation of α Leonis (Regulus). The disappearance takes place at 10h. 1m. aft., 24° from the vertex; the reappearance at 10h. 10m. aft., 8° from the vertex.

May 29. (6h. 35m. aft.) Mercury at greatest elongation East = 23°.

May 21. Sun enters Gemini, 1h. 39m. morn.

In this month the mornings increase 43m., and the afternoons 42m.

* The Temperature column gives the daily average of the Thermometer for 50 years.

Days of		Fasts and Festivals. Remarkable Days—Events.	THE SUN.			THE MOON.			Days to end of the year.
M.	W.		Rises.	Sets.	Before Clock.	Rises. morn.	Souths morn.	Sets morn.	
			H. M.	H. M.	M. S.	H. M.	H. M.	H. M.	
1	S	S Philip & S Jas. P. Arth. b. 1850	4 35	7 19	3 4	0 7	4 22	8 37	244
2	S	Rogation Sunday.	4 33	7 21	3 11	0 55	5 13	9 34	243
3	M	Invention of the Cross. Rog. d.	4 31	7 23	3 18	1 34	6 2	10 36	242
4	Tu	Rogation Day.	4 29	7 24	3 24	2 5	6 48	11 38	241
5	W	Rogation Day.	4 28	7 25	3 30	2 32	7 33	Aftn.	240
6	Th	Ascension Day. Holy Thursday	4 26	7 26	3 34	2 55	8 16	1 46	239
7	F	Length of day 15h. 3m.	4 25	7 28	3 39	3 16	8 58	2 49	238
8	S	EASTER TERM ENDS.	4 23	7 30	3 43	3 36	9 40	3 56	237
9	S	Sunday after Ascension. Half	4 21	7 31	3 46	3 57	10 23	5 1	236
10	M	[quarter day.	4 20	7 33	3 48	4 19	11 7	6 8	235
11	Tu	Spencer Perceval assass., 1812.	4 18	7 34	3 50	4 43	11 53	7 15	234
12	W	Earl of Strafford beheaded, 1641.	4 16	7 36	3 52	5 11	Aftn.	8 24	233
13	Th		4 15	7 37	3 52	5 44	1 33	9 30	232
14	F	Oxf. T. ends. Camb. T. div. N.	4 13	7 39	3 53	6 26	2 27	10 32	231
15	S	Oxf. T. beg. Whitsund. Scot.	4 12	7 41	3 52	7 15	3 22	11 28	230
16	S	Whit Sunday.	4 10	7 42	3 52	8 14	4 18	Morn	229
17	M	Whit Monday.	4 9	7 44	3 50	9 22	5 14	0 15	228
18	Tu	Whit Tuesday.	4 8	7 45	3 48	10 35	6 9	0 56	227
19	W	Dunstan. Ember Week.	4 6	7 46	3 46	11 52	7 2	1 29	226
20	Th	♃ rises 3h. 15m. morn.	4 5	7 48	3 43	Aftn.	7 55	1 57	225
21	F	Ember Day.	4 3	7 49	3 39	2 30	8 47	2 24	224
22	S	TRINITY TERM. Ember Day.	4 2	7 51	3 35	3 50	9 39	2 50	223
23	S	Trinity Sunday.	4 0	7 52	3 31	5 10	10 32	3 15	222
24	M	Q. VICTORIA BORN, 1819.	3 59	7 54	3 26	6 29	11 25	3 43	221
25	Tu	Princess Helena born, 1846.	3 58	7 56	3 20	7 43	Morn.	4 13	220
26	W	Augustin. Epsom Derby Day.	3 57	7 57	3 14	8 53	0 20	4 50	219
27	Th	CORPUS CHRISTI, Ven. Bede.	3 56	7 58	3 8	9 56	1 15	5 34	218
28	F	☽'s Ascending Node 10° 53′ ♌	3 55	7 59	3 1	10 49	2 10	6 24	217
29	S	Restoration K. Charles II. 1660	3 54	8 0	2 53	11 32	3 3	7 19	216
30	S	1st Sunday after Trinity.	3 53	8 1	2 45	Morn.	3 54	8 21	215
31	M	Obliquity of Eclip. 23° 27′ 16″.	3 52	8 1	2 37	0 7	4 42	9 24	214

PHASES OF THE MOON.

(Last Quarter   3d. 1h. 41m. After.
● New Moon   11   4   7 After.
) First Quarter 18   9   30 After.
○ Full Moon   25   3   23 After.

In Apogee 6d. 6h. M. | In Perigee 21d. 10h. A.

RAINFALL IN MAY, 1868.

In this month rain fell during 6 days. The total fall for the month was 1 58 inch; an amount *less* than the average since 1860 of 0·82 inches.

MORNING AND EVENING STARS.

♀ VENUS an evening star near the end of the month; in conjunction with the Moon on the 11th at 2h. 55m. *aft.*

♂ MARS visible in the evening; near to Regulus on the 24th; in conjunction with the Moon on the 18th at 10h. 25m. *aft.*

♃ JUPITER, a morning star, in conjunction with the Moon on the 10th at 2h. 32m. *morn.*

♄ SATURN rises at 9h. 57m. *aft.* on the 5th, visible through the night, in conjunction with the Moon on the 26th at 8h. 29m. *morn.*

Time of High Water at the undermentioned Ports—

Day of Month	Week	Average daily Temperature.	LOND. BDGE. Morn.	After.	LIVERPOOL. Morn.	After.	S'HAMPTON. Morn	After.	NEWCASTLE. Morn.	After.	HULL. Morn.	After.	DOVER. Morn.	After.	BRISTOL. Morn.	After.	Day of the Year.
		Deg.	H. M.	H. M.	H. M.	H. M.	H. M.	H. M.	H. M.	H. M.	H. M.	H. M.	H. M.	H. M.	H. M.	H. M.	
1	Tu	57	6 27	6 52	3 36	4 2	2 44	3 8	9 5	9 34	11 2	11 32	3 25	3 48	11 37	11 59	152
2	W	58	7 17	7 45	4 29	5 0	3 33	4 0	10 4	10 37	..	0 3	4 12	4 38	..	0 23	153
3	Th	58	8 16	8 51	5 35	6 12	4 31	5 3	11 13	11 46	0 35	1 7	5 6	5 35	0 52	1 26	154
4	F	57	9 26	9 58	6 47	7 18	5 35	6 6	..	0 16	1 38	2 7	6 3	6 32	2 0	2 35	155
5	S	57	10 27	10 57	7 48	8 16	6 37	7 7	0 45	1 14	2 35	3 3	7 3	7 33	3 11	3 43	156
6	S	57	11 27	11 55	8 41	9 4	7 35	8 1	1 40	2 3	3 30	3 56	8 1	8 25	4 13	4 39	157
7	M	57	..	0 19	9 24	9 44	8 23	8 45	2 25	2 44	4 19	4 40	8 45	9 8	5 2	5 25	158
8	Tu	57	0 40	1 1	10 4	10 23	9 7	9 28	3 3	3 23	4 59	5 19	9 31	9 53	5 48	6 11	159
9	W	58	1 22	1 41	10 43	11 3	9 46	10 7	3 42	4 1	5 39	5 59	10 14	10 35	6 33	6 56	160
10	Th	58	2 1	2 20	11 23	11 44	10 27	10 48	4 19	4 38	6 20	6 41	10 57	11 20	7 18	7 39	161
11	F	58	2 40	3 0	..	0 5	11 10	11 31	4 59	5 19	7 2	7 23	11 43	..	8 0	8 21	162
12	S	59	3 19	3 40	0 26	0 47	11 53	..	5 40	6 1	7 44	8 4	0 5	0 27	8 41	9 1	163
13	S	58	4 0	4 20	1 9	1 30	0 15	0 37	6 23	6 46	8 25	8 47	0 51	1 15	9 21	9 42	164
14	M	57	4 42	5 5	1 53	2 17	1 0	1 24	7 11	7 36	9 11	9 37	1 40	2 5	10 4	10 26	165
15	Tu	59	5 29	5 53	2 41	3 6	1 49	2 15	8 1	8 29	10 0	10 27	2 30	2 56	10 49	11 13	166
16	W	59	6 21	6 49	3 33	4 2	2 42	3 10	8 59	9 34	10 56	11 31	3 23	3 51	11 39	..	167
17	Th	59	7 18	7 50	4 35	5 8	3 40	4 9	10 10	10 45	..	0 9	4 20	4 47	0 6	0 33	168
18	F	59	8 24	9 0	5 44	6 23	4 40	5 14	11 22	11 56	0 43	1 16	5 15	5 44	1 1	1 37	169
19	S	59	9 35	10 8	6 57	7 32	5 46	6 21	..	0 27	1 48	2 17	6 13	6 47	2 13	2 52	170
20	S	59	10 42	11 13	8 4	8 33	6 55	7 27	0 59	1 29	2 47	3 17	7 21	7 52	3 30	4 4	171
21	M	60	11 45	..	9 1	9 28	7 59	8 29	1 55	2 22	3 47	4 16	8 22	8 51	4 37	5 8	172
22	Tu	60	0 14	0 41	9 53	10 17	8 56	9 22	2 48	3 13	4 44	5 9	9 19	9 46	5 37	6 4	173
23	W	60	1 8	1 34	10 41	11 5	9 46	10 9	3 37	3 59	5 33	5 57	10 12	10 37	6 31	6 57	174
24	Th	61	1 58	2 21	11 28	11 50	10 31	10 53	4 21	4 43	6 21	6 45	11 2	11 26	7 22	7 44	175
25	F	61	2 44	3 4	..	0 12	11 15	11 36	5 4	5 25	7 8	7 29	11 49	..	8 6	8 26	176
26	S	62	3 24	3 44	0 32	0 52	11 57	..	5 45	6 6	7 49	8 8	0 11	0 32	8 45	9 2	177
27	S	62	4 4	4 22	1 11	1 29	0 16	0 36	6 25	6 45	8 26	8 45	0 52	1 13	9 19	9 37	178
28	M	62	4 42	5 0	1 47	2 6	0 55	1 14	7 5	7 25	9 5	9 25	1 34	1 54	9 55	10 13	179
29	Tu	61	5 18	5 37	2 26	2 46	1 35	1 55	7 46	8 7	9 45	10 5	2 15	2 36	10 31	10 48	180
30	W	61	5 57	6 19	3 6	3 26	2 15	2 35	8 29	8 52	10 26	10 48	2 56	3 16	11 6	11 25	181

RISING and SETTING of SEVEN PRINCIPAL PLANETS on the 5th, 15th, and 25th.

D.	MERCURY ☿ Rises h. m.	Sets h. m.	VENUS ♀ Rises h. m.	Sets h. m.	MARS ♂ Rises h. m.	Sets h. m.	JUPITER ♃ Rises h. m.	Sets h. m.	SATURN ♄ Rises h. m.	Sets h. m.	URANUS ♅ Rises h. m.	Sets h. m.	NEPTUNE ♆ Rises h. m.	Sets h. m.
5	7 17M	9 49A	4 15M	8 45A	10 43M	0 35M	2 20M	4 42A	7 45A	4 5M	6 2M	10 22A	1 45M	2 49A
15	4 59M	8 57A	4 25M	9 3A	10 33M	0 3M	1 45M	4 15A	7 1A	3 24M	5 26M	9 44A	1 7M	2 11A
25	4 11M	7 45A	4 44M	9 12A	10 24M	11 29A	1 9M	3 47A	6 19A	2 41M	4 50M	9 8A	0 28M	1 32A

ECLIPSES, OCCULTATIONS, AND OTHER CELESTIAL PHENOMENA.

June 1. In this month there is no real night, but either constant daylight or twilight, the length of the day being 16h. 15m.

June 4. Saturn in opposition with the Sun, 0h. 32m. aft.

June 11. Mercury stationary in the heavens, 10h. 39m. aft.

June 17. Mercury and Venus in conjunction, 2h. 22m. aft.

June 18. Mercury in Aphelion, 9h. 11m. morn.

June 21. Sun enters Cancer, 10h. 4m. morn. Summer commences.

June 23. Occultation of μ Sagittarii. The disappearance takes place at 10h. 53m. aft., 110°

from the vertex; the reappearance at 11h. 56m. aft. 228° from the vertex.

June 24. Mercury in inferior conjunction with the Sun, 9h. 46m. aft.

June 28. Venus in Perihelion 3h. 39m. aft.

To the 20th of this month the mornings increase 6m., and the afternoons 13m., and from the 20th to the 30th, the mornings decrease 4 m. and the afternoons 0 m.

* The Temperature column gives the daily average of the Thermometer for 50 years.

Days of		Fasts and Festivals. Remarkable Days—Events.	THE SUN.			THE MOON.			Days to end of the year.
M.	W.		Rises.	Sets.	Before Clock.	Rises morn.	Souths morn.	Sets morn.	
			H. M.	H. M.	M. S.	H. M.	H. M.	H. M.	
1	Tu	*Nicomede.*	3 50	8 5	2 28	0 36	5 28	10 29	213
2	W	♃ rises 2h. 30m. morn.	3 50	8 6	2 19	1 0	6 12	11 32	212
3	Th	Pr. Geo. Fred. of Wales b. 1865	3 49	8 7	2 9	1 21	6 54	Aftn.	211
4	F	Battle of Magenta, 1859.	3 48	8 8	1 59	1 41	7 36	1 41	210
5	S	*Boniface.*	3 47	8 9	1 49	2 1	8 18	2 46	209
6	☙	2d Sunday after Trinity.	3 47	8 10	1 38	2 24	9 2	3 53	208
7	M	☉ Semidiameter 15′ 47″.	3 46	8 11	1 27	2 46	9 47	5 1	207
8	Tu	Ascot Races.	3 46	8 12	1 16	3 12	10 35	6 10	206
9	W	♄ rises 8h. 3m. morn.	3 46	8 12	1 4	3 42	11 25	7 17	205
10	Th	♀ ☌ ☾ 8h. 34m. aft.	3 45	8 13	0 52	4 22	Aftn.	8 23	204
11	F	St. Barnabas.	3 45	8 14	0 40	5 9	1 15	9 23	203
12	S	Trinity Term ends.	3 45	8 14	0 28	6 6	2 12	10 14	202
13	☙	3d Sunday after Trinity.	3 44	8 15	0 15	7 11	3 9	10 58	201
14	M	Battle of Marengo, 1800.	3 44	8 16	0 3	8 24	4 5	11 33	200
15	Tu	Wat Tyler killed, 1381.	3 44	8 16	After.	9 41	5 0	Morn.	199
16	W	Length of day 16h. 33m.	3 44	8 17	0 23	10 59	5 52	0 5	198
17	Th	St. Alban, First Eng. Martyr.	3 44	8 17	0 36	Aftn.	6 43	0 30	197
18	F	Battle of Waterloo, 1815.	3 44	8 17	0 49	1 35	7 34	0 56	196
19	S	Magna Charta, 1216.	3 44	8 18	1 1	2 52	8 25	1 21	195
20	☙	4th Sunday after Trin. Queen's	3 44	8 18	1 14	4 11	9 17	1 46	194
21	M	Longest day. [Accession.	3 45	8 18	1 27	5 26	10 10	2 14	193
22	Tu	Cambridge Commencement.	3 45	8 19	1 40	6 38	11 4	2 47	192
23	W	☾'s Ascending Node, 9° 31′ ♌	3 45	8 19	1 53	7 42	11 58	3 26	191
24	Th	St. John Baptist. Midsum. D.	3 45	8 19	2 6	8 40	Morn.	4 12	190
25	F	Cambridge Term ends.	3 46	8 19	2 18	9 27	0 52	5 5	189
26	S	Corn Law repealed, 1846.	3 46	8 19	2 31	10 6	1 44	6 4	188
27	☙	5th Sunday after Trinity.	3 47	8 19	2 43	10 37	2 34	7 8	187
28	M	Q. Victoria Crowned, 1838.	3 47	8 19	2 56	11 4	3 21	8 12	186
29	Tu	St. Peter.	3 47	8 18	3 8	11 28	4 6	9 17	185
30	W	Battle of Oudenarde, 1708.	3 48	8 18	3 19	11 48	4 50	10 22	184

PHASES OF THE MOON.

☾ Last Quarter	2d.	7h. 22m.	Morn.
● New Moon	10	3 52	Morn.
☽ First Quarter	17	2 15	Morn.
○ Full Moon	24	1 39	Morn.

In Apogee 3d. 0h. M. | In Perigee 16d. 10h. M.
In Apogee 30d. 6h. A.

RAINFALL IN JUNE 1868.

In this month rain fell during 4 days. The total fall for the month was 0·78 inch; an amount *less* than the average, since 1860, of 2·27 inches.

MORNING AND EVENING STARS.

♀ Venus an evening star during this month; in conjunction with the Moon on the *10th*, at 8h. 34m. aft.

♂ Mars visible in the evening in the north-west quarter of the heavens; in conjunction with the Moon on the *16th*, at 0h. 58m. morn.

♃ Jupiter a morning star during this month; in conjunction with the Moon on the *6th*, at 10h. 44m. aft.

♄ Saturn will be visible in the south-east quarter of the heavens soon after sunset; in conjunction with the Moon on the *22nd*, at 1h. 13m. aft.

Time of High Water at the undermentioned Ports—

Day of Month	Week	Average daily Temperature*	Lond. Bdge. Morn	After.	Liverpool Morn.	After.	S'hampton Morn.	After.	Newcastle Morn.	After.	Hull Morn.	After.	Dover Morn	After.	Bristol Morn.	After.	Day of the Year
		Deg.	H. M.	H. M.	H. M.	H. M.	H. M.	H. M.	H. M.	H. M.	H. M.	H. M.	H. M.	H. M.	H. M.	H. M.	
1	Th	61	6 40	7 3	3 47	4 10	2 55	3 16	9 17	9 43	11 14	11 41	3 36	3 57	11 45	..	182
2	F	62	7 27	7 53	4 36	5 4	3 40	4 5	10 11	10 41	..	0 10	4 19	4 42	0 6	0 29	183
3	S	62	8 23	8 55	5 36	6 9	4 32	5 2	11 14	11 45	0 39	1 8	5 7	5 34	0 53	1 23	184
4	S	62	9 28	9 58	6 44	7 18	5 33	6 5	..	0 15	1 37	2 6	6 2	6 32	1 56	2 34	185
5	M	62	10 28	10 58	7 48	8 18	6 36	7 8	0 46	1 15	2 35	3 3	7 3	7 35	3 9	3 44	186
6	Tu	62	11 28	11 57	8 45	9 9	7 39	8 6	1 42	2 7	3 31	4 0	8 4	8 34	4 16	4 44	187
7	W	62	..	0 23	9 32	9 55	8 32	8 58	2 30	2 53	4 24	4 48	8 55	9 21	5 11	5 38	188
8	Th	62	0 46	1 11	10 18	10 41	9 23	9 46	3 15	3 38	5 11	5 34	9 47	10 18	5 56	6 17	189
9	F	62	1 35	1 58	11 4	11 27	10 8	10 31	4 0	4 21	5 58	6 21	10 36	11 1	6 56	7 21	190
10	S	62	2 19	2 42	11 50	..	10 54	11 17	4 42	5 4	6 45	7 8	11 26	11 50	7 45	8 8	191
11	S	61	3 5	3 27	0 13	0 36	11 41	..	5 27	5 50	7 30	7 53	..	0 14	8 30	8 52	192
12	M	62	3 48	4 10	0 59	1 21	0 4	0 27	6 13	6 36	8 15	8 37	0 39	1 4	9 13	9 34	193
13	Tu	62	4 32	4 57	1 44	2 7	0 51	1 15	7 0	7 25	9 0	9 25	1 29	1 55	9 56	10 18	194
14	W	63	5 20	5 45	2 31	2 55	1 40	2 4	7 51	8 16	9 51	10 15	2 20	2 45	10 39	11 1	195
15	Th	63	6 9	6 36	3 20	3 46	2 29	2 54	8 43	9 13	10 41	11 9	3 10	3 35	11 24	11 49	196
16	F	62	7 4	7 32	4 13	4 43	3 20	3 47	9 44	10 17	11 41	..	4 1	4 27	..	0 14	197
17	S	62	8 1	8 33	5 15	5 49	4 14	4 44	10 51	11 26	0 16	0 49	4 53	5 19	0 39	1 6	198
18	S	62	9 6	9 39	6 25	7 3	5 17	5 51	11 59	..	1 20	1 50	5 47	6 17	1 39	2 17	199
19	M	62	10 13	10 48	7 38	8 12	6 26	7 3	0 31	1 4	2 21	2 53	6 51	7 29	2 57	3 38	200
20	Tu	61	11 23	11 57	8 45	9 14	7 39	8 12	1 37	2 7	3 26	4 0	8 5	8 35	4 17	4 50	201
21	W	61	..	0 29	9 41	10 6	8 42	9 8	2 35	3 1	4 29	4 57	9 4	9 32	5 21	5 49	202
22	Th	61	0 57	1 22	10 29	10 52	9 33	9 56	3 25	3 48	5 21	5 45	9 50	10 24	6 16	6 42	203
23	F	62	1 46	2 9	11 15	11 36	10 19	10 40	4 10	4 31	6 8	6 32	10 48	11 11	7 7	7 30	204
24	S	61	2 30	2 51	11 56	..	11 0	11 20	4 51	5 10	6 54	7 14	11 33	11 53	7 51	8 11	205
25	S	62	3 10	3 28	0 16	0 34	11 39	11 57	5 29	5 48	7 33	7 52	..	0 12	8 29	8 45	206
26	M	62	3 46	4 2	0 51	1 8	..	0 15	6 5	6 23	8 8	8 24	0 31	0 50	9 1	9 17	207
27	Tu	62	4 20	4 38	1 25	1 43	0 33	0 50	6 41	6 59	8 41	8 59	1 10	1 29	9 33	9 48	208
28	W	62	4 56	5 13	1 59	2 16	1 6	1 24	7 17	7 35	9 17	9 35	1 46	2 4	10 3	10 20	209
29	Th	62	5 29	5 46	2 34	2 52	1 42	2 0	7 54	8 13	9 53	10 11	2 23	2 41	10 36	10 51	210
30	F	62	6 6	6 24	3 9	3 27	2 18	2 36	8 32	8 53	10 30	10 50	2 59	3 17	11 7	11 23	211
31	S	62	6 43	7 5	3 47	4 11	2 55	3 17	9 17	9 43	11 14	11 41	3 36	3 58	11 46	..	212

Rising and Setting of Seven Principal Planets on the 5th, 15th, and 25th.

D.	Mercury ☿ Rises	Sets	Venus ♀ Rises	Sets	Mars ♂ Rises	Sets	Jupiter ♃ Rises	Sets	Saturn ♄ Rises	Sets	Uranus ♅ Rises	Sets	Neptune ♆ Rises	Sets
	h. m.	h. m.	h. m.	h. m.	h. m.	h. m.	h. m.	h. m.	h. m.	h. m.	h. m.	h. m.	h. m.	h. m.
5	3 20M	6 46A	5 10M	9 12A	1017M	10 59A	0 34M	3 18A	5 56A	2 0M	4 13M	8 29A	11 45A	0 53A
15	2 46M	6 32A	5 40M	9 6A	10 11M	10 59A	11 55A	2 49A	4 55A	1 19M	3 37M	7 53A	11 6A	0 14A
25	2 48M	6 56A	6 10M	8 54A	10 5M	9 57A	11 20A	2 17A	4 14A	0 38M	3 1M	7 15A	10 27A	11 35M

ECLIPSES, OCCULTATIONS, AND OTHER CELESTIAL PHENOMENA.

July 1. No real night until the 20th, before which, either constant daylight or ... length of the Day being 16h. 29m.

July 3. The earth at greatest distance from the Sun, 8h. 16m. aft.

July 4. Occultation of ξ Ceti. The disappearance takes place at 2h. 31m. morn. 122° from the vertex; the reappearance at 3h. 13m. morn. 208° from the vertex.

July 6. Mercury stationary in the heavens, 6h. 35m. morn.

July 17. (5h. 18m. morn.) Mercury at greatest West = 20°.

July 22. Occultation of ξ2 Sagittarii. The disappearance takes place at 2h. 20m. morn., 161° from the vertex; at the reappearance the star will be below the horizon.

July 22. The Sun enters Leo, 9h. 16m. morn.

July 22-23. A partial eclipse of the Moon, invisible at Greenwich.

* The Temperature column gives the daily average of the Thermometer for 50 years.

Days of M.	Days of W.	Fasts and Festivals. Remarkable Days—Events.	THE SUN. Rises. H. M.	Sets. H. M.	After Clock. M. S.	THE MOON. Rises after. H. M.	Souths morn. H. M.	Sets morn. H. M.	Days to end of the year.
1	Th	Princess Alice married, 1862.	3 49	8 18	3 31	Morn.	5 32	11 26	183
2	F	*Visitation B. Virgin Mary.*	3 50	8 18	3 42	0 8	6 13	Aftn.	182
3	S	Dog-days begin.	3 50	8 17	3 54	0 28	6 56	1 36	181
4	S	**6th Sunday after Trinity.**	3 51	8 17	4 4	0 49	7 39	2 43	180
5	M	☾'s Ascending Node 8° 53′ ☊	3 52	8 16	4 15	1 12	8 25	3 50	179
6	Tu	Sir Thos. More beheaded, 1535.	3 53	8 16	4 25	1 41	9 14	4 59	178
7	W	*Translation of Thomas A'Becket.*	3 54	8 15	4 35	2 16	10 7	6 8	177
8	Th	Dividends due.	3 55	8 15	4 45	2 58	11 2	7 11	176
9	F	Fire Insurance expires.	3 56	8 14	4 54	3 51	Aftn.	8 7	175
10	S	Oxford Term ends.	3 57	8 13	5 3	4 55	0 59	8 54	174
11	S	**7th Sunday after Trinity.**	3 58	8 13	5 11	6 7	1 57	9 35	173
12	M	Crimea evacuated, 1856.	3 59	8 12	5 19	7 26	2 54	10 8	172
13	Tu	Richard Cromwell died, 1712.	4 0	8 11	5 26	8 45	3 48	10 36	171
14	W	Bastille taken, 1789.	4 1	8 10	5 33	10 5	4 40	11 2	170
15	Th	*St. Swithin.*	4 2	8 9	5 39	11 25	5 32	11 27	169
16	F	Flight of Mahomet, 622.	4 3	8 8	5 45	Aftn.	6 22	11 50	168
17	S	☿ greatest elong. 5*h.* 18*m. morn.*	4 5	8 7	5 50	1 57	7 13	Morn.	167
18	S	**8th Sunday after Trinity.**	4 6	8 6	5 55	3 13	8 5	0 17	166
19	M	♄ ☌ ☾ 4*h.* 52*m. aft.*	4 7	8 5	5 59	4 26	8 58	0 48	165
20	Tu	*Margaret.*	4 8	8 4	6 3	5 32	9 51	1 25	164
21	W	Robert Burns died, 1796.	4 10	8 2	6 6	6 31	10 44	2 7	163
22	Th	*Mary Magdalene.*	4 11	8 1	6 9	7 21	11 36	2 56	162
23	F	☾ Eclipsed, invis. at Greenwich.	4 12	8 0	6 10	8 4	Morn.	3 52	161
24	S	Window tax repealed, 1851.	4 14	7 59	6 12	8 38	0 27	4 55	160
25	S	**9th Sund. aft. Trin. St. James**	4 15	7 57	6 13	9 6	1 15	5 59	159
26	M	*St. Anne.*	4 17	7 56	6 13	9 30	2 1	7 3	158
27	Tu	Atlantic Cable laid, 1866.	4 18	7 54	6 12	9 52	2 45	8 9	157
28	W	Length of day 15*h.* 33*m.*	4 20	7 53	6 11	10 12	3 28	9 13	156
29	Th	William Wilberforce died, 1833	4 21	7 51	6 10	10 32	4 9	10 16	155
30	F	Thomas Gray died, 1771.	4 22	7 50	6 8	10 52	4 51	11 22	154
31	S	Royal Academy closes.	4 24	7 48	6 5	11 14	5 33	Aftn.	153

PHASES OF THE MOON.

☾ Last Quarter	2*d.*	0*h.*	46*m.*	Morn.
● New Moon	9	1	38	After.
☽ First Quarter	16	6	48	Morn.
○ Full Moon	23	1	55	After.
☾ Last Quarter	31	5	6	After.

In Perigee 12*d.* 5*h.* A. | In Apogee 28*d.* 0*h.* A.

RAINFALL IN JULY, 1868.

In this month rain fell during three days. The total fall for the month was 0.45 inch; an amount *less* than the average, since 1860, of 1·34 inches.

MORNING AND EVENING STARS.

☿ Mercury, a morning star, rising about an hour before the Sun; in conjunction with the Moon on the 8*th*, at 6 *h.* 32*m. morn.*

♀ Venus an evening star; in conjunction with the Moon on the 10*th*, at 8*h.* 58*m. aft.*

♂ Mars in conjunction with the Moon on the 14*th*, at 7*h.* 39*m. morn.*

♃ Jupiter visible all night; in conjunction with the Moon on the 4*th*, at 6*h.* 0*m. aft.*

♄ Saturn will be visible after sunset in the south-eastern quarter of the heavens; in conjunction with Moon on the 19*th*, at 4*h.* 52*m. aft.*

AUGUST EIGHTH MONTH. [1869.

Time of High Water at the undermentioned Ports—

Month	Week	Ave race daily Temperature*	LOND. BDGE. Morn.	After.	LIVERPOOL Morn.	After.	S'HAMPTON Morn.	After.	NEWCASTLE Morn.	After.	HULL Morn.	After.	DOVER Morn.	After.	BRISTOL Morn.	After.	Day of the Year.
		Deg.	H. M.	H. M.	H. M	H. M	H. M.	H. M.	H. M.	H. M	H. M.	H. M.	H. M.	H. M.	H. M.	H. M.	
1	S	63	7 27	7 52	4 37	5 5	3 40	4 5	10 11	10 41	..	0 10	4 20	4 44	0 7	0 30	213
2	M	63	8 21	8 56	5 38	6 15	4 35	5 7	11 15	11 49	0 40	1 11	5 10	5 38	0 56	1 30	214
3	Tu	62	9 32	10 6	6 53	7 30	5 41	6 18	..	0 23	1 42	2 14	6 10	6 44	2 6	2 48	215
4	W	63	10 41	11 16	8 4	8 37	6 54	7 30	0 57	1 30	2 46	3 19	7 20	7 55	3 29	4 6	216
5	Th	62	11 50	..	9 6	9 33	8 3	8 33	2 0	2 28	3 51	4 21	8 27	8 56	4 41	5 12	217
6	F	62	0 20	0 48	9 58	10 22	9 1	9 27	2 54	3 18	4 50	5 14	9 24	9 51	5 41	6 9	218
7	S	62	1 15	1 42	10 46	11 10	9 51	10 15	3 42	4 5	5 38	6 3	10 17	10 43	6 36	7 3	219
8	S	62	2 6	2 27	11 34	11 58	10 38	11 2	4 27	4 49	6 27	6 51	11 9	11 35	7 28	7 52	220
9	M	63	2 50	3 12	..	0 21	11 26	11 49	5 12	5 35	7 15	7 39	11 59	..	8 16	8 38	221
10	Tu	63	3 35	3 55	0 43	1 6	..	0 12	5 57	6 20	8 1	8 22	0 23	0 47	8 59	9 19	222
11	W	63	4 18	4 42	1 28	1 50	0 35	0 57	6 43	7 7	8 44	9 7	1 12	1 36	9 40	10 0	223
12	Th	62	5 3	5 26	2 12	2 35	1 20	1 43	7 31	7 55	9 31	9 54	2 0	2 24	10 21	10 43	224
13	F	62	5 51	6 14	2 59	3 22	2 7	2 30	8 20	8 46	10 18	10 43	2 48	3 11	11 3	11 24	225
14	S	62	6 37	7 2	3 46	4 12	2 54	3 19	9 13	9 44	11 11	11 42	3 35	4 0	11 47	..	226
15	S	62	7 29	7 59	4 41	5 15	3 45	4 15	10 16	10 52	..	0 15	4 25	4 51	0 11	0 37	227
16	M	61	8 33	9 10	5 53	6 35	4 48	5 25	11 30	..	0 49	1 23	5 21	5 55	1 9	1 48	228
17	Tu	61	9 47	10 27	7 16	7 54	6 5	6 44	0 8	0 45	1 58	2 34	6 31	7 10	2 33	3 17	229
18	W	61	11 6	11 43	8 31	9 3	7 22	7 59	1 21	1 54	3 10	3 45	7 49	8 24	3 59	4 37	230
19	Th	61	..	0 16	9 31	9 56	8 30	8 58	2 25	2 51	4 18	4 47	8 53	9 21	5 9	5 37	231
20	F	61	0 45	1 12	10 18	10 39	9 22	9 44	3 16	3 38	5 12	5 34	9 46	10 10	6 3	6 27	232
21	S	61	1 36	1 56	10 59	11 18	10 4	10 23	3 59	4 17	5 55	6 15	10 31	10 52	6 50	7 12	233
22	S	60	2 15	2 35	11 36	11 54	10 41	10 58	4 35	4 52	6 35	6 55	11 12	11 31	7 31	7 49	234
23	M	60	2 53	3 8	..	0 11	11 15	11 33	5 9	5 25	7 12	7 29	11 49	..	8 6	8 23	235
24	Tu	60	3 25	3 41	0 28	0 44	11 50	..	5 42	5 58	7 46	8 1	0 7	0 24	8 38	8 53	236
25	W	60	3 56	4 12	0 59	1 14	0 6	0 21	6 14	6 29	8 16	8 31	0 41	0 57	9 6	9 20	237
26	Th	60	4 28	4 43	1 29	1 45	0 37	0 52	6 45	7 2	8 46	9 2	1 14	1 31	9 34	9 48	238
27	F	60	4 57	5 13	2 0	2 16	1 8	1 24	7 19	7 36	9 19	9 35	1 48	2 5	10 3	10 18	239
28	S	60	5 29	5 45	2 32	2 49	1 41	1 58	7 53	8 11	9 52	10 9	2 22	2 40	10 33	10 49	240
29	S	60	6 3	6 22	3 7	3 27	2 16	2 36	8 31	8 55	10 28	10 51	2 58	3 17	11 6	11 25	241
30	M	59	6 42	7 5	3 48	4 15	2 57	3 22	9 20	9 50	11 18	11 49	3 38	4 2	11 48	..	242
31	Tu	59	7 31	8 3	4 46	5 22	3 49	4 20	10 22	11 0	..	0 22	4 27	4 55	0 12	0 41	243

RISING and SETTING of SEVEN PRINCIPAL PLANETS on the 5th, 15th, and 25th.

D.	MERCURY ☿ Rises h.m.	Sets h.m.	VENUS ♀ Rises h.m.	Sets h.m.	MARS ♂ Rises h.m.	Sets h.m.	JUPITER ♃ Rises h.m.	Sets h.m.	SATURN ♄ Rises h.m.	Sets h.m.	URANUS ♅ Rises h.m.	Sets h.m.	NEPTUNE ♆ Rises h.m.	Sets h.m.
5	3 42M	7 32A	6 45M	8 35A	10 0M	9 24A	10 40A	4 1A	3 29A	11 49A	2 21M	6 35A	9 44A	10 52M
15	5 2M	7 38A	7 16M	8 16A	9 57M	8 35A	10 2A	3 8A	2 50A	11 10A	1 44M	5 58A	9 4A	10 12M
25	6 12M	7 28A	7 47M	7 55A	9 55M	8 25A	9 24A	2 32A	2 11A	10 31A	1 8M	5 20A	8 24A	9 32M

ECLIPSES, OCCULTATIONS, AND OTHER CELESTIAL PHENOMENA.

August 1. Day breaks at 1h. 31m. morn., and twilight ends at 10h. 41m. aft., the length of the day being 15h. 21m.

Aug. 1. Mercury in Perihelion, 8h. 50m. morn.

Aug. 3. Occultation of α Tauri (Aldebaran). The disappearance takes place at 0h. 22m. morn. 56° from the vertex. The reappearance at 1h. 13m. morn., 259° from the vertex.

Aug. 7-8. A Total Eclipse of the Sun, invisible at Greenwich, begins on the earth generally at 7h. 38m. aft. Longitude 144° 20' E., and latitude 36° 54' N. Ends on the 8th, at 0h. 24m. morn., in longitude 90° 11' W., and latitude 14° 53' N.

Aug. 12. Mercury in superior conjunction with the Sun, 4h. 40m. morn.

Aug. 14. Saturn stationary in the heavens, 11h. 26m. aft.

Aug. 23. Sun enters Virgo, 3h. 43m. morn.

In this month the mornings have decreased 48m., and the afternoons 59m.

* The Temperature column gives the daily average of the Thermometer for 50 years.

Days of		Fasts and Festivals. Remarkable Days—Events.	THE SUN.			THE MOON.			Days to end of the year.
M.	W.		Rises.	Sets.	After Clock.	Rises after.	Souths morn.	Sets after.	
			H. M.	H. M.	M. S.	H. M.	H. M.	H. M.	
1	S	10th Sunday after Trinity.	4 26	7 47	6 1	11 39	6 18	1 33	152
2	M	[*Lammas Day.*	4 27	7 45	5 58	Morn.	7 4	2 40	151
3	Tu	Bank of England founded, 1732.	4 28	7 44	5 53	0 10	7 54	3 47	150
4	W	Oyster season commences.	4 30	7 42	5 48	0 49	8 47	4 52	149
5	Th	[b. 1844.	4 31	7 40	5 42	1 37	9 44	5 53	148
6	F	*Transfiguration.* D. of Edinburgh	4 33	7 38	5 36	2 35	10 42	6 45	147
7	S	*Name of Jesus.*	4 35	7 37	5 29	3 44	11 42	7 29	146
8	S	11th Sunday after Trinity.	4 36	7 35	5 22	5 0	Aftn.	8 6	145
9	M	♀ ☌ ☾ 3h. 57m. aft.	4 38	7 33	5 14	6 23	1 37	8 37	144
10	Tu	St. Lawrence.	4 39	7 31	5 5	7 45	2 32	9 5	143
11	W	Half quarter day.	4 41	7 29	4 56	9 7	3 26	9 30	142
12	Th	Grouse shooting begins.	4 42	7 27	4 46	10 28	4 18	9 55	141
13	F	♃ rises 10h. 10m. aft.	4 44	7 25	4 36	11 47	5 10	10 22	140
14	S	♄ stationary 11h. 26m. aft.	4 46	7 23	4 25	Aftn.	6 2	10 51	139
15	S	12th Sunday after Trinity.	4 47	7 21	4 13	2 16	6 54	11 26	138
16	M	Length of day 14h. 29m.	4 50	7 19	4 1	3 24	7 47	Morn.	137
17	Tu	Gower died, 1402.	4 50	7 17	3 49	4 26	8 40	0 6	136
18	W	Earl Russell born, 1792.	4 52	7 15	3 36	5 19	9 32	0 53	135
19	Th	♄ sets 10h. 54m. aft.	4 53	7 13	3 22	6 3	10 22	1 46	134
20	F	Blackcock shooting commences.	4 55	7 11	3 8	6 38	11 11	2 45	133
21	S	♂ sets 8h. 37m. aft.	4 57	7 9	2 54	7 9	11 57	3 48	132
22	S	13th Sunday after Trinity.	4 58	7 7	2 39	7 35	Morn.	4 54	131
23	M	Treaty of Prague, 1866.	5 0	7 5	2 23	7 57	0 42	5 59	130
24	Tu	St. Bartholomew.	5 1	7 3	2 7	8 17	1 25	7 2	129
25	W	Chatterton died, 1770.	5 3	7 1	1 51	8 36	2 7	8 6	128
26	Th	Prince Albert born, 1819.	5 5	6 59	1 34	8 57	2 48	9 10	127
27	F	Landing of Julius Cæsar, B.C. 55	5 6	6 57	1 17	9 18	3 30	10 16	126
28	S	*Augustine.*	5 9	6 54	1 0	9 42	4 13	11 20	125
29	S	14th Sunday after Trinity.	5 9	6 52	0 42	10 9	4 58	Aftn.	124
30	M	Peace with China, 1842.	5 11	6 50	0 24	10 42	5 45	1 31	123
31	Tu	John Bunyan died, 1688.	5 14	6 48	0 6	11 25	6 35	2 35	122

PHASES OF THE MOON.

● New Moon   7d. 10h. 8m. After.
☽ First Quarter 14   0 41 After.
○ Full Moon   22   4 24 Morn.
☾ Last Quarter 30   7 58 Morn.

In Perigee 9d. 1h. A. | In Apogee 25d. 2h. M.

RAINFALL IN AUGUST, 1868.

In this month rain fell during 10 days. The total fall for the month was 2·28 inches; an amount, more than the average, since 1860, of 0·64 inches.

MORNING AND EVENING STARS.

☿ Mercury, a morning star, may be seen, for a few mornings, early in this month; in conjunction with the Moon on the 7th, at 1h. 57m. aft.

♀ Venus an evening star; in conjunction with the Moon on the 9th, at 3h. 57m. aft.

♂ Mars in conjunction with the Moon on the 11th, at 6h. 20m. aft. near Spica Virginis on 23rd.

♃ Jupiter in conjunction with the Moon on the 1st, at 10h. 38m. morn., and again on the 28th, at 10h. 37m. aft.

♄ Saturn in conjunction with the Moon on the 15th, at 9h. 19m. aft.

Time of High Water at the undermentioned Ports—

Day of Month	Week	Average daily Temperature.*	LOND. BDGE. Morn.	LOND. BDGE. After.	LIVERPOOL. Morn.	LIVERPOOL. After.	S'HAMPTON. Morn.	S'HAMPTON. After.	NEWCASTLE. Morn.	NEWCASTLE. After.	HULL. Morn.	HULL. After.	DOVER. Morn.	DOVER. After.	BRISTOL. Morn.	BRISTOL. After.	Day of the Year.
		Deg.	H. M.	H. M.	H. M.	H. M	H. M.	H. M.	H. M.	H. M.	H. M	H. M	H. M.	H. M.	H. M.	H. M.	
1	W	59	8 40	9 20	6 4	6 49	4 57	5 37	11 39	..	0 56	1 31	5 28	6 5	1 19	2 2	244
2	Th	59	10 1	10 41	7 32	8 11	6 21	7 1	0 19	1 0	2 9	2 48	6 47	7 27	2 51	3 36	245
3	F	58	11 20	11 55	8 46	9 15	7 40	8 13	1 36	2 8	3 25	4 0	8 4	8 36	4 17	4 51	246
4	S	58	..	..	9 41	10 5	8 43	9 9	2 36	3 2	4 30	4 58	9 6	9 33	5 22	5 50	247
5	S	58	0 55	1 20	10 28	10 51	9 33	9 56	3 25	3 47	5 22	5 45	9 59	10 23	6 17	6 43	248
6	M	58	1 44	2 6	11 14	11 38	10 18	10 41	4 8	4 29	6 8	6 32	10 48	11 14	7 8	7 32	249
7	Tu	58	2 30	2 53	..	0 1	11 5	11 29	4 52	5 15	6 55	7 18	11 38	..	7 55	8 18	250
8	W	58	3 14	3 37	0 24	0 47	11 52	..	5 38	6 1	7 41	8 3	0 3	0 27	8 41	9 2	251
9	Th	58	3 59	4 21	1 9	1 30	0 15	0 37	6 24	6 46	8 25	8 46	0 51	1 15	9 21	9 40	252
10	F	58	4 42	5 3	1 51	2 12	0 58	1 20	7 8	7 31	9 8	9 30	1 38	2 0	9 59	10 19	253
11	S	58	5 24	5 46	2 33	2 55	1 41	2 3	7 53	8 17	9 52	10 14	2 22	2 45	10 38	10 57	254
12	S	57	6 9	6 32	3 17	3 41	2 26	2 50	8 43	9 11	10 39	11 8	3 7	3 31	11 19	11 43	255
13	M	57	6 58	7 27	4 10	4 43	3 16	3 43	9 43	10 19	11 42	..	3 57	4 24	..	0 9	256
14	Tu	57	7 58	8 32	5 22	6 6	4 19	4 58	11 0	11 41	0 17	0 54	4 54	5 29	0 41	1 21	257
15	W	57	9 21	10 4	6 53	7 35	5 42	6 24	..	0 23	1 32	2 13	6 9	6 50	2 7	2 55	258
16	Th	57	10 47	11 27	8 14	8 49	7 5	7 43	1 2	1 39	2 51	3 28	7 31	8 8	3 40	4 21	259
17	F	57	..	0 1	9 17	9 41	8 15	8 42	2 11	2 48	4 3	4 32	8 38	9 8	4 53	5 21	260
18	S	56	0 30	0 54	10 2	10 20	9 5	9 24	3 1	3 21	4 57	5 17	9 28	9 48	5 45	6 6	261
19	S	56	1 16	1 37	10 37	10 54	9 42	9 59	3 40	3 56	5 36	5 54	10 8	10 27	6 27	6 47	262
20	M	56	1 55	2 11	11 11	11 27	10 16	10 32	4 12	4 27	6 12	6 29	10 45	11 3	7 5	7 22	263
21	Tu	56	2 27	2 43	11 43	11 59	10 47	11 3	4 43	4 58	6 45	7 1	11 20	11 37	7 38	7 54	264
22	W	56	2 57	3 12	..	0 14	11 19	11 35	5 13	5 29	7 17	7 33	11 54	..	8 10	8 24	265
23	Th	55	3 28	3 42	0 29	0 45	11 51	..	5 44	6 0	7 47	8 2	0 10	0 26	8 39	8 53	266
24	F	55	3 58	4 13	1 0	1 14	0 6	0 22	6 15	6 30	8 16	8 31	0 43	0 59	9 6	9 19	267
25	S	55	4 26	4 41	1 29	1 44	0 36	0 51	6 46	7 2	8 46	9 2	1 15	1 31	9 33	9 47	268
26	S	55	4 58	5 14	2 0	2 16	1 7	1 24	7 19	7 36	9 18	9 35	1 48	2 6	10 2	10 18	269
27	M	54	5 30	5 48	2 34	2 53	1 42	2 2	7 55	8 17	9 53	10 14	2 24	2 43	10 35	10 53	270
28	Tu	54	6 9	6 33	3 15	3 40	2 23	2 47	8 42	9 12	10 39	11 9	3 4	3 28	11 16	11 41	271
29	W	54	6 58	7 28	4 11	4 48	3 15	3 48	9 45	10 24	11 44	...	3 53	4 25	..	0 11	272
30	Th	54	8 4	8 46	5 32	6 19	4 27	5 9	11 9	11 51	0 22	1 2	5 1	5 39	0 48	1 32	273

Rising and Setting of Seven Principal Planets on the 5th, 15th, and 25th.

D.	MERCURY ☿ Rises h. m.	Sets h. m.	VENUS ♀ Rises h. m.	Sets h. m.	MARS ♂ Rises h. m.	Sets h. m.	JUPITER ♃ Rises h. m.	Sets h. m.	SATURN ♄ Rises h. m.	Sets h. m.	URANUS ♅ Rises h. m.	Sets h. m.	NEPTUNE ♆ Rises h. m.	Sets h. m.
5	7 15M	7 7A	8 20M	7 30A	9 54M	7 54A	8 42A	11 50M	1 30A	9 48A	0 26M	4 38A	7 40A	8 48M
15	8 1M	6 41A	8 57M	7 9A	9 52M	7 28A	3 A	11 11M	0 52A	9 10A	11 46A	4 0A	7 0A	8 8M
25	8 32M	6 16A	9 24M	6 50A	9 53M	7 1A	7 23A	10 29M	0 16A	8 32A	11 9A	3 22A	6 20A	7 26M

ECLIPSES, OCCULTATIONS, AND OTHER CELESTIAL PHENOMENA.

September 1. Day breaks at 3h. 9m. morn., and twilight ends at 8h. 51m. aft., the length of the Day being 13h. 32m.

Sept. 9. Jupiter stationary in the heavens, 9h. 20m. aft.

Sept. 13. Occultation of μ_1 Sagittarii. The disappearance takes place at 5h. 34m. aft., 141° from the vertex. The reappearance at 6h. 4m. aft., 190° from the vertex.

Sept. 14. Mercury in Aphelion, 8h. 28m. morn.

Sept. 23. Sun enters Libra, 0h. 28m. morn. Autumn commences.

Sept. 24. Occultation of ξ^2 Ceti. The disappearance takes place at 0h. 20m. morn., 62° from the vertex. The reappearance at 1h. 27m., 320° from the vertex.

Sept. 25. (4h. 52m. aft.) Mercury at greatest elongation East = 26°.

In this month the mornings decrease 47m., and the afternoons 1h. 7m.

* The Temperature column gives the daily average of the Thermometer for 50 years.

Days of M.	Days of W.	Fasts and Festivals. Remarkable Days—Events.	THE SUN. Rises. H. M.	THE SUN. Sets. H. M.	THE SUN. Before Clock. M. S.	THE MOON. Rises after. H. M.	THE MOON. Souths morn. H. M.	THE MOON. Sets after. H. M.	Days to end of the year.
1	W	*St. Giles.* Partridge shooting com.	5 14	6 46	0 13	Morn.	7 29	3 37	121
2	Th	London burnt, 1666, O. S.	5 16	6 43	0 32	0 17	8 25	4 32	120
3	F	Battle of Dunbar, 1650.	5 17	6 41	0 51	1 20	9 23	5 19	119
4	S	☿ in ☋ 4*h.* 10*m. morn.*	5 19	6 39	1 10	2 33	10 22	5 59	118
5	**S**	**15th Sunday after Trinity.**	5 21	6 37	1 30	3 54	11 20	6 33	117
6	M	Commenc. of Jewish year 5630.	5 22	6 34	1 50	5 15	Aftn.	7 3	116
7	Tu	*Enurchus.* Sevastopol tkn. 1855	5 24	6 32	2 10	6 40	1 13	7 30	115
8	W	*Nativity of the B. Virgin Mary.*	5 25	6 30	2 30	8 5	2 7	7 56	114
9	Th	Battle of Flodden Field, 1513.	5 27	6 28	2 51	9 28	3 1	8 22	113
10	F	☉ Semidiameter 15′ 56″.	5 29	6 25	3 11	10 49	3 55	8 52	112
11	S	Mahomet born, 569.	5 30	6 23	3 32	Aftn.	4 49	9 25	111
12	**S**	**16th Sunday after Trinity.**	5 32	6 21	3 53	1 17	5 43	10 5	110
13	M	Charles J. Fox died, 1806.	5 33	6 18	4 14	2 21	6 36	10 49	109
14	Tu	*Holy Cross Day.* Holy Rood.	5 35	6 16	4 35	3 17	7 29	11 42	108
15	W	Ember week.	5 37	6 14	4 56	4 4	8 19	Morn.	107
16	Th		5 38	6 12	5 17	4 41	9 8	0 38	106
17	F	*Lambert.* Ember Day.	5 40	6 9	5 39	5 12	9 55	1 40	105
18	S	Ember Day.	5 41	6 7	6 0	5 39	10 40	2 44	104
19	**S**	**17th Sunday after Trinity.**	5 43	6 5	6 21	6 1	11 23	3 49	103
20	M	☿ sets 6*h.* 28*m. aft.*	5 44	6 2	6 42	6 22	Morn.	4 54	102
21	Tu	**St. Matthew.**	5 46	6 0	7 3	6 42	0 5	5 59	101
22	W	Virgil died, 19 B.C.	5 48	5 57	7 24	7 2	0 47	7 3	100
23	Th	New Post Office opened, 1829.	5 49	5 55	7 45	7 23	1 29	8 7	99
24	F	Samuel Butler died, 1680.	5 51	5 53	8 6	7 46	2 11	9 11	98
25	S	Lucknow relieved, 1857.	5 53	5 51	8 27	8 11	2 55	10 16	97
26	**S**	**18th Sunday aft Trin.** *Cyprian.*	5 54	5 48	8 47	8 41	3 41	11 23	96
27	M	♀ sets 6*h.* 47*m. aft.*	5 56	5 46	9 7	9 18	4 29	Aftn.	95
28	Tu	☾'s Ascending Node 4° 23′ ☊	5 57	5 44	9 27	10 5	5 20	1 27	94
29	W	**St. Michael.** Michaelmas Day.	5 59	5 42	9 47	11 2	6 14	2 23	93
30	Th	*St. Jerome.*	6 1	5 39	10 6	Morn.	7 9	3 12	92

PHASES OF THE MOON.

● New Moon	6*d.*	6*h.*	7*m.*	Morn.
☽ First Quarter	12	9	23	After.
○ Full Moon	20	8	41	After.
☾ Last Quarter	28	9	10	After.

In Perigee 6*d.* 8*h.* A. | In Apogee 21*d.* 8*h.* M.

RAINFALL IN SEPTEMBER, 1868.

In this month rain fell during 10 days. The total fall for the month was 1·74 inch; an amount less than the average, since 1860, of 0·52 inch.

MORNING AND EVENING STARS.

♀ Venus an evening star; in conjunction with the Moon on the 8*th*, at 9*h.* 22*m. morn.*

♂ Mars visible in the south-west after sunset; in conjunction with the Moon on the 9*th*, at 9*h.* 10*m. morn.*

♃ Jupiter rises on the 15*th*, at 8*h.* 3*m. aft.*, and will be visible all the night; in conjunction with the Moon on the 25*th*, at 4*h.* 39*m. morn.*

♄ Saturn visible in the South-west for a short time after sunset; in conjunction with the Moon on the 12*th*, at 4*h.* 42*m. morn.*

Time of High Water at the undermentioned Ports—

Day of Month	Week	Average daily Temperature*	LOND. BDGE. Morn.	LOND. BDGE. After.	LIVERPOOL Morn.	LIVERPOOL After.	S'HAMPTON Morn.	S'HAMPTON After.	NEWCASTLE Morn.	NEWCASTLE After.	HULL Morn.	HULL After.	DOVER Morn.	DOVER After.	BRISTOL Morn.	BRISTOL After.	Day of the Year
		Deg.	H. M.	H. M.	H. M.	H. M.	H. M.	H. M.	H. M.	H. M.	H. M.	H. M.	H. M.	H. M.	H. M.	H. M.	
1	F	54	9 32	10 16	7 5	7 46	5 53	6 35	..	0 32	1 42	2 22	6 19	7 1	2 22	3 9	274
2	S	54	10 58	11 36	8 25	8 54	7 16	7 51	1 12	1 47	3 1	3 28	7 41	8 15	3 53	4 28	275
3	S	54	..	0 7	9 20	9 44	8 19	8 47	2 15	2 40	4 9	4 36	8 42	9 10	4 58	5 27	276
4	M	54	0 34	0 59	10 7	10 29	9 12	9 34	3 4	3 27	5 0	5 23	9 36	10 0	5 54	6 20	277
5	Tu	53	1 22	1 46	10 52	11 15	9 56	10 18	3 47	4 8	5 46	6 9	10 24	10 49	6 45	7 9	278
6	W	53	2 7	2 29	11 37	11 59	10 41	11 4	4 30	4 52	6 32	6 55	11 13	11 37	7 32	7 55	279
7	Th	52	2 51	3 14	...	0 22	11 28	11 50	5 14	5 36	7 17	7 39	...	0 2	8 17	8 38	280
8	F	52	3 35	3 56	0 44	1 6	..	0 12	5 58	6 21	8 0	8 22	0 26	0 49	8 58	9 18	281
9	S	52	4 17	4 39	1 27	1 48	0 34	0 56	6 44	7 6	8 44	9 6	1 12	1 35	9 37	9 54	282
10	S	52	5 0	5 21	2 9	2 30	1 16	1 38	7 27	7 50	9 27	9 49	1 56	2 19	10 13	10 34	283
11	M	52	5 42	6 5	2 52	3 16	2 1	2 25	8 16	8 44	10 14	10 41	2 43	3 6	10 55	11 18	284
12	Tu	51	6 32	7 0	3 42	4 13	2 49	3 17	9 14	9 48	11 12	11 47	3 30	3 56	11 43	..	285
13	W	51	7 31	8 8	4 51	5 35	3 50	4 30	10 29	11 12	..	0 26	4 27	5 3	0 13	0 51	286
14	Th	50	8 51	9 36	6 25	7 9	5 13	5 56	11 55	..	1 6	1 46	5 43	6 23	1 27	2 26	287
15	F	50	10 20	10 59	7 48	8 23	6 36	7 14	0 37	1 14	2 25	3 3	7 3	7 40	3 11	3 50	288
16	S	50	11 34	..	8 51	9 14	7 46	8 12	1 45	2 13	3 36	4 6	8 11	8 36	4 24	4 51	289
17	S	50	0 3	0 27	9 34	9 53	8 35	8 56	2 35	2 54	4 30	4 50	8 58	9 19	5 14	5 36	290
18	M	50	0 48	1 7	10 9	10 25	9 13	9 29	3 12	3 29	5 8	5 25	9 37	9 55	5 55	6 14	291
19	Tu	49	1 25	1 42	10 41	10 57	9 45	10 1	3 44	3 58	5 41	5 57	10 13	10 30	6 32	6 50	292
20	W	49	1 57	2 12	11 13	11 28	10 17	10 32	4 13	4 28	6 14	6 31	10 47	11 4	7 7	7 22	293
21	Th	49	2 28	2 43	11 44	12 0	10 48	11 4	4 43	4 58	6 46	7 1	11 21	11 38	7 38	7 55	294
22	F	49	2 58	3 14	...	0 16	11 21	11 37	5 14	5 30	7 17	7 33	11 55	..	8 11	8 25	295
23	S	49	3 29	3 43	0 31	0 47	11 53	..	5 45	6 1	7 47	8 3	0 11	0 28	8 40	8 55	296
24	S	48	3 59	4 15	1 3	1 19	0 10	0 27	6 18	6 35	8 19	8 36	0 46	1 5	9 10	9 24	297
25	M	48	4 30	4 47	1 36	1 54	0 43	1 2	6 53	7 13	8 54	9 13	1 23	1 42	9 40	9 58	298
26	Tu	48	5 5	5 24	2 13	2 33	1 22	1 42	7 34	7 56	9 33	9 54	2 3	2 24	10 16	10 35	299
27	W	48	5 46	6 10	2 55	3 20	2 4	2 28	8 21	8 50	10 17	10 45	2 45	3 9	10 58	11 22	300
28	Th	47	6 36	7 6	3 49	4 25	2 55	3 28	9 22	10 1	11 20	12 0	3 36	4 6	11 52	..	301
29	F	47	7 42	8 24	5 7	5 54	4 4	4 46	10 45	11 28	..	0 40	4 39	5 17	0 26	1 8	302
30	S	47	8 9	9 52	6 43	7 23	5 31	6 11	..	0 10	1 21	2 1	5 57	6 37	1 57	2 43	303
31	S	47	10 33	11 11	7 58	8 28	6 49	7 23	0 49	1 22	2 37	3 11	7 15	7 48	3 24	4 1	304

RISING and SETTING of SEVEN PRINCIPAL PLANETS on the 5th, 15th, and 25th.

D.	MERCURY ☿ Rises	MERCURY ☿ Sets	VENUS ♀ Rises	VENUS ♀ Sets	MARS ♂ Rises	MARS ♂ Sets	JUPITER ♃ Rises	JUPITER ♃ Sets	SATURN ♄ Rises	SATURN ♄ Sets	URANUS ♅ Rises	URANUS ♅ Sets	NEPTUNE ♆ Rises	NEPTUNE ♆ Sets
	h. m.	h. m.	h. m.	h. m.	h. m.	h. m.	h. m.	h. m.	h. m.	h. m.	h. m.	h. m.	h. m.	h. m.
5	8 38M	5 44A	9 55M	6 33A	9 53M	6 39A	6 42A	9 46M	11 47M	7 55A	10 30A	2 43A	5 40A	6 46M
15	8 38M	5 6A	10 26M	6 22A	9 54M	6 16A	6 1A	9 1M	11 6M	7 18A	9 52A	2 4A	5 1A	6 5M
25	5 47M	5 6A	10 53M	6 17A	9 54M	5 58A	5 19A	8 15M	10 31M	6 43A	9 13A	1 25A	4 22A	6 24M

ECLIPSES, OCCULTATIONS, AND OTHER CELESTIAL PHENOMENA.

October 1. Day breaks at 4h. 9m. morn., and twilight ends at 7h. 31m. aft., the length of the day being 11h. 35m.

Oct. 8. Mercury stationary in the heavens, 2h. 55m. aft.

Oct. 17. Occultation of Ψ1 Aquarii. The disappearance takes place at 0h. 43m. morn., 90° from the vertex. The reappearance at 1h. 22m. morn., 22° from the vertex.

Oct. 18. Venus in Aphelion, 10h. 55m. aft.

Oct. 20. Mercury in inferior conjunction with the Sun, 8h. 56m. morn.

Oct. 23. Sun enters Scorpio, 8h. 48m. morn.

Oct. 26. Occultation of ν Geminorum. The disappearance takes place at 0h. 25m. morn., 22° from the vertex. The reappearance at 1h. 22m. morn., 279° from the vertex.

Oct. 26. Venus and Saturn in conjunction, 2h. 7m. morn.

Oct. 28. Mercury in Perihelion, 8h. 9m. morn.

Oct. 28. Mercury stationary in the heavens, 9h. 6m. aft.

In this month the mornings decrease 52m., and the afternoons 1h. 3m.

* The Temperature column gives the daily average of the Thermometer for 50 years.

Days of M.	Days of W.	Fasts and Festivals. Remarkable Days—Events.	THE SUN. Rises. H. M.	Sets. H. M.	Before Clock. M. S.	THE MOON. Rises morn. H. M.	Souths morn. H. M.	Sets after. H. M.	Days to end of the year.
1	F	*Remigius.* Cambridge Term com.	6 2	5 37	10 25	0 9	8 6	3 53	91
2	S	[Pheasant shooting.	6 4	5 35	10 44	1 23	9 3	4 29	90
3	S	**19th Sunday after Trinity.**	6 6	5 32	11 3	2 43	9 59	5 0	89
4	M	New River finished, 1614.	6 7	5 30	11 21	4 7	10 55	5 27	88
5	Tu	First English Bible print., 1536	6 9	5 28	11 38	5 31	11 50	5 54	87
6	W	*Faith, Virg. and Mart.*	6 11	5 26	11 56	6 56	Aftn.	6 21	86
7	Th	Treaty of Aix-la-Chapelle, 1748	6 12	5 23	12 13	8 20	1 41	6 49	85
8	F	☿ stationary *2h. 55m. aft.*	6 14	5 21	12 29	9 43	2 36	7 21	84
9	S	*St. Denys.*	6 16	5 19	12 46	11 0	3 32	7 58	83
10	S	**20th Sunday after Trinity.**	6 17	5 17	13 1	Aftn.	4 28	8 42	82
11	M	Oxford Term commences.	6 19	5 15	13 17	1 11	5 22	9 32	81
12	Tu	Robert Stephenson died, 1859.	6 21	5 12	13 31	2 2	6 15	10 29	80
13	W	*Transl. K. Edward Conf.*	6 23	5 10	13 46	2 42	7 5	11 31	79
14	Th	Fire Insur. ceases. Divid. due.	6 24	5 8	14 0	3 16	7 53	Morn.	78
15	F	Length of day *10h. 40m.*	6 26	5 6	14 13	3 43	8 38	0 35	77
16	S	Houses of Parlm. burnt, 1834.	6 28	5 4	14 26	4 8	9 22	1 40	76
17	S	**21st Sun. after Trin.** *Etheldreda.*	6 29	5 1	14 38	4 30	10 4	2 45	75
18	M	**St. Luke Evangelist.**	6 31	4 59	14 49	4 49	10 46	3 49	74
19	Tu	Dean Swift died, 1745.	6 33	4 57	15 0	5 8	11 27	4 53	73
20	W	Battle of Navarino, 1827.	6 35	4 55	15 11	5 29	Morn.	5 57	72
21	Th	Bat. Trafalgar; Nelson k., 1805	6 36	4 53	15 20	5 49	0 10	7 4	71
22	F	Revoc. Edict of Nantes, 1685.	6 38	4 51	15 29	6 14	0 53	8 9	70
23	S	Battle of Edgehill, 1642.	6 40	4 49	15 38	6 42	1 39	9 17	69
24	S	**22nd Sunday after Trinity.**	6 42	4 47	15 45	7 17	2 26	10 19	68
25	M	*St. Crispin.*	6 43	4 45	15 52	8 0	3 16	11 22	67
26	Tu	Wreck of Royal Charter, 1859.	6 45	4 43	15 58	8 53	4 8	Aftn.	66
27	W	M. Servetus burned, 1553.	6 47	4 41	16 4	9 53	5 2	1 9	65
28	Th	**St. Simon and St. Jude.**	6 49	4 39	16 8	11 3	5 57	1 52	64
29	F	Hare Hunting begins.	6 50	4 37	16 12	Morn.	6 52	2 29	63
30	S	King Alfred died, 900.	6 52	4 35	16 15	0 18	7 46	2 59	62
31	S	**23rd Sunday after Trinity.**	6 54	4 34	16 17	1 38	8 40	3 27	61

PHASES OF THE MOON.

● New Moon	*5d.*	*2h.*	*20m.*	After.
☽ First Quarter	12	10	3	Morn.
○ Full Moon	20	1	57	After.
☾ Last Quarter	28	8	34	Morn.

In Perigee *5d. 7h.* M. | In Apogee *18d. 10h.* M.

RAINFALL IN OCTOBER, 1867.

In this month there were 16 days on which rain fell. The total rainfall was 1·92 inch; being 0·68 inch *less* than the average of the preceding seven years.

MORNING AND EVENING STARS.

♀ VENUS an evening star; in conjunction with the Moon on the *8th*, at *5h. 42m. morn.*; and with Mars on the *6th*, at *10h. 32m. morn.*

♂ MARS an evening star, setting nearly at the same time as Venus; in conjunction with the Moon on the *8th*, at *4h. 9m. morn.*

♃ JUPITER rises soon after sunset; in conjunction with the Moon on the *22nd*, at *5h. 34m. morn.*

♄ SATURN may be seen for a short time after sunset in the south-west; in conjunction with the Moon on the *9th*, at *4h. 3m. aft.*

Time of High Water at the undermentioned Ports—

Month	Week	Average daily Temperature	Lond. Bdge. Morn.	Lond. Bdge. After.	Liverpool Morn.	Liverpool After.	S'hampton Morn.	S'hampton After.	Newcastle Morn.	Newcastle After.	Hull Morn.	Hull After.	Dover Morn.	Dover After.	Bristol Morn.	Bristol After.	Day of the Year
		Deg.	H. M.	H. M.	H. M.	H. M.	H. M.	H. M.	H. M.	H. M.	H. M.	H. M.	H. M.	H. M.	H. M.	H. M.	
1	M	46	11 43	..	8 56	9 20	7 55	8 22	1 50	2 16	3 43	4 12	8 18	8 45	4 33	5 1	305
2	Tu	46	0·10	0 36	9 43	10 5	8 47	9 10	2 40	3 3	4 36	4 59	9 10	9 35	5 28	5 54	306
3	W	46	1 0	1 22	10 28	10 51	9 33	9 56	3 25	3 45	5 22	5 45	10 0	10 24	6 19	6 45	307
4	Th	46	1 44	2 6	11 14	11 37	10 18	10 41	4 8	4 30	6 9	6 32	10 49	11 14	7 9	7 32	308
5	F	46	2 27	2 50	12 0	..	11 5	11 28	4 52	5 14	6 55	7 18	11 38	..	7 55	8 17	309
6	S	45	3 13	3 34	0 22	0 44	11 50	..	5 36	5 58	7 40	8 1	0 2	0 25	8 37	8 57	310
7	S	45	3 56	4 17	1 5	1 26	0 12	0 33	6 21	6 43	8 22	8 43	0 49	1 12	9 16	9 35	311
8	M	45	4 37	4 59	1 47	2 8	0 54	1 16	7 5	7 28	9 5	9 27	1 34	1 57	9 54	10 14	312
9	Tu	45	5 21	5 43	2 31	2 54	1 39	2 3	7 52	8 18	9 50	10 15	2 20	2 44	10 34	10 56	313
10	W	44	6 8	6 35	3 19	3 47	2 27	2 53	8 47	9 19	10 44	11 17	3 8	3 34	11 20	11 46	314
11	Th	44	7 3	7 35	4 18	4 55	3 21	3 54	9 54	10 33	11 53	..	4 0	4 30	..	0 15	315
12	F	44	8 13	8 53	5 38	6 21	4 32	5 10	11 14	11 52	0 30	1 7	5 4	5 39	0 53	1 34	316
13	S	43	9 32	10 11	7 0	7 35	5 48	6 24	..	0 28	1 43	2 17	6 14	6 50	2 17	2 57	317
14	S	43	10 47	11 18	8 7	8 34	6 58	7 28	1 1	1 31	2 50	3 21	7 24	7 53	3 34	4 5	318
15	M	43	11 45	..	8 57	9 17	7 53	8 16	1 56	2 18	3 48	4 12	8 18	8 40	4 31	4 55	319
16	Tu	42	0 9	0 31	9 35	9 53	8 37	8 56	2 37	2 55	4 33	4 51	9 0	9 19	5 16	5 36	320
17	W	42	0 50	1 9	10 9	10 25	9 13	9 30	3 12	3 28	5 8	5 25	9 37	9 56	5 55	6 15	321
18	Th	42	1 28	1 44	10 42	10 59	9 47	10 3	3 44	3 59	5 42	5 59	10 15	10 32	6 34	6 52	322
19	F	42	2 0	2 16	11 16	11 33	10 20	10 37	4 15	4 31	6 16	6 34	10 51	11 10	7 10	7 28	323
20	S	42	2 32	2 48	11 50	..	10 54	11 13	4 48	5 5	6 15	7 8	11 28	11 47	7 45	8 3	324
21	M	41	3 4	3 22	0 8	0 26	11 31	11 49	5 22	5 40	7 26	7 43	..	0 6	8 20	8 36	325
22	M	41	3 39	3 56	0 43	1 1	..	0 8	5 58	6 16	8 0	8 18	0 25	0 45	8 53	9 10	326
23	Tu	41	4 13	4 31	1 19	1 38	0 27	0 46	6 36	6 57	8 36	8 57	1 5	1 26	9 27	9 46	327
24	W	41	4 51	5 13	1 59	2 21	1 7	1 29	7 19	7 42	9 19	9 41	1 48	2 11	10 6	10 27	328
25	Th	40	5 36	6 1	2 44	3 10	1 53	2 18	8 7	8 37	10 5	10 33	2 34	2 59	10 49	11 14	329
26	F	41	6 27	6 56	3 38	4 10	2 45	3 15	9 9	9 44	11 6	11 43	3 26	3 55	11 41	..	330
27	S	41	7 27	8 3	4 47	5 28	3 48	4 24	10 23	11 6	..	0 22	4 25	4 58	0 11	0 45	331
28	S	42	8 43	9 23	6 10	6 51	5 1	5 39	11 43	..	1 0	1 35	5 32	6 6	1 24	2 6	332
29	M	41	10 1	10 38	7 26	7 59	6 16	6 51	0 19	0 53	2 9	2 41	6 41	7 17	2 48	3 26	333
30	Tu	42	11 12	11 41	8 28	8 55	7 24	7 55	1 23	1 50	3 13	3 47	7 49	8 18	4 1	4 33	334

RISING and SETTING of SEVEN PRINCIPAL PLANETS on the 5th, 15th, and 25th.

D.	Mercury ☿ Rises h. m.	Sets h. m.	Venus ♀ Rises h. m.	Sets h. m.	Mars ♂ Rises h. m.	Sets h. m.	Jupiter ♃ Rises h. m.	Sets h. m.	Saturn ♄ Rises h. m.	Sets h. m.	Uranus ♅ Rises h. m.	Sets h. m.	Neptune ♆ Rises h. m.	Sets h. m.
5	5 9M	4 1A	11 16M	6 20A	9 55M	5 39A	4 32A	7 24A	9 53M	6 3A	8 30A	0 42A	3 38A	4 40M
15	5 45M	3 45A	11 27M	6 31A	9 54A	5 26A	3 49A	6 37M	9 20M	5 28A	7 50A	0 2A	2 58A	3 58M
25	6 37M	3 35A	11 28M	6 50A	9 51A	5 17A	3 8A	5 50M	8 46M	4 52A	7 9A	11 23M	2 19A	3 17M

ECLIPSES, OCCULTATIONS, AND OTHER CELESTIAL PHENOMENA.

November 1. Day breaks at 5h. 1m. *morn,* and twilight ends at 6h. 27m. *aft.,* the length of the Day being 9h. 36m.

Nov. 5. (4h. 29m. *morn.*) Mercury at greatest elongation West = 19°.

Nov. 8. Jupiter in opposition with the Sun, 6h. 20m. *morn.*

Nov. 9. Mars and Saturn in conjunction, 2h. 37m. *aft.*

Nov. 17. Occultation of μ Ceti. The disappearance takes place at 9h. 49m. *aft.,* 99° from the vertex, the reappearance at 11h. 10m. *aft.,* 305° from the vertex.

Nov. 22. Sun enters Sagittarius, 5h. 36m. *morn.*

Nov. 22. Occultation of ζ2 Geminorum. The disappearance takes place at 8h. 51m. *aft.,* 74° from the vertex. The reappearance at 9h. 46m. *aft.,* 215° from the vertex.

In this month the mornings decrease 49m., and the afternoons 39m.

The Temperature column gives the daily average of the Thermometer for 50 years.

M.	W.	Fasts and Festivals. Remarkable Days—Events.	Rises. H. M.	Sets. H. M.	Before Clock. M. S.	Rises morn. H. M.	Souths morn. H. M.	Sets after. H. M.	Days to end of the year.
1	M	**All Saints Day.** Hallowmas.	6 56	4 32	16 19	3 0	9 34	3 53	60
2	Tu	MICHAELMAS TERM. *All Souls.*	6 58	4 30	16 19	4 24	10 28	4 20	59
3	W	Battle of Oltenitza, 1853.	6 59	4 28	16 19	5 48	11 23	4 45	58
4	Th	☿ rises 5h. 5m. *morn.* [landed.	7 1	4 26	16 18	7 14	Aftn.	5 15	57
5	F	Gunpowder Plot, 1605. K. W.	7 3	4 25	16 16	8 35	1 16	5 50	56
6	S	*St. Leonard.*	7 5	4 23	16 14	9 50	2 13	6 31	55
7	�§	24th **Sunday after Trinity.**	7 6	4 21	16 10	10 58	3 10	7 20	54
8	M	Camb. Term div. noon. [Day.	7 8	4 20	16 6	11 56	4 6	8 16	53
9	Tu	PR. OF WALES b. 1841. L. Mayor's	7 10	4 18	16 1	Aftn.	4 58	9 18	52
10	W	John Milton died, 1674.	7 12	4 16	15 55	1 19	5 48	10 22	51
11	Th	*St. Martin.* Martinmas.	7 14	4 15	15 48	1 49	6 35	11 28	50
12	F	♀ sets 6h. 28m. *aft.*	7 15	4 13	15 40	2 15	7 20	Morn.	49
13	S	*Britius.*	7 17	4 12	15 32	2 35	8 2	0 35	48
14	�§	25th **Sunday after Trinity.**	7 19	4 11	15 23	2 55	8 44	1 39	47
15	M	*Machutus.*	7 21	4 9	15 12	3 15	9 25	2 44	46
16	Tu	♂ sets 5h. 25m. *aft.*	7 22	4 8	15 1	3 33	10 7	3 48	45
17	W	*Hugh, Bishop of Lincoln.*	7 24	4 6	14 50	3 54	10 50	4 53	44
18	Th	Cardinal Pole died, 1558.	7 26	4 5	14 37	4 19	11 35	5 58	43
19	F	☽'s Ascending Node 1° 37′ ♌	7 27	4 4	14 24	4 44	Morn.	7 5	42
20	S	*Edmund, King and Martyr.*	7 29	4 3	14 9	5 18	0 23	8 13	41
21	�§	26th **Sunday after Trinity.** Pr.	7 31	4 2	13 54	5 58	1 13	9 17	40
22	M	*Cecilia.* [Royal b. 1840	7 32	4 0	13 38	6 48	2 5	10 16	39
23	Tu	*Clement.*	7 34	3 59	13 22	7 45	2 59	11 10	38
24	W	John Knox died, 1574.	7 36	3 58	13 4	8 52	3 53	11 55	37
25	Th	MICHMAS. TERM ENDS. *Catherine.*	7 37	3 57	12 46	10 5	4 47	Aftn.	36
26	F	☉'s Hor. par. 8″ 7.	7 39	3 56	12 27	11 21	5 41	1 3	35
27	S	Pr. Mary Camb. (Teck) b. 1833.	7 40	3 55	12 7	Morn.	6 33	1 30	34
28	�§	**Advent Sunday.**	7 42	3 55	11 47	0 40	7 25	1 55	33
29	M	Length of day 8h. 11m.	7 43	3 54	11 26	1 59	8 17	2 20	32
30	Tu	**St. Andrew.** Andermas.	7 45	3 53	11 4	3 20	9 9	2 44	31

PHASES OF THE MOON.

● New Moon	3d.	11h.	36m. After.
☽ First Quarter	11	2	56 Morn.
○ Full Moon	19	7	18 Morn.
☾ Last Quarter	26	6	14 After.

In Perigee 2d. 6h. ⌀. | In Apogee 14d. 9h. ⌀.
In Perigee 30d. 9h. ⌀.

RAINFALL IN NOVEMBER, 1867.

In this month there were four days on which rain fell. The total rainfall was 0·86 inch; being 1·55 inch less than the average of the preceding seven years.

MORNING AND EVENING STARS.

☿ MERCURY a morning star; is well situated for observation about the 5th, rising 1h. 50m. before the Sun; in conjunction with the Moon on the 2nd, at 2h. 17m. aft.

♀ VENUS an evening star; in conjunction with the Moon on the 7th, at 6h. 5m. morn.

♃ JUPITER rises about sunset, and will continue visible through the night; in conjunction with the Moon on the 18th, at 4h. 50m. morn.

♄ SATURN an evening star; sets soon after the Sun; is unfavourably situated for observation.

Time of High Water at the undermentioned Ports—

Day of Month	Week	Average daily Temperature	LOND. BDGE. Morn.	After.	LIVERPOOL. Morn.	After.	S'HAMPTON. Morn.	After.	NEWCASTLE. Morn.	After.	HULL. Mo n.	After.	DOVER. Morn.	After.	BRISTOL. Morn.	After.	Day of the Year
		Deg	H. M.	H. M.	H. M.	H. M.	H. M.	H. M.	H. M.	H. M.	H. M.	H. M	H. M.	H. M.	H. M.	B. M.	
1	W	43	..	0 9	9 21	9 45	8 22	8 48	2 16	2 40	4 12	4 37	8 45	9 11	5 1	5 28	335
2	Th	42	0 35	1 0	10 8	10 31	9 13	9 36	3 3	3 27	5 0	5 24	9 37	10 3	5 55	6 22	336
3	F	43	1 26	1 50	10 54	11 18	9 59	10 22	3 49	4 11	5 48	6 12	10 28	10 53	6 48	7 12	337
4	S	42	2 11	2 35	11 42	..	10 46	11 10	4 33	4 56	6 36	6 59	11 19	11 44	7 36	8 0	338
5	S	42	2 56	3 19	0 5	0 27	11 33	11 55	5 19	5 41	7 22	7 45	..	0 8	8 22	8 42	339
6	M	42	3 41	4 4	0 49	1 10	..	0 17	6 4	6 26	8 6	8 28	0 31	0 54	9 2	9 21	340
7	Tu	42	4 24	4 44	1 31	1 52	0 38	1 0	6 48	7 11	8 49	9 11	1 17	1 40	9 40	10 0	341
8	W	42	5 4	5 27	2 14	2 35	1 22	1 44	7 34	7 57	9 33	9 55	2 3	2 25	10 19	10 38	342
9	Th	42	5 49	6 12	2 56	3 19	2 5	2 27	8 20	8 46	10 18	10 42	2 46	3 8	10 57	11 19	343
10	F	41	6 37	7 0	3 44	4 10	2 51	3 15	9 15	9 45	11 12	11 43	3 31	3 55	11 41	..	344
11	S	40	7 25	7 55	4 39	5 13	3 41	4 10	10 16	10 51	..	0 14	4 19	4 45	0 5	0 32	345
12	S	40	8 29	9 5	5 49	6 26	4 42	5 15	11 24	11 57	0 46	1 17	5 14	5 44	1 4	1 39	346
13	M	40	9 39	10 10	7 1	7 32	5 50	6 22	..	0 29	1 48	2 18	6 16	6 47	2 17	2 53	347
14	Tu	41	10 43	11 14	8 2	8 32	6 53	7 24	0 59	1 28	2 48	3 17	7 19	7 49	3 28	4 0	348
15	W	41	11 42	..	8 55	9 16	7 51	8 15	1 54	2 17	3 45	4 10	8 16	8 38	4 28	4 53	349
16	Th	40	0 7	0 29	9 36	9 55	8 37	8 58	2 37	2 56	4 32	4 51	8 59	9 20	5 16	5 38	350
17	F	40	0 48	1 9	10 13	10 31	9 17	9 36	3 15	3 33	5 10	5 28	9 41	10 1	5 59	6 20	351
18	S	40	1 28	1 48	10 50	11 9	9 55	10 14	3 50	4 8	5 47	6 7	10 22	10 42	6 42	7 3	352
19	S	40	2 7	2 26	11 29	11 49	10 33	10 53	4 26	4 45	6 27	6 47	11 4	11 26	7 23	7 44	353
20	M	39	2 46	3 3	..	0 10	11 14	11 35	5 4	5 24	7 7	7 28	11 48	..	8 5	8 25	354
21	Tu	38	3 23	3 43	0 30	0 51	11 57	..	5 44	6 5	7 48	8 8	0 9	0 31	8 44	9 3	355
22	W	38	4 3	4 23	1 11	1 32	0 18	0 39	6 26	6 48	8 28	8 49	0 54	1 17	9 22	9 42	356
23	Th	38	4 45	5 6	1 53	2 15	1 0	1 23	7 11	7 34	9 11	9 34	1 40	2 3	10 2	10 23	357
24	F	38	5 29	5 53	2 38	3 2	1 47	2 12	7 59	8 25	9 58	10 23	2 27	2 52	10 45	11 8	358
25	S	38	6 19	6 44	3 28	3 55	2 37	3 4	8 54	9 26	10 51	11 23	3 18	3 43	11 32	11 57	359
26	S	37	7 12	7 43	4 26	4 58	3 31	3 59	9 59	10 34	11 58	..	4 12	4 37	..	0 23	360
27	M	37	8 17	8 52	5 34	6 12	4 31	5 5	11 12	11 47	0 33	1 7	5 6	5 36	0 52	1 27	361
28	Tu	38	9 30	10 2	6 51	7 28	5 40	6 16	..	0 21	1 39	2 11	6 8	6 42	2 1	2 46	362
29	W	38	10 36	11 12	8 1	8 33	6 51	7 27	0 54	1 26	2 44	3 16	7 17	7 52	3 26	4 3	363
30	Th	38	11 45	..	9 2	9 29	7 59	8 28	1 55	2 23	3 48	4 17	8 23	8 52	4 37	5 8	364
31	F	38	0 15	0 42	9 54	10 18	8 56	9 23	2 49	3 14	4 45	5 10	9 20	9 47	5 37	6 5	365

RISING and SETTING of SEVEN PRINCIPAL PLANETS on the 5th, 15th, and 25th.

D.	MERCURY ☿ Rises h. m.	Sets h. m.	VENUS ♀ Rises h. m.	Sets h. m.	MARS ♂ Rises h. m.	Sets h. m.	JUPITER ♃ Rises h. m.	Sets h. m.	SATURN ♄ Rises h. m.	Sets h. m.	URANUS ♅ Rises h. m.	Sets h. m.	NEPTUNE ♆ Rises h. m.	Sets h. m.
5	7 29M	3 33A	11 19M	7 13A	9 44M	5 12A	2 25A	5 5M	8 13M	4 17A	6 28A	10 42M	1 39A	2 37M
15	8 18M	3 42A	11 32M	7 35A	9 34M	5 10A	1 44A	4 21M	7 38M	3 42A	5 46A	10 2M	1 0A	1 55M
25	8 53M	9A	11 39M	7 55A	9 21M	5 11A	1 3A	3 39M	7 5M	3 7A	5 6A	9 22M	0 20A	1 15M

ECLIPSES, OCCULTATIONS, AND OTHER CELESTIAL PHENOMENA.

December 1. Day breaks at 5h. 42m. morn, and twilight ends at 5h. 56m. aft., the length of the Day being 8h. 7m.

Dec. 8. Occultation of δ Capricorni. The disappearance takes place at 5h. 36m. aft., 164° from the vertex. The reappearance at 6h. 35m. aft., 270° from the vertex.

Dec. 11. Mercury in Aphelion, 7h. 44m. morn.

Dec. 11. Saturn in conjunction with the Sun, 1h. 8m. aft.

Dec. 12. Mercury and Saturn in conjunction, 0h. 8m. aft.

Dec. 13. Mercury in superior conjunction with the Sun, 5h. 0m. aft.

Dec. 14. (3h. 42m. morn.) Venus at greatest elongation East=47°.

Dec. 14. Occultation of ξ2 Ceti. The disappear-ance takes place at 0h. 21m. aft., 75° from the vertex. The reappearance at 10h. 15m. aft., 2° from the vertex.

Dec. 20. Occultation of ζ2 Geminorum. The disappearance takes place at 5h. 27m. morn., 121° from the vertex. The reappearance at 6h. 27m. morn., 302° from the vertex.

Dec. 21. The Sun enters Capricornus, 6h. 23m. aft. Winter commences.

Dec. 21. Occultation of δ Cancri. The disappearance takes place at 9h. 39m. aft., 12° from the vertex. The reappearance at 10h. 32m. aft., 257° from the vertex.

Dec. 31. The Earth at least distance from the Sun, 6h. 0m. aft.

In this month to the 21st, the mornings decrease 20m. and the afternoons 2m.

DECEMBER XXXI DAYS.

Days of M.	Days of W.	Fasts and Festivals. Remarkable Days—Events.	THE SUN. Rises. H. M.	THE SUN. Sets. H. M.	THE SUN. Before Clock. M. S.	THE MOON. Rises morn. H. M.	THE MOON. Souths morn. H. M.	THE MOON. Sets after. H. M.	Days to end of the year.
1	W	Princess of Wales born, 1844.	7 46	3 53	10 41	4 43	10 3	3 11	30
2	Th	Battle of Austerlitz, 1805.	7 48	3 52	10 18	6 5	10 58	3 42	29
3	F	Battle of Hohenlinden, 1800.	7 49	3 51	9 54	7 24	11 55	4 20	28
4	S	♀ sets 7*h.* 11*m. aft.*	7 50	3 51	9 30	8 37	Aftn.	5 5	27
5	S	**2nd Sund. in Advent.** Ramadân.	7 52	3 50	9 5	9 42	1 50	5 59	26
6	M	*Nicholas.*	7 53	3 50	8 39	10 35	2 46	7 0	25
7	Tu	☾'s Ascending Node 0° 40′ ☊	7 54	3 50	8 13	11 17	3 39	8 6	24
8	W	*Conception of Virgin Mary.*	7 55	3 49	7 47	11 51	4 28	9 12	23
9	Th	Grouse shooting ends.	7 56	3 49	7 20	Aftn.	5 14	10 18	22
10	F	First Gold from Australia, 1851	7 57	3 49	6 52	0 41	5 58	11 24	21
11	S	♄ ☌ ☉ 1*h.* 8*m. aft.*	7 58	3 49	6 25	1 2	6 40	Morn.	20
12	S	**3rd Sunday in Advent.**	7 59	3 49	5 57	1 22	7 22	0 30	19
13	M	*Lucy.*	8 0	3 49	5 28	1 39	8 3	1 35	18
14	Tu	Prince Albert died, 1861.	8 1	3 49	5 0	1 58	8 45	2 38	17
15	W	Ember week.	8 2	3 49	4 31	2 22	9 30	3 44	16
16	Th	Cambridge Term ends.	8 3	3 49	4 1	2 46	10 16	4 51	15
17	F	Oxford Term ends.	8 4	3 49	3 32	3 17	11 6	5 59	14
18	S	Ember Day.	8 4	3 49	3 3	3 54	11 58	7 5	13
19	S	**4th Sunday in Advent.**	8 5	3 50	2 33	4 41	Morn.	8 7	12
20	M	♅ ☌ ☾ 7*h.* 13*m. aft.*	8 6	3 50	2 3	5 37	0 52	9 5	11
21	Tu	**St. Thomas.** Shortest day.	8 6	3 51	1 33	6 41	1 48	9 54	10
22	W	☉ Semidiameter 16′ 18″.	8 7	3 51	1 3	7 53	2 43	10 35	9
23	Th	♅ rises 5*h.* 14*m. aft.*	8 7	3 52	0 33	9 10	3 38	11 10	8
24	F	Hugh Miller died, 1856.	8 8	3 52	0 4	10 28	4 31	11 36	7
25	S	**Christmas Day.**	8 8	3 53	After.	11 46	5 22	Aftn.	6
26	S	**Sunday aft. Xmas. St. Stephen**	8 8	3 54	0 56	Morn.	6 13	0 27	5
27	M	**St. John the Evangelist.**	8 8	3 55	1 26	1 4	7 3	0 49	4
28	Tu	**Innocents' Day.**	8 9	3 55	1 55	2 25	7 55	1 15	3
29	W	♆ sets 0*h.* 59*m. morn.*	8 9	3 56	2 25	3 44	8 47	1 41	2
30	Th	Royal Society instituted, 1660.	8 9	3 57	2 54	5 3	9 42	2 15	1
31	F	*Silvester.*	8 9	3 58	3 23	6 16	10 38	2 55	0

PHASES OF THE MOON.

● New Moon	3*d.*	10*h.*	41*m.*	Morn.
☽ First Quarter	10	11	12	After.
○ Full Moon	18	11	50	After.
☾ Last Quarter	26	2	34	Morn.

In Apogee 12*d.* 3*h.* A. | In Perigee 27*d.* 7*h.* A.

RAINFALL IN DECEMBER, 1867.

The total rainfall for 1867, in England, was 30·86 inches, or 0·12 inch less than the average of eight preceding years. Rainfall for this month 1·40 inch, or 1·20 less than the average.

MORNING AND EVENING STARS.

♀ VENUS an evening star; in conjunction with the Moon on the *7th*, at *5h. 12m. morn.*

♂ MARS an evening star; sets on the *25th* about an hour after the Sun; in conjunction with the Moon on the *5th*, at *4h. 0m. morn.*

♃ JUPITER well situated for observation; rising about 2 hours before sunset on the *15th*; in conjunction with the Moon on the *15th*, at *6h. 43m. morn.*

♄ SATURN unfavourably situated for observation this month; in conjunction with the Moon on the *31st*, at *1h. 42m. aft.*

THE TIME OF HIGH WATER

At the undermentioned Ports and Places may be approximately found by adding to or subtracting from the time of high water at London Bridge the quantities annexed.

Place	Country	+/−	h. m.	Place	Country	+/−	h. m.
Aberdeen Bar	Scotland	sub.	1 7	Guernsey Pier	Eng. Chan	add	4 30
Aberdovey	Wales	add	5 53	Hartlepool	England	add	1 21
Aberystwith	Wales	add	5 24	Harwich	England	sub.	2 1
Agnes (St.)	Scilly Isles	add	2 23	Hastings	England	sub.	4 16
Aldborough	England	sub.	3 22	Hâvre de Grâce	France	sub.	4 16
Alderney Pier	Eng. Chan	add	4 39	Heligoland	Germ. Ocean	sub.	2 34
Antwerp	Belgium	add	2 18	Holyhead	Wales	sub.	3 56
Arran Isle	Scotland	sub.	2 52	Holy Island Harbour	England	add	0 23
Arundel Bar	England	sub.	2 32	Honfleur Harbour	France	sub.	4 38
Banff	Scotland	sub.	1 39	Howth Harbour	Ireland	sub.	2 58
Bantry Harbour	Ireland	add	1 40	Ipswich	England	sub.	1 32
Barnstaple Bar	England	add	3 23	Jersey (St. Helier)	Eng. Chan	add	4 22
Beachy Head	England	sub.	2 47	King's Road	Bristol Chan.	add	5 6
Beaumaris	Wales	sub.	3 35	Kingstown Harbour	Ireland	sub.	2 57
Belfast	Ireland	sub.	3 24	Kinsale Harbour	Ireland	add	2 36
Berwick	England	add	0 11	Land's End	England	add	2 23
Blakeney Harbour	England	add	4 23	Leith Pier	Scotland	add	0 10
Boulogne	France	sub.	2 42	Lerwick Harbour	Shetland	sub.	3 37
Brest Harbour	France	add	1 40	Margate Pier	England	sub.	2 27
Bridgewater Bar	England	add	4 43	Milford Haven Entrance	Wales	add	3 49
Bridlington	England	add	2 32	Minehead Pier	England	add	4 23
Bridport	England	add	3 58	Needles Point	Isle of Wight	sub.	4 21
Brielle	Holland	add	0 53	Newhaven	England	sub.	2 16
Brighton	England	sub.	2 52	Newport	South Wales	sub.	5 3
Caernarvon Bar	Wales	sub.	4 34	Nore Light	River Tham.	sub.	1 37
Calais	France	add	2 18	Ostend	Belgium	sub.	1 42
Cardigan Bar	Wales	add	4 54	Pembroke Dockyard	Wales	add	4 5
Chatham	England	sub.	0 56	Penzance	England	add	2 23
Cherbourg	France	add	5 42	Peterhead	Scotland	sub.	1 33
Chichester Harbour	England	sub.	2 37	Portland (Breakwater)	England	add	4 54
Christchurch Harbour	England	sub.	5 7	Portsmouth Dockyard	England	sub.	2 26
Cork Harbour	Ireland	sub.	2 54	Ramsgate Harbour	England	sub.	2 23
Cowes	I. of Wight	sub.	3 22	Rye Bay	England	sub.	2 47
Cromer	England	add	4 53	Salcombe	England	add	3 54
Dartmouth Harbour	England	add	4 9	Scarborough	England	add	2 4
Deal	England	sub.	2 42	Scilly Islands (St. Mary)	England	add	2 11
Devonport Dockyard	England	add	3 36	Selsea Bill	England	sub.	2 22
Dieppe	France	sub.	3 1	Sheerness Dockyard	England	sub.	1 30
Dingle Bay	Ireland	add	1 44	Shields (North)	England	add	1 16
Douglas Harbour	Isle of Man	sub.	2 55	Shoreham Harbour	England	sub.	2 33
Dublin Bar	Ireland	sub.	2 55	Spithead (Anchorage)	England	sub.	2 47
Dundalk Bar	Ireland	sub.	3 11	Spurn Point	England	add	3 19
Dundee	Scotland	add	0 25	St. Ives	England	add	2 37
Dungeness	England	sub.	3 22	St. Malo	France	add	3 58
Dunkerque	France	add	1 59	Sunderland	England	add	1 15
Eddystone	Eng. Chan.	add	3 8	Swansea Bay	Wales	add	3 54
Exmouth Bar	England	add	4 14	Tees River Bar	England	add	1 38
Falmouth	England	add	2 50	Torbay	England	add	3 53
Flamboro' Head	England	add	2 23	Tynemouth Bar	England	add	1 13
Flushing	Holland	sub.	0 47	Valentia	Ireland	add	1 35
Fowey	England	add	3 7	Waterford Harbour	Ireland	add	3 59
Galway Bay	Ireland	add	2 28	Weymouth	England	add	4 53
Granville	France	add	4 6	Whitby	England	add	1 38
Gravesend	England	sub.	0 57	Wisbeach	England	add	0 57
Greenock	Scotland	sub.	1 59	Yarmouth Roads	England	sub.	4 52

Ex. 1.—Required the time of high water at Aberdeen on January 1st.

Time of high water at London Bridge 3h. 46m. Morn.
Subtract tide interval 1 7

Time of high water at Aberdeen ...... 2 39 Morn.

Ex. 2.—Required the time of high water at Scarborough on Jan. 2nd.

Time of high water at London Bridge 4h. 32m. Morn.
Add tide interval 2 4

Time of high water at Scarborough.. 6 36 Morn.

It may happen that the "tide interval" to be subtracted is greater than the quantity from which it has to be taken, in which case 12 hours must be added to the London Bridge time, the resulting difference will be the preceding day's Afternoon tide where the London morning tide was used. Sometimes the sum "high water at London Bridge" + "tide interval" will exceed 12 hours; in this case, the excess will be the time of high water after the noon or midnight following, according as the London high water was either morning or afternoon.

Ex. 3.—Required the time of high water at Aberdeen, Jan. 9th, aft.

Time of high water at London Bridge on Jan. 10th, + 12 hours .... 12h. 4m. Morn.
Subtract tide interval 1 7

Time of high water at Aberdeen, Jan. 9th, 10 57 After.

Ex. 4.—Required the time of high water at Scarborough, Jan. 9th, aft.

Time of high water at London Bridge, Jan. 9th .... 11h. 31m. Morn.
Add tide interval 2 4

Time of high water at Scarborough, Jan. 9th .... 1 35 After.

A Calendar

For ascertaining Any Day of the Week for any given time within the Present Century.

Years 1801 to 1900	31 Jan.	28 Feb.	31 Mar.	30 Apr.	31 May.	30 June.	31 July.	31 Aug.	30 Sept.	31 Oct.	30 Nov.	31 Dec.
1801 1807 1818 1829 1835 1846 1857 1863 1874 1885 1891	4	7	7	3	5	1	3	6	2	4	7	2
1802 1813 1819 1830 1841 1847 1858 1869 1875 1886 1897	5	1	1	4	6	2	4	7	3	5	1	3
1803 1814 1825 1831 1842 1853 1859 1870 1881 1887 1898	6	2	2	5	7	3	5	1	4	6	2	4
1805 1811 1822 1833 1839 1850 1861 1867 1878 1889 1895	2	5	5	1	3	6	1	4	7	2	5	7
1806 1817 1823 1834 1845 1851 1862 1873 1879 1890 ...	3	6	6	2	4	7	2	5	1	3	6	1
1809 1815 1826 1837 1843 1854 1865 1871 1882 1893 1899	7	3	3	6	1	4	6	2	5	7	3	5
1810 1821 1827 1838 1849 1855 1866 1877 1883 1894 1900	1	4	4	7	2	5	7	3	6	1	4	6
LEAP YEARS.	...	29	...	...	...	...	...	...	...	...	...	...
1804 1832 1860 1888	7	3	4	7	2	5	7	3	6	1	4	6
1808 1836 1864 1892	5	1	2	5	7	3	5	1	4	6	2	4
1812 1840 1868 1896	3	6	7	3	5	1	3	6	2	4	7	2
1816 1844 1872 ...	1	4	5	1	3	6	1	4	7	2	5	7
1820 1848 1876	6	2	3	6	1	4	6	2	5	7	3	5
1824 1852 ... o ...	4	7	1	4	6	2	4	7	3	5	1	3
1828 1856 1884 ...	2	5	6	2	4	7	2	5	1	3	6	1

NOTE.—To ascertain any day of the week in any year of the present century, first look in the table of years for the year required, and under the months are figures which refer to the corresponding figures at the head of the columns of days below. For Example:—To know what day of the week Sept. 2 will be on in the year 1869, in the table of years look for 1869, and in a parallel line under Sept., is fig. 3, which directs to col. 3, in which it will be seen that Sept. 2 falls on Thursday.

1	2	3	4	5	6	7
Monday 1	Tuesday 1	Wedns. 1	Thursday 1	Friday 1	Saturday 1	Sunday 1
Tuesday 2	Wedns. 2	Thursday 2	Friday 2	Saturday 2	Sunday 2	Monday 2
Wedns. 3	Thursday 3	Friday 3	Saturday 3	Sunday 3	Monday 3	Tuesday 3
Thursday 4	Friday 4	Saturday 4	Sunday 4	Monday 4	Tuesday 4	Wedns. 4
Friday 5	Saturday 5	Sunday 5	Monday 5	Tuesday 5	Wedns. 5	Thursday 5
Saturday 6	Sunday 6	Monday 6	Tuesday 6	Wedns. 6	Thursday 6	Friday 6
Sunday 7	Monday 7	Tuesday 7	Wedns. 7	Thursday 7	Friday 7	Saturday 7
Monday 8	Tuesday 8	Wedns. 8	Thursday 8	Friday 8	Saturday 8	Sunday 8
Tuesday 9	Wedns. 9	Thursday 9	Friday 9	Saturday 9	Sunday 9	Monday 9
Wedns. 10	Thursday 10	Friday 10	Saturday 10	Sunday 10	Monday 10	Tuesday 10
Thursday 11	Friday 11	Saturday 11	Sunday 11	Monday 11	Tuesday 11	Wedns. 11
Friday 12	Saturday 12	Sunday 12	Monday 12	Tuesday 12	Wedns. 12	Thursday 12
Saturday 13	Sunday 13	Monday 13	Tuesday 13	Wedns. 13	Thursday 13	Friday 13
Sunday 14	Monday 14	Tuesday 14	Wedns. 14	Thursday 14	Friday 14	Saturday 14
Monday 15	Tuesday 15	Wedns. 15	Thursday 15	Friday 15	Saturday 15	Sunday 15
Tuesday 16	Wedns. 16	Thursday 16	Friday 16	Saturday 16	Sunday 16	Monday 16
Wedns. 17	Thursday 17	Friday 17	Saturday 17	Sunday 17	Monday 17	Tuesday 17
Thursday 18	Friday 18	Saturday 18	Sunday 18	Monday 18	Tuesday 18	Wedns. 18
Friday 19	Saturday 19	Sunday 19	Monday 19	Tuesday 19	Wedns. 19	Thursday 19
Saturday 20	Sunday 20	Monday 20	Tuesday 20	Wedns. 20	Thursday 20	Friday 20
Sunday 21	Monday 21	Tuesday 21	Wedns. 21	Thursday 21	Friday 21	Saturday 21
Monday 22	Tuesday 22	Wedns. 22	Thursday 22	Friday 22	Saturday 22	Sunday 22
Tuesday 23	Wedns. 23	Thursday 23	Friday 23	Saturday 23	Sunday 23	Monday 23
Wedns. 24	Thursday 24	Friday 24	Saturday 24	Sunday 24	Monday 24	Tuesday 24
Thursday 25	Friday 25	Saturday 25	Sunday 25	Monday 25	Tuesday 25	Wedns. 25
Friday 26	Saturday 26	Sunday 26	Monday 26	Tuesday 26	Wedns. 26	Thursday 26
Saturday 27	Sunday 27	Monday 27	Tuesday 27	Wedns. 27	Thursday 27	Friday 27
Sunday 28	Monday 28	Tuesday 28	Wedns. 28	Thursday 28	Friday 28	Saturday 28
Monday 29	Tuesday 29	Wedns. 29	Thursday 29	Friday 29	Saturday 29	Sunday 29
Tuesday 30	Wedns. 30	Thursday 30	Friday 30	Saturday 30	Sunday 30	Monday 30
Wedns. 31	Thursday 31	Friday 31	Saturday 31	Sunday 31	Monday 31	Tuesday 31

		Begins
Vikramâditya Samvat........	1925-26	Mar. 14.
'Sálivâhana 'Saka (Hindu)..	1790-91	
Malabar	1044-45	
Yezdijird or Naoroz (Parsi)	1238-39	Sept. 22.
Hijra............................	1285-86	April 13.
Fasli (Upper India)............	1278-79	
Shahur San	1269-70	
Jewish Era	5628-29	
Buddhist Era, (Ceylon, Ava,)	2412-13	Mar. 14.

Parsi reckoning.

The Ancient Persians reckoned a new era from the accession of each monarch; and, as Yezdijird had no successor, the date of his accession has remained the era from which they count down to the present time. This dated 16th June, A.D. 632 (ten years after the Hijra). They make the year to consist of 365 days, and say that a month is added at the end of 120 years, and make up the difference between their year and the solar year. They name 12 months of 30 days each, and add five days to bring the number up to 365.

The Mohammedans reckon from the *Hijra*, or Flight of Mohammed from Mecca on the evening of Thursday, the 15th of July, A.D. 622. Their year is lunar; the months have 30 and 29 days alternately. 163 Gregorian years are equal to 168 Mohammedan years by less than a day. By this system of reckoning, each year begins about 10 or 11 days earlier than that which preceded it.

The Hindus have several eras. The principal era is *Vikramâditya*, after the name of a king who exists in historical memory only as the founder of an era. The years are luni-solar, and are called *Samvat*.

Jan.   1 is 18th of *Ramazan* (9th Mohamd. mo.).
,,   is 12th of *Tir* (4th Parsi m. Rasimi rec.).
,,   is 19th of *Pausha* (10th Hindu month).
,,   is 18th of *Tebet* (4th Jewish month).
,,   13 is 1st of *Mágha* (11th Hindu mnth).
,,   is 1st of *Shebat* (5th Jewish month).
,,   15 is 1st of *Shawal* (10th Mohamd. mo.).
,,   20 is 1st of *Amardad* (5th Parsi mo. Ras.).
Feb. 12 is 1st of *Phálguna* (12th Hindu month).
,,   is 1st of *Adar* (6th Jewish month).

Feb. 12 is 1st of *Zu'lkadah* 11th Mohamd. mo.).
,,   19 is 1st of *Sharivar* (6th Parsi mo. Ras.).
Mar. 13 is 1st of *Nisan* or *Abib* (7th Jewish mo.).
,,   14 is 1st of *Chaitra* (1st Hindu m.) V.S.1926.
,,   15 is 1st of *Zu'lhijjah* (12th Moham. mo.).
,,   21 is 1st of *Meher* (7th Parsi mo. Ras.).
Apl.   12 is 1st of *Iyar* or *Zius* (8th Jewish mo.).
,,   13 is 1st of *Vais'âkha* (2nd Hindu month).
,,   is 1st of *Muharram* (1st Mohamd. mo.).
A.H. 1286, (Fête of Hasan and Husain).
,,   20 is 1st of *Aban* (8th of Parsi mo.   Ras.).
May 11 is 1st of *Sivan* (9th Jewish month).
,,   13 is 1st of *Safar* (2nd Mohamd. month).
,,   14 is 1st of *Jyaishtha* (3rd Hindu month).
,,   20 is 1st of *Adar* (9th Parsi month. Ras.).
June 10 is 1st of *Tammuz* (10th Jewish month).
,,   11 is 1st of *Rabiu'luwal* (3rd Mohamd. m.).
,,   14 is 1st of *Ashâdh* (4th Hindu month).
,,   19 is 1st of *Deh* (10th Parsi month).
July   9 is 1st of *Ab* (11th Jewish month).
,,   11 is 1st of *Rabiu'lakhir* (3rd Moham. mo.)
,,   15 is 1st of *Srávana* (5th Hindu month).
,,   19 is 1st of *Bahman* (11th Parsi month).
Aug.   8 is 1st of *Elul* (12th Jewish month).
,,   9 is 1st of *Jamada'lawal* (5th Moh. mo.).
,,   15 is 1st of *Bhádrapada* (6th Hindu month).
,,   18 is 1st of *Asfandyar* (12th Parsi month).
Sep.   6 is 1st of *Tisri* (1st Jewish month), 5630.
,,   8 is 1st of *Jamada'lakhir* (6th Moh. mo.).
,,   15 is 1st of *Aswina* (7th Hindu month).
,,   17—21, inclusive are the 5 added days (Gathas) to the Parsi year.
,,   22 is 1st of *Favardin* (1st Parsi month, A. Y. 1239).
Oct.   6 is 1st of *Heshran* (2nd Jewish month).
,,   7 is 1st of *Rajab* (7th Mohamm. month).
,,   15 is 1st of *Kárttika* (Hindu month).
,,   22 is 1st of *Ardibehisht* (2nd Parsi month).
Nov.   5 is 1st of *Kislev* (3rd Jewish month).
,,   6 is 1st of *Shaban* (8th Mohamm. mo.).
,,   13 is 1st of *Margas'irsha* (Hindu mo.).
,,   21 is 1st of *Khurdad* (3rd Parsi month).
Dec.   4 is 1st of *Tebet* (4th Jewish month).
,,   5 is 1st of *Ramazan* (9th Moham. month).
Roza or *Fast* commences.
,,   12 is 1st of *Pausha* (10th Hindu month).
,,   21 is 1st of *Tir* (4th Parsi month)

MEMORANDA FOR THE YEAR 1870.

January.	April.	July.	October.
1 Saturday.	1 Friday.		1 Saturday.
2 ii. Sunday aft. Christ.	3 Passion Sunday.	3 iii. Sun. aft. Trin.	2 xvi. Sun. aft. Trin.
6 Th. Epiphany.	10 Palm Sunday.	10 iv. Sun. ,, ,,	9 xvii. Sun. ,, ,,
9 i. Sunday aft. Epiph.	15 Good Friday.	17 v. Sun. ,, ,,	16 xviii. Sun. ,, ,,
16 ii. Sunday ,, ,,	17 Easter Day.	24 vi. Sun. ,, ,,	23 xix. Sun. ,, ,,
23 iii. Sunday ,, ,,	23 Sat. St. George.	31 vii. Sun. ,, ,,	30 xx. Sun. ,, ,,
30 iv. Sunday ,, ,,	24 i. Sunday aft. Easter		

February.	May.	August.	November.
1 Tuesday.	1 ii. Sun. aft. Easter.		1 Tuesday.
6 v. Sunday aft. Epiph.	8 iii. Sun. ,, ,,	1 Monday.	6 xxi. Sun. aft. Trin.
13 Septuagesima.	15 iv. Sun. ,, ,,	7 viii. Sun. aft. Trin.	9 P. Wales' Birthday.
20 Sexagesima.	22 v. Sun. ,, ,,	14 ix. Sun. ,, ,,	13 xxii. Sun. aft. Trin.
27 Quinquagesima.	24 Tu. Qn's. Birthday.	21 x. Sun. ,, ,,	20 xxiii. Sun. ,, ,,
	26 Ascension day.	28 xi. Sun. ,, ,,	27 Advent Sunday.
	29 Sunday aft. Ascen.		30 Wed. St. Andrew.

March.	June.	September.	December.
1 Tu. St. David.	1 Wednesday.		1 Thursday.
2 Ash Wednesday.	5 Whit Sunday.	1 Thursday.	4 ii. Sun. in Advent.
6 i. Sunday in Lent.	12 Trinity Sunday.	4 xii. Sun. aft. Trin.	11 iii. Sun. ,, ,,
13 ii. Sunday ,, ,,	16 Corpus Christi.	11 xiii. Sun. ,, ,,	18 iv. Sun. ,, ,,
17 Th. St. Patrick.	19 i. Sunday aft. Trin.	18 xiv. Sun. ,, ,,	21 Wed. St. Thomas.
20 iii. Sunday in Lent.	20 M. Q. Accession.	25 xv. Sun. ,, ,,	25 Sun. Christmas.
25 F. Lady Day.	24 F. Midsummer d.	29 Th. Michaelmas.	31 Saturday.
27 iv. Sunday in Lent.	26 ii. Sunday aft. Trin.		

THE variety of our agricultural and natural products favours the perfection of birds common in temperate climates ; whilst our insular position invites many foreign visitants that flock to us during the winter and spring seasons.

The following list gives the names of the chief birds, either indigenous or foreign, that may be found in each month. The names given are those in most popular use, but many birds are known under others in certain localities.

JANUARY.

Bird, &c.	Resorts.
Coot	Mud-banks on coasts.
Curlew	Sea-shore.
Duck (Wild)	Sea-coasts.
Fieldfare	Hedges.
Goose (Wild)	Water-meadows.
Grouse, Black Game	Moors, &c.
Gull	Sea-coasts.
Hare	Hedges, fields, &c.
Knot	Coasts.
Lark	Fields.
Partridge	Fields generally.
Pheasant	Open and covert.
Pigeon (Wood)	Turnip-fields, woods, &c.
Rabbits	Sand-banks, hedges, &c.
Rockbirds (Puffins)	Sea-coasts, on rocks.
Snipe	Marshes.
Teal	Rivers and large ponds.
Widgeon	ditto.
Woodcock	Open and covert.

FEBRUARY.

As a general rule, taking the average of seasons, the sportsman will find that the list of birds at his disposal for February is as nearly as possible that already given for the preceding month. Of course all depends on the temperature of the season, which may induce an early visit of some birds, or delay that of others.

MARCH and APRIL.

Coot	Rivers, marshes, &c.
Curlew	Sea-shore.
Duck (Wild)	Fens, marshes, coasts, &c.
Goose (Wild or Grey)	Open plain.
Godwit	Marshes.
Gull	Sea-shores.
Hare	Hedges, &c.
Heron	Marshes.
Pigeon (Wood)	Woods, &c.
Rabbit	Warrens, &c.
Rockbirds	Coasts, rivers, &c.
Snipe	Marshes, &c.
Teal and Widgeon	Rivers and marshes.

MAY and JUNE.

Duck (Wild)	Streams.
Gannet	Rocky shores
Godwit	Coasts.
Gull	Sea-shores.
Heron	Marshes, &c.
Rockbirds, Auks, &c.	Rocky coasts.
Rook	Trees, &c.

JULY.

Duck, Mallards, &c.	Rushes.
Gannet	Rocky shores
Garganet	Fens.
Gull	Sea-shores.
Heron	Marshes, &c.
Landrail	Corn-fields.
Rockbirds	Rocky coasts.

AUGUST.

Bird, &c.	Resorts.
Duck	Corn-fields.
Duck (Velvet)	Marshes, &c.
Grouse	Moors, &c.
Gull	Sea-shores.
Heron	Marshes, &c.
Landrail	Corn-fields.
Oxbird	Sea-coasts, &c.
Partridge	Fields, &c.
Rabbit	Fields, &c.

SEPTEMBER.

Black Game	Moors, &c.
Duck (Wild)	Marshes, &c.
Grouse	Moors, &c.
Gull	Sea-coast.
Hare	Fields.
Heron	Marshes.
Landrail	Corn-fields.
Partridge	Fields, furrows, &c.
Pigeon (Wood)	Pea-fields.
Plover	Marshes.
Quail (rarely)	With Partridges.
Rabbit	Warrens, &c.
Snipe	Marshes, &c.
Starling	ditto.

OCTOBER.

Black Game	Moors.
Duck (Wild)	Marshes, &c.
Grouse	Moors, &c.
Gull	Sea-coasts.
Hare	Fields.
Heron	Marshes.
Partridge	Fields, &c.
Pheasant	Open and covert.
Pigeon (Wood)	Turnip-fields.
Plover	Marshes.
Rabbit	Warrens, &c.
Snipe	Marshes, &c.
Starling	ditto.
Teal, &c.	ditto.
Woodcock	Covers near sea.

NOVEMBER and DECEMBER.

Black Game	Moors, &c.
Duck (Wild)	Marshes, &c.
Grouse	Moors.
Gull	Sea-coast.
Hare	Fields, &c.
Heron	Marshes.
Partridge	Fields, &c.
Pheasant	Open and covert.
Pigeon (Wood)	Turnip-fields.
Plover	Marshes.
Rabbit	Warrens, &c.
Snipe	Marshes, &c.
Starling	ditto.
Swan (Wild)	ditto.
Teal, Widgeon, &c.	ditto.
Woodcock	Hedges, furze, moors, &c.

Hares, rabbits, snipe, swan, wild-duck, and all wild water-fowl, woodcocks, and plovers, are not included under the game-law restrictions.

Game licences for shooting may be taken out for different periods of the year. One, from April 5, and before November 1, to expire on April 5 following, costs £3. If taken to expire on October 31st of the same year, or from 1st November to the 5th April following, the cost is £2. For a gamekeeper, being an assessed servant, the charge is £2. Dealers in game must also pay £2 for a licence.

The following Tables give the close time for different kinds of Game for England, Scotland, and Ireland. During the periods therein named, it is illegal to pursue the kinds mentioned.

Bird.	England.	Scotland.	Ireland.
Black Game	10th Dec. & 20th Aug., or 1st Sept. in Somerset, Devon, and New Forest.	As "Heath Fowl."	As "Heath Fowl."
Deer . .	None.	None.	10th June & 20th Oct.
Grouse, or Red Game	10th Dec. & 12th Aug.	As "Heath Fowl."	10th Dec. and 20th Aug.
Heath Fowl	......	10th Dec. & 20th Aug.	Ditto.
Heath, or Moor Game	None.	......	Ditto.
Landrail .	None.	None.	10th Jan.& 20th Sep.
Muirfowl, or Ptarmigan	......	10th Dec. & 12th Aug.	10th Dec. and 12th Aug.
Partridge .	1st Feb. and 1st Sept.	As in England.	10th Jan.& 20th Sep.
Pheasant .	1st Feb. and 1st Oct.	As in England.	10th Jan.& 1st Sept.
Quail . .	None.	None.	10th Jan.& 20th Sep.

The Angler's Calendar.

FOR some years past, constant complaints have been made of the scarcity of animal food, and its consequent high price. Despite our natural position and resources in respect to the productions of seas and rivers, little has been done to cultivate, artificially, the production of fish. But with a little care, our fresh-water fish might be almost indefinitely increased, and made a valuable source of food. The prejudice against that article has no foundation, for all lies in the art of cooking, as in the hands of a Frenchman, carp, tench, pike, &c., become savoury and nutritious food. The following is a list of the fish frequenting our streams at different periods of the year, with brief directions for their capture, omitting any mention of the casting net, now so largely used, to the detriment of the angler.

JANUARY.—In this month fresh-water fish are extremely scarce, only Chub, Pike or Jack, and Roach being within reach of the angler. Trolling and bottom fishing alone can be had resort to.

FEBRUARY.—Carp, Chub, Gudgeon, Minnow, Pike, and Roach.

MARCH.—Carp, Chub, Gudgeon, Pike, Roach, and Trout.

For *fly-fishing*, various artificial and natural flies may be used; but as the natural are scarce, the choice of the artificial is arbitrary.

APRIL.—Barbel, Bleak, Bream, Carp, Chub, Eels, Flounders, Gudgeon, Minnows, Pike or Jack, Roach, Rudd, Ruff, Tench, and Trout.

Fly-fishing.—Imitation of the Green Drake fly, Red fly, Blue Dun fly, Red Spinner, &c.

MAY.—Much as last month. Bleak, Barbel, Carp, Chub, Roach, and Tench spawn during this month.

Fly-fishing.—Use the Golden Dun-midge, Sandfly, Stone-fly, and imitation Little Yellow May Dun, Black Gnat, Downhill fly, Green Drake, &c.

JUNE.—In this month Trout are in best condition, other fresh-water fish having but recently spawned.

Fly-fishing.—Green Drake, Grey Drake, &c.

JULY.—All fresh-water fish may be taken, morning and evening, or on cloudy days.

Fly-fishing. — Pale and July Dun, Gold-eye, Gauze-wing, &c.

AUGUST.—Fresh-water fishing as in July.

Fly-fishing.—August Dun, Orange and Cinnamon fly, Red, Brown, and Black Palmer.

Note.—Whilst the variety of flies for Trout and other fishing is all but unlimited, a general rule may be considered to hold good, that the fly of the season, natural or artificial, is the most killing. The former will depend for its presence on the temperature, climate, and locality, and the latter must be made to correspond thereto.

SEPTEMBER.—Barbel, Chub, Dace, and Roach resort to deep water. All fresh-water fish may be caught during the day.

OCTOBER.—Bleak, Dace, Gudgeon, Perch, Pike, Roach, Tench, and Trout.

NOVEMBER.—Chub, Grayling, Pike, and Roach caught by bottom-fishing or trolling.

DECEMBER.—A month generally adverse to the art of angling; but on favourable days, Chub, Pike, and Roach may be occasionally taken.

The only fish strictly preserved by law in our islands is the Salmon, and every variety of its genus and species. The acts define "Salmon" as including all migratory fish of the genus *Salmo*, and give an epitome of all kinds of fish recognized as of the Salmon tribe, by general or local names in different parts of the kingdom. Any attempt to poison, stupefy, or otherwise injure the fish, is visited by heavy penalties. Lights and spears are forbidden, as is also the use of other engines, their sale or possession. Nets employed must have a diameter of not less than two inches from knot to knot. No fixed engine shall be employed. Net fishing is unlawful between the 1st of September and the 1st of February following. But a rod and line may be employed between the 1st of September and the 1st of November following. The intervals here named as forbidden are known as the close season for salmon, &c. As regards selling Salmon, &c., it is prohibited, under penalties, between 3rd of September and the 2nd of February following. Net fishing for salmon is prohibited between twelve o'clock at noon on Saturday, and six o'clock on Monday morning. During this interval, however, in the open season, rod-fishing may be legally followed. The preservation of salmon varies practically on most rivers, and local authorities alone can instruct the angler on such points, and in getting and properly using "passes."

ANGLING STATIONS.—On the Lea: *Lea Bridge, Tottenham, Park* and *Angel Road* stations; *Ponder's End, Ordnance Factory* at Waltham Abbey, all accessible by Great Eastern Railway. On the Thames: *Wandsworth, Putney, Barnes, Mortlake, Kew, Isleworth, Richmond, Twickenham, Bushey Park, Hampton Wick, Teddington, Kingston, Hampton Court, Sunbury,* by boat, omnibus, or South-Western Railway. On the Colne: *West Drayton, Windsor, Maidenhead,* and *Marlow,* by the Great Western Railway. The New River, extending on the N.E. of London as far as Ware.

THE time given in this Almanack is Greenwich Mean Time, or the time which should be shown by a well-regulated clock; the column headed, Sun before or after Clock, gives the difference between this, and apparent time, or the time as shown by the real Sun. The exceptions are the times of High Water at Liverpool, Southampton, Newcastle, Hull, Dover, and Bristol, where the *local* time is given.

The Astronomical Symbols made use of are:—

SIGNS OF THE ZODIAC.

♈	Aries	The Ram.
♉	Taurus	The Bull.
♊	Gemini	The Twins.
♋	Cancer	The Crab.
♌	Leo	The Lion.
♍	Virgo	The Virgin.
♎	Libra	The Balance.
♏	Scorpio	The Scorpion.
♐	Sagittarius	The Archer.
♑	Capricornus	The Goat.
♒	Aquarius	The Water-Bearer.
♓	Pisces	The Fishes.

h. Hours.
m. Minutes of time.
s. Seconds of time.
° Degrees of Arc, or Fahrenheit's Thermometer.
′ Minutes of Arc.
″ Seconds of Arc.

SIGNS OF THE PLANETS.

1. ☉ Sun.	6. ♂ Mars.
2. ☿ Mercury.	7. ♃ Jupiter.
3. ♀ Venus.	8. ♄ Saturn.
4. ⊕ or ⊕ The Earth.	9. ♅ Uranus.
5. ☽ Moon.	10. ♆ Neptune.

N. North. S. South. E. East. W. West.

CONJUNCTION ☌.   OPPOSITION ☍.

Conjunction.—A Planet is in conjunction with another body, when it has the same longitude, and is seen in the same direction in the heavens. This state may happen to all the planets; those whose orbits lie between the Sun and Earth, as well as those whose orbits are exterior to that of the Earth; the former class being called inferior, and the latter superior planets. It is obvious that in the case of the inferior planets, this conjunction will be of two kinds; the one when the planet is between the Earth and the Sun, called inferior conjunction, and the other, when at the opposite point of its orbit, with the Sun between the planet and Earth, called superior conjunction. This latter is the only kind of conjunction that can happen to the superior planets, Mars, Jupiter, Saturn, Uranus, and Neptune; the inferior planets, Mercury and Venus, being subject to both kinds.

Opposition.—A planet is said to be in opposition, when it is distant from the Sun 180° of longitude, at which time it is most brilliant, souths about midnight, and is at its least distance from the Earth. This can only be said of planets whose orbits are external to that of the earth.

Elongation.—The inferior planets, in their revolution round the Sun, appear to an observer on the Earth, to swing pendulum-like from side to side of the sun, being alternately east and west of it; the greatest elongation is the termination of one of the swings, either east or west, and at these times the planet appears, when viewed through a telescope, like the moon in her first quarter, if the elongation be in east; and her last quarter if west; both Mercury and Venus exhibit these phases, passing from new to full, while moving from inferior to superior conjunction, and from full to new again, while passing from superior to inferior conjunction.

Occultation.—It often happens that the Moon in her motion in orbit passes before, and hides from a spectator on the Earth, some of the fixed stars, and occasionally one or other of the planets; these occurrences are called occultations. Among the celestial phenomena are given the times at which certain of these occultations take place, as well as the exact point on the Moon's limb where the observer is to look for the phenomenon; this point is counted from the vertex, or highest upper portion of the Moon's image, towards the right hand, as seen in an inverting telescope, counting continuously from 0° up to 360°. The disappearance always takes place on the right-hand side of the Moon, and the re-appearance on the left, when viewed through an inverting or Astronomical telescope. Such stars only have been included in this list as may be observed with very moderate telescopic power. Should the instrument used not be of the inverting kind, the vertex may still be used as the point to count from, and in the same direction, only adding 180° to the distance given from vertex for the inverting telescope, if the number be less than 180°, and subtracting 180° if greater; bearing in mind, in this case, that the disappearances will take place on the left-hand side of the Moon's image, and the re-appearances on the right.

METEORS.

These remarkable bodies, once supposed to have their birth in our atmosphere, and there, after a short but often brilliant existence to die, have of late years been proved to be bodies obeying the law of universal gravitation, like the other bodies of the Solar System, and consisting of a ring of Meteorites revolving round the Sun once in about 33 years, inclined at a small angle to the ecliptic or Earth's path. From an investigation of the accounts that have come down to us of extraordinary "Star showers," Professor Newton, in America, suggested that this ring of Meteorites was considerably thicker and more dense in one part than in another, so that although the Earth must pass through the November node of the ring every year, yet the Earth could only encounter the thick part once in 33 years, the time of revolution of the ring round the Sun; but, since the ring is inclined at only a slight angle to the ecliptic, the thicker portion may require two or three years to escape the Earth entirely, so that for a year or two before or after the chief display, there may be showers of more or less magnitude, such as occurred after the magnificent shower of November, 1866, in the following November. Although the annual fall of Meteors which takes place between the 10th and 15th of November is that most generally known, from their number and frequency, there are other Meteor periods that occur with a marked regularity, such as the "fiery tears" of St. Laurence, between the 9th and 14th of August. These are generally larger than the November Meteors, but fall in much less number, and at greater intervals of time. Another epoch, about the 23rd of April, regularly occurs.

A very strong presumption that Meteors come

to us from very distant regions of space, is afforded by the interesting discovery of Schiaparelli, that the positions of the orbits of several of the late Comets, and the Meteor rings, are almost identical, leading us to conclude that space, so far from being "empty space," is crowded with matter.

ECLIPSES.

In the year 1869 there will be two Eclipses of the Sun, and two of the Moon.

I. A partial Eclipse of the Moon, January 27, visible at Greenwich.

	D.	H.	M.
First contact with penumbra...	27	11	18 aft.
First contact with shadow	28	0	29 morn.
Middle of Eclipse	28	1	38 morn.
Last contact with shadow	28	2	47 morn.
Last contact with penumbra...	28	3	58 morn.

The first contact with the shadow occurs 53° from the northernmost point of the Moon's limb towards the East: the last contact 31° towards the West, viewing with the naked eye.

II. An Annular Eclipse of the Sun, February 10—11, invisible at Greenwich. Visible as a partial Eclipse at the Cape of Good Hope.

	D.	H.	M.	
Eclipse begins	...	11	2	42 aft. } Cape
Greatest portion eclipsed.	11	4	12 aft. } Mean
Eclipse ends	...	11	5	29 aft. } time.

The first contact with the Moon occurs 118° from the northernmost point of the Sun's limb towards the West, and the last contact 72° towards the East, as seen with the naked eye.

III. A Partial Eclipse of the Moon July 22—23, invisible at Greenwich.

IV. A Total Eclipse of the Sun, August 7, invisible at Greenwich.

An eclipse may be defined, in general terms, as the interposition of one heavenly body between another and the Sun: according to this definition, therefore, an occultation of a star or planet by the Moon, as well as a transit of Mercury or Venus across the Sun's disc, may be said to be eclipses; but astronomers use the term only in speaking of solar and lunar eclipses.

A lunar eclipse, is when the Sun, Earth, and Moon are in a straight line in the order in which they are here mentioned, the shadow of the Earth being thrown on to the Moon; from this it will be seen that a lunar eclipse can only occur at full moon, and then only when, at the full, the moon is in, or very near to, her node (the place where her orbit intersects the ecliptic), and the more or less near agreement of these phenomena will determine the magnitude of the eclipse. It is a prevailing and popular notion that lunar, are of more frequent occurrence than solar, eclipses, an idea favoured by the fact that an eclipse of the moon is universal, and is seen of the same character and magnitude at all places on the earth where the Moon is above the horizon. On the other hand, a solar eclipse may be total in one part of Europe, partial in another, and not eclipsed at all in Africa.

Solar Eclipses are occasioned when the same bodies are in a straight line, but the Moon and Earth change places, the order being Sun, Moon, Earth; and now the light of the Sun will be cut off from the Earth by the interposition of the opaque body of the Moon. This, it will easily be seen, can only happen under similar conditions to those necessary to occasion a lunar eclipse; that is, at the time of new moon, the latter body must be near her node. If this occur at the same time that the Moon is in apogee, or at its greatest distance from the earth, the sun will, at the greatest phase, not be totally eclipsed, but the centre only will be covered by the black body of the Moon, leaving an "annulus," or ring of sunlight, round the border; whence the name "annular" eclipse. Should the Moon, at the node, be in perigee (at its least distance from the earth), the eclipse will be total, and the whole of the Sun be hidden from view. An eclipse of the Sun may be partial, as well as annular or total; the two former kinds offer no phenomena worthy of remark; but, in the latter case, at the moment of totality, some very remarkable appearances present themselves, among which may be mentioned the "red flames," or "protuberances," as they have been called by different observers; these consist of red or rose-coloured projections seen around the discs of the Sun and Moon, some of them in shape like conical hills, others crooked like the Australian "boomerang," and occasionally irregular masses of the same character have been observed, separated from the discs a short distance. Previous to the observation of the eclipse of 1860, it was a matter of doubt, whether these prominences belonged to the Sun or Moon, a doubt most satisfactorily cleared up by the photographs taken in Spain, where the eclipse was total. From these it may be seen that the advancing Moon gradually covered up the prominences in the direction of her motion, uncovering those in her rear, thus proving them to have had their origin in the Sun. This eclipse was very fully observed by the astronomers sent out to Spain by the English Government. Their observations were afterwards sent to Greenwich to (it was understood) be drawn up in the form of a "Report," which is still looked for.

A total eclipse of a very favourable kind happened in 1868, August 17—18, the Moon being at the time in perigee. It was total across the centre of India, Suez, and the South of China. One of the principal objects in observing this eclipse was to ascertain, if possible, by means of spectrum analysis, the physical nature of the prominences, for which purpose this eclipse was very suitable, the totality being increased by the Moon's proximity to the Earth. Though the weather was generally unfavourable some valuable results were obtained, and the gaseous nature of the prominences established by all the observers who used the spectroscope, several bright lines (the evidence of gaseous nature) being seen, the majority of which were coincident with the dark ones seen in the Sun spectrum, while some of the observers suspected new ones. The light of the prominences could not be polarized, but that of the corona could be, in a plane passing through the centre of the sun. Another remarkable phenomenon always accompanying a total eclipse is the above-mentioned corona, a beautiful silvery ring of light surrounding the Sun and Moon, through the circumference of which several large rays or beams of light are seen, as if radiating from its centre, to stretch for a considerable distance beyond the circumference, some of them straight, and others curved like a scimitar.

Meteorology of the Year 1867–68.

The following observations of the barometer, thermometer, and rain gauge, are extracted from those taken at Kew Observatory.* Generally speaking, they vary, either way, about two degrees from those made at the Royal Observatory, Greenwich. The elevation of that place above the water or sea level is such as to cause greater radiation of heat than at Kew. The air there contains also less moisture; hence a lower average temperature is generally observed. The Kew observations, however, are now universally taken as the standard of comparison with those of foreign observatories.

To enable the reader to judge more accurately of the remarkable character of the year ending September, 1868, the months of July, August and September, 1867, are included. It will be perceived that the spring and summer of 1868 present some most remarkable features yet unobserved by meteorologists during the present century. An early and mild spring was followed by a summer of absolutely tropical heat; the corrected temperature in the shade having, on more than one occasion, exceeded 92° Fah., whilst a range from 82° to 88° was of common occurrence during July. Another remarkable fact was that during the whole of the hot period little rain fell, and scarcely any dew was deposited. The effect on vegetation was to cause the ripening of the cereals at least from three weeks to a month before the usual period, whilst grass and green crops were almost destroyed. Refreshing rains in September, however, restored the fields to a spring-like appearance, and remedied the evils of the preceding drought.

Possibly many of the readers of this Almanack may be desirous of commencing personal observations on the barometer, thermometer, and rain-fall. The following brief words of advice will be of value:—In purchasing the two former, a condition should be made that they have been verified at Kew; otherwise, as a general rule, they will be of little value. The instruments should be fixed to a frame at a height of about five feet from the ground, so that the eye of the observer shall be level with the indications of the mercury in each. Neither the thermometer nor barometer should be exposed to the sun's rays, as such would cause erroneous indications. Hence both should face the North, and the sides of the frame should be protected by a projecting ledge, so as to shelter them from the sun when out at its farthest north declination. The frame should not be fixed over a grass plot, because of the radiation produced thereby, but rather over a gravel or pebble bed. Certain corrections, as for capillary attraction, expansion of the glass of the instruments, height above sea level, and several others, have to be made. The limits of our space prevent giving detailed instructions on such matters, but reference to the works of Lowe, Symons, Glaisher, Galton, and other meteorologists will supply every necessary information, together with tables ready calculated, in some cases, for such purposes. The rain gauge is so simple an instrument as to require no advice respecting its use, with the exception that it should not be placed on the ground, because in a heavy rain-storm the rain would be beaten off, and erroneously increase the amount of fall indicated. It must be also borne in mind that its position must not be too elevated. About two inches less rain falls annually at a height of 50 feet from the ground, than on its surface. The gauge may be properly placed, therefore, at a height of three or four feet, and away from walls, in an open situation.

1867.	Barom. (mean.)	Thermom. Min.	Max.	Rnfall. Inches.	1867.	Barom. (mean.)	Thermom. Min.	Max.	Rnfall. Inches.	1867.	Barom. (mean.)	Thermom. Min.	Max.	Rnfall. Inches.
July 1	30·796	53·0	80·4	0·257	July 17	29·708	53·1	68·6	0·381	Aug. 2	30·014	48·9	58·5	0·000
,, 2	30·685	56·7	58·2	0·009	,, 18	29·591	55·6	68·7	0·047	,, 3	30·051	42·3	67·9	0·000
,, 3	29·999	54·9	71·0	0·146	,, 19	29·681	51·6	64·9	0·003	,, 4	30·076	51·4	69·5	0·000
,, 4	29·855	54·9	70·8	0·006	,, 20	29·806	52·0	69·8	0·094	,, 5	29·983	49·6	70·2	0·000
,, 5	30·055	57·5	67·5	0·000	,, 21	29·673	57·6	70·1	0·010	,, 6	29·753	56·3	64·4	0·306
,, 6	30·157	45·7	70·8	0·000	,, 22	29·694	54·5	72·2	0·224	,, 7	29·753	47·9	64·7	0·320
,, 7	30·175	49·5	69·0	0·000	,, 23	29·615	55·3	70·1	0·020	,, 8	29·719	54·8	71·5	0·060
,, 8	30·267	47·0	70·1	0·000	,, 24	29·703	51·7	68·8	0·000	,, 9	29·846	57·7	70·0	0·000
,, 9	30·253	46·1	70·8	0·000	,, 25	29·771	44·1	70·7	1·328	,, 10	30·110	48·8	72·7	0·000
,, 10	30·189	48·3	74·4	0·000	,, 26	29·626	51·9	57·7	0·158	,, 11	—	48·4	76·1	0·000
,, 11	30·076	46·4	73·8	0·000	,, 27	30·026	48·8	59·8	0·000	,, 12	30·075	57·8	81·0	0·000
,, 12	29·812	55·1	73·0	0·000	,, 28	30·114	45·1	66·1	0·000	,, 13	30·003	57·4	83·2	0·000
,, 13	29·732	53·6	69·6	0·334	,, 29	30·042	45·3	66·2	0·000	,, 14	29·915	59·1	85·9	0·180
,, 14	29·716	54·5	70·1	0·120	,, 30	30·020	44·9	66·1	0·000	,, 15	29·700	61·5	64·9	0·210
,, 15	29·499	52·7	64·9	0·241	,, 31	29·984	47·4	68·6	0·000	,, 16	29·748	55·3	69·7	0·001
,, 16	29·512	55·0	65·8	0·228	Aug. 1	29·983	49·2	58·7	0·000	,, 17	29·890	53·7	70·0	0·000

* Kew, Surrey. Lat., 51° 29′ 29″ N. Long., 0° 18′ W. Height above sea level, 34 feet.
Time of observation, 10 A.M.

1867.	Barom. (mean.)	Thermom. Min.	Thermom. Max.	Rnfall. Inches.	1867.	Barom. (mean.)	Thermom. Min.	Thermom. Max.	Rnfall. Inches.	1868.	Barom. (mean.)	Thermom. Min.	Thermom. Max.	Rnfall. Inches.
Aug 18	30·044	59·9	73·0	0·000	Oct. 30	29·795	51·5	56·7	0·066	Jan. 8	30·118	27·3	34·0	0·000
,, 19	30·010	57·3	77·3	0·830	,, 31	29·937	52·9	57·5	0·000	,, 9	30·235	29·1	30·4	0·000
,, 20	29·378	63·0	71·2	0·000	Nov. 1	29·918	52·5	60·9	0·003	,, 10	30·202	28·7	32·8	0·000
,, 21	30·004	53·8	70·7	0·000	,, 2	30·428	37·2	49·9	0·000	,, 11	29·870	30·1	32·7	0·283
,, 22	30·020	49·3	73·1	0·000	,, 3	30·332	25·9	48·3	0·000	,, 12	29·958	31·1	46·9	0·090
,, 23	30·031	48·0	74·9	0·000	,, 4	30·277	35·5	52·8	0·000	,, 13	29·539	36·7	49·3	0·047
,, 24	30·062	49·7	74·0	0·000	,, 5	30·419	39·9	46·9	0·000	,, 14	29·898	39·9	52·4	0·075
,, 25	30·027	55·5	75·0	0·000	,, 6	30·460	29·7	47·1	0·000	,, 15	29·982	43·1	51·0	0·005
,, 26	29·965	57·0	69·3	0·145	,, 7	30·562	29·5	49·2	0·004	,, 16	30·140	36·6	50·8	0·000
,, 27	30·042	48·0	68·3	0·000	,, 8	30·589	29·3	51·8	0·000	,, 17	29·801	45·1	52·6	0·142
,, 28	30·159	45·1	65·7	0·000	,, 9	30·593	29·2	47·1	0·000	,, 18	29·256	42·7	49·7	0·584
,, 29	30·165	57·5	70·9	0·000	,, 10	30·546	40·2	50·2	0·000	,, 19	29·053	40·6	47·9	0·035
,, 30	30·038	55·3	70·7	0·005	,, 11	30·300	35·6	40·1	0·000	,, 20	29·235	38·4	42·7	0·003
,, 31	29·843	55·8	75·7	0·001	,, 12	30·175	31·0	44·2	0·000	,, 21	29·666	30·2	41·3	0·800
Sept. 1	29·851	59·4	75·7	0·000	,, 13	29·969	35·5	34·0	0·020	,, 22	29·100	36·5	37·9	0·147
,, 2	30·092	52·3	75·0	0·000	,, 14	29·601	35·0	55·6	0·060	,, 23	29·905	32·6	36·1	0·000
,, 3	29·966	60·8	72·1	0·390	,, 15	29·643	47·4	60·0	0·000	,, 24	30·135	27·0	38·4	0·300
,, 4	29·820	58·0	70·0	0·148	,, 16	29·684	46·9	48·5	0·000	,, 25	29·641	31·4	47·5	0·000
,, 5	29·850	57·6	68·6	0·013	,, 17	29·874	37·9	42·5	0·000	,, 26	30·108	37·9	42·9	0·000
,, 6	29·773	51·1	67·5	0·000	,, 18	30·292	33·0	43·0	0·000	,, 27	30·191	28·8	45·3	0·390
,, 7	29·955	54·3	69·3	0·000	,, 19	30·317	39·3	48·1	0·000	,, 28	29·992	37·1	50·4	0·400
,, 8	30·052	47·8	69·1	0·020	,, 20	30·435	33·7	40·5	0·000	,, 29	30·314	35·3	45·3	0·000
,, 9	29·860	52·6	70·1	1·010	,, 21	30·510	36·3	42·7	0·000	,, 30	30·197	35·0	46·7	0·000
,, 10	29·885	52·4	67·0	0·325	,, 22	30·509	32·5	45·5	0·000	,, 31	29·872	40·7	52·3	0·023
,, 11	29·930	47·3	66·8	0·000	,, 23	30·489	32·5	45·5	0·000	Feb. 1	29·415	47·5	55·9	0·031
,, 12	29·795	52·7	70·5	0·000	,, 24	30·652	31·0	42·2	0·000	,, 2	29·919	40·3	52·5	0·273
,, 13	29·936	52·6	67·1	0·000	,, 25	30·476	32·0	39·7	0·008	,, 3	30·011	44·1	45·4	0·000
,, 14	30·019	47·8	64·5	0·076	,, 26	30·176	35·4	46·1	0·000	,, 4	30·374	30·5	48·4	0·000
,, 15	29·968	51·1	64·8	0·015	,, 27	30·276	31·0	42·1	0·000	,, 5	30·270	38·3	48·5	0·000
,, 16	29·200	45·5	60·7	0·000	,, 28	30·371	25·0	41·8	0·000	,, 6	30·301	38·6	43·7	0·004
,, 17	30·378	43·3	57·9	0·036	,, 29	30·322	22·6	43·7	0·000	,, 7	29·894	30·7	46·6	0·108
,, 18	30·296	49·7	63·7	0·000	,, 30	29·894	28·5	42·5	*0·686	,, 8	29·925	41·9	43·4	0·000
,, 19	30·136	51·0	65·6	0·000	Dec. 1	29·265	38·6	51·5	0·523	,, 9	30·568	37·5	45·2	0·000
,, 20	30·156	51·5	62·6	0·000	,, 2	29·670	28·0	31·7	0·005	,, 10	30·519	32·3	51·8	0·000
,, 21	30·124	45·5	61·6	0·160	,, 3	30·124	25·6	38·2	0·000	,, 11	30·499	41·9	50·0	0·000
,, 22	29·900	50·5	64·6	0·065	,, 4	30·311	29·5	38·7	0·185	,, 12	30·459	30·2	45·7	0·000
,, 23	29·954	45·5	64·8	0·000	,, 5	29·829	27·0	42·5	*0·010	,, 13	30·371	34·5	48·5	0·000
,, 24	30·188	47·3	59·8	0·000	,, 6	29·857	32·2	39·2	0·014	,, 14	30·121	41·4	47·8	0·020
,, 25	30·455	35·5	59·3	0·000	,, 7	30·120	29·5	36·5	0·000	,, 15	30·171	43·4	46·5	0·021
,, 26	30·435	38·9	61·9	0·000	,, 8	30·133	30·8	35·5	0·126	,, 16	30·557	28·9	37·1	0·000
,, 27	30·324	46·6	60·6	0·000	,, 9	30·274	21·6	30·2	0·000	,, 17	30·204	31·2	49·4	0·000
,, 28	30·226	49·3	62·4	0·000	,, 10	30·041	19·8	38·8	0·005	,, 18	30·082	31·2	48·1	0·030
,, 29	30·206	49·3	61·7	0·000	,, 11	30·054	33·0	50·8	0·000	,, 19	29·638	42·4	46·4	0·000
,, 30	30·035	50·3	63·1	0·000	,, 12	30·147	44·9	52·1	0·000	,, 20	30·119	31·7	38·2	0·037
Oct. 1	30·421	43·3	56·3	0·000	,, 13	30·267	39·4	46·4	0·000	,, 21	29·963	37·7	53·3	0·000
,, 2	29·961	39·1	56·8	0·040	,, 14	29·970	36·4	48·5	0·130	,, 22	29·759	42·5	51·0	0·014
,, 3	29·895	37·6	52·6	0·000	,, 15	29·768	43·1	53·7	0·105	,, 23	30·257	37·0	45·3	0·015
,, 4	30·138	33·5	48·3	0·000	,, 16	29·823	49·7	52·4	0·005	,, 24	30·217	37·0	54·8	0·000
,, 5	30·073	31·5	49·0	0·000	,, 17	29·617	48·1	52·5	0·000	,, 25	30·344	47·8	60·9	0·000
,, 6	29·967	30·2	53·2	0·172	,, 18	29·510	36·1	42·3	0·000	,, 26	30·271	41·3	54·8	0·000
,, 7	29·617	43·6	57·0	0·010	,, 19	29·778	29·0	38·8	0·000	,, 27	30·039	46·2	49·6	0·000
,, 8	29·590	39·5	51·2	0·005	,, 20	30·012	22·0	32·9	0·118	,, 28	29·882	42·0	55·1	0·000
,, 9	29·819	32·5	47·9	0·280	,, 21	29·862	25·5	42·4	0·040	,, 29	29·490	44·1	50·4	0·510
,, 10	29·910	42·1	52·2	0·000	,, 22	29·812	37·6	51·4	0·000	Mar. 1	29·886	36·2	50·4	0·013
,, 11	30·172	30·0	47·1	0·153	,, 23	30·205	25·4	43·0	0·013	,, 2	30·050	49·8	54·3	0·050
,, 12	29·814	37·4	52·2	0·000	,, 24	30·125	25·0	47·5	0·000	,, 3	30·220	44·5	54·4	0·000
,, 13	29·602	38·1	57·3	0·030	,, 25	30·180	28·5	38·9	0·000	,, 4	30·114	46·6	56·6	0·000
,, 14	99·747	38·1	61·5	0·004	,, 26	30·255	27·0	32·2	0·103	,, 5	29·640	48·5	56·2	0·000
,, 15	29·800	50·0	63·2	0·353	,, 27	30·371	28·0	37·9	0·000	,, 6	29·760	38·3	49·6	0·010
,, 16	29·895	50·8	59·9	0·010	,, 28	30·255	29·2	33·8	0·000	,, 7	29·691	34·5	50·5	0·180
,, 17	29·739	48·8	62·4	0·030	,, 29	30·143	26·4	40·4	0·004	,, 8	29·158	35·8	44·7	0·000
,, 18	29·750	45·1	59·3	0·080	,, 30	30·344	30·2	36·1	0·000	,, 9	29·559	32·4	48·3	0·000
,, 19	29·691	41·3	55·7	0·005	,, 31	30·243	25·5	31·2	0·000	,, 10	29·447	32·3	50·7	0·017
,, 20	29·916	33·2	56·0	0·000	**1868.**					,, 11	29·640	34·3	50·8	0·083
,, 21	30·118	38·1	61·1	0·000	Jan. 1	30·156	26·5	31·8	0·000	,, 12	29·757	38·8	54·3	0·060
,, 22	30·217	52·7	64·6	0·000	,, 2	30·198	27·5	34·3	0·012	,, 13	30·163	44·6	55·7	0·020
,, 23	29·984	54·1	61·0	0·000	,, 3	30·160	23·8	29·8	0·000	,, 14	30·227	45·3	52·3	0·025
,, 24	29·875	48·5	58·8	0·000	,, 4	29·991	26·7	30·3	0·000	,, 15	30·239	33·8	51·5	0·000
,, 25	30·160	46·6	57·7	0·000	,, 5	30·006	26·8	33·0	0·113	,, 16	30·018	37·1	52·4	0·025
,, 26	30·110	40·1	59·5	0·000	,, 6	29·880	31·0	34·6	*0·010	,, 17	29·985	44·3	50·2	0·000
,, 27	29·488	46·7	55·4	0·340	,, 7	30·045	31·0	33·2	*0·243	,, 18	30·210	35·6	48·4	0·000
,, 28	29·966	35·0	55·0	0·023						,, 19	29·887	31·2	48·3	0·015
,, 29	29·837	38·0	60·7	0·014	* Melted snow and rain.					,, 20	29·922	32·2	46·5	0·003

1868.	Barom. (mean)	Thermom. Min.	Thermom. Max.	Rnfall Inches
Mar 21	30·059	43·8	56·5	0·000
,, 22	30·015	40·4	52·6	0·015
,, 23	29·816	37·6	47·7	0·025
,, 24	29·963	33·5	42·3	0·000
,, 25	30·114	29·5	45·9	*0·405
,, 26	29·956	33·0	55·6	0·000
,, 27	30·149	42·7	55·9	0·000
,, 28	30·469	38·5	48·8	0·000
,, 29	30·593	32·5	42·1	0·000
,, 30	30·461	28·5	51·2	0·000
,, 31	30·382	28·7	57·7	0·000
Apr. 1	30·362	47·6	54·3	0·000
,, 2	30·391	38·6	54·2	0·000
,, 3	30·197	39·1	62·5	0·000
,, 4	30·028	32·7	66·4	0·000
,, 5	30·055	36·2	64·6	0·000
,, 6	29·948	41·5	61·4	0·000
,, 7	29·709	41·4	62·6	0·000
,, 8	29·412	43·2	53·0	0·040
,, 9	29·821	35·7	45·8	0·015
,, 10	30·015	33·3	48·8	0·000
,, 11	30·037	35·0	46·9	0·000
,, 12	30·029	29·4	42·6	0·000
,, 13	30·024	32·5	49·2	0·000
,, 14	30·216	39·3	54·1	0·000
,, 15	30·319	31·9	61·6	0·000
,, 16	30·085	44·2	61·9	0·000
,, 17	29·916	49·6	58·3	0·020
,, 18	29·831	39·0	55·2	0·063
,, 19	29·454	42·4	55·8	0·377
,, 20	29·150	45·7	55·7	0·420
,, 21	29·617	46·4	60·0	0·025
,, 22	29·696	49·8	59·7	0·034
,, 23	29·721	40·9	58·7	0·240
,, 24	29·523	44·9	56·4	0·026
,, 25	30·036	44·6	56·5	0·006
,, 26	30·153	43·8	58·2	0·000
,, 27	30·069	38·0	59·1	0·134
,, 28	30·030	39·4	59·6	0·000
,, 29	30·115	47·8	61·8	0·000
,, 30	30·115	48·1	64·5	0·000
May 1	30·261	50·2	63·5	0·000
,, 2	30·113	39·1	69·6	0·000
,, 3	29·871	43·9	78·8	0·000
,, 4	30·020	47·7	61·7	0·000
,, 5	30·156	42·1	55·1	0·000
,, 6	30·153	40·3	53·7	0·000
,, 7	29·948	35·8	63·7	0·000
,, 8	29·807	37·3	74·1	0·042
,, 9	29·758	50·8	66·6	0·081
,, 10	29·785	41·0	64·1	0·030
,, 11	29·844	42·0	62·6	0·000
,, 12	29·894	45·3	65·7	0·000
,, 13	30·162	43·6	63·8	0·000
,, 14	30·311	50·1	69·8	0·000
,, 15	30·170	46·7	73·4	0·000
,, 16	30·043	53·2	67·3	0·000
,, 17	30·110	51·6	57·8	0·000
,, 18	30·086	48·7	71·9	0·000
,, 19	29·957	53·9	83·0	0·000
,, 20	29·962	56·8	69·5	0·000
,, 21	29·913	44·6	66·4	0·035
,, 22	29·783	51·8	63·3	0·082

1868.	Barom. (mean)	Thermom. Min.	Thermom. Max.	Rnfall Inches
May 23	29·567	52·9	61·8	0·203
,, 24	29·666	39·6	59·7	0·157
,, 25	29·804	52·5	66·4	0·000
,, 26	30·008	46·9	67·4	0·000
,, 27	30·168	45·9	70·2	0·000
,, 28	30·181	45·1	75·9	0·000
,, 29	29·940	54·9	74·0	0·135
,, 30	29·995	53·9	67·9	0·000
,, 31	30·087	50·9	69·6	0·000
June 1	20·942	45·1	71·9	0·000
,, 2	29·945	53·2	69·9	0·000
,, 3	30·069	45·3	67·3	0·000
,, 4	30·012	48·8	60·7	0·097
,, 5	30·140	48·5	70·2	0·000
,, 6	30·170	47·8	74·8	0·000
,, 7	30·158	52·6	67·5	0·090
,, 8	30·192	47·5	55·6	0·000
,, 9	30·161	45·1	67·0	0·000
,, 10	30·143	44·3	71·1	0·000
,, 11	30·197	46·3	70·5	0·000
,, 12	30·221	54·6	74·7	0·000
,, 13	30·184	50·8	80·8	0·000
,, 14	30·204	54·9	80·2	0·000
,, 15	30·212	63·1	74·8	0·000
,, 16	30·222	52·6	75·4	0·000
,, 17	30·153	55·3	78·0	0·000
,, 18	30·242	55·3	73·4	0·000
,, 19	30·148	50·8	68·8	0·000
,, 20	30·019	54·9	76·5	0·000
,, 21		56·6	78·9	0·171
,, 22	29·683	55·1	69·5	0·000
,, 23	29·777	47·8	70·1	0·122
,, 24	30·037	48·0	71·5	0·004
,, 25	30·178	56·5	71·7	0·000
,, 26	30·313	49·3	77·0	0·000
,, 27	30·221	49·9	85·0	0·000
,, 28	30·222	58·8	73·3	0·000
,, 29	30·318	50·8	71·4	0·000
,, 30	30·280	48·9	72·4	0·035
July 1	30·246	52·3	69·4	0·000
,, 2	30·107	54·8	74·4	0·000
,, 3	29·980	57·7	77·3	0·000
,, 4	29·993	53·3	55·8	0·000
,, 5	30·012	49·7	69·3	0·000
,, 6	30·039	49·7	69·3	0·000
,, 7	30·103	51·2	75·7	0·000
,, 8	30·091	52·8	82·7	0·000
,, 9	30·121	55·5	81·2	0·000
,, 10	30·149	53·1	79·5	0·000
,, 11	30·115	54·7	79·7	1·034
,, 12	30·068	55·5	78·4	0·400
,, 13	30·020	55·6	81·0	0·000
,, 14	30·015	53·3	81·9	0·000
,, 15	29·904	58·4	85·3	0·000
,, 16	29·923	58·6	86·0	0·000
,, 17	29·975	62·5	79·4	0·000
,, 18	29·989	59·9	82·1	0·000
,, 19	30·005	61·5	77·7	0·000
,, 20	30·027	53·7	85·2	0·000
,, 21	30·023	60·9	89·2	0·000
,, 22	29·929	60·6	90·2	0·000
,, 23	30·165	61·6	76·1	0·000
,, 24	30·373	50·7	72·1	0·000
,, 25	30·223	52·8	74·7	0·000
,, 26	29·982	56·3	77·2	0·010
,, 27	29·831	58·2	85·7	0·000

1868.	Barom. (mean)	Thermom. Min.	Thermom. Max.	Rnfall. Inches
July 28	29·674	58·5	85·3	0·170
,, 29	29·714	54·0	62·5	0·010
,, 30	30·003	49·9	77·8	0·000
,, 31	30·155	63·8	75·2	0·000
Aug. 1	30·244	47·7	80·5	0·000
,, 2	30·156	52·0	82·1	0·000
,, 3	30·003	60·5	80·4	0·000
,, 4	29·873	61·3	84·5	0·000
,, 5	29·817	58·6	85·4	0·210
,, 6	29·716	61·2	75·7	0·160
,, 7	29·725	64·6	76·8	0·005
,, 8	30·018	55·3	75·7	0·000
,, 9	30·147	52·8	74·3	0·000
,, 10	29·874	57·4	81·5	0·000
,, 11	29·571	63·0	73·7	0·098
,, 12	29·681	52·7	73·1	0·021
,, 13	29·517	55·3	64·6	0·269
,, 14	29·753	51·5	72·2	0·000
,, 15	29·863	54·3	75·3	0·000
,, 16	29·709	60·9	70·9	0·220
,, 17	29·702	60·1	68·2	0·645
,, 18	29·588	58·8	72·1	0·328
,, 19	29·778	60·1	68·4	0·135
,, 20	29·965	56·9	62·0	0·000
,, 21	29·944	54·3	70·2	0·334
,, 22	29·249	52·1	66·4	0·052
,, 23	29·547	52·6	64·5	0·023
,, 24	29·839	49·3	64·1	0·000
,, 25	30·065	48·3	63·8	0·000
,, 26	30·114	45·7	64·5	0·020
,, 27	30·007	57·8	69·2	0·000
,, 28	30·177	47·3	63·0	0·000
,, 29	30·245	50·7	64·6	0·000
,, 30	30·170	49·5	70·5	0·000
,, 31	30·101	55·6	72·4	0·000
Sept. 1	30·194	48·8	74·3	0·000
,, 2	30·248	48·5	75·8	0·000
,, 3	30·125	48·8	78·5	0·000
,, 4	30·112	50·4	80·3	0·000
,, 5	37·203	50·6	85·7	0·000
,, 6	30·030	53·8	84·7	0·000
,, 7	30·012	53·1	86·4	0·000
,, 8	30·190	53·3	64·6	0·000
,, 9	30·319	52·7	69·2	0·000
,, 10	30·151	48·5	71·5	0·000
,, 11	29·976	44·1	73·3	0·000
,, 12	29·966	55·8	66·9	0·000
,, 13	29·986	48·0	63·7	0·000
,, 14	29·911	43·3	61·5	0·000
,, 15	29·954	50·7	62·0	0·000
,, 16	29·895	47·5	66·4	0·000
,, 17	29·675	51·3	66·3	0·010
,, 18	29·532	54·3	64·6	0·060
,, 19	29·497	46·6	63·9	0·020
,, 20	29·608	54·9	66·0	0·010
,, 21	29·686	48·8	69·9	0·000
,, 22	29·689	53·7	66·1	0·000
,, 23	29·670	45·7	63·6	0·000
,, 24	29·676	47·7	65·0	0·060
,, 25	29·418	43·6	63·3	0·160
,, 26	29·666	47·2	67·3	0·560
,, 27	29·433	52·8	63·8	0·080
,, 28	29·387	51·7	61·8	0·220
,, 29	29·295	52·9	63·7	0·160
,, 30	29·289	49·8	61·9	0·350

* Melted snow and rain.

Meteorology is the science of the weather, and treats of the phenomena which occur in the atmosphere, their causes and effects. The phenomena to which it refers are accounted for by natural laws disclosed in the study of chemistry, electricity, the atmospheric properties, &c.

Rain.—The waters of the earth yield up a certain quantity of moisture into the air, which being condensed, assumes the form of clouds. These clouds, on being affected by a diminution of temperature, lose their suspensory property, and fall to the ground in the form of a shower of rain.

In the old Almanacks, and in some of recent date, will be found predictions of the weather twelve months in advance. Thus, Moore's Almanack for 1868 warned farmers that in July there would be heavy rain and showery weather, "interrupting the gathering in of the hay." How this prediction was *verified* is notorious. We, therefore, will only venture to examine, and endeavour to explain those signs which may frequently be found to precede atmospheric changes.

In our islands, variable winds, and many other causes, tend to render any predictions that can be relied on simply impossible. We know that, as a rule, an easterly wind usually brings cold, dry weather; while one from the south, or south-west, is warm and moist. When these two winds meet, a circumstance of common occurrence, rain is almost sure to result, simply because the cold east wind condenses the moisture of the south, south-westerly, or westerly winds, and thus makes the water previously held in the air take the form of rain.

Only those who are accustomed to watch daily the external signs of changes of the weather can, as a rule, give anything like a prediction of coming changes. Hence farmers, shepherds, and sailors have always been proverbially "weather-wise." The indications on which they depend refer chiefly to those causes that arise from changes of the amount of moisture in the atmosphere. These are derived from the contrary influences of hot and moist air mixing with cold and dry air. For example,—a long ribbon of dry seaweed becomes moist as damp weather approaches, because it contains a salt that attracts the excessive moisture of the atmosphere. For somewhat similar reasons painted walls or iron rails become moist as wet weather comes on. In dry weather the stairs of houses creak if stood on, whilst in wet weather, or during its approach, they emit no sound. On the wind changing to the south-west from a drier quarter, the paving of the streets, tiles or slates on houses, become moist; the window-frames and doors "stick"; ropes become tight, if previously they were loosely stretched; the steam is abundantly visible from a locomotive as it travels along; smoke falls to the ground; and many other familiar signs of change of weather appear.

Animals of all kinds are amongst the earliest indicators of a change. Sea-birds, such as gulls, fly inland in search of food as stormy weather comes on. Wild-fowl forsake marshy ground, and seek higher localities, often flying towards towns. Swallows and rooks fly low, and keep near "home," both before and during bad weather. Frogs are unusually noisy before rain. Worms and leeches generally appear at the surface of the ground or water,—in fact, a leech is an excellent weather indicator. Moles throw up much earth before rain; ants close up their nests to preserve their larvæ or early stage of their young; cattle, sheep, and other quadrupeds huddle together near bushes and trees; while horses and asses assume an amusing, thoughtful aspect, just as if they were studying the probable changes of the weather. If a piece of catgut, or a human or horse hair, be hung over a little pulley, with a weight attached at one end, whilst the other is fixed to a nail, the contraction of the hair, or its stretching, will indicate coming changes of weather. Hence it is impossible for women to keep the hair in curl during wet, whilst it curls well in dry weather.

All such, and many others, are what may be called, for the sake of clearness, *natural* indications of a change of weather. Equally so are the following; but because they are not commonly noticed, and require careful observation, they are considered more scientific:—

1. If the mercury of a Barometer rise gradually, while the Thermometer falls, and dampness becomes less, a north-west, north, or north-east wind may be expected, with less rain or snow according to the season of the year.

2. If the Barometer fall, and the Thermometer rises, with increased dampness, wind and rain may be expected from the south-east, south, or south-west. A fall in winter, with a low Thermometer, foretells snow.

3. The Barometer almost always rises as a northerly wind comes on. Yet rain may occur, but in no great quantity, except on our west coasts.

4. In our islands, if the Barometer gradually rise above 29½ inches, as a rule a northerly wind may be expected. If it rise fast, then squalls from the north-west, north, or north-east may be expected. If the Thermometer fall at the same time, dry and open weather generally follows. A sudden rise of the Barometer may, however, be afterwards followed by a south-west wind and wet.

5. The quicker the rise of the Barometer, the more unsettled will the weather be; whilst a steady or slow rise indicates settled weather to follow.

6. Great and sudden falls of the Barometer show that violent gales may be expected. These generally occur, under such circumstances, from the south-east, south, or south-west.

7. Great elevations of the Barometer, maintained for some time, are almost always accompanied with northerly winds.

8. A sudden fall of the Barometer, with a westerly wind, is often followed by a storm from the north-west, north, or north-east.

9. The Barometer is always highest with a north-east, and lowest with a south-west wind, in all parts of our islands.

To observe these indications, a Barometer and Thermometer of good construction are required. Wheel-barometers, it must be borne in mind, are never to be trusted.

The clouds afford many indications of changes of the weather, for of course the latter depends on them. A rosy sky at sunset foretells fine weather, whilst a dark reddish tint indicates rain. A red sky in the morning shows bad weather, or much rain or wind; but a grey sky, fine weather; a dawn high in the sky, wind; if a low dawn, fair weather. The softer-looking the clouds, the less wind may be expected; the harder, more rolled, and tufted or ragged, the stronger the coming wind. Inky clouds foretell rain; light, scudding clouds, driving across heavy masses, foretell wind and rain; but if alone, wind only. High upper clouds, crossing the "face" of the sun, moon, or stars in a different direction to that of the lower clouds, or the wind felt on the earth at the moment, foretell a change of wind towards that direction. Streaks, wisps, &c., of clouds, indicate wind and rain. The higher the clouds, the more gradual and lasting the change. Misty clouds, hanging on heights, bushes, &c., foretell rain, if they stay, increase, or descend; if they rise or disperse, fine weather may be expected.

A Key to the Calendar,

CONTAINING AN ACCOUNT OF THE VARIOUS SAINTS' DAYS* AND ANNIVERSARIES,
WITH THE LEGENDS AND POPULAR SUPERSTITIONS CONCERNING THEM.

January.

> "When the grass grows in Janiveer,
> It grows the worse for't all the year."

The month is so named from the Roman deity Janus, who was supposed to preside over doors. He was represented with two faces, one of which looked back, over the old year; the other forward, to the new. The Roman year originally commenced in March; at first it had but ten months, till Numa Pompilius, who died 672 B.C., added January and February. It is usually the coldest month of the twelve, hence the adage,

> "As the day lengthens,
> So the cold strengthens."

A warm January is regarded by the farmer with anything but satisfaction.

1. *Circumcision.*—Instituted to commemorate our Saviour's obedience to the ceremonial law on the eighth day after the Nativity. This feast was one of the latest introduced into the Calendar, and does not appear to have been observed till towards the end of the 11th century.

The first day of the year is generally observed as a season of rejoicing, not only in England but throughout the world. In Scotland it is a general holiday; in France *le jour de l'an* is celebrated by making presents to both young and old, and Paris presents all the appearance of an immense fair.

6. *Epiphany*, or Manifestation.—On this day, the Wise Men of the East, following the guiding of a star, found the infant Saviour in the manger at Bethlehem, and there offered Him gifts. According to tradition, the Wise Men were three kings—Gaspar, Melchior, and Balthazar; they were later in life baptized by St. Thomas, and spent their days in preaching the Gospel; after death their relics were removed to Cologne, and may to this day be seen in the noble cathedral there. Following their example, the Queen, through the Lord Chamberlain, annually on this day present gold, frankincense, and myrrh at the Chapel Royal, St. James's.

Old Christmas Day.—Until the alteration of the Calendar in the year 1752, the anniversary of Christ's birth was held on this day.

Twelfth Day.—This is a high festival with young people, not only in England, but in most parts of Europe also; a cake is prepared for the occasion, and the king is drawn by lot.

8. *St. Lucian.*—But little is known of this saint, who is supposed to have been a native of Syria, and to have suffered martyrdom on the rack in Nicomedia. By others he is supposed to have been a priest associated with St. Denys in missionary work in France, and to have suffered martyrdom at Beauvais, A.D. 312.

Plough Monday.—The first Monday after the

Epiphany is still observed as a day of conviviality in many parts of the country. In former times the ploughmen kept lights burning before favourite shrines, in order to obtain a blessing on their labours; they also went from house to house, begging money to "speed the plough," by paying for the tapers, but money so collected is now too frequently spent in dissipation.

13. *St. Hilary*, Bishop of Poictiers, was an eminent defender of the truth in opposition to the Arians; for so doing he was banished to Phrygia by the Emperor Constantius, but after some years returned to his see, where he died in peace, A.D. 368.

18. *St. Prisca, Virgin and Martyr*, is said to have been a noble Roman maiden of about twelve, who on refusing to sacrifice to the gods was thrown into the amphitheatre; but the lions, recognizing her sanctity, lay down at her feet, and refused to touch her; she was then beheaded, upon which an eagle descended and watched her corpse till it was buried.

20. *St. Fabian* succeeded St. Anterus as bishop of Rome, A.D. 236. He suffered in the Decian persecution, A.D. 250. This is also the eve of St. Agnes, a day celebrated by poets and dear to maidens, who, on using certain charms are favoured with dreams of their future husbands:—

> "They told her how, upon St. Agnes' eve,
> Young virgins might have visions of delight,
> And soft adornings from their loves receive
> Upon the honied middle of the night,
> If ceremonies due they did aright;
> As, supperless to bed they must retire,
>   *   *   *   *   *   *
> Nor look behind, nor sideways, but require
> Of heaven, with upward eyes, for all that they
>   desire."

21. *St. Agnes* having devoted herself to the service of God, refused to become the bride of a noble Roman; she was charged with being a Christian, and suffered many brutal indignities rather than sacrifice to the gods. She suffered martyrdom A.D. 304, first by being thrust into the flames, and then being beheaded. Shortly afterwards, while her parents were bewailing her death, she appeared to them with a glorified aspect, and a spotless lamb by her side, and bade them dry their tears, for she was now for ever united to her dear Saviour.

22. *St. Vincent*, a Spaniard, suffered an amount of refined cruelty such as fell to the lot of few. He was half roasted on a kind of gridiron covered with sharp spikes, and salt was sprinkled upon him during the process; when nearly exhausted, he was taken off by his persecutors, to be reserved for another day, but he almost immediately expired, A.D. 304.

The state of the weather is now a matter of anxiety to the farmer, and many will

> "Remember on St. Vincent's day,
> If that the sun his beames display."

25. *Conversion of St. Paul.*—This was also a favourite day of observation with weather prophets, some of whom, probably of the monkish order, proposed the following scheme,—

"Clara dies Pauli bona tempora denotetanni,"&c., which took the following form in English,—

"If St. Paule's day be faire and cleare,
It doth betyde a happy yeare;
But if perchance it then should raine,
It will make deare alle kinds of graine;
And if ye clouds make dark ye skie,
Then neate and fowles this year shall dye;
If blustering winds doe blowe aloft,
Then warre shall vex ye realm full oft."

With few exceptions, other saints are commemorated only when they suffered martyrdom, but of St. Paul we celebrate not only the anniversary of his death, but also that of his conversion—the greatest triumph of Christianity up to that time, when Saul the persecutor became Paul the apostle. He now devoted all his energies to the propagation of that Gospel which he had before endeavoured to eradicate; his former glory he now accounted shame. His perils and dangers, his voyages and travels, his writings, and the chief events of his life, are all known to Bible readers. According to some traditions, he visited Britain, but of this there is no trustworthy record; there were Christians in the island at a very early period, but there are other traditions that St. Joseph of Arimathea was the first to plant the Gospel; certain it is that from the earliest records St. Paul was the patron saint of London, whose shield bears his emblem—a sword or dagger, and whose cathedral is dedicated to him. It is recorded that in company with St. Peter he suffered martyrdom at Rome. After decapitation his head rebounded three times, and a fountain gushed out from each place touched. In the Church of the Three Fountains, at Rome, fountains may still be seen.

30. *King Charles the Martyr.*—Till 1859 this was a red-letter day in the English Calendar, and a service appointed for the day. How such a service could have been retained for nearly two hundred years will probably serve for a subject of discussion by future antiquaries. The service found many defenders; even the impiety and profanity of some of the allusions were regarded as the most appropriate that could be selected, and the whole office was regarded as being almost inspired. Upon this subject even good Mr. Wheatley says: "How much reason, then, had our state to punish those impious Rebels who murdered the best of Kings, *only for adhering to the best of Religions*: and also to set apart a day of Humiliation for Fasting and Prayer, and to draw up a mournful office, after the example of David."

February.

"February fill dike, be it black or be it white;
But if it be black, it's the better to like."

February is so named from Februa, supposed to be the same as Juno; "and the evident relation between the Februata Juno and the Purificata Virg. Maria is one of the most striking instances of the connection between Pagan and Christian rites and festivities as to the periods of their occurrence."—*Dr. Forster.*

The weather is usually intensely cold and frosty at the commencement of the month, but frequently towards the middle or end there are some warm days; trees begin to bud, and plants to sprout, but the return of frost too frequently nips the promised bloom.

1. *St. Bride* (Bridget or Brigida), although not in the Prayer Book Calendar, is too important a personage to be overlooked in the Almanack. From her we derive the honoured name of Bride, and cakes are still sacrificed at her shrine. All Christmas decorations of churches, schools, and private houses must be removed previous to the morrow, this being the eve of the

2. *Purification.*—The presentation of Christ in the Temple, commonly called the Purification of St. Mary the Virgin. The Reformers, desirous that our Saviour should attract more attention than His mother, reversed the order of the festival, but the popular voice never recognized the change; consequently the day has always been regarded as the Feast of the Purification, in commemoration of the Blessed Virgin's appearance in the Temple to make the accustomed offering of a pair of turtle-doves. The Feast of Candlemas dates from Anglo-Saxon times, and was celebrated with many candles—our Saviour being termed "A Light to lighten the Gentiles"—although the Virgin was herself regarded as a light: thus John Lydgate addresses her—"Haile luminary and benynge lanterne."

Candlemas is one of the recognized half-yearly terms in Scotland. Many a farmer will regard this day with an anxious gaze and, regardless of the truth or falsehood of the prediction in former years, will be elevated or depressed as the weather may be propitious or otherwise:—

"If Candlemas Day be fair and bright,
Winter will have another flight;
But if Candlemas Day be clouds and rain,
Winter is gone, and will not come again."

3. *St. Blaise,* Bishop of Sebaste, in Armenia, suffered martyrdom A.D. 316. He was cruelly tortured, his flesh being dragged off by means of iron combs with curved teeth, such as are used by wool-combers. In consequence of this he has been regarded as the patron saint of wool-workers, and formerly his day was observed in Bradford, Leeds, and other centres of the manufactures as a holiday; processions were formed, and those who took part in them were termed Blazers—hence the term "As drunk as Blazers," or blazes.

5. *St. Agatha.*—Of this saint but little is known. She is said to have suffered martyrdom A.D. 253. Her flesh was nipped off with pincers, and burning torches were applied to her body. Her sufferings have afforded much scope for the ingenuity of painters.

9. *Shrove Tuesday,* 1869.—In Roman Catholic times it was compulsory upon the people to confess their sins, and be *shriven* by the priest on this day. A barbarous custom was prevalent, that of throwing sticks or stones at cocks; cock-fighting was also common till prohibited by Act of Parliament. The only custom now remaining is that of eating pancakes. The earliest day on which Shrove Tuesday can fall in any year is February 3, and latest March 9.

10. *Ash Wednesday.*—The first of the forty days of Lent, instituted about the year 130, in reference to the miraculous fasts of Moses, Elias, and our Lord. Ashes were placed on the heads of penitents, and flesh was forbidden to be eaten: eggs, milk, and wine were also at times interdicted. After the Litany, the Commination Service is this day said in church.

12. In the Old Durham Kalendar there is an entry, "On this day the birds begin to sing."

14. *St. Valentine,* bishop, martyred A.D. 270. "On this day the birds begin to pair," was another adage applied to this anniversary. Many young persons date their pairing from this

festival, for festival it is, whether it fall in or out of the Lenten season. In pagan Rome it was customary for youths to draw names in honour of the goddess Februato Juno on the 15th of February, and when paganism was abolished the honour was conferred upon St. Valentine.

17, 19, 20. *Ember Days.*—On these days young men intended for the ministry of the Church are solemnly set apart for their office, and prayers are offered up that the "Bishop may lay hands suddenly upon no man; but faithfully and wisely make choice of fit persons to serve in the sacred Ministry."

24. *St. Matthias*, one of the seventy-two disciples sent out by our Lord, was, upon the apostacy of Judas, chosen to be one of the twelve. We have no authentic account of his life; by St. Jerome he is said to have preached the Gospel to a nation of cannibals, and to have died at Sebastopolis; by others he is said to have been stoned in Judea.

March.

"Comes in as a Lion and goes out like a Lamb," or "Comes in as a Lamb and goes out like a Lion."

1. *St. David:* Patron saint of Wales—hence the name Taffy. St. David was born of a princely family, and was celebrated for his learning and sanctity of life. He was Bishop of Menevia, since called St. David's. On this day natives of Wales wear leeks in their hats, it is by their historians said in commemoration of a victory gained over the Saxons, although there is another version of the story by no means complimentary to the beauty of the primitive inhabitants of the Principality.

2. *St. Cedde* or *Chad.*—An early English Bishop, who fixed his see at Lichfield. He died of a pestilence in the year 673.

3. *St. Perpetua* was thrown into the Amphitheatre at Carthage, A.D. 203, and tossed, but not quite killed, by a wild cow; eventually she was put to death by the young gladiators.

12. *St. Gregory the Great*, consecrated Pope in 590, was regarded with much favour in this country, on account of his having despatched St. Augustine for the purpose of Christianizing it. Although austere, St. Gregory was in every sense a pious, amiable man, devoted to good works. Dr. Chambers, in his "Book of Days," traces some connection between St. Gregory and the Highland clan Gregor, of which Rob Roy was an active and illustrious member.

17. *St. Patrick.*—The patron saint of Ireland is claimed by the Scotch as a native of their country. They say that he was born near Dumbarton, and that he founded many churches in North Britain before sailing from Port Patrick for Ireland. Arrived there he energetically set to work converting the heathen and founding churches. In explaining the doctrine of the Trinity, he plucked a leaf of trefoil, and showed how three leaves might be united and yet be but one. The Shamrock has therefore been recognized as the national emblem ever since. The saint is also said to have charmed all reptiles from the island so that none can exist there, and also to have taught the natives the true art of mixing their liquor—an art which has never since been lost. He died A.D. 432, at the good old age of 123, and was buried in the cathedral city of Down. For some pious reason the Reformers left St. Patrick's name out of the calendar, but an Order of Knighthood was established in his honour by King George III., and there appears but little likelihood of the day being forgotten by the saint's adopted countrymen.

The Church of Rome commemorates one who should have been the patron saint of England instead of St. George—St. Joseph of Arimathea. The "Episcopal Almanack" for 1674, thus describes "the British Apostle":— "St. Joseph of Arimathea, who entertained the body of Christ into his tomb, and His doctrine into his heart, was a ruler amongst the Jews, who for his faith so hated him that, as reported, he was banished his country, and came over into Britain in the time of King Arviragus, with eleven others, his associates, where they found such entertainment that, though the king himself would not be dissuaded from his idolatry by their preaching, yet he allowed them twelve hides of ground in a desolate island, full of fens and brambles, called the Ynis-Witrin—since by translation, Glastonbury. Here they built a small church, made of rods wattled or interwoven, living there many years, devoutly serving God, by watching, praying, fasting, and preaching; having high meditations under a low roof, and large hearts betwixt narrow walls. Many were converted by them to the Christian faith, which doctrine was so rooted in their hearts that it was in great force when Austin the Monk first came over into England. St. Joseph is said to have died and been buried there, as is witnessed by divers learned authors." Other "learned authors" also have described the dry thorn walking-staff of St. Joseph, how he struck it into the ground, how it grew, and how it still blossoms every year at Christmas.

18. *St. Edward, King and Martyr*, was son of King Edgar, and ascended the throne at the early age of twelve, in 975, but four years afterwards was foully murdered by order of his stepmother, Elfrida, at Corfe Castle. His body was privately buried in unconsecrated ground, but could not rest, and on the 20th June, 982, it was translated to Shaftesbury with great pomp.

21. *Palm Sunday*, so named in memory of the triumphal entry of our Lord into Jerusalem, a few days before His passion. Branches of willow are now gathered and placed in many churches.

21. *St. Benedict*, or Benet, patron of the Western monks and founder of the Benedictine order, was born in Umbria in 480, and when only fourteen retired to the desert in order to enjoy a solitary religious life. He founded his first monastery on Mount Casino, and then drew up a stringent code of rules for the government of the inmates. He died A.D. 534.

25. *Maundy Thursday* is the day before Good Friday. On this day Christ washed the feet of His disciples, and gave them a command to love one another; hence it is called *Dies Mandati*, Mandate, or Maundy Thursday. Formerly the church doors used to stand open for the whole day, signifying that all who would might come in. The ceremony first commenced in 1362, and for a long time the English Kings observed the custom of washing the feet of a number of poor men equal to the years of their age, and of giving them shoes, stockings, and money. Money and clothing are still given by deputy, but the feet-washing has long been discontinued.

25. *The Annunciation* commemorates the visit paid by the angel Gabriel to the Blessed Virgin when he revealed the purpose of God, and told her of the Saviour who should be born.

26. *Good Friday*, so named from the good and blessed work performed by Jesus Christ in sub-

mitting to a shameful, ignominious, and painful death on the cross for the salvation of mankind. Next to the first day of the week and Easter, this was the earliest of the days set apart in commemoration of the chief events in the life of Christ; but when first celebrated we have no record. By the Roman Catholics and by the Greeks, as well as by the English Church, it is regarded as a strict fast. It is also a close holiday at the Bank, and in all Government offices; but in Scotland it is not observed by Presbyterians. Hot cross buns are probably a relic of paganism. In London they are eaten for breakfast on this day; and the superstition that a cross bun preserved from one Good Friday to another will prevent an attack of whooping-cough has some believers still.

28. *Easter Sunday* has always been regarded as the very queen or the highest of all the Christian festivals. The mournful season of Lent is past, the Saviour has been crucified and buried, and "now is Christ risen indeed," "the first-fruits of them that slept." The name is derived from Eostre, a goddess to whom the Saxons and other northern nations sacrificed at about this season. The Paascha, or Jewish Passover, celebrated at this time, lent its name to the Christian Paschal season, but the precise time for keeping Easter has been a cause of contention between Eastern and Western Christians. Customs peculiar to the season are dying out in England, but on the Continent paschal eggs, with coloured shells, and toys in the shape of gigantic eggs, are given amongst all classes.

April.

"March winds and April showers
Bring forth May flowers."

April, the fourth month of the year, was by the Romans dedicated to Aphrodite Venus, the goddess of all budding beauties; but there is some difficulty in tracing the origin of the name, some believing the root to be Aphrodite —Aphrilis—Aprilis; others that it is derived from the festival Fortuna Virilis, celebrated April 1.

1. *All Fools' Day.*—The "Public Advertiser" for April 13, 1789, contains the following paragraph:—"*Humorous Jewish Origin of the Custom of Making Fools on the First of April.*—This is said to have begun from the mistake of Noah in sending the Dove out of the Ark before the water had abated, on the first day of the month among the Hebrews, which answers to the 1st of April; and to perpetuate the memory of this deliverance, it was thought proper, whoever forgot so remarkable a circumstance, to punish them by sending them upon some sleeveless errand similar to that ineffectual message upon which the bird was sent by the Patriarch. The custom appears to be of great antiquity, and to have been derived by the Romans from some of the Eastern nations."

3. *St. Richard*, Bishop of Chichester, was born at Droitwich, and educated at Oxford and Paris; he then travelled to Bologna, and on his return was elected Bishop of Chichester, although King Henry III. had nominated another. Richard was supported by the Pope, and the King was compelled to give way, and restore the revenues which he had sequestered. Richard died in the full odour of sanctity in 1253, and was canonized eight years after.

4. *Low Sunday* is so called because it was the custom to celebrate the Sunday next after Easter

as a feast of the same kind, but somewhat lower in degree.

4. *St. Ambrose*, Bishop of Milan, one of the great early Fathers, was born at Treves in 340, and although he had not then been baptized, he was chosen Bishop of Milan. He was a strenuous opponent of Arianism, and a staunch defender of the rights of the Church; on one occasion he went so far as to refuse to admit the Emperor Theodosius to his cathedral. He is the reputed author of the *Te Deum*.

19. *St. Alphege* was stoned to death on the spot where a church is built and dedicated to his memory at Greenwich. He was an Englishman of noble family, and was appointed Archbishop of Canterbury in 1006. In 1012 the Danes invaded and ravaged Canterbury, took the good Archbishop prisoner, and after seven months' confinement, finding that he would not pay the heavy ransom which was demanded, they took away his life.

23. *St. George.*—The history of this redoubtable warrior-saint will not bear too close an examination. He is the patron saint of England, and has ever been held in great honour; his deeds are fully recorded in the *Veritable History of the Seven Champions of Christendom.*

25. *St. Mark*, one of the four Evangelists, is supposed to be the same as John Mark, mentioned Acts xii. xv. He was a disciple of St. Peter, and founded a church at Alexandria, where, unable to look on quietly while the heathens were worshipping Serapis, he denounced their idolatry, and so incensed them, that he was immediately seized, bound with cords, and dragged through the streets till he died, A.D. 68. St. Mark is the Patron Saint of Venice, and is usually depicted with a winged lion by his side.

There is a superstition in some parts of the country that if persons sit in the church porch from eleven o'clock at night, on St. Mark's Eve, till one o'clock in the morning, they will see the ghosts of such of their neighbours as will die during the next year. In order to see the ghosts it is necessary to watch three years successively, and sometimes they who watch will see their own, and thus be warned of their impending fate.

May.

"Hail, bounteous May! that dost inspire
Mirth and youth, and fond desire;
Woods and groves are of thy dressing;
Hill and dale doth boast thy blessing."

1. *St. Philip and St. James.*—The St. James commemorated this day is the one who was cousin, and has been called the brother of our Lord; to distinguish him from the other James, he is styled the Less, possibly because he was the smaller, or the younger. He was remarkable for his simplicity and piety, and gained great influence in Jerusalem, of which city he was the first bishop. This so enraged the Jews, that they hurled him from a pinnacle of the Temple. He was not killed by the fall, but was able to get upon his knees, and in this posture was killed by clubs and stones. Of St. Philip but little is known beyond what is stated of him in the New Testament. Tradition says that he was married, had several daughters, and that he preached the Gospel in Phrygia.

2. *Rogation Sunday*, so called from *rogare*, to beseech. The three rogation days are the Mon-

day, Tuesday, and Wednesday before Holy Thursday. No special service has been provided for them, but one of the Homilies is enjoined to be read.

3. *Invention of the Cross.*—The word invention here means discovery; but Protestants will prefer the ordinary meaning to the true one. The day is in commemoration of the Empress Helen finding the true cross. She undertook a journey to the Holy Land in 326 for the purpose. On arriving at Jerusalem, she commenced digging at the spot where it was supposed to be buried, and at some depth discovered three crosses. A dead body was applied to them, and it came to life the moment it touched the cross on which our Lord had been crucified.

6. *Ascension Day*: Holy Thursday, in commemoration of the day Christ "ascended into Heaven, led captivity captive, and opened the Kingdom of Heaven to all believers." It is celebrated forty days after Easter. Members of the High Church party have endeavoured to get this day set apart as a general holyday, in the same manner as the days of the Birth, Passion, and Resurrection; but their efforts have not been attended with any large amount of success. On this day the parochial bounds are beaten by the charity children, who are attended by the beadle and other officials. Formerly it was the custom to flog or bump some of the children at the bounds, in order that those localities might be impressed on their memories.

St. John Ante Port. Latin.—See Dec. 27.

15. *Quarter-day in Scotland.* In that country the term, *Whit-Sunday*, is fixed, and may fall on any day in the week.

16. *Whit Sunday* commemorates the descent of the Holy Ghost upon the Apostles immediately after the Ascension. It derives its name from the Saxon word Witte, or wisdom, which the Holy Spirit imparted. It is also called Pentecost, a Jewish term for the feast which fell fifty days after Easter. Monday and Tuesday are also holydays, a fact of which people in general are willing to avail themselves. The weather at this time is mostly fine, and working men and women are but too glad to get away from their close homes for a few hours.

19. *St. Dunstan* was born in the isle of Avalon, and early assumed the monastic habit, with all its austerities; he built a cell near the Abbey of Glastonbury, and employed himself in goldsmith's work. The great enemy of souls, foreseeing his future greatness, tried in various ways to seduce St. Dunstan, who on one occasion seized the fiend by the nose with a pair of red-hot tongs. At the age of 21 he restored Glastonbury Abbey, then in ruins, and became abbot. He was banished by Edwy, but recalled by Edgar, and made Archbishop of Canterbury, in which office he died, A.D. 988.

23. *Trinity Sunday.*—On this day the Church commemorates the mystery of the Holy Trinity. It will be noticed that while the life and death of Christ form the subject of many commemorations, of the Holy Spirit there is but one, and of the Father none; all the remaining Sundays of the year are in the English Church named after the Holy Trinity, while in the Church of Rome they are named after Pentecost.

26. *St. Augustine.*—When Pope Gregory determined to send a mission to England, he selected St. Augustine, then prior of a Roman monastery, to head the forty monks. Apparently neither St. Augustine nor St. Gregory were aware that England had been, more or less, a Christian country, although at that time in a retrograde condition. St. Augustine landed in Kent, and converted King Ethelbert. He was consecrated Archbishop of Canterbury in 597, and died in 604.

27. *Corpus Christi* is not in the Anglican calendar, but is a high day in that of Rome. It was instituted in honour of the doctrine of transubstantiation by Pope Urban IV., about the year 1263, and confirmed by the Council of Vienne in 1311.

27. *Venerable Bede* was born at Jarrow. He was regarded as a prodigy of learning, and was much esteemed for his saintly life, but does not appear to have conformed in all things to the established usages of the Church of Rome. He died 735. One of the monks commenced an epitaph, but was puzzled to find the proper epithet to fit in with the words he had written—

> "Hac sunt in fossa,
> Bedæ   ossa."

While thinking about it he fell asleep, and when he awoke he found that an angel had filled up the blank with the word "*Venerabilis.*"

29. *Restoration of King Charles II.*: Royal Oak Day, in memory of Charles II. having sought safety by hiding in the thick branches of an oak. Oak-apples used to be worn on this day, which was also a red-letter day in the calendar, having been set apart as a day of public thanksgiving for "that signal and wonderful Deliverance vouchsafed to our then most gracious sovereign King Charles the Second and all the Royal Family, and in them to this whole Church and State, and all orders and degrees of men in both, from the unnatural Rebellion, Usurpation, and Tyranny of ungodly and cruel men, and from the sad confusion and ruin thereupon ensuing." But like the service for King Charles' execution it was set aside in 1859.

June.

Although poets in all ages have sung the praises of May, June is, in reality, the most pleasant month of the year. The day reaches its full length, flowers make their appearance, birds are in song; earth, air, and water teem with life, and all nature is gay and joyous.

1. *St. Nicomede*, who is said to have been a disciple of St. Peter, was discovered to be a Christian by giving burial to Felicula, a maiden who had been martyred in the Domitian persecution. He was scourged to death by means of a whip heavily laden with lead, A.D. 90.

5. *St. Boniface*, the apostle of Germany, was born in Devonshire about the year 680. He had a strong desire to spread abroad a knowledge of the Gospel, and having obtained the sanction of Pope Gregory II. he proceeded on a mission to Germany, and was made first Archbishop of Mayence in 745. He appears to have laboured in Bavaria and on and about the Rhine, and in the year 755, having previously resigned his bishopric in order that he might carry on his missionary work without impediment, he suffered martyrdom at Utrecht with fifty-two of his companions.

11. *St. Barnabas.*—One of the most active of the disciples was Joses, surnamed Barnabas, the Son of Consolation. He is said to have been one of those who, having possessions, sold them and laid down the price at the apostles' feet. He for some time laboured with St. Paul; but after

awhile disputes arose, and he pursued his own course, choosing Cyprus for the field of his labours. He was stoned to death at Salamis, and was buried with a copy of St. Matthew's Gospel on his breast. This was the longest day, old style; hence the saying,

"Barnaby bright, Barnaby bright,
Longest day and the shortest night."

17. *St. Alban,* the first English martyr: suffered in 303. He was converted to Christianity by Amphibalus, a priest of Caerleon, who, flying from persecution, was hospitably entertained by St. Alban at Verulam. Being closely pursued, he made his escape in his host's clothes. This being discovered exposed St. Alban to the fury of the pagans, and on his refusing to sacrifice to their gods, he was first miserably tortured, and then put to death.

20. *Queen's Accession.*—This is the only day now set apart for a religious State service being the day on which Her Majesty began her happy reign, in 1837. This is also the day of the translation of King Edward, (*see* March 18.)

24. *St. John the Baptist.*—Unlike most other saints in the calendar, whose deaths alone are commemorated, the Church celebrates the birthday of St. John, for the reason, says an old writer, that even before his birth he was canonized. He was son of Zacharias, a priest, and Elizabeth, the cousin of Mary, and, like his prototype Elijah, was a recluse, and also a preacher of righteousness.

29. *St. Peter,* brother of St. Andrew, and son of Jonas, was a fisherman, who left all to follow Christ. He appears to have been one of the most zealous and attached of all the disciples, and although frequently rebuked, was one of those most honoured by the friendship of his Master. He was married, and is said to have had a daughter, Petronilla. St. Paul having founded a church at Rome, of which Linus was the first bishop, went there again accompanied by St. Peter, and as a Roman citizen suffered death by decapitation, A.D. 65. St. Peter, regarded as a Jewish slave, was crucified, but, at his own request, with his head downwards, not conceiving himself worthy of suffering in the same manner as his Master.

July.

"Now comes July, and with his fervid noon
Unsinews labour. The swinkt mower sleeps;
Tho weary maid rakes feebly; the warm swain
Pitches his load reluctant; the faint steer,
Lashing his sides, draws sulkily along
The slow encumbered wain in mid-day heat."

This Month, originally named Quintilis, or fifth, received its present name in honour of Julius Cæsar.

2. *Visitation of the Blessed Virgin Mary.*—This festival was instituted by Pope Urban VI. in commemoration of the journey which the Virgin Mary took to the hill country of Judea, in order to visit her cousin Elizabeth, mother of John the Baptist.

4. *Translation of St. Martin's* relics from their humble resting-place to the noble cathedral at Tours.

15. *St. Swithin's Day.*—" If on St. Swithin's Day it proves fair, a temperate winter will follow; but if rainy, stormy, or windy, then the contrary." So says the author of the "Shepherd's Kalendar." That it should rain for forty days

after a wet St. Swithin appears to have been an article of popular belief, even in Anglo-Saxon times. The legend of the day is that the Saint, who died in 868, desired to be buried in the open churchyard, not in the chapel of the minster, as was usual with bishops; this desire was complied with; but, on his being canonized, the monks thinking it disgraceful for the saint to lie in the open cemetery, determined to remove his body into the choir. This was attempted with solemn procession on the 15th July; it rained, however, so violently for forty days together that the design was abandoned. The monks finding it vain to contend with one who had the elements so entirely under his control, like discreet and prudent men, let him have his own way; he, to show his opinion of their conduct, and to warn others against interfering with the wishes of the dead, still continues the forty days' rain. Unfortunately, for the truth of the legend, the saint's relics were in 971 translated by St. Athelwold to a shrine, and in 1094 retranslated to Winchester Cathedral by Bishop Walkelin.

20. *St. Margaret* was one of the most popular saints in England. She was the daughter of a pagan priest at Antioch, but was educated as a Christian. She refused to marry a Roman governor, and, in consequence, was exposed to the most dreadful tortures, and at last beheaded, A.D. 278.

22. *St. Mary Magdalene* is believed to have been the saint to whom much had been forgiven, and who loved much. She was the most constant of all our Lord's followers,

"Not she with traitorous kiss her Master stung,
Not she denied Him with unfaithful tongue;
She, when Apostles fled, could danger brave,
Last at His cross, and earliest at His grave."

After the Ascension she is said to have lived for some time in Judea, and then to have retired to Ephesus, where she resided with the Virgin Mary. Painters have represented her as a lovely woman, in a large number of repentant attitudes, some of them being only such as unrepentant "Magdalenes" could be induced to assume.

25. *St. James,* surnamed the Great, Apostle and Martyr. He was originally a fisherman, brother of St. John; he is the patron saint of Spain, where, after the death of his Master, he is said to have preached the Gospel. On his return to Jerusalem he received the crown of martyrdom, being beheaded by order of Herod the Great, A.D. 43. He was the first martyred of all the apostles, and is regarded as the patron saint of pilgrims.

26. *St. Anne,* mother of the Virgin Mary, was daughter of Matthew the priest and Mary his wife; she married Joachim, and after twenty years was made happy by the birth of a daughter, who has been called blessed by all generations.

August.

The ancient Roman name of this month was Sextilis, the sixth from March, till the Emperor Augustus changed the name to his own, because in this month Cæsar Augustus took possession of his first consulate, reduced Egypt, and put an end to civil war.

1. *Lammas Day* should rather have been Loafmass, of which Saxon name it is a corruption. On this day the Ancient Britons celebrated the gift of Ceres by offering a loaf made of new corn; this custom was adopted by the early Christians, and the first fruits were presented at the altar.

In the Salisbury Missal the day is called *Benedictis novorum fructuum.*

Lammas is one of the Scottish Quarter-days.

6. *Transfiguration.*—This festival, instituted by the Greek Christians in 700, was introduced into the Roman Calendar in 1455; it commemorates the Transfiguration of Christ in the presence of the three disciples on Mount Tabor.

7. *Name of Jesus.*—This day, says Wheatley, "was formerly dedicated to the memory of Afra, a courtezan of Crete, who, being converted to Christianity by Narcissus, Bishop of Jerusalem, suffered martyrdom. How it came afterwards to be dedicated to the name of Jesus I cannot find."

10. *St. Laurence* suffered martyrdom in 258. He was a Spaniard, and was treasurer to Pope Sixtus II. After the martyrdom of his master, he was called upon to give up the keys of his charge; refusing to do so, he was grilled over a slow fire: the saint appears rather to have liked the process, for after awhile "he, in triumph, bade his executioners turn him over, for that the side downward was broiled enough." His countrymen say that it was not so much on account of religion that he bore his sufferings with such fortitude, as from the innate nobility of his soul; he felt that he was a Spaniard! The symbol of St. Lawrence, a gridiron, is to be found used as a vane on some of the churches dedicated to his memory.

24. *St. Bartholomew* is supposed to be the apostle called Nathaniel. His surname being Tolmai —thus, Bar-Tolmai—the son of Tolmai. He preached the Gospel in Armenia and India, and suffered martyrdom in the former country by being flayed alive; hence he is always represented with a butcher's or currier's flaying-knife. At Croyland Abbey a curious custom existed of presenting flaying-knives to all visitors on this day. This is the anniversary of the fearful massacre of Protestants at Paris in 1572, and also of the ejection of the Nonconforming Ministers in 1662. St. Bartholomew displaces St. Swithin, for—

> "All the tears St. Swithin can cry,
> St. Bartlemy's mantle wipes dry."

28. *St. Augustine,* Bishop of Hippo, one of the great doctors of the Christian Church. His writings are read with reverence at the present day alike by members of the Greek, Roman, and Protestant Communions. He was an African, and was converted from heathenism by St. Ambrose at Milan. On his return he was chosen Bishop of Hippo, in Africa, and died, at the age of seventy-seven, in 430. St. Monica, his mother, should have had a place in the Anglican Calendar; her conduct deserves the admiration of all Christian mothers.

29. *St. John the Baptist Beheaded.*—The birth of St. John is celebrated June 24. The Anglo-Saxons, with more truthfulness than elegance, say that the daughter of Herodias "tombtyle" to please Herod, and so far succeeded that he promised to give anything she liked to ask. Her choice was the head of the Baptist, in revenge for his having reproved or spoken in public of her improper conduct.

September.

When the year commenced with March *September* was in reality the seventh month, but now the name is a misnomer, as also are those of October, November, and December.

1. *St. Giles,* the patron of cripples, was a native of Athens. He visited France in the year 715, where he lived a hermit's life for some time. A monastery was built on the site of his hermitage. Of this he became abbot, and died in 725.

2. *London Burnt,* 1666.—A religious service was formerly appointed for this day.

7. *St. Enurchus,* while on a mission at Orleans, was selected as bishop, the attention of the people being directed to him by a dove alighting on his head. He converted 7,000 infidels in three days, and foretold the time of his own death.

8. *Nativity of the Blessed Virgin Mary.*—This day was set apart in the year 695, in consequence of a concert of angels being held in the air.

14. *Holy Cross Day.* When the Emperor Heraclius had recovered the wood of the Holy Cross from the sacrilegious hands of Chosroes, King of Persia, he, on his return to Jerusalem, determined to convey it to Mount Calvary. Attired in his imperial robes, he in vain essayed to move the venerated relic from the ground. A voice from Heaven explained the mystery. Christ himself had entered Jerusalem lowly and meek, riding upon an ass, while the emperor, in all his pomp, had endeavoured to defile the Cross. He thereupon disrobed himself, and accomplished the removal without difficulty.

17. *St. Lambert* was Bishop of Utrecht in the time of King Pepin I.; but, for reproving the king's grandson for irregularities, he was murdered at the instigation of an abandoned woman, A.D. 704.

21. *St. Matthew,* Apostle and Evangelist, was a Jew, the son of Alpheus. His Hebrew name was Levi. He was an officer employed to collect the hateful Roman public taxes, hence the name publican. Too frequently the publicans were harsh and dishonest; consequently, to be a publican was to be hated by the people generally. Our Lord saw him sitting at the receipt of custom, and said, "Follow me." This was sufficient. After the Ascension, Matthew preached the Gospel in Judea, and afterwards in Parthia and Ethiopia. He wrote his Gospel in Hebrew, and this is said to have been translated into Greek by one of the other disciples.

26. *St. Cyprian,* Archbishop of Carthage, his native city. He appears to have been an earnest devout believer in the Christian faith, and was one of the staunchest upholders of the rights and dignities of the episcopal office. Many of his writings are extant, and he was fortunate in having a deacon who acted as his biographer. He was beheaded A.D. 258, in the persecution under Decius.

29. *St. Michael and All Angels.*—This is the only day set apart in commemoration of the angels. The theme offers great scope to the imagination of a poetic preacher, inasmuch as Scripture is all but silent respecting the hierarchy of heaven. St. Dionysius, Milton, Fletcher and many other writers have described the different orders, and the MSS. of the middle ages will supply every variety of sketches and finished drawings, some of which might pass for actual portraits. Louis XI., in 1469, dubbed St. Michael a knight.

This is one of the regular quarter days; geese are now in season.

30. *St. Jerome,* one of the most learned and most voluminous of the early Fathers, studied divinity under Gregory Nazianzen and Epiphanius; and also studied Hebrew in Bethlehem. He collected and translated the books of the Bible into Latin, in the version known as the Vulgate, and appears to have passed a busy

literary life, which, at an advanced age, he ended in peace, A.D. 420.

October.

> "A good October and a good blast,
> To blow the hog acorn and mast."

The days begin to draw in apace. We have tea by candlelight, and fires are frequently not only pleasant, but necessary. Young men resume their studies, and home again becomes homely.

1. *St. Remigius* was chosen Archbishop of Rheims when but twenty-two years of age. The French king Clovis, a pagan, had married Clotilda, a Christian, and, at his wife's request, had invoked the aid of the God of Christians, in a battle, which he won. He thereupon sought baptism at the hands of St. Remigius, who afterwards performed the ceremony of coronation. On this occasion the holy oil was brought in a cruse, or ampulla, by a dove. This cruse was made use of in France at the coronation of princes, down to that of Charles X in 1825. St. Remigius died at the age of 95, A.D. 535.

Pheasant shooting commences, and every kind of game may be legally killed till February.

6. *St. Faith*, a remarkably beautiful maiden, was born at Agen, in Aquitaine. Refusing to sacrifice to Diana, she was forced to undergo the most dreadful torments, being first beaten with twigs and then half-roasted over a slow fire, after which she was beheaded, A.D. 290.

9. *St. Denys*, the patron saint of France, is usually represented carrying his head in his hand, the tradition being that it was cut off on Monte-martre, upon which he took it up and carried it two miles, when, being tired, he sat down to rest. Both his body and his head were afterwards enshrined at St. Denis, near Paris, of which city he was Bishop at the time of his martyrdom, in 272.

13. *Translation of King Edward the Confessor.*—This king ranks with Alfred as a lawgiver, or rather law collector, the Code Edward being at the time of the Norman Conquest what the Code Napoleon has been in later times; it still forms the basis of our Common Law. He succeeded to the crown in 1042, and received the title of Confessor from the Pope, in gratitude for settling Rome scot or Peter pence. He rebuilt the church at Westminster, and when Henry III replaced it by the present edifice he translated the Saint's remains, A.D. 1269. Edward was the first Royal personage that "touched" for the king's evil—Queen Anne was the last.

17. *St. Etheldreda*, "twice a widow and always a virgin," was daughter of Anna, king of the East Angles. She fled from her second husband first to Coldingham, a priory under the superintendence of St. Ebba, and then to Ely, where she built an abbey, where she was celebrated as St. Audry. A fair was held there annually, and a flimsy kind of lace made in the neighbourhood was much in demand. This gave rise to the designation "tawdry."

18. *St. Luke*, Evangelist, is supposed to be "the beloved physician" mentioned by St. Paul. In other respects Scripture is silent about St. Luke. Tradition, however, says that he was one of the seventy; that he preached the Gospel in Egypt and Greece; that he was an artist, and took portraits of the Virgin Mary and of Christ. He lived to the age of eighty-four, and was then hanged upon an olive tree. The only things about St. Luke of which we are tolerably certain are

that he wrote the Gospel which goes by his name, and also the "Acts of the Apostles."

25. *St. Crispin*, and his brother, Crispianus, were born at Rome, whence they travelled to France, spreading the Gospel as they went, and, like honest men, earning their living by their hand-labour—shoemaking. They were enabled to sell shoes at a very low price, as their leather cost nothing; it was supplied by angels direct from heaven. The governor of Soissons, hearing that they were Christians, had them beheaded. Their bodies were thrown into the sea, but were washed ashore at Romney Marsh, in Kent. St. Crispin is the patron of cordwainers, by many of whom he is commemorated every Monday. On this day, in the year 1415, was fought the celebrated battle of Agincourt, between the English and the French, who outnumbered the former in the proportion of six to one. King Henry is represented as saying to his soldiers:—

> "He that shall live this day, and see old age,
> Will yearly on the vigil feast his neighbours,
> And say, 'To-morrow is St. Crispian.'
> Then will he strip his sleeve, and show his scars,
> And say, 'These wounds I had on St. Crispian's day.'"

28. *St. Simon and St. Jude*, Apostles, are generally represented together—Simon with a saw in his hand, emblematic of the death he underwent, being sawn asunder; and Jude with a carpenter's square, or with a boat. Nothing certain is known of either. Until the change of style in 1752, this was Lord Mayor's day in London, and wet weather was commonly expected. A waiting woman in an old play says of something that we fear will be found out, "'Tis as certain as that it will rain on Simon and Jude's day."

November.

1. *All Saints.*—In this festival the Church honours all the saints not otherwise commemorated, the reason given by one of our liturgists being, "because we cannot particularly commemorate every one of those saints in whom God's graces have been eminent, for that would be too heavy a burden; and because in those particular feasts which we do celebrate, we may justly be thought to have omitted some of our duty through infirmity or negligence; therefore Holy Church appoints this day in commemoration of the saints in general." The festival was instituted in 610, when the Pantheon at Rome was consecrated as a Christian church.

2. *All Souls* is in the calendar of the Church of Rome, but not in that of the English. On this day they commemorate the faithful departed this life, and special prayer is made for those souls which are undergoing in an intermediate state a purgatorial cleansing from sin by means of punishment. Many members of the Church of England hold the doctrine in a modified form. The passing bell is a relic of the olden times.

> "When thou dost hear a bell or knell,
> Then think upon thy Passing Bell.
> When the bell begins to toll,
> 'Lord, have mercy on the soul.'"

A pleasing custom connected with All Souls' Day, prevalent on the Continent, is likely to become a more frequent practice here, now that cemeteries are superseding the old churchyards, namely, that of placing wreaths of flowers, or *immortelles*, on the graves of the departed. If the festival of ALL SAINTS were set apart for the practice here, there could be no objection on the ground of doctrine; Churchman and Dissenter alike would equally be willing to pay some mark of respect to the memory of the departed.

5. *Gunpowder Plot*, 1605.

"Please to remember the fifth of November,
   Gunpowder treason and plot,
I see no reason why gunpowder treason
   Should ever be forgot:
A stick and a stake for our Queen's sake.
Halloo! halloo, boys, God save the Queen!"

This is now the only recognized service for the day; yet, till 1859, it was one of our red-letter days! The clergy were ordered to give notice of its observance the Sunday before. Coupled with the thanksgiving for the deliverance of King James from the "unnatural conspiracy" and "popish treachery" was also a thanksgiving for bringing King William to deliver the nation from King James's grandson and namesake; and the clergy were commanded, "after morning prayer or preaching," to read the Act of Parliament of the 3rd of James I. for the observance of the day, *i.e.*, for dethroning his grandson!! Even the days of "poor old Guy" are numbered. The police order to "move *on*," moves *off* many recollections of the past.

6. *St. Leonard*, the patron saint of prisoners, was born at Le Mans, in France, and became a pupil of St. Remigius. According to some, he was made Bishop of Limosin; according to others, he would receive no higher dignity than that of deacon. He obtained a favour from the newly-converted King, Clovis, that all the prisoners he saw should be set free; thereupon he visited all the prisons, and as soon as he heard of any prisoner, claimed his freedom. Perhaps this general gaol delivery may not have proved an unmitigated blessing.

9. *Lord Mayor's Day.*—In the first Charter granted to the Londoners, their chief magistrate was designated the Portreeve, which by Richard I. was altered to Bailiff, and by King John, in 1209, to Mayor: the prefix "Lord" was given by Richard II. on the death of Wat Tyler. On this day the newly-chosen Lord Mayor publicly assumes his dignity; the feast at Guildhall remains, but the "Show" has sunk to very modest dimensions.

11. *St. Martin*, Bishop of Tours, is one of the best known of the French saints, from the picture in which he is represented as dividing his cloak with the beggar. He died in 397. St. Martin is more frequently invoked than most people are aware, the vulgar expression "my eye and Betty Martin" being a corruption of *Mihi beate Martini*.

Martinmas. One of the Scottish quarter-days.

11. *St. Britius* succeeded St. Martin in the bishopric of Tours. He is remarkable for having been cleared, by a miracle, from a charge of immorality. A child thirty days old, after having been duly admonished, declared in the presence of many witnesses, that St. Britius was *not* his father! Upon this the people charged him with sorcery, and he was driven from his see, but after seven years' absence regained it.

15. *St. Machutus* was Bishop of St. Malo, in France. He appears to have led a restless life, and is said to have performed many miracles.

17. *St. Hugh*, Bishop of Lincoln, also was a Frenchman, but rendered his name famous in this country by rebuilding Lincoln Cathedral in

A.D. 1200. He died in London, but was taken to Lincoln and borne to his grave on the shoulders of King John of England and King William of Scotland, assisted by a host of nobles, three archbishops, fourteen bishops, one hundred abbots, and an innumerable company of common people. A story is told of St. Hugh, that on his visit to Godstow, he saw a hearse in the midst of the choir with lights burning round it, and was informed that it was that of Fair Rosamond, who had obtained of King Henry many favours for the nunnery. Whereupon he ordered her corpse to be removed from a place "much too good for her," and buried in the churchyard.

20. *St. Edmund* is now our one royal martyr. He was king of the East Angles, and had the misfortune to be taken prisoner by the Danes, who used their utmost endeavours to induce him to renounce his religion. Finding their efforts fruitless, they first scourged him, then bound him to a tree, and then shot at him until his body was completely full of arrows; finally, they struck off his head and threw it into a wood hard by. The Saxons sought for it, but probably would not have discovered it had it not called out, "Here! here!" On reaching the head, they found that it was being guarded by a wolf. His body was buried at St. Edmundsbury, or Bury St. Edmunds, A.D. 870.

22. *St. Cecilia's* day used to be a popular anniversary in England. Dryden, Pope, and others wrote odes in honour of it. Recently, too, there was a St. Cecilia Society. The saint, the patroness of music, is usually represented with a musical instrument of some kind. She was a Roman lady; immediately after her marriage she converted her husband, his brother, and a friend, who were all subsequently put to death in 230, in consequence.

23. *St. Clement*, the third Bishop of Rome, was martyred in the year 100 by being cast into the sea with an anchor round his neck. He is the author of an epistle which in the early ages of the Church was publicly read, and was regarded as almost equal in authority to those of St. Paul.

25. *St. Catherine* is known by her wheel. She was born at Alexandria, and early in life displayed a passion for polite literature. On her conversion she spared no pains in publishing the truths of Christianity, and openly rebuked the pagans for their idolatry. Naturally this gave much offence, and she was condemned to suffer death by being torn to pieces by wheels having hooked spikes. Tradition says that her would-be torturers were disturbed by a direct interposition from heaven; and, being foiled in this, they were content to behead her outside the city.

28. *Advent Sunday.*—The Christian year now commences. There are four Sundays in Advent. These are intended as preparations for the commemorations of the advent of Christ. On the first Sunday we pray to be enabled to cast away the works of darkness; on the second, return thanks for the first means of grace, the Holy Scripture; on the third, for the ministry; and on the fourth, pray for the more direct interposition of God's great might. There are always four Sundays in Advent, the first being that nearest St. Andrew's day, either before or after, as the case may be.

30. *St. Andrew*, Apostle, patron saint of Scotland, was first a disciple of St. John the Baptist, and appears to have been the first to follow

Christ: for this reason it is supposed that the place of honour has been given to him in the Anglican prayer-book, where he comes first of all those commemorated. But little is known of him, although he is believed to have suffered martyrdom at Patra, in Greece, A.D. 70, by being crucified on a cross in the form of X.

December.

December, although the twelfth month, retains its old Roman name of the tenth. It is the dullest and dreariest of the twelve. In November we feel, and console ourselves by thinking that there is, or may be, worse weather to come; in January, we think that the worst is over; yet even in December there are some bright spots. In this month we have Christmas, with all its mirth; and during the few short bright crisp days that every December brings forth, the healthy pedestrian enjoys an amount of exhilaration which he is a stranger to in warmer days, and on his return he will exclaim, Fine bracing weather! There is, unfortunately, a reverse to this. The "fine bracing weather" can only be enjoyed by those who are well clad, well shod, warmly housed, and are well cared for when they return. The poor, who are without these comforts, find themselves cramped, and pinched, and miserable; but to them December is not without some joy, for it is a season of almsgiving; the wealthy open their purses to their poorer brethren, and the more inclement the season the more liberal are their gifts.

6. *St. Nicholas* is the patron saint of Russia; also of New York. In the last-named place, the inhabitants, with that practical good sense which characterises so many of their actions, have dedicated a large hotel, one of the largest in the world, to the memory of good St. Nicholas. The saint was a native of Asia Minor. Even as a babe he evidenced his piety by refusing his natural maternal nourishment on Fridays and other appointed fasts. He is the patron of the young, who, in some parts of the world, expect him to visit them on his day, and bring them presents. St. Nicholas is commonly represented with a tub containing three naked children, in memory of one of his miracles performed in a time of great scarcity, when a certain man, being short of provisions, seized some little children, cut them up, salted their limbs, and served them up to his guests. He set a dish before St. Nicholas, who, at once perceiving what it contained, went to the tub where the limbs were in salt, offered up some prayers, and restored the children alive and whole. He performed many other good and pious works, and died Bishop of Myra, A.D. 326.

8. *Conception of the Blessed Virgin Mary.*— "This day," Dr. Forster says, "is a solemn festival, held by the Church in commemoration of the miraculous Conception of the Immaculate, Holy and Blessed Virgin Mother of God; and is, as Butler assures us, the joyful dawning of the bright day of mercy, refulgent in the birth of our Lord Jesus Christ." The festival was instituted by St. Anselm, afterwards Archbishop of Canterbury, in 1070.

13. *St. Lucy*, martyred 305. She was born at Syracuse, and having determined to devote herself to a religious life, she declined the addresses of a young nobleman, who declared that her brilliant eyes haunted him night and day. She thereupon cut out her eyes and sent them to him. She also gave the whole of her fortune to the poor. In order to reward her for the sacrifice, God gave her a fresh pair of eyes, more beautiful than before. Her suitor, enraged at his repulse, and at the loss of his expected fortune, denounced her to the heathen judge, who ordered her to be put to death.

21. *St. Thomas*, Apostle and Martyr.—The Gospel narrative of Thomas, surnamed Didymus, relates that he was hard of belief; he would see and judge for himself—and he believed. After the Ascension he appears to have gone to India, and to have preached the Gospel to the Parthians, Medes, and Persians, and was martyred at Melapore, on the Coromandel coast, being first stoned, and then run through with a spear.

25. *Christmas Day.*—This is the greatest holyday in the year, in every sense. On this day we celebrate the birth of the Saviour, and even those who care little about religion make the day and season a time of rejoicing. Even before breakfast we are saluted with—

" God bless you, merry gentlemen,
　　Let nothing you dismay,
　Remember Christ our Saviour
　　Was born on Christmas Day."

A custom which was inaugurated by the angels,

" While shepherds watched their flocks by night,
　All seated on the ground."

26. *St. Stephen*, the first Martyr.—Of St. Stephen nothing is known except that he was chosen one of the first deacons, that he was devout and eloquent, and that he was the first martyr, having been stoned to death by the fanatical Jews, some of whom, as St. Paul says, thought that by so acting they did God service. St. Stephen ought to be regarded as the patron of 'prentice lads, who this day go round collecting Christmas boxes, as also do the dustmen, postmen, and bellmen, with almost all classes of tradesmen's assistants. Being a day of rest, our forefathers turned it to account by making it a practice to bleed their horses, as recommended by good old Thomas Tusser:—

" Ere Christmas be passed, let horse to let blood,
For many a purpose it doth them much good;
The day of St. Stephen old fathers did use;
If that do mislike thee, some other day chuse."

Bishop Hall says, " On St. Stephen's Day blessings are implored upon pastures."

27. *St. John*, Apostle, Evangelist, and Martyr.— St. John, the beloved disciple, was one of Zebedee's children, and brother to St. James the Great. He was the youngest of the twelve, and to his charge was committed the Mother of Jesus at the foot of the Cross. It is supposed that he remained in Judea as long as she lived, and then preached in various parts of the world. In his old age he was sent to Rome by Domitian, and there, before the gate *Porta Latina*, was put into a cauldron of boiling oil, from which he not only suffered no injury, but acquired a more juvenile appearance. He had previously had a cup of poison offered him, but before putting his lips to it, the poison, in the form of a snake, escaped from the cup. He was banished to the isle of Patmos, where he wrote the Book of Revelations. After Domitian's death he returned to Ephesus, where he wrote his Gospel. At this

time a report got abroad that he would not die but would await the second coming of Christ. But on reaching the age of 100 he fell asleep.

28. *Holy Innocents.*—Childermas Day, in commemoration of the children slain by order of the impious Herod. It has been well observed that the Church commemorates three kinds of martyrs, each being exemplified in the three days past. 1. Those who, like St. Stephen, are martyrs both in the will and the deed—this is the highest kind of martyrdom. 2. Those who, like St. John, are martyrs in will but not in deed. 3. Those who are martyrs in deed, but not in will, as were those innocent babes commemorated this day.

31. *St. Silvester*, Bishop of Rome, died 335. He succeeded Miltiades in the Papacy, A.D. 314, and was the first to introduce palls, corporals, unctions, mitres, &c. Many miracles are recorded of him.

DATES OF SOME FASTS AND FESTIVALS.

Cent. I. Sundays, Easter, Pentecost.
,, II. Lent, Christmas.
,, III. Ember Days.
,, IV. Saints' Days, Annunciation.
,, V. Rogation, Circumcision, Advent.
,, VI. Felicitas, Marcellinus, Pancras.
,, VII. Nativity, B. V. M. All Saints.
,, VIII. Presentation, Transfiguration, Boniface.
,, IX. Easter Monday and Tuesday, and Whit-Monday and Tuesday.
,, X. All Souls', Evens or Vigils.
,, XI. All Popes that had been Martyred.
,, XII. Thomas of Canterb. 11,000 Virgins.
,, XIII. Epiphany, Circumcision, Conception, Conv. of St. Paul.
,, XIV. Thomas Aq., Bridget, Corp. Christi.
,, XVI. The VII. Sorrows of Our Lady Bruno.
,, XIX. Immaculate Conception of the B.V.M.

The Chinese and Japanese Calendars.

THE Almanack of the Chinese holds a very important place among the natives. It is prepared under a special commission appointed by the Emperor, who has made it a penal offence to issue any pirated edition. A large part of it is taken up with tables of the lucky and unlucky days, with which astrologers amuse the people. Besides this cabalistic part, there are tables to show the rising of the sun according to the latitudes of the different places, the times of the new and full moon, the beginning and length of the 24 terms, eclipses, conjunctions of the planets, &c. Two or three editions are published by Government, the prices of which vary from 3 to 10 cents. (1d. to 3d.) per copy. Everybody buys it, lest misfortune should overtake him by transacting important affairs on unlucky days.

The Chinese civil year is lunar, consisting of 12 months of 29 and 30 days alternately. But every three years a thirteenth month has to be added; or, to state it more exactly, in every nineteen years there are seven years which have thirteen months. This, however, contains a slight error. The Chinese have, therefore, formed a cycle of 60 years, in which period 22 intercalary months occur.

The 15th degree of *Aquarius* is the starting point for the lunar year. Why this was fixed upon is not quite clear; but we may suppose that it was connected with the first efforts at agriculture after the winter months. They have, moreover, an annual festival at this season. The Chinese may also be said to have a solar year as well as a lunar, and the winter solstice marks its annual limit. This solar year is divided into 24 periods of 15 days each on an average.

The day is divided into twelve parts or watches, called *shiu*, each equal to two hours of our reckoning. They begin at 11 o'clock p.m., and go by the name of Tsz, (11 p.m.—1 a.m.) chen, (1—3 a.m.) yin, (3—5 a.m.) mau, shin, sz, wu, wi, shin, yin, siu, and hai, which are called horary characters. Each part or watch is divided into eight parts, called *kĕ*, equivalent to 15 minutes of our time. At Canton, in the south of China, most people understand the European ystem of clocks and watches. As in Japan, the Chinese have a method of measuring time by *time sticks* (as they are called), which are long sticks made of clay and sawdust. By slow combustion of these sticks, they are made to measure hours or days, the longest lasting a week. Dials are in common use, and are frequently attached to the mariner's compass. In former times clepsydras of various forms were employed.

The Chinese Imperial Almanack is a curious medley of science and superstition. The Jesuit fathers in the Ming Dynasty received authority to regulate the astronomical portion with exactitude. But from Adam Schaal and Verbiest down to the last of the Romish missionaries (dismissed in 1826), who had this special duty, none were allowed to interfere with the peculiar institutions, which appeared in the almanack as lucky days and ruling stars. Astrology has, up to the present hour, considerable influence on the daily life and conduct of the millions of China.

The book itself consists of 40 to 50 closely-printed pages, under a yellow cover, the mark of the Imperial auspices under which it is published. The first few pages are in red letter. The first two are occupied by a description of the positions of two or more of the stars, which are supposed to be ever wandering, and always exerting great influence on human affairs.

Next comes a table of the fast days to be observed in memory of former emperors and worthies. Then we have the birthdays of the lesser deities of the Chinese Pantheon. These number more than a hundred. A table follows of the lucky hours in each day of the sixty-year cycle, and another of the unfavourable winds, accompanied by the names of the evil spirits who cause them.

The book itself bears the seal of the Astronomical Board, and the first article is a list of the dates of the commencement of the 24 periods into which the year is divided. In other words, for the times when the sun enters the twelve signs of the Zodiac, and when it reaches the middle points of them. They are calculated, of course, for Peking, and include the equinoxes and solstices, and correspond to hours in right ascension of European astronomy.

After this there is a map of astrological mysteries, the positions of the presiding spirit and his subordinate genii, are given, showing the days on which it would be dangerous to build, &c. Then there is a table of the 24 terms for every province of the empire, the figures supplying the place of a table of longitudes. Thus: Hangchow differs from Peking 15, Nanking 9, and Foochow 12 minutes. Such a table is essential in a country where longitudes differ to the extent of about 50 degrees.

Here Chinese superstition creeps in, and the direction of the heavens is said to be north, south, east, or west, in different months, and warnings are given against taking a journey or building in any other than the given direction.

Various notes of the month, taken from the ancient Book of Rites, are here printed, e. g. :—

First Month.—The east wind breaks up the frost. Torpid animals begin to move. The otter sacrifices his first caught fish to the ancestor of the otters. Grass and trees bud.

Second Month.—The peach blossoms. The falcon is transformed into a pigeon. Swallows arrive. Thunder and lightning begin.

Third Month.—The *Wootung* tree blossoms. Mice are transformed into pigeons. Rainbows are first seen. The *Tai-shing* bird alights on the mulberry. Wild doves shake their wings.

Fourth Month.—The mole-cricket chirps. The wheat autumn arrives.

Fifth Month.—The butcher-bird calls. Stags' horns fall off. The *mantis* appears.

Sixth Month.—Warm winds. Grass decomposes and produces glow-worms.

Seventh Month.—Cool winds. Dew falls. Grain ripens.

Eighth Month.—Worms close up their holes with earth. Swallows go away. Wild geese come for a time. Thunder ceases.

Ninth Month.—Sparrows are transformed to oysters. The wolf is the animal to be sacrificed. Insects become torpid and collect in holes. Chrysanthemums bloom.

Tenth Month.—Frosts. Pheasants go to the sea and are transformed to oysters. Rainbows cease.

Eleventh Month.—Fountains move. Worms make holes.

Twelfth Month.—The falcon goes northward. Pheasants call.

The Chinese civil year is lunar. New-year's day falls on the first new moon after the sun enters *Aquarius* (i.e., not before Jan 21, nor after Feb. 19).

The year 1869 will be the 4,506th of the Chinese Era. It will be called in Chinese, VIIth of Tung-chi, which is *wu-chen*, the 5th year of the cycle, and VIIIth of Tung-chi, which is *ki-sz*, the 6th year of the cycle.

The months bear no special name; they are called 1st, 2nd, &c. The length varies between 29 and 30 days.

mn.	day.	
12	8	Ancient Festival, also day sacred to Julai Buddha. (*Tathagata.*)
15° of Aquarius.		Lih-chun. Opening of Spring,
12	19	kept with great celebrations and pomp.
1	1	New-year's day, called *yuen-tan*, is universal holiday in China. All accounts are settled on New-year's eve.
1	9	*Yuh-wang Shangte*. Jupiter of the Greek.
1	15	Feast of Lanterns.
1	19	*Chang-chun*, a Physician, deified by the Tauists. Worshipped specially by the doctors, druggists, &c.
2	2	The household gods born. Great display of fireworks.
2	15	*Lau-kiun*, the founder of Tauists born, B.C. 604; 54 years before Confucius.

The Japanese Calendar.

AN important branch of Japanese education consists in learning the almanack: the chronological system being most complicated. The year is divided into twelve months, distinguished by the twelve signs of the zodiac, which, according to Japanese astronomy, are named after twelve animals; but these twelve months vary in length year by year, and the Mikado, or sacred emperor, at his court of Miako, arranges the number of the intercalary days and the months to which they are to be added.

Even an answer to the ordinarily simple question of "What's o'clock?" requires the exertion of much thought and calculation, before it can be answered according to the Japanese system.

The diurnal revolution of the earth is divided into twelve parts, and if these divisions were reckoned consecutively there would not be much difficulty in ascertaining the time of the day or night: but owing to the peculiar sacredness attached to the number nine, the principal epochs of day and night, namely, noon and midnight, are both known by the number nine. And the whole system of numbering the divisions of time is based upon the multiples of this perfect number, and upon the circumstance that sunset and sunrise are always called by the number six. Thus: if we begin to reckon from noon, that is called the hour of nine; for the next division of time we take twice nine, or eighteen; subtracting the decimal, eight remains; it is therefore called the hour of eight. That is 2 o'clock of our reckoning. For the next or third hour, the third multiple of nine is used, i. e., twenty-seven. The decimal number is again subtracted, and seven remains; for the fourth division, the fourth multiple, thirty-six; and again subtracting the tens, we have six left, which must be the hour of sunset: next the fifth multiple, or forty-five; subtracting the forty leaves five, or the fifth hour; and so with the sixth multiple, or the hour of four. The succeeding division is midnight, at which point the numbering recommences, with nine and its multiples; the fourth division is again six, or sunrise, and so the circle is completed at noon.

In order to distinguish the divisions of the day from those of the night, besides the number belonging to each division of time, it is also called by the name of one of the twelve signs of the zodiac: thus: midnight, or nine, is the hour of the mouse; sunrise, or six, the hour of the hare; noon, that of the horse; sunset, that of the cock. The subjoined table may make these daily divisions of time more clear:—

Noon	9th hour, called also	......	The Horse.
	8 ,,	,,	...... The Goat.
	7 ,,	,,	...... The Monkey.
Sunset ...	6 ,,	,,	...... The Cock.
	5 ,,	,,	...... The Dog.
	4 ,,	,,	...... The Boar.
Midnight	9 ,,	,,	...... The Mouse.
	8 ,,	,,	...... The Bull.
	7 ,,	,,	...... The Tiger.
Sunrise	6 ,,	,,	...... The Hare.
	5 ,,	,,	...... The Dragon.
	4 ,,	,,	...... The Snake.

As sunrise and sunset must always be called the sixth hour, this introduces another element to complicate the calculation, in order to allow for the variation constantly taking place in the relative length of the day and night.

It is one of the duties of the priests in the temples to mark the lapse of time by sounding their beautiful bells, and the practised ear soon recognizes, even in the depth of night, whether it is the hour of the boar or the bull that has just been rung out on the silver-toned bells.

Years since.		B.C.
5873	The Creation of the world	4004
4217	The Deluge	2348
3790	The Call of Abraham	1921
3731	Joseph was sold into Egypt	1862
3494	The Exodus under Moses	1625
3449	Canaan divided among the tribes	1580
3052	The Fall of Troy	1183
2951	Era of Cheops; Great Pyramid	1082
2918	David became King of Israel	1049
2882	The Temple of Jerusalem founded	1013
2845	Division of Solomon's kingdom	976
2831	Probable era of Homer (from 915 to	962
2741	Carthage was founded	878
2639	The Olympic era commenced	776
2616	Foundation of Rome; era A. U. C.	753
2274	The Babylonian Captivity commenced	605
2456	Jerusalem taken by Nebuchadnezzar	587
2398	Death of Cyrus	529
2378	Expulsion of the Tarquins	509
2349	Xerxes was defeated at Thermopylæ	480
1924	Cæsar's invasion of Britain	55
1913	The murder of Cæsar	44
1896	Octavius became Emperor	27
1873	Birth of Our Lord, 4 years bef. Ch. era	4
		A.D.
1840	The Crucifixion of Our Lord	29
1826	Invasion of Brit. by Aulus Plautius	43
1808	Revolt of the Britons under Boadicea	61
1799	Jerusalem was destroyed	70
1749	The Emperor Hadrian visited Britain	120
1556	Constantine embraced Christianity	313
1539	Constantinople made the capital	330
1460	Rome sacked by Alaric	409
1451	The Romans finally quitted Britain	418
1420	Vortigern called in the aid of Saxons	449
1415	Saxon kingdom founded in Kent	454
1042	Egbert, first king of all England	827
998	Alfred the Great succeeded to the Crown	871
957	The Norsemen conquered Neustria	912
890	King Edward the Martyr murdered	979
852	Canute of Denmark king of England	1017
803	The Battle of Hastings	1066
783	The Domesday survey completed	1086
773	The Crusades commenced	1096
769	William Rufus was killed	1100
689	The Murder of Thomas à Becket	1170
679	Richard I. went to the Crusades	1190
654	King John granted Magna Charta	1215
604	First Representative Parliament	1265
587	Wales was conquered by Edward I.	1282
564	Wallace was captured and executed	1305
563	Robert Bruce King of Scotland	1306
542	Edward II. deposed and murdered	1327
523	Battle of Crécy; the French defeated	1346
523	Battle of Nevill's Cross	1346
522	Calais captured by Edward III.	1347
513	The French were defeated at Poictiers	1356
488	Wat Tyler's rebellion	1381
481	Battle of Otterburn (or Chevy Chase)	1388
470	Richard II. was deposed	1399
454	The Battle of Agincourt	1415
440	Joan of Arc raised the siege of Orleans	1429
414	The Wars of the Roses commenced	1455
408	The House of York came to the Throne	1461
398	Warwick was killed at Barnet	1471
384	Richard III. killed at Bosworth	1485
356	Battle of Flodden; Scots defeated	1513
330	Monasteries were dissolved	1539
314	The Marian persecution began	1555
313	Archbishop Cranmer burnt	1556
311	Calais was taken from the English	1558
311	Accession of Queen Elizabeth	1558
297	The St. Bartholomew Massacre	1572
282	Mary Queen of Scots was beheaded	1587
281	The Spanish Armada was defeated	1588

Years since.		A.D.
264	The Gunpowder Plot	1605
229	The Long Parliament assembled	1640
227	The Battle of Edgehill	1642
224	Battle of Naseby; the king defeated	1645
220	Charles I. was beheaded, 30th January	1649
216	Oliver Cromwell Lord Protector	1653
209	The Monarchy was restored	1660
184	Duke of Monmouth's rebellion	1685
180	Parliament elected William and Mary	1689
179	The Battle of the Boyne	1690
177	The Glencoe Massacre	1692
165	The Battle of Blenheim	1704
165	Gibraltar was taken by the English	1704
156	The Treaty of Utrecht	1713
155	The Accession of the House of Hanover	1714
149	The South Sea Bubble	1720
126	The Battle of Dettingen	1743
124	The Battle of Fontenoy	1745
124	The Scotch Rebellion	1745
94	Battle of Lexington, first American	1775
87	Independence of the United States	1782
76	Louis XVI. of France was executed	1793
72	The Mutiny at the Nore	1797
71	The Irish Rebellion	1798
71	The Battle of the Nile	1798
68	The Union of Great Brit. and Ireland	1801
68	The British expedition to Egypt	1801
67	The Treaty of Amiens	1802
66	The war with France resumed	1803
64	Buonaparte Emperor of the French	1805
64	Battle of Trafalgar; death of Nelson	1805
60	The Battle of Corunna	1809
57	The French expedition to Russia	1812
55	The Restoration of the Bourbons	1814
54	The Battle of Waterloo; 18th June	1815
53	The Bombardment of Algiers	1816
49	The Trial of Queen Caroline	1820
47	The Greek Revolution broke out	1822
45	The first Burmese war commenced	1824
43	The Insurrection of the Janissaries	1826
42	The Battle of Navarino	1827
39	Revolution in France; Charles X. exp.	1830
37	The first Reform Act passed, 7th June	1832
36	The Carlist war in Spain	1833
35	English Poor Law Amendment Act	1834
35	The Houses of Parliament were burnt.	1834
32	Accession of Queen Victoria, 20th June	1837
31	The Rebellion in Canada	1838
30	The War with China	1839
30	The Affghan war commenced	1839
30	The Chartist riots at Newport	1839
29	Marriage of Queen Victoria	1840
28	Birth of the Prince of Wales, 9th Nov.	1841
27	The Imposition of the Income Tax	1842
26	Scinde was conquered	1843
25	The Civil war in Switzerland	1844
24	Sir John Franklin sailed	1845
24	The Sikhs were defeated at Moodkee	1845
23	Repeal of the Corn Laws, 26th June	1846
20	War between the U. S. and Mexico	1847
21	Chartist assemblage, 10th April	1848
21	Fr. Revolution, Louis Philippe exp.	1848
18	International Exhibition in London	1851
17	Louis Napoleon Emperor of French	1852
15	The Battle of Inkerman	1854
14	The Capture of Sebastopol	1855
12	The Indian Mutiny broke out	1857
8	The Death of the Prince Consort	1861
7	The Second International Exhibition	1862
5	War between Germany and Denmark	1864
4	The Death of Lord Palmerston	1865
3	The Seven Weeks War	1866
2	Fenian outrages at Manchester, &c.	1867
2	The New Reform Act passed	1867
1	Terrible earthquake in Peru	1868

THE FARM: THE FRUIT, FLOWER, & KITCHEN GARDEN.

January.

THE FARM.—January is the real month of winter, although, according to astronomers the season is supposed to commence in December. The outdoor operations of the farm are consequently often at a standstill, so far as the fields are concerned. But this may be turned to great account by the farmer. While the frost does much work in breaking up his soil into fine fragments that can never be effected by the plough, destroys insects and vermin generally, and otherwise does the work of nature, he may be well employed in many indoor operations. Should the month prove wet, he will find the necessity of following out an entire system of land-drainage. The kitchen garden may also claim his attention, as may also the orchard and flower garden if the weather prove open. Of course all operations of an outdoor nature must be regulated by the position of the farm. Hedges should be repaired, and other similar preparations made in anticipation of the spring. The dung beds or pits may be prepared for spring manure. Cattle while housed should be allowed sufficient access to light and fresh air. Farm machinery should be got into proper working order for spring operations. Potatoes and carrots, &c. &c., must be kept from frost. Watercourses kept open for fear of spring floods, ditches banked up and cleared as the weather permits. Spare labour will thus be utilized, and all necessary preparations made to avert the consequences of floods arising from sudden thaws or violent rains.

THE KITCHEN GARDEN.—Work done in this department must necessarily, like farming operations, depend on the weather. If this prove open, digging, trenching, ridging, and other preparation of the ground should be vigorously carried on. It is not sufficiently known that the more the soil is exposed to air, light, and thoroughly drained, the more productive it becomes. The effect of a frost on well-drained land is of incalculable advantage. It pulverizes the soil, opening out little channels for the passage of moisture, and also for the radicles of the growing seed to push their way through in search of food. Whilst the soil is soft, the roots, &c., of decayed plants of the previous year's growth may be removed. Hotbeds should be prepared for forcing plants, such as Cucumbers, Melons, &c. &c. Indeed, as a rule, every opportunity should be taken of utilizing the time that the severity of the season leaves for indoor work. The following seeds may be sown. In hotbeds, *Cucumbers, Melons, &c., &c.* In the open ground, *Beans, Peas, Cabbage, Radish,* and other *cruciferous seeds.* In a warm border, *Carrots* may also be sown. But in all cases, the temperature of the air, the condition of the season and soil, with other concomitant circumstances, must be kept in mind. The great variations that occur in our climate render specific directions for this and the next month impossible. They call for the vigilant intelligence of man to adapt them to his purposes.

FRUIT GARDEN.—The general instructions already given under the preceding headings are equally applicable. All outdoor operations must depend on the state of the weather. If practicable—that is, in the absence of frost—plant fruit trees, presuming that the ground has been already prepared in the autumn. The antecedent manuring must have had either the object of promoting the growth of wood to produce large trees, or, on the other hand, to produce much fruit on small trees. Here we may remark on the value of *wood-charcoal* as an ingredient of manure. It has the effect of absorbing both the beneficial and harmful gases, &c., that the soil of previous growing plants possesses; in the one case storing food, and in the other preventing injury to the growing plant. Hence the common but less beneficial use of coal-ashes, the mineral constituents of which, together with those of charcoal, afford potash, silica, and other minerals, for the use of the plant. In setting plants a common error is to put them in too deep. The roots or radicles will always find their own way *downwards* in search of moisture and food. A good rule is to plant so that the top of the radiating branch of the root shall only be two or three inches below the surface of the soil, which can easily be earthed up if washed away by rain. It should be remembered that all the vitalizing influence of the soil depends on the ready access of atmospheric air. As all plants at this period of the year are only in a semi or half-vital state, pruning of most fruit trees may be extensively practised. If this be delayed until spring arrives, injurious results from bleeding may occur.

FLOWER GARDEN.—The attention of the florist is generally directed to indoor plants that are to be forced for early flowering. *Crocuses* and other bulbs may be planted, if not already sufficiently done. *Verbenas* and *Dahlias* intended to supply cuttings may be placed in a gentle heat. Decaying or decayed leaves should be removed from them. Some *Annuals* may be sown, if the weather be open. *Carnations, Calceolarias* and *Cinerarias* will require occasional watering. Bulbs already sown in open ground will require shelter from frost, by means of matting &c., a point of especial importance in regard to *Hyacinths* and *Tulips. Roses* and other shrubs may be judiciously pruned, and certain kinds may be planted if the state of the soil permit. *Manuring* should be attended to, especially in regard to beds for *Ranunculuses,* which may be planted towards the end of the month. Green-fly and other insects should be kept off by smoking. Give air to plants as far as safely can be done, in the absence of frost, and during sunlight. Prepare labels, sticks, and other material ready for spring use.

February.

THE FARM.—This month, with the increasing heat of the sun, induces generally plenty of outdoor work on the farm. First in importance is the duty of keeping open all watercourses, ditches, &c., so that superfluous water or freshes may be drawn off from the land. The melting of the snow, and heavy rains, that frequently occur in February, render every precaution in these respects of the greatest necessity. Manure may be carted to the fields, and, if the weather prove open, ploughing may be pursued. The soil should be got ready for oats and barley. *Spring Wheat* (Talavera, &c.), *Peas, Beans, &c.,* should be sown; and *Rye* replaced where it has failed in autumn sowing. In respect to manures, the great variety now offered to the farmer leaves an almost unlimited choice.

Phosphates, guano, and animal manures artificially prepared, stand first in value; salt, sulphate of ammonia, and lime or chalk, with nitrate of soda, are also in great use. For peas, beans, and other leguminous crops lime is absolutely essential. Hedges should be repaired, trimmed, and planted. Hop grounds should be dug up, and well manured. Cattle require care this month, owing to the changeable character of the weather. Oilcake is a good admixture of food for them and sheep. *Cabbage-seed* may be sown for subsequent planting out, and the land ploughed for carrots, mangold, turnips, &c. Grass land should be dressed, and as the weather permits every preparation should be made to anticipate the requirements of the coming spring.

KITCHEN GARDEN.—The first duties of this month comprise the preparation of the soil. The frost will have broken up hard masses, and this should be followed up by spade work, manuring, trenching, ridging, and other such operations. Even the stiffest clay-land may thus be made highly productive, especially for *Pea* and *Bean crops*, which may be now sown abundantly. *Cabbages* may be transplanted. *Cauliflowers* thinned out; *Carrots* sown on warm borders; *Cucumbers* and *Melons* sown in hotbeds. *Radishes*, *Lettuces*, and *small Salads* should be sown for early supply, as also various *Sweet Herbs*. Plant *early kinds of Potatoes* in warm situations. Shelter *Artichokes*, and other plants liable to injury from frost. *Seakale* may be forced. *Peas* and *Celery* should be earthed up, *Parsley* sown in drills, and *Onions* on a warm border, for salads.

FRUIT GARDEN.—When possible, plant out cuttings of *Gooseberries, Currants, Raspberries*, and other plants of a similar nature. Prune all plants that require it, keeping back such as are too luxuriant, whilst stimulating those which are backward by judicious manuring. Most of the seed-shops sell suitable manures for such purposes, and the advice of an intelligent seedsman should be sought in regard to such objects. The pruning of *Vines* should be concluded in the course of February, otherwise bleeding and consequent loss of fruit and plant may result. The nut tribe, as of *Filberts, Hazel*, &c., may be planted. Discretion is required in retarding the growth of many fruit trees, lest the possibly succeeding cold east wind of March may prove seriously harmful. Fork over all borders. Remove stones, and the stems of last year. Dress borders with well-rotted dung, decayed leaves, with the addition in many cases of lime, salt, and nitrate of soda, dependent on the requirements of the soil. Do not forget the value of charcoal as an under-dressing, the uses of which have been already pointed out. Drain stiff soil by trenching up. The addition of a quantity of broken crockery, tiles, &c., will assist draining operations. It is a serious error to remove all the stones found in some soils, for they greatly assist draining.

FLOWER GARDEN.—The gradual increasing heat of the weather induces fresh operations in this department. *Crocuses* and other *bulbous* or *bulb-like plants* will now appear, and their growth should be assisted by hoeing or raking the intermediate soil. As already pointed out, access of air and moisture is an essential condition of the growth in perfection of all plants. Sow *Anemones*. Look to *Calceolarias, Carnations*, &c., watering when required, and remove, by smoking, green fly and other vermin. The seedsmen supply a supposed specific for such purposes. By the end of the month, if the weather prove favourable, flowering plants should be abundantly planted in the open ground. Of late years *Geraniums, Verbenas*, and *Calceolarias* have been the most favourite plants for popular use; hence great attention has been paid to them amongst the nurserymen for the purpose of sale; they have been in fact a kind of stock, together with *Fuchsias*, and the variety and beauty of the flowers of each fully justify the choice that popular taste has made of them. *Calceolarias* that have advanced may be replanted. *Verbenas* should be trimmed, removing decayed leaves, be occasionally watered, and judiciously exposed to the air, so that whilst avoiding frost, they may be hardened for early sale when requisite. Protect *Hyacinths, Tulips*, &c., from frost by matting, or throw straw on the beds, removing it as a genial sunshine appears. Many cuttings made in the end of the previous year will have so far progressed that on warm days they may be freely exposed to the sun on a border having a southern aspect. The time-limits of such exposure should be ten in the morning and not later than three in the afternoon, due regard being had to the possibility of injury by frost. All plants propagated by cuttings may now be safely dealt with by planting in a moderate heat.

March.

THE FARM.—*Spring Corn* should be sown early in this month, if the weather prove open, including *Wheat, Oats, Barley*, and in certain districts *Flax* and *Hemp*. It is to be regretted that the two last named crops, beside that of *Buck-wheat*, have been so neglected in many districts where they might have been economically grown. Generally such, by prudence, may be made profitable crops, especially as during recent years the failure of the cotton crop has largely stimulated the linen trade in all its branches. Artificial manures, phosphates, nitrate of soda, gypsum or sulphate of lime, common salt, sulphate of ammonia, made from gas-tar liquor, are all valuable manures for graminaceous crops that include wheat, oats, rye, barley, grass, &c. *Carrots* and *Parsnips* may be sown on light lands. Top-dress *Wheat* with soot, ashes, and chalk; the addition, in moderate amount, of superphosphate will be of value. Remember that although gypsum or sulphate of lime has, comparatively speaking, of itself little nutritious power, indirectly it possesses great power as an absorbent of ammonia—the sole nitrogenous nutriment of plants. It is, in fact, one of the farmer's bankers. *Potato* ground should be prepared early in, and planted at the end, of this month. Be particular about the soil, as the potato will only grow in one well drained, open, and free from surface water. Look to ditches and drainage in general. When possible, weed and stone the ground. Keep cattle and sheep well sheltered, but with abundant access of air. Cleanliness in the stable or byre is essential. Mash your turnip and other feeds, as being most economical in use. Commence making water-meadows in suitable situations. Attend to poultry, lime-washing their houses, and setting them on other stock-eggs than your own, to obtain good broods.

KITCHEN GARDEN.—Much should be made of this department during the month of March. In the absence of previous sowing, sow *Angelica*,

Basil, Borage, Brocoli, Carrots, Capsicum, Celery and *Celeriac, Cress,* and other salad plants, *Leeks, Onions,* and all of that family. *Melons* and *Cucumbers* may be sown, and those already advanced carefully looked to. Sow *Orach* and other kinds of *Spinach, Parsnips, Pompions, Vegetable Marrows,* and other similar members of the *Gourd family; Nasturtiums, Parsley, Rosemary, Rampion, Rapeseed,* for salads; *Rhubarb, Tomatoes,* and generally most plants required for late spring or early summer use. We presume that from previous instructions everything has been done to prepare the ground, in respect to digging, trenching, &c., &c., for the now increasing vitalizing influence of spring. This must naturally have been effected by every intelligent gardener. In regard to early crops, fork up *Asparagus* beds; plant out *Cauliflower* and *Cabbage* plants; plant *Jerusalem Artichokes. Kohl Rabi,* an excellent stock food for cattle, may be sown. Generally, all the main crops for man or beast should either be planted, thinned out, or otherwise attended to, depending on the circumstances of weather, temperature, &c.

FRUIT GARDEN. - Planting, and, according to the temperature (if low), pruning may be proceeded with. The violent winds that often come in March have the advantage of loosening the soil about the roots of plants, but some of them require protection, not only against the force of the wind, but also from its drying and cooling effects. Plants, like animals, have a temperature when growing which exceeds that of the average external temperature of the atmosphere; hence Providence has assigned to all plants of temperate climes that produce stems an outer protector, familiarly known as *bark.* But the leaf and flower buds in March are all but destitute of such protection, hence the necessity of vigilance on the part of the horticulturist. Wall-plants, such as peaches, apricots, &c., should be trained and nailed to walls. In pruning vines, owing to the stimulus of increased air and light, much caution is necessary. Grafting may be carried on. *Strawberry* beds should be dressed, cleaned, and otherwise looked to; and nut trees may be occasionally shaken to distribute the fertilizing male pollen. Nature, however, generally does this most effectually at this period of the year by means of the violent winds that are the usual characteristic of March.

FLOWER GARDEN.—The uncertain character of this month prevents the appearance of many flowers. In respect to *Fuchsias, Geraniums, Calceolarias, Cinerarias,* and plants grown for similar purposes, the directions of last month may still be followed. Protect all bulb or bulb-like plants from frost. Top-dressing *Pansies.* Sow tender *annuals,* such as *Lobelias,* &c., on warm borders. *Roses* should not be planted out later than March. Pruning, owing to the advance of the season, cannot be carried on beyond this month, but its temperature must rule this and all other operations of the flower garden. Pot *Cinerarias,* and smoke them to destroy the aphis or green fly. Plant out last year's *Hollyhocks.* Clear dead leaves off all bedding plants, and give plenty of air during warm days, avoiding risk from frost.

April.

THE FARM.—By the beginning of this month all spring *Corn* should have been sown. Grass land may be stoned, rolled, and manured, if the latter has not been attended to. Top-dressings of nitrate of soda, sulphate of ammonia, soot, and other stimulating manures, may be applied on all corn lands. They give strength and vitality of growth to the straw. In part, the same observation holds good in respect to grass land. *Turnips* also are much benefited by a top-dressing of nitrate of soda. The main crop of *Potatoes* should be planted, the ground being first manured with decayed vegetable matter or stable dung. *Paring* and *burning* of waste ground may be followed, especially on peat or bog lands. Clay lands should be dressed with such substances as will diminish their stiffness, as sand, ashes, old mortar, &c. *Cattle* may be, with *sheep,* put in pastures, being housed at night if frost prevail. *Lucerne* should be sown in rich deep soil.

KITCHEN GARDEN.—The advance of spring requires that all seeds intended for early crops should soon be sown. *Scarlet Runners* are found to succeed well, and crop early, if sown in this month in open soil containing plenty of lime salts. Clear the beds, so as to prevent the propagation of weeds that might grow to seed. The surface soil, as an absorbent of air and moisture, should be kept well hoed or raked; this plan greatly assisting the germination and growth of seeds and plants. All varieties of the *Cabbage* or *Brassica* tribe should be sown in warm beds for subsequent transplanting, including *Cabbage* proper, *Brocoli, Brussels Sprouts, Cauliflower,* &c. The same applies to each variety of *Peas* and *Beans;* the gourd tribe, such as the *Cucumber, Melon, Pumpkin,* &c.; *Salads,* including *Lettuce* of all varieties. *Cress* should be sown for fresh crops, and seedlings transplanted. *Celery* plants may be pricked out. Sow *Seakale, Vegetable Marrows* (the latter in rich soil in pots or hotbeds), *Spinach, Radish, Carrots, Cardoon,* and *Savoys.* Walks and beds should be kept well dressed. Worms may be destroyed on gravel walks, and the appearance of the latter improved, by watering with a solution of one pound of copperas (sulphate of iron) to two gallons of water. Some use salt for the same purpose. Soot is an excellent preventive of worms, so applied on beds, round the stems of plants.

FRUIT GARDEN.—Many fruit trees, depending on the state of the weather, are now in bloom; hence pruning is all but out of the question. Grafting may still be pursued, and in certain cases planting may be followed. Wall trees are liable to attacks of insects; many specifics have been proposed as a remedy. The removal of the larva, or insect, should be done by hand. A good lime-wash on the walls prevents, to a large extent, the encroachment of all insects. Tobacco liquor has also been strongly recommended. Unnecessary shoots on *Vines* should be rubbed off. *Strawberry* plants that have been covered may now be exposed to the air, and the adjacent soil dressed with decayed leaves or the waste of the cucumber frame. All the *Peach* or *Almond* tribe (*Drupaceous trees*) should be carefully looked to, and superfluous buds removed. The trimming of hedges should be attended to.

FLOWER GARDEN.—The care of the preceding winter month devoted by the florist will now show some signs of repayment. Keep *Tulips,* and other *bulb* or *bulb-like* plants, sheltered from frost. Prick out tender *annuals,* and sow those of a hardy kind. Pot out the *Pink* tribe, as also *Calceolarias, Cinerarias,* and *Dahlias.* The same may be remarked in respect to *Fuchsias,* which can yet be propagated by cuttings. If the heat be strong, shelter *Hyacinths*. Plant out *Pansies*, *Auriculas*, again, with *Polyanthuses*, should be sheltered. Sow *Mignonette*, *Major* and *Minor Convolvulus*, *Sweet Pea*, *Calliopsis*, *Nasturtium*, and other summer flowering plants. *Roses* should be finally pruned and planted, and the ground round the growing trees kept open. In the greenhouse, the *Lily of the Valley*, *Azaleas*, *Pelargoniums*, *Heaths*, *Fuchsias*, *Begonias*, *Petunias*, &c., will now be advancing rapidly, and should be mostly in full bloom. In respect to the *Petunia*, a beautiful double variety has been introduced of late years. The *Hollyhock* should be sown or replanted, and *Chrysanthemums* potted, fresh cuttings being also made. Plant out strong *Dahlia* roots. Keep hedges and walks in a trimmed condition.

May.

THE FARM.—*Barley* and *Grass* seeds should be finished sowing by this month. *Wheat* and other *cereal crops* should be hoed. As opportunity offers, continue draining the land by tiles or other contrivances. Nothing is so important as thorough drainage, and it is a great mistake to suppose that draining diminishes the goodness of the soil, for by extended experiments with the richest sewage water, it has been found that the soil absorbs most of the valuable substances; the water drained from it scarcely containing a percentage of either organic or inorganic matter. *Water meadows* may be prepared during this month. Hoe *Peas* and *Beans*. Keep up the production of dung-pits. If seaweed is procurable, work it into the soil. Sow *Lucerne* and *Buckwheat*. Hoe *Potatoes*, *Cabbages*, and *Carrot* land. *Swede Turnips* may be sown early in the month; *White Turnips*, with *Rape*, &c., towards the end. In ordinary seasons, grass will now be rapidly advancing towards the period of cutting; preparations should therefore be made for all hay harvesting operations. Cattle and horses may have green feed with advantage. If *Oaks* are on the farm, the stripping of the *bark* may be proceeded with. Mind chances of rot with sheep if left in damp meadows.

KITCHEN GARDEN.—In the latter portion of April or beginning of May, *Asparagus* becomes a favourite vegetable. The bed should be kept well open by means of the fork. Sow *Sweet Herbs* for winter use. Hoe *Beans*, cutting off the tops that are coming into flower; this is *said* to prevent the attack of blight, &c., on the plants. Thin out *Red Beet*, sow and plant out *Brocoli*, *Borecole*, and other members of the *Cabbage* tribe. Thin *Carrots*. Plant out *Celery*, *Capsicum*, and *Cauliflowers*. Earth up *Endive*, *Lettuces*, &c. Sow *Beans* and *Peas* for succession of crops. Plant out *Lettuces*. Thin *Leeks* and weed *Onions*. The same may be said in regard to *Parsnips*, *Turnips*, and other so-called root-crops. Plant out *Vegetable Marrows*, *Cucumbers*, and other members of the gourd tribe. Keep up a succession of *Small Salads* by weekly sowing. *White* and *Red Radishes* are also to be sown. Sow *Spinach*, and thin preceding crop. Weed beds carefully, for this preserves the plants from loss of nutriment, that unchecked weeds always cause.

FRUIT GARDEN. — *Peaches*, *Nectarines*, and *Apricots* require attention in the removal of superfluous blossoms, and the general retardation of growth which tends to weaken the trees. Follow the same plan in respect to all fruit trees; for no matter how luxuriant the bearing power of a tree may appear to be, there is a limit to its strength. All leading shoots, except wanted for next year, should be stopped, and a large proportion of buds pinched off. Insects will commence vigorous attacks on trees; all should therefore be carefully examined for the removal of vermin, and the plans already suggested for their extermination be incessantly applied. Divest *Apples*, *Pears*, *Cherries*, and other wall or espalier trees of useless wood and shoots. Water *Strawberries* while in flower, and remove useless runners.

FLOWER GARDEN.—Generally, May is considered as the initiator of the flower season. Bedding out is usually extensively followed. *Bulb plants*, such as *Tulips*, *Hyacinths*, &c., should be removed from the ground, and dried in the shade, to put away for the next season. *Auriculas* may also be changed to a cool bed for the same reason. Sow, for succession, *Sweet Peas*, *Nasturtiums*, *Lupins*, and other *annuals*. *Fuchsias*, *Calceolarias*, *Geraniums*, &c., may now be planted out. Much depends on taste for the effect that may arise in the garden, and much may be learned by the florist paying a visit to Kew Gardens, or those of leading floriculturists. A judicious arrangement of a few plants in the beds will greatly excel in effect a careless assortment of much larger resources. *Mignonette* may still be sown. *Pinks*, *Carnations*, &c., should have the ground stirred up, and sticks provided to support the stems of the latter. *Roses* are now greatly liable to the attacks of *aphis*, which should be smoked off. Plant out *Verbenas*, they form a pretty alternation with geraniums and calceolarias. Only three natural colours exist; now red with yellow are afforded by flowers of the plants named, whilst the green leaves supply a substitute for the third. Hence full scope is left with such materials for tasty arrangement. Sow *Wallflowers* for next year. *Water Anemones*. Plant out *Dahlias*, *Pansies*, and *Chrysanthemums*. Pot off *Cinerarias*, and sow fresh seed, as also of *Polyanthus*. Sow both *perennials* and *biennials* generally. Keep grass and gravel walks in good order, mowing the grass weekly, and frequently sweeping the gravel when dry, and rolling it after rains. Beds should also be well raked, to give a smooth appearance.

June.

THE FARM.—Most of the farmer's crops having now been sown, he can leave them to the course of nature, but he will have many matters requiring his attention. Generally the *Hay* harvest becomes universal. One word on the stacking of hay. If so done in a wet condition, or during heavy rain, the chances are that the rick will catch fire spontaneously; it is therefore a matter of great importance that dry weather should be taken advantage of for that purpose. *Paring* and *burning* of the soil, and *burning clay* and *lime*, should be carried out. Plough, cleanse, and manure fallows. *Swede Turnips*, sow in drills, with artificial manures, as bone-dust, &c. Plant out *Cabbages*; weed *Wheat*, *Pea*, and *Bean* fields. Plough in stable manure on spare land, so that its valuable constituents may not be lost by evaporation. Tie up *Hop vines*, weed *Flax*, hoe *Carrots* and *Potatoes*. *Bees* now about to swarm require attention. A few handfuls of mustard seed, sown near their hives, will yield abundance of flowers, to which the bees gladly resort, and the plan has the advantage of keeping them near home. Keep up the storing of liquid manure in tanks. Repair ponds, and use the waste mud as manure. Sheep-shearing will be among the operations of the farm.

KITCHEN GARDEN.—In June, this department becomes usually very productive, affording *Peas, Beans, Potatoes, Cauliflowers*, &c., &c. The ground then previously occupied, and that which has been lying fallow, may now be utilized, and crops of *Beans, Brocoli, Brussels Sprouts, Cabbage*, &c., may be sown for autumn and winter use. Trench *Celery*, plant out *Endive* and *Jerusalem Kale*. WATER newly planted *Asparagus* beds; indeed, if the season be dry, generally, watering must be had recourse to. Thin out *Seakale*. Sow *Early Turnips, Small Salads, Spinach, Radish*, &c. Thin *Parsnips*, and hoe *Potatoes, Onions*, &c. *Lettuce, Leeks, Kidney Beans*, and *Runner Beans* may be sown. Thin *Scorzoneras*. Plant out *Vegetable Marrows* and *Pumpkins* in a good deep and rich soil, also *Capsicums* and *Tomatoes*. Plant out *Cabbage, Savoy*, and *Cauliflowers*.

FRUIT GARDEN.—Green fly will infect wall-trees. Use tobacco water, or some of the numerous compounds recommended to keep down the pest. Sulphur, in the form of vapour, or from a burning match, answers well for small trees, which should be first moistened by a syringe. Pinch off superfluous shoots on fruit trees, to direct general and stop harmful growth. *Ripening fruit* will attract birds, which may be kept away by nets and many other devices. *Strawberry beds* should be neatly covered between the rows with straw, to prevent injury to the fruit by rain. Plant out *early forced Strawberries*, as they generally yield abundantly in the ensuing season. Clear *Gooseberry* and *Currant* bushes of insects by a wash of lime or soot water. Stop leading shoots of *Fig trees*. Carefully go over *Vines*, thinning out what wood is not required. *Raspberry beds* should also be thinned out. Lay *Strawberries* in pots, for next year's forcing, in rich soil.

FLOWER GARDEN.—In a hot season watering must be constantly had recourse to. Sow *Biennials* and *Perennials*; transplant *large Annuals* to their intended permanent beds. Dry and lay up *bulbs*, including *Anemones, Tulips, Ranunculus*, &c., &c. Plant out *Dahlias, Chrysanthemums*, &c. Propagate *Wallflowers, Rockets, Sweet Williams*, &c., by slips. Plant out *Carnations* and *Pinks* in their proper places. Sow *Stocks* of quick growth. Keep *Roses* from insects by fumigation as far as possible. Give *Heaths* plenty of air. Sow *Hollyhocks*, and stake them, *Sunflowers*, and other plants requiring support. Trim all *Biennials* and *Perennials*, and look carefully to the neatness in appearance of beds, walks, &c.

July.

THE FARM.—The year 1868 presented the most extraordinary feature of corn harvest, even threshing having been general throughout England in this month. The dryness and heat of the season were perhaps unparalleled in our islands. Usually, July is a month of anxiety to the farmer, owing to the prevalence of storms, especially from the middle to the end of the month. The turnip field is often infested with the "fly." In case of failure of the crop it is advisable to be prepared with a good stock of cabbage plants. In respect to *Turnips* it is best by every possible means to force them into early

large leaf. *Turnip sowing* should be diligently followed as a winter crop for cattle. Drilling is, perhaps, the best method, and a free use of the numerous manures now offered. It must be remembered that turnips are constituted of about 90 per cent. of water; they consequently do not greatly exhaust the soil of mineral and organic constituents. Sow *Rape, Tares*, and *Cole seed*. Hoe *Potatoes* and *Carrots*. Prepare everything for the coming harvest, as carts, waggons, tarpaulins. Repair roofs of sheds. Cattle and sheep require plenty of water, and ewes intended for early lambing should be liberally fed.

KITCHEN GARDEN.—The instructions for last month generally serve for July. All kinds of *Cabbage, Cauliflower, Brussels Sprouts, Borecole*, &c. may be planted for winter and spring use. Earth up *Celery*, watering occasionally. Many or most *sweet herbs*, being in flower, may be gathered. Attend to *Cucumbers* and *Melons*. Sow succession of *various salads*. *Leeks* should be earthed up, whilst *Shalots*, and many of the *Onion tribe*, may be gathered and stored. Last crops of quick-growing *Peas* and *Beans* may be sown. Sow *Turnips* (see preceding article). Transplant *Lettuces*. Supply plants generally with plenty of water, if rain be deficient, and also liquid manure. Usually, however, July is a very wet month.

FRUIT GARDEN.—The instructions given for the preceding month will, if they have been judiciously carried out, leave comparatively little to be done in July. Abundant and forcible watering will remove most insects from fruit trees. Superfluous growth of wood must be checked by pinching off buds or shoots. *Gooseberry* bushes may be thinned, and *Raspberries* may be similarly treated. Train *Vines* carefully. Thin *Nectarines* and *Peaches*, as also *Plums, Cherries, Figs*, and *Apricots*. Summer training is of high importance. Make new plantations of *Strawberries*. Loosen as far as possible the earth about the roots of fruit trees, as their productiveness is much influenced thereby.

FLOWER GARDEN.—The garden is now in full flower-bearing vigour. Many plants, as *Carnations, Piccotees*, &c., require shading from extreme heat of the sun. *Seedling Auriculas* and *Polyanthuses* may be transplanted; as also *Cinerarias* and *Calceolarias*. Remove all *bulbs*, and store away. Attend carefully to *Dahlias*. Generally, plentiful watering is requisite for most plants in the absence of rain. *Roses, Fuchsias*, and other plants in flower, keep neatly trimmed from decaying or dead leaves, and remove insects by fumigation. Stake *Hollyhocks* and other tall-growing stems.

August.

THE FARM.—This is the principal harvest month throughout nearly all England. In July, 1868, however, as already stated, the usual period of harvest was anticipated by about three weeks. Oats and barley, early sown, generally become ripe before wheat. The latter should be cut when dead ripe. The inconveniences of local want of labour are now largely overcome by aid of steam machinery, which is at once economical and effective in action. Harvest operations and threshing will occupy most of the attention of the farmer, but the following matters should also be attended to. Carry *Peas* and *Beans*, as also cut *Tares*. Hoe *Turnips*. Pull up *Mangold, Carrots*, &c., that are running to seed, and give as food to pigs. *Clover* and *Lucerne* will serve as part food for cattle and sheep. Harrow and plough up land for sowing wheat, &c., especially fallows, forming the soil into ridges. Pasturage will begin to fail in many cases, especially if the summer has been dry. Where possible, therefore, sewage may be beneficially applied to stimulate the growth of meadow and Italian rye grass. Its effects are astonishing. The houses of live-stock should be well cleaned out during leisure time, and the refuse carried to the fields. In the dairy, butter and cheese making will give occupation. The advance of autumn improves the quality of milk in respect to its richness. Poultry will find much food in the stubble of the fields that have been reaped, and also in the stack-yard. Ducks may also be thus partly fed.

THE KITCHEN GARDEN.—Sowing and planting out members of the *Cabbage* tribe should be made for spring crops early in this month, including different varieties of the *Cabbage proper, Borecole, Brocoli, Cauliflowers, Coleworts, Savoys,* &c. *Salads,* including *Lettuce, Radish, Endive,* &c., should also be sown. *Onions, Shalots,* and others of the tribe will be ready for gathering and storing; and a winter supply of *Onions* should be sown. Earth up *Leeks* and *Celery. Spinach, Turnips, Fennel,* and *Lovage* may be sown. Some *sweet herbs,* such as *Marjoram, Thyme,* &c., may be plucked and dried. Where *Peppermint* is grown, the plants may be cut, and at once distilled, if required for the oil. Keep *Asparagus* beds free from weeds. Remove the *waste* of *Peas* and *Beans.* Weed and hoe *Parsnips.* Trim *Tomatoes* of all superfluous growth.

FRUIT GARDEN.—In this and preceding month a large quantity of fruit will have become ready for gathering, preserving, and storing. Its condition for such purposes will of course entirely depend on the state of the weather, which if wet is unfit for fruit-gathering. Insects of all kinds now attack fruit trees, which consequently should be defended by all possible means. The removal of blighted fruit will lead to the improvement of that remaining sound. *Budding* and *grafting* are generally pursued in this month and the close of the preceding. Plant fresh *Strawberry* beds as soon as the runners are sufficiently rooted.

FLOWER GARDEN.—Much has here to be done in this month in preparation for the next year, especially in propagating all kinds of plants. *Petunias, Verbenas, Lobelias,* and *Calceolarias* should be struck early. Sow *Tulips* and other bulb-roots, *Anemones, Auriculas, Mignonette, Polyanthuses, Stocks,* &c. Pot out *Chrysanthemums. Rose* budding may be carried on. Plant out *Pinks, Double Wallflowers,* and *Pansies. Geraniums, Pelargoniums,* and *Cinerarias* should be abundantly propagated by cuttings. Transplant *biennial* and *perennial* seedlings. Generally prepare all plants intended for early spring blossoming. In the absence of rain and dew, watering should be freely practised; lawns rolled and mowed. Gravel walks will require constant weeding, and an occasional watering with salt and water, to keep down worms, mosses, &c.; and they should be frequently rolled after moisture by rain or watering.

September.

THE FARM.—Harvest work continues in this month for all corn crops. In stacking be careful about damp, which may cause spontaneous combustion in the rick. When the crops are carried, *ploughing* and *manuring* should be vigorously carried on during fine weather. In many cases *paring* and *harrowing* the stubble will be desirable before manuring. *Lime* should be applied when required, and in the chalk districts *lime-burning* should be carried on. Cut *Clover* for seed by end of month. *Threshing* should be followed, both of Wheat and Winter Beans. Fallow *Wheat* may be sown by the end of the month, and the early portion of Winter *Tares* and *Rye. Fences* should be cropped. *Hedges* and *ditches* looked to. *Hop* gathering becomes general in the districts of its growth. *Mustard* will be ready for gathering. *Thin pastures*—sending sheep on some, with an eye to the fostering of breeding ewes. *Cattle* should now be fat, and ready for sale. In the dairy, *Cheese* and *Butter* are still profitable products, although cows generally give less milk. The farmer will wisely see to his stock of winter food for cattle, in regard to quantity, condition, &c., and regulate his purchases according to his wants and market prices. Practically, this month may be considered as the end of the farmer's year, for the majority of his crops will have been gathered, and he can, following the example of the manufacturer, take stock, and balance his accounts—a practice, unfortunately, too rare among agriculturists.

THE KITCHEN GARDEN.—As on the farm, this harvest is in course of completion; and preparation for the next year will be desirable. Plants already in growth for winter and spring use should be hoed and well stirred. *Vermin* removed by dressings of lime, sulphate of ammonia, or soot. The latter is often valueless when purchased, owing to adulterations with sawdust, &c. Transplant July sowings of *Celery,* and earth-up all others in dry weather. Plant out *Cabbage, Brocoli, Cauliflower, Coleworts, Savoy, Endive,* &c. Hoe *Turnips,* and dress with lime or soot, to kill slugs. Make new plantations of *Asparagus. Cardoons*—at least the early crop—will be ready for use; they should be earthed-up for blanching. Make *Mushroom beds.* Sow *Salads* for winter use; as also *Onions* and *Spinach. Potatoes,* and some kinds of *Onions,* will be ready for taking up and storing. Plant out *Brussels Sprouts* and other winter greens (some already noticed).

FRUIT GARDEN.—Many store fruits are in perfection this month. They require careful gathering for immediate use and preserving. *Insects* become a pest in the garden, especially earwigs. They are readily trapped, however, by beanstalks and other contrivances (set over-night), into which they creep for shelter from dew, and from which they can be removed early in the morning. Nail the future fruit shoots of *Nectarines* and *Peaches* in closely, removing decayed leaves, and protecting the ripening fruit by netting. *Vines* should be similarly protected in regard to the *Grapes,* and leaves removed that would prevent ripening. The *pruning* of roots may be proceeded with by removing superfluous root-branches. *Apple, Pear, Cherry, Plum, Gooseberry, Currant,* and other fruit trees done bearing, may be judiciously pruned. Gather *Apples* and *Pears* a day or two before ripe, laying the Pears singly in storing them, keeping out all bruised fruit, for that would soon spread great injury to all that is sound. *Nuts* should be stored in a dry place, or they will become mildewed and spoiled.

FLOWER GARDEN.—The operations of the last month may in most cases be continued. The general effect of arrangement in the garden should be carefully attended to, both as regards its present and intended state for next season. The layering of *Carnations* and *Piccotees* should be proceeded with. Prepare fresh *Tulip Beds*, and plant out *bulbous roots* generally for early flowering next year. Cut *Roses*. Insert trimmings of *Fuchsias, Geraniums, Calceolarias, &c.,* as cuttings. Pot *Cinerarias, Verbenas, &c.,* and remove *Ranunculuses* and *Auriculas*. *Chrysanthemums* will require liquid manure to stimulate early blooming. Tie up *Dahlias*, and manure in dry weather. *Hollyhocks* may be dealt with in the same way. Selections should be made of choice plants of each for next year's growth. Plant out *Pinks* in rich soil; also early *Pansy cuttings*, pricking out seedlings of the latter. *Polyanthus seedlings* may be planted in rich beds. Plant out and sow *Anemones*. Plant out various hardy *annuals* to stand the winter in the open air. *Insects* should be removed, as already directed under the head of the Fruit Garden. Generally, this and the following month should be one of constant preparation by the floriculturist.

October.

THE FARM.—At times this month proves almost as fine as September, but such occasions are too rare to be trusted to. *Wheat* sowing becomes the chief occupation of the farmer, he having, of course, prepared the soil by means already alluded to. The choice of seed, as also its quality, that of manures, &c., should be all regulated by the qualities of the soil, a knowledge of which can only be arrived at by an acquaintance with chemistry, as an aid to agriculture, and long experience. Agriculture has only become a really scientific art since the teachings of chemistry have been followed out. The mode of sowing must be left to the judgment of the farmer, but by all means avoid thick sowing. Beside wasting seed, it lessens the producing power of the soil, and the roots choke one another. *Winter Beans* should be sown in well-harrowed and manured furrows. *Rye, Winter Tares*, or *Vetches* should also be sown. Stubble fields should be well ploughed, and manuring fully carried out for early spring crops of all kinds, as on the break-up of the weather, with great rain, these operations are not only impeded, but much of their utility destroyed. For similar reasons, the state of the *ditches, hedges,* and *fences* should be well looked to; and preparations made for extending any system of *drainage* that may be required; which, if properly done throughout the land, would not only improve the farmer's prospects, but also the sanitary condition of the country. Much that has been done in this respect has only indicated how much has yet to be effected. *Hop-poles* should be stacked away for next season, being first cleared of the haulm. *Potatoes, Turnips, Carrots,* and *Mangold* will be harvested this month, and should be carefully protected from damp. *Water meadows* and *pasturage* land may be fed off by horses, cattle, and sheep, to economize the winter stock. Any repairs required in the water meadows should now be effected, to provide against the harm or utilize the benefits of coming floods. *Live Stock* will require much care, as owing to the arrival of the rainy season, long and cold nights, and other causes, affections of the lungs and

windpipe become prevalent. Oilcake may be given to cattle and sheep in addition to the usual food. Pigs will consume small potatoes that are otherwise useless. *Poultry* will require care. Geese and turkeys may be fattened, with an eye to the wants of Christmas. Cows, owing to less green food, lessen the quantity of milk, hence the production of butter and cheese in the dairy diminishes. The cows will also be advancing in calf.

KITCHEN GARDEN.—The lowering temperature of the air gradually diminishes the vital powers of most plants. Decayed leaves fall, and afford a valuable manure for next year's crops. The preparation of the ground by *digging, draining, trenching, &c.,* should now be vigorously carried on, every available spot being got ready for future crops. Earth-up *Celery*, both for protection and blanching. Plant out *Cabbages, Coleworts,* and *Cauliflower*, weeding carefully, and looking after the caterpillars that infest them. Prick out *Lettuces* under a frame or on warm borders, and tie up those and *Endive* already planted out. Take up *Potatoes, Carrots, Beet, Turnips,* and *Parsnips*, for store. Early *Mazagan Beans* may be planted in warm situations. Earth-up *Chardoons* in dry weather. Thin out *Spinach*. *Seakale* may be forced in a bed or by covering with pots at the end of this month. *Lavender, Pennyroyal,* and *Rosemary* may be transplanted. *Asparagus* beds may be cleared of the decayed haulm, and their tops well manured. Continue the formation of *Mushroom* beds. Plant *Chives* and *Rocambole*.

FRUIT GARDEN.—Planting may now be vigorously followed in already prepared ground, *root pruning* being simultaneously performed. The garden should have a thorough overhaul for the improvement of good plants, and the removal of others. *Apples* and *Pears* should be carefully gathered on fine days, and after storing should be as carefully looked over to remove any bruised or decaying fruit. *Strawberry* plants clear of runners, and manure between the rows. Plant out *Gooseberry* and *Currant* trees, trimming those already in their intended position. Trim *wall trees* of dead leaves. Remove superfluous shoots from *Peach* and *Nectarine* trees. Keep a constant watch on all fruit stored during the preceding and present month.

FLOWER GARDEN.—The beauty of this department is gradually waning for the year, especially if frost set in. Preparations should be made for extensively potting *Calceolarias, Geraniums, &c.,* intended for early bloom next year. Shelter *Auriculas, Polyanthuses, Cinerarias,* choice *Pinks, Fuchsias, &c.,* from frost, or put them into the place intended for their wintering. Plant various *bulbous roots*, including *Anemones, Hyacinths, &c.* In dry weather water *Chrysanthemums* as required, especially such as are about to bloom. Take up, dry, and store *Dahlia* and *Marvel of Peru* roots. Pot *Pansies* and *Hollyhocks* for early flowering. Generally in the garden the refuse of dead annuals should be removed, new beds prepared, borders and walks trimmed and cleaned, and other preparations made for the frost and storms of winter.

November.

THE FARM.—Generally, the operations of last month may be recommended for November. *Wheat sowing* is to be continued, as also *ploughing, manuring, draining, &c.,* according to the state of the weather, or the climate in which the farm is situated. All so-called "*root-crops*," as *Potatoes, Turnips, Carrots, Mangold*, &c., should be removed and stored. The subsoil plough should now be employed on stubble ground. Fields intended for *Peas* and *Beans* carefully got ready for sowing in spring. Fences, ditches, and hedges should be well looked to. Indoors, *threshing* will form a constant occupation. Sheep pastures will be too poor to feed much stock, and consequently these animals, cattle, and horses must depend on indoor feed. Poultry are best kept in the yard, with an occasional turn into the field. The *dairy produce* will still further diminish as grass becomes scarce, but cabbage and turnip-tops, with mangold, will in part supply the deficiency of this for cows. *Hop-gardens* should be well drained, and if so prepared young hop-plants may be set.

KITCHEN GARDEN.—Vegetation has now ceased in many respects, consequently all ground from which the crops have been removed should be *dug, trenched*, and otherwise prepared for future use. Thorough *drainage* is a matter of the highest importance, for in its absence the soil will get cold and unproductive; besides, the roots of standing plants and crops will be seriously injured. Keep the *stems* of *plants* warm by surrounding them with litter. All *root-crops* ripe for removal should be taken up and stored. *Asparagus* beds should be kept well dressed, &c., as noted in the preceding month, and the crowns of *Artichokes* protected from frost by a mulching of leaves. Certain varieties of *Peas* and *Beans* may be sown, depending on the state of the soil and temperature. Keep earthing up *Celery, Cardoons*, and *Leeks*. Tie up *Lettuce* and *Endive* for blanching. Plant out *Cabbage* for summer crop, and protect young *Cauliflower* plants from frost. Clear *Brussels Sprouts, Savoys*, and *Borecole* of dead leaves. *Rhubarb* and *Seakale* may be forced for early use; *Spinach* may be gradually thinned for house use as a vegetable; *Parsnips, Scorzoneras*, and *Salsafy* may be left in the ground till required for use, or stored up, as may be most convenient.

FRUIT GARDEN.—The directions for last month may be here repeated to a large extent. All changes or removals in the garden should be completed. *Digging, draining, planting, pruning*, &c., should be actively followed. *Currant* and *Gooseberry* trees should be planted and pruned. *Strawberries* may be treated as directed in October, but if removed and replanted in the same ground, it is said that their bearing powers are greatly increased. It is presumed that *fruit* trees have been completely cleared. It will be necessary to keep a careful watch over the store-room, to prevent mildew, &c., which is best done by keeping it dry and well ventilated. After the removal of the fruit, *Apple, Pear, Plum*, and *Cherry trees* should all be pruned. Wash the stems of such trees with hot lime and water, after removing moss, &c. *Dwarf fruit trees* should now be pruned into the desired shape.

FLOWER GARDEN.—Occasionally the garden presents some specimens of flower, of which the *Chrysanthemum* is in most perfection; but as a rule, especially if frost prevail, its beauty is destroyed, dead and dying leaves and flowers being predominant. Hence the necessity of clearing all ground so occupied, and preparing it for future and fresh crops by digging, &c. As each bed thus "falls in," it becomes a fresh opening for the gardener's skill, which ought to be im-

proved each year by additional experience and study. All dead leaves should be collected into a pit, to serve in part for future mould and manure, for both of which they are invaluable, and also for heat in forcing. *Auriculas* and other plants named as placed in winter quarters during October should have abundance of air, but not if the weather be frosty. Various "*bulbous*" *roots*, as *Anemones, Hyacinths, Tulips*, &c., may be planted, depending on the state of the weather. *Dahlias* and *Marvel of Peru* should be removed, dried, and stored after the first frost, although still in bloom. *Hollyhocks* may be cut down, and others propagated from the old plant, or by eyes from the flowering stems. Pot off *Pansies*, prune *Roses* and *Fuchsias*. Pot *Crocuses* for forcing into early flower. Layer *Carnations* and pot them, protecting them from damp, but yet giving plenty of air in fine weather. Look to *Pinks* that they are not injured by storms of rain or wind. The garden walks should be kept clean from dead leaves, as these soon discolour the gravel. Frequent rolling is desirable. Spare time or labour may be occupied by collecting all materials, such as old mortar, hedge sweepings, &c., to form manure for the beds. Turf should be pared from loamy soil for this purpose, and, indeed, everything gathered that is calculated to render the soil more fertile, whether in the form of manures or as alteratives.

December.

THE FARM.—Whilst all vegetation lies in apparent death, it falls to the lot of man to prepare many conditions for its revival. At the farm, therefore, as the weather permits, *ploughing* should be carried on, with *subsoiling, carting lime, making roads, draining, manuring*, &c. *Draining* should be especially attended to, because of the rains, melted snows, &c., that during this and the following months tend to flood undrained land, first securing a good outfall at the lowest part of the farm, so that the water may be readily carried off. A knowledge of the art of taking levels, as practised by surveyors, will be found of great advantage, and economy of labour. *Digging*, and *carting manure* to *Hop* grounds, may be done. Comparatively little pasturage will be found except for a few sheep, and generally the fields will be exceedingly wet, and therefore prejudicial to their health. Top-dressing of *grass lands*, and manuring generally, may therefore be advantageously carried on; where necessary, *draining* should also be effected. Cattle should be kept warm and clean, yet with plenty of air, their manure being carted to the fields on frosty days. The addition of *sulphate of lime*, or *gypsum*, tends to fix the *ammonia* in stable dung, and so "saves the loss" of one of its most valuable constituents. *Turnips*, with *hay*, will now be the staple food of all the domestic animals. Owing to the condition of the cows, and their scanty yield of milk, but little can be done in the dairy. The poultry yard, including *Fowls, Ducks, Geese*, and *Turkeys*, becomes a source of profit, if *fattening* has been carefully attended to, the season of the year creating a great demand for them. Care should be paid to the feeding of *breeding Cows* and *Ewes*, they requiring nourishing diet.

KITCHEN GARDEN.—But little variation from the instructions for the preceding month need be made in respect to outdoor operations. The earthing up of *Celery* should be continued. *Peas* and *Beans* may be sown early in warm situations.

Seakale and *Rhubarb* may be covered for forcing. *Parsnips*, &c., in the ground, and *Celery*, should be protected by litter from frost. *Cauliflower* plants should be well aired in the absence of frost. The *stores of Onions, Potatoes*, &c., examined occasionally, and kept dry ; *manures* prepared and carted to the ground. *Spinach* will still, with *Cabbages*, &c., form winter greens for domestic use. *Parsley*, often in great request during this month, should be sheltered from frost. An early and small crop of *Carrots* may be sown, for subsequent planting out. Generally, the month is favourable for carrying out alterations in the arrangement of the gardens. Trees may be lopped, and the larger sticks selected for peas, beans, &c., whilst the twigs will economize fuel.

FRUIT GARDEN.—Generally, the weather is too uncertain to permit of planting, but *pruning* may be extensively carried out. This remark extends to all kinds of trees ; those growing against the wall should have the choice shoots nailed in. By judicious pruning alone can a tree be stimulated to its utmost producing power in regard to fruit ; for without this, the best soil and manure will only produce straggling branches that will absorb the chief strength of the plant, and produce nothing but wood. *Strawberry* plants, if choice, should be protected in severe weather by a covering of straw, or other light, cheap material. The fruit room should be looked to ; labels prepared and fixed on choice trees ; and such operations as will lessen the amount of work required in the coming spring.

FLOWER GARDEN.—All outdoor work will depend on the state of the weather. It has been already indicated, under the preceding heads for this month and November. Beds may be roughed up and top-dressed, the advantage of frost being great in pulverizing the soil. The lawn, gravel walks, edgings, &c., should be kept trim and in neat order. A general rule in respect to all kinds of plants for this and following months is to allow access of air, but to protect from frost, and to water sparingly. It is useless to enumerate the variety of such plants, as they have already been named in the directions given for the three preceding months. *Hyacinths* may be stimulated by gentle heat for early flowering. *Tulip* beds should be protected from frost. *Lobelias, Cinerarias*, &c., may be repotted. *Dahlia* roots that have been stored away must be carefully looked to, lest they may be injured from damp or frost. The same remarks apply also to the *Marvel of Peru*. Stimulate *Chrysanthemums* with a little liquid manure. Planting *hardy Roses* may be continued, mulching over the stems with litter on the surface of the soil. *Pinks, Carnations*, and *Pansies* planted in open beds will require care lest they be loosened by frost. They also require protection from vermin. The stock of manures should be stirred up to promote equal decomposition of all parts, and to prevent excessive heating.

ANNUAL AVERAGE PRICES OF WHEAT, BARLEY, AND OATS, IN ENGLAND AND WALES DURING THE PRESENT CENTURY.

Years.	Wheat.	Barley.	Oats.	Years.	Wheat.	Barley.	Oats.	Years.	Wheat.	Barley.	Oats.
1800	113 10	59 10	39 4	1823	53 4	36 6	22 11	1846	54 8	32 8	23 8
1801	119 6	68 6	37 0	1824	63 11	36 4	24 10	1847	69 9	44 2	28 8
1802	69 10	33 4	20 4	1825	68 6	40 0	25 8	1848	50 6	31 6	20 6
1803	58 10	25 4	21 6	1826	58 8	34 4	26 8	1849	44 3	27 9	17 6
1804	62 3	31 0	24 3	1827	58 6	37 7	28 2	1850	40 3	23 6	16 5
1805	89 9	44 6	28 4	1828	60 5	32 10	22 0	1851	38 6	24 9	18 7
1806	79 1	38 8	27 7	1829	66 3	32 6	22 9	1852	40 9	28 6	19 1
1807	75 4	39 4	28 4	1830	64 3	32 7	24 5	1853	53 3	33 2	21 0
1808	81 4	43 4	33 4	1831	66 4	38 0	25 4	1854	72 5	36 0	27 11
1809	97 4	47 0	31 5	1832	58 8	33 1	20 5	1855	74 8	34 9	27 5
1810	106 5	48 1	28 7	1833	52 11	27 6	18 5	1856	69 2	41 1	25 2
1811	95 3	42 3	27 7	1834	46 2	29 0	20 11	1857	56 4	42 1	25 0
1812	126 6	66 9	44 6	1835	39 4	29 11	22 0	1858	44 2	34 8	24 6
1813	109 9	58 6	38 6	1836	48 6	32 10	23 1	1859	43 9	33 6	23 2
1814	74 4	37 4	25 8	1837	55 10	30 4	23 1	1860	53 3	36 7	24 5
1815	65 7	30 3	23 7	1838	64 7	31 9	22 5	1861	55 4	36 1	23 9
1816	78 6	33 11	27 2	1839	70 8	39 6	25 11	1862	55 5	35 1	22 7
1817	96 11	49 4	32 5	1840	66 4	36 5	25 8	1863	44 9	33 9	21 2
1818	86 3	53 10	32 5	1841	64 4	32 10	22 5	1864	40 2	29 11	20 1
1819	74 6	45 9	28 2	1842	57 3	27 6	19 3	1865	41 10	29 9	21 10
1820	67 10	33 10	24 2	1843	50 1	29 6	18 4	1866	49 11	37 5	24 7
1821	56 1	26 0	20 6	1844	51 3	33 8	20 7	1867	64 5	39 11	26 0
1822	44 7	21 10	28 1	1845	50 10	31 8	22 6	1868	63 9	41 1	27 7

HIGHEST AND LOWEST PRICES OF WHEAT, since the passing of Sir Robert Peel's Corn Bill, 1846, with the annual Tithe Rentcharge payable during the same period.

	Highest Price.	Lowest Price.	Difference.	Tithe Rentcharge		Highest Price.	Lowest Price.	Difference.	Tithe Rentcharge
1845	60 1	45 1	15 0	102 17 8¾	1857	56 3	42 6	13 9	105 16 3½
1847	102 5	49 5	52 11	99 18 10¾	1858	54 4	39 10	14 6	108 19 6¼
1848	56 10	46 10	10 6	102 1 0	1860	62 11	42 5	20 6	110 17 1½
,,	52 3	41 9	10 6	100 3 7¾	,,	61 1	50 0	11 1	112 3 4¾
1850	44 1	36 11	7 2	98 16 10	1862	62 1	53 2	8 11	109 13 6
1851	43 6	36 7	6 11	96 11 4¾	,,	51 1	43 9	7 4	107 5 2
1852	44 9	35 6	9 3	93 16 11¾	1864	44 1	38 9	5 4	103 3 10¾
1853	59 5	37 10	21 7	91 13 5¾	1865	46 7	37 10	8 9	98 15 10½
1854	83 3	52 2	31 1	90 19 5	1866	55 10	40 10	15 0	97 7 9¾
1855	78 2	56 7	21 7	89 15 8¾	1867	68 4	52 2	16 2	98 13 3
,,	83 1	64 4	18 9	93 18 1¼	1868	74 7	53 7	21 0	100 13 8
1856	66 4	53 0	13 4	99 13 7¾					

Name.	Title.	Acces.	Died.	Age.	Rgned.
	SAXONS AND DANES.				
EGBERT	First King of all England	827	837	—	10
ETHELWULF	Son of Egbert	837	858	—	21
ETHELBALD	Son of Ethelwulf	858 }	860	—	2
ETHELBERT	Second son of Ethelwulf	858 }	866	—	8
ETHELRED	Third son of Ethelwulf	866	871	—	5
ALFRED	Fourth son of Ethelwulf	871	901	—	30
EDWARD THE ELDER	Eldest son of Edward	901	925	—	24
ATHELSTAN	Eldest son of Edward	925	940	—	15
EDMUND	Brother of Athelstan	940	946	—	6
EDRED	Brother of Edmund	946	955	—	9
EDWY	Son of Edmund	955	958	—	3
EDGAR	Second son of Edmund	958	975	—	17
EDWARD THE MARTYR	Son of Edgar	975	979	—	4
ETHELRED II.	Half-brother of Edward	979	1016	—	37
EDMUND IRONSIDE	Eldest son of Ethelred	1016	1016	—	1
CANUTE	By conquest and election	1017	1035	—	16
HAROLD I.	Son of Canute	1035	1040	—	5
HARDICANUTE	Another son of Canute	1040	1042	—	2
EDWARD THE CONFESSOR	Son of Ethelred II.	1042	1066	—	24
HAROLD II.	Brother-in-law of Edward	1066	1066	—	0
	THE HOUSE OF NORMANDY.				
WILLIAM I.	Obtained the Crown by Conquest	1066	1087	60	21
WILLIAM II.	Third son of William I.	1087	1100	43	13
HENRY I.	Youngest son of William I.	1100	1135	67	35
STEPHEN	Third son of Stephen, Count of Blois, by Adela, fourth daughter of William I.	1135	1154	49	19
	THE HOUSE OF PLANTAGENET.				
HENRY II.	Son of Geoffrey Plantagenet, by Matilda, only daughter of Henry I.	1154	1189	56	35
RICHARD I.	Eldest surviving son of Henry II.	1189	1199	42	10
JOHN	Sixth and youngest son of Henry II.	1199	1216	51	17
HENRY III.	Eldest son of John	1216	1272	65	56
EDWARD I.	Eldest son of Henry III.	1272	1307	67	35
EDWARD II.	Eldest surviving son of Edward I.	1307	1327	43	20
EDWARD III.	Eldest son of Edward II.	1327	1377	65	50
RICHARD II.	Son of the Black Prince, eldest son Edw. III.	1377	Dep.1399	33	22
	THE HOUSE OF LANCASTER.				
HENRY IV.	Son of John of Gaunt, fourth son of Ed. III.	1399	1413	46	14
HENRY V.	Eldest son of Henry IV.	1413	1422	34	9
HENRY VI.	Only son of Henry V.	1422 {	Dep. 1461 / Dep. 1471	49	39
	THE HOUSE OF YORK.				
EDWARD IV.	His grandfather was Richard, son of Edmund, fifth son of Edward III. ; and his grandmother, Anne, was great-granddaughter of Lionel, third son of Ed. III.	1461	1483	41	22
EDWARD V.	Eldest son of Edward IV.	1483	Dep.1483	12	0
RICHARD III.	Younger brother of Edward IV.	1483	1485	33	2
	THE HOUSE OF TUDOR.				
HENRY VII.	Son of Edmund, eldest son of Owen Tudor and Catherine, widow of Henry V.; his mother Margaret Beaufort, was great-grand-daughter of John of Gaunt.	1485	1509	52	24
HENRY VIII.	Only surviving son of Henry VII.	1509	1547	55	38
EDWARD VI.	Son of Henry VIII. by Jane Seymour	1547	1553	16	6
MARY	Daughter of Henry VIII. by Cath. of Arragon	1553	1558	42	5
ELIZABETH	Daughter of Henry VIII. by Anne Boleyn	1558	1603	69	45
	THE HOUSE OF STUART.				
JAMES I.	Son of Mary Queen of Scots, grand-dau. of James IV. and Margaret, dau. of Hen. VII.	1603	1625	58	22
CHARLES I.	Only surviving son of James I.	1625	1649	48	24
COMMONWEALTH	Commonwealth declared May 19	1649	—	—	—
	Oliver Cromwell, Lord Protector	1653	1658	—	—
	Richard Cromwell, Lord Protector	1658	Res.1659	—	—

Name.	Title.	Acces.	Died.	Age.	Rgned.
	THE HOUSE OF STUART—RESTORED.				
CHARLES II.	Eldest son of Charles I.	1660	1685	54	25
JAMES II.	Second son of Charles I.	1685	Dep. 1688 D. 1702	68	
WILLIAM III. and	Son of William of Orange, by Mary, daughter of Charles I.	1689	1702	51	13
MARY	Eldest daughter of James II.		1694	32	6
ANNE	Second daughter of James II.	1702	1714	49	12
	THE HOUSE OF HANOVER.				
GEORGE I.	Son of the Elector of Hanover, by Sophia, daughter of Fred. V., King of Bohemia, and Elizabeth, daughter of James I.	1714	1727	67	13
GEORGE II.	Only son of George I.	1727	1760	77	33
GEORGE III.	Grandson of George II.	1760	1820	82	60
GEORGE IV.	Eldest son of George III.	1820	1830	68	10
WILLIAM IV.	Third son of George III.	1830	1837	72	7
VICTORIA	Daughter of Edward, 4th son of George III.	1837	WHOM GOD PRESERVE.		

Sovereigns of Scotland from A.D. 1067, to the Union of the Crowns.

Names.	Began to reign.	Names.	Began to reign.	Names.	Began to reign.
Malcolm *(Ceanmohr)*	1057, Apr.	Alexander III.	1249, July 8	James IV.	1488, Jun. 11
Donald *(Bane)*	1092, Nov.	Margaret	1286, Mar. 19	James V.	1513, Sept. 9
Duncan	1094, May	John (Baliol)	1292, Nov. 17	Mary	1542, Dec. 16
Donald *(Bane)* rest.	1095, Nov.	Robert I. (Bruce)	1306, Mar. 27	Francis and Mary	1558, Apr. 24
Edgar	1097, Sept.	David II.	1329, June 7	Mary	1560, Dec. 5
Alexander I.	1107, Jan. 8	Robert II. (Stewart)	1371, Feb. 22	Henry and Mary	1565, July 29
David I.	1124, Apr. 27	Robert III.	1390, Apr. 12	Mary	1567, Feb. 10
Malcolm *(Maiden)*	1153, May 24	James I.	1406, Apr. 4	James VI.	1567, July 29
William *(The Lion)*	1165, Dec. 9	James II.	1457, Feb. 20	(Ascended the throne of Eng.	
Alexander II.	1214, Dec. 4	James III.	1480, Aug. 3	as James I., 24th March, 1603)	

Styles of English Architecture.

Name.	Prevailed.	Characteristics.
NORMAN	1066 to 1154	Round-headed doorways and windows, heavy pillars, and zig-zag ornaments. (Example, Nave, Rochester Cathedral.)
TRANSITION	1154 to 1189	Same, but with pointed windows.
EARLY ENGLISH	1189 to 1272	Narrow-pointed windows, generally plain; clustered pillars. (Example, Choir, Westminster Abbey.)
TRANSITION	1272 to 1307	Tracery introduced into windows.
DECORATED	1307 to 1377	Geometrical tracery in windows, enriched doorways, beautifully arranged mouldings. (Example, Lady Chapel, Ely.)
TRANSITION	1377 to 1399	Lines less flowing. (Example, Choir, York Minster.)
PERPENDICULAR	1399 to 1547	Upright lines of mouldings in windows and doorways; combination of square heads with pointed mouldings. (Example, King's College Chapel, Cambridge).
TUDOR	1550 to 1600	A debased species of Perpendicular, mostly employed in domestic architecture.
JACOBEAN	1603 to 1641	An admixture of Classical with all kinds of Gothic or Pointed.

DATES OF DIGNITIES.

The Saxons, in the fifth and sixth centuries, founded the Heptarchy, meaning the seven States, though there really were nine; these were all subdued by Egbert, King of Wessex, who in consequence took the title of King of England in 827. The Norman Kings, beginning with William I. in 1066, were also Dukes of Normandy. Henry II. in 1172 styled himself Lord of Ireland, which title Henry VIII. changed into King, in 1541. Edward III. assumed the title of King of France in 1337. Anne, on the union of England and Scotland in 1707, became Queen of Great Britain; and George III., on the union with Ireland in 1801, dropped the empty style of King of France, and took the title of King of Great Britain and Ireland. Her present Majesty, in 1859, altered her official designation to Queen of Great Britain and Ireland, and of the Colonies and Dependencies thereof, Empress of India, Defender of the Faith, Sovereign of the Order of the Garter, &c.

The first English DUKE was Edward the Black Prince; he was created Duke of Cornwall by his father, Edward III. in 1337. The title of MARQUIS was first bestowed by Richard II. on his favourite, Robert de Vere, Earl of Oxford, created Marquis of Dublin in 1386. The Saxon titles of ALDERMAN or EORL, and THANE, were changed into EARL and BARON by William I. The title of VISCOUNT was long in use in France before it was bestowed on any person in England; the first person who held it was John Beaumont, created Viscount Beaumont and Count of Boulogne in France, in 1440. The order of BARONETS was established by James I. in 1611, and exists only in the British Dominions.

GEORGE WILLIAM FREDERICK, eldest son of Frederick Lewis, Prince of Wales (eldest son of George II., *born* 20th January, 1707; *died* 20th March, 1751) by Augusta, youngest daughter of Frederick, duke of Saxe Gotha (*born* 30th Nov., 1719; *died* 8th Feb. 1772), was born at Norfolk House, St. James's Square, 4th June, 1738. He succeeded to the throne as George III. on the death of his grandfather, 25th Oct., 1760. On 8th Sept., 1761, he married Sophia Charlotte, daughter of Charles, duke of Mecklenburg Strelitz (*born* 19th May, 1744; *died* 17th Nov., 1818), and was crowned with her on 22nd September following: he had by her a family of nine sons and six daughters. Early in his reign he showed symptoms of insanity, and after recovering from two serious attacks (1788, 1804), his mind entirely gave way: many of his latter years were consequently passed in seclusion, and the government was carried on, from 5th Feb., 1811, until his death, by his eldest son George, under the title of Prince Regent. He died at Windsor, 29th Jan., 1820. His family were as follows:—

I. GEORGE AUGUSTUS FREDERICK, Prince of Wales, born 12th August, 1762. On 8th April, 1795, he married his cousin Caroline, daughter of Charles, duke of Brunswick Wolfenbuttel (*born* 17th May, 1768; *died* 7th Aug., 1821), by whom he had a daughter, Charlotte, Princess of Wales (*born* 7th Jan., 1796; *died* in childbirth, 6th Nov., 1817, having married 2nd May, 1816, Prince Leopold, of Saxe Coburg, afterwards King of the Belgians). The Prince became Regent, 5th Feb., 1811, and succeeded to the throne as George IV., 29th Jan., 1820. He died at Windsor, 26th June, 1830.

II. FREDERICK, born 16th Aug., 1763, was at the age of six months declared Prince-bishop of Osnaburgh. On 27th Nov., 1784, he was created Duke of York and Albany, and Earl of Ulster. On 29th Sept., 1791, he married Frederica, daughter of Frederick William II. of Prussia (*born* 7th May, 1767; *died*, without issue, 6th Aug., 1820). The duke, who was for many years Commander-in-chief of the Army, died 5th Jan., 1827.

III. WILLIAM HENRY, born 21st Aug., 1765, was, on 20th May, 1789, created Duke of Clarence and St. Andrews, and Earl of Munster. He for many years lived with Mrs. Jordan, an actress, and had by her a numerous family, who took the name of Fitzclarence. On 11th July, 1818, he married Adelaide, daughter of George, Duke of Saxe Meiningen (*born* 13th Aug., 1792; *died* 2nd Dec., 1849), by whom he had two daughters, Charlotte Augusta Louisa *born* and *died* 27th March, 1819, and Elizabeth Georgina Adelaide *born* 20th December, 1820, *died* 4th March, 1821. The duke, who had entered the Royal Navy in 1779, held the office of Lord High Admiral in 1827-28, and succeeded to the throne as William IV. 26th June, 1830. He died at Windsor, 20th June, 1837.

IV. CHARLOTTE AUGUSTA, Princess Royal, born 29th September, 1766; married, 18th May, 1797, Frederick, Prince (afterwards King) of Wurtemburg (*born* 6th Nov., 1754; *died* 30th Oct., 1816). She died, without issue, 6th Oct., 1828.

V. EDWARD AUGUSTUS, born Nov., 1767, was on 23rd April, 1799, created Duke of Kent and Strathearn, and Earl of Dublin. He married at Coburg, 29th May, 1818 (and again at Kew Palace, 11th July) Victoria, daughter of Francis, Duke of Saxe Coburg, sister of Prince Leopold, and widow of Charles, Prince of Leiningen (*born* 17th Aug., 1786; *died* 16th March, 1861), by whom he had one daughter, Her Majesty Queen Victoria. The duke died at Sidmouth, 23rd Jan., 1820.

VI. AUGUSTA SOPHIA, born 8th Nov., 1768. She died unmarried, 22nd Sept., 1840.

VII. ELIZABETH, born 22nd May, 1770. She married 7th April, 1818, Frederick, Landgrave of Hesse Homburg (*born* 30th July, 1769; *died* 2nd April, 1829), and died, without issue, 10th Jan., 1840.

VIII. ERNEST AUGUSTUS, born 5th June, 1771, was on 24th April, 1799, created Duke of Cumberland, and Earl of Armagh. He married at Strelitz, 29th May, 1815 (and again at Carlton-House, 29th Aug.), Frederica, third daughter of Frederick V., Grand-Duke of Mecklenburg-Strelitz, widow, 1st, of Prince Frederick Louis Charles, of Prussia, and 2nd, of Frederick William, Prince of Salms-Braunfels (*born* 2nd March, 1778; *died* 21st June, 1841), by whom he had issue George, ex-King of Hanover. The duke became King of Hanover on the decease of his brother William IV., and died 18 Nov., 1851.

IX. AUGUSTUS FREDERICK, born 27th Jan. 1773. Created Duke of Sussex 27th Nov., 1801. He married at Rome, 4th April, 1793, and at St. George's, Hanover Square, 5th Dec. following, Lady Augusta Murray, daughter of John, Earl of Dunmore; but this being contrary to the provisions of the Royal Marriage Act (12 Geo. III. c. 11), the union was pronounced invalid in Aug., 1794. By Lady Augusta—who afterwards took by royal license the name of D'Ameland—he had a son and a daughter; Augustus Frederick, known afterwards as Sir Augustus Frederick D'Este (*born* 13th Jan., 1794; *died*, unmarried, 20th Dec., 1848), and Augusta, known as Mademoiselle D'Este (*born* 11th August, 1801; married 13th Aug., 1845, Sir Thomas Wilde, afterwards Lord Truro; *died* 21st May, 1866). Lady D'Ameland died 5th March, 1830, and the duke shortly after contracted a morganatic marriage with Lady Cecilia Underwood, now Duchess of Inverness. He died at Kensington Palace, 21st April, 1843; and was, by his own desire, buried in the Kensal-Green Cemetery 4th May following.

X. ADOLPHUS FREDERICK, born 24th Feb., 1774, was on 27th Nov., 1801, created Duke of Cambridge, Earl of Tipperary, and Baron Culloden. He married at Hesse Cassel, 1st May, 1818, (and again at the Queen's Palace, 1st June) Augusta, daughter of Frederick, Landgrave of Hesse (*born* 25th July, 1797), by whom he had issue, George, Duke of Cambridge; Augusta, Duchess of Mecklenburg Strelitz; and Mary, Princess Teck. The duke, who acted as Viceroy of Hanover until the death of William IV., died at Kew, 8th July, 1850.

XI. MARY, born 25th April, 1776. She married 22nd July, 1816, her cousin William Frederick, Duke of Gloucester (*born* 15th May, 1776; *died* 30th Nov., 1834), and died without issue, 30th April, 1857.

XII. SOPHIA, born 3rd Nov., 1777; died unmarried, 27th May, 1848.

XIII. OCTAVIUS, born 23rd Feb., 1779; died 3rd May, 1783.

XIV. ALFRED, born 22nd Sept., 1780; died 26th August, 1782.

XV. AMELIA, born 7th August, 1783; died unmarried, 2nd Nov., 1810.

Her Majesty ALEXANDRINA VICTORIA, of the United Kingdom of Great Britain and Ireland, Queen, Defender of the Faith, born 24th May, 1819; succeeded to the throne 20th June, 1837, on the death of her uncle, King William IV.; crowned 28th June, 1838; and married, 10th February, 1840, to his late Royal Highness Francis ALBERT Augustus Charles Emmanuel, PRINCE CONSORT, DUKE OF SAXONY, PRINCE OF COBURG AND GOTHA, who was born 26th August, 1819; died 14th December, 1861. Her Majesty is the only child of his late Royal Highness Edward Duke of Kent, fourth son of King George III., and has issue—

1. Her Royal Highness VICTORIA Adelaide Mary Louisa, PRINCESS ROYAL, born 21st November, 1840; married 25th January, 1858, to his Royal Highness the Crown Prince (only son of the King of Prussia), and has had issue his Royal Highness Prince Frederick William Victor Albert, born 27th January, 1859; her Royal Highness Princess Victoria Elizabeth Augusta Charlotte, born 24th July, 1860; his Royal Highness Prince Albert William Henry, born 14th August, 1862; his Royal Highness Prince Francis Frederick Sigismund, born 15th September, 1864, died 18th June, 1866; and her Royal Highness Princess Frederika Wilhelmina Amelie Victoria, born 12th April, 1866.

2. His Royal Highness ALBERT EDWARD, PRINCE OF WALES, DUKE OF SAXONY, CORNWALL AND ROTHESAY, EARL OF DUBLIN, K.G., K.T., K.P., G.C.S.I., K.T.S., G.C.B., P.C., General, Colonel of the 10th Hussars, and Colonel-in-chief of the Rifle Brigade, born 9th November, 1841; married, 10th March, 1863, to the Princess Alexandra Caroline Mary Charlotte Louisa Julia (born 1st December, 1844), eldest daughter of the King of Denmark, and has issue his Royal Highness Prince Albert Victor Christian Edward, born 8th January, 1864; his Royal Highness Prince George Frederick Ernest Albert, born 3rd June, 1865; her Royal Highness Louise Victoria Alexandra Dagmar, born 20th February, 1867; and her Royal Highness Victoria Alexandra Olga Mary, born 6th July, 1868.

3. Her Royal Highness ALICE Maud Mary, born 25th April, 1843; married, 1st July, 1862, to his Royal Highness Prince Frederick William Louis of Hesse Darmstadt, K.G., and has issue Princess Victoria Alberta Elizabeth Matilda Mary, born 5th April, 1863; Princess Elizabeth Alexandrina Louise Alice, born 1st November, 1864; and Irene Marie Louise Anna, born 11th July, 1866.

4. His Royal Highness ALFRED Ernest Albert, Duke of Edinburgh, Earl of Kent, and Earl of Ulster, K.G., K.T., P.C., born 6th August, 1844; Captain Royal Navy, 23rd February, 1866.

5. Her Royal Highness HELENA Augusta Victoria, born 25th May, 1846; married, 5th July, 1866, to Major-General his Royal Highness Prince Frederick Christian Charles Augustus of Schleswig Holstein Sonderbourg Augustenbourg, K.G., and has issue Prince Christian Victor Albert Ludwig Ernest Anton, born 14th April, 1867.

6. Her Royal Highness LOUISA Caroline Alberta, born 18th March, 1848.

7. His Royal Highness ARTHUR William Patrick Albert, K.G., born 1st May, 1850; Lieutenant Royal Artillery, 30th October, 1868.

8. His Royal Highness LEOPOLD George Duncan Albert, born 7th April, 1853.

9. Her Royal Highness BEATRICE Mary Victoria Feodore, born 14th April, 1857.

Royal Princes and Princesses.

His Royal Highness GEORGE Frederick Alexander Charles Ernest Augustus, DUKE OF CUMBERLAND (EX-KING OF HANOVER), K.G., G.C.H., cousin to Her Majesty; born 27th May, 1819; married 18th February, 1843, Princess Mary of Saxe-Altenberg, and has issue a son, born 21st September, 1845, and two daughters.

Her Royal Highness AUGUSTA Wilhelmina Louisa, DUCHESS OF CAMBRIDGE, daughter of the Landgrave of Hesse Cassel, born 25th July, 1795; married 7th May, 1818, the Duke of Cambridge (who died 8th July, 1850), and had issue—

1. His Royal Highness GEORGE William Frederick Charles, DUKE OF CAMBRIDGE, Field-Marshal Commanding-in-Chief, K.G., K.P., G.C.B. G.C.H., G.M.M.G., G.C.L.H., P.C., D.C.L., cousin to Her Majesty, born March 26th, 1819.

2. Her Royal Highness AUGUSTA Caroline Charlotte Elizabeth Mary Sophia Louisa, cousin to Her Majesty, born 19th July, 1822; married, 28th June, 1843, Frederick, reigning Duke of Mecklenburg Strelitz, G.C.B., and has issue a son, born 22nd July, 1848.

3. Her Royal Highness MARY Adelaide Wilhelmina Elizabeth, cousin to Her Majesty, born 27th November, 1833; married, 12th June, 1866, H.S.H. Francis Paul Charles Louis Alexander, Prince of Teck, G.C.B., and has issue a daughter, born 26th May, 1867, and a son, born 13th August, 1868.

Her Majesty's Near Relatives.

Half-Sister.—Daughter of the late Duchess of Kent by her first husband the reigning Prince of Leiningen, Anne Feodorowna Augusta Charlotte Wilhelmina, born 7th December, 1807, married 18th February, 1828, Ernest Christian, Prince of Hohenlohe Langenberg, who died 12th April, 1860, and by him had issue—

1. Charles Louis William Leopold, born 25th October, 1829.

2. Herman Ernest Francis Bernard, reigning Prince of Hohenlohe Langenberg, born 31st August, 1832, an officer in the Austrian service.

3. Victor Ferdinand Francis Eugène Gustave Adolphus Constantine Frederic, Count Gleichen, born 11th November, 1833, Captain in the Royal Navy, Governor of Windsor Castle, married 26th January, 1861, Laura Williamina, youngest daughter of Admiral Sir George Seymour, and has issue a daughter born 20th Dec., 1861; and a son born 15th Jan., 1863.

4. Adelaide Victoire, born 20th July, 1835, married 11th September, 1856, Prince Frederick of Schleswig Holstein Sonderbourg Augustenbourg.

5. Feodore Victoire, born 7th July, 1839, married 23rd October, 1858, Prince George of Saxe Meiningen.

Nephews.—1. His Serene Highness Ernest Leopold, reigning Prince of Leiningen, Captain in the Royal Navy, born 9th November, 1830, married 11th September, 1858, Princess Maria Amelia of Baden, and has issue a daughter born 24th July, 1863, and a son born 1865.

2. Edward Frederic, born 5th January, 1833, Captain Royal Imperial Guard of Austria.

LORD STEWARD'S DEPARTMENT.—Board of Green Cloth, Buckingham Palace.

Lord Steward, Earl of Bessborough.
Treasurer of the Household,

Comptroller of the Household,
Master of the Household, Major Sir John Clayton Cowell, K.C.B., R.E.

Secretary to the Board, Edward M. Browell, Esq.
Paymaster of the Household, W. Hampshire, Esq.
Lord High Almoner, Bishop of Oxford.
Sub-Almoner, Rev. Richard William Jelf, D.D.

LORD CHAMBERLAIN'S DEPARTMENT.—Office, Stable Yard, St. James's Palace.

Lord Chamberlain, Viscount Sydney, G.C.B.
Vice-Chamberlain, Viscount Castlerosse.
Comptroller, Lord Otho Fitzgerald.
Chief Clerk, Thomas Charles March, Esq.
Inspector of Accounts, Daniel Tupper, Esq.
First Clerk, George Hertslet, Esq.
Second Clerk, F. W. Jennings, Esq.
Priv. Sec. to Her Majesty, Gen. Hon. Chas. Grey.
Keeper of the Privy Purse, Maj.-Gen. Sir Thos. Myddelton Biddulph, K.C.B.
Master of the Ceremonies, Gen. Hon. Sir E. Cust.
Assistant-Master of the Ceremonies, Colonel C. Bagot.
Marshal of the Ceremonies, Hon. Spen. Lyttelton.
Groom of the Robes, Maj.-Gen. F. H. Seymour.
Lords in Waiting, Marquis of Normanby; Viscount Torrington; Earl of Camperdowne; Lord Camoys; Lord Suffield; Lord Methuen

Grooms in Waiting, Hon. Mortimer Sackville West; Lieut.-Col. William Henry Frederick Cavendish ; Col. the Hon. Augustus F. Laddell; Col. Lord James Charles Plantagenet Murray; Sir Henry Seton, Bt. ; Maj.-Gen. Francis Seymour, C.B. ; Capt. Lord Frederick Herbert Kerr, R.N.
Extra Grooms in Waiting, Hon. Sir Charles Aug. Murray, K.C.B. ; Lieut. Walter George Stirling.
Gentlemen Ushers of the Privy Chamber, Hon. Frederick Byng ; Chas. Heneage, Esq. ; Gen. Sir John M. F. Smith ; Algernon West, Esq.
Black Rod and Deputy Great Chamberlain, Adm. Sir Augustus Wm. James Clifford, Bt., C.B.
Gentlemen Ushers Daily Waiters, Sir William

Martins ; Hon. Spencer Cecil Brabazon Ponsonby; Edward Hamilton Anson, Esq.
Grooms of the Privy Chamber, Arthur Johnstone Blackwood, Esq. ; John Francis Campbell (of Islay), Esq. ; Col. Edward Stopford Claremont, C.B. ; Hon. Roden Berkeley W. Noel.
Gentlemen Ushers Quarterly Waiters, Henry Greville, Esq. ; Alfred Montgomery, Esq. ; Maj.-Gen. Henry Sykes Stephens ; Wilbraham Taylor, Esq. ; Col. George Howard Vyse ; Capt. William Ross ; Comm. Chas. Gudgeon Nelson, R.N. ; Francis Knollys, Esq.
Extra Gentleman Usher Quarterly Waiter, John George Green, Esq.
Assistant Gentleman Usher, Sir Alexander Cornewall Duff Gordon, Bt.
Poet Laureate, Alfred Tennyson, Esq., D.C.L.
Examiner of Plays, Wm. Bodham Donne, Esq.
Librarian, B. B. Woodward, Esq.
Governor and Constable of Windsor Castle, Capt. Count Gleichen, R.N.
Her Majesty's Body Guard of the Yeomen of the Guard—Captain, Rt. Hon.
Lieutenant, Lieut.-Col. Sir John Henry Cooke, knt. ; *Ensign*, Col. William Paston Furnell, C.B. ; *Adjutant*, Lieut.-Col. William Griffin Sutton ; *Exons*, Lieut.-Col. Charles Doyle Patterson ; Col. Oliver Paget Bourke ; Lieut.-Col. John Augustus Todd.
Hon. Corps of Gentlemen-at-Arms—Captain, Lord Foley; *Lieutenant*, Sir William Topham, knt. ; *Standard-Bearer*, David James Harmar, Esq. ; *Clerk of the Cheque and Adjutant*, Lieut.-Col. William M'Call.
Master of the Buckhounds, Rt. Hon. Earl of Cork.

DEPARTMENT OF THE MASTER OF THE HORSE.—Office, Royal Mews, Pimlico.

Master of the Horse, Marquis of Ailesbury, K.G.
Clerk Marshal and Chief Equerry, Colonel Lord Alfred Paget.
Crown Equerry, Secretary to the Master of the Horse, and Superintendent of the Royal Stables, Col. George Ashley Maude, C.B., R.A.
Equerries in Ordinary, Col. Lord Augustus C. Lennox FitzRoy; Maj.-Gen. Viscount Bridport; Lieut.-Gen. Francis Hugh George Seymour;

Col. the Hon. D. C. Fitzgerald de Ros; Col' Charles Taylor du Plat; Col. F. H. Ponsonby ; Col. the Hon. A. E. Hardinge, C.B.
Honorary Equerry, Maj.-Gen. the Hon. Alexander Gordon, C.B.
Pages of Honour, Hon. Spencer Frederick Jocelyn; Hon. Frederick William Stopford; George Walter Grey, Esq. ; Hon. G. F. H. Somerset.

CHAPELS ROYAL.

Dean of the Chapels Royal, The Bishop of London.
Sub-Dean and Chaplain at St. James's Palace, Rev. Francis Garden, M.A.
Clerk of the Queen's Closet, The Bishop of Worcester.

Domestic Chaplain, Very Rev. Dean of Windsor.
Hereditary Grand Almoner, The Marquis of Exeter.
Lord High Almoner, The Bishop of Oxford.
Sub-Dean, Chapels Roy., Rev. Francis Garden, M.A.

MEDICAL DEPARTMENT.

Physicians in Ordinary, Sir James Clark, bt. ; Sir Henry Holland, bt. ; Sir Wm. Jenner, bt.
Physicians Extraordinary, Peter Mere Latham ; Neill Arnott; Sir Thomas Watson, bt.
Physician-Accoucheur, Sir Charles Locock, bt.
Sergeant Surgeons, Sir William Ferguson, bt. ; Cæsar Henry Hawkins, Esq.
Sergeant Surgeon Extraordinary, James Paget, Esq.

Surgeons Extraordinary, Richard Quain, Esq. John Hilton, Esq. ; Prescott Gardner Hewett, Esq.
Physician to the Household, F. Hawkins, M.D.
Surgeon to the Household, Thomas Spencer Wells, Esq.
Apothecary to Her Majesty and the Household, Claudius Francis Du Pasquier, Esq.

MEDICAL DEPARTMENT—*continued.*
Surgeons and Apothecaries in Ordinary to the Household at Windsor, James Ellison, Esq.; Thomas Fairbank, Esq. (jointly).
Surgeon Oculist, William White Cooper, Esq.

Surgeon Dentist, Edwin Saunders, Esq.
Cupper, John Mapleson, Esq.
Dentist to the Household, Edwin Truman, Esq.
Chemists and Druggists in Ordinary, Mr. Peter Squire; Mr. Peter Wyatt Squire (jointly).

LADIES OF HER MAJESTY'S HOUSEHOLD.

Mistress of the Robes, The Duchess of Argyll.

Ladies of the Bedchamber, The Duchess (Dowager) of Athole; Marchioness (Dowager) of Ely; Countess of Gainsborough; Countess of Caledon; Viscountess Clifden; the Dowager Lady Churchill; the Dowager Lady Waterpark; the Duchess of Roxburghe.

Extra Ladies of the Bedchamber, The Duchess (Dowager) of Norfolk; the Countess (Dowager) of Mount Edgcumbe; Viscountess Jocelyn.

Bedchamber Women, Lady Caroline Barrington; Viscountess Forbes; Hon. Mrs. George Campbell; Viscountess Chewton; Hon. Mrs. Alexander Gordon; Lady Codrington; Lady Sarah Elizabeth Lindsay; Hon. Mrs. Robert Bruce.

Extra Bedchamber Women, Lady Augusta Frederica Elizabeth Stanley; Mrs. Pratt; Lady Charlotte Copley.

Honorary Bedchamber Woman in Ordinary, Hon. Lady Biddulph.

Maids of Honour, Hon. Lucy Maria Kerr; Hon. Caroline Fanny Cavendish; Hon. Flora Clementina Isabella Macdonald; Hon. Emily Cathcart; Hon. Horatia Charlotte Stopford; Hon. Harriet Lepel Phipps; Hon. Florence Catherine Seymour; Hon. Mary Louisa Lascelles.

Extra Maid of Honour, Hon. Eleanor Stanley.

H.R.H. THE PRINCE OF WALES'S HOUSEHOLD.

Groom of the Stole, Vacant.
Lords of the Bedchamber, Lord Alfred Hervey; Viscount Hamilton, M.P.
Extra Lord of the Bedchamber, Earl of Mount Edgcumbe.
Comptroller and Treasurer, General Sir William Thomas Knollys, K.C.B.
Grooms of the Bedchamber, Hon. Charles Lindley Wood; Hon. Alexander Temple Fitzmaurice.
Extra Groom of the Bedchamber, Hon. Robert Henry Meade.

Equerries, Major Christopher C. Teesdale, C.B., R.A.; Major George Henry Grey, Northumberland Militia; Lieutenant-Colonel Frederick Charles Keppel, Grenadier Guards; Captain Arthur Edward Augustus Ellis.
Extra Equerry, Colonel Robert Nigel F. Kingscote, C.B.
Private Secretary and Keeper of the Privy Seal, Herbert W. Fisher, Esq.
Attorney-General, Sir William Alexander, Bart.
Chaplain, Rev. William Lake Onslow, M.A.

HOUSEHOLD OF H.R.H. THE PRINCESS OF WALES.

Chamberlain, Lord Harris, G.C.S.I.
Ladies of the Bedchamber, Marchioness of Carmarthen; Countess of Morton; Countess of Macclesfield; Viscountess Walden.

Bedchamber Women, Hon. Mrs. William George Grey; Hon. Mrs. Edward Coke; Hon. Mrs. Francis Stonor; Hon. Mrs. Arthur Hardinge.
Extra Bedchamber Woman, Hon. Mrs. R. Bruce.

HOUSEHOLD OF H.R.H. THE DUKE OF EDINBURGH.

Treasurer, Colonel the Hon. Augustus Frederick Liddell.

Equerries, Hon. Eliot Thomas Yorke; Lieutenant Arthur Balfour Haig, R.E.

HOUSEHOLD OF H.R.H. THE PRINCESS CHRISTIAN.
Honorary Bedchamber Woman.—Mrs. G. Gordon.

Orders of Knighthood.

KNIGHTS OF THE GARTER.
Ribbon, Garter Blue.   *Motto*, Honi soit qui mal y pense.
THE SOVEREIGN.
H.R.H. THE PRINCE OF WALES.

H.R.H. the Duke of Edinburgh.
H.R.H. the Prince Arthur.
Ex-King of Hanover.
Duke of Cambridge.
Emperor of the French.
Emperor of Austria.
Emperor of Russia.
The Sultan.
King of Italy.
King of Prussia.
King of Portugal.
King of Denmark.
King of the Belgians.
Duke of Saxe Meiningen.
Duke of Brunswick.
Duke of Saxe-Coburg Gotha.
Gd. Du. of Mecklenburg-Strelitz.
Grand Duke of Hesse.

Crown Prince of Prussia.
Prince Louis of Hesse.
Prince Christian of Holstein.
Duke of Buccleuch.
Duke of Abercorn.
Marquis of Hertford.
Earl of Clarendon.
Earl Granville.
Marquis of Westminster.
Duke of Wellington.
Duke of Devonshire.
Earl of Harrowby.
Earl of Derby.
Duke of Somerset.
Earl Russell.
Earl of Shaftesbury.
Earl Fitzwilliam.
Earl Grey.

Duke of Sutherland.
Marquis of Ailesbury.
Earl Spencer.
Duke of Cleveland.
Earl Cowper.
Earl Cowley.
Duke of Richmond.
Duke of Rutland.
Duke of Beaufort.
Duke of Marlborough.
Prelate of the Order, Bishop of Winchester.
Chancellor, Bishop of Oxford.
Registrar, Dean of Windsor.
Garter Principal King of Arms, Sir Charles George Young.
Gentleman-Usher of the Black Rod, Sir Augustus Clifford, Bart.

KNIGHTS OF THE THISTLE.
Ribbon, Green. *Motto,* Nemo me impune lacessit.
THE SOVEREIGN.
H.R.H. THE PRINCE OF WALES. **H.R.H. THE DUKE OF EDINBURGH.**

Marquis of Tweeddale.
Duke of Roxburghe.
Earl of Mansfield.
Duke of Montrose.
Earl of Dalhousie.
Duke of Argyll.
Lord Kinnaird.
Marquis of Ailsa.

Earl of Fife.
Earl of Zetland.
Lord Belhaven and Stenton.
Earl of Airlie.
Lord Napier.
Lord Lovat.
Earl of Stair.
Duke of Athole.

Dean of the Order, W. Muir, D.D.
Sec., Sir J. S. Richardson, Bart.
Deputy, Albert W. Woods, Esq., F.S.A., *Lancaster Herald.*
Lyon King of Arms, George Burnett, Esq.
Gentleman Usher of the Green Rod, Frederic Peel Round, Esq.

KNIGHTS OF THE ORDER OF ST. PATRICK.
Ribbon, Sky-blue. *Motto,* Quis separabit?
THE SOVEREIGN.
The Lord Lieutenant, *Grand Master.*

Duke of Cambridge.
Earl of Roden.
Marquis of Clanricarde.
Marquis of Conyngham.
Earl of Howth.
Marquis of Headfort.
Earl of Arran.
Earl of Wicklow.
Earl of Fingall.
Earl Dartrey.
Marquis of Londonderry.

Earl of Granard.
Viscount Gough.
Marquis of Donegal.
Earl of Cork and Orrery.
Lord Dufferin.
Lord Lurgan.
Earl of Charlemont.
Earl of Dunraven.
Marquis of Drogheda.
Marquis of Waterford.
Earl of Erne.

Earl of Mayo (extra).
Prelate of Order. The Lord Primate.
Chancellor, Archbishop of Dublin.
Registrar, Dean of St. Patrick's.
Genealogist, Sir W. Leeson.
Sec., Lowry V. T. Balfour, Esq.
Usher of the Black Rod, Sir Geo. Burdett L'Estrange.
Ulster King of Arms, Attendant on the Order, Sir J. B. Burke, C.B.

KNIGHTS OF THE BATH.
Ribbon, Crimson. *Motto,* Tria juncta in uno.
THE SOVEREIGN.
General H. R. H. THE PRINCE OF WALES.
Field-Marshal H.R.H. THE DUKE OF CAMBRIDGE.

Military Knights Grand Cross.

F.M. Viscount Gough, G.C.S.I.
Gen. Sir G. Pollock, G.C.S.I.,I.A.
F.M. Sir Alexander Woodford.
F.M. Sir J. Fox Burgoyne, Bt.
Gen. Sir De Lacy Evans.
Gen. Sir Richard England.
Adm. Sir Jas. A. Gordon.
F.M. Sir Hew D. Ross.
Gen. Ld. Straithnairn, G.C.S.I.
Adm. Sir Michael Seymour.
F.M. Sir William M. Gomm.
Adm. Sir Thomas J. Cochrane.
Adm. Sir George F. Seymour.
Gen. Sir John Bell.
Gen. Sir Charles Yorke.
Lt.-Gen. Sir J. Hope Grant.
Lt.-Gen. Sir Patrick Grant.
Gen. Sir Arthur B. Clifton.
Gen. Sir James A. Hope.
Gen. Sir John F. Fitzgerald.
Adm. Sir Fairfax Moresby.
Gen. Sir William Rowan.
Adm. Sir Houston Stewart.
Gen. Sir W. J. Codrington.
Gen. Sir James Jackson.
Gen. Sir John Cheape.
Gen. Viscount Melville.
Adm. Hon. Sir Fred. W. Grey.
Vice-Adm. Sir James Hope.
Adm. Sir George R. Lambert.
Adm. Sir Stephen Lushington.
Gen. Sir J. L. Pennefather.
Lt.-Gen. Sir Richard Airey.
Adm. Sir C. Howe Fremantle.
Lt.-Gen. Sir A. Wilson, Bart.
Lt.-Gen. Sir Edward Lugard.
Gen. Sir John Aitchison.
Gen. Hon. Sir Charles Gore.
Gen. The Marqs. of Tweeddale.
Lt.-Gen. Ld. Napier of Magdala, G.C.S.I.

Civil Knights Grand Cross.

Viscount Stratford de Redcliffe.
Earl of Clarendon.
Rt. Hon. Sir John McNeill.
Earl of Ellenborough.
Rt. Hon. Sir Geo. H. Seymour.
Rt. Hon. Sir George Grey, Bart.
Rt. Hon. Sir H. L. Bulwer.
Lord Broughton.
Earl Cowley.
Earl of Dalhousie.
Viscount Halifax.
Earl of St. Germans.
Rt. Hon. Sir John L. Mair Lawrence, Bart., G.C.S.I.
Lord Howden.
Lord Bloomfield.
Earl of Malmesbury.
Rt. Hon. Sir J. Pakington, Bart.
Lord Lyons.
Viscount Sydney.
Sir James Hudson.
Maj.-Gen. Rt. Hon. Sir H. Knight Storks.   [ingen, R.N.
Capt. H.S.H. the Prince of Leiningen, R.N.
Rt. Hon. Sir Robert Peel, Bart.
Rt. Hon. Sir Andrew Buchanan.
Lord Aug. W. F. S. Loftus.
Rt. Hon. Sir John Young, Bart.
Honorary Knights Grand Cross.
Dk. de la Victoria y de Morella.
The Reigning Grand Duke of Mecklenburgh-Strelitz. (*Civil*).
F.M. H.H. Omar Lutfâ Pacha.
Gen. H.I.H. Prince Napoleon.
Marshal Certain Canrobert.
Marshal Count Vaillant.
Gen. Alphonso La Marmora.
Marshal M. E. P. M. De Mac-Mahon, Duke de Magenta.
Marshal Auguste M. E. R. de St Jean D'Angely.
The King of Prussia.

H.H. The Maharajah Jung Bahadoor Koonwar Ranajee.
The King of Denmark. (*Civil*).
H.H. The Bey of Tunis. (*Civil*).
H.S.H. The Prince of Teck. (*Cl.*)
H.H. The Viceroy of Egypt. (*Cl.*)
H.S.H. Prince of Hohenlohe-Langenburg. (*Civil*).
SECOND CLASS.
Military Knights Commanders.
Major-Gen. Sir J. G. Woodford.
Gen. Sir G. Bowles.
Gen. The Earl of Lucan.
Gen. Sir H. J. W. Bentinck.
Lt.-Gen. Hon. Sir J. Y. Scarlett.
Lt.-Gen. Sir George Buller.
Gen. Sir Richard J. Dacres.
Adm. Sir Henry Prescott.
Gen. Sir W. F. Williams, Bt.
Lt.-Gen. Lord Rokeby.
Lt.-Gen. Sir Robert Garrett.
Vice-Adm. Hon. Sir H. Keppel.
Lt.-Gen. Sir Sydney J. Cotton.
Lt.-Gen. Sir Wm. R. Mansfield.
Lt.-Gen.Sir C.T.VanStraubenzee.
Adm. Sir Henry J. Leeke.
Col. Sir John Jones.
Lt.-Gen. Sir John Michel.
Major-Gen. Sir Robert Walpole.
Col. Sir John Douglas.
Major-Gen. Sir D. Edw. Wood.
Major-Gen. Sir A. H. Horsford.
Adm. Sir Provo W. P. Wallis.
Adm. Sir Robert L. Baynes.
Col. Sir Anthony C. Sterling.
Major-Gen. Sir R. Denis Kelly.
Adm. Sir Will. F. Martin, Bart.
Vice-Adm. Sir L. T. Jones.
Col. The Earl of Longford.
Lt.-Gen. Sir Thomas S. Pratt.
Adm. Sir Lucius Curtis, Bart.
Adm. Sir William Bowles.
Gen. Sir Charles G. Ellicombe.

ORDER OF THE BATH—cont.

Adm. Sir W. J. H. Johnstone.
Gen. Sir J. C. Chatterton, Bart.
Adm. Sir James Scott.
Lt.-Gen. Sir Abraham J. Cloeté.
Adm. Sir Charles Talbot.
Lt.-Gen. Sir William H. Elliott.
Vice-Adm. Sir George R. Mundy.
Lt.-Gen. Sir S. Robert Wesley.
Lt.-Gen. Sir D. A. Cameron.
Vice-Adm. Sir Alexander Milne.
Vice-Adm. Sir Aug. L. Kuper.
Major-Gen. Sir John Garvock.
Gen. Sir William Wood.
Adm. Sir Geo. Rose Sartorius.
Gen. Sir Abraham Roberts.
Gen. Sir Thomas Reed.
Gen. Sir John Scott.
Gen. Sir William Wyllie.
Gen. Sir Chas. A. Windham.
Adm. The Earl of Lauderdale.
Vice-Adm. Sir Robert Smart.
Vice-Adm. Sir John Kingcome.
Lt.-Gen. Sir John E. Dupuis.
Gen. Sir Fortescue Graham.
Vice-Adm. Sir Sydney C. Dacres.
Lt.-Gen. Lord William Paulet.
Lt.-Gen. Hon. Sir A. A. Spencer.
Major-Gen. Sir John W. Gordon.
Col. Sir Edward H. Greathed.
Major-Gen. Sir C. W. D. Staveley.
Inspector-Gen. of Hospitals, Sir William Linton.
Comm. Gen.-in-Chief, Sir William J. T. Power.
Adm. Sir Edward Collier.
Adm. Sir Peter Richards.
Adm. Sir Henry J. Codrington.
Adm. Sir Joseph Nias.
Vice-Adm. Sir Edw. Belcher.
Gen. Sir E. Finucane Morris.
Gen. Sir Patrick E. Craigie.
Lt.-Gen. Sir John B. Gough.
Lt.-Gen. Sir G. H. Lockwood.
Major-Gen. Sir John R. Smyth.
Adm. Sir Fred. T. Michell.
Vice-Adm. Sir T. M. Symonds.
Rear-Adm. Sir Wm. H. Hall.
Lt.-Gen. Sir George Bell.
Major-Gen. Sir F. E. Chapman.
Insp-General Hospitals and Fleets, Sir David Deas, M.D.
Lt.-Gen. Sir T. Holloway, R.M.
Capt. Sir W. S. Wiseman, Bt.,R.N.
Lt.-Gen. Sir William Bell.
Lt.-Gen. Sir John Bloomfield.
Lt.-Gen. Sir A. B. Stransham.
Lieut.-Gen. Sir W. B. Ingilby.
Major-Gen. Sir Trevor Chute.
Capt. Sir George L. Heath, R.N.

Officers in the Indian Army.

Lt.-Gen. Sir Rob. J. H. Vivian.
Major-Gen. Sir Thomas Seaton.
Major-Gen. Sir C. S. Stuart.
Gen. Sir Henry G. A. Taylor.
Gen. Sir Alexander Lindsay.
Gen. Sir John Low.
Gen. Sir David Capon.
Major-Gen. Sir N. B. Chamberlain.
Gen. Sir P. Montgomerie.
Lt.-Gen. Sir Maurice Stack.
Major-Gen. Sir Edward Green.
Lt.-Gen. Sir George Brooke.
Major-Gen. Sir Henry Tombs.
Maj.-Gen. Sir George Malcolm.

Civil Knights Commanders.

Sir Geo. Russell Clerk, G.C.S.I.
Sir Henry Light.
Sir George Grey.
Sir Charles E. Trevelyan.
Gen. Sir Duncan M'Gregor.
Sir Richard Mayne.
Sir Henry Barkly.
Sir John Francis Davis, Bart.
Col. Sir Probyn T. Cautley, I.A.
Major-Gen. Sir Justin Sheil, I.A.
Lt.-Col. Sir H. C. Rawlinson, I.A.
Col. Sir William T. Denison.
Adm. Sir Charles Elliot.
Hon. Sir John Duncan Bligh.
Sir John Fiennes Crampton, Bt.
Sir James Macaulay Higginson.
Sir John Shaw Lefevre.
Sir Andrew Smith, M.D.
Vice-Adm. Sir Alexander Milne.
Adm. Sir Thomas Hastings.
Sir Henry B. E. Frere, G.C.S.I.
Sir Robert Montgomery, G.C.S.I.
Sir Rowland Hill.
Sir Fred. Jas. Halliday.
Sir Rob. N. C. Hamilton, Bart.
Lt.-Gen. Sir Rich. J. H. Birch.
Major-Gen. Sir Peter M. Melvill.
Maj.-Gen. Sir H. B. Edwardes.
Sir Charles Lennox Wyke.
Major-Gen. Rt. Hon. Sir Thos. A. Larcom, Bart.
Lord Dufferin and Claneboye.
Major-Gen. Sir G. H. Macgregor, I.A.
Sir John Peter Grant.
Sir John H. Drummond Hay.
Sir Harry Smith Parkes.
Sir Rutherford Alcock.
Sir Philip E. Wodehouse.
Sir Charles H. Darling.
Lt.-Gen. Sir Edward Macarthur.
Sir R. I. Murchison, Bart.
Sir Henry F. Howard.
Major-Gen. Sir T. M. Biddulph.
Sir Aug. Berkeley Paget.
Sir James Douglas.
Major-Gen. Sir W. M. Coghlan.
Sir Robert G. Colquhoun.
Major Sir John C. Cowell.
Lt.-Gen. Sir J. G. Le Marchant.
Rt. Hon. Sir William Hutt.
Sir Alexander Malet, Bart.
Hon. Sir Chas. Aug. Murray.
Hon. Sir J. H. T. Manners-Sutton.
Sir James Clark, Bart.
Sir Thomas Erskine May.
Sir Charles Pressly.
Gen. Sir W. T. Knollys.
Sir John Alexander Macdonald.
Sir William Rose.
Rear-Adm. Sir J. C. Caffin.
Vice-Adm. Sir R. S. Robinson.

Civil Companions.

Aldham, Capt. W. Cornwallis R.N.
Alexander, Robert, Esq.
Alison, Charles, Esq.
Archibald, Edw. Mortimer, Esq.
Armstrong, Sir W. George.
Ashby, James W. M., Esq., R.N.
Balfour, Major-Gen. George, I.A.
Bartlin, Geo. Gregory, Esq.
Bayley, Charles John, Esq.
Becher, Col. John Reid.
Black, Henry, Esq.

Bonham, Edward W., Esq.
Booth, James, Esq.
Bowring, Edgar Alfred, Esq.
Brown, William, Esq.
Browne, George, Esq.
Brownrigg, Sir Henry John.
Bryson, Alexander, M.D., Director Gen. Med. Dep. of the Navy,
Burke, Sir J. Bernard.
Campbell, Thomas Edmd., Esq.
Carnegie, Major John W., I.A.
Chadwick, Edwin, Esq.
Churchill, Henry Adrian, Esq.
Clarke, Sir Robert B.
Cleeve, Frederick, Esq.
Cocks, Arthur Herbert, Esq.
Cole, Henry, Esq.
Colebrooke, Gen. Sir W. M. G.
Coles, Capt. Cowper P., R.N.
Commerell, Capt. John E., R.N.
Cooper, Frederick Henry, Esq.
Couper, Sir G. E. Wilson, Bart.
Crichton, Lt.-Col. W. H., I.A.
Crofton, Major Sir Walter Fred.
Crowe, John Rice, Esq.
Cumberbatch, A. Carlton, Esq.
De Rottenburg, Col. George.
De Strzelecki, Paul Edm., Esq.
Dingli, Dr. Sir Adriano.
Donnelly, William, Esq.
Doyle, Percy William, Esq.
Draper, William Henry, Esq.
Dunlop, Robert Henry, Esq.
Dunlop, Rear-Adm. Hugh.
Eastwick, Edward B., Esq.
Edye, John, Esq.
Eliot, Major Charles, I.A.
Elphinstone, Lt.-Col. H. Craufrd.
Ellis, Robert Staunton, Esq.
Farnall, Henry Burrard, Esq.
Fitzgerald, Capt. Charles, R.N.
Forbes, William A., Esq.
Forsyth, John, Esq.
Forsyth, Thomas Douglas, Esq.
Foster, Morgan H., Esq.
Fraser, Lt.-Col. Alexander, R.A.
Galton, Capt. Douglas.
Gibbs, Frederick W., Esq.
Goldsmid, Lt.Col. Fred. I.
Gordon, Henry William, Esq.
Grant, Major James Aug., C.S.I.
Greathed, Lt.-Col.W.W.H., I.A.
Green, Lt.-Col. Sir W. H. R.,I.A.
Green, John, Esq.
Greene, Col. Godfrey Thomas.
Greig, Major John James.
Griffith, Philip, Esq.
Gubbins, Frederick Bebb, Esq.
Hamilton, Ker Baillie, Esq.
Harris, Vice-Adm. Hon. E. A. J.
Hay, Jas. deV. Drummond,Esq.
Henderson, Lt.-Col. E.
Herbert Chas. St. John S., Esq.
Hervey, Col. Charles R. West.
Hill, Col. Stephen John.
Hincks, Francis, Esq.
Horsford, Sir Robert.
Howland, William Pearce, Esq.
Hume, Alan Octavian, Esq.
Ironside-Bax, John H., Esq.
Jeans, William David, Esq.
Jervois, Col. William F. D.
Jordan, Edward, Esq.
Kellie, Col. Earl of, I.A.
Kennedy, Sir Arthur Edward.

Langevin, Hector Louis, Esq.
La Trobe, Charles J., Esq.
Lawrence, *Lt.-Gen.* Sir G. St. Patrick, I.A.
Lawrence, *Col.* Rich. Chas., I.A.
Lay, Horatio Nelson, Esq.
Lloyd, Thomas, Esq.
Loch, Henry Brougham, Esq.
Longworth, John Aug., Esq.
Lumsden, *Col.* Harry B., I.A.
MacDonnell, Sir Richard G.
McDougall, William, Esq.
Maclean, John, Esq.
McLeod, Sir Donald F., K.C.S.I.
Mallet, Louis, Esq.
Marsden, *Lt.-Col.* F. C., I.A.
Martin, Sir James Ranald.
Mathew, Geo. Buckley, Esq.
Mayne, Francis Otway, Esq.
Merewether,*Col.*SirW.L.,K.C.S.I.
Merivale, Herman, Esq.
Metcalfe, Sir T. J., Bart.
Money, Alonzo, Esq.
Moore, Niven, Esq.
Moriarty, *Com.* H. A., R.N.
Morier, Robert B. D., Esq.
Northcote, Rt. Hon. Sir S.H.,Bt.
Ord, *Col.* Sir Harry St. George.

Osborne, *Capt.* J. W. W., I.A.
Palliser, *Major* William.
Pelly, Saville Marriott, Esq.
Petrie, Samuel, Esq.
Phayre, *Col.*SirA.P.,I.A.,K.C.S.I.
Playfair, Lyon, Esq.
Preedy, *Capt.* George W., R. N.
Ramsey, *Col.* Henry, I.A.
Rawlinson, Robert, Esq.
Rawson, William Rawson, Esq.
Read, Edw. Anderton, Esq.
Reed, Edward James, Esq.
Richmond, *Major* Matthew.
Ricketts, Geo. Hen. M., Esq.
Robe, *Major-Gen.* Fred. H.
Robertson, David B., Esq.
Romaine, Will. Govett, Esq.
Rowe, Sir Joshua.
Sapte, Brand, Esq.
Saunders, Chas. Burslem, Esq.
Scarlett, Hon. Peter Campbell.
Skey, F. C., Esq.
Smith, Sir Peter.
Smith, Thomas, Esq.
Stephen, Sir Alfred.
Tayler, *Col.* Reynell G., I.A.
Taylor, *Col.* Robert Lewis.
Thomson, Edward Deas, Esq.

Thornton, Edward, Esq. (*a.*)
Thornton, Edward, Esq. (*b.*)
Tilley, Samuel L., Esq.
Tucker, Henry Carre, Esq.
Tulloh, *Major-Gen.* Alexander.
Tupper, Charles, Esq.
Verdon, George F. Esq.
Wade, Thomas Francis, Esq.
Wake, Herwald Craufurd, Esq.
Walker, James, Esq.
Ward, John, Esq.
Warner, Charles William, Esq.
Watts, Isaac, Esq.
Wauchope, Samuel, Esq.
Williams, *Col.* Geo. Walter, I.A.
Wilson, John Cracroft, Esq.
Wingfield, Sir Chas. J., K.C.S.I.
Wood, Richard, Esq.
Young, Sir Henry Edw. Fox.
Yule, Sir George Udny, K.C.S.I.
Yule, *Col.* Henry, I.A.
Dean of the Order, Dean of Westr.
Bath King of Arms, Adm. Hon. George Grey.
Registrar & Secretary, Albert W. Woods, Esq., *Lancaster Herald.*
Gent.-Usher of the Scarlet Rod, G. C. Barrington, Esq.

ORDER OF ST. MICHAEL AND ST. GEORGE.

Ribbon, Saxon blue, with a scarlet stripe. *Motto,* Auspicium melioris ævi.

THE SOVEREIGN.

Gd. Master, and First and Principal Kt. Gd. Cr., F.M. H.R.H. The Duke of Cambridge, K.G., K.P.

Knights Grand Cross.

F.M. Sir Alexander Woodford.
Demetrio Count Salomon.
Candiano Count Roma.
Demetrio Count Caruso.
Sir Alessandro Damaschini.
Rt. Hon. Sir John Young, Bart.
Sir Giuseppe Maria Bar. de Piro.
Sir Demetrio Valsamachi.
Sir Dionisio Count Flambariari.
*M.-Gen.*Rt.Hon.SirH.K.Storks.
Lt.-Gen. Sir J. G. Le Marchant.
Sir George Fergusson Bowen.
Sir Pietro Armeni Braila.

Sir Georgio Marcoran.
*Lt.-Gen.*Sir Patrick Grant.
Sir Adriano Dingli.
Sir Victor Houlton.

Knights Commanders.

Sir Joseph Rudsdell.
Sir Hector Greig.
Sir Anto Count Lefcochilo Dusmani.
Sir Spiridione Valsamachi.
Sir Demetrio Comte Curcumelli.
Sir James Philip Lacaita.
Sir Charles E. Douglas, Kt.

Sir Antonio Micallef.
Sir Peter Smith.
Sir Spiridione Valaoriti.
Sir Henry Drummond Wolff.
Sir Charles Sebright.
Major Sir Wilford Brett.
Count Nich. Suberias Bologna.
*Chancery of Order,*Colonial Office.
Prelate, The Archbishop of Corfu.
*Sec.& Reg.*Chief Clerk, Col. Office.
King of Arms, Sir H. Drummond Wolff, K.C.M.G.
Officer of Arms, Malta, Lt.-Col. Bertram Charles Mitford.

ORDER OF THE STAR OF INDIA.

THE SOVEREIGN.

Grand Master and First and Principal Knight Grand Commander, Viceroy and Gov. Gen. of India. H.R.H. The Prince of Wales.

H.H. The Nizam of Hydrabad.
Field-Marshal Viscount Gough.
H.H. The Maharajah of Gwalior.
Lord Harris.
H.H.TheMaharajahDuleepSingh
H.H.TheMaharajahof Cashmere.
Sir George Russell Clerk.
H.H. The Maharajah of Indore.
H.H. The Guicowar of Baroda.
Rt. Hon. Sir John L. M. Lawrence, Bart.
Gen. Lord Strathnairn.
Gen. Sir George Pollock.
H.H. The Maharajah of Jeypore.
H.H.TheRajahofKuppoorthulla.
H.H. The Rajah of Rewah.
Sir H. B. E. Frere.
H.H.TheMaharajahofJoudhpore
Sir Robert Montgomery.
H.H. The Maharajah of Travancore.
Sir W. Rose Mansfield.
H.H. TheMaharajahofKerowlee.
*Lt.-Gen.*Lord Napier of Magdala.
Honorary.
H.H. the Viceroy of Egypt.

Knights Commanders.
Sir Cecil Beadon.
The Nawab of Hyderabad.
Sir Donald F. McLeod.
The Maharajah of Deo in Behar.
Sir Henry Ricketts.
The Maharajah of Vizianagram.
Sir Henry Byng Harington.
The Maharajah of Bulrampore.
Sir Walter Elliot.
Sharf-ul-Omrah, Bahadoor.
Sir Thomas Pycroft.
The Rajah Gidhore.
Sir John M. Macleod.
The Rajah Dinker Rao.
Major-Gen Sir J. C. Coffin.
Lt.-Gen. Sir. G. St.P. Lawrence.
The Rajah of Drangadra.
Major-Gen. Sir Geo. M. Sherer.
The Rajah of Benares.
Lt.-Gen. Sir Arthur T. Cotton.
MeerSheerMahomedofMeerpore.
M.-Gen. Sir N. B. Chamberlain.
The Rajah Sahib Dyal Missar.
Sir George Udny Yule.
Tranjore Madava Rao Dewan.

Sir Charles J. Wingfield.
The Thakoor of Bhownugger.
Maj.-Gen. Sir H. B. Edwardes.
Col. Sir Arnold B. Kemball.
Sirdir Nihal Singh Chachi.
Major-Gen. Sir Robert Wallace.
Lt.-Col. Sir Wm. H. R. Green.
Major Sir George Wingate.
The Maharajah of Johore.
Major-Gen. Sir Hen. M. Durand.
Sir Wm. Muir. [Chief of Edur.
The Maharajah Sree Jowan Sinje
Sir Daniel Eliott.
Sir George Fred. Hervey.
Major-Gen. Sir William Hill.
M.-Gen. Sir V. Eyre. [Nadown.
The Rajah Jodhbir Chund of
Sir Henry Lacon Anderson.
Sir Richard Temple.
Col. Sir Arthur P. Phayre.
TheMaharajahMaunSingofOnde.
Col. Sir Edward R. Wetherall.
Col. Sir W. W. Turner.
Rt. Hon. Sir W. Fitzgerald.
Maj.-Gen. Sir George L. Russell.
Col. Sir William L. Merewether.

H.R.H. Prince of Wales.
H.R.H. Duke of Edinburgh.
H.R.H. Duke of Cambridge.
Archbishop of Canterbury.
Bishop of London.
Archbishop of York.
Duke of Marlborough.
Earl of Malmesbury.
Duke of Somerset.
Duke of Richmond and Lennox.
Duke of Beaufort.
Duke of Buccleuch.
Duke of Argyll.
Duke of Montrose.
Duke of Northumberland.
Duke of Leinster.
Duke of Wellington.
Duke of Buckingham & Chandos.
Duke of Abercorn.
Marquis of Salisbury.
Marquis of Donegal.
Marquis of Exeter.
Marquis of Anglesey.
Marquis of Cholmondeley.
Marquis of Londonderry.
Marquis of Conyngham.
Marquis of Ailesbury.
Marquis of Clanricarde.
Marquis of Westminster.
Marquis of Normanby.
Marquis of Hartington.
Earl of Tankerville.
Earl of Bradford.
Earl of Shrewsbury and Talbot.
Earl of Derby.
Earl of Devon.
Earl of Sandwich.
Earl of Dalhousie.
Earl of Rosebery.
Earl of Hardwicke.
Earl de la Warr.
Earl Spencer.
Earl of Clarendon.
Earl of Carnarvon.
Earl Cadogan.
Earl of Cork and Orrery.
Earl of Bessborough.
Earl of Roden.
Earl of Mayo.
Earl of Wilton.
Earl Grey.
Earl of Lonsdale.
Earl Harrowby.
Earl of St. Germans.
Earl de Grey and Ripon.
Earl Howe.
Earl Granville.
Earl of Ducie.
Earl of Ellenborough.
Earl of Strafford.
Earl Cowley.
Earl Russell.
Earl of Kimberley.
Viscount Falkland.
Viscount Sydney.

Viscount Gough.
Viscount Stratford de Redcliffe.
Viscount Eversley.
Viscount Halifax.
Viscount Bury.
Viscount Royston.
Viscount Castlerosse.
Lord Edward G. F. Howard.
Lord Charles Fitzroy.
Lord John J. R. Manners.
Lord Robert Montagu.
Lord Otho Fitzgerald.
Lord Stanley.
Lord Proby.
Lord Claud Hamilton.
Lord Clarence Paget.
Lord Ernest Bruce.
Lord de Ros.
Lord Colville.
Lord Napier.
Lord Kinnaird.
Lord Foley.
Lord Forester.
Lord Bloomfield.
Lord Stanley of Alderley.
Lord Broughton.
Lord St. Leonards.
Lord Lyons.
Lord Belper.
Lord Ebury.
Lord Chelmsford.
Lord Lyveden.
Lord Taunton.
Lord Westbury.
Lord Athlumney.
Lord Romilly (*Master of Rolls*).
Lord Lytton.
Lord Hylton.
Lord Colonsay.
Lord Cairns.
Lord Hatherley.
Lord Dufferin and Clandeboye.
Lord Augustus Loftus.
Sir John S. Pakington, bart.
Sir Stafford H. Northcote, bart.
Sir George Grey, bart.
Sir Thomas F. Fremantle, bart.
Sir William G. Hayter, bart.
Sir David Dundas, bart.
Sir John Trollope, bart.
Sir John Young, bart.
Sir Alex. J. E. Cockburn, bart.
Sir Robert Peel, bart.
Sir William Gibson Craig, bart.
Sir Edward Ryan.
Sir Frederick Pollock.
Sir Henry Lytton Bulwer.
Sir George H. Seymour.
Sir Lawrence Peel.
Sir John McNeill.
Sir John Taylor Coleridge, kt.
Sir William Erle, kt.
Sir James W. Colvile.
Sir William Hutt.
Sir Andrew Buchanan.

Sir James Plaisted Wilde.
Sir Edward V. Williams.
Sir Fitz Roy Kelly.
Sir Richard T. Kindersley.
Sir H. Knight Storks, G.C.B.
Sir William Bovill.
Sir W. R. S. V. Fitzgerald.
Sir John Rolt.
Sir Robert G. Phillimore.
Sir Francis Bond Head.
Sir Colman O'Loghlen.
Sir Joseph Napier, Bart.
Sir James Fergusson, Bart.
Sir Charles Jasper Selwyn.
Hon. Percy E. Herbert.
Hon. William Francis Cowper.
Hon. Edward Pleydell Bouverie.
Hon. Charles Pelham Villiers.
Hon. Henry G. Elliot.
Hon. Henry T. Lowry Corry.
Hon. James A. Stuart Wortley.
Hon. George C. W. Forester.
Hon. Henry B. W. Brand.
John Evelyn Denison.
Holt Mackenzie.
Stephen Lushington.
William Ewart Gladstone.
Thomas Milner Gibson.
Richard More O'Ferrall.
Spencer Horatio Walpole.
Benjamin Disraeli.
Joseph Warner Henley.
Robert Adam C. N. Hamilton.
William Beresford.
Edward Cardwell.
John Parker.
Henry Unwin Addington.
Edward Horsman.
Robert Lowe.
William Monsell.
Frederick Peel.
Jonathan Peel.
Thomas H. S. S. Estcourt.
Charles Bowyer Adderley.
John Robert Mowbray.
John Inglis.
Thomas E. Headlam.
Chichester Samuel Fortescue.
Henry Austin Bruce.
William Nathaniel Massey.
George Joachim Goschen.
Edmund Hammond.
Russell Gurney.
Stephen Cave.
Henry James Baillie.
Colonel J. Wilson Patten.
George Patton.
George Ward Hunt.
Colonel J. E. Taylor.
John Thomas Ball.
H. C. E. Childers.
A. H. Layard.
William Forster.
John Bright.

Privy Council Office, Downing Street, S.W.

Lord Pres. of Council, Earl de Grey and Ripon.
Clerk of the Council, Arthur Helps, Esq., D.C.L.
Deputy Clerk of the Council and Chief Clerk, Edmund Stephen Harrison, Esq.
Senior Clerks, Charles George Villiers Bayly and Herbert Manson Suff, Esqrs.

Registrar of the Privy Council, Henry Reeve, Esq.
Clerk to the Registrar, Robert Lemon, Esq.
Medical Officer, John Simon, Esq., F.R.S.
Clerk for Clergy Returns, Rev. W. Harness, M.A.
Private Sec. to Lord President, B. M. Seton, Esq.

Consists of the whole Peerage of Great Britain and of certain representatives of the Peerages of Scotland and Ireland, but many members of these latter have also English titles which give them seats in the House. For instance, the Duke of Buccleuch sits as Earl of Doncaster, and the Duke of Leinster, as Viscount Leinster. It is under these inferior titles that they will be found in this list, but for convenience of reference such Peers are separately enumerated. Including 13 minors, the assembly contains 4 Princes of the Blood, 2 Archbishops, 21 Dukes, 17 Marquises, 109 Earls, 22 Viscounts, 24 Bishops (one of whom is also a temporal peer), 219 Barons, 16 Scottish representative Peers elected for each Parliament, 28 Irish representative Peers elected for life, and 4 Irish spiritual Peers, (1 Archbishop and 3 Bishops), who sit in rotation, session by session. There are also 13 ladies who are Peeresses in their own right, and whose titles and names are given at the end of this list.*

* b., signifies born; s., succeeded; m., married; w., widower or widow; M., minor.

PRINCES OF THE BLOOD.

Style, His Royal Highness the Duke of ——. *Addressed as,* Sir, or more formally, May it please your *Creat.* Royal Highness.

1841 Albert Edward Prince of Wales, Duke of Cornwall, &c., b. 1841, m.
1866 Alfred Ernest Albert, Duke of Edinburgh, Earl of Kent, &c., b. 1844.
1799 George Fred. A.C.E.A. Duke of Cumberland (Ex-King of Hanover), &c., b. 1819, s. 1851, m.
1801 George William Frederick Charles, Duke of Cambridge, &c., b. 1819, s. 1850.

ARCHBISHOPS.—*Style,* The Most Rev. His Grace the Lord Archbishop of ——. *Addressed as,* My Lord Archbishop, or, Your Grace.

1868 *Canterbury.* Rt. Hon. Archibald Campbell Tait, *D.C.L.,* formerly Bishop of London.
1862 *York,* William Thomson, *D.D.,* formerly Bishop of Gloucester and Bristol.

DUKES.—*Style,* His Grace the Duke of——, *Addressed as,* My Lord Duke, or Your Grace. The eldest sons of Dukes and Marquises take, by courtesy, their father's second title. The other sons and the daughters are styled Lord Edward, Lady Caroline, &c.

			Eldest Sons.
1483	Norfolk	H. Fitzalan-Howard, Earl Marshal, b. 1847, s. 1860	E. Arundel & Surrey
1547	Somerset	Ed. Adolphus Seymour, K.G. b. 1804, s. 1855, m.	E. St. Maur
1675	Richmond	Chas. H. Gordon-Lennox, K.G. (Scotch Duke, Lennox) b. 1818, s. 1860, m.	E. March
1675	Grafton	William Henry Fitzroy, b. 1819, s. 1863; m.	E. Euston
1682	Beaufort	H. C. Fitzroy Somerset, K.G., b. 1824, s. 1853; m.	M. Worcester
1684	St. Albans	W. A. A. de Vere Beauclerc, b. 1840, s. 1849; m.	E. Burford
1694	Leeds	Geo. Godolphin Osborne, (Scotch Viscount, Dunblane), b. 1802, s. 1859; w.	M. Carmarthen
1694	Bedford	William Russell, b. 1809, s. 1861	M. Tavistock
1694	Devonshire	William Cavendish, K.G., b. 1808, s. 1858; w.	M. Hartington
1702	Marlborough	J. W. Spencer-Churchill, b. 1822, s. 1857; m.	M. Blandford
1703	Rutland	Charles Cecil J. Manners, K.G., b. 1815, s. 1857.	M. Granby
1711	Brandon	Wm. Alex. L. S. Douglas-Hamilton, (Scotch Duke, Hamilton,) b. 1845, s. 1863.	M. Douglas
1716	Portland	W. J. Cavendish Bentinck-Scott, b. 1800, s. 1854.	M. Titchfield
1719	Manchester	William Drogo Montagu, b. 1823, s. 1855, m. ...	V. Mandeville
1756	Newcastle	H. P. A. Pelham-Clinton, b. 1834, s. 1864, m. ...	E. Lincoln
1766	Northumberland	Algernon George Percy, b. 1810, s. 1867, m.	E. Percy
1814	Wellington	Arthur R. Wellesley, (Irish Earl, Mornington), b. 1807, s. 1852, m.	M. Douro
1822	Buckingham & Chandos	Richard P. C. T. N. B. C. Grenville, (Irish Earl, Nugent), b. 1823, s. 1861, m.	M. Chandos
1833	Sutherland	George Gran. W. Suth. Leveson-Gower, K.G. (Scotch Earl, Sutherland), b. 1828, s. 1861, m.	M. Stafford
1833	Cleveland	Harry Geo. Powlett, K.G., b. 1803, s. 1864, m. .	E. Darlington
1868	Abercorn	James Hamilton, K.G., (Scotch Earl, Abercorn; Irish Viscount, Strabane), b. 1811, s. 1818, m...	V. Hamilton

MARQUISES.—*Style,* The Most Hon. the Marquis of —— *Addressed as,* My Lord Marquis.

1551	Winchester	John Paulet, b. 1801, s. 1843, m.	E. Wiltshire
1784	Lansdowne	Henry C. K. P. Fitzmaurice, (Irish Earl, Kerry and Shelburne), b. 1845, s. 1866	E. Shelburne
1786	Townshend	John Villiers S. Townshend, b. 1831, s. 1863, m.	V. Raynham
1789	Salisbury	Robert Arthur T. Cecil, b. 1830, s. 1868, m.	V. Cranborne
1789	Bath	John Alexander Thynne, b. 1831, s. 1837, m. ...	V. Weymouth
1793	Hertford	Rich. Seymour-Conway, K.G., (Irish Baron, Conway), b. 1800, s. 1842	E. Yarmouth
1796	Bute	John Patrick Crichton-Stuart, (Scotch Earl, Dumfries), b. 1847, s. 1848	E. Windsor
1801	Exeter	William Alleyne Cecil, b. 1825, s. 1867, m.	L. Burghley
1812	Northampton	Charles Douglas Compton, b. 1816, s. 1851, w.	E. Compton
1812	Camden	John Charles Pratt, b. 1840, s. 1866, m.	E. Brecknock
1815	Anglesey	Henry Paget, b. 1797, s. 1854, m.	E. Uxbridge
1815	Cholmondeley	Geo. Horatio Cholmondeley, (Irish Viscount, Cholmondeley), b. 1792, s. 1827, m.	E. Rocksavage
1821	Ailesbury	G. W. F. Brudenell-Bruce, K.G., b. 1804, s. 1856, m.	E. Bruce
1826	Bristol	Frederick Wm. J. Hervey, b. 1834, s. 1864, m....	E. Jermyn

1831	Ailsa	Archibald Kennedy, *K.T.*, *(Scotch Earl, Cassillis),* b. 1816, s. 1846, m.	E. Cassillis
1831	Westminster	Richard Grosvenor, *K.G.*, b. 1795, s. 1845, m.	E. Grosvenor
1838	Normanby	G.A.C.Phipps,*(I.Baron,Mulgrave)b.*1819,s. 1863.m.	E. Mulgrave

EARLS.—*Style*, The Right Hon. the Earl of —— *Addressed as*, My Lord. The eldest sons of Earls take, by courtesy, their father's second title, but the younger sons are only styled the Hon. George, &c. The daughters, however, like those of Dukes and Marquises, are called Lady Isabella, &c.

1442	Shrewsbury and Talbot..	Charles J. C. Talbot, *(Irish Earl, Waterford),* b. 1830, s. 1868, m.	V. Ingestre
1485	Derby	Edw. G. Stanley, *K.G.*, b. 1799, s. 1851, m. ...	L. Stanley
1529	Huntingdon	Fran. Theo. Hen. Hastings, b. 1808, s. 1828, w.	L. Hastings
1551	Pembroke & Montgomery	1605 Geo. Robt. Chas. Herbert, b. 1850, s. 1862,*M.*	L. Herbert
1553	Devon	Wm. Reginald Courtenay, b. 1807, s. 1859, w.	L. Courtenay
1603	Suffolk & Berkshire	Charles John Howard, b. 1804, s. 1851, m.	V. Andover
1622	Denbigh	Rudolph W. Basil Feilding, *(Irish Earl, Desmond),* b. 1823, s. 1865, m.	V. Feilding
1624	Westmorland	Francis Wm. Henry Fane, b. 1825, s. 1859, m. .	L. Burghersh
1626	Lindsey	Geo. A. F. Albemarle Bertie, b. 1814, s. 1818 ...	L. Bertie
1628	Stamford & Warrington	George Harry Grey, b. 1827, s. 1845, m.	L. Grey of Groby
1628	Winchilsea & Nottingham	Geo. James Finch-Hatton, b. 1815, s. 1858, m. .	V. Maidstone
1628	Chesterfield	Geo. P. C. A. Stanhope, b. 1831, s. 1866	L. Stanhope
1660	Sandwich	John William Montagu, b. 1811, s. 1818, m......	V. Hinchingbrook
1661	Essex	Arthur Algernon Capel, b. 1803, s. 1839, m ...	V. Malden
1661	Carlisle	Rev. William George Howard, b. 1808, s. 1864.	V. Morpeth
1662	Doncaster	W. F. Mont.-Douglas-Scott, *K.G.*, *(Scotch Duke, Buccleuch & Queensberry.)* b. 1806, s. 1819, m.	E. Dalkeith
1672	Shaftesbury	A. Ashley-Cooper, *K.G.*, b. 1801, s. 1851, m. ...	L. Ashley
1679	Berkeley	[*Title not claimed*].	V. Dursley
1682	Abingdon	Montagu Bertie, b. 1808, s. 1854, w.	L. Norreys
1690	Scarborough	Richard George Lumley, *(Irish Viscount, Lumley),* b. 1813, s. 1856, m.	V. Lumley
1696	Albemarle	George Thomas Keppel, b. 1799, s. 1851, m. ...	V. Bury
1697	Coventry	George William Coventry, b. 1838, s. 1843, m. .	V. Deerhurst
1697	Jersey	Victor A. Geo. Child-Villiers, *(Irish Viscount, Grandison),* b. 1845, s. 1859	V. Villiers
1706	Poulett	William Henry Poulett, b. 1827, s. 1864, m......	V. Hinton
1711	Ferrers	Sewallis Edward Shirley, b. 1847, s. 1859	V. Tamworth
1711	Dartmouth	William Walter Legge, b. 1823, s. 1853, m.	V. Lewisham
1714	Tankerville	Charles Bennet, b. 1810, s. 1859, m.	L. Ossulston
1714	Aylesford	Heneage Finch, b. 1824, s. 1859, m.	L. Guernsey
1718	Cowper	F. T. De Grey Cowper, *K.G.*, b. 1834, s. 1856..	V. Fordwich
1718	Stanhope	Philip Henry Stanhope, b. 1805, s. 1855, m. ...	V. Mahon
1721	Macclesfield	Thos. Augustus W. Parker, b. 1811, s. 1850, m.	V. Parker
1722	Graham	Jas. Graham, *K.T.*, *(Scotch Duke, Montrose),* b. 1799, s. 1836, m.	M. Graham
1729	Waldegrave	William Fred. Waldegrave, b. 1851, s. 1859,*M.*	V. Chewton
1730	Ashburnham	Bertram Ashburnham, b. 1797, s. 1830, m.	V. St. Asaph
1742	Harrington	Chas. Wyndham Stanhope, b. 1809. s. 1866, m.	V. Petersham
1743	Portsmouth	Isaac Newton Wallop, b. 1825, s. 1854, m.	V. Lymington
1746	Brooke & Warwick	George Guy Greville, b. 1818, s. 1853, m. :	L. Brooke
1746	Buckinghamshire	Rev. Aug. Edward Hobart, b. 1793. s. 1849. m.	L. Hobart
1746	Fitzwilliam	Wm. Thos. S. Wentworth-Fitzwilliam, *K.G.*, *(Irish Earl, Fitzwilliam),* b. 1815, s. 1857, m.	V. Milton
1752	Guildford	Dudley Francis North, b. 1851, s. 1861, *M.*	L. North
1754	Hardwicke	Charles Philip Yorke, b. 1799, s. 1834, m.	V. Royston
1756	Ilchester	Hen. E. Fox-Strangeways, b. 1847, s. 1865, m.	V. Stavordale
1761	De La Warr	George J. Sackville-West, b. 1791, s. 1795, m...	L. West
1765	Radnor	William Pleydell Bouverie, b. 1779, s. 1828, w.	V. Folkestone
1765	Spencer,	John Poyntz Spencer, *K.G.*, b. 1835, s. 1857, m.	V. Althorp
1772	Bathurst	William Lennox Bathurst, b. 1791, s. 1866	L. Apsley
1772	Hillsborough	Arthur W. B. T. S. R. Hill, *(Irish Marquis, Downshire.)* b. 1844, s. 1868	E. Hillsborough
1776	Clarendon	G.W.F. Villiers, *K.G.*, *G.C.B.*, b.1800,s.1838, m.	L. Hyde
1776	Mansfield	Wm. David Murray, *K.T.*, *(Scotch Viscount, Stormont),* b. 1800, s. 1840, m.	V. Stormont
1784	Abergavenny	William Nevill, b. 1826, s. 1868, m.	V. Nevill
1786	Strange	John James H. H. Stewart-Murray, *(Scotch Duke, Atholc),* b. 1840, s. 1864, m.	M. Tullibardine
1789	Mount-Edgcumbe	William Henry Edgcumbe, b. 1832, s. 1861, m.	V. Valletort
1789	Fortescue	Hugh Fortescue, b. 1818, s. 1861, w.	V. Ebrington
1793	Carnarvon	Henry Howard M. Herbert, b. 1831, s. 1849, m.	L. Porchester
1800	Cadogan	Henry Charles Cadogan, b. 1812, s. 1864, m. ...	V. Chelsea
1800	Malmesbury	James H. Harris, *G.C.B.*, b. 1807, s. 1841, m. ...	V. Fitzharris
1801	Rosslyn	F. R. St. Clair-Erskine, b. 1833, s. 1866, m.	L. Loughborough

1801	*Craven*	George Grimston Craven, *b.* 1841, *s.* 1866, *m.*...	V. Uffington
1801	*Onslow*	Arthur George Onslow, *b.* 1777, *s.* 1827, *m.* ...	V. Cranley
1801	*Romney*	Charles Marsham, *b.* 1808, *s.* 1845, *w.*	V. Marsham
1801	*Chichester*	Henry Thomas Pelham, *b.* 1804, *s.* 1826, *w.* ...	L. Pelham
1801	*Wilton*	Thomas Egerton, *b.* 1799, *s.* 1814, *m.*	V. Grey de Wilton
1804	*Powis*	E. J. Herbert, *(Irish Baron, Clive), b.* 1818, *s.* 1848	V. Clive
1805	*Nelson*	Horatio Nelson, *b.* 1823, *s.* 1835, *m.*	V. Trafalgar
1806	*Manvers*	Sydney Wm. H. Pierrepont, *b.* 1825, *s.* 1860, *m.*	V. Newark
1806	*Orford*	Horatio Walpole, *b.* 1813, *s.* 1858, *m.*	L. Walpole
1806	*Grey*	Henry Grey, *K.G., b.* 1802, *s.* 1845, *m.*	V. Howick
1807	*Lonsdale*	William Lowther, *b.* 1787, *s.* 1844	V. Lowther
1809	*Harrowby*	Dudley Ryder, *K.G., b.* 1798, *s.* 1823, *w.*	V. Sandon
1812	*Harewood*	Henry Thynne Lascelles, *b.* 1824, *s.* 1857, *m.* ...	V. Lascelles
1813	*Minto*	W. H. E. M. Kynynmound, *b.* 1814, *s.* 1859, *m.*	V. Melgund
1814	*Cathcart*	Alan Frederick Cathcart, *(Scotch Baron, Cathcart), b.* 1828, *s.* 1859, *m.*	L. Greenock
1815	*Verulam*	James W. Grimston, *(Irish Viscount, Grimston; Scotch Baron, Forrester), b.* 1809, *s.* 1845, *m.*.	V. Grimston
1815	*Brownlow*	Adelbert Wellington Cust, *b.* 1844, *s.* 1867	V. Alford
1815	*St. Germans*	E. Granville Eliot, *G.C.B., b.* 1798, *s.* 1845, *w..*	Lord Eliot
1815	*Morley*	Albert Edmund Parker, *b.* 1843, *s.* 1864	V. Boringdon
1815	*Bradford*	Orlando Geo. C. Bridgeman, *b.* 1819, *s.* 1865, *m.*	V. Newport
1815	*Beauchamp*	Frederick Lygon, *b.* 1830, *s.* 1866	V. Elmley
1816	*De Grey & Ripon,* 1833.	George Fred. S. Robinson, *b.* 1827, *s.* 1859, *m.* .	V. Goderich
1821	*Eldon*	John Scott, *b.* 1845, *s.* 1854	V. Encombe
1821	*Howe*	R.W.P.Curzon-Howe, *G.C.H., b.*1796, *s.*1820, *m.*	V. Curzon
1821	*Somers*	Charles S. Somers-Cocks, *b.* 1819, *s.* 1852, *m...*	V. Eastnor
1821	*Stradbroke*	John Edw. Cornwallis Rous, *b.* 1794, *s.* 1827, *m.*	V. Dunwich
1823	*Vane*	G. H. R. C. W. Vane-Tempest, *b.* 1821, *s.*1854, *m.*	V. Seaham
1826	*Amherst*	William Pitt Amherst, *b.* 1805, *s.* 1857, *m.*	V. Holmesdale
1827	*Cawdor*	J. F. Vaughan Campbell, *b.* 1817, *s.* 1860, *m.* ..	V. Emlyn
1831	*Munster*	William Geo. Fitzclarence, *b.* 1824, *s.* 1842, *m.*	V. Fitzclarence
1831	*Camperdown*	R. A. P. H. Duncan Haldane, *b.* 1841, *s.* 1867 ..	V. Duncan
1831	*Lichfield*	Thomas George Anson, *b.* 1825, *s.* 1854, *m.*	V. Anson
1833	*Durham*	Geo. F. D'Arcy Lambton, *b.* 1828, *s.* 1840, *m...*	V. Lambton
1833	*Granville*	G. G. Leveson-Gower, *K.G., b.* 1815, *s.*1846, *m.*	L. Leveson
1837	*Effingham*	Henry Howard, *b.* 1806, *s.* 1845, *m.*	L. Howard.
1837	*Ducie*	Henry John Moreton, *b.* 1827, *s.* 1853, *m.*	L. Moreton
1837	*Yarborough*	Charles Anderson-Pelham, *b.* 1835, *s.* 1862, *m.* .	L. Worsley
1837	*Innes*	Jas. Hen. Rob. Innes-Ker, *K.T., (Scotch Duke, Roxburghe), b.* 1816, *s.* 1823, *m.*	M. Bowmont
1837	*Leicester*	Thomas William Coke, *b.* 1822, *s.* 1842, *m......*	V. Coke
1838	*Lovelace*	William King-Noel, *b.* 1805, first Earl, *m.*	V. Ockham
1838	*Zetland*.	Thomas Dundas, *K.T., b.* 1795, *s.* 1839, *w.* ...	L. Dundas
1841	*Gainsborough*	Charles George Noel, *b.* 1818, *s.* 1866, *w.*	V. Campden
1844	*Ellenborough*	Edward Law, *G.C.B., b.* 1790, *s.* 1818, *m.*	V. Southam
1846	*Ellesmere*	Francis C. Granville Egerton, *b.* 1847, *s.* 1862 ..	V. Brackley
1847	*Strafford*	George Stevens Byng, *b.* 1806, *s.* 1860, *m.*	V. Enfield
1850	*Cottenham*	William John Pepys, *b.* 1825, *s.* 1863	V. Crowhurst
1857	*Cowley*	Henry R. C. Wellesley, *K.G., G.C.B., b.* 1804, first Earl, *m.*	V. Dangan
1859	*Winton*	Arch. W. Montgomerie, *S.E., b.* 1841, *s.* 1861, *m.*	L. Montgomerie
1860	*Dudley*	William Ward, *b.* 1817, first Earl, *m.*	V. Ednam.
1861	*Russell*	John Russell, *K.G., b.* 1792, first Earl, *m.*	V. Amberley
1866	*Kimberley*	John Wodehouse, *b.* 1826, first Earl, *m.*	L. Wodehouse
1866	*Dartrey*	Richard Dawson, *K.S.P., (Irish Baron, Cremorne), b.* 1817, *s.* 1827, *m.*	L. Cremorne.
1868	*Feversham*	William E. Duncombe, *b.* 1829, first Earl, *m.*	

VISCOUNTS.—*Style,* The Right Hon. the Viscount ——. *Addressed as,* My Lord. The eldest sons of Viscounts and Barons have no distinctive title; they, as well as the younger and the female branches of the family, are styled the Hon. Robert, Hon. Mary, &c.

1550	*Hereford*	Robert Devereux, *b.* 1843, *s.* 1855, *m.*
1712	*Bolingbroke & St. John,*	1716 Henry St. John, *b.* 1820, *s.* 1851.
1720	*Falmouth*	Evelyn Boscawen, *b.* 1819, *s.* 1852, *m.*
1721	*Torrington*	George Byng, *b.* 1812, *s.* 1831, *m.*
1747	*Leinster*	Augustus Fred. Fitzgerald, *(Irish Duke, Leinster), b.* 1791, *s.* 1804, *w.*
1789	*Sydney*	John Robert Townshend, *G.C.B., b.* 1805, *s.* 1831, *m.*
1795	*Hood*	Francis Wheler Hood, *(Irish Baron, Hood), b.* 1838, *s.* 1846, *m.*
1801	*St. Vincent*	Carnegie Robert John Jervis, *b.* 1825, *s.* 1859, *m.*
1802	*Melville*	Henry Dundas, *G.C.B., b.* 1801, *s.* 1851.
1805	*Sidmouth*	William Wells Addington, *b.* 1824, *s.* 1864, *m.*
1814	*Gordon*	George Hamilton Gordon, *(Scotch Earl, Aberdeen), b.* 1841, *s.* 1864.
1816	*Exmouth*	Edward Pellew, *b.* 1811, *s.* 1833, *m.*
1821	*Hutchinson*	J. L. G. Hely-Hutchinson, *(IrishEarl,Donoughmore), b.* 1848, *s.* 1866, *M.*
1823	*Clancarty*	William T. Le Poer-Trench, *(Irish Earl, Clancarty), b.* 1803, *s.* 1837, *m.*

1826	Combermere	Wellington H. Stapleton-Cotton, *b.* 1818, *s.* 1865, *m.*
1835	Canterbury	Charles John Manners-Sutton, *b.* 1812, *s.* 1845.
1842	Hill	Rowland Hill, *b.* 1800, *s.* 1842, *m.*
1846	Hardinge	Charles Stewart Hardinge, *b.* 1822, *s.* 1856, *w.*
1849	Gough	Hugh Gough, *K.S.P., G.C.B., K.S.I., b.* 1779, first Viscount, *w*
1852	Stratford de Redcliffe	Stratford Canning, *G.C.B., b.* 1788, first Viscount, *m.*
1857	Eversley	Charles Shaw-Lefevre, *b.* 1794, first Viscount, *w.*
1866	Halifax	Charles Wood, *G.C.B., b.* 1800, first Viscount, *m.*

BISHOPS.—*Style,* The Right Rev. the Lord Bishop of ——. *Addressed as,* My Lord.

Appointment.		
1868	London	John Jackson, *D.D. Translated from Lincoln.*
1861	Durham	Charles Baring, *D.D. Translated from Gloucester and Bristol.*
1827	Winchester	Richard Sumner, *D.D. Translated from Llandaff.*
1837	Exeter	Henry Philpotts, *D.D.*
1840	St. David's	Connop Thirlwall, *D.D.*
1842	Chichester	Ashhurst Turner Gilbert, *D.D.*
1845	Oxford	Samuel Wilberforce, *D.D.*
1846	St. Asaph	Thomas Vowler Short, *D.D. Translated from Sodor and Man.*
1848	Manchester	James Prince Lee, *D.D.*
1849	Llandaff	Alfred Ollivant, *D.D.*
1854	Salisbury	Walter Kerr Hamilton, *D.D.*
1854	Bath and Wells	Rt. Hon. R.J. Eden (Ld. Auckland), *D.D. Translated from Sodor and Man.*
1857	Ripon	Robert Bickersteth, *D.D.*
1857	Norwich	Hon. John Thomas Pelham, *D.D.*
1859	Bangor	James Colquhoun Campbell, *D.D.*
1860	Carlisle	Hon. Samuel Waldegrave, *D.D.*
1861	Worcester	Henry Philpott, *D.D.*
1863	Gloucester and Bristol.	Charles John Ellicott, *D.D.*
1864	Ely	Edward Harold Browne, *D.D.*
1865	Chester	William Jacobson, *D.D.*
1867	Rochester	Thomas Legh Claughton, *D.D.*
1868	Lichfield	George Augustus Selwyn, *D.D.*
1868	Hereford	James Atlay, *D.D.*
1868	Peterborough	William Cotton Magee, *D.D.*
1868	Lincoln	Christopher Wordsworth, *D.D.* (*without seat*).

Creat.   BARONS.—*Style,* The Right Hon. Lord ——.   *Addressed as,* My Lord.

1264	De Ros	William L. L. Fitzgerald-de-Ros, *b.* 1797, *s.* 1839, *m.*
1290	Hastings	Jacob Henry Delaval Astley, *b.* 1822, *s.* 1859, *m.*
1295	Fitzwalter	Brook William Bridges, *b.* 1801, title called out of abeyance, 1868, *m.*
1296	Audley	George Edward Thicknesse-Touchet, *b.* 1817, *s.* 1837, *w.*
1299	Clinton	Charles Henry Rolle Trefusis, *b.* 1834, *s.* 1866, *m.*
1309	Beaumont	Henry Stapleton, *b.* 1848, *s.* 1858, *M.*
1313	Willoughby D'Eresby	Alberic Drummond-Willoughby, *b.* 1821, *s.* 1865.
1321	Dacre	Thomas Crosbie William Brand-Trevor, *b.* 1808, *s.* 1853, *m.*
1383	Camoys	Thomas Stonor, *b.* 1797, title called out of abeyance, 1839, *m.*
1448	Stourton	Charles Stourton, *b.* 1802, *s.* 1846, *m.*
1455	Berners	Henry William Wilson, *b.* 1797, *s.* 1851, *m.*
1492	Willoughby de Broke	Henry Verney, *b.* 1844, *s.* 1862, *m.*
1509	Conyers	Sackville George Lane-Fox, *b.* 1827, *s.* 1859, *m.*
1523	Vaux of Harrowden	George Mostyn, *b.* 1804, title called out of abeyance, 1838, *m.*
1529	Wentworth	Ralph Gordon Noel Noel-Milbanke, *b.* 1839, *s.* 1862.
1547	Seymour	Edw. Adolphus F. Seymour, *b.* 1835, called to his father's barony, 1863.
1558	St. John of Bletshoe	St. Andrew Beauchamp St. John, *b.* 1811, *s.* 1817, *m.*
1597	Howard de Walden, & Seaford,	1826, Frederick George Ellis, *b.* 1830, *s.* 1868.
1603	Petre	William Bernard Petre, *b.* 1817, *s.* 1850, *m.*
1603	Saye and Sele	Rev. Frederick Twisleton-Wykeham-Fiennes, *b.* 1799, *s.* 1847, *m.*
1605	Arundell of Wardour	John Francis Arundell, *b.* 1831, *s.* 1862, *m.*
1608	Clifton	John Stuart Bligh, (*Irish Earl, Darnley*), *b.* 1827, *s.* 1835, *m.*
1615	Dormer	Joseph Thaddæus Dormer, *b.* 1790, *s.* 1826, *m.*
1616	Teynham	George Henry Roper-Curzon, *b.* 1798, *s.* 1842, *m.*
1640	Stafford	Henry Valentine Stafford Jerningham, *b.* 1802, *s.* 1851, *m.*
1643	Byron	George Anson Byron, *b.* 1818, *s.* 1868, *M.*
1672	Clifford of Chudleigh	Charles Hugh Clifford, *b.* 1819, *s.* 1858, *m.*
1711	Boyle	R. E. St. L. Boyle, *K.P.* (*Irish Earl, Cork & Orrery*), *b.* 1829, *s.* 1856, *m.*
1711	Hay	George Hay, (*Scotch Earl, Kinnoul*), *b.* 1827, *s.* 1866, *m.*
1711	Middleton	Henry Willoughby, *b.* 1817, *s.* 1856, *m.*
1728	Monson	William John Monson, *b.* 1829, *s.* 1862.
1749	Ponsonby	Geo. John B. Ponsonby, (*Irish Earl, Bessborough*), *b.* 1809, *s.* 1847, *m.*
1760	Sondes	George John Milles, *b.* 1794, *s.* 1836, *m.*
1761	Scarsdale	Rev. Alfred Nathaniel Holden Curzon, *b.* 1831, *s.* 1856, *m.*
1761	Boston	George Ives Irby, *b.* 1802, *s.* 1856, *m.*
1762	Lovell and Holland	George James Perceval, (*Irish Earl, Egmont,*) *b.* 1794, *s.* 1840, *m.*
1762	Vernon	Augustus Henry Vernon, *b.* 1829, *s.* 1866, *m.*
1765	Digby	Edward St. Vincent Digby, (*Irish Baron, Digby*), *b.* 1809, *s.* 1856, *m.*
1766	Sundridge & Hamilton,	1776, G. D. Campbell, *K.T.,* (*Scotch Duke, Argyll*), *b.* 1823, *s.* 1847, *m.*

1766	Hawke	Edward William Harvey Hawke, *b.* 1799, *s.* 1824, *m.*
1776	Foley	Thomas Henry Foley, *b.* 1808, *s.* 1833, *m.*
1780	Dynevor	George Rice Rice-Trevor, *b.* 1795, *s.* 1852, *m.*
1780	Walsingham	Thomas de Grey, *b.* 1804, *s.* 1839, *m.*
1780	Bagot	William Bagot, *b.* 1811, *s.* 1856, *m.*
1780	Southampton	Charles Fitzroy, *b.* 1804, *s.* 1810, *m.*
1782	Grantley	Fletcher Norton, *b.* 1798, *s.* 1822, *m.*
1782	Rodney	George Brydges H. D. Rodney, *b.* 1857, *s.* 1864, *M.*
1784	Berwick	William Noel Hill, *b.* 1802, *s.* 1861.
1784	Sherborne	James Henry Legge Dutton, *b.* 1804, *s.* 1862, *m.*
1786	Tyrone	J. H. de la Poer Beresford, *K.P.* (*Irish Marquis, Waterford*), *b.* 1844, *s.* 1866.
1786	Carleton	Richard Boyle, (*Irish Earl, Shannon*), *b.* 1809, *s.* 1842, *m.*
1786	Suffield	Charles Harbord, *b.* 1830, *s.* 1853, *m.*
1786	Dorchester	Guy Carleton, *b.* 1811, *s.* 1826, *w.*
1788	Kenyon	Lloyd Kenyon, *b.* 1805, *s.* 1855, *m.*
1788	Braybrooke	Charles Cornwallis Neville, *b.* 1823, *s.* 1861, *m.*
1790	Fisherwick	G.H.Chichester, *K.P.*, *G.C.H.* (*Irish Marquis, Donegall*), *b.* 1798, *s.* 1844, *m.*
1790	Gage	Henry Hall Gage, (*Irish Viscount, Gage*), *b.* 1791, *s.* 1808, *w.*
1792	Thurlow	Edward Thos. Hovell-Thurlow, *b.* 1837, *s.* 1857.
1793	Auckland	Rt. Rev. R. J. Eden, Bishop of Bath & Wells, (*Irish Baron, Auckland*), *b.* 1799, *s.* 1849, *m.*
1794	Lyttelton	George Wm. Lyttelton, (*Irish Baron, Westcote*), *b.* 1817, *s.* 1837, *w.*
1794	Mendip	H. G. Agar-Ellis, (*Irish Viscount, Clifden*), *b.* 1863, *s.* 1866, *M.*
1796	Stuart of Castle Stuart	Archibald George Stuart, (*Scotch Earl, Moray*,) *b.* 1810, *s.* 1867.
1796	Stewart of Garlies	Randolph Stewart, (*Scotch Earl, Galloway*), *b.* 1800, *s.* 1834, *m.*
1796	Saltersford	Jas. Geo. H. Stopford, (*Irish Earl, Courtown*), *b.* 1823, *s.* 1858, *m.*
1796	Brodrick	Very Rev. W.J.Brodrick, (*Irish Viscount, Midleton*), *b.* 1798, *s.* 1863, *m.*
1796	Calthorpe	George Stephens Gough, *b.* 1815, *s.* 1868, *m.*
1797	Carington	Charles Robert Carington, (*Irish Baron, Carington*), *b.* 1843, *s.* 1868.
1797	Bolton	William Henry Orde-Powlett, *b.* 1818, *s.* 1850, *m.*
1797	Northwick	George Rushout, *b.* 1811, *s.* 1859.
1797	Lilford	Thomas Lyttelton Powys, *b.* 1833, *s.* 1861, *m.*
1797	Ribblesdale	Thomas Lister, *b.* 1828, *s.* 1832, *m.*
1801	Moore	Hen. Fras. S. Moore, (*Irish Marquis, Drogheda*), *b.* 1825, *s.* 1837, *m.*
1801	Loftus	John Henry W. G. Loftus, (*Irish Marquis, Ely*), *b.* 1849, *s.* 1857, *m.*
1801	Carysfort	Granville Leveson Proby, (*Irish Earl, Carysfort*), *b.* 1825, *s.* 1868, *m.*
1801	Abercromby	George Ralph Campbell Abercromby, *b.* 1838, *s.* 1852, *m.*
1802	Redesdale	John Thomas Freeman-Mitford, *b.* 1805, *s.* 1830.
1802	Rivers	Horace Pitt-Rivers, *b.* 1814, *s.* 1867, *m.*
1802	Sandys	Augustus Fred. Arthur Sandys, *b.* 1840, *s.* 1863.
1802	Sheffield	G. A. Fred.Charles Holroyd, (*Irish Earl, Sheffield*,) *b.* 1802, *s.* 1821, *m.*
1806	Erskine	Thomas Americus Erskine, *b.* 1802, *s.* 1855, *w.*
1806	Mont-Eagle	George John Browne, (*Irish Marquis, Sligo*), *b.* 1820, *s.* 1845, *w.*
1806	Granard	Geo. A. H. Forbes, *K.P.*, (*Irish Earl, Granard*), *b.* 1833, *s.* 1837, *m.*
1806	Crewe	Hungerford Crewe, *b.* 1812, *s.* 1835.
1806	Gardner	Alan Legge Gardner, (*Irish Baron, Gardner*) *b.*1810, *s.* 1815, *m.*
1807	Manners	John Thomas Manners, *b.* 1852, *s.* 1864, *M.*
1809	Hopetoun	John Alexander Hope, (*Scotch Earl, Hopetoun*,) *b.* 1831, *s.* 1843, *m.*
1814	Stewart	F. W. R. Stewart,*K.P.*, (*Irish Marquis, Londonderry*,) *b.* 1805, *s.* 1854, *m.*
1815	Meldrum	Charles Gordon, (*Scotch Marquis, Huntly*), *b.* 1847, *s.* 1863.
1815	Ross	James Carr-Boyle, (*Scotch Earl, Glasgow*,) *b.* 1792, *s.* 1843, *m.*
1815	Grinstead	Wm. Willoughby Cole, (*Irish Earl, Enniskillen*,) *b.* 1807, *s.* 1840, *m.*
1815	Foxford	William Hale John C. Pery, (*Irish Earl, Limerick*), *b.* 1840, *s.* 1866, *m.*
1815	Churchill	Francis George Spencer, *b.* 1802, *s.* 1845, *m.*
1815	Harris	George Francis Robert Harris, *K.S.I.*, *b.* 1810, *s.* 1845, *w.*
1817	Colchester	Reginald Charles Edward Abbot, *b.* 1842, *s.* 1867.
1821	Ker	Wm. S. Robt. Kerr, (*Scotch Marquis, Lothian*), *b.* 1832, *s.* 1841, *m.*
1821	Minster	Fras. Nath. Conyngham, *K.P.*, *G.C.H.*, (*Irish Marquis, Conyngham*,) *b.* 1797, *s.* 1832, *m.*
1821	Ormonde	Jas. Edw. Wm. T. Butler, (*Irish Marquis, Ormonde*), *b.* 1844, *s.* 1854.
1821	Wemyss	F. W. Charteris-Douglas, (*Scotch Earl, Wemyss*), *b.*1796, *s.* 1853, *m.*
1821	Clanbrassill	Robert Jocelyn, *K.P.*, (*Irish Earl, Roden*,) *b.* 1788, *s.* 1820, *m.*
1821	Kingston	James King, (*Irish Earl, Kingston*,) *b.* 1800, *s.* 1867, *m.*
1821	Silchester	W. L. Pakenham, *K.C.B.*, (*Irish Earl, Longford*), *b.* 1819, *s.* 1860, *m.*
1821	Oriel	Clotworthy J.E. F. Foster-Skeffington, (*Irish Viscount, Massereene and Ferrard*), *b.* 1842, *s.* 1863.
1821	Ravensworth	Henry Thomas Liddell, *b.* 1797, *s.* 1855, *w.*
1821	Delamere	Hugh Cholmondeley, *b.* 1812, *s.* 1855, *m.*
1821	Forester	John George Weld Forester, *b.* 1801, *s.* 1828, *m.*
1821	Rayleigh	John James Strutt, *b.* 1796, *s.* 1836, *m.*
1824	Gifford	Robert Francis Gifford, *b.* 1817, *s.* 1826, *m.*
1825	Penshurst	P.E.A.F.W.S.Smythe, (*Irish Viscount, Strangford*,) *b.* 1825, *s.*1857, *m.*
1826	Somerhill	U. J. De Burgh, *K.P.*, (*Irish Marquis, Clanricarde*), *b.* 1802, *s.* 1808, *m.*
1826	Wigan	James Lindsay, (*Scotch Earl, Crawford & Balcarres*) *b.* 1783, *s.* 1825, *w.*

1826	Ranfurly	Thos. G. H. Stuart Knox, (*Irish Earl, Ranfurly,*) b. 1849, s. 1858, M.
1826	De Tabley	George Warren, b. 1811, s. 1827, m.
1826	Wharncliffe	Edw. Mont. S. G. Stuart-Wortley, b. 1827, s. 1855, m.
1826	Feversham	William Ernest Duncombe, b. 1829, s. 1867, m.
1827	Tenterden	John Henry Abbott, b. 1796, s. 1832.
1827	Plunket	John Span Plunket, b. 1793, s. 1866, m.
1828	Heytesbury	Wm. Henry Ashe àCourt Holmes, b. 1809, s. 1860, m.
1828	Rosebery	Arch. J. Primrose, K.T. (*Scotch Earl, Rosebery,*) b. 1783, s. 1814, m.
1828	Clanwilliam	R. C. F. Meade, G.C.H. (*Irish Earl, Clanwilliam*), b. 1795, s. 1805, w.
1828	Skelmersdale	Edward Bootle-Wilbraham, b. 1837, s. 1853, m.
1829	Wynford	William Samuel Best, b. 1798, s. 1845, m.
1830	Brougham and Vaux	William Brougham, b. 1795, s. 1868, m.
1831	Kilmarnock	William Harry Hay, (*Scotch Earl, Erroll*), b. 1823, s. 1846, m.
1831	Fingall	Arthur James Plunkett, K.P., (*IrishEarl, Fingall,*), b. 1791, s. 1836, m.
1831	Sefton	William Philip Molyneux, (*Irish Earl, Sefton*), b. 1835, s. 1855, m.
1831	Clements	William Sydney Clements, (*Irish Earl, Leitrim*), b. 1806, s. 1854.
1831	Rossie & Kinnaird, 1860	G. W. F. Kinnaird, K.T., (*Scotch Baron, Kinnaird*), b. 1807, s. 1826, m.
1831	Kenlis	Thomas Taylour, K.P., (*Irish Marquis, Headfort*), b. 1787, s. 1829, m.
1831	Chaworth	William Brabazon, b. 1803, s. 1851, m.
1831	Dunmore	Charles Adolphus Murray, (*Scotch Earl, Dunmore,*) b. 1841, s. 1845, m.
1831	Hamilton	R.M.Hamilton,K.T.(*ScotchBaron,Belhaven &Stenton*),b.1793,s.1814, m.
1831	Howden	J. H. Caradoc, G.C.B., K.H., (*Irish Baron, Howden*), b. 1799, s. 1839, w.
1831	Panmure	F.M.Ramsay,K.T.,G.C.B.(ScotchEarl,Dalhousie)b.1801,s.1852&1860, w.
1831	Poltimore	Aug. Fred. Geo. Warwick Bampfylde, b. 1837, s. 1858, m.
1831	Mostyn	Edward Mostyn Lloyd-Mostyn, b. 1795, s. 1854, m.
1831	Templemore	Henry Spencer Chichester, b. 1821, s. 1837, m.
1831	Cloncurry	Edward Lawless, (*Irish Baron, Cloncurry*,) b. 1816, s. 1853, m.
1831	De Saumarez	John St. Vincent Saumarez, b. 1806, s. 1863, .m.
1832	Hunsdon	L. B. Cary, G.C.H., (*Scotch Viscount, Falkland*) b. 1803, s. 1809, m.
1834	Denman	Thomas Denman, b. 1805, s. 1854, m.
1835	Abinger	William Frederick Scarlett, b. 1826, s. 1861, m.
1835	De L'Isle & Dudley	Philip Sidney, b. 1828, s. 1851, m.
1835	Ashburton	Francis Baring, b. 1800, s. 1864, m.
1835	Hatherton	Edward Richard Littleton, b. 1815, s. 1863, m.
1835	Worlingham	Archib. Brabazon S. Acheson, (*Irish Earl, Gosford*), b. 1841, s. 1864.
1836	Stratheden	William F. Campbell, (also *Baron Campbell*), b. 1824, s. 1860 and 1861.
1837	Portman	Edward Berkeley Portman, b. 1799, first Baron, w.
1837	Lovat	Thos. A. Fraser, K.T., (*Scotch Baron, Lovat*), b. 1802, first Baron, m.
1837	Bateman	Wm. Bateman Bateman-Hanbury, b. 1826, s. 1845, m.
1837	Charlemont	James M. Caulfeild, K.P., (*Irish Earl, Charlemont*), b. 1820, s. 1863, m.
1838	Kintore	Francis A. Keith-Falconer, (*Scotch Earl, Kintore*), b. 1828, s. 1844, m.
1838	Lismore	G. P. O'Callaghan, K.P. (*Irish Viscount, Lismore*), b. 1815, s. 1857, m.
1838	Rossmore	Henry Cairns Westenra, (*Irish Viscount, Rossmore*), b. 1851, s. 1860, M.
1838	Carew	Robert Shapland Carew, (*Irish Baron, Carew*), b. 1818, s. 1856, m.
1838	De Mauley	Chas. Frederick Ashley C. Ponsonby, b. 1815, s. 1855, m.
1838	Wrottesley	Arthur Wrottesley, b. 1824, s. 1867, m.
1838	Sudeley	Sudeley Charles G. Hanbury Tracy, b. 1837, s. 1863.
1838	Methuen	Frederick Henry Paul Methuen, b. 1818, s. 1849, m.
1839	Stanley of Alderley	Edward John Stanley, (also *Baron Eddisbury*), b. 1802, s. 1850, m.
1839	Stuart de Decies	Henry Villiers Stuart, b. 1803, first Baron, w.
1839	Leigh	William Henry Leigh, b. 1824, s. 1850, m.
1839	Wenlock	Beilby Richard Lawley, b. 1818, s. 1852, m.
1839	Lurgan	Charles Brownlow, K.P., b. 1831, s. 1847, m.
1839	Monteagle of Brandon	Thomas Spring-Rice, b. 1849, s. 1866, M.
1839	Seaton	James Colborne, b. 1820, s. 1863, w.
1839	Keane	Edw. Arthur Wellington Keane, b. 1815, s. 1844, m.
1841	Oxenfoord	John H. Dalrymple, K.T., (*Scotch Earl, Stair*), b. 1819, s. 1864, m.
1841	Vivian	Charles Crespigny Vivian, b. 1808, s. 1842, m.
1841	Congleton	John Vesey Parnell, b. 1805, s. 1842, m.
1849	Elgin	Victor A. Bruce, (*Scotch Earl, Elgin & Kincardine*) b. 1849, s. 1863, M.
1850	Clandeboye	F. T. Blackwood, K.P., K.C.B., (*I.D., Dufferin*). b. 1826, s. 1841, m.
1850	Londesborough	William Henry Forester Denison, b. 1834, s. 1860, m.
1850	Overstone	Samuel Jones Loyd, b. 1796, first Baron, w.
1850	Truro	Charles Robert Claude Wilde, b. 1816, s. 1855, m.
1851	Broughton	John Cam Hobhouse, G.C.B., b. 1786, first Baron, w.
1851	De Freyne	Charles French, b. 1792, s. 1863, m.
1852	St. Leonards	Edward Burtenshaw Sugden, b. 1781, first Baron, w.
1852	Raglan	Richard Henry Fitzroy Somerset, b. 1817, s. 1855, w.
1856	Aveland	Gilbert Henry Heathcote, b. 1830, s. 1867, m.
1856	Kenmare	Thomas Browne, (*Irish Earl, Kenmare*), b. 1789, s. 1853, w.
1856	Lyons	Richard Bickerton Pemell Lyons, G.C.B., b. 1817, s. 1858.
1856	Belper	Edward Strutt, b. 1801, first Baron, m.
1856	Talbot de Malahide	James Talbot, (*Irish Baron, Talbot de Malahide*), b. 1805, s. 1850, m.
1857	Ebury	Robert Grosvenor, b. 1801, first Baron, m.
1857	Skene	James Duff, K.T., (*Scotch Earl, Fife*), b. 1814, s. 1857, m.

1858	Chesham	William George Cavendish, b. 1815, s. 1863, m.
1858	Chelmsford	Frederic Thesiger, b. 1794, first Baron, m.
1858	Churston	John Yarde-Buller, b. 1799, first Baron, w.
1858	Strathspey	John Chas. Grant-Ogilvie, (Scotch Earl, Seafield), b. 1815, s. 1853, m.
1859	Leconfield	George Wyndham, b. 1787, first Baron, w.
1859	Egerton of Tatton	William Tatton Egerton, b. 1806, first Baron, m.
1859	Tredegar	Charles Morgan Robinson Morgan, b. 1793, first Baron, m.
1859	Lyveden	Robert Vernon Vernon, b. 1800, first Baron, m.
1859	Taunton	Henry Labouchere, b. 1798, first Baron, m.
1861	Westbury	Richard Bethell, b. 1800, first Baron, w.
1861	Fitzhardinge	Francis W. Fitzhardinge Berkeley, b. 1826, s. 1867, m.
1863	Annaly	Henry White, b. 1791, first Baron, m.
1863	Houghton	Richard Monckton Milnes, b. 1809, first Baron, m.
1865	Romilly	John Romilly, b. 1802, first Baron, w.
1865	Northbrook	Thomas George Baring, b. 1826, s. 1866, w.
1866	Barrogill	James Sinclair, (Scotch Earl, Caithness), b. 1821, s. 1855, m.
1866	Clermont	Thomas Fortescue, (Irish Baron, Clermont), b. 1815, s. 1840, m.
1866	Meredyth	Wm. M. Somerville, (Irish Baron, Athlumney), b. 1802, first Baron, m.
1866	Kenry	E. R. W. Wyndham-Quin, K.P., (Irish Earl, Dunraven), b. 1812, s. 1850, w.
1866	Monck	Charles Stanley Monck, (Irish Viscount, Monck), b. 1819, s. 1849, m.
1866	Hartismere	John Henniker-Major, (Irish Baron, Henniker), b. 1801, s. 1832, m.
1866	Lytton	Edward G. E. L. Bulwer-Lytton, b. 1806, first Baron, m.
1866	Hylton	William G. Hylton-Jolliffe, b. 1800, first Baron, m.
1866	Strathnairn	Hugh Henry Rose, G.C.B., K.S.I., b. 1803, first Baron.
1866	Penrhyn	Edward Gordon Douglas-Pennant, b. 1800, first Baron, m.
1867	Brancepeth	G. F. Hamilton-Russell, (Irish Viscount, Boyne), b. 1797, s. 1855, m.
1867	Colonsay	Duncan McNeill, b. 1793, first Baron.
1867	Cairns	Hugh McCalmont Cairns, b. 1819, first Baron, m.
1868	Kesteven	John Trollope, b. 1800, first Baron, m.
1868	Ormathwaite	John Benn-Walsh, b. 1798, first Baron, m.
1868	O'Neill	Rev. William O'Neill, b. 1800, first Baron.
1868	Napier of Magdala	Robert Napier, K.C.B., b. 1810, first Baron, m.
1868	Hatherley	William Pagewood, Lord Chancellor,, first Baron, m.

PEERESSES IN THEIR OWN RIGHT.

Creation.		Title
1840	Cecilia Letitia Underwood, Duchess, w.	Inverness.
1633	Edith Maud Abney Hastings, Countess, b. 1833, w.	Loudoun.
1861	Anne Leveson-Gower, Countess, b. 1829, m.	Cromartie.
1868	Mary Anne Disraeli, Viscountess, m.	Beaconsfield.
1663	Anne Florence Cowper, Baroness, b. 1806, w.	Lucas.
1264	Mary Frances Elizabeth Boscawen, Baroness, b. 1822, m.	Le Despencer.
1299	Sophia Russell, Baroness, b. 1791, w.	De Clifford.
1308	Harriet Anne Curzon, Baroness, b. 1787, w.	De la Zouche.
1529	Harriet Windsor-Clive, Baroness, b. 1797, w.	Windsor.
1554	Susan North, Baroness, b. 1797, m.	North.
1803	Margaret Elphinstone-De Flahault, Baroness, w.	Keith.
1834	Sophia Elizabeth Wykeham, Baroness, b. 1790	Wenman.
1864	Elizabeth Sackville-West, Baroness, b. 1795, m.	Buckhurst.

THE IRISH REPRESENTATIVE PEERS (Two vacant).

Creation.	
1822	George Thomas John Nugent, Marquis (and Earl, 1621) of Westmeath, b. 1785, s. 1814, m.
1781	Stephen Moore, Earl of Mount-Cashell, b. 1792, s. 1822, m.
1785	Henry J. R. Dawson-Damer, Earl of Portarlington, b. 1822, s. 1845, m.
1789	William Richard Annesley, Earl Annesley, b. 1830, s. 1838.
1789	John Crichton, Earl of Erne, K.P., b. 1802, s. 1842, m.
1793	William Howard, Earl of Wicklow, K.P., b. 1788, s. 1818, w.
1795	George Charles Bingham, Earl of Lucan, K.C.B, b. 1800, s. 1839, m.
1797	Somerset Richard Lowry-Corry, Earl of Belmore, b. 1835, s. 1845, m.
1800	Francis Bernard, Earl of Bandon, b. 1810, s. 1856, m.
1816	Richard White, Earl of Bantry, b. 1800, s. 1851, w.
1743	Mervyn Wingfield, Viscount Powerscourt, b. 1836, s. 1844, m.
1776	Thomas Vesey, Viscount de Vesci, b. 1803, s. 1855, m.
1781	James Hewitt, Viscount Lifford, b. 1811, s. 1855, m.
1781	Edward Ward, Viscount Bangor, b. 1827, s. 1837.
1785	Hayes St. Leger, Viscount Doneraile, b. 1818, s. 1854, m.
1793	Cornwallis Maude, Viscount Hawarden, b. 1817, s. 1856, w.
1806	George Frederick Upton, Viscount Templetown, b. 1802, s. 1863, m.
1461	Edward Plunkett, Lord Dunsany, b. 1808, s. 1852, w.
1543	Lucius O'Brien, Lord Inchiquin, b. 1800, s. 1855, m.
1621	Cadwallader Davis Blayney, Lord Blayney, b. 1802, s. 1834.
1789	John Cavendish Browne, Lord Kilmaine, b. 1794, s. 1825, m.
1790	Robert Dillon, Lord Clonbrock, b. 1807, s. 1826, w.
1797	Edward Crofton, Lord Crofton, b. 1806, s. 1817, m.
1800	Eyre Massey, Lord Clarina, b. 1798, s. 1810, m.
1812	Richard Handcock, Lord Castlemaine, b. 1791, s. 1840, m.
1845	Denis St. George Daly, Lord Dunsandle, b. 1810, s. 1847.

SIXTEEN SCOTTISH REPRESENTATIVE PEERS,

ELECTED FOR THE PRESENT PARLIAMENT.

1639 Airlie, Earl of	David Graham-Drummond Ogilvy.
1606 Blantyre, Baron	Charles Stuart.
1455 Caithness, Earl of	James Sinclair.
1604 Colville of Culross, Baron	Charles-John Colville.
1510 Elphinstone, Baron	William-Buller-Fullerton Elphinstone.
1619 Haddington, Earl of	George Baillie-Hamilton.
1605 Home, Earl of	Cospatrick-Alexander Home.
*1619 Kellie, Earl of	Walter Grimby Erskine.
1624 Lauderdale, Earl of	Thomas Maitland.
1458 Morton, Earl of	Sholto-John Douglas.
1656 Orkney, Earl of	Thomas-John-Hamilton Fitz-Maurice.
*1651 Rollo, Baron	John-Rogerson Rollo.
1445 Saltoun, Baron	Alexander Fraser.
1646 Selkirk, Earl of	Dunbar-James Douglas.
1686 Strathallan, Viscount	William-Henry Drummond.
1480 Sinclair, Baron	James St. Claire.
1694 Tweeddale Marquis of	George Hay.

SCOTCH AND IRISH PEERS WHO SIT IN PARLIAMENT UNDER BRITISH TITLES.

Title.	Sit and vote as	Title.	Sit and vote as	Title.	Sit and vote as
Aberdeen, E.	Gordon, B.	Eglinton, E.	Winton, E.	Leitrim, E.	Clements, B.
Argyll, D.	Sundridge, B.	Egmont, E.	Lovell & Holland, B.	Limerick, E.	Foxford, B.
Athole, D.	Strange, B.	Elgin, E.	Elgin, B.	Londonderry, M.	Stewart, B.
Bessborough, E.	Ponsonby, B.	Ely, M.	Loftus, B.	Longford, E.	Silchester, B.
Boyne, V.	Brancepeth, B.	Enniskillen, E.	Grinstead, B.	Lothian, M.	Kerr, B.
Buccleuch, D.	Doncaster, E.	Erroll, E.	Kilmarnock, B.	Massereene, V.	Oriel, B.
Caithness, E.	Barrogill, B.	Falkland, V.	Hunsdon, B.	Meath, E.	Chaworth, B.
Carysfort, E.	Carysfort, B.	Fife, E.	Skene, B.	Midleton, V.	Brodrick, B.
Charlemont, E.	Charlemont, B.	Fingall, E.	Fingall, B.	Monck, V.	Monck, B.
Clancarty, E.	Clancarty, V.	Gage, V.	Gage, B.	Montrose, D.	Graham, E.
Clanricarde, M.	Somerhill, B.	Galloway, E.	StewartofGarlies, B.	Moray, E.	Stuart, B.
Clanwilliam, E.	Clanwilliam, B.			Mornington, E.	Marybro', B.
Clifden, V.	Mendip, B.	Glasgow, E.	Ross, B.	Ormonde, M.	Ormonde, B.
Conyngham, M.	Minster, B.	Gormanston, V.	Gormanston.B.	Ranfurly, E.	Ranfurly, B.
Cork & Orrery, E.	Boyle, B.	Gosford, E.	Worlingham, B.	Roden, E.	Clanbrassill, B.
Courtown, E.	Saltersford, B.	Granard, E.	Granard, B.	Rosebery, E.	Rosebery, B.
Crawford & Balcarres, E.	Wigan, B.	Hamilton, D.	Brandon, D.	Roxburghe, D.	Innes, B.
		Headfort, M.	Kenlis, B.	Seafield, E.	Strathspey, B.
Dalhousie, E.	Panmure, B.	Hopetoun, E.	Hopetoun, B.	Sefton, E.	Sefton, B.
Darnley, E.	Clifton, B.	Huntly, M.	Meldrum, B.	Shannon, E.	Carleton, B.
Donegall, M.	Fisherwick, B.	Kenmare, E.	Kenmare, B.	Sheffield, E.	Sheffield, B.
Donoughmore, E.	Hutchinson, V.	Kingston, E.	Kingston, B.	Sligo, M.	Monteagle, B.
Downshire, M.	Hillsbro', E.	Kinnoul, E.	Hay, B.	Stair, E.	Oxenfoord, B.
Drogheda, M.	Moore, B.	Kintore, E.	Kintore, B.	Strangford, V.	Penshurst, B.
Dunmore, E.	Dunmore, B.	Lauderdale, E.	Lauderdale, B.	Waterford, M.	Tyrone, B.
Dunraven, E.	Kenry, B.	Leinster, D.	Leinster, V.	Wemyss, E.	Wemyss, B.

OFFICERS OF THE HOUSE OF PEERS.

Clerk of Parliaments, Sir J. G. S. Lefevre, K.C.B.
Dep. do. (Clerk-Assist.) Sir Wm. Rose, K.C.B.
Read. Clerk & Clerk of Priv. Com., Hon. S. Bethell.
Counsel to Chairman of Com., Thos. F. Kent, Esq.
Chief Clerk, H. Stone Smith, Esq.
Principal Clerk for Bills, W. E. Walmisley, Esq.
Clerk attend. Table and Cashier, W. A. Green, Esq.
Other Clerks in the Office, P. Birch, E. M. Parratt, B. S. R. Adam, M. F. Halliday, W. H. Haines, F. Vane, C. Congreve, O. E. Grant, J. H. Robinson, A. W. Dubourg, H. Walmisley, W. Malony, Esqrs., Hon. F. Stonor, L. Birch, F. G. Green, A. Pechell, G. J. Webb, H. Brougham, M. A. Thoms, W. H. Palk, H. C. Malkin, Esqrs., Hon. E. P. Thesiger, R. W. Monro, A. Harrison, E. F. Taylor, Esqrs.

PRIVATE BILL OFFICE.
Prin. Clerk & Taxing Officer, B. S. R. Adam, Esq.
Peers' Printed Paper Office, O. E. Grant, Esq.
Summoning Officer and Receiver of Fees, Parliamentary Office, W. A. Malony, Esq.
Examiners for Standing Orders, C. Frere, Esq., R. Palgrave, Esq. *Clerk*, E. Webster, Esq.
Gentleman Usher of the Black Rod, Admiral Sir A. W. Clifford, Bart., C.B.
Yeoman Usher, Col. R. C. Spencer Clifford.
Serj.-at-Arms, Lt.-Col. Hon. W. P. M. C. Talbot.
Deputy, G. Wallace Goodbody, Esq.
Receiver of Fees, House of Lords, G. J. Oldrini, Esq.
Short-Hand Writer, Joseph Gurney, Esq.
Principal Doorkeepers, Messrs. G. J. Oldrini, R. Moody, W. Howard, W. H. Brophoy.

---

* New Members. † New Constituencies.

Abingdon—Hon. C. H. Lindsay, C.
Andover—Hon. D. F. Fortescue, L.
ANGLESEA—*R. Davies, L.
Ashton-under-Lyne—*T. Mellor, C.
Aylesbury—N. M. de Rothschild, L. S. G. Smith, C.
Banbury—B. Samuelson, L.
Barnstaple—T. Cave, L. *Capt. Williams, C.
Bath—W. Tite, L. *D. Dahrymple, L.
Beaumaris—Hn. W. O. Stanley, L.
Bedford—*J. Howard, L. S. Whitbread, L.
BEDS.—Col. Gilpin, C. F. C. H. Russell, L.
BERKS.—R. Benyon, C. R. J. Loyd-Lindsay, C. *John Walter, L.
Berwick—*Lord Bury, L. *J. Stapleton, L.
Beverly—Sir H. Edwards, C. *Capt. Kennard, C.
Bewdley—*Sir R. A. Glass, C.
Birkenhead—John Laird, C.
Birmingham—G. Dixon, L. *P. H. Muntz, L. J. Bright, L.
Blackburn—W. H. Hornby, C. *Joseph Feilden, C.
Bodmin—Hon. E. L. Gower, L.
Bolton—*J. Hick, C. W. Gray, C.
Boston—J. W. Malcolm, C. *T. Collins, C.
Bradford—W. E. Forster, L. *H. W. Ripley, L.
Brecknock, H. Gwyn, C.
BRECKNOCK—Hn. Maj. Morgan, C.
Bridgnorth—H. Whitmore, C.
Bridgewater—A. W. Kinglake, L. P. Vanderbyl, L.
Bridport—T. A. Mitchell, L.
Brighton—J. White, L. H. Fawcett, L.
Bristol—Hon. F. H. F. Berkeley, L. *S. Morley, L.
Buckingham—Sir H. Verney, L.
BUCKS.—Rt. Hon. B. Disraeli, C. C. G. Du Pre, C. *N. G. Lambert, L.
†Burnley—*R. Shaw, L.
Bury (Lanc.)—R. N. Philips, L.
Bury St. Edmund's—E. Greene, C. J. A. Hardcastle, L.
Calne—*Lord E. Fitzmaurice, L.
Cambridge—*Col. Torrens, L. *W. Fowler, L.
Cambridge Univ.—Rt. Hon. S. H. Walpole, C. A. J. B. Hope, C.
CAMBRIDGE—Lord G. Manners, C. Lord Royston, C. *Rt. Hon. H. Brand, L.
Canterbury—A. Butler - Johnstone, C. *T. H. Brinckman, L.
Cardiff—Colonel Stuart, L.
CARDIGAN—*E. M. Richards, L.
Cardigan—Sir T. D. Lloyd, L.
Carlisle—*Sir W. Lawson, L. E. Potter, L.
Carmarthen—*Col. C. Stepney, L.
CARMARTHEN—*J. Jones, C. *E. J. Sartoris, L.
Carnarvon—W. B. Hughes, L.
CARNARVON—*Capt. Parry, L.

Chatham—A. J. Otway, L.
†Chelsea—*C. W. Dilke, L. *Sir H. A. Hoare, L.
Cheltenham—*H. B. Samuelson, L.
CHESHIRE (East)—W. J. Legh, C. *E. C. Egerton, C.
†CHESHIRE (Mid)—*Hon. W. Egerton, C. *G. C. Legh, C.
CHESHIRE (West)—Sir P. Egerton, C. J. Tollemache, C.
Chester—Earl Grosvenor, L. *H. C. Raikes, C.
Chichester—Lord H. Lennox, C.
Chippenham—G. Goldney, C.
Christchurch—*E. Haviland-Burke, L.
Cirencester—Hon. A. Bathurst, C.
Clitheroe—*R. Assheton, C.
Cockermouth—*I. Fletcher, C.
Colchester—J. G. Rebow, L. * W. Brewer, L.
CORNWALL (East)—Sir John S. Trelawny, L. *E. B. Williams, C.
CORNWALL (West)—J. St. Aubyn, L. *A. P. Vivian, L.
Coventry—H. W. Eaton, C. *A. S. Hill, C.
Cricklade—*Hon. F. Cadogan, L. Sir D. Gooch, C.
CUMBERLAND (East)—Hon. C. W. G. Howard, L. W. N. Hodgson, C.
CUMBERLAND (West)—Col. Lowther, C. Hon. P. Wyndham, C.
†Darlington—*E. Backhouse, L.
Denbigh—*W. Williams, L.
DENBIGH—Sir W. Wynne, C. *G. O. Morgan, L.
Derby—M. T. Bass, L. *S. Plimsoll, L.
†DERBY (East)—*Hon. Capt. Egerton, L. *Hon. H. Strutt, L.
DERBY (South)—*Sir T. Gresley, C. *Rowland Smith, C.
DERBY (North)—Lord G. Cavendish, L. *A. P. Arkwright, C.
Devizes—Sir T. Bateson, C.
DEVON (North)—Sir S. H. Northcote, C. T. Dyke Acland, L.
†DEVON (East)—*Sir L. Palk, C. Lord Courtenay, C.
DEVON (South)—Sir L. M. Lopes, C. S. T. Kekewich, C.
Devonport—M. Chambers, L. *J. D. Lewis, L.
†Dewsbury—* J. Simon, L.
Dorchester—Colonel Sturt, C.
DORSET.—W. H. B. Portman, C. H. G. Sturt, C. J. Floyer, C.
Dover — Major Dickson, C. *G. Jessel, L.
Droitwich—Sir J. Pakington, C.
Dudley—H. B. Sheridan, L.
Durham—J. Henderson, L. *J. R. Davison, L.
DURHAM (North)—Sir H. Williamson, L. *G. Elliot, C.
DURHAM (South)—J. W. Pease, L. *Capt. F. E. B. Beaumont, L.
ESSEX (East)—*J. Round, C. *Lt.-Col. Ruggles-Brise, C.
†ESSEX (West)—*Lord E. Cecil, C. *H. J. Selwin-Ibbetson, C.

ESSEX (South)—*R. W. Baker, L. *A. Johnston, L.
Evesham—Colonel Bourne, C.
Exeter—J. D. Coleridge, L. *E. A. Bowring, L.
Eye—Viscount Barrington, C.
Finsbury—W. M'Cullagh Torrens, L. A. Lusk, L.
Flint—Sir J. Hanmer, L.
FLINT.—Lord R. Grosvenor, L.
Frome—T. Hughes, L.
Gateshead—Rt. Hn. Sir W. Hutt, L.
GLAMORGAN—C. R. M. Talbot, C. H. H. Vivian, L.
Gloucester—W. P. Price, L. C. J. Monk, L.
GLOUCESTER (East)—R. S. Holford, C. Sir M. Beach, C.
GLOUCESTER (West)—R. N. F. Kingscote, L. *S.S. Marling, C.
Grantham—*Hn. F. J. Tollemache, *Capt. Cholmeley, L.
†Gravesend—*Sir C. Wingfield, L.
Greenwich—Ald. Salomons, L. Rt. Hon. W. E. Gladstone, L.
Grimsby—*G. Tomline, L.
Guildford—G. J. H. Onslow, C.
†Hackney—*C. Reed, L. *J. Holms, L.
Halifax—J. Stansfeld, L. E. Akroyd, C.
HANTS (South) — Rt. Hon. W. F. Cowper, L. Lord H. Scott, C.
HANTS (North)—W. W. B. Beach, C. G. Sclater-Booth, C.
*Hartlepool—*R. W. Jackson, C.
Harwich—Colonel Jervis, C.
Hastings—*T. Brassey, L. *F. North, L.
Haverfordwest—*Col. Edwards, L.
Helston—*A. W. Young, L.
Hereford—G. Clive, L. *J. W. S. Wyllie, L.
HEREFORD.—Sir J. R. Bailey, C. *Sir H. D. Croft, C. R. M. Biddulph, L.
Hertford—R. Dimsdale, C.
HERTS.—Abel Smith, C. Hon. H. F. Cowper, L. *H.R. Brand, L.
Horsham—*Major Aldridge, C. R. H. Hurst, L. (Double return).
Huddersfield—*E. A. Leatham, L.
Hull—C. M. Norwood, L. J. Clay, L.
Huntingdon—T. Baring, C.
HUNTS—E. Fellowes, C. Lord R. Montagu, C.
Hythe—Baron M. Rothschild, L.
Ipswich—H. E. Adair, L. *H. W. West, L.
Kendal—*J. Whitwell, L.
KENT (East)—E. L. Pemberton, C. *Hon. G. W. Milles, C.
†KENT (Mid)—*Lord Holmesdale, C. *W. Hart Dyke, C.
KENT (West)—*C. H. Mills, C. *J. G. Talbot, C.
Kidderminster—*T. Lea, L.
King's Lynn—Rt. Hon. Lord Stanley, C. *Hon. R. Bourke, C.
Knaresboro'—*A. Illingworth, L.
Lambeth—* Ald. J. C. Lawrence, L. *W. M'Arthur, L.

LANCASHIRE (North) —Rt. Hon. J. Wilson Patten, C. *Captain Stanley, C.
†LANCASHIRE (North-East) *J. M. Holt, C. *J. P. Starkie, C.
†LANCASHIRE (Sou.-West) — C. Turner, C. *R. A. Cross, C.
†LANCASHIRE (South East)—Hon. A.F.Egerton,C. *J.S.Henry,C.
Launceston—*H. C. Lopes, C.
Leeds—E. Baines, L. *Ald.Carter, L. *W. St. J. Wheelhouse, C.
Leicester—P. A. Taylor, L. J. D. Harris, L.
LEICESTER (North) — Rt. Hon. Lord J.R. Manners, C. *S.W. Clowes, C.
LEICESTER (South) — Lord Curzon, C. *A. Pell, C.
Leominster— R. Arkwright, C.
Lewes—Lord Pelham, L.
Lichfield—Colonel R. Dyott, C.
Lincoln—C. Seely, L. *J. H. Palmer, L.
†LINCOLN (Mid)—*H. Chaplin, C. *Colonel Amcotts, C.
LINCOLN (North) — Sir M. J. Cholmeley, L. *R. Winn, C.
LINCOLN (South)—W. E. Welby, C. *E. Turnor, C.
Liskeard—Sir A. W. Buller, L.
Liverpool—S.R. Graves, C. *Lord Sandon, C. *W. Rathbone, L.
London—Rt. Hon. G. J. Goschen, L. Ald. W. Lawrence, L. R. W. Crawford, L. *C. Bell, C.
†London University — Rt. Hon. R. Lowe, L.
Ludlow—Hon. Col. Clive, C.
Lymington—Lord G. Lennox, C.
Macclesfield—*W.C.Brocklehurst, L. *D. Chadwick, L. [man,L.
Maidstone—W. Lee, L. J. What-
Maldon—*E. H. Bentall, L.
Malton—Hon.C.W.Fitzwilliam,L.
Malmesbury—*W. Powell, C.
Manchester—*H. Birley, C. T. Bazley, L. Jacob Bright, L.
Marlborough—Lord E. Bruce, C.
Marlow—*T. O. Wethered, C.
Marylebone— H. Lewis, L. T. Chambers, L.
MERIONETH—*D. Williams, L.
Merthyr Tydvil—*H. Richard, L. *R. Fothergill, L.
MIDDLESEX—*Lord GeorgeHamilton, C. Viscount Enfield, L.
†Middlesborough — *H. W. F. Bolckow, L.
Midhurst—W. T. Mitford, C.
Monmouth—*Sir J. Ramsden, L.
MONMOUTH—C.O.S. Morgan, C. Col. Somerset, C. [Tracy,L.
Montgomery—Hon. C. Hanbury-
MONTGOMERY—C.W.W.Wynn, C.
Morpeth—Rt. Hon.SirG.Grey, L.
Newark—G. Hodgkinson, L. *E. Denison, L. [T.E.Headlam,L.
Newcastle-on-Tyne—J. Cowen, L.
Newcastle-under-Lyne—E. Buckley, C. *W. S. Allen. L.
Newport (I.W.)—C. Wykeham Martin, L.
†NORFOLK (North-East)—Hon. F.Walpole,C. *Sir E.Lacon,C.

†NORFOLK (South-East) — C. S. Read, C. E. Howes, C.
NORFOLK (West)- SirW.Bagge,C. Hon. T. De Grey, C.
Northallerton—*J. Hutton, L.
Northampton—Lord Henley, L. C. Gilpin, L.
NORTHAMPTON (North)—Rt. Hon. G. W.Hunt, C. S. G.Stopford,C.
NORTHAMPTON (South) — Sir R. Knightley, C. *Major F. W. Cartwright, C.
NORTHUMBERLAND (South) —W. B. Beaumont, L. Hon. H. G. Liddell, C.
NORTHUMBERLAND(North)—Earl Percy, C. *M. W. Ridley, C.
Norwich—SirW. Russell, L. *Sir H. J. Stracey, C.
Nottingham—*Sir R. Clifton, C. *Colonel Wright, C.
NOTTS (North)—Rt. Hon. J. E. Denison, L. *F. C. Smith, C.
NOTTS (South)—W. H. Barrow, C. T. B. Hildyard, C. [Platt, L.
Oldham—J. T. Hibbert, L. J.
Oxford University—Rt. Hon. G. Hardy, C. Rt.Hon. J. R. Mowbray, C.
Oxford—Rt. Hon. E. Cardwell, L. *W. G. Vernon Harcourt, L.
OXFORD—Rt.Hon.J.W.Henley,C. Colonel J. S. North, C. *W. C. Cartwright, L.
Pembroke—*T. C. Meyrick, C.
PEMBROKE—J. H. Scourfield, C.
Penrhyn & Falmouth—*R. N.Fowler, C. *E. B. Eastwick, C.
Peterborough—G. H. Whalley, L. *W. Wells, L.
Petersfield—W. Nicholson, L.
Plymouth—Sir R. Collier, L. C. W. Morrison, L.
Pontefract—H. C. E. Childers, L. Major Waterhouse, C.
Poole—*A. Guest, C.
Portsmouth—*Sir J. Elphinstone, C. W. H. Stone, L.
Preston—*E. Hermon, C. Sir T. G. Hesketh, C.
Radnor—R. G. Price, L.
RADNOR—Hon. A. Walsh, C.
Reading—Sir F. H. Goldsmid, L. G. J. Shaw Lefevre, L.
Retford (East)—F. J. S.Foljambe, Viscount Galway, C.
Richmond—Sir R. Palmer, L.
Ripon—Lord J. Hay, L.
Rochdale—T. B. Potter, L.
Rochester—P.W. Martin, L. Serj. Kinglake, L.
RUTLAND—Hon. G. J. Noel, C. *G. H. Finch, C.
Rye—*J.S.Hardy,C. [Charley,C.
Salford—*C.E.Cawley,C. *W.T.
Salisbury—*J.A. Lush, L. *E.W. T. Hamilton, L.
SALOP (North) — J. R. Ormsby Gore, C. Viscount Newport, C.
SALOP (South)—Gen. P. E. Herbert, C. *Col. E. Corbett, C.
Sandwich—E.Knatchbull-Hugessen, L. *H. A. Brassey, L.
Scarborough—Sir J.Johnstone, L. J. D. Dent, L.

Shaftesbury—G. G. Glyn, L.
Sheffield—G. Hadfield, L. *A. J. Mundella, L.
Shoreham—Rt. Hon. S. Cave, C. Sir P. Burrell, C.
Shrewsbury—W. J. Clement, L. *J. Figgins, C.
SOMERSET(East)—*R. Bright, C. *Major R. S. Allen, C.
SOMERSET (West)—Hon. Capt. A. Hood, C. W. Gore Langton, C.
†SOMERSET (Mid.)—R. N. Grenville, C. R. H. Paget, C.
Southampton—R. Gurney, C. *P. M. Hoare, C.
Southwark—J. Locke, L. A. H. Layard, L.
South Shields—*J.C.Stevenson, L.
Stafford—Col. Meller, C. *H.D. Pochin, L.
†STAFFORD (West)— *Sir H. M. Ingram, C. *Sir Smith Child,C.
†STAFFORD(East)—*J.R.M'Lean, L. M. A. Bass, L.
STAFFORD(North)—*Rt. Hon. C. B. Adderley, C. Sir E. M. Buller, L.
†Stalybridge—*J. Sidebottom, C.
Stamford—Rear-Ad.Sir J.Hay,C.
St. Ives.—*C. Magniac, L.
Stockport—*W. Tipping, C. J. B. Smith, L.
†Stockton—*J. Dodds, L.
Stoke-on-Trent —*G. Melly, L. *W. S. Roden, L.
Stroud—*S.S.Dickinson,L. H.S. P. Winterbotham, L.
SUFFOLK (East)—Hon. J. Henniker-Major, C. F.Corrance,C.
SUFFOLK (West)—Maj.Parker,C. Lord A. Hervey, C.
Sunderland—J. Candlish, L. *E. T. Gourley, L.
SURREY (East)—Hon. P. J. Locke King, L. C. Buxton, L.
†SURREY (Mid)—*Hon. W. Brodrick, C. *H. W. Peek, C.
SURREY (West)—G. Cubitt, C. J. I. Briscoe, L.
SUSSEX (East) J. G. Dodson, L. *G. B. Gregory, C.
SUSSEX (West)—Col. Barttelot, C. Hon. H. Wyndham, C.
Swansea—L.L. Dillwyn, L.
Tamworth—Sir R. Peel, L. *Sir H. L. Bulwer, L.
Taunton—A. C. Barclay, L. *E. W. Cox, L.
Tavistock—A. Russell, L.
Tewkesbury—*W. E. Price, L.
Thirsk—Sir W. P. Gallwey, C.
Tiverton— Hon. G. Denman, C. *J. H. Amory, L.
Tower Hamlets—A. S. Ayrton, L. *J. D'A. Samuda, L.
Truro—F. M. Williams, C. Hon. Capt. Vivian, L.
Tynemouth—*T. E. Smith, C.
Wakefield—*S. A. Beaumont, L.
Wallingford—*S. Vickers, C.
Walsall—C. Forster, L.
Wareham—Vacant.
Warrington—*P. Rylands, L.
Warwick—A. W. Peel, L. *E. Greaves, C.

WARWICK (North)—C. N. Newdegate, C. W.B.Davenport, C.
WARWICK (South)—H. C.Wise, C. J. Hardy, C.
†Wednesbury—*A. Brogden, L. *A. H. Brown, L.
Wenlock—Rt. Hn. G. Forester, C.
Westbury—*J. L. Phipps, C.
Westminster—*W. H. Smith, C. Hon. R. W. Grosvenor, L.
WESTMORELAND — Earl Bective, C. W. Lowther, C.
Weymouth—*C. J. T. Hambro, C. H. Edwards, L.
Whitby—*W. H. Gladstone, L.
Whitehaven—*G. Bentinck, C.
Wigan—H. Woods, L. *J. Lancaster, L.
Wight (Isle of)—Sir J.Simeon, L.
Wilton—E. Antrobus, L.
WILTS (North)—LordC.Bruce, L. *Sir G. S. Jenkinson, C.
WILTS (South)—LordH.Thynne, C. T. F. Grove, L.
Winchester—W. B. Simonds, C. J. Bonham Carter, L.
Windsor—R. Eykyn, L.
Wolverhampton—Rt. Hon. C. P. Villiers, L. T. M.Weguelin, L.
Woodstock—H. Barnett, C.
Worcester—*W. Laslett, C. A. C. Sherriff, L.
WORCESTER (E.)—*Hon. C. Lyttelton, L. *R. P. Amphlett, C.
WORCESTER (West)—W. E. Dowdeswell, C. F. W. Knight, C.
Wycombe—*H.Capt.Carington, L.
York—J.Lowther, C. *J. P. B. Westhead, L.
YORKS—(W. R., N. Div.)—Sir F. Crossley,L.Ld.F.Cavendish,L.
YORKS—(W. R., S.)—Viscount Milton, L. H. F. Beaumont, L.
YORKS(W.R.,E.)—*C.B.Denison, C. *Joshua Feilden, L.
YORKS (N.R.)—Hon. W. E. Duncombe, C. F. A. Milbank, L.
YORKS (E.R.) — *C. Sykes, C. *W. H. Broadley, C.

SCOTLAND.
Aberdeen—Colonel Sykes, L.
ABERDEEN (East)—W. D. Fordyce, L. [L.
†Aberdeen (W.)—*W.M'Combie
ARGYLE—Marquise' Lorne, L.
Ayr—E. H. Craufurd, L.
AYR (North)—*W. Finnie, L.
†AYR (South)—*Sir D. Wedderburn, L.
BANFF—R. Duff, L.
BERWICK—D. Robertson, L.
BUTE—*C. Dalrymple, C.
CTHNSS.—G.Traill, L. [Adam, L.
CLACKMANNAN & KINROSS—W.P.
DUMBARTON—*A. Orr-Ewing, C.
Dumfries—*R. Jardine, L.
DUMFRIES—Sir S. Waterlow, L.
Dundee—*G. Armitstead, L. Sir J. Ogilvy, L.
Edinburgh—D. M'Laren, L. *J. Miller, L.
Edinburgh and St. Andrew's Universities—*L. Playfair, C.B., L.
EDINBURGH—*Sir A.Maitland, L.
Elgin—M. E. Grant Duff, L.

ELGIN AND NAIRN—*Hon. J. O. Grant, C.
Falkirk—J. Merry, L.
FIFE—Sir R. Anstruther, L.
FORFAR—Hon. C. Carnegie, L.
Glasgow — W. Graham, L. R. Dalglish, L. *G. Anderson, L.
†Glasgow and Aberdeen Universities—*Jas. Moncreiff, L.
Greenock—*J. J. Grieve, L.
Haddington—Sir H. Davie, L.
HADDINGTON—Lord Elcho, C.
†Hawick—G. O. Trevelyan, L.
Inverness—*Æ.W. Macintosh, L.
INVERNESS—*D. Cameron, L.
Kilmarnock—Rt. Hon. E.P. Bouverie, L.
KINCARDINE—J. D. Nicol, L.
Kirkcaldy—R. S. Aytoun, L.
KIRKCUDBRIGHT—*W. H. Maxwell, C.
LANARK(N.)—SirT.Colebrooke,L
†LANARK (S.)—*Maj. Hamilton.
Leith—*R. A. Macfie, L.
LINLITHGOW—P. M'Lagan, C.
Montrose—W. E. Baxter, L.
ORKNEY AND SHETLAND—F.Dundas, L.
Paisley—H. E. Crum-Ewing, L.
PEEBLES AND SELKIRK—*Sir G. G. Montgomery, C.
Perth—Hon. A. Kinnaird, L.
PERTH—*C. S. Parker, L.
RENFREW—A. A. Spiers, L.
ROSS AND CROMARTY—*A. Matheson, L.
ROXBURGH—Sir W. Scott, L.
St. Andrew's—E. Ellice, L.
Stirling—*H. Campbell, L.
STIRLING—Admiral Erskine, L.
SUTHERLAND—Ld.R.L.Gower,L.
Wick—*G. Loch, L.
Wigton—G. Young, L.
WIGTON—*Lord Garlies, C.

IRELAND.
ANTRIM—Hon. E.O'Neill, C. Admiral Seymour, C.
Armagh—J. Vance, C.
ARMAGH—Sir J. M. Stronge, C. *W. Verner, C.
Athlone—*J. Ennis, L.
Bandon—*W. Shaw, L.
Belfast—*W. Johnston, C. *T. M'Clure, L.
Carlow—*Captain Fagan, L.
CARLOW—H. Bruen, C. *A. Kavanagh, C.
Carrickfergus—*M. R. Dalway, C.
Cashel—J. L. O'Beirne, L.
CAVAN—Hon. Col. Annesley, C. E. J. Saunderson, L.
CLARE—Colonel Vandeleur, L. Sir C. O'Loghlen, L.
Clonmel—J. Bagwell, L.
Coleraine—Sir H. H. Bruce, C.
CORK—*Mc C. Downing, L. *A. H.S. Barry, L.
Cork — J. F. Maguire, L. N. D. Murphy, L.
DONEGAL—Viscount Hamilton, C. T. Conolly, C.
Down—Colonel W. B. Forde, L. Lord A. Hill Trevor, C.
Downpatrick—*W. Keown, C.
Drogheda—B. Whitworth, L.

Dublin—Sir A. Guinness, C. J. Pim, L. [Hamilton, C.
DUBLIN—Col. Taylour, C. I. T.
Dublin University—A. Lefroy, C. *Dr. J. T. Ball, C.
Dundalk—*P. Callan, L.
Dungannon—Hon. C. S. Knox, C.
Dungarvan—*H. Matthews, C.
Ennis—Captain Stacpoole, L.
Enniskillen—*Visct. Crichton, C.
FERMANAGH—Hon. Col. Cole, C. Captain Archdall, C.
Galway—Sir R. Blennerhasset, *Lord St. Lawrence, L.
GALWAY— W. H. Gregory, L. Viscount Burke, L.
KERRY—Lord Castlerosse, L. H. A. Herbert, L.
KILDARE—Rt. Hon. W. Cogan, L. Lord O. Fitzgerald, L.
Kilkenny—Sir J. Gray, L.
KILKENNY—G. L. Bryan, L. Hn. L. Agar Ellis, L.
KING'S COUNTY—Sir P. O'Brien, L. *D. Sherlock, L.
Kinsale—Sir G. Colthurst, L.
LEITRIM—Dr. J. Brady, L. W. Ormsby Gore, L.
Limerick—Major Gavin, L. F. W. Russell, L.
LIMERICK—Rt. Hon. W. Monsell, L. E. J. Synan, L.
Lisburn—E. W. Verner, C.
Londonderry—*R. Dowse, L.
LONDONDERRY—R. Peel Dawson, C. Sir F.W. Heygate, C.
LONGFORD—Col. S. Greville Nugent, L. Major O'Reilly, L.
LOUTH—Rt. Hon. C. Fortescue, L. *M. O'Reilly Dease, L.
Mallow—E. Sullivan, L.
MAYO—Lord Bingham, C. *G. H. Moore, L.
MEATH—M. E. Corbally, L. E. F. M'Evoy, L.
MONAGHAN—Col. O'C. P. Leslie, C. * S. E. Shirley, C.
New Ross—*P. M'Mahon, L.
Newry—*W. Kirk, L.
Portarlington—*Capt. Damer, C.
QUEEN'S Co.—Rt.Hon. J.W.Fitzpatrick, L. *K. T. Digby, L.
ROSCOMMON—C. O. O'Connor, L. Rt. Hon. Col. French, L.
SLIGO—*D. M. O'Connor, L. Sir R. G. Booth, C.
Sligo—* Major L. Knox, C.
TIPPERARY—C. Moore, L. Hon. Capt. White, L.
Tralee—D. O'Donoghue, L.
TYRONE—Lord C. Hamilton, C. Rt. Hon. H. T. L. Corry, C.
Waterford—J.A.Blake, L. *J.Delahunty, L.
WATERFORD—J. Esmonde, L. E. De la Poer, L.
WESTMEATH—W. Pollard-Urquhart, L. W. F. Greville-Nugent, L.
Wexford—R. J. Devereux, L.
WEXFORD—*J. T. Power, L. *M. P. Darcey, L.
WICKLOW—W. Fitzwilliam Dick, C. *H. W. Fitzwilliam, L.
Youghal—*C. Weguelin, L.

OFFICERS OF THE HOUSE OF COMMONS.

Clerk of the House of Commons, Sir Denis Le Marchant, Bart., Palace of Westminster.

Clerk Assistant, Sir T. Erskine May, K.C.B. Palace Yard.

Second do., Henry Ley, Esq., 51, Chester Square.

CLERKS ON THE ESTABLISHMENT OF THE OFFICE OF THE CLERK OF THE HOUSE OF COMMONS.

Chief Clerk Public Bill Office, and Clerk of the Fees, William Rose, Esq.

Clerk of the Journals, Charles Rowland, Esq.

Chief Clerk, Committee Clerks' Office, Charles William Pole, Esq.

Chief Clerk Private Bill Office, W. Hodgkin, Esq.

Senior Clerks, J. L. Postlethwaite, Esq., F. H. Gray, Esq., H. B. Mayne, Esq., R. Marriott, Esq., J. B. Bull, Esq., S. B. Gunnell, Esq., C. Eales, Esq.

Assistant do., W. Glyn, Edw. H. Ley, W. D. Hawes, M. C. Conry, G. J. Stone, C. E. A. Leigh, F. H. Webber, W. A. F. Davie, A. J. S. Milman, A. Turner, W. M. Molyneux, G. Laughton, Esqrs.

Junior Clerks, F. E. Villiers, S. C. Smith, A. F. Kingscote, W. Gibbons, C. Forster, R. G. Lind-

say, W. Dickinson, F. B. G. Jenkinson, R. C. Walpole, F. Tupper, R. F. Craig, B. W. Harrison, F. R. Keollys, Esqrs.

Accountants, G. Broom, Esq., W. O. Mayne, Esq.

Short-Hand Writer, Joseph Gurney, Esq.

Assistant, W. H. Salter, Esq.

VOTE OFFICE.

Deliver. of Votes & Print. Papers, J. J. Collins, Esq.

Assistants, R. M. Baily, F. C. N. Franco, H. A. M. Killick, Esqrs.

Serjeant-at-Arms, Lord Charles J. Fox Russell.

Deputy-Serjeant, R. A. Gosset, Esq.

Assistant do., Col. C. W. Forester.

Chaplain to the House, Rev. Chas. Merivale, M.A.

Secretary to the Speaker, Alfred Denison, Esq.

Counsel to Speaker, and Examiner of Election Recognizances, G. K. Rickards, Esq.

Clerk, M. M. Ainslie, Esq.

Examiners of Petitions for Private Bills, Charles Frere, Esq., Reginald Palgrave, Esq.

Taxing Master of the House, Charles Frere, Esq.

Clerk, E. Webster, Esq.

Librarian, G. Howard, Esq.

At the time of the union with Scotland, in 1707, the English House of Commons consisted of 513 members; 45 were then added for Scotland, and in 1801, 100 for Ireland, making the present total of 658. This total number was preserved by the first Reform Act (1832), as well as by the recent one (30 and 31 Vict. cap. 102), but in each case the apportionment was altered, and it now stands, England and Wales 498 members, Scotland 60, and Ireland 100. By the Reform Act of 1867, 11 English boroughs were totally disfranchised, and 23 others lost 1 member each, but 25 seats were bestowed on new boroughs and universities, and 28 on counties, some receiving 1 additional member, and others being so subdivided that Yorkshire now returns 10 members, and Lancashire 8, whilst the majority of the rest have 4 or 6. Taking the three kingdoms, there are now 375 members for boroughs and universities, and 283 for counties; but up to 1867 the numbers were, boroughs and universities, 402 ; counties, 256. Though much inferior in antiquity to the other branches of the Legislature, and in theory merely equal to them, the House of Commons, by its constitutional power of alone granting or withholding the supplies by means of which the functions of Government are carried on, has in reality a preponderance which makes it impossible for any policy to be long pursued that does not meet with its approbation. This position is entirely the growth of comparatively modern times, for, neither in the Saxon Witanagemot, nor in the Norman King's Court, (*Curia Regis*), was the voice of the people, as distinct from the privileged orders of priests and nobles, heard. Simon de Montfort it was, who, having seized on the government from the feeble Henry III., first called on the people of the towns to send representatives to the great council of the nation, in 1265, and they responded so readily, and granted money so much more freely than their noble associates would do, that Edward I., in spite of the origin of the custom, about 30 years after laid the regular foundation of the present system. The Crown long possessed great influence over the House, and exercised it in a way that would not now be tolerated ; for even down to the reign of Elizabeth, the issuing or withholding of the writ of summons was dependent on the pleasure of the Court, and a town whose representative had been "in opposition" in one Parliament often found itself deprived of its members in the next.

The Peerage and the House of Commons, Alphabetically Arranged.

New Members with an Asterisk (*). c. for County.

Abercorn, *D.,* Chesterfield House, South Audley Street, W.

Abercromby, *L.,* Brooks's Club, S.W.

Aberdeen, *E.,* Haddo House, Aberdeenshire.

Abergavenny, *E.,* 58, Portland Place, W.

Abingdon, *E.,* 18, Grosvenor Street, W.

Abinger, *L.,* 48, Chester Sq., S.W.

Acland, T. Dyke........*Devon, N.*

Adair, Hugh E. ....*Ipswich*

Adam, W. P., ...*Clackmannan*

Adderley, Right Hon. C. B. ....*Stafford N.*

Ailesbury, *M.,* 78, Pall Mall, S.W.

Ailsa, *M.,* 30, Old Burlington Street, W.

Airlie, *E.,* Airlie Lodge, Kensington, W.

Akroyd, E. ....*Halifax*

Albemarle, *E.,* Brooks's Club.

Aldborough, *E.,* Belan Hall, Kildare

*Aldridge, Major ....*Horsham*

Allen, W.S. *Newcastle-under-Lyme*

*Allen, Major ....*Somerset, E.*

*Amcotts, Col. ....*Lincoln (Mid)*

Amherst, *E.,* 43, Grosvenor Sq.

*Amphlett, R. P....*Worcester, E.*

*Amory, J. H. ....*Tiverton*

*Anderson, G.............*Glasgow*

Anglesey, *M.,* 25, Berkeley Sq.

Annaly, *L.,* 48, Grosvenor Place.

Annesley, *E.,* 25, Norfolk Street, Park Lane, W.

Annesley, Hon. Col. H. ....*Cavan*

Anstruther, Sir R. ......*Fifeshire*

Antrim, *E.,* Glenarm Castle, Antrim

Antrobus, E. ....*Wilton*

Arbuthnott, *V.,* Arbuthnott House, Kincardine

Archdall, Capt. ....*Fermanagh*

*Armitstead, G. ....*Dundee*

*Arkwright, A. P. ....*Derby, N.*

Arkwright, R. ....*Leominster*

Argyll, *D.,* Campden Hill, Kensington, W.

Arran, *E.,* Pavilion, Hans Pl., W.

Arundell, *L.,* 2, Savile Row, W.

Ashbrook, V., Castle Durrow, Queen's County
Ashburnham, E., 30, Dover St., W.
Ashburton, L., 82, Piccadilly, W.
Ashtown, L., Woodlawn, Galway
*Assheton, R. .... Clitheroe
Athlumney, L., Brooks's Club.
Athole, D., 22, Dover St., W.
Auckland, L. (Bp. Bath & Wells), 13, Queen's Square, S.W.
Audley, L., 15, Gloucester Sq.
Aveland, L., 12, Belgrave Sq.
Avonmore, V., Rosaca, Tipperary
Aylesford, E., 48, Grosvenor St.
Aylmer, L., Melbourne, Canada
Ayrton, A. S. ......Tower Hamlets
Aytoun, R. S. .... Kirkcaldy
*Backhouse, E. .... Darlington
Bagge, Sir W. .... Norfolk, W.
Bagot, L., 54, Lowndes Sq., S.W.
Bagwell, J. .... Clonmel
Bailey, Sir J. R. ...Herefordshire
Baines, E. .... Leeds
*Baker, R. W. .... Essex, S.
*Ball, J. T. ... Dublin University
Bandon, E., Palace Hotel, Buckingham Gate
Bangor, V., 42, Brook St., W.
Bangor, Bp., 27, Parliament St.
Bantry, E., Thomas's Hotel, Berkeley Square, W.
Barclay, A. C. .... Taunton
Baring, T. .... Huntingdon
Barnett, H. .... Woodstock
Barrington, V., Shrivenham, Berks.
Barrington, Lord .... Eye
Barrow, W. H. .... Notts, S.
*Barry, A. H. Smith......Cork, c.
Barttelot, Col. W. B...Sussex, W.
Bass, M. A. ....Stafford, E.
Bass, M. T. .... Derby
Bateman, L., Palace Hotel, Buckingham Gate.
Bateson, Sir T. .... Devizes
Bath, M., 48, Berkeley Sq., W.
Bathurst, E., 38, Half-moon St.
Bathurst, A. A. .... Cirencester
Baxter, W. E. .... Montrose
Bazley, T. .... Manchester
Beach, Sir M. H...Gloucester, E.
Beach, W. B. ....Hants, N.
Beauchamp, E., 13, Belgrave Sq.
Beaufort, D., 29, Belgrave Sq.
Beaumont, L.—a minor, b. 1848
Beaumont, H. F. West Riding, S.
*Beaumont, Capt. F. Durham, S.
*Beaumont, S. .... Wakefield
Beaumont, W. B. Northumber., S.
*Bective, Earl .... Westmoreland
Bedford, D., 6, Belgrave Sq.
Belhaven, L., 31, Dover St., W.
*Bell, C. ....London
Bellew, L., Barmeath, Ireland.
Belmore, E.—abroad.
Belper, L., 88, Eaton Sq., S.W.
*Bentall, E. H. .... Maldon
Bentinck, G. ....Whitehaven
Benyon, R. .... Berks
Berkeley, E. ..Cranford, Middlesex
Berkeley, Hon. F. H. F. .... Bristol
Berners, L., 22, Pk. Cres., Reg. Pk.
Berwick, L., Army & Navy Club.
Bessborough, E., 40, Charles St., Berkeley Square.

Biddulph, M. ......Herefordshire
Bingham, Lord .... Mayo.
*Birley, H. .... Manchester.
Blake, J. A. .... Waterford
Blantyre, L., 3, Cromwell Houses.
Blayney, L., Carlton Club, S.W.
Blennerhasset, Sir R. ...... Galway.
Bloomfield, L. .... abroad.
*Bolckow, H. W. F. Middlesborough
Bolingbroke, V., 38, St. James's St.
Bolton, L., 46, Prince's Gardens, W
Booth, G. Sclater .....Hants, N.
Booth, Sir R. Gore ......Sligo, c.
Boston, L., 4, Belgrave Sq., S.W.
*Bourke, Hon. R. ...King's Lynn.
*Bourne, Col. .... Evesham.
*Bowring, E. A. .... Exeter.
Boyne, V. 22, Belgrave Sq., S.W.
Bouverie, Right Hon. E. P.
.... Kilmarnock.
Bradford, E., 43, Belgrave Sq. S.W.
Brady, Dr. .... Leitrim, c.
*Brand, H. R. .... Herts.
*Brassey, H. A. .... Sandwich.
*Brassey, T. .... Hastings.
Braybrooke, L., 42, Upper Brook Street, W.
Breadalbane, E., Carlton Club.
*Brewer, W. .... Colchester.
Bridport, L., 12, Wimpole St., W.
Bright, Jacob .... Manchester.
Bright, John .... Birmingham.
*Bright, R. .... Somerset, E.
*Brinckman, T. H....Canterbury.
Briscoe, J. I. .... Surrey, W.
*Brise, Lieut-Col. R., Essex, N.E.
Bristol, M., St. James's Sq. S.W.
*Broadley, W. H. ...Yorks, E.R.
*Brocklehurst, W.C. Macclesfield.
*Brodrick, Hon. W., Surrey, Mid.
*Brogden, A. .... Wednesbury.
Brougham & Vaux, L.
Broughton, L., 42, Berkeley Sq. W.
*Brown, A. H. .... Wenlock.
Brownlow, E., 11, Prince's Gate.
Bruce, Sir H. H............Coleraine.
Bruce, Lord C. B. ......Wilts, N.
Bruce, Lord E. ......Marlborough.
Bruen, H. .... Carlow, c.
Bryan, G. L. ....Kilkenny, c.
Buccleuch, D., Montague House, Whitehall. [gowshire.
*Buchan, E., Kirkhill, Linlith-
Buckingham, D., Chandos House, Cavendish Square.
Buckley, E. Newcastle-undr-Lyme.
Buckinghamshire, E....Sidmouth.
Buller, Sir A. W. ......Liskeard
Buller, Sir E. M. ...Stafford, N.
*Bulwer, Sir H. L. ......Tamworth
Burke, Viscount ......Galway, c.
*Burke, E. H. .... Christchurch
Burrell, Sir P. .... Shoreham
Bury, Lord .... Berwick
*Bute, M.,
Buxton, C. .... Surrey, E.
Byron, L., 48, Eaton Place, S.W.
Cadogan, E., Chelsea House, Cadogan Place.
*Cadogan, Hon. F. ......Cricklade
Cairns, L., 5, Cromwell Houses.
Caithness, E., 17, Hill Street, Berkeley Sq. [Terrace.
Caledon, E., 5, Carlton House
*Callan, P. ....Dundalk

Calthorpe, L., 33, Grosvenor Sq.
Cambridge, D., Glo'ster House, Piccadilly.
Camden, M., 96, Eaton Sq., S.W.
*Cameron, D.......Inverness-shire
Camoys, L., 31, Dover St., W.
Campbell, L., 17, Bruton St., W.
*Campbell, H. .... Stirling
Camperdown, E., 39, Charles St., Berkeley Square
Candlish, J., ... Sunderland
Canterbury, Abp., Lambeth Pal.
Canterbury, V., 13, Chesterfield Street, W.
Carbery, L., Castle Freke, Cork.
Cardwell, Rt. Hon. E......Oxford
Carew, L., 28, Belgrave Sq., S.W.
Carington, L., 8, Whitehall Yard
*Carington, Hon. Capt., Wycombe
Carlisle, Bp., 10, Hurley St., W.
Carlisle, E., Castle Howard, Yorkshire.
Carnarvon, E., 66, Grosvenor St.
Carnegie, Hon. C. ... Forfarshire
Carter, J. Bonham ... Winchester
Carnwath, E. .... [kenny.
Carrick, E., Thomas Town, Kil-
*Carter, Alderman ....Leeds
*Cartwright, Maj., Northampton, S.
*Cartwright, W. C...Oxfordshire
Carysfort, E., 14, Halkin St., W.
Cashel, Bp. .... [lone.
Castlemaine, L., Moydrum, Ath-
Castlerosse, Viscount ......Kerry
Castle-Stuart, E., Stuart Hall, Tyrone.
Cathcart, E., 1, Regent St., S.W.
Cavan, E., 47, Onslow Sq., S.W.
Cave, Rt. Hon. S......... Shoreham
Cave, T. .... Barnstaple.
Cavendish, Lord F. ...W.R., N.
Cavendish, Lord G. H. Derby, N.
Cawdor, E., 74, South Audley St.
*Cawley, C. E. .... Salford
*Cecil, Lord E. ......Essex, N.W.
Chambers, M. ....Devonport
Chambers, T. .... Marylebone
Charlemont, E., 49, Eaton Place
*Chaplin, H. .... Lincoln, Mid.
*Chadwick, D. .... Macclesfield
Charleville, E. Tullamore King's County
*Charley, W. T. .... Salford
Chelmsford, L., 7, Eaton Sq., S.W.
Chesham, L., Brookes's Club, S.W
Chesterfield, E., White's Club.
Chetwynd, V.
*Child, Sir Smith ...Stafford, W.
Childers, H. .... Pontefract
Chichester, Bp., 3, Qn. Anne St.
Chichester, E., 11, Whitehall Pl.
Cholmeley, Sir M. J., Lincoln, N.
*Cholmeley, Capt. ......Grantham
Cholmondeley, M., 12, Carlton House Terrace.
Churchill, L., 5, Bury Street, S.W.
Churston, L., 38, Lowndes Sq.
Clancarty, E., Palace Hotel, Buckingham Gate.
Clanmorris, L., Newbrook, Mayo.
Clanricarde, M., 17, Stratton Street, W.
Clanwilliam, E., 32, Belgrave Sq.
Clarendon, E., 1, Grosvenor Crescent, S.W.

Clarina, L., Elm Park, Limerick.
Clay, J. ....*Hull*
Clermont, L., 45, Brook St., W.
Clement, W. J. ......*Shrewsbury*
Cleveland, D., 17, St. James's Square, S.W.
Clifden, V., a minor, b. 1863.
Clifford, L., Ugbrooke Park, Devon.
*Clifton, Sir R. ......*Nottingham*
Clinton, L., 16, Park Street, W.
Clive, Hon. Col. ....*Ludlow*
Clive, G. ....*Hereford*
Clonbrock, L., 34, Duke Street, W.
Cloncurry, L., White's Club, S.W.
Clonmell, E.. Bishop's Ct., Naas.
*Clowes, S. W. ......*Leicester, N.*
Cogan, Rt. Hon. W....*Kildare, c.*
Colchester, L., 34, Berkeley Sq.
Cole, Hon. Col. ....*Fermanagh, c.*
Colebrooke, Sir T. E. *Lanark, N.*
Coleridge, J. D................*Exeter*
*Collins, T. ....*Boston*
Colonsay, L., 125, Piccadilly, W.
Collier, Sir R. P. ....*Plymouth*
Colthurst, Sir G. ....*Kinsale*
Colville, L., 42, Eaton Pl., S.W.
Combermere, V., 48, Belgrave Square, S.W. [Street, W.
Congleton, L., 47, Cumberland
Conolly, T. ....*Donegal*
Conyers, L., 55, Jermyn St., S.W.
Conyngham, M., 5, Hamilton Place, W.
Corbally, M.E.............*Meath, c.*
*Corbett, Col. E. ...*Shropshire, S.*
*Cork and Orrery, E., 1, Grafton Street, W.
Corrance, F. S. ......*Suffolk, E.*
Corry, Rt. Hon. H. T. L., *Tyrone*
Cottenham, E., Arthur's Club.
Courtenay, Lord ....*Devon, E.*
Courtown, E., 97, Eaton Pl., S.W.
Coventry, E., 40, Great Cumberland Street.
Cowen, J......*Newcastle-on-Tyne*
Cowley, E., 20, Albemarle Street.
Cowper, Rt. Hon. W.F. *Hants, S.*
Cowper, Hon. H. F. ......*Herts*
*Cox, E. M. ....*Taunton*
Cranstoun, L., Sandridge, Kent.
Craven, E., 16, Charles Street, Berkeley Square.
Craufurd, E. H. ....*Ayr*
Crawford and Balcarres, 9, Grosvenor Square.
Crawford, R. W. ....*London*
Crewe, L., 28, Hill Street, Berkeley Square.
*Crichton, Viscount..*Enniskillen*
*Croft, Sir H. D. ...*Herefordshire*
Crofton, L., 32, Bruton Street, W.
*Cross, R. A. ...*Lancashire, S.W.*
Crossley, Sir F....*Yorks, W.R., N.*
Cubitt, G. ....*Surrey, W.*
Cumberland, D., abroad.
Crum-Ewing, H. E..........*Paisley*
Curzon, Viscount ......*Leicester*
Dacre, L., Thomas's Hotel, Berkeley Square.
Dalglish, R. ....*Glasgow*
Dalhousie, E., 53, Lancaster Gate.
*Dalrymple, C...........*Buteshire*
*Dalrymple, D................*Bath*
*Dalway, M. R. ...*Carrickfergus*

*Damer, Capt......*Portarlington*
*Darcey, M. P. ......*Wexford, c.*
Darnley, E., 29, Hill Street.
Dartmouth, E., 40, Grosvenor Sq.
Dartrey, E., 30, Curzon Street, W.
Davenport, W. B....*Warwick, N.*
Davie, Sir H. ....*Haddington*
*Davies, R. ....*Anglesea*
*Davison, J. R. ....*Durham*
*Dawson, R. P. ...*Londonderry, c.*
*Dease, M. O'Reilly .. *Louth, c.*
De Blaquiere, L., 9, Strafford Pl.
Decies, L., Bolam House, Newcastle-on-Tyne.
De Freyne, L., 54, Parliament St.
De Grey and Ripon, E., 1, Carlton Gardens, S.W.
De Grey, Hon. T. ...*Norfolk, W.*
*Delahunty, J. ....*Waterford*
Delamere, L., 14, Bruton St., W.
De la Poer, E. ......*Waterford, c.*
De la Warr, E., 17, Upper Grosvenor Street.
De L'Isle and Dudley, L., 32, Albemarle St. [W.
De Mauley, L.,12, So. Audley St.
*Denbigh, E., 49, Eaton Sq., S.W.
*Denison, C. B....*Yorks, W.R.E.*
*Denison, E. ....*Newark*
Denison, Rt. Hon. J. E. *Notts, N.*
Denman, L., 28, Sackville St., W.
Denman, Hon. G. ....*Tiverton*
Dent, J. D..............*Scarborough*
Derby, E., 23, St. James's Square.
De Ros, L., 19, Eaton Place, S.W.
Derry, Bp.
De Saumarez, L., 41, Prince's Gt.
De Tabley, L., 32, Brook St., W.
Devercux, R. J. ....*Wexford*
De Vesci, V., 4, Carlton House Terrace.
Devon, E., 23, Brook Street, W.
Devonshire, D., 78, Piccadilly, W.
Dick, W. F. ....*Wicklow, c.*
*Dickinson, S. S. ....*Stroud*
Dickson, Major ....*Dover*
Digby, L., 39, Belgrave Sq., S.W.
*Digby, K. T.......*Queen's County*
*Dilke, C. W. ....*Chelsea*
Dillon, V., 34, Hill Street, W.
Dillwyn, L. L. ....*Swansea*
Dimsdale, L. ....*Hertford*
Disraeli, Rt. Hon. B. ......*Bucks*
Dixon, G. ....*Birmingham*
*Dodds, J. ....*Stockton*
Dodson, J. G. ....*Sussex, E.*
Donegall, M., 22, Grosvenor Sq.
Doneraile, V., 83, Grosvenor St.
Donoughmore,E., a minor,b.1848.
Dorchester, L., Greywell Hall, Hants.
Dormer, L., Brooks' Club, S.W.
Dowdeswell, W. E., *Worcester, W.*
Downe, V., Baldersby Park, Thirsk.
*Downing, McC. ....*Cork, c.*
Downshire, M., 24, Belgrave Sq.
*Dowse, R. ....*Londonderry.*
Dragoda, M., 48, Dover St., W.
Dublin, Abp.
Ducie, E., 1, Belgrave Sq., S.W.
Dudley, E., Dudley House, Park Lane.
Dufferin, L., 8, Grosvenor Sq., W.
Duff, M. E. Grant ....*Elgin*

Duff, R. W. ....*Banffshire*
Duffus, L., Hempriggs, Wick.
Dunalley, L., Kilboy, Tipperary.
Dunboyne, L., 75, Queen's Gt..W.
Duncombe, Hon. W. E. *N.R.*
Dundas, F....*Orkney and Shetland.*
Dundonald, E. ....[Street.
Dunmore, E., 2, Great Stanhope
Dunraven, E., 5, Buckingham Gt.
Dunsandle, L., Carlton Club.
Dunsany, L., Travellers' Club.
Du Pré, C. G. ....*Bucks*
Durham, Bp.
Durham, E., 6, Cromwell Houses, S.W.
*Dyke, W. Hart ...*Kent, Mid.*
Dynevor, L., 19, Prince's Gardens, W.
Dysart, E., Ham House, Richm.
Dyott, Col. R. R...........*Lichfield*
*Eastwick, E. B. ....*Penrhyn*
Eaton, H. W. ....*Coventry*
Ebury, L., 35, Park Street, Grosvenor Square.
Edinburgh, D., abroad.
Edwardes, Col. ...*Haverfordwest*
Edwards, H. ....*Weymouth*
Edwards, Sir H...........*Beverley*
Effingham, E., 57, Eaton Place.
Egerton, L., 7, St. James's Sq.
*Egerton, E. C. ......*Cheshire, E.*
Egerton, Sir P. ......*Cheshire, W.*
Egerton, Hon. A. F. *Lanc., S.E.*
*Egerton, Hon. Capt...*Derby, E.*
Egerton, Hon. W., *Cheshire, Mid.*
Eglington, E., 3, Upper Belgrave Street.
Egmont, E., 26, St. James's Pl.
Elcho, Lord ......*Haddingtonshire.*
Eldon, E., 1, Hamilton Place, W.
Elgin, E., a minor, b. 1849.
Elibank, L., Darn Hall, Peeblesh.
Ellenborough, E. 108, Eaton Sq.
Ellesmere, E., Bridgwater House
Ellice, E. ....*St. Andrew's*
Elliott, G. ....*Durham, N.*
Ellis, Hon. L. A.......*Kilkenny, c.*
Elphinstone, L., 21, Chesham St.
*Elphinstone, Sir J. *Portsmouth*
Ely, Bp.
Ely, M., a minor, b. 1849.
Enfield, Viscount ....*Middlesex*
Enniskillen, E., 65, Eaton Place.
*Ennis, J. ....*Athlone*
Erne, E., 95, Eaton Square.
Erroll, E., 5, Grafton Street, W.
Erskine, L.,
Erskine, Admiral ...*Stirlingshire*
Esmonde, J. ....*Waterford, c.*
Essex, E., 21, Chesham Street.
Eversley, V., 69, Eaton Place.
Exeter, Bp.,
Exeter, M., Burlington Hotel, Cork Street, W.
Exmouth, V., 1, Prince of Wales Terrace, W.
*Ewing, A. Orr...*Dumbartonshire*
Eykyn, R. ....*Windsor*
*Fagan, Capt. ....*Carlow*
Fairfax, L., Maryland, U. S.
Falkland, V., 4, Prince's Gate.
Falmouth, V., 2, St. James's Sq.
Farnham, L., Farnham, Cavan.
Fawcett, H. ....*Brighton*
Fellowes, E.................*Hunts*

Feilden, Joseph ....Blackburn
*Feilden, Joshua, Yorks.W.R.,E.
Fermoy, L., 5, Pembridge Square.
Ferrers, E., Staunton Harold, Leicestershire.
Feversham, L., 2, Albert Gate.
Ffrench, L., Castle Ffrench, Galway.
Fife, E., 4, Cavendish Square, W.
*Figgins, J. ....Shrewsbury
*Finch, G. H. ....Rutland
Fingall, E., Brooks' Club, S.W.
*Finnie, W. ....Ayrshire, N.
Fitzgerald, Lord O. ...Kildare, c.
Fitzhardinge, L., 32, LowndesSq.
*Fitzmaurice, Lord E. ......Calne
Fitzpatrick, Right Hon. J. W. Queen's County
Fitzwalter, L., 23, Park Street, W.
Fitzwilliam, E., 19, Grosvenor Sq.
Fitzwilliam, Hon. C. W. ...Malton
*Fitzwilliam, Hon. W., Wicklow, c.
*Fletcher, I. ....Cockermouth
Floyer, J. ....Dorset, c.
Foley, L., 26, Grosvenor Square.
Foljambe, F. J. S. ...East Retford
Forbes, L., 22, Palmyra Square, Brighton.
Forde, Col. W. B. ......Down, c.
Fordyce, W. D...Aberdeensh., E.
Forester, L., 6, Audley Square.
Forester, Rt. Hon. G. ...Wenlock
Forster, C. ....Walsall
Forster, W. E. ....Bradford
Fortescue, Rt. Hon. C...Louth, c.
Fortescue, Hon. D. F ......Andover
Fortescue, E., 43, Lowndes Sq.
*Fothergill, R. ...Merthyr Tydvil
*Fowler, R. N. ....Penryn
*Fowler, W. ....Cambridge
Frankfort, V.,
French, Right Hon. Colonel, Roscommon, c.
Gage, V., 4, Whitehall Yard.
Gainsborough, E., 9, Cavendish Square, W.
Galloway, E., 85, Eaton Square.
Gallwey, Sir W. P. ....Thirsk
Galway, V., Serlby Hall, Notts.
Galway, Viscount ...East Retford
Gardner, L., 46, Dover Street, W.
*Garlies, Lord ...Wigtown, c.
Gavin, Major ....Limerick
Garvagh, L., Garvagh House, Londonderry.
Gifford, L., 49, Pall Mall, S. W.
Gilpin, C. ....Northampton
Gilpin, Col. R. T. ...Bedford, c.
Gladstone, Right Hon. W. E. Greenwich
Gladstone, W. H. ....Whitby
Glasgow, E., 32, Albemarle St.
*Glass, Sir R. ....Bewdley
Gloucester and Bristol, Bp., 27, Portman Square.
Glyn, G. G. ....Shaftesbury
*Goldney, G. ....Chippenham
Goldsmid, Sir F. H. ......Reading
Gooch, Sir D. ....Cricklade
Gore, J. R. O. ......Shropshire, N.
Gore, W. O. ....Leitrim, c.
Gormanston, V., Gormanston Castle, Balbriggan.
Gort, V., 10, WarwickSquare, S.W
Goschen, Rt. Hon. G. J....London

Gosford, E., 59, Grosvenor Street.
Gough, V., 29, HydeParkGardens.
*Gourley, E. T. ....Sunderland
Gower, L. ....Bodmin
Gower, Lord R.C.L...Sutherland, c.
Grafton, D., 47, Clarges Street.
Graham, W. ....Glasgow
Granard, E., 45, Brook Street, W.
*Grant, Hon. J. O., Elgin & Nairn
Grantley, L, 10, Wilton Place.
Granville, E., 16, Bruton Street.
Graves, L., Thanckes House, Devonport.
Graves, S. R. ....Liverpool
Gray, Lt.-Col ....Bolton
Gray, Sir J. ....Kilkenny
*Greaves, E. ....Warwick
Greene, E. ...Bury St.Edmund's
*Gregory, G. B. ....Sussex, E.
Gregory, W. H. ....Galway, c.
Grenville, R. N....Somerset (Mid).
Greville-Nugent, S. ...Longford, c.
Greville-Nugent, W.F. Westmeath
Grey, E., 13. Carlton House Ter.
Grey, Rt. Hon. Sir G. ...Morpeth
*Grieve, J. J. ....Greenock
Grosvenor, Earl ....Chester
Grosvenor, Lord R......Flintshire
Grosvenor, Hn.R.W. Westminster
Grove, T. F. ....Wilts, S.
Guilford, E., a minor, t. 1851.
Guillamore, V., Caher Guillamore, Bruff.
*Guest, A. ....Poole
Gurney, Rt.Hon. R., Southampton
Gwyn, H. ....Brecknock
Haddington, E., Boodle's Club
Hadfield, G. ....Sheffield
*Hambro, C. J. T. ...Weymouth
Halifax, V., 10, Belgrave Sq.
Hamilton, D., 22, Arlington St.
Hamilton, Viscount ...Donegal
Hamilton, Lord Claude ...Tyrone
*Hamilton, Lord Geo...Middlesex
Hamilton, I. T. ......Dublin, c.
Hamilton, E. W. T. ...Salisbury
Hanbury Tracey, Hon. C. Mont-gomeryshire
Hanmer, Sir J. ....Flint
Harberton, V., University Club
*Harcourt, G. Vernon ...Oxford
Hardcastle, J.A.Bry.St.Edmund's
Hardinge, V., 36, South St. W.
Hardwicke, E., 44, Portman Sq.
Hardy, Rt. Hon. G. ......Oxford University
Hardy, J. ....Warwick, S.
*Hardy, J. S. ....Rye
Harewood, E., 13, Hanover Sq.
Harrington, E., 4, Craig's Court
Harris, L., 28, South St., Prk.Ln.
Harris, J. D. ....Leicester
Harrowby, E., 39, Grosvenor Sq.
Hastings, L., 24, Kensington Palace Gardens
Hatherley, L.
Hatherton, L., 16, Eaton Place South, S.W.
Hawarden, V., 5, Prince's Gar-
Hawke, L., Boodle's Club, S.W.
Hay, Lord John ....Ripon
Hay, Rear.-Ad.Sir J...Stamford
Headlam, Right Hon. T. E. Newcastle-on-Tyne

Headley, L., Carlton Club, S.W.
Headfort, M., Brooks's Club.
Henderson, J. ....Durham
Henley, Lord ......Northampton
Henley, Rt. Hon. J. ...Oxford, c.
Henniker, L., 6, Grafton St., W.
Henniker-Major Hn. J.Suffolk, E.
*Henry, J. S. ...Lancashire. S.E.
Herbert, H. A. ....Kerry
Herbert, Gen. P. E. Shropshire, S.
Hereford, V., Trefoyd, Brecon.
*Hermon, E. ....Preston
*Herries. L., Everingham Park.
Hertford, M., 20, Manchester Sq.
Hervey, Lord A. ......Suffolk, W.
Hesketh, Sir T. G. ......Preston
Heygate, Sir F...Londonderry, c.
Heytesbury, L., 41, Eaton Place
Hibbert, J. T. ....Oldham
*Hick, J. ....Bolton
Hildyard, T. B. ......Notts, S.
Hill, V., Thomas's Hotel, Grosvenor Square
Hill, S. ....Coventry
*Hoare, Sir H. A. ....Chelsea
*Hoare, P. M. ......Southampton
Hodgkinson, G. ....Newark
Hodgson, W. N. ......Cumberland
Holford, R. S. ...Gloucester, E.
Holmesdale, Lord ...Kent, Mid
*Holms, J. ....Hackney
*Holt, J. M....Lancashire, N.E.
Home, E., 6, Grosvenor Sq., W.
Hood, V., 40, South Street, W.
*Hood, Hon. Capt. Somerset, W.
Hope, A. J. B. ...Cambridge University
Hopetoun, E., 24, Carlton House Terrace
Hornby, W. ....Blackburn
Hotham, L., 45, Grosvenor St.
Houghton, L., 16, UpperBrook St.
Howard de Walden, L.
Howard, Hon. C. Cumberland, E.
*Howard, J. ....Bedford
Howden, L., Athenæum Club.
Howe, E., 8, South Audley St.
Howes, E. ....Norfolk, S.E.
Howth, E., Howth Castle, Dublin
Hugessen, E. K. ....Sandwich
Hughes, T. ....Frome
Hughes, W. B. ....Carnarvon
Hunt, Rt. Hon. G. W. ...North-ampton, N.
Huntingdon, E., 64, Gloucester Place, W. [Hall, Suffolk
Huntingfield, L., Heningham
Huntly, M., Aboyne Castle.
Hurst, R. H. ....Horsham
Hutt, Rt. Hon.Sir W...Gateshead
*Hutton, J. ....Northallerton
Hylton, L., 16, Stratton St., W.
*Ibbetson, H. J. S. ...Essex, W.
Ilchester, E., Melbury House, Dorsetshire
*Illingworth, A. ...Knaresborough
Inchiquin, L.,47, Prince's Grdns.
*Ingram, Sir Meynell, Stafford W
*Jackson, R. W. ......Hartlepool
*Jardine, R. ....Dumfries
*Jenkinson, Sir G. S...Wilts, N.
Jersey, E., Long's Hotel, BondSt.
Jervis, Col. ....Harwich
*Jessel, G. ....Dover
*Johnston, A. ....Essex, S.

*Johnston, W. .....*Belfast*	Limerick, *E.*, Great West. Hotel.	Marlborough, *D.*, 19, St. James's
Johnstone, Sir J ...*Scarborough*	Lincoln, *Bp.* Riseholme.	Square, S. W.
Johnstone, A. B. ....*Canterbury*	Lindsay, Hon. C. H. ....*Abingdon*	Martin, C. W. ....*Newport, I.W.*
*Jones, J......*Carmarthenshire*	Lindsey, *E.*, Uffington House,	Martin, P. W. ....*Rochester*
*Kavanagh, A. ....*Carlow, c.*	Stamford,	Masserene, *V.*, Athenæum Club.
Keane, *L.*, United Service Club	Lisle, *L.*, Mountnorth, Cork.	Massy, *L.*, Duntry League,
Kekewich, S. T. ....*Devon, S.*	Lismore, *V.*, 31, Old Burlington	Limerick.
Kellie, *E.*, Alloa Park, Clackmannan	Street, W.	Matheson, Sir J.,*Ross & Cromarty*
Konmare, *E.*,54, Eaton Pl., S.W.	Listowell, *E.*, Convamore, Cork.	*Matthews, H. ....*Dungarvan*
*Kennard, Capt. ....*Beverly*	Llandaff, *Bp.*, 27, Parliament St.	Maxwell, W. H ....*Kircudbright, c.*
Kensington, *L.*, Sandhill Park,	Lloyd, Sir T. D.....*Cardigan*	Mayo, *E.*, abroad.
Taunton	*Loch, G.... ....*Wick*	Meath, *E.*, 28, Cavendish Sq., W.
Kenyon, *L.*, 12, Portman Sq. W.	Locke, J. ....*Southwark*	Meller, Col. ....*Stafford*
Keown, W. ....*Downpatrick*	Locke-King,Hon. P. J.,*Surrey,E.*	*Mellor, T. ....*Ashton-under-Lyne*
Kesteven, *L.*, 6, Cavendish Sq.	Londesborough, *L.*, 3, Grosvenor	Melly, G. ....*Stoke-upon-Trent*
Kilmaine, *L.*, Carlton Club	Square, W.	Melville *V.*, 7, Portugal St., W.
Kilmorey, *E.*, Shavington, Salop	London, *Bp.*, 22, St. James's Sq.	Meredyth, *L.*, 22, Dover St., W.
Kimberley, *E.*, 48, BryanstonSq.	Londonderry, *M.*, 37, Grosvenor	Merry, J. ....*Falkirk*
Kinglake, A. W. ....*Bridgewater*	Square, W.	Methuen, *L.*, 8, Prince's Gate.
Kingsale, *L.*, Ringrone, Devon.	Longford, *E.*, 24, Bruton Street.	*Meyrick, T. C. ....*Pembroke*
Kingscote, R.N.F. *Gloucester, W.*	Lonsdale, *E.*, 14, Carlton House	Mexborough, *E.*, 33, Dover St.
Kingston, *E.*, 42, Brook St. W.	Terrace.	Middleton, *L.*, 32, Albemarle St.
Kinnaird, *L.*, 2, Pall Mall East.	*Lopes, H. C.....*Launceston*	Midleton, *V.*, 4, Upper Grosvenor Street.
Kinnaird, Hon. A. ....*Perth*	Lopes, Sir L. M. ....*Devon, S.*	Milbank, F. A. ....*Yorks, R.N.*
Kinnoul, *E.*, 30, Wilton Crescent	Lorne, Marquis of.....*Argyllshire*	*Miller, J. ....*Edinburgh*
Kintore, *E.*, 61, Jermyn St., S.W.	Lorton, *V.*, Rockingham, Roscommon.	*Milles, Hon. G. ....*Kent, E.*
*Kirk, W. ....*Newry*	Lothian, *M.*, 36,Belgrave Square.	Milltown, *E.*, Russborough,
Knight, F. W. ....*Worcester, W.*	*Louth, *L.*, Louth Hall, Ireland.	Wicklow.
Knightley,Sir R.,*Northampton, S.*	*Lovat, *L.*, 13, Bury Street, W.	*Mills, C. H. ....*Kent, W.*
Knox, Hon. C. S. ....*Dungannon*	Lovelace, *E.*, Brooks's Club,	Milton, Viscount. *Yorks, W.R., S.*
*Knox, Major L. ....*Sligo*	S.W.	Minto, *E.*, 48, Eaton Square, S.W.
Lacon, Sir E. ....*Norfolk, N.E.*	Lowe, Right Hon. R. ....*London	Mitford, W. T. ....*Midhurst*
Laird, John ....*Birkenhead*	University*	Molesworth, *V.*, 13, Grand Parade, Brighton.
*Lancaster, J. ....*Wigan.*	Lowther, Col. ....*Cumberland, W.*	Monck, *V.*
Lanesborough, *E.*, Lanesborough Lodge, Cavan. [Meath.	Lowther, J. ....*York*	Moncreiff, J....*Glasgow & Aberdeen*
Langford,*L.*,SummerfieldHouse,	Lowther, W. ....*Westmoreland*	Monk, C. J. ....*Gloucester*
Lansdowne, *M.*, 54, Berkeley Sq.	Loyd-Lindsay, R. J. ....*Berks*	Monsell, Rt. Hon.W...*Limerick, c.*
*Laslett, W. ....*Worcester*	Lucan, *E.*, 36, South Street, W.	Monson, *L.*, 3a, King Street, St.
Lauderdale, *E.*, 83, Lancaster	Lurgan, *L.*, Brooks's Club, S.W.	James's.
Gate, W.	*Lush, J. A. ....*Salisbury*	Montagu, Lord R. ....*Hunts*
*Lawrence, J. C. ....*Lambeth*	Lusk, A. ....*Finsbury*	Monteagle, *L.*, a minor, b. 1849.
Lawrence, W. ....*London*	Lyons, *L.*, abroad.	Montgomery, Sir G. G.
*Lawson, Sir W. ....*Carlisle.*	Lyttelton, *L.*, 12, Stratton Street.	*Peebles and Selkirk, c.*
Layard, A. H. ....*Southwark*	Lyttelton,Hon.C.G. *Worcester,E.*	Montrose, *D.*, 45, Belgrave Sq.
*Lea, T. ....*Kidderminster*	Lytton, *L.*, 12,Grosvenor Square.	Moore, C. ....*Tipperary, c.*
*Leatham, E. A....*Huddersfield*	Lyveden, *L.*, 20, Savile Row, W.	*Moore, G. H. ....*Mayo*
Leconfield, *L.*, 44, Belgrave Sq.	*M'Arthur, W. ....*Lambeth*	Moray, *E.*.Donibristle, Fifeshire.
Lee, W. ....*Maidstone*	Macclesfield, *E.*, 94, Eaton Sq.	Morgan, C. O. S., *Monmouthshire*
Leeds, *D.*, 15, Portman Square.	*M'Clure, T. ....*Belfast*	*Morgan, G. O. ....*Denbighshire*
Lefevre, G. J. S. ....*Reading*	*M'Combie, W. ....*Aberdeen, W.*	Morgan,Hon. Major.*Brecknock,c.*
Lefroy, A. ....*Dublin University*	Macdonald, *L.* ...*Armadale, N.B.*	Morley, *E.*, 2, Milton Ter., S.W.
Legh, G. C. ....*Cheshire, Mid.*	M'Evoy, E. F. ....*Meath*	*Morley, S. ....*Bristol*
Legh, W. J. ....*Cheshire, East*	*Macfie, R. A. ....*Leith*	Morrison, W. ....*Plymouth*
Leicester, *E.*, Holkham Hall, Norfolk.	*Macintosh, Æ. W. ....*Inverness*	Morton, *E.*, 16, Lowndes St., S.W.
Leigh, *L.*, 37, Portman Square.	M'Lagan, P. ....*Linlithgow, c.*	Mostyn, *L.*, 9, Lower Seymour
Leinster, *D.*, 6, Carlton House	M'Laren, D. ....*Edinburgh*	Street, W. [Club, Kilkenny.
Terrace.	*M'Lean, J. R. ....*Stafford, E.*	Mount - Cashell, *E.*, National
Leitrim, *E.*, 1, Suffolk Place, S.W.	*Magniac, C. ....*St. Ives*	Mount-Edgcumbe, *E.*, Carlton
Lennox, Lord G. ....*Lymington*	Maguire, J. F. ....*Cork*	Club, S.W. [Kilkenny.
Lennox, Lord H ....*Chichester*	*M'Mahon, P. ....*New Ross*	Mount-Garrett, *V.*, Ballyconra,
Leslie, Col. C. P. ....*Monaghan*	*Maitland, Sir A....*Edinburgh, c.*	Mountmorres, *V.*, Achonry, Irel.
Leven and Melville, *E.*, 17, Dover Street, W.	Malcolm, J. W. ....*Boston*	*Mowbray, Rt. Hon. J. R.
Lewis, H. ....*Marylebone*	*Marling, S. S. ...*Gloucester, W.*	*Oxford University*
Lewis, J. D. ....*Devonport*	Malmesbury, *E.*,19, Stratford Pl.	Muncaster, *L.*, Muncaster Castle, Ravenglass.
Lichfield, *Bp.*	Manchester, *Bp.*, 55, Jermyn St.	Munster, *E.*, White's Club, S.W.
Lichfield, *E.*, Shugborough, Staffordshire.	Manchester, *D.*, 1, Great Stanhope Street, W.	*Mundella, A. J. ....*Sheffield*
Liddell,Hon.H.,*Northumberland S*	Manners, *L.*, a minor, b. 1852.	*Muntz, P. H. ....*Birmingham*
Lifford, *V.*, Cecil House, Wimbledon.	Manners, Lord G. ....*Cambs.*	Murphy, N. D. ....*Cork*
Lilford, *L.*, Boodle's Club, S. W.	Manners, Lord J. ...*Leicester, N.*	Muskerry, *L.*, 3, Upper Wimpole Street, W.
	Mansfield, *E.*, Caen Wood, Highgate, N.	Napier, *L.*, abroad.
	Manvers, *E.*, 6, Tilney Street,W.	Napier of Magdala, *L.*, abroad.
	Mar, *E.*, Junior Athenæum Club.	

Nelson, E., 3, Seamore Place,W.
Netterville, V.,Cruicerath,Meath.
Newborough, L., Glynellifon, N. Wales. [Terrace, S.W.
Newcastle, D, 18, Carlton House
Newdegate, C. N....Warwick, N.
Newport, Viscount Shropshire, N.
Nicholson, W............Petersfield
Nicol, J. D................Kincardine
Norbury,E.,34,Belgrave Square.
Noel, Hon. G. J............Rutland
Norfolk, D., 21, St. James's Sq.
Normanby, M., Palace Hotel, Pimlico.
Normanton, E.,Somerley,Hants.
*North, F. ....Hastings
North, Col. S. J......Oxfordshire
Northampton, M.,145,Piccadilly.
Northbrook, L., 45, St. James's Place, W. [Devon, N.
Northcote, Rt. Hon. Sir S. H.
Northesk, E., Ethie, Forfarshire.
Northumberland, D., Charing Cross, S.W.
Northwick, L., 22, Park St., W.
Norwich, Bp.
Norwood, C. M. ....Hull
O'Brien, Sir P......King's County
O'Connor, O. O. ...Roscommon, ^.
O'Connor, D. M. ......Sligo, c.
O'Donoghue, D...........Tralee
Ogilvy, Sir J.............Dundee
O'Loghlen, Sir C. ......Clar,ec.
O'Neill, L., 19, Belgrave Square.
Ongley, L., Old Warden, Beds.
Onslow, G. ....Guildford
Onslow, E., Richmond, Surrey.
Oranmore, L.,Castle Macgarrett, Mayo.
Orford, E., 45, Brook Street, W.
Orkney, E., 3, Ennismore Place.
Ormathwaite, L., 28, Berkeley Square, W.
Ormonde, M., 17, Park Lane, W.
O'Reilly, Major......Longford, c.
Otway, A. J. ....Chatham
Overstone, L., 2, Carlton Gardens, S.W.
Oxford, Bp., 26, Pall Mall, S.W.
Paget, R. H.......Somerset, Mid.
Pakington, Rt. Hon. Sir J. S. Droitwich
Palk, Sir L. ....Devon, E.
*Palmer, J. H............Lincoln
Palmer, Sir Roundell, Richmond
Parker, Major ....Suffolk, W.
*Parry, Capt. ......Carnarvon, c.
Patten, Rt. Hon. J. W. Lanc., N.
Pease, J. W. ......Durham, S.
*Peek, H. W. ....Surrey, Mid.
Peel, A. W. ....Warwick
Peel, Sir R. ....Tamworth
Pelham, Lord ....Lewes
*Pell, A. ....Leicester, S.
Pemberton, E. L. ......Kent, E.
Pembroke, E., a minor, b. 1850.
Penrhyn, L., Mortimer House, Halkin Street, W.
*Percy, Earl, Northumberland,N.
Perth, E.
Peterborough, Bp.
Petre, L., 57, Portland Place, W.
Philips, R. N....Bury, Lancashire
Pim, J.....................Dublin
Platt, J...................Oldham.

Playfair, Lyon ......Ed. & St. A.
*Plimsoll, S. ....Derby
Plunket, L., Bray, Dublin.
*Pochin, H. D.............Stafford
Pollard-Urquhart, W. Westmeath, c.
Poltimore,L.,Brooks's Club,S.W.
Polwarth, L., Mertoun House, Berwick.
Portarlington,E.,Draper'sHotel, Sackville Street.
Portland, D., 19, Cavendish Sq.
Portman, L., 5, Prince's Gate, W.
Portman, Hon. W. ....Dorsetshire
Portsmouth, E., Brooks' Club.
Potter, E. ....Carlisle
Potter, T. B. ....Rochdale
Poulett, E., 3, Buckingham Gate.
*Powell, W. ....Malmesbury
*Power, J. T. ....Wexford, c.
Powerscourt, V., 37, Grosvenor Square, W.
Powis, E., 45, Berkeley Sq., W.
Price, R. G. ....Radnor
*Price, W. E. ....Tewkesbury
Price, W. P.............Gloucester
Queensberry, M., Kinmount, Dumfries.
Radnor, E., 44, Wilton Crescent.
Radstock, L., 30, Bryanstone Square, W.
Raglan, L., 9, Wilton Crescent.
*Raikes, H. C. ....Chester
*Ramsden, Sir J. ......Monmouth
Ranelagh, L., 7, New Burlington Street, W.
Ranfurly, E., a minor, b. 1849.
*Rathbone, W. ....Liverpool
Rathdonnell, L.
Ravensworth, L., Carlton Club.
Rayleigh, L., University Club.
Read, C. S...........Norfolk, S.E.
Reay, L., 10, Windsor Terrace, Plymouth.
Rebow, J. G. ....Colchester
Redesdale, L., 6, Park Place, St. James's.
*Reed, C.................Hackney
Rendlesham, L., Rendlesham, Suffolk. [Yorkshire.
*Richard, H. ......Merthyr Tydvil
*Richards, E. M...Cardiganshire
Richmond, D., 49, Belgrave Sq.
*Ridley, W., Northumberland,N.
*Ripley, H. W...........Bradford
Ripon, Bp., National Club, S.W.
Rivers, L., a minor, b. 1849.
Robertson, D. ......Berwickshire
Roden, E., National Club, S.W.
*Roden, W. S........Stoke-on-Trent
Rodney, L., a minor, b. 1857.
Rokeby, L., 22, Portman Sq.,W.
Rollo, L., 1, Regent Street, W.
Romilly, L., 14, Hyde Park Ter.
Romney, E., 48, Green Street, Grosvenor Square, W.
Rosebery, E., 139, Piccadilly.
Rosse, E., Birr Castle, King's County.
Rosslyn, E., 7, New Burlington Street.
Rossmore, L., a minor, b. 1851.
Rothschild, Baron M. ......Hythe
Rothschild, N. M. ......Aylesbury

*Round, J...............Essex, N.E.
Roxburghe, D., Clarendon Hotel, Bond Street.
Royston, Lord ...Cambridgeshire
Russell, E., 37,Chesham Pl.,S.W.
Russell, A. ....Tavistock
Russell, F. C. H. ....Beds
Russell, E. W. ....Limerick
Russell, Sir W. ....Norwich
Ruthven, L., Freeland House, Perthshire.
Rutland, D., Bute House, Kensington, W.
*Rylands, P. ....Warrington
St. Albans, D., 53, Brook Street.
St. Asaph, Bp., 14, Jermyn St.
St. Aubyn, J..........Cornwall, W.
St. David's, Bp., 1, Regent St.
St. Germans, E., 36, Dover St.
St. John, L., Melchbourne Park, Beds.
*St. Lawrence, Viscount, Galway
St. Leonards, L., Carlton Club.
St. Vincent, V., Long's Hotel, Bond Street.
Salisbury, Bp., 9, Half-moon St.
Salisbury, M., 1 Mansfield St.
Salomons, Ald., D. ...Greenwich.
Saltoun, L., 9, Gt. Stanhope St.
*Samuda, J. D'A., Tower Hamlets.
Samuelson, B. ....Banbury.
*Samuelson, H. B. ...Cheltenham.
*Sandon, Lord........Liverpool.
Sandwich, E., 46, Grosvenor Sq.
Sandys, L., 61, South Audley St.
*Sartoris, E. J. ...Carmarthen, c.
Saunderson, E. J........Cavan, c.
Saye and Sele, L., Brookes'Club.
Scarborough, E. 102, Eaton Sq.
Scarsdale, L., Kedleston Hall, Derby.
Scott, Lord H. ....Hants, S.
Scott, Sir W. ......Roxburghshire.
Scourfield, J. H. Pembrokeshire.
Seafield, E., 169, New Bond St.
Seaton, L., 34, Albany, W.
Seely, C. ....Lincoln.
Sefton, E., 37, Belgrave Square.
Selkirk, E., 43, Berkeley Square.
Seymour, Admiral ......Antrim, c.
Shaftesbury, E.,24,GrosvenorSq.
Shannon, E., CastleMartyr,Cork.
*Shaw, W. ....Bandon.
Sheffield, E., 20, Portland place.
Sherard, L., Carlton Club.
Sherborne, L., 45, Grosvenor Sq.
Sheridan, H. B. ....Dudley.
*Sherlock, D. ......King's County.
Sherriff, A. C. ....Worcester.
*Shirley, S. E. ......Monaghan, c
Shrewsbury, E.,36,Belgrave Sq.
*Sidebottom, J. ......Stalybridge.
Sidmouth, V., 36, Chester Sq.
Simeon, Sir J., ... Isle of Wight.
*Simon, J...............Dewsbury.
Simonds, W. B. ......Winchester.
Sinclair, L., Hermanstown, Haddington.
Skelmersdale, L.,41,Wilton Cres.
Sligo, M.,Clarendon Hotel, W.
Smith, Abel ....Herts.
*Smith, F. C. ....Notts, N.
Smith, J. B. ....Stockport.
*Smith, R. ....Derby, S.
Smith, S. G. ....Aylesbury

*Smith, T. E............*Tynemouth.*
*Smith, W. H. ...... *Westminster.*
Somers, E., 33, Princes' Gate.
Somerset, D., 20, Dover Street.
Somerset, Col. ...*Monmouthshire.*
Somerville, L., Arthur's Club.
Sondes, L., 32 Grosvenor Sq.
Southampton, L., Carlton Club.
Southesk, E., Kinnaird Castle, Forfarshire.
Southwell, V.
Spencer, E.,27, St. James'Place.
Stacpoole, Capt., ...*Ennis.*
Stafford, L., Palace Hotel, Pimlico.
Stair, E., 32, Albermarle Street.
Stamford, E., 33, Hill Street, Berkeley Sq.   [Houses.
Stanhope. E.,3, Grosvenor Place
*Stanley, Capt. ...*Lancashire, N.*
Stanley, Rt. Hon. Lord *King's Lynn*
Stanley, Hon. W. O....*Beaumaris*
Stanley of Alderley, L., 40, Dover Street, W.
Stansfeld, J................*Halifax*
*Stapleton, J.............*Berwick*
*Starkie, J. P. *Lancashire, N.E.*
*Stepney, Col. ....*Carmarthen*
*Stevenson, J. C....*South Shields*
Stone, W. H. ....*Portsmouth*
Stopford, S. G....*Northampton, N.*
Stourton, L., Brooks' Club. S.W.
*Stracey, Sir H. J. *Norfolk, N.E.*
Stradbroke, E., 33, Belgrave Sq.
Strafford, E., 5, St. James's Sq.
Strangford, V., 58, Cumberland Street, W.
Stratford de Redcliffe, V., 29a, Grosvenor Square, W.
Strathallan, V., 34, Thurloe Sq.
Strathmore, E., Glammis, Forfarshire.
Strathnairn, L., 47, Brook Street.
Stronge, Sir J. ....*Armagh, c.*
*Strutt, Hon. H. ....*Derby, E.*
Stuart, Colonel ....*Cardiff*
Stuart de Decies, L., Dromana, Waterford.
Sturt, Colonel............*Dorchester*
Sturt, H. G............*Dorsetshire*
Sudeley, L., 5, Bolton Row, W.
Suffield, L., 12, Berkeley Square.
Suffolk, E., Limmer's Hotel, W.
Sullivan, E. ....*Mallow*
Sutherland, D., Stafford House. St. James's, S. W.
Sydney, V., 3, Cleveland Square.
Sykes, Colonel ....*Aberdeen*
*Sykes, C............*Yorks, E.R.*
Synan, E. J. ....*Limerick, c.*
Taaffe, V., abroad.
Talbot, C. R. M., *Glamorganshire.*
*Talbot, J. G. ....*Kent, West*
Talbot de Malahide, L., 81, Jermyn Street, W.
Tankerville, E., 19, Curzon St.
Taunton, L., 27, Belgrave Square.
Taylor, P. A. ....*Leicester*
Taylour, Colonel........*Dublin, c.*

Teignmouth, L., Langton Hall, Yorkshire.
Templemore, L., 32, Bruton St.
Templetown, V., 9, Half-Moon Street, W.
Tenterden, L., Carlton Club, S.W.
Teynham, L., West Barnet, Herts.
Thurlow, L., 63, St. James's St.
Thynne, Lord H. ....*Wilts, S.*
*Tipping, W.............*Stockport*
Tite, W.....................*Bath*
*Tollemache, Hon. F. J. *Grantham*
Tollemache, J.........*Cheshire, W.*
*Tomline, G. ....*Grimsby*
Torphichen, L., Brooks' Club.
*Torrens, Colonel .....*Cambridge*
Torrens, W. M'C. ....*Finsbury*
Torrington, V., 4, Warwick Square, Pimlico.
Townshend, M., 39, Dover Street.
Traill, G....................*Caithness*
Tredegar, L., 39, Portman Sq.
Trelawny, Sir J. ...*Cornwall, E.*
Trevelyan, G. O...........*Hawick*
Trevor, Lord A. Hill ...*Down, c.*
Trimleston, L., 24, Park Lane, W.
Truro, L., 29, Dover Street, W.
Tuam, *Bp.*
*Turner, C...........*Lancashire, S.W.*
*Turnor, E.............*Lincoln, S.*
Tweeddale, M., 42, Brook St., W.
Valentia, V., Bletchington Park, Oxfordshire.
Vance, J.....................*Armagh*
Vandeleur, Col. ....*Clare, c.*
Vanderbyl, N..........*Bridgewater*
Vane, E., Holdernesse House, Park Lane, W.
Vaux of Harrowden, L., 2, Albermarle Street.
Ventry, L., Dingle, Kerry.
Verner, E. W. ....*Lisburn*
*Verner, W. ....*Armagh, c.*
Verney, Sir H........*Buckingham*
Vernon, L., 20, Hanover Sq., W.
Verulam, E., 24, Great Stanhope Street, W.
*Vickers, S.............*Wallingford*
Villiers, Rt. Hon. C. P.
...............*Wolverhampton*
Vivian, L., 17, Queen's Gate Terrace, W.
*Vivian, A. P. ......*Cornwall, W.*
Vivian, Hon. Capt. ....*Truro*
Waldegrave, E., a minor, b. 1851.
Wales, Prince of, Marlborough House, S.W.
Wallscourt, L., 31, Chester Sq.
Walpole, Rt. Hon. S. H.
..............*Cambridge University*
*Walpole, Hon. F., *Norfolk, N.E.*
*Walsh, Hon. A. ......*Radnorshire*
Walsingham, L., 23, Arlington Street, W.
*Walter, John..............*Berks*
Warwick, E., 1, Stable Yard, St. James's.
Waterford, M., 30, Charles St.,
Waterhouse, Major ...*Pontefract*

*Waterlow, Sir S. H. *Dumfries, c.*
Waterpark, L., Brooks' Club.
*Wedderburn, Sir D.......*Ayr, S.*
*Weguelin, C. ....*Youghal*
Weguelin, T. M., *Wolverhampton*
Wellington, D., Apsley House, Hyde Park.
*Wells, W. ....*Peterborough*
Wemyss, E., St. James's Place.
Wenlock, L., 29, Berkeley Sq.
Wentworth, L., 86, St. James's Street, S.W.
*West, H. W................*Ipswich*
Westbury, L., 75. Lancaster Gt.
*Westhead, J. P. B. ....*York*
Westmeath, M., 39, Devonshire Place, W.
Westminster, M., 33, Upper Grosvenor Street.
*Wethered, T. O. ....*Marlow*
Whalley, G. H. .....*Peterborough*
Wharncliffe, L., 15, Curzon St.
Whatman, J. ....*Maidstone*
*Wheelhouse, W. St. J....*Leeds*
Whitbread, S. ....*Bedford*
White, Hon. Col....*Tipperary, c.*
White, J. ....*Brighton*
Whitmore, H. ....*Bridgnorth*
*Whitwell, J. ....*Kendal*
Whitworth, B. ....*Drogheda*
Wicklow, E., 2, Cavendish Sq.
*Williams, Capt. .....*Barnstaple*
*Williams, D. ....*Merioneth*
Williams, F. M. ....*Truro*
*Williams, W. ....*Denbigh*
Williamson, Sir H...*Durham, N.*
Willoughby de Eresby, L.,*Grimsthorpe, Lincolnshire*
Willoughby de Broke, L., Junior Carlton Club.
*Willyams, E. B....*Cornwall, E.*
Wilton, E., 7, Grosvenor Sq.
Winchester, *Bp.*, 19, St. James's Square, S.W.
Winchester, M., 2a, Albany, W.
Winchilsea, E., 32, Albemarle St.
*Wingfield, Sir C. ......*Gravesend*
*Winn, R. ....*Lincoln, N.*
Winterbotham, H. S. P....*Stroud*
Winterton, E., Shillingleo Park, Sussex
Wise, H. C. ....*Warwick, S.*
Woods, H. ....*Wigan*
Worcester, *Bp.*
*Wright, Col. ....*Nottingham*
Wrottesley, L., 18, Chapel Street Park Lane.
*Wyllie, J. W. S. ......*Hereford*
Wyndham, Hon. H...*Sussex, W,*
Wyndham, Hn. P. *Cumberland, W.*
Wynford, L., 7, Park Place, St. James's, S.W.
Wynn, C. W. W. *Montgomeryshire*
Wynn, Sir W. ......*Denbighshire*
Yarborough, E.,17, Arlington St.
York, *Abp.*, Athenæum Club.
*Young, A. W..............*Helston*
Young, G. ....*Wigton*
Zetland, E., 91, Arlington St.

The Ministry.

THE PRESENT MINISTRY.		THE LATE MINISTRY.
Rt. Hon. Wm. Ewart Gladstone	*First Lord of the Treasury*	Rt. Hon. Benjamin Disraeli
Rt. Hon. Lord Hatherley	*Lord High Chancellor*	Rt. Hon. Lord Cairns
Rt. Hon. Earl de Grey and Ripon	*Lord President of the Council*	His Grace the D. of Marlborough
Rt. Hon. Earl of Kimberley	*Lord Privy Seal*	Rt. Hon. Earl of Malmesbury
Rt. Hon. Henry Austin Bruce	*Sec. of State Home Dept.*	Rt. Hon. Gathorne Hardy
Rt. Hon. Earl of Clarendon	*Sec. of State Foreign Dept.*	Rt. Hon. Lord Stanley
Rt. Hon. Earl Granville	*Sec. of State Colonial Dept.*	His Grace the Duke of Buckingham and Chandos
Rt. Hon. Edward Cardwell	*Sec. of State War Dept.*	Rt. Hon. Sir J. S. Pakington, bt.
His Grace Duke of Argyll	*Sec. of State Indian Dept.*	Rt. Hon. Sir Staff. H. Northcote
Rt. Hon. Robert Lowe	*Chancellor of the Exchequer..*	Rt. Hon. George Ward Hunt
Rt. Hon. H. Childers	*First Lord of the Admiralty*	Rt. Hon. Hen. Th. Lowry Corry
(Not in the Cabinet)	*First Commissioner of Works*	Rt. Hon. Lord John Manners
Rt. Hon. John Bright	*Pres. of the Board of Trade..*	His Grace the Dk. of Richmond
Rt. Hon. Chichester Fortescue	*Chief Secretary for Ireland*	(Not in the Cabinet.)
Rt. Hon. Marquis of Hartington	*Postmaster-General*	(Not in the Cabinet.)
Rt. Hon. G. Joachim Goschen	*Pres. of Poor-Law Board.....*	(Not in the Cabinet.)

THE ABOVE FORM THE CABINET.

F.M. H.R.H. Dk. of Cambridge	*Commanding-in-Chief*	F.M. H.R.H. Dk. of Cambridge
Rt. Hon. Lord Dufferin & Claudeboye	*Chancellor Duch. of Lancaster*	Col. Rt. Hon. Jn. Wilson Patten
Now in the Cabinet	*Chief Commis. Poor Law Bd.*	Rt. Hon. Earl of Devon
	Paym.-Gen. V.-P.B. of Trade	Rt. Hon. Stephen Cave
Austen Henry Layard	*Works and Public Buildings...*	Lord John Manners
William E. Forster	*V.-P. Committee of Council ..*	Rt. Hon. Lord Robert Montagu
James Stansfeld	*Third Lord of the Treasury ..*	(A New Office.)
W. P. Adam		Hon. Gerard James Noel
Capt. Hon. J. Vivian	*Jun. Lords H.M.'s Treasury*	Sir Graham G. Montgomery, Bt.
Marquis of Lansdowne		Henry Whitmore, Esq.
George Glyn	*Joint Secs. to the Treasury*	Lieut.-Col. Thomas Edw. Taylor
A. S. Ayrton		George Sclater-Booth, Esq.
Rt. Hon. Sir Colman O'Loghlen	*Jdge.Adv.Gen. & Jdge.Marsh.*	Rt. Hon. John Robert Mowbray
		Vice-Adm. Sir Alexander Milne
		Vice-Adm. Sir Sydney C. Dacres
	Jun. Lords of the Admiralty	Rear-Adm. George H. Seymour
		Rear-Adm. Sir J. C. D. Hay, Bt.
		Hon. Frederick A. Stanley
	Secretary to the Admiralty ...	Lord Henry Lennox
	Parl. Sec. to Poor Law Board	Sir Mich. E. Hicks Beach, Bt.
E. H. Knatchbull Hugessen	*Und. Sec. of State Home Dep.*	Sir James Fergusson, Bt.
A. J. Otway	*Und. Sec. of State Frgn. Dep.*	Edward C. Egerton, Esq.
William Monsell	*Und. Sec. of State Colon. Dep.*	Rt. Hon. Charles B. Adderley
M. E. Grant Duff	*Und. Sec. of State War Dep.*	Earl of Longford, K.C.B.
	Und.Sec. of State Indian Dep.	Lord Clinton
Sir Robert Collier	*Attorney-General*	Sir John Burgess Karslake, Knt.
Sir John Duke Coleridge	*Solicitor-General*	Sir Wm. Baliol Brett

Ireland.

Lord Lieutenant, Earl Spencer.	*Solicitor-General*, Serjeant Barry.
Under Secretary,	*Law Adviser*, Charles Shaw, Esq.
Lord Chancellor, Rt. Hon. — O'Hagan.	*Commander of the Forces*, General the Rt. Hon.
Vice-Chancellor, Rt. Hon. H. E. Chatterton.	Lord Strathnairn, G.C.B., K.S.I.
Lord Justice of the Court of Appeal, Rt. Hon.	*Hereditary Lord High Steward*, Admiral Rt. Hon.
Jonathan Christian.	Earl of Shrewsbury, Talbot, and Waterford.
Attorney-General, Rt. Hon. — Sullivan.	

Scotland.

Lord Justice General, Rt. Hon. John Inglis.	*Hereditary Master of the Household*, D. of Argyll.
Keeper of Great Seal, Earl of Selkirk.	*Hereditary Grand Constable*, Earl of Erroll.
Keeper of Privy Seal, Earl of Dalhousie.	*Knight Marischal*, Dk. of Hamilton & Brandon.
Lord Advocate, Rt. Hon. J. Moncreiff.	*Keeper of the Great Seal of the Prince of Wales in*
Lord Justice Clerk, Rt. Hon. George Patton.	*Scotland*, Sir William Dunbar, Bt.
Lord Clerk Register, Rt. Hon. Sir W. G. Craig.	*Commander of the Forces*, Major-General Randal
Solicitor-General, George Young, Esq.	Rumley.
Heritable Standard-Bearer, ViceAdmiral the Earl	
of Lauderdale, K.C.B.	

TREASURY, Whitehall.

Hours, 11 to 5.

Lords Commissioners.—*First Lord*, Right Hon. W. E. Gladstone, £5,000; *Chanc. Exch.*, Right Hon. Robert Lowe, M.P., £5,000; *Third Lord*, Rt.Hon. J. Stansfeld, £2,000; W. P. Adam, Esq., £1,000; Capt. Hon. J. Vivian, £1,000; Marq. of Lansdowne (without salary).

Joint Secretaries.—G. G. Glyn, Esq., £2,000; W. S. Ayrton, Esq., £2,000.

Permanent Secretary, G. A. Hamilton. £2,500.

Assistant to Secretaries and Auditor of Civil List, Wm. Law, Esq., £1,500.

Principal Clerks, Charles Walter Stronge, £1,500; James Henry Cole, £1,200; Morgan H. Foster, C.B., £1,500; and Sir Wm. Clerke, Bart., £1,050.

Private Secretaries to First Lord, W. H. Gladstone, Esq., M.P.), and W. B. Gurdon.

Private Secretary to Mr. Lowe, C. Rivers Wilson, Esq.

Private Secretary to Mr. Stansfeld, R. E. Welby, Esq.

Private Secretary to Mr. A. S. Ayrton, G. L. Ryder, Esq.

Private Secretary to Mr. Adam, ———

Private Secretary to Mr. Hamilton, V. D. Broughton, Esq.

Private Secretary to Mr. Glyn, F. E. Clay, Esq.

Assist. Private Sec., H. A. D. Seymour, Esq.

Private Sec. to Chanc. Exc., C. R. Wilson, Esq.

Solicitor, John Greenwood, Esq., Q.C., £2,500.

Assistant Solicitor, A. K. Stephenson, Esq., £1,200.

Accountant, Richard Mills, Esq., £680.

Legal Offices.

Lord Chancellor, Lord Hatherley.

Attorney-General, Rt. Hon. Sir Robert Collier, M.P.

Solicitor-General, Sir John Duke Coleridge, M.P.

[For other Legal Offices, Judges, &c. &c., See *Law List* following this.]

HOME OFFICE, Whitehall.

Principal Secretary for Home Affairs, The Right Hon. Henry Austin Bruce, £5,000.

Under Secretaries, Hon. A. F. O. Liddell, Q.C., £2,000; E. H. Knatchbull Hugessen, M.P., £1,500.

Chief Clerk, Fras. Seymour Leslie, Esq.

Senior Clerks, John Streatfeild, and Chas. Erskine, Esqrs., and Hon. Arthur Dillon.

Private Secretary to the Secretary of State, Albert Rutson, Esq., £300.

Clerk for Criminal Business, George Everest, Esq.

Clerk for Signet Business, Henry Wm. Sanders, Esq., £600.

Accountant, A. G. Pennefather, Esq.

Clerk for Highway and Turnpike Trusts Accounts, W. Harrison, Esq.

Parliamentary Counsel, Henry Thring, Esq.

LOCAL GOVERNMENT ACT OFFICE,

8, Richmond Terrace, Whitehall.

Secretary, Tom Taylor, Esq., £1,000.

Inspectors, Robert Rawlinson, C.E., C.B.; R. Morgan, C.E., and A. Taylor, Esqrs.

FACTORY DEPARTMENT, 10, Whitehall.

Inspector, Alexander Redgrave, Esq., £1,000.

Sub-Inspectors, Chas. Trimmer, Esq., London; Daniel Walker, Esq., Broughtyferry, Dundee; Chas. Patrick, Esq., Rawtenstall, Lancashire; Robt. Wm. Coles, Esq., Manchester; John D. Campbell, Esq., Glasgow; George H. L. Rickards, Esq., Leeds; G. H. Whymper, Esq., London; R. E. S. Oram, Esq., London; James Henderson, Esq., Blackburn; J. B. Lakeman, Esq., Halifax; ———, Esq., Huddersfield; T. S. Oswald, Esq., Nottingham; E. Gould, Esq., Sheffield.

Inspector, Robert Baker, Esq., £700.

Sub-Inspectors, Samuel Savil Kent, Esq., Llangollen; Joseph Ewings, Esq., Penworthen, Preston; David Jones, Esq., Bolton; William Straker Darkin, Esq., Belfast; Thomas Steen, Esq., Stockport; ———, Esq., Limerick; G. F. Buller, Esq., Frome; Commander May, R.N., Stoke-upon-Trent; Chas. Nassau-Girardot, Esq., Leicester; E. B. Fitton, Esq., Worcester; H. G. Earnshaw, Esq., Stroud, Gloucester; W. H. Beadon, Coventry; John Bailey, Esq., South Wales.

INSPECTORS OF COAL MINES.

Inspector of Mines, H. Seymour Tremenheere, Esq., £800.

Inspectors, W. Alexander, Esq., Glasgow; John J. Atkinson, Esq., Chilton Moor, Fence Houses; James Philip Baker, Esq., The White House, Whitmore Reans, Wolverhampton; Joseph Dickinson, Esq., Pendleton, Manchester; Frank Newby Wardell, Esq.; T. E. Wales, Esq., Swansea; T. Evans, Esq., Belper; Peter Higson, Esq., Manchester; Lionel Brough, Esq., Clifton, Bristol; George Wm. Southern, Esq., Pontefract; Ralph Moore, Esq., Glasgow; Thomas Wynne, Esq., Stone.

FOREIGN OFFICE, *Downing Street.*

Secretary of State.—Right Hon. The Earl of Clarendon, K.G., G.C.B., £5,000.

Under Secs.—Right Hon. Edmund Hammond, £2,000, and A. J. Otway, Esq., M.P., £1,500.

Assist. Under Sec.—James Murray, Esq., £1,300.

Commercial & Consular.—Hon. Chas. Spring Rice, £976.

Chief Clerk.—Francis Beilby Alston, £1,067.

Senior Clerks.—Wm. Hy. Wylde, John Bidwell, Thomas George Staveley, John Bodger Hole, John W. G. Woodford, & Hon. Edward Scott Gifford, £4,957.

Librarian & Keeper of the Papers.—Edw. Hertslet. Esq., £800.

Sub-Librarian.—Alfred Scrimshire Green, £488.

Superintendent of the Treaty Department.—John B. Bergne, Esq., £800.

Assistant.—Richard Bury, Esq., £500.

Translator.—Charles Cannon, Esq., £500.

Priv. Sec. to Lord Clarendon.—T. V. Lister, Esq., £300.

Priv. Sec. to Mr. W. Otway.— £150.

Précis Writer.—H. A. W. Hervey, Esq., £300.

Passport Dep. Clerk.—F. Bernhardt, Esq., £200.

COLONIAL OFFICE,

14, Downing Street.

Secretary of State for the Colonies, Earl Granville, £5,000.

Under Secs., Sir Frederic Rogers, Bart., £2,000; Rt. Hon. W. Monsell, £1,500.

Assist. Und. Sec. Sir F. R. Sandford, £1,500.

Law Adviser, H. T. Holland, Esq., £1,200.

Chief Clerk, Gordon Gairdner, Esq., £1,250.

Senior Clerks, Henry Taylor, D.C.L., Sir George Barrow, Bart., Charles Cox, and W. Dealtry, Esqrs., £3,628.

Private Sec., Hon. R. Meade, £300.

Librarian, William Halksworth, Esq., £769.

Assistant Librarian, Wm. W. Woods, Esq., £400.

Precis Writer, William Strachey, Esq., £1,000.

Registrar, William Anthony Nunes, Esq., £430.

Emigration Board, 8, Park Street, Westminster.
Commissioners, Thomas William Clinton Murdock, Esq., and Stephen Walcott, Esq.
Assistant Secretary, Richard Bell Cooper, Esq.

WAR OFFICE, Pall Mall.

Secretary of State for War, the Rt. Hon. E. Cardwell, M.P., £5,000.
Parliamentary Under Secretary of State, Lord Northbrook, £1,000.
Permanent Under Sec. of State, Lieut.-Gen. Sir E. Lugard, G.C.B., £2,000.
Controller-in-Chief, Maj.-Gen. Sir H. K. Storks, G.C.B., £2,000.
Assistant Under Sec. of State, D. Galton, Esq. C.B., F.R.S., £1,500.
Military Assistant, Colonel L. Shadwell, £792.
Chief Clerk, Clere Talbot, Esq., £1,200.
Private Sec., S. G. Osborne, Esq., £300.
Ditto to Lord Northbrook, F. G. Faithfull, Esq. £150.
Ditto to Sir E. Lugard, W. R. Buck, Esq., £150.
Ditto to Mr. Galton, J. W. Cooper, Esq., £150.
Ditto to Sir H. Storks, G. Lawson, Esq., £150.

COMMANDER-IN-CHIEF'S OFFICE, HORSE GUARDS.

Whitehall, S.W.—Hours 11 to 5.

Commander-in-Chief, Field Marshal H.R.H. the Duke of Cambridge, K.G., K.P., G.C.B., G.C.M.G., P.C., Colonel of the Grenadier Guards, £4,132.
Military Secretary, Lieut.-Gen. Wm. Frederick Forster, K.H., £9,243.
Assistant Military Secretary, Colonel E. B. Johnson, C.B., Royal Artillery.
Private Secretary, Col. the Hon. Jas. W. B. Macdonald, C.B., £365.
Assistants to the Military Secretary, John Drake and W. Freeth, Esqrs.
Private Sec. to Mil. Sec., J. A. F. Forster, Esq.

INDIA OFFICE.

St. James's Park.

Secretary of State, The Duke of Argyll, K.T., £5,000.
Under-Secretaries of State, Herman Merivale, Esq., C.B., £1,500; M. E. Grant Duff, Esq., M.P., £1,200.
Assistant Under-Secretary of State, James Cosmo Melvill, Esq., £2,000.

COUNCIL.

Henry T. Prinsep, *(Vice-President)*; Sir Henry C. Montgomery, Bart. Lieut.-Gen. Sir Robert J. H. Vivian, K.C.B.; Sir Jas. Weir Hogg, Bart.; Elliot Macnaghten, Esq.; Ross D. Mangles, Esq.; Sir Frederick Currie, Bart.; Wm. Urquhart Arbuthnot, Esq.; Sir T. Erskine Perry, Knt.; Major-Gen. William Erskine Baker; Sir George Russell Clerk, K.S.I., K.C.B.; and Sir Henry Bartle Edward Frere, G.C.S.I., K.C.B.; Sir K. Montgomery, K.C.B., G.C.S.I.; Sir F. Halliday, K.C.B.; Sir H. Rawlinson, K.C.B.
Private Secretary to the Secretary of State, Marquis of Lorne, £300.
Assistant Private Secretary and Precis Writer, W. N. Sturt, Esq.
Assistant Precis Writer,
Priv. Sec. to Mr. Grant Duff, £150.
Priv. Sec. to Mr. Merivale, H.G. Walpole, Esq., £150.
Clerk of the Council, John Davison, Esq.
Secretary for Military Correspondence, Major-Gen. T. T. Pears, C.B.

SECRETARIES OF DEPARTMENTS.
Financial, Thomas L. Seccombe, Esq.
Judicial and Public, Sir H. L. Anderson, K.C.S.I.
Political and Secret, J. W. Kaye, Esq.
Public Works, Railway, and Electric Telegraph, W. T. Thornton, Esq.
Revenue, Francis W. Prideaux, Esq.

ADMIRALTY.

NAVAL DEPARTMENT—Whitehall.

LORDS COMMISSIONERS:—
Right Hon. Henry Childers, M.P., £4,500.

In course of reconstruction.

Secretary, £2,000.
Second Sec., William Govett Romaine, Esq., C.B., £1,500.
Chief Clerk, John Henry Briggs, Esq., £1,100.
Private Secretary to First Lord, £300.
Private Secretary to

WORKS AND PUBLIC BUILDINGS,

12, Whitehall Place.

First Commissioner, Rt. Hon. Austen Henry Layard, M.P., £2,000.
Secretary, Alfred Austin, Esq., £1,200.
Assistant Sec., George Russell, Esq., £800.
Priv. Sec. to Com., Edmund Oldfield, Esq., £150.
Chief Examiner, Joseph Bedder, Esq., £600.
Assistant Examiner, William John Barker, Esq., £400.
Examiner of Furniture Accounts, John Miniken, Esq., £369.
Accountant, Frederick George Gibbins, Esq.
Surveyor of Works and Public Buildings, Henry Arthur Hunt, Esq., £1,000.
Salaried Architect and Surveyor, James Pennethorne, Esq., £1,500.
Assistant Surveyor of Works in London, John Taylor, Esq., £644.
Assistant Surveyor of Works, Country District, Wm. Starie, Esq., £700.
Itinerant Assistant Surveyors for Post Offices and Probate Registries, George Buckler & James Williams, Esqrs, £1,244.
Land Surveyor, Thomas Alexis Dash, Esq., £400.
Clerk of the Furniture, James Robinson Sanders Cox, Esq., £600.
Inspector of Rates, V. Griffiths, Esq., £400.
Solicitor, Philip Henry Lawrence, Esq., £1,500.

In Scotland.

Assistant Surveyor of Works, Robert Matheson, Esq., £1,000.

WOODS, FORESTS, AND LAND REVENUES,

Whitehall Place.

Commissioners, The Hon. Charles A. Gore, and the Hon. James K. Howard, £1,200 each.
Principal Clerks, James Frazer Redgrave, Esq., £800; and J. R. Sowney, Esq., £641.
Receiver-General and Paymaster, Warner Chas. Higgins, Esq., £700.
Solicitor for England, &c., Horace Watson, Esq., £1,800.
Solicitor for Scotland, Andrew Murray, Esq., Edinburgh
Solicitors for Ireland, Messrs. Hallowes and Hamilton, Dublin.
Chief Mineral Inspector, W. W. Smyth, Esq., £800.
Surveyor, James Pennethorne, Esq.

Land Revenue Records and Enrolments,
24, Spring Gardens.

Keeper of the Records, Henry G. Hewlett, Esq.
Deputy Keeper, William Impey, Esq.
Assistant Keeper, Alexander D. Young, Esq.

BOARD OF TRADE, Whitehall, S.W.

President, Rt. Hon. John Bright, M.P., £2,000.
Parliamentary Secretary, John Shaw Lefevre, Esq., M.P., £2,000.
Permanent Secretary, T. H. Farrer, Esq. £1,500.
Assistant Secretaries:—
 Commercial, Sir Louis Mallet, C.B., £1,800.
 Harbour, C. Cecil Trevor, Esq., £900.
 Railway, Robert G. Wyndham Herbert, Esq., £900.
 Marine, Thomas Gray, Esq., £800.
Chief of Statistical Department and Compt. of Corn Returns, Albany W. Fonblanque, Esq., £900.
Accountant, Henry R. Williams, Esq., £1,000.
Assistants in the Harbour, Railway, and Statistical Departments, Walter F. Larkins, Duncan Macgregor, Richard Valpy, Esqrs., each £800.
Priv. Sec. to Pres., Henry G. Calcraft, Esq., £300.
Priv. Sec. to Sec. Jemmett Browne, Esq., £150.
Priv. Sec. to Parliamentary Sec., A. E. Pearson, Esq.
Professional Members of Marine and Harbour Departments, Capt. W. H. Walker. H.C.S.; Capt. G. A. Bedford, R.N.
Surveyor General of Steam Vessels, Capt. R. Robertson, R.N.
Inspectors (Railway Department), Capt. Tyler, R.E.; Col. Yolland, R.E.; Col. F.H. Rich. R.E.; and Col. C. S. Hutchinson, R.E.; each £1,000.
Draftsman, Finlay McKenzie, Esq., £700.
Librarian, Wm. M. Bucknall, Esq., £556.
Law Clerk, F. J. Hargrave Hamel, Esq., £369.
Registrar, J. Whiting Parsley, Esq., £370.

POOR LAW COMMISSION,
Whitehall, S.W.

President, The Rt. Hon. G. Joachim Goschen, M.P. £2,000.
Secretaries, Henry Fleming, Esq., £1,500, and Arthur Wellesley Peel, M.P., £1,000.
Assist. Secretaries, Wm. Golden Lumley, Esq., £1,200, and Francis Fletcher, Esq., £900.
Inspectors, William Henry Toovey Hawley, Esq.; John Thomas Graves, Esq., F.R.S., Barrister-at-law; Andrew Doyle, Esq., Barrister-at-law; Harry Burrard Farnall. Esq., C.B.; Richd. Basil Cane, Esq.; JohnLambert, Esq.; Uvedale Corbett, jun., Esq., Barrister-at-law; Edward Smith, M.D.; Wm. Orlando Markham, M.D.; William Peel, Robert Hedley, Joseph J. Henley, Lt.-Col. Ward, and Henry Longley, Esqrs., £700 each.
Inspector of Workhouse Schools, Edward Carleton Tufnell, Henry Granville Bowyer, Thomas Browne Browne, Esqrs., £600 each; and Edmond Henry Wodehouse, Barrister-at-Law, £300.
Priv. Sec. to Pres. , £150.
Chief Clerk Office, Hugh Owen, Esq., £700.
Chief Clerk Correspondence, E. Sutton, Esq., £700.

COMMITTEE OF COUNCIL ON EDUCATION,
Council Office, Downing Street—11 to 5.

Lord President, Earl de Grey and Ripon.
Vice-President, Rt. Hon. Wm. Edward Foster, M.P., £2,000.
Secretary, Ralph R. W. Lingen, Esq, £1,500.
Assistant Secretaries, J. Sykes, A. T. Cory, Esqrs., each £1,000.
Examiners, F. T. Palgrave, W. Severn, H. S.

Bryant, W. F. Edwards, G. Miller, H. S. Drewry, F. C. Hodgson, S. Joyce, G. W. Kekewich, H. L. Whateley, Esqrs., in all £5,400.
Clerks, J. G. Hickson, H. D. Wardrop, Esqrs. £660.
Counsel, William Golden Lumley, Esq, £400.
Architect, Major Rhode Hawkins, Esq, £400.
Accountant, R. G. C. Hamilton, Esq., £405.

INSPECTORS OF SCHOOLS, £63,653.

For Church of England Schools, Rev. H. W. Bellairs, Rev. J. J. Blandford, Rev. W. J. Kennedy, Rev. M. Mitchell, Rev. D. J. Stewart, Rev. E. D. Tinling, Rev. W. P. Warburton, Rev. F. Watkins, Rev. G. R. Moncreiff, Rev. B. M. Cowie, Rev. J. G. C. Fussell, Rev. J. W. D. Hernaman, Rev. R.L. Koe, Rev. H. R. P. Sandford, Rev. E. P. Arnold, Rev. W. Campbell, Rev. W. W. Howard, Rev. H. B. Barry, Rev. B. J. Binns, Rev. T. W. Sharpe, Rev. S. J. G. Fraser, Rev. H. M. Capel, Rev. R. Temple, Rev. F. Meyrick, Rev. C. J. Robinson, Rev. N. Gream, Rev. R. F. Wilkinson, Rev. J. R. Byrne, Rev. Capel Sewell, Rev. W. F. Tregarthen, Rev. H. A. Pickard, Rev. C. F. Routledge, Rev. C. W. King, Rev. G. French, Rev. C. H. Parez, Rev. C. F. Johnstone, Rev. J. R. Blakiston, Rev. H. G. Alington, M.A., Rev. C. D. DuPort, M.A., Rev. E. T. Watts, M.A., Rev. E. W. Crabtree, M.A., Rev. G. Steele, M.A., Rev. S. Pryce, B.A., Rev. J. Lomax, Rev. R. Wilde, Rev. H. Smith, Rev. F. F. Cornish.
For Dissenters' Schools, M. Arnold, Esq. J. Bowstead, Esq.; C. H. Alderson, Esq.; W. Scoltock, Esq.; E. H. Brodie, Esq.; D. R. Fearon, Esq.; J. G. Fitch, Esq.; H. Waddington, Esq.; H. E. Oakeley, Esq.
For Roman Catholic Schools, S. N. Stokes, Esq.; H. J. Lynch. Esq.; P. le Page Renouf, Esq.
For Church of Scotland, E. Woodford, Esq., LL.D.; J. Gordon, Esq.; D. Middleton, Esq.; W. Williams, Esq.; John Hall, Esq; J. Kerr, Esq.
For other Schools in Scotland, J. Cumming, Esq., LL.D.; C. E. Wilson, Esq; James Scougall, Esq.
Episcopal, Rev. T. Wilkinson.

Science and Art Department.
Cromwell Road, South Kensington.
Secretary, Henry Cole, C.B., £1,500.
Assistant Secretary, Norman MacLeod, £800.
Chief Clerk, G. F. Duncombe, £450.
Accountant, A. L. Simkins, £450.

SCIENCE DIVISION.
Official Inspector, Capt. J. F. D. Donnelly, R.E,
Occasional Inspectors, F. J. Sidney, LL.D., and Capt. Harris, E.I.C. (Navigation).
Official Examiner, G. C. T. Bartley.

ART DIVISION.
Inspector-General for Art, Richard Redgrave, R.A.
Official Inspector, H. A. Bowler,
Official Examiner, E. P. Bartlett.
Inspectors of Local Schools, R. G. Wylde, and J. F. Iselin, M.A.

South Kensington Museum.
Mondays, Tuesdays, and Saturdays, Free. Wednesdays, Thursdays, and Fridays, Students' days, on payment of 6d. each person. Hours, 10 A.M. till 10 P.M. on Mondays, Tuesdays, and Saturdays, and on Wednesdays, Thursdays, and Fridays, from 10 till 4, 5, or 6, according to the season.
Director, Henry Cole, Esq., C.B.

Assistant Directors, R. A. Thompson, P. Cunliffe Owen, Capt. E. R. Festing, R.E., each £600.
Director of New Buildings, Lieut-Col. Scott, R.E.
Editor of Catalogues, Rev. J. H. Pollen, M.A.
Museum Keeper (Art Collection), G. Wallis.
Museum Keeper (Art Library). R. H. Soden Smith, M.A., £350.

School of Mines and Museum of Practical Geology, Jermyn Street.

Museum open on Mondays and Saturdays from 10 A.M. to 10 P.M.; on Tuesdays, Wednesdays, and Thursdays, from 10 A.M. to 4 P.M. or 5 P.M. according to the season. Museum closed on Fridays, and from 10th Aug. to 10th Sept.
Director, Sir Roderick Impey Murchison, Bart., K.C.B., F.R.S., LL.D.
Keeper of Mining Records, Robert Hunt, F.R.S.
Registrar, Curator, and Librarian, Trenham Reeks.
Professors, Thomas H. Huxley, LL.D., F.R.S. (Natural History); Warington W. Smyth, M.A., F.R.S. (Mining and Mineralogy); Edward Frankland, LL.D., F.R.S. (Chemistry); John Percy, M.D., F.R.S. (Metallurgy); Robt. Willis, M.A., F.R.S. (Applied Mechanics); Andrew C. Ramsay, F.R.S. (Geology).

GEOLOGICAL SURVEY OF THE UNITED KINGDOM.
Director-General, Sir Roderick Impey Murchison, Bart, K.C.B., F.R.S., LL.D.
Director for Great Britain, Andrew C. Ramsay, F.R.S.
Director for Ireland, J. Beete Jukes, M.A., F.R.S.
Director for Scotland, Arch. Geikie, F.R.S.
Palæontologist, R. Etheridge.
Naturalist, T. H. Huxley, F.R.S.
Geologists on the British Survey, Henry W. Bristow, F.R.S., William T. Aveline, Henry H. Howell E. Hull, B.A., E. Best, William Whitaker, B.A., T. McK. Hughes, A. H. Green, M. A. W. Topley, and J. Roche Dakyns.
Geologists on the Irish Survey, G. V. Du Noyer. W.H. Baily, F. Foot, G. H. Kinahan, and J. O'Kelly.
Geologists on the Scotch Survey, E. Hall, F.R.S., J. Geikie, B. N. Peach.

EDINBURGH MUSEUM OF SCIENCE AND ART.
Director, Professor Thomas C. Archer.
Keeper of Nat. Hist., Professor George J. Allman.

ROYAL COLLEGE OF SCIENCE FOR IRELAND. Stephen's Green, Dublin.
Dean of Faculty, Sir Robt. Kane, LL.D., F.R.S.
Secretary, Fredk. J. Sidney, LL.D., M.R.I.A.

DUCHY OF CORNWALL OFFICE,
Buckingham Gate.

THE PRINCE OF WALES' COUNCIL.
Lord Warden of the Stannaries, Lord Portman.
Attorney-Gen., Sir W. J. Alexander, Bt., Q.C.
Receiver-Gen.. Maj.-Gen. Sir T. M. Biddulph.
Comptroller of the Household, General Sir William Thomas Knollys, K.C.B.
Keeper of the Privy Seal, Herbt. W. Fisher, Esq. The Earl of Leicester.
Sec. and Keeper of Records, J. W. Bateman, Esq.
Auditor, William George Anderson, Esq.
Assistant-Secretary, George Wilmshurst, Esq.
Law Clerk, A. G. Lloyd, Esq.
Clerk Accnt. and Dep. Receiver, J. Lamond, Esq.

DUCHY OF LANCASTER OFFICE,
Lancaster Place, Strand.
Chancellor, Lord Dufferin and Claneboye, K.P., K.C.B.

Vice Chancellor of the County Palatine, William Milbourne James, Esq., Q.C.

COUNCIL OF THE DUCHY.
Admiral Right Hon. Earl of Hardwicke, P.C.
Lord Portman.
Right Hon. Lord Belper.
Right Hon. Sir George Grey, Bt., G.C.B., M.P.
Maj.-Gen. Sir T. Myddelton Biddulph, K.C.B.
Attorney.Gen., Henry Wynd. West, Esq., Q.C.
Receiver-Gen., General Charles Richard Fox.
Auditor, Francis Alfred Hawker, Esq.
Clerk of Council & Registrar, J. H. Gooch, Esq.
Coroner, William John Payne, Esq.
Queen's Serjeant, Charles Purton Cooper, Esq.
Queen's Counsel, Gordon Whitbread, Esq.
Clerk in Court & Solicitor, E. T. Whitaker, Esq.
Clerk of the Records, William Hardy, Esq.

LORD ADVOCATE'S OFFICE,
1, New Street, Spring Gardens.
Lord Advocate of Scotland, The Right Hon. James Moncreiff.
Secretary,

CUSTOMS ESTABLISHMENT,
Custom House, Lower Thames Street.
Chairman, Rt. Hon. Sir Thos. Fras. Fremantle, Bart., £2,000.
Deputy-Chairman, Fredk. Goulburn, Esq., £1,600.
Commissioners, Grenville Chas. Lennox Berkeley, Esq., Ralph William Grey, Esq., and Colonel F. Romilly, £1,200 each.
Secretary, George Dickins, Esq., £1400.
Assistant Secretary, John B. Hale, Esq., £850.
Committee Clerks, Thomas John Pittar, Joah F. Bates, and Robert Bates, Esqs., £700 each.
London Petition Clerk, W. Douglas Chester, £500.
Chief Clerks, W. Dugdale Thring, H. J. Maclean, J. Smith, and Fredk. G. Walpole, Esqrs.
Solicitor, Felix John Hamel, Esq., £2,000.
Assistant Solicitor, A. Ramsey, Esq., £800.
Assistant Solicitor for Merchant Shipping, J.O'Dowd, Esq., £800.
Surveyors General, Henry Charles Brown, Esq., and Robert A. Ogilvie, Esq., £900 each.
Receiver General, Sir Fras. Hastings Doyle, Bart., £1,200.
Assistant, Charles S. Cartwright, Esq., £600.
Comptroller-General, Henry W. Dobell, Esq., £800.
Assistant, Robert Grimes Hast, Esq., £550.
Inspector General, Imports and Exports, Edward Bernard, Esq., £800.
Assistant, Richard Whitmore, Esq., £475.
Examiner, Watkin Williams Taylor, Esq., £300.
Assistant, Henry Walter World, Esq., £550.
Comptroller of Accounts, Custom House and Victoria Docks, J. Lalor, Esq., £500.
Assistant Comptroller, J. Maggs, Esq., £380.
London Docks, Thomas Perkins, Esq., £440.
Assistant, Malcolm D. Crosbie, Esq., £400.
St. Katharine Docks, Edward Jones. Esq., £500.
Assistant, Henry Cumming, Esq., £400.
E. and W. India Docks, J. R. Squirrell, Esq., £450.
Assistant, George Haggar, Esq., £400.

TEA AND EAST INDIA DEPARTMENT.
Custom House Comptroller, S.J.Louttit, Esq., £500.
Assistant, Robert Dixon, Esq., £400.

LONG ROOM.
Collector and Chief Registrar of British Shipping, William Wybrow, Esq., £1,200.
Principals of Branches, J.S. Willimott, E.Sheppard, W. Malraison, H. Beser, G. Evans, £500 each.
Chief Clerks, Fredk. Rich, Robt. Mackay, J. R. Hawkins, E. Boyd, T. D. Thorpe, R. Main.

SEARCHERS' DEPARTMENT.

Principal, H. Caulier, Esq., £500.
Chief Clerk, Edward King, Esq., £400.

OUT-DOOR DEPARTMENT.

Comptroller, Charles E. Hunt, Esq., £700.
Inspectors-General, Samuel Brent, J. Thorpe, J.H.
Lilley (Liverpool), Esqs., £600 each.
Assist. Ins. Gen., J. E. Burt, Esq., £550.
Principal Inspector of Gaugers, Jas. L. Johnston,
£500.
Registrar for Out-door Officers, Watermen, &c.,
Robert Seath.
Principal Surveyor for Tonnage, W.H.Moore, £500.

CUSTOMS BENEVOLENT FUND (AND OFFICE OF THE BILLS OF ENTRY OF CUSTOMS.

Secretary and Manager of the Bill of Entry Office,
Robert S. Butterfield, Esq.
*Queen's Warehouse Keeper and Receiver of Wreck
for the Port of London*, Parker Stanley, Esq.
Registrar of Aliens for Port of London, J.Tribe, Esq.

INLAND REVENUE OFFICE,
Somerset House.

Chairman, Wm. Henry Stephenson, Esq., £2,000.
Deputy Chairman, Chas. J. Herries, Esq., £1,600.
Commissioners, Alfred Montgomery, Esq.; Henry
Roberts, Esq.; Sir Alex. Cornewell Duff Gordon, Bart.; James Disraeli, Esq., each £1,200.
Joint Secretaries, Thomas Sargent and William
Corbett. Esqrs., each £1,200.
Assistant Secretaries, Adam Young and William
Lomas, Esqrs., each £800.
Solicitor, William Henry Melville, Esq., £2,000.
Assistant Solicitor, Stephen Dowell, Esq., £1000.
Receiver-General, Jas. Brotherton, Esq., £1,000.
Chief Clerk, William Rea, Esq., £510.
Accountant and Comptroller-General., Frederick
Gripper, Esq., £1,000.
Assistant Do. Thomas Stair, Esq., £675.
Registrar of Licenses and Bankers' Returns, William
W. Dalbiac, Esq., £590.
Chief Clerk, John Halse, Esq., £390.
Registrar of Warrants, H. C. Reding, Esq., £425.
Chief Clerk, James Boulton, Esq., £290.
Warehouse-keeper, George Evett, Esq., £570.
Assistant Do., Dugald M'Intyre, Esq., £440.
Chief Clerk, Henry C. Elliott, Esq., £335.

STAGE AND HACKNEY CARRIAGE, RAILWAY AND
RACE HORSE DUTIES OFFICE, Somerset House.

Assessor, William W. Sutherland, Esq., £500.

STAMPING DEPARTMENT.

Comptroller, Edwin Hill, Esq., £770.
Deputy Do. Ormond Hill, Esq., £520.

SURVEYORS OF TAXES (METROPOLITAN.)

City of London, 1st district: Edward Welsh; *2nd.
dis.*, A. J. Deane; *3rd dis.*, H. W. Noble; *4th
dis.*, F. Cheeseman, 1 and 2, Great Winchester
Street Buildings.
Tower, 1st district: Charles Gross, Alma Villas,
Dalston; *2nd dis.*, S. Knott, 17, Arbour Terrace, Commercial Road East.
Mile End, Augustus Samson, 118, Mile End Road.
Finsbury, 1st district: Evan Lloyd, 18, Charterhouse Square; *2nd dis.*: F. W. Clarke, 6, Pullin's Row, Upper Street, Islington; *3rd dis.*:
F. W. Gribble, 2, Market Place, Upper Holloway Road.
St. Pancras part of Hampstead: Ralph Heslop Silversides, 21, Harrington Street, Hampstead
Road; *St. Pancras*: Joseph Welsh, 28, Red
Lion Square.
Kensington, 1st district: William Mayne, 25, Upper

Phillimore place, Kensington; *2nd dis.*: Henry
Sibley Hodgson, 12, Broadway, Hammersmith.
Paddington: David Cumberland, 18, Paddington
Green.
Marylebone 1st district: Rob. W. Ramsay; *2nd dis.*:
Arthur G. Day, 43, Somerset Street, Portman
Square.
Bloomsbury: H. Sach, 26, Gt. Russell Street.
St. Margaret's, Westminster: Augustus Samson,
13, Charlotte Street, Pimlico.
St. George's, Hanover Square: Francis Blake, 43,
Somerset Street, Portman Square.
St. Martin's-in-the-Fields: C. Robinson, 3, King
Street, Covent Garden.
St. James's, Westminster: E. H. Row, 13, Air
Street, Regent Street.
East Brixton, 1st district: John Robert Cottell, 2,
Gloucester Place, Brixton; *2nd dis.*: Henry
Haworth, 6, Hanover Place, Clapham Road;
3rd dis.: Roger Bourne, Elephant Buildings,
Walworth.
Clapham: W. Henry Cottell, 2, Gloucester Place,
Brixton.
West Brixton: Richard Pearce, New Wandsworth.
Southwark: Alf. A. Gracewood, Elephant Buildings, Walworth.
Principal of the Laboratory, G. Phillips, Esq.,
£450.
Deputy, James Bell, Esq., £450.
Surveyor of Buildings, H. Witherden Young, Esq.
Chief Inspector of Stamps and Taxes Department,
Edward Hyde, Esq., £800.
Assistant, Frederick B. Garnett, Esq., £600.
First Class Inspector, T. Fawcitt, Esq., £650.
Registrar of Land Tax, H. E. Harvey, Esq.
Deputy Registrar of Land Tax, J. Salter, Esq.
Comptroller Legacy and Succession Duty Department, Alfred Hanson, Esq., £1,500.
Assistant Comptroller, C. Walpole, Esq., £1,000.
Chief Clerks, Henry E. A. Dalbiac, £800; Frank
H. Stephenson, £700; and T. G. Godby, £650.
Superintendents, John Parker, £750, (Edinburgh),
and B. N. Hindes (Ireland), £500.

CANCEL AND SPOILED STAMP OFFICE.

Allowance Days, Tuesday and Thursday, 12 to 2;
Saturday, 10 to 12.
Examiner, Richard P. Walker, Esq., £680.

SEA POLICY STAMP OFFICE.

1 and 2, Great Winchester Street Buildings.
Distributor, John Harrison, Esq.
Chief Clerk, vacant.

SPECIAL COMMISSIONERS' DEPARTMENT.

Richard M. Lynch, Daniel O'Connell, Esqrs., and
Viscount Sudeley, each £600.
Chief Examiner of Claims, Walter B. Long, Esq.,
£640.
Assistant Examiner, A. J. Gibbs, Esq., £430.
Chief Assessment Clerk, C. F. Leith, Esq., £540.

INLAND REVENUE (COLLECTORS') OFFICES.
Where all Licences and Excise duties are paid
and all description of Licences granted. Attendance from 9 a.m. to 3 p.m. Saturdays,
close at 2 p.m.
London Central Collection, 1 and 2, Winchester
Buildings, London Wall, E.C., J. Harrison, Esq.
London East Collection, Tower Hill, J. Weddle,
Esq.
London North Collection, 40, Gloucester Street,
Camden Town, N., C. R. Solomon, Esq.
London South Collection, Elephant Buildings, S.
H. Tarrant, Esq.
London West Collection, Somerset House, W.C.,
M. Hargreaves, Esq.

INLAND REVENUE OFFICES.

Where Supervisors attend from 9 to 11 a.m., Grant Dog Licences, and occasional Licences to Publicans and Refreshment-house Keepers.

Gresham House (Room No. 23), Mr. Ord, Supervisr.

19, *Bridgewater Sq., Barbican,* Mr. Scott, do.
229, *Hackney Road.* Mr. Craven, do.
11, *Bruce Rd., Bromley-by-Bow,* Mr. Marriott, do.
Tower Hill, Mr. Snelgrove .... do.
40, *Gloucester St., Camden Tn.,* Mr. Barrett, do.
6, *Pallin's Row, Islington,* Mr. Scattergood, do.
183, *Gt. Portland Street,* Mr. Townsend, do.
384, *Kennington Road,* Mr. Harper, do.
Elephant Buildings, Mr. Peake, do.
153, *Lupus Street, Pimlico,* Mr. Newman, do.
26, *Gt. Russell St., Bloomsbury,* at which office Game and Hawkers' Licences are granted, Mr. Weller .... do.

PROVINCIAL COLLECTORS OF INLAND REVENUE.

Aylesbury, William Wells Page, Esq.
Bangor, David Lawton, Esq.
Barnstaple, Charles Dudgeon, Esq.
Bath, George Augustus Mason, Esq.
Birmingham, Andrew Cowie, Esq.,
Bolton, Charles Sheriff, Esq.
Brighton, William Llewellin, Esq.
Bristol, Josh. Drinkwater, Esq.
Cambridge, William S. Welsman, Esq.
Canterbury, John Shea, Esq.
Cardiff, Richard Hill, Esq.
Carlisle, George Whitehead, Esq.
Carmarthen, John Ambrose Edgar, Esq.
Chester, Walter Butler, Esq.
Colchester, William Coomber, Esq.
Coventry, William Hickling, Esq.
Derby, Charles Frederick Oding, Esq.
Exeter, Andrew Wilson, Esq.
Gloucester, Robert Moffat, Esq.
Halifax, Stephen Mallison, Esq.
Hereford, William Coles, Esq.
Hull, Arthur Gerald Geoghegan, Esq.
Ipswich, Robert Burton, Esq.
Kingston, Colin Campbell, Esq.
Lancaster, John Booth, Esq.
Leeds, John Bailey, Esq.
Leicester, John Raw Gill, Esq.
Lichfield, Robert Pape, Esq.
Lincoln, John Davis, Esq.
Liverpool, Alexander Fraser, Esq.
Lynn, John W. Priestman, Esq.
Maidstone, Horatio Standley, Esq.
Manchester, James Chevalier, Esq.
Newcastle-on-Tyne, John Miller, Esq.
Northampton, James Leighton Acklam, Esq.
Norwich, Thomas Drinkwater, Esq.
Nottingham, William Cronin, Esq.
Oxford, David Hammond, Esq.
Plymouth, John Harris, Esq.
Portsmouth, Robert East, Esq.
Reading, William Ritson, Esq.
Ripon, James Walton, Esq.
Salisbury, David William Richards, Esq.
Sheffield, James Fairlie, Esq.
Shrewsbury, George Scott Gillitlic, Esq.
Southampton, John Jolliffe, Esq.
Stafford, Nathaniel Cresswell, Esq.
Stamford, James Hudson, Esq.
Stourbridge, George Thorne, Esq.
Sunderland, William Kelman, Esq.
Swansea, Frederick Clarkson, Esq.
Taunton, Andrew Cornwall, Esq.
Truro, Walter Coath, Esq.
Ware, John Harrison, Esq.
Warrington, William Ball, Esq.

Welchpool, William Fisher, Esq.
Weymouth, George Chapple, Esq.
Worcester, Thomas Watts, Esq.
York, James Macfadzean, Esq.

POST OFFICE,

Chief Office, St. Martin's-le-Grand.

Postmaster-General, Marquis of Hartington, £2,500.
Secretary to the Post Office, J. Tilley, Esq., £1,500.
Assist. Secs., Fredk. Hill and F. Ives Scudamore, Esqs., £1,200 each.

Secretary's Office.

Chief Clerk, Rodie Parkhurst, Esq., £800.
Foreign and Colonial, Wm. Jas. Page, Esq., £900.
Home Mails, Arthur Benthall, Esq., £793.
Priv. Sec. to Postm.-Gen., J. L. Du Plat Taylor, Esq., £300.
Medical Officer, Dr. Waller Lewis.
Solicitor, William Henry Ashurst, Esq., £1,500.
Assistant Solicitor, R. W. Peacock, Esq., £1,000.
Surveyor, Metropolitan District, A. M. Cunynghame, Esq., £800.
Surveyors, Provincial Districts, George Hen. Creswell, William John Godby, John Warren, John Patten Good, Wm. Gay, James H. Newman, Ernest Milliken, Wm. Barnard, Henry James, Edward Burckhardt, A. A. Burckhardt, E. Maberly, C. Rea, and T. B. Harkness, Esqrs., £700 each.
Inspector-Gen. of Mails, E. J. Page, Esq., £900.
Principal Clerk, Lachlan Maclean, Esq., £500.
Surveyor, Travelling Post Office Department, John West, Esq., £643.
Receiver and Accountant-General, Geo. Chetwynd, Esq., £825.
Chief Examiner, Charles Court, Esq., £575.
Cashier, Charles Burges Fyfe, Esq., £575.
Principal Bookkeeper, William Court, Esq., £550.
Controller, Money Order Office, Frederic Rowland Jackson, Esq., £850.
Chief Clerk, William Farmer, Esq., £550.
Bookkeeper, Henry Thomas Palmer, Esq., £450.
Examiner, Charles John Croke, Esq., £417.
Controller, Savings' Bank Department, A. C. Thomson, Esq., £580.
Assistant Controller, J. Ramsey, Esq., £470.
Controller, Circulation Department, T. Boucher, Esq., £900.
Chief Clerk, G. E. Stow, Esq., £575.
Controller, Returned Letter Office, G. R. Smith, Esq., £600.

INLAND BRANCH.

Sub-Controller, H. Mellersh, Esq., £600.

LOMBARD STREET BRANCH OFFICE.

Postmaster, W. Hillmer, Esq., £500.

CHARING CROSS BRANCH OFFICE.

Postmaster, W. Tull, Esq., £500.

NEWSPAPER BRANCH.

*Assist. Superintendt. in Charge.—*H. Pannett, Esq.
Inspectors of Sorting, A. Swift, J. Robinson, and J. Steel.

FOREIGN BRANCH.

Sub-Controller, J. C. Lovett, Esq. £600.

REGISTERED LETTER BRANCH.

Sub-Controller, W. H. Grey, Esq., £600.

EAST CENTRAL OFFICE, St. Martin-le-grand.
Postmaster, F. Salisbury, Esq., £600.

WEST CENTRAL OFFICE, Charing Cross.
Postmaster, G. Tuck, Esq., £500.

Metropolitan District Offices.

1. WESTERN DISTRICT OFFICE, 3, Vere Street.
Postmaster, J. Milton, Esq., £600.
2. EASTERN DISTRICT OFFICE, Nassau Place, Commercial Road.
Postmaster, C. J. Potter, Esq., £500.
3. SOUTH-WESTERN DISTRICT OFFICE, 8, Buckingham Gate.
Postmaster, T. W. Angell, Esq., £550.
4. SOUTH-EASTERN DISTRICT OFFICE, Borough.
Postmaster, J. Lawson, Esq., £550.
5. NORTHERN DISTRICT OFFICE, Essex Road.
Postmaster, H. Wilson, Esq., £450.
6. NORTH-WESTERN DISTRICT OFFICE, Seymour Street.
Postmaster, W. F. Potts, Esq., £450.

BRITISH MUSEUM,

Great Russell Street, Bloomsbury.

Principal Librarian and Secretary, John Winter Jones, Esq., F.S.A., £800, and £400 as *Secretary*.
Assistant Secretary, Thomas Butler, Esq., £500.
Accountant, John Cleave, Esq., £500.
Keeper of Printed Books, Thomas Watts, Esq.
Assistant Keepers, William Brenchley Rye and George Bullen (Superintendent of Reading Room), Esqrs.
Keeper of Maps and Charts, R. H. Major, Esq., F.R.G.S.
Keeper of Manuscripts and Egerton Librarian, Edward Augustus Bond, Esq.
Keeper of Oriental MSS., C. Rieu, Esq., Ph.D.
Superin. of Nat. Hist., Prof. R. Owen, F.R.S., £800.
Keeper of Zoology, Dr. John E. Gray, F.R.S.
Keeper of Geology, Geo. R. Waterhouse, Esq.
Keeper of Mineralogy, N. S. Maskelyne, Esq., M.A.
Keeper of Botany, J. J. Bennett, Esq. F.R.S.
Keeper of Oriental Antiquities, Samuel Birch, Esq., LL.D., F.S.A.
Keeper of Greek and Roman Antiquities, Charles T. Newton, Esq., M.A.
Keeper of British and Mediæval Antiquities and Ethnography, Augustus W. Franks, Esq., M.A., F.S.A.
Keeper of Coins and Medals, William Sandys Wright Vaux, Esq., M.A., F.R.S.
Keeper of Prints and Drawings, G. W. Reid, Esq.
The Salaries of Keepers of Departments, thirteen, vary from £300 to £600 annually, and those of three Assistant Keepers are £450 each.
Solicitors, Messrs. Bray, Warren, Harding, and Warren.

The Museum is open on Mondays, Wednesdays, and Fridays—

Nov. Dec. Jan. and Feb. ...... 10 to 4
Sept. Oct. Mar. and Apr. ...... 10 to 5
May, June, July, and Aug. ... 10 to 6

The Reading Room is open to persons holding tickets of admission every day—

Nov. Dec. Jan. and Feb. ...... 9 to 4
Sept. Oct. Mar. and Apr. ...... 9 to 5
May, June, July, and Aug. ... 9 to 6

The Museum is also open during the Easter, Whitsun, and Christmas weeks, every day, except Saturday.

The Museum and Reading Room are closed on Sundays, Ash Wednesday, Good Friday, and Christmas Day; also from the 1st to 7th January, the 1st to 7th May, and the 1st to 7th September, inclusive.

The total estimates voted for the Museum for 1868–69 were £99,380, showing a net increase on the previous year of £3,934. Of this amount £49,135 is absorbed in salaries and wages, £24,035 in purchases and acquisitions; £10,500 in bookbinding; the remainder being for various incidental expenses. The total number of persons, exclusive of readers, who visited the Museum in 1867, was 445,036. The number of visits to the Reading-room by students and others, 103,469, which, with other visitors on the closed days to the Sculpture and other Galleries, for the purpose of study, make a total of 556,317 for the year. In 1868, in addition to the regular open days for general visitors, as stated above, the public were admitted on Saturdays from the 8th of May to the 31st of August between twelve and six o'clock, a plan which will most probably be adopted in the summer of 1869. The number of volumes catalogued in the Library is 139,111. The additions to the Library in 1867, amounted to 32,645 volumes.

CHARITY COMMISSIONERS.

8, York Street, St. James's Square.

Unpaid, Rt. Hon. William Edward Forster, M.P.
Chief Com. Peter Erle, Esq., Q.C., £1,500.
Commissioners, James Hill, Esq., and Arthur Hobhouse, Esq., Q.C., £1,200 each.
Secretary, Henry Morgan Vane, Esq., £800.
Inspectors, Thos. Hare, Walker Skirrow, Francis Offley Martin, and W. Good, Esqrs., £800 each.
Chief Clerk, George Henry Gauntlett, Esq., £500 to £700.

CIVIL SERVICE COMMISSIONERS,

4, Broad Sanctuary, Westminster.

First Commissioner, Rt. Hon. Sir E. Ryan, £1,500.
Secretary, Theodore Walrond, Esq., £800.
Registrar, Horace Mann, Esq., £600.
Assistant Examiners, E. Headlam, Esq., £700, and E. Poste, Esq., £500.

COPYHOLD, INCLOSURE, AND TITHE COMMISSION, 3, St. James's Square.

Commissioners, George Darby, George Ridley, and James Caird, Esqrs., each £1,500.
Assistant Commissioners, Lieut.-Col. George A. Leach, R.E., £1,000; and Henry Pyne Esq., £700.
Architectural Surveyors, George B. Mayo, Esq., John James Thomson, Esq., M.I.B.A.
SURVEY AND MAP DEPARTMENT under Lieut.-Col. Leach, R.E.
Secretary, Henry Morgan Vane, Esq., £800.

ECCLESIASTICAL AND CHURCH ESTATES COMMISSIONERS, 10, Whitehall Place.

Church Estates Commissioners, The Earl of Chichester; the Right Hon. John Robert Mowbray, M.P., and Edward Howes, Esq., M.P.
Treasurers, The Earl of Chichester, the Right Hon. John Robert Mowbray, M.P., and Edwd. Howes, Esq., M.P.
Auditor, W. G. Anderson, Esq.
Secretary, James Jell Chalk, Esq.
Assistant Secretary, George Pringle, Esq.
Architect, E. Christian, Esq., 8A, Whitehall Place.
Surveyors, Mess. Clutton, 9, Whitehall Place, and Smith & Watkins, 14, Whitehall Place.

GOVERNMENT EMIGRATION OFFICE,
65, Fenchurch Street.

Chief Officer, Capt. John S. Forster, R.N.
Assistants, Capt. Westbrook, R.N.; Capt. Barnard, R.N.; Capt. Stanbridge, R.N.
AT THE OUTPORTS :—*Liverpool*, Rear-Ad. Robert Kerr. *Assistants*, Capt. Bourchier, R.N.; Lieut. H. J. Edwards, I.N.; Capt. Hoblyn, R.N.—*Plymouth*, Capt. Stoll, R.N.—*Glasgow and Greenock*, Capt. Mackenzie, R.N.—*Queenstown*, Capt. Gibbons, R.N.—*Londonderry*, Capt. Gough, R.N.; Capt. Geary, and Capt. J. R. St. Albans.

EXCHEQUER AND AUDIT DEPARTMENT,
Somerset House.—(Hours 10 to 4.)

Comptroller-General of Her Majesty's Exchequer, and Auditor-General of Public Accounts, Sir William Dunbar, Bt., £2,000.
Assistant Comptroller and Auditor, William George Anderson, Esq., £1,500.
Secretary, Chas. Lister Ryan, Esq., £800 to £1,000.
Chief Clerk, Henry Treherne, Esq.
Inspectors, first section, Henry Thomas Dundas Bathurst, Francis Alfred Hawker, John Williams Soady, John Llewelyn, Charles Mallet, Henry Treherne, £600 to £800 each.
Private Secretary to the Comptroller and Auditor General, Wm. Cospatrick Dunbar, Esq., £100.

FRIENDLY SOCIETIES' REGISTRATION OFFICE, 28, Abingdon Street.

Registrar, J. Tidd Pratt, Esq., £1,000.
Chief Clerk, H. Tompkins, Esq., £300.

GENERAL REGISTER OFFICE,
Somerset House, W.C.

Registrar-General, George Graham, Esq., £1,200.
Secretary, E. Edwards, Esq., £800.
Superintendents, William Farr, M.D., F.R.S.; James Thomas Hammick, W. H. W. Tytheridge, William Clode, Thomas Oakes, and John Shoveller, Esqs., in all £3,210.
Inspectors of Registration, John Stevens Thornton and E. Whitaker, Esqrs., in all £946.

GREENWICH ROYAL OBSERVATORY.

Astronomer Royal, George Biddel Airy, Esq., LL.D., D.C.L., M.A., F.R.S., &c., £1,000.
First Assistant, Edward James Stone, Esq., M.A., F.R.S., F.R.A.S., £400.
Sen. Assistants, J. Glaisher, F.R.S., F.R.A.S., £300; and Edwin Dunkin, F.R.A.S., Esqls., £230.
Junior Assistants, William Ellis, F.R.A.S., £180; George Strickland Criswick, £170; William Thynne Lynn, B.A., Lond., F.R.A.S., £170; and James Carpenter, F.R.A.S., £150., Esqrs.
Additional Assistant for Magnetical & Meteorological Observatory, William C. Nash, Esq., £120.

HERALDS' COLLEGE,
Bennet's Hill, Doctors' Commons.

Earl Marshal, Duke of Norfolk.

KINGS OF ARMS :—

Garter, Sir Charles G. Young, D.C.L., F.S.A.
Clarenceux, Robert Laurie, Esq.
Norroy, Walter Aston Blount, Esq.

SIX HERALDS :—

Lancaster, Albert William Woods, Esq., F.S.A.
Richmond, Matthew C. H. Gibbon, Esq.
York, Thomas William King, Esq., F.S.A.
Windsor, G. H. Rogers-Harrison, Esq.
Chester, Henry Murray Lane, Esq.
Somerset, James Robinson Planché, Esq.

FOUR PURSUIVANTS :—

Portcullis, George William Collen, Esq.
Rouge Dragon, George E. Adams, Esq., M.A.
Blue Mantle, H. H. Molyneux Seel, Esq.
Rouge Croix, John Haviland, Esq.
Registrar, Albert William Woods, Esq.
Earl Marshal's Secretary, Henry Matthews.

IRISH OFFICE,
17 and 18, Great Queen Street.

Chief Secretary to the Lord Lieutenant of Ireland, Right Hon. Chichester Fortescue, M.P., £4,425.
Private Secretary to Chief Secretary, T. H. Burke, Esq.

LONDON GAZETTE OFFICE,
45, St. Martin's Lane. Hours, on Monday, Wednesday, Thursday, and Saturday 10 to 5; on Tuesday and Friday 10 to 3; and 6 to 7 for publication *only*.

Editor, Manager, and Publisher, Thomas Lawrence Behan, Esq., £800.
Chief Clerk, Walter Coates, Esq., £400.
Total expenditure, £8,398; receipts, £23,237.

LORD GREAT CHAMBERLAIN'S OFFICE,
Royal Court, House of Lords.

Joint Hereditary Lord Great Chamberlain, Lord Willoughby de Eresby.
Secretary, Robert Burrell, Esq.
** Tickets are issued gratis to the public every Saturday between 10 and 4 o'clock, to view the Houses of Parliament.

MARINE LOCAL BOARD.
Office for Examinations, 5, East India Avenue. *Mercantile Marine Office for the Entry and Discharge of Crews*, Hammet Street, Minories.
Chairman, Henry Green, Esq.
Secretary, John Domett.

MARINE OFFICE,
7, New Street, Spring Gardens.

Inspector-General, Major-Gen. J. O. Travers, C.B.
Deputy Adjutant-General, Col. S. N. Lowder, C.B.
Assistant Adjutant-General, Col. J. W. C. Williams.

GENERAL REGISTER OFFICE OF SHIPPING AND SEAMEN.
6, Adelaide Place, London Bridge.

Registrar-General, John J. Mayo, Esq., £1,000.
Inspector, J. Hughes, Esq., £567.

SURVEYORS OF STEAM SHIPS UNDER THE MERCHANT SHIPPING ACT. 1854,
5, East India Avenue, Leadenhall Street.

Chief Surveyors, R. Galloway, Esq. C.E.; George Barber, Esq., M.I.N.A.
Surveyors of Steam Vessels for the Port of London, G. J. Gladstone, Robert Taplin, C.E.; T. W. Traill, R.N., C.E.; and S. W. Snowden, C.E., Esqrs.
Surveyors at the Outports :—Bristol, Walter Hannah; *Hull*, Orme Hamerton; *Liverpool*, W. C. Taylor, Robert Murray, Alexander Elder, and William Campbell (for wood only); *Newcastle*, William Burroughs, 1 vacant; *Plymouth*, H.D. Grey; *Southampton*, vacant.
SCOTLAND—*Glasgow*, James Grier and Alexander M'Kinlay; *Leith*, Leighton Mills.
IRELAND—*Dublin*, F. W. Wyner; *Cork*, H. S. Bone.

METEOROLOGICAL OFFICE,
2, Parliament Street.

Chairman of Committee, Lieut-General Sabine, R.A., F.R.S.
Secretary, Balfour Stewart, LL.D., F.R.S.
Director, Robert H. Scott, M.A., F.G.S.
Marine Superintendent, Captain H. Toynbee, F.R.A.S.

METROPOLIS ROADS NORTH of the THAMES,
Office, 32, Craven Street, Strand.
Secretary, George Labalmondiere, Esq.
Accountant, Vincent Charles Wright, Esq.
Surveyor-General and Inspector, H. Browse, Esq.
Superintendent of Tolls, Murray Anderson.

MINT,
Tower Hill. 10 to 4.
Master Worker, Thos. Graham, Esq., F.R.S., £1,500.
Deputy Master and Comptroller (vacant), £1,000.
Registrar and Accountant, Rbt. F. Suft, Esq., £354.
Senior Clerks, Robert Mushet, Charles Sterry, W. J. Aberdein, and R. A. Hill, Esqrs., £631.
Superintendent of Coining and Die Department, John Graham, Esq., £531.
Foreman of the Press-Room, Mr. J. Newton, £290.
Queen's Assay Master—resident, H. W. Field, Esq.
Assistant Assayer, E. J. Ridsdale, Esq.
Non-Resident Assayers. Dr. Miller, Dr. J. Stenhouse, and Messrs. Johnson.
Modeller and Engraver to the Mint, Leonard Wyon, Esq., £
Resident Engraver, T. J. Minton, Esq., £230.
Cost of Establishment, 1868-69, £18,000.

NATIONAL DEBT OFFICE,
19, Old Jewry.
Secretary and Comptroller-General, Sir Alexander Young Spearman, Bart., £1,500.
Assistant Do., Charles Henry Wyndham A'Court Repington, Esq., £1,000.
Actuary, Alexander Glen Finlaison, Esq., £900.
Chief Clerk, William Taylor, Esq., £700.
Principal Check Officer, Chas. J. Bott, Esq., £600.
Principal Clerks, Chas Lee, Robt. L. Fenn, William Barnett, and Henry Court, Esqrs., £2,210.
Private Secretary to the Comptroller-General, Geo. J. Haffenden, Esq., £100.
Consulting Barrister, John Tidd Pratt, Esq.
Brokers, William Herbert Mullens, John Henry Daniell, John Ashley Mullens, and William Edward Marshall, Esqrs., £750.

NATIONAL GALLERY,
Trafalgar Square and South Kensington.
Director, William Boxall, Esq., R.A., £1,000.
Keeper and Secretary, Ralph Nicholson Wornum, Esq., £750.

NATIONAL PORTRAIT GALLERY,
29, Great George Street.
Public days (admission free), Mondays, Wednesdays, and Saturdays, from 10 to 4; and, in summer months, from 10 till 6.
Secretary and Keeper, Geo. Scharf, Esq., F.S.A., £470.

PARKS, CHASES, AND GARDENS.
Ranger of St. James', Green and Hyde Parks, and Richmond, H.R.H. the Duke of Cambridge, K.G.
Superintendent Department of the Ranger, Colonel the Hon. James MacDonald, C.B.
Superintendent Department of the Commissioners of Works, Mr. John Mann, Palace entrance, Kensington.
Richmond, Col. the Hon. Augustus Liddell, *dep.*
Ranger of Greenwich Park (vacant).
Greenwich and Victoria Parks, Mr. G. Merrett, the Lodge, Victoria Park.
Hampton Court Park, Dowager Lady Bloomfield.
Ranger of Bushy Park, Her Majesty the Queen.
Head Keeper of do., Mr. Rowe Sawyer.
Regent's Park, Mr. Charles Edwards, North Lodge.

Battersea and Kennington Parks, and Chelsea Asylum Grounds, Mr. John Gibson.
Director of the Royal Botanical Gardens, Kew, Joseph D. Hooker, Esq. F.R.S., £800.
Curator, John Smith, Esq., £280.
Brompton Cemetery, John H. Ruddick.

PATENT OFFICE.—*See page 104.*

PATRIOTIC FUND,
19, New Street, Spring Gardens.
Treasurer, The Paymaster-General.
Trustees, The First Lord of the Admiralty, Secretary of State for War, and The Paymaster General.
Secretary to Commission and to Executive and Finance Committee, Wm. Hy. Mugford.

PRIVY SEAL OFFICE,
1, New Street, Spring Gardens.
Lord Privy Seal, Rt. Hon. the Earl of Kimberley, G.C.B., £2,000.
Chief Clerk and Keeper of the Records, Wm. Goodwin, Esq., £400.
Private Sec. to Earl of Kimberley, Edmond Rob. Wodehouse, Esq., £300.

PUBLIC WORKS LOAN BOARD.
3, Bank Buildings.
Chairman, John Gellibrand Hubbard, Esq., M.P.
Secretary, Wm. Williamson Willink, Esq., £1,400.
Assistant Sec., Edmd. Robt. Spearman, Esq., £650.
Solicitor, £600.
Accountant, Robt. Foster Shattock, Esq., £430.

QUEEN ANNE'S BOUNTY.
First Fruits and Tenths Office,
Dean's Yard, Westminster.
Secretary & Treasurer, Christopher Hodgson, Esq.
Assistant Secretary, John Holford, Esq.
Cashier and Accountant, George Aston, Esq.
Assistant, Joseph Keech Aston, Esq.
Auditor, Charles Ansell, Esq.
Counsel, Samuel Pepys Cockerell, Esq.
Solicitors, Messrs. Burder and Dunning, 27, Parliament Street.

RECORD OFFICE,
Rolls Yard, Chancery Lane.
Keeper of the Records, The Master of the Rolls.
Deputy Keeper, Thos. Duffus Hardy, Esq., £1,000.
Secretary, John Edwards, Esq., £638.
Assistant Keepers, 1st Class, Henry James Sharpe, Joseph Burtt, John James Bond, Hans Claude Hamilton, F.S.A.; Joseph Redington, Jas. Gairdner, and William Hardy, Esqrs., £2,970.
Do., 2nd Class, Wm. Basevi Sanders, Esq., £400.

REGISTRY OF DESIGNS OFFICE,
1, Whitehall
Registrar, Wm. Wybrow Robertson, Esq., £600.
Assist.-Registrar, James Hill Bowen, Esq., £338.
Chief Clerk, R. D. Spinks, Esq., £225.
Designs and Transfers registered, 11 till 3.

ROYAL ACADEMY, Trafalgar Square.
President, Sir Francis Grant, Knt., R.A.
Secretary, John Prescott Knight, Esq., R.A.
Keeper, Charles Landseer, Esq., R.A.
Treasurer, Sydney Smirke, Esq., R.A.
Librarian, Solomon A. Hart, Esq., R.A.
Registrar, Henry Eyre. Esq.
Open from early in May till the end of July.

STATIONERY OFFICE.

Princes Street, Storey's Gate. 10 to half-past 4.

Comptroller, Wm. Rathbone Greg, Esq., £1,430.
Chief Clerk, Hugh G. Reid, Esq.

Clerks, First Class, Joseph James Wickwar, William Robinson, Geo. Thos. Parson, Samuel Page, Leopold Charles Martin, Esqrs., £2,341.
Second Class, Frederick Bryan, Charles Mitchell, John Boddington Gill, William Henry Gardner, and Thomas Lewis Fox, Henry Erskine K. Fullerton, and Stephen Fisher, Esqrs., £2,388.
Examiners of Printers' Accounts, William Lawrence and William Strachan, Esqrs., each £500.
Assistant ditto, Frederick John Brodie, Esq., £347.
Receiver of Printed Forms, Walter Bentley, £200.
Examiner of Binding, John Young, Esq., £450.
Assistant ditto, Thomas Hy. Croysdill, Esq., £220.
Examiner of Paper, James Diggens, Esq., £495.
Assistant ditto, Joseph Sandell, Esq., £250.
Assistant ditto in Dublin, W. J.Wickwar, Esq., £350.
Secretary to Comptroller, Jas. S. Lewis, Esq., £318.
Amount voted for 1869, £395,909; 1868, £384,226.
Cost of Establishment, 1868-69, £18,315.

TOWER OF LONDON.

Chief Governor and Constable, F.M. Sir John Fox Burgoyne, Bart., G.C.B.
Lieutenant of the Tower, General Sir George Bowles, K.C.B., £768.
Deputy Lieutenant, Lieut.-Gen. Right Hon. Lord de Ros, £786.
Major, Col Frederick Amelius Whimper, £300.
Chaplain, Rev. W. G. Green, M.A., £150.
Steward & Coroner, Thomas Wrake Ratcliff, Esq.
Keeper of the Regalia, Lieut.-Col. C. Wyndham.

TRINITY HOUSE, Tower Hill.

Master, Capt. H.R.H. The Duke of Edinburgh.
Deputy, Capt. Frederick Arrow.

Elder Brethren.—Capt. William Pixley, Sir Frederick Snow, Adm. Rob. Gordon, Capt. William E. Farrer, Capt. H. Bonham Bax, Capt. Gabriel J. Redman, Rt. Hon. Earl Russell, Capt. J. Fulford Owen, Rt. Hon. Lord Taunton, Capt. William Pigott, Capt. H. Shuttleworth, Capt. James Drew, Capt. Thomas N. Were, Rt. Hon. Earl of Derby, Capt. Richard W. Pelly, Capt. M. Currie Close, Capt. John Fenwick, Capt. George Bayly, Capt. John S.Webb, Capt. E. Parry Nisbet, Rt. Hon. Sir J. S. Pakington, Bt., The Duke of Somerset, Rt. Hon. T. M. Gibson, Rt. Hon. W. E. Gladstone, Rear-Adm. R. Collinson, The Duke of Argyll, K.T., Capt. Charles Granger Weller, Capt. Geo. Patrick Lambert, Rt. Hon. Sir S. H. Northcote, Rt. Hon. Benjamin Disraeli.
Secretary, Robin Allen, Esq.
Assistant Secretary, John Inglis, Esq.
Accountant, H. L. Farrer, Esq.
Pilotage Clerks, J. H. Hart, H. F. Fremont, and D. Keigwin, Esqrs.
Clerks of Estates, &c., E. J. Seaton and R. D. Morewood, Esqrs.

WEST INDIAN INCUMBERED ESTATES COMMISSION,

8, Park Street, Westminster.

Chief Commissioner, James Fleming, Esq., Q.C.
Assistant Commissioner, Reginald John Cust, Esq.
Secretary, Reginald John Cust, Esq.

WESTMINSTER ABBEY DEAN AND CHAPTER OFFICE.

Receiver-General, John Charles Thynne, Esq., Little Cloisters.
Auditor, Henry A. Hunt, Esq.
Chapter Clerk, Charles St. Clare Bedford, Esq., Broad Sanctuary.

Chambers of Agriculture, &c.

CENTRAL CHAMBER OF AGRICULTURE.—Office: Salisbury Hotel, Fleet Street, London. *Chairman*—R. Jasper More, Esq., M.P., Linley Hall, Bishop's Castle, Salop. *Vice-Chairman*—Clare Sewell Read, Esq., M.P., Honingham Thorpe, Norwich. *Treasurer*—Charles Clay, Esq., Walton, Wakefield. *Secretary*—John Algernon Clarke, Esq., Long Sutton, Lincolnshire.

Banbury Dis., C. Simmons, Farnboro', Banbury.
Brecknockshire, H. de Winton, Syncar, Brecon.
Carmarthenshire, David Prosser, Carmarthen.
Cheshire, Thomas Rigby, Over, Winsford.
North Cheshire, George W. Clarke, Macclesfield.
Cirencester, Robert Ellett, Cirencester.
Cornwall County. H. Tresawna, Lamellyn, Probus.
Croydon, John Wood, The College, Croydon.
Devon and Cornwall, John Moon, Plymouth.
Devon Central, Chas. H. S. Veale, Newton Abbot.
Devonshire, B. J. Ford, Solicitor, Exeter.
Dorsetshire. Henry Lock, Dorchester.
Durham (North), F. T. Wharam, Durham.
Durham (South), S. Richardson, Darlington.
Essex, C. H. Branwhite, Gestingthorpe, Halstead.
Faringdon, F. H. Barfield, Faringdon.
Gloucestershire, Alfred C. Wheeler, Gloucester.
Hampshire, Henry Downs, Basingstoke.
Herefordshire, J. T. Owen Fowler, Hereford.
Hertfordshire, G. Chambers, Standon Friars, Ware.
Hungerford, W. Chandler, Aldbourne, Hungerford.
Kent (East), George Slater, Canterbury.
Kent (West), S. Godding Reader, Maidstone.
Leicestershire, T. Willson, Knaptoft Hall, Rugby.
Lincolnshire, Fred. Andrew, Solicitor, Lincoln.
Loughborough, John Henry Gray, Loughborough.
Midland, J. B. Lythall, 39.New St., Birmingham.

Monmouthshire, J. Pybus, Court Farm, Magor.
Newbury, J. R. Evans, Ridgemoor, Burghclere.
Norfolk, C. R. Gilman, Norwich.
North of England, G. Armstrong, Newcastle.
Northamptonshire, J. M. Lovell, Harpole, Weedon.
Penrith, T. Robinson, Clifton, Penrith, Westmrlnd.
Peterborough, William Barford, Peterborough.
Shropshire, William Edwards, Shrewsbury.
Somerset, H. G. Andrews, Rimpton, Sherborne.
Staffordshire, W. Tomkinson, Newcastle, Staffish.
Suffolk (East), H. Biddell, Playford, Ipswich.
Suffolk (West), G. Blencowe, Bury St. Edmunds.
Sunderland, R. Thompson, Solicitor, Sunderland.
Swindon, J. H. Piper, Swindon, Wiltshire.
Warwickshire, Hugh Suffolk, Coventry.
Wigton, T. M'Mechan, Wigton, Cumberland.
Worcestershire, John Blick, Solicitor, Droitwich.
Yorkshire (East Riding), T. Turner, Sol., Beverley.
    ,,   *(North Riding),* J. Soulby, Malton.
    ,,   *(West Riding),* M. B. Hick, Wakefield.
   Branches—Malton, J. Soulby, Malton, Yorksh.
   Ripon, G. M. Lomas, Dishforth, Thirsk.
   Bedale, J. Teale, Solicitor, Bedale.
   Whitby, James Wilkinson, Whitby.
   Thirsk, W. R. West, Solicitor, Thirsk.
   York, James Grayston, jun., Solicitor, York.
   Scarboro', G. Leighton, jun., MoorHo., Seamer.

HIGH COURT OF CHANCERY.

Lord High Chancellor of Great Britain, The Right Hon. William Page, Baron Hatherley, £10,000.
Principal Secretary, Gordon Whitbread, Esq.
Office, Quality Court, Chancery Lane.
Secretary of Presentations, The Hon. Edward P. Thesiger, £400.
Secretary of Commissions of Peace, The Hon. Hallyburton G. Campbell, £400.
Gentleman of the Chamber, Samuel Smith, Esq.
Registrar in Lunacy, Charles Norris Wilde, Esq.
Purse Bearer, William Goodbody, Esq.
Trainbearer, Mr. Elscy.
Serjeant-at-Arms, Lieut.-Colonel the Hon. Wellington Patrick Manvers Chetwynd Talbot.
Deputy Sergeant-at-Arms, G. Goodbody, Esq.
Messenger or Pursuivant, G. S. Ridgway, Esq.
Deputy Messenger or Pursuivant, Mr. H. Chouler.

COURT OF APPEAL IN CHANCERY, Lincoln's Inn.

The Lord Chancellor, The Rt. Hon. William Page, Lord Hatherley.
Lord Justice, The Right Hon. Sir Charles Jasper Selwyn, Knt., £6,000.
Secretary, Charles Samuel Bagot, Esq.

ROLLS COURT, Chancery Lane.

Master of the Rolls, The Right Hon. John, Lord Romilly, £6,000.
Chief Secretary, Wilford George Brett, Esq.
Secretary of Causes, Algernon Cox, Esq.
Gentleman of the Chamber, E. S. Newman, Esq.
Clerk of the Papers, A. Grayson Madders, Esq.
Chief Clerks, Edmund Boyle Church, John Wm. Hawkins, and R. Marshall, Esqrs.

VICE-CHANCELLORS' COURTS, Lincoln's Inn.

Vice-Chanc., The Hon. Sir John Stuart, Knt., £5,000.
Secretary, Dugald Stuart, Esq.
Chief Clerks, Alfred Hall, Robert Wm. Peake, and Henry Francis Church, Esqrs.
Vice-Chanc., The Hon. Sir R. Malins, Knt., £5,000.
Secretary, Edward Borton, Esq.
Chief Clerk (Div. A to K), F. E. Edwards, Esq.
Chief Clerk (Div. L to Z) J. A. Buckley, Esq.
Vice-Chancellor, The Hon. Sir George Markham Giffard, Knt., £5,000.
Secretary, Francis Bacon, Esq.
Chief Clerks, H. Leman and E. Bloxam, Esqrs.

ACCOUNTANT-GENERAL'S OFFICES, Chancery La.

Accountant-General, William Russell, Esq.
Chief Clerk, Samuel Parkinson, Esq.
Senior Clerks, Benjamin Lewis, John Headland, Henry John Haines, and Thomas Wellington Jeffcott, Esqrs.

TAXING MASTERS IN CHANCERY, 12, Staple Inn.
Robert B. Follett, Richard Mills, John Wainewright, Richard Bloxam, Alfred H. Shadwell, Charles F. Skirrow, and G. Hume, Esqrs.

CLERKS OF RECORDS AND WRITS, Chancery La.
Edward Grubb, Esq. (A to F); James A. Murray, Esq. (G to N); S. C. Ward, Esq. (O to Z).

REPORT OFFICE.

First Clerk, Thomas Coghlan, Esq.
Second Clerk, Edwin J. Abraham, Esq.
Account.-General's Certificate Clerk, J. Skeen, Esq.
Search Clerk, Edward King, Esq.

CHANCERY REGISTRARS' OFFICE, Chancery Lane.
Registrars, Richard Howell Leach, Henry Latham, John Lewis Merivale, Edward Dod Colville, Frank Milne, Ralph Disraeli, Paul John King, Pearce Wm. Rogers, George Farrer, James Michael Holdship, Frederic Symes Teesdale, and Arthur Ellis, Esqrs.
Principal Clerks, Hall Plumer, N. Ward, L. L. Pemberton, William Clowes, R. Pemberton Koe, Edward John Cobby, H. J. Jackson, Charles Carrington, Edward Richard Colville, Germain Lavie, Warren Pugh, Chas. Beale, Richard Howell Walker Leach, and Robert Seppings Godfrey, Esqrs.
Clerk of Entries (A to K), Edward Ansell.
Ditto (L to Z), George Lindley.

ENROLMENT OFFICE, Chancery Lane.

Clerk of Enrolments, The Hon. Wm. Romilly.
PETTY BAG OFFICE, Rolls Yard, Chancery Lane.
Clerk of the Petty Bag, A. Murray, Esq.
EXAMINERS' OFFICE, Rolls Yard, Chancery La.
Examiner (A to K), Charles Beavan, Esq.
Sworn Clerk, Mr. George Anderson Croft.
Examiner (L to Z), Charles Otter, Esq.
Sworn Clerk, Thomas Hughes Greenland, Esq.
PRESENTATION OFFICE, Quality Court.
Secretary of Presentations, Hon. E. P. Thesiger.

OFFICE OF THE REGISTRAR IN LUNACY, Quality Ct.
Registrar in Lunacy to the Lord Chancellor, Chas. Norris Wilde, Esq.

OFFICES OF THE MASTERS IN LUNACY,

45, Lincoln's Inn Fields.

Masters in Lunacy, Francis Barlow, Esq., and Samuel Warren, Esq., Q.C., D.C.L.
Chief Clerk, John Stewart, Esq.
Visitors of Lunatics, William Norris Nicholson, Esq.; Sir William Charles Hood, M.D.; John C. Bucknill, M.D.; and (*ex officio*) the Masters in Lunacy.
Secretary, Easton J. Cox, Esq.

OFFICES OF THE COMMISSIONERS IN LUNACY.

19, Whitehall Place.

Commissioners, Right Hon. Earl of Shaftesbury, K.G. (*Chairman*); Francis Barlow, Esq.; Col. Henry Morgan Clifford,; Hon. Dudley Francis Fortescue, M.P.; Bryan Waller Procter, Esq.; James Wilkes, Esq., F.R.C.S.; R. Nairne, M.D.; John Davies Cleaton, Esq., F.R.C.S.; William George Campbell, Robert Wilfred Skeffington Lutwidge, and John Forster, Esqrs., each £1,500.
Secretary, C. P. Phillips, Esq., £800.
Chief Clerk, Thomas Martin, Esq., £500.

GREAT SEAL PATENT OFFICE, AND OFFICE OF THE COMMISSIONERS OF PATENTS FOR INVENTIONS, 25, Southampton Buildings, Chancery Lane.
Office hours, 10 to 4; except Christmas Day and Good Friday.
Commissioners of Patents for Inventions, The Lord Chancellor, the Master of the Rolls; the Attorney-General and the Solicitor-General for England, £10,500; the Lord Advocate, £850; the Attorney-General for Ireland, £1,200; the Solicitor-General for Ireland, £800; and others.
Clerk of the Commissioners, Bennet Woodcroft, Esq., F.R.S., £1,000.

PATENT DIVISION.

First Class Clerks, Alfred John Prothero, Richd. John Sheppard, and Thomas A. Sims, Esqrs., each £450.

SPECIFICATION DIVISION.

First Class Clerks, Robert Lucas, Thos. Duffield, William Marwick Michell, and Jeken Jas. V. Elwin, Esqrs., each £450.
Library Clerk, William G. Atkinson, Esq., £400.
Financial Clerk, A. P. Gipps, Esq., £385.
Translator, A. Tolhausen, Esq., £500.

PATENT OFFICE MUSEUM, South Kensington.
Superintendent, B. Woodcroft, Esq., F.R.S.
Curator, Francis P. Smith, Esq., £435.

JUDICIAL COMMITTEE OF THE PRIVY COUNCIL.

The Committee is composed of the Lord President, Lord Chancellor, the Archbishops of Canterbury and York, Lords Justices of the Court of Appeal in Chancery, Master of the Rolls, Vice Chancellor, Lords Chief Justices of Queen's Bench and Common Pleas, Lord Chief Baron of Exchequer, Judges of the Queen's Bench, Common Pleas, Barons of the Exchequer, Judges of the Court of Probate and High Court of Admiralty, and all Privy Councillors who have held any of the offices before mentioned. and two appointed under sign manual.
Indian Assessors, The Right Hon. Sir Lawrence Peel, and the Right Hon. Sir J. W. Colvile.

COURT OF QUEEN'S BENCH.

JUDGES.

Lord Chief Justice of England, The Right Hon. Sir Alexander James Edmund Cockburn, Bart., £8,000.
Clerks, Henry Wm. Frayling, £700, Francis Algernon Cobham, Charles Barnes, Esqrs., £400 each.
Puisne Justices, The Hon. Sir Colin Blackburn, Knt., £5,000.
Clerks, J. Payne, £600; H. Thornton, £400.
The Hon. Sir John Mellor, Knt., £5,000.
Clerks, W.J. Cleave, £600; W.G. Bower, £400.
The Hon. Sir Robert Lush, Knt., £5,000.
Clerks, W. E. Coe, £600; F. Waters, £400.
The Hon. Sir James Hannen, Knt., £5,000.
Clerks, George J. Widdicombe, £600; Fredk. Morris, £400.

ASSOCIATE'S OFFICE, 19, Chancery Lane.
Associate, The Hon. H. G. Campbell, £1,000.
Chief Clerk, E. Eldred, £300.

QUEEN'S BENCH OFFICE, Temple.
Masters, Charles Robert Turner; Henry John Hodgson, John Unthank, John Hibberd Brewer, Charles M. Smith, Esqrs., £1,125 each.

MASTERS' DEPARTMENT.
Masters' Chief Clerk, Charles Thomas Sansom, Esq., £350.
Error and Outlawry Office, W. L. Kerton, Esq., £505.
Rule Office, George Augustus Le Maire, £600.
Writ Office, Henry Wm. Southwell, £310.
Appearances, Edward Rose, £260.

CROWN OFFICE, 2, King's Bench Walk.
Queen's Coroner and Attorney, T. Norton, £1,200.
Master, John George Malcolm, Esq. £1,200.
Clerk, James Winning, £500, and others.

COURT OF COMMON PLEAS.

JUDGES.

Lord Chief Justice, The Right Hon. Sir William Bovill, Knt., £7,000.
Clerks, Thomas Turner, £700. W. G. Bower, John Tingey, £400 each.
Puisne Justices, The Hon. Sir Jas. Shaw Willes, Knt., £5,000.
Clerks, John James Barnes, £600, Stephen Minot, £400.
The Hon. Sir John Barnard Byles, Knt., £5,000.
Clerks, Charles Levick Ruse, £600, George H. Parkinson, £400.
The Hon. Sir Hen. Singer Keating, Knt., £5,000.
Clerks, S. J. Masters, £600, E. Phelan, £400.
The Hon. Sir Montague E. Smith, Knt., £5,000.
Clerks, Thomas H. Knott, £600, Henry Simpson, £400.

ASSOCIATE'S OFFICE, 18, Chancery Lane.
Associate, T. W. Erle, Esq., £1,000.

COMMON PLEAS OFFICE, Chancery Lane.
Masters, Alexander A. Park, £1,500; Henry Methold, John Gordon, Julius Talbot Airey. William Morgan Benett, Esqrs., £1,125 each,
Chief Clerk, Charles John Tootell, Esq., £700.

OFFICE FOR FILING CERTIFICATES OF THE ACKNOWLEDGMENT OF DEEDS BY MARRIED WOMEN, 7, Lancaster Place, Strand.
Registrar, Mayow Short, Esq., £700.
First Clerk, Daniel Millard, £300.

COURT OF EXCHEQUER.

BARONS.

Lord Chief Baron, The Right Hon. Sir Fitzroy Kelly, Knt., £7,000.
Clerks, Jas. F. Browning, £700, J. B. S. Coleman, £400.
Puisne Barons, The Hon. Sir Samuel Martin, Kt., £5,000.
Clerks, G. Lovejoy, £650, Wm. Whyman Jiggins, £624.
The Hon. Sir George William Wilshere Bramwell, Knt. £5,000.
Clerks, Joseph Capp, £600, Jas. Edwd. Saunders, £400.
The Hon. Sir Wm. Fry Channell, Knt., £5,000.
Clerks, Nathaniel Whisson, £600, John Meacher, £400.
The Hon. Sir Gillery Pigott, Knt., £5,000.
Clerks, R. F. Fenning, £600, Thomas Lovell, £400.
Commissioner for taking Special Bail, John Boucher, Serjeants' Inn.

ASSOCIATE'S OFFICE, 18 and 19, Chancery Lane.
Associate, Henry Pollock, Esq., £1,000.

EXCHEQUER OFFICE (OF PLEAS), 7, Stone Bldgs.
Masters, William Henry Walton, £1,500; Wm. Frederick Pollock, John Charles Templer, and Marcus Henry Johnson, Esqrs., £1,125 each.
Clerks, Suitors' Fund and Taxing Department, Mr. W. E. Jennings, and Mr. A. Vincent.
Sealer of Executions, William Weller, £350.
Judgment Department, Messrs. F. Redman, £500, H. H. Walker, G. Stonhouse, and E.H. Hallett.
Writ Department, Messrs. W. Trinder, £350, E. W. Lipscombe, and J. F. Townsend.
Rule Department, Messrs. C. H. Rule, £600, W. Stratford, E. T. Dax, F. H. Mitchell, and P. E. Vizard.
Filazers Department, Messrs. S. Richards, £350, W. J. Weller. and W. G. Chapman.

THE QUEEN'S REMEMBRANCER'S OFFICE.
58, Chancery Lane.

The Queen's Remembrancer, William Hen. Walton, Esq.
Chief Clerk, Charles Panton, Esq.

LAND REGISTRY OFFICE, 34, Lincoln's Inn Fields.

Registrar, Brent S. Follett, Esq., Q.C., £2,500.
Assistant Registrar, R. H. Holt, Esq., £1,500.
Examiners of Title, Charles Davidson, Esq.; A. Burrows, Esq.
Chief Clerk, Octavius Dillingham Mordaunt, £400.

FOR THE COUNTY OF MIDDLESEX.
8, Serle St., Lincoln's Inn.

Registrars, The Right Hon. Lord Truro; Fredk. Villiers Meynell, Esq.
Deputy Registrar and Chief Clerk, Thos. Roberts Williamson.

REGISTRY OF JUDGMENTS, EXECUTIONS, &c.,
OPERATING AS CHARGES ON LAND.

Terrace, Serjeants' Inn, Chancery Lane.
Registrar, Alexander A. Park, Esq., £1.500.
Clerks, James Pask, William Harris, John James Harris, and A. T. Pask.

EXAMINERS OF CRIMINAL LAW ACCOUNTS AND AUDITORS OF SHERIFFS' ACCOUNTS,

2, New Street, Spring Gardens.
Examiners, George Wilkin, and John Hughes Preston, Esqrs., £1,000 each.
Principal Clerk, Alfred Pike, Esq., £435.

COMPANIES' REGISTER OFFICE,

13, Serjeants' Inn, Fleet Street.
Registrar, Hon. Edward Cecil Curzon, £700.
Chief Clerk, George Deane, Esq., £400.

COURTS OF PROBATE, AND DIVORCE AND MATRIMONIAL CAUSES.

COURT OF PROBATE, Westminster Hall.

Judge, The Rt. Hon. Sir J. P. Wilde, Knt. £5,000.
Registrars, Augustus Frederic Bayford, LL.D.; £1,600; Charles John Middleton, Esq., £1,500; Edward Francis Jenner, Esq., £1,500; and Henry Linwood Strong, Esq., £1,000.
Secretary, Edward Archer Wilde, jun., Esq., £300.
Crier and Principal Clerk, Geo. T. Billinge, £600.
PRINCIPAL REGISTRY OF THE COURT OF PROBATE.
Great Knightrider Street.
Record Keepers, J. Smith, J. F. Coleman, each £600.
Sealer, Mr. G. R. Harman, £300.

COURT OF DIVORCE, Westminster.
Judge Ordinary, Rt. Hon. Sir J. P. Wilde, Knt.

ADMIRALTY and ECCLESIASTICAL COURTS.

HIGH COURT OF ADMIRALTY, Westminster.

Judge, The Rt. Hon. Sir Robert Joseph Phillimore, Knt., D.C.L., £4,000.
Secretary, Walter G. F. Phillimore, Esq., £300.
REGISTRY, Godliman Street.
Registrar, Henry C. Rothery, Esq., M.A., £2,095.
Assist. Registrar, H. A. Bathurst, Esq., M.A., £1,200.
Chief Clerk, R. G. M. Browne, Esq., £700.
MARSHAL'S OFFICE, Paul's Bakehouse Court.
Marshal, Evan Jones, Esq., £700.
Clerk, Henry John Hunter, £290.
Queen's Advocate-General, Sir Travers Twiss, Knt., D.C.L., Q.C.
Admiralty Advocate, J. Parker Deane, D.C.L., Q.C.
Queen's Proctor, Francis Hart Dyke, Esq.
Admiralty Proctor, Henry Graham Stokes, Esq.

COURT OF ARCHES, Westminster.

Dean of the Arches, The Rt. Hon. Sir Robert Joseph Phillimore, Knt., D.C.L.
Registrar, John Shephard, Esq., Godliman Street.
Clerk and Record Keeper, J. Collis.

COURT OF FACULTIES OF THE ARCHBISHOP OF CANTERBURY.

10, Great Knightrider Street.
Master of the Faculties, The Rt. Hon. Stephen Lushington, D.C.L.
Registrar, Hon. Sir John Henry Thomas Manners Sutton, K.C.B.
Deputy Registrars, Edmund Charles Currey, Esq., and William Price Moore, Esq.
Clerk and Record Keeper, Mr. Henry Tayler.

COURT OF PECULIARS OF THE ARCHBISHOP OF CANTERBURY.

Bell Yard, Doctors' Commons.
Vicar-General, Sir T. Twiss, Knt., D.C.L., Q.C.
Registrar of the Province, Fras. Hart Dyke, Esq.
Registrar of the Diocese, William H. Cullen, Esq.
Apparitor-General and Proctor, F. Knyvett, Esq.

VICAR-GENERAL'S OFFICE, Bell Yd., Doctors' Com.
Vicar-General, The Rt. Worshipful Sir Travers Twiss, Knt., Q.C., D.C.L.
Registrar, Francis Hart Dyke, Esq.
Record Keeper, Mr. Henry Watts.
Assistant Record Keeper, Mr. S. T. Ryder.

DEAN AND CHAPTER OF ST. PAUL'S, London.
Commissary, Rt. Hon. Sir Robert Joseph Phillimore, Knt., D.C.L.
Chapter Clerk and Registrar, C. Hodgson, Esq.
Receiver and Steward, William Sellon, Esq., Chapter House.
Deputy Registrar, John B. Lee, Esq.

DEAN AND CHAPTER OF WESTMINSTER ABBEY.
Receiver-General, John Charles Thynne, Esq., Little Cloisters.
Auditor, Henry A. Hunt, Esq.
Chapter Clerk, Charles St. Clare Bedford, Esq., Broad Sanctuary.

THE BISHOP OF LONDON'S CONSISTORY COURT.
Judge, Sir Travers Twiss, Knt., D.C.L., Q.C., 3, Paper Buildings, Temple.
Registrars, John Shephard Esq.; J. B. Lee, Esq.
Apparitor, John Hassard, Esq.
Deputy Apparitor and Record Keeper, Mr. J. Collis.

BISHOP OF LONDON'S REGISTRY OFFICE, FOR GRANTING MARRIAGE LICENCES, &c., 3, Godliman Street.
Registrars, John Shephard, Esq., and John B. Lee, Esq.
Apparitor, John Hassard, Esq.
Record Keeper, Mr. John Collis.

INNS OF COURT, &c.

THE TEMPLE (MIDDLE AND INNER).

Master, Ven. Archdeacon Robinson, D.D.
Reader, Rev. Alfred Ainger, B.A.
Assistant Preacher, Rev. G. F. Maclear, B.A.
Organist, Mr. E. J. Hopkins.

INNER TEMPLE.

Treasurer, vacant.
Master of the Library, vacant.
Librarian, John Edward Martin, Esq.
Sub-Treasurer, George Edwards, Esq.

MIDDLE TEMPLE.

Treasurer, Thos. W. Greene, Esq., Q.C.
Sub-Treasurer, Chas. Shaw, Esq.
Clerk, Mr. Thomas Purdue.
Library Keeper, R. Goodhall Smith, Esq.
Master of the Library, T. W. Greene, Esq., Q.C.
Master of the Garden, J. Greenwood, Esq., Q.C.

LINCOLN'S INN.

Treasurer, James Bacon, Esq.
Master of the Library, Montagu Chambers, Esq., Q.C., M.P.
Preacher, Rev. Canon Cook, M.A.
Chaplain, Rev. Charles J. D'Oyly, M.A.
Assistant Preacher, Rev. James G. Lonsdale, M.A.
Steward, Michael Doyle.
Librarian, William H. Spilsbury, Esq.

GRAY'S INN.

Treasurer, N. Huddleston, Esq., Q.C.
Dean of the Chapel, Samuel Turner, Esq.
Preacher, Rev. James Augustus Hessey, D.C.L.
Reader and Afternoon Preacher, Rev. Alexander Taylor, M.A.
Reader on the Law of Real Property, &c., Frederick Prideaux, Esq.
Steward, Charles Edmund Banks.
Clerk, F. N. Musgrave.
Master of the Library, William M. Best, Esq.
Librarian, W. Douthwaite, Esq.

COUNCIL OF LEGAL EDUCATION.

Chairman, Rt. Hon. Lord Westbury.

READERS.

Constitutional Law and Legal History, Thomas Collett Sandars, Esq.
Equity, William Lloyd Birkbeck, Esq.
Law of Real Property, &c., Fred. Prideaux, Esq.
Jurisprudence and the Civil Law, J. Sharpe, LL.D.
Common Law, Herbert Broom, LL.D.
Clerk of the Council, Edward Davey, Steward's Office, Lincoln's Inn.

ROLLS CHAPEL.

Preacher, Rev. John S. Brewer, M.A.
Reader, Rev. William Henry Brookfield, M.A.

SHERIFFS' OFFICES AND OFFICERS.

SHERIFFS, ETC., LONDON AND MIDDLESEX.

Sheriffs of London and Middlesex, Alderman Cotton, and C. W. C. H. Hutton, Esq.
Under Sheriffs of Middlesex,

SHERIFFS' AND SECONDARY'S OFFICE,
20, Basinghall Street.

Officers to Sheriffs of London—["*Serjeants at Mace.*"]—Heywood, Saml., 63, Coleman Street; Hildyard, Nathaniel, 10, Tokenhouse Yard; Jackson Nicholas Lane, 77, Basinghall Street; Macpherson, Alex., 3, Guildhall Chambers, 31, Basinghall Street; Whittle, John Edward, 3, Guildhall Chambers, Basinghall Street.

SHERIFF OF MIDDLESEX OFFICE,
24, Red Lion Street, Holborn.

Agents.—Messrs. Burchell and Hall.
Officers to Sheriff of Middlesex.—Hemp, William, 41, Burton Crescent; Levy and Co., 62, Chancery Lane; Nathan and Co., 22, Chancery Lane; Slowman and Co., 22, Chancery Lane; Bower and Luckett, 1, Bream's Buildings; Strong and Taylor, 22, Castle Street, Holborn.

SHERIFF OF SURREY OFFICE, New Inn, Strand.

Under Sheriffs.—Messrs. Abbott, Jenkins, and Abbott.

Officers.—George Seal, 57, George Street, Blackfriars Road; Henry Herrick, 26, Stamford Street; Wm. Keene and Francis Edwin Keene, 99, Upper Stamford Street; James Hutton and Henry Hutton, Guildford; James Nichols and Alfred Joyes, Reigate.

SHERIFF OF KENT OFFICE, 24, Bedford Row.

Acting Under Sheriffs.—Messrs. Charles James Palmer and Charles Bull.
Officers.—John Smith, Gravesend; Richard John Smith, Alma Villa, New Cross; Edward Bigg, Sittingbourne; Charles Horatio Smith, Alma Villa, New Cross; Chas. Thame Armitage, Dover.

SHERIFF OF ESSEX OFFICE,
13, Furnival's Inn, Holborn.

London Agents.—Messrs. Probert and Wade.
Officers.—G. C. Matthams, Chelmsford; Nathaniel Cobb, Colchester.

SHERIFF OF SUSSEX OFFICE, 24, Bedford Row.

Acting Under Sheriffs.—Messrs. Charles James Palmer and Charles Bull.
Officers.—Charles Horatio Smith, Alma Villa, New Cross; Samuel Smith, Brighton; William Death, Petworth.

SHERIFF OF HERTS OFFICE, 40, Chancery Lane.

London Agents.—Messrs. Hawkins, Paterson, Snow, and Burney.
Officer, John Orridge, Hertford.

COURT OF BANKRUPTCY.

LONDON COMMISSIONERS, &c., 82, Basinghall St.

Senior Commissioner, Edward Holroyd, Esq.
Commissioners, Thomas Ewing Winslow, Esq.; James Bacon, Esq., Q.C.
Chief Registrar, John Fisher Miller, Esq.
Registrars, William Hazlitt, Henry Philip Roche, James Rigg Brougham, William Powell Murray, Philip Henry Pepys, Hon. William Cecil Spring-Rice.

OFFICIAL ASSIGNEES, MESSENGERS, &c.

In Mr. Commissioner Holroyd's Court:
Assignee, Edward Watkin Edwards.
Messenger, Thomas Edward Stubbs.
In Mr. Commissioner Bacon's Court:
Assignee, George John Graham.
Messenger, James Cooper.
In Mr. Commissioner Winslow's Court:
Assignee, Mansfield Parkyns.
Messenger, John Drewett Austin.
Provisional Assignee and Official Assignee, Hatton Hamer Stansfeld, 33, Lincoln's Inn Fields.
Unattached:—Messenger, Thomas Hamber.
Registrar of Meetings, Mr. John Frederick Bucclough.

CHIEF REGISTRAR'S OFFICE, Basinghall Street.

Chief Registrar, John Fisher Miller, Esq.
Secretary, Duncan Stewart, Esq.

APPEALS AND TRUST DEEDS, Quality Court.

Registrar in Attendance, Charles H. Keene, Esq.
The Accountant in Bankruptcy, Rd. Clarke, Esq.
Chief Clerk, John Saffery, Esq.
Taxing Master, William Frederick Higgins, Esq.

LATE COURT FOR RELIEF OF INSOLVENT DEBTORS IN ENGLAND.

The jurisdiction is vested in the Bankruptcy Court, under "The Bankruptcy Act, 1861." The business is still carried on at 33, Lincoln's Inn Fields, (entrance in Portugal Street).

Provisional and Official Assignee, Hatton Hamer Stansfeld, Esq.
Law Clerk and Examiner, A. S. Twyford, Esq.
Clerks, William Notson, Richard Humphries, and William F. Burden.
Taxing Master, W. Henry Hester, Esq.

CITY, BOROUGH, & WESTMINSTER COURTS.

LORD MAYOR'S COURT, Guildhall.
Judge, the Recorder of London, Right Hon. Russell Gurney, Q.C.
Registrar, Woodthorpe Brandon, Esq.
Deputy Registrar, Richard James Pawley, Esq.

CITY OF LONDON COURT, Guildhall.
Judge, Robert Malcolm Kerr, Esq., LL.D.
Treasurer, The Chamberlain of London.
Chief Clerk, A. White.
Registrar, Thomas James Nelson, Esq.
Clerk of the Judgments, William James Grant.
Clerk Accountant, James Deacon.
Process Clerk, George James Mitchell.
Cash Clerk, James Cutler Tilt.
Ledger Clerk, William Henry White.
Serjeant-at-Mace, C. Fitch.

SOUTHWARK BOROUGH COURT OF RECORD.
Steward and Judge, Mr. Serjt. William Payne, 2, Serjeants' Inn.
Prothonotary, Henry Devereux Pritchard, Esq.
Deputy, Henry Simpson, Esq.
High Bailiff and Returning Officer, William Gresham, Esq., 24, Basinghall Street.

COUNTY COURTS.

BLOOMSBURY COUNTY COURT.
Great Portland Street, Regent's Park, W.
Judge, George Lake Russell, Esq., £1,500.
Registrar, John Wright, Esq.
High Bailiff, R. Wright, Esq.

BOW COUNTY COURT, Bow Road.
Judge, John Bury Dasent, Esq., £1,500.
Registrar, Charles Frederick Hore, Esq.
High Bailiff, Henry Plater, Esq.

BROMPTON COUNTY COURT.
Whitehead's Grove, Chelsea.
Judge, Sir J. Eardley Eardley Wilmot, Bart.
Registrar, Richard Wright, Esq.
High Bailiff, John Bellas Rogers, Esq.

CLERKENWELL COUNTY COURT.
33, Duncan Terrace, Islington.
Judge, Thomas Hull Terrell, Esq., £1,500.
Registrar, Robert Cheere, Esq.
High Bailiff, William Sladden, Esq.

LAMBETH COUNTY COURT, Camberwell New Road.
Judge, John Pitt Taylor, Esq., £1,800.
Registrar, Charles Twamley, Esq.
High Bailiff, Henry Devereux Pritchard, Esq.

MARYLEBONE COUNTY COURT, 179, Marylebone Road.
Judge, Sir John E. Eardley Wilmot, Bart., £1,500.
Registrar, Charles Burrows, Esq.
High Bailiff, John Rogers, Esq.

SHOREDITCH COUNTY COURT, 12, Charles Square.
Judge, John Bury Dasent, Esq.
Registrar, Thomas Luxmore Wilson, Esq.
High Bailiff, William Ghrimes Kell, Esq.

SOUTHWARK COUNTY COURT, 50, Swan Street, Borough.
Judge, Charles S. Whitmore, Esq., Q.C., £1,500.
Registrar, Thomas Kemmis Bros, Esq.
High Bailiff, Edward Lambert, Esq.

WESTMINSTER COUNTY COURT, 82, St. Martin's Lane.
Judge, Francis Bayley, Esq., £1,800.
Registrar, Christopher Cuff, Esq.
High Bailiff, John Arthur Bayley, Esq.

WHITECHAPEL COUNTY COURT, 16, Great Prescot Street.
Judge, Sir W. Buchanan Riddell, Bart., £1,500.
Registrar, Edward Charles Ryley, Esq.
High Bailiff's, Richard Barton le Gros, and Samuel Benjamin Williams, Esq.

REGISTRY OF COUNTY COURTS JUDGMENTS, &c., 2, New Street, Spring Gardens.
Registrar, Thomas Hamilton, Esq.
Chief Clerk, Henry Whiting Brider, Esq.

CORONERS.

For the Queen's Household, William Thomas Manning, Esq., 20, Great George Street, Westminster.
City of London and Borough of Southwark, Mr. Serjeant Payne, 2, Serjeants' Inn, Chancery Lane.—*Deputy*, William John Payne, Esq.
Liberty of the Tower, Thomas Wrake Ratcliff, Esq., White Horse Street, Commercial Road.
City of Westminster, Charles St. Clare Bedford, Esq., Broad Sanctuary.—*Deputy*, Samuel Fred. Langham, jun., Esq., 10, Bartlett's Buildings.
Duchy of Lancaster, William John Payne, Esq., 2, Serjeants' Inn.
County of Middlesex: Eastern District, John Humphreys, Esq., Manor House, Westbourne Gardens; *Deputy*, James George Richards, Esq., 13, Lancaster Road, Kensington; *Coroner's Office*, 33, Spital Square.—*Central District*, Edwin Lankester, M.D., F.R.S., 25, Great Marlborough Street.—*Western District*, Thos. T. Bramah Diplock, M.D., 35, Oakley Square.— *Deputy*, Frederick James Hand, Esq., 5, New Inn.
County of Surrey: Eastern Division, William Carter, Esq., Wandsworth Common. — *Western Division*, Charles John Woods, Esq., Charles Street, Godalming.
Guildford, John Rand Capron, Esq., 55, Quarry Street, Guildford.
County of Kent, Charles Joseph Carttar, Esq., Greenwich; John Noble Dudlow, Esq., West Malling; William Tanner Neve, Esq., Cranbrook; Thomas Hills, Esq., Chatham.
Canterbury, Thomas Thorpe De Lassaux, Esq.
County of Essex, Charles Carne Lewis, Esq., Maldon.—*Deputy*, Charles Carne Lewis, jun., Esq.

POLICE COURTS, CITY OF LONDON.
MANSION HOUSE.
Magistrate, The Lord Mayor, or one of the Aldermen.
Principal Clerk, George Colwell Oke, Esq.
Assistant Clerk, Mr. T. Holmes Gore.
Cashier, Mr. William Ball.
Junior Clerk, Mr. Alnutt.

GUILDHALL.
Magistrate, An Alderman (in rotation).
Chief Clerk, George Martin, Esq.
Assistant Clerk, Mr. Joseph David.
Clerk of Special Sessions, Mr. Henry Fred. Youle.
Cashier and Accountant, Mr. G. H. Griffin.

CITY POLICE CHIEF OFFICE, 26, Old Jewry.
Commissioner, Col. James Fraser.
Chief Superintendent, Capt. Charles G. Hodgson.

Surgeon, George Borlase Childs, Esq., F.R.C.S.
Receiver, Frederick White Saunders.
Chief Clerk, Robert Cousins.

The force comprises 1 Superintendent, 1 Chief Inspector, 1 Inspector of Detective Department, 12 ditto of Divisions, 14 Station Sergeants, 12 Detective Sergeants, 56 Sergeants, and 560 Constables.

METROPOLITAN POLICE COURTS.

Bow Street, Covent Garden.

Magistrates, Sir Thomas Henry, Knt., £1,500; James Vaughan, Esq., £1,200; Frederick Flowers, Esq., £1,200.
Chief Clerk, William Dyott Burnaby, Esq., £500.

Clerkenwell, King's Cross Road.

Magistrates, John Henry Barker, Esq., £1,200; William Major Cooke, Esq., £1,200.
Chief Clerk, John Alexander, Esq., £500.
Lambeth, Lower Kennington Lane.
Magistrates, George Percy Elliott, Esq., £1,200; Edmund Humphrey Woolrych, Esq., £1,200.
Chief Clerk, J. P. Perry, Esq., £500.

Marlborough Street.

Magistrates, Robert P. Tyrwhitt, Esq., £1,200; Alexander Andrew Knox, Esq., £1,200.
Chief Clerk, J. F. Nokes, Esq., £500.

Marylebone, 86, High Street.

Magistrates, John Smith Mansfield, Esq., £1,200; Louis C. Tennyson d'Eyncourt, Esq., £1,200.
Chief Clerk, Wilfred Tate, Esq., £500.

Southwark, Blackman Street.

Magistrates, Thomas B. Burcham, Esq., £1,200; William Partridge, Esq., £1,200.
Chief Clerk, A. H. Safford, Esq., £500.

Thames, Arbour Street East, Stepney.

Magistrates, John Paget, Esq., £1,200; Ralph Augustus Benson, Esq., £1,200.
Chief Clerk, John Pyer, Esq., £500.

Westminster, Vincent Square.

Magistrates, Thomas Jas. Arnold, Esq., £1,200; Henry Selfe, Esq., £1,200.
Chief Clerk, William Taylor, Esq., £500.

Worship Street.

Magistrates, Cuthbert E. Ellison, Esq., £1,200; Robert Milnes Newton, Esq., £1,200.
Chief Clerk, Edward Leigh, Esq., £500.

Hammersmith, Vernon Street, and Wandsworth, Love Lane.

Magistrates, James Taylor Ingham, Esq., £1,200; C. Orchard Dayman, Esq., £1,200.
Chief Clerk, J. S. Leigh, Esq., £500.

Greenwich and Woolwich.

Magistrates, Daniel Maude, Esq., £1,200; James Henry Patteson, Esq., £1,200.
Chief Clerk, John A. G. Boustred, Esq., £500.

METROPOLITAN POLICE OFFICE,
4, Whitehall Place.

Commissioner, Sir Richard Mayne, K.C.B., £1,500.
Assistant Commissioners, Captain William C. Harris and Lt.-Col. D. W. P. Labalmondiere, £800 each.
Receiver, Maurice Drummond, Esq.
Chief Clerk, Edmund George May, Esq.
Surgeon, Timothy Holmes, Esq.
Inspector of Public Carriages and Property left therein, Lieut.-Col. G. F. Paschal.

Veterinary Surgeon, Mr. Arthur Cherry.
Inspectors of Drivers and Conductors, Timothy Cavanagh and Edward Ware.
Inspectors of Common Lodging Houses and Inspecting Dangerous Structures, Robert W. Roberts, Richard Reason, and James Francis Bundey.
Police Force, Superintendents, Inspectors, Sergeants, and Constables.
Surveyor, F. H. Caiger, Esq.

PRISONS.
City Prison, Holloway.

Governor, John Weatherhead, Esq.
Chaplain, Rev. John Owen, B.D.
Surgeon, Mr. Thomas Graham.

Debtors' Prison, Whitecross Street.

Keeper, Benjamin Constable, Esq.
Chaplain, Rev. Thomas Pugh.
Surgeon, Mr. William Butler Langmore.

House of Correction, Coldbath Fields.

Governor, Lieut.-Col. Thomas Harpur Colvill.
Chief Warder, Mr. George Hoare.
Surgeon, William Smiles, Esq., M.D.
Chaplain, Rev. Edward Arthur Illingworth, M.A.
Assistant Chaplain, Rev. W. F. Stocken, M.A.

House of Correction, Tothill Fields.

Matron, Mrs. Susanna Maria Billiter.
Principal Warder and Storekeeper, Mr. T. Crea.
Chaplain, Rev. George Henry Hine, M.A.
Surgeon, vacant.

House of Detention, Clerkenwell.

Governor, Capt. Rowland Bentinck Codd.
Chaplain, Rev. Geo. D'Urban John Hough, M.A.
Surgeon, William Smiles, Esq., M.D.

Newgate.

Governor, Edmund James Jonas, Esq.
Ordinary, Rev. F. E. Lloyd Jones, M.A.
Surgeon, John Rowland Gibson, Esq.
Clerk, Mr. Sidney R. Smith.

Surrey County Gaol, Horsemonger Lane.

Governor, John Keene, Esq.
Chaplain, Rev. John Jessop, M.A.
Surgeon, Thomas H. Waterworth, Esq., M.D.
Governor's Clerk, Mr. John Keene, jun.
Matron, Mrs. Rebecca Langbridge.

Surrey House of Correction, Wandsworth.

Governor, Richard Onslow, Esq.
Chaplain, Rev. J. W. H. L. Gilbert.
Assistant Chaplain, Rev. Joseph Gegg.
Surgeon, Thomas Poyntz Wright, Esq.

Convict Prisons.

Pentonville.—*Governor,* J. C. A. Bones, Esq.
Deputy, W. E. Buller, Esq.
Chaplain, Rev. Ambrose Sherwin, M.A.
Medical Officer, C. L. Bradley, Esq., F.R.C.S.
Millbank.—*Governor,* William Morrish, Esq.
Deputy, Capt. H. J. Wallack.
Medical Officer, R. M. Gover, Esq.
Chaplain, Rev. George B. De Renzi.
Dartmoor.—*Governor,* Capt. W. L. Stopford.
Deputy, Capt. Elliot Salter.
Chaplain, Rev. James Frances.
Medical Officer, H. F. Askham, Esq.
Female Prison, Parkhurst, Isle of Wight.—
Lady Superintendent, Mrs. Sarah Gibson.
Medical Officer, Henry Roome, Esq., M.D.
Portland.—*Governor,* George Clifton, Esq.
Deputy Governors, Major R. Hickey, Major J. Farquharson.

Chaplain, Rev. Arthur Hill, M.A.
Assistant do., Rev. H. A. Taylor, M.A.
Visiting Priest, Rev. George Poole.
Medical Officer, E. S. Blaker, Esq.
Assistant Surgeon, D. Nicolson, Esq.
Steward, Mr. E. P. Driver.
Clerk of Works, Mr. John Rhodes.
Chief Clerk, Mr. James Hary.
Chief Warden, Mr. W. Brooks.
Superintendent of the Guard, Mr. B. Durley.
Engineer, Mr. George Waters.

PORTSMOUTH.—*Governor,* Capt. Walt. J. Stopford.
Deputy Governor, Major F. Noott.
Chaplain, Rev. John W. Banks.
Medical Officer, V. C. Clarke, Esq., M.D., R.N.
Assistant Surgeon, R. E. Power, M.D.

CHATHAM.—*Governor,* Capt. T. F. Powell.
Deputy Governors, Capt. W. Talbot Harvey, and
     Capt. Campbell Hardy.

Chaplain, Rev. W. H. Duke.
Assistant Chaplain, Rev. F. A. Gardiner.
Visit. Roman Cath. Priest, Rev. M. O'Sullivan.
Visit. Presbyterian Minis., Rev. A. I. B. Baxter.
Medical Officer, J. D. Burns, Esq., M.D., R.N.
Assistant do., J. D. Steele, Esq.
Chief Clerk, Mr. Henry Whitmore.

WOKING.—*Governor,* Capt. Richard D. J. Bramly.
Chaplain, Rev. Raymond Blathwayt.
Medical Officer, John Campbell, Esq., R.N.

FEMALE PRISON, BRIXTON.—*Lady Superintendent,*
     Mrs. Emma Mary Martin; *Dep.* Mrs. Rendle.
Chaplain, Rev. Frederick W. Batchelor.
Medical Officer, James D. Rendle, Esq.

REFUGE, FULHAM.—*Superintendent,* Mrs. S. Seale.
Chaplain, Rev. J. K. Walshaw.
Medical Officer, H. P. Ree, Esq.

Judicial Statistics.

ENGLAND AND WALES.

THE following is a brief summary of the statistics of criminal and civil law in respect to England and Wales during the year 1867. The whole of the police staff numbered 26,073 persons, and the entire cost was £1,920,508. The number of known thieves and other offenders at large was 97,313, of whom 14,491 lived in the metropolis. Houses of bad character amounted to 20,197. The number of indictable offences or crimes committed was 55,538, and 28,132 persons were apprehended on that account. Of these 17,753 were committed for trial. 135 murders were committed during the year, 3,038 burglaries, 38,300 larcenies, 1,971 breaking into shops, &c. The summary convictions amounted to 335,359, out of 474,665 proceeded against. The coroners' inquests numbered 24,648, involving 1,356 cases of suicide and 11,172 of accidental death. The total number of committals for trial was 18,971. There were 26 persons sentenced to death, 10 males were executed and no females. There were 145,184 commitments to prison, including debtors, &c. Of these 1,362 were cases in which the person had been committed ten times. 78 per cent. was of persons born in England; 46,462 could neither read nor write, and 17,320 had no occupation. There were 167,252 persons in prison on 29th September, 1867. The total cost of prisons was £657,130. The personal cost of each prisoner was £26 13s. There were at the end of the year 7,586 persons in Convict Prisons, and 3,979 in Reformatories. The criminal lunatics numbered 1,244, of whom 155 were for murder. There were 322 coroners in England and Wales.

The Statistics of the Common Law, Equity, Civil Law, &c., are as follows: At the three Westminster Common Law Courts 127,221 writs of summons were issued, 41,704 judgments, 29,283 executions, and 471 writs of capias. There were 1,158 defended and 395 undefended causes at the three courts. The chief causes of action were contracts, compensation for personal injury, actions on bills, &c., and for goods sold and delivered. The total amount recorded was £524,127. Only 13¾ per cent. of actions brought went to trial, making 5,253. The total of County Court plaints issued was 942,181, involving a sum of £2,194,836. The judgments given were 542,560, in which only 856 cases were decided by a jury. The amount of debts so recovered was £1,151,629; of costs, £47,184; of fees on all proceedings, £311,835. The number of proceedings in equity were 613, the amount in dispute being £82,622. The orders for winding-up public companies amounted to 23, the pending orders and petitions 116. In the Bankruptcy Courts there were 3,072 cases in the London district; 1,857 in the country district Courts, and 4,065 before the County Courts, making a total of 8,994, being an increase of nearly 11 per cent. on 1865-6. Of these in 3,787 cases the debts exceeded £300, and 5,207 were below that amount in each case. The gross produce realized from the bankrupts' estates was £583,520, or 20 per cent. less than in the preceding year. In 1,649 cases a dividend was declared, but in 5,876 there was none. Only 40 cases gave a dividend of 20s. in the pound; one half of all cases gave less than 2s. 6d. The number of discharges granted was 6,902, suspended 345, and refused 109. There were 6,912 trust deeds registered, 3,971 being composition deeds. The revenue of the Court of Bankruptcy was £145,414. In the Court of Chancery 2,099 cases were heard during the year. The amount of debts proved was £12,490,346. The calls made on orders for winding-up companies, £4,497,831, the amount ordered to be paid to creditors, £7,310,339. In Lunacy 66 petitions for hearing were presented. In the Court of Admiralty 594 cases in connection with shipping were instituted, involving claims to the amount of £922,030, one half of which sum was for damages by collisions, and £188,690 was claimed for salvage. In the Divorce Court 321 petitions were filed, 224 being for dissolution of marriage, and 70 for judicial separation. 159 causes were tried, 119 decrees for dissolution of marriage were made, and 11 for judicial separation. 9,722 probates, and 4,604 administrations of wills were granted; the total property involved amounting, with that passed by the Chief Registrars, to £92,302,570. The number of suits in the Ecclesiastical Courts were 14, besides 176 for faculties. From all courts 59 appeals came before the House of Lords, and 101 before the Privy Council.

SCOTLAND.

Owing to a peculiarity of form and other causes, the judicial statistics of Scotland are not so readily capable of being summarized as those of England, Wales, and Ireland. The following, however, is a brief *resumé* of some important points for the year ending March, 1868. The total of vagrants, "tinkers" and unlicensed hawkers was 62,076, showing an increase of 12,702 on the previous year. County police numbered 1,021. The number of persons charged with offences was 3,305, of whom 2,534 were convicted, and one executed. Of offences against the person there were 864; against property with violence, 445; and without violence, 1,633; other offences of all kinds, 363. Of the number of committals, 714 persons could neither read nor write. The total return of criminal trials was 2,811. The latest return in regard to civil cases applies only to the year ending 1st January, 1865, and has consequently ceased to be of interest. The total number of cases in that year amounted to 1,149, including matters of debt, trespass, contract, divorce, &c.

IRELAND.

The judicial statistics for Ireland in 1866 are afforded by a return from the Statistics Office, Dublin, in August of the following year (the latest published) and give results as stated below. The police establishment of Ireland is divided into three kinds, namely, the Constabulary, the Dublin Metropolitan Police, and the Local Force in Towns (excepting Dublin). The totals of each in 1866 were Constabulary, 11,906; Dublin Force, 1,067; Local Forces, 382; the latter showing a decrease of 207 on the preceding year, arising chiefly from the abolition of the local force in Belfast, and the substitution of men under the denomination of Constabulary, as just stated. The returns also include the Fire Brigade establishment. The only town in Ireland possessing any local force corresponding to the English Borough Police in 1866 was Londonderry. The Constabulary and Local Forces correspond generally with the English Borough Police, and the Dublin Force does so with that of the City of London. The total cost of the whole forces in 1866 is returned at £779,917, being an increase of £13,230 on the preceding year. The average cost per man was about £55, against £75, the cost in England and Wales (both 1865). The greatest proportion of the cost of police in Ireland is paid by the Treasury, only about £60,000 out of the precedingly named sum being provided by other sources. The report states, however, that the constabulary are really entitled to be considered as equivalent to a standing army, as evinced by their services during the Fenian outbreaks. The total of known thieves and depredators under 16 was 414, and above that age 2,231; receivers of stolen goods, 1,060; prostitutes, 37 under 16 and 3,120 above 16 years of age. Suspected persons under 16 years old, 494; above, 2,763; making a total of all ages (excepting vagrants and tramps) of 10,118. Of the latter, there were 3,227 under 16 and 1,351 above that age, showing a total of 11,500 that can only be practically considered as a kind of recruiting ground for the criminal class, and exceeding the latter in number. The traveller in Ireland cannot help, on the most cursory observation, to notice the number of vagrants, &c., in all the large towns and suburbs in an all but destitute condition. In 1866 there was a decrease of vagrants below 1865 of 580 persons of all ages. Compared with a similar population in England and Wales, however, Ireland appears favourably, at least in 1865; and the total of all classes in Ireland was 10,118 against a similar population in England of 21,826; whilst in respect to vagrants, Ireland had 11,500 against 8,890, a shocking proof of the general effects of poverty in Ireland. Whilst, therefore, the criminal population in Ireland is less than one half of that of a corresponding population in England the proportion of vagrants is reversed. The total absence of Industrial Schools in 1865-66 in Ireland in part accounts for this result. The total of houses of bad character in 1866 for the whole of Ireland was 2,489, to which is to be added 3,552 as tramps and vagrants' lodging-houses, also as a rule of questionable character. The general proportion of criminals to the entire population in Ireland in 1866 was as 1 to 266; of prostitutes, 1 in 1,829. It is a remarkable fact that in 1865 the workhouse relief in Ireland was 14,751 above the number corresponding to the same proportion of population in England and Wales, while the out-door relief was 118,475 less. Truly, Ireland is a statistical anomaly in many respects. The total of criminals in confinement, in 1866, in Ireland was: in the local prisons, 2,343; in convict prisons, 1,432; in reformatories, 632; giving a grand total, with 11,578 tramps, of 26,103, against 38,169 in an equivalent population of England and Wales; so that Ireland, thus far, appears in a very creditable position, the result being 31 per cent. in favour of Ireland. The number of crimes returned by the police were 9,082, and persons apprehended, 6,252; the major portion of both being in the first and last quarters of the year, all in regard to indictable offences not summarily disposed of. Of these there were, in 1866, murders of infants, 36; of adults, 30; attempts to murder, &c., 118; manslaughter, 47; various "immoral" offences, 180; assaults with bodily harm, 413; common assaults, 506; offences against property with violence, 424; ditto without violence, 5,153; malicious offences against property, 627; forgery, &c., 108; miscellaneous, 1,450. Of treasonable and seditious offences, 283 constituted treason-felony: 34 sedition: 13 administration of seditious oaths: 95 seditious language: 159 having arms in a proclaimed district, making, with other treasonable charges, a total of 694, all arising from the Fenian conspiracy. The chief characteristics of Irish criminal offences were consequently malicious offences against life and property; riots and assaults, inflicting bodily harm. The proportion of murders are 66 in Ireland against 36 in a corresponding population of England and Wales. The total of coroners' inquests was 3,092, or about one-half of that corresponding to a similar population of England and Wales. The total cost of criminal prosecutions was £56,547, being an increase of about £7,000 on 1865, and chiefly attributable to the cost of Fenianism. Only two persons were executed in 1866. Of the total committents, about one-third of the persons could neither read nor write. Of 28,480 persons in the Irish County Prisons there were only one per cent. of women and girls, and less than four per cent. of men and boys *not* of Irish birth; at the same period, there were in English gaols no less than 12 per cent. of men and boys, and 21 per cent of women, men and girls of Irish birth. Including debtors and all others, there were 32,280 persons in prison in Ireland at the commencement of 1867. The number of lunatics sent to gaol was 553 against 36 in England and Wales for a proportionate population. The total cost of each prisoner was £33 12s. 8d. against £30 15s. 3d. per head in England.

In regard to civil law, &c., there were 16,136 writs issued from the Superior Courts of all kinds, in the first instances; 1,523 executions against the body, and 2,534 against the property of debtors. The number of judgments registered was 5,160 The total chancery cases was 1,863. There was only one winding-up case; namely, that of the Tipperary Bank, commenced in court in 1856. The total value of estates sold in the Landed Estates Court was £1,258,585, with a net rental of £63,350, the number of sales being 281. The total of property sworn under probates of wills, &c., was £6,307,880, the duty paid being £99,212. In the Divorce Courts the petitions for divorce in six months ending September, 1866, were but four, with only three petitions for alimony. The total number of persons declared bankrupt was 176, and there were 496 petitions of insolvency lodged. About 100,000 civil cases were disposed of at Petty Sessions in 1866, allowing an estimate of 10 per cent. for places from which no returns had been made.

In the present condition of the "Irish Question," as it is politically termed, the following facts, derived from a return to Parliament in July, 1868, for the year 1866, will be of considerable interest in regard to the ten-ure of land in that island. The proceedings against "Cottier" tenants, that is, such persons who hold an agreement in writing in respect to a dwelling-house without land or with any portion of land less than half an acre, at a rent not exceeding £5 annually, whether of monthly or yearly tenancy, were as follows:—Proceedings for waste, 23; for non-payment of rent, 130; for overholding possession, 1,018; the complaints in such cases that were heard amounted to 761; warrants to special bailiffs, 285; stay of execution for 14 days, 239. The number of civil ejectments served in all amounted to about 1,000; but the returns on this point seem defective, as great irregularity prevailed in reference to the mode of service. The aggregate of replevins amounted only to 41, an insignificant number compared to the total civil processes in Ireland for the year, which numbered 193,142. The total of ejectments, estimated for the year 1866 was 1,383, but actual returns were made from only 19 counties out of 32, and from only 6 counties of cities and towns out of 9. Adding the previously given number of 285 to the above, it appears that the number of ejectments of all kinds (except of weekly tenants) amounted to 1,668. The general result shows a disinclination to resort to distraint for rent, and the absence of necessity in disturbing sub-tenants. About 100 families were saved from such disturbances by the change of law effected by the Landlord and Tenant Act of 1860.

Educational Statistics.

The most recent report that has been issued by the Committee of Council on Education is that dated 27th June, 1868, and embraces the statistics for the year ending 31st August, 1867. The report refers only to Great Britain, excluding Ireland. The number of schools inspected in the twelve months was 14,591; the number of children present at inspection, 1,391,100. The annual average attending the schools amounted to 1,147,463; the number of teachers certificated, 12,613; of assistant teachers, 1,203; and of pupil teachers, 11,519. By an addendum making up the returns to 31st December, 1867, the numbers of certificated teachers were: of males, 7,099; females, 5,738; total, 12,837: assistant teachers: male, 529; female, 650: total, 1,179; and of pupil teachers, male, 5,374; female, 6,312; total, 11,686. On an average, there were from five to six certificated pupil teachers in England to one of either of those in Scotland. The returns show a general and gratifying progress on those of 1866, the increase in the number of children being no less than 103,496, including 45,835 evening scholars. The increase of certified teachers (31st August, 1867) was 742; of assistant teachers, 163; and of pupil teachers, 564. For the professional instruction of teachers, Great Britain had 37 colleges, the certified expenditure of which for the year ending 31st December, 1867, was £100,125. To these may be added six colleges affording instruction separately to male and female students, making a total of 43 colleges for teaching and training. These colleges afforded far more than ample accommodation for a large excess in number beyond those persons actually studying in them—14,600 against 21,400 that might be accepted. The average annual salary of a certificated teacher was £89, and of an uncertificated one from £52 to £70 for masters. The salary of a certificated mistress was about £55, averaging from £30 to £33 for those uncertificated. Out of every 11 children of the labouring classes attending school, the average number inspected and aided by the Committee of Education was 4. The Report of the Commissioners of National Education in Ireland, made up to the end of 1867, gives the following facts. The number of schools in operation was 6,520. The total number of children whose names were put on the rolls of the school books during the year was 913,198; the average daily attendance, 321,515. The increase over the previous year on the rolls was 2,379, and the daily average increase, 5,290. The schools are connected with all persuasions. The Established Church had 65,146; Catholics, 707,267; Presbyterians, 102,768; and other persuasions, 6,564; making a total of 912,745, the religious opinions of 453 pupils not having been stated. The largest number of Roman Catholics attending were in Munster (234,719) and Leinster (194,507). The number of teachers in the Board's Service was 8,326, of whom 3,480 were trained; besides these were 348 workmistresses and technical teachers. In certain parts of Ireland model schools and school farms are in active work. The total amount of receipts by the Commissioners for the year was £438,267, and the expenditure £370,504, carrying forward a balance in hand to 1868 of £67,763. The total number of teachers trained during the year was 299, besides 12 who supported themselves. Of the 299, there were 50 belonging to the Established Church, 167 Roman Catholics, 68 Presbyterians, and 14 of other persuasions. From the preceding facts it is evident that the schools rightly deserve the term "National" as applied to them in Ireland.

THE frequent mistakes made by public men when speaking of the national expenditure, and the subsequent corrections of the facts and figures they advance, with the reassertions in reply, evidence an amount of ignorance which cannot be considered as wilful, but which arises from the simple fact that no member of parliament, opposition or ministerial, whether Liberal or Conservative, has yet been able to master the details of the finances of this country. This will afford an abundant apology for any shortcomings, in the following attempt to unravel some of the mysteries of the subject. To the "outsider" the details furnished in the reports of any government are simply unintelligible, and to those practically acquainted with some divisions of such details, the rest are insoluble problems received with partial doubtings, but yet with an amount of faith that despairing ignorance can alone give rise to.

The chief divisions of the expenditure of the United Kingdom are those of the army, navy, and civil service, omitting for the moment the consideration of the interest of the national debt, which for general purposes may be considered as an annual charge equal to 23 millions sterling, increased by annuity charges by about 3¾ millions more. The army service absorbs at least 15½ millions annually, and the navy about 11 millions, taking the account of expenditure furnished for the year ending March 31st 1868, and omitting the accidental extraordinary charge due to the Abyssinian expedition. The civil service, for effective and non-effective expenditure, reached in the same year the sum of 11 millions, exclusive of the superannuations and post-office service, which of all the government departments alone affords a profit by its transactions in the legitimate commercial sense of the term. With the superannuations the total of civil service reached 12½ millions. Omitting, therefore, the item of national debt, which under present circumstances can only be considered as an unavoidable charge, the three departments of army, navy, and civil service present a total expenditure of about 40 millions sterling in round numbers. The exact amounts will be found in the following tables, which give an account of the total revenue of the United Kingdom for the year ending 31st March, 1868, after deducting a variety of items in the nature of drawbacks, and also of the general expenditure in the same period, omitting the amount applied to the reduction of the national debt, which will be considered in a subsequent article.

REVENUE for 1867–68.		
Heads of Income.	Net Receipts.	Total.
Balances, bills, and advances outstanding on the 31st March 1867		£ 3,180,498
Customs	22,664,980	
Excise .... ⎫		
Stamps .... ⎬	39,302,680	
Taxes (Land & Assess. ⎪		
Income and Prop. Tax... ⎭		
Post-office	4,558,962	
Crown Lands..................	449,252	
Miscellaneous.................	2,586,218	
		69,562,092
		72,742,590
Deduct,—Balances and Bills, outstanding	1,734,958	
Advances repayable and outstanding	1,311,634	
		3,046,592
		69,695,998
Excess of Expenditure over Income		2,166,024
Excess of Expenditure, as above	2,166,024	
Balances, Bills, &c., 31 March 1867 £3,180,497		
Balances, Bills, &c., 31 March, 1868 £3,046,592		
	133,905	
Actual Excess of Expenditure over Income	2,299,929	
		£71,862,022

EXPENDITURE FOR 1867–68.		
Heads of Payments.		Amounts.
Payments from Income of Crown Lands		£ 95,781
Interest and Management of the Permanent Debt	22,868,924	
Terminable Annuities......	3,447,270	
Interest of Exch. Bonds...	87,250	
Ditto Exchequer Bills......	165,919	
Ditto Bank Advances	2,387	
		26,571,750
Civil List	405,721	
Annuities and Pensions ...	286,839	
Salaries and Allowances	143,419	
Diplomatic Sals. and Pens.	174,053	
Courts of Justice	672,560	
Miscellaneous Charges ...	211,306	
		1,893,898
Army	15,418,582	
Navy	11,168,949	
Abyssinian Expedition ...	2,000,000	
Miscellaneous Civil Serv...	8,491,342	
Salaries, Superannuations, &c. of Customs and Inland Revenue............	2,481,152	
Ditto ditto, Post-office......	2,402,051	
Post-office Packet Service	808,517	
		42,770,593
Total Ordinary Expenditure		71,332,022
Expenses of Fortifications..................		530,000
		£71,862,022

The total of the cost of the three services, added to that of the interest of the national debt, disposes of about 66 out of 70 millions of the annual expenditure, and presents the most prominent features for remark.

The actual cost of the army and navy may be justly compared to that of the manufacture of any article, such as cotton, linen, &c. Three elements come into operation, namely, the raw material, its conversion into a useful condition, and, thirdly, the cost of superintending the operation. In respect to the army and navy, the raw material consists of men, ammunition, &c.; the second head of cost is found in keep, clothing, making ammunition, &c.; and the third is what is technically termed the "civil estimates," equivalent to the managership, clerkship, &c., of the manufactory. Taking this view of our national expenditure, the question becomes simplified, because the items are segregated into three essential and chief elements. As regards the two first great divisions, the raw material and its conversion into a useful commodity, they should be simply one of purchase—on the principle of buying in the cheapest market (not that of the lowest price), and converting the material by consummate management, at the least possible ordinary cost, into what is required by the State's wellbeing. Practically, we regard these two points in the light of recruiting and maintaining the active service in army and navy; and in procuring all the possible requirements which the exigencies of those services call for.

In all ordinary commercial transactions it will be found that the two divisions immediately under notice are the subject of the greatest outgoing cost. In every branch of industry in the country the cost of material and its reduction to serviceable purposes forms about 90 per cent. of the expenditure of the firm. But if we turn to the national balance sheet, already given, it will be found that the dead weight or cost of managing the national debt, the army and navy, including pensions, &c., for non-effective service, amounts to something like 25 per cent. of the total expenditure. In the margin of 10 per cent. that has been supposed to exist between the purchase of raw material, its conversion, &c., in the hands of the manufacturer, and his receipts, no notice has been taken of the interest of his capital nor of the profit he should make beyond that. It is only, indeed, reasonable to suppose that on an average the actual dead weight cost for management of such a concern does not exceed 2 or 3 per cent. of the returns, whilst the management of the national receipts and expenditure shows at least eight times that amount, or 25 per cent.

An analysis of some items of this cost will therefore be given.

During the early part of the present and the latter portion of the preceding century, whilst we were at war with nearly every nation on the face of the globe, the import trade was so diminished as to make the customs an exceedingly uncertain source of income. Consequently the Chancellors of the Exchequer of those days relied mainly on the excise department. Almost every available chance of taxation was had recourse to. A relative of the writer of this article, who entered the excise in 1781, used often to remark that Pitt would have willingly granted a pension of £150 per annum to any one who could invent a new source of excise tax. The return of peace and the eventual changes inaugurated by free trade changed the aspect of affairs, and now the customs stand at the head of our national sources of revenue, a result arising from the great imports and exports that have accompanied the enormous extension of our manufactures. In presenting the Budget for 1868-69 in April, 1868, Mr. Ward Hunt, the Chancellor of the Exchequer, relied on receiving during the current year the sum of £22,800,000

from the customs and £20,330,000 from the exciso, or, as it is now termed, the Inland Revenue department. Comparable with these estimates are those for 1866 and 1867, a summary of which is given in the following tables:—

CUSTOMS DUTIES.

Amounts received for	1866.	1867.
Chicory	£109,066	£111,272
Cocoa and Chocolate	21,332	21,549
Coffee	386,762	394,521
Corn	824,442	854,761
Fruit, dried : Currants	265,448	265,472
,, Figs & Prunes	31,666	36,226
,, Raisins	106,026	109,405
Pepper	28,634	free.
Spirits : Rum	2,098,454	2,192,620
,, Brandy	1,627,639	1,659,694
,, Geneva & other sorts	292,337	445,937
Sugar	5,552,838	5,764,460
,, Molasses	97,587	56,119
Tea	2,558,148	2,776,520
Tobacco and Snuff	6,535,576	6,549,282
Wine	1,410,944	1,425,009
Wood and timber	27,717	free.
All other articles	21,735	22,336
AGGREGATE GROSS RECEIPT	21,996,351	22,684,283
Deduct drawbacks, &c.	254,812	249,508
NET RECEIPT	£21,741,539	£22,434,775

EXCISE, 1867.
Heads of Duty.

Chicory	£21,907
Hackney Carriages	102,519
Licenses (including to kill & sell game)	2,650,237
Malt	6,302,418
Race Horses	9,263
Railways	486,742
Stage Carriages	35,556
Spirits	10,511,530
Sugar	94,117
	20,173,289
Law Costs recovered	501
Fines and Forfeitures	5,631
Miscellaneous	10,917
Total Excise	£20,190,338

Officially connected with the Inland Revenue department but essentially distinct in their source, are the Income and Property Tax, Stamps, Assessed, and other taxes. For many years the Property Tax has been a favourite resource of most Chancellors of the Exchequer, as a means of extricating themselves from financial difficulties, and of preventing the necessity of a loan. The last instance of the kind was the imposition of a sixpenny income tax, or rather an increase of a formerly existing fourpenny tax, by twopence, to cover the expenses incidental to the Abyssinian expedition, and which was a prominent feature in the Budget of 1868-69. For this period Mr. Hunt estimated hence an income of £6,900,000. The amounts received in previous years were as follows :—

PROPERTY AND INCOME TAX.

	1866.	1867.
Schedule A	£2,882,938	£2,510,731
,, B	327,351	276,445
,, C	612,228	538,808
,, D	2,105,203	1,957,374
,, E	393,972	353,936
Total	£6,321,692	£5,637,294

The stamp duties form an important item of revenue; they embrace a great variety of sources. In 1868-69, the estimate of revenue from all these sources was £9,650,000, against the following amounts, actually received in the years named.

STAMPS.

	1866.	1867.
Deeds and other Instruments	1,633,923	1,619,313
Bills of Exchange, &c.	768,531	730,070
Bankers' Notes	1,589	1,815
Bankers' Composition	130,585	127,847
Receipts, Drafts, &c.	531,324	547,583
Probates of Wills, &c.	1,580,776	1,623,273
Legacy Duty	2,604,332	2,568,044
Fire Insurances	1,178,385	952,338
Marine Insurances	472,562	482,167
Patent Medicines	57,336	59,601
Cards	8,941	9,161
Probate Court Fees	135,546	142,879
Licences and Certificates	134,018	133,297
Gold and Silver Plate	65,183	64,959
Newspapers	120,784	115,495
Admiralty Court Fees	9,867	11,066
Divorce Cause's Fees	2,701	2,467
Patents for Inventions	114,331	114,815
Land Registry Fees	1,275	1,690
Law (Ireland)	30,780	31,865
Registration (Ireland)	10,895	11,453
Companies Registration	—	2,843
Record (Ireland)	—	44

Total £9,593,664 £9,354,085

Assessed and other taxes produce on an average 3½ millions yearly, while from Crown lands and miscellaneous sources another 3½ millions are raised.

Last in the item of receipts is a department of Government—the post-office,—which, financially and socially, meets with approval on all hands. It yields a profit in its working expenses equal to about 1¼ millions annually. The method of conducting its business is the most perfect of any branch of the service, and there is little doubt that when the telegraphic system is amalgamated with the post-office, the present advantages of the latter will be greatly improved in regard to our national, commercial, and social requirements.

So far for the income of the country, which may be supplemented by a tabular statement of Mr. Hunt's Budget for 1868-69, both in regard to estimated income and expenditure; it is as follows :—

REVENUE, 1868-69.

Customs	£22,800,000
Excise	20,330,000
Income Tax	6,900,000
Stamps	9,650,000
Taxes	3,540,000
Post-office	4,650,000
Crown Lands	350,000
Miscellaneous	3,130,000
	£71,350,000

EXPENDITURE.

Interest on Debt	£26,700,000
Consolidated Fund	1,865,000
Army	15,456,000
Navy	11,177,000
Civil Services	9,174,000
Customs and Inland Revenue	2,598,000
Post-office and Packet Service	3,458,000
	£70,428,000

Leaving an estimated surplus of revenue beyond expenditure of £922,000, for the year ending 31st March, 1869.

At the close of the quarter, September 30, 1868, the results of the Budget were a net increase of £205,265 on the quarter's, and of £837,091 for the year ending the same date. During the latter period customs increased slightly; there was a decrease of nearly half-a-million in excise, a slight decrease in assessed taxes; an increase of 2½ millions in income tax; no change in the Post-office, nor in the miscellaneous sources worthy of notice. The total Income for the year ending September 30, was £70,307,562.

EXPENDITURE.—Whatever points of party attack are open, accidentally or recurrently, that of the National Expenditure, from its extent and the variety of its details, is one most commonly resorted to, hence the vote-of-supply nights in the House of Commons are generally enlivened with very animated discussions. It would be evidently impossible here to give even a brief outline of the details of our National Expenditure. The "Blue Book" for the Civil Service Estimates alone, for 1868-69, is a volume of some hundred pages, folio size. A few salient points of expenditure can only therefore be noticed.

Army and Navy.—By reference to pages 138, 148, the amount expended for 1867-68, and voted for 1868-69, will be found in detail. The amount includes all expenses, in providing, keeping, and clothing the men, the expenditure on fortifications, shipbuilding, dockyards and arsenals ; the manufacture of small-arms, ordnance, artillery, &c.; in fact every expense incidental to the two services, independent of the Abyssinian war of 1867-68. These estimates have been gradually increased for several years past. In 1865-66, the total national expenditure was but 66 millions, and the great difference between that amount and the present expenditure is almost entirely due to the great cost of modern armaments, including armour-plated ships, new fortifications, new ordnance and small arms. In the latter department an immense deal of money has been spent in what is termed conversion of the ordinary rifle or musket into the Enfield or Snider form. Again, each improvement in the manufacture of heavy ordnance, has led to further expenditure in armour-plating our vessels, and the end of these two opposing causes seems utterly out of view, until the nation, unable, will no longer bear the constantly increasing burden of this kind of expenditure. In the years since 1860, no less than 3 millions sterling were simply wasted in useless gun conversion ; and the experiments, still carried on at Shoeburyness in Essex, attest the utter want of security which can be expected either from the new gun or armour-plating systems constantly brought forward. Each charge of a twelve-inch gun, including powder and shot, costs about £12, so that each time it is discharged, that amount of the nation's money is sent to the winds. Guns of still larger calibre, or more refined workmanship, cost about £40 at each discharge. The cost of testing a twelve-inch gun is about £2,000, and the cost of some employed in the service has been £4,000 each.

The efficiency of our armour-clad navy, despite the enormous amount it has cost, has been greatly disputed. In the House of Commons, in May, 1868, an eminent authority declared that those vessels "rolled so heavily that they could not use their guns with anything like precision." Many of the gun-boats were so defective as to be unable to go to sea safely. Supplies were voted for 35,700 men for the navy, being a reduction of about 2,000 on the year 1867-68. But, despite all complaints, 7,748 tons of armoured, and 6,931 tons of unarmoured vessels were ordered to be built in 1868-69. The expenditure on armoured ships in 1865-66, was £792,000; in 1867-68, £824,000; whilst in 1868-69, it was proposed to expend £1,360,000. In the navy votes for 1868-69 there was required £3,036,634 for wages of seamen and marines, whilst for their victuals and clothing, a sum of £1,336,000 was asked for. The remaining details of navy cost are given elsewhere; but it was stated that while the cost of the French navy was 6.35 per cent. value of the trade of France, the cost of the British navy was but 2.73 per cent. of our trade.

The total estimate of fortifications already completed or in progress, was £11,850,000, of which sum the fortifications at Portsmouth, which must extend over a length of 17 miles, will cost £1,192,000, requiring an army of 30,000 men for their defence.

The details of the army estimates are given at another page. They only vary in character with the different nature of the service. A general statement may be here made to the effect that, including officers and men, the total cost of each individual is at the rate of about 30s. per week; an amount far in excess of the weekly wages of the ordinary class of skilled workmen in this country.

Civil Service.—This we have reckoned as the third great division of the cause of expenditure of our national finances.

The general nature of the civil service expenditure will be best understood by extracts from the estimates for the year 1868-69, printed by order of the House of Commons, in February, 1868. In that document the several heads of expenditure are classified as follows :—

1. Public works and buildings.
2. Salaries and expenses of public departments.
3. Law and justice.
4. Education, science, and art.
5. Colonial, consular, and other foreign services.
6. Superannuation and retired allowances, and gratuities for charitable and other purposes.
7. Miscellaneous, special, and temporary purposes.

A supplemental heading is entitled "Revenue Department and Packet Service."

Under the first head, public works, &c. is included the cost of maintenance of all public buildings belonging to the treasury, foreign office, commissioners of works, &c., &c. The vote for the royal palaces was £56,000; parks, &c., £137,500; houses of parliament, £54,900. The total of Class I. amounted to £1,260,782, being nearly £200,000 in excess of 1867-68.

Under class II. (salaries, &c.) the treasury absorbed £84,600; the home office, £89,400; foreign office, £74,450; colonial, £32,900; board of trade, £97,725; secretary of Ireland, &c., £29,000; paymaster-general's office, £19,500; public works, £34,700; board of works in Ireland, £26,500; besides these is a long list of miscellaneous public officers, &c., &c. The poor law commission cost is £209,000; and a sum of £395,000 is set down as cost of stationery and printing. The Irish poor law commission cost

£95,000; privy council, £42,500; the exchequer and audit, £38,500. The total of votes for salaries in class II. of certain public officers was £1,661,179, a sum about £120,000 less than in 1867-68.

Under the next heading, III., or Law and Justice, a total sum of £3,581,586 forms the estimate. The chief items are—criminal prosecutions, £188,776; police, £266,000; county prisons, &c., £240,000; metropolitan police, £190,500; Ireland, law, £150,000; Scotland, £136,000; English government prisons, £296,000; constabulary in Ireland, £884,000, and government prisons in that country, £63,400.

In striking contrast with the preceding, which may be called the punitive department, is that included in class IV., or education, science, and art. The total of the estimate is £1,618,527, or somewhat less than the half of that of class III. In other words, we nationally spend less than half in preventing than in punishing or detecting crime. The learned societies in Great Britain receive £13,000; of Ireland, £8,000; Scottish universities, £18,000. In public education in Great Britain, £842,500; science and art departments, £239,000; British museum, £99,400; public education in Ireland, £360,195, are the sums estimated.

Class V. absorbs £486,277, which includes, with several other items, for numerous consuls abroad, £171,000; China and Japan service, £117,600; ministers at foreign courts, &c., £56,300; colonial offices, St. Helena, &c. £79,000; emigration, £14,000.

Class VI.. superannuations, &c., absorbs an amount of £426,825, its chief item being superannuations and retired allowance of public officers, £256,000; merchant seamen's fund, £51,000; non-conforming clergy, £41,386.

Class VII. absorbs £132,000 for expenses of commissions, and a variety of miscellaneous expenses too numerous to detail.

The estimates for revenue departments and post-office, &c. are as follows :

Customs	£1,024,653
Inland Revenue	1,574,210
Post-office	2,369,235
Post-office Packet Service	1,089,349
Total	£6,057,447

The grand total of all the preceding Civil classes for 1868-69 is	9,173,032
Revenue Department	6,057,447
	15,230,479

Or a net actual increase on 1867-68 of £418,112.

Under the educational heading it is stated that the number of children on the books of the schools under the supervision of the government was 1,359,019 in England and Wales, and 212,628 in Scotland—a total of 1,571,647, whilst the average attendance for the year was 911,681 in England, and 169,708 in Scotland, giving a total of 1,081,389.* In the United Kingdom there were 10,530 persons under scientific instruction in May 1867. The sub-headings of Class VI., or superannuation and retired allowances, is a mass of minute details, involving many curious items. As specimens of this, may be mentioned the following recipients—Toulonese and Corsican emigrants, £594; Polish refugees, £1,750; distressed Spaniards, £714; French refugees,

---

* Detailed information on this head will be found in another page of the Almanack.

£520; Her Majesty's charities, &c., in Scotland, £2,000, &c., Refuge for the Destitute, significantly forming a conclusion, at a cost of £325. The estimate for the relief of Distressed Seamen is one that will commend itself to every Briton. The amount is £45,000, exclusive of a sum granted towards defraying the expenses of an establishment at Sable Island, Nova Scotia, for the relief of persons shipwrecked. The larger sum is applied for the subsistence and conveyance home of British seamen left destitute abroad, or taken off wrecks at sea, as well as of British subjects other than seamen; also for remunerating owners for detention and loss, and as rewards to masters and crews for saving life. Under the head of superannuation and retired allowances are embraced all the pensions paid to officers of every department of governmental service, including somewhat singularly, the " Household of the late Princess Charlotte of Wales," £900; and the same of the late King of the Belgians, £646. The total of the estimate is £255,867, being a net increase of £13,413 on the year 1867-68. Of the vote for Princess Charlotte's household Lady Gardiner receives £600 as bedchamber woman; and although H.R.H. has been dead for more than half a century, this allowance only commenced December 11,1865. The amount of new allowances, placed for the first time on the estimates, in 1868-69, is stated at £20,353.

In Class VII. the expenses of temporary commissioners is stated at £40,000, being a net decrease of £12,000 on the previous year. The Malta and Alexandria Telegraph is charged for £500, as part of the expenses of the government superintendent, whose labours had not commenced at the time of the estimates being voted, the line never having been got to work until September, 1868. The sum of £280 is charged for the use of the Electric Telegraph Company's line to Balmoral.

The miscellaneous estimates of Class VII. include expenses of Royal Households not provided for in the civil list, fees on appointments, &c., and a great variety of items and repayments to the Civil Contingencies Fund. In the latter the expense of the cattle plague is stated at about £16,000, in connection with the orders of the Privy Council. The least amount, 34s. 10d., is charged as the expense of removing a British lunatic from France. Under this head is included an estimate of £47,600 for payments of local dues on shipping through the conditions of sundry treaties of reciprocity. The last of the

chief items is that for the cultivation of flax in Ireland. The sum of £4,000 is spent in payment of salaries to about 40 flax instructors, with travelling, and incidental expenses.

The last of the civil estimates is that for the revenue department customs, excise, &c., and post-office. Under this head the salaries of the officers are charged in respect to each department, as also a variety of incidental expenses. The total and separate amounts for each department have been already given at a previous page. The total sum charged for the conveyance of mails at home and abroad is stated at £775,500; but this does not include many subsidies named in the Post-office Packet Service. A sum of about £580,000 of the above is paid to railway companies in the United Kingdom for the conveyance of mails. The total cost of salaries, wages, and allowances, in connection with the Post-office Savings' Banks is returned as £50,350. The amount voted for superannuations in 1868-69, was £66,409. Under the head of the Post-office Packet Service is included all the contracts entered into with public companies or private individuals for the conveyance of mails abroad; £383,000 is charged as the cost of all American mails; £541,300 for the Asian and Australian; £96,950 for the Packet Service in the United Kingdom; and £43,700 for conveyance of mails to Africa. A net increase of the estimate of £280,000 above that of 1867-68 is stated, the total vote being £1,089,349.

Such is a brief analysis of the Civil Service estimates for 1868-69. The great variety of charges renders it impossible to enter into further details. It is to be regretted that no return is made of the total number of persons paid in this service. The whole is in a most unsatisfactory condition in regard to its financial aspects; and a vigorous hand is required to lessen the expenses which are out of all proportion to the work performed.

THE CONSOLIDATED FUND.—The next subject of importance in connection with the finance of our kingdom is the *Consolidated Fund*, a statement of which presents the balance-sheet of the national transactions, with certain exceptions that have been or will be noticed. The inexperienced eye will perceive little difference between the account of the Consolidated Fund and that of the National Revenue and Expenditure; but, financially, and in the question of the audit, many differences arise. The following table gives the principal heads of receipts and expenditure.

THE CONSOLIDATED FUND for the Year ending March 31st, 1868.

RECEIPTS.	£	s.	d.	PAYMENTS.	£	s.	d.
Income	69,600,218	4	1	Interest and Management of the National Debt	26,316,193	16	9
Money raised by Annuities 28 & 29 Vict.	480,000	0	0	Sinking Fund	1,790,404	9	4
Money raised by Excheq. Bonds	1,700,000	0	0	Interest on Unfunded Debt	255,556	5	0
Repayments on account of advances for the Purchase of Bullion, Local Works, &c. ...	1,573,063	18	10	Civil List and other ordinary charges on the Consol. Fund	1,893,898	3	5
For New Courts of Justice	375,000	0	0	Fortifications, 28 & 29 Vict. ...	530,000	0	0
For Greenwich Hospital	115,445	8	7	Advances for Purchase of Bullion and for Local Works, &c.	1,422,880	2	2
Amount of Sinking Fund applied in payment of Bank of England Advances	901,638	9	4	Exchequer Bonds paid off	1,700,000	0	0
				Exchequer Bills paid off	45,700	0	0
					33,954,632	16	8
				Surplus, viz., £43,303,039 18. 0d. Less, 2,512,305 16s. 10d.	40,790,733	4	2
	74,745,366	0	10		74,745,366	0	10

Another statement is furnished in the Parliamentary Papers published in 1868, showing an account of monies applicable to the payment of the Consolidated Fund, and of the charges thereon; but as it really furnished nothing different to the preceding, except mere accountants' items it needs no special consideration.

In the first of the two preceding tables an account is given of the receipts properly due to and included in the Consolidated Fund Dr. account. This need not be here discussed, as it has already been generally considered under the broad heading of the Income and Expenditure of the United Kingdom. The object of the following analysis will be rather to show the expenditure in certain departments in respect to the charges on the Consolidated Fund.

From Nos. 10 to 30 of the finance accounts, ending March 31st, 1868, and ordered to be printed by the House of Commons on the 2nd July of that year, are occupied by a statement of the expenditure of various departments chargeable on the Consolidated Fund; but these have already been in general dealt with at a preceding page under the heads of Customs, Inland Revenue, Post Office Packet Service, and Superannuation of Revenue Departments, to which may be added that in regard to the woods and forests, a sum of £95,780 10s. 9d. is charged as a payment out of the Public Income, which includes a charge of collection, amounting to £16,815 18s. 1d.; and "other" charges which, amounting to £78,964 12s. 8d., include payments for ancient pensions and payments to schools, churches, &c., payments of land revenue, payments transferred from the civil list, in all amounting to £10,952 4s. 6d.; salaries to wardens and others, £2,526 6s. 6d.; payments for repairs, taxes, &c., in all £26,221 8s. 3d.; and, lastly, the cost of maintaining buildings, walls, fences, roads, &c., &c., stated at £39,524 13s. 5d. The total gross receipt of the woods and forests department for the year ending March 31, 1868, was £449,252 6s. 10d., of which sum £345,000 was paid into the Exchequer during the year. These amounts, together with the cash balances of the preceding and current year, made the Dr. and Cr. accounts stand respectively as amounting on each side to £513,098 13s.

Under the head of miscellaneous receipts, forming part of the Consolidated Fund, and amounting to £2,586,218, are the following, as paid into the Exchequer for the year ending 31 March, 1868. Small branches of the Hereditary Revenue, £10,697; Profits of issue of the Bank of England in regard to the suspension of the Bank-Note Restriction Act, £138,578; fees of public officers, £271,180; sale of old stores, £866,580; extraordinary receipts in the civil departments, £205,560; income of the London, Edinburgh, and Dublin Gazettes, £28,269; contribution from India for military charges, £850,000; ditto for diplomatic and consular services, £23,553; and for the Red Sea Telegraph Co.'s Annuity, (for doing nothing, the cable having been a dead failure), £18,027; unclaimed wages of seamen, &c., £8,820; savings of grants of Parliament, and over issues repaid, £30,691; money returned by various individuals for "conscience sake," £4,638; treasury chest, £2,738; Greenwich Hospital, £15,480; Isle of Man, £12,389; Greek loan, £7,937; casual receipts, £9,733; Japan indemnity (moiety), £68,532; and others of smaller amounts.

Repayments of advances from the Consolidated Fund, of a miscellaneous but frequently important character may next be analyzed, all for the year ending 31 March, 1868. Amongst them are the following: bullion purchased for coinage, £250,000; colonial docks, £840; county gaols, Ireland, £6,986; drainage advances, £247,000; ditto annuities, &c., £10,527; re-building of London bridge, £19,559; building and support of lunatic asylums in Ireland, £128,702; Menai and Conway bridges, £3,260; New Zealand loan (interest, &c.), £1,500; public works loan fund, Great Britain, £584,017; Ireland, £59,636; inland loan improvements, £109,992; employment of poor, £914; bridges and roads in Ireland, £1,730; Sardinian loan, £80,000; valuation of land, Ireland, £13,341; West Indian relief, £36,089; wide streets, Dublin, £1,112.

Civil List Annuities and Pensions, chargeable on Consolidated Fund.—This department of the annual charge on the fund and the revenue of the country, has always been a point of soreness and complaint on the part of the nation. The total sum may practically be considered as a payment for non-effective services, with the exception of the "Civil List," in which Her Majesty's annual allowance is included, embracing the privy purse, household, &c., &c.

The Queen's Civil List was established by 1–2 Vict., cap. 21, which provides that during her life all the revenues of the crown shall be part of the Consolidated Fund, but that a *Civil List* shall be set apart for the Queen. In 1837 this was fixed at £385,000, with the following limitations: £60,000 annually is to provide for Her Majesty's privy purse; £231,260 for the salaries of the royal household; £44,240 for retiring allowances and pensions to servants; and £13,200 for royal bounty, alms, &c.; leaving a surplus of £36,300 for the general purposes of the court. Whenever the civil charges exceed the sum of £400,000, an account of the expenditure must be laid before Parliament, within thirty days after the excess of expenditure has been incurred, or the payments audited. This privilege, lodged by way of demand in any member of the House of Commons, and in consequence equally so of the House of Lords, has not been acted on. In the account of the sum appropriated to the civil list as furnished in the parliamentary papers of 1868, the amount of £405,721 5s. is charged, of which £385,000 is set aside for the use of Her Majesty, as already explained. The balance £20,721 5s. is stated to be a charge for pensions granted by 1. Vict. c. 2. Class V.

Next in importance is an account of annuities and pensions paid out of the Consolidated Fund for the use of the royal family and numerous individuals who have, in some way or other, served the state. First in order in the return is an annuity to H.R.H. the Duchess of Cambridge of £6,000, granted in the reign of George III. and IV. The Princess Augusta of Mecklenburgh-Strelitz receives £3,000; H.R.H. the Duke of Cambridge, £12,000, besides other sources of income as Commander-in-Chief, &c.; H.R.H. Princess Mary of Teck, £3,000, and another sum of £2,000 granted on her marriage in 1866, as an additional allowance, making in all £5,000 annually; H.R.H. the Princess Royal (crown princess of Prussia), receives £8,000; on her marriage in 1857, she received also a dowry of £40,000, at which time there was considerable feeling in both Houses of Parliament that the most advisable course would have been to have granted a much larger dowry and no annuity. The Princess Alice Maud (of Hesse), received on her marriage a dowry of £30,000 in 1861, and since then an annuity of £6,000; H.R.H. the Prince of Wales has an annuity of £40,000, but with the addition of the revenues that fall to him from the Stannaries, as Duke of Cornwall, and his army connections, his income exceeds £100,000; the Duke of Edinburgh has an annuity of £15,000, besides his naval pay; H.R.H. the Princess Helena (Schleswig-Holstein), has an annuity of £6,000, voted to her on her marriage with Prince Christian. The Princess of Wales receives £10,000 annually, which in the event of her becoming a widow, is to be increased to £30,000. The total present amount, and future charges of the royal family, exclusive of Her Majesty, is £111,000.

Next in order to the above, and chargeable on the Consolidated Fund, are numerous salaries and pensions granted for naval and military, civil, judicial, and other services; the salaries and allowances of officers of the House of Commons; grants, &c., to the Scottish clergy, and various institutions in Scotland; the salary of the lord-lieutenant of Ireland; the grant to Maynooth College of £26,300 per annum; the salaries and pensions of the diplomatic service, amounting with pensions, &c., to £174,053; salaries of the judges and others connected with the courts of justice, &c., in England, Scotland, and Ireland, amounting to £672,560; and miscellaneous services of £211,305, which, with £530,000 for the construction of fortifications, make a total of £741,305.

As explicatory details of some of the items of our National Expenditure, the following will be read with interest :—

DUCHY OF CORNWALL.

The statement of revenue, &c., of the Duchy of Cornwall for the year ending 31st December, 1867, as affecting the income of H.R.H. the Prince of Wales, presents the following items :—*Receipts,* —Balance in hand, £8,100; rents and profits secured to the Prince of Wales, £49,031; royalties of coal mines in Somerset, £2,174; of mines in Cornwall, £3,471; annuity received from the Consolidated Fund in lieu of tin coinage duties, &c., £16,216; dividends on stock, &c., £1,784, which, with some minor items, make a total of £80,787. *Expenditure.*—Paid to H.R.H., £54,927; various charges on outlay, taxes, pensions, &c., £9,700; expenses of management, £7,530; balance in hand, £8,636. The capital account shows a balance in favour of the estate of £74,640, in cash and Consolidated 3 per cent. Annuities.

DUCHY OF LANCASTER.

Her Majesty, as Duchess of Lancaster, claims the net revenues of the Duchy. In the year ending 21st December, 1867, the total *Revenues* amounted to £48,796, commencing with a balance in hand of £4,536; rents and profits accruing to Her Majesty, £30,102; royalties of mines and quarries, £7,727; sale of wood, £1,894; dividends on stock, £1,059; transfer of capital for repair of Savoy Chapel, £1,056, and other items of minor importance. *Payments* were: £29,000 to Her Majesty; expenses of management, &c., £13,362; restoration of the Savoy Chapel, London, £1,245; leaving, with small items, a balance in favour of

the estate, of £5,168. In the expenses are various charges of pensions, salaries, donations, repairs, taxes, &c., &c.

WORKS AND PUBLIC BUILDINGS.

The annual return for 1866-67 gives the following particulars as to the amount of money expended on public works, &c. The total amount voted was £1,313,310, and the expenditure was as follows: Royal Palaces, £49,127; Public Buildings, £103,024; Royal Parks and Pleasure Gardens, £110,053; Houses of Parliament, £51,411; Furniture of Public Offices, £11,995; Embassy Houses at Paris and Madrid, £1,106; Westminster Bridge, £6,176; New Foreign Office, £54,998; Public Offices' Site, £22,550; Probate Court, £5,347; Public Record Repository, £21,500; Nelson Column (Lions), £6,000, including £1,000 balance due to Sir E. Landseer; Patent Office, £8,269; National Gallery, £39,144; University of London. £9,253; Chapter House, Westminster, £2,835; Office of Works, (Salaries, and Expenses), £33,425; Advance for New Courts of Justice, £436,145; Burlington House Designs, £1,575; Wellington Monument, £2,800; South Kensington Roads, £1,285; leaving a balance of £336,486 unexpended of the vote.

WOODS, FORESTS, AND LAND.

The following present some of the leading items of the income and expenditure of the Woods, Forests, &c., Commission for 1866-67, ending 31st March, 1867. *Revenue* from Lands, Manors, Mines, &c., £386,049; expenditure, £49,935; Windsor Park receipts, £6,182, payments, £29,194; Royal forests and woodlands, £40,225, payments, £25,218, showing a total income of £491,194. Of the balance, 330,000 was paid into the Exchequer, and a sum of £63,846 kept in hand for the following year. An amount of £28,815 was voted in the Civil Service estimates for 1866-67, of which £27,911 was paid in salaries, legal expenses, &c., leaving £904 as balance in hand. The legal expenses alone amounted to £10,309, or about two-thirds of the sum paid for salaries.

MERCANTILE MARINE FUND.

This fund had a gross income for the year ending 31st December, 1867, of £383,092, derived from the following sources :—Fees received under the Merchant Shipping Act for examination of masters and mates, engagement and discharge of crews, renewal of certificates, &c., &c.; in all £56,387; light dues received per Trinity House Corporation, £272,551; per Port of Dublin Corporation, £19,836; and Commissioners of Northern Lighthouses (Scotland) £34,319. The expenditure includes the following items :—By salaries, fees, &c., at the various ports of the United Kingdom, £48,838; expenses of maintaining the lighthouses by the three corporations just named, £301,356; Excess of income over working expenditure, £32,898. The amount expended for new works, in building lighthouses, &c., was, in England, £20,629; Scotland, £12,593; and Ireland, £17,125. An advance to relieve distressed seamen abroad amounted to £1,934. The Japanese lighthouses cost £12,242.

MORTALITY IN THE MERCANTILE MARINE.

The following interesting statistics are afforded by the Board of Trade returns for the year 1867.

The total number of deaths reported was 5,283. Of these 932 sailors were under 20 years of age; 2,442 between 20 and 30; 799 between 31 and 40; 353 between 41 and 50; 99 between 51 and 60; 7 over 60 years old; and 651 ago unknown. The cause of diseases were as follows: Yellow fever, 346; other forms of fever, 415; brain and nervous system, 109; heart, &c., 88; lungs, &c., 66; consumption, 147; stomach, liver, &c., 521, of which 212 were from cholera, and 214 from dysentery; urinary organs, &c., 27; skin diseases, 15; rheumatism, 7; scurvy, 52; various other diseases, 82; natural causes, 31; drowned by wreck, 1,808; drowned by accidents other than wrecks, 1,105; other accidental causes, 275; murder and homicide, 16; suicide, 16; unknown causes, 157.

GREENWICH HOSPITAL.

By an Act of Parliament passed in 1865, the administration of Greenwich Hospital was entirely changed. A very large proportion of the inmates were pensioned off at an annual allowance of £15 per head, only those being retained at the Institution who were either incapable of leaving it, or, not having any friends living, did not choose to leave. The capital account for the year ending 31 March, 1867, showed as assets, cash £182,871; money on loan, £139,957; stock in the 3 per cent. annuities, &c., £1,635,243; in the consols, 3 per cent. £1,195,382; and £10,000 invested in the Hexham and Allendale Railway Company; it therefore presented a total of £3,163,453.

The Receipts and Expenditure for 1866-67 amounted to £180,135. The first was constituted of a balance from 31 March, 1866, of £11,672; the dividends of funded property brought in £81,917; interest on loans, £4,243; Transfers from Consolidated Fund in place of seamen's sixpences, £20,000; rents, £4,385; proportion of freightage on conveyance of treasure in Her Majesty's ships, £2,404; old stores, £1,512; percentage for use of Greenwich Hospital furniture, £50; miscellaneous receipts, £38. The produce of the northern estates in Northumberland, &c., consisting of farms, lands, quarries, lime and clay works, fisheries, wood, mines, &c., was £50,912, making a grand total of income of £180,135. Under the head of expenditure for 1866-67, are the following chief items: management of property in the north of England, £9,273; cost of the establishment at the Admiralty, £1,261; offices of the comptroller and solicitor, £1,493; Greenwich Household and Infirmary, £40,213; school, £21,630; pensions to flag and other officers, £3,698; pensions and allowances to seamen, £46,501; gratuities to widows of persons slain, &c., in the service of the crown, transfer of £15,480 to the Consolidated Fund at the rate of £15 per head on 1,032 men in 1867, or the average number of inmates in the Hospital, and short of 1,400; investment of surplus income in the consols, £10,000. Balance of income account, £28,672; making as *per contra* a total of £180,135.

National Debt.

If it be the privilege of great nations to be in debt, the United Kingdom has much to be proud of in that respect, standing at the head of all others in regard to its funded debt. In former times the government of this country depended chiefly on moderate loans, obtained from the rich merchants, especially of the city of London, which, by thus aiding the monarchs in the pressure of money matters arising from ordinary or extraordinary causes, secured to itself many privileges, some of which it still retains. The goldsmiths and quasi-bankers of a few centuries ago were, in fact, the national bankers in regard to the advance of money. But in the course of time the exigencies of the public service, arising from wars abroad and heavy expenses at home, far outstripped the power of those individuals to meet the financial demands of the government. The nation was then appealed to, and a public debt was created for the payment of which, in respect to interest and principal, the national honour was pledged. The early loans were of only short duration, but in 1664 public securities bearing interest were negotiated, a portion of the revenue being set aside for the payment of principal and interest. In 1672, Charles II. was the first to break national faith, shutting up the exchequer and announcing that a sum of £1,328,000 due to the goldsmiths could not be paid for a year. A universal panic set in, and much private ruin was the consequence. The principal was never redeemed, but the interest was duly paid in 1684. In 1699 an act was passed allowing interest at the rate of 3 per cent.; but a moiety of the then debt still forms part of our present funded debt.

Gradually the national debt grew in amount. In the time of William and Mary it rose from 3 to 12 millions. In the days of Queen Anne it arrived at 36 millions. At the conclusion of the reign of George II. it reached 102 millions. It was reserved, however, for the reign of George III. to raise the debt to its maximum. In 1760, when that monarch came to the throne, the total was as just stated; but in 1815, when peace was declared, the whole funded debt amounted to 861 millions. Subsequently a gradual reduction was effected till in 1834 the debt was reduced to 773 millions. It oscillated for about 25 years between that sum and 805 millions—the amount it reached in 1859. The Russian war of 1854-55 added to it no less than 33 millions in three years. Since that period it has been the constant endeavour of financialists to reduce the debt, and the consequent annual charge on the revenue of the country, by the creation of a sinking fund, that, although to a comparatively small extent, has lessened the amount of principal and interest. Plainly, in fact, the savings of the nation, like those of an individual, are applied to the payment of the debts. Another happy feature of our present financial economy is that of charging extraordinary expenses on revenue instead of creating new loans. Thus in 1867-68 the expense of the Abyssinian war was entirely defrayed out of the revenue by the imposition of an extra tax on income and property.

The subsequent statements in respect to the present condition of the national debt are extracted from a parliamentary paper published in May, 1868.

The following tables show the state of the debt at the periods named, together with the annual charge—in other words, the principal and interest :—

NATIONAL DEBT AND CHARGE—1867 AND 1868.

	Debt.	Charge.
Total unredeemed Debt on 31st March, 1867 :—		
Great Britain	£729,916,314	£24,688,862
Ireland	39,624,690	1,201,560
	£769,541,004	£25,890,422
Debt created or transferred between 31st March, 1867, and 31st March, 1868 :—		
Great Britain	£1,209,978	£2,078,445
Ireland	483,978	14,520
	£1,693,956	£2,092,965
Total............	£771,234,960	£27,983,387

	Debt.	Charge.
Debt reduced or transferred between 31st March, 1867, and 31st March, 1868 :—		
Great Britain	£28,891,984	£1,522,378
Ireland	1,152,648	36,446
	£30,044,632	£1,558,824
Total unredeemed Debt on the 31st March, 1868 :—		
Great Britain	£702,234,309	£25,244,930
Ireland	38,956,019	1,179,633
	£741,190,328	£26,424,563
Total............	£771,234,960	£27,983,387

	Debt.	Charge.
Total unredeemed Debt and Charge on 31st March, 1868, as above	£741,190,328	£26,424,562
Total unredeemed Debt and Charge on 31st March, 1867, as above	769,541,004	25,890,422
Between 31st March, 1867, and 31st March, 1868... Decrease	£28,350,676	Increase... £534,140

The preceding figures refer only to the funded debt of the kingdom, and are independent of exchequer bills, &c., to which allusion will more particularly be made.

By the provisions of an act passed in the reign of George IV., which came into operation in 1829, the annual surplus revenue beyond the expenditure of the United Kingdom was to be applied to the reduction of the national debt. In the year ending March, 1868, the sum of £1,797,311 3s. 11d. became applicable for that purpose. Of this money, £895,672 was expended in the purchase of stock, the price of 3 per cents. being 93¾. The sum of £901,638 9s. 4d., the balance, was paid into the Bank of England for advances made on account of the deficiencies of the consolidated fund. These items afford particulars relating to the sinking fund already alluded to.

The UNFUNDED DEBT is comprised of exchequer bills and bonds. Of bills, there were outstanding on the 31st March, £5,611,100, bearing a charge on interest of £139,750, or estimated at that sum. Of bonds there were outstanding, at the same date, £2,300,000, at an estimated interest of £76,250. It need scarcely be stated that exchequer bills are similar in character to the promissory note of the merchant, being issued by the Chancellor of the Exchequer for a limited period to meet present necessities. As they are always convertible in the markets they are much sought after, as a temporary investment of large sums by bankers and others. They are never allowed to go below par, and as a rule are generally at a slight premium. The following table shows the different departments or divisions of the national debt, and the sums due on each ; from the total, however, the sum of £654,652 has to be deducted as standing in the name of commissioners, which will reduce the amount to that stated as £741,190,328, &c., as given in the general view of the national debt in the above balance-sheet.

DESCRIPTION, &c., OF EACH BRANCH OF THE NATIONAL DEBT.

	CAPITALS.
GREAT BRITAIN.	£
New Annuities at 2½ per cent.	3,843,974
Exchequer Bonds, created per 16 Vict. c. 23, at 2½ per cent.............	418,300
Debt due to the Bank of England at £3 per cent............................	11,015,100
Consolidated Ann. at £3 per cent....	389,806,767
Reduced Annuities at £3 per cent....	106,184,994
New Annuities at £3 per cent.........	190,928,801
Total at £3 per cent.	697,935,662
New Annuities at £3½ per cent.......	240,746
Ditto at £5 per cent...................	430,250
Total, Great Britain...................	702,868,932
IRELAND.	
New Annuities at £2½ per cent.....	3,081
Consolidated Ann. at £3 per cent...	5,952,167
Reduced Annuities at £3 per cent....	111,148
New Annuities at £3 per cent........	30,275,383
Debt due to the Bank of Ireland at £3 per cent................................	2,630,769
New Annuities at £5 per cent.........	3,500
Total, Ireland..........................	38,976,048
Total, United Kingdom, at 31st March 1868	741,844,980

Many schemes have been proposed for a rapid extinction of this enormous incubus on the resources of the nation, but that it will be ever paid off is more than doubtful. Still, when it is remembered that about 500 million sterling capital have been paid for the construction of railways, &c., during the last thirty years, the possibility cannot be questioned, however the probability may be.

The following statistics in respect to the national debt of our own and other countries in 1866, are extracted from the report of the board of trade, presented to Parliament in 1868. A few only of the items are given, the most important nations having been selected.

AMOUNT PER HEAD OF POPULATION FOR PUBLIC DEBT AND REVENUE.

Country.	Debt per head.			Revenue per head.		
	£	s.	d.	£	s.	d.
United Kingdom	26	15	9	2	5	7
Holland	21	17	10	2	9	2
United States	8	8	9	8	8	5
France	14	18	9	1	19	1
Spain	10	4	6	1	14	4
Portugal	9	17	6	0	16	4
Greece	9	15	3	0	18	4
Italy	9	8	3	1	8	3
Austria	7	5	3	0	17	3
Belgium	5	0	7	1	6	4
Russian Empire	3	14	1	0	18	11
Brazil	3	1	3	0	13	0
Turkey (1867–68)	1	19	1	0	8	3
Prussia	1	15	8	1	1	6
Norway	1	1	10	0	12	7
Sweden	1	0	0	0	9	1

The estimates, in regard to population of the United States, are founded on the census of 1860, and hence are liable to correction. From the preceding statistics it would seem, as a rule, that the heavier the debt the more prosperous the kingdom, although such a view is somewhat anomalous if applied to individuals in place of nations. This point, however, may be further elucidated by the following statistics in relation per head to imports and exports of a few nations for 1866. The value of such information would be greatly enhanced if, besides the items of population, exports and imports, we could arrive at some estimate of the entire natural produce of each country, in respect to its consumption, money value, &c.

EXPORTS AND IMPORTS PER HEAD OF POPULATION.

	Exports.			Imports.		
	£	s.	d.	£	s.	d.
Holland	7	9	1	8	12	5
United Kingdom	5	10	9	7	5	9
Belgium	4	16	7	6	1	5
France	3	5	2	2	15	9
Greece	0	16	6	1	15	10
Italy	0	16	6	1	14	4

PAUPERISM AND POOR RATES.

The latest returns, published in June, 1868, give the following general results for the year ending Lady-day, 1867, in respect to England and Wales. There were relieved, in-door, 137,310, and out-door, 794,236 cases or persons, giving a grand total of 931,546, of whom 24,379 were pauper lunatics confined in asylums and licensed houses. This shows an excess in grand total of 15,500 nearly over the preceding year, and an increase of nearly 1,000 lunatics. The return for the metropolis alone gives the following result for 1867. Relieved, in-door, 33,070; out-door, 89,384; giving a total of 122,454, of whom 4,430 were lunatics. The excess over the preceding year in grand total was 22,000, and of lunatics about 200. At the end of the official year (Lady-day) 1867, the total expenditure from poor-rates, and from sums received in aid of rates, was £10,905,173, of which £6,959,840 was devoted to the relief of the poor only; £2,511,511 for county, borough, and police rates; £792,522 for other purposes unconnected with poor relief, leaving a balance of £641,300, expended miscellaneously, all in England and Wales. The total rates received in the metropolis was £1,844,765, of which £1,175,353 was expended exclusively in poor relief; £504,728 in county, &c., rates; £26,009 in objects unconnected with poor relief, and £138,665 in miscellaneous matters. In July, 1868, so far as returns had been made, there were in England and Wales 655 unions, and 14,695 parishes chargeable with poor-rates, making returns, but the total of parishes was 14,886. In the last week of July, 1868, there were in England and Wales, 916,170 persons on the books, receiving relief, of whom 126,021 were in the metropolis. The proportion receiving in-door relief was as one to five of those receiving out-door relief. The total increase for the metropolis was 8,283; for England and Wales, 37,291, compared with the corresponding week in 1867. The increase per cent. for the metropolis was 7, and for England and Wales 4·2 per cent. The causes of such an increase of pauperism cannot here be discussed, but as the recipients of relief generally belong to the industrial and agricultural classes, the following statements will be read with interest. Of every 100 persons, aged 20 years and upwards, in England and Wales, the occupations were as follows:—professional, 3·8; domestic, 37·4; commercial, 4·6; agricultural, 14·6; industrial, 34·1; inefficient and non-productive, 5·5, according to the last census.

ACCIDENTS IN COAL MINES.

The year 1867 was not characterized by so heavy a loss of life as in some previous years in respect to coal-mines. The computed number of males employed in the mines was 333,166. 105,077,743 tons of coal were raised, and the total loss of life was 1,190. The most serious catastrophe was the explosion at the Ferndale Colliery, when 178 lives were lost. The total of the year gives the loss of one life for every 88,300 tons of coal raised. In the preceding year, 1866, the loss of life was 1,484, of which number 361 lives were sacrificed at the Oaks Colliery explosion. Comparing the several coal districts of Great Britain, the following results are arrived at:— In the Northumberland, Cumberland, and North Durham districts, there was in 1865, one life lost to every 258 males employed; in 1866, one in every 259; and in 1867, one in every 325. In South Durham, a most dangerous locality for coal-mines, the numbers for the respective years were 414, 310, and 481. In North and East Lancashire one in 238, 200, and 224. In Yorkshire, one in 636, 83, and 411. In Derby, Notts, Leicester, and Warwick shires, one in 330, 467, and 422. In North Staffordshire, Cheshire, and Shropshire, one in 403, 112, and 284. In South Staffordshire and Worcestershire, one in 296, 248, and 244. In Monmouthshire, Gloucestershire, Somersetshire, and Devonshire, one in 325, 321, and 366. In South Wales, one in 182, 243, and 95. In East Scotland, one in 450, 662, and 483. In West Scotland one in 340, 445, and 602. Total in Great Britain for the three years respectively, one in 321, 216, and 280. It has been satisfactorily shown that the fall of the barometer generally, if not always, preceeds an explosion,

RELATIVE RANK IN ARMY AND NAVY.

	Rank with
Field Marshals	Admirals of the Fleet.
Generals	Admirals.
Lieut.-Genls.	Vice-Admirals.
Major-Genls.	Rear-Admirals.
Brigadier-Genls.	Captains of the Fleet, and Commodores.
Colonels	Captains over 3 yrs.
Lieut-Cols.	Captains under 3 yrs. and Staff Capt. (late Masts. of the Fleet).

According to date of Commission.

Majors, according to date of Commsn. or Order.	Lieutenants, and Navigating Lieutenants of 8 yrs. standing.
Capts, according to date of Commsn. or Order.	Lieutenants, and Navigating Lieutenants und. 8 yrs.' standng.
Lieuts. according to date of Commsn. or Order.	Sub-Lieutenants, and Nav. Sub.-Lieutnts.
Ensigns, according to seniority in their ranks.	Midshipmen, and Navigating Midshipmen, above 17 years of age, and 2 years' service at sea in Navy or Merchant Service.

Lieut.-Cols., but jun. of that rank.	Commanders and Staff Commanders.

ARMY AGENTS.

Barron & Smith, Messrs. 26, Duke St., Westmr.

Borough, Sir Edwd. R. Bt., Armit, & Co., No. 4, Nassau Street, Dublin.

Cane & Sons, Messrs. R., Dawson Street, Dublin.

Clack, Henry Tucker, Esq., 50, Leicester Square.

Codd, Edward S., Esq., 35, Craven St. Strand.

Cox & Co., Messrs., Craig's Court, Charing Cross.

Downes & Son, Messrs., 26, King William Street, West Strand.

Draper, Edward Thomson, Esq. (for Royal Marines), 12, Buckingham Street, W.C.

Grindlay & Co., Messrs., 55, Parliament St., S.W.

Holt, V. W., Esq., 17, Whitehall Place, S.W.

Hopkinson, Messrs. Charles & Co., Regent Street, St. James's.

Kirkland, Sir John, 17, Whitehall Place, S.W. also General Agent for Recruiting Service, &c.

Lawrie, A., Esq., 10, Charles St., St. James's Sq.

M'Grigor, Sir Charles R., Bt., & Co., 17, Charles Street, St. James's Square.

Price & Boustead, Messrs., 34, Craven St., Strand.

A. F. Ridgway & Sons, Messrs., 2, Waterloo Pl., Pall Mall, S.W.

Thacker & Co., Messrs., 87, Newgate Street, E.C.

General Agent for the Recruiting Service, &c., Sir John Kirkland, 17, Whitehall Place, S.W.

NAVY AND PRIZE AGENTS.

Banton and Mackrell, Messrs. (*late John P. Muspratt*), 33, Abchurch Lane.

Burnett, Messrs. & Co., 17 Surrey St., Strand.

Case & Loudonsack, Messrs., 1 James St., Adelphi.

Chard, William & Edward, Messrs., 3, Clifford's Inn, Fleet Street.

Hallett & Co., Messrs., 7, St. Martin's Place, Trafalgar Square.

Ommanney, Octavius, 41, Norfolk St., Strand.

O'Byrne Brothers, 58, Pall Mall, S.W.

Vernon, Henry C., Esq., 6, New Inn, Strand.

Stilwell, John Gilliam, Thomas, John Pakenham, and Henry, 22, Arundel Street, Strand.

Tory, Hildreth, & Ommanney, Messrs., 41, Norfolk Street, Strand.

Woodhead, Messrs., & Co., 44, Charing Cross.

Military Service.

Amount Voted for the Year 1868-69, £15,455,400.

Department of the Secretary of State for War—Salaries, £166,487. Contingencies, £3,000.

WAR OFFICE, PALL MALL, S.W. 10 to 4.

Sec. of State for War, Rt. Hon. Edward Cardwell, M.P., £5,000. *Priv. Sec.,* S. G. Osborne, Esq., £300. *Assist. Priv. Sec.,* £150.

Under Sec., Parl., Lord Northbrook, £1,500. *Priv. Sec.,* F. G. Faithfull, Esq., £150.

Under Sec., Perm., Lt.-Gen. Sir E. Lugard, G.C.B., £2,000. *Priv. Sec.,* W. R. Buck, Esq., £150.

Under Sec., Controller-in-Chief, Major-Gen. Rt. Hon. Sir H. K. Storks, G.C.B., G.C.M.G., £2,000. *Priv. Sec.,* George Lawson, Esq., £150.

Assist. Under Sec., Douglas Galton, Esq., C.B., F.R.S., £1,500. *Priv. Sec.,* J. W. Cooper, Esq., £150.

Mil. Assist., Col. L. Shadwell, £792.

Chief Clerk, Clere Talbot, Esq., £1,200.

Director of Works, Major-Gen. E. Frome, R.E., £1,200.

Clerks, R.E. Dept., Second Class, A. G. Bragg, H. F. Kirkman, D. Blackmore, and W. J. Creighton, Esqrs.

Dep. (Fortifications), Col. W. F. D. Jervois, C.B., R.E., £1,083.

Dep. (Barracks), Lieut.-Col. T. A. L. Murray, R.E., £700.

Clerks, R.E. Dept., First Class, J. H. Lawson and W. B. Hambly, Esqrs.

Surveyor, R. O. Mennie, Esq.

Chief Draughtsman, W. H. Tregallas, Esq.

Director of Ordnance, Major-Gen. Lefroy, £1,000

Assist., Col. T. W. Milward, C.B., R.A., £727.

Insp. Gen. Reserve Forces, Major-Gen. Hon. James Lindsay, £914.

Deputy, Col. E. W. C. Wright, £347.

Chap. Gen., Rev. G. R. Gleig, M.A., £1,000.

Director of Clothing, G. D. Ramsay, Esq., £1,000.

First Clerk, L. N. Choveaux, Esq., £575.

Clerks, F. Ram, M. O'Hea, and H. D. Fellowes, Esqrs., £1,168.

Director of Contracts, Thos. Howell, Esq., £1,500.

Sup. Barrack Dept., Lieut.-Col. B. H. Martindale, R.E., £990.

Barrack Masters, Capt. F. W. Smith, Lieut. G. H. Sanders.

Accountant General, W. Brown, Esq., C.B., £1,200.

Assist. A.G., John Milton, Esq., £990.

Chief Auditor, Army Accounts, H. W. S. Whiffin, Esq., £1,200.

MILITARY SERVICE—*continued.*
Solicitor, C. M. Clode, Esq., £400.
Assist. Sol., John Clulow, Esq., £975.
Exam. Military Service, Major W. Marvin, £460.

CLERKS.

CENTRAL DEPARTMENT.—*First Class,* 1st *section,* C. Talbot (Chief Clerk), E. Pennington, R. Gwyn, F. Crafer, C. C. Hutchins, W. W. Veasey, G. V. Dunbar, R. Thompson, and D. Harrison, Esqrs., £6,340.
Second Section, W. H. Cheetham, L. S. K. Bird, J. F. Allen, C. J. Borrow, H. A. Greene. T. D. Cater, H. Baker, and S. H. Payne, Esqrs., £5,090.

ACCOUNTANT-GENERAL'S DEPARTMENT. — *First Class,* 1st *section,* W. H. White, J. Hanby, M. N. Girdlestone, A. Austin, and T. E. Ripley, Esqrs., £3,670.
Second Section, H. S. Hood, H. Minney, H. A. March, and W. Alexander, Esqrs., £2,325.
CHIEF AUDITOR'S DEPARTMENT.—*First Class,* 1st *section,* J. Maclean, E. Stillwell, F. W. Kirby, T. Dowling, W. A. Cockburn, and C. G. H. Furlonge, Esqrs., £4,490.
Second Section, H. Bynam, G. Byham, T. B. Branwell, A. A. Gibbon, J. J. Bourne, J. N. Gladstone, C. F. Freer, H. Edmonds, and C. T. J. Jones, Esqrs., £5,325.
Accountant, J. O. Hurst, Esq., £453.

DEPARTMENT OF THE COMMANDER-IN-CHIEF, £55,091.

Salaries, £54,091.   Contingencies, £1,000.
Horse Guards, Whitehall. 10 to 4.

COMMANDER-IN-CHIEF'S OFFICE, £9,466.
Commander in Chief, Field Marshal H.R.H. the Duke of Cambridge, K.G., Colonel of the Grenadier Guards, £4,432. *Private Sec.,* Col. the Hon. Jas. W. B. Macdonald, C.B., £365.
Military Secretary, Lieut-Gen. Wm. Frederick Forster, K.H., £2,243.
Assistant Military Secretary, Colonel E. B. Johnson, C.B., Royal Artillery.
Assistants to the Military Secretary, John Drake and Walter Freeth, Esqrs.

ADJUTANT-GENERAL'S DEPARTMENT, £13,379.
Adj.-Gen., Lt.-Gen. Lord Wm. Paulet, K.C.B., £1,887.
Deputy Adj.-Gen., Col. C. R. Egerton : *Royal Art.,* Col. Gloucester Gambier, R.A. ; *Roy. Engs.,* Col. Hon. H. F. Keane, £3,069.
Assist. Adj.-Gens., Col. E. A. Whitmore; Col. A. J. Herbert, C.B.; Col. W. A. Middleton, C.B., R.A.; Col. J. F. M. Browne, C.B., R.E., £2,337.
Dep. Assist. Adj.-Gens., Major Robert C. Stewart, Capt. G. H. A. Forbes, R.A., £806.
Chief Clerk, E. Houndle, Esq., £700.

QUARTERMASTER-GENERAL'S DEPARTMENT, £4,245.
Quartermaster-General, Lieut-General Sir James Hope Grant, G.C.B., £1,877.
Dep. Q.M.G. (vacant).
Assist. Q.M.G., Col. Hon. H. H. Clifford, V.C.; Lieut.-Col. J. M. Grant, R.E., £1,137.
Dep. Assist. Q.M.G., Lt.-Col. F. S. Vacher, £403.
Chief Clerk, Charles W. Mather, Esq., £566.
Inspector-General of Cavalry, Major-General Lord G. A. F. Paget, C.B., £692.
Insp.-Gen. Art., Major-Gen. A. J. Taylor, £692.
Insp.-Gen. Engs., Major-Gen. E. Froome, £1,200.
Attached to Foot Guards, Major-Gen. Hamilton, C.B., £692.
Dep. Judge Adv., Col. J. H. Laye.
Comm. Roy. Eng., London, Lt.-Col. C. B. Ewart.

Insp. of Regtl. Colours (Heralds' College, Doctors' Commons), Albert William Woods, Esq., Lancaster Herald, £60.

DEPARTMENTS.

ARMY MEDICAL DEPARTMENT, 6, Whitehall Yard. £217,650.
Sal. £216,098.   Contingencies, £1,552.
Director Gen., T. G. Logan, M.D., C.B., £1,500.
Sanitary Branch, Dep. Insp. Gen. H.H. Massy, M.D.
Statistical Branch, Dep. Insp. Gen. T. G. Balfour, M.D.
Medical Branch, Staff Surg. Maj. T. Crawford, M.D.

COMMISSARIAT DEPARTMENT, 5, New Street, Spring Gardens, S.W., £103,810.
Sal., £86,861. Conting., £2,889. Wages, £14,060.
Comm. Gen. in Chief, Sir W. J. Tyrone Power, K.C.B., £1,095.
Dep. Comm. Gen., E. B. de Fonblanque.
Assist. Comm. Gen., J. B. Price.

JUDGE ADVOCATE GENERAL'S DEPARTMENT, Great George Street, S.W., £6,175.
Sal., £5,125.   Contingencies, £1,050.
Judge Adv. Gen., Rt. Hon. John R. Mowbray, M.P., £2,000.
Dep. do., Vernon Lushington, Esq., £1,100.
Dep. Judge Adv., Col. J. H. Laye, London ; Col. C. L. Nugent, Dublin ; Col. G. Mein, £780.

MILITARY STORE AND MANUFACTURING DEPARTMENTS, £776,918.
Sal., £109,653. Conting., £8,797. Rents, £1,670. Wages, £656,798.
Princ. Sup. of Stores, H. W. Gordon, C.B., Woolwich, £803.
H. Tatum, War Office, £803.

PURVEYOR'S DEPARTMENT, 109, Victoria Street, S.W., £22,361.
Sal., £20,862. Conting., £1,499.
Purveyor in Chief, J. Scott Robertson, £848.

TOPOGRAPHICAL DEPARTMENT, 4, New Street, Spring Gardens, £5,556.
Director, Col. Sir Henry James, R.E., £1,345.
Executive Off., Lt.-Col. Cooke, C.B., R.E., £728.
Assist., Capt. Barrington, R.A., £502.

ORDNANCE SELECT COMMITTEE, (£8,133).
President, Brig.-Gen. J. H. Lefroy, R.A., £933.
Vice-Pres., Capt. W. G. Luard, R.N., £500.
Sec., Lt.-Col. H. Heyman, R.A., £758.
Assist. Sec., Capt. R. W. Haig, R.A., £471.

COUNCIL OF MILITARY EDUCATION, 13, Great George Street, S.W., (£8,205).
President, The Commander in Chief, ex officio.
Vice Pres., Major-Gen. W. C. E. Napier, £1,000.
Sec., Capt. D. D. Greentree, £400.

COMMANDANTS OF MILITARY DISTRICTS.

Chatham.—Major Gen. F. Murray, £692, Chatham.
Eastern.—   Colchester.
Guernsey and Alderney.'—Major Gen. Scott, £954, Guernsey.
Jersey.—Major Gen. P. M. N. Guy, C.B., £954, Jersey.
Northern.—Major Gen. Sir John Garvock, K.C.B., £692, Manchester.
South Eastern.—Major-Gen. D. Russell, C.B., £692, Dover.
South Western.—Lt. Gen. Sir George Buller, K.C.B., £1,557, Portsmouth.
Western.—Lt. Gen. Hon. Sir A. A. Spencer, K.C.B., £865, Devonport.
Woolwich, Major Gen. E. C. Warde, C.B., £692, Woolwich.

RECRUITING DISTRICTS.

Insp. Gen. Recruiting, Mr.Gn.Edwards,c.b.,£914.

Bristol.—*Insp. F. Off.*, Col. L. Fyler. *Adj.*, Lt. Connell.

Leeds.—*Insp. F. O.*, Col. H. Bingham. *Adj.*, Lt. Goodman.

Liverpool.—*Insp. F. O.*, Col. Sir J. Jones, k.c.b., *Adj.*, Lt. Clarke.

London.—*Insp. F. O.*, Col. R. C. H. Taylor, c.b., *Adj.*, Lt. Windowe.

Glasgow.—*Insp. F. O.*, Col. R. Gardiner. *Adj.*, Lt. Gilby.

Belfast.—*Insp. F. O.*,Col.R.Budd. *Adj.*,Lt.Griffin.

Dublin.—*Insp. F. O.*, Col. A. C. Bentinck. *Adj.*, Lt. Hamilton.

MILITARY PRISONS.

Office, 45, Parliament Street, S.W., £24,269.

Insp. Gen. Lt. Col. E. Y. W. Henderson, r.e.

Insp., Capt. Edmond F. Du Cane, r.e., £400.

Aldershot.—*Gov.*, Capt. A. P. Miller, £400. *Med. Off.*, Thomas Fox, Esq., m.d., £137.

Cork.—*Gov.*, Major H. W. Campbell, £331. *Med. Off.*, Dr. J. W. Johnston, £91.

Devonport.—*Chief Warder*, Mr. J. Martin, £116. *Med. Off.*, Assist. Surg. R. W. Woollcombe, £91.

Dublin.—*Gov.*, Major F. K. Bacon, £285. *Med. Off.*, T. Joliffe Tufnell, Esq., £91.

Fort Clarence.—*Gov.*, Capt. Edwards, £400. *Med. Off.*, C. Cowen, Esq., £91.

Gosport.—*Gov.*, Col. W. H. C. Wellesley, £290. *Med. Off.*, J. T. Telfer, Esq. £91.

Greenlaw (Pennycuick).—*Gov.*, Capt. D. F. Allen, £285. *Med. Off.*, J. G. Wood, Esq., m.d., £91.

Limerick.—*Chief Warder*, Mr. R. Forsyth, £119.

Shorncliffe.—*Chief Warder*, W. Tucker, £104.

Southwark.—*Gov.*, Capt. C. Clerk, £300. *Med. Off.*, E. Mockler, Esq., £91.

Weedon.—*Gov.*, £349. *Med. Off.* Dr. Swann, £91.

STAFF, &c., OF SCOTLAND.

In Command. Maj. Gen. R. Rumley, Edinburgh.

Assist. Adj. Gen.,Col.Hon.F. Colborne,Edinburgh.

Com. R. Artil., Col. J. L. Elgee, Leith Fort.

Com. R. Eng.. Col. H. A. White, Edinburgh.

Fort Major, Lt. Col. J. H. Cox, Edinburgh.

STAFF, &c., OF IRELAND.

Comm. the Forces, Gen. the Rt. Hon. Hugh H. Lord Strathnairn, g.c.b., g.c.s.i.

Mil. Sec., Bt. Col. Hon. L. Smyth, c.b.

ADJUTANT GENERAL'S DEPARTMENT. (*Head Quarters—Dublin*.)

Dep. Adj. Gen., Col. K. D. Mackenzie, c.b.

Dep. Assist. Adj. Gen., Capt. G. Hay.

QUARTERMASTER-GENERAL'S DEPARTMENT. (*Head Quarters—Dublin*.)

Dep. Q. M. Gen., Bt. Col. G. W. Mayow.

Dep. Assist. Q. M. Gen. Capt. W. T. Stuart.

ROYAL ARTILLERY AND ROYAL ENGINEERS. (*Head Quarters—Dublin*.)

Col. on Staff., Col. T. B. F. Marriott, R. Art.

Assist. Adj. Gen., Lt. Col. A. C. Pigou, R. Art.

Com. R. Eng., Col. G. Wynne.

Assist. Adj. Gen., Bt. Col. Nicholson, c.b., R.Eng.

Comm. the Division at the Curragh, Major Gen. A. A. T. Cunynghame, c.b.

Assist. Adj. Gen., Lt.-Col. Hon. W. H. A. Feilding.

Assist. Q. M. Gen., Col. E. Seager.

Dep. Judge Adv., Col. C. L. Nugent.

Com. Roy. Art., Col. C. S. Henry, c.b.

Com. Roy. Eng., Lt.-Col. F. R. Chesney.

Com. Northern Dis., Major Gen. A. A. T. Cunynghame, c.b., Dublin.

Com.South Westn.Dis., Maj.Gen.G.Campbell,Cork.

Com. Curragh Dis., Major Gen. A. Borton, c.b., The Camp, Curragh.

FIELD MARSHALS.

Hugh, Viscount Gough, g.c.b., k.p., g.c.s.i. Roy. Horse Gds., and Colonel in Chief 60 Rifles.

H.R.H. George William Frederick Charles, Duke of Cambridge, k.g., g.c.b., k.p., g.c.m.g. Gren. Guards, Roy. A. and Roy. Eng., Commanding-in-Chief the Forces.

Sir Alexander Woodford, g.c.b., g.c.m.g. Sc. Fus. Gds. Gov. of Chelsea Hospital.

Sir William Maynard Gomm g.c.b. Co.,Gds.

Sir John Fox Burgoyne, Bt., g.c.b. Royal Eng., Constable of the Tower.

GENERALS.

Sir J. F. FitzGerald, g.c.b. 18 F.

Sir A. B. Clinton g.c.b., 1 Dr.

Marq.Tweeddale,k.t.,g.c.b. 2LG.

Sir Wm. Wood, k.c.b., k.h. 14 F.

E. M. G. Showers, Royal Artill.

G. Swiney, Royal Artillery.

Sir G. Pollock, g.c.b.,g.c.s.i.R.A.

Sir Jas. A. Hope, k.c.b. 9 Foot.

Sir A. Lindsay, k.c.b. Rl. Art.

Sir John Bell, g.c.b. 4 Foot.

Sir J. Aitchison, g.c.b. 72 Foot.

Sir DeLacy Evans, g.c.b. 21 F.

Sir C. G. Ellicombe, k.c.b. R. En.

Sir W. Rowan, g.c.b., 52 F.

Sir G. Bowles, k.c.b. 1 W.I.R.

Hon. H. F. C. Cavendish. 2 D.G.

H.R.H. Prince of Wales k.g., 10 Huss.& Col. in Chief Rifle Br.

Hon.SirCGore,g.c.b.,k.h.,6F.

Chas. Richard Fox, 57 Foot.

Chas. Aug. Shawe, 74 Foot.

Sir R. England, g.c.b.,k.h., 41 F.

Sir W.J.Codrington, g.c.b., 23 F.

Sir J. M. F. Smith, k.h., R. Eng.

Sir A. Roberts, k.c.b., 101 Foot.

Sir D. M'Gregor, k.c.b.

C. G. J. Arbuthnot, 91 Foot.

John Spink, k.h., 2 Foot.

Sir J. Jackson,g.c.b.,k.h. 1D.G.

John Drummond.

Sir C. R. O'Donnell, 18 Huss.

Robert B. Coles, 65 Foot.

E. P. Buckley, 83 Foot.

G. C. Earl of Lucan, k.c.b., 1 L.G.

Sir C. Yorke, g.c.b., Rif. Br.

Sir W.M.G.Colebrooke, c.b.,k.h., Royal Artillery.

Hon. Sir E. Cust, k.c.h., 16 Lanc.

Francis John Davis, 67 Foot.

M. Beresford, 20 Foot.

Sir J. C. Chatterton, Bt.,k.c.b., k.h., 5 Lancers.

Sir W. T. Knollys, k.c.b., 62 Ft.

Sir H.R.Ferguson Davie, Bt.73F.

H. I. Delacombe, Royal Mar.

Wm. Wylde, c.b., Royal Art.

J. G. Griffith, Royal Artillery.

Sir F. Graham, k.c.b., R.M.Art.

Sir J. Cheape, g.c.b., Royal En.

E. F. Gascoigne, 69 Foot.

HughH.Lord Strathnairn,g.c.b., g.c.s.i., 92 F. Com. Forces Irel.

J. T. Brown, Royal Marines.

SirP.Montgomerie,k.c.b., R.Art.

E. Garstin, Royal Engineers.

St. J. A. Clerke, k.h., 75 Foot.

SirH. J.W.Bentinck, k.c.b., 28 F.

Sir T. Reed, k.c.b., 44 Foot.

Hen. Visct. Melville, g.c.b., 60 F.

Wm. R. Ord, Royal Engineers.

F. R. Chesney, Royal Artillery.

Sir P. E. Cragie, k.c.b., 55 Foot.

Sir R. J. Dacres, k.c.b., Roy. Art.

Sir E. F. Morris, k.c.b., 49 Ft.

Henry Colvile, 12 Foot.

EverardW.Bouverie, 15 Huss.

Hon. T. Ashburnham, c.b., 82 F.

Sir J. Scott, k.c.b., 7 Huss.

Sir J. L.Pennefather, g.c.e.,22 F.

E. Wells Bell, 66 Foot.

SirW.R.Williams,Bt.,k.c.b., R.A.

Sir D. Capon, k.c.b., 106 Foot.

John Eden, c.b., 34 Foot.

Hon. C. Grey. 71 Foot.

W. L. L. F. Lord de Ros, 4th Huss. Dep. Lt. of the Tower.

Philip S. Stanhope, 13 F.

LIEUTENANT GENERALS.

F. Schuler, R. Art.
Hen. Ld Rokeby, K.C.B., 77 F.
Henry Edward Porter.
Wm. Beckwith, K.H., 14 Huss.
Hen. Wm. Breton, 56 F.
Allan T. Maclean, 13 Huss.
Thomas Ger. Ball, 8 F.
C. M. Carmichael, C.B. 20 Huss.
George Dixon, 104 F.
F. Maunsell, 85 F.
John Hall, 19 Huss.
Sir G. H. Lockwood, K.C.B. 12 La.
Sir P. Grant, G.C.B., G.C.M.G., 78 F. Gv. & Cm.-in-Chf, Malta,&c.
Sir R. J. H. Vivian, K.C.B. 102 F.
Sir W. Wyllie, K.C.B. 109 F.
Sir Richard Airey, G.C.B. 7 F. Gov. & Cm.-in-Chief, Gibraltar.
Hon. Sir J.Yorke Scarlett, K.C.B. 5 D. Gds. Com.Troops, Aldrsht.
Sir Geo. Buller, K.C.B. Rifle Brigade. s. S. W. District.
Sir John B. Gough, K.C.B. 2 Drs.
Hon. Arthur Upton.
Sir A. J. Cloeté, K.C.B.,K.H. 19 F.
G. Macdonald, 16 F.
Sir G. Ash Windham, K.C.B. 46 F. Com. Forces B. N. America.
Jas. R. Craufurd, 27 F.
W. S. Balfour.
Richard Greaves, 40 F.
Sir W.H. Elliott, K.C.B., 51 F.
Pringle Taylor, K.H., 24 F.
Thos. H. Johnston, 87 F.
H. Aitchison Hankey, 3 Huss.
John Campbell, 97 F.
Hen. D. Townshend, 25 F.
Thomas Wood, 84 F.
Wm. H. Eden, 90 F.
Sir Jas. Hope Grant, G.C.B., 9 Lanc. Quarter Master Gen.
Joseph Clarke, 76 F.
Sir J.G.LeMarchant, K.C.B.11 F.

Chas. Gascoyne, 89 F.
Sir W. R. Mansfield, K.C.B., G.C.S.I. 38 F. Com.-in-Ch. E. I.
George Moncrieff.
Sir E. Lugard, G.C.B. 31 F. Under Sec. of State for War.
G. Conran, R. Artillery.
Marcus J. Slade, 50 F.
Sir J. E. Dupuis, K.C.B., R. Art.
G. H. MacKinnon, C.B. 26 F.
G. F.Visc. Templetown, C.B. 60 F.
Hon. Art. Alex. Dalzell, 48 F.
Sir Thos. S. Pratt, K.C.B. 37 F.
W. N. Hutchinson, 33 F.
Simcoe Baynes, 35 F.
Mont. C. Johnstone, 88 F.
Edw. Sabine, R. Art.
Wm. F. Forster, K.H., 81 F. Mil. Sec. to F. M. Com.-in-Chief.
Thos. Gordon Higgins, R. Art.
Fred. Johnston.
Sir Ed. Macarthur, K.C.B. 100 F.
Thos. Foster, R. Eng.
Sir Wm. Bell, K.C.B. R. Art.
D. H. Macdowall, 3 F.
Sir Rt. Garrett, K.C.B., K.H. 43 F.
G. T. Colomb, 4 W. L. R.
Poole V. England, R. Art.
SirSydney J. Cotton, K.C.B. 10 F.
Maurice Barlow, 3 W. I. Reg.
E. H. D. E. Napier, 61 F.
Sir J. Bloomfield, K.C.B. R.A.
Sir G. Brooke, K.C.B. R. Art.
Sir J. Michel, C.B. 86 F.
Sir A.B. Stransham, K.C.B. R.M.
Fra. Warde, R. Art.
Alex. Anderson, R. Marines.
Sir T. Holloway, K.C.B., R.M. Ar.
Sir R. P. Douglas, Bt. 98 F. s. Cape of Good Hope.
C. C. Hay, 93 F.
Thos. Lemon, C.B., R. Mar.

H. Goodwyn, R. Eng.
Rob. Cornelis Lord Napier, G.C.B. R. Eng. Com. Forces, Bombay.
W. Scott, R. Eng.
Sir A. T. Cotton, K.C.S.I. R. Eng.
G. A. Malcolm, C.B., 105 F.
F. F. Whinyates, R. Art.
Hen. Eyre, 59 F.
Montgomery Williams, R. Eng.
Lord W. Paulet, K.C.B. 68 F.A.-G.
John Patton, 47 F.
Sir Duncan A. Cameron, K.C.B., 42 F. Gov. R. M. Coll.
Sir W.B. Ingilby, K.C.B. R.Ar.
Rich. J. Stotherd, R. Eng.
Tho. Matheson.
Sir George Bell, K.C.B., 1 F.
R. Richardson Robertson, C.B., 3 Dragoon Gds.
Burke Cuppage, R. Art.
Samuel Braybrooke, 99 F.
J. Alexander, C.B. R. Art.
J. T. Lane, C.B. R. Art.
E. Huthwaite, C.B. R. Art.
Sir A. Wilson, Bt., G.C.B. R. Art.
R. Law, K.H. 2 W. I. Reg.
B. S. Stehelin, R. Eng.
Sir C. T. Van Straubenzee, K.C.B. 39 F.
W, G. Gold, 53 F.
A. C. Pole, 63 F.
E. W. F. Walker, C.B., 94 F.
T. A. Drought, 15 F.
Chas. Stuart.
Hon. Sir A. A. Spencer, K.C.B., 96 F. s. W. District.
Chas Ashmore, 30 F.
Robt. Burn, R. Art.
H. K. Bloomfield, 64 F.
John Lawrenson, 8 Huss.
Studholme J. Hodson, 54 F. s. Ceylon and Straits Sett.
H. Servante, R. Eng.

MAJOR GENERALS.

G. Campbell, C.B. R. Art.
C. Grant, C.B. R. Art.
G. Twemlow, R. Art.
F. H. G. Seymour.
W. A. M'Cleverty, 108 F. Comm. Forces, Madras.
Lewis D. Williams.
Robt. Blucher Wood, C.B.
Chas. E. Gold.
J. Hale, 103 F.
Chas. A. Lewis.
Wm. Parlby, 21 Huss.
J. Thos. Hill
John Longfield, C.B. 29 F.
C. W.M. Balders, C.B. 17 Lanc.
F. W. Hamilton, C.B. s. Ft. Gds.
Ch.Hastings Doyle, s. N. S., 70 F.
Fred. Horn, C.B. 45 F.
John F. G. Campbell, C.B., 79 F.
Lord Fred. Paulet, C.B., 32 F.
Sir J. R. Smyth, K.C.B., 6 Dr. Gds., s. Madras.
W. J. D'Urban, 107 F.
Hen. John French, 80 F.
R. Horsford, R. Art.
John ffolliott Crofton, 95 F.
John Grattan, C.B., 17 F.
Hn. J. Lindsay, Insp.-Gn. ofR. F.
Wm. Sullivan, C.B., 58 F.

A. A. T. Cunynghame, C.B. s.Irld.
J. Fordyce, R. Art. s.
Edw. B. Brooke.
Fred. Hope.
Joshua S. Smith.
Hen. A. O'Neill.
Richard Parker.
C. Trollope, C.B.
Lord G. A. F. Paget, C.B., 7 Dr. Gds., Inspector-Gen. of Cav.
Brook Taylor, s. Bengal.
George T. C. Napier, C.B.
E. Rowley Hill, 5 F.
Geo. Wm. Key, 11 Huss.
Edward Pole.
F. Holt Robe, C.B.
Sir R. Walpole, K.C.B.
Art. J. Lawrence, C.B.
C. P. Ainslie, s. W. and L. Islands.
Freeman Murray, s.
Alexander Nelson Visc. Bridport
D. Russell, C.B. s.
Horatio Shirley, C.B.
Wm. S. Newton.
E. C. W. M. Milman, s.Mauritius.
Spencer Perceval.
Henry Cooper.
Randal Rumley, s.

Rt. Hon. Sir H. K. Storks, G.C.B. G.C.M.I., Undr Sec.of St. for Wr.
A. Rowland, R. Art.
Rt. Hon. G. C. Weld Forester.
Edw.C.Hodge, C.B., s. Aldersht.
Thos. Crombie.
Hen. E. Doherty, C.B.
Aug. H. Ferryman, C.B.
W. R. Faber.
Thos. J. Galloway.
Sir John Garvock, K.C.B., Comm. Troops, N. District.
Wm. Jones, C.B.
W. B. Goodfellow, R. Eng.
Sir W.M. Coghlan, K.C.B., R. Art.
Hon.A.H.Gordon, C.B.,s.Bombay.
Corbet Cotton.
Henry Servante, R. Eng.
Matthew Smith.
Henry Bates.
Edw. Frome, Director of Works and Insp. Gen. of Eng.
T. M. Wilson.
Geo. Staunton.
C. Crutchley, s. Gibraltar.
W. Hamilton, C.B.
Chas. Rochfort Scott, Lt. Gov., &c., Guernsey.
Mark K. Atherley, s. Malta.

MAJOR-GENERALS—*continued.*

Sir Trevor Chute, K.C.B., s.
Wm. G. Brown.
Henry Jervis.
Michael W. Smith, C.B.
Daniel Thorndike, R. Art.
T. P. Flude, R. Art.
John M. Perceval, C.B.
Hen. W. Stisted, C.B., s. Canada.
P. M. N. Guy, C.B. Lt. Gov. Jersey.
Fran. Seymour, C.B.
Chas. Steuart, C.B.
J. L. Dennis.
Chas. R. S. Lord West, C.B.
Fred. P. Haines. s. Madras.
Hen. Geo. Teesdale, R. Art.
A. A. Shuttleworth, R. Art.
J. A. Lambert.
W. O'Grady Haly, C.B., s. Bengl.
C. S. Reid, R. Art.
Hen. Phipps Raymond.
John M'Coy, R.A.
ƁƇLord H. H. M. Percy.
W. C. E. Napier, Council of Mil.E.
Chas. H. Ellice, C.B., s.
R. C. Moore, C.B., R. Art.
Hen. R. Jones, C.B.
Sir T. M. Biddulph, K.C.B.
G. Balfour, C.B., R. Art.
Chas. Hagart, C.B.
W. E. Baker, R. Eng.
Thos. M. Steele, C.B.
James Creagh.
R. F. Crawford, R. Art.
Edward Last.
J. St. George, C.B. R. Art. D. of O.
Jas. P. Sparks, C.B.
Hen. Carr Tate, Royal Mar. Art.
H. B. Turner, R. Eng.

Robert Lewis.
Thos. Williams, C.B.
Rich. Wilbraham, C.B., s. Netley.
Chas. E. Wilkinson, R. Eng.
E. C. Warde, C.B. R. Art., s. Wool.
Wm. Irwin.
F. Adams, C.B., s.
J. R. Brunker, s. China.
Hen. Darby Griffith, C.B.
J. W. Ormsby, R. Art., R. Mil. A.
Wm. T. Renwick, R. Eng.
Jas. W. Smith, C.B.
Luke S. O'Connor, C.B., s. Jam.
C. Lucas, R. Art.
F. Darley George, C.B.
Hon. Geo. Cadogan, C.B.
J. C. Hope Gibsone.
A. J. Taylor, Inspec.-Gen. of Art.
J. W. Croggan, R. Art.
John Yorke, C.B.
J. Abbott, R. Art.
Hen. D. O'Halloran.
H. R. H. Prince Frederic Christian
  Ch. Aug. Schleswig.-Hols. K.G.
Sir J. W. Gordon, K.C.B., R. Eng.
J. H. Gascoigne, C.B., R. Mar.
ƁƇCollingwd. Dickson, C.B. R.A.
J. H. E. Dalrymple.
Geo. C. Langley, R. Mar.
J. O. Travers, C.B., R. Mar.
W. R. Maxwell, R. Mar.
D. Rainier, s. India.
Frank Turner, C.B., R. Art.
H. H. Graham, C.B.
Henry Renny, s. Aldershot.
G. Campbell, C.B., s.
Hayes Marriott, R. Mar.
Sir H. M. Durand, R. Eng., C.B.
E. Lawford, R. Eng.

C. W. Tremenheere, C.B., R. Eng.
John J. Bissett, C.B., s.
ƳƇ Sir H. Tombs, K.C.B., R. Art.
H. W. Trevelyan, C.B., R. Art.
Jas. Brind, C.B., R. Art.
John Armstrong, C.B., s.
Sir D. E. Wood, K.C.B., R. Art.
R. R. Kinleside, R. Art.
E. A. Holdich, C.B. :
Sir F. E. Chapman, K.C.B., R. E. s.
Sir C. W. D. Staveley, K.C.B.
A. Huyshe, R. Art.
R. N. Phillips.
J. W. Fitzmayer, C.B., R. Art.
Sir Alf. H. Horsford, K.C.B. s. Ald.
W. D. P. Patton.
W. H. Askwith, R. Art.
W. E. D. Broughton, R. Eng.
G. J. Carey, C.B., s. Aldershot.
Hon. P. E. Herbert, C.B.
Arth. Borton, C.B., s., Ireland.
D. E. Mackirdy.
Ths. Kensington Whistler, R. Ar.
J. S. Brownrigg, C.B., s. Shorncl.
J. L. A. Simmons, C.B., R. Eng.
W. M. S. M'Murdo, C.B., s.
Wm. Munro, C.B.
A. C. Errington.
C.A.Edwards, C.B., Ins.-G.of Rec.
S. T. Christie, C.B.
Chas. Jas. Dalton, R. Art.
W. M. Wood.
Hen. Smyth, C.B.
Lord Mark Kerr, C.B.
F. M. Eardley-Wilmot, R. Art.
Hen. Wase Whitfeild.
John Wilkie.
Hon. P. de Bathe.
Sir W. T. Denison, K.C.B. R. Eng.

AIDES-DE-CAMP TO THE QUEEN.

Col. John Le Couteur, Jersey Militia.
Col. G. H. Marquis of Donegal, K.P., G.C.H. Antrim Militia.
Col. Geo. R. Lord Dynevor, R. Carmarthen Mil.
Col. William S. R. Norcott, C.B. Unattached.
Col. H. S. H. Prince W. A. E. of Saxe-Weimar, C.B. Grenadier Guards.
Col. Sir E. R. Wetherall, C.B., K.C.S.I. Unatt.
Col. W. F. Duke of Buccleuch, K.G. Edin. Mil.
Col. John W. Patten, 3 Royal Lancashire Mil.
Col. R. A. Shafto Adair, Suffolk Artillery Mil.
Col. G. W. F. Marquis of Aylesbury, Roy. Wilts Yeomanry Cavalry.
Col. John A. Ewart, C.B., h.p. late 78 Foot.
Col. William Parke, C.B., h.p. 53 Foot.
Col. Thomas Tapp, C.B., 10½ Foot.
Col. E. Wodehouse, C.B., Royal Artillery.
Col. George Bent, C.B., Royal Engineers.
Col. Chas. Viscount Eversley, Hants Yeo. Cav.

Col. F. H. P. Lord Methuen, Royal Wilts Mil.
Col. The Marquis of Exeter, Northampton and Rutland Militia.
Col. Wm. Adam Orr, C.B., Royal Artillery.
Col. S. N. Lowder, C.B., Royal Marines.
Col. Hen. Wylie Norman, C.B., H.M. Ind. F.
Col. Alfred T. Wilde, C.B., H.M. Ind. F.
Col. George Lambrick, Royal Marines.
Col. Hon. H. F. Keane, Royal Engineers.
Col. W. J. E. Grant, Royal Artillery.
Col. Sir R. T. Gerard, Bt., Lan. Huss. Yeo. Cav.
Col. William Bell, Royal Guernsey Militia.
Col. T. F. Wilson, C.B., Bengal S. C.
Col. Hon. F. A. Thesiger, C.B., 95 Foot.
Col. John Field, C.B., 10 Bombay N. I.
Col. Robert Phayre, C.B., Bombay S.C.
Col. Martin Dillon, C.B., Rifle Brigade.
Col. Thomas Walter Milward, C.B., Royal Artil.
Col. Hen. St. Clair Wilkins, Royal Engineers.

Cavalry.

[The names of Supernumerary or Seconded Officers are printed in *Italics*. In the Royal Artillery *A* to *F*, and 1 to 25, denote the Brigades. In the Infantry, 1 to 4 show the Battalions. Where two Stations are given, as "*Madras—Chatham,*" the second is the depôt.]

1ST LIFE GUARDS.
Windsor.
Col. G. C. Earl of Lucan, K.C.B., *g.*
L. Col. Hon. D. Fitz Geraldde Ros, *c.*
Major &L.Col. Richard Bateson.
Adjutant. Thomas Cox.
Agents. Messrs. Cox & Co.

2ND LIFE GUARDS.
Regent's Park.
Col. Marq. Tweeddale, K.T., G.C.B., *g.*
L. Col. Frederick Marshall, *c.*
Major & L. Col. Roger Palmer.
Adjutant. Robert Reid, *lt.*
Agents, Messrs. Cox & Co.

ROYAL HORSE GUARDS.
Hyde Park.
Col. Viscount Gough, G.C.B., K.P. *f.m.*
L. Col. Duncan James Baillie.
Major, Owen L. C. Williams, *l.c.*
Adjutant, R. M'Alpine, *lt.*
Ag. Sir C. R. M'Grigor, Bt. & Co.

CAVALRY—continued.

1ST DRAGOON GUARDS.
Sheffield.
Col. ☰ Sir J. Jackson, G.C.B., K.H. g
L.Col. Herbert Dawson Slade.
Majors, Henry Alexander; Jas. Gunter.
Adjutant, H. Barker, lt.
Agents. Messrs. Cox & Co.

2ND DRAGOON GUARDS.
Bombay—Canterbury.
Col. Hon. H. F. C. Cavendish, g.
L.Col. Wm. H. Seymour, c.B. c.
Majors, C. Synge Hutchinson, c.; Anthony M. Fawcett.
Adjutant. B. Edmonds, lt.
Agents. Messrs. Cox & Co.

3RD DRAGOON GUARDS.
Chichester.
Col. R. R. Robertson, c.B., l.g.
L.Col. Conyers Tower, c.B., c.
Majors, John Miller, l.c.; Fredk. J. S. Lindesay.
Adjutant, G. F. Robertson, lt.
Agents, Messrs. Hopkinson & Co.

4TH DRAGOON GUARDS.
Brighton.
Col. ☰ Sir J. C. Chatterton, Bt., K.C.B., K.H., g.
L.Col. C. Cameron Shute, c.
Major, Frank Chaplin.
Adjutant, P. E. Poppe, lt.
Agent, A. Lawrie, Esq.

5TH DRAGOON GUARDS.
Aldershot. [l.g.s.
Col. Hn. Sir J. Y. Scarlett, K.C.B.,
L.Col. Hon. S. J. G. Calthorpe, c.
Major, Fred. Hay Swinfen.
Adjutant, T. H. Hartnell, cor.
Agents, Messrs. Cox & Co.

6TH DRAGOON GUARDS.
Longford.
Col. Sir J.R. Smyth, K.C.B., m.g., s.
L.Col. Courtenay W. Bruce.
Majors, Edward Lennox Jervis; William Thomas Betty.
Adjutant, W. W. Graham, lt.
Agent, A. Lawrie, Esq.

7TH DRAGOON GUARDS.
Colchester.
Col. Ld.G.A.F. Paget, c.B., m.g., s.
L.Col. Robert Clarke.
Majors, Christopher Barton; W. B. Armstrong.
Adjutant, David Scotland, lt.
Agents, Messrs. Cox & Co.

1ST DRAGOONS.
Dublin. [K.C.H. g.
Col. ☰ Sir Ar. B. Clifton, G.C.B.,
L.Col. James Ainslie.
Major, Walter John Coney.
Adjutant, John Lee, lt.
Agents, Messrs. Cox & Co.

2ND DRAGOONS.
Cahir.
Col. Sir J. B. Gough, K.C.B., l.g.
L.Col. Geo. Calvert Clarke, c.
Major, Andrew Nugent.
Adjutant, J.W. Hozier, lt.
Agents, Messrs. Cox & Co.

3RD HUSSARS.
Bombay—Canterbury.
Col. Henry A. Hankey, l.g.

L.Col. Edward Howard Vyse.
Majors, Wm. Morrison Bell; R. B. H. Blundell.
Adjutant, C. E. Nettles, lt.
Agents, Messrs. Cox & Co.

4TH HUSSARS.
Bengal—Canterbury.
Col. W. L. L. F. Lord de Ros, g.
L.Col. James Swinburne.
Majors, A. G. M. Moore; Hon. Fred. George Ellis.
Adjutant, J. W. Lay, cor.
Agents, Messrs. Cox & Co.

5TH LANCERS.
Bengal—Canterbury.
Col. E. Pole, m.y.
L.Col. W. Hicks Slade, c.
Majors, W. G. Dunham Massy; Fred. Walter Carden.
Adjutant, F. Sedley, lt.
Agent, Henry T. Clack, Esq.

6TH DRAGOONS.
Manchester.
Col. L. D. Williams, m.y.
L.Col. Hon. C. W. Thesiger.
Majors, Theodore Wirgman; Hon. E. R. Bourke, s.
Adjutant, J. L. Bland, lt.
Agents, Messrs. Cox & Co.

7TH HUSSARS.
Bengal—Canterbury.
Col. Sir John Scott, K.C.B., g.
L.Col. Harington A. Trevelyan.
Majors, T.H.Stisted; F.Garforth.
Adjutant, H. A. Bushman, lt.
Agents. Messrs. Hopkinson & Co.

8TH HUSSARS.
Edinburgh.
Col. John Lawrenson, l.g.
L.Col. Fra. E. Macnaghten.
Majors, J. Puget; W. Mussenden.
Adjutant, W. St. Lo Malet, lt.
Agents, Messrs. Cox & Co.

9TH LANCERS.
Newbridge.
Col.Sir J.Hope Grant,G.C.B., l.g.s.
L.Col. Chardin P. Johnson.
Majors, Hon. Ivo de Vesci T. W. Fiennes; Henry Marshall.
Adjutant, F. De la G. Grissell, lt.
Agents, Messrs. Cox & Co.

10TH HUSSARS.
Aldershot.
Col. H.R.H.AlbertEdwardPrince of Wales and Duke of Cornwall, K.G., g.
L.Col. Valentine Baker, c.
Major, John Fife.
Adjutant, J. C. Russell, lt.
Agents, Messrs. Cox & Co.

11TH HUSSARS.
Bengal—Canterbury.
Col. Geo. Wm. Key, m.g.
L.Col. ☰ C. C. Fraser, c.B., c.
Majors, Art. Lyttleton Annesley; Edward Harnett.
Adjutant, St. J. S. Taylor, lt.
Agents, Messrs. Cox & Co.

12TH LANCERS.
Dundalk.
Col.Sir G.H.Lockwood. K.C.B.,l,g.
L.Col. Thos. G. A. Oakes, c.B., c.
Major, Adolphus U. Wombwell.

Adjutant, B. V. Denneby, lt.
Agents, Messrs. Cox & Co.

13TH HUSSARS.
Canada—Canterbury.
Col. ☰ A. T. Maclean, l.g.
L.Col. S. G. Jenyns, c.B., c.
Major, FitzRoy D. Maclean.
Adjutant, P. Morrisey, cor.
Agents, Messrs. Cox and Co.

14TH HUSSARS.
Dublin.
Col.☰ Wm. Beckwith, K.H., l.g.
L.Col. Pearson S. Thompson, c.
Majors, Fred. B. Chapman; E. Pemberton Campbell.
Adjutant, J. Harpur, lt.
Agents, Messrs. Cox & Co.

15TH HUSSARS.
York.
Col.☰ Everard W. Bouverie, g.
L.Col. F.W.J.FitzWygram, c.
Major, Bryan Burrell.
Adjutant, R. M. Briscoe, lt.
Agents, Messrs. Cox & Co.

16TH LANCERS.
Madras—Canterbury.
Col. Hon. Sir E. Cust, K.C.H., g.
L.Col. Wm. T. Dickson, c.
Majors, T. Woollaston White,l.c.; Hugh D'A. P. Burnell.
Adjutant, R. T. Maillard, lt.
Agents, Messrs. Cox & Co.

17TH LANCERS.
Hounslow.
Col. C. W. M. Balders, c.B., m.g.
L.Col. Drury C. Drury-Lowe.
Majors, Hon. W. H. Curzon. Henry A. Sarel, l.c.
Adj., J. Brown, cor.
Agents, Messrs. Cox & Co.

18TH HUSSARS.
Madras—Canterbury.
Col. Sir C. R. O'Donnell, g.
L.Col. Richard Knox, c.
Majors, Wm. W. Arbuthnot. R. B. Prettejohn, l.c.
Adj., F. A. Baines, it.
Agents, Messrs. Cox & Co.

19TH HUSSARS.
Bengal—Canterbury.
Col. John Hall, l.g.
L.Col. Charles V. Jenkins, c.
Majors, Roland Richardson, l.c. H. Cadogan Craigie.
Adj., A. H. Chapman, lt.
Agents, Messrs. Cox & Co.

20TH HUSSARS.
Bengal—Canterbury.
Col. C. M. Carmichael, c.B., l.g.
L.Col. Henry James Staunus, c. s.
Edward Charles Warner.
Majors, C. M'Clintock Cotton. Robert Alexander.
Adj., R. G. Loch, lt.
Agents, Messrs. Thacker & Co.

21ST HUSSARS.
Bengal—Canterbury.
Col. William Parlby, m.g.
L.Col. R. Bannatyne M'Leod.
Majors, E. Armitage Hardy. H. Erskine Forbes.
Adj., A. W. Twyford, lt.
Ag. Messrs. A.F.Ridgway&Sons.

Royal Regiment of Artillery.

Col. *F.M.* H.R.H. Geo. W. F. C. Duke of Cambridge, K.G.

A. *Br. Horse Art.* Col.Com.

Adj., Hn. A. Stewart. *Meerut.*
B. *Br.* Col. Com. ꟿ *Lt. Gen.* Sir W. Bell, K.C.B. [*Woolwich.*
Adj., Capt. F. A. Whinyates.
C. *Br.* Col. Com. Gen. Sir George Pollock, G.C.B., G.C.S.I.
Adj., Capt. G.B. Traill. *Aldershot.*
D. *Br.* Col. Com. Gen. E. M. G. Showers.
Adj., Capt. W.H. Caine. *Bangalore.*
E. *Br.* Col. Com. Lt.Gen. F. Schuler.
Adj., Capt. H.W. Stockley. *Kirkee.*
F. *Br.* Col.Com. *Major Gen.* Sir A. Wilson, Bt., G.C.B. [*Umballa.*
Adj., Capt. D. MacFarlane.
Depôt. Maidstone, *Adj.,* Capt. Æ. de V. Tupper.
1st *Br.Gar.* & *Field.* Col. Com. Gen. Sir W. M. G. Colebrooke, C.B.
Adjutant, Capt. D. R. Cameron. *Halifax.*
2nd *Br.* Col. Com. Lt.Gen. P. V. England.
Adj., Capt. H.B. Maule. *Mauritius.*
3rd *Br.* Col. Com. Lt. Gen. T. G. Higgins.
Adj., Capt. H.C. Farrell. *Montreal.*
4th *Br.* Col.Com. Gn. Sir R. J. Dacres, K.C.B.
Adj., Capt. R. Sandham. *Toronto.*
5th *Br.* Col. Com. ꟿ Lt.Gen. Sir W. B. Ingilby, K.C.B. [*Madras.*
Adj., Capt. R. W. C. Campbell.
6th *Br.* Col.Com ꟿ Lt.Gen. Sir J. Bloomfield, K.C.B.
Adj., Capt. R.N. Young. *Ptsmouth.*
7th *Br.* Col.Com. Lt. Gen. R. Burn.
Adj., Capt. F. Duncan. *Woolwich.*
8th *Br.* Col. Com. ꟿ Lt.Gn. Burke Cuppage.
Adj., Cap. F.G. Baylay. *Lucknow.*
9th *Br.* Col. Com.

Adj., Capt. F. A. Mant. *Dublin.*
10th *Br.* Col.Com. Gen. W. Wylde, C.B.
Adj., Cap. C.G. Johnson. *Malta.*
11th *Br.* Col.Com. Lt. Gen. Sir J. E. Dupuis, K.C.B. [*Woolwich.*
Adj., Capt. P. H. Sandilands.
12th *Br.* Col. Com. Gen. Sir W. F. Williams, Bart., K.C.B.
Adj., Capt. H.Y. Wortham. *Gosport.*
13th *Br.* Col. Com. Lt. Gen. E. Sabine. [*Plymouth.*
Adj., Capt. W. H. Newcome.
14th *Br.Cl.Com.Gen.* F.R. Chesney.
Adj., Major H. Le G. Geary. *Ahmedabad.*

15th *Br.* Col. Com. ꟿ Lt. Gen. F. Warde. [*Gibraltar.*
Adj., Capt. F. A. Anley.
16th *Br.* Col. Com. *Major-Gen.* E. Huthwaite, C.B. [*Barrackpore.*
Adj., Capt. S. A. Bazalgette.
17th *Br.* Col. Com. Lt. Gen. F. F. Whinyates. [*Dover.*
Adj., Capt. W. H. M'Causland.
18th. *Br.* Col. Com. *Major-Gen.* A. Rowland. [*Kurrachee.*
Adj., Capt. T. P. Berthon.
19th *Br.* Col.Com. Gen. G. Swiney.
Adj., Capt. F. W. Ward. *Peshawur.*
20th *Br.* Col. Com. Gen. Geo. Curran.
Adj., Capt. H.M. Finlay. *Kamptee.*
21st *Br.* Col. Com. Gen. J. G. Griffith. [*Mhow.*
Adj., Capt. T. H. Ouchterlony.
22nd *Br.* Col. Com. Gen. Sir A. Lindsay, K.C.B.
Adj. Capt. C.G. Robinson. *Morar.*
23rd *Br.* Col. Com. Gen. Sir P. Montgomerie, K.C.B.
Adj., Capt. H. M'Leod. *Secunderabad.*
24th *Br.* Col. Com. *Major-Gen.* G. Twemlow.
Adj., Capt. A. Dixon. *Meen Meer.*
25th *Br.* Col.Com. Lt. Gen. Sir G. Brooke, K.C.B.
Adj. Capt. E.C. Griffin. *Allahabad.*
Depôt Br. 1st *Div. Com.*
Adj. Capt. A.D. Burnaby. *Sheerness*
Depôt Br. 2nd *Div. Com.*
Adj. Capt. C.D. Gilmour. *Woolwich*
Depôt Br. 3rd *Div. Com.*
Adj. Capt. J. M. Burn. *Warley.*
Coast Br. Com. Lt.Col. J. Campbell.
Adj. W. Crawford, *Woolwich.*
Cols. 3 G. R. H. Kennedy, *s.*
1 J. H. Francklyn, C.B.
9 G. Gambier, C.B., *s.*
8 G. J. L. Buchanan, *s.*
5 Henry S. Rowan, C.B.
9 P. B. Feilding Marriott, *s.*
1 Thomas Elwyn.
11 Charles James Wright.
7 Anthony Benn.
14 Wm. James Smythe.
3 John Henry Lefroy.
14 James W. Domville, *s.*
12 Edwin Wodehouse, C.B. *s.*
15 Evan Maberly, C.B., *s.*
4 W. M. Hall Dixon.
13 John M. Adye, C.B.
6 Frederick Alex. Campbell.
10 H. P. Goodenough, *s.*
5 G. B. Shakespear.
B *Br.* H. L. Gardiner.

4 Robert Parker Radcliffe.
15 C. W. Younghusband.
13 R. Corcyra Romer, *s.*
11 C. L. D'Aguilar, C.B.
7 Arnold Thompson.
2 Henry Clerk.
12 ꟿ Matthew C. Dixon.
A. *Br.* J. Turner, C.B.
2 Edward Henry Fisher.
8 R. F. Mountain.
10 E. M. Boxer.
6 C. S. Longden.
(Late Bengal).
Cols. 24 Arthur Broome, *s.*
22 Reg. E. Knatchbull.
24 H. A. Carleton, C.B.
22 William H. Delamain.
25 David Reid.
C. *Br.* J. Hall Smyth, C.B., *s.*
F. *Br.* Ernle Kyrle Money.
19 William Maxwell.
19 H. E. L. Thuillier.
19 Charles Douglas.
16 Edward Kaye, *s.*
19 Thomas Brougham.
24 John Eliot.
25 Henry Lewis.
F. *Br.* H. P. de Teissier.
C. *Br.* C. Vyvyan Cox.
25 C. Hildesley Dickens.
16 Henry Hammond.
(Late Madras).
20 *Cols.* G. W. M. Simpson.
26 John Maitland.
D. *Br.* George Rowlandson.
17 William Adam Orr, C.B.
23 W. Kinnaird Worster.
23 Joseph Lyon Barrow.
17 Gerard P. Eaton, *s.*
D. *Br.* John Desbrisay Mein.
23 James George Balmain.
23 George Selby.
D. *Br.* A. W. Macintire, C.B.
20 Thomas Hay Campbell.
23 C. H. Hutchinson.
(Late Bombay).
Col. *having rank of Col.* Com. 21, Sir W. M. Coghlan, K.C.B., *m.g.*
Cols. 18 George Prince Sealy, *s.*
21 A. B. Kemball, C.B., K.C.S.I.
21 William David Aitkin.
E. *Br.* C. Bondler Fuller.
21 John Worgan.
21 Edward Wray, C.B.
21 John Gordon Petrie, C.B.
18 J. D. Woolcombe, C.B.
Coast Brigade of Artillery, Lt.Col. J. Campbell.
Adj. W. Crawford, *lt.*
Riding Establishment.
Capt., A. M. Calvert, *m.*
Agents, Messrs. Cox & Co.

Corps of Royal Engineers.

Col. *F.-M.* H.R.H. Geo. W. F. C. Duke of Cambridge, K.G.

A Trp., R.E.Trp. Aldershot.	4th, Bermuda.	18th, Bermuda	26th, Weymou.	34th, Hlifx., N.S.
B Trp., Aldersh.	5th, Halifax, N.S.	19th, Glasgow.	27th, Malta.	35th, Chatham.
1st Co., Canada.	6th, Aldershot.	20th, Cork.	28th, Curragh.	36th, do.
2nd, Cape of G.H.	7th, Woolwich.	21st, Shorncliffe	29th, Portsmou.	37th, do.
3rd, Aldershot.	8th, do.	22nd, Ca. of G.H.	30th, Gibraltar.	38th, do.
	9th, Bermuda.	23rd, do.	31st, do.	39th, do.
10th, Chatham.		24th, Mauritius.	32nd, S.Helena.	40th, do.
11th, Dover.		25th, Dover.	33rd, Malta.	
12th, Chatham.				
13th, Edinb. (su)				
14th, London (s)				
15th, Canada.				
16th, Dublin (s)				
17th, Gibraltar				

ROYAL ENGINEERS—*continued.*
Cols.-Com., Sir J. F. Burgoyne, Bart., G.C.B., *f.m.*
Sir C. G. Ellicombe, K.C.B., *g.*
Sir J. M. F. Smith, K.H.; *g.*
Wm. Redman Ord, *g.*
Thomas Foster, *l.g.*
Montgomery Williams, *l.g.*
Richard John Stotherd, *i.g.*
B. S. Stehelin, *l.g.*
Colonels, E. Wm. Durnford, *s.*
Sir Henry James.
George Wynne.
William Crawley Stace.
H. Drury Harness, C.B.
Charles Erskine Ford, *s.*
Rob. Gorges Hamilton, *s.*
William Charles Hadden, *s.*
Roger Stewart Beatson.
Sampson Freeth.
William George Hamley.
Edmund Ogle, *s.*
John Cameron.
John S. Hawkins.
James Holt Freeth.
Charles Fanshawe.
Gother E. Mann, C.B.

(Late Bengal,)
Cols.Com., Sir J. Cheape, G.C.B. *g.*
Edward Garstin, *g.*
Henry Goodwyn, *l.g.*
Maj-Gen., having rank as Col. Com.
Wm. Erskine Baker, *m.g.*
Cols., Henry Rigby.
Richard Strachey, C.S.I.
John Reid Becher, C.B.
Robert Maclagan.
John Harley Maxwell.
John Douglas Campbell.
(Late Madras.)
Cols. Com., Sir A.T. Cotton, K.C.S.I.
Edward Lawford, *m.g.*   [*l.g.*
Cols., Charles Alexander Orr.
Arch. J. M. Boileau.
Henry W. Hitchins.
John Carpendale.
(Late Bombay.)
Cols. Com., W.B. Goodfellow, *m.g.*
Walter Scott, *l.g.*
Maj.Gen. having rank as Col. Com.
Henry Blois Turner, *m.g.*
Cols., Harry W. B. Bell.
William Kendall.
M. K. Kennedy.
W. R. Dickinson.

Adj. Bruce Brine, *2nd capt.*
Roy. Eng. Trn. Adj.A.K. Haslett, *lt.*
Agents, Messrs. Cox and Co.

MILITARY TRAIN.

Troops 1, 5, 6, 7, 20, 23, 24, Aldsht | 9 & 10, Curragh
2, 4, 11, Dublin, 12, Shorncliffe
3, Kensington, 17, Chatham
8, 13, 14, 15, 16, 18, Portsmouth
& 19, Woolwich 21, Devonport
22, Hilsea
Col. Com., George Erskine.
Brig. Maj. Bt. Lt.-Col. C. R. Shervinton, Unat.
Lt. Cols., J. P. Robertson, C.B., *c.*
Bartholomew O'Brien, *c.*
Henry Bird, *c.*
Majors, John M'Court.
James Hornby Buller.
James Henry Wyatt, C.B.
Adjs., W. Shackleton, *lt.* Dublin.
J. Taylor, *lt., Aldershot.*
John Devine, *lt., Woolwich.*
Agent, Sir John Kirkland.

Infantry.

GRENADIER GUARDS.
1. *Wellington Barracks*; 2. *Tower*; 3. *Dublin.*
Col., H.R.H .Geo. W. F. C. Duke of Cambridge, K.G., *f.m.s.*
Lt. Col., Michael Bruce, *c.*
Majors, 3, H.S.H. Prince Wm. A. E. of Saxe Weimar, C.B., *c.*
1 Henry F. Ponsonby, *c.*
2 John Hynde King, *c.*
Adjs., 2 Visc. Hinchinbrook, *capt.*
1 L. R. Seymour, *capt.*
3 T. F. Fairfax, *capt.*
Solicitor, W. J. Farrer, Esq.
Agents, Messrs. Cox and Co.

COLDSTREAM GUARDS.
1. *Chelsea*; 2. *Windsor.*
Col., Sir William M. Gomm, G.C.B., *f.m.*
L.Ct., 1 Hon.A.E.Hardinge,C.B.C.
Majors, 1 Hon. P.R.B.Feilding, *c.*
2 Charles Baring, *c.*
Adj., 2 G. J. F. Smyth, *capt.*
1 Hon. F. A. Wellesley, *capt.*
Solicitor, R. J. P. Broughton, Esq.
Agents, Messrs. Cox and Co.

SCOTS FUSILIER GUARDS.
1. *Wellington Barracks*; 2. *Chelsea.*
Col. Sir Alexdr. Woodford, G.C.B., G.C.M.G., *f.m.*
L.Col., 2 F.C.A. Stephenson, C.B.C.
Majs., 1 Hen. Poole Hepburn, *c.*
2 Lord Abinger, *l.c.*
Adjs., 1 C. A. Wynne-Finch, *capt.*
2 Hon. P. S. Methuen, *capt.*
Solicitor, Fredk. Ouvry, Esq.
Agents, Messrs. Cox and Co.

1ST FOOT.
1 *Madras—Chatham.*
2 *Bombay—Chatham.*
Col., Sir George Bell, K.C.B., *l.g.*
L. Col., 2 Richard George Coles.
1 Fred. Wells.

Majors, 2 George Rowland.
2 George Frederick Berry.
1 E. T. St. L. M'Gwire.
1 W. F. J. Rudd.
Adjs., 1 F. R. Stanton, *lt.*
2 F. C. H. Brooke, *lt.*
Agents, Messrs. Cox and Co.

2ND FOOT.
1 *Bombay—Chathm.* 2 *Aldrsht.*
Col., John Spink, K.H., *g.*
L. Cols., 1 Thos. Addison, C.B., *c.*
2 Henry Reynolds Werge.
Majors, 1 James Rose, *l.c.*
2 Richard H. Rocke.
1 John Charles Weir.
2 John Thompson.
Adjs., 2 G. H. Woodard, *lt.*
1 B. A. Beale, *lt.*
Agents, Messrs. Cox and Co.

3RD FOOT.
1 *Bengal—Shorncliffe.*
2 *Bristol.*
Col., Day Hort Macdowall, *l.g.*
L.Cols., 1 Thomas Geo. Gardiner
2 Chas. Knight Pearson.
Majors, 2 John Otway Wemyss.
2 Talbot Ashley Cox.
1 Francis Morley.
1 C. Sutherland Dowson.
Adjs., 2 John Cotter, *lt.*
1 F. W. Kane, *lt.*
Agents, Messrs. Cox and Co.

4TH FOOT.
1 *Dover*; 2 *Dublin.*
Col., Sir John Bell, G.C.B., *g.*
L. Cols., 1 William Wilby, C.B., *c.*
2 Thomas Martin.
Majors, 1 W. G. Cameron, C.B., *c.*
2 Fras. Fisher Hamilton.
2 James Paton.
1 Edward Wm. Bray, *c.*
Adjs., 2 J. H. M'Ewen, *lt.*
1 C. M. Davidson, *lt.*
Agents, Messrs. Cox and Co.

5TH FOOT.
1 *Bengal—Shorncliffe.*
2 *Aldershot.*
Col., Edward Rowley Hill, *m.g.*
L. Cols., 2 J. A. V. Kirkland, *c.*
1 William Roberts.
Majors, 2 J. C. Bartley, *l.c.*
2 George Carden.
1 Thomas Scovell Bigge.
1 Thomas Rowland.
Adjs., 1 W. S. Darley, *lt.*
2 C. Hackett, *lt.*
Agents, Messrs. Cox and Co.

6TH FOOT.
1 *Bengal—Colchester.* 2 *Aldrsht.*
Col., 1 Hon. Sir Charles Gore, G.C.B., K.H., *g.*
L. Cols, 1 C. O. Creagh-Osborne.
2 John H. F. Elkington, *c.*
Majors, 1 Thomas Lynden Bell.
1 Philip Aug. Mosse.
2 Henry B. Feilden.
2 Charles Burch Phillipps.
Adjs., 2 H. Kitchener, *lt.*
1 G. de C. Morton, *lt.*
Agent, A Lawrie, Esq.

7TH FOOT.
1 *Bengal—Walmer*; 2 *Bury.*
Col., Sir Rchd. Airey, G.C.B., *l.g.s.*
L. Cols., 1 Hugh Robt. Hibbert.
2 Joshua H. Cooper.
1 Thomas W. Marten.
Majors, James Fras. Hickie.
2 George Henry Waller.
1 James Menzies Clayhills.
1 G. F. Herbert.
Adjs., 2 J. Smith, *lt.*
1 J. Potham, *lt.*
Agents, Messrs. Cox and Co.

8TH FOOT.
1 *Bombay—Chatham.*
2 *Aldershot.*
Col., Thomas Gerrard Ball, *l.g.*

INFANTRY—*continued.*

L. Cols., 2 Alex. C. Robertson, *c.*
1 Henry George Woods.
Majors, 1 William F. A. Colman.
1 John V. W. H. Webb.
2 Fred. Bradford M'Crea.
2 Fras. Barry Drew.
Adjs., 1 L. J. Hamilton, *lt.*
2 J. M. Batten, *lt.*
Agents, Messrs. Cox and Co.

9TH FOOT.
1 *Cape of Good Hope—Pem-broke;* 2 *Dublin.*
Col., Sir J. Arch. Hope, G.C.B., *g.*
L. Cols., 1 Henry Disney Ellis, *c.*
2 Thomas E. Knox, C.B., *c.*
Majors, 2 William Sankey, *c.*
1 George H. Hawes, *l.c.*
1 Henry James Buchanan, *l.c.*
2 Sydney Darling.
Adjs., 2 A. F. B. Wright, *lt.*
1 Z. S. Bayly, *lt.*
Agents, Messrs. Cox and Co.

10TH FOOT.
1 *Japan—Shorncliffe.*
2 *Madras—Shorncliffe.*
Col., Sir S. J. Cotton, K.C.B., *l.g.*
L. Cols., Wm. Fenwick, C.B., *c.s.*
1 Henry R. Norman, *c.*
2 Stephen F. C. Annesley, *c.*
Majors, 2 Cuthbert Barlow.
1 Patrick Brown Lucas.
1 J. P. H. Crowe.
2 W. H. P. Gordon Bluett.
Adjs., 2 J. C. Little, *lt.*
1 G. C. Helme, *lt.*
Agents, Messrs. Cox and Co.

11TH FOOT.
1 *Bengal—Parkhurst.*
2 *Cape—Parkhurst.*
Col., Sir J. G. Le Marchant, K.C.B. G.C.M.G., *l.g.*
L. Cols., 2 Aug. F. Jenner, *c.*
1 A. H. Louis Wyatt, *c.*
Majors, 2 Thomas Peebles.
1 John Roe.
1 James Williams.
2 Chas. Peregrine Teesdale.
Adjs., 2 H. H. Skill, *lt.*
1 H. Bamfield, *lt.*
Agents, Messrs. Cox and Co.

12TH FOOT.
1 *Devonport.*
2 *Bengal—Gosport.*
Col., Henry Colvile, *g.*
L. Cols., 1 H. Meade Hamilton, *c.*
2 Richard Atkinson.
Majors, 2 James Wm. Espinasse.
1 John M'Kay.
1 Robert Cecil Dudgeon.
2 Edward Foster.
Adjs., 2 W. J. Boyes, *lt.*
1 H. D. A. Cutbill, *lt.*
Agents, Messrs. Cox and Co.

13TH FOOT.
1 *Gibraltar—Shorncliffe.*
2 *Gosport Forts.*
Col., Philip S. Stanhope, *l.g.*
L. Cols., 1 W. F. MacBean, *c.*
2 Thos. Maunsell.
Majors, 2 R. B. Montgomery.
1 Arthur Bainbrigge.
1 Charles Poore Long.
2 Robert Douglas.

Adjs., 2 R. S. Clarke, *lt.*
1 R. F. King, *lt.*
Agents, Messrs. Cox and Co.

14TH FOOT.
1 *Bombay—Chatham.*
2 *Melbourne—Chatham.*
Col., Sir W. Wood, K.C.B., K.H., *g.*
L. Cols., 2 W. Cosmo Trevor, C.B.
1 John Dwyer.
Majors, 1 Wm. H. Hawley.
1 Chas. Edward Grogan.
2 John G. Maycock.
2 Edward Kent Jones.
Adjs., 1 H. M'L. Hutchison, *lt.*
2 F. W. Harington, *lt.*
Agents, Messrs. Downes and Son.

15TH FOOT.
1 *Bermuda—Chatham.*
2 *Cork.*
Col., T. Armstrong Drought, *l.g.*
L. Cols., 2 John H. Wingfield, *c.*
1 Henry Grierson, *c.*
Majors, Johnson Wilkinson.
2 Fras. P. Hopkins.
1 Sylvester W. F. M. Wilson.
2 P. A. A. Twynam.
Adjs., 1 J. M'Murray, *lt.*
2 C. J. Burnett, *lt.*
Agents, Messrs. Cox and Co.

16TH FOOT.
1 *Nova Scotia—Colchester.*
2 *Barbados—Colchester.*
Col., George Macdonald, *l.g.*
L. Cols., 1 George J. Peacocke, *c.*
2 William C. Bancroft.
Majors, 2 John Oct. Chichester.
2 James William Bostock.
1 J. W. Helyar.
1 S. G. C. Hogge.
Adjs., 1 J. L. Price, *lt.*
2 J. Pyne, *lt.*
Agents, Sir J. Kirkland; V. W. Holt, Esq.

17TH FOOT.
1 *Newry.* 2 *Dublin.*
Col. John Grattan, C.B., *m.g.*
L. Cols., 1 Alex. M'Kinstry, *c.*
Majs., 2 David LatoucheColthurst
1 George Tito Brice, *l.c.*
1 William Affleck King.
2 Jas. B. H. Boyd.
Adjs., 2 W. M. Rolph, *lt.*
1 R. K. Watson, *lt.*
Agents, Messrs. Cox and Co.

18TH FOOT.
1 *Curragh.*
2 *New Zealand—Colchester.*
Col., Sir J. F. FitzGerald, G.C.B., *g.*
L. Cols., 1 George F. S. Call, *c.*
2 George Aug. Elliot.
Majors, 2 James H. Rocke, *l.c.*
1 Lumley Graham, *c.*
2 Richard P. Bishopp.
1 George Henry Pocklington.
Adjs., 1 W. H. Herbert, *lt.*
2 A. J. A. Jackson, *lt.*
Agents, Messrs. Cox and Co.

19TH FOOT.
1 *Bengal—Sheffield.*
2 *Madras—Sheffield.*
Col., Sir A. J. Cloeté, K.C.B., K.H., *l.g.*
L. Cols., 1 Rob. O. Bright, *c.*
2 G. Bingham Jennings.

Majors, Edward Chippindall, *l.c.*
2 Henry de R. Pigott.
Bonar Millett Deane, *s.*
2 Richard Doyle Barrett.
1 Edward St. J. Griffiths.
Adjs., 2 B. Colclough, *lt.*
1 J. G. Moir, *lt.*
Agent, Sir John Kirkland.

20TH FOOT.
1 *Aldershot.*
2 *C. of Good Hope—Shorncliffe.*
Col., M. Beresford, *g.*
L. Cols., 2 Henry R. Browne, *c.s.*
1 Alex. H. Cobbe.
Majors, 1 W. L. Devenish Meares.
2 George Edward Francis.
1 Fredk. Lockwood Edridge.
2 Augustus William Ord.
Adjs., 2 D. O'Neill Power, *lt.*
1 C. E. Hussey, *lt.*
Agents, Messrs. Cox and Co.

21ST FOOT.
1 *Curragh.*
2 *Madras—Preston.*
Col., Sir DeLacy Evans, G.C.B *g.*
L. Cols., 2 J. E. Robertson, *c.s.*
1 John Thomas Dalyell.
2 Edwin A. T. Steward.
Majors, 1 Fred. Torrens Lyster.
1 W. P. Collingwood, *l.c.*
2 Alfred Templeman.
2 S. W. H. Hawker.
Adjs., 2 J. Ferguson, *lt.*
1 C. E. Bovill, *lt.*
Agents, Messrs. Cox and Co.

22ND FOOT.
1 *New Brunsw.—Chatham.*
2 *Newcastle-on-Tyne.*
Col., Sir J.L.Pennefather, G.C.B., *g.*
L. Cols., 1 F. P. Harding, C.B., *c.*
2 David Anderson, *c.*
Majors, 1 J. H. Graham.
1 Thomas Tyacke.
1 Herbert G. Panter.
2 George Fuller Walker.
Adjs., 2 J. D. C. Thomas, *lt.*
1 J. H. Hamersley, *lt.*
2 E. Straton, *lt.*
Agents, Messrs. Cox and Co.

23RD FOOT.
1 *Bombay—Walmer.*
2 *Newport, Monmouth.*
Col., Sir William J. Codrington, G.C.B., *g.*
L. Cols., 1 Robert Pratt, C.B., *c.*
2 E. W. D. Bell, C.B., *c.*
Majors, James Gubbins, *l.c.*, *s.*
1 Henry D. Torrens, C.B., *c.*
1 Charles Elgee, *l.c.*
2 Hon. Savage Mostyn.
2 G. P. Prevost.
Adjs., 1 J. M. Clayton, *lt.*
2 R. F. Williamson, *lt.*
Agents, Messrs. Cox and Co.

24TH FOOT.
1 *Malta—Sheffield.*
2 *Burmah—Sheffield.*
Col., Pringle Taylor, K.H., *l.g.*
L. Cols., 2 Thomas Ross, *c.*
1 Richard T. Glyn.
Majors, 1 Rich. Henry Travers.
2 And. J. Macpherson.
2 F. C. D'Epinay Barclay.
1 Henry J. Hitchcock.

INFANTRY—*continued.*

Adjs., 2 C. J. Bromhead, *lt.*
　1 H. R. Farquhar, *lt.*
Agents, Messrs. Barron & Smith.

25TH FOOT.
　1 *Aldershot.*
　2 *Bengal—Preston.*
Col., Henry Dive Townshend, *l.g.*
L. Cols., 1 H. Torrens Walker, *c.*
　2 Chas. J. Stewart Wallace.
Majors, 2 George Bent.
　1 Henry Pears.
　1 Fras. Henry Pender.
　2 James A. Ruddell-Todd.
Adjs., 1 C. P. Heigham, *lt.*
　2 S. R. B. Partridge, *lt.*
Agents, Messrs. Cox and Co.

26TH FOOT.
　Bengal—Dundee.
Col., Geo. H. M'Kinnon, c.b., *l.g.*
L. Col., Shurlock Henning.
Majors, William Mosse.
　Simpson Hackett.
Adj., H. M. E. Brunker, *lt.*
Agents, Messrs. Cox and Co.

27TH FOOT.
　Chatham.
Col., James R. Craufurd, *l.g.*
L.Col., R. J. Baumgartner, c.b.,*c.*
Majors, Richard Freer.
　Fras. Eastwood Murphy.
Adj., K. D. Murray, *lt.*
Agents, Messrs. Cox and Co.

28TH FOOT.
　Gibraltar—Parkhurst.
Col., Sir H.J.W.Bentinck, k.c.b., *g.*
L.Col., Charles F. T. Daniell.
Majors, C. R. Berkeley Calcott.
　Philip Philpot.
Adj., T. Horniblow, *lt.*
Agents, Messrs. Cox and Co.

29TH FOOT.
　Canada—Colchester.
Col., John Longfield, c.b., *m.g.*
L. Col., Lindsay Farrington, *c.*
Majors, Hales Wilkie.
　Nathaniel P. Ledgard.
Adj., W. Winn, *lt.*
Agents, Messrs. Cox and Co.

30TH FOOT.
　Nova Scotia—Chatham.
Col., Charles Ashmore, *l.g.*
L.Col., Thos. Hen. Pakenham, *c.*
Majors, Wm. John Brook.
　Henry Prim Hutton, *l.c.*
Adj., N. Bannatyne, *lt.*
Agnts, Sir C.R. M'Grigor, Bt.&Co.

31ST FOOT.
　Malta—Chatham.
Col., Sir Edw. Lugard, g.c.b., *g.*
L. Col., Robt. J. Eagar, *c.*
Majors, W. D. S. Dickins.
　Thomas E. Swettenham.
Adj., R. Hill, *lt.*
Agents, Messrs. Price & Boustead.

32ND FOOT.
　Mauritius—Colchester.
Col., Lord Frdk.Paulet, c.b., *m.g.*
L. Col., Patrick Johnston.
Majors, Hon. B. M. Ward.
　Alfred Bassano, *c.*
Adj., D. Bond, *lt.*
Agents, Messrs. Cox and Co.

33RD FOOT.
　Portsmouth.
Col., Wm. N. Hutchinson, *l. g.*
L. Col., A. Sisson Cooper, c.b.,
Majors, Thos. Basil Fanshawe.
　Richard Lacy.
Adj., W. Everett, *lt.*
Agents, Messrs. Cox and Co.

34TH FOOT.
　Aldershot.
Col., John Eden, c.b., *g.*
L. Col., John Gwilt, c.b., *c.*
Majors, Joseph Jordan, *l.c.*
　Granville William Puget.
Adj., J. O. Gage, *lt.*
Agents, Messrs. Cox & Co.

35TH FOOT.
　Portsmouth.
Col., Simcoe Baynes, *l. g.*
L. Col., J. M'N. Walter, c.b., *c.*
Maj., T. E. Blomfield. A. Tisdall.
Adj., Rob. H. Ross, *lt.*
Agent, Sir John Kirkland.

36TH FOOT.
　Bengal—Pembroke Dock.
Col.,
L. Col., Pat.W. McMahon, c.b., *c.*
Majors, FitzWm. F. Hunter, *l. c.*
　Rickard Lloyd.
Adj., W. A. Smail, *lt.*
Agents, Messrs. Cox and Co.

37TH FOOT.
　Bengal—Pembroke Dock.
Col., Sir T. S. Pratt, k.c.b., *l. g.*
L. Col., John Davis.
Majors, George W. Savage.
　Wm. Worsley Worswick.
Adj., W. E. Gilbert, *lt.*
Agents, Messrs. Cox and Co.

38TH FOOT.
　Bengal—Gosport.
Col., Sir W. R. Mansfield, k.c.b.
　g.c.s.i., *l. g.*, *s.*
L. Col., Fred. Art. Willis, c.b., *c.*
Majors, Hor. Page Vance.
　Hon. C. J. Addington.
Adj., A. Stokes, *lt.*
Agents, Messrs. Cox and Co.

39TH FOOT.
　Fermoy.
Col., Sir C. T. Van Straubenzee,
　k.c.b., *l.g.*
L.Col., Robert H. Currie.
Majors, William Leckie, *l.c.*
　Robert B. Baker.
Adj., C. F. Oldfield, *lt.*
Agents, Messrs. Price & Boustead.

40TH FOOT.
　Carlisle.
Col., Richard Greaves, *l.g.*
L.Col., Frederick Samuel Blyth.
Majors, Hon. F. Le P. Trench.
　Thomas Clowes Hinds.
Adj., J. T. Whelan, *lt.*
Agents, Messrs. Cox and Co.

41ST FOOT.
　Bengal—Colchester.
Col., Sir R. England, g.c.b., k.h., *g.*
L. Cols., Julius E. Goodwyn, c.b., c.s.
　Ỹ Ẹ Hugh Rowlands.
Majors, William Allan.
　A. H. Wavell.
Adj., M. T. B. Michell, *lt.*
Agents, Messrs. Cox and Co.

42ND FOOT.
　Edinburgh.
Col., Sir D.A.Cameron, k.c.b.,*l.g.*
L.Col., John C. M'Leod.
Majors, Duncan Macpherson.
　Francis C. Scott.
Adj., J. E. Christie, *lt.*
Agents, Messrs. Cox and Co.

43RD FOOT.
　Jersey.
Col., Sir R.Garrett, k.c.b., k.h.,*l.g.*
L.Col., Francis H. Synge.
Majors, F. M. Colvile, c.b., *l.c.*
　Ỹ Ẹ F. A. Smith.
Adj., St. V. A. Hammick, *lt.*
Agents, Messrs. Cox and Co.

44TH FOOT.
　Kilkenny.
Col., Sir Thomas Reed, k.c.b.,*g.*
L.Col., John J. Hort, *c.*
Majors, Andrew Browne, c.b., *c.*
　John Geddes.
Adj., A. J. Roberts, *lt.*
Agents, Messrs. Cox and Co.

45TH FOOT.
　Madras—Chatham.
Col., Fred. Horn, c.b., *m.g.*
L.Col., H. Woodbine Parish, c.b.
Majors, George Lamont Hobbs.
　Charles Lewis Griffin.
Adj., J. O. Gage, *lt.*
Agents, Messrs. Cox and Co.

46TH FOOT.
　Parkhurst.
Col., Sir C. Ash Windham, k.c.b.,
　l.g., *s.*
L.Col.,
Major, Charles Parker Catty.
Adj., F. Grieve, *lt.*
Agents, Messrs. Cox and Co.

47TH FOOT.
　Nova Scotia—Pembroke.
Col., John Patton, *l.g.*
L.Col., Robt. Wm. Lowry, *c.*
Majors, Charles C. Villiers, *l.c.*
　William FitzRoy.
Adj., S. Lang, *lt.*
Agents, Messrs. Cox and Co.

48TH FOOT.
　Malta—Colchester.
Col., Hon. Art. A. Dalzell, *l. g.*
L. Col., J. Guise R. Aplin, *c.*
Majors, Wm. R. Williamson.
　John Richard Lovett.
Adj., R. Pennell, *lt.*
Agents, Messrs. Cox and Co.

49TH FOOT.
　Bombay—Colchester.
Col., Sir E. F. Morris, k.c.b., *g.*
L. Col., Cadwallader Adams, *c.*
Majors, F. Wm. Gostling.
　Charles FitzGerald.
Adj., W. H. Thomas, *lt.*
Agents, Messrs. Cox and Co.

50TH FOOT.
　Sydney—Chatham.
Col., Marcus J. Slade, *l.g.*
L. Col., H. Edwin Weare, c.b., *c.*
Majors, Fras. G. Hamley, *l.c.*
　A. C. K. Lock, *l.c.*
Adj., W. H. Barker, *lt.*
Agents, Messrs. Cox and Co.

INFANTRY—*continued.*

51ST FOOT.
Portland. [K.H., *l.g.*
Col., ㉟ Sir W. H. Elliott, K.C.B.,
L.Col., William Agg.
Majors, Sam. Alexander Madden.
    Charles Acton.
Adj., A. S. Wynne, *lt.*
Agent, A. Lawrie, Esq.

52ND FOOT.
Malta—Shorncliffe.
Col. ㉟ Sir Wm. Rowan, G.C.B.,*g.*
L. Col., Art. Lennox Peel.
Majors, Hon. Ernest G. Curzon.
    George Charles Synge.
Adj.,
Agents, Messrs. Cox and Co.

53RD FOOT.
Canada—Shorncliffe.
Col., William George Gold, *l.g.*
L. Col., Arch. Rich. Harenc.
Majors, John A. Dalzell.
    Brownlow N. Garnier.
Adj., C. H. Bonney, *lt.*
Agents, Messrs. Cox and Co.

54TH FOOT.
Belfast.
Col., Studholme J. Hodgson,*l.g.,s.*
L. Col., Jas. Sinclair Thomson.
Majors, Edw. Thos. Shiffner.
    F. G. C. Probart.
Adj., J. H. Tarleton, *lt.*
Agents, Messrs. Cox and Co.

55TH FOOT.
Bengal—Sheffield.
Col.,SirPatrk.E.Craigie, K.C.B.,*g.*
L. Col., Robert Hume, C.B., *c.*
Majors, Thomas S. Brown, *l.c.*
    John Richard Hume.
Adj., F. Barnston, *lt.*
Agents, Messrs. Cox and Co.

56TH FOOT.
Waterford.
Col., Henry Wm. Breton, *l.g.*
L. Col., Richard W. Lacy, *c.*
Majors, George Wm. Patey, *l.c.*
    Richard Anderson, *l.c.*
Adj. M. C. Garsia, *lt.*
Agents, Messrs. Cox and Co.

57TH FOOT.
Aldershot.
Col., Charles Rich. Fox, *g.*
L. Col., Edward Bowen.
Majors, Robt. A. Logan, C.B., *l.c.*
    Henry Butler, *l.c.*
Adj., W. A. R. Thompson, *lt.*
Agents, Messrs. Cox and Co.

58TH FOOT.
Bengal—Pembroke.
Col., Wm. Sullivan, C.B., *m.g.*
L. Col., Charles Hood, *c.*
Majors, Robt. C. Whitehead.
    H. G. O. Burningham.
Adj., O. W. Hill, *lt.*
Agents, Messrs. Cox and Co.

59TH FOOT.
Ceylon—Gosport.
Col., Henry Eyre, *l.g.*
L. Col., Chas. Kendal Bushe.
Majors, Joseph de Montmorency
    Edward F. Chadwick.
Adj., W. G. Small, *ens.*
Agents, Messrs. Cox and Co.

60TH ROYAL RIFLE CORPS.
1 *Canada*; 2 *Bengal*; 3 *Madras*; 4 *New Brunswick.*
Depot of Corps, *Winchester.*
Col.-in-Chief, Hugh Visc. Gough,
    G.C.B., K.P., G.C.S.I., *f. m.*
Col.-Com., 2 George Fredk. Visc.
    Templetown, C.B., *l.g.*
1 Henry Visc. Melville, G.C.B.*g.*
L.Cols., 2 Fras. R. Palmer, C.B.,*c.*
    4 Robt. B. Hawley, *c.*
    3 Peter Burton Roe, *c.*
    1 R. Joseph Feilden.
Majors, 3 Hon. F. Kennedy, *l.c.*
    2 Gibbes Rigaud, *c.*
    Sir E. Fitz-Gerald Campbell,
        Bart., *c. s.*
    4 Charles A. B. Gordon, *l.c.*
    1 Henry Fras. Williams, *l.c.*
    2 A. John FitzGerald.
    4 Edward T. Wickham.
    J. P. Battersby, *s.*
    1 Bernard E. Ward, *l.c.*
    3 R. Wilmot Brooke.
Adjs., 4 L. C. Brownrigg, *lt.*
    1 N. W. Wallace, *lt.*
    2 C. P. Cramer, *lt.*
    3 A. H. Bircham, *lt.*
Ag., Sir C. R. M'Grigor,Bt., & Co.

61ST FOOT.
Bermuda—Gosport
Col. E. H. D. E. Napier, *l.g.*
L.Col., John P. Redmond, *c.*
Majors, Alexander Wm. Gordon.
    Wm. F. Brett, *c.*
Adj., H. H. A. Stewart, *lt.*
Agents, Messrs. Cox and Co.

62ND FOOT.
Cork.
Col. Sir W. T. Knollys, K.C.B.,*g.*
L. Col. W. Lenox Ingall, C.B., *c.*
Majors, C. M. S. L. Gwynne.
    Bradney Todd Gilpin.
Adj., T. H. Forsyth, *lt.*
Agents, Messrs. Cox and Co.

63RD FOOT.
Curragh.
Col. Arthur Cunliffe Pole, *l.g.*
L.Col. Vere Hunt Bowles.
Majors, Arch. Wyberly.
    Frederick Miller, *l.c.*
Adj., W. S. Ward, *lt.*
Agent, E. S. Codd, Esq.

64TH FOOT.
Malta—Parkhurst.
Col. ㉟ H. K. Bloomfield, *l.g.*
L.Col. ㉟ T. de O. Hamilton.
Major, Thomas Anderson.
    Robert Mockler.
Adj., E. J. Jekyll, *lt.*
Ag. Sir C. R. M'Grigor, Bt., & Co.

65TH FOOT.
Dublin.
Col. Robert B. Coles, *g.*
L.Col. A. F. W. Wyatt, C.B., *c.*
Majors, Robert H. MacGregor.
    F. Beaumaris Bulkeley.
Adj., V. Butler, *lt.*
Agent, E. S. Codd, Esq.

66TH FOOT.
Dublin.
Col. Edward W. Bell, *g.*
L.Col. Algernon R. Garrett.

Majors, George Vincent Watson.
    Charles Perrin.
Adj., W. L. Beattie, *lt.*
Agents, Messrs. Cox and Co.

67TH FOOT.
Portsmouth.
Col. Francis J. Davies, *g.*
L.Col. John W. Thomas, C.B., *c.*
Majors, Dugald S. Miller.
    Frederick W. Jebb.
Adj., A. J. Poole, *lt.*
Agents, Messrs. Cox and Co.

68TH FOOT.
Manchester.
Col. Lord Wm. Paulet, K.C.B., *l.g.s.*
L.Col. H. Harpur Greer, C.B., *c.*
Majors, Joshua Henry Kirby.
    Charles U. Shuttleworth, *l.c.*
Adj., Charles Covey, *lt.*
Agents, Messrs. Cox and Co.

69TH FOOT.
Canada—Preston.
Col. E. F. Gascoigne, *g.*
L.Col. George Hughes Messiter.
Majors, George Bagot.
    Francis G. Blood.
Adj., R. B. Clarke, *lt.*
Agents, Messrs. Cox and Co.

70TH FOOT.
Kinsale.
Col. Charles H. Doyle, *m.g., s.*
L.Col. William Cooper.
Majors, Arthur Saltmarshe.
    William Henry Ralston.
Adj., N. Huskisson, *lt.*
Agents, Messrs. Cox and Co.

71ST FOOT.
Gibraltar
Col. Hon. Charles Grey, *g.*
L.Col. John I. Macdonell.
Majors, Frederick W. Lambton.
    Charles J. Mounsey.
Adj., H. J. T. Hildyard, *lt.*
Agents, Messrs. Cox and Co.

72ND FOOT.
Limerick.
Col. Sir J. Aitchison, G.C.B., *g.*
L.Col. Wm. Payn, C.B., *c.*
Majors, Cecil Rice.
    Charles Fleming Hunter.
Adj., J. Thomson, *lt.*
Agents, Messrs. Cox and Co.

73RD FOOT.
China—Shorncliffe.
Col. Sir H. R. F. Davie, Bt., *g.*
L.Col. Godfrey J. Burne.
Majors, John Cox Gawler, *c.*
    Frederick Reeve.
Adj. W. Clarke, *lt.*
Agents, Messrs. Cox and Co.

74TH FOOT.
Gibraltar—Stirling.
Col. Charles A. Shawe, *g.*
L.Col. Wm. Kelty M'Leod.
Majors, John Jago.
    Leonard H. L. Irby.
Adj., S. H. Hardy, *lt.*
Agents, Messrs. Cox and Co.

75TH FOOT.
Hong Kong—Shorncliffe.
Col. St. John A. Clerke, K.H., *g.*
L.Col., Thomas Milles.

INFANTRY—*continued.*
Majors, Thomas C. Dunbar, *s.*
  Chas. H. Malan ; G. G. Suttie.
Adj., A. S. Leatham, *lt.*
Agent, E. S. Codd, Esq.

76TH FOOT.
Burmah—Shorncliffe.
Col. Joseph Clarke, *l.g.*
L.Col. Henry C. Brewster, *c.*
Majors, John Hackett, *l.c.*
  Christopher R. Richardson.
Adjs., G. D. Cookson, *lt.*
Agents, Messrs. Cox and Co.

77TH FOOT.
Bengal—Gosport.
Col. Lord Rokeby, K.C.B., *l.g.*
L.Col. Henry Kent.
Majors, William N. M. Orpen.
  H. M. L. Colquhoun.
Adj., G. A. White, *lt.*
Agents, Messrs. Cox and Co.

78TH FOOT.
Canada—Aberdeen. [*l.g.*
Col. Sir P. Grant, G.C.B., G.C.M.G.
L.Col. Alexander Mackenzie.
Majors, Oswald Barton Feilden.
  Augustus E. Warren.
Adj, E. P. Stewart, *lt.*
Agents, Messrs. Cox and Co.

79TH FOOT.
Bengal—Stirling.
Col. J. F. G. Campbell, C.B., *m.g.*
L.Cols. William C. Hodgson, *c.*
  Richard M. Best, *c.*
Majors, Keith R. Maitland.
  George Murray Miller.
Adj., A. Hume, *lt.*
Agents, Messrs. Barron & Smith

80TH FOOT.
Fleetwood.
Col. Henry John French, *m.g.*
L.Col. Robert Prescott Harrison.
Majors, Hamilton Charles Smith.
  Wm. George Margesson.
Adj., S. G. Huskisson.
Agents, Messrs. Cox and Co.

81ST FOOT.
Buttevant.
Col. William Fred.Forster, K.H., *l.g.*
L.Col. John Arthur Gilden.
Majors, R. Bruce Chichester.
  John Bourchier.
Adj., M. Curry, *lt.*
Agents, Messrs. Cox and Co.

82ND FOOT.
Aden—Chatham.
Col. Hon. Th. Ashburnham,C.B.,*g.*
L.Col. David Watson, *c.*
Majors, C. T. V. Bunbury, *l.c.*
  Henry Chandler Wilkinson.
Adj., W. A. Dixon, *lt.*
Agents, Messrs. Cox and Co.

83RD FOOT.
Gibraltar—Colchester.
Col. Edward P. Buckley, *g.*
L.Col. Augustus B. Hankey, *c.*
Majors, Edward Meurant.
  Julian Wakefield.
Adj., W. C. Collis, *lt.*
Agents, Messrs. Cox and Co.

84TH FOOT.
Jamaica—Colchester.
Col. Thomas Wood, *l.g.*

L.Col. Thomas Lightfoot, C.B., *cl.*
Majors, Frederick Hardy.
  James Hudson.
Adj., G. J. Smallpeice, *lt.*
Agents, Messrs. Cox and Co.

85TH FOOT.
Bengal—Shorncliffe.
Col. Frederick Maunsell, *l.g.*
L.Col. F. Ernest Appleyard.
Majors, George Thompson.
  Edward Smyth Mercer.
Adj., William H. Drage, *lt.*
Agents, Messrs. Cox and Co.

86TH FOOT.
Mauritius—Parkhurst.
Col. Sir J. Michel, K.C.B., *l.g.*
L.Col. E. W. D. Lowe, C.B., *c.*
Majors, John Jerome.
  Charles Darby.
Adj.,H. R. S. Chatfield, *lt.*
Agents, Messrs. Cox and Co.

87TH FOOT.
Malta—Walmer.
Col. Thos. H. Johnston, *l.g.*
L.Col. Thomas Casey Lyons.
Majors, John Hallowes.
  Thomas W. Sheppard.
Adj., J. M. F. England, *lt.*
Agents, Messrs. Cox and Co.

88TH FOOT.
Bengal—Parkhurst.
Col. Montague C. Johnstone, *l.g.*
*L.Col.*G. VaughanMaxwell,C.B.,*c.s*
  Edward H. Maxwell, *c.*
Majors, B. B. Mauleverer, *l.c.*
  William Thomas Betts.
Adj., H. G. Moore, *lt.*
Ag., Sir C. R. M'Grigor,Bt.,& Co

89TH FOOT.
Athlone.
Col. Charles Gascoyne, *l.g.*
L.Col. Wm. Boyle, *c.*
Majors, Edward Buller Thorp.
  James Buchanan Kirk.
Adj., R. G. Newbigging, *lt.*
Agents, Messrs. Cox and Co.

90TH FOOT.
Bengal—Preston.
Col. William H. Eden, *l.g.*
L.Col. James Clerk Rattray.
Majors, L. N. D. Hammond.
  Henry W. Palmer.
Adj., R. I. Ward, *lt.*
Agents, Messrs. Cox and Co.

91ST FOOT.
Madras—Fort George.
Col. C. G. J. Arbuthnot, *g.*
L.Cols. Bertie E. M. Gordon, *c.*
  W. T. L. Patterson, *c.*
Majors, William B. Battiscombe.
  John Penton.
Adj., W. Grant, *lt.*
Agent, Sir John Kirkland.

92ND FOOT.
Bengal—Aberdeen.
Col. Hugh H. Lord Strathnairn,
  G.C.B., G.C.S.I., *g. s.*
L. Col. Christian M. Hamilton.
Majors, Forbes MacBean.
  Arthur Wellington Cameron.
Adj. R. B. M'Ewen, *lt.*
Agents, Messrs. Cox and Co.

93RD FOOT.
Bengal—Perth.
Col. C. Craufurd Hay, *l.g.*
L.Cols. Fred. W. Burroughs.
  E. S. F. G. Dawson.
Majors, James M. Brown.
  Reg. S. Williams.
Adj., FitzRoy M'Pherson, *lt.*
Agents, Messrs. Cox and Co.

94TH FOOT.
Dover.
Col. E. W. F. Walker, C.B., *l.g.*
L.Col. Septimus Lyster.
Majors, Lord John Henry Tay-
  lour, Haydon L. Cafe.
Adj.,
Agents, Messrs. Cox and Co.

95TH FOOT.
Bombay—Pembroke.
Col. John ffolliott Crofton, *m.g.*
L.Cols. J. A. R. Raines, C.B., *c., s.*
  Hon. F. A. Thesiger, C.B., *c.*
Majors, G. C. Vialls, *c.*
  Hon. E. C. H. Massey, *c.*
Adj., E. W. Golding, *lt.*
Agents, Messrs. Cox and Co.

96TH FOOT.
Bombay—Colchester.[*l.g.,s.*
Col. Hon. Sir A.A. Spencer, K.C.B.,
L.Col. W. A. M. Barnard.
Majors, G. F. C. Bray, *l.c.*
  James Briggs.
Adj., W. Newbigging, *lt.*
Agents, Messrs. Cox and Co.

97TH FOOT.
Aldershot.
Col. John Campbell, *l.g.*
L.Col. Edward T. Gloster, *c.*
Majors, Martin Petrie.
  O. Barwell Cannon.
Adj., F. H. Vigne, *lt.*
Agents, Messrs.Hopkinson & Co.

98TH FOOT.
Aldershot.
Col. Sir R. P. Douglas, Bt., *l.g.s.*
L.Col. Francis Peyton, *c.*
Majors, G. D. D. Cleveland.
  T. F. Lloyd.
Adj., A. H. A. Gordon, *lt.*
Agents, Messrs. Cox and Co.

99TH FOOT.
Cape Good Hope—Preston.
Col. Samuel Braybrooke, *i.g.*
L.Col. John Hart Dunne.
Majors, W. H. D. R. Welman.
  Henry Frederick W. Elly.
Adj., C. J. Greenham, *lt.*
Agents, Messrs.Price & Boustead.

100TH FOOT.
Canada—Glasgow.
Col. Sir E. Macarthur, K.C.B., *l.g.*
L.Col. William Campbell.
Majors, Henry Cook.
  Henry George Browne.
Adj., B. M. Dawes, *lt.*
Agents, Messrs. Cox and Co.

101ST FOOT.
Bengal—Walmer.
Col. Sir A. Roberts, K.C.B, *g.*
L.Col. Fred. O. Salusbury,C.B.,*c.*
Majors, Edward Brown.
  George Craster Lambert.
Adj., T. Macleane, *lt.*
Agents, Messrs. Barron & Smith.

INFANTRY—*continued.*

102ND FOOT.
Bengal—Walmer.
Col. Sir R. J. H.Vivian,K.C.B.,*l.g.*
L.Col. Thomas Raikes, *c.*
Majors, John Blick Spurgin, *c.*
Henry Joseph Jepson.
Adj., R. C. Parry, *lt.*
Agents, Messrs. Cox and Co.

103RD FOOT.
Bengal—Shorncliffe.
Col. Joseph Hale, *m.g.*
L.Cols. Thomas Tapp, C.B., *c. s.*
William Stuart Furneaux.
Majors, Francis Seton Kempt.
George Edward Herne.
Adj., A. A. Godwin, *lt.*
Ag., Sir C. R. M'Grigor,Bt., & Co.

104TH FOOT.
Bengal—Walmer.
Col. George Dixon, *l.g.*
L.Col. Walter Birch, *c.*
Majors, Webber D. Harris.
C. H. E. Græme.
Adj., C.V. E. Parker, *lt.*
Agent, Sir J. Kirkland.

105TH FOOT.
Bengal—Shorncliffe.
Col. G. A. Malcolm, C.B., *l.g.*
L.Col. J. R. Mackenzie.
Majors, C. Wallis Lethbridge.
Henry Adolphus Graham.
Adj., T. Kelly, *lt.*
Agents, Messrs. Cox and Co.

106TH FOOT.
Bengal—Shorncliffe.
Col. Sir David Capon, K.C.B., *g.*
L.Col. Henry Philip Tyacke.
Majors, W. M. Sloane Bolton.
R. R. Gillespie.
Adj., W. Ainsworth, *lt.*
Ag., Messrs.A.F.Ridgway&Sons.

107TH FOOT.
Bengal—Preston.

Col. Wm. James D'Urban, *m.g.*
L.Col. Robert Patton, *c.*
Majors, John D'Oyly Baring.
Albert Locke Nicholson.
Adj., W. G. Mansergh, *lt.*
Agents, Messrs. Cox and Co.

108TH FOOT.
Bombay—Gosport.
Col. W. A. M'Cleverty, *m.g., s.*
L.Col. Charles Wilson Moore.
Majors, ArthurJames Shuldham.
H. E. Thesiger Williams.
Adj., A. S. Tollemache, *lt.*
Agents, Messrs. Cox and Co.

109TH FOOT.
Bengal—Chatham.
Col. Sir W. Wyllie, K.C.B., *l.g.*
L.Col. A. A. P. Browne.
Majors, Edward Valintine.
August Schmid.
Adj., O. Schmidt, *lt.*
Agents, Messrs.Price & Boustead.

RIFLE BRIGADE.
1 *Canada—Winchester* ; 2 *Devon-*
port; 3 *Bengal — Winchester* ;
4 *Chester.*
Col. in Chief. H.R.H. Albert Ed.
Prince of Wales and Duke of
Cornwall, K.G., *g.*
Cols. Com. 1 Sir G. Buller, K.C.B.,
l.g. s.
2 Sir C. Yorke, G.C.B., *g.*
L.Cols., A. Macdonell, C.B., *c.*
4 F. R. Elrington, *c.*
1 Lord A. G. Russell, *c.*
3 Julius E. Glyn, C.B., *c.*
2 W. A. Fyers, C.B., *c.*
Majors, 2 Hercules Walker, *l.c.*
1 Edmund M. Buller.
3 John Ross, C.B., *c.*
4 Arthur James Nixon.
1 Arthur F. Warren, *l.c.*
3 H. J. Maclean.

4 H. R. L. Newdigate.
2 A. H. Stephens.
Adjts., 4 L. V. Swaine, *lt.*
2 E. H. Chamberlin, *lt.*
1 Sir A. R. Palmer, Bt., *lt.*
3 F. E. Kerr, *lt.*
Agents, Messrs. Cox and Co.

1ST WEST INDIA REGT.
Sierra Leone.
Col. Sir G. Bowles, K.C.B., *g.*
L.Cols. G. Nigel K. A. Yonge, *c.*
Henry Anton.
Majors, John M'Auley.
Wm. W. W. Johnston.
Adj., J. W. Arrowsmith, *it.*
Agents, Messrs. Cox and Co.

2ND WEST INDIA REGT.
Bahamas.
Col. Sir Robert Law, K.H., *l.g.*
Lt.Cols., William Hill.
James D. Mends.
Majors, John Deane Reece.
H. J. W. Wise.
Adj., J. Dalgleish, *ens.*
Agents, Messrs. Barron & Smith.

3RD WEST INDIA REGT.
Jamaica.
Col. Maurice Barlow, *l.g.*
L.Cols. W. J. Chamberlayne, *c.*
Robert Hughes, *c.*
Majors, Robert Wm. Harley, *l.c.*
John E. Dickson Hill.
Adj., R. Wilson, *lt.*
Agents, Messrs. Cox and Co.

4TH WEST INDIA REGT.
Barbados.
Col. Geo. Thos. Colomb, *l.g.*
L.Col. George James Ivcy.
Hon. Wm. Henry Herbert.
Majors, Christopher J. Barnard.
R. E. D. Ness.
Adj., C. O. Bulger.
Agent, E. S. Codd, Esq.

COLONIAL CORPS.

CEYLON RIFLE REGIMENT.
Ceylon & Hong Kong.
L.Cols. William T. Layard, *c.*
James M. Macdonald, *c.*
Majors, Lionel Hook.
Edward F. Tranchell.
Adjs., R. Calvert, *ens.*
J. Quarry, *lt.*
Agent, Sir John Kirkland.

CAPE MOUNTED RIFLEMEN.
L.Col. Lewis Edward Knight.
Major, George Francis Morant.
Adj., H. S. Pasley, *lt.*
Agent, Sir John Kirkland.

ROY. CANADIAN RIFLE REG.
Kingston, Canada.
Col. The Lt. Gen. com.for the time
being the Forces in Canada.
L.Cols. Francis Gordon Hibbert.
John Thomas Campbell.
Majors, W. H. Sharpe.
Edward Whyte.
Adj., H. Givins, *lt.*
Agent, Sir John Kirkland.

ROYAL MALTA FENCIBLE
ARTILLERY.
L.Col. Antonio Mattei, *c.*
Saverio Gatt, *c.*
Adj., P. Bernard, *lt.*
Agent, Sir John Kirkland.

COMMISSARIAT STF. CORPS
*Hd. Quar.,*109,*Victoria St.,Westr.*
Stations.
A. Company ....Montreal.
B. Company ....Curragh.
C. Company ....Ireland.
D. Company ....Aldershot.
E. Company ....Aldershot.
Detachments, *Chatham,Woolwich,*
Bermuda, China and Gibraltar.
Staff Officer, Matthew B. Irvine,
(Assist. Comm. Gen.).

MIL. STORE STAFF CORPS.
Hd. Quar.,Roy.Arsenal, Woolwich.
Staff Officer, W. H. Parkyn, (Sup.
of Stores).

PAY OF THE ARMY.

Staff Appointments.	Pr. Ann.		Per Ann.
Field-Marshal Gen. Command.-in-Chief	£5,999	Adjt.-Gen.—When held by a Gen. Officer..	£1,383
General ditto	3,458	Ditto When held by a Colonel	1,095
General	2,075	Deputy Adjutant-General	691
Lieutenant-General	1,383	Assistant Adjutant-General	346
Major-General	691	Deputy Assistant Adjutant-General	260
Brigadier-General	520	Qtrmr.-Gen.—When held by a Gen. Officer	1,383
Colonel	415	Ditto When held by a Colonel ...	1,095

	Per Ann.
Deputy Quartermaster-General	£691
Assistant Quartermaster-General—	
If serving at Head Quarters, when no D.Q.-M.-G. is employed there	501
If serving at Head Quarters, on half-pay of his Regimental Rank, when a D.Q.-M.-G. is employed there	346
Otherwise	260
Deputy Assist. Quartermaster-General—	
If serving at Head-Quarters, when no D.Q.-M.-G. is employed there	319
If serving at Head-Quarters when a D.Q.-M.-G. is employed there	260
If serving elsewhere	173
Military Sec. (other than at Hd. Quart.)	346
Assistant Military Secretary	173
Aide-de-Camp—To the Sovereign	190
Ditto To a General Officer	173
Major of Brigade	173
Inspector of Musketry	173
Deputy Judge Advocate	260
Recruiting District—Inspecting Fld. Off.	501
Ditto Adjutant	155
Volunteers' Staff—Inspector-General	691
Ditto Deputy Inspector	346
Assistant Inspector	173

DEPARTMENTAL PAY.	Pr. Ann.
Commissary-General	£1,095
Deputy Commissary-General	547
Assistant Commissary-General	273
Ditto (after 5 years' service as such)	365
Deputy Assistant Commissary-General	182
Ditto (after 5 years' service as such)	228
Acting Deputy Assist. Commissary-Gen.	136
1st Class Clerk or Storekeeper	82
2nd Class ditto	73
3rd Class ditto	63
(Increasing 6d. a-day after three years' service in the Class.)	
Civilian Commissariat Clerk, on appoint.	109
(Increasing 1s. 6d. a-day after each 5 years' service, to 12s. a-day.)	

Inspector-General of Hospitals	£730
Do. (after 25 years' service on full pay)	821
Do. " 30 years' " "	857
Do. " 35 years' " "	912
Deputy Inspector-General	547
Do. (after 25 years' full-pay service)	584
Do. " 30 years' " "	638
Do. " 35 years' " "	675
Surgeon-Major	438
Do. (after 25 years' full-pay service)	492
Surgeon	319
Do. (after 15 years' full-pay service)	365
Assistant-Surgeon	182
Do. (after 5 years' full-pay service)	228
Do. " 10 years' " "	273
Do. " 15 years' " "	319

Staff Veterinary Surgeon	383
Do. (after 20 years' service)	401
Do. " 25 years' "	419
Veterinary Surgeon, 1st Class	228
Do. (after 10 years' service)	264
Do. " 15 years' "	282
Do. " 20 years' "	310
Do. " 25 years' "	365
Veterinary Surgeon	182

	Per Ann.
Veterinary Surg. (after 5 years' service)	£209
Do. " 10 years' "	237
Do. " 15 years' "	255
Principal Purveyor	346
Do. (after 20 years' service)	392
Do. " 25 years' "	438
Purveyor	246
Do. (after 15 years' service)	273
Do. " 20 years' "	301
Do. " 25 years' "	328
Deputy Purveyor	173
Do. (after 10 years' service)	209
Do. " 15 years' "	228
Do. " 20 years' "	255
Assist. Purveyor (increasing to 9s. a-day)	91
Probationary Clerks	91

Barrackmaster, 1st Class	319
Do. (after 5 years' service in rank)	365
Do. " 10 years' " "	410
Do. " 15 years' " "	456
Barrackmaster, 2nd Class	136
Do. (after 5 years' service in rank)	182
Do. " 10 years' " "	228
Do. " 15 years' " "	273

Chaplains, 1st Class	365
Do. (after 25 years' service)	410
Chaplains, 2nd Class	319
Do. 3rd Class	273
Do. 4th Class	182
Do. (after 5 years' service)	228

Principal Superintendent of Stores	803
Superintendent of Stores	547
Deputy Superintendent of Stores	365
Do. (after 5 years' full-pay ser. in rank)	438
Assistant Superintendent of Stores	246
Do. (after 5 years' full-pay ser. in rank)	301
Deputy Assist. Superintendent of Stores	100
Do. (after 5 years' on full-pay)	146
Do. " 10 years' "	191

PRICES OF COMMISSIONS.

LIFE GUARDS.	£
Lieutenant-Colonel	7,250
Major	5,350
Captain	3,500
Lieutenant	1,785
Cornet	1,260

ROYAL REGIMENT OF HORSE GUARDS.	
Lieutenant-Colonel	7,250
Major	5,350
Captain	3,500
Lieutenant	1,600
Cornet	1,200

FOOT GUARDS.	
Captain, with rank of Lieutenant-Colonel	4,800
Lieutenant, with rank of Captain	2,050
Ensign, with rank of Lieutenant	1,200

CAVALRY AND INFANTRY OF THE LINE.	
Lieutenant-Colonel	4,500
Major	3,200
Captain	1,800
Lieutenant	700
Cornet or Ensign	450

In passing from one rank to another, the sum payable is the difference between the original price of the two commissions.

The above are the "regulation" prices, but it is notorious that the sums actually paid are much higher.

RANK.	Horse Artillry	LifeGds. &H.Gds.	Cavalry.	Artillry	Enginrs.	Foot Guards.	Infantry.
	£	£	£	£	£	£	£
Colonel of Regiment	1082	1800	1350	994	990	2200	1000
Colonel	584	...	...	474	474	...	...
Lieutenant-Colonel	488	532	419	326	326	419	292
Major	...	445	351	305	200	282	211
Captain	290	275	266	220	200	...	...
Second Captain	290	...	...	200	124	133	118
Lieutenant	179	188	164	124	124	133	118
Cornet	...	146	146	...	...	...	...
Ensign	...	...	...	...	...	100	95
Paymaster	228	...	228	228	228	...	228
Adjutant	320	237	209	231	179	182	182
Quartermaster	197	173	155	142	146	118	118
Riding Master	179	164	164	164	...	...	...
Veterinary Surgeon	182	182	182	182	182	...	...
Regimental Corporal or Serjeant Major	84	79	69	80	88	63	60
Troop or Company Serj.-Maj. or Corp.-Maj.	...	69	60	...	...	...	...
Quartermast., Corp.-Maj., &Quatmast.-Serj.	74	69	60	71	79	54	51
Colour and Company Serjeant	...	...	...	...	64	51	48
Staff Farrier and Carriage Smith	...	...	...	71	...	...	...
Serj. Farrier & Carriage or Shoeing ditto	65	...	...	...	63	...	...
Field Battery Serjeant Major	74	...	...	71	...	...	...
Armourer-Serjeant	57	50	45	54	55	94	94
Paymaster-Serjeant	57	...	45	54	...	...	...
Field Battery Quartermaster-Serjeant	74	...	...	...	...	...	...
Farrier Major (or Farrier Serjeant)	...	74	69	...	...	...	...
Farrier	...	59	48	...	...	...	...
Serjeant Instructor of Musketry	...	57	57	...	...	57	57
Saddler Serjeant	...	50	63	...	...	...	...
Hospital Serjeant	...	...	45	54	...	...	42
Orderly-room Clerk	...	50	45	...	...	42	39
Bandmaster	...	79	69	106	...	...	60
Battery Serjeant-Major	...	...	...	63	...	...	...
Battery Quartermaster-serjeant	...	...	...	71	...	...	...
Staff Collar Maker and Staff Wheeler	...	...	...	61	...	...	...
Farriers' and Carriage Smith	...	...	...	61	...	...	...
Serjeant of the Band	...	...	...	58	...	...	...
Corporals of the Band	...	...	...	46	...	...	...
Musicians	...	...	...	30	...	...	...
Master Gunners......£57, £66, and	...	...	...	94	...	...	...
Troop Staff Serjeant	...	...	...	...	74	...	...
Serjeant Tailor	...	...	...	...	...	...	...
Serjeants (Corporals in Household Cavalry)	57	50	45	54	55	42	39
Trumpet, Drum, Fife, Bugle, & Pipe Major	57	54	45	54	79	42	39
Kettledrummers	...	47	36	...	...	...	...
Trumpeters, Buglers, Fifers,Pipers,& Drum.	41	36	28	26	25	24	22
Corporals	45	...	32	42	{ 48	28	27
2nd Corporals	...	...	...	...	{ 37 }	...	...
Bombardiers	42	...	...	39	...	...	...
Collar Makers, Wheelers, Shoeing Smiths, Saddlers, and Harness Makers	{ 44 40 }	48	37	{ 41 37 }	36	...	...
Privates, Roughriders, Gunners, & Drivers	{ 29 26 }	36	25	26	{ 28 25 }	22	21
Boys	...	...	...	...	...	...	...

RESERVE FORCES.

These consist of the Militia, the Yeomanry Cavalry, the Volunteers, also a body of Enrolled Pensioners, and an Army Reserve Force recently created. Beside Staff Officers of Pensioners, 86 in number, whose duties mainly consist in paying the men's pensions and allowances, and preventing the frauds by personation (these were formerly not uncommon), the whole of the Reserve Forces are under the supervision of an Inspector-General, who takes the place of the former Inspector-General of Militia, and, in consequence of the much larger sphere of action, has a Deputy-Inspector to assist him, and eleven Assistant-Inspectors. The staff of the Reserve Forces is as follows:—

Inspector-General of Reserve Forces, Maj.-Gen. Hon. James Lindsay.

Deputy-Inspector of Reserve Forces, Bt.-Col. E. W. C. Wright.

I. DISTRICT.—West Central, East, North, and South Census Districts of London.—Bt. Col. James Daubeny, C.B.

II. DISTRICT.—Berks, Cinque Ports, Hants, Isle of Wight, Kent, rural parts of Surrey, Sussex, —Bt. Lt.-Col. Hon. William James Colville.

III. DISTRICT. Bedford, Berks, Cambridge, Essex, Hertford, Hunts. rural part of Middlesex, Norfolk, Oxford, Sussex,—Bt. Lt.-Col. Alex. J. H. Elliott, Unatt.

IV. DISTRICT.—Cornwall, Devon, Dorset, Gloucester, Somerset, Wilts,—Bt.-Col. Rob. Bruce.

V. DISTRICT.—Brecknock, Cardigan, Carmarthen, Glamorgan, Haverfordwest, Hereford, Monmouth, Pembroke, Northampton, Radnor, Rutland, Warwick, Worcester,—Bt.-Col. Sir F. Fitz-Gerald Campbell, Bart.

VI. DISTRICT.—Anglesea, Carnarvon, Cheshire, Denbigh, Derby, Flint, Isle of Man, Merioneth, Montgomery, Salop, Stafford,—Bt. Lt.-Col. Fred. George Thomas Deshon.

VII. DISTRICT.—Leicester, Lincoln, Nottingham, York, Bt. Lt.-Col. Arthur Wombwell.

VIII. DISTRICT.—Lancashire,—Bt.-Col. F. Green Wilkinson.

IX. DISTRICT. — Ayr, Berwick, Berwick-on-Tweed, Cumberland, Dumfries, Durham, Haddington, Kirkcudbright, Newcastle-on-Tyne, Northumberland, Roxburgh, Selkirk, Westmoreland, Wigton,—Bt.-Col. E. Roche.

X. DISTRICT. — Argyle, Bute, Clackmannan, Dumbarton, Lanark, Perth, Renfrew, Stirling,—Bt.-Col. E. G. Bulwer, C.B.

XI. DISTRICT.—Aberdeen, Banff, Caithness, Cromarty, Edinburgh, Elgin, Fife, Forfar, Kincardine, Kinross, Linlithgow, MidLothian, Nairn, Orkney, Peebles, Ross, Shetland, Sutherland,—Bt. Lt.-Col. George N. Boldero.

Full particulars of the constitution, strength, expense, &c., of the various bodies forming the Reserve Forces will be found in the article on the Army Estimates, under Votes 8, 9, 10, and 11.

The Naval and Military Estimates for 1868-69.

With Illustrations from other Parliamentary Papers.

ARMY.

THE Army Estimates for the year ending 31st March, 1869, amount to the sum of £15,455,400, and provide for a force of 137,530 men and 13,000 horses. This shows an additional charge of £203,200, and an increase of 245 men and 170 horses on the estimates of 1867-8, and is an advance on the actual expenditure of 1866-67 of £1,066,921, when 137,400 men (only 130 fewer) were employed. The total British establishment amounts to 136,650; but the force whose cost is to be defrayed out of the Army funds is 138,691—an excess of 2,041. The forces in India (British) number 64,466; in the colonies, 40,929; at home, 32,255. These numbers are made up of 6,549 officers, 345 regimental medical officers, 10,035 non-commissioned officers, 3,056 trumpeters and drummers, and 116,665 rank and file. The general staff numbers 251, and costs in pay and allowances, £101,815. The great heads of charge are:—

1. Pay and Allowances	£5,749,200
2. Commissariat	1,292,500
3. Clothing	496,900
4. Barracks	706,300
5. Divine Service	42,800
6. Martial Law	23,000
7. Hospitals	380,800
Total, Regular Forces	£8,691,500
8. Militia and Inspection of Reserve	986,800
9. Yeomanry Cavalry	88,000
10. Volunteer Corps	385,000
11. Enrolled Pensioners and Reserve	64,600
Total Reserve Forces	£1,524,500
12, 13. Military Store Departments ...	1,491,400
14. Works and Buildings	968,400
15. Military Education	169,300
16. Surveys of the United Kingdom...	118,600
17. Miscellaneous Services	142,700
18. Administration of the Army	224,600
Total Effective Services	£13,331,000
19. Rewards for Distinguished Services	26,700
20. Pay of General Officers	72,000
21. Retired Full and Half-Pay	470,800
22. Widows' Pensions, &c.	157,000
23. Pensions for Wounds	23,800
24. Chelsea and Kilmainham In-Pensions	33,600
25. Out-Pensions	1,184,600

26. Superannuation Allowances	£135,200
27. Militia, Yeomanry, &c.	20,700
Total Non-Effective Services	£2,124,400
Total	£15,455,400

In detail these votes are as follows:—
1. *Pay and Allowances.*—Increase, £49,168; decrease, £139,478—net decrease, £90,310. Staff pay and contingencies (cost £101,815) have increased £3,524; and regimental extra pay, mainly good conduct pay or for skill in arms (cost £215,141), £1,887; but the ordinary regimental pay (£4,825,119) has the large decrease of £104,446. There is a charge of £30,000 for a body of Indian troops (in number 880) for service in China, now first introduced. The whole cost of recruiting (£103,248) is £21,550 less than last year, the bounty to recruits having sunk from £82,000 to £60,000. The veterinary department (£5,248) is slightly increased in charge, and 1,443 horses are purchased at a cost of £53,300. The gunnery and engineering schools show an increase: gunnery (cost £7,855) of £2,101; engineering (cost £21,658) of £3,600; but musketry (cost £10,546) is reduced by £2,244; gymnastics (cost £2,321) by £129; and instruction in cookery (cost £369) by £31. Working pay for miscellaneous duties (as fire brigade, musketry warders, &c. cost £1,500) is increased by £500; and pay of 674 native military labourers in tropical climates (cost £7,100) by £100. Military Savings' Banks cost, for additional interest as before, £2,000. Expenses of discharged soldiers (£28,000—a decrease of £7,000) are made up of £1,000 gratuities to soldiers settling in the colonies; £7,000 gratuities to soldiers discharged by indulgence; and £20,000 to discharged soldiers and their families to take them home, and temporary allowance to widows and children. Travelling expenses of regimental officers (£10,000) show an increase of £1,210; and miscellaneous and unforeseen charges (£1,000), a decrease of £100. There are 3 lieutenant-generals, 12 major-generals, 8 brigadier-generals, and 8 colonels on the staff employed at home; total, 31; and 4, 11, 1, and 5 in the colonies; total, 21. The pay of the privates is as follows:—Household Cavalry, 2s. 0¼d.; Horse Artillery, 1s. 7¼d. or 1s. 5¼d.; Cavalry, 1s. 5d.; Foot Artillery, 1s. 5¼d.; Foot Guards, 1s. 3d.; Infantry, 1s. 2d.; Military Train, Commissariat Staff Corps, and

Military Store Staff Corps, 1s. 5d.; Army Hospital Corps, 1s. 2d.; West India Regiments, 1s.; Ceylon Rifles, 11d.; Cape Mounted Rifles, 1s.; Malta Fencible Artillery, 11d.; Canadian Rifles, 1s. 2d.; African Artillery, 1s. 3¼d.; Gun Lascars, 11d.

2. *Commissariat.*—Increase, £39,461; decrease, £36,900—net increase, £2,561. Pay, contingencies, and wages of the department (cost £103,810) have decreased £1,193; purchase of tools (cost £5,652), £241; cost of provisions and allowances in lieu (£514,114), £18,416, and colonial allowances, mainly for extra cost of provisions in China and Japan (£95,750), £17,050. But forage (cost £443,388) shows an increase of £36,265; and transport of troops (cost in the colonies, £62,914; at home, £67,500), £3,196. The commissariat establishment consists of 206 officers: 73 at home, 133 abroad.

3. *Clothing, &c.*—Increase, £53,409; decrease, £126,538—net decrease, £73,129. Pay, contingencies, rent and taxes, fuel and light of the various clothing establishments (cost £16,147) have decreased £235; but wages (£102,719) have increased £725. Materials for the manufacture of clothing (cost £509,746) have also increased £46,379; compensation in lieu of clothing (i.e., services performed at regiments—cost £50,693), £4,140; and implements and miscellaneous expenses (cost £4,000), £2,000; but manufactured clothing (value £418,288) has decreased £107,587; machinery (cost £534), £316; and packing and freight (cost £12,000), £1,500. The charge for buildings and police (£3,389) is transferred to Votes 14 and 17. The clothing establishments consist of a factory at Pimlico and another at Woolwich; inspection, store, and account departments, employing 58 officers and clerks, and 285 foremen, viewers, &c. The establishment performs many services for other departments, on payment, as supplying clothing for the troops in India, the Marines, the Volunteers, and the Militia, and inspects and issues clothing for the London and Dublin Metropolitan Police, the General Post Office, and the Custom House. The clothing supplies for the Army vary in value, per man, from £8 15s. 3d. in the Life and Horse Guards, "certain articles of saddlery and accoutrements" included; Horse Artillery, £4 14s. 4d.; Cavalry, £4 2s. 6d.; Foot Artillery, £3 13s. 4d.; Engineers, £4 9s. od.; ditto, Mounted Troops, £6 19s. 4d.; Military Train, £4 6s. od.; Foot Guards, £4 6s. od.; to Infantry of the Line, £3 7s. 6d. Of the various special services, the Military Store Staff Corps costs the highest, £4 10s. 6d, and the West India Regiments the lowest, £2 11s. 7d. A parliamentary paper (H. C. 115) gives, in much detail, the accounts of the clothing factories for the year 1866-67. Besides a general balance-sheet, amounting for Pimlico to £442,821 15s. 8d., and for Woolwich to £102,727 8s. od., there are given statements of manufactures, and also of repairs and alterations, in which the charges on every article are apportioned as follows:—Cost of material; labour, divided into cutting, and making by hand or machinery; indirect expenditure, i.e., portion of the establishment charges, total expenditure, and rate per garment. The enormous amount of "clerical work" that such returns as these must occasion, may be seen from such entries as these, it being noticed that the whole amount is only 5½d. "Military clerk's tunic altered and repaired, with 2d. of materials, at the charge of 3d. by piece-work—' total

direct labour,' 3d.; indirect expenditure, ½d.; grand total, 5½d." "Commissariat Staff Corps private's trousers repaired and altered, with 1d. of material, 2d. labour, and ¼d. indirect expenditure; grand total, 3¼d."

4. *Barracks.*—Increase, £60,272. Every item of this vote shows an increase. Pay, contingencies, and wages of labourers (cost £47,367) have increased £3,179; clothing of barrack sergeants, &c. (cost £2,100), £100; purchase and repair of furniture and stores (cost £116,000), £30,000; washing and repairing bedding, and purchase of palliasse straw (cost £42,672), £1,442; miscellaneous services, mainly sanitary (cost £27,621), £3,581; fuel and light (cost £270,000), £14,500; lodging allowance (cost £92,000), £1,500; rents, taxes, &c. (cost £98,000), £5,700. There are 52 barrack masters and 45 clerks employed.

5. *Divine Service.*—Increase, £1,989; decrease, £1,172—net increase, £817. Pay and contingencies (cost £24,122) have decreased £1,081, and rent of buildings hired for the performance of divine service, and payments for accommodation to the soldiery (cost £492), £91; but the allowances to officiating clergymen (cost £18,227) have increased £1,989. Beside the Chaplain-General, there are 83 chaplains (66 at home, 17 abroad) and 297 officiating clergymen (184 at home, 113 abroad).

6. *Martial Law.*—Increase, £2,325; decrease, £325—net increase, £2,000. Pay and contingencies of the Judge Advocate-General's establishment (cost £6,175) have increased £175; allowances to acting judge advocates and other expenses of courts martial remain, as before, at £2,000; pay and contingencies of military prisons, 18 in number (cost £24,269), have decreased £195; but the subsistence and other expenses of the prisoners (cost £24,139) have increased £493; expenses of confinement of men in civil gaols stand as in 1867-68 at £4,000; but the expenses of confinement of men in barrack-cells (cost £14,860) show a decrease of £140; and the expenses incurred for deserters (cost £13,270) have decreased £1,000. The establishment of the Judge Advocate-General consists of four deputy judges and three clerks. The expenses for deserters are divided in about equal proportions between a military police in garrisons and camps (£4,770); expenses on routes of deserters and their escorts (£4,000), and rewards for apprehension (£4,900). The number of men flogged between April 12 and December 31, 1867, was, Army, 17; Royal Marines, 2 (H. C. 102).

7. *Hospitals.*—Increase, £107,340; decrease, £2,158—net increase, £105,182. This increase is almost entirely due to the pay and contingencies of the medical department. The pay has been raised, so that though the numbers are now reduced from 680 to 673, the charge has risen from £114,072 to £218,660. Extra pay to compounders of medicine and orderlies (cost £4,664) has increased £133; but the cost of medicines (£21,200) and the allowances to private medical practitioners (£4,000) stand the same as in 1867-68. The pay of the staff (34 in number) of the General Hospitals at Netley and Woolwich (cost £4,450) has an increase of £66; and the charge for treatment of lunatics (cost £5,200) one of £700; the gross charge is £11,900, but £6,700 of this is met by the half-pay or pension of the patients. The pay and contingencies of the purveying department, (148 in number—cost £22,361) show a decrease of £137; and the purchase of furniture and stores (cost £6,000) one of £2,000; but all the

remaining items, as wages of orderlies and nurses, diet, &c., washing, rents, water supply, fuel and light, and miscellaneous services (cost altogether £104,246) give an increase of £2,562. The medical department consists of 329 staff and 345 regimental officers, total, 673. Of the staff 189 are employed at home, and 140 abroad; of the regimental officers, the greater number are abroad. The Army Hospital Corps numbers 1,003 men; 743 at home, 260 abroad.

8. *Militia and Inspection of Reserve.*—Increase, £82,588; decrease, £657—net increase, £81,931. Pay of inspecting staff of reserve forces (cost £5,565) has increased £4,972; but the pay of inspecting staff of militia in Ireland (cost £1,000) has decreased £407. The regimental, extra, and extra duty pay and allowances of the militia (cost £433,350) have increased £10,819; and the bounty and expenses of enrolment (cost £181,500) £8,000; travelling expenses, as in 1867-58 £24,000; but provisions and forage (cost £21,800) have increased £3,400. Clothing (cost £213,397) has increased £40,397; expenses of prison staff, mainly for apprehension of offenders under the Militia Acts (cost £1,800) have increased £200; hospital expenses (cost £11,200) £500; but divine service remains as in 1867-68 at £500; and contingent expenses (£5,100) show a decrease of £200. The staff of the militia numbers 160 adjutants, 130 quartermasters, and 4,776 non-commissioned officers and drummers. The Irish militia were not trained in 1867; but of the English and Scotch militias, numbering 3,485 officers, 3,765 non-commissioned officers, and 93,912 privates, there were absent from the training, 263 officers, 17 non-commissioned officers and 1,312 privates with leave, and 16 officers, 4 non-commissioned officers, and 3,959 privates without leave; and 1,347 officers, 340 non-commissioned officers, and 26,202 privates were wanting to complete the establishment. But this is mainly caused by the appointment of ensigns having been suspended since July, 1860, and the reduction of privates to 600 effectives in all regiments made in August, 1864 (H. C. 300).

9. *Yeomanry Cavalry.* — Increase £91; decrease, £91. Pay, &c., yeomanry cavalry (cost £55,837) shows a decrease of £91; but an exactly similar sum has been added to the extra pay and allowances (cost £31,513.) The miscellaneous charges (cost £650) remain as in 1867-68. The permanent staff consists of 362 individuals, (132 adjutants, 8 sergeant-majors, 276 sergeants, and 44 trumpeters), and the various corps amount to 15,823 officers and men.

10. *Volunteer Corps.*—Increase, £31,340; decrease, £7,190 — net increase, £24,150. Pay of adjutants to corps (cost £94,400), and of sergeant instructors (cost £58,000) show increases of £1,980 and £6,810 respectively. The capitation grant (cost £228,050) has increased £22,550; but the miscellaneous charges (cost £4,700) have decreased £200. The number of adjutants is 283, (with 108 more belonging to the corps) and the number of corps, 1,297—11 light horse, 221 artillery, 19 engineers, 7 mounted rifles, and 1,039 rifles, having a total establishment of 215,812 men. Of these, 187,864 are enrolled; 155,216 are efficient, 32,648 non-efficient, and 90,588 have earned the additional 10s. for extra efficiency. On 22 occasions in the year 1867 there were reviews, field-days, or camps sanctioned, at which not fewer than 1,000 volunteers were present. The highest number (24,450)

was at Dover, 22 April, and the lowest (1,064) at Cadbury, 17 August. (H. C. 382.)

11. *Enrolled Pensioners and Reserve.*—Increase, £9,600; decrease, £13,000—net decrease, £3,400. Pay, &c. of enrolled pensioners (cost £32,100) is an increase of £2,100; it includes £2,960 for command allowance to staff officers, £12,000 pay of pensioners during training, and £14,000 bounty money, at £1 a head. Pay, &c., of the reserve force (cost £21,000) shows a decrease of £13,000; it includes £2,400 for pay during training, £11,600 bounty money, at £4 a head, and £7,000 for men expected to engage under the provisions of the Army Reserve Act, 1867. The clothing for pensioners, &c. (cost £11,500) is an increase of £7,500. The army reserve is governed by a series of regulations drawn up under the authority of 30 & 31 Vict., c. 110, by the Secretary for War. It is to be composed of 50,000 men, in two classes. Class I., in number 20,000, are liable, when on permanent service, to duty in any part of the world; they must be soldiers who have not served more than one term of enlistment; they are to engage for a term of five years, and to receive £3 per annum bounty. Class II., in number 30,000, are liable only to service within the United Kingdom, and must be soldiers who decline to take a second engagement, or military or marine pensioners. No limit of age is fixed for Class I., but that of Class II. must not exceed 45 at the time of enrolment; their bounty is £2 per annum, and their period of service varies according to the time that they have already been in the army or marines. The pay is on the scale of 2s. per day for privates, up to 3s. 6d. for the sergeant-major, when called out for training or exercise, with 6d. additional if called out in aid of the civil power. Each man has also £1 per annum for boots, shirts, &c., but is provided with other clothing. The offences of the men of the reserve, as making away with necessaries, absence from training, &c., are to be punished by the deduction of fines from their pay, allowance, or pension. (H. C. 320.)

12, 13. *Military Store Departments.*—Increase, £122,925; decrease, £187,087—net decrease, £64,162. The departments comprised are 15 in number at home, and 3 abroad. Pay of establishments, with contingencies and rents (cost £120,120), show a decrease of £1,994; and wages (cost £656,798), one of £113,900. The establishments cost altogether £776,918. The materials employed (cost £396,161) show an increase of £47,191. The departments cost, for purchase or repair of stores, £494,068, against £499,557 in 1867-68—a decrease of £5,489. Small arms (cost £76,000) have decreased £55,000, and most of the other items of that year show a decrease, more or less considerable, amounting to £24,250 in the whole; but against this there is an increase of £9,830 for gun carriages (cost £40,830); of £22,490 for saddlery (cost £40,890), and of £42,841 for miscellaneous stores (cost £238,098)—a total increase of £74,761. The various charges of horse hire, freight, and machinery (cost £84,770) have decreased £16,547, machinery standing for £16,028 of the amount, and the charges for buildings and police have been removed to Votes 14 and 17. The departments are as follows:—

Woolwich Arsenal.—Carriage department. Salaries £10,156; wages, £127,35. Gun factories, £8,670 and £69,985. Laboratory, £7,814 and £189,990. Chemical and photographic establishment, £2,415 and £439. Gas factory, £91 and £2,981. Medical establishment, £1,309. School, £526.

Small Arms Establishments.—Enfield, £5,486 and £94,902. Birmingham, £1,878 and £13,390. *Waltham Abbey.*—Gunpowder factory, £2,912 and £11,048.

Portsmouth.—Ordnance factories, £1,118 and £9,716.

Devonport.—Laboratory, £966 and £5,841.

Machinery establishment, £1,654 and £514. There are also 18 instructors, from captains to sergeants, in the various departments, costing (with £120 for labourers) £2,944.

The Military Store department, numbering 270, costs, in pay and allowances, £89,348 ; and the War department has in its employ, vessels manned by 157 persons, whose pay and allowances amount to £10,191.

The Parliamentary paper referred to under Vote 3, gives very full details of the accounts of the manufacturing departments.

14. *Works and Buildings.*—Increase, £151,961 ; decrease, £26,912—net increase, £125,049. This estimate is for superintending all military works, buildings, and repairs, as well as for executing many of them. The Royal Engineer department, which is the supervising power, costs, in pay and contingencies, £95,894, an increase of £5,405. The survey of defensive positions, and incidental expenses, remain as before, £2,500 and £2,000 ; but photographic services (cost £150) have decreased £50. Fortifications and Military Store buildings (cost £253,075) have increased by £30,475 ; barracks (cost £213,868) by £20,768 ; but manufacturing establishments (cost £24,925) have decreased £19,900. Works on such buildings in amount less than £1,000 each, amount to £82,450, being a decrease of £6,952 ; but the ordinary and current repairs— fortifications, £60,000 ; barracks, £209,921 ; manufacturing establishments, £23,664 — together, £293,585, have increased £11,237. Beside the Royal Engineer officers employed (5 only of whom are charged in this estimate) there are 355 civilian surveyors, clerks, &c., and 93 military clerks and foremen. The chief charges at home are, at Windsor, £18,000 for additional land and buildings at the Infantry barracks ; £15,000 for the purchase of Warley barracks ; and £10,000 for reforming the river defences of Tilbury and New Tavern Forts. But abroad, £70,000 are required for defences at Bermuda ; £25,000 for the same service in Nova Scotia and New Brunswick ; £35,000 for Quebec ; and £15,000 each for Malta and Gibraltar. Huts at Hongkong stand for £12,000, and a new hospital at Halifax for £10,000, beside many minor charges. Special services at various stations cost £146,650. Among these are, adapting works to modern armaments, £10,000 ; defence of harbours, £35,000 ; £30,000 for married soldiers' quarters ; and £20,000 for lock hospitals (Contagious Diseases Act).

As connected with this vote, a Parliamentary paper (H. C. 488) shows that the sum of £5,950,000 was authorized to be raised for the expenses of fortification in the United Kingdom, by Acts 23 and 24 Vict. c. 109 ; 25 and 26 Vict. c. 78 ; 26 and 27 Vict. c. 80 ; 27 and 28 Vict. c. 109 ; 28 and 29 Vict. c. 61 ; and 30 and 31 Vict. c. 45. The sum of £5,030,000 has been raised, and terminable annuities at 3¼ per cent. to the amount of £347,153 created ; the annuities will expire 5th April, 1885. £920,000 still remains to be raised. The sum of £5,004,884 18s. 5d. has

been expended up to April 1, 1868. The fortifications on which it has been laid out, are at Portsmouth, Plymouth, Pembroke, Portland, Gravesend, Chatham, Sheerness, Dover, and Cork.

15. *Military Education.*—Increase, £5,876 ; decrease, £1,496—net increase, £4,290. The Council of Military Education (cost £8,205), shows an increase of £8 ; the Woolwich Academy (cost £38,581) one of £1,856 ; the Cadet College, Sandhurst (cost £36,731), one of £1,577 : the department for instruction of Artillery officers (cost £2,943) one of £53; and the Military Medical School (cost £9,600) one of £185. But the Staff College, Sandhurst (cost £7,955) has decreased by £641; the Chelsea Military Asylum and Normal School (cost £14,917) by £299; and the Hibernian School, Dublin (cost £11,378), by £556. On the other hand, the charge for regimental and garrison schools and libraries (£39,015) has increased by £2,107. The Council of Military Education consists of 6 members, a secretary, and a board of examiners, whose pay amounts to £3,220. There are 34 professors and masters and 200 cadets at Woolwich ; 29 professors and masters and 300 cadets at Sandhurst ; and 9 professors and masters and 30 students at the Staff College. The department for instruction of Artillery officers has a director and an assistant director, and 6 instructors, professors, and masters. The Military Medical School has 4 professors and 4 assistant professors, and the allowance to the examiners of candidates for the Army medical service is £400. As to regimental and garrison schools, there are 2 inspectors and 5 assistants, 221 schoolmasters, and 176 schoolmistresses. For libraries and reading-rooms there is an allowance of £2 10s per annum for each troop, battery, or company, on the British establishment (cost £4,000), £603 for librarians, and special allowances £168, making the whole charge—for schools £34,244, and for libraries, and games for troops proceeding to the colonies, £4,771.

16. *Surveys of the United Kingdom.*—Increase, £30,255. Pay and extra pay, &c., of the staff (cost £6,975) has increased by £557; of non-commissioned officers and sappers (cost £13,818) by £1,380; of civil assistants, meresmen, and labourers (cost £77,777) by £19,458; travelling expenses (cost £1,700) by £500; rents, stores, buildings and repairs, and contingencies (cost £18,330) by £8,380. The establishment has been increased in number, and now consists of 20 members of the staff, 454 non-commissioned officers and sappers, 800 civil assistants, and 450 labourers—a total of 1,724.

17. *Miscellaneous Services.*—Increase, £26,330; decrease, £32,830—net decrease, £6,500. The cost of the Ordnance Committee (£8,133) has decreased £208, and the rewards to inventors (£6,500) £18,600; the Special Experimental Committees, which cost £1,031 in 1867-68, do not appear in the present estimates. Expenses arising from the Contagious Diseases Act (cost £20,795) show an apparent decrease of £7,476, but £21,583 more appears under other heads, making a real increase of £14,107. Many of the items are fixed charges, as grants to certain hospitals, churches, &c., pay of military attachés abroad, law charges, instruction of soldiers in trades, &c. But advertisements (cost £5,000) show an increase of £1,000 ; and £13,419 is the cost of police for various Government establishments, formerly charged to each establishment,

but now for the first time brought under the Miscellaneous vote. The Guernsey and Jersey militia (cost £12,432) show an increase of £3,324; maintenance of telegraph and signal stations (cost £2,267) one of £815; compensation for losses (cost £1,800) one of £200; the magnetic and meteorological department, Woolwich (cost £686) one of £536; equipping a ship for hospital and sanitary purposes at Hong Kong (cost £9,500) one of £3,500; field allowances in the colonies (cost £1,000) one of £1,915; and medals (cost £100) one of £100. The remaining items, of Tower Armouries (cost £1,185), Royal Artillery Institution (cost £180), and Miscellaneous (cost £276), show small increases of £2, £11, and £23 respectively. The Ordnance Committee (with a sub-committee on small arms) consists of 7 members, a secretary and an assistant secretary, and has 10 clerks, a draughtsman, an armourer, and 5 printers attached to it. Among the experimental services appear £15,000 for rifled guns and ammunition, and £13,000 for shields, targets, and iron plates. The telegraphic establishments are at Head Quarters and the London barracks, Aldershot, Portsmouth, Bermuda, Gibraltar, Malta, and St. Helena. The Tower Armouries, which cost £1,185, produced as fees in 1867 the sum of £2,046 14s. 10d.; 15 warders, 1 collector, and 2 armoury keepers are employed.

18. *Administration of the Army.*—Increase, £6,979; decrease, £961—net increase, £6,011. This is divided into 3 departments. *Secretary of State for War*: salaries, contingencies, &c. (cost £169,487), shows an increase of £6,033. *Commander-in-Chief*: salaries, contingencies, &c. (cost £49,435), one of £187. *Topographical*: salaries, contingencies, &c. (cost £5,556), one of £171. The Secretary at War's department numbers 28 members, with a chief and 433 other clerks, and 103 office keepers, messengers, &c. The Commander-in-Chief's department numbers 23 members, with 1 principal and 80 other clerks, a military draughtsman, and 20 office keepers, messengers, &c. The Topographical department numbers 24 members, of whom 18 are civil assistants, and 7 labourers.

19. *Rewards for Distinguished Services.*—Increase, £600. Rewards to officers (cost £21,500) show an increase of £500, and to sergeants (cost £4,365) of £70. The Victoria Cross pensions (cost £840) have increased £30. The rewards are enjoyed by 181 officers and 319 sergeants, and the Victoria Cross pensions of £10 each are held by 111 non-commissioned officers and men. 27 of these pensions are paid by the Indian Government, and 70 of the recipients are now serving with their regiments; the remaining 41 have been discharged.

20. *Pay of General Officers.*—There is no alteration in the sum (£72,000) for the payment of General Officers who are not colonels of regiments. The number is 153, the same as in 1867-68.

21. *Retired Full and Half-pay.* — Increase, £9,700; decrease, £1,700—net increase, £8,000. Full pay of reduced and retired officers (cost £127,000) shows an increase of £5,000; and half-pay and military allowances (cost £331,500) one of £4,700; but the half-pay, &c., to officers of disbanded foreign corps (cost £12,300) gives a decrease of £1,700. The number of officers retired on full-pay is 381; of those on half-pay, 2,073; and of those on foreign half-pay, 286.

22. *Widows' Pensions, &c.*—Decrease, £1,636. Widows' pensions (cost £115,950) have decreased by £921; compassionate allowances (cost £23,466) by £69; and Royal bounty and relief fund (cost £17,563) by £646. There are 2,056 widows pensioned; 1,726 individuals who receive compassionate allowances, being the children of deceased officers; and 175 individuals who share in the Royal bounty, being widows, mothers, or sisters of officers who have been killed or mortally wounded in action.

23. *Pensions for Wounds.*—Decrease, £1,370. The number of wounded officers receiving pensions is 235. It was 249 in 1867-68.

24. *Chelsea and Kilmainham Hospitals.* — Decrease, £2,212. Chelsea Hospital (cost £26,754) shows a decrease of £2,005; and Kilmainham (cost £6,808) one of £207. Chelsea has beside, a secretary and 14 clerks, 11 military officers, 25 ward orderlies, 30 nurses, and 538 in-pensioners. Kilmainham has 4 military officers, 7 nurses, and 137 in-pensioners.

25. *Out-Pensioners.*—Increase, £100; decrease, £2,267—net decrease, £2,167. The out-pensions (cost £1,156,000) have decreased £2,267; but the allowances to staff officers and others for paying and superintending the pensioners (cost £28,610) have increased £100. The out-pensioners are in number 61,748 (62,730 in 1867-68), at rates varying from 1½d. to 3s. 10d. per diem. The sum of £1,350 is the amount of pensions granted to men who commuted their former pensions, with a view of settling in the colonies.

26. *Superannuation Allowances.* — Decrease, £809. The sum (£133,200) is divided among 1,038 individuals of very various ranks, and £2,000 is held in hand for gratuities.

27. *Militia, Yeomanry, &c.* — Increase, £219; decrease, £2,500—net decrease, £2,281. Retired allowances to militia officers (cost £15,500) show a decrease of £1,000, and militia out-pensions (cost £4,500) one of £1,500. Retired allowances to yeomanry cavalry and volunteer officers (cost £475 and £279) have increased £110 and £100 respectively. There are 309 pensioned militia officers, 484 pensioned militiamen, and 5 retired adjutants of yeomanry, and 4 of volunteers.

From the foregoing, it appears that £90,250 is saved on pay, &c.; £73,100 on clothing; £3,400 on the enrolled pensioners and Army reserve; £64,100 on military store departments; £6,500 on miscellaneous services; and £10,500 on pensions and other non-effective services. On the other hand, works and buildings show an increase of £125,049; hospital establishments, £105,182; militia and reserve, £81,931; and volunteers, £24,150; the surveys of the United Kingdom, £30,255. The administration of the Army shows an increase of £6,011; administration of martial law, £2,000; divine service, £817; rewards for distinguished services, £600; the commissariat, £2,561. It must also be noticed that the sum of £539,806 15s. was paid into the Treasury during the year 1867 by the War Office, being military contributions from some of the colonies, payments by the students of the Military Colleges, rent of lands belonging to the department, sale of old clothing, fines levied on contractors, &c., &c.

16 Votes, Increase..................		£451,050
11 ,, Decrease..................		247,850
Net Increase		£203,200

𝔑𝔞𝔟𝔞𝔩 𝔖𝔢𝔯𝔟𝔦𝔠𝔢.

Amount Voted for the Year 1868-69, £11,177,290.

ADMIRALTY (£182,364).

NAVAL DEPARTMENT.—Whitehall. 10 to 4.

LORDS COMMISSIONERS :—
Right Hon. Henry Childers, M.P., £4,500.

Private Sec.,	
Private Sec.,	£300.
Private Sec.,	
Private Sec.,	
Private Sec.,	
Private Sec.,	

First Sec. Private Sec.,
Second Sec. Private Sec., H. J. V. S.Neale, Esq.

Chief Clerk, John Henry Briggs, Esq., £1,100.

Acting Director-Gen. of Naval Ordnance, Rear-Admiral A. Cooper Key, C.B., F.R.S.

HYDROGRAPHIC DEPARTMENT, Whitehall. £19,042.
Hydrographer, Capt. G. H. Richards, R.N., £1,000.
Chief Naval Assistant, Magnetic Department, Staff Commander F. J. O. Evans, R.N., F.R.S., £500.
Civil Assistants, Commander Edward Dunsterville, £600, William Blackney, Esq.,Paymaster, R.N., £450, and D. Griffiths Dimsey, Esq. (for pilotage duties) £338.
Naval Assistants, Staff Commanders John Burdwood, £422, James Penn, John E. Davis, George F. McDougall, and Thomas A. Hull.
Superint. of Compasses, Staff Com. W. Mayes.
Superint. of Charts, Capt. Richard Hoskin, £400.
COMPTROLLER OF THE NAVY, Whitehall. £19,138.
Comptroller, Vice-Ad. Sir R. S. Robinson, £1,300.
Private Sec., R. B. Yorke, Esq.
Chief Constructor, Edward J. Reed, C.B., £1,000.
Assistant Constructors, Frederick K. Barnes, Nathaniel Barnaby, and James B. C. Crossland, Esqrs., each £500.
Surveyor and Inspector of Contract Work, James Luke, Esq. £752.
Valuer and Inspector of Dockyard Work, Wm. B. Robinson, Esq., £752.
Chief Clerk, Walter D. Eden, Esq., £850.
STEAM BRANCH, 22, New St., Spring Gardens.
Engineer in Chief of the Navy, Thomas Lloyd, Esq., C.B., £900.
Assistant, James Wright, Esq., £550.
Inspecting Officer, James Steil, Esq., R.N., £200.
First-class Chief Clerk, Chas. Edward Lang, Esq.
Chief Draughtsman, James Graff, Esq.

DEPARTMENTS.

ACCOUNTANT-GENERAL, Somerset House. £53,278.
Accountant-General, Jas. Beeby, Esq, £1,300.
Assistant Accountant, Pay, J.Whiffin, Esq., £1,000.
Ditto, *Cash*, H. W. R. Walker, Esq., £1,000.
Chief Clerk, Pay, James Reddie, Esq.
Chief Clerk, Cash, Henry Butler, Esq.
Inspector of Yard Accounts, Henry Brady, Esq.
First-class Clerks, Charles Spence, Robert Atkinson, James Bowden, G. C. Harrison, Joseph Nash, John Matson, E. H. Hay, G. H. Johnson, Esqs.
STOREKEEPER-GENERAL, Somerset House. £7,726.
Storekeeper-Gen., Hon. Robert Dundas, £1,300.
First-class Clerk, Nelson Girdlestone, Esq.

Registrar of Contracts & Public Securities, Antonio Brady, Esq., £850.
Chief Clerk, A. S. Stuart, Esq.
COMPTROLLER OF VICTUALLING, Somerset House. £15,315.
Comptroller of Victualling, Charles Richards, Esq., R.N., £1,300.
Chief Clerk, Charles Champ, Esq., £850.
Clerk, Frederick Perigal, Esq., £800.
Clerks, first class, Anthony Pike, Samuel S. Lewis, and Matthew G. Jefferson, Esqrs., each £650.
MEDICAL DIRECTOR-GENERAL, Somerset House. £4,480.
Director Gen., Alexander Bryson, Esq., M.D., C.B., F.R.S., £1,300.
Chief Clerk, William King Fossett, Esq., £800.
TRANSPORTS, Somerset House (£7,590).
Director, Capt. W. R. Mends, R.N., C.B., £1,200.
Deputy, Capt. Charles Cruttenden, £365.
Chief Clerk, William Willis, Esq., £850.
ENGINEERING AND ARCHITECTURAL WORKS, 2 & 3, Spring Gardens Terrace. £5,255.
Director, Lt.-Col. A. Clarke, R.E., £1,300.
Examiner of Accounts, George Higgs, Esq., £500.
Principal Clerk, J. Russell, Esq., £399.
Chief Draftsman, E. J. Woodhead, Esq., £422.
Clerks and Accountants, J. Davis, C. F. Wootton, Esqrs., £500.
COAST GUARD OFFICE, 26, Spring Gardens. £6,441.
Comptroller General, Rear-Adm. J. Walter Tarleton, C.B., A.D.C., £1,264.
Deputy, Capt. George Wodehouse, R.N., £700.
First-class Clerk, John Coltson, Esq., £543.
Surveyor of Buildings, Henry Case,.Esq., £400.

Director of Education for the Admiralty, Rev. Joseph Woolley, LL.D., £964.
ROYAL NAVAL COLLEGE, PORTSMOUTH. £3,037.
Gov., Right Hon. T. L. Corry, M.P.
Capt.-Superint., Capt. Arthur W. A. Hood, £258.
Professor, Rev. T. J. Main, M.A., F.R.A.S., £600.
Instructor in Fortification, Maj. Hen. B. Roberts, R.M.A., £200.
Assist. Observatory, John Deans, Esq., £120.
Clerk, Henry F. Kirkham, Esq., £200.
ROYAL OBSERVATORY AT GREENWICH. £4,736.
Astron. Royal, G. Biddel Airy, Esq., M.A., £1,000.
First Assist., Edward J. Stone, £400.
Sup. of Chronometer, G. B. Airy, Esq.
Sup. of Nautical Almanac, J. R. Hind, Esq., £500.

FLAG OFFICERS IN COMMISSION AND THEIR SECRETARIES.

Nore	*Vice-Ad.* Sir B. W. Walker, Bart., K.C.B.	Formidable	*Sec.*, C. A. Pritchard.
Portsmouth	*Admiral* Sir Thomas S. Pasley, Bart.	Victory	*Sec.*, Arthur Price.
Devonport	*Adm.* Sir William F. Martin, Bart.,K.C.B.	RoyalAdelaide.	*Sec.*, F. F. Fegen.
Queenstown, Ireland	*Rear-Admiral* F. Warden, C.B.	Mersey	*Sec.*, G. W. Underhill
Woolwich	*Commodore* William Edmondstone, C.B.	Fisgard	*Sec.*, Francis J. Lory.

FLAG OFFICERS IN COMMISSION AND THEIR SECRETARIES—*continued.*

Channel Squadron.	*Vice-Admiral* Sir T. Symonds, K.C.B.	Minotaur	... *Sec.*, F. Love.
	Rear-Ad. Alfred P. Ryder, *Second*	Penelope	... *Sec.*, Thomas Royle.
Mediterranean........	*Vice-Ad.* Lord Clarence E. Paget, C.B. ...	Caledonia	... *Sec.*, H. H. Shanks.
North America and West Indies	*Vice-Ad.* Sir George R. Mundy, K.C.B......	Royal Alfred	*Sec.*, J. Ashby, C.B.
	Commodore A. Phillimore, *Jamaica*	Aboukir	...... *Sec.*, R. J. B. Smart.
Pacific.	*Rear-Ad.* Hon. G. F. Hastings, C.B.	Zealons	...... *Sec.*, Henry Perry.
	Comm. R. A. Powell, C.B. *Southern Division.*	Topaze	...... *Sec.*, R. Sainthill.
S. E. Coast of Amer.	*Rear-Admiral* George Ramsay, C.B.	Narcissus	... *Sec.*, Edwin Harris.
China	*Vice-Ad.* Hon. Sir H. Keppel, K.C.B.	Rodney	...... *Sec.*, Wm. B. Risk.
	Comm. Oliver J. Jones, *Hong Kong.......*	P. Charlotte.	*Sec.*, Fra. A. Carter
East Indies	*Commodore* Leopold G. Heath, K.C.B.	Octavia	... *Sec.*, H. H. Wyatt.
Australia	*Commodore* Rowley Lambert, C.B.	Challenger...	*Sec.*, F.W.S.Ponsonby
Cape of Good Hope ...	*Commodore* George G. Randolph	Seringapatm	*Sec.*, Silas Waymouth
W. Coast of Africa ...	*Commodore* William M. Dowell, C.B.	Rattlesnake .	*Sec.*, W. J. C. Row.
Admiral Super. Portsmouth	*Rear-Admiral* Geo. G. Wellesley, C.B. ...	Asia.............	*Sec.*, G. H. Harvey. (civilian).
Admiral Super-Devonport	*Rear-Admiral* Hn. J. R. Drummond, C.B......	Indus	*Sec.*, John Besley. (civilian).
Admiral Super. Malta	*Rear-Admiral* Edward G. Fanshawe	Hibernia.......	*Sec.*, Fredk. Penfold.

FLAG OFFICERS.

ADMIRALS OF THE FLEET.

Sir Lucius Curtis, Bart., K.C.B.
Sir Thos. J. Cochrane, G.C.B.
Sir G. F. Seymour, G.C.H., G.C.H.

ADMIRALS.

Sir W. Bowles, K.C.B., V.-Ad. U.K.
Sir George Rose Sartorius, K.C.B.
Sir Fairfax Moresby, G.C.B., *Rear-Admiral U.K.*
Sir Houston Stewart, G.C.B.
Sir Provo W. Parry Wallis, K.C.B.
Sir W. J. Hope Johnstone, K.C.B.
Sir W. F. Martin, Bart., C.B.
Sir Henry J. Leeke, K.C.B., K.H.
Sir Chs. Howe Fremantle, G.C.B.
Sir Michael Seymour, G.C.B.
Henry Eden.
Hon. Sir Fred. Wm. Grey, G.C.B.
Sir Rbt. Lambert Baynes, K.C.B.
John Alexander Duntze.
C. R. Drinkwater Bethune, C.B.
Sir Charles Talbot, C.B.
Sir Thomas Sabine Pasley, Bart.
Rt. Hon. Lord E. Russell, C.B.
Sir Henry J. Codrington, K.C.B.
Rt. Hon. Thos. Earl of Lauderdale, K.C.B.

VICE-ADMIRALS.

Sir Robert Smart, K.C.B., K.H.
Sir Geo. Rodney Mundy, K.C.B.
Hon Sir Henry Keppel, K.C.B.
John Elphinstone Erskine.
Sir James Hope, G.C.B.
Sir R. W. Walker, Bart., K.C.B.
Sir Alexander Milne, K.C.B.
Rt. Hon. Lord C. E. Paget, C.B.
Richard Laird Warren.
George Elliot.
Sir Sydney C. Dacres, K.C.B.
Sir Lewis Tobias Jones, K.C.B.

Robert Fanshawe Stopford.
Robert Spencer Robinson.
Sir T. M. C. Symonds, K.C.B.
Woodford John Williams.
Sir Augustus L. Kuper, K.C.B.
Charles Eden, C.B.
Hon. Charles G. J. B. Elliot, C.B.
Hon. Joseph Denman.
George St. Vincent King, C.B.
Edward Pellew Halsted.
Charles Frederick.
Henry Kellett, C.B.

REAR ADMIRALS.

William Hy. A. Morshead, C.B.
Richard Collinson, C.B.
George Ramsay, C.B.
Hastings R. Yelverton, C.B.
George Henry Seymour, C.B.
George Greville Wellesley, C.B.
Hon. George F. Hastings, C.B.
Hon. Swynfen T. Carnegie, C.B.
Frederick Warden, C.B.
Arthur Lowe.
Edward Gennys Fanshawe.
Claude Hy. Mason Buckle, C.B.
Hon. Thomas Baillie.
George Giffard, C.B.
Sir F. W. E. Nicolson, Bart., C.B.
Hon. James R. Drummond, C.B.
John Lort Stokes.
Arthur Forbes.
Frederick Henry H. Glasse, C.B.
Charles Gepp Robinson.
George Thomas Gordon.
Erasmus Ommanney, C.B., F.R.S.
Douglas Curry.
George W. D. O'Callaghan, C.B.
Thomas Pickering Thompson.
Wallace Houstoun.
William John C. Clifford, C.B.

William Loring, C.B.
John Fulford.
Alfred Phillipps Ryder.
Henry Chads.
Francis Scott, C.B.
Arthur Farquhar.
Edwin Clayton T. D'Eyncourt.
Thomas Henry Mason.
Sidney Grenfell, C.B.
Richard Strode Hewlett, C.B.
Sir John C. D. Hay, Bart., F.R.S.
James Horsford Cockburn.
James Wilcox, C.B.
Hugh Dunlop, C.B.
Astley Cooper Key, C.B., F.R.S.
Frederick Byng Montresor.
Charles Farrel Hillyar.
Edward Southwell Sotheby, C.B.
Michael De Courcy, C.B.
John Walter Tarleton, C.B.
Rt. Hon. Lord F. Herbert Kerr.

NAVAL AIDES-DE-CAMP TO THE QUEEN.

Adm. Rt. Hon. T. Earl of Lauderdale, K.C.B.
Capts., Hon. Francis Egerton.
William R. Mends, C.B.
Arthur P. E. Wilmot, C.B.
Charles F. A. Shadwell, C.B.
William Edmonstone, C.B.
Frederick A. Campbell.
Frederick B. P. Seymour, C.B.
Geoffrey T. P. Hornby.
William Houston Stewart, C.B.
Sir F. L. McClintock, Kt., F.R.S.

MARINE AIDES-DE-CAMP TO THE QUEEN.

Cols., Samuel N. Lowder, C.B.
George Lambrick.

SHIPS IN COMMISSION, WITH THEIR CAPTAINS. [Nov. 1, 1868.]

Aboukir, 86, screw, receiving-ship, Commodore Augustus Phillimore, Jamaica.
Achilles, 26, sc., armour-plated, Capt. E. W. Vansittart, C.B., Channel Squadron. [China.
Adventure, 2, sc. trp. sh., Capt. H. J. Raby, V.C.,
Antelope, 3, paddle s.-ves. Lt.-Com. J. Buchanan, Mediterranean.
Arethusa, 35, sc. fri., Capt. R. Coote, Mediterranean.
Argus, 6, pad. slp., Com. F. W. Hallowes, China.

Asia, st. grd. shp. of res., Rear-Adm. G. G. Wellesley, C.B., Capt. E. B. Rice, Portsmouth.
Avon, 2, double-sc. composite gun-vessel, Com. G. D. Fitzroy, China and Japan.
Banterer, sc. gn.-bt., Lt.-Com. J. E. Pringle, China.
Barracouta, 6, paddle-sloop, Com. G. D. Bevan, North America and West Indies.
Basilisk, 6, pad.-sl., Capt. W. N. W. Hewett, V.C., China, ordered home.

SHIPS IN COMMISSION, &c.—*continued.*

Beacon, 2, sc. gunboat, Com. E. T. Parsons, South-east Coast of America.

Bellerophon, 14, sc. armour-plated, Capt. R. J. J. G. Macdonald, Channel Squadron.

Black Prince, 41, sc. iron armour-plated, Capt. A. C. Gordon, Greenock. [Australia.

Blanche, 6, sc.-sloop, Capt. J. E. Montgomerie,

Boscawen, 20, train.-sh., Com. R. O. Leach, Portland.

Brilliant, 16, Naval Reserve drill-ship, Com. F. M. Prattent, Dundee.

Brisk, 16, sc.-corvette, Capt. C. W. Hope, Australia, ordered home.

Bristol, 31, sc.-frigate, Capt. F. W. Wilson, particular service.

Britannia, 8, tr.-sh., Capt. J. Corbett, Dartmouth.

Britomart, sc.-gunboat, Lt.-Com. A. H. Alington, Lake Erie. [China.

Bustard, sc.-gunboat, Lt.-Com. C. F. W. Johnson,

Buzzard, 6, paddle-sloop, Staff-Com. J. G. H. Thain, particular service.

Caledonia, 30, sc., armour-plated, Capt. A. H. Gardiner, flagship of Vice-Admiral the Rt. Hon. Lord Clarence E. Paget, C.B., Mediterranean.

Cambridge, gunnery-ship, Capt. Hon. F. A. C. Foley, Devonport.

Cameleon, 17, sc.-sl., Com. W. H. Auncsley, Pacific.

Caradoc, 2, paddle st.-vessel, Lt.-Com. Hon. H. H. A'Court, Mediterranean.

Castor, 22, Naval Reserve drill-ship, Com. Charles G. Nelson, North Shields.

Challenger, 18, sc.-corvette, Commodore Rowley C. Lambert, C.B., Australia.

Chanticleer, 17, sc.-sloop, Com. W. W. S. Bridges, Pacific. [Pacific.

Charybdis, 17, sc.-corvette, Capt. A. M'L. Lyons,

Cherub, sc.-gunboat, Lt. S. R. Huntley, Lk. Huron.

Cockatrice, sc.-gunboat, Com. James Ferris Prowse, Mediterranean.

Cockchafer, sc.-gunboat, Lt.-Com. H. Kerr, China.

Constance, 35, sc.-frigate, Capt. H. T. Burgoyne, F. G, North America and West Indies.

Cormorant, 4, sc. gun-ves. Com. G. D. Broad, China.

Cracker, 2, double-sc. composite gun-ves., Com. Hawksworth Fawkes, S. E. Coast of America.

Crocodile, 3, Indian troop-ship, Capt. George W. Watson, Portsmouth.

Cruiser, 5, sc.-sl., Com. M. Singer, Mediterranean.

Cumberland, 24, guard-ship of Reserve, Capt. the Hon. A. A. Cochrane, C.B., Sheerness.

Dædalus, 16, Naval Reserve drill-ship, Com. Iltid T. M. Nicholl, Bristol.

Danae, 6, sc.-sloop, Capt. Sir Malcolm Macgregor, Bart., West Coast of Africa.

Daphne, 4, sc.-sloop, Com. G. L. Sullivan, E.Indies.

Dart, 5, sc. gun-vessel, Com. Marcus Lowther, North America and West Indies.

Dasher, 2, st.-ves., Com. J. H. Bushnell, Chan. Is.

Dauntless, 31, sc.-frigate, Capt. E. P. B. Von Donop, Coast-guard, Humber.

Defence, 18, sc., armour-plated, Capt. Charles H. May, Channel Squadron.

Donegal, 81, sc.-ship, Capt. E. W. Turnour, Coast-guard, Birkenhead.

Doris, 24, sc.-frigate, Capt. Henry Carr Glyn, North America and West Indies.

Dove, sc. gunboat, Lt.-Com. M. J. Dunlop, China.

Drake, sc. gunboat, Lt.-Com. C. Crowdy, China.

Dromedary, 2, sc. iron store-ship, Staff-Com. James Kiddle, West Coast of Africa.

Dryad, 4, sc.-sloop, Com. P. H. Colomb, E.Indies.

Duke of Wellington, 49, sc., receiving-ship, Capt. Thomas Cochran, Portsmouth.

Duncan, 81, sc.-ship, Capt. C. Fellowes, Coast-guard service, Queensferry, North Britain.

Durham, 20, Naval Reserve drill-ship, Com. G. G. Duff, Sunderland.

Dwarf, 2, double-sc. composite gun-vessel, Com. C. F. Walker, China.

Eagle, 16, Naval Reserve drill-ship, Com. E. C. Symons, Liverpool.

Eclipse, 6, sc.-sloop, Capt. Henry Harvey, North America and West Indies.

Egmont, 4, receiving and store-ship, Capt. H. F. W. Ingram, Rio de Janeiro.

Endymion, 21, sc.-fri., Capt. C. Wake, Mediterran.

Enterprise, 4, sc.-sloop, armour-plated, Com. G. S. Bosanquet, Mediterranean.

Euphrates, 3, Indian troop-ship, Capt. Montagu B. Dunn, Bombay. [Portsmouth.

Excellent, gunnery-ship, Capt. A. W. A. Hood,

Falcon, 17, sc.-sl., Com. H. L. Perceval, Woolwich.

Favorite, 10, sc.-corvette, armour-plated, Capt. J. D. M'Crea, North America and W. Indies.

Firm, sc.-gunboat, Lieut.-Com. Horace W. Rochfort, China. [wich.

Fisgard, 42, Comm. W. Edmonstone, C.B., Wool-

Flora, 40, sailing-ship, Capt. A. Wilmshurst, Ascension.

Formidable, 26, Vice-Adm. Sir B. W. Walker, Bart., K.C.B., Capt. D. McL. Mackenzie, flagship, Sheerness.

Forte, 29, sc.-frigate, Capt. John H. J. Alexander, C.B., East Indies.

Forward, sc.-gunboat, Lt. T. H. Larcom, Pacific.

Fox, 2, sc.-store-ship, Staff-Com. Robert B. Batt, particular service.

Galatea, 26, sc.-frigate, Capt. H.R.H. the Duke of Edinburgh, K.G., particular service.

Ganges, 20, train.-sh., Com. J. E. M. Wilson, Falmth.

Gannet, 3, sc. surv.-sl. Com. W. Chimmo, Devnport.

Gnat, 2, double-sc. composite gun-vessel, Com. C. B. Theobald, China.

Greyhound, 5, sc.-sloop, Capt. Charles Stirling, South-east Coast of America.

Havock, sc.-gunboat, Lt.-Com. Y. O'Keefe, China.

Hector, 20, sc. iron-ship, Capt. A. F. R. de Horsey, Coast-guard, Southampton Water.

Helicon, pad.-des. ves., Com. E. Field, Ch. Squad.

Hercules, 12, sc. iron armour-plated, Capt. Lord Gilford, Chatham.

Heron, sc.-gunboat, Lieut.-Com. L. B. Solly, Lake Ontario.

Hibernia, 104, sailing-ship, Com. Wm. L. Partridge, flagship of Rear-Adm. E. G. Fanshawe, Malta.

Himalaya, 2, sc. troop-ship, Capt. S. B. Piers, particular service.

Icarus, 3, sc.-sloop, Com. Lord C. Scott, China.

Implacable, 24, tr.-sh., Com. P. W. Pellew, Dvnport.

Impregnable, 78, tr.-sh., Capt. W. G. Jones, Dvnport.

Indus, guard-ship of reserve, Rear-Adm. the Hon. J. R. Drummond, C.B., Capt. G. O. Willes, C.B., Devonport.

Industry, 2, iron sc.-storeship, Staff-Com. C. J. Polkinghorne, particular service.

Investigator, 2, paddle-vessel, Lieut. John H. O'Brien, West Coast of Africa.

Irresistible, 60, sc.-ship, Com. Arthur G. R. Roe, Bermuda.

Jackal, 1, iron paddle-vessel, Lieut.-Com. A. E. Dupuis, West Coast of Scotland.

Janus, sc.-gunboat, Lt.-Com. L. C. Keppel, China.

Jaseur, 5, gun-vessel, Com. C. F. Hotham, West Coast of Africa.

Jason, 17, sc.-corvette, Capt. C. M. Aynsley, North America and West Indies.

Jumna, 3, Indian troop-ship, Capt. B. S. Pickard, Bombay.

Juno, 6, sc.-corvette, Capt. W. A. R. Pearse, particular service.

Ships in Commission, &c.—*continued.*

Lapwing, 3, double-sc. gun-vessel, Com. Philip R. Sharpe, particular service.

Lee, 5 sc. gun-vessel, Com. C. W. Andrew, West Coast of Africa.

Leven, 2, gun-vessel, Lt. O. S. Cameron, China.

Liffey, 31, screw-frigate, Capt. John O. Johnson, North America and West Indies.

Linnet, sc. gunboat, Lt.-Com. C. P. Bushe, South-east Coast of America.

Lion, 60, screw ship, Capt. Gerard J. Napier, Devonport, receiving-ship for seamen of reserve.

Lord Warden, 20, armour-plated, Capt. W. R. Rolland, Mediterranean.

Malabar, 3, Ind. tr.-sh., Cpt. F. D. Rich, Bombay.

Malacca, 13, sc. corvette, Cpt. R. B. Oldfield, Pacif.

Manilla, iron sc. st.-ves., Nav.-Lt. F. A. Johnston, Hong Kong.

Medusa, pad. st.-ves., Staff-Com. G. B. F. Swain, part. service.

Meeanee, hosp.-sh. at Hong Kong, Cm. H.M. Miller

Megæra, 4, iron sc.-storeship, Staff-Com. Jabez Loane, part. service.

Mersey, 36, sc.-frig, flagsh. of Rear-Ad. Claude H.M. Buckle, c.b., Cpt. R. D. White, Queenstown

Minotaur, 34, iron sc.-sh., flagship of Rear-Ad. F. Warden, c.b., Capt. Jas. G. Goodenough, Channel Squadron.

Minstrel, sc. gunboat, Lt.-Com. M. B. Medlycott, North America and West Indies.

Mullet, 5, sc. gunboat, Comm. Edw. Kelly, N. America and West Indies.

Mutine, 17, sc. sloop., Com. Hen. M'C. Alexander, Pacific, ordered home.

Myrmidon, 4, sc. gun-vessel, Com. Hen. B. Johnstone, West Coast of Africa.

Nankin, 50, Capt. R. Hall, Pembroke.

Narcissus, 35, sc. frigate, flagship of Rear-Adm. G. Ramsay, c.b., Cpt. J. C. Wilson, S. E. C. Amer.

Nassau, 5, sc., surveying-ves., Capt. R. C. Mayne, c.b., Straits of Magellan.

Nereus, 6, st. dep., St-Cm. J. P. Dillon, Valparaiso

Newport, 5. sc. surveying-ves., Com. George S. Nares, Mediterranean.

Niger, 13, sc. corvette, Capt. J. M. Bruce, North America and West Indies, ordered home.

Niobe, 4, sc. sloop, Com. T. K. Mackenzie, North America and West Indies.

Northumberland, 26, sc. armour-plated sh., Capt. Devonport.

Nymph, 4, sc. sl., Com. Edw. S. Meara, East Ind.

Oberon, 3, iron-pad. steam-ves., Lt. John Shortt, South-east Coast of America. [hope, China.

Ocean, 24, sc., armour-plated, Capt. C. S. S. Stan-

Octavia, 35, sc. frigate, Capt. Basil de R. S. Hall, flagship of Comm. Sir L. Heath, c.b., East Indies

Opossum, sc. gunboat, Lt.-Com. John E. Stokes, Hong Kong.

Orwell, gunboat, Lieut.-Com. A. F. Marescaux, Queenstown.

Pallas, 6, sc. corvette, armour-plated, Capt. E. H. C. Lambert, Channel Squadron.

Pandora, 5, sc. gun-ves., Com. John Burgess, West Coast of Africa.

Pearl, 21, sc. corvette, Capt. J. F. Ross, China.

Pembroke, 25, sc. block sh., Rear-Adm. J. W. Tarleton, c.b., Capt. the Hon. J. W. S. Spencer, Coast Guard, Harwich.

Penelope, 10, iron double sc. cor., armour-plated, flagship of Rear-Adm. Alfred P. Ryder, Capt. F. Marten, Channel Squadron.

Penguin, 5, sc. gun-ves., Lt.-Com. John J. Martin, Devonport.

Perseus, 15, sc. sloop, Com. C. E. Stevens, China.

Peterel, 3, sc. sloop, Com. Hon. E. G. L. Cochrane, Cape of Good Hope.

Philomel, 3, double-sc. gun-ves., Com. J. H. Coxon, North America and West Indies.

Phœbe, 35, sc.-frigate, Capt. J. Bythesea, VC North America and West Indies.

Pigmy, 1, paddle st.-ves., St.-Com. W. H. Petch, Portsmouth.

Plover, 3, double sc. gun-ves., Com. James A. Poland, West Coast of Africa.

President, 16, Naval Res. drill-sh., Com. H. W. Comber, City Canal.

Princess Charlotte, 12, receiving-ship, Commodore O. J. Jones, Hong Kong.

Prince Consort, 31, sc. ship, armour-plated, Capt. W. Armytage, Mediterranean.

Psyche, 2, paddle-wh. despatch ves., Lieut.-Com. Sir F. Blackwood, Bart., Mediterranean.

Pylades, 17, sc. corvette, Capt. Cecil W. Buckley VC Pacific.

Racoon, 22, sc. corvette, Capt. R. Purvis, Cape of Good Hope.

Rapid, 11, sc. sloop, Com. Hon. F. Wood, Mediter.

Rattler, 17, sc. sl., Com. H. F. Stephenson, China.

Rattlesnake, 19, sc. corvette, Commo. Wm. M. Dowell, c.b., West-coast of Africa.

Reindeer, 7, sc. sloop, Com. Edw. Nares, Pacific.

Revenge, 73, sc. sh., Capt. W. J. S. Pullen, Coast-guard, Pembroke Dock.

Rifleman, 8, sc. surveying-ves., Nav. Lt. John W. Reed, China Sea.

Rinaldo, 7, sc. sloop, Com. W. K. Bush, China.

Rodney, 78, sc.-sh., Capt. A. C. F. Heneage, flagsh. of Vice-Adm. the Hon. Sir H. Keppel, China.

Rosario, 11, sc. sl., Com. Geo. Palmer, Australia.

Royal Adelaide, 26, Cpt. G. W. Preedy, c.b., flagsh. of Adm. Sir W. F. Martin, Bt., k.c.b., Devonport.

Royal Alfred, 18, sc., armour-plated sh., Capt. the Hon. W. C. Carpenter, flagsh. of Vice-Adm. Sir G. R. Mundy, k.c.b., N. Amer. and W. Indies.

Royal George, 72, sc. sh., Capt. R. Jenkins, c.b., Coast-guard, Kingstown.

Royal Oak, 24, sc. sh., armour-plated, Capt. H. S. Hillyar, c.b., Channel Squadron.

Royalist, 11, sc. sl., Com. Loftus F. Jones, North America and West Indies.

St. George, 72, sc. sh. Capt. M. S. Nolloth, Coast-guard, Portland.

St. Vincent, 26, training-sh. for boys, Com. R. Carter, Portsmouth. [China.

Salamis, paddle des.-ves., Com. Edw. B. Pusey.

Satellite, 21, sc. corvette, Capt. J. Edye, c.b., Pacif.

Scout, 21, sc. corvette, Capt. J. A. P. Price, Pacific, ordered home. [Portsmouth.

Serapis, 3, Indian troop-sh., Capt. John C. Soady.

Seringapatam, receiving-sh., Commo. George G. Randolph, Cape of Good Hope.

Serpent, 4, sc. gun-ves., Com. C. J. Bullock, China, ordered home.

Simoom, 4, iron sc. troop-sh., Capt. T. B. Lethbridge, particular service.

Skylark, sc. gunboat, Lt.-Com. A. J. Collins, Gibr.

Slaney, 1, sc. gun-ves., Lieut.-Com., W. F. L. Elwyn, China.

Sparrowhawk, 4, sc. gun-ves., Com. Edwin A. Porcher, Pacific.

Speedwell, 5, sc. gun-ves., Com. J. P. J. Parry, West Coast of Africa.

Sphinx, 6, paddle sloop, Capt. J. E. Parish, North America and West Indies, ordered home.

Spider, sc. gunboat, Lieut. F. W. Prosser, South-east Coast of America.

Spiteful, 6, paddle sl., Com. B. L. Lefroy, E. Ind.

Star, 4, sc. gun-ves., Com. Walter S. de Kantzow, East Indies.

SHIPS IN COMMISSION, &c.—*continued.*

Starling, gunboat, Lt.-Com. R. E. Stopford, China

Sylvia, 5, sc. surveying-ves., Com. E. W. Brooker, China and Japan Seas.

Terrible, 19, paddle frigate, Capt. Treveven P. Coode, particular service.

Terror, 16, sc. iron floating battery, armour-plat., Capt. Jas. F. B. Wainwright, Bermuda.

Topaze, 31, sc. frigate, Commo. R. A. Powell, C.B., Pacific. [Swilly.

Trafalgar, 60, sc. sh., Capt. E. K. Barnard, Lough

Trinculo, sc. gunboat, Lt.-Com. F. de V. Sanders, Mediterranean.

Trincomalee, 16, Naval Reserve drill-ship, Com. E. T. Nott, Hartlepool.

Tyrian, sc. gunbt., Lt.-Com. E. J. Church, Devonp.

Urgent, 4, sc. iron troop-sh., Capt. S. H. Henderson, particular service.

Valiant, 24, iron sc. armour-plated sh., Capt. J. J. Kennedy, C.B., Coast-guard, River Shannon.

Vestal, 4, sc. sloop, Com. J. E. Hunter, N. Amer. and West Indies.

Victoria and Albert, paddle Royal yacht, Capt. H.S.H. Prince of Leiningen, G. C. B., Portsmouth.

Victory, 12, flagsh. of Adm. Sir Thos. Pasley, Bt., Capt. F. B. P. Seymour, C.B., Portsmouth.

Vigilant, 4, sc. gun-ves., Com. R. A. O. Brown, E.I.

Vindictive, store-sh., Nav. Lt. Geo. Stovin, Bight of Benin, Jellah Coffee.

Viper, 2, iron double sc. gunboat, armour-plated, Com. H. E. Crozier, Bermuda.

Virago, 6, pad.-sloop, Com. H. M. Bingham, Aust.

Vixen, 2, iron and wood double sc. gunboat, armour-plated, Com. L. H. Versturme, Bermuda.

Warrior, 32, iron sc., armour-plated, Capt. Hen. Boys, Channel Squadron. [China.

Weazel, sc. gunboat, Lt.-Com. W. H. Richards,

Winchester, 12, drill-sh. for Naval Reserve, Com G. M. Balfour, Aberdeen.

Wizard, sc. gunboat, Lieut.-Com. P. J. Murray, Mediterranean.

Zealous, 20, sc. armour-plated ship, Capt. R. Dawkins, flagsh. of Rear-Adm. the Hon. G. F. Hastings, C.B., Pacific.

Zebra, 7, sc. sloop, Com. H. A. Trollope, China.

SHIPS BUILDING.

Private yards marked thus *

Active, iron sc. corv., cased with wood, *Blackwall

Bittern, 3, double sc. gun-ves., Pembroke.

Briton, 10, sc. corvette, Sheerness.

Bulwark, 81, sc. ship, Chatham.

Captain, 6, iron double sc. turret-ship, armour-plated, *Birkenhead.

Despatch, iron-tank vessel, *Greenwich.

Druid, 10, screw corvette, Deptford.

Glatton, double-sc. turret-sh., armour-pl., Chath.

Growler, 2, double-screw composite gun-vessel, *Glasgow (Lawrie).

Inconstant, 16, iron sc. frigate, cased with wood, Pembroke.

Invincible, 14, double-sc. iron ship, armour-pl., *Glasgow (Napier).

Iron Duke, 14, double-sc. iron ship, armour-pl., Pembroke.

Robust, 81, screw ship, Devonport.

Spartan, 6, screw gun-ves., Deptford.

Sultan, 13, iron sc. sh., armour-plated, Chatham.

Swiftsure, 14, iron sc. sh. armour-pl.,*Jarrow-on-Tyne.

Triumph, 14, ir. sc. sh., arm.-pl.,*Jarrow-on-Tyne.

Vanguard, 14, double-sc. iron ship, armour-pl., *Birkenhead.

Volage, 8, iron sc. corvette, cased with wood, *Blackwall.

Vulture, 3, double-sc. gun-vessel, Sheerness.

Royal Marine Forces.

GENERAL OFFICERS. — ARTILLERY.

Gen., Sir F. Graham, K.C.B.
Lt.-Gen., Sir Thomas Holloway, K.C.B.
Major-Gen., Henry Carr Tate.

LIGHT INFANTRY.

Gens., Henry Ivatt Delacombe.
John Tatton Brown.
Lt.-Gens., Sir Anth. Blaxland Stransham, K.C.B.
Alexander Anderson.
Thomas Lemon, C.B.
Major-Gens., John Hawkins Gascoigne, C.B.
George Colt Langley.
Joseph Oates Travers, C.B.
William Robert Maxwell.
Hayes Marriott.

STAFF.

Insp.-Gen.—Major-Gen., Joseph O. Travers, C.B.
Dep.Adj.-Gen.—Col.-Com.S.N.Lowder, C.B.,A.D.C.
Assist.Adj.-Gen.—Col. John Wm. C. Williams.

ARTILLERY.

Head Quarters, Portsmouth.

Col., Sir Fortescue Graham, K.C.B., *g.*
Col. Com., G. A. Schomberg, C.B.
Col. 2nd Com., Charles L. Barnard.
Lt.-Cols., J. W. Collman Williams, *c.*, *As.-Adj.Gen.*
George S. Digby, C.B. *c.*
Henry Adair.
Henry Way Mawbey.
Frederick L. Alexander.
Adj., H. I. De Kantzow, *2nd capt.*
C. C. Suther, *2nd capt.*

LIGHT INFANTRY.

[1. *Chatham;* 2. *Portsmouth;* 3. *Plymouth;* 4. *Woolwich Divisions.*]

Cols., 2, John Tatton Brown, *g.*
4 Sir Anthony B. Stransham, K.C.B., *l. g.*
1 Alexander Anderson, *l. g.*
3 Thomas Lemon, C.B., *l. g.*
Cols. Com., Sam. N. Lowder, C.B., *Dep. Adj. Gen.*
1 George Lambrick.
2 William Stratton Aslett.
3 William Fra. Foote.
4 William G. Suther, C.B.
Cols. 2nd. Com., 2 Charles Louis.
1 Richard King Clavell.
3 Penrose C. Penrose, C.B.
4 George Brydges Rodney.
Lt.-Cols., 2 Jermyn C. Symonds, *c.*
1 Peregrine H. Fellowes, *c.*
1 Charles William Adair, *c.*
4 Charles Frederick Menzies.
4 John Henry Stewart.
3 James Pickard.
2 W. A. G. Wright.
3 G. Wentworth Forbes.
2 Fleetwood J. Richards.
2 Arthur Butcher.
3 George Drury.
1 Edward Andrée Wylde.
4 J. W. A. Kennedy.
1 Robert Boyle, C.B., *c.*
3 John Elliott.
4 Charles M'Arthur.
Ag., E. T. Draper, Esq.,

The Naval and Military Estimates for 1868-69.

With Illustrations from other Parliamentary Papers.

NAVY.

THE sum required for Naval services for the year ending 31st March, 1869, is £11,177,290, against £10,976,253 granted for the year 1867-68, showing an increase of £201,037; but as certain services amounting to £11,735, which appeared in the Navy Estimates for the latter year, are now, by direction of the Treasury, transferred to the Civil Service or Post Office, the real increase is £212,772, and £10,964,518 is the total charge for 1867-68. The directions of the Treasury (by minute of 2nd November, 1867) have caused supplies and services valued at £203,292 to be rendered to other departments, which will be paid for direct into the Exchequer, instead of being, as hitherto, appropriated as credits in aid of these votes. This sum, deducted from that of £212,772, leaves £9,480 only as the increase for 1868-69.

The total force in the fleet and coast-guard service is 67,120, a decrease of 2,242; but the charge, as above, is greater. The chief part of the excess arises in relation to iron armour-plated ships, which, though more costly than wood, require fewer men.

The various Votes are as follows:—

	£
1. Wages for Seamen and Marines ...	3,036,634
2. Victuals and Clothing	1,335,842
3. Admiralty Office	182,364
4. Coast Guard, Volunteers, and Reserve	263,926
5. Scientific Branch	63,565
6. Dockyards and Naval Yards	1,223,562
7. Victualling Yards and Transport Establishments	87,179
8. Medical Establishments..............	64,824
9. Marine Divisions	20,709
10. Naval Stores	1,985,408
11. New Works, Machinery, and Repairs	814,237
12. Medicine and Medical Stores	78,164
13. Martial Law and Law Charges ...	20,365
14. Miscellaneous Services	175,800
Total for the Effective Service...	£9,352,579
15. Half Pay, Reserved Half Pay, and Retirement	700,166
16. Pensions and Allowances	773,945
Total for the Naval Service......	£10,826,690
17. Conveyance of Troops	350,600
Grand Total........................	£11,177,290

The details of these votes must now be given.

1. *Wages, &c., to Seamen and Marines.*—Increase, £132,286; decrease, £46,604; net increase, £85,682. The force to be paid (67,120) consists of 45,670 seamen (including officers), 14,700 marines (ditto), 7,400 boys, and 350 civilians for coast-guard service, a reduction of 842 seamen, 1,700 marines, and 100 civilians. The naval officers employed consist of 21 flag officers (8 at home, 13 abroad), 3,478 commissioned officers (captains to sub-lieutenants), 736 subordinate officers (midshipmen, clerks, naval cadets), 1,093 warrant officers (gunners, boatswains, carpenters). The marine officers are 436 in number; and of the boys, 4,300 are on service, and 3,100 under instruction in training-ships. 136 naval cadets were admitted in the year 1867. The coast-guard employs 3,200 officers, seamen, and boys afloat, and 4,500 officers and men on shore, beside 350 civilians; total, 8,050. There are 5 troop ships employed in the Indian service

2 in the Mediterranean have crews of 472 officers and men; and 3 in the Red Sea have 758. The cost in wages for this service is £62,296, an increase of £3,207. The total wages and allowances for seamen (cost £2,560,980) show an increase of £33,139, and for marines (cost £527,249) a decrease of £23,078, but the Indian Government is to pay £37,342 for seamen and £1,016 for marines employed in the Red Sea troopships. The expense of raising seamen, and bounty (cost £1,700), is an increase of £1,100. As to the marines on shore, the subsistence of commissioned and staff officers (cost £80,981) has increased £13,858; but of non-commissioned officers and privates (cost £183,184) has decreased £44,752. The prizes for good shooting to the marines (cost £1,163) have increased by £783; the colonial and field pay, &c., to marines at San Juan, who receive "double personal pay," (cost £4,000) by £2,000, and the contingencies of the marine service (cost £22,000), by £1,000. But further charges for the corps occur under 7 other votes, making its whole cost £991,309. The ships in commission on 1st December, 1867, were 150 effective steamships for general service, 45 sailing and 205 steam ships employed in special services, and 41 sailing and 29 steam vessels in the coast-guard (which also possesses some vessels of its own); a total of 320, or 5 less than on 1st December, 1866.

2. *Victuals and Clothing.*—Increase, £113,374; decrease, £19,146; net increase, £94,228. Provisions received under contract (cost £628,590) show an increase of £1,622; allowances in lieu of provisions and fuel (cost £173,323) one of £10,826; lights and culinary fuel for service afloat (cost £64,286) one of £696; victualling stores received under contract (cost £33,400) one of £3,400; freight, &c., on provisions and victualling stores (cost £17,000) one of £500; marine clothing and appointments (cost £53,825) one of £5,386; and marine barrack stores (cost £19,021) one of £444. Savings (i. e., payments for provisions not taken up by persons entitled to them, amount £128,253) show a decrease of £16,137; allowances in lieu of lights to officers, &c., afloat (cost £19,315) one of £794; seamen's clothing, soap, and tobacco (cost £37,126) one of £1,834; and allowances in lieu of marine clothing, &c. (cost £5,019) one of £381. The mess allowances in lieu of rations, and mess traps, furniture, &c., remain at their former amounts of £56,184 and £10,000. The estimated value of issues of provisions (£84,977) and clothing (£5,523) to other departments forms part of the sum of £203,292 already mentioned. The provisions supplied are for 5,000 coast volunteers and 10,000 Naval Reserve men when on drill afloat, and 717 men and boys in yard service afloat, in addition to the seamen and marines of the fleet and the coast-guard, a total of 88,837 persons. The coast volunteers afloat receive provisions valued at £4,586, an increase on 1867-68 of £34, but the money allowance in lieu of provisions to the Naval Reserve remains at its former amount of £29,867. Gratuitous issues of bedding on first entry, of clothing to coaling and other working parties, &c., amounts to £42,518, an increase of £2,382. Marines when afloat receive annually a pair of half boots (cost £2,408), and the Naval Reserve are supplied gratuitously with caps (cost £290).

It appears from a Parliamentary Paper (H. C.

353) that the quantity of navy beef cured at the Victualling Yard, Deptford, in the five years 1863-64 to 1867-68 amounted to 14,200 tierces and 15,337 barrels, at an average cost of £9 18s. 10½d. per tierce, and £6 17s. 7d. per barrel. Old beef was sold (quantity not stated) at an average price of £2 8s. 7d. per tierce. 1,868,910 lbs. of preserved boiled beef were prepared at Deptford at an average price of 11d. per lb. in the seasons 1866-67 and 1867-68.

3. *Admiralty Office.*—Increase, £6,356. Salaries, &c., (cost £171,064) show an increase of £5,346; and contingencies (cost £3,000), one of £1,000; but travelling expenses stand at £3,300, rents, rates, and taxes at £2,600, and fuel and light at £2,400, as in 1867-68. The salaries of the six Lords of the Admiralty amount to £9,700; that of the First Secretary to £2,000; of the Second Secretary to £1,500. The Controller and five other principal Officers of the Navy, who are heads of departments, receive £1,300 each. The departments are :—

1. *Secretary*—50 clerks (£21,370) ; 6 literary employés, 30 messengers, &c. ; total, £26,759.

2. *Controller*—26 clerks (£7,861) ; Chief Constructor, £1,000; 3 assistants £500 each ; Surveyor, £700; Chief Engineer of the Navy, £900; assistant, £550; 7 messengers, &c. ; total, £10,138.

3. *Accountant-General* — 155 clerks (£44,859) ; 2 Assistant Accountant-Generals, £1,000 each; an Inspector of yard accounts, £850 ; 26 messengers, &c. ; total, £53,276.

4. *Storekeeper-General*—21 clerks (£5,979) ; a committee of 3 for checking accounts (£1,283) ; 3 messengers, &c. ; total, £7,726.

5. *Comptroller of Victualling*—41 clerks (£13,514); 9 messengers, &c. ; total, £15,315.

6. *Medical Director-General*—14 clerks (£4,389); 3 messengers, &c. ; total, £4,480.

7. *Director of Transports* (£1,200)—17 clerks (£5,373) ; an Assistant (£365) ; 4 messengers, &c. ; total, £7,590.

8. *Director of Engineering and Architectural Works*—7 clerks and draughtsmen (£2,276) ; 2 messengers, &c. ; total, £5,255.

There is also a Registrar of Contracts, &c. (£850), with 7 clerks (£2,122), and 1 messenger ; total, £3,267.

The chief clerks in each department receive from £850 to £1,100 each, and the sum of £11,252 appears to be required for clerks, draughtsmen, &c., temporarily employed. The messengers, porters, &c., are 102 in number, and their pay and allowances amount to £9,524 ; beside £760 for a housekeeper and servants.

4. *Coast Guard, Volunteers, and Reserve.*—Increase, £3,271 ; decrease, £6,412 ; net decrease, £3,141. Salaries, &c., Coast-Guard Office (cost £5,394) show a decrease of £141 ; and pay and allowances to officers and men on shore (those afloat are provided for under Votes 1, 2), cost £23,546, one of £6,271. The items of rent, rates, and taxes for the office, travelling expenses, and contingencies, stand at the sums, respectively, of £167, £700, and £180, as in 1867-68 ; as is the case with fuel and light (cost £4,800) ; but the rents, &c., of the coast-guard stations (cost £35,800) show an increase of £200 ; the travelling expenses of officers and men and their families on removal (cost £18,890) one of £1,000 ; and contingencies (cost £5,264), one of £71. The drill of coast-guard and reserve, and the wages, bounty, &c., of the coast volunteers, stand, as in 1867-68, at £4,150 and £20,000 respectively ; but the wages, &c., of the naval reserve (cost £145,035)

show an increase of £2,000. The coast-guard is governed by a Controller-General and Deputy (£1,264 and £700) ; 3 other officers are employed in the office, and 16 clerks (£3,871). The coasts of the United Kingdom are divided into 11 districts, in each of which is a guard and drill ship; there are also 45 cruisers and 33 watch vessels, and about 500 stations on shore, where 4,850 officers, seamen, and civilians are employed. The sea force is 2,840 officers and men, and 360 boys. The stations are regularly visited by the inspecting officers, 16 in number, at rates of pay of from £219 to £146, and their allowances on visiting duty amount to £7,890. There is also a mounted guard of 17 men (cost £2,318), and forage for them and the inspecting officers costs £7,000. 285 chief and other boatmen (wages from £54 15s. to £73), cost £16,316. The total cost of the coast-guard is £762,438 ; and ships valued at £36,138 have been lent for its service since its transfer to the Admiralty. The coast volunteers average 5,000 in number; they receive bounty at from £1 1s. to £1 6s. per man, per annum, with wages at 1s. 7d. per day when afloat, beside conduct and billetting money, the total cost being about £4 each man. The naval reserve, estimated at 16,000, beside 130 lieutenants and 90 sub-lieutenants, though put in this vote at only £145,035, causes a further charge, under other heads, of £68,084 ; a total of £213,119. On and April, 1868, the strength of the reserve was stated by the Admiralty at 15,358, but only 12,890 had presented themselves for drill in the year 1867 (II. C. 238 and 218).

5. *Scientific Branch.* Increase, £1,389; decrease, £2,930; net decrease, £1,541. Salaries, &c., at the Royal Observatory, Greenwich (cost £2,732), show an increase of £85 ; the Observatory at the Cape of Good Hope, one of £44, in incidental expenses ; the Nautical Almanac (cost £2,399), one of £83; salaries, &c., hydrographical department (cost £6,042), one of £35; and Naval College, Portsmouth (cost £3,037), one of £52. The magnetic and meteorological department (cost £1,090), is a charge transferred from other estimates. Contingencies, Royal Observatory (cost £2,004) show a decrease of £81 ; the School of Naval Architecture (cost £1,360), one of £209; and surveys (cost £26,452), one of £2,640. The charges for chronometers (£1,000), compass department (£762), rewards, experiments, &c., for scientific purposes (£500), Royal United Service Institution (£300), libraries and museums at Haslar and Plymouth Hospitals (£100), drawing, engraving, &c., charts (£12,000), contingencies in the hydrographical department (£1,000), and the pay of the Director of Education for the Admiralty (£960), remain as in 1867-68.

The staff of the Greenwich Observatory consists of the Astronomer Royal (£1,000), and 6 assistants at from £400 to £170; and that of the observatory at the Cape, of an Astronomer (£600), and 2 assistants (£400 and £250), with 2 other assistants (£150 and £100), in the Magnetic department. The Magnetic department at Greenwich has a Superintendent (£300), with assistants (£270). The Nautical Almanack has a Superintendent (£500), a chief assistant (£300), and 10 computers (£1,399) ; the number of Nautical Almanacks sold in the five years, 1863 to 1867, was 106,883. The Hydrographical department consists of the Hydrographer (£1,000), chief naval assistant (£500), 3 civil and 5 naval assistants, 5 draughtsmen, 4 messengers, &c. During the five years 1863 to 1867, it has paid over £25,333 4s. 10d. to the Exchequer, for 3,866 books and 467,262 charts sold; but since 1864 the books that it has issued are accounted for by the Stationery Office. 369 officers, men, boys, and marines, are employed in the survey service, whose pay and allowances amount to £30,667; their victuals to £7,203; stores, medicine, and pilotage, £17,075; making the total charge £81,397. Surveys are in progress on the English coast, in the Mediterranean, Straits of Magellan, China and Japan, West Indies, Newfoundland, British Columbia, and the Cape of Good Hope; and soundings are being made for submarine cables. The Australian Colonies also are in course of survey by the department, the greater part of the cost being borne by the Colonial authorities.

6. *Dockyards and Naval Yards.*—Increase, £8,708; decrease, £160,514; net decrease, £151,806.

The dockyards at home are (1) *Deptford*: salaries £10,770, wages £39,858; total £50,628—a decrease of £10,415. (2) *Woolwich*: salaries £22,743, wages £126,847; total £149,590—a decrease of £28,973. (3) *Chatham*: salaries £24,193, wages £186,338; total £210,531—a decrease of £3,898. (4) *Sheerness*: salaries £19,786, wages £112,563; total £132,349—a decrease of £8,896. (5) *Portsmouth*: salaries £35,648, wages £225,317; total £260,965—a decrease of £85,689. (6) *Devonport*: salaries £36,766, wages £197,992; total £234,758—a decrease of £20,993. (7) *Pembroke*: salaries £12,827, wages £77,090; total £89,917—a decrease of £251. (8) *Haulbowline*: salaries *nil*, wages £670—an increase of £255. Sum total for dockyards at home, £1,102,357, against £1,259,779, a decrease of £157,422. The decrease is entirely in wages (£159,997), and the increase occurs in salaries (£857), rents, &c. (£101), gas lighting (£65), hire of teams (£18), wages of police (£1,534), survey valuation of stock (£1,000), and a new item, work in connection with gunnery fittings (£4,000).

The dockyards abroad are (1) *Gibraltar*: salaries £2,339, wages £2,676; total £5,015—an increase of £520. (2) *Malta*: salaries £10,851, wages £19,010; total £29,861—an increase of £186. (3) *Halifax*: salaries £1,593, wages £2,457; total £4,050—an increase of £66. (4) *Bermuda*: salaries £4,127, wages £11,710; total £15,837—a decrease of £755. (5) *Antigua*: salaries £386, wages £580; total £966, as in 1867-68. (6) *Jamaica*: salaries £1,359, wages £5,179; total £6,538—a decrease of £50. (7) *Ascension*: salaries *nil*, wages £861; total £861, as in 1867-68. (8) *Sierra Leone*: salaries *nil*, wages £60; total £60, as in 1867-68. (9) *Cape of Good Hope*: salaries £2,339, wages £2,382; total £4,721—an increase of £25. (10) *Trincomalee*: salaries £1,395, wages £693; total £2,088—an increase of £123. (11) *Singapore*: salary £100—a new charge for care of naval coal depôt and stores. (12) *Hongkong*: salaries £6,861, wages £11,019; total £17,880—an increase of £850. (13) *Esquimault*: salaries *nil*, wages £240; total £240, as in 1867-68. Sum total for dockyards abroad, £87,205 against £86,589—an increase of £1,065, leaving net decrease on dockyards £151,806.

Each home dockyard has an admiral, commodore or captain superintendent, whose pay and allowances are respectively £1,642 10s. and £691 19s. 7d. Other officers are, the master attendant, master shipwright, chief engineer, storekeeper, accountant, each usually about £600 or £650; surgeon, chaplain, each £350 or

£400. There are also 155 clerks (from £90 to £450) and 9,174 "established" artisans and labourers, i.e., entitled to pensions for service, and a number of hired men (6,101 in 1868), varying with the exigencies of the service. The superintendents of the dockyards abroad have salaries and allowances of amounts varying with the importance of their charge, from £1,930 at Malta to £341 at Hong Kong; and minor stations are in charge of storekeepers or clerks at from £350 to £600. The "established" shipwrights, &c., in these dockyards number only 179, whilst the hired workmen are 367; total, 546. The cost of the police for the home dockyards (450) is £34,123, an increase of £1,534, and for that abroad £5,888, an increase of £582, the whole charge being £40,011. The number of police in the dockyards abroad is not given in the estimates.

On 1st February, 1868, there were 330 screw and 73 paddle steamers afloat, 32 screw and 2 paddle steamers building, and 29 effective sailing ships afloat, making a total of 466 vessels. Seven iron and 12 wooden vessels are building in the dockyards, and 12 contract-built vessels are being completed there.

7. *Victualling Yards and Transport Establishments.*—Increase £1,387, decrease £603; net increase £784. The victualling yards at home are (1) *Royal Victoria*, Deptford: salaries £10,275, wages £27,466; total £37,723—an increase of £368. (2) *Royal Clarence*, Gosport: salaries £4,977, wages £10,262; total £15,239—an increase of £379. (3) *Royal William*, Plymouth: salaries £5,438, wages £9,782; total £15,220—an increase of £228. (4) *Haulbowline*, Cork: salaries £1,501, wages £1,392; total £2,893—an increase of £37. There are employed in these yards, 21 clerks, 64 police, and 411 "established" artisans, &c. Sum total for victualling yards at home, £71,075 against £69,973—an increase of £1,102.

The victualling yards abroad are 14 in number, viz.: Ascension, Auckland, Barbadoes, Bermuda, Cape of Good Hope, Esquimault, Gibraltar, Halifax, Hong Kong, Jamaica, Malta, Sierra Leone, Sydney, and Trincomalee; but at only 4 of them does the expenditure exceed £1000. These are Malta (£4,983), with storekeeper (£600), 3 clerks, and 107 workmen. *Esquimault*, Vancouver's Island (£1,821), with paymaster in charge (£600), clerk (£303), and 2 artificers (£365). *Ascension* (£1,811) allowances to the captain, paymaster, chaplain, surgeon, and chief engineer of H.M.S. *Meander* (£385), gardener (£100), and Kroomen and other labourers (£1,250). *Jamaica* (£1,289), with paymaster in charge (£250), clerk (£305), and 9 workmen (£560). The total cost for these yards (£14,249), shows a decrease of £301.

The transport establishment at Deptford, salaries £1,268, wages £487; total £1,755—shewing a decrease of £17; has a resident transport officer (£400), senior clerk (£381), and four carpenters, R.N. (£183). There are also labourers whose wages amount to £487, an increase of £20 on 1867-68, but their number is not stated.

8. *Medical Establishments.*—Increase £2,180; decrease £42; net increase £2,138. The medical establishments at home are, (1) *Haslar Hospital*, Gosport: salaries £9,059, wages £9,993; total £19,052—an increase of £615. (2) *Plymouth Hospital*: salaries £5,597, wages £6,123; total £11,720—an increase of £524. (3) *Haulbowline Hospital*, Cork: salaries £869, wages £739; total, £1608—an increase of £24. (4) *Yarmouth Hospital*, Lunatic Asylum: salaries £2,204, wages £1,834; total £4,038

—an increase of £433. Sum total for hospitals at home £36,418 against £34,822—an increase of £1,596. The medical establishments abroad are (1) *Malta*: salaries £2,268, wages £1,576; total £3,844—a decrease of £13. (2) *Bermuda*: salaries £1,787, wages £965; total £2,752—an increase of £103. (3) *Jamaica*: salaries £2,090, wages £840; total £2,930—an increase of £22. (4) *Ascension*: wages only, £402, as in 1867-68. (5) *Cape of Good Hope*: salaries £1,074, wages £590; total £1,664—a decrease of £1. (6) *Hong Kong*, "Melville" hospital ship: salaries £2,841, wages £811; total £3,652—an increase of £152. Sum total for hospitals abroad, £15,244 against £14,981—an increase of £263.

The Marine Infirmaries are (1) *Woolwich*: salaries £1,877, wages £2,460; total £4,337—an increase of £11. (2) *Chatham*: salaries £1,801,wages £2,234; total £4,035—an increase of £129. (3) *Portsmouth*, Forton, salaries £1,197, wages £53; total £1,250—an increase of £12. (4) *Portsmouth*, Fort Cumberland: salaries £1,321, wages £271; total £1,592—an increase of £63. (5) *Plymouth*: salaries £1,220, wages £430; total £1,650—an increase of £44. (6) *Deal*: wages and contingencies only, £298—an increase of £20. Sum total for Marine Infirmaries, £13,162 against £12,883—an increase of £179.

The increase in charge is almost entirely in salaries and wages, (£607 and £1,213). There are 28 police employed in the hospitals at home, and 12 in the infirmaries; their cost is £2,897.

9. *Marine Divisions.*—Increase £3,261. Salaries and allowances to paymasters, barrack masters, &c., (cost £3,536 7s. 6d.) show an increase of £1,740 17s. 6d.; rents, rates, &c. (cost £8,227), one of £935; lighting the barracks with gas, (cost £3,945), one of £505; contributions and grants, as for church and chapel accommodation, schools, divisional bands, &c., (cost £1,996), one of £80; and contingencies, (cost £3,004 12s. 6d.), one of £8. 2s. 6d. The sum of £20,709 is thus apportioned among the divisions:—*Woolwich*, £4,507; *Chatham*, £3,667; *Portsmouth*, Forton, £3,722; *Portsmouth*, Fort Cumberland, £4,149; *Plymouth*, £3,634; *Deal*, recruiting depôt, £1,030. The total number of marines is, artillery, 2,700, light infantry, 12,000. Of these 8,000 are employed afloat, and 6,700 ashore. There are 6,510 men receiving good-conduct pay (£16,450); and 705 marksmen receiving extra pay (£1,163). Each man on re-engaging after 8 years' service receives £3 bounty, and a free kit valued at £4.

10. *Naval Stores.*—Increase £269,338.

Sec.I.—*Storekeeper-General.*—Increase £52,860; decrease £15,463—net increase £37,397. The stores to be purchased consist mainly of timber, masts, &c. (cost £78,731), hemp and canvas (cost £102,875); and coal and other fuel (cost £225,354); which show increases of £7,106, £21,931, and £17,823 respectively; and of metals and metal articles (cost £166,585); iron armour-plates, beams and masts (cost £103,800); and pitch, paint, &c. (cost £184,563); which show decreases of £11,775, £28,200, and £2,631. Local purchases of stores at coast-guard stations (£5,000), and freight (£20,000), stand as in 1867-68; and value of stores for other departments (£6,000), is a new item.

Sec. II.—*Controller.*—Increase £262,820; decrease £30,079—net increase £231,941. Three iron armour-plated ships and 8 gun-boats building by contract (cost £435,000, part of £851,300 required), show an increase of £83,170; experimental purposes, &c. (cost £12,000), one of

£2,000; and repairs of ships in private yards (cost £36,000), one of £16,000. The charge for steam machinery for the fleet (£35,000), shows a decrease of £4,279. Building and repairing coast-guard tenders (£12,000), and subsistence, &c., of officers superintending ships building by contract (£2,000), stand as in 1867-68. There are also charges for part of the expense of new iron armour-plated ships (£150,000); and of Captain Coles' turret ship "Captain," (£90,000). These two items will eventually amount to £540,000 and £275,000.

11. *New Works, Machinery, and Repairs.*—Increase, £52,305; decrease, £126,656; net decrease, £74,351. These amount, in the naval yards at home, to £533,270 for works and buildings, and £70,198 for machinery; total, £603,468; divided thus: *Deptford*, £3,895; *Woolwich*, £8,982; *Chatham*, £229,705; *Sheerness*, £7,951; *Portsmouth*, £279,858; *Devonport*, £15,304; *Keyham*, £22,300; *Plymouth Breakwater*, £6,000—total for "Plymouth," £44,204; *Pembroke*, £11,693; *Haulbowline, &c.*, £23,780. Naval yards abroad, works and buildings, £106,100; machinery, £4,969; total, £111,069. Victualling yards at home and abroad, £8,460; medical establishments ditto, £11,760; marine barracks, £23,640; coast-guard buildings, £20,000; Admiralty offices, £6,000. Temporary superintendence of the various dockyards costs £13,840; and contingencies, £10,000.

12. *Medicines and Medical Stores.*—Increase, £1,500; decrease, £4,000; net decrease, £2,500. Hospital and infirmary stores (cost £38,564) show an increase of £500; and miscellaneous disbursements of the medical service, which include freight of medical stores, funerals of seamen, &c. (cost £2,500), one of £1,000. The expense of carrying out the Contagious Diseases Act (£12,500) shows a decrease of £4,000. The charges for medicines and surgical instruments (£8,500), and for sick quarters (£5,100 for the fleet, £11,000 for the coast-guard and reserve), remain as in 1867-68.

13. *Martial Law and Law Charges.*—Increase, £33; decrease, £1,000; net decrease, £967. The legal department (cost £13,014) shows a decrease of £1,000, saved on fees to counsel, &c. The Naval Prison at Lewes (cost £2,891) shows an increase of £33; but that at Malta, and the conveyance of prisoners (£1,760 and £1,200), stand as in 1867-68. Lewes Prison has a governor (£389), a chaplain (£250), a local medical practitioner (£100), and allows £26 to a Roman Catholic priest, at Malta the governor has £300, and two sums of £50 each are allowed to the chaplain of the dockyard and the medical officer of the flagship for services to the prisoners.

14. *Miscellaneous Services.*—Increase, £10,600; decrease, £3,250; net increase, £7,350. The majority of these are fixed charges, as pilotage, £9,000; expenses for furniture, postage, &c., for commanders-in-chief, £4,000; passage-money, officers and men, £55,000; telegraphs, £6,000; contributions to institutions, £1,500; per centage to banks for transmission of money, £1,500; "Warner" floating light-vessel, £370; medals for seamen and marines, £100; hire of vessels, £200; assistance to H.M. ships in distress, £500; compensation for damage done by H.M. ships, £4,000; books and stationery for schools, £3,500; loss by exchange on the East India and China stations, £4,000; part of expense of iron-clad ship for the colony of Victoria, £50,000; and miscellaneous payments, as freight of specie,

payment of interpreters, conveyance of the Royal household by sea ($£1,942\ 3s.\ 4d.$ in 1866-67), &c., £7,455. The rewards for services against pirates (£2,000 awarded to the "Osprey" and the "Opossum" for service in China, 18th July, 1866) show a decrease of £200; compensation to owners of merchant vessels for excess of wages paid to substitutes for such of their crews as may enter the Navy, by 16 & 17 Vict. cap. 131 (cost £150), one of £100. Compensation for losses by shipwreck or action (cost £3,000) shows an increase of £1,500; contributions to Sailors' Homes (cost £525) one of £100; stamps on contracts and officers' commissions (cost £7,000) one of £3,000; gratuities for wounds and special services (cost £5,000) one of £1,000; expense of committees to investigate or report on naval matters (cost £3,000) one of £1,000; lodging allowances to officers, &c., in case of stress of weather or special service (cost £7,000) one of £3,000. A vote of £1,000 for interest and extra pay in connection with naval savings' banks is a new item.

15. *Half-pay, Reserved Half-pay, and Retirement.*—Decrease, £4,771. Half-pay for 1,022 officers on the active list (82 admirals, 177 captains, 215 commanders, 176 lieutenants, 83 staff-commanders and navigating lieutenants, 34 chaplains, 90 surgeons, &c., 109 paymasters, 37 chief engineers, and 19 others of various classes), £204,795, against 1,049 and £210,189; decrease, 29 officers, £5,388. Reserved half-pay for 358 officers, £90,492, against 401 and £100,128; decrease, 43 officers, £9,836. Retirement for 1,743 officers, £352,348, against 1,734 and £338,253; increase, 9 officers, £14,095; ditto for 248 marine officers, £52,531, against 259 and £56,373; decrease, 11 officers, £4,842.

16. *Pensions and Allowances.* (a) *Military.*—Increase, £21,918; decrease, £138; net increase, £21,780. Many of these items are fixed charges; as pensions for good and meritorious services (£6,150) paid to 8 flag officers, 28 captains, 6 marine officers, and 3 medical officers; 10 of the pensions have been granted within the year. Pensions for conspicuous bravery (£190) are amounts of £10 each to 19 Naval or Marine Victoria Cross men. Flag officers' retired service pensions (£1,500) are amounts of £150 each paid to 7 admirals and 3 vice-admirals. The compassionate list (£15,500) affords allowances to children of naval and marine officers. Pensions to old and disabled commissioned officers (£5,025) are paid to 10 captains (£80 each), 6 commanders (£65 each), 50 lieutenants (£50 each), and 15 staff commanders and masters (£50 each), in all, 90 officers. Pensions to 586 commissioned and warrant officers for injuries received on service (£40,595) show an increase of £1,784. Pensions to 209 widows and relatives of officers slain, drowned, &c., on service (£11,113) show one of £393. Pensions to widows of 2,982 naval officers (£154,060) show one of

£31. Pensions to widows of 224 marine officers (£11,396) have decreased by £138. Pensions and gratuities to 9,078 seamen and 5,851 marines (£304,918) have increased by £19,708.

(b) *Civil.*—Increase, £5,723; decrease, £1,140—net increase, £4,583. Pensions and superannuations to 463 salaried officers (£91,435) have decreased £1,140. To 3,075 artificers, &c. (£87,507), have increased £3,099. To 1,058 coast-guard officers and men, and 68 widows and 146 children of men who have met their deaths on duty (£43,433), have increased £2,440. The contribution in aid of the pension fund for the Metropolitan Police, on account of police employed in naval establishments at home (£1,123), has increased £184.

17. *Non-Naval Services.*—Increase, £66,964; decrease, £122,340; net decrease, £55,376. These services are rendered to the Army Department in the conveyance of troops. The troopships, under the heads of wages, victuals, coals, medicines, and pilotage (cost £113,100), show an apparent decrease of £43,626; but as £74,191 are charged for wages under Vote 1, they really cost £30,565 more than in 1867-68. Mess allowances to army officers (cost £37,800) show an increase of £25,150; army passage-money (£cost £43,000) one of £5,000; bedding and other stores for troops (cost £6,800) one of £1,700; and provisions for troops (cost £60,600) one of £23,700. Conveyance of troops (cost £14,200) shows a decrease of £69,750; freight of army and ordnance stores (cost £42,000) one of £3,000; inter-colonial conveyance of troops and stores (cost £24,000) one of £6,000; freight of ships on short services (cost £7,800) one of £3,550; fitting transports and freight ships (cost £200) one of £900; and pay and contingent expenses of transport officers afloat (cost £700) one of £800. Forage and stores for horses (cost £400) is the only item which remains as in 1867-68.

From the foregoing it may be seen that £3,141 is saved on the coast-guard, coast volunteers, and reserve; £1,541 on the scientific branch; £151,806 on the dockyards and naval yards; £74,351 on new works and machinery; £2,500 on medicines; £967 on martial law and law charges; £4,771 on half-pay; and £55,376 on conveyance of troops; a total of £294,453. But there is an increase of £85,682 on wages; £94,228 on victuals and clothing; £6,346 on the Admiralty Office; £784 on victualling yards and the transport establishment; £2,138 on medical establishments; £3,261 on marine divisions; £37,397 on naval stores; £231,941 on naval construction; £7,350 on miscellaneous services; £21,780 on military pensions; and £4,583 on civil pensions.

8 Votes, Decrease £294,453
9   „   Increase 495,490

Net Increase 201,037

Naval and Military Directory.

GARRISONS, DOCKYARDS, VICTUALLING YARDS, BARRACKS, DEPOTS, HOSPITALS, PRISONS, PENSION OFFICES, &c.

In the following List will be found the Names and Stations of the Principal Military and Naval Officers, such as the public have most frequent occasion to communicate with on matters of business.

ABERDEEN.—15th *Depôt Battalion.* — *Majors,* Chas. H. Gordon, c.b., c. ; A. Pitcairn, l.c. *Adjt.* G. W. Northey, *capt. Surgeon,* A. R. Smith (Staff). *Staff Officer Pens.,* Capt. W. A. Godley. *Barrack Master,* Capt. J. Forbes.

ALDERSHOT CAMP.

In Command, Lieut.-Gen. Hon. Sir J. Y. Scarlett, k.c.b. *Asst. Adj.-Gen.,* Col. E. Newdigate. *Asst. Q.M.-Gen.,* Col. Jas. Conolly. *Brigade Major, R.A.,* Major W. H. Goodenough. *Insp.-*

Gen. Hosp., R. Lawson. *Comm. R. Eng.*, Col. R. M.
Laffan. *Chaplains*, Rev. J. E. Sabine, W. M.
Wright, C. Craven, J. B. Rowlands, J. O'Dwyer
(R.C.), J. O'Flaherty (R.C.), J. Milne (P.).
Dep. Comm. Gen., R. Routh. *Assist. Sup. Stores*,
A. C. Macduff. *Staff Vet. Surgeon*, B. C. R.
Gardiner. *Barrack Masters*, Col. T. Smith, Capt.
Frith. *Gov. Mil. Prison*, Capt. A. P. Miller.
ARMAGH.—*Staff Officer Pens.*, Major M. W. de la
Poer Beresford. *Barrack Master*, Lieut. J. Nagel.
ASHTON.—*Barrack Master*, Capt. Brickenden.
ATHLONE.—*Staff Officer Pens.*, Major J. Baillie.
Barrack Master, Lieut.-Col. J. Campbell.
BALLINCOLLIG.—*Com. R. Art.*, Col. N. M'I.
Mackay. *Barrack Master*, Major J. N. Gosset.
BALLYMENA.—*Staff Off. Pens.*,Capt.T.N.Woodall
BATH.—*Staff Officer Pens.*, Capt. J. T. Chandler.
BELFAST.—*Com. R. Eng.*, Col. H. C. B. Moody.
Staff Officers Pens., Col. W. M'Pherson; Lieut.-
Col. W. Child. *Barrack Master*, A. Gall.
BERWICK.—*Barrack Master*, F. Landers.
BIRMINGHAM.—*Asst. Sup. Small Arms Factories*,
Major H. T. Arbuthnot, R.A. *Staff Officer Pens.*,
Major H. M. Smyth. *Barrack Master*, E. Wilson.
BIRR.—*Staff Officer Pens.*, Capt. R. W. Woods.
Barrack Master, H. Brill.
BRADFORD.—*Barrack Master*, Capt. Boothby.
BRECON.—*Barrack Master*, Capt. W. Watson.
BRIGHTON.—*Staff Officer Pens.*, Capt. A. H.
Hull. *Barrack Master*, J. Riley.
BRISTOL.—*Staff Surgeon*, George Saunders.
Staff Officer Pens., Major A. Maclean. *Barrack
Master*, Capt. W. Watson.
BROMPTON (CHATHAM).—*Barrack Master*, Capt.
Buckley.
BURY (LANC.).—*Barrack Master*, Capt. Brick-
enden.

CANTERBURY.—*Cavalry Depôt.*

Comm., E. B. Cureton, I.C. *Asst. Comm.*, J. R.
Steadman Sayer, C.B., c. *Majors*, Peter Withing-
ton; J. E. Swindley. *Adj.*, G. S. Davies. *Surgeon*,
J. S. Chartres (Staff). *Vet. Surg.*, Wm. C. Lord.
Staff Officer Pens., Capt. E. R. Berry. *Barrack
Master*, J. Lamont.
CARDIFF.—*Staff Officer Pens.*, Capt. R. H.
Lewis. *Barrack Master*, Capt. W. Watson.
CARLISLE.—*Staff Officer Pens.*, Major T. W.
Prevost. *Barrack Master*, Major H. W. Dennie.
CARLOW.—*Staff Officer Pens.*, Capt. R. Reid.
CAVAN.—*Staff Officer Pens.*, Capt. G. G. Mac-
kenzie.

CHATHAM.

In Command, Major Gen. F. Murray. *Comm.
R. Eng.*, Lt. Col. E. W. Ward. *Dep. Insp.-Gen.*,
R. Bowen. *Chaplains*,Rev.T. Coney, T.C. Stanley,
M. Cuffe, (R.C.), J. B. Wilson, (P.) *Sup. of Stores*,
A. Gun. *Assist. Comm. Gen.* J. H. Sale, *Brigade
Major*, Major W. W. Lynch. *Staff Off. Pens.*, Col.
R. Jenkins. *Barrack Master*, J. Buckley. *Gov.
Military Prison (Fort Clarence)*, Capt. Edwards.
1st Depôt Batt.—Lt. Col. J. W. S. Smith, C.B., c,
Major, H. A. Welman. *Adj.*, D. Reid, *capt. Surg.*,
J. W. Hulseberg (Staff). *2nd Depôt Batt.*—Lt.
Col., W. Rickman. *Majors*, W. A. Armstrong,
I.c.; W. H. Kerr. *Adjt.*, J. Heywood, *capt.
Surg.*, G, Mc G. Cardlan (Staff).
CHATHAM.—*Royal Engineer Establishment.*£21,472.
Director, Col. T. L. J. Gallwey, £1,100. *Instruc-
tor in Construction*, Col. H. Wray, £800. *Instruc-
tor in Field Works*, Col. W. C. Lennox, V.C.,
C.B., £650. *Instructor in Surveying*, Col. A.
A'Court Fisher, C.B. £650. *Instructor in Tele-
graphy*, Capt. R. H. Stotherd, £650. *Field Officer
for Discipline*, Col. F. Somerset, £383. *Brigade
Major*, Major R. Harrison, £173.

CHATHAM DOCKYARD. £210,531.
Sal. £24,193. *Wages*, £136,338.
Capt.-Superintendent, W. C. Chamberlain,
£1,250. *Master Attendant*, Staff Capt. R. Stokes,
£600. *Master Shipwright*, P. Thornton, Esq.,£630.
Chief Engineer, T. Baker, Esq., £650. *Naval
Storekeeper*, A. P. Cooper, Esq., £600. *Accountant*,
E. Clatworthy, Esq., £600. *Cashier*, B. H.
Churchward, Esq., £500. *Clerk of Works*, W. T.
Rivers, Esq. *Chaplain*, Rev. J. S. Robson,
£350. *Staff Surg.*, J. King, Esq., £493. *Inspector
of Stores*, W. A. Hatton, Esq., £350.
CHATHAM MARINE INFIRMARY. £4,035.—*Sal.*,
£1,801. *Wages*, £2,234. *Dep. Insp.-Gen.*, C. A.
Anderson, Esq., M.D., £584. *Purceyor*, Capt. J.
Huskisson, R.M., £100. *Chaplain*, Rev. J. F.
Schön, £100. *Assist. Surgs.*, M. Rodgers, Esq., M.D.,
T. Kipling, Esq., £496.

ROYAL HOSPITAL, CHELSEA. £26,754.
Governor, F. M. Sir A. Woodford, G.C.B., £500.
Lt. Gov., £400.
Sec., Major-Gen. G. Hutt, C.B., £700. *Chaplain*,
Rev. G. Mathias, *Principal Med. Off. Dep. Insp.-
Gen.* W. Lucas. *Adj.* Capt. J. J. C. Irby, £210.
CHELSEA, ROYAL MILITARY ASYLUM. £14.917.—
Comm., Col. E. A. G. Muller, £300. *Sec. & Adj.*,
Col. E. Adams, £183.
CHELSEA.—*Staff Offs. Pens.*, Col. M. Whitmore,
Capt. T. P. Wright. *Barrack Master*, Capt. W.
Peel.
CHESTER.—*Staff Offs. Pens.*, Capt. J. C. Clarke.
Barrack Mast. and Assist. Sup. Stores, J. Durnford.
CHICHESTER.—*Barrack Masters*, Capt. F. F.
Laye, Lt. W. F. Le Poer Trench.
CLONMEL.—*Staff Off. Pens.*, Major W. J.
Dorehill.

COLCHESTER CAMP.

Staff Col., *Brigade Major*,
Capt. R. A. Leggett. *Comm. R. Art.*, Lt. Col. E.
Moubray. *Comm. R. Eng.*, Col. H. W. Montagu.
Chaplains, Rev. G. Dacre, C. J. Duthie, J. Virtue,
(R.C.) *Surg.*, J. Hannan. *Assist. Comm. Gen.*,
J. S. C. Sutherland. *Barrack Master*, Capt. Sir
W. O'Malley, Bart. *4th Depôt Batt. Lt. Col.*,
R. T. Farren, C.B.,c. *Major*, G. S. Coxon. *Adj.*
H. Brackenbury, *capt. Surg.*,
8th Depôt Batt. Lt. Col., P. Robertson-Ross.
Majors, L. J.P. Jones, H. R. Cowell. *Adj.*, F.
Drage, *capt.* *Surg.*, R. Webb (Staff).
CORK.—*In Command*, Major-Gen. G. Campbell,
C.B. *Comm. R. Eng.*, Lt. Col. V.T. Marris. *Assist.
Adj.-Gen.* Lt.-Col. A. A. Nelson. *Dep. Insp.Gen.*,
R. K. Prendergast. *Staff Off. Pens.*, Lt. Col. J.
W. Graves, Lt.-Col. Thomson, C.B. *Chaplain*,
Rev. C. J. Hort. *Dep. Assist. Sup. Stores*, S. L. D.
Smith. *Barrack Master*, Major Gosset. *Gov.Mil.
Prison*, Major H. W. Campbell.
COVENTRY.—*Staff Off. Pens.*, Major J. T. Ussher.
Barrack Master, E. Wilson.
CREMILL.—See ROYAL WILLIAM YARD.

CURRAGH CAMP.

In Command, Major Gen. A.A.T. Cunynghame,
C.B. *Assist. Adj. Gen.*, Lt. Col. Hon. W. H. A.
Feilding, Coldst. Gds. *Assist. Qua. Mast. Gen.*,
Bt. Col. E. Seager. *Dep. Judge Advo.*, Bt. Col.
C. L. Nugent, *(Dublin).* *Comm. Roy. Art.*, Bt.
Col. O. S. Henry, C.B. *Comm. Roy. Eng.*, Lt.Col.
F.R.Chesney. *Chapls.*,Rev.M.Crooke, T.Molouy,
(R.C.) J. M'Whinny, (P.) *Barrack Master*, Col.
Evelegh, C.B.
DEAL MARINE INFIRMARY. £298.—*Contingencies*,
£48. *Wages*, £250. *Staff Surg.*, D. J. Duigan, M.D.
Assist. Surg., J. V. N. Blake.

DEPTFORD DOCKYARD. £50,628.

Sal., £10,770. *Wages*, £39,858.

Capt. Sup., A. P. E. Wilmot, C.B., £100. *Master Attendt.*, Staff Capt. R. C. Allen. *Master Shipwright*, R. P. Saunders, Esq., £300. *Storekeeper and Cashier*, E. I. Brietzcke, Esq., £600. *Accountant*, J. Breaks, Esq. (*Paymaster, R.N.*), £600. *Engineer*, C. Pemberton, Esq., R.N. *Clerk of Works*, C. Brown, Esq., £300. *Staff Surg.*, J. H. Patterson, Esq., M.D., £405. *Insp. of Stores*, J. Easthope, Esq., £450.

DEPTFORD VICTUALLING YARD. £37,723.

Sal., £10,257. *Wages*, £27,466.

Capt. Sup., A. P. E. Wilmot, C.B., £800. *Master Attendt.*, Staff Capt. R. C. Allen, £600. *Accountant*, J. Breaks, Esq., (*Paymaster, R.N.*) *Vict. Storekpr.*, E. Ede, Esq., £600. *Store Receiver*, E. Wilkinson, £500. *Engineer*, C. Pemberton, Esq., R.N. *Staff Surg.*, R. Grigor, Esq., M.D., £558. *Transport Off.*, Comm. W. A. de V. Brownlow.

DERBY.—Staff Off. Pens., Capt. J. A. Brockman.

DEVONPORT.

In Command, Lt. Gen. Hon. Sir A. A. Spencer, K.C.B. *Comm. Roy. Eng.*, Col. S. Westmacott. *Dep. Insp. Gen.*, G. T. Ferris. *Chaplain*, Rev. D. Somerville. *Sup. of Stores*, W. L. Penno. *Brigade Major*, Major G. P. Colley. *Laboratory, Assist. Sup.*, Capt. K. Keate, R.A., £421. *Barrack Master*, Major J. Daniell.

DEVONPORT DOCKYARD. £234,738.

Sal., £36,766. *Wages*, £197,992.

Rear Admiral Sup., The Hon. J. R. Drummond. C.B., £1,683. *Master Attendt.*, Staff Capt. T. C. Pullen, £600. *Assist.*, Staff Capt. S. Spain, £500. *Add.*, Staff Capt. J. F. Loney. *Master Shipwright*, A. Moore, Esq., £650. *Assists.*, H. R. Herbert. Esq., £400; J. Angear, Esq., £400. *Engineer*, T. W. Miller, Esq., £650. *Assist.*, R. Nicoll, Esq., £500. *Naval Storekpr.*, A. Eliott, Esq., £600. *Accountant*, R. P. Chaplin, Esq., £600. *Cashier*, H. Innes, Esq., £500. *Cicil Engineer*, (*at Keyham*), R. Townshend, Esq.£550. *Clerk of Works*, S. L. Churchward, Esq., £300. *Chaplain*, Rev. R. B. Howe, B.A., £350. *Staff Surg.*, C. T. S. Kevern, Esq., £529. *Assist. Surg.*, Matthew Coates, Esq., £228. T. B. Forster, Esq., M.D., (*for service at Keyham*), £300. *Queen's Harbour-Master*, Staff Capt. J. R. Aylen, R.N., £500. *Insp. of Stores*, J. J. Crealock, Esq., £350.

DORCHESTER.—Staff Off. Pens., Major C. E. Astell. *Barrack Master*, E. Schrimshaw.

DOVER.—In Command, Major Gen. D. Russell, C.B. *Assist. Adj. Gen.*, Col. J. W. Cox. *Comm. Roy. Art.*, Col. G. P. Eaton. *Comm. Roy. Eng.*, Col. R. G. Hamilton. *Brigade Major*, Lt. Col. Greaves. *Dep. Insp. Gen.*, J. Mure, M.D. *Chaplains*, Rev., C. Green, H. N. Wheeler, J. Daly, (R.C.) *Assist. Comm. Gen.*, Hon. J. A. Erskine. *Dep. Sup. of Stores*, W. M. King. *Barrack Master*, J. G. Wright.

DUBLIN.

In Command, Gen. the Rt. Hon. Hugh H. Lord Strathnairn, G.C.B., G.C.S.I. *Mil. Sec.*, Col. Hon. L. Smyth, C.B. *Dep. Adj. Gen.*, Bt. Col. K.D. Mackenzie, C.B. *Dep. Q. M. Gen.* Bt. Col. G. W. Mayow, C.B. *Col. on Staff.* Col. T. B. F. Marriott, R. Art. *Comm. Roy. Eng.*, Col. G. Wynne *Staff Offs. Pens.*, Col. R. R. Harris, Major G. B. Stoney. *Dep. Insp. Gen.*, W. Home, M.D. *Chaplain*, Rev. R. L. M'Ghee. *Princ. Sup. Stores*, T. C. Martelli. *Barrack Master*, Capt. Munns. *Gov. Mil. Prison*, Major F. K. Bacon.

DUBLIN, ROYAL HOSPITAL, Kilmainham. £6,808. —*Master*, Gen. Lord Strathnairn, G.C.B., £100.

Joint Dep. Masters, Col. K. D. Mackenzie, C.B., Col. G. W. Mayow, C.B. *Chaplain*, Rev. G. Hare, £250. *Sec.*, G. F. Dunn, Esq., £300.

DUBLIN, ROYAL HIBERNIAN MILITARY SCHOOL. £11,378.—*Comm.*, Col. H. B. J. Wynyard, £329 *Sec. & Adj.*, Lt. Col. T. B. Speedy, £227.

DUMBARTON.—Barrack Master, Major R. D. Barbor.

DUNRAR.—Barrack Master, F. Landers.

DUNDALK.—Barrack Master, Lt. J. Nagel.

DUNDEE.—Staff Off. Pens., Capt. A. C. Young. *Barrack Master*, Capt. J. Forbes.

EASTBOURNE.—Assist Surgeon, V.S.Gouldsbury, M.D. *Barrack Master*, J. Riley.

EDINBURGH.

In Command, Major Gen. R. Rumley. *Comm. Roy. Art.*, Col. J. L. Elgee, (*Leith Fort*). *Comm. Roy. Eng.*, Col. H. A. White. *Assist. Adj. Gen.*, Hon. F. Colborne. *Dep. Insp. Gen.*, W. Home, M.D. *Chaplain*, (*Castle*), Rev. J. Millar. *Dep. Sup. of Stores*, G. G. Munro. *Assist. Comm. Gen.*, R. Cumming. *Staff Off. Pens.*, Major W. J. Kirk. *Barrack Master*, F. Landers.

ENFIELD, *Small Arms Factory.—Sup.*, Col.W.H. Dixon, R.A., £975. *Assist. Sup.*, Capt. M. P. Eden, R.A., £451.

ENNIS.—Staff Off. Pens., Capt. R. G. Charlton.

ENNISKILLEN.—Staff. Off. Pens., Capt. R. H. Brooke. *Barrack Master*, R. T. Wolfe.

EXETER.—Staff Off. Pens., Lt. Col. A. Pigott. *Barrack Master*, Major F. Daniell.

FALMOUTH.—Staff Off. Pens., Capt. E. C. Domville.

FERMOY.—Barrack Master, Lt. Col. Heyland.

FLEETWOOD.—Assist. Surg., G. Ashton, M.B. *Barrack Master*, Major H. W. Dennie.

FORT CLARENCE, Rochester.—*Gov. Mil.Prison*, Capt. Edwards. *Barrack Master*, Capt. Buckley.

FORT GEORGE.—*Dep. Assist. Sup. of Stores*, J. J. Lake. *Assist. Surg.*, G. N. Irvine, M.D. *Barrack Master*, J. J. Lake.

FORT PITT, Chatham.—*Barrack Master*, Capt. Buckley.

GALWAY.—Staff Off. Pens., Capt. R.G.S. Mason.

GLASGOW.—Staff Surg., A. D. Home, C.B., H.C., *Staff Offs. Pens.*, Major G. F. Moore, Capt. J. Stewart. *Barrack Master*, Major R. D. Barbor.

GLOUCESTER.—Staff Off. Pens., Lt. Col. H. C. C. Somerset.

GOSPORT.—11th *Depôt Battalion*. Lt. Col., J. Nason. *Major*, W. Little. *Adj.*, A. M. Cardew, *capt. Surg.*, S. Roch, (Staff.) *Chaplains*, Rev. T. Molesworth, G. A. Vandeleur, A. McCarthy, (R.C.) *Surg.*, S. Roch. *Barrack Masters*, Capt. F. F. Laye, Lt. W. F. Le Poer Trench. *Gov. Mil. Pris.*, Col. W. H. C. Wellesley.

GOSPORT VICTUALLING YARD. — *See* ROYAL CLARENCE YARD.

GRAVESEND.—Comm. R. Eng., Lieut.-Col. C. G. Gordon, C.B. *Assist. Surg.*, T. O'Farrell, M.D.; R. Turner. *Barrack Master*, W. Boulger.

GREENLAW, Edinburgh.—*Gov. Mil. Prison*, Capt. F. D. Allen. *Barrack Master*, F. Landers.

ROYAL HOSPITAL, GREENWICH.

Gov., Admiral of the Fleet Sir J. A. Gordon, G.C.B. *Capt. Sup.*, Thomas Wilson, C.B. *Lieuts.*, Hen. Bainbridge, J. C. Clarke. *Chaplain*, Rev. Wm. G. Tucker, M.A. *Dep. Insp.-Gen.*, W. R. E. Smart, C.B., M.D. *Assisting Surgeon*, Robert Grahame, M.D. *Steward*, Arthur Jones, Esq., R.N. *Controller and Solicitor*, John C. Lethbridge, Esq.

GREENWICH SCHOOLS.—*Principal and Chaplain*, Rev. Robert Holme. Nautical Division, (80 boys)— *Head Master*, George S. Bourne, Esq., R.N. *Se-*

cond *Master*, Edward W. Snell.—*Section A* (240 boys). *Head Master*, Rev. J. Hill, B.D. *Second Master*, William F. Card.—*Section B* (240 boys). *Head Master*, Dr. Edw. Purcell. *Second Master*, Robert Mustart.—*Section C* (240 boys). *Head Master*, Henry R. Baillie. *Second Master*, Albert Escott. *French Master*, M. Quesnel.

GUERNSEY.—*In Command*, Major-Gen. C. R. Scott. *Comm. R. Art.*, Lieut.-Col. R. K. Freeth. *Comm. R. Eng.*, Col. J. H. Freeth. *Fort Major*, Col. J. Miller. *Staff Officer Pens.*, Capt. J. E. Harvey. *Barrack Master*, W. R. Jenney.

HALIFAX.—*Staff Officer Pens.*, Col. J. E. Orange.

HAMPTON COURT.—*Barrack Master*, J. Lynas.

HARWICH.—*Barrack Master*, J. Bacon.

HASLAR HOSPITAL, PORTSMOUTH. £19,052. *Sal.*, £9,059. *Wages*, £9,993.

Capt. Sup., Charles F. A. Shadwell, C.B. *Lieuts.*, Harry T. Veitch, £200. Charles G. Fegen, £200. *Chaplain*, Rev. Geo. Jackson, M.A., £350. *Insp.-Gens.*, Sir David Deas, K.C.B., M.D., Geo. Burn, Esq., M.D., £1,825. *Dep. Insp.-Gens.*, George Mackay, Esq., M.D., R. D. Mason, Esq., £1,314. *Agent and Steward*, John Russell, Esq., £500. *Staff Surgeon*, James Vaughan, Esq., £518.

HAULBOWLINE NAVAL HOSPITAL, Cork. £1,608. *Sal.*, £869. *Wages*, £739.

Staff Surgeon, Wm. Loney, Esq., M.D., £493.

HAULBOWLINE VICTUALLING YARD. £2,893. *Sal.*, £1,501. *Wages*, £1,392.

Storekeeper and Accountant, John Rose Paris, Esq., £500. 18 Shipwrights, &c., *Wages*, £670.

HERBERT HOSPITAL.—See WOOLWICH.

HOLY ISLAND.—*Barrack Master*, F. Landers.

HOUNSLOW.—*Barrack Master*, J. Lynas.

HULL.—*Staff Officer Pens.*, Capt. C. H. Fresson.

HYTHE. *School of Musketry.* £10,546.—*Comm. and Insp.-Gen.*, Col. W. R. Haliday, £892. *Chief Instructor*, Lieut.-Col. H. F. Bythesea, £260. *Capt. and D.A.A. Gen.*, Capt. D. R. Barnes, £365. *Barrack Master*, Lieut. E. Harrison.

INVERNESS.—*Staff Officer Pens.*, Maj. J.P. Stuart.

IPSWICH.—*Staff Officer Pens.*, Capt. W. E. Todd. *Barrack Master*, Capt. Sir W. O'Malley, Bart.

ISLE OF MAN.—*Staff Off. Pens.*, Major Dickson.

JERSEY.—*In Command*, Major-Gen. P. M. N. Guy, C.B. *Comm. R. Art.*, Col. Hon. E. T. Gage. *Comm. R. Eng.*, Lieut.-Col. E. C. A. Gordon. *Staff Surgeon-Major*, E. W. Bawtree, M.D. *Fort Major and Adj.*, Col. John Fraser. *Assist. Super. of Stores*, J. Greig. *Staff Officer Pens.*, Capt. J. E. Harvey. *Barrack Master*, Lieut. W. Fuller.

KILKENNY.—*Staff Officer Pens.*, Capt. R. J. Spofforth. *Barrack Master*, Capt. W. B. Park.

KNELLER HALL, Twickenham.—*Barrack Master*, J. Lynas.

LEEDS.—*Staff Officer Pens.*, Major W. Pilsworth. *Barrack Master*, Capt. B. C. Boothby.

LEITH FORT.—*Comm. R. Art.*, Col. J. L. Elgee. *Barrack Master*, F. Landers.

LEWES NAVAL PRISON. £2,891.—*Gov.*, Comm. C. M. Luckraft, R.N., £381. *Chaplain*, Rev. Geo. A. M. Little, £200.

LIMERICK.—*Comm. R. Eng.*, Lieut.-Col. R. D. Kerr. *Staff Officer Pens.*, Capt. H. H. Pratt. *Barrack Master*, W. Barton.

LITTLEHAMPTON.—*Barrack Masters*, Capt. F. F. Laye, Lieut. W. F. Le Poer Trench.

LIVERPOOL.—*Insp. Field Officer*, Col. Sir John Jones, K.C.B. *Adj.*, Lieut. M. Clarke. *Staff Offs. Pens.*, Major H. C. Faulkner; Capt. J. F. Birch. *Barrack Master*, J. Durnford.

LONDON.

Staff Officers Pens., Lt.-Col. J. P. Pigott. Major F. F. Dore, Tower Hill. Col. M. R. S. Whitmore

and Capt. T. P. Wright, *Chelsea Hospital.* Major D. H. MacKinnon and Capt. R. C. D. Bruce, *Regent's Park Barracks.* Col. F. P. Nott, *Kennington Park.* Major H. T. Richmond, *Deptford.*

LONDON.—*Insp. Field Officer, Recruiting*, Col. R. C. H. Taylor. *Adj.*, Lieut. W. F. Wyndowe.

LONDON.—*Chaplain, Chelsea Hospital*, Rev. G. Mathias. *Other Mil. Chaplains*, Rev. W. G. Green (*Tower*), R. Halpin, G. Hare, L. J. Parsons, P. Beaton (P.).

Barrack Master (in charge of all the London Barracks), Capt. W. Peel, Regent's Park Barracks.

Gov. Military Prison (Southwark), Capt. C. Clerk.

LONDON, The Tower.—*Constable*, F.M. Sir J. Burgoyne, Bt., G.C.B. *Lieut.*, Gen. ⚔ Sir George Bowles, K.C.B. *Dep. Lieut.*, Gen. Lord De Ros. *Major*, Bt. Col. F. A. Whimper, Unatt. *Chaplain*, Rev. Wm. Graham Green, B.A. *Med. Officer*, Dep. Insp. Gen. J. S. Graves, h.p.

Military Store Department.—*Sup. in Charge*, Robt. R. Pringle, Esq., £684. *Deputies*, William O'Neill and J. B. Cole, Esqrs., £365 each. *Sup. of Inspectors*, John J. Lardner, Esq.

Army Clothing Depôt, Pimlico.—*Sup.*, Col. J. Hudson, £500. *Inspector*, Col. H. C. B. Daubeney, C.B., £500. *Storekeeper*, Capt. G. Grant, £500. *Small Arms Factory, Millbank.*—*Asst. Sup.* Major H. S. C. Dyer, R.A., £589.

LONDONDERRY.—*Staff Officer Pens.*, Major D. Hamilton. *Barrack Master*, A. Gall.

LONGFORD.—*Staff Officer Pens.*, Lt.-Col. W. Mauleverer. *Barrack Master*, Capt. Adam.

LYNN.—*Staff Officer Pens.*, Capt. J. S. Cannon.

MAIDSTONE.—*Adj. R. Horse Art. Depôt*, Lt. Æ. De V. Tupper. *Barrack Master*, W. Thompson.

MANCHESTER.

In Command, Major Gen. Sir John Garvock, K.C.B. *Assist. Adj. Gen.*, Col. J. W. Reynolds. *Assist. Q.M. Gen.*, Col. H. L. Maydwell. *Dep. Judge Adv. Gen.*, Lieut. Col. G. Mem. *Comm. R. Art.*, Col. C. L. D'Aguilar, C.B. *Comm. R. Eng.*, Col. W. G. Hamley. *Dep. Insp. Gen.*, J. Bent. *Dep. Comm. Gen.*, G. D. Lardner. *Staff Officers Pens.*, Col. A. F. Bond; Major J. F. Sharp. *Barrack Master*, Capt. L. Brickenden.

MARCHWOOD MAGAZINE.— *Dep. Assist. Sup of Stores and Barrack Master*, A. Montanaro.

NETLEY, ARMY MEDICAL SCHOOL. £9,600.

President, Thos. G. Logan, M.D., C.B., *Direct.-Gen. Army Med. Dept. Physician to the Council of India*, Sir Jas. Ranald Martin, C.B.

Professors.—*Mil. Surgery*, Dep. Insp. Gen. T. Longmore, C.B., £850. *Mil. Medicine*, Dep. Insp. Gen. W. C. Maclean, M.D., £850. *Mil. Hygiene*, E. A. Parkes, Esq., M.D., F.R.S., £850. *Pathology*, W. Aitken, Esq., M.D., £850.

Assistant Professors.—*Mil. Surgery*, Staff Surg. Maj. W. A. Mackinnon, C.B. *Mil. Medicine*, Staff Surg. W. J. Fyffe, M.D. *Mil. Hygiene*, Staff Surg. F. S. B. F. de Chaumont, M.D. *Pathology*, Staff Assist. Surg. Vivian Wearne, £1,064. *Sec.*, H. F. T. G. Borchert, Esq., £200.

NETLEY, ROYAL VICTORIA HOSPITAL. £5,516. *Gov. and Comm.*, Maj.-Gen. Rich. Wilbraham, C.B., £600. *Staff Capt. and Assist. Comm.*, Maj. Thos. A. Rawlins, £303. *Chaplain*, Rev. W. F. Hobson. *Q.M. and Adj.*, Army Hosp. Corps, Henry Saville, *ll.*

NEWBRIDGE.—*Barrack Master*, J. Barber.

NEWCASTLE-ON-TYNE.—*Staff Officer Pens.*, Capt. D. Beere. *Barrack Master*, J. Short.

NEWCASTLE-UNDER-LYNE.—*Staff Officer Pens.*, Capt. J. H. Lawrence-Archer.

NEWPORT (MON.).—*B. Master*, Capt. W. Watson.
NEWRY.—*Staff Officer Pens.*, Capt. W. H. Graves.
Barrack Master, Lieut. J. Nagel.
NORTHAMPTON.—*Staff Officer Pens.*, Capt. C.
W. St. John. *Barrack Master*, H. H. R. Hewitt.
NORWICH.—*Pens.*, Col. J. Cockburn. *Barrack Master*, Capt. Sir W. O'Malley, Bart.;
NOTTINGHAM.—*Off. Pens.*, Lieut.-Col. Story.
OMAGH.—*Staff Off. Pens.*, Capt. Wedderburne.
PAISLEY.—*Staff Officer Pens.*, Major M. E.
Smith. *Barrack Master*, Major R. D. Barbor.
PARKHURST. 5th *Depôt Battalion.*—Lt.-Col., E.
R. Jeffreys, C.B., *c. Major*, Hen. W. Meredith,
l.c. Adj., Wm. C. Justice. *capt. Surgeon*, A. E.
T. Longhurst, M.D. (Staff), *Chaplain*, Rev. H.
E. Maskew. *Barrack Master*, Capt. E. J. Otway.

PEMBROKE DOCKYARD. £89,917.

Sal., £12,827. *Wages*, £77,090.
Capt. Sup., Robert Hall, £1000. *Harbour Master*,
Staff Comm. George H. Blakey. *Master Shipwright*, John I. Fincham, Esq., £650. *Storekeeper and Cashier*, Edgecumbe Chevallier, Esq.,
£600. *Accountant*, Chas. J. Pringle, Esq., £450.
Inspector of Stores, Theophilus Scott, Esq., £350.
Staff Surgeon, David Lyall, Esq., M.D., £530.
Chaplain, Rev. Samuel Beal, B.A., £400.

PEMBROKE DOCK.

13th *Depôt Batt.*, *Lt. Col.*, W. L. Stewart. *Major*,
J. Hare. *Adj.*, Rob. Bennett, *capt. Surgeon*,
W. H. Harris (Staff).
Comm. R. *Eng.*, Col. G. F. Mann, C.B. *Chaplains*, Rev. S. Beal and J. A. Bayley. *Assist.
Comm. Gen.*, W. Hewetson. *Surgeon*, W. H.
Harris. *Barrack Master*, W. C. Moore.
PENALLY, Pembroke.—*Assist. Surgeon*, Arthur
Chester. *Barrack Master*, W. C. Moore.
PERTH.—*Staff Officer Pens.*, Major J. W. Boyd.
PIERSHILL, Edin.—*Barrack M.*, F. Landers.

PLYMOUTH.

In Command, Lieut.-Gen. Hon. Sir A. A. Spencer, K.C.B. *Comm.* R. *Art.*, Col. R. C. Romer.
Chaplains, Rev. W. Sykes; L. Parsly (R.C.).
Town Major, Major B. Ramsay. *Staff Officers
Pens.*, Col. H. Rogers; Major R. Law. *Barrack
Master*, Major J. Daniell.

PLYMOUTH NAVAL HOSPITAL. £11,720.

Sal., £3,597. *Wages*, £6,123.
Capt. Sup., Edward Tatham. *Lieuts.*, Robert
S. Moore; John P. Cheyne, £400. *Chaplain*,
Rev. Nathaniel Proctor, B.A., £350. *Insp.-Gen.*,
John Davidson, Esq., C.B., M.D., £913. *Dep.
Insp. Gen.*, Henry J. Domville, Esq., C.B., M.D.,
£599. *Agent and Steward*, John Grant, Esq.,
£400. *Staff Surgeon and Medical Storekeeper*,
Robert Pottinger, Esq., £493.
PLYMOUTH VICTUALLING YARD. — *See* ROYAL
WILLIAM YARD.
PLYMOUTH MARINE INFIRMARY. £1,650.
Sal., £1,220. *Wages*, £430.
Staff Surgeon, James Jenkins, Esq., C.B., M.D.,
£496. *Assistant Surgeons*, Charles J. Devonshire,
Esq., B.A.; Thomas S. Burnett, Esq., £513.

PORTSMOUTH.

In Command, Lieut.-Gen. Sir G. Buller, K.C.B.
Assist. Adj. Gen., Lieut.-Col. J. Peel. *Assist. Q.M.
Gen.*, Col. G. H. S. Willis. *Comm. R. Art.*, Col.
E. Wodehouse, C.B. *Comm. R. Eng.*, Col. W. C.
Hadden. *Dep. Insp. Gen.*, G. A. Gordon, M.D.,
C.B. *Chaplains*, Ven. Archdeacon Wright, Rev.
R. Orr, E. Butler (R.C.). *Sup. of Stores*, W. L.
M. Young, C.B. *Sup. of Ordnance Factories*, Maj.
Fraser, R.A., £557. *Assist. Comm. Gen.*, H.

Maule; D. C. Napier. *Town Major*, Major E.
Breton. *Staff Officers Pens.*, Lieut. Col. G. W.
Meehan; Capt. C. R. De la Bere. *Barrack
M.* Capt. F. F. Laye ; Lieut. W. T. Le PoerTrench.

PORTSMOUTH DOCKYARD. £260,965.

Sal., £35,648. *Wages*, £225,317.
Rear-Adm. Sup., Geo. G. Wellesley, C.B., £1,683.
Master Attendant, Staff Capt. William T. Mainprise, R.N., C.B., £600. *Assist.*, Staff Capt. H. A.
Morinarty, C.B., £500. *Master Shipwright*, Henry
Cradock, Esq., £700. *Chief Eng., &c.*, Andrew
Murray, Esq., £650. *Assist.*, William Lynn, Esq.,
£400. *Naval Storekeeper*, John Martin, Esq.,
£600. *Accountant*, George E. Gittens, Esq., £550.
Cashier, William M. Richards, Esq., £500.
Sup. Civil Eng., Henry Wood, Esq., £600. *Chaplain*, Rev. Edw. S. Phelps, B.A., £350. *Staff Surgeon*, Edw. H. Cree, Esq., M.D., £493. *Insp. of
Stores*, Alfred Penfold, Esq., £350.
PORTSMOUTH MARINE ARTILLERY INFIRMARY,
Fort Cumberland. £1,592. *Sal.*, £1,321. *Wages*,
£271. *Staff Surgeon*, John F. Charlton, Esq.,
M.D., £496.
PORTSMOUTH MARINE INFIRMARY, Forton.
£1,250. *Sal.*, £1,197. *Wages*, £53. *Staff Surgeon*, Charles D. Steel, Esq., £518.
PORTSMOUTH NAVAL HOSPITAL.—*See* HASLAR.
PRESTON. 9th *Depôt Battalion.*—Lieut.-Col.,
Wm. Hardy, *c. Major*, Robt. Maunsall, *l.c. Adj.*,
Wm. H. Paul, *capt. Chaplain*, Rev. Edwin Smith.
Sur., John Wood (Staff). *Staff Off. Pens.*, Capt. M.
Browne. *Barrack Master*, Major H. W. Dennie.
PRIDDY'S HARD, Gosport.—*Dep. Sup. of Stores*,
C. K. Cleeve.
PURFLEET MAGAZINE.—*Dep. Sup. of Stores and
Barrack Master*, W. H. H. Scott.
ROYAL CLARENCE VICTUALLING YARD, Weevil,
Gosport. £15,239. *Sal.*, £4,977. *Wages*, £10,262.
Capt.-Sup., Charles F. A. Shadwell, C.B., £800.
Master-Attendant, Staff Captain George H. K.
Bower, R.N., C.B., £500. *Storekeeper*, Thomas G.
Grant, Esq., £550.
ROYAL WILLIAM VICTUALLING YARD, Cremill,
Plymouth. £15,220. *Sal.*, £5,448. *Wages*,
£9,782. *Capt. Sup.*, Edw. Tatham, £800. *Master-
Attendant*, Staff Capt. William T. Wheeler, R.N.,
£500. *Storekeeper*, Thomas Jamieson, Esq., £600.

SANDHURST.

ROYAL MILITARY COLLEGE. £36,731.—*Gov.* Lt.-
Gen. Sir D. A. Cameron, K.C.B., £1,250. *Comm.*,
Col. E. G. Hallewell, £637. *Chap.*, Rev. E. J.
Rogers, £464. *Adj.*, Capt. W. Patterson, £354.
STAFF COLLEGE. £7,955.—*Comm.*, Col. T. E.
Lacy, £648. *Adjutant*, Major A. S. Jones, F.C.,
£353. *Barrack Master*, Quartermaster Davis.
SCARBOROUGH.—*Barrack Mast.*, Capt. Boothby

SHEERNESS DOCKYARD. £132,349.

Sal., £19,786. *Wages*, £112,563.
Capt.-Sup., William K. Hall, C.B. *Master Attendant*, Staff Captain Henry Paul, R.N., £600.
Master Shipwright, Alfred B. Sturdee, Esq., £600.
Assist. Master Attendant, Staff Capt. Valentine G.
Roberts, £500. *Assist. Master Shipwright*, William
Mitchell, Esq., £400. *Engineer*, John Ward, Esq.,
R.N., £500. *Storekeeper*, J. Creasey, Esq., £600.
Accountant, James Horsey, Esq., £450. *Cashier*,
Robert G. Hobbes, Esq., £500. *Clerk of Works*,
Frederick Turner, Esq., £300. *Chaplain*, Rev.
Roland Wilson, B.A., £350. *Staff Sur.*, Robert
T. C. Scott, Esq., £503. *Inspector of Stores*, Chas.
Pennell, Esq., £300. *Barrack Master*, Walter
Gillies, 2nd Lieut. R.M.

SHEERNESS.—*Comm. R. Eng.*, Lt.-Col. J. W. Lovell. *Garr. Chap.*, Rev. G. Lawless. *Barrack Master and Dp.-Assist. Sup. of Stores*, G. Wilgress.

SHEFFIELD.—*14th Depôt Battalion.—Lieut.-Col.*, J. C. H. Jones, *c. Major*, B. H. Heathcote. *Adj.*, W. J. Tarte, *capt. Chaplain*, Rev. G. C. Williams. *Assist. Surg.*, J. A. Shaw, M.D. (Staff). *Staff Off. Pens.*, Major G. Wolfe. *Barrack Master*, J. Harbourne.

SHOEBURYNESS SCHOOL OF GUNNERY. £7,855. *In Comm.*, Major-Gen. F. M. Eardley-Wilmot, R.A., £415. *Brigade Major*, Col. R. Curtis, R.A., £173. *Sups. of Experiments*, Capt. H. J. Alderson; Lieut. C. H. F. Ellis, £237. *Adj.*, Capt. Dugdale, R.A. *Chaplain*, Rev. George Wylde. *Barrack Master*, W. Boulger.

SHORNCLIFFE CAMP.

In Command, Major-Gen. J. S. Brownrigg, C.B. *Brigade Maj.*, Capt. A. E. Ross. *Chaplains*, Revs. H. St. George; J. B. H. Harris; J. M'Sweeny, (R. C.); F. Cannon, (P.) *Surgeons*, W. Sinclair; A. Semple, M.D. *3rd Dep. Batt.*—Hon. J. J. Bourke, *Major*, T. H. Clarkson. *Adjt.*, J. N. Colthurst, *capt. Surg.*, H. J. Rose (Staff). *10th Dep. Bat.* — *Lt.-Col.* R. W. M. Fraser, *c. Maj.* J. Hare. *Adj.*, J. M'Queen, *capt. 12th Dep. Batt.*—*Lt. Col.*, A. C. Goodenough, C.B., *c. Major*, F. E. Drewe, *l. c. Adj.*, W. Wood, *capt. Assist. Surg.*, P. T. Frazer (Staff). *Barrack Master*, Lt. E. Harrison. *Warder, Mil. Prison*, W. Tucker.

SHREWSBURY.—*Staff Officer Pens.*, Capt. J. G. M'D. Tulloch.

SLIGO.—*Staff Officer Pens.*, Capt. H. Kean. *Barrack Master*, Capt. W. Adam.

SOUTHAMPTON. ORDNANCE SURVEY DEPARTMENT.—*Executive Officer*, Col. Cameron, R.E. *Trigonometrical Branch*, Capt. Clarke, R.E., F.R.S. *Publication do.*, Capt. Parsons, R.E., F.R.A.S.

SOUTHAMPTON.—*Staff Officer Pens.*, Lt.-Col. W. Lacy. *Barrack Master*, George Allan.

STIRLING.—*Staff Officer Pens.*, Capt. D. Stewart. *Assist. Sup. of Stores, and Barrack Master*, W. E. Webster.

SUNDERLAND.—*Barrack Master*, J. Short.

TAUNTON.—*Staff Officer Pens.*, Capt. H. G. E. Somerset.

TEMPLEMORE.—*Barrk. Mas.*, Capt. J. E. Acklom.

TILBURY FORT.—*Barrack Master*, W. Boulger.

TIPNER, Portsmouth.—*Dep. Assist. Super. of Stores*, J. F. Edwards. *Barrack Masters*, Capt. F. F. Laye; Lt. W. F. Le Poer Trench.

TRALEE.—*Staff Officer Pens.*, Lt.-Col. Stokes. *Barrack Master*, Lt.-Col. Heyland.

TROWBRIDGE.—*Staff Officer Pens.*, Capt. J. Lawson. *Barrack Master*, Capt. W. Watson.

TULLAMORE.—*Staff Off. Pens.*, Capt. Kekewich.

TYNEMOUTH.—*Barrack Master*, J. Short.

UPNOR, Chatham.—*Assist. Sup. of Stores*, G. C. Holden. *Barrack Master*, Capt. J. Buckley.

WALMER.—*6th Depôt Battalion.—Lt.-Col.*, Fowler Burton, C.B., *c. Major*, R. J. Hughes. *Adj.*, A. H. Godfrey, *capt. Chaplain*, Rev. J. A. Walsh Collins. *Surgeon*, Frederick Douglas, M.D. (Staff). *Barrack Master*, Capt. W. K. Fraser.

WALTHAM ABBEY GUNPOWDER FACTORY.—*Sup.*, Col. C. W. Younghusband, R.A., £993. *Assist. Sup.*, Capt. F. M. Smith, R.A., £401. *Clerk 1st. Class*, G. E. Durnford, Esq., £350.

WARLEY.—*Chaplain*, Rev. E. L. Walsh. *Assist. Surgeon*, Geo. W. L'Estrange. *Barrack Master*, Major E. Sutherland.

WATERFORD.—*Staff Officer Pens.*, Captain H. L. Searle. *Barrack Master*, Capt. W. B. Park.

WEEDON.—*Barrack Master and Assist. Sup. of Stores*, H. H. R. Hewitt. *Gov. Mil. Prison*, Capt. F. Brome.

WEEVIL.—See ROYAL CLARENCE VICTUALLING YARD.

WEYMOUTH.—*Comm. R. Eng.*, Lieut.-Col. Belfield. *Barrack Master*, E. Schrimshaw.

WINCHESTER.—*7th Depôt Battalion.—Lieut.-Col.* A. M. M'Donald, *c. Majors*, Rupert B. Deering; E. W. Blackett. *Adj.*, A. Morrah, *capt. Surgeon-Major*, W. Lapsley (Staff). *Chaplain*, Rev. H. Hare. *Barrack Master*, A. Montanaro.

WHITEHAVEN.—*Barrack Master*, Major H. W. Dennie.

WINDSOR.—*Barrack Master*, J. Lynas.

WOOLWICH.

In Comm. Major-Gen. E. C. Warde. *Dep. Assist. Q.M. Gen.*, Lieut.-Col. R. Biddulph. *Com. R.E.*, Col. W. D. Gosset. *Brigade Major*, Major R. J. Hay. *Dep. Insp.-Gen.*, J. G. Inglis, M.D., C.B. *Chaplains*, Revs. H. Hulcatt, F. F. Thomson, T. L. Coghlan, R.C. *Assist. Comm.-Gen.*, T. F. Moore. *Principal Sup. of Stores*, H. W. Gordon, C.B. *Staff Veter. Surgeon*, W. Thacker. *Staff Officer Pens.*, Lieut.-Col. D. W. Tench. *Barrack Master*, Major E. Sutherland.

WOOLWICH DOCKYARD. £149,590. *Sal.*, £22,743. *Wages*, £126,847. *Comm.* Capt. Wm. Edmonstone, C.B., £1,250. *Master Attendant*, Staff Captain Francis H. May, £600. *Master Shipwright*, William Ladd, Esq., £650. *Assist.* W. H. Henwood, Esq., £400. *Naval Storekeeper*, O. B. Piers, Esq., £600. *Accountant*, Henry G. B. Johnson, Esq., £500. *Cashier*, Robert Harwood, Esq., £450. *Engineer*, John Trickett, Esq., £650. *Clerk of Works*, D. Patridge, Esq., £400. *Assist. Civil Eng.*, Edwin A. Bernays, Esq., £300. *Chaplain*, Rev. Jas. C. Connolly, R.A., £350. *Staff Surgeon*, John I. Acheson, Esq., £493. *Insp. of Stores*, W. R. de Montmorency, £300.

WOOLWICH ROYAL MILITARY ACADEMY. £38,581. *Governor*, H.R.H. Duke of Cambridge, K.G. *Lieut.-Gov. Comm.*, Major-Gen. Ormsby, R.A., £1,000. *Chaplain*, Rev. A. C. Fraser, £263. *Adj.*, Major South, £572.

WOOLWICH MANUFACTURING DEPARTMENTS.—Carriage Department: *Sup.*, Col. H. Clerk, R.A., £845. *Assist. Sup.*, Capt. F. Close, R.A., £421. *Principal Clerk*, F. J. Fullom, Esq., £552.

Chemical Department.—*Chemist to War Department*, F. A. Abel, Esq., F.R.S., £800. *Senior Assist.*, W. Y. Dent, Esq., F.C.S., £350.

Gun Factory.—*Sup.*, Col. F. A. Campbell, R.A., £993. *Assist. Sup.*, Capt. G. M. Molony, R.A., £451. *Dep. Assist. Sup.*, R. S. Fraser, Esq., £500. *Principal Clerk*, J. Baker, Esq., £500.

Laboratory.—*Sup.*, Col. E. M. Boxer, R.A., £845. *Assist. Sup.*, Capt. V. D. Majendie, R.A., £419. *Principal Clerk*, W. E. Oram, Esq., £500.

WOOLWICH HERBERT HOSPITAL. £1,010.—*Gov.*, Col. H. J. Shaw, £350.

WOOLWICH MARINE INFIRMARY. £4,337. *Sal.*, £1,877. *Wages*, £2,460.—*Dep. Insp.-Gen.*, James Salmon, Esq., M.D., £639. *Purveyor*, Capt. J. C. Travers, R.M., £100. *Assist. Surgeons*, William S. Fisher, Esq., M.B., R.A., Saml. Grose, Esq., £456.

YARMOUTH NAVAL HOSPITAL (Lunatic Asylum). £4,038. *Sal.*, £2,204. *Wages*, £1,834.—*Dep. Insp. Gen.*, Wm Macleod, Esq., M.D., £584. *Agent and Steward*, James R. Constantine, Esq., £300. *Assisting Staff Surgeon*, James Whicher, Esq., M.D., £439

ALL religions and all forms of worship are tolerated in the British Empire, but two Christian Churches receive from the Government a degree of support that is not extended to other religions bodies. These are, the Episcopal Church in England and Ireland, and the Presbyterian Church in Scotland, and they are in consequence termed the Established or State Churches of their respective countries.

The ESTABLISHED CHURCH IN ENGLAND, a Protestant Episcopal institution, is governed by 2 archbishops and 26 bishops, who, though nominally elected by the clergy of each diocese, are in reality appointed by the Premier for the time being. The 2 archbishops and 24 of the bishops have seats in the House of Peers, and the last appointed bishop having a seat is ex officio the chaplain of their Lordships' House. A very large proportion of the episcopal property is managed by a body of Ecclesiastical Commissioners appointed in 1836, who pay therefrom fixed incomes to the prelates, ranging from £15,000 to the Archbishop of Canterbury, and £10,000 to the Archbishop of York and the Bishops of London and Winchester, and £8,000 to the Bishop of Durham, to £5,500, £5,000, £4,200, £2,700, and £2,000, which last is the income of the Bishop of Sodor and Man, who, however, is not a lord of Parliament. The inferior dignitaries of the Church are the Deans, of whom there are 30, with incomes varying from £3,000 to the Dean of Durham, to £700 to the Dean of Bangor, £1,000 each being about the average. As assistants to the bishops there are 71 archdeacons, who commonly hold other preferments, as their archidiaconal incomes are but small. Under the archdeacons there are 610 rural deans, who exercise an unpaid supervision over the parochial clergy. The number of benefices is now about 13,000 (12,628 is the return from the Bishops' Registrars in 1861), and the clergy of every class, from the archbishops to the stipendiary curates, are estimated at 18,000. The revenues of the Church are not accurately known, but they are usually greatly exaggerated, from the fact of all the tithes (£5,000,000 on a rough estimate) being supposed to be devoted to their professed object; but Parliamentary returns show that up to 31st December, 1866, rent-charges in lieu of tithes had been settled by the Tithe Commissioners to the amount of £4,053,000. Of this sum, lay impropriators, and schools, and colleges received £962,000, and clerical appropriators and lessees £679,000; leaving less than £2,500,000 to be divided among the parochial clergy. Some estimates have placed the Church property at the rate of £10,000,000 per year, but it is more probably put at about double the amount of the tithe—glebe, pew rents in towns, and surplice fees being taken with the account—or something less than £5,000,000. No religious census has been officially taken in England, but the Church population is estimated on reliable data at about 12,500,000, and 5,500,000 church sittings are available for them. In towns a charge of from 5s. to 10s. or upwards, per year, is made for the great majority of the seats; but in most of the churches built or enlarged of late years a certain number of free sittings are provided.

In theory the Church of England is governed by means of its Convocation of Bishops and Clergy, but practically, Convocation is at present, a merely deliberative body. There is a House of Convocation for each province, Canterbury and York, also another for the whole Irish Church, each differently constituted. That of Canterbury consists of two Houses, the upper confined to the bishops, the lower is composed of the dean of each cathedral, the archdeacons, and proctors elected from every cathedral chapter, and one or more elected by the clergy of every diocese. In York there is but one House, the bishops, deans, archdeacons and proctors sitting together. In Ireland, Convocation is practically in abeyance. In England a fresh election of proctors is made with every new parliament.

For the Established Church in Ireland see p. 164.

The Established Church in the Colonies now numbers 45 bishops and about 2,000 clergy. The first colonial see established was that of Nova Scotia in 1787; next came Quebec in 1793. The first East Indian see was Calcutta, founded in 1813; to which succeeded Jamaica, the first of the West Indian sees, in 1824. The episcopate of Australia dates from the establishment of the see now called Sydney, in 1836; that of New Zealand from 1841; and that of Africa from 1850. Taking the sees in order of groups of colonies we have :—

(1.) *North American Sees*, 9, with 657 clergy. Montreal (Metropolitan), Columbia, Fredericton, Huron, Newfoundland, Nova Scotia, Ontario, Quebec, Rupert's Land and Toronto.

(2.) *Indian Sees*, 7, with 543 clergy. Calcutta (Metropolitan), Bombay, Colombo, Labuan, Madras, Mauritius, Victoria.

(3.) *West Indian Sees*, 6, with 264 clergy. Antigua, Barbados, Guiana, Jamaica, Kingston, Nassau.

(4.) *Australian Sees*, 9, with 371 clergy. Sydney (Metropolitan), Adelaide, Brisbane, Goulburn, Grafton and Armadale, Melbourne, Newcastle, Perth, Tasmania.

(5.) *New Zealand Sees*, 6, with 105 clergy. New Zealand (Metropolitan), Christchurch, Dunedin, Nelson, Waiapua, Wellington.

(6.) *African Sees*, 5, with 165 clergy. Capetown (Metropolitan), Grahamstown, St. Helena, Natal, Sierra Leone.

(7.) *Gibraltar*; clergy, 58.

(8.) *Falklands*; clergy, 23.

There are also 7 missionary bishops, whose sees are Jerusalem, Melanesia, Honolulu, Central Africa, Orange River, Niger Region, Ningpo.

The population of the various colonies where sees have been planted (with the exclusion of India), is about 9,000,000, but there is no satisfactory census of the numbers belonging to the Established Church.

Before the independence of the United States the Protestant Episcopal clergy in America were under the supervision of the Bishop of London; but in 1784 an American clergyman, Dr. Seabury, was consecrated Bishop of Connecticut by some Scottish bishops, and in 1787, the Archbishop of Canterbury (Dr. Moore) consecrated Dr. White and Dr. Provoost as bishops of Pennsylvania and New York, and these prelates afterwards consecrated others. From this beginning has sprung the existing Protestant Episcopal Church in America. It now numbers 34 sees, 4 assistant bishops, and 8 missions—each under a prelate; the number of clergy is above 2,000. The affairs of the Church are managed by a General Convention, which meets triennially, and in which the bishops form an Upper House after the model of the English Convocation; the Lower

House is composed of 4 clerical and 4 lay deputies from each diocese. The Church has no state aid, but it has very considerable property from endowments and annual subscriptions, pew rents, &c.; tithes, except as a free-will offering, are unknown.

The Roman Catholic Church had no legal existence in England from the death of Mary (A.D. 1558), till the year 1778, when the penal laws were considerably mitigated. Vicars Apostolic were, however, appointed by the Popes from 1623 to 1688, when England was divided into 4 districts. These were again divided into 8 in 1840, and in 1851, by what was stigmatized as the "Papal Aggression," a hierarchy of 1 archbishop and 12 bishops was erected. In Ireland the 4 archbishops and 24 bishops of Catholic times have kept up their succession to the present day. But in Scotland, as in England, Vicars-Apostolic took the place of the bishops, and the country is divided into 3 districts, over which 4 bishops *in partibus* (i.e., having titles taken from sees in infidel regions) preside. At present the Roman Catholic Church in the British dominions numbers 9 archbishoprics, 69 bishoprics, and 32 vicariates. In Great Britain there are 1,639 clergy, 1,283 churches, chapels, and stations, 67 communities of men, 227 convents, and 21 colleges. But many of the chapels are those of religious houses, and not open for public use, which may account for only 575 being returned by the Registrar-General in England and Wales, and several of the colleges are really only advanced schools. The number of Roman Catholics in Ireland was ascertained by the census of 1861 to be 4,490,583, including 1,419 bishops and clergy, but the inquiry into religious persuasions was not carried out in Great Britain.

The ESTABLISHED CHURCH IN SCOTLAND is Presbyterian in discipline, and is governed by a General Assembly, presided over by a Royal Commissioner, and consisting of both clerical and lay deputies. The country for Church purposes is divided into 16 synods and 84 presbyteries, and there are about 1,300 ministers. The churches number 1,250, the schools 1,800, the scholars 140,000, and the Church population is estimated at 1,000,000, by whom the sum of £140,000 is annually raised for home and missionary purposes. The Presbyterian form of church government was first set up in Scotland in 1560, but was superseded by the Episcopal Church under the Stuarts. At the Revolution in 1688 the Episcopal Church was disestablished and disendowed, though it still exists as a sect with 7 bishops and about 160 clergy, and 165 churches; and Presbyterianism gained the legal establishment which it still preserves. The patronage of the benefices is in the hands of various bodies or individuals, but the wishes of the parishioners are usually consulted. A dispute, however, arose on this point in 1840, and the Assembly and the law courts came into collision. The Assembly at last gave way, when Dr. Cook, Dr. Chalmers, and about 400 other ministers resigned their preferments in 1843, and formed what is now known as

THE FREE CHURCH OF SCOTLAND, the great principle of which is, that no minister shall be "intruded" on a congregation—that is, that congregations shall have the power of refusing admission to any one of whose life or doctrine they disapprove. The sum of £357,000 was raised in the first year of the secession, which was divided between a sustentation and a church and school

building fund, and by 1853 no less than 850 congregations had been formed. At the present day the Free Church is a fully organized body, consisting of 16 synods and 71 presbyteries. There are 880 ministers with 923 congregations, many of them meeting in well-appointed churches built for them; and there are upwards of 130,000 scholars in the Free Church schools. Having no endowments, the clergy are supported by the sustentation fund, which gives on an average £140 to each minister, but whether they have "manses" (parsonages) in addition, depends on local circumstances. The sum of £368,527 was raised in 1867 for the various purposes of the Church, among which several missions, especially to India, Africa, and to the Jews in Turkey, Hungary, and Holland, are included.

Presbyterianism is the prevalent form of Church government in Scotland, as also in the North of Ireland, but with several subdivisions. The chief of these in probable number of adherents are :—

(1) *The United Presbyterian Church*, which has 31 presbyteries, 593 churches, 575 ministers, and about 160,000 members in Scotland, England, and Ireland, who raise £260,000 per annum for its purposes. It has many missionaries in the West Indies (especially in Jamaica), and in the East Indies and Africa.

(2) *The Presbyterian Church in Ireland* has 37 presbyteries (one of them in India), 598 ministers, and 560 congregations, 123,000 members, and 58,000 Sunday scholars. The church raised £84,000 in the year 1867, and supports missions to the Roman Catholics as well as to India and to the Jews.

(3) *The Presbyterian Church in England* has 7 presbyteries, 113 churches, 110 ministers, 20,000 communicants, and 15,500 scholars. Its adherents are most numerous in the North of England, and 5 of the presbyteries are found there; the other 2 are in London and Birmingham.

(4) *The Church of Scotland in England* has 4 presbyteries, 20 churches, and 19 ministers, beside 6 military chaplains, stationed in London, Aldershot, Chatham, and Shorncliffe.

(5) The less numerous divisions are, the Reformed Presbyterian Synod, with 6 presbyteries, 43 churches, 40 ministers, and 5 missionaries to the New Hebrides; Reformed Presbyterian Synod in Ireland, 5 presbyteries, 32 churches, 32 ministers; Eastern Reformed Synod in Ireland, 2 presbyteries, 9 churches, 8 ministers; United Original Seceders, 4 presbyteries, 23 ministers; Secession Presbytery in Ireland, 10 churches, 10 ministers.

After the two Established Churches and their branches, we have to mention the Dissenting communities. Foremost in numbers stand,

(1) *The Wesleyan Body*, often called Methodists, which was organized in 1738, by the Rev. John Wesley, of Lincoln College, Oxford, assisted by his brother Charles, and the Rev. George Whitfield. In 1796, shortly after the death of the founder, a New Connexion was formed; in 1810 arose the Primitive Methodists, and in 1815 the Bible Christians, called also Bryanites. The Wesleyan Association, formed in 1834, and the Wesleyan Reform Association, founded in 1849, joined in 1857 in founding the United Free Church Methodists. Notwithstanding these separations the original body is still the most numerous; it possesses 5,024 chapels, and 2215 ministers, 3172 members, and 826,775 scholars. The New Connexion has 261 chapels, 250 circuit and 1,244 local preachers, 550,055 members, and

826,775 scholars. The Primitive Methodists have 2,879 chapels, 155,000 members, about 14,000 itinerant and local preachers, and 230,000 scholars. The Bible Christians have 417 chapels, 65 itinerant and 957 local preachers, 14,500 members, and 22,000 scholars. The Methodist Free Church has 817 chapels, 271 itinerant and 3,246 local preachers, 70,000 members, and 140,000 scholars. The missionary operations of the Wesleyans are very extensive.

(2) *The Independents, or Congregationalists,* maintain that each church is its own ruler, and thus dispense with both bishops and presbyteries. They first appeared in the time of Elizabeth, and were then known as Brownists, from one Robert Browne, their leader. They were at first very harshly treated in England, and in consequence great numbers of them repaired to North America; but their principles triumphed under the Commonwealth. In 1831 the majority of their churches were formed into the Congregational Union, which, whilst affirming the Scriptural independence of each, seeks to promote evangelical religion, and to maintain and enlarge the civil rights of Protestant Dissenters. The Union is composed of 76 Associations at home and in the colonies, with 3,300 churches, of which 2,946 are at home, and 384 abroad, 113 being foreign mission churches; the ministers and missionaries are 2,876. There are also Congregational Unions in Scotland (100 churches), and in Ireland (27 churches). The number of members is supposed to be about 340,000. The Countess of Huntingdon's Connexion, and the Welsh Calvinistic Methodists, who hold the Congregational rule, have 31, and 728 chapels, about 700 ministers and local preachers, 95,000 members, and 140,000 scholars.

(3) *The Baptists,* like the Congregationalists, are grouped in Associations of churches, and the majority of these belong to the Baptist Union. The Union was formed in 1832, and consists of 40 Associations and 1,459 churches; and there are 952 churches not in union, being, in England, 1,819; in Wales, 464; in Scotland, 98; and in Ireland, 30; total, 2,411. The number of ministers is 2,000, of members, 221,524; and of scholars, 192,334. The sums raised for missionary and benevolent purposes by the Baptists are estimated at nearly £140,000; their missionaries are almost exclusively employed in India and China, but there are also missions in the West Indies, on the West Coast of Africa, in Brittany, and in Norway.

(4) The chief of the minor religious sects are, the Unitarians, with 289 ministers, 93 chapels, and about 250 mission stations. The Society of Friends, which consists of about 17,000 members, and has 265 recorded ministers, and about 400 unrecorded; their places of worship in England and Wales are 365. The Moravians, with 91 churches, 58 ministers, 5,500 members, and 5,800 scholars. The Catholic and Apostolic Church (Irvingites), with 19 churches; the New Jerusalem Church (Swedenborgians), with 18; and the Latter-Day Saints (Mormons), with 82. Other sects exist, which, according to the Registrar-General's return in 1868, had registered places of worship. Their names occur, together with those already mentioned, in the following list:—

RELIGIOUS SECTS IN ENGLAND AND WALES.

Apostolics.
Armenian New Society.
Baptists.
Baptized Believers.
Believers in Christ.
Bible Christians.
Bible Defence Association.
Brethren.
Calvinists.
Calvinistic Baptists.
Catholic and Apostolic Church.
Christians.
Christians who object to be otherwise designated.
Christian Believers.
Christian Brethren.
Christian Eliasites.
Christian Israelites.
Christian Teetotallers.
Christian Temperance Men.
Christian Unionists.
Church of Scotland.
Church of Christ.
Countess of Huntingdon's Connexion.
Disciples in Christ.
Eastern Orthodox Greek Church.
Eclectics.
Episcopalian Dissenters.
Evangelical Unionists.
Followers of the Lord Jesus Christ.
Free Catholic Christian Church.
Free Christians.
Free Church.
Free Grace Gospel Christians.
Free Gospel Church.

Free Church (Episcopal).
Free Church of England.
Free Union Church.
General Baptist.
General Baptist New Connexion.
German Lutheran.
German Roman Catholic.
Glassites.
Greek Catholic.
Hallelujah Band.
Independents.
Independent Religious Reformers.
Independent Unionists.
Inghamites.
Jews.
Latter Day Saints.
Modern Methodists.
Mormons.
New Connexion of Wesleyans.
New Jerusalem Church.
New Church.
Old Baptists.
Original Connexion of Wesleyans.
Plymouth Brethren.
Peculiar People.
Presbyterian Church in England.
Primitive Methodists.
Progressionists.
Protestants adhering to Articles of Church of England, 1 to 18 inclusive, but rejecting Order and Ritual.
Providence.
Quakers.

Ranters.
Reformers.
Reformed Presbyterians or Covenanters.
Recreative Religionists.
Refuge Methodists.
Reform Free Church of Wesleyan Methodists.
Revivalists.
Revival Band.
Roman Catholics.
Salem Society.
Sandemanians.
Scotch Baptists.
Second Advent Brethren.
Separatists (Protestant).
Seventh Day Baptists.
Strict Baptists.
Swedenborgians.
Testimony Congregational Church.
Trinitarians.
Union Baptists.
Unionists.
Unitarians.
Unitarian Baptists.
Unitarian Christian.
United Christian Church.
United Free Methodist Church.
United Brethren or Moravians.
United Presbyterians.
Welsh Calvinistic Methodists.
Welsh Free Presbyterians.
Wesleyan Methodist Association.
Wesleyan Reformers.
Wesleyan Reform Glory Band.

Among the inhabitants of the United Kingdom are nearly 60,000 Jews, mainly in London and other large towns, who possess about 100 synagogues, and perhaps as many as 150 ministers and readers. A few Mohammedans are also found, but they possess no place of worship. The more numerous Greeks have churches, which are usually richly decorated, in London, Manchester, Liverpool, &c.

The Established Church of England.

1 Canterbury. £15,000.

Archbishop, Right Hon. and Most Rev. Archibald Campbell Tait, D.C.L. (1868.)
Dean, Very Rev. H. Alford, D.D., (1857), £2,000.

Canons.

Archd. Croft ... £1,000	J. C. Robertson ... £1,000
Archd. Harrison £1,000	John Thomas ... £1,000
W. Stone £1,000	J. W. Blakesley.. £1,000

Archds., Ven. Jas. Croft, M.A., *Canterbury* (1825); Ven. Benj. Harrison, M.A., *Maidstone* (1845).
Secretary, J. B. Lee, Esq., 3, Dean's Yard, Westminster.

2 York. £10,000.

Archbishop, Right Hon. and Most Rev. William Thomson, D.D. (1862).
Dean, Hon. and Very Rev. Aug. Duncombe, D.D. (1858), £2,000.

Canons.

C. Johnstone £700	Archd. Creyke...... £700
Hon. John Baillie £700	William Hey £700

Archdeacons, Ven. Edward Churton, M.A., *Cleveland* (1846), £200; Ven. Charles M. Long, M.A., *East Riding* (1854), £200; Ven. W. B. T. Jones, M.A., *York.* (1867), £200.
Archbishop's Secs., J. B. Lee, Esq., 3, Dean's Yard, Westminster; T. S. Noble, Esq., York.

3 London. £10,000.

Bishop, Right Rev. John Jackson (1868).
Dean of St. Paul's, Very Rev. Henry L. Mansel, D.D., (1868), £2,000.

Canons.

W. Hale Hale, M.A. £666	H. Melvill, B.D.... £1000
T. Dale, M.A. £1000	R. Gregory, M.A. £1000

Archds., Ven. W. Hale Hale, M.A., *London,* (1842), £230; Ven. John Sinclair, M.A., *Middlesex,* (1843), £374.
Sec., J. B. Lee, Esq., 3, Dean's Yard, Westminster.

4 Durham. £8,000.

Bishop, Rt. Rev. Charles Baring, D.D. (1861).
Dean, Very Rev. George Waddington, D.D. (1840), £3,000.

Canons.

Bishop of Exeter, D.D.	Arc. Prest, M.A. £1,000
H. Jenkyns, D.D.	Temple Chevallier, B.D.
Arc. Bland, M.A. £1,000	£1,000.
T. S. Evans, M.A. £1,000	

Archds., Ven. Edward Prest, M.A., *Durham,* (1863), £210; George Bland, M.A., *Northumberland,* (1853); George Hans Hamilton, M.A., *Lindisfarne* (1865), £835.
Sec., J. B. Lee, Esq., 3, Dean's Yard, Westminster.

5 Winchester. £10,500.

Bishop, Rt. Rev. C. R. Sumner, D.D. (1827).
Dean, Very Rev. T. Garnier, D.C.L. (1840), £1,400.

Canons.

W. Wilson, D.D. ... £700	T. Woodrooffe, M.A. £700
Ven. Philip Jacob, M.A.	W. Carus, M.A. ...£700
£700	J. S. Utterton, M.A. £700

Archds. Ven. J. S. Utterton, M.A., *Surrey,* (1859); Ven. Philip Jacob, M.A., *Winchester* (1860), £200.
Secs., Burder and Dunning, 27, Parliament St.

6 Bangor. £4,200.

Bishop, Rt. Rev. J. C. Campbell, D.D., (1859).
Dean, Very Rev. J. Vincent Vincent, (1862), £700.

Canons.

Henry Magendie, A.M. (1818) £386	Thomas Thomas, M.A. (1864) £350
Arc. WynneJones, M.A. (1863) £350	Arc. Evans, M.A. (1866) £350

Archds., Ven. John Wynne Jones, M.A., *Bangor,* (1863); Ven. J. Evans, *Merioneth,* (1866).
Secs., Burder & Dunning, 27, Parliament Street, Hugh B. Roberts, and A. Stowe, Bangor.

7 Bath and Wells. £5,000.

Bishop, Rt. Hon. and Rt. Rev. Robert John Lord Auckland, D.D., (1845).
Dean of Wells, Very Rev. G. H. S. Johnson, M.A., (1854), £1,000.

Canons of Wells.

F. Beadon, M.A. ...£600	R. J. Meade, M.A.£600
R. W. Browne, M.A. £600	T. D. Bernard, M.A.£600

Archds., Ven. George A. Denison, M.A., *Taunton,* (1851), £400; Ven. R. W. Browne, M.A., *Bath,* (1860), £200; Ven. A. O. Fitzgerald, M.A. *Wells,* (1863).
Secs., Burder & Dunning, 27, Parliament Street, Henry Bernard, Esq., Wells.

8 Carlisle. £4,500.

Bishop.—Hon. and Rt. Rev. S. Waldegrave, D.D.
Dean.—Very Rev. F. Close, D.D., (1856), £1,425.

Canons.

C. G. V. Harcourt, M.A., (1837) £700	Henry Gipps, M.A. £700
Henry Percy, M.A. £700	Archd. Boutflower (1867) £700

Archdeacons.—Ven. John Cooper, M.A., *Westmorland,* (1864), £200; Ven. Samuel P. Boutflower, M.A., *Carlisle,* (1867).
Bishop's Secretaries.—John B. Lee, Esq., 3, Dean's Yard, Westminster; G. G. Mounsey, Esq., Carlisle.

9 Chester. £4,500.

Bishop.—Right Rev. W. Jacobson, D.D., (1865).
Dean.—Very Rev. J. S. Howson, D.D. (1867), £1,000.

Canons.

G. B. Blomfield, M.A., (1827) £500	T. Hillyard, M.A. £500
Thos. Eaton, M.A. £500	G. Moberly, D.D. £500

Archdeacons.—Ven. John Jones, M.A., *Liverpool,* (1855), £200; Ven. William Pollock, M.A., *Chester,* (1867), £200.
Secretaries, Burder and Dunning, 27, Parliament Street; C. J. R. Parry and Gamon, Chester.

10 Chichester. £4,200.

Bishop.—Rt. Rev. Ashhurst T. Gilbert, D.D. (1842).
Dean.—Very Rev. W. F. Hook, D.D. (1859), £940.

Canons.

C. E. Hutchinson, M.A. £497	C. Pilkington, B.C.L. £498
C. A. Swainson, D.D. £502	S. Douglas, M.A., £496.

Archdeacons.—Ven. J. Garbett, M.A. *Chichester,* £200; Ven. W. B. Otter, M.A., *Lewes,* £200.
Secs., Burder and Dunning, 27, Parliament St.

11 Ely. £5,500.

Bishop.—Rt. Rev. E. H. Browne, D.D. (1864).
Dean.—Vy. Rev. H. Goodwin, D.D. (1858), £1,000.

Canons.

J. H. Sparke, M.A. £600	E. B. Sparke, M.A. £600
W. Selwyn, D.D. £600	T. Jarrett M.A. ... £600
Archdcn. Yorke, M.A.	B. H. Kennedy, D.D.
£600.	£600

Archdeacons.—Ven. and Hon. H. R. Yorke, M.A., *Hunts.* (1855), £ ; Ven. Lord A. C. Hervey, M.A., *Sudbury* (1862), £ ; Ven. W. Emery, B.D., *Ely* (1864), £ ; Ven. H. J. Rose, B.D., *Beds.* (1866), £.
Secretaries.—J. B. Lee, Esq., 3, Dean's Yard, Westminster; H. R. Evans, Esq., Ely.

12 Exeter. £2,700.

Bishop.—Rt. Rev. H. Philpotts, D.D. (1830).
Dean.—Very Rev. A. Boyd, D.D. (1867), £2000.

Canons.

The Bishop £1,000	E. C. Harington, M.A.
H. Woollcombe, M.A.	£1,000
£1,000	F. C. Cook, M.A.£1,000
P. Freeman, M.A.£1,000	S. U. B. Lee, M.A.£1,000

Archdeacons.—Ven. P. Freeman, M.A., *Exeter* (1865), £65; Ven. W. J. Philpotts, M.A., *Cornwall* (1845), £330; Ven J. Downall, M.A., *Totnes* (1859), £200; Ven. H. Woollcombe, M.A., *Barnstaple* (1865), £117.
Secretaries.—Burder and Dunning, 27, Parliament Street; E. Barnes, Esq., Exeter.

13 Gloucester and Bristol. £5,000.

Bishop.—Rt. Rev. C. J. Ellicott, D.D. (1863).

14 Gloucester.

Dean.—Very Rev. H. Law, M.A. (1862), £1,000.

Canons.

Sir J. H. C. Seymour, Bt. M.A. ....£430 | R. Harvey, M.A. £430
E. Evans, M.A. ....£430 | E. D. Tinling, M.A. £430
Archdeacon.—Sir G. Prevost, Bt., M.A., (1865), £200
Chapter Clerk, G. Whitcombe, Esq.
Registrar, Thomas Holt, Esq.
Bishop's Secretary, B. Bonnor, Esq.

15 Bristol.

Dean.—Very Rev. G. Elliot, D.D. (1850), £1,300.

Canons.

H. Moseley, M.A....£650	J. P. Norris, M.A. £650
E. Girdlestone M.A. £650	J. Randall, M.A. £500

Archdeacon.—Ven. T. Thorp, B.D. (1836), £180.
Registrar & Secretary, C. S. Clarke, Esq., Bristol.

16 Hereford. £4,200.

Bishop.—Right Rev. J. Atlay, D.D. (1868).
Dean.—Hon. and Vy. Rev. G. Herbert, M.A.£1,000.

Canons.

Lord Saye and Sele, D.C.L., £612. [£585. | W. E. Evans, M.A. £600
W. P. Musgrave, M.A. | W. Waring, M.A....£587

Archdeacons.—Ven. Lord Saye and Sele, D.C.L., *Hereford* (1863), £200; Ven. W. Waring, M.A., *Salop* (1851), £200.
Secs.—J. B. Lee, Esq., 3, Dean's Yard, Westminster; Messrs. Evans and Beddoe, Hereford.

17 Lichfield. £4,500.

Bishop.—Rt.Rev.G.A.Selwyn, D.D., D.C.L. (1867).
Dean.—W. W. Champneys, M.A. (1868), £1,000.

Canons.

J. G. Lonsdale, M.A (1855) £500	J. Latham, B.D. £500
H. D. Ryder, M.A....£500	H. Moore, M.A.......£500

Archdeacons.—Ven. H. Moore, M.A., *Stafford* (1865), £200; Ven. T. Hill, B.D. *Derby* (1847); Ven. J. Allen, M.A., *Salop* (1847), £200.
Secretary.—Rev. F. Thatcher, Palace, Lichfield.

18 Lincoln. £5,000.

Bishop.—Rt. Rev. C. Wordsworth, D.D. (1868).
Dean.—Very Rev. J. A. Jeremie, D.D., D.C.L., (1864), £2,000.

Canons.

F.C. Massingberd, M.A. | Ven.H.Mackenzie,M.A
Ven.W.F.J. Kaye, M.A. | E. Venables, M.A.

Archdeacons.—Ven. W. F. J. Kaye, M.A., *Lincoln* (1863), £30; Ven. E. Trollope, M.A., *Stow* (1867), £170; Ven. H. Mackenzie, *Notts.* (1866), £40.
Secs., Burder and Dunning, 27, Parliament Street; William Moss, Esq., Lincoln.

19 Llandaff. £4,200.

Bishop, Right Rev. Alfred Ollivant, D.D. (1849).
Dean, Very Rev. T. Williams, M.A. (1857), £700.

Canons.

Achd.Crawley, M.A.£350	E. Hawkins, M.A. £350
Archd. Blosse..........£350	W. Bruce, M.A. £350

Archd., Ven. William Crawley, M.A., *Monmouth* (1843), £ ; Ven. H. L. Blosse, M.A., *Llandaff* (1859), £.
Secs., Burder and Dunning, 27, Parliament St.

20 Manchester. £4,200.

Bishop, Rt. Rev. J. P. Lee, D.D., F.R.S. (1848).
*Dean,*Very Rev. G. H. Bowers, D.D. (1847), £2,000.

Canons.

C. Richson, M.A....£600	N. W. Gibson, M.A. £600
J. H. Marsden, B.D.£600	Archd. Durnford £600

Archd., Ven. Richard Durnford, M.A., *Manchester* (1867), £200.
Secs., J. Burder, Esq., Manchester, and Burder and Dunning, 27, Parliament Street.

21 Norwich. £4,500.

Bishop, Hon. and Rt. Rev. J.T.Pelham, D.D. (1857).
Dean, V. Rev. E. M. Goulburn, D.D. (1866), £1,600.

Canons.

A. Sedgwick, LL.D. £800 | C. K. Robinson, D.D.
J. W. L. Heaviside, M.A., | £800
£800 | J. M. Nisbet, M.A. £800

Archds., Ven. A. M. Hopper, M.A., *Norwich* (1868), £200; Ven. W. A. Bouverie, B.D., *Norfolk* (1850), £200; Ven. and Rt. Rev. V. W. Ryan, D.D., late Bishop of Mauritius, *Suffolk* (1868), £184.
Secs., J. B. Lee, Esq., 3, Dean's Yard, Westminster; John Kitson, Esq., Norwich.

22 Oxford. £5,000.

Bishop, Right Rev. S. Wilberforce, D.D. (1845).
Dean of Christ Church, Very Rev. Henry G. Liddell, D.D. (1855) £2,500

Canons.

E. B. Pusey, D.D. £1,250	C. A. Heurtley, D.D.,
R. W. Jelf, D.D. £1,250	£1,250
Ven.Arch.Clerke £1,250	R. P. Smith, D.D. £1,250
C.A.Ogilvie, D.D. £1,250	W. Bright, M.A. £1,250

Archds., Ven. C. Carr Clerke, D.D., *Oxford* (1830); Ven. Edw. Bickersteth, D.D., *Buckingham,* (1853), £300; Ven. J. Randall, M.A., *Berks.* (1855), £200.
Sec., John M. Davenport, Esq., Oxford.

23 Peterborough. £4,500.

Bishop, Right Rev. W. C. Magee, D.D. (1868).
Dean, Very Rev. A.P.Saunders, D.D. (1853) £1,160.

Canons.

John James, D.D.....£548	M. Argles, M.A. £548
O. Davys, M.A. £548	H. Pratt, M.A. £548

Archds., Ven. H. Fearon, B.D., *Leicester* (1863), £200; O.Davys, M.A., *Northampton* (1842), £88.
Sec. and Chapter Clerk, H. P. Gates, Esq., Peterborough.
Secs. in London, Day and Hassard, 28, Great George Street.

24 Ripon. £4,500.

Bishop, Right Rev. R. Bickersteth, D.D. (1857).
Dean, Very Rev. H. M'Neile, D.D (1868), £1,000.

Canons.

P. W. Worsley, M.A. £500|H. M. Birch, B.D. ...£500
S. Holmes, M.A. ...£500|Ven. E. Cust £500
Archds., Ven. C. Musgrave, D.D., *Craven* (1836)
£200; Ven. E. Cust, *Richmond,* (1868), £
Secs., J. B. Lee, Esq., 3, Dean's Yard, Westminster; Samuel Wise, Esq., Ripon.

25 Rochester. £5,000.

Bishop, Rt. Rev. T. L. Claughton, D.D. (1867).
Dean, Very Rev. R. Stevens, D.D. (1820), £1,200.

Canons.

J. Griffith, D.D. ...£600|T.Robinson,D.D. ...£600
E.Hawkins,D.D....£600|A. Grant, D.C.L. ...£600
Archds., Ven. A. Grant, D.C.L., *Rochester and St. Alban's* (1863), £200; Ven. C. A. St. John Mildmay, M.A., *Essex* (1861), £200; Ven. W. B. Ady, M.A., *Colchester* (1864), £600.
Secs., Day and Hassard, 28, Great George Street.

25 St. Asaph. £4,200.

Bishop, Rt. Rev. Thos Vowler Short, D.D. (1846).
Dean, V. Rev. R. B. M. Bonnor, M.A. (1859), £700.

Canons.

Ar. Wickham, M.A. £350|Archd. Ffoulkes ...£350
Hugh Jones, M.A. £350|R. W. Edwards ...£350
Archs.—Ven. R. Wickham, M.A., *St. Asaph* (1854);
H. P. Ffoulkes, M.A., *Montgomery* (1861).
Secs., C. W. Wyatt, Esq., and R. J. Sisson, Esq.

26 St. David's. £4,500.

Bishop, Rt. Rev. Connop Thirlwall, D.D. (1840).
Dean, Very Rev.L.Llewellin, D.C.L., (1840), £250.
Canons, W. B. Thomas, M.A. (1859), £350; W. Reed, M.A. (1865), £350; Rev. Sir E. G. Williams, Bart. (1858), £350; Rev. W. Richardson, M.A. (1854), £350.
Archs., Ven. Geo. Clark, M.A., *St. David's* (1864), £200; R. W. P. Davies, M.A., *Brecon* (1859), £250; Ven. W. North, M.A., *Cardigan* (1860), £200; D. A. Williams, M.A., *Carmarthen* (1865), £200.
Secs., Burder and Dunning, 27, Parliament-street; John Thirlwall, Esq., Abergwili.

27 Salisbury. £5,000.

Bishop, Right Rev. W. K. Hamilton, D.D. (1854).
Dean, Very Rev. H. Parr Hamilton, M.A., F.R.S., (1850), £1,000.

Canons.

Wm. Fisher, M.A. ...£500|Hon. D. H. Gordon £500
Arch. Hony, B.D. ...£500|Fran. Lear, M.A. ...£500
Archdeacons.—Ven. W. E. Hony, B.D., *Sarum* (1846), £180; Ven. T. Sanctuary, M.A., *Dorset* (1862), £200; Ven. T. Stanton, M.A., *Wilts* (1868), £200.
Sec., Fitzherbert Macdonald, Esq., Salisbury.

28 Worcester. £5,000.

Bishop, Right Hon. Henry Philpott, D.D. (1861).
Dean, Very Rev. John Peel, D.D. (1845), (1,450).

Canons.

Hon. J. Fortescue £725|Sir G. F. Lewis......£725
J. R. Wood, M.A. £725 | Philip Wynter,D.D.£725
Archdeacons, Ven. R. B. Hone, M.A., *Worcester* (1849), £200; Ven. John Sandford, B.D., *Coventry* (1851), £200.
Secs., J. B. Lee, Esq., 3, Dean's Yard, Westminster; A. C. Hooper, Esq., Worcester.

29 Sodor and Man. £2,000.

Bishop, Hon. and Rev. H. Powys, D.D., 1854.
Archdeacon, Ven. J. C. Moore, M.A. (1844), £700.
Sec., Samuel Harris, Esq.

The Irish Establishment.

Sees.	ARCHBISHOPS.	Appointed.
Armagh	M. G. Beresford, D.D.	1862
Dublin	R. C. Trench, D.D.	1864

	BISHOPS.	
Meath	S. Butcher, D.D.	1866
Cashel	R. Daly, D.D.	1843
Cork	John Gregg, D.D.	1862
Derry	W. Alexander, D.D.	1867
Down	R. Knox, D.D.	1849
Killaloe	W. Fitzgerald, D.D.	1862
Kilmore	H. Verschoyle, D.D.	1862
Limerick	Charles Graves, D.D.	1866
Ossory	J. T. O'Brien, D.D.	1842
Tuam	C. B. Bernard, D.D.	1866

Colonial Bishops.

Sees.		Appointed.
Adelaide	A. Short, D.D.	1847
Antigua	W. W. Jackson, D.D.	1860
Barbados	Thomas Parry, D.D.	1842
Bombay	H. A. Douglas, D.D.	1868
Brisbane	E. W. Tufnel, D.D.	1859
Calcutta	R. Milman, D.D.	1867
Capetown	R. Gray, D.D.	1847
Christ Ch. N.Z.	H. J. C. Harper, D.D.	1866
Colombo	P. C. Claughton, D.D.	1862
Columbia	George Hills, D.D.	1859
Dunedin	H. L. Jenner, D.D.	1866
Falklands	Vacant.	
Fredericton	John Medley, D.D.	1845
Gibraltar	Hon. A. C. Harris, D.D.	1868
Goulburn	Mesac Thomas, D.D.	1863
Grafton and Armadale	J. Francis Turner, D.D.	1868
Grahamstown	H. Cotterill, D.D.	1856
Guiana	W. P. Austin, D.D.	1842
Huron	B. Cronyn, D.D.	1857
Jamaica	A. G. Spencer, D.D.	1843
Kingston	R. Courtenay, D.D.	1856
Labuan	Vacant.	
Madras	Frederick Gell, D.D.	1861
Mauritius	T. G. Hatchard, D.D.	
Melbourne	Charles Perry, D.D.	1847
Montreal		
Nassau	A. R. P. Venables, D.D.	1863
Natal	J. W. Colenso, D.D.	1853
Nelson	A. B. Suter, D.D.	1866
Newcastle	W. Tyrrell, D.D.	1847
Newfoundland	Edw. Feild, D.D.	1844
	J. B. Kelly, D.D., Coadjutor	1867
New Zealand	Vacant.	
Nova Scotia	H. Binney, D.D.	1851
Ontario	J. T. Lewis, D.D.	1862
Perth	M. B. Hale, D.D.	1857
Quebec	J. W. Williams, D.D.	1863
Rupert's Land	R. Mackray, D.D.	1865
Sierra Leone	E. H. Beckles, D.D.	1860
St. Helena	T. E. Welby, D.D.	1862
Sydney	F. Barker, D.D.	1854
Tasmania	C. H. Bromby, D.D.	1864
Toronto	A. N. Bethune, D.D.	1867
Victoria	C. R. Alford, D.D.	1867
Wellington	C. J. Abraham, D.D.	1858
Waiapua	W. Williams, D.C.L.	1858

Missionary Bishops.

Central Africa	W. G. Tozer, D.D.	1863
Honolulu	T. N. Staley, D.D.	1861
Jerusalem	S. Gobat, D.D.	1846
Melanesia	J. C. Patteson, D.D.	1861
Niger Region..	S. A. Crowther, D.D.	1864
Ningpo	W. A. Russell, M.A.	1867
Orange River	E. Twells, D.D.	1863

Scottish Episcopal Church.

Moray	Robert Eden, D.D.	1851
Aberdeen	J. G. Suther, D.C.L.	1857
Argyll	A. Ewing, D.D.	1847
Brechin	A. P. Forbes, D.C.L.	1847

Edinburgh	C. H. Terrot, D.D.	1841
	T. B. Morrell, D.D., Coadjutor.	1863
Glasgow	W. S. Wilson, D.D.	1859
St. Andrew's	Chas. Wordsworth, D.C.L.	1853

Roman Catholic Church.

ARCHBISHOP AND METROPOLITAN.

The Most Rev. Henry Edward Manning, Archbishop of Westminster, cons. 1865. Clergy, 221.

SEES.	BISHOPS.	CONSC.	CLERGY.
Beverley	Rob. Cornthwaite	1861	119
Birmingham	Wm. Ber. Ullathorne	1850	153
Clifton	William Clifton	1857	66
Hexham and Newcastle	Jas. Chadwick	1866	106
Liverpool	Alexander Goss	1853	208
Meneria, Wales	Thos. Jos. Brown	1850	53
Nottingham	Rd. Butler Roskell	1853	62
Plymouth	William Vaughan	1855	39
Salford	William Turner	1851	121
Shrewsbury	James Brown	1851	83
Southwark	Thomas Grant	1851	160
Northampton	Fras. Kerril Amherst	1858	31

IRELAND.

Cardinal, The Most Eminent and Most Rev. Paul Cullen, Consecrated Archbishop of Armagh 1850, translated to Dublin 1852, created Cardinal 1866.

SEES.	ARCHBISHOPS.	CONS.	CLERGY.
Armagh	Michael Kieran	1867	205
Dublin	Cardinal Paul Cullen	1852	217
Cashel & Emly	Patrick Leahy	1857	102
Tuam	John MacHale	1834	101

	Bishops.		
Achonry	Patrick Durcan	1852	36
Ardagh			90
Clogher	James Donnelly	1865	89
Clonfert	John Derry	1847	35
Cloyne	William Keane	1851	121

SEES.		CONS.	CLERGY.
Cork	William Delany	1847	81
Derry	Francis Kelly	1849	94
Down & Connor	Patrick Dorian	1860	87
Dromore	John P. Leahy	1854	37
Elphin	Laurence Gillooly	1856	88
Ferns	Thomas Furlong	1857	111
Galway	John McEvilly	1857	58
Kerry	David Moriarty	1854	101
Killaloe	Michael Flannery	1858 }	121
	Coadjutor N. Power	1865 }	
Killala	Thos. Feeny	1839	35
Kildare and Leighlin	James Walshe	1856	119
Kilmacduagh & Kilfenora	Patrick Fallon	1853	17
Kilmore	Nicholas Conaty	1865	73
Limerick	George Butler	1861	110
Meath	Thomas Nulty	1864	136
Ossory	Edward Walsh	1845	98
Raphoe	Daniel McGettigan	1856	51
Ross	Michael O'Hea	1858	24
Waterford & Lismore	Dominic O'Brien	1855	98

In Ireland Bishops, like Archbishops, are addressed as MOST REVEREND.

SCOTLAND.

John Strain, Bp. of Abila, cons. 1864. Clergy 60.
John Gray   ,,   Hypsopolis ,, 1866. }
James Lynch ,,   Arcadiopolis,, 1866. } ,, 107.
James Kyle ,,   Germanicia ,, 1828.   ,,   30.

The Roman Catholic Hierarchy throughout the world consists of 12 Patriarchates; 188 Archbishoprics; 892 Bishoprics.

The Established Church in Ireland.

EVER since the time of the Reformation the Established Church in Ireland has differed in many important respects from the sister Establishment in England. For instance, the sees were much more numerous, there being 4 archbishoprics and 31 bishoprics, but several of these latter, even in Catholic times, were held in couples, and in 1833 there were 4 archbishops and 18 bishops. In that year the Irish Church Temporalities Act (3 & 4 Will. IV., c. 37) was passed under the auspices of Lord Stanley, the Irish Secretary (now Earl of Derby), and a most important change was effected, the various dioceses being prospectively so united, that in a few years the prelacy was reduced to 2 archbishops and 10 bishops; but the deans and chapters of the cathedrals and the archdeacons of the dioceses were not interfered with, though a body of Ecclesiastical Commissioners was formed, on which many of their duties were devolved.

Another and more important point of difference was, and is, found in the fact that the originally numerous body of prelates had never succeeded in bringing anything more than a minority of the Irish people to accept their spiritual guidance. Without going further back, where statistical information is hard to obtain and scarcely reliable, we learn from the Report of the Commissioners of Public Instruction that in 1834 the members of the Established Church were only 852,064 against 6,427,712 of Roman Catholics (a proportion of 8 to 1), and in 1861 the census showed that the numbers stood at about 7 to 1, the Roman Catholics being returned at 4,490,583, and the members of the Established Church at 678,661—the famine of 1845 and 1846 and emigration having reduced the population of Ireland from 8,175,124 in 1841 to 6,552,385 in 1851, and to 5,764,543 in 1861.

Another point of difference up to 1837 was the manner in which tithes were levied. These were in many cases of necessity collected by force, and lives were not unfrequently lost on such occasions. To ameliorate this state of things, an Act was passed (1 & 2 Vict. c. 109), which reduced the tithe by one-fourth, and directed the remainder to be paid by the landlord instead of by the tenant.

Before the passing of the Church Temporalities Act, the Irish episcopate stood thus:—

PROVINCE OF ARMAGH.	
Sees.	Revenue.
Armagh (archbishopric)	£17,670
Meath and Clonmacnoise	5,220
Clogher	10,371
Down and Connor	5,896
Derry	14,193
Raphoe	5,787
Kilmore	7,478
Dromore	4,813
PROVINCE OF DUBLIN.	
Dublin (archbishopric) and Glandelagh	9,321
Kildare	6,452
Ossory	3,859
Ferns and Leighlin	6,550
PROVINCE OF CASHEL.	
Cashel (archbishopric) and Emly	7,354
Limerick, Ardfert, and Aghadoe	5,369
Waterford and Lismore	4,323
Cork and Ross	4,346
Cloyne	5,009
Killaloe and Kilfenora	4,041
PROVINCE OF TUAM.	
Tuam (archbishopric) and Ardagh	8,206
Elphin	7,034
Clonfert and Kilmacduagh	3,261
Killala and Achonry	4,082
Total	£150,635

By the operation of the Act the following changes were effected, as vacancies allowed, the change being in every case accompanied by a reduction of income. The provinces of Cashel and Tuam were consolidated with those of Dublin and Armagh, Cashel and Tuam being thus reduced to bishoprics, and the only archbishoprics left were Armagh and Dublin. The bishoprics were grouped in twos and threes, and the episcopate stood thus in 1854, when the whole of the contemplated changes had been effected, and so continues in 1868, except as to revenue.

PROVINCE OF ARMAGH AND TUAM.	
Sees	Gross revenue.
Armagh (archbishopric) and Clogher	£12,087
Meath and Clonmacnoise	4,068
Derry and Raphoe	8,000
Down, Connor, and Dromore	4,204
Kilmore, Elphin, and Ardagh	6,253
Tuam, Killala, and Achonry	4,600
PROVINCE OF DUBLIN AND CASHEL.	
Dublin (archbishopric) Glandelagh, and Kildare	7,786
Ossory, Ferns, and Leighlin	4,200
Cashel, Emly, Waterford, and Lismore	5,000
Killaloe, Kilfenora, Clonfert, and Kilfenora	3,870
Limerick, Ardfert, and Aghadoe	4,973
Cork, Cloyne, and Ross	2,498
Total	£67,539

To carry the Act into effect, a body of Ecclesiastical Commissioners was appointed, and by them the revenues of the suppressed sees were received, and applied to certain purposes pointed out in the statute. As, however, nothing was receivable until the death or removal of the prelates then in possession, a loan of £100,000 was granted by the Board of Works, and the Commission commenced its operations. Its functions are, first, to provide church requisites; second, to pay parish clerks, organists, &c.; third, to build and repair churches; fourth, to pay

the sums known as ministers' money to certain incumbents, and the salaries of certain Dublin curates. It also has to manage the lands in its possession, granting leases or converting leaseholds into perpetuity holdings, as may be agreed on, and it has also built a number of residentiary houses for the clergy, but the period for repayment has been complained of as too short, thus making a needlessly heavy demand on the incumbents. Indeed, the proceedings of the commission have failed to find satisfaction. Its expenses, amounting at present to 12½ per cent. of its gross receipts, have been considered far too heavy; they amounted to £15,247 in 1841; sunk to £8,023 in 1844, and to £5,528 in 1852, but were returned in 1868 as £14,008 16s. on the average of years. These working expenses paid, any surplus that may remain is to be devoted to augmenting small livings; a sum of £7,880 is stated to be so applied annually. Beside receiving the whole clear proceeds of the suppressed sees (£58,631), and £4,450 from Armagh and £6,080 from Derry, the Commission levies a tax which produces £18,175 on the existing ones and on all livings, varying with their value from 2½ to 15 per cent., and the proceeds of 90 suspended parishes (£20,652) are likewise received by it. The following is its constitution at present: the Archbishop of Armagh, Lord Chancellor, Archbishop of Dublin, the Bishops of Meath, Ossory and Cashel, the Lord Chief Justice, all unpaid; and Dr. Gayer, Q.C., and Mr. Quin, who receive salaries. There are also a secretary, treasurer, 25 clerks, architects, agents, &c., and yet a part of the income is left to be collected by an agency firm at a charge of 10 per cent.

The Church continues under the system introduced in 1833, but an impression having gained ground that some alteration and improvement in the management and distribution of its revenues might yet be made, a Royal Commission of Inquiry was issued on the 30th of October, 1867. The commissioners were Earl Stanhope, Earl of Meath, Sir Joseph Napier, Bart., Colonel Robert A. S. Adair, Dr. T. J. Ball, and E. P. Shirley, George Clive, and E. Howes, Esqrs., with Dr. Elrington as secretary. The Commissioners issued queries addressed to nearly 2,000 persons, as to every particular relating to Church property, and also examined witnesses and records, and eventually, on the 27th of July, 1868, presented a Report with very elaborate tables; but whilst they were pursuing their inquiries, the Irish Church question was brought under the notice of Parliament by Mr. Gladstone, and an unsuccessful attempt was made to legislate thereon.

In March, 1868, the Irish Reform Bill was in discussion in the House of Commons, and on the resumption of the debate on March 23, Mr. Gladstone, who had a week before intimated his opinion that an emphatic declaration regarding the Irish Church was required, now moved three resolutions. The first declared that the Irish Church should cease to exist as an Establishment; the second, that new personal interests should not, for the present, be created by public patronage, and that the Ecclesiastical Commission should confine their inquiries to objects only of immediate necessity, or involving individual rights, pending the decision of Parliament; and the third, that an Address be presented to Her Majesty, asking that, with a view to the purposes aforesaid, she would place at the disposal of Parliament her interest in all Church temporalities belonging to the dignitaries, &c., of the Irish Church. Mr. Gladstone entered into all particulars of the Irish Church, denouncing it as an anomaly and unnecessary, confirming his statements by statistics, history, &c. Lord Stanley moved an amendment, opposing Mr. Gladstone's resolutions, and defended the existence of the Irish Church, denouncing the resolutions as a mere electioneering cry. His amendment admitted the necessity of modification in regard to the temporalities, but urged that any attempt at disestablishment or disendowment should be left for the decision of a new Parliament.

After a vehement debate of three days the first resolution was carried against the Government amendment by a majority of 56 : ayes, 328 ; noes, 272. The resolutions were next debated at full length, and on April 30 the first carried by a majority of 65 : ayes, 330 ; noes, 265. The two remaining resolutions being considered the necessary consequence of the first, were then allowed to pass comparatively unopposed ; and Mr. Gladstone then, on the 14th May, brought in a bill to suspend all appointments in the Irish Church, pending further legislation on the subject. After a severe struggle, the bill was read a third time, and passed ; but it was rejected in the House of Lords on June 29, on the second reading by a majority of 93 : ayes, 97 ; noes, 192. The matter thus stands over, but may be expected to occupy a large share of notice as soon as the Reformed Parliament has got into working order.

Shortly after the debates on the Suspensory Bill were brought to a close, the Commissioners' Report was presented to the Queen, and printed for presentation to the Houses of Parliament. The following abstract of its contents gives the exact state of the Irish Church at the present day, and will afford the means of judging of the justice and advisability of Mr. Gladstone's proposals for its disendowment and disestablishment, although those questions had not been openly mentioned when the Commission was issued.

The following are the names, extent, Church population, and numbers of benefices and clergy of the 12 united dioceses, and the net incomes of their bishops at the present day.

DIOCESES.	Extent in Acres.	Church population.	No. of Benefices.	Clergy.	Net Income of Bishops.
Armagh and Clogher	1,758,852	150,778	165	170	£9,798
Meath	1,264,995	16,289	105	105	3,782
Tuam, Killala, and Achonry	2,687,705	17,157	77	77	4,767
Down, Connor, and Dromore	1,329,974	146,136	150	150	3,763
Derry and Raphoe	1,945,896	65,951	112	112	6,171
Kilmore, Elphin, and Ardagh	1,959,620	53,196	118	118	5,255
Dublin and Kildare	1,282,160	112,766	154	154	7,387
Ossory, Ferns, and Leighlin	1,745,247	36,663	171	171	3,579
Cashel, Emley, Waterford, and Lismore	1,405,769	13,853	104	104	4,347
Limerick, Ardfert, and Aghadoe	1,769,017	15,103	95	95	3,874
Killaloe, Kilfenora, Clonfert, and Kilmacduagh	2,707,851	15,906	89	89	3,130
Cork, Cloyne, and Ross	1,744,260	43,228	170	170	2,174
Exempt Jurisdiction of Newry and Mourne		7,733			
	20,701,795	693,357	1,518	1,515	£58,031

Beside the 12 prelates, there are 30 corporations of deans and chapters ; 12 minor corporations connected with cathedrals, 32 deans, 33 archdeacons, 1,509 beneficed incumbents (perpetual curates included), and more than 500 stipendiary curates. The total revenues of the Church amount to £613,984 ; made up of : (1) rent of lands, £204,933 ; (2) tithe rent-charge, £364,244 ; (3) other sources, £12,675 ; and (4) value of houses and lands occupied by the clergy, £32,152. Nearly one-fifth of the gross sum of £613,984 is administered by the Ecclesiastical Commission. The balance-sheet, published with this Report of their average net income and outlay, is as follows, and bears out the remark of the Royal Commissioners, that " the proportion which the expenses of administration and management bear to the revenues is high, and, in their opinion, is capable of being reduced without prejudice to efficiency."

AVERAGE NET INCOME.

	£
See Estates, after deducting Poor-rates.	58,631
Suspended Benefices	20,652
Charge on See of Armagh	4,450
" " Derry	6,080
Tax on Bishoprics and Benefices	18,175
Interest on Perpetuity Mortgages	1,033
" Glebe House Mortgage Loans	1,743
Dividends on Insurance Fund, Consols	542
Carried forward	£111,306

	£
Brought forward	£111,306
,, Perpetuity Fund, Consols.	2,325
Rent of Premises in rear of House	31
	£113,662

AVERAGE ANNUAL EXPENDITURE.

Parochial Estimates :	£	s.	d.
Parish Clerks' Salaries	14,513	17	10
Sextons'	9,668	5	9
Organists'	1,440	4	8
Organ-blowers	132	17	0
Tuning Organs	139	3	4
Communion elements	2,039	11	3
Church requisites	3,040	17	4
Lighting and Fuel	6,013	17	1
	£37,258	14	3

	£
Dublin Curates' Stipends	£2,210
Curates' Stipends, suspended Benefices	1,685
Augmentation of small Benefices	7,880
Ministers' money	13,128
Salaries to Incumbents, Curates, and Vicars choral	2,719
Salaries to Diocesan Schoolmasters	259
Quit and Crown Rents, &c.	383
Payment to Auditors of Registrars' Accounts	250
Salaries to Incumbents of Tullow and Kill	200
Carried forward	£28,714

Brought forward £28,714			0

Establishment, &c. :

Office Salaries................................	6,665	0
Salaries of two Architects	1,000	0
„ eight Inspectors	2,002	16
„ two Drawing Clerks	275	0
Supernumerary Clerks and Messengers	405	10
Superannuation Salaries	292	10
Salary and office expenses of Solicitor	800	0
Postage, Printing, Stationery, &c....	700	0
Survey and Valuation of Lands......	122	0
Rent of House	250	0
Incidents (Repairs, Insurance, Taxes, &c., of House)	480	0
Travelling Agents' expenses, and Registrars' fees, about	16	0

	£14,008	16
Church Repairs £24,000	0	0
Leaving for Buildings, Enlargements, &c............................... £10,690	9	9
	£113,662	0	0

The Account then stands thus :

Bishops	£61,147
Deans and Chapters	10,749
Minor Corporations	10,176
Cathedral Dignitaries......................	10,940
Beneficed Clergy	366,264

	£459,274
Ecclesiastical Commission, as above...	£113,662
	£572,936

There is a balance of £40,048, of which £19,546 is stated to be available for the purpose of maintaining the Cathedrals and choral services ; the destination of the remaining £20,592 we have failed to trace.

The houses and lands in the occupation of the Bishops (12 in number) are valued at £3,715 15s. 9d.; of the Dignitaries (4), £292 10s. ; and of the Clergy (1,509,) £28,143 17s. 7d. Of the other lands, some are leased in perpetuity, to the amount of £72,354 8s. 10d. per annum ; and others for lives or terms of years to the amount of £66,699 10s. 7d.

Of the benefices, 1,484 are parishes, properly so called ; 27 are chapelries, whose incumbents are styled perpetual curates, but have no districts ; and 7 are sinecure rectories. 146 are in royal, 988 in ecclesiastical, and 309 in college and lay patronage ; 73 are royal, ecclesiastical or lay in turn : 90 of the benefices are vested in the Ecclesiastical Commissioners, for various causes, the most frequent being the non-performance of Divine service therein for 3 years or more before their taking possession. There are 64 appropriate or impropriate parishes without incumbents ; and there are 10 extra-parochial districts with a total Church population of 404.

The benefices are classified thus, as regards Church population and net annual value :

Under	20 persons	92	Under	£100	297
„	30 „	48	„	£200	421
„	40 „	59	„	£300	367
„	100 „	287	„	£400	225
„	200 „	254	„	£500	107
„	500 „	336	„	£600	53
„	750 „	122	„	£700	23
„	1000 „	100	„	£800	17
„	2000 „	115	„	£900	9
„	5000 „	63	„	£1000	3
Above 5000 „		4	„	£1100	7

After a full consideration of the circumstances of each diocese, the Commissioners came to the conclusion that a further consolidation of dioceses and a reduction of episcopal incomes was desirable.

They would reduce the number of Deans and Chapters and Cathedral Establishments to that of the Sees (8,) and convert the remaining Cathedrals to the use of parish churches. They would make residence, and the conduct of a daily choral service, incumbent on the Deans, whose salaries should be £1,000 a year each; the Dean of Dublin, however, being allowed £1,200. They would reduce the Archdeacons to 17; that is, two for each Diocese, with one extra for Kilmore. As to the Ecclesiastical Commissioners, they would enlarge their powers, especially as regards leasing the Church lands ; but would reduce their expense by substituting clerks in many cases for highly-paid officials, and abolishing the office of treasurer.

The Commissioners thus sum up their principal recommendations :

"1. A further consolidation of dioceses and a reduction in the number and (with one exception) in the incomes of the bishops.

"2. A corresponding reduction in the number of cathedral establishments, so that they shall not exceed the number of bishoprics.

"3. A reduction in the number of archdeacons.

"4. The suppression of all dignities and offices in the dissolved cathedral corporations.

"5. A re-arrangement of benefices to meet the exigencies of the Church population, and a more equitable adjustment of income to services.

"6. That with a view to re-arrangement, the duty be imposed upon the Board of Ecclesiastical Commissioners of taking the necessary proceedings for the union, division, or alteration of benefices.

"7. That the existing powers of suspending appointments to benefices be extended to all cases where for twelve months next before the time of suspension Divine service shall not have been performed, and also to benefices in royal or ecclesiastical patronage where the Church population is under 40 in number. In each case provision to be made for such spiritual duties as are requisite.

"8. That an additional ad valorem tax be imposed upon all benefices above £300 a year in which the Church population does not amount to 100 in number.

"9. The payment of the expenses of providing the elements for the Holy Communion, or for music in any churches not cathedral, out of the funds of the Ecclesiastical Commissioners, be discontinued, and that in no cases, except where the parishioners are unable to provide for the services of a parish clerk, shall a salary to a parish clerk be paid by the Commissioners, and that in such cases the offices of parish clerk and sexton be consolidated, if practicable.

"10. That the expense of maintaining the ecclesiastical courts and registries be defrayed by the general fund vested in the Ecclesiastical Commissioners, and that the clergy be thereupon relieved from the visitation fees.

"11. That the period for repayment of building loans from the Ecclesiastical Commissioners be extended.

"12. That the estates of all the capitular bodies, and such estates of the bishoprics as shall not be allocated for the endowment of those retained, shall be transferred to the Board of Ecclesiastical Commissioners.

"13. That the surplus arising from all property

vested in the Ecclesiastical Commissioners shall be applicable at their discretion for the suitable augmentation of benefices inadequately endowed.

"14. That with a view to carry out these recommendations and others of a subordinate character, and for the purposes of a more effective management of Church property, the constitution of the Board of Ecclesiastical Commissioners be improved and its powers enlarged.

"15. That the expense of converting leaseholds into perpetuities be diminished; and with this object, that the amount of purchase-money be ascertained, with such alterations of the present system as have been suggested.

"16. That increased facilities be given for leasing lands belonging to the parochial clergy, and

that the power to lease be vested in the Ecclesiastical Commissioners.

"17. That the owners of land liable to pay tithe-rent charge be empowered to redeem their liability.

"19. That provision be made to prevent ecclesiastical persons alienating or encumbering by deed their official incomes.

"20. That more stringent and summary powers of enforcing residence be given to the bishop and ecclesiastical courts."

Should the recommendations of the Commissioners be carried out, the following will be the conjoined sees, with their Church Population and number of benefices, and the salaries of the Bishops and Deans.

Sees.		Composed of the Dioceses of—	Church Populatn.	Bene-fices	Bishop	Dean
Armagh	Composed of the Dioceses of	Armagh, Clogher, Kilmore	182,000	221	£6,000	£1,000
Derry	,,	Derry and Raphoe	66,000	112	3,000	1,000
Down	,,	Down and Connor and Dromore	152,000	153	3,000	1,000
Tuam	,,	Tuam, Killala, Achonry, Clonfert, Ardagh, Elphin, and Kilmacduagh	40,000	161	3,000	1,000
Dublin	,,	Dublin, Meath, and Kildare	128,000	259	4,500	1,200
Limerick	,,	Kilfenora, Killaloe, Cashel, Emly, and Limerick	28,000	178	3,000	1,000
Cork	,,	Cork, Ross, Cloyne, Ardfert, and Aghadoe	47,000	212	3,000	1,000
Ossory	,,	Ossory, Leighlin, Ferns, Waterford and Lismore	50,000	222	3,000	1,000
			693,000	1,518	£28,500	£8,200

Some of the Commissioners desire that Dublin should remain an archbishopric, with a salary of £5,000; and an additional allowance of £500 is recommended for each of the Prelates attending Parliament.

Members of Convocation.

PROVINCE OF CANTERBURY.

The Most Reverend the Lord Archbishop.
The Right Rev. the Lords Bishops.
The Very Rev. the Deans.
The Venerable the Archdeacons.

Also the following Proctors elected by the Chapters and Clergy of the several Dioceses.

CANTERBURY.—*Chapter*, J. W. Blakesley. *Clergy*, Ashton Oxenden, J. C. B. Riddell.

LONDON.—*Chapter*, No Election. *Clergy*, M. Gibbs, J. E. Kempe. *Westminster Chapter*, W. Conway.

WINCHESTER.—*Chapter*, W. Carus. *Clergy*, G. H. Sumner, Robert Gregory. *Vicar General*, Sir Travers Twiss, D.C.L. *Registrar*, F. Hart Dyke, Esq. *Actuary*, Francis Cobb, Esq.

BANGOR.—*Chapter*, T. Thomas. *Clergy*, E. Lewis, J. C. Vincent.

BATH & WELLS.—*Chapter*, R. J. Meade. *Clergy*, J. S. H. Horner, G. H. U. Fagan.

CHICHESTER.—*Chapter*, C. A. Swainson. *Clergy*, C. B. Wollaston, R. S. Sutton.

ELY.—*Chapter*, W. Selwyn. *Clergy*, W. B. Hopkins, F. Bathurst.

EXETER.—*Chapter*, E. C. Harington. *Clergy*, A. Tatham, H. S. Clerk.

GLOUCESTER & BRISTOL.—No returns made.

HEREFORD.—*Chapter*, Sir F. A. G. Ouseley, Bt. *Clergy*, J. Jebb, J. W. Joyce.

LINCOLN.—*Chapter*, F. C. Massingberd. *Clergy*, R. W. Miles, G. G. Perry.

LICHFIELD.— *Chapter*, E. J. J. G. Edwards. *Clergy*, W. Fraser, E. H. Abney.

LLANDAFF.—*Chapter*, E. Hawkins. *Clergy*, C. R. Knight, W. Feetham.

NORWICH.—*Chapter*, J. W. L. Heaviside. *Clergy*, W. Potter, H. Howell.

OXFORD.—*Chapter*, R. W. Jelf. *Clergy*, F. K. Leighton, C. Lloyd.

PETERBOROUGH.—*Chapter*, M. Argles. *Clergy*, Lord A. Compton, G. E. Gillett.

ROCHESTER.—*Chapter*, T. Robinson. *Clergy*, no returns.

SALISBURY.—*Chapter*, no returns. *Clergy*, E. A. Dayman, J. L. Topham.

ST. ASAPH.—*Chapter*, H. Glynne. *Clergy*, D. Williams, W. W. How.

ST. DAVIDS.—*Chapter*, W. B. Thomas. *Clergy*, J. Hughes, H. de Winton.

WORCESTER.—*Chapter*, J. R. Wood. *Clergy*, H. A. Woodgate, R. Seymour.

University of Oxford.

Elected.

Chancellor, Rt. Hon. the Earl of Derby, D.C.L., Ch. Ch. 1852
High Steward, Rt. Hon. the Earl of Carnarvon, D.C.L., Ch. Ch. 1859
Vice-Chancellor, F. K. Leighton, D.D., Warden of All Souls 1866
Pro-Vice-Chancellors, F. C. Plumptre, D.D., Univ.; J. P. Lightfoot, D.D., Exeter; H. G. Liddell, D.D., Ch. Ch.; J. E. Sewell, D.D., New.
Proctors, Rev. C. H. Cholmely, M.A., Magdalen; Rev. W. G. Cole, M.A., Trinity.
Pro-Proctors, Rev. G. S. Ward, M.A., Magdalen Hall; Rev. T. H. R. Shand, M.A., Brasenose; Rev. C. Eddy, M.A., Queen's; Rev. J. E. Henderson, M.A., Magdalen.
Representatives in Parliament, Rt. Hon. Gathorne Hardy, D.C.L., Oriel, (1865); Rt. Hon. J. R. Mowbray, Ch. Ch. 1868
Assessor of the Chancellor's Court, M. Bernard, B.C.L., All Souls 1859
Deputy Steward, Sir Roundell Palmer, D.C.L., M.P., Magdalen College 1852
Public Orator, Richard Michell, D.D., Magdalen Hall 1848
Member of the Medical Council of the United Kingdom, H. W. Acland, D.M., late Fel. of All Souls.
Bodley's Librarian, H. O. Coxe, M.A., Corpus 1860
Sub-Librarians, A. Hackman, M.A., Ch. Ch. 1862
„ J. Nutt, M.A., All Souls ... 1867
Keeper of the Archives, J. Griffiths, M.A., Wadham 1857
Keeper of the Museum, J. Phillips, D.C.L., Magdalen 1854
Radcliffe's Librarian, H. W. Acland, M.D., All Souls 1851
Radcliffe Observer, Robert Main, M.A. 1860
Bampton Lecturer for 1869, R. P. Smith, D.D., Ch. Ch. 1868
Registrar of the University and of the Chancellor's Court, E. W. Rowden, D.C.L., New College 1853
Proctors in the Chancellor's Court, F. J. Morrell, J. C. Dudley, T. Mallam, J. D. Davenport, F. P. Morrell, M.A., St. John's.
Coroners of the University, F. Symonds, F.R.C.S., Eng., F. P. Morrell, M.A., St. John's.
University Counsel, Sir R. Palmer, M.A., D.C.L., Magdalen 1861
Solicitor, Fred. J. Morrell.
Esquire Bedel, W. W. Harrison, M.A., Brasenose.
Yeomen Bedels, H. S. Harper; John Haines.
Organist, John Stainer, D. Mus., M.A.
Bailiff, William F. Perkins.
Bellman and Marshal, T. B. Brown.
Clerk of the University, G. Parker.
Verger, M. Holliday.
Keeper of the University Galleries, J. Fisher.
Librarian of the Taylor Institution, J. Macray.

HEBDOMADAL COUNCIL.

Official Members, The Chancellor, Vice-Chancellor, ex-Vice-Chancellor, and the Proctors.
Heads of Houses, Provost of Oriel, Pres. of St. John's, Pres. of Magdalen, Dean of Ch. Ch., Princ. of Brasenose, Warden of New College.
Professors, Rev. E. B. Pusey, D.D.; Rev. C. A. Heurtley, D.D.; Rev. R. Scott, D.D.; Rev. H. Wall, M.A.; Rev. B. Price, M.A.; M. Bernard, Esq., B.C.L.
Members of Convocation, Rev. H. L. Mansel, D.D.; Rev. R. Michell, D.D.; Rev. J. M. Wilson, B.D.; Rev. J. Griffiths, M.A.; Rev. E. T. Turner, M.A.; Rev. H. P. Liddon, M.A.

PUBLIC EXAMINERS.

In Literis Humanioribus (for Honours), Wm. W. Capes, M.A., Fellow of Queen's; C. S. Parker, M.A., Fellow of University; F. W. Walker, M.A., late Fellow of C. C. C.; G. E. Thorley, M.A., Fellow of Wadham.
In Lit. Humanioribus, G. Marshall, M.A., late Student of Ch. Ch.; C. L. Wingfield, M.A., Fellow of All Souls; W. C. Sidgwick, M.A., Fellow of Merton.
In Scientiis Math. et Phys., F. Harrison, M.A., Fellow of Oriel; D. Thomas, M.A., Fellow of Trinity; H. Deane, M.A., Fellow of St. John's.
In Scientia Naturali, G. W. Child, D.M., Fellow of Exeter; A. G. V. Harcourt, M.A., Senior Student of Ch. Ch.; R. B. Clifton, M.A., Wadham.
In Jurisprudentia et Hist. Modern, J. H. Ramsay, M.A., late Student of Ch. Ch.; M. Burrows, M.A., Fellow of All Souls; T. E. Holland, M.A., Fellow of Exeter.

MODERATORS.

In Schola Litt. Gr. et Lat. (for Honours), C. W. Sandford, M.A., Student of Ch. Ch.; J. Y. Sargont, M.A., late Fellow of Magdalen; J. R. King, M.A., late Fellow of Merton. Robt. S. Wright, M.A., Fellow of Oriel.
In Schola Litt. Gr. et Lat., H. L. Thompson, M.A., Senior Student of Ch. Ch.; I. Bywater, M.A., Fellow of Exeter; E. R. Bernard, M.A., Fellow of Magdalen.
In Schola Discipl. Math., T. H. R. Shand, M.A., Fellow of Brasenose; B. Price, M.A., Fellow of Pembroke; F. S. Evans, M.A., Magdalen.

MASTERS OF THE SCHOOLS.

T. F. Dallin, M.A., Pembroke; E. Hatch, M.A., Pembroke; A. Plummer, M.A., Fellow of Trinity; A. Robinson, M.A., Fellow of New College.

COLLEGES AND HALLS.

	Members on Books.
All Souls, F. K. Leighton, D.D., Warden. 1858	118
Balliol, Robert Scott, D.D., Master. 1854	409
Brasenose, E. Hartopp Cradock, D.D., Principal. 1853	464
Christ Church, Very Rev. Henry G. Liddell, D.D., Dean. 1855	1010
Corpus Christi, James Norris, D.D., President. 1843	225
Exeter, John P. Lightfoot, D.D., Rector. 1854	672
Jesus, C. Williams, D.D., Principal. 1857	204
Lincoln, M. Pattison, B.D., Rector. 1861	219
Magdalen, F. Bulley, D.D., Pres. 1855....	304
Merton, R. Bullock-Marsham, D.C.L., Warden. 1826	226
New College, J. E. Sewell, D.D., War. 1860	229
Oriel, E. Hawkins, D.D., Provost. 1828..	411
Pembroke, Evan Evans, M.A., Master. 1864	274
Queen's, Ven. W. Jackson, D.D., Provost. 1862	336
St. John's, P. Wynter, D.D., Pres. 1828..	413
Trinity, S. Wayte, B.D., President. 1866	342
University, Fred. C. Plumptre, D.D., Master. 1836	352
Wadham, B. P. Symons, D.D., Ward. 1831.	369
Worcester, R. L. Cotton, D.D., Provost. 1839	343
St. Alban Hall, W. C. Salter, M.A., Principal. 1861	68
St. Edmund Hall, E. Moore, B.D., Principal. 1864	91
Magdalen Hall, R. Michell, D.D., Principal. 1868	279

	Members on Books.
St. Mary Hall, D. P. Chase, M.A., *Principal.* 1857	114
New Inn Hall, H. H. Cornish, D.D., *Principal.* 1866	36
Charsley's Hall (Private)	21
Benson's Hall (Private)	6
Total	**7,728**

PROFESSORS.	Elected.
Anatomy (*Aldrich's and Tomlin's*), Annexed to Linacre Professorship of Physiology	1860
Ang.-Saxon, Rev. J. Bosworth, D.D., *Ch.Ch.*	1858
Arabic (*Laud's*), Rev. R. Gandell, M.A., *Magdalen Hall*	1861
Arabic (*Lord Almoner's*), T. K. Chenery	1868
Astronomy (*Savilian*), W. F. Donkin, M.A., *University*	1842
Botany and Rural Economy, M. A. Lawson, M.A., *Magdalen*	1868
Chemistry (*Waynflete*), Sir B. C. Brodie, Bart., M.A., *Balliol*	1865
Civil Law (*Regius*), Sir Travers Twiss, D.C.L., *University*	1855
Clinical (*Lord Lichfield's*), H. W. Acland, M.D., *All Souls*	1857
Comparative Philology, Max Müller, M.A., *All Souls*	1868
Divinity (*Margaret*), Rev. Charles Abel Heurtley, D.D., *Canon of Ch. Ch.*	1853
Divinity (*Regius*), Rev. E. Payne Smith, D.D., *Canon of Ch. Ch.*	1865
Ecclesiastical History (*Regius*), Rev. W. Bright, M.A., *Canon of Ch. Ch.*	1868
Exegetical (*Ireland*), Rev. R. Scott, D.D., *Master of Balliol*	1862
Experimental Philosophy, Robert Bellamy Clifton, M.A., *Wadham*	1865
Geology, J. Phillips, M.A., *Magdalen*	1856
Geometry (*Savilian*), H. J. S. Smith, M.A., *Balliol*	1861
Greek (*Regius*), Rev. Benj. Jowett, M.A., *Balliol*	1855
Hebrew (*Regius*), Rev. Edward Bouverie Pusey, D.D., *Canon of Ch. Ch.*	1828
History (*Camden*), Rev. G. Rawlinson, M.A., *Exeter*	1861
International Law (*Chichele*), M. Bernard, B.C.L., *All Souls*	1859
Latin Literature, J. Conington, M.A., *Ch.Ch.*	1854
Law (*Vinerian*), K. E. Digby, M.A., *Corpus*	1868
Logic, Rev. Henry Wall, M.A., *Balliol*	1359
Medicine (*Aldrich's*), Annexed to Regius Professorship of Medicine	1861
Medicine (*Regius*), H. W. Acland, M.D., *All Souls*	1857
Mineralogy, M. H. Nevil Story-Maskelyne, M.A., *Wadham*	1854
Modern History (*Chichele*), Montagu Burrows, M.A., *Magdalen Hall*	1862
Modern History (*Regius*), Rev. William Stubbs, M.A., *Oriel*	1866
Moral Philosophy (*Waynflete*), Rev. H. W. Chandler, M.A., *Pembroke*	1867
Moral Philosophy, Rev. J. M. Wilson, B.D., *Corpus*	1858
Music, Rev. Sir Fred. A. Gore Ouseley, Bart., D.Mus., *Ch. Ch.*	1855
Music (*Choragus*), C. W. Corfe, D.Mus.	1860
Natural Philosophy, Rev. B. Price, M.A., *Pembroke*	1853
Pastoral Theology (*Regius*), Rev. C. Atmore Ogilvie, D.D., *Canon of Ch. Ch.*	1842

	Elected.
Physiology (*Linacre*), George Rolleston, M.D., *Pembroke*	1860
Poetry, Sir F. H. Doyle, Bart., B.C.L., *All Souls*	1867
Political Economy (*Drummond's*), Bonamy Price, M.A., *Worcester*	1868
Sanskrit (*Col. Boden's*), M. Williams, M.A., *University*	1860
Septuagint (*Grinfield*), Rev. J. A. Hessey, D.C.L., *St. John's*	1865
Zoology (*Hope's*), J. O. Westwood, M.A., *Magdalen*	1861

TEACHERS.—*Hindustani*, Joseph Chambers, M.A.; *German*, Robert Bertram; *French*, Jules Bué, M.A.; *Italian*, Vital De Tivoli; *Spanish*, Rev. Lorenzo Lucena.

Reader in *Indian Law*, S. J. Owen, M.A., *Ch. Ch.*

University of Cambridge.

Chancellor, His Grace The Duke of Devonshire, K.G., LL.D. ... 1861

High Steward, The Earl of Powis, LL.D., *St. John's* ... 1863

Vice-Chancellor, E. Atkinson, D.D., *Master of Clare* ... 1868

Representatives in Parliament, Right Hon. S. H. Walpole, M.A., *Trinity*, (1868). A. J. B. Beresford-Hope, LL.D., *Trinity*, (1868).

Commissary, W. Forsyth, Q.C.

Deputy High Steward, Francis Barlow, M.A., *Trinity Hall* ... 1856

Public Orator, Rev. W. G. Clark, M.A., *Trinity* ... 1857

Registrar, Rev. H. R. Luard, M.A., *Trinity* 1862

Librarian, H. Bradshaw, M.A., *King's* ... 1867

Assessor to the Chancellor, J. Tozer, LL.D., *Caius* ... 1852

Counsel, Hon. G. Denman, *Trinity*; G. Druce, M.A., *St. Peter's*.

Council, The Chancellor; the Vice-Chancellor; H. W. Cookson, D.D., *Master of St. Peter's*; R. Okes, D.D., *Provost of King's*; W. H. Thompson, D.D., *Master of Trinity*; W. H. Bateson, D.D., *Master of St. John's*; Professor Lightfoot, D.D., *Trinity*; Professor Humphry, M.D., *Downing*; Professor C. C. Babington, M.A., *St. John's*; Prof. Stokes, *Pembroke*; J. Power, M.A., *Pembroke*; N. M. Ferrers, M.A., *Caius*; J. L. Hammond, *Trinity*; R. Burn, M.A., *Trinity*; W. G. Clark, *Trinity*; W. M. Gunson, *Christ's*; H. A. Morgan, *Jesus*; S. G. Phear, *Emmanuel*.

Every University Grace must pass the Council before it can be introduced to the Senate.

Sex Viri, Dr. Phelps; Dr. Bateson; Professor Stokes; Dr. Paget; J. Power, *Pembroke*; Professor Liveing.

Auditors of the Chest, Dr. Cookson, *St. Peter's*; J. Porter, *St. Peter's*; E. W. Crabtree, *Cath. Coll.*

Proctors, W. H. Whitting, M.A., *King's*; T. Hewitt, M.A., *Emmanuel.*

Pro-Proctors, J. Porter, M.A., *St. Peter's*; R. B. Somerset, M.A., *Trinity.*

Moderators, P. Frost, M.A., *St. John's*; R. B. Hayward, M.A., *St. John's.*

Esquire Bedel, H. Godfray, M.A., *St. John's* 1854
,, ,, W. H. Besant, M.A., *St. John's* 1866

EXAMINERS.

Classical Tripos, F. C. Hodgson, M.A., *King's*; J. Peile, M.A., *Christ's*; A. G. Day, M.A., *Caius*; R. C. Jebb, M.A., *Trinity*; R. C. A. Tayler, M.A., *Trinity*; C. W. Moule, M.A., *Corpus.*

Moral Sciences Tripos, W. M. Campion, B.D.,

Queen's; F. J. A. Hort, M.A., *Trinity*; F. D. Maurice, M.A., *Trinity*; T. Webster, M.A., *Trinity.*

Natural Science Tripos, Professor G. M. Humphry, M.D.; O. Fisher, M.A., *Jesus*; G. Henslow, M.A., *Christ's*; P. T. Main, M.A., *St. John's.*

Theology, Professor J. B. Lightfoot, D.D.; Professor T. Jarrett, M.A.; H. Russell, B.D., *St. John's*; T. R. Birks, M.A., *Trinity*; G. F. Browne, M.A., *St. Catharine's*; W. E. Churton, M.A., *King's.*

Civil Law, Professor J. T. Abdy, LL.D.; E. C. Clark, M.A., *Trinity*; R. S. Ferguson, M.A., *St. John's*; B. Walker, M.A., *Corpus.*

COLLEGES AND HALLS.	Members on Books.
Christ's, Jas. Cartmell, D.D., *Master.* 1849	450
Clare College, Edward Atkinson, D.D., *Master.* 1856	278
Corpus Christi, Jas. Pulling, D.D., *Master.* 1850	451
Downing, T. Worsley, D.D., *Master.* 1836	103
Emmanuel, G. Archdall-Gratwicke, D.D., *Master.* 1835.	442
Gonville and Caius, E. Guest, LL.D., F.R.S., *Master.* 1852	532
Jesus, Geo. E. Corrie, D.D., *Master.* 1849	287
King's, R. Okes, D.D., *Provost.* 1850	156
Magdalene, Hon. and Rev. Latimer Neville, M.A., *Master.* 1853	224
Pembroke College, Gilbert Ainslie, D.D., *Master.* 1828	165
Queens', G. Phillips, D.D., *President.* 1857	265
Sidney-Sussex, Robert Phelps, D.D., *Master.* 1843	183
St. Catharine's College, Charles Kirby Robinson, D.D., *Master.* 1861	209
St. John's, W. H. Bateson, D.D., *Master.* 1857	1591
St. Peter's College, H. W. Cookson, D.D., *Master.* 1847	252
Trinity, William H. Thompson, D.D., *Master.* 1866	3033
Trinity Hall, Thomas C. Geldart, LL.D., *Master.* 1852	353
Members not on the College Boards	127
Total	8,974

PROFESSORS.	Elected.
Anatomy, G. M. Humphry, M.D., *Downing*	1866
Arabic, Rev. Henry G. Williams, B.D., *Emmanuel*	1854
Arabic (*Lord Almoner's*) Rev. T. Preston, M.A., *Trinity*	1855
Archæology (*Disney*), Rev. Churchill Babington, B.D., *St. John's*	1865
Astronomy (*Lowndes's*), J. C. Adams, M.A., *Pembroke*	1858
Astronomy (*Plumian*) Rev. J. Challis, M.A., F.R.S., *Trinity*	1836
Botany, C. C. Babington, M.A., *St. John's*	1861
Chemistry, G. D. Liveing, M.A., *St. John's*	1862
Civil Law (*Regius*), John Thomas Abdy, LL.D., *Trinity Hall*	1854
Divinity (*Hulsean*), Rev. J. B. Lightfoot, D.D., *Trinity*	1861
Divinity (*Margaret*), Rev. W. Selwyn, D.D., *St. John's*	1855
Divinity (*Norrisian*), Rev. C. A. Swainson, D.D., *Christ's*	1864
Divinity (*Regius*), Very Rev. James Amiraux Jeremie, D.D., *Trinity*	1850
Geology (*Woodwardian*), Rev. A Sedgwick, LL.D., F.R.S., *Trinity*	1818

	Elected.
Greek (*Regius*), Rev. B. H. Kennedy, D.D., *St. John's*	1867
Hebrew (*Regius*), Rev. Thos. Jarrett, M.A., *Trinity*	1854
Hulsean Lecturer, Rev. J. J. S. Perowne, B.D., *Corpus*	1868
Lady Margaret Preacher, Rev. W. G. Clark, Public Orator, *Trinity*	1863
Law (*Downing*), W. L. Birkbeck, M.A., *Trinity*	1860
Mathematics (*Lucasian*), George Gabriel Stokes, M.A., *Pembroke*	1849
Medicine (*Downing*), W. W. Fisher, M.D., *Downing*	1841
Mineralogy, William Hallows Miller, Esq., M.A., F.R.S., *St. John's*	1832
Modern History (*Regius*), Charles Kingsley, M.A., *Magdalene*	1860
Moral Philosophy, Rev. F. D. Maurice, M.A., *Trinity*	1866
Music, W. Sterndale Bennett, Mus. D., *St. John's*	1856
Natural Philosophy (*Jacksonian*), Rev. R. Willis. M.A., F.R.S., *Caius*	1837
Physic (*Regius*), Henry J. Hayles Bond, M.D., *Corpus Christi*	1851
Political Economy, H. Fawcett, M.A., *Trinity Hall*	1864
Pure Mathematics (*Sadlerian*), A. Cayley, M.A., *Trinity*	1863
Sanskrit, E. B. Cowell, M.A.	1867
Zoology, A. Newton, M.A., *Magdalene*	1866

University of London.

Temporary Offices, 17, Savile Row, W.

THE SENATE.

Chancellor, Rt. Hon. Earl Granville, K.G., D.C.L., F.R.S.

Vice-Chancellor, G. Grote, LL.D., D.C.L., F.R.S. Duke of Devonshire, K.G., LL.D., F.R.S.; Rt. Hon. Earl of Kimberley, M.A.; Bp. of St. David's, D.D.; Lord Overstone, M.A.; Sir J. E. E. Dalberg Acton, Bt.; N. Arnott, M.D., F.R.S.; Arch. Billing, M.D., A.M., F.R.S.; Geo. Burrows, M.D., F.R.S.; Rt. Hon. E. Cardwell, M.A., M.P., D.C.L.; Sir P. de M. G. Egerton, Bt., M.P., F.R.S.; R. N. Fowler, M.A. M.P.; Rt. Hon. G. J. Goschen, M.P.; W. W. Gull, M.D.; J. Heywood, M.A., F.R.S.; R. Holt Hutton, M.A.; G. Jessel, M.A., M.P.; G. Johnson, M.D.; F. Kiernan, F.R.S.; Sir John G. Shaw Lefevre, K.C.B., D.C.L., F.R.S.; Sir C. Locock, Bt., M.D.; Rt. Hon. Robt. Lowe, M.A., M.P.; Sir John Lubbock, Bt., M.A., F.R.S.; Sir W. Stirling Maxwell, Bart., M.A.; W. A. Miller, M.D., Treasurer R.S.; T. S. Osler, LL.B.; J. Paget, F.R.S.; E. Quain, M.D.; P. M. Roget, M.D., F.R.S.; Rt. Hon. Sir E. Ryan, M.A., F.R.S.; W. Sharpey, M.D., F.R.S.; F. Sibson, M.D., F.R.S.; Wm. Spottiswoode, M.A., F.R.S.; Rt. Hon. Lord Stanley, D.C.L., M.P., F.R.S.; J. Storrar, M.D.; Hon. E. T. B. Twisleton, M.A.; F. J. Wood, LL.D.

Representative in Parliament, Rt. Hon. R. Lowe, M.A.

Representative on Med. Coun. J. Storrar, M.D.

Registrar, W. B. Carpenter, M.D., F.R.S.

Clerk to the Senate, Thomas Douce, B.A.

Chairman of Convocation, John Storrar, M.D.

Clerk of do., John Robson, M.A.

EXAMINERS.

Anatomy, Prof. W. Turner, M.B., F.R.S.E.; and John Wood, F.R.C.S.

Botany, Rev. M. J. Berkeley, M.A.; T. Thomson, M.D., F.R.S.

Chemistry, H. Debus, Ph.D., F.R.S.; Prof. A. W. Williamson, Ph.D., F.R.S.

Classics, F. A. Paley, M.A.; Wm. Smith, LL.D.

English Language, Literature and History, Rev. J. Angus, D.D.; C. K. Watson, M.A.

Experimental Philosophy, Prof. R. B. Clifton, M.A.; Prof. G. Carey Foster, B.A.

Forensic Medicine, E. H. Greenhow, M.D.; Thos. Stevenson, M.D.

French Language, Rev. P. H. E. Brette, B.A., B.D.; Th. Karcher, LL.B.

Geology and Palæontology, A. Geikie, F.R.S., F.G.S.; Prof. T. Rupert Jones, F.G.S.

German, F. Althaus, Ph.D.; Prof. Buchheim, Ph.D.

Hebrew Text of the Old Testament, Greek Text of the New Testament, and Scripture History, Rev. S. Davidson, D.D., LL.D., Rev. J. J. S. Perowne, B.D.

Law and Principles of Legislation, Prof. M. Bernard, B.C.L., M.A.; J. R. Quain, LL.B.

Logic and Moral Philosophy, Prof. A. Bain, M.A.; Prof. G. Croom Robertson, M.A.

Materia Medica, &c., Prof. A. B. Garrod, M.D., F.R.S.; S. O. Habershon, M.D.

Mathematics and Natural Philosophy, E. J. Routh, M.A.; I. Todhunter, M.A., F.R.S.

Medicine, Prof. J. Russell Reynolds, M.D.; Samuel Wilks, M.D.

Midwifery, J. B. Hicks, M.D., F.R.S.; W. O. Priestley, M.D.

Physiology, Comparative Anatomy, and Zoology, Prof. T. H. Huxley, Ph.D., F.R.S.; Henry Bower, M.B.

Political Economy, Prof. W. Stanley Jevons, M.A.; Prof. J. Waley, M.A.

Surgery, F. Le Gros Clark; Prof. J. E. Erichsen.

UNIVERSITY COLLEGE, LONDON.

President, George Grote, Esq., D.C.L., LL.D., F.R.S.

Vice-President, Rt. Hon. Lord Belper, D.C.L.

Treasurer, pro tem. G. Grote, Esq.

COUNCIL.

President; Vice-President; Treasurer; H. M. Bompas, M.A.; J. Booth, C.B.; *G. Buchanan, M.D.; H. H. Cozens-Hardy, LL.B.; Hon. G. Denman, Q.C., M.P.; *E. Enfield; *T. H. Farrer; E. W. Field; *R. N. Fowler, M.A., M.P.; W. Fowler, LL.B., M.P.; *Sir F. H. Goldsmid, Bart., M.P.; J. Goldsmid, Esq., M.A.; J. C. Gooden, Esq.; J. Hodgkin, Esq.; C. Z. Macaulay, Esq.; Hen. Matthews, LL.B., Q.C., M.P.; *E. Romilly; Rt. Hon. Sir Edw. Ryan; *Samuel Sharpe; John Tyndall, Esq., F.R.S.; F. J. Wood, LL.D.

Auditors, R. B. Hayward, M.A.; T. C. Watson; Henry Sharpe; Alfred Taylor.

Note.—The Asterisks denote the Committee of Management.

SENATE.

Pres., Sir F. H. Goldsmid, Bt. Q.C., M.P.

Vice-Pres., Edw. Romilly; Jas. Booth, C.B.

Secretary, J. Robson, B.A.

PROFESSORS.

Faculty of Arts and Laws.

Ancient and Modern History, E. S. Beesly, M.A.

Arabic and Persian, Chas. Rieu, Ph.D.

Architecture, T. H. Lewis, F.A.S., F.I.B.A.

Botany, Daniel Oliver, F.L.S., F.R.S.

Chemistry, &c., A. W. Williamson, F.R.S.

Engineering, George Fuller, C.E.

Comparative Grammar, T. H. Key, M.A., F.R.S.

English Lan. and Lit., Henry Morley, Dean.

English Law, John A. Russell, Q.C.

French, Charles Cassal, LL.D.

Geology and Mineralogy, J. Morris, F.G.S.

German, Adolph Heimann, Ph.D.

Greek, Henry Malden, M.A.

Hebrew, Rev. D. W. Marks.

Italian, G. Volpe.

Jurisprudence, H. J. Roby, M.A.

Latin, John R. Seeley, M.A.

Pure Mathematics, T. A. Hirst, Ph.D., F.R.S., Vice Dean.

Applied Mathematics and Mechanics, B. T. Moore, M.A., C.E.

Phil. of Mind, &c., G. Croom Robertson, M.A.

Physics, G. C. Foster, B.A.

Political Economy, J. E. Cairnes, M.A.

Sanskrit, T. Goldstäcker, Ph.D.

Telugu, C. P. Brown.

Zoology, Robert E. Grant, M.D., F.R.S.

Faculty of Medicine.

Anatomy, Geo. V. Ellis.

Anatomy and Physiology, Wm. Sharpey, M.D. LL.D., F.R.S.

Chemistry, &c., A. W. Williamson, F.R.S.

Clinical Medicine, Sir Wm. Jenner, Bart, M.D., F.R.S.

Clinical Medicine (Holme), Wilson Fox, M.D.

Clinical Surgery (Holme), J. E. Erichsen.

Clinical Surgery, Sir Henry Thompson.

Comparative Anatomy, R. E. Grant, M.D., F.R.S.

Forensic Medicine, George Harley, M.D., F.R.S.

Materia Medica, Sydney Ringer, M.D., Vice Dean.

Medicine and Clinical Med., J. R. Reynolds, Dean.

Obstetric Med., Graily Hewitt, M.D.

Ophthalmic Med., &c., T. W. Jones, F.R.S.

Pathological Anaty., H. C. Bastian, M.D., F.R.S.

SCHOOL.

Head Master, T. Hewitt Key, M.A., F.R.S.

Vice Master, E. R. Horton, M.A.

KING'S COLLEGE, LONDON.

Official Governors, Lord Chancellor, Abp. of York, Bp. of London, Lord Chief Justice Queen's Bench, Secretary of State Home Department, Speaker of House of Commons, Lord Mayor, Deans of St. Paul's and Westminster.

Life Governors, Duke of Cambridge, K.G.; Marq. of Cholmondeley; Earl Howe; Earl of Harrowby, K.G.; Earl of Powis; Rt. Hon. Sir J. T. Coleridge; Sir T. Watson, Bt., M.D.

The Council, The Governors and Treasurer; Bishops of Winchester and Ely; Rt. Hon. W. E. Gladstone, D.C.L., M.P.; R. Cheere; The Master of the Temple, D.D.; C. P. Serocold; Sir W. Heathcote, Bart., D.C.L.; T. G. Sambrooke; Rev. C. D'Oyly, M.A.; Hon. G. W. Leslie Waldegrave; Rev. John G. Lonsdale, M.A.; J. Coleridge, Q.C.; Edmd. Beckett Denison, Q.C.; H. Acland, M.D.; R. Hudson; A. Farre, M.D.; W. H. Smith, M.P.; C. Austen-Leigh, Esq.; Rev. G. Currie, D.D.; Colonel Ouseley; A. J. Beresford-Hope, Esq., M.P.

Treasurer, E. Wigram.

Principal of College, Rev. A. Barry, D.D.

Chaplain,

Censor, Rev. W. H. White.

Secretary, J. W. Cunningham.

Librarian, J. Lamb.

PROFESSORS.

Divinity, Rev. E. H. Plumptre, M.A.; Rev. Canon Robertson, M.A.; Rev. S. Leathes, M.A.; Rev.

S. Cheetham, M.A.; Rev. A. I. M'Caul, B.A.; and Rev. Henry Jona.
Classical Literature, Rev. J. G. Lonsdale, M.A.; Rev. J. J. Heywood, M.A.; and J. R. Mozley, Esq., M.A.
English Language and Modern History, Rev. J. S. Brewer, M.A.; Rev. J. J. Heywood; and J. R. Mozley, Esq.
Mathematics, Rev. T. C. Hall, M.A.; Rev. T. A. Cock, M.A.; and Rev. W. Howse, M.A.
Nat. Philosophy and Astronomy, W. G. Adams, M.A.
Experimental Philosophy, C. Wheatstone, Esq.
Law and Jurisprudence, John Cutler, Esq.
Geology and Mineralogy, James Tennant, Esq.
Zoology, T. Bell, Esq.
Chemistry, W. A. Miller, M.D., F.R.S.; J. T. Bottomley, B.A.
Practical Chemistry, C. L. Bloxam, Esq.
Architecture, R. Kerr, Esq.
Hebrew, Rev. S. Leathes, M.A.
Sanskrit,
Arabic, A. Ameuney.
Hindustani, Thomas Howley, Esq.
Chinese, Rev. J. Summers.
Tamil and Telugu, Thomas Howley, Esq.
Bengali, Rev. J. Campbell.
Gujarati and Marathi, Rev. H. Prestonji.
French, MM. Mariette and Stievenard.
German, A. Buchheim, Ph.D.
Italian, V. Pistrucci.
Vocal Music, J. Hullah, Esq.
Geometrical Drawing, T. Bradley, Esq., and W. J. Glenny, Esq.
Machinery, C. P. B. Shelley, Esq.
Surveying, H. J. Castle, Esq.; E. Marshall, Esq.
Drawing, Ph. De La Motte, Esq.

PROFESSORS, MEDICAL SCHOOL.

Anatomy, R. Partridge, Esq.
Physiology and Morbid Anatomy, L. S. Beale, M.B.
Comparative Anatomy, T. R. Jones, Esq.
Botany, R. Bentley, Esq., F.L.S.
Chemistry, W. A. Miller, M.D., F.R.S., and C. L. Bloxam, Esq.
Materia Medica, A. B. Garrod, M.D.
Medicine, G. Johnson, M.D.
Medicine, Forensic, W. A. Guy, B.M.
Midwifery, W. O. Priestley, M.D.
Surgery, Sir W. Fergusson, Bart.
Demonstrator, John Wood, Esq., F.R.C.S.
Librarian, R. H. G. Tritton, Esq.

University of Durham.

Governors, The Dean and Chapter of Durham.
Warden, Very Rev. George Waddington, D.D., Dean of Durham.
Sub-Warden, Rev. Temple Chevallier, B.D.
Senate, The Warden, the Professors, the Proctors, one representative of the Chapter, one elected by the Convocation, and one by the Fellows of the University.
Proctors, Rev. J. Barmby, B.D., and Rev. Joseph Waite, M.A.

PROFESSORS.

Divinity & Eccles. Hist., Rev. A. S. Farrar, D.D.
Greek & Classical Lit., Rev. T. S. Evans, M.A.
Math. & Astronomy, Rev. T. Chevallier, B.D.
Tutors, Rev. Joseph Waite, M.A.; Rev. J. Barmby, B.D.; Rev. F. J. Copeman, B.A.
Hebrew, Rev. T. Chevallier, B.D.
Law, William Gray, M.A.
History, Political Literature, T. Greenwood, M.A.
Medicine, Dennis Embleton, M.D.
Chemistry, A. F. Maneco.

Civil Engineering & Mining, A. Beanlands, M.A.
Registrar & Librarian, Rev. T. T. Thornton, M.A.
Observer, John Isaac Plummer.
Treasurer, A. Beanlands, M.A.
Auditor, John Fogg Elliot.

UNIVERSITY COLLEGE.

Master, Rev. J. Waite, M.A.
Censors, Rev. F. S. Copeman, M.A.; Rev. T. T. Thornton, M.A.
Bursar & Chaplain, Rev. F. F. Walrond, M.A.

BISHOP HATFIELD'S HALL.

Principal, Rev. J. Barmby, B.D.
Censor & Chaplain, Rev. J. D. Hepple, M.A.

SCOTLAND.

University of Aberdeen, 1494.

Chancellor, Duke of Richmond.
Vice-Chancellor, Principal Campbell.
Rector, M. E. Grant Duff, M.P.
Principal, P. C. Campbell, D.D.
Assessors, J. Webster, Adv.; E. Woodford, LL.D.; A. Kilgour, M.D.; Rev. Prof. Pirie, D.D.
Secretary, David Thomson, M.A.
Librarian, Rev. John Fyfe, A.M.

PROFESSORS.

Greek, W. D. Geddes, A.M.
Humanity, John Black, M.A.
Logic, A. Bain, A.M.
Mathematics, F. Fuller, M.A.
Moral Philosophy, W. Martin, A.M.
Natural Philosophy, D. Thomson, M.A.
Natural History, J. Nicol.
Systematic Theology, S. Trail, D.D., LL.D.
Church History, W. R. Pirie, D.D.
Biblical Criticism, W. Milligan, D.D.
Oriental Languages, A. Scott, A.M.
Law, P. Davidson, LL.D.
Institutes of Medicine, G. Ogilvie, M.D.
Practice of Medicine, J. Macrobin, M.D.
Chemistry, J. S. Brazier.
Anatomy, John Struthers, M.D.
Surgery, W. Pirrie, F.R.S.E.
Materia Medica, R. Harvey, M.D.
Midwifery, R. Dyce, M.D.
Med. Jurisprudence, F. Ogston, M.D.
Botany, G. Dickie, M.D.

University of St. Andrew's, 1411.

Chancellor, Duke of Argyll, LL.D., K.T.
Vice-Chancellor, Principal Tulloch, D.D.
Rector, John Stuart Mill, LL.D.
Senior Principal, Principal Tulloch, D.D.
Dean of Faculty of Arts, Prof. Campbell, M.A.
Joint Librarians, R. Walker and W. Troup.
Registrar and Clerk, William Troup.

THE UNIVERSITY COURT.

John S. Mill; Principal Tulloch, D.D.; John Hunter, LL.D. (*Auditor of the Court of Session*); A. Findlater, LL.D.; Hon. Charles Baillie (Lord Jerviswoode); Professor Fischer.

UNITED COLLEGE OF ST. SALVATOR AND ST. LEONARD.

Principal, J. C. Shairp, M.A.

PROFESSORS.

Humanity, John C. Shairp, M.A.
English Lit.,
Greek, Rev. Lewis Campbell, M.A.
Mathematics, W. L. F. Fischer, M.A., F.R.S.
Logic, Thomas Spencer Baynes, LL.D.

Moral Philosophy, Robert Flint.
Natural Philosophy, William Swan, F.R.S.E.
Civil History, W. M'Donald, M.D.
Anatomy & Medicine, Oswald H. Bell, M.D.
Chemistry, M. Foster Heddle, M.D.
Clerk & Factor, W. F. Ireland.

COLLEGE OF ST. MARY.

Principal, John Tulloch, D.D.

PROFESSORS.

Systematic Theology, John Tulloch, D.D.
Biblical Criticism & Theology, W. Brown, D.D.
Ecclesiastical History, John Cook, D.D.
Oriental Languages, A. F. Mitchell, D.D.
Secretary and Factor, S. Grace.

University of Edinburgh, 1589.

Chancellor, The Right. Hon. the Lord Justice General.
Rector, Jas. Moncrieff, Esq., M.P.
Vice-Chancellor and Principal, Sir A. Grant, Bart., LL.D., &c.
Secretary of Senatus, Professor Wilson.

PROFESSORS.
Faculty of Arts.

Latin, William F. Sellar, LL.D.
Greek, John Stuart Blackie, M.A.
Mathematics, Philip Kelland, M.A., F.R.S.
Logic, Rev. Alexander Campbell Fraser, M.A.
Moral Phil. & Polit. Economy, Henry Calderwood, LL.D.
Natural Philosophy, Peter Guthrie Tait, M.A.
Rhetoric, David Masson, M.A.
Universal History, Cosmo Innes, M.A.
Astronomy, Charles Piazzi Smyth, F.R.S.
Agriculture, John Wilson, F.R.S.E.
Music, Herbert S. Oakeley, M.A.
Sanskrit, Theodore Aufrecht, M.A.
Engineering, Fleeming Jenkin, F.R.S.

Faculty of Divinity.

Divinity, Thomas Jackson Crawford, D.D.
Church History, William Stevenson, D.D.
Hebrew, David Liston, M.A.
Biblical Criticism, A. H. Charteris, D.D.

Faculty of Law.

Public Law, James Lorimer, M.A.
Civil Law, James Muirhead.
Scotch Law, Norman Macpherson, LL.D.
Conveyancing, James Stuart Tytler.
Constitutional Law & History, Cosmo Innes, M.A.

Faculty of Medicine.

Materia Medica, Robert Christison, M.D., D.C.L.
Medical Police, Douglas Maclagan, M.D.
Chem., Lyon Playfair, C.B., F.R.S., LL.D., M.D.
Surgery, James Spence.
Practice of Physic, Thomas Laycock, M.D.
Anatomy, William Turner, M.B.
Pathology, William Henderson, M.D.
Midwifery, Sir Jas. Y. Simpson, Bt., M.D., D.C.L.
Clinical Surgery, James Syme.
Botany, Jno. Hutton Balfour, M.A., M.D., F.R.S.
Institutes of Medicine, J. H. Bennett, M.D.
Natural History, Geo. Jas. Allman, M.D., F.R.S.

University of Glasgow, 1450.

Chancellor, Duke of Montrose, K.T.
Vice-Chancellor, The Principal.
Rector, Rt. Hon. Lord Stanley, M.P.
Dean of Faculties, Sir James Fergusson, Bart.
Principal, Thomas Barclay, D.D.
Clerk & Secretary, Rev. Duncan H. Weir, D.D.

PROFESSORS.

Humanity, George G. Ramsay, M.A.
Greek, Edmund Law Lushington, M.A.
Mathematics, Hugh Blackburn, M.A.
Civil Engineering and Mechanics, William J. M. Rankine, LL.D., F.R.S.
Logic, John Veitch, M.A.
Moral Philosophy, Edward Caird, B.A.
Natural Philosophy, Sir William Thomson, LL.D.
English Language and Literature, J. Nichol, B.A.
Astronomy, Robert Grant, LL.D.
Divinity, John Caird, D.D.
Church History, Thomas T. Jackson, D.D.
Biblical Criticism, W. P. Dickson, D.D.
Oriental Languages, Rev. D. H. Weir, D.D.
Law of Scotland, R. Berry, M.A.
Conveyancing, James Roberton, LL.D.
Materia Medica, J. Cowan, M.D.
Chemistry, Thomas Anderson, M.D.
Surgery, Joseph Lister, M.B., F.R.S.
Practice of Medicine, William Gairdner, M.D.
Midwifery, William Leishman, M.D.
Anatomy, Allen Thomson, M.D.
Botany, Alexander Dickson, M.D.
Institutes of Medicine, A. Buchanan, M.D.
Forensic Medicine, Harry Rainy, M.D.
Natural History, John Young, M.D.
Waltonian Lec. Eye, George Rainy, M.D.
Keeper of Hunterian Museum, Prof. Young, M.D.
Librarian, R. B. Spears.
Clerk of Senate, Professor Weir, D.D.
Registrar, T. Moir.

IRELAND.
University of Dublin. 1591.

Chancellor, Right Hon. Lord Cairns, LL.D. T.C.D., D.C.L. Oxon., LL.D. Cantab. 1867.
Vice-Chancellor, Right Hon. Sir Joseph Napier, Bart., LL.D. 1867.
Members for the University, Anthony Lefroy, LL.D. (1868) ; Rt.Hon.John T.Ball,M.P.(1868).
Provost, Humphrey Lloyd, D.D. 1867.
Vice-Provost, John Lewis Moore, D.D. 1867.
Proctors, Andrew S. Hart, LL.D.; Rev. J. Leslie.
Censor, Rev. William Roberts, M.A.
Deans, J. H. Todd, D.D.; Rev. T. T. Gray, M.A.
Registrar, John Toleken, M.D.
Bursar, Rev. Joseph Carson, D.D.
Auditor, Andrew S. Hart, LL.D.
Librarian, James Henthorn Todd, D.D.
Secretary to the Senate, Rev. John H. Jellett, B.D.

PROFESSORS AND LECTURERS.

	Elected.
Divinity (Regius), George Salmon, D.D....	1866
Divinity (Archbp. King's Lecturer), William Lee, D.D.	1864
Civil Law (Regius), Thos. E. Webb, LL.D.	1867
Feudal and English Law (Regius), Mountiford Longfield, LL.D.	1834
Greek (Regius), John Kells Ingram, LL.D.	1866
Oratory and English Literature, Edward Dowden, M.A.	1867
Natural Philosophy, John H. Jellett, B.D....	1848
Natural Philosophy (Erasmus Smith), Joseph A. Galbraith, M.A.	1854
Mathematics (Erasmus Smith), Michael Roberts, M.A.	1862
Modern History (Erasmus Smith), James W. Barlow, M.A.	1860
Hebrew (Regius), James H. Todd, D.D.....	1849
Astron. Royal, Francis Brünnow, Ph.D....	1865
Political Economy, James Slattery, M.A....	1865
Moral Philosophy, Thomas K. Abbott, M.A.	1867
Biblical Greek, George Sidney Smith, D.D.	1838

	Elected.
Ecclesiastical Hist., Richd. Gibbings, D.D.	1863
Irish, Thaddeus O'Mahony, M.A.	1861
Arabic, Meer Owlad Allee	1861
Sanskrit, Carl Friedrich Lottner	1863
Physic (Regius), William Stokes, M.D.	1845
Anatomy, Benj. Geo. M'Dowell, M.D., Ch.M.	1853
Surgery (Regius Prof.) Robert Adams, M.D.	1861
Surgery, Robert Smith, M.D., Ch.M.	1849
Chemistry, James Apjohn, M.D.	1850
Botany, Vacant.	
Geology, Samuel Haughton, M.D., F.R.S.	1851
Mineralogy, James Apjohn, M.D.	1845
Civil Engineering, Samuel Downing, LL.D.	1852
Music, Robert P. Stewart, Mus.D.	1862
Professor of German, A. M. Selss, M.A.	1866
Lecturer in Italian, Robert Atkinson, M.A.	1867
Lecturer in Zoology, E. P. Wright, M.D.	1858
Lecturer in Anatomy, Edw. H. Bennett, M.D.	1864
Director of Museum, E. P. Wright, M.D.	1857
Curator of Anatoml. Museum, John Connor	1858

SCHOOL OF ENGINEERING.

Mathematics, William Roberts, M.A.	1867
Mechanics, Richard Townsend, M.A.	1862
Principles of Physics, J. A. Galbraith, M.A.	1842
Geology, Samuel Haughton, M.D.	1842
Civil Engineering (Ext.) Sir J. MacNeill, LL.D	1842
Pract. Engineering, Saml. Downing, LL.D.	1852
Chemistry, Constructive, J. Apjohn, M.D.	1842
Drawing and Surveying, S. Downing, LL.D.	1842

The Queen's University in Ireland.

Chancellor, Right Hon. the Earl of Clarendon, K.G.
Vice-Chancellor, Right Hon. M. Brady, P.C.
Secretary, G. J. Stoney, Esq., M.A., F.R.S.
Clerk of Convoc, Jas. Wilson, Esq., M.A., LL.B.

QUEEN'S COLLEGE, BELFAST.

President, Rev. P. Shuldham Henry, D.D.
Vice-President, Thomas Andrews, M.D., F.R.S.
Registrar, Rev. Richard Oulton, B.D.
Bursar, Alexander Dickey, Esq.
Librarian, Rev. George Hill.

Deans of Residences.
Church of England, Rev. Robert Hannay.
Presb. Church, Rev. Henry Cooke, D.D., LL.D.
Non-Subscribing Presbyterians, Rev. John Porter.
Wesleyan Methodists, Rev. William M'Kay.

QUEEN'S COLLEGE, CORK.

President, Sir Robert Kane, M.D., F.R.S.
Vice-President, John Ryall, LL.D.
Registrar, Robert J. Kenny, Esq.
Bursar, Edward M. Fitzgerald, Esq.
Librarian, Matthias O'Keefe, A.M., M.D.

Deans of Licensed Residences.
Church of England, Rev. George Webster.
Presbyterian Church, Rev. William Magill.
Wesleyan, Rev. Mr. Best.
Non-Subscribing Presbyterians, Rev. W. Whitelegg.

QUEEN'S COLLEGE, GALWAY.

President, Edward Berwick, A.B.
Registrar, William Lupton, A.M.
Bursar, George Johnston Allman, LL.D.
Librarian, John H. Richardson, A.B.,

Deans of Licensed Residences.
Church of England, Rev. J. Treanor, B.A.
Presbyterian Church, Rev. W. Adair.
Wesleyan Methodist Church, Rev. Hugh Moore.
Independent Church, Rev. John Lewis.

Royal College of St. Patrick, Maynooth.

President, Rev. Charles William Russell, D.D.
Vice-Pres., Rev. Robt. Ffrench Whitehead, D.D.

Dean, Rev. James O'Kane.
Junior Deans, Revs. Richard Quinn, Thomas Hammond, and James Hughes.
Prefect & Librarian, Rev. John O'Hanlon, D.D.
Bursar, Rev. Thomas Farrelly, D.D.
Secretary, Rev. Walter M. Lee, D.D., P.P., Bray.

The Catholic University, Dublin.

Chancellor, Cardinal Archbishop Paul Cullen, D.D., Apostolic Delegate.
Vice-Chancellor, Archbishop John M'Hale, D.D.
Rector, Monsig. Bartholomew Woodlock, D.D.

Deans of Houses.
St. Patrick's House, Very Rev. A. O'Loughlin.
St. Mary's, Very Rev. T. O'Donohue.
Our Lady's, Very Rev. John Leterrier, S.M.
Secretary & Librarian, Thomas Scratton, B.A.

Colleges and Schools.

METROPOLITAN.

CHARTER HOUSE.

Master, Ven. William Hale Hale, M.A.
Preacher, Rev. G. Currey, D.D.
Master of School, Rev. W. Haig Brown, LL.D.
Second Master, Rev. F. Poynder, M.A.
Reader and Librarian, Rev. J. J. Halcombe, M.A.
Assistants, Rev. T. Vyvyan, M.A.; Rev. H. J. Evans, M.A.; Rev. S. W. Skeffington, M.A.; F. W. K. Girdlestone, B.A.

CHRIST'S HOSPITAL.

Head Master, Rev. G. Bell, M.A.
Assistant Masters in Upper Grammar School, Rev. James Thomson, M.A.; Rev. C. Hawkins, B.C.L.; Fras. A. C. Hooper, M.A.
Master Latin School, Rev. J. T. White, D.D.
Masters of Lower Grammar School, Rev. Samuel Gall, B.A.; John Wingfield, M.A.; Malcolm Laing, B.A.; Rev. E. G. Peckover, M.A.; Rev. E. B. Penny, M.A.
Head Math. Master, Rev. T. J. Potter, M.A.
Assistant ditto, J. H. Newman, B.A.
Second Ditto, E. S. Carlos, B.A.
Warden, Capt. E. G. Mainwaring.
Head Mast., English Depart., Vacant.
Ditto, Commercial Ditto, H. Sharp.
Ditto, Drawing Ditto, W. H. Back.
Ditto, French Ditto, Rev. Dr. E. Bretto.
Music Master, George Cooper.

HERTFORD BRANCH.

Master, Rev. N. Keymer, M.A.
First Assistant Ditto, J. Dyson.
Second Assistant Ditto, A. Stoddart.
Third Assistant Ditto, J. Staples.
Girls' Mistress, Miss S. A. Peacock.
Steward, George Ludlow.
Matron, Miss Dora M. Peile.

CITY OF LONDON.

Head Master, Rev. E. A. Abbott, M.A.
Second Master, F. Cuthbertson, M.A.
Assistant Masters, Rev. J. Harris, M.A.; Rev. A. Richard Vardy, M.A.; Rev. C. Braddy, M.A.; C. N. Woodroffe; T. Sharpe; J. T. Ablett.

Junior Department.
Principal Master, T. St. Clair Macdougal.
Assistant Masters, Thomas Todd; G. E. Dodson; W. J. Richardson.
Secretary, Thomas Brewer.

DULWICH COLLEGE.

Master of College, Rev. A. J. Carver, D.D.
Chaplain, Rev. Samuel Cheetham, M.A.

Under Master, Upper School, Vacant.
Assistant Masters ditto, Rev. G. Voigt, M.A.; Rev. T. Gwatkin, M.A.; Rev. R. B. Gardiner, M.A.; G. B. Doughty.
Mast. of Low. School, Rev. W. F. Greenfield, M.A.
Assistant Masters of Lower School, Rev. B. O. Huntly, M.A.; E. Ewer.
Assistant Masters in both Schools, M. Darqué (*French*), J. C. L. Sparkes (*Drawing*), Henry Baumer (*Music*), F. W. Mellor, (*Writing*).
Clerk to the Board of Governors, R. J. Dennen.

HIGHGATE.

Head Master, J. B. Dyne, D.D.
Assistant Master, Rev. R. Fletcher, M.A.

KING'S COLLEGE SCHOOL, LONDON.

Head Master, Rev. G. F. Maclear, M.A.
Vice-Master, Rev. John Twentyman, M.A.
Master of Lower School, Rev. G. Rust, M.A.
Masters, T. S. Carr, Esq.; Rev. T. O. Cockayne, M.A.; Rev. W. Hayes, M.A.; Rev. J. H. Standen, M.A.; Rev. O. Adolphus, M.A.; T. S. Carte, Esq., M.A.; Rev. B. Jackson, M.A.; Rev. C. W. Kett, M.A.; C. H. Cunningham, Esq., M.A.
Math. Master, John Shackleton, Esq., B.A.

MANCHESTER NEW COLLEGE, GORDON-SQUARE, LONDON, W.C.

President, S. D. Darbishire, Esq.
Principal, Rev. J. J. Tayler, B.A.
Theology, Professor Rev. J.J. Tayler.
Philosophy, Professor Rev. James Martineau.
Hebrew Language & Literature, Prof. Martineau.

MERCHANT TAYLORS'.

Head Master, Rev. J. A. Hessey, D.C.L.
Classic. & Math. Masters, Rev. J. A. L. Airey, M.A.; Rev. C. Scott, M.A.; Rev. R. Whittington, M.A.; Rev. A. J. Church, M.A.
Assistant to Head Master, J. R. Hall, B.A.

ROYAL NAVAL SCHOOL, NEW CROSS, KENT.

Head Master & Chaplain, Rev. C. W. Arnold, M.A.
Mathematical Master, Wm. Hogg.
Second & Third Classical Masters, Rev. G. F. Heather, B.A.; Rev. T. M. Tidy, M.A.
Secretary, Alfred Eames.

ROYAL FEMALE NAVAL SCHOOL, St. Margaret's, Isleworth.

Pres., Earl of Shrewsbury and Talbot. *Sec.,* Arthur Ellis, R.N., 32, Sackville Street, W.

ST. PAUL'S.

High Master, Rev. Herbert Kynaston, D.D.
Sur-Master, Rev. J. H. Lupton, M.A.
Chaplain or 3rd Do., Rev. E. T. Hudson, M.A.
Fourth Master, Rev. J. W. Shepard, M.A.
Mathematical Master, E. A. Hadley, M.A.
Examiners, Rev. T. W. Steel, M.A.; Ven. Archdeacon R. W. Browne, M.A.; W. Besant, M.A.; M. Dupont.
French Masters, M. Tito Pagleardini; M. Stievenard.

WESTMINSTER.

Head Master, Rev. C. B. Scott, D.D.
Under Master, Rev. H. M. Ingram, M.A.
Assistant Masters, Classics, Rev. James Marshall, M.A.; Rev. B. F. James, M.A.; E. Gilliat, B.A.
Ditto, Mathematics, Rev. C. A. Jones, M.A.; C. H. H. Cheyne, M.A.

NEW COLLEGE, ST. JOHN'S WOOD, N.W.
Faculty of Theology.

Principal & Professor of Theology & Homiletics, Rev. Robert Halley, D.D.

Criticism & Interpretation of Greek Testament, Professors Halley and Goodwin.
Hebrew & Oriental Langs., Prof. Rev. M. Nenner.
Eccles. Hist., Prof. Rev. S. Newth, M.A., F.R.A.S.
Faculty of Arts.
Greek & Latin Languages, Prof. Wm. Smith, LL.D.
Pure & Mixed Mathematics, Prof. Newth, M.A.
Mental & Moral Philos, Prof. Rev. J. H. Godwin.
Chemistry & Natural History Lecturer, Edwin Lankester, M.D., F.R.S.
German, Professor Nenner.
Librarian & Secretary, Rev. W. Farrer, LL.B.

PROVINCIAL.
(*Grammar Schools, unless otherwise stated.*)

ABINGDON.
Head Master, Rev. E. T. H. Harper, M.A.

APPLEBY.
Head Master, C. Thelkeld, M.A.

BATH.
Head Master, Rev. H. S. Fagan, M.A.

BEDFORD.
Head Master, Rev. F. Fanshawe, M.A.
Sec. do., Rev. H. Le Mesurier, M.A.
Commercial School.
Head Master, W. Finlinson.
Second do., W. J. Porter, B.A.

BIRKENHEAD (St. Aidan's College).
Principal, Rev. J. Baylee, D.D.
Chaplain, Rev. S. H. Ireson.

BIRMINGHAM (Queen's College).
Principal, The Earl of Lichfield.
Vice-Prin., Hon. and Rev. G. Yorke, M.A.
Warden, Rev. T. E. Espin, B.D.
Sub-Warden, Rev. W. H. Poulton, M.A.

Professors, &c.
Classics, H. G. Cundy, B.A.
Mathematics, Rev. W. H. Poulton, M.A.
French, Jean O'Flanagan.
German, Dr. Karl Dammann.
Drawing, Charles Docker.

Department of Medicine.
Anatomy, Professor Lloyd, M.R.C.S.
Botany, Professor Hinds, M.R.C.S.
Chemistry, Professor Alfred Anderson, F.C.S.
Forensic Medicine, Prof. John Postgate, F.R.C.S.
Materia Medica, Professor Divers.
Medicine, Professor Nelson.
Midwifery, Professors John Clay, M.R.C.S., and Suckling, M.R.C.S.
Physiology, Professor Norris, M.R.C.S.
Surgery, Professors, W. S. Cox, F.R.S., F.R.C.S.; O. Pemberton, M.R.C.S., & F. Jordan, F.R.C.S.
Medical Tutor, Dr. James Hinds.
Clinical Medicine, Drs. Fleming and Forster.
Clinical Surgery, Professors West, Gamgee, Jordan and Wilders.
Clinical Midwifery, Professor Berry, F.R.C.S.
Department of Law.
Law, G. J. Johnson.
Medical Jurisprudence, John Postgate, F.R.C.S.
Department of Engineering.
Architecture, J. H. Chamberlain.
Chemistry, Alfred Anderson, F.C.S.
Engineering [Vacant.]
Geology, Descriptive, Alfred Anderson, F.C.S.
Geology, Practical, Professor Beckett, F.G.S.
Mathematics, Rev. W. H. Poulton, M.A.
Department of Agriculture.
Agriculture, Henry Tanner, M.R.A.C.
Vegetable Physiology, Dr. Hinds.
Practical Chemistry, Alfred Anderson, F.C.S.

Department of Theology.
Theology, Pastoral, Rev. Professor Espin, B.D.

BIRMINGHAM GRAMMAR SCHOOL.
Head Master, Rev. Charles Evans, M.A.
Second do., Rev. E. F. MacCarthy, M.A.

BLACKBURN.
Head Master, T. Ainsworth, Esq., M.A.
Second do., G. Ainsworth, Esq., B.A.

BOGNOR, (St. Michael's School).
Lady Warden, Miss Wheeler.

BRADFIELD (St. Andrew's College).
Warden, Rev. T. Stevens, M.A.
Head Master, Rev. S. P. Denning, M.A.
Second do., Rev. G. B. Morley, M.A.

BRIGHTON COLLEGE.
Principal, Rev. J. Griffith, M.A.
Vice-Principal, Rev. J. Newton, M.A.

BRISTOL.
Head Master, Rev. J. W. Caldicott, M.A.
Second do., Rev. T. W. Openshaw, M.A.

BROMSGROVE.
Head Master, Rev. G. J. Blore, M.A.

BRUTON.
Head Master, Rev. S. Middleton, M.A.
Second do., Rev. J. Creeser, M.A.

BURY ST. EDMUNDS.
Head Master, Rev. A. H. Wratislaw, M.A.
Second do., Rev. G. H. Statham, B.A.

BURY, LANCASHIRE.
Head Master, Rev. Ch. F. Hildyard, B.A.
Second do., Rev. W. Haslam, B.A.

CAMBRIDGE.
Head Master, Rev. F. Heppenstall, M.A.
Second do., Rev. John Wisken, M.A.
Third do., Rev. G. W. Asplen, M.A.

CANTERBURY (St. Augustine's College).
Warden, Rev. Canon Bailey, B.D.
Sub-Warden, Rev. Edward Redman Orger, M.A.
Fellows, Rev. G. U. Withers, D.D.; Rev. J. B. Trend, M.A.; Rev. Gavin F. Saxby, B.A.
Lecturer in Practical Med., Alfred Lochée, M.D.
Professor of Sanskrit, Reinhold Rost, Ph.D.

CANTERBURY (King's School).
Head Master, Rev. John Mitchinson, D.C.L.
Second do., J. S. Lipscomb, M.A.

CANTERBURY (Clergy Orphan School).
Head Master, Rev. C. Matheson, M.A.

CARLISLE HIGH SCHOOL.
Head Master, Rev. T. C. Durham, M.A.
Second do., Rev. A. C. Whitley, M.A.

CHELTENHAM COLLEGE.
Principal, T. W. Jex-Blake, M.A.
Classical Department.
Head Master, Rev. C. Bigg, M.A.
Mathematical do., Rev. J. C. Turnbull; J. Birkett; W. Boyce.
Assistant do., Revs. P. Gantillon, J. Mugliston, H. T. Price, G. W. Smyth, J. Wood.
Military and Civil Department.
Head Master, Rev. T. A. Southwood, M.A.
Vice and Assistant do., H. E. Bayly; G. T. Watts; W. Inchbald; J. Leighton.
Junior Department.
Head Master, Rev. T. M. Whittard.
Second do., J. T. Thorn.

CHELTENHAM GRAMMAR SCHOOL.
Head Master, H. M. Jeffrey, M.A.
Second Master, Vacant.
Comm. Dept., John Waterworth.

CHICHESTER (Theological College).
Principal, Rev. Canon Swainson, D.D.
Vice-Principals, Rev. G. W. Pennethorne, M.A.; Rev. J. S. Pater, M.A.

CIRENCESTER (Royal Agricultural College).
Principal, Rev. J. Constable, M.A.
Professor of Agriculture, John Wrightson.
Chemistry, A. H. Church, M.A.
Natural History, W. T. T. Dyer, B.A.
Anatomy, &c., J. A. McBride, Ph.D., M.R.C.V.S.
Mathematics, &c., The Principal.
Drawing Master, James Miller.

CLIFTON COLLEGE.
Head Master, Rev. J. Percival, M.A.,
Classical do., H. G. Dakyns, M.A.

CLITHEROE.
Head Master, Rev. E. Boden, M.A.

COVENTRY.
Head Master, Rev. J. Grover, M.A.
Second do., Rev. J. J. Soden, M.A.

COWBRIDGE.
Head Master, Rev. T. Williams, M.A.
Assist. do., T. C. Donkin, B.A.

CRANBROOK.
Head Master, Rev. C. Crowden, M.A.

CRANLEIGH (Surrey County School).
Head Master, Rev. J. Merriman, M.A.

CUDDESDEN THEOLOGICAL COLLEGE.
Principal, Rev. E. King, M.A.
Vice-Princ., Rev. O. J. Reichel, M.A., B.C.L.
Chaplain, Rev. H. T. Morgan, M.A.

DARTFORD.
Head Master, Rev. S. F. Creswell, M.A.

DERBY.
Head Master, Rev. Walter Clark, M.A.
Second Do., Rev. Wm. Page Oldham, M.A.

DONCASTER.
Head Master, Rev. W. Gurney, M.A.

DORCHESTER (County School).
Head Master, Rev. R. G. Watson, M.A.

DURHAM.
Head Master, Rev. H. Holden, D.D.
Second Do., Rev. B. C. Caffin, M.A.

EDINBURGH ACADEMY.
Rector, Rev. James Stephen Hodson, D.D.
Classical Masters, H. Weir, M.A.; J. Carmichael; James Clyde, LL.D.; and John Banks, M.A.

ELY.
Head Master, Rev. J. Chambers, M.A.
Second Do., J. Greenwood, M.A.

EPSOM COLLEGE.
Head Master, Rev. R. Thornton, D.D.
Assist. Masters, Revs. A. Hackman, E. Dix, W. H. Harrison; Messrs. F. H. Barham, T. W. Thomas, H. H, Evans, J. Jeffery.

ETON COLLEGE.
Provost, C. O. Goodford, D.D.
Fellows.
Vice-Provost, Rev. T. Carter, M.A.; Rev. G. J. Dupuis, M.A.; Rev. J. Wilder, M.A.; Rev. E. Coleridge, M.A.; Bishop Chapman, D.D.; Rev. W. Eliot, M.A.; Rev. W. A. Carter, M.A.; Rev. E. Balston, D.D.
Conducts—Rev. G. Baker, M.A.; Rev. J. Shepherd, M.A.; Rev. F. F. Vidal.
Head Master—
Lower Master—Rev. F. E. Durnford, M.A.
Assist. Upper School, Rev. J. E. Yonge, M.A.; W. Johnson, M.A.; Rev. J. L. Joynes, M.A.; Rev. C. Wolley, M.A.; Rev. S. T. Hawtrey,

M.A.; Rev. Russell Day, M.A.; Rev. Wm. Wayte, M.A.; Rev. C. C. James, M.A.; Rev. E. D. Stone, M.A.; Rev. F. St. J. Thackeray, M.A.; Rev. H. Snow, M.A.; Rev. E. Warre, M.A.; O. Browning, M.A.; F. W. Cornish, M.A.; E. A. Leigh, M.A.; Rev. G. R. Dupuis, M.A.; A. C. Ainger, B.A.; H. W. Mozeley, B.A.; A. C. James, B.A.
Assist. Lower School, Rev. J. W. Hawtrey, M.A.; Rev. W. L. Hardisty, M.A.; G. E. Marindin, B.A.; R. B. A. Mitchell, B.A.
Assist. Master in Coll., H. E. Luxmore, B.A.
Math. Masters, Rev. G. Frewer, M.A.; Rev. F. J. Ottley, M.A.; Rev. E. Hale, M.A.; E. P. Rouse, M.A.; Rev. T. Dillon; T. Dalton, B.A.
Steward of the Courts, A. Hobhouse, Q.C.
Organist, John Mitchell.

TRINITY COLLEGE, GLENALMOND, PERTHSHIRE.
Warden, Rev. John Hannah, D.C.L.
Sub-Warden, Rev. R. H. Witherby, M.A.
Tut. in Theol., The Warden, Rev. O. Orton, M.A.
Assistants in Public School Department, Rev. W. H. Bolton, B.A.; M. T. Park, B.A.; Rev. J. Turner; Dr. Ph. Hangen; T. Knowles, B.A.
Honorary Secretary, William Smythe, M.A.

GLOUCESTER (Cathedral School).
Head Master, Rev. H. Fowler, M.A.

GLOUCESTER (Crypt Grammar School).
Head Master, Rev. U. Naylor, B.A.

GUERNSEY (Elizabeth College).
Principal, Rev. J. Oates, M.A.
Vice-Prin., H. C. Watson.
Master, Lower School, Rev. W. Manning.

HALSTEAD.
Head Master, Rev. S. J. Eales, M.A.

HAMPTON LUCY.
Head Master, Rev. H. P. Kendall, M.A.

HARROW SCHOOL.
Head Master, Rev. H. M. Butler, D.D.
Lower Master, G. F. Harris, M.A.

Assistant Masters.
Classics, Rev. F. Rendall, M.A.; Rev. T. H. Steel, M.A.; Rev. B. F. Westcott, B.D.; C. F. Holmes, M.A.; W. J. Bull, M.A.; A. G. Watson, D.C.L.; Rev. J. Smith, M.A.; Rev. F. W. Farrar, M.A., F.R.S.; H. E. Hutton, M.A.; E. E. Bowen, B.A.; R. B. Smith, M.A.; Rev. L. Sanderson, M.A.; E. M. Young, M.A.; J. A. Cruikshank, M.A.; H. Nettleship, M.A.
Mathematics, Rev. R. Middlemist, M.A.; R. B. Hayward, M.A.; Rev. W. D. Bushell, M.A.; J. F. Marillier.
Natural Science, G. Griffith, M.A.
Mod. Lang., Mons. G. Ruault; Mons. G. Masson.

HOUGHTON-LE-SPRING.
Head Master, Rev. A. Bennett, B.A.
Second Master, S. J. Rowton, M.A.

HUDDERSFIELD COLLEGIATE SCHOOL.
Principal, Rev. A. Smith, M.A.
Vice-Prin., Rev. J. H. Lorimer, M.A.

HURSTPIERPOINT.
Head Master, Rev. E. C. Lowe, D.D.
Lower Master, Rev. G. O. L. Thomson, B.A.

ISLINGTON (Church Missionary College).
Principal, Rev. T. Green, M.A.
Tutor, Rev. G. W. F. Munby, M.A.

IPSWICH.
Head Master, Rev. Hubert Holden, M.A., LL.D.
Mathematical Master, Rev. Thomas Ashe, M.A.

ISLE OF MAN, (King William's College).
Principal, Rev. Joshua Jones, D.C.L.
Vice-Prin., Rev. William Heaton, M.A.
Bursar, Rev. Edward Scott, M.A.
Modern Depart., Rev. Hugh C. Davidson.
Math. Master, G. Metcalf, Esq., M.A.
Modern Lang., Mast., M. V. Pleignier.
Assist. Masts., J. E. Lewis, B.A.; E. Smith, Esq.
Drawing Master, J. T. Kiddell, Esq.

JERSEY (Victoria College).
Principal, Rev. W. O. Cleave, LL.D.
Prof. Math. Rev. J. Le Sueur, B.A.
Prof. Eng. Lit., Rev. J. N. Hammond, M.A.
Classical Master, Rev. D. E. Norton, M.A.

KIDDERMINSTER.
Head Master, Rev. J. G. Sheppard, D.C.L.

LAMPETER, (St. David's Theological College).
Prin. Prof. of Greek, Very Rev. L. Lewellin, D.C.L., Dean of St. David's.
Vice Prin., Prof of Hebrew, and Prof. of Divinity, Rev. J. J. S. Perowne, B.D.
Latin Liter., Rev. C. G. Edmondes, M.A.
Physical Sciences, Rev. J. Matthews, M.A.
Professor of Welsh, Rev. J. Hughes, B.D.
Prof. of Mod. Lang., Rev. D. M. Spence, M.A.
Board of Examiners, Rev. J. W. Burgon, M.A., Oxford; Rev. J. W. Josling, M.A., Cambridge.

LANCASTER.
Head Master, Rev. T. Faulkner Lee, D.D.

LANCING (St. Nicholas College).
Provost, Rev. N. Woodard, M.A.
Vice Provost, Rev. E. C. Lowe, D.D.
Chaplain, Rev. E. Field, M.A.

LEEDS.
Head Master, Rev. W. G. Henderson, D.C.L.
Scientific Depart., Thomas Fairleigh.
Modern Depart., Rev. H. Williams, B.A.

LICHFIELD (Theological College).
Principal, Rev. G. H. Curteis, M.A.
Vice-Principal, Rev. S. Latham, M.A.

LINCOLN.
Head Master, Rev. John Fowler, M.A.

LIVERPOOL, (Queen's College).
President, Isaac Hadwen, Esq.
President of the Senate, J. T. Danson, Esq.
Prin. of College, Rev. J. Sephton, M.A.
Dean, Rev. Professor Whitworth, M.A.
Secretary, Charles Sharp, Esq.
Latin and Greek, Prof. Rev. F. B. Watkins, M.A.
Math. and Nat. Phil., Rev. W. A. Whitworth, M.A.
Experimental Physics, E. Davies, F.C.S.
Chemistry, Prof. G. Hamilton, F.C.S., F.R.A.S.
English Lang., Prof. Rev. T. England, M.A.
French, Professor Eugene Husson.
German, Herr Sachs. *Hebrew*, Rev. Dr. Baar.
Italian, Dr. Spola.
Spanish, Mr. J. B. Thwaites.
Geology, G. H. Morton, F.G.S.
Zoology and Botany, W. B. Carter, M.B., B.S.C., F.R.C.S.I.
Drawing and Painting, John Finnie.

LIVERPOOL (Royal Institution School).
Head Master, Rev. D. W. Turner, D.C.L.

LOUTH.
Head Master, Rev. G. C. Hodgkinson, M.A.

LUDLOW.
Head Master, Rev. W. C. Sparrow, M.A.
Second do., Rev. E. P. Wellings, B.A.

LYNN REGIS.
Head Master, Rev. T. White, M.A.
Second do., Rev. T. A. Kershaw, M.B.

MACCLESFIELD.
Head Master, Rev. T. B. Cornish, M.A.
Second do., Rev. J. G. Tiarks, M.A.

MALVERN.
Head Master, Rev. A. H. Faber, M.A.

MANCHESTER (Owen's College).
Principal, J. G. Greenwood, B.A.
Prof. Lang. and Lit., Greece and Rome, J. G. Greenwood, B.A.
English Lang. and Liter. Ancient and Modern History, A. W. Ward, M.A.
Mathematics, Thos. Barker, M.A.
Natural Philosophy, Wm. Jack, M.A.
Logic, &c., W. Stanley Jevons, M.A., F.S.S.
Jurisprudence, R. C. Christie, M.A., F.S.S.
Chemistry, H. E. Roscoe, B.A., Ph.D., F.R.S.
Laboratory Assist., C. Schorlemmer, F.C.S.
Natural History, W. C. Williamson, F.R.S.
Oriental and Modern Lang. and Lit., T. Theodores.
Free Hand Drawing, W. Walker.
Assistant Lecturer in Classics and Mathematics, Alfred T. Bentley, B.A.
Hon. Sec. to Trustees, J. P. Aston.
Reg. and Sec., J. H. Nicholson.
Sub-Librarian, J. Hill.

MANCHESTER (Grammar School).
High Master, F. W. Walker, M.A.
Second do., Rev. G. Perkins, M.A.

MARLBOROUGH COLLEGE.
Head Master, Rev. G. G. Bradley, M.A.
Assist. Masters, Rev. C. W. Tayler, B.A.; Rev. J. Sowerby, M.A.; Rev. G. W. De Lisle, M.A.; Rev. J. F. Bright, M.A.; Rev. T. A. Preston, M.A.; Rev. J. S. Thomas, M.A.; Rev. H. E. Booth, M.A.; Rev. H. Bell; Rev. C. E. Thorpe, B.A.

MARLBOROUGH (Grammar School).
Head Master, Rev. F. H. Bond, M.A.

MONMOUTH.
Head Master, Rev. C. M. Roberts, M.A.

NORWICH.
Head Master, Rev. Augustus Jessopp, M.A.
Sub-Master, Rev. W. G. Macdonald, M.A.

NEWPORT (Salop).
Head Master, Rev. C. W. Saxton, D.D.

NEWPORT (I. W.)
Head Master, Rev. A. Wallace, M.A.

OAKHAM.
Head Master, Rev. W. S. Wood, D.D.

OTTERY ST. MARY.
Head Master, Rev. George Smith, M.A.
Second do., Rev. Herbert Candy, M.A.

OXFORD (The Cathedral School, Ch. Ch).
Head Master, Rev. W. Price, M.A.

OXFORD (St. Edward's School).
Head Master, Rev. F. W. Fryer, M.A.

OXFORD (Magdalen College School).
Head Master, Rev. Canon Hill, D.C.L.

PETERBOROUGH.
Head Master, Rev. E. B. Whyley, M.A.

PLYMOUTH.
Head Master, W. Bennett, M.A.

POCKLINGTON.
Head Master, Rev. F. J. Gruggen.

PORTSMOUTH (Royal Naval College).
Capt. Supt., Capt. Arthur W. A. Hood, R.N.
Professor, Rev. T. J. Main, M.A., F.R.A.S.
Math. Master, C. R. Tompkins, R.N.
Instructor Fortifications and Mechanical Drawing, Major H. B. Roberts, R.M.A.
Assist. in the Observatory, John Jeans.
Clerk, H. F. Kirkham.

RADLEY (St. Peter's College).
Warden, Rev. W. Wood.
Sub-Warden, Rev. W. H. Ranken, M.A.
Assist. Masters, Rev. J. B. Jones, M.A.

REPTON.
Head Master, Rev. S. A. Pears, D.D.
Second do., Rev. G. M. Messiter, M.A.
Mathemat. Master, Rev. G. P. Clarke, M.A.

RICHMOND (Yorkshire).
Head Master, Rev. T. H. Stokoe, M.A.
Assist. Masters, Rev. J. Snowdon, and others.

RIPON.
Head Master, Rev. J. F. MacMichael, B.A.
Second do., Robert Jamblin, Esq., B.A.

ROCHESTER CATHEDRAL (Grammar School).
Head Master, Rev. R. Whiston, M.A.
Second do., Rev. J. Espin, M.A.

ROSSALL SCHOOL (near Fleetwood).
Head Master, Rev. W. A. Osborne, M.A.
Second do., Rev. S. J. Phillips, M.A.

RUGBY.
Head Master, Rev. Fred. Temple, D.D.
Assist. Masters, Rev. H. J. Buckoll, M.A.; Rev. C. T. Arnold, M.A.; Rev. L. F. Burrows, M.A.; Rev. P. B. Smith, M.A.; Rev. T. W. Jex Blake, M.A.; Rev. C. B. Hutchinson, M.A.; Rev. C. E. Moberly, M.A.; J. M. Wilson, B.A.; E. A. Scott, M.A.; Rev. C. Elsee, M.A.; A. W. Potts, B.A.; J. S. Philpotts, B.A.; J. Kitchener, B.A.; Rev. J. Robertson, M.A.; A. Sidgwick, B.A.; H. Lee Warner, B.A.; E. F. Grenfell, B.A.; Rev. T. N. Hutchinson, M.A.; Rev. C. J. E. Smith, M.A.; R. Whitelaw, B.A.

RUTHIN SCHOOL.
Head Master, Rev. J. W. Freeborn, M.A.
Second do., Rev. D. Hughes, M.A.

ST. BEES THEOLOGICAL COLLEGE.
Principal, Rev. G. H. Ainger, D.D.
Tutor, Rev. J. E. Middleton, M.A.
Lecturer, Rev. J. E. Smallpeice, M.A.

ST. BEES GRAMMAR SCHOOL.
Head Master, Rev. G. H. Heslop, M.A.

SALISBURY THEOLOGICAL COLLEGE.
Principal, Rev. Chancellor Eddrup, M.A.
Vice-Principal, Rev. H. T. Kingdon, M.A.

SALISBURY CATHEDRAL SCHOOL.
Head Master, Rev. E. Dowland, M.A.

SANDBACH GRAMMAR SCHOOLS.
Head Master, Rev. Lewis Evans, M.A.

SANDHURST ROYAL MILITARY COLLEGE.
Governor, Lieut.-Gen. Sir D. A. Cameron, K.C.B.
Commandant, Col. E. G. Hallewell.
Major and Superin. of Studies, Col. J. E. Addison.
Chaplain, Rev. E. J. Rogers, M.A.
Paymaster, Major W. L. Hilton.
Quartermaster, J. Davies.
Surgeon, Deputy-Inspector-Gen. Maclean, M.D.
Assistant-Surgeon, J. Greig, M.B.
Riding Master, Capt. Charles C. Brooke.
Capts. of Companies of Gent. Cadets, Maj. W. R. Farmar; Maj. A. P. Bowlby.
Adjutant, Captain W. Patterson.
CADETS' COLLEGE.—*Professors and Masters.*
Mathematics, Rev. J. W. Vinter, M.A.; Rev. A. Deck, M.A.; G. Hester; R. H. Greer; J. P. Ketley.
Fortification, Col. W. H. Adams; Capt. G. Philips; Capt. L. Griffiths; Lieut.-Col. W. Porter; Capt. H. Cardew; Capt. L. A. Hale.
Mil. Surveying, Maj. R. Petley; Capt. W. Pater-

son; Capt. W. H. Richards; Capt. E. A. Anderson; Capt. T. H. Pitt; Capt. Fothergill.
Mil. Hist., Capt. E. M. Jones; Lieut. H. G. Mo Gregor; Lieut. C. W. Robinson.
Landscape Drawing, E. Delamotte; R. Harley.; A. A. A. de Charente; J. Balagné; J. C. J. Bornacier, E. Clavequin.
German, Carl Dresner.
Lect. in Geology and Mineralogy, T. R. Jones.
Lecturer on Chemistry, Dr. E. Atkinson.
Librarian, G. Clarke.

STAFF COLLEGE.

Commandant, Col. T. E. Lacy.
Adjutant, Major A. S. Jones, V.C.

Professors and Masters.
Mathematics, Rev. J. F. Twisden, M.A.; T. Savage. M.A.
Military History, Major C. Adams.
Fortification, &c., Capt. H. Schaw.
Military Topography, Captain S. B. Farrell, R.E.
Military Administration, Capt. W. Walker.
French, A. Talambier.
German, J. J. Overbeck, D.D.
Hindustani, John Dowson.

SEDBERGH.

Head Master, Rev. H. G. Day, M.A.
Second do., Rev. I. Green, M.A.

SEVENOAKS.

Head Master, Rev. C. Crofts, M.A.

SHERBORNE.

Head Master, Rev. H. D. Harper, M.A.
Second do., A. M. Curteis, M.A.

SHOREHAM MIDDLE SCHOOL.

Head Master, Rev. F. M. D. Mertens, M.A.

SHREWSBURY.

Head Master, Rev. H. W. Moss, M.A.
Second do., Rev. John Rigg, B.D.
Assistant do., Rev. G. Preston, M.A.; Rev. G. W. Fisher, M.A.; Rev. J. Chapman, M.A.; Rev. G. T. Hall, B.A.; T. A. Bentley; T. N. Henshaw.

SOLIHULL.

Head Master, Rev. J. H. Bennett, M.A.

SUTTON COLDFIELD.

Head Master, Rev. Albert Smith, M.A.

TAUNTON.

Head Master, Rev. W. Tuckwell, M.A.

TENBURY.

Head Master, Rev. F. Millard, M.A,

THAME.

Head Master, Rev. T. B. Fooks, D.C.L,

TIVERTON.

Head Master, Rev. J. B. Hughes, M.A.

TONBRIDGE.

Head Master, Rev. James Ind Welldon, D.C.L.
Second do., Rev. Edward I. Welldon, M.A.
Assistant do., Rev. J. R. Little, M.A.; Rev. J. Langhorne, B.A.; Rev. J. Stroud, M.A.; C. Walters, M.A.; E. H. Goggs, B.A.; C. G. Gepp, M.A.; M. Berncastle; W. McGill, B.A.

UPPINGHAM.

Head Master and Warden, Rev. E. Thring, M.A.
Usher and Sub-Warden, Rev. W. J. Earle.
Chaplain, Rev. W. F. Witts, M.A.
Mast. of Low. Sch., Rev. R. J. Hodgkinson, M.A.

WARWICK.

Head Master, Rev. H. Hill, M.A.

WELLINGTON COLLEGE, (near Wokingham, Berks.)

Head Master, Rev. E. W. Benson, D.D.
Tutors and Assist. Masters, H. W. Eve, Esq., Rev. A. Carr, M.A.; Rev. C. W. Penny, M.A.; Rev. T. H. Freer, M.A.; A. F. Griffith, Esq., M.A. (*Mathematical*); Rev. S. N. Tebbs, M.A.; Rev. J. D. Lester, B.A.; Rev. J. H. Merriott, B.A.; W. Charnley, Esq., B.A. (*Mathematical*); Rev. P. H. Kempthorne, B.A.; Rev. J. H. D. Matthews, B.A.; Rev. E. Davenport, B.A.; B. C. Hammond, Esq., M.A.
Bursar, Rev. C. W. Penny, M.A.

WELLS THEOLOGICAL COLLEGE.

Principal, Rev. C. M. Church, M.A.
Vice-Principals, Rev. A. W. Grafton, M.A.; Rev. F. S. Moberly, M.A.

WIMBORNE.

Head Master, Rev. W. Fletcher, D.D.
Second do., Rev. H. Pix, M.A.

WINCHESTER COLLEGE.

Warden, Rev. G. B. Lee, M.A.
Fellows, Harry Lee, B.D.; Robert Grant, B.C.L.; Geo. C. Rashleigh, M.A.; G. W. Heathcote, B.C.L.; C. H.Ridding, B.C.L.; H. B. Williams, M.A.; T. F. A. P. Hodges, D.C.L.; Rev. G. Moberly, D.C.L.
Head Master, Rev. G. Ridding, M.A.
Second do., Rev. W. Awdry. M.A.
Masters of Houses, Rev. H. J. Wickham, M.A.; Rev. H. E. Moberly, M.A.; Rev. J. T. H. Du Boulay, M.A.; Rev. W. A. Fearon; F. Morshead, Esq.; Rev. C. H. Hawkins; Rev. E. Serjeant; Rev. J. T. Bramston.
Assistants, J. D. Walford, M.A.; Rev. H. E. Moberly, M.A.; Rev. J. T. H. Du Boulay, M.A.; Rev. E. H. Sergeant, M.A.; C. Griffith, M.A.; Rev. C. H. Hawkins, M.A.; C. L. Stonhouse, B.A.
Lec. in Phys. Science, Rev. G. Richardson, M.A.
Chaplains, Rev. J. Baker, M.A.; Rev. C. H. Hawkins, B.A.; Rev. G. Beckwith, M.A.

WOOLWICH (Royal Military Academy).

Lt.-Gov. Com., Maj.-Gen. J. W. Ormsby, R.A.
2nd Commandant, Lieut.-Col. G. T. Field, R.A.
Assist. Inspector, Capt. E. J. Bruce, R.A.
Captains of Companies of Gent. Cadets, Capt. O. R. Stokes,‡R.A.; Lt.-Col. G. A. Milman, R. A.; Capt. W. H. McCausland, R.A.
Chaplain, Rev. A. C. Fraser.
Paymaster and Adj., Major C. South.
Quartermaster, Geo. Alex. Shepherd.
Surgeon, E. S. Protheroe.

CIVIL BRANCH.—Professors and Masters.
Mathematics, J. J. Sylvester, M.A., F.R.S.
Fortification, Capt. J. J. Wilson, R.E.
Artillery, Lt.-Col. C. H. Owen, R.A.
Surveying, Major A. W. Drayson.
Mechanics, T. M. Goodeve.
Math. Masters, S. Fenwick, F.R.A.S.; Rev. G. Y. Boddy, M.A.; Wm. Racster; M.W. Crofton.
Fortification, Major W. J. Stuart; Capt. C. N. Martin; Capt. E. L. Bland; Capt. Lewin.
Geometrical Drawing, T. Bradley; G. S. Pritchard; F. Bradley.
Landscape Drawing, G. B. Campion; A. Penley.
Instructor in Artillery, Capt. O. H. Goodenough.
Assist. Instructor in do., Capt. H. W. Briscoe; Capt. W. H. Wardell.
Prof. Mil. Hist., Capt. H. Brackenbury.
Surveying and Topographical Drawing, Major A. W. Drayson; Capt. G. A. Crawford; Capt. A.

H. Hutchinson; Capt. F. E. Pratt; Lieut.
W. H. Collins.
French, A. Lovey; T. Karcher, B.A.; E.Valentin.
German, C. A. Feiling; F. Schlutter; C. H.
Schaible, Ph.D.
Hindustani, Major R. Robertson.
Geology and Mineralogy, J. Tennant.
Chemistry, C. L. Bloxam.
Chief Clerk, William M'Gee.

WOOTTON-UNDER-EDGE.
Head Master, Rev. B. R. Perkins, B.C.L.

WORCESTER.
Head Master, Rev. F. J. Eld, M.A.

WORCESTER CATHEDRAL SCHOOL.
Head Master, Rev. M. Day, M.A.
Second do., T. Baxter, Esq., F.G.S.

WYCOMBE.
Head Master, Rev. J. Poulter, M.A.

WYE.
Head Master, Rev. J. R. Major, M.A.

YARMOUTH (Great).
Head Master, Rev. J. J. Raven, B.D.

YORK (St. Peter's School).
Head Master, Rev. R. Elwyn, M.A.

YORK (Abp. Holgate's School.)
Head Master, Rev. R. Daniel, B.D.

Societies and Institutions.

ACCLIMATIZATION AND ORNITHOLOGICAL, the Cottage, St. James's Park.—*Hon. Sec.*, E. C. Ryley.

ADDITIONAL CURATES S., 7, Whitehall.—*Sec.*, Rev. E. Cutts,B.A. *Assist.Sec.*,Rev.A. J.Ingram,M.A.

AERONAUTICAL,Argyll Lodge, Kensington.—*Hon. Sec.*, F. W. Brearey, Blackheath.

ANGLO-BIBLICAL, 22, Hart Street, W.C.—*Hon. Home Sec.*,Rev. J.Mills,F.R.G.S.,&c. *Hon. Lib. and Foreign Sec.*, Rev. W. H. Black, F.S.A.

ANTHROPOLOGICAL, 4, St. Martin's Place, W.C.— *President*, Dr. Jas. Hunt, F.S.A. *Director*, E. W. Brabrook. F.S.A. *Sec.*, J. F. Collingwood.

ART-UNION OF LONDON, 444, West Strand. *Hon. Secs.*, L. Pocock, F.S.A.; E. E. Antrobus, F.S.A. *Assist. Sec.*, T. S. Watson, B.A.

BIRKBECK LITERARY AND SCIENTIFIC INSTITUTION, SouthamptonBuildings.—*Pres.*,W.L.Birkbeck, M.A. *Treas.*, Jas. Gowland. *Sec.*, G. M. Norris.

BRITISH ARCHÆOLOGICAL ASSOCIATION, 32, Sackville Street. *Pres.*, Earl Bathurst. *Treas.*, Gordon M. Hills. *Secs.*, Edw. Roberts, F.S.A.; Edw. Levien, M.A., F.S.A.

BRITISH ASSOCIATION FOR THE ADVANCEMENT OF SCIENCE.—*Pres.*, Dr. Hooker, F.R.S. *Pres.* (*Elect.*), Prof. G. G. Stokes. F.R.S. *Gen. Secs.*, Francis Galton, M.A., F.R.S.; Prof. Hirst, F.R.S. *Assist. Do.*, Geo. Griffith, M.A., Harrow. *Gen. Treas.* Wm. Spottiswoode, F.R.S., 50, Grosvenor Place. *Meeting* in 1869 to be held at Exeter.

BRITISH INSTITUTION, 52, Pall Mall.—*Pres.* Marq. of Westminster, K.G. *Vice Pres.*, Lord Broughton,G.C.B. *Sec. and Keeper*, Geo. Nichol.

BRITISH AND FOREIGN BIBLE, Earl Street, Blackfriars.—*Pres.*, Earl of Shaftesbury. *Secs.*, Rev. C. Jackson, S. B. Bergne.

BRITISH AND FOREIGN SCHOOL,Borough Rd. *Pres.*, Earl Russell, K.G. *Sec.*, Rev. A. Bourne, B.A.

CAMDEN SOCIETY, 25, Parliament Street.—*Pres.*, W. Tite, M.P., F.R.S., V.P.S.A. *Director*, J. Bruce,F.S.A. *Hon. Sec.*, W. J. Thoms,F.S.A.

CAVENDISH S., 19. Montague Street, W.C.—*Pres.*, T. Graham, F.R.S. *Sec.*, T. Redwood.

CHEMICAL SOCIETY.—*Pres.*, W. De la Rue. *Hon. Sees.*, W. Odling,M.B.; A. V. Harcourt.

CHURCH MISSIONARY S., Salisbury Square, Fleet St.—*Pres.*, Earl of Chichester. *Treas.*, Capt. Hon. F. Maude, R.N. *Secs.*, Rev. H. Venn, B.D. (*Hon.*); Rev. C. C. Fenn, M.A.; Rev. J. Mee, M.A.; E. Hutchinson. *Assist. Clerical Sec.*, Rev. H. Venn, Jun., *Asst. Sec.*, J. M. Holl.

CLERGY PROVIDENT SOCIETY, 7, Whitehall.— *Sec.* Rev. Arthur J. Ingram, M.A.

COLLEGE OF PRECEPTORS, 42, Queen Sq., Bloomsbury.—*Pres.*,Rev. W. Haig-Brown, LL.D. *Vice-Pres.*, C. H. Pinches, Ph.D.; Rev. H. A. Holden, LL.D.; J. Templeton, M.A. *Dean*, Rev. G. A. Jacob, D.D. *Sec.*, John R. O'Neil, M.A.

ECCLESIOLOGICAL, 78, New Bond Street.—*Sec.*, Rev. B. Webb, M.A.

ENTOMOLOGICAL, 12, Bedford Row.—*Pres.*, H. W. Bates. *Secs.*, J. W. Dunning; R. McLachlan. *Lib.*, E. W. Janson.

EPIDEMIOLOGICAL SOCIETY, 37, Soho Square.— *Pres.*, Dr. Seaton. *Hon. Sec.*, J. N. Radcliffe.

ETHNOLOGICAL SOCIETY, 4, St. Martin's Place. —*Pres.*, Prof. Huxley. *Hon. Secs.*, T. Wright, M.A.; D. W. Nash.

GENEALOGICAL SOCIETY, 208, Piccadilly.—*Sec.*, Rycroft Reeve.

GEOLOGICAL SOCIETY, Somerset House.—*Pres.*, Prof. Huxley, LL.D., F.R.S. *Secs.*, P. M. Duncan, M.B., F.R.S.; John Evans, F.R.S. *Foreign Sec.*, Prof. D. J. Ansted, M.A., F.R.S. *Treas.*, J. Gwyn Jeffreys, F.R.S. *Assist. Sec.*, *Librarian*, &c., H. M. Jenkins. *Clerk*, W. W. Leighton.

GEOLOGISTS' ASSOCIATION, University Coll. — *Pres.*, Prof. J. Morris, F.G.S. *Hon. Sec.*, J. Cumming.

GRESHAM COLLEGE, Gresham Street.—*Profs.*— *Divinity*, Rev. H. J. Parker, M.A. *Astronomy*, Rev. J. Pullen, B.D., F.A.S. *Geometry*, Rev. Morgan Cowie, B.D. *Law*, J. T. Abdy, D.C.L. *Rhetoric*, Rev. Charlton Lane, M.A. *Music*, Henry Wylde, Mus. Doc. *Physic*, E. L. Thompson.

HAKLUYT SOCIETY, 37, Gt. Queen St.—*Pres.*, Sir R. I. Murchison, K.C.B., D.C.L., F.R.S., &c. *Hon. Sec.*, Clement R. Markham.

HARVEIAN SOCIETY, Stafford Rooms, Tichborne Street, W.—*Pres.*, J. E. Pollock, M.D. *Treas.*, H. W. Fuller, M.D. *Hon. Secs.*, J. B. Curgenven; C. R. Drysdale, M.D.

HUNTERIAN SOCIETY, Finsbury Circus.—*Pres.*, T. B. Peacock, M.D. *Hon. Secs.*, W. Allingham, F.R.C.S.; J. J. Phillips, M.D.

INCORPORATED CHURCH BUILDING SOCIETY, 7, Whitehall.—*Treas.*, Henry G. Hoare. *Sec.*, Rev. Geo. Ainslie, M.A. *Chief Clerk*, M. H. Dunning.

INCORPORATED LAW SOCIETY, Chancery Lane.— *Pres.*, J. H. Bolton. *Vice Pres.*, E. Lawrance. *Sec.*, E. W. Williamson. *Lib.*, J. Lapworth.

INSTITUTE OF ACTUARIES, 12, St. James's Square.
—*Pres.,* Samuel Brown, F.S.S. *Hon. Secs.,*
A. H. Bailey; A. Day. *Assist. Sec.,* F. Gover.

INSTITUTE OF PAINTERS IN WATER COLOURS, 53,
Pall Mall, S.W.—*Pres.,* H. Warren. *Vice-Pres.,*
L. Haghe. *Treas.,* J. Absolon. *Sec.,* Jas.
Fahey.

INSTITUTION OF CIVIL ENGINEERS, 25, Gt. George
Street, S.W.—*Pres.,* C. H. Gregory. *Hon.
Sec.,* C. Manby, F.R.S. *Sec.,* James Forrest.

LINNÆAN SOCIETY.—*Pres.,* G. Bentham, F.R.S.
Treas., W. W. Saunders, F.R.S. *Secs.,* G. Busk,
F.R.S.; F. Currey, F.R.S. *Lib.,* Richd. Kip-
pist, A.L.S.

LONDON INSTITUTION, Finsbury Circus.—*Pres.,*
T. Baring, M.P., F.R.S. *Treas.,* H. C. Robarts.
Lib., E. W. Brayley, F.R.S. *Assist. Sec. and
Sub.-Lib.,* H. T. Williams.

LONDON LIBRARY, 12, St. James's Square.—*Pres.,*
Earl of Clarendon. *Sec. and Lib.,* R. Harrison.

LONDON AND MIDDLESEX ARCHÆOLOGICAL S.,
22, Hart Street, Bloomsbury.—*Pres.,* Lord
Talbot de Malahide. *Hon. Secs.,* T. Milbourn,
11, Poultry, E.C.

LONDON MISSIONARY SOCIETY, 8, Blomfield St.,
Finsbury.—*Treas.,* Hon. A. Kinnaird, M.P.
For. Sec., Rev. J. Mullens, D.D. *Home Secs.,*
Rev. W. Fairbrother; Rev. Robert Robinson.

MATHEMATICAL SOCIETY.—*Pres.,* J. J. Sylvester.
Hon. Secs., G. C. De Morgan; M. Jenkins.

MEDICAL SOCIETY OF LONDON, 32A, George St.,
Hanover Square.—*Pres.,* B. W. Richardson,
F.R.S. *Hon. Secs.,* Francis Mason, F.R.C.S.;
A. E. Sansom, M.D. *Regist. & Sub.-Lib.,* W. E.
Poole.

METEOROLOGICAL SOCIETY, 25, Gt. George Street,
Westminster. — *Pres.,* Jas. Glaisher, F.R.S.,
F.R.A.S. *Treas.,* Henry Perigal, F.R.A.S.
Secs., C. Brooke, M.A., F.R.S.; J. W. Tripe,
M.D. *Lib.,* Fred. Gaster. *Foreign Sec.,* Lieut.-
Col. Strange, F.R.A.S.

METROPOLITAN SANITARY ASSOCIATION, 1, Adam
Street, Adelphi.—*Treas.,* W. Hawes. *Hon. Sec.,*
Arthur Hall.

NATIONAL ASSOCIATION FOR THE PROMOTION OF
SOCIAL SCIENCE, 1, Adam Street, Adelphi, W.C.
—*Pres.,* Rt. Hon. Earl of Carnarvon. *Chair-
man of the Council and Gen. Sec.,* G. W. Hast-
ings, LL.B. *Assist. Sec.,* J. Robinson. *Foreign
Sec.,* J. Westlake. *Treas.,* W. S. Cookson; W.
Hawes.

NATIONAL SOCIETY FOR PROMOTING THE EDUCA-
TION OF THE POOR IN THE PRINCIPLES OF THE
ESTABLISHED CHURCH, Sanctuary, Westmin-
ster. — *Pres.,* the Archbishop of Canterbury.
Treas., Archdeacon Sinclair. *Sec.,* Rev. Alex.
Wilson, M.A. *Depot Sup.,* E. Simpson.

NAVAL AND MILITARY BIBLE SOCIETY, 32, Sackville Street.—*Sec.,* Richard Mouat.

NUMISMATIC SOCIETY, 13, Gate Street, Lincoln's
Inn Fields.—*Pres.,* Wm. Sandys W. Vaux,
F.R.S., F.S.A. *Hon. Secs.,* J. Evans, F.S.A.;
B. V. Head. *Foreign Sec.,* Jn. Yonge Aker-
man, F.S.A. *Lib.,* S. F. Corkran.

OBSTETRICAL SOCIETY OF LONDON, 53, Berners St.
—*Pres.,* John H. Davis, M.D. *Treas.,* Alfred
Meadows, F.R.C.S. *Hon. Secs.,* C. P. Murray, M.D.,
Henry Gervis, M.D.

PALÆONTOGRAPHICAL SOCIETY, 13, Granville Park,
Lewisham. — *Pres.,* Dr. J. S. Bowerbank,
F.R.S. *Hon. Sec.,* Rev. T. Wiltshire, F.G.S.

PATHOLOGICAL SOCIETY, 53, Berners Street.—
Pres., John Simon, D.C.L., F.R.S. *Hon. Secs.,*
Chas. Murchison, M.D.; John W. Hulke,
F.R.S.

PHILHARMONIC SOCIETY, St. James' Hall, Piccadilly.—*Sec.,* Stanley Lucas.

PHILOLOGICAL SOCIETY, University College.—
Pres. Bp. of St. David's. *Hon. Sec.,* F. J. Fur-
nivall.

QUEKETT MICROSCOPICAL, University College.—
Pres., A. E. Durham. *Sec.,* W. M. Bywater.

RAY SOCIETY.—*Pres.,* Sir P. De G. M. Egerton,
Bart. *Sec.,* H. T. Stainton, Lewisham.

ROYAL ACADEMY, Trafalgar Square.—*Pres.,* Sir
Francis Grant. *Secs.,* John P. Knight. *Keeper,*
Charles Landseer. *Treasurer,* S. Smirke.
Librarian, Solomon A. Hart. *Regis.,* H. Eyre.

ROYAL ACADEMY OF MUSIC, 4, Tenterden Street,
Hanover Square.—*Pres.* Earl of Dudley.
Chairman and Principal, Professor Sterndale
Bennett. *Sec.,* J. Gill.

ROYAL AGRICULTURAL SOCIETY OF ENGLAND, 12,
Hanover Square. —*Pres.,* H.R.H. the Prince of
Wales, K.G. *Sec.,* M. Jenkins.

ROYAL ARCHÆOLOGICAL INSTITUTE, 16, New
Burlington Street.—*Pres.,* Rt. Hon. Lord Tal-
bot de Malahide, F.S.A. *Treas.,* J. Henderson,
F.S.A. *Hon. Secs.,* A. Way; C. Tucker; J.
Burtt. *Sec.,* B. Willsher.

ROYAL ASIATIC S. 5, New Burlington Street.—
Pres., Viscount Strangford. *Director,* Sir H.
Rawlinson, K.C.B., D.C.L. *Sec.* Dr. R. Rost.

ROYAL ASTRONOMICAL SOCIETY, Somerset House.
—*Pres.,* Admiral Manners. *Secs.,* W. Huggins;
E. J. Stone, M.A. *Foreign Sec.,* Lt.-Col.
Strange. *Assist. Sec.,* J. Williams.

ROYAL BOTANIC SOCIETY, Regent's Park.—*Pres.,*
Rt. Hon. Earl-De-La-Warr, D.C.L. *Sec.,* J.
de Carle Sowerby, F.L.S. *Curator,* R. Mar-
nock.

ROYAL COLLEGE OF PHYSICIANS, Pall Mall East.
—*Pres.,* Jas. Alderson, M.D. *Treas.,* F. J.
Farre, M.D. *Registrar,* Henry Alfred Pitman,
M.D. *Res. Off.,* William Copney.

ROYAL COLLEGE OF SURGEONS, Lincoln's-inn-
fields.—*Pres.,* Richard Quain. *Vice-Pres.,* Edward Cock; Samuel Solly. *Sec.,* Edward Trimmer. *Clerk,* Thomas Madden Stone. *Conserv.
of Museum,* W. H. Flower. *Librarian,* John
Chatto.

ROYAL GEOGRAPHICAL SOCIETY, 15, Whitehall
Place.—*Pres.,* Sir R. I. Murchison, Bt., K.C.B.,
D.C.L., F.R.S., &c. *Secs.,* C. R. Markham; R. H.
Major. *Assist. Sec.,* H. W. Bates. *Cur. of Maps,*
Capt. C. George. *Accountant,* H. W. Farley.

ROYAL HORTICULTURAL SOCIETY, South Kensing-
ton and Chiswick.—*Pres.,* Duke of Buccleuch,
K.G. *Treas.,* John Clutton. *Sec.,* Lt.-Col.
Scott, R.E. *Assist. Sec.,* James Richards.
Clerk, J. Douglas Dick. *Kensington Garden
Supt.,* George Eyles. *Chiswick do.,* A. F. Barron.

ROYAL INSTITUTE OF BRITISH ARCHITECTS, 9,
Conduit Street, W.—*Pres.,* William Tite, M.P.,
F.S.A., &c. *Hon. Sec.,* J. P. Seddon. *Hon.
Sec. Foreign Corr.,* T. L. Donaldson. *Assist.
Sec.,* Charles L. Eastlake. *Librarian,* S. W.
Kershaw. *Clerk,* Edward Freeman.

ROYAL INSTITUTION, Albemarle Street.—*Pres.,*
Sir Henry Holland, Bart. *Treas.,* W. Spottis-
woode, F.R.S. *Hon. Sec.,* H. Bence Jones,
M.D., F.R.S. *Assist. Sec. and Lib.,* B. Vincent.

ROYAL LITERARY FUND, 4, Adelphi Terrace. —*Pres.*, Earl Stanhope. *Treas.*, Sir Henry Ellis, Lord Houghton, W. F. Pollock. *Sec.*, Octavian Blewitt.

ROYAL MEDICAL AND CHIRURGICAL SOCIETY, 53, Berners Street.—*Pres.*, Samuel Solly, F.R.S. *Hon. Secs.*, William Ogle, M.D.; G. G. Gascoyen. *Hon. Librarians*, Alex. P. Stewart, M.D.; Charles Brooke, M.A., F.R.S. *Assist. Resident do.*, B. R. Wheatley.

ROYAL MICROSCOPICAL SOCIETY, King's College, Strand.—*Pres.*, J. Glaisher. *Treas.*, R. Mestayer. *Assist. Sec.*, Walter W. Reeves. *Hon. Secs.*, Jabez Hogg; H. J. Slack.

ROYAL NATIONAL LIFEBOAT INSTITUTION, 14, John Street, Adelphi.—*Chairman*, T. Baring, M.P., F.R.S., V.P. *Deputy do.*, Thos. Chapman, F.R.S., V.P. *Sec.*, Richard Lewis.

ROYAL SCHOOL OF MINES.—*Director*, Sir R. I. Murchison, Bt., K.C.B., D.C.L., M.A., F.R.S., &c. *Lecturers*, Dr. Frankland, F.R.S.; J. Percy, M.D., F.R.S.; A. C. Ramsay, F.R.S.; W. W. Smyth, M.A., F.R.S.; Robt. Willis, M.A., F.R.S.; T. H. Huxley, F.R.S.; J. H. Edgar, M.A. *Regis.*, Trenham Reeks. *Museum of Practical Geology, Jermyn Street, London.*

ROYAL SOCIETY.—*Pres.*, Lt.-Gen. Edw. Sabine, R.A., D.C.L., LL.D. *Vice-Pres. and Treas.*, W. A. Miller, M.D., LL.D. *Secs.*, W. Sharpey, M.D., LL.D.; Prof. G. G. Stokes, M.A., D.C.L. *For. Sec.*, Prof. W. H. Miller, M.A. *Assist. Sec. and Lib.*, W. White.

ROYAL SOCIETY FOR THE PREVENTION OF CRUELTY TO ANIMALS, 172, New Bond Street.—*Sec.* John Colam.

ROYAL SOCIETY OF LITERATURE, 4, St. Martin's Place.—*Pres.*, Bishop of St. David's. *Treas.*, J. Godfrey Teed, Q.C. *Librarian*, N. E. S. A. Hamilton. *For. Sec.*, James Hunt. *Hon. Sec.*, Wm. S. W. Vaux, F.S.A. *Res. Clerk*, J. Ayres.

ROYAL SOCIETY OF MUSICIANS, 12, Lisle Street, Leicester Square.—*Sec.*, Stanley Lucas.

ROYAL UNITED SERVICE INSTITUTION, Whitehall Yard.—*Pres.*, Gen. Lord Hotham, M.P. *Chairman of Council*, 1868-9, Major-Gen. Hon. Jas. Lindsay. *Vice do.*, Rear-Adm. Sir John C. D. Hay, Bart., M.P., F.R.S. *Sec. and Curator*, Capt. B. Burgess. *Assist. Sec. and Lib.*, C. R. Low, late Lt. I.N.

ROYAL VETERINARY COLLEGE, College Street, Camden Town.—*Treas.*, J. W. Bosanquet. *Principal Sec.*, *Lecturer on the Anatomy, &c., of the Horse*, Prof. C. Spooner. *Lecturer on Cattle Pathology, &c.*, Prof. J. B. Simonds. *Descriptive Anatomy with Physiology*, Assist. Professor Pritchard. *Lect. on Chemistry, &c.*, Prof. R. V. Tuson. *Demonstr. Anat.*, J. W. Axe. *Clerk, Dispenser, and Collector*, Edw. Cooke.

RUSSELL INSTITUTION, 55, Great Coram Street.— *Pres.*, Earl Russell. *Sec. and Librarian*, E. A. McDermot.

SOCIETY FOR THE ENCOURAGEMENT OF ARTS, MANUFACTURES, AND COMMERCE, 18 and 19, John Street, Adelphi.—*Pres.*, The Prince of Wales, K.G. *Chairman of the Council*, Lord Henry G. Lennox, M.P. *Sec.*, P. Le Neve Foster, M.A. *Assist. Sec.*, Chas. Critchett, R.A. *Financial Officer*, S. T. Davenport.

SOCIETY FOR PROMOTING CHRISTIAN KNOWLEDGE, 67, Lincoln's-Inn-Fields.—*Treasurers*, Rev. W. G. Humphry, B.D.; J. S. Gilliat; J. R. Kenyon, Q.C.; W. H. Smith, M.P. *Secs.*, Rev. J. Evans, M.A.; Rev. J. D. Glennie, M.A.; Rev. Hy. Swabey, M.A. *Accountant*, James D. Trigge. *Superintendent of Depositories*, T. Burt. *Collector*, Edw. Drew.

SOCIETY FOR THE PROPAGATION OF THE GOSPEL IN FOREIGN PARTS, 5, Park Place, St. James's Street.—*Sec.*, Rev. W. T. Bullock, M.A. *Assist. Secs.*, W. F. Kemp, Esq., M.A.; Rev. H. W. Tucker, M.A.; Rev. G. C. Campbell, M.A. (*Hon.*) *Travelling Sec.*, Rev. G. L. Towers, M.A.

SOCIETY FOR THE PROTECTION OF WOMEN AND CHILDREN, 20, Haymarket.—*Treas.*, Marquis Townshend. *Sec.*, J. W. Motum.

SOCIETY OF ANTIQUARIES, Somerset House.— *Pres.*, Earl Stanhope. *Treas.*, F. Ouvry. *Dir.*, C. S. Perceval, LL.D. *Sec.*, C. Knight Watson, M.A.

SOCIETY OF BRITISH ARTISTS, Suffolk Street.— *Pres.*, F. Y. Hurlstone. *Vice-Pres.*, J. J. Hill. *Treas.*, J. Noble. *Sec.*, T. Roberts.

SOCIETY OF ENGINEERS, 6, Westminster Chambers.—*Pres.*, *Sec.*, G. W. Harris.

SOCIETY OF PAINTERS IN WATER COLOURS, Pall Mall East.—*Pres.*, Fred. Taylor. *Treas.*, W. C. Smith. *Sec.*, W. Callow.

SOCIETY OF SCHOOLMASTERS, 4, Adelphi Terrace. *Chairman*, Rev. Dr. Spyers. *Treas.*, Rev. Dr. Mortimer. *Sec.*, Octavian Blewitt.

STATISTICAL SOCIETY, 12, St. James's Square.— *Pres.*, Rt. Hon. W. E. Gladstone, M.P. *Hon. Secs.*, W. A. Guy, M.B., F.R.S.; W. G. Lumley, LL.M.; Fred. Purdy. *Assist. Sec.*, F. Grove.

SURREY ARCHÆOLOGICAL SOCIETY, 8, Danes' Inn, Strand.—*Pres.*, The Duke of Buccleugh. *Hon. Sec.*, E. V. Austin.

SYRO-EGYPTIAN SOCIETY, 22, Hart Street, Bloomsbury.—*Treas.*, Dr. W. Camp. *Sec.*, Rev. J. Mills.

VICTORIA INSTITUTE, 9, Conduit Street, W.—*Pres.*, Earl of Shaftesbury. *Hon. Treas.*, Capt. E. Gardiner Fishbourne, R.N., C.B. *Hon. Sec.*, J. Reddie, Esq.

WIDOWS' RELIEF SOCIETY, 32, Sackville Street, W.—*Pres.*, The Marquis Cholmondeley. *Sec.*, S. Rayson.

ZOOLOGICAL SOCIETY OF LONDON, 11, Hanover Square.—*Pres.*, Viscount Walden. *Treas.*, R. Drummond, Esq. *Sec.*, Dr. P. L. Sclater, M.A.

DATES OF FOUNDATION OF LEARNED SOCIETIES.

	Year.		Year.		Year.
Antiquaries	1707	Edinburgh Royal	1783	Philological	1842
Archæological Institute	1843	Geographical	1830	Royal Society	1660
Ashmolean	1828	Geological	1807	Scottish Antiquaries	1780
Asiatic	1823	Harveian	1831	Society of Arts	1753
British Association	1831	Hunterian	1819	Statistical	1834
Camden	1838	Linnean	1788	United Service	1831
Chemical	1841	Meteorological	1821	Zoological	1826

BANK OF ENGLAND, FOUNDED 1694.

Capital, £14,553,000.　　Rest, £3,610,597 ex. div.

The Total Dividends for the year ending 1st October, 1868, were at the rate of £8 per cent. The Price of Bank Stock, 1st October, £241 ex. div.

THE GOVERNOR, DEPUTY-GOVERNOR, AND OTHER OFFICERS FOR THE YEAR 1868-69.

Governor, Thomas Newman Hunt, Esq. | *Deputy Governor,* Robt. Wigram Crawford, Esq.

Henry Hulse Berens, Esq.	Charles Herman Goschen, Esq.	George Lyall, Esq.
Arthur Edward Campbell. Esq.	James Alexander Guthrie, Esq.	Thomas Masterman, Esq.
Edwd. Henry Chapman, Esq.	Thomson Hankey, Esq.	James Morris, Esq.
James Pattison Currie, Esq.	Baron Heath.	George Warde Norman, Esq.
Benjamin Buck Greene, Esq.	Kirkman Daniel Hodgson, Esq.	Edward Howley Palmer, Esq.
Henry Riversdale Grenfell, Esq.	Henry Lancelot Holland, Esq.	Alfred Chas. de Rothschild, Esq.
Henry Hucks Gibbs, Esq.	John Gellibrand Hubbard, Esq.	Christopher Weguelin, Esq.
John Saunders Gilliat, Esq.	Alfred Latham, Esq.	Clifford Wigram, Esq.

Principal Officers.

Chief Accountant, George Earle Grey, Esq. | *Assistant Sec.,* George F. Glennie, Esq.
Deputy do., John Francis, Esq. | *Principal Discount Office,* John Green Elsey, Esq.
Assistant do., Henry G. Aylmer, Esq. | *Do. Branch Banks Office,* Richd. A. Marsden, Esq.
Chief Cashier, George Forbes, Esq. | *Do. Private Drawing Office,* John Fradgley, Esq.
Deputy do., Frank May, Esq. | *Do. Public do.,* Robert Curtis, Esq.
Assistant do. Samuel C. Gray. Esq. | *Do. Bill Office,* Peter Hingeston, Esq.
Secretary, Hammond Chubb, Esq. | *Do. Issue Office,* James Robinson, Esq.
Deputy do., John T. Horley, Esq.

Western Branch, Burlington Gardens.

Agent, Robert R. Pym, Esq. | *Sub-Agent,* Charles D. MacCarthy, Esq.

Country Branches.

MANCHESTER	*Agent,* Geo. A. Shee, Esq.	PLYMOUTH	*Agent,* Charles K. Lee, Esq.
Do.	*Sub-Agent,* Vacant	Do.	*Sub-Agent,* O. De B. Bryck, Esq.
LIVERPOOL	*Agent,* Robt. Davidson, Esq.	NEWCASTLE-ON-TYNE	*Agent,* D. H. Goddard, Esq.
Do.	*Sub-Agent,* Capt.G.R. Lempriere	Do.	*Sub-Agent,* F. F. Fairley, Esq.
BIRMINGHAM	*Agent,* W.Chippendale, Esq.	HULL	*Agent,* Col. P. M. Francis
Do.	*Sub-Agent,* G.A.K.Howman,Esq.	Do.	*Sub-Agent,* Capt.P. R. Lempriere
BRISTOL	*Agent,* JoshuaSaunders,Esq.	PORTSMOUTH	*Agent,* H. S. J. Ross, Esq.
Do.	*Sub-Agent,* Walter Nisbet, Esq.	Do.	*Sub-Agent,* F. F. Barnham, Esq.
LEEDS	*Agent,* R. B. Turner, Esq.	LEICESTER	*Agent,* Thos. T.Wright, Esq.
Do.	*Sub-Agent,* Hy. M.Franck, Esq.	Do.	*Sub-Agent,* F. B. Maule, Esq.

The Bank of England was the first Joint Stock Bank established in England, and having exclusive privileges in the Metropolis, granted by Royal Charter, it continued the only Joint Stock Bank in London until 1834. At this date the London and Westminster Bank was founded, and proceeded so successfully, that it was quickly followed by the formation of the London Joint Stock Bank, and the Union Bank of London. Some of the privileges claimed by the Bank of England, in opposition to the new Banks, were found, after litigation, to be untenable. The private Bankers, who were very powerful, combined in their endeavours to hinder the development of their new rivals, by curtailing their usefulness to the public; and the fact of having excluded them from the facilities of the Bankers' Clearing House for twenty years, shows to what an extent their opposition was carried. The paid-up Capital of the Joint Stock Banks carrying on the London business, now amounts to £12,000,000; and the subscribed Capital to £41,650,000; an overwhelming proof of the public need they have supplied, and a token of the pre-eminence which Joint Stock Banking seems destined to occupy in the future.

The Bankers' Clearing House is situated near the Post Office, Lombard Street, and is the medium through which many Bankers obtain the amount of Cheques, &c., in their hands for collection from other Bankers.

Instead of presenting their Cheques, &c., at each Banking House, and receiving cash and notes in payment, Clearing Bankers settle the whole amount delivered during the day at this establishment by receiving or paying the difference in their amount by a single Cheque on the Bank of England.

Every Bank in London and the Country is represented by Clearing Bankers, and as their agents send through the Clearing Houses all Drafts payable in the City, the vast amount passing daily through this channel is explained—it frequently exceeds £10,000,000.

CLEARING BANKERS.

Private Banks.	*Joint Stock Banks.*
Barclay, Bevan, & Co.	Alliance Bank.
Barnett, Hoares, Hanburys, & Co.	Ditto Southwark Branch.
Bosanquet, Salt, & Co.	City Bank.
Brown, Janson, & Co.	Consolidated Bank.
Dimsdale, Fowler, & Barnard.	Imperial Bank.
Fuller, Banbury, & Co.	London and County Banking Co.
Glyn & Co.	London Joint Stock Bank.
Martin & Co.	London and Westminster Bank.
Prescott, Grote, Cave, & Co.	Ditto Southwark Branch.
Robarts, Lubbock, & Co.	Metropolitan Bank.
Smith, Payne, & Smith.	National Bank.
Williams, Deacon, & Co.	National Provincial Bank of England.
Willis, Percival, & Co.	Union Bank of London.

Bank of England clears on one side only.

JOINT-STOCK BANKS.

NAME OF BANK. L are with Limited Liability.	When estab.	Capital Subscribed.	Shrs.	Paid-up Capital.	Per Share.	Reserve.	Dividend.	Price Oct. 1 1868.
		£	£	£	£	£	Per cent.	
Agra Bank...	1867	1,000,000	10	1,000,000	10	—	8 A cap.	12
							B	6¼
Albion Bank, L....	1864	28,500	50	57,000	15	5,000	4	10
Alliance Bank, L	1862	4,000,000	100	1,000,000	25		4	12
Anglo-Italian Bank, L......	1866	400,000	20	200,000	10	No dividend 30 June 1868, £8,000 undvd.	Held in suspense.	5
Anglo-Austrian Bank	1863	2,000,000	20	750,000	7½	33,791	35	13½
Anglo-Egyptian, L.	1864	800,000	20	800,000	20	—	10 per ann. interim divd.	18¼
Australian Joint Stock B.	1853	1,211,110	20	605,555	10	2,000	8	
Bank of Australasia.........	1834	1,200,000	40	1,200,000	40	200,000	10	52
Bank of British Columbia	1862	500,000	20	298,000	20	20,000	No dividend 31 Dec. 1868	9
B. of British Nth. America.	1836	1,000,000	50	1,000,000	50	150,000	6 per ann. & 1½ bonus.	50
Bank of Egypt	1856	250,000	25	250,000	25	55,000	10 per ann.	36
Bank of New South Wales	1817	1,000,000	20	1,000,000	20	333,333	15 per ann.	44
Bank of Otago, L.	1863	465,040	20	232,520	10	—	No div. £10,000 held over.	5
Bank of Scotland	1695	1,500,000	100	1,000,000	100	275,000	......	
Bk. of Victoria (Australia)	1852	1,000,000	50	500,000	25	100,000	10	38
Bank of South Australia...	1841	500,000	25	500,000	25	106,000	10	31
Bank of New Zealand	1861	500,000	10	500,000	10	150,000	15 div. & bonus	18
Chartered Bank of India, Australia and China.	1853	800,000	20	800,000	20	10,000	5	21
Chartered Merc. B. of Ind., London, and China.	1854	750,000	25	750,000	25	145,900	14	30½
City Bank......................	1855	1,000,000	20	500,000	10	80,000	6	32
Colonial Bank.................	1836	2,000,000	100	500,000	25	136,000	7	12
Colonial B. of Australasia	1856	1,000,000		437,500	7	47,000	8	—
Consolidated Bank, L.	1863	2,000,000	10	800,000	4	100,000	5 per ann.	4½
Delhi & London Bank, L...	1844	675,250	50	337,625	25	15,000	5	—
East London Bank, L.......	1863	1,000,000	50	100,000	5	5,000	5	4½
Eng.B.of Rio de Janeiro,L.	1863	1,000,000	20	500,000	10	1867-8, profits absorbed in depreciation of capital.	—	8½
Eng.Scot.& Aust.Chart.B.	1852	600,000	20	600,000	20	45,000	7	17
General London Bank, L.	1863		1	4,356	5		6	—
		Dollars.		Dollars.	Dols.	Dollars.		
Hong Kong and Shanghai Banking Corporation ...	1865	5,000,000	250	3,000,000	125	375,000	12	26
		£	£	£	£	£		
Imperial Bank, L.............	1862	2,250,000	100	448,940	20	46,000	5 per ann.	16¼
Imperial Ottoman Bank ...	1863	4,050,000	20	2,025,000	10	106,305	11	11
Ionian Bank, old	1839	300,000	25	180,000	25	53,000	10	26
Ditto, new	—	—	25	—	5		None.	5
Land Mortgage B. of India	1863	2,000,000	20	400,000	4	6,000	None.	4 dis.
Lond.B.of Mexico&S.Ame.	1864	1,000,000	20	400,000	20	21,000	6	13
Lond. & Brazil. B., L., old	1862	1,940,000	100	750,000	45	20,000	None.	54¾
Ditto, new			20	—	7½			
London & River Plate, L...	1862	1,500,000	100	600,000	40	145,000	12½	53

JOINT STOCK BANKS—*Continued.*

NAME OF BANK. L are with Limited Liabiltiy.	When estab.	Capital Subscribed.	Shrs.	Paid-up Capital.	Per Share.	Reserve.	Dividend.	Price Oct. 1, 1868.
Lond. & River Plate, L. new	—	—	25	—	10	—	—	10½
Lond. & S. African Bank...	1860	500,000	20	500,000	20	—	3½	12½
Lond. & Sth. Western B., L.	1862	1,000,000	100	200,000	20	3,000	2½	—
London & Westminster B.	1854	10,000,000	100	2,000,000	20	1,000,000	24 per ann.	65½
London & County Bk., old	1836	2,500,000	50	1,000,000	20	800,000 1 Feb. 1868	16	49½
London Joint Stock Bank	1836	4,000,000	50	1,200,000	15	418,000	12½	31½
Lon. Chart. B. of Australia	1852	1,000,000	20	1,000,000	20	105,000	8 per ann.	24
Merch. Banking Co. of Lon.	1863	1,500,000	100	375,000	25	25,000	—	19
Ditto, new		—	100	—	20	—	5	—
Metropolitan Bank, L.......	1865	200,000	10	200,000	10	—	5 per ann.	6
Midland Banking Co., L...	1863	804,000	100	158,625	20	10,000	6	19
National B. of Australia...	1858	1,000,000	5	540,000	4	150,000	10 bonus 2½ per annum.	6½
National Bank	1835	2,500,000	50	1,500,000	30	522,240	10	65
National Bank of India ...	1863	927,400	26	463,700	12½	34,400	8	—
National Bank of Scotland	1825	1,000,000	100	1,000,000	100	294,879	12	—
National Provin. B. of Eng.	1833	2,100,000	100	1,080,000	42	259,700	21	134½
Ditto, new		—	20	—	12	—	—	39½
Oriental Bank..............	1851	1,500,000	25	1,500,000	25	444,000	12	45
Provin. Banking Corp., L.	1864	1,113,450	50	157,503	10	12,000	7½	7 to 5 dis.
Provincial Bank of Ireland	1825	—	100	—	25	248,717	20 per ann.	90
		—	10	—	10	—	—	—
Standard B. of Brit. S. Africa	1862	2,149,800	100	464,730	25	16,000	4	13–11 dis.
New, issued at 6 per. cent.		—	100	—	10	—	—	
Union Bank of Australia	1837	1,250,000	25	1,250,000	25	250,000	16 per ann.	47½
Union Bank of London ...	1839	4,000,000	50	1,200,000	15	300,000	15	34½
West Lond. Commercial B.	1866	30,870	10	10,203	3	—	5	—

Banks and Bankers in London.

1 Agra Bank, 35, Nicholas Lane.
Agra and Masterman's, 8, Walbrook *(in liquidation.)*
2 Albion Bank, 2, Bank Buildings, City; 16, West Smithfield; and 12, Bank Buildings, Metropolitan Cattle Market.
3 Alliance Bank, Alliance Buildings, Bartholomew Lane; *Southwark Branch*, Boro' High St.
4 Alexanders, Cunliffes, &Co., 30, Lombard Street.
5 Anglo-Italian Bank, 16, Leadenhall Street.
6 Anglo-Austrian Bank, St. Mildred's Court, Poultry.
7 Anglo-Egyptian Banking Company, Limited, 27, Clement's Lane, Lombard Street.
Asiatic Banking Corporation, 52, Threadneedle Street *(in liquidation)*.
8 Australian Joint Stock Bank, 18, King William Street.
9 Bank of Australasia, 4, Threadneedle Street.
10 Bank of British North America, 124, Bishopsgate Street Within.
11 Bank of British Columbia, 5, East India Avenue, Leadenhall Street.
12 Bank of England, Threadneedle Street; *Western Branch*, 1, Burlington Gardens.
13 Bank of Egypt, 26, Old Broad Street.
Bank of India, 11, New Broad Street, *(in liquidation)*.
Bank of London, 17, Tokenhouse Yard *(in liquidation)*.
14 Bank of New South Wales, 64, Old Broad St.
15 Bank of Otago, 5, Adam's Court, Old Broad St.
16 Bank of Scotland, 11, Old Broad Street.
17 Bank of Victoria, 3, Threadneedle Street.
Bank of Queensland, 33, Walbrook *(in liquidation)*.
Bank of Hindustan, China, and Japan, 1, Bank Buildings *(in liquidation)*.
18 Bank of New Zealand, 50, Old Broad Street.
19 Barber, James, Son, and Co., 136, Leadenhall Street.
20 Barclay, Bevan, Tritton, Twells, and Co., 54, Lombard Street.
21 Barnetts, Hoares, Hanburys, and Lloyds, 60 and 62, Lombard Street.
22 Baum, Sons, and Co., 58, Lombard Street.
23 Bennett, W., 8, Bank Buildings, Metropolitan Cattle Market.
24 Biggerstaff, W. and J., 63, West Smithfield, and 6, Bank Buildings, Metrop. Cattle Market.
Bombay City Bank, 7, East India Avenue, *(in liquidation)*.
25 Bosanquet, Salt, and Co. 73, Lombard Street.
26 Brazilian & Portuguese Bank (or Eng. Bank of Rio de Jan., Limited), 13, St. Helen's Place.
British and Californian Banking Company, 72, Lombard Street *(in liquidation)*.
27 Brooks and Co., 18, Lombard Street.
28 Brown, Janson, and Co., 32, Abchurch Lane.
29 Brown, John, and Co., 25, Abchurch Lane.
30 Chartered Bank of India, Australia, and China, Hatton Court, Threadneedle Street.
31 Chartered Mercantile Bank of India, London and China, 65, Old Broad Street.
32 Child and Co., 1, Fleet Street, City.
33 City Bank, 5, Threadneedle Street, corner of Finch Lane. *Branches*, 34, Old Bond Street; 159 and 160, Tottenham Court Road; and 25, Ludgate Hill.
Clearing House, Post Office Court, Lombard St.
34 Cocks, Biddulph, and Co., 43, Charing Cross.
35 Colonial Bank, 13, Bishopsgate Street Within.
36 Colonial Bank of Australasia, 10, New Broad Street.
Commercial Bank Corporation of India and the East, 64, Moorgate Street *(in liquidation)*.

Continental Bank Corporation, 10, Clement's Lane (*in liquidation*).

37 Consolidated Bank, 52, Threadneedle Street. Charing Cross Branch, 450, West Strand.

38 Commercial Banking Company of Sydney, New South Wales, 33, Cornhill.

39 Coutts and Co., 57, 58, and 59, Strand.

40 Cunliffe, Roger, Sons, and Co., 6, Prince's Street, Mansion House.

41 Delhi and London Bank, 76, King William St.

42 Dimsdale, Fowler, and Barnard, 50, Cornhill.

43 Dobree and Sons, 6, Tokenhouse Yard.

44 Drummond and Co., 42, Charing Cross.

45 East India Bank, 12, Leadenhall Street.

46 East London Bank, 52, Cornhill; *Shoreditch*, 31, High Street; *Whitechapel*, 110, High Street; *Borough*, 26, Tooley Street.

English and American Bank, 40, Threadneedle Street (*in liquidation*).

47 English Bank of Rio de Janeiro, Limited (late Brazilian and Portuguese Bank), 1, St. Helen's Place.

English Joint Stock Bank, 29, Clement's Lane, Lombard Street (*in liquidation*).

48 English, Scottish, and Australian Chartered Bank, 73, Cornhill.

English and Swedish Bank, 13, St. Helen's Place (*in liquidation*).

European Bank, 8, Old Jewry (*in liquidation*).

49 Fuller, Banbury, and Co., 77, Lombard Street.

50 General London Bank, 27, James Street, Covent Garden.

51 Glenn and Co., 32, New Broad Street.

52 Glyn, Mills, Currie, and Co., 67, Lombard St.

53 Goslings and Sharpe, 19, Fleet Street.

54 Grindlay and Co., 55, Parliament Street.

Hallett, Ommanney, & Co., 14, George Street, Westminster (*in liquidation*).

55 Harwood, Knight, & Allen, 33, Abchurch La.

56 Herries, Farquhar, and Co., 16, St. James's St.

57 Hill, Charles, and Sons, 17, West Smithfield, and 2, Bank Buildings, Metrop. Cat. Market.

58 Hoare and Co., 37, Fleet Street.

59 Hongkong and Shanghai Banking Corporation, 32, Nicholas Lane, Lombard Street.

60 Hopkinson, Charles, & Co., 3, Regent Street.

61 Hoyland, E., and Son, 113, Leadenhall Street.

62 Imperial Bank, 6, Lothbury. *Westminster Branch*, Victoria Street.

63 Imperial Ottoman Bank, 4, Bank Buildings.

64 India, Peninsula, London, and China Bank, Limited, Gresham House.

65 Ionian Bank, 31, Finsbury Circus.

King & Co., *see* Smith, Elder and Co.

66 Lacy and Son, 60, West Smithfield, and 11, Bank Buildings, Metropolitan Cattle Market.

67 Land Mortgage Bank of India, 17, Change Alley, Cornhill.

68 Layard, Edward, 81, Moorgate Street.

69 London Bank of Mexico and South America, 16, King William Street.

London and Bombay Bank, 10, Clement's Lane (*in liquidation*).

London and Exchange Bank (*in liquidation*).

70 London Joint-Stock Bank, 5, Princes Street, Bank; *Chancery Lane Branch*, 124, Chancery Lane; *Western Branch*, 69, Pall Mall.

71 London and Westminster Bank, 41, Lothbury. *City Office*, 41, Lothbury; *Country Department*, 41, Lothbury; *Westminster Branch*, 1, St. James's Square; *Bloomsbury Branch*, 214, High Holborn; *Southwark Branch*, 3, Wellington Street, Borough; *Eastern Branch*, 130, High Street, Whitechapel; *St. Marylebone Branch*, 4, Stratford Place, Oxford Street;

Temple Bar Branch, 217, Strand; *Lambeth Branch*, 91, Westminster Bridge Road.

72 London and Brazilian Bank, 2, Old Broad St.

73 London & River Plate Bank, 40, Moorgate St.

74 London & S. African Bank, 10, King Wm. St.

75 London and South-Western Bank, 29, Lombard Street; *Regent Street*, 27, Regent Street; *Brixton*, 10, Loughborough Place; *Camden Town*, 67 and 68, Park Street; *Chelsea*, 24, King's Road; *Clapham*, Crescent Place; *Hampstead*, High Street; *Kilburn*, Manor Terrace; *Norwood*, 2, Woodman Terrace; *Peckham*, 98, High Street; *Putney*, High Street; *St. John's Wood*, Circus Road; *Wandsworth*, High Street; *Stepney*, Commercial Rd.

76 London Chartered Bank of Australia, 88, Cannon Street, City.

77 Lond. & County Banking Co., 21, Lombard St. *Bayswater*, Westbourne Grove; *Blackheath*, 5, Spencer Place; *Caledonian Road*, 193. Caledonian Road; *Covent Garden*, Henrietta Street; *Deptford*, Broadway; *Greenwich*, Nelson Street; *Hackney*, 1, Amherst Road; *Hanover Square*, 21, Hanover Square; *Holborn*, 324 and 325, High Holborn; *Islington*, 19, High Street; *Kensington*, High Street; *Knightsbridge*, Albert Gate; *Lambeth*, 165, Westminster Bridge Road; *Limehouse*, 1, Providence Place; *Newington*, High Street; *Oxford Street*, 441, Oxford Street; *Paddington*, 6, Berkeley Place, Edgware Road; *Shoreditch*, 181 and 182, Shoreditch; *Southwark*, High Street, Borough; *Stratford*, *Essex*, Broadway; *Westminster*, 3, Victoria Street; *Woolwich*, Powis Street.

London and Mediterranean Bank, 10, Clement's Lane, (*in liquidation*).

78 London & Venezuela Bank, 9, Tokenhouse Yd.

Marryat, Price, & Co., 3, King William Street, City, (*in liquidation*).

80 Martins, 68, Lombard Street.

81 Merchant Banking Company of London, 112, Cannon Street.

82 Metropolitan Bank, 75, Cornhill; *Hammersmith*; *Woolwich*.

83 Midland Banking Compy., 38, New Broad St.

84 National Bank, 13, Old Broad Street; *Bayswater*, 19, Gloucester Gardens; *Camden Town*, 189, High Street; *Charing Cross*, 9 and 10, Charing Cross; *Oxford Street*, 23, Old Cavendish Street; *Pimlico*, 4, Arabella Row.

85 National Bank of Australasia, 47, Cornhill.

86 National Bank of India, 80, King William St.

87 National Provincial Bank of England, 112, Bishopsgate Street, corner of Threadneedle Street; *St. Marylebone Branch*, 28, Baker Street; *St. James's Branch*, 14, Waterloo Place, Pall Mall; *Islington Branch*, 173, Upper Street.

88 National Bank of Scotland, 37, Nicholas Lane.

New Zealand Banking Corporation, 1, Cushion Court, Old Broad Street, (*in liquidation*).

89 Oriental Bank Corpor., 40, Threadneedle St.

Peninsular, West Indian, and Southern Bank, Lawrence Lane, (*in liquidation*).

90 Praeds and Co., 189, Fleet Street.

91 Prescott, Grote, Cave, and Co., 92, Threadneedle Street.

92 Provincial Banking Corporation, 7, Bank Buildings, Lothbury; *Edgware Road*, 80, Connaught Ter.; *Kingsland*, 560, Kingsland Rd.

93 Provincial Bank of Ireland, 12, Old Broad St.

Puget, Bainbridges, and Co., 17, Tokenhouse Yard (*in liquidation*).

94 Ransom, Bouverie, and Co., 1. Pall Mall East.

95 Richardson & Co., 13, Pall Mall, & 23, Cornhill.

96 Robarts, Lubbock, and Co., 15, Lombard St.
97 Robertson, George, 11, New Broad Street.
    Royal Bank of India, 13, Leadenhall Street, *(in liquidation).*
98 Samuel Montagu and Co., 60, Old Broad St.
    Scinde, Punjaub, and Delhi Bank Corporation, 80, King William St. *(in liquidation).*
99 Scott, Sir Sam., Bart, & Co., 1, Cavendish Sq.
100 Seale, Low, and Co., 7, Leicester Square.
101 Shank, J., 4, Bank Buildings, Metro.Cat.Mkt.
102 Sillar, W. C., and Co., 62, Cornhill
103 Smith, Elder, and Co., 41, Pall Mall, now H. S. King and Co.
104 Smith, Payne, and Smiths, 1, Lombard St.
105 South Australian Banking Company 54, Old Broad Street,
106 Standard Bank of British South Africa, 10, Clement's Lane, Lombard Street.
107 Stoy, J., & Co., 7, Victoria St., Westminster.
108 Stride, J. & W. S., 41, West Smithfield, and 8, Bank Buildings, MetropolitanCattle Market
109 Twining, R., and Co., 215, Strand.
110 Union Bank of Australia, 38, Old Broad St.
111 Union Bank of Ireland, 52, Moorgate Street.
112 Union Bank of London, 2, Prince's Street, Mansion House; *Charing Cross Branch*, 4, Pall Pall East; *Regent Street Branch*, Argyll Place, Regent Street; *Temple Bar Branch*, Chancery Lane.
113 United Service Co., 9, Waterloo Place.
114 West Lon.Com. Bank, 34, Sloane Sq.,Chelsea.
115 Williams, Deacon, Labouchere, Thornton, and Co., 20, Birchin Lane.
116 Willis, Percival, and Co., 76, Lombard Street.

LIST OF COUNTRY BANKS IN ENGLAND AND WALES, WITH THEIR LONDON AGENTS.

The numbers refer to the London agents, a list of which will be found at pages 186–188.

BANKS AND THEIR BRANCHES IN SCOTLAND.

BANK OF SCOTLAND.—*Head Offices*, in Edinburgh in Bank Street; in Glasgow, 65 Ingram Street. *Branches*, Aberdeen, Airdrie, Alyth, Annan, Arbroath, Ardrossan, Auchtermuchty, Ayr, Ballachulish, Barrhead, Beauley, Blairgowrie, Broadford, Callander, Castle-Douglas, Coldstream, Cumnock, Dumfries, Dundee, Dunfermline, Dunse, Dysart, Falkirk, Forfar, Fraserburgh, Galashiels, Gatehouse, Glasgow (head office and branches), Greenock, Haddington, Helensburgh, Innerkeithen, Inverness, Jedburgh, Kelso, Kilmarnock, Kirkcaldy, Kirkcudbright, Lauder, Leith, Lossiemouth, Moffat, Montrose, Motherwell, Oban, Paisley, Peebles, Perth, Portree, St. Andrews, Stirling, Stonehaven, Strathaven, West Linton. *London Agents*: Bank of England, Coutts & Co., Smith, Payne & Co., National Provincial Bank of England, and London and County Bank.

ROYAL BANK OF SCOTLAND.—*Head Offices*: in Edinburgh, 36 St. Andrew's Square in Glasgow; Royal Exchange Square. *Branches*: Aberdeen, Alyth, Arbroath, Ardrossan, Ayr, Ayton, Bathgate, Biggar, Barrowstowness, Brechin, Broughty-Ferry, Buckhaven, Campbelton (Argyllshire), Cumpsie, Catrine, Coatbridge, Cumnock, Cupar, Dalkeith, Dalmellington, Doune, Drymen, Dumfries, Ecclefechan, Elgin, Falkirk, Forfar, Galashiels, Girvan, Glasgow (and branches), Granton (near Edinburgh), Grantown, Greenock, Haddington, Hamilton, Hawick, Irvine, Jedburgh, Johnstone, Kilmarnock, Kinross, Lanark, Largo, Leith, Lesmahagow, Leven, Lochee, Lockerbie, Maybole, Meigle, Melrose, Montrose, Musselburgh, Newmilns, Perth, Port Glasgow, Portobello, Rothesay, St. Andrews, Saltcoats, Sanquhar, Stewarton, Stirling, Strathaven, Wishaw. *London Agents:* Bank of England, Coutts & Co.

BRITISH LINEN COMPANY.—*Head Offices:* Edinburgh, 36 St. Andrew Square; Glasgow, 110, Queen Street. *Branches:* Aberdeen, Annan, Arbroath, Balfour, Brechin, Carluke and Wishaw, Castle-Douglas, Coldstream, Cupar, Dumfries, Dunbar, Dundee, Dunfermline, Dunse, Elgin, Forres, Fort-William, Glasgow (and branches), Golspie, Greenock, Haddington, Hamilton, Hawick, Inverness, Irvine, Jedburgh, Kelso, Kilmarnock, Kingussie, Kinross, Kirriemuir, Langholm, Leith, Melrose, Moffat, Montrose, Nairn, Newton-Stewart, Port-Berwick, Paisley, Peebles, Perth, Sanquhar, Selkirk, Stranraer, Tain, Thornhill, Wigtown. *London Agents:* Bank of England, and Smith, Payne & Co.

COMMERCIAL BANK OF SCOTLAND.—*Head Offices:* Edinburgh, George Street; Glasgow, 10, Gordon Street, *Branches:* Aberdeen, Alloa, Annan, Anstruther, Arbroath, Ayr, Ayton, Balmacara, Banff, Beauley, Beith, Biggar, Blairgowrie, Bonhill, Callender, Campbelton, Carnwath, Colinsburgh, Crieff, Cromarty, Cupar, Dalkeith, Douglas, Dumbarton, Dumfries, Dunbar, Dundee, Dunfermline, Dunkeld, Earlston, Elgin, Falkirk, Forfar, Galashiels, Girvan, Glasgow (and branches), Grangemouth, Greenock, Haddington, Hamilton, Hawick, Invergordon, Inverness, Jedburgh, Kelso, Kilmarnock, Kirkcaldy, Kirkwall, Lanark, Leith, Lerwick, Leven, Linlithgow, Lockerbie, Musselburgh, Newburgh, (Fifeshire), Perth, Peterhead, Pitlochrie, St. Andrews, Stirling, Stromness, Tain, Thurso, Turriff, Whitburn, Wick. *Sub-Branches:* Abingdon, Comrie, Crail, Eyemouth, Kilwinning, Kincardine, Markinch, Mauchline, St. Clairtown. *London Agents:* Coutts & Co., and London and Westminster Bank.

NATIONAL BANK OF SCOTLAND.—*Head Offices:* in Edinburgh, 42, St. Andrew Square; in Glasgow, Queen Street. *Branches:* Aberdeen, Airdric, Alloa, Anstruther, Ayr, Banff, Bathgate, Berwick-on-Tweed, Biggar, Burntisland, Castle-Douglas, Coatbridge, Coupar-Angus, Cupar-Fife, Dalkeith, Denny, Dingwall, Dumfries, Dundee, Dunfermline, East Linton, Elie, Falkirk, Forfar, Forres, Fort William, Galashiels, Girvan, Glasgow (and branches), Grantown, Greenock, Hawick, Inverary, Inverness, Islay, Jedburgh, Kelso, Kilmarnock, Kilsyth, Kirkcaldy, Kirkcudbright, Kirkintilloch, Kirkwall, Kirriemuir, Langholm, Largo, Leith, Lochmaben, Montrose, Nairn, Newton-Stewart, Oban, Paisley, Partick, Perth, Pittenweem, Portree, Selkirk, Stirling, Stornoway, Stranraer, Stromness, Thurso, Ullapool, Whithorn. *London Agents:* Glyn & Co., Coutts & Co., and Union Bank of London.

UNION BANK OF SCOTLAND.—*Head Offices:* in Edinburgh, Parliament Square; in Glasgow, 97, Ingram Street; Aberdeen; and Perth. *Branches:* Aberfeldy, Aberdour, Alloa, Alva, Auchterarder, Auchtermuchty, Ayr, Ballater, Banchory, Banff, Barrhead, Bathgate, Beith, Blair-Athole, Blairgowrie, Brechin, Bridge of Allan, Broxburn, Buckie, Castle-Douglas, Coatbridge, Coupar-Angus, Crieff, Cullen, Dalbeattie, Dalry (Kirkcudbrightshire), Doune, Dumbarton, Dumfries, Dunblane, Dundee, Dunkeld, Dunning, Dunoon, Edzell, Elgin, Ellon, Errol, Fochabers, Forfar, Fraserburgh, Galston, Gatehouse, Girvan, Govan, Greenock, Helensburgh, Huntly, Innerleithen, Inveraray, Inverurie, Irvine, Johnston, Keith, Killin, Kilmarnock, Kincardine, Kincraigie Tough, Kirkcaldy, Kirkwall, Kirriemuir, Leith, Lerwick, Leslie, Lochgelly, Lochgilphead, Lumsden, Macduff, Maryhill, Maybole, Mintlaw, Moffat, Monivie, Montrose, Neilston, New Pitsligo, Paisley, Peebles, Peterhead, Pitlochrie, Port Glasgow, Portsoy, Renfrew, Rosehearty, Selkirk, Stewarton, Stirling, Stranraer, Strathaven, Stromness, Tarbert (Loch-Fine), Thornhill, Tillicoultry, Thurso, Turriff, Wick. *London Agents,* Coutts & Co., Glyn & Co.

CLYDESDALE BANKING COMPANY.—*Head Offices:* in Edinburgh, 29 George Street and High Street; in Glasgow, Miller Street. *Branches:* Airdrie, Alexandria, Alloa, Anstruther, Arbroath, Ayr, Bathgate, Beith, Borrowstounness, Brechin, Campbelton, Coatbridge, Cumnock, Cupar, Dalkeith, Dalmellington, Dalry, Denny, Dollar, Dumbarton, Dumfries, Dundee, Eaglesham, Falkirk, Greenock, Hamilton, Helensburg, Inverkeithing, Irvine, Kilmarnock, Kilwinning, Kinross, Lanark, Leith, Lochgilphead, Lockerbie, Mid-Calder, Montrose, Muirkirk, Neilston, New Galloway, Newton-Stewart, Paisley, Penicuik, Pittenween, Pollockshaws, Portobello, Rothesay, St. Andrew's, Stewarton, Stirling, Stranraer, Tillicoultry, Tobermory, Wemyss Bay, Whithorn, Wigtown. *London Agents,* Barnetts, Hoare, Hanbury, Lloyd & Co., London and Westminster Bank.

CITY OF GLASGOW BANK.—*Head Office:* 24, Virginia Street, Glasgow; Edinburgh Branch, 12, South Hanover Street. *Branches:* Airdrie, Ardrossan, Auchinblae, Ayr, Banff, Barrhead, Bonhill, Brechin, Broughty-Ferry, Buckie, Carluke, Carnoustie, Crieff, Cupar, Dalry (Ayrshire), Dingwall, Douglas, Dunbar, Dundee, Dunoon, Dunse, Elgin, Falkland, Ferryport-on-Craig, Fettercairn, Forres, Girvan, Glenluce, Gorebridge, Govan, Greenlaw, Greenock, Gourock, Haddington, Hamilton, Inverness, Islay, Jedburgh, Johnstone, Kelso, Kilbirnie, Kilsyth, Kirkcaldy, Kirkintilloch, Kirriemuir, Lamlash, Lanark, Largo, Larkall, Lasswade, Lauder, Lesmahagow, Leven, Linlithgow, Lochwinnoch, Millport, Milnathorpe, Motherwell, New Cumnock, Newton-Stewart, Newton, Oban, Paisley, Partick, Peterhead, Pollockshaws, Port Ellen (Islay), Port-Glasgow, Port-William, Rothes, Rothesay, Rutherglen, Saltcoats, Stirling, Shotts, Stornoway, Stranraer, Tranent, West Calder, West Kilbride, Whitburn, Wigtown, Wishaw. In the ISLE OF MAN, Douglas, Castletown, Ramsey, and Peel as the BANK OF MONA. *London Agents:* London Joint Stock Bank.

ABERDEEN AND COUNTY BANK.—Aberdeen. *Branches:* Alford, Banchory, Banff, Bervie, Dufftown, Durno, Echt, Ellon, Fraserburgh, Fyvie, Golspie, Huntly, Insch, Inverary, Keith, Kildrummy, Laurencekirk, Lumphanan, Lybster, Mintlaw, Montrose, New Deer, Old Meldrum, Peterhead, Rhynie, Stonehaven, Tarland, Tarves, Thurso, Turriff, Wick. *Agents in Edinburgh,* Royal Bank; *in London,* The London Joint Stock Bank.

CALEDONIAN BANKING COMPANY.—Inverness.

Branches: Bonar Bridge, Cromarty, Dingwall, Dornoch, Elgin, Forres, Fortrose, Gairloch, Garmouth, Grantown, Kingussie, Lairg, Lochcarron, Nairn, Rothes, Ullapool. *Agents in Edinburgh,* Union Bank of Scotland; *in London,* Barclay, Bevan, & Co.

CENTRAL BANK OF SCOTLAND.—Perth. *Branches:* Aberfeldy, Auchterarder, Blackford, Coupar Angus, Crieff, Dunkeld, Killin, Newburgh, Pitlochrie. *Agents in Edinburgh,* Commercial Bank; *in London,* Glyn, Mills & Co.

NORTH OF SCOTLAND BANKING COMPANY.—Aberdeen. *Branches:* Aberchirder, Aboyne, Alford, Auchinblae, Banchory, Banff, Bervie, Buckie, Cullen, Dufftown, Elgin, Ellon, Fraserburgh, Huntley, Insch, Invergordon, Inverurie, Keith, Kintore, Laurencekirk, Longside, Macduff, Methlick, Montrose, New Deer, Old Deer, Old Meldrum, Peterhead, Portree, Portsoy, Rhynie, Stonehaven, Strichen, Turriff. *Agents in Edinburgh,* Commercial Bank; *in London,* Barclay and Co. and Union Bank of London.

BANKS AND THEIR BRANCHES IN IRELAND.

PRIVATE BANKS IN DUBLIN.

LA TOUCHE, DAVID AND Co.—Castle Street, Dublin. *London Agents,* National Provincial Bank of England.

BALL & Co.—31, Henry Street. *London Agents,* Ransom, Bouverie and Co.

BOYLE, LOW, MURRAY AND Co.—35, College Green. *London Agents,* Williams, Deacon and Co.

GUINNESS, MAHON AND Co.—17, College Green. *London Agents,* London and County Bank.

JOINT STOCK BANKS.

BANK OF IRELAND.—*Head Office,* College Green, Dublin. *Branches:* Armagh, Ballinasloe, Ballinrobe, Bandon, Belfast, Callan, Carlow, Clonmel, Cork, Derry, Drogheda, Dundalk, Galway, Gorey, Kilkenny, Limerick, Longford, Maryborough, Navan, Newry, New Ross, Omagh, Queenstown, Roscrea, Sligo, Thurles, Tipperary, Tralee, Tullamore, Waterford, Westport, Wexford, Youghal. *Sub-agencies:* Arklow, Bagnalstown, Cahir, Castlebar. *London Agents:* Bank of England, Coutts and Co.

HIBERNIAN JOINT STOCK BANKING COMPANY.—25, College Green, Dublin, and Castle Street. *Branches:* Abbeyleix, Athy, Bray, Drogheda, Kells, Kilkenny, Mullingar, Naas, Parsonstown, Tullamore. *London Agents:* Barnetts, Hoare, and Co.

ROYAL BANK OF IRELAND.—*Head Office,* Foster Place, Dublin. *Smithfield Branch,* 24, Arran Quay. *Corn Market Branch,* 14 and 15, Corn Market. *London Agents:* The London and Westminster Bank.

PROVINCIAL BANK OF IRELAND. — *Head Office,* 42, Old Broad Street, London. *Dublin Office,* College Street. *Branches:* Armagh, Athlone, Ballina, Ballymena, Ballyshannon, Banbridge, Bandon, Belfast, Carrick-on-Shannon, Carrick-on-Suir, Cavan, Clogheen, Clonmel, Coleraine, Cootehill, Cork, Drogheda, Dungannon, Dungarvan, Ennis, Enniscorthy, Enniskillen, Fermoy, Galway, Kilkenny, Kilrush, Limerick, Londonderry, Mallow, Monaghan, Nenagh, Newcastle (Limerick), Newry, Omagh, Parsonstown, Skibbereen, Sligo, Strabane, Templemore, Tralee, Waterford, Wexford, Youghal. *London Agents,* Barclay and Co.

NATIONAL BANK.—*Head Office,* 13, Old Broad Street, London. *Dublin Office,* 34, College Green. *Branches:* Athlone, Athy, Ballina, Ballinasloe, Ballymahon, Belfast, Boyle, Bruff, Carlow, Carrickmacross, Carrick-on-Suir, Cashel, Castlerea, Charleville, Clonakilty, Clonmel, Cork, Dundalk, Dungarvan, Ennis, Enniscorthy, Fermoy, Galway, Kanturk, Kells, Kilkenny, Killarney, Kilrush, Kingstown, Limerick, Lismore, Listowel, Longford, Loughrea, Macroom, Mallow, Midleton, Mitchelstown, Moate, Montmellick, Mullingar, Nenagh, Newcastle, New Ross, Rathkeale, Roscommon, Roscrea, Thurles, Tipperary, Tralee, Tuam, Waterford, Wexford, Wicklow. *London Agents:* Head Office, 13, Old Broad Street.

NORTHERN BANKING COMPANY.—*Head Office,* Belfast. *Branches:* Armagh, Ballibay, Ballybofey, Ballycastle, Ballymena, Ballynahinch, Banbridge, Carndonagh, Carrickfergus, Carrick-on-Shannon, Castlewellan, Clones, Coleraine, Comber, Downpatrick, Dromore, Fintona, Kilrea, Lisburn, Londonderry, Largan, Magherafelt, Mohills, Newry, Newtownlimavady, Newtownstewart, Ramelton, Virginia. *London Agents:* Glyn and Co.; London Joint Stock Bank.

BELFAST BANKING COMPANY.—*Head Office,* Belfast. *Branches:* Antrim, Armagh, Ballybay, Ballymena, Ballymoney, Bangor, Caledon, Castleblayney, Coleraine, Cookstown, Drogheda, Dundalk, Dungannon, Enniskillen, Kilkeel, Larne, Londonderry, Lurgan, Magherafelt, Monaghan, Navan, Newry, Newtownards, Newtownlimavady, Portadown, Portaferry, Rathfriland, Saintfield, Strabane, Tandragee. *London Agents,* Union Bank of London.

ULSTER BANKING COMPANY. — *Head Office,* Belfast. *Branches:* Antrim, Ardee, Armagh, Aughnacloy, Ballymena, Ballymoney, Banbridge, Belturbet, Castleberg, Cavan, Cookstown, Cootehill, Donegal, Downpatrick, Dublin, Edenderry, Enniskillen, Lisburn, Londonderry, Longford, Lurgan, Maghera, Monaghan, Newtownards, Omagh, Portadown, Sligo, Strabane, Trim. *London Agents:* Prescott, Grote and Co., and London and Westminster Bank.

MUNSTER BANK (Limited).—*Head Office,* 66, South Mall, Cork. *Branches:* Bandon, Bantry, Bruff, Cahirciveen, Charleville, Fermoy, Fethard, Kilmallock, Kinsale, Limerick, Macroom, Midleton, Rathkeale, Skibbereen, Tipperary. *London Agents:* Union Bank of London.

COLONIAL AND FOREIGN BANKS, WITH THEIR LONDON AGENTS.

N.B. The numbers given in the following List refer to the Banks in London on which the Colonial or Foreign Banks draw. See List of London Bankers at p. 186, ante. The addresses given are those of the head offices in London. Most Bankers in the United Kingdom issue draughts on all the leading Colonial and Foreign Banks.

ACAPULCO.—Agency of London Bank of Mexico and South America, 69.

ADELAIDE.—Bank of Adelaide, 112; Bank of Australasia, 9; Bank of South Australia, 54, Old Broad Street; English, Scottish and Australian Chartered Bank, 48; National Bank of Australasia, 85; Union Bank of Australia, 110.

AGRA.—Branch of Agra Bank, 1; Bank of Bengal, 39; Bank of Upper India, 112.

ALEXANDRIA.—Anglo-Egyptian Bank, 7; Bank of Egypt, 13; Imperial Ottoman Bank, 62.

ALLAHABAD.—Bank of Bengal, 39; Delhi and London Bank, 112.

ANCONA.—Le Mesurier and Co., 112,

ANTIGUA.—Colonial Bank, 35.

ANTWERP.—Nottebohn, Bros.; Van Lith and Co. J. B. Bischoffsheim; Lemme and Co.

ARARAT.—Bank of New South Wales, 14; London Chartered Bank of Australia, 76.

ATHENS.—Ionian Bank, 65.

AUCKLAND (New Zealand).—Bank of Australia, 9; Bank of New S. Wales, 14; Bank of New Zealand, 18; Union Bank of Australia, 110.

BADEN-BADEN.—Müller and Co.

BADULLA (Ceylon).—Oriental Bank, 112.

BAHIA.—London and Brazilian Bank, 72.

BALLARAT (Victoria).—Bank of Australasia, 9; Bank of New South Wales, 14.

BARBADOS.—Colonial Bank, 35.

BAREILLY.—Oriental Bank Corporation, 12, 112.

BATAVIA.—Chartered Bank of India, 33.

BATHURST (N. S. Wales).—Aust. Jnt. Stock, Bk, 8.

BELLEVILLE.—Bank of Montreal, 112.

BENARES.—Delhi and London Bank, 112; Bank of Bengal, 39.

BERBICE.—British Guiana Bank, 104.

BERLIN.—T. Abel, jun., 112; A. Paderstein, 112.

BERNE.—Marcuard and Co.

BESANÇON.—Jacquard and Co.

BILBOA.—Allan T. Jones.

BOGOTA.—London Bank of Mexico, 69.

BOLOGNA.—C. B. Renoli.

BOMBAY.—Agra Bank, 1; Bank of Bombay, 39; Chartered Mercantile Bank, 70; Comptoir d'Escompte de Paris, 112; Forbes and Co., 39; Hongkong Bank, 77; National Bank of India, 87; Oriental Bank Corporation, 12, 112.

BONN.—Jonas Cahn, 112.

BORDEAUX.—J. Violett and Co., 112.

BOSTON, U.S.—Bank of the Metropolis, 112; Blake, Bros., 12; Page and Co., 33; Wells and Co., 112.

BOULOGNE-SUR-MER.—Adam and Co., 39, 71.

BREMEN.—Lang and Co.; Bremen Bank; Schröder and Sons; Laman and Sons.

BRESLAU.—Eichborn and Co.

BREST.—E. Pesron; Lemonier and Co.

BRISBANE (Queensland).—Bank of Australasia, 9; Australian Joint Stock, 8; Bank of New South Wales, 14; Union Bank of Australia, 110.

BRUSSELS.—T., C., and J. Bigwood, 112.

BUENOS AYRES.—London & River Plate Bank, 73.

CADIZ.—John D. Shaw.

CAEN.—Guibert and Co.

CAIRO.—Anglo-Egyptian Bank, 7.

CALAIS.—Bellart and Sons, 71.

CALCUTTA.—Agra Bank, 1; Bank of Bengal, 39; Chartered Bank of India, &c., 10; Chartered Mercantile Bank, 31; Comptoir d'Escompte, 112; Delhi and London Bank, 41; National Bank of India, 86; Oriental Bank, 89.

CALLAO.—London Bank of Mexico, 68.

CANADA.—Bk. of Montreal, 10, 12; Bk. of Cnda., 112.

CANTERBURY (New Zealand).—Union Bank of Australia, 110.

CANTON.—Gilman and Co., 112.

CAPE-TOWN.—Cape of Good Hope Bank, 71; London and South African Bank, 74; South African Bank. 3; Union Bank, 3.

CARLSBAD.—A. T. Seifert; B. Schwalb.

CARLSRUHE.—G. Müller and Co.

CARTHAGENA (New Granada).—London Bank of Mexico, 69.

CASSEL (Hesse).—Goldschmidt, Bros.

CAWNPORE.—Bank of Upper India, 112.

CEPHALONIA.—Ionian Bank, 65.

CEYLON.—Oriental Bank, 89.

CHAMOUNIX.—H. Brodhag.

CHARLESTON, U.S.—Heriot and Co., 112.

CHICAGO.—Bank of Montreal, 10, 12.

CINCINNATI, U.S.—Gilmore and Co., 112.

COBLENTZ.—A. Jordan.

COLOGNE.—Schaaffhausen's Union Bank, 112.

COLOMBO (Ceylon).—Chart. Mercantile Bank, 31.

COLUMBIA, (British).—10.

CONSTANCE.—Macaire and Co., 112.

CONSTANTINOPLE.—Imperial Ottoman Bank, 63.

COPENHAGEN.—Bank of Copenhagen, 112.

DACCA.—Bank of Bengal, 39.

DELHI.—Delhi and London Bank, 41.

DEMERARA.—Colonial Bank, 55; British Guiana Bank, 104.

DIEPPE.—G. Chapman; Osmond and Co., 112.

DIJON.—Maloir and Co.

DRESDEN.—R. Thode and Co., 112.

DUNEDIN, (Otago).—Bank of Australasia, 9; Bank of New South Wales, 14; Bank of New Zealand, 18.

D'URBAN, (Natal).—London and South African Bank, 74; Natal Bank, 71.

EMS.—Becker and Jung, 112.

FLORENCE. — Anglo-Italian Bank, 5 ; Maquay and Pakenham. 112.

FRANKFORT-ON-MAINE.—Rothschilds and Sons.

GALATZ.—Bk. of Roumania, 13, King's Arms Yd.

GALLE, (Ceylon).—Chartered Mercantile Bank, 30; Oriental Bank, 89.

GEELONG, (Victoria).—Bank of Australasia, 9; Bank of New South Wales, 14; Colonial Bank of Australasia, 36; London Chartered Bank, 76; &c.

GENEVA.—L. Pavrin; H. Brodhay; (both) 112.

GENOA.—Anglo-Italian Bank, 112, 5.

GHENT.—Bank of Flanders. 112.

GIBRALTAR.—Johnson and Towers.

GOTTENBURG.—Scandinavian Credit Company.

GÖTTINGEN.—Klettwig and Co.

GOULBURN, (N.S.W.).—Australian Joint Stock, 8; Bank of New South Wales, 14; &c.

GUERNSEY.—Guernsey Banking Company; Dobree and Sons, Tokenhouse Yard; Guernsey Commercial Banking Company, 71.

GUADALAJURA and GUANAJUATO.—London Bank of Mexico, 69.

HAGUE.—Scheurleer and Sons.

HALIFAX, (Nova Scotia).—Bank of British North America, 10.

HAMBURG.—A. Behn; Berenberg and Co.; Vereins Bank; all on 112.

HAMILTON, (Canada).—Bank of Montreal, 112; Bank of British North America, 10.

HAMILTON, (Victoria).—Bank of Victoria, 17.

HAMILTON, (New Zealand).—Bank of Otago, 15.

HANKOW.—Chartered Bank of India, 30; Chartered Mercantile Bank, 31.

HANOVER.—Bank of Hanover, 112.

HAVANA.—Fesser and Co., 112.

HEIDELBERG.—Köster and Co., 112.

HOBART TOWN.—Bank of Australasia, 9; Bank of Van Dieman's Land, 71; Bank of New South Wales, 14; &c.

HOMBOURG.—Goldschmidt, 112.

HONG KONG.—Agra, 1; Chartered Bank of India, &c. 30; Comptoir d'Escompte, 112; Oriental Bank, 89.

INSPRUCK.—F. J. H. Holtman.

JERUSALEM.—M. P. Bergheim.

JUBBULPORE.—Delhi and London Bank, 41.

KANDY, (Ceylon).—Chartered Mercantile Bank, 31; Oriental Bank, 89.

KINGSTON, (Jamaica).—Colonial Bank, 35.

KINGSTON, (Canada West.)—Bank of Montreal, and Royal Canadian Bank, (both) 112.

KURRACHEE.—Chartered Bank, 30; Agra Bank, 31.

LAHORE.—Agra, 1; Delhi and London, 41.

LAUNCESTON, (Tasmania).—Bank of Australasia, 9; Bank of Van Diemen's Land, 71; Bank of New South Wales, 14.

LEGHORN.—Maquay and Co., 112.

LEIPSIC.—Trege and Co.; Becker and Co., 112.

LIEGE.—De Sauvage and Co., 112.

LILLE.—R. Mathon, 112.

LIMA.—London and Mexico Bank, 69.

LISBON.—London and Brazilian Bank, 72; Unino De Porto, 37.

LUBECK.—Müller Brothers.

LUCERNE.—E. Knoerr and Sons.

LUCKNOW.—Bank of Bengal, 39; Delhi and London Bank, 41.

LYTTELTON, (New Zealand).—Bank of New South Wales, 14; Bank of New Zealand, 18.

MADEIRA.—Cossart, Gordon, and Co.

MADRAS.—Agra Bank, 1; Arbuthnot and Co., 39; Chartered Mercantile, 31; Lecot and Co., 70; Oriental Bank, 89.

MADRID.—Bayo and Co., 70.

MAITLAND, (N. S. W.)—Bank of Australasia, 9; Bank of New South Wales, 14.

MALAGA.—Crooke, Bros., Clemmans & Son, 112.

MALTA.—James Bell and Co.; Rose and Co.; Duckworth and Co., 112.

MANILA.—Hongkong Bank, 77; J. M. Tuason and Co., 112.

MARSEILLES.—Folsch and Co.; Salary and Co.; Liquier and Co., 112.

MAURITIUS.—Commercial Bank, 21; Oriental Bank, 89.

MAZATLAN.—London and Mexico Bank, 69.

MAYENCE.—G. L. Kayser, 112.

MELBOURNE.—Bank of Australasia, 9; English, Scottish, &c., Bank, 48; Bank of New South Wales, 14; Bank of Victoria, 17; Colonial Bank of Australasia, 36; London Chartered Bank, 76; National Bank, 85; Oriental Bank, 89; Union Bank, 110.

MESSINA.—Cailler & Co.; Melardi & Sons, 112.

METZ.—M. Goudchaux, nephew of F. G. Simon.

MEXICO.—London Bank of Mexico and South America, 69; Hongkong and Shanghai Banking Company, 59.

MILAN.—Ulrich and Co.; C. F. Brot; A. Comerio; Anglo-Italian Bank, 5.

MODENA.—A. Verona, 112.

MONTE VIDEO.—London & River Plate Bank, 73.

MONTPELLIER.—E. Blonquier, Sons, and Leeuhardt; Tissie Sarrus, 112.

MONTREAL (Canada).—Bank of British North America, 10; Commercial Bank of Canada; City Bank of Montreal, 52; Bank of Montreal, 52; Merchants Bank, 52; Ontario Bank, 52.

MOSCOW.—Wogan and Co.; Zanker & Co.; Ludwig, Prehn, and Grabe, 112.

MUNICH.—R. de Froelich and Co., 112.

MUSSOORIE.—The Delhi and London Bank, 41.

NANCY.—Jules Elic; Longlet and Co., 70.

NANTES.—Broussett and Sons; Rousselot, Allion, and Sons, 112.

NAPLES.—Anglo-Italian Bank, 5; Iggulden and Co.; W. J. Turner and Co.; Clauson & Co.; Rogers, Brothers, and Co., 70.

NEGAPATAM.—Oriental Bank Corporation. 89.

NELSON (New Zealand).—Union Bank of Australia, 110; Bank of New Zealand, 18; Bank of New South Wales, 14.

NEUFCHATEL.—Pury & Co.; N. du Pasquier & Co.

NEWCASTLE, HUNTER'S RIVER (N. S. W.)—Bank of Australasia, 9; Bank of New South Wales, 14; Bank of New Zealand, 18; Australian Joint-Stock Bank, 8.

NEWFOUNDLAND. — Union Bank, 70; Harvey, Tucker, and Co., 112.

NEW ORLEANS.—Southern Bank, 70; Canal and Banking Company, 70; Citizens' Bank, 70.

NEW YORK.—Bank of California, 89; Bank of Montreal, 112; Bank of New York, 112; Blake, Brothers, 52; Chemical Bank, 70; Duncan, Sherman, and Co., 112; &c., &c.

NICE.—Garlone and Co.; Lacroix, Brothers, 112.

NINGPO.—Hongkong Bank, 59.

NUREMBERG.—Loedel and Merkel; Kalb, 112.

OPORTO.—Banco Alliança, 70; Banco Lusitano, 3.

ORLEANS.—Richanli and Co.; Forges & Co., 112.

OSTEND.—Bach and Co. 112.

OTAGO.—Union Bank of Australia, 110.

OTTAWA, (Canada).—Bank of British N. America, 10; Bank of Montreal, 70.

PALERMO.—Thomas Brothers; Lehn, Denniger, and Co.; Morrison and Co., 112.

PARIS.—Rothschild Brothers; F. M. Chaigneau, 112; Callagan and Co, 31; Charles Lafitte and Co., 70; E. Blount and Co., 52, 70, 112; M. André and Co.; Pedro Gil; Vanden Brock Brothers and Co.; Bowles, Drevet, and Co., 112; Comptoir d'Escompte, 112.; &c. &c.

PARMA.—G. B. Campolonghi, 112.

PATRAS.—Barff, Hancock, and Co.; Ionian Bk, 65.

PAU.—Bergerot and Co.; The English Bank; Musgrave Clay, 112.

PERNAMBUCO.—English Bank of Rio de Janeiro, 47; London and Brazilian Bank, 71; Mills, Latham, and Co, 112.

PENANG.—Chartered Mercantile Bank of India, London, and China, 31.

PERU.—London Bank of Mexico and S. America, 69.

PHILADELPHIA.—G. C. Carson and Co.; Wells, Fargo, and Co., 112.

PICTOU.—Bank of Montreal, 112.

PIETERMARITZBURG.—Natal Bank, 71; London and South African Bank, 74; Standard Bank of British South Africa, 106.

PISA.—F. Pevereda; Maquay, Pakenham, and Smyth, 112.

PONDICHERRY.—Oriental Bank Corporation, 89.

PORT ADELAIDE, (South Australia).—Union Bank of Australia, 112; Bank of South Australia, 112; National Bank of Australasia, 85.

PORT ALBERT.—Bank of Victoria, 17.

PORT AUGUSTA.—National Bank of Australasia, 85.

PORT CHALMERS, (Otago).—Bank of Otago, 15.

PORT ELLIOT.—Bank of South Australia, 105.

PORT ELIZABETH.—London and South African Bank, 74; Standard Bank of British South Africa, 106; Port Elizabeth Bank, 70.

PORT MACDONNELL.—National Bank of Australasia, 85.

PORTLAND, (Victoria).—United Bank of Australia, 112; Bank of Australasia, 9; Bank of Victoria, 17.

PORT LOUIS, (Mauritius).—Oriental Bank Corporation, 89; Chartered Bank of India, London, and China, 30.

PRAGUE.—M. Block and Son; E. Rosenfeld; L. Söhne.

PRINCE EDWARD ISLAND, Bank of. 112.

QUEBEC, (Canada).—City Bank; Bank of British North America, 10; Bank of Montreal, 112; Bank of Quebec, 112.

QUEENSLAND, (New South Wales).—Union Bank of Australia, 112; Bank of New South W., 14.

QUEENSTOWN, (Otago).—Bank of Otago, 15; Bank of New Zealand, 18.

RANGOON.—Chartered Bank of India, Australia, and China, 30.

RHEIMS.—Ruinart; A. Camuset and Co., 112.

RICHMOND, (New South Wales).—Bank of New South Wales, 14.

RICHMOND. (South Africa).—Standard Bank of British South Africa, 106.

RIGA.—Mitchell; Wöhrmann and Son, 112.

RIO DE JANEIRO.—Bank of Brazil; London and Brazilian Bank, 72; English Bank of Rio de Janeiro, Limited, 47.

RIO GRANDE DO SUL.—London and Brazilian Bank, 72.

ROCKHAMPTON.—Union Bank of Australia, 110; Australian Joint Stock Bank, 8; Bank of New South Wales, 14.

ROUEN.—Delafosse; Pécuchet and Lainé, 112.

ROME.—Freeborn and Co.; Maquay, Pakenham, and Hooker, 112; Plowman, Cholmeley, and Co., 112.

ROSARIO.—London and River Plate Bank, 73.

ROTTERDAM, Bank of, 112.

SALONICA.—Imperial Ottoman Bank, 73.

SALZBURG.—J. Spath, jun., and Co.; Spangler and Trauner, 112.

SANDHURST, BENDIGO, (Victoria).—Bank of Victoria, 17; Bank of Australasia, 9; Union Bank of Australia, 110; Bank of New South Wales, 14; Colonial Bank of Australasia, 36; Oriental Bank Corporation, 89.

SAN FRANCISCO.—Messrs. F. H. Grain and Thos. Menzies, Agents of Bank of British North America, 10; Bank of British Columbia, 11; London and San Francisco Bank; Wells, Fargo, and Co., 112.

SCHAFFHAUSEN.—C. G. Hunter; Zündel and Co.

SEVILLE.—Cahill, White, and Beck; J. P. Lacave and Co., 112.

SHANGHAI, (China).—Chartered Mercantile Bank of India, London, and China, 31; Oriental Bank Corporation, 89; Hongkong and Shanghai Banking Corporation, 59; Comptoir d'Escompte, 112.

SINGAPORE.—Chartered Mercantile, 31; Oriental Bank Corporation, 89; Australia and China; Hamilton, Gray, and Co., 30; Hongkong and Shanghai Banking Corporation, 59.

SPA.—Henri Hayemal.

ST. CROIX.—Colonial Bank, 35.

ST. GALL.—J. J. Mayer, jun.; G. Zyli.

ST. JOHN'S (Newfoundland).—Commercial Bank of Newfoundland, 77.

ST. JOHN (N.B.)—Bank of British North America, 10; Bank of New Brunswick, 115.

ST. KITTS.—Colonial Bank, 35.

ST. LUCIA.—Colonial Bank, 35.

ST. MALO.—P. Fontan; Lemoine, 112.

ST. OMER.—A Caffieri; E. Deneuville, 112.

ST. PETERSBURG. — Blessig and Co.; Anderson and Co.; St. Petersburg Commercial Joint Stock Bank, 112.

ST. SEBASTIAN.—J. and F. Brunet, 112.

ST. THOMAS.—Colonial Bk.; Bk. of St. Thomas, 112.

ST. VINCENT.—Colonial Bank, 35.

STOCKHOLM.—Tottie and Co.; Stockholm's Enskilda Bank, 112.

STRALSUND.—F. A. Spalding and Son, 112.

STRASBURG.—E. Klose & Co., 112.

STUTTGARD.—Sons of G. H. Keller; Benedict Bros.; Hahl and Federer, 112.

SUEZ.—G. West, 112.

SYDNEY (N.S.W.)—Union Bk. of Australia, 110; London Chartered Bank of Australia, 76; Oriental Bank Corporation, 89; Commercial Banking Company of Sydney; Bank of New South Wales, 14; Australian Jnt. Stock Bk., 8; Bank of Australasia, 9; English, Scottish, and Australian Chartered Bank, 48.

TASMANIA.—Union Bank of Australia, 110.

TORONTO (Upper Canada).—Bank of British North America, 10; City Bank of Montreal, 52; Commercial Bk. of Canada, 77; Bk. of Toronto, 33; Bank of Montreal, 112.

TOULON.—Trabaud Bros.; Fauchier and Co., 112.

TOULOUSE.—Courtois and Co., 112.

TOURS.—Gouin Brothers, 112.

TRIESTE.—T. G. Sirovich; Moore and Co., 112.

TRINIDAD.—Colonial Bank, 35.

TURIN.—Nigra Brothers; Vincent, Teja and Co. Anglo-Italian Bank, 5.

UTRECHT.—Vlaer and Kol, 112.

VALENCIENNES.—Dupont and Co.; E. Lefebvre and Co., 112.

VALENCIA.—White, Llano, and Morand, 112.

VENICE.—Schielin Brothers; S. and A. Blumenthal and Co., 112.

VERA CRUZ.—C. Markoe; McCalmont, Bros. & Co.

VICHY.—G. Pommier and Co.; A. Butin and Co.

VICTORIA (Port Philip).—Union B. of Austral., 110.

VICTORIA WEST.—Standard Bank of British South Africa, 106.

VICTORIA (Vancouver Island).—Bank of British North America, 10; Chartered Bank of British Columbia, 11; Wells, Fargo and Co., 112.

VIENNA.—H. M. Weikersheim and Co.; Henikstein and Co.; L. Epstein; M. L. Biedermann and Co.; Fred. Schey; Anglo-Austrian Bk., 6.

VIRGINIA (U. S.)—Wells, Fargo and Co., 112; Bank of California, 89.

WARSAW.—S. A. Fraenkel, 112.

WASHINGTON.—Biggs & Co.

WELLINGTON (New Zealand). — Union Bank of Australia, 110; Bank of New Zealand, 18; Bank of N. South Wales, 14; Bank of Australasia, 9.

WIESBADEN. —Marcus Berle; Bernhard Berle; C. Kalb, jun., 112.

WILDBAD.—W. Klumpp, 112.

WOOLONGONG.—English, Scottish, and Australian Chartered Bank, 48.

WORMS.—J. P. Valckenberg, 112.

YOKOHAMA.—Chartered Mercantile Bank of India, London and China, 31; Oriental Bank Corporation, 89; Hongkong and Shanghai Banking Corporation, 59.

ZANTE.—Ionian Bank, 59; Barff & Co., 39.

ZURICH.—G. Schultess; M. Pestalozzi, 112.

DISCOUNT, FINANCE, AND LAND COMPANIES.

AUSTRALIAN MORTGAGE LAND AND FINANCE COMPANY (Limited).—72, Cornhill.

CITY DISCOUNT COMPANY (Limited).—3, Sun Court, Cornhill. *Managers*, John Cooper, R. T. Craig.

CREDIT FONCIER OF ENGLAND (Limited).—St. Clement's House, Clement's Lane, Lombard Street. *Governor*, James Levick.

CREDIT FONCIER OF MAURITIUS (Limited).—17, Change Alley, Cornhill. *Secretary*, W. G. Dick.

EAST INDIA LAND CREDIT AND FINANCE COMPANY (Limited).—5, East India Avenue. *Manager*, C. L. Nicholson.

ENGLISH AND FOREIGN CREDIT COMPANY (Lim.) —3, Winchester Buildings. *Manager*, J. W. Batton.

GENERAL CREDIT AND DISCOUNT COMPANY (Lim.) —7, Lothbury. *Manager*, J. Macdonald.

INTERNATIONAL FINANCIAL SOCIETY (Limited).— 60, Threadneedle St. *Manager*, W. Hope.

LONDON FINANCIAL ASSOCIATION (Limited).— South Sea House, Threadneedle Street. *Manager*, A. Wildy.

NATIONAL DISCOUNT COMPANY (Limited).—33, Cornhill. *Manager*, R. P. Wobber.

NEW CONSOLIDATED DISCOUNT COMPANY (Lim.)— 28, Clement's Lane, Lombard Street. *Manager*, S. Baker.

UNITED DISCOUNT CORPORATION (Limited.)—34, Abchurch Lane. *Managing Directors*, J. Bruce, H. S. Coulson.

WARRANT FINANCE COMPANY (Limited).—62, Gresham House, Old Broad Street. *Secretary*, J. A. Mann.

PRIVATE BILL OR DISCOUNT BROKERS.

Alexanders, Cunliffes and Co., 30, Lombard St.
Brightwen and Co., 8, Finch Lane.
Harwood, Knight and Allen, 33, Abchurch Lane.
R. Lawes and Co., 26, Birchin Lane.
B. S. Phillips and Co., 19, Birchin Lane.
Roger Cunliffe, Sons & Co., 6, Princes St., Bank.
Sanderson and Co., 7, Nicholas Lane.
Spencer, Hobbs and Co., 11, George Yard, Lombard Street.
Gillett, Bros. and Co., 72, Lombard Street.
John Green, 6, Nicholas Lane.
W. Shipman and Co., 12, Clement's Lane.

N.B. The above are recognized discount or bill brokers; but there are many other firms that pursue the same business in the City.

IMPORTS AND EXPORTS OF BULLION, FOR 1867.

The total Imports of gold and silver bullion and specie for the year 1867, amounted in computed real value to £23,821,047, being in the following proportions:

Gold	£15,800,159
Silver	8,020,888
	£23,821,047

This amount gives a value of about 10½ millions sterling less than in 1866, and in excess of about 2¾ millions over that of 1865. In 1867, there were 8⅓ millions less of gold imported and about 2¼ millions less silver than in 1866.

The Exports for 1867 were as follows:

Gold	£7,890,079
Silver	6,437,210
	£14,327,289

or, 7¾ millions less than in 1866, in the proportions of nearly 5 millions gold and 2¾ silver.

Of the total Imports of gold and silver in 1867, the following amounts, in computed real value, were received from each country named:

Russia, £61,446; Hanse Towns, £216,682; Holland, £37,142; Belgium, £23,338; France, £1,388,462; Portugal, &c., £341,244; Spain, &c., £26,751; Gibraltar, £89,978; Malta, £54,312; Turkey, £52,328; Egypt, £106,388; West Coast of Africa, £149,430; British Possessions in Africa, £22,425; British India, £205,328; Australia, £5,801,720; British Columbia, £2,335; British North American Provinces, £148,718; Mexico, South America (except Brazil), and West Indies, £7,840,862; Brazil, £688,141; United States, £6,498,006; and from other countries, £66,005. The maximum Imports of gold into the United Kingdom from all parts, during the last nine years, was in 1866: whilst the minimum was in 1861. The largest Imports of silver occurred in 1859, and the smallest in 1861, during the same period. The recent discoveries of deposits of gold at the Cape of Good Hope will most probably much modify the statement of imports of gold during the next few years, should the statements of the richness of the gold-bearing districts be borne out by facts.

COINAGE OF 1867.

An interesting return was made to Parliament in June, 1868, giving an account of the weight of metal, number and nature of the pieces, value, &c., of the money coined at the British Mint during the years from 1858 to 1867 inclusive. The following extracts are for the year 1867 alone. No silver groats, or fourpenny pieces, have been coined during the last eleven years, nor any half-crowns since 1851. In 1867 no sovereigns were coined. Fractions of an ounce are omitted in the following table.

GOLD COINAGE, 1867.

	Weight in Ounces.	Number of Pieces.	Value in pounds Sterling.
Half-Sovereigns...	127,485 ...	992,795 ...	496,397

SILVER COINAGE.

Florins	154,080 ...	423,720 ...	42,372
Shillings	393,140 ...	2,166,120 ...	108,306
Sixpences	123,840 ...	1,362,240 ...	34,056
Threepences	32,604 ...	717,288 ...	8,966

The total value of silver coined during 1867 was £193,842, and the actual cost of the metal employed amounted to £195,446. In the ten years 1858 to 1867 inclusive, the total value of the gold coinage issued was £47,112,569, and the number of pieces 13,338,143. The total value of the silver coinage for the same period was £3,554,722. In respect to the copper coinage in 1867, there were 5,483,520 pence, worth £22,848; of half-pence, 2,508,800, worth £5,226; and of farthings, 5,017,600, worth £5,226; the total value of copper coinage being £33,301. No half-farthings have been coined during the last eleven years. In 1867 worn silver coins, weighing 376,142 ounces, were re-coined; of the nominal value of £120,000; the loss being £16,560. The yearly average cost of silver to the Mint was 60¾d. per ounce troy.

BANK OF ENGLAND NOTE ISSUES.

A Parliamentary paper issued in July, 1868, gives the weekly issue of notes by the Bank during 1867 and 1868, stating also the value of each note; the amount held by the public; and that held by the Bank, with the weekly stock of bullion. As a resumé, it may be stated, that the total weekly issue of notes varied from about 33 to 38 millions sterling; the amount of bullion from 18 to 22 millions; the notes held by the public from 22 to 25 millions; by the Bank from 10 to 15 millions; the securities being constantly estimated at 15 millions. The number of £5 notes issued weekly was from 8 to 9 millions; of £10 notes, between 4 and 5 millions; of £20 to £100 notes, about 7 millions; £200 to £500 notes, 2 millions; and £1,000 notes about the same value in pounds sterling. The weekly averages of each varied, comparatively speaking, but little, considering the amount of the transactions during the whole period of sixteen months.

THE year 1867 was an anomaly in the history of trade. A low rate of discount—not 2 per cent. during the latter half of the year—a general depression of trade and consequent lowness of prices in every department of manufactures and commerce—universal retrenchment of expenditure in respect to domestic management, with all the signs of "want of business," may be considered as an epitome of the commercial position of the year. But the cause of all these commercial and social misfortunes is easily arrived at. In 1866 and 1867, some of the most gigantic failures that ever occurred took place. In financial circles, it is only necessary to refer to the stoppage of Overend, Gurney, & Co., a firm that had previously held a position second only to one of the first-rate banks. Following this, were failures of several banking establishments, and of a great number of Limited Liability Companies, that shook the confidence of the entire community. The panic thus occasioned has in its effects yet to be recovered from. The sufferers were chiefly of a class who depended on the dividends arising from such companies as a constant means of support. The absence of these dividends, the calls to fulfil engagements of the bankrupt companies, and a decline in the value of nearly all but Government securities, added to a deficient harvest and other causes, prevented the possibility of fresh investments, or of ordinary expenditure in retail trade ; consequently, those who had money to invest dared not run any risk beyond that afforded by first-rate securities, which were sought for with avidity by large capitalists ; and securities of a lower nature were beneath the notice of all but the most venturous speculators.

It need scarcely be remarked, that all investors exercised the greatest caution. Whether in financial or in commercial circles, the utmost absence of speculation was manifested. The great stimulus to trade is the usual method of advances made on warrants and other securities, representing saleable goods, such as cotton, hemp, wool, wines, &c. But the want of confidence, not only in regard to the variation of prices, but even the reliability on the solvency of those promoting such transactions, rendered nugatory all attempts to create either an ordinary natural or artificial demand. To these causes may be added the *laches* of certain railway companies ; foremost in which, financially speaking, were the London, Chatham, and Dover ; the Brighton ; and Great Eastern lines. With respect to the results of these causes on private individuals, it may be sufficient to state, that early in the year 1868, the Inland Revenue Department at Somerset House received notice from 1600 persons that they should discontinue keeping private carriages, claiming to be exempt from the tax incidental thereto, in the year 1868-9, a step that will cause a loss of revenue equivalent to £10,000 per annum. The year 1867 may with justice be characterized as a "black year" in a commercial sense ; happily, however, so far as can be at present judged, relieved by the prospects which the excellent and early harvest of 1868 seemed to afford.

CORN AND SEED FOOD TRADE.

The seasons of 1867 were generally unfavourable to all kinds of grain. April opened with an almost summer-like aspect, whilst it will be remembered that the "Derby-day" was characterized by a snow-storm never equalled in severity during the previous winter. The harvest time, August, unlike that of 1868, was cold and cheerless. Throughout Europe, extreme changes of temperature were constant, and consequently the harvest products, as a whole, fell below an average, extending in some cases to between 33 and 50 per cent. In respect to the United Kingdom, the imports of grain and flour were of value equal to £40,000,000, against £29,800,000 in 1866, an amount causing an extra charge of about 6s. 8d. on each member of the population for the year. The average yield per bushel of wheat did not exceed 60 lbs., a loss equal to 3 per cent. on the average of ordinary years. Oats, rye, and other cereal crops were equally defective. Barley afforded an excellent average in consequence of a greater breadth of land having been sown.

BEANS and PEAS suffered greatly from the weather.

POTATOES.—This crop, like those already named, suffered greatly from the extremes of temperature, and inconstant, or more properly speaking, constant changes of the weather. The average result of the harvest was estimated at half that of an ordinary one.

FLOUR.—America and Russia largely supplied the deficiency of our wheat in grain, the latter country alone affording 14,000,000 cwts. In this respect, Australia also assisted. The importation of flour in 1867, from all sources, was about 3,600,000 cwts., of which the greater portion came from the United States.

The following table gives the total imports of corn or cereals during the year, for the United Kingdom :—

IMPORT OF CEREALS, &c., DURING 1867.

	cwts.
Wheat	34,505,206
Barley	5,728,208
Oats	9,415,335
Peas	1,580,710
Beans	1,983,928
Indian Corn, or Maize	8,506,181
Flour	3,589,116

The total importation of wheat and wheaten flour from all countries in 1867, was 38,238,742 cwts., against 28,128,609 cwts., or 36 per cent. in excess of the quantity imported in 1866.

Taking the whole year, the average price of wheat, in England and Wales, was 64s. 5d., or

14*s.* 5*d.* above that of 1866; the average, in 1866, being 50*s.*, in 1865, 41*s.* 1½*d.*, in 1864, 40*s.* 3*d.*, and in 1863, 44*s.* 8*d.*

The total arrivals of wheat during the first seven months of 1868 were in excess of those of 1867 to the extent of about 17 per cent. The total importation for the period was 20,706,791 cwts., of which Russia contributed 26 per cent., the United States 22 per cent., Germany 19 per cent., Turkey and Egypt each 12 per cent., the remainder being of minor importance. Russia and Germany supplied less than in 1867, whilst there was a great increase from the United States and Egypt. According to the returns of the Board of Trade, published in September, 1868, there were in the United Kingdom a total of 3,933,924 acres under cultivation for wheat, 2,337,037 acres of barley land, and 4,452,060 acres of oat land, all showing an increase on the statistics of 1867. The fall of wheat in the Autumn of 1868 was equal to 33 per cent. on the prices at the same period in 1867, a result owing to the productive harvest of 1868.

CATTLE TRADE.

The abundant moisture of the early part of 1867 and some later portions of the year, while greatly inimical to the production of corn crops, improved those for pasturage. The season was, in fact, favourable for rearing and feeding all kinds of domestic animals. The imports from abroad fell off; partly, no doubt, owing to the unfavourable reports of the cattle plague, and the stringent regulations of our Government, in respect to cattle importation from the Continent. Formerly, the supply of the metropolis was chiefly maintained by driving cattle by road; but the facilities of the railroad system have not only caused almost all the cattle to be thus conveyed, but an immense number of slaughtered animals is thus sent up from even the north of Scotland. Generally, prices of live and dead stock ruled low. The fall of sheep was 14*d.* per stone of 8lbs. Calves fetched higher prices than in 1866, partly because the season proved good for rearing. Pork was by no means in good demand, and fell some 25 per cent. in price on an average. On this, it may be remarked, that the careless mode now adopted of feeding pigs degenerates their quality; and although for the present enhancing the profit, will soon have a bad influence on the market.

The *Metropolitan Cattle Market* is necessarily a test of the annual products of the kingdom, there being the greatest demand. The following table gives the amount of

HEAD STOCK ON SALE, 1867.

	Beasts.	Sheep and Lambs.	Calves.	Pigs.
January	18,150	82,400	756	1,508
February	17,140	79,710	1,091	1,970
March	14,460	95,600	1,100	1,800
April	16,250	113,770	977	1,805
May	19,860	160,370	1,709	2,260
June	16,270	146,650	2,609	2,048
July	18,870	136,480	3,117	1,755
August	20,030	124,190	2,653	2,205
September	25,290	127,510	1,565	2,979
October	28,340	103,870	1,129	2,865
November	24,080	109,960	1,016	2,350
December	21,910	92,490	943	1,880
Total	240,650	1,373,000	18,665	25,425

The preceding table, compared with 1866, shows a decrease in all respects. In that year, 256,855 beasts, 1,386,180 sheep and lambs, 19,012 calves, and 30,433 pigs, were sold at the Metropolitan market.

The current price of beef varied in 1867 from 3*s.* 2*d.* to 3*s.* 6*d.* for low; and from 5*s.* to 5*s.* 6*d.* for best qualities; of mutton from 3*s.* 2*d.* to 3*s.* 8*d.* and from 4*s.* 10*d.* to 6*s.* 2*d.* for respective qualities, per 8lb. stone, sinking the offal. Generally, the "cattle disease" had little effect. The imports for 1867 show a total of head stock equal to 765,080, being about 350,000 fewer than in 1866.

Of dead meat, either fresh or preserved, the imports of 1867 were 213,607 cwts., those of 1866 being 144,064 cwts., and 1865, 49,824 cwts. Further information on these subjects will be found at a subsequent page, for 1868.

TEA TRADE.

There are few articles of consumption that have been so much affected by a reduction of import duty as Tea. It is a matter of all but universal consumption in our country, and, in fact, has become a necessary of life by force of habit. Conventionally a "cup of tea" is a social requirement: hence the amount of its consumption, taken correlatively with other commodities, such as coffee, sugar, and malt liquors, may be taken as a test of commercial prosperity. Yet such a test may become deceptive, because a resort to the use of tea may supplant that of ordinary food, and malt liquors. A judicious examination, however, of the statistics afforded by the trade must be of great advantage to the political economist. The sale of tea by licensed victuallers introduced a new, and to their trade an anomalous element in respect to its consumption, and possibly will tend simultaneously to an increased consumption of that article, and to that of spirits, &c., for reasons that need not be here discussed.

In January, 1867, there was an advance in the price of Congou of from ½*d.* to 1*d.* per pound. February was characterized by large arrivals, and prices slightly receded. March showed great depression in respect to prices; while in April there was a partial revival. May witnessed a more gloomy period for the trade; whilst June, perhaps with its improved temperature, indicated a revival. The average for Black leaf in this month was about 1*s.* per pound. July showed a decline, owing to heavy shipments, amounting to 6*d.* per pound on "new make Congous," which were sold at from 2*s.* 2½*d.* to 2*s.* 3*d.*, compared to prices fetched May 23rd. The quality, however, was inferior. In August the market was in a depressed state. In September, on the arrivals of new teas, the prices of Oopecks varied from 1*s.* 6½*d.* to 2*s.* 5½*d.*, the teas above 2*s.* being good. October was a busy month in the trade. Fine Kaisows advanced considerably in value, 3*s.* 2*d.* being paid for best qualities for export. In November a fair business was done, Monings and Kaisows fetching from 2*s.* 2*d.* to 2*s.* 6*d.* per pound. Some parcels of Red-leaf were disposed of at from 14*d.* to 16*d.* per pound; but at a loss to the importers. In December the cargoes of the *Agamemnon* and *Lennox Castle*, consisting chiefly of Monings and Oopecks, were sold at from 1*s.* 6*d.* to 1*s.* 11*d.*, according to quality, showing a decline of from 1*d.* to 2*d.* per pound. The finest fetched 2*s.* 7*d.* Kaisows ranged from 2*s.* to 2*s.* 5*d.*, showing a decline of about 1½d. Common Red and Black-leaf fetched from 11½d. to 12½d. per pound.

The estimated imports of Tea into the United Kingdom for 1867 were 128,022,007 lbs., those for 1866 being 139,610,044 lbs. The delivery for home consumption, 112,500,000 lbs.; for exports 31,500,000 lbs. The average monthly delivery, 12,000,000 lbs. and the average price in bond, all considered as "Sound Common Congou," was 11¼d. per pound. The duty charged per pound was 6d., and the average stock on 31st December, 1867, was estimated at 84,000,000 lbs. The lowest price Congou fetched 5d.; the highest 1s. 10d.; Souchong varied from 11d. to 2s. 10d; Pekoe from 8d. to 1s. 10d.; best to 3s.6d.; scented Orange, from 13d. to 2s. 6d. per pound.

Generally speaking, the tea trade was dull during the early part of 1868. At the public sales of the new season's tea in September, 30,146 packages were offered for sale. Of these, some parcels were sold by private contract, and about 27,000 packages were sold by auction without reserve. Souchongs fetched from 1s 2d. per lb. for inferior to 1s. 6d. for fair quality, showing a reduction of 2d. to 4d. per lb. Other qualities were reduced in price from ½d. to 1d. per lb.

SUGAR TRADE.

The consumption of Sugar in this country is large, as it has different purposes. As a condiment to tea and coffee, and preserving vegetable and animal substances, in brewing, &c., it is an article of great commercial importance. In the early part of 1867 the trade was in a favourable condition; but in March, April, and May, depression existed. In June, an increase of prices, to the extent of 2s. or 3s. per cwt., was realized. But in subsequent months the trade became again depressed, to be revived, however, in September and October. In the middle of November, prices were 4s. 6d. above the highest range in January, giving an average rise of 25 per cent. on the lowest value. The markets then became dull, the prices closing for the year at an average advance of 1s. to 1s. 6d. per cwt. above those current in January. The prices between January 1st, 1867, and January 1st, 1868, for each quality of sugar, were as follows :—

	1867.	1868.
West India Muscovado, fine	34s. to 35s. 6d.	36s. to 36s. 6d.
Good	33s. to 33s. 6d.	35s. to 35s. 6d.
Middling	32s. to 32s. 6d.	34s. to 34s. 6d.

The prices of Demerara scarcely differed materially from the above. East India sugar fetched lower prices. Crystallized Mauritius varied from 34s. to 39s.; Ditto Yellow, 31s. 6d. to 33s. 6d.; low to brown, 26s. or 28s. to 30s. 6d. and 32s. 6d.; Penang, 27s. 6d. and 28s. 6d. to 34s. and 36s.; Natal, from 27s. 6d. to 35s. 6d.; Java, 34s. to 39s.; Manilla clayed, from 28s. 6d. to 31s. 6d.; unclayed, 24s. 6d. to 29s. All duty paid, per cwt. The importation in 1867 was as follows :—

	Tons.
Colonial	230,000
Foreign (raw)	290,000
Foreign (refined)	40,000
	560,000

Home consumption amounted, in all, to 590,500 tons; exportation, to 9,000 tons of raw, and

10,700 British refined; leaving an estimated stock of 127,500 tons on January 1st, 1868.

In 1868 the sugar trade was generally weak, owing to considerable stocks being on hand, which, however, were run down by the end of August. On the 31st of that month the stock amounted in the United Kingdom to 2,435,962 cwts. against 3,378,244 cwts. at the same date in 1867. Considerable business was done in the two following months, with a recovery of prices. Similar remarks apply to all descriptions of foreign sugar offered in our markets.

Of late years sugar produced from *beet root* has become a large import, and great quantities have been sent to various English ports from the continent, chiefly for the purpose of the distiller. In 1867-68 there were imported into England 2,244,884 loaves, 16,714 casks, 162,640 barrels and cases, and 160,839 sacks. The manufacture has long been pursued on the continent, which obtains its chief supplies from the beet as Great Britain does from the cane. Attempts have been made to produce this article on a large scale in New South Wales. The present area there under cultivation is 622 acres, and the absence of machinery is the only bar to still more extended operations.

The prices of sugar were as follows at the close of September, 1868 :— Jamaica, poor to fine, 34s. 6d. to 35s. 6d.; Demerara, 31s. to 34s.; Barbadoes, 31s. 6d. to 37s. 6d.; Mauritius, 34s. to 36s.; Antigua, 30s. to 34s. 6d.; Benares, 36s. to 40s. (white); Madras, 34s. to 41s.; Penang, 28s. 6d. to 38s.; and Natal, 28s. 6d. to 36s.

COFFEE TRADE.

Coffee, like tea, has become a necessary of the household; but the amount of its consumption is less than that of tea. They both exercise a great physiological effect on the human system. Tea acts as a sedative, whilst coffee is of a more exciting character. Each contains a peculiar principle, called either *Caffeine* or *Theine* according to its source, coffee or tea, but identical in character. The effect of coffee, however, is varied, owing to many chemical principles that it derives during the operation of roasting. From the commencement of 1867 to the close, the coffee trade was in a depressed condition. The year opened with an active demand, prices varying from 78s. to 82s. per cwt., though an advance of 2s. on previous rates. In February prices receded, recovering slightly in March, followed by a decline in April. May showed some improvement, checked by large arrivals in June. July showed a slight improvement, but excess of supply in August and September was followed by a reduction in prices. October showed slight improvement, lost in November, when prices ranged 1s. per cwt. less. In December, prices reached from 4s. 6d. to 6s. 6d. less than those current in 1867. The imports, estimated in 1867, were :—

	Tons.
Colonial	44,500
Foreign	19,000
	63,500

Entered for home consumption, 14,200 tons; for export, 44,000 tons; leaving an estimated stock, December 31st, of 20,000 tons. Current prices were: Ceylon, 63s. to 85s. 6d.; Mocha (in garbled), 106s. to 115s.: ungarbled, 70s. to 85s.; Java. 55s. to 88s.; Brazil, 48s. to 78s.; Costa Rica, 75s. to 83s. per cwt.

The coffee, like the tea trade, was generally dull in 1868. The stocks towards the close of the year were heavy, and the markets had little buoyancy. At the autumn sales most qualities fell in price. The receipts of East Indian coffee were in excess of those of 1867, but there were also large deliveries to the trade. Other kinds suffered a reduction in price.

RICE TRADE.

Of late years, Rice has become much more an article of food than formerly, still it is of comparatively small importance in that respect in temperate climes of Europe, compared to what it is in India, China, and Japan, where, to a large extent, it takes the place of our wheat and other cereals. Generally, throughout 1867, the trade was good. The total imports amounted to 106,620 tons; the delivery to 118,197 tons; and the estimated stock, December 31st, was 41,187 tons. Bengal fetched from 13s. 6d. to 16s. 6d.; other Indian species lower rates, running down to 10s. 6d. per cwt. The total amount landed in the first 44 weeks of 1868 was 97,038 tons against 36,133 tons in the same period in 1867. The estimated stock at the end of October, 1868 was 33,024 tons, against 13,072 at the same period in 1867. The prices on October 31, 1868 were as follows: Carolina kind, 32s. to 38s.; Java, 24s. to 34s.; Patna, 22s. to 24s.; Rangoon, 17s. 6d. to 21s., all of good qualities, per cwt.

SPICE TRADE.

This trade is of too limited a nature to require detailed remarks. *Ginger*, imported from Jamaica, fell in 1867 from 15s. to 18s. per cwt. common, and 5s. to 10s. per cwt. good. Cochin was generally steady; Bengal rose, in consequence of limited supply, from 2s. 6d. to 3s. per cwt., attaining a price of about 29s. African fluctuated much, running from 13s. to 30s. per cwt. *Cassia* varied from 107s. to 128s. *Cinnamon* rose from 3d. to 4d. per pound. *Cloves* were similarly affected. The same may be remarked in respect to *Nutmegs* and *Mace*. *Pepper* slightly above the average of previous years' quotations. The following are the total deliveries for the first 44 weeks of 1868. *Cassia Lignea*, 5,108 packages; *Cinnamon*, 10,493 packages; *Cloves*, 9,240 do.; *Ginger*, W.I., 14,078, E.L., 6,653 cases, and 5,140 bags, African, 7,032 bags; *Mace*, 334 packages; *Nutmegs*, 1,326 do.; *Black Pepper*, 4,888, *White do.*, 795 tons; *Pimento*, 10,202 bags. The prices in October, 1868 were as follows: *Cassia*, best, 144s. to 148s. per cwt.; *Cinnamon*, 2s. 6d. to 3s. 6d. per lb.; *Cloves*, 9½d. to 11d. per lb.; *Ginger*, Jamaica, 5s. 10d. to 10s. per cwt. African, 24s.; Cochin, finest, 120s. to 180s. per cwt.; *Mace*, 2s. 4d. to 3s. 2d. per lb.; *Nutmegs*, 2s. 6d. to 4s. 3d. per lb.; *Pepper*, best black, 4¼d. to 4⅝d.; White, 1s. to 1s. 9d.; *Cayenne*, 2¼d. to 8½d. per lb. In all the preceding quotations the prices of the higher qualities alone are named, the variations in the lower qualities being too numerous to mention.

FRUITS (Dried).

The trade was dull in the early part of the year. But towards May an advance of 2s. on all sorts of currants, and from 4s. to 6s. on Valentia raisins was obtained. Towards the close of the year the markets drooped. The prices of *Currants* varied from 24s. to 34s. per cwt.; of *Figs*, from 21s. to 65s. *Raisins*: *Valentia*, 23s. to 45s.; *Muscatel*, 42s. to 100s.; *Sultanas*, 40s. to 52s. *Almonds*, £6 to £12, all per cwt., according to

quality. In twenty years the consumption of currants has risen from 14,000 to 39,000 tons, thanks to the reduction of duty on import.

The total imports of *Currants* up to October, 1868, were 10,768 tons against 18,827 tons during the same period of 1867. Demand generally was active, with advancing prices. *Valentia raisins* imported during the same period were 6,499 tons against 6,828 for 1867. The deliveries in 1868 for home consumption were 20 per cent. less than in 1867. The supply of *Sultanas* was scanty, with improved prices. *Good Figs* were in demand, while inferior kinds were dull of sale. Average price of currants, 24s. per cwt.; raisins, 25s., the best fetching 52s. per cwt., duty paid.

WINE TRADE AND FOREIGN SPIRITS.

This department of commerce was an exception to the general depression witnessed in 1867. The trade was generally brisk and profitable, despite that the hope of a reduction of duty on Portuguese wines was disappointed. The home delivery of foreign wines showed a slight increase on that of 1866; the consumption was decidedly larger. The total estimated imports of all kinds of wines for 1867 amounted to about 145,000 pipes, 128,000 of which were entered for home consumption, 17,500 for export, leaving an estimated stock of 129,000 pipes. The imports of brandy were estimated at 39,500 puncheons. The home consumption 27,700; export, 3,250; leaving an estimated stock of 60,000 puncheons. In Port Wines there was a falling off to the extent of 1,500 pipes cleared compared with 1866. Marsala showed an increase. Prices generally ruled at a lower average, due to the abundant production of 1861 and 1865. The consumption of low spirit wines gained on that of strong wines. *Rum* showed a decided increase in home and export deliveries, with rise of prices. Brandy also showed an increase in home consumption; although there was a falling off in the imports of both, prices advanced. German spirits also advanced in price.

In the first seven months of 1868, ending July 31, there was an increased consumption of 864,161 gallons of wine in the United Kingdom, compared with the same period of 1867. Of this quantity, 672,528 gallons were passed as under 26° strength. The total of home-made spirits for the first six months of the year, entered for home consumption, amounted to 9,571,842 gallons; showing a decrease of 605,315 gallons for the corresponding half-year of 1867. Of the total, England consumed 5,317,574 gallons; Scotland, 2,048,640 gallons; and Ireland, 2,205,628, each showing a decrease. In the same period, 1,454,198 proof gallons of foreign brandy were entered for home consumption, being a slight increase on the similar half-year of 1867. The importation of rum was 1,898,168 proof gallons, showing a decrease of 216,614 gallons. Much depression ruled in the wine and spirit trades, arising from a variety of causes. Adulteration, generally, was greatly influential, by which, whilst more spirits are really consumed, the actual quantity of the pure article is decreased. Sherry was in good demand; port, slack; French wines were held in abeyance until the result of the '68 vintage was known, which turned out favourable. The Oporto vintage turned out small, the produce being estimated at 40,000 against 45,000 pipes in 1867. Oïdium never appeared, hence the condition of the grapes was excellent. In other parts of Portugal the yield was good and abundant.

MALT, HOPS, BEER, &c.

There can be little doubt that malt liquors are gradually superseding other kinds of fermented drinks. It is stated that on the continent, and especially in France, where wine is generally so cheap, the consumption of beer is steadily progressing. In England, if not in the whole of the United Kingdom, malt liquors are an undoubtedly favourite beverage. In the year 1867-68, ending March 31, the gross amount of duty collected on malt, and paid into the Exchequer, was £6,518,900, of which only about £325,000 was collected in Ireland. Of course a considerable proportion of the malt was employed in Scotland for the distillation of whisky, still a very large portion was used for the manufacture of malt liquors. Despite the general growth of barley produced in the United Kingdom, much is imported from abroad. In the seven months ending July 31st, 1868, there were imported 3,339,989 cwts., or about 330,000 less than in 1867, and 1,000,000 cwts. less than in 1866. The barley harvest in 1868 succeeded that of wheat, contrary to usual custom. According to general opinion the majority of the crop was inferior, and from 48s. to 50s. per quarter was the estimated price of good malting barley for the brewing season. In the western and south-western districts of England the crop was a fair average, but in Norfolk and Suffolk it was inferior. The estimate for the whole country placed the crop at 20 per cent. below the average. In Scotland the crop bore a fair average. Hops, although produced of the finest quality and in abundance in our own country, in Kent, Surrey, &c., are largely imported from abroad. In the period extending from August, 1867, to end of June, 1868, there were imported from all parts into the United Kingdom 316,501 cwts. against 84,396 in 1866-67 and 60,997 in 1865-66. The produce in England was generally good and abundant for the season of 1868.

The estimate crop of hops in 1868 was fixed at about 450,000 cwt., and prices were expected to range from 75s. for inferior to 105s. for best, per cwt.

According to the "declared or real" value of beer and ale exported in 1867, the value was fixed at £1,909,033. The official rates of valuation, however, only mention £479,849. The exports of British beer in the six months ending June, 1868, are stated as 295,881 barrels, with a declared value of £1,052,953, against £1,110,718 and £1,159,530 for the years 1867 and 1866 respectively, during the same period. The best customer for beer is British India. The following table gives the number of barrels exported and their declared value for the countries named during the first six months of 1868:—

	Barrels.	Declared Value.
United States	10,807	£51,744
British W. Indies and Guiana	13,036	45,750
British India	117,212	319,648
Australia	66,746	267,709
Other Countries	88,080	368,102
Total	295,881	£1,052,953

With the exception of the United States and Australia, our exports to all other countries decreased during the first six months of 1868, compared to a like period of 1867, and in some cases still more so when compared with the exports of 1866. A remarkable feature of the trade is, that although the number of breweries in the United States is gradually increasing, our exports of beer to that country are also on the increase.

WOOL TRADE.

This being one of the staple trades and manufactures of our country, exhibited the common characteristics of the year, it sharing in the general stagnation of commerce. The tendency of prices of the raw material was downwards throughout the year. The imports for 1867 were about 4,000,000 lbs. in excess of those of 1866. The exports were much larger than in that year, being an excess of £22,000,000 beyond those of 1866. Accumulation of stocks was not large. The exports of woollen yarn and manufactures, in value, for the first eleven months, reached £24,050,642 against £24,106,357 in 1866. The total import of *Australian and Tasmanian* wools amounted to 533,143 bales; of *East Indian* and *Persian* 46,461. In *Domestic wools* there was a considerable decline in prices throughout the year, amounting to about 30 per cent., the range being lower than in any other year since 1856. Of sheep-skins, 8,783 bales were imported from the River Plate districts. The import of Cape wools amounted to about 135,000 bales. Alpaca and Peruvian wools were less in import than in 1866. Prices were greatly reduced, amounting to about 30 per cent.

Generally speaking, the prices of all kinds of wool fell during 1868. New South Wales, that fetched 1s. 4d. to 2s. in March, fell 1d. in September. Port Phillip slightly increased in price, whilst Van Dieman's Land were stationary. New Zealand fell; East India advanced about 10 per cent. Peruvians were steady. Domestic wools, English, Scotch, and Irish, were only in languid request; but, as holders generally showed no disposition to sell, prices did not undergo material alteration. Sheep skins were in only limited demand, owing to the low prices of fine colonial wools, which affected those pulled from skins. Generally speaking, in August and September prices were in favour of buyers. The following are the comparative imports of all kinds of wool into Liverpool:—

	Bales.
From 1st January to 29th Sept., 1868	115,436
" " to 30th " 1867	164,764

Showing a decrease of about 50,000 bales as regards the imports for the similar period in 1867. There were 208,223 bales of wool sold at the London sales in August and September, 1868.

SILK TRADE.

This branch of industry, like other textile manufactures, experienced in 1867 great depression, owing to the general state of trade. The imports showed an increase of 500,284 lbs., an increased consumption of 73,062, and an increased stock, December 31st, 1867, of 265,222, and a great reduction in prices. The export of raw and thrown silk showed an increase of 100,000 lbs. The American demand for manufactures was very limited. China silk, for making satins, was in increased demand; and Japan sold well. European silk was in demand for best qualities. The average monthly deliveries for 1867 were:— of Bengal, 643 bales; China, 2,044; Canton, 390; Chinese thrown, 6; and of Japan, 662 bales. The prices of Bengal varied from 15s. to 24s. 6d. per pound; of China, from 18*s.* to 25*s.*; Canton, 15*s.* 6*d.* to 26*s.*; Japan, 32*s.* to 35*s.*; and of Italian Raw, from 40*s.* to 45*s.* Generally, prices at the end of 1867 were about 15 per cent. less than those fetched at the commencement of the year, the most steady being in respect to Italian silks, others showing considerable fluctuations.

The year 1868 opened with great dulness of trade, which continued for the first nine months. Towards the close of September, 1868, the stock of best and good China silk was by no means larger than a healthy trade would require, good prices being realized for the article when required, but purchasers only supplied themselves with just bare requirements. The prices of all other sorts were but nominal. In Japan silks the finest qualities were alone saleable at previous rates; other sorts were difficult of sale at a reduction of from 1*s.* to 2*s.* per pound. In Italian nothing was doing, and Bengal silks shared in the general reduction. The imports of silks from January 1 to September 23, 1868, were:

	Bales.
Bengal	5,976
China	25,111
Canton	3,941
Chinese (Thrown)	625
Japan	5,624
Bales	41,277

COTTON.

This, the chief staple of our manufactures, exhibited great signs of depression. As a rule, there was an uninterrupted fall in value, causing great loss to importers, the total fall in value on raw cotton averaging nearly 50 per cent. Uplands, that fetched 15*d.* in December, 1866, were sold at 10¼*d.* in April, 1867. Pernambuco fell from 15¾*d.* to 12*d.*; Egyptian, from 17*d.* to 13¾*d.*; and fine Bengal, from 9*d.* to 7*d.* In yarns, 40*s.*-weft fell during the same period from 20¼*d.* to 17½*d.*; 30*s.* twist from 20¼*d.* to 17¼*d.* Seven-pound shirtings from 11*s.* 6*d.* to 9*s.* 9*d.*, and 8¼lbs. from 13*s.* 3*d.* to 11*s.* 3*d.* The closing rates for 1867, compared with 1866, for raw cotton, were as follows:—

	1866	1867
Orleans	15⅜*d.*	7⅜*d.*
Pernambuco	15¾	7⅞
Egyptian	17	7¾
Smyrna	12¼	6
Dhollerah	12½	5½
Bengal	9	4⅝

The import of raw cotton for the year reached 3,500,771 bales, weighing 1,275,216,000 pounds; being a decrease of 248,270 bales, or 81,735,988 pounds, compared with 1866. The actual home consumption was 2,552,498 bales, weighing 954,517,505 pounds; being an increase of 7 per cent. over 1866. The weekly deliveries to the trade averaged 48,317 bales; the actual consumption (spinners having stocks in hand) was at the rate of 49,086 bales. The total export was returned as equal to 1,015,940 bales, showing a decrease of 121,525 bales. The estimated stock, officially declared at the close of the year, was 554,803 bales. The exports of cotton goods in 1867 were the largest on record, the excess over 1866 being 10 per cent. Yarns were exported in excess of that year to the extent of 17 per cent. It was estimated that the total import of raw cotton into Europe reached, in 1867, to about 4,213,000 bales. The estimated real consumption for Europe, in respect to countries, was:—Great Britain 954½, and the Continent 618½ millions of pounds. The total weight of yarns and manufactures produced in 1867 was estimated at 840 million pounds in Great Britain, being an increase of 8 per cent. on 1866. The value of the entire production was estimated at about £87,200,000, giving an average value of 24¾*d.* per pound; and the cost of production was estimated at £74,600,000, or at the rate of 21¼*d.* per pound.

Generally, throughout the first nine months of 1868, the cotton trade was dull. Prices, however, for the raw material, yarns, and manufactured goods experienced an advance on those of 1867, varying from 10 to 15 per cent. The total imports of raw cotton during the first nine months were as follows:—

		Bales.
From 1st January to 30th Sept.,	1868	2,590,186
,, ,, ,, ,,	1867	2,853,595

Showing a deficiency for 1868 of about 260,000 bales. In respect to prices for the comparative periods of the two years: Sea Island rose in 1868 to 24*d.* from 16*d.*; New Orleans from 9*d.* to 10½*d.*; Peruvians, from 8½*d.* to 10*d.*; Egyptian, from 8½*d.* to 10*d.* In East India cottons there was a general rise of at least 15 per cent. In yarns 30*s.*, water twist fetched 13*d.* against 10¾*d.* in 1867. Shirtings 39in. were quoted at 8*s.* 6*d.* in 1868 against 8*s.* 3*d.* in 1867. Domestics at 3*d.* against 2⅝*d.* in the latter year. The exports of both yarns and goods were in excess of 1867 in regard both to quantity and price.

LINEN.

This, like other textile trades and manufactures, was characterized by general dulness and depression throughout the year, with only occasional interruption. In preceding years, during the American Civil War, when the supply of cotton was so scanty, each department of flax, hemp, and jute manufactures was in the most flourishing condition. Hence the reaction that subsequently arose was the more severely felt. Various causes, beside the general depression of trade, also led to that of the linen manufacture. There was an inadequate supply of raw material; an over production of yarns and goods took place, stimulated by previous prosperity, and although the supply of raw material was diminished, yet manufacturers were compelled to keep their mills going by reducing the prices asked for yarns; and a similar cause also operated on manufacturers of cloth, who desired to keep from undue accumulation of stock. Short time and partial stoppage of machinery have since tended to mitigate this state of things. It must also be borne in mind, as already stated in our review of the cotton trade, that the reduction in the price of that article, equal to 50 per cent. on the prices of 1866, exercised perhaps the principal adverse action against the linen trade. Flax and jute did not greatly fluctuate in price during 1867, but the general tendency was to a fall in price. Jute kept a better and steadier price in the market. The imports of hemp were 70,637 tons, against 72,308 in the previous year. The demand for linen was generally languid. In eleven months ending November 30, 1867, there were imported but 65,943 tons against 68,028 in 1866. In respect to prices obtained for yarns, it may be remarked that generally they ruled in that year about the same as in 1860, that is, preceding the great rise in cotton, caused by its diminished supply. In the first eleven months of 1867, the total declared weight of linen yarns exported amounted to 31,598,000 pounds, of the value of £2,277,000 ; and of linen cloth, 198,070,000 yards, valued at £6,593,000. According to the report of the Board of Customs, there was a total falling off in value in regard to linen exports of all kinds, equal in round numbers to £2,000,000, during 1867. For the year the declared value of linen yarns for export was on an average 1s. 5d. per lb. ; of white and plain cloths, 7¾d. per yard ; of printed, checked, or dyed, 13d. ; and of sail cloth, 13d. per yard ; whilst thread for sewing was declared at 2s. 6d. per lb. It is estimated that in 1867, about 854,000 spindles were at work in about 86 factories, whilst in 44 factories for weaving, 15,000 power looms were in operation.

The year 1868 was by no means a prosperous one. The demand for most descriptions of goods was extremely sluggish, but the price of the raw material was not depressed, its supply having been inadequate to the consumption. Much Russian flax that used to be sent to Great Britain, was imported into France and Ireland, to supply the failure of the crops ; hence to Scotland (Dundee), the amount imported was deficient. Although the importation of the first nine months of 1868 exceeded the average of five preceding years, still the stock kept small. The great drought of 1868 much affected the growth of flax throughout Europe, inducing the possibility of great increase in price, that must unavoidably affect the prospects of spinners and manufacturers. Prices of Russian hemp advanced at least ten per cent. in the middle of the year, remaining afterwards without much fluctuation.

INDIGO.

This article, of so great importance in dyeing calicoes, afforded a remunerative trade to the importers, a somewhat remarkable circumstance, considering the extent to which gas colours have superseded it and other colour-sources. Central American Indigo was largely sold and consumed during 1867. Bengal advanced from 3d. to 4d. per pound during the May sales, and a further advance of from 3d. to 6d. occurred in August, with a fall at the October sales ; prospects very gloomy. The consumption of East India in Europe was estimated at 40,000 chests in 1867 ; and prices varied, according to quality, from 3s. 10d. to 9s. 3d. per pound. The trade in 1868 was similarly characterized.

LEATHER.

The trade was generally quiet, the demand, however, being steady throughout 1867, with reduction of stocks. Prices were, as a rule, uniform. The imports of foreign decreased to the extent of 440,000 cwts. compared with 1866, whilst the exports of our wrought slightly increased. In shipment of boots and shoes, there was a decrease, the amount being 3,238,414 against 3,739,304 in 1866. The prices of *English butts* varied from 13½d. to 31d. ; of *Foreign*, from 12d. to 24d. per pound.

718,031 salted hides were imported from the River Plate and the Rio Grande, showing an increase of 53,174 beyond 1866. In London hides there was a rise during the autumn of from 3s. to 5s. per hide, with a good supply.

The leather trade was generally dull during the first nine months of 1868. *English butts* held their prices, as did some of foreign supply. *Dressing hides* were generally scarce. *English horse hides* sold freely, whilst the *Spanish* were in less demand. *Curried leather* was in demand, some of the best shoe being scarce, causing a rise of price. *Foreign leather* scarcely varied in price. Generally speaking, prices were comparatively steady for the year in respect both to the raw and manufactured materials, no violent fluctuations in any department having occurred.

OIL AND TALLOW.

These trades ruled quiet and depressed, purchases being only made for immediate wants. In *Linseed* (seed) prices ran from 60s. to 62s. The oil ranged from £35 10s. to £37 in the early part of 1867, advancing to £39 in August, followed by a rapid decline in October to £34 10s. *Oil-cakes* met with an increased consumption. *Rape* and other oil-seeds greatly fluctuated. *Olive-oils* ranged from £55 to £66. Imports for the year were 20,273 tons. *Cocoa-nut Oil* ranged from £51 to £61. *Palm-oil* was steady at from £40 to £42 per ton, with imports to the extent of 38,088 tons.

Prices of tallow fluctuated to the extent of 3s. per cwt., varying from 42s. 9d. to 45s. 9d. The stock in hand on 31st December, 1867, was 39,400 casks. *Fish-oils* were unsatisfactory. *Sperm* varied from £125 in January to £110 at the close of the year.

The prices of most oils fell during 1868 for the first nine months. *Fish oils* suffered to the extent of 10 per cent. ; *Olive*, about 2 per cent. ; *Seed oils*, such as rape, &c., 25 per cent. ; cocoanut, 4 per cent. *Tallow* advanced about 10 per cent. in September. *Seeds* for producing oil also fell in price, varying from 10 to 20 per cent. *Turpentine* and *Resin* also fell, but comparatively to only a small extent in price. The imports of *Linseed* were 50 per cent. beyond those of 1867. *Palm oil* advanced in price, owing to the demand for tallow, it being largely employed in the candle and soap manufactures.

TANNING MATERIALS.

English oak bark, after advancing till March, and receding in price in June, 1867, maintained the opening quotations till the close of the year. *Foreign bark* was nearly stationary throughout the year. The import of *Mimosa bark* was large, with a greatly increased consumption and advanced prices. *Valonia* was greatly diminished in import, but prices fell. *Terra Japonica* fell in regard to import stock, and prices, as regards *Gambier Cutch*, greatly advanced, with diminished import and stock in hand. Similar remarks apply to this branch of trade in respect to the first nine months of 1868.

PETROLEUM.

This oil has been so abundantly produced from varied sources, in recent years, as to have greatly affected the oil market generally. Its uses as an illuminating agent, and also possibly as a substitute for coal, show its importance. The chief supply is drawn from the United States. The total shipment from America in 1867 amounted (to all ports of the kingdom) to 63,201,634 gallons, a trifle in excess of 1866. Prices varied from 13d. to 20d. or 22d. per gallon. *Petroleum Spirit*, at one time a drug, has become of value through the invention of a new kind of lamp, by which it may be safely burnt. This caused an advance of something like 300 per cent. on its value. *Paraffin oil* was dull of sale owing to the competition of American petroleum. The production of Scotland and Wales for 1867 was estimated at about 200,000 barrels, an amount far below the capabilities of our mineral and manufacturing resources in those districts.

Petroleum was in better demand during 1868 than in the previous year. The prices of different kinds were and will continue to be affected by the attempts that have been made to substitute various kinds of mineral oil for coal as fuel. In October, 1868, however, prices were slightly lower than at the same period in 1867 for all kinds except crude American. *Refined Paraffin* fell, while the *Coarse* rose in price. The same remarks apply to lubricating rock-oil and grease. *Paraffin Wax* was about 25 per cent. cheaper than in 1867.

CHEMICALS.

Generally the trade in 1867 was unsatisfactory, depending, as it does, on most branches of textile manufactures. *Soda-ash* declined from 2⅜d. per cent. to 2d. At the close of the year prospects not encouraging. *Caustic Soda* fell from 19s. to 15s. 6d. per cwt. *Crystal Soda* varied downwards from £5 15s. to £4 10s. per ton. *Bicarbonate* fell from 18s. 6d. to 13s. per cwt. *Bleaching Powder*, or *Chloride of Lime*, fell from 14s. 6d. to 10s. per cwt. *Bichromate of Potash* stood at about 5d. *Chlorate*, 1s. *Prussiate* (yellow), 1s. to 1s. 0½d. *Quicksilver* averaged about £7 per bottle for the year. *Saltpetre* ruled from 17s. 6d. to 19s. 6d. per cwt.; *Refined do.*, 22s. to 24s. *Nitrate of Soda*, so largely in demand as a manure, was steady, prices varying from 11s. 6d. to 12s. 6d., with an increased stock (3,565 tons) at the end of the year. *Brimstone*, or *Sulphur*, varied from £6 15s. to £7, the importation being 50,000 tons. *Refined do.*, £10 5s. per ton. *Flowers of S.* from 12s. to 14s. per cwt. *Crude Turpentine*, with low stocks, fetched from 9s. to 10s. per cwt. *Spirits of Turpentine* varied from 27s. to 28s. 6d., and the low price stimulating consumption led to increased shipments from America and the Continent. The early part of 1868 presented similar aspects in regard to the trade in Chemicals. Prices generally did not greatly fluctuate. At the end of September the following were current quotations: *Argol*, 60s. to 82s. per cwt.; *Ashes*, pot (Canada) 31s. 6d., pearl, (do.) 32s.; *Brimstone*, rough, 140s. to 142s. 6d., roll, 200s. to 218s., flour, 280s. to 290s. per ton; *Alum*, 150s. to 155s. per ton; *Borax*, 60s. per cwt.; *Potash*, bichromate, 5d.; chlorate, 13d.; *Prussiate*, 1s.; *Red do.* 1s. 10d.; *Prussian Blue*, 1s. to 1s. 10d. per lb.; *Saltpetre*, refined, 23s. 6d. to 24s. per cwt.; *Soda*, ash, per degree, 1¾d., bicarbonate, 11s. 6d. per cwt.; *Crystals*, 90s. per ton; *Sulphate of Quinine*, 4s. 3d. to 4s. 9d. per oz.; *Sulphate of Copper*, 24s. per cwt.; *Copperas*, green, per ton, 55s. to 60s.; *Iodine*, 9¾d. to 10d. per oz.; *Bleaching Powder*, £11 to £11 5s. per ton; *Common Salt*, 7s. 6d.. 11s., 13s. per ton; *Rock Salt*, 4s. to 6s. per ton; *Nitrate of Soda*, £14 to £14 10s. per ton for manuring and other purposes.

TIMBER.

The import into the port of London was one-fifth less, or 20 per cent. than the average of the four preceding years, in 1867. An increase of Swedish and Norwegian timber took place to the extent of 13 per cent. over 1866, and 8 per cent. of the four preceding years. Prussian timber fell off 55 per cent.; Russian was a fair average. From British America only one-half of the usual export arrived. Teak and hard woods fell off considerably. Colonial supplies were in general greatly contracted, owing to an increased demand in those countries to supply local wants. Generally, the tendency is to send timber sawn into deals, battens, &c., in place of the log, as was formerly the custom. Prices generally were steady. The total imports of Wood for the whole kingdom were estimated in 1867, as follows :—

	Loads.
Colonial sawn (deals, &c.)	670,000
Colonial and hewn (timber and hard woods)	430,000
Foreign sawn (deals, battens, boards, &c.)	1,200,000
Foreign hewn (timber and hard woods)	730,000
Colonial and Foreign Stores	58,000
Total in loads	3,088,000

In 1868 the timber trade was in a similar position to that of 1867.

TOBACCO.

This article of trade is of so universal consumption and productive to revenue as to place it amongst the most important of our imports and manufactures. In 1867, there was a total import from all parts of 57,586,287 pounds; of this quantity the United States furnished 37,547,166 pounds, being an increase of about 8,000,000 pounds on the preceding year, which arose from an improved condition of the labour market in that country, and a consequent increase of cultivation of the plant. A remarkable feature was in the export from Japan, which, while only 262,631 pounds in 1866, rose to 2,193,951 pounds in 1867. Holland ranked next in export, sending us 7,692,614 pounds; from Turkey we received about 2,300,000 pounds, and the total from all countries, excepting the United States, amounted to 20,039,121 pounds. The quantities of tobacco entered for *home consumption* showed a most trifling increase not exceeding one-tenth per cent. The quantities so entered were as follows :—

	Lbs.
Unmanufactured *stemmed*	18,292,768
Ditto *unstemmed*	21,816,315
Total	40,109,083
Manufactured	938,844
Total of all tobaccos	41,047,927

A feature in the trade is the increased rise of *stemmed* tobacco, equal in 1867 to 29 per cent.; and a decrease of *unstemmed*, equal to 16 per cent.

The imports of tobacco for the first eight months of 1868 were as follows :—

Stemmed	12,461,412 lbs.
Unstemmed	14,027,988 lbs.
	26,489,400 lbs.

Showing a trifling decrease compared with the same period of 1867; but, as in that year, indicating an increased importation of stemmed tobacco in preference to unstemmed. Trade was generally quiet during the year, but the crop for 1869 use was considered as highly satisfactory in regard to American sources of supply. The prices of stemmed tobacco advanced on those of 1867, while other qualities remained almost stationary.

MACHINE TRADE.

As regards machines required for manufacturing purposes generally, the business was dull throughout 1867. In Leeds alone one-fifth of the hands usually at work, in total amounting to over 2,500, were out of employ. From the commencement of the year to the close, a gradual decrease of work was experienced. The stagnation of trade at home, and the uncertain condition of Continental politics, alike influenced this result. Agricultural machines, however, were in great demand, and in this department business was generally good, owing to the adoption of steam machinery by farmers becoming universal.

SHIPPING TRADE.

In both wood and iron shipbuilding general and great depression, existed in 1867. On the Thames, this almost amounted to a suspension of the latter, causing the greatest distress in the eastern parts of the metropolis, at least 40,000 persons being rendered destitute of employ. The relative totals of shipbuilding in 1866 and 1867 were as follows for all parts of the kingdom:—

	Vessels.		Tons.
1866	2,734		736,499
1867	2,180		465,899
Decrease	554		270,600

Facts and figures that require no further remarks to impress with the discouraging character of the trade for the year. Shipbuilding on the Clyde—in respect to iron vessels—suffered less than at other ports, owing to the material being on the spot, and abundance of skilled labour at hand. The same may be remarked in reference to the Ports in the North of England; while the Mersey suffered similar depression to that of the Thames district, owing to many foreign vessels having passed into British hands. The total registered vessels show an increase for the year 1867 over that of 1866. The registered tonnage &c. were for—

	Vessels.	Tons.	Men.
1867	40,942	7,277,098	346,606
1866	40,912	7,297,984	346,799

The chief source of the increase of vessels was due to the sale of many belonging to the United States to British owners. In the first eleven months of 1867, British shipping decreased to the extent of 378 vessels, but increased in tonnage to the extent of 29,116 tons *entered inwards.* It increased by 1,309 vessels, registering 673,910 tons, *cleared outwards*; while *Foreign* tonnage decreased in comparison with 1866 to the extent of 1,034 vessels, registering 120,543 tons *entered inwards*; and increased 573 vessels, registering 160,990 tons, *clearing outwards* with cargo. In respect to the value of British shipping an improvement arose with a return of confidence in the money market. In respect to freights for long voyages, improvement was evident, but as emigration fell off the freights for Australia and New Zealand declined. The increased export of coal told favourably on shipping engaged in the trade. There were of course numerous causes that affected the shipping interest generally in 1867 and 1868, but, as will be seen by reference to the preceding accounts of our export and import trade, however depressed the home markets were, that depression had not so great an effect on our Colonial and Foreign business, all of which from our insular position can alone be carried on by shipping.

TRADE OF THE UNITED KINGDOM, BOTH FOR IMPORTS AND EXPORTS, AND IN TRANSIT, DURING 1867 and 1868.

The greatness of our manufactures is attested by the fact that there is scarcely a spot of civilized or savage world in which they are found unused. Even in mid-Africa, among the most uncivilized tribes, a knife, a piece of cloth, or some other article, attests the industrial activity of our country. The grand total value therefore of our imports and exports becomes a matter of interest to all, whether engaged in trade or not, and the following table, furnished by the Report of the Customs in 1868, gives all particulars for 1867:—

IMPORTS.	1867.
Merchandise from foreign countries	£214,466,719
Merchandise from British possessions	60,783,134
Bullion	23,821,047
Total	299,070,900

EXPORTS.	
MERCHANDIZE, viz.: BRITISH AND IRISH PRODUCE.	
To foreign countries	131,303,770
To British possessions	49,880,201
Foreign and colonial produce	44,873,165
Bullion	14,324,517
	240,381,653

There were transhipments the value of which was	6,555,527

By adding these three sets of figures together, viz., imports, exports, and transhipments, a grand total is obtained, representing the value of the entire trade of 1867 for the United Kingdom as equal to £546,008,080. This result indicates a decrease beneath the value of the most prosperous known year of £551,734,406, or about 8·6 per cent. Hence it follows that however much our internal or domestic trade may have suffered, this has not attained to an equal extent on home, foreign, and colonial trade taken *en masse.* The chief falling off in value in regard to exports existed in cotton, linen, woollen and worsted manufactures (cloth, hosiery, &c.), haberdashery and millinery, hardware and cutlery, and silk manufactures. There was a counterbalancing increased value of exports in cotton, linen, woollen and worsted yarn, copper and brass manufactures, coals, iron, unwrought steel, and steam-engines. The largest decrease, about £5,000,000, was in cotton manufactures. This was not owing to less quantity, which had an increase, but to depreciation of price, already noticed in the article on the cotton trade. The greatest falling off in exports to foreign countries was to the United States. The decrease for 1867, compared with 1866, was £6,673,811. The percentage of falling off in value of exports to all foreign countries was in 1867, against 1866, about 3 per cent., whilst the decrease in respect to exports to British possessions amounted to about 7 per cent. An increased value of about £7,500,000 took place generally in respect of exports to Continental Europe, excepting Turkey and Italy: the largest increase (£4,000,000) being to the Hanse Towns. There was also an increase in respect to exports to British India equal to about £1,800,000. The decrease in the value of foreign and colonial exports was equal to 10 per cent., that is about £5,000,000, chiefly arising from the reduced value of raw cotton exported by us to the Continent, which decrease to France alone equalled £3,100,000.

In respect to imports, the decrease of those brought from foreign countries was 4 per cent., or about £8,620,000. The decrease of British possessions imports was 16 per cent. or £11,420,000. The reduction of the price of cotton largely accounts for the amount of the first item. France and the United States are among our best customers, and from which we largely import. In 1867 our imports from France of all commodities, including corn, amounted in value to £33,740,660. The declared value of British and Irish exports to that country for the year was £12,121,010. The value of our exports to the United States in 1867 was £21,825,703, whilst the imports into this country from the States amounted to £41,047,949. It must be borne in mind that all the preceding figures for both countries refer only to the value of *produce* and *manufacture*, questions of coin, bullion, &c., not being included either in imports or exports. The preceding articles on each subject of produce or manufacture give detailed information in respect to each. The limits of our space forbid our entering into minute details of many others, but at the same time of minor importance than those already dealt with.

The Board of Trade Returns, published in September, 1868, show a general falling-off in business for the first eight months in the year. During that period the exports of British and Irish produce amounted in value to £116,777,023, or about £4,500,000 less than in the corresponding period of 1867; and £3,500,000 less than in 1866. Cotton manufactures, especially, show a decrease, but this does not so much affect the quantity as the price, for reasons already stated above. Next to cotton, the woollen and worsted manufactures, silk, hardware, cutlery, machinery, iron, and the metal trades suffered. The exports of beer, ale, leather, and fire-arms were improved. In goods imported free of duty there was a decrease in the following, compared with the similar period of 1867; viz: raw cotton, manufactures of cotton, guano, hemp, hides, gloves, metals, petroleum, paper and tallow. A small increase occurred in raw silk, Indian silk manufactures, wool and

woollen rags, Indian corn, cocoa, oats, brandy, molasses, and wine, which indicate increased home consumption; with important diminution in coffee, refined sugar, and tea. The value of wheat received was £15,320,539, but the import was at once checked on the favourable harvest which this country produced. The computed value of the imports for the seven months ending July 31 was £132,283,806, against £128,935,900 in 1867, and £143,544,759 in 1866.

The following were the estimated stocks of the articles named, in the bonded warehouses of this country, on August 31st 1868:—

Cocoa	6,612,345 lbs.
Coffee	62,216,713 „
Rum	7,093,964 galls.
Brandy	7,590,902 „
Sugar, unrefined	2,435,262 cwts.
Molasses	172,037 „
Tea	64,250,505 lbs.
Tobacco	58,483,741 „
Wine	13,736,613 galls.

In the above, coffee is greatly increased, rum suffered a decrease; brandy was in advance of 1867, sugar 33 per cent less, molasses nearly three times the stock of 1867; tea 14 per cent. decrease; tobacco nearly the same, and wine an almost equal stock to that of the corresponding period of the preceding year. Generally the prospects of trade would have been adverse, had it not been for the excellent harvest of 1868; and in closing these remarks it may be observed that, owing to the abundant supply of wheat, great hopes were held in October, 1868, that the future of trade would gradually become prosperous, and employment at last found for the large number of workmen unoccupied in nearly all the manufacturing districts. The fall in the price of bread, due to the harvest, prevented much suffering, and the mildness of the autumn also aided in that respect. An additional reason for the general improvement in trade, was traceable to the production of abundant pasturage, due to refreshing rains that succeeded the drought of summer. Added to, and consequent on, these causes, was a return of confidence in the money markets.

WHOLESALE PRICES OF MEAT IN THE LONDON MARKETS,

Per Stone of 8 lbs. to sink offal.

1867.

October.—Beef, 3s. 2d. to 4s. 6d.; Mutton, 3s. 4d. to 4s. 6d.; Veal, 3s. 10d. to 4s. 8d.; Pork, 3s. 10d. to 4s. 2d.

November.—Beef, 3s. 2d. to 4s. 6d.; Mutton, 3s. 2d. to 4s. 6d.; Veal, 3s. 8d. to 4s. 6d.; Pork, 3s. 2d. to 4s. 4d.

December.—Beef, 3s. 0d. to 4s. 6d.; Mutton, 3s. 0d. to 4s. 6d.; Veal, 3s. 8d. to 4s. 6d.; Pork, 3s. 0d. to 4s. 2d.

1868.

January.—Beef, 4s. 4d. to 5s. 0d.; Mutton, 4s. 4d. to 5s. 2d.; Veal, 5s. 0d. to 6s. 0d.; Pork, 3s. 8d. to 4s. 4d.

February.—Beef, 4s. 4d. to 5s. 0d.; Mutton, 4s. 6d. to 5s. 4d.; Veal, 5s. 0d. to 5s. 8d.; Pork, 3s. 8d. to 4s. 4d.

March.—Beef, 4s. 4d. to 5s. 2d.; Mutton, 4s. 8d. to 5s. 4d.; Veal, 5s. 0d. to 5s. 8d.; Pork, 3s. 8d. to 4s. 4d.

April.—Beef, 4s. 4d. to 5s. 2d.; Mutton, 4s. 8d. to

5s. 6d.; Veal, 5s. 0d. to 5s. 8d.; Pork, 3s. 8d. to 4s. 4d.; Lamb, 7s. 0d. to 8s. 0d.

May.—Beef, 4s. 4d. to 5s. 2d.; Mutton, 4s. 2d. to 4s. 10d.; Lamb, 6s. 8d. to 7s. 4d.; Veal, 4s. 8d. to 5s. 4d.; Pork, 3s. 8d. to 4s. 4d.

June.—Beef, 4s. 4d. to 5s. 2d.; Mutton, 4s. 0d. to 4s. 10d.; Lamb, 5s. 8d. to 6s. 6d.; Veal, 4s. 8d. to 5s. 6d.; Pork, 3s. 8d to 4s. 4d.

July.—Beef, 4s. 4d. to 5s. 0d.; Mutton, 4s. 4d. to 5s. 6d.; Lamb, 4s. 8d. to 5s. 8d.; Veal, 4s. 2d. to 5s. 0d.; Pork, 3s. 8d. to 4s. 4d.

August.—Beef, 4s. 2d. to 5s. 0d.; Mutton, 4s. 2d. to 4s. 10d.; Lamb, 4s. 8d. to 5s. 6d.; Veal, 4s. 0d. to 5s. 0d.; Pork, 3s. 8d. to 4s. 4d.

September.—Beef, 4s. 8d. to 5s. 8d.; Mutton, 4s. 6d. to 5s. 6d.; Lamb, 4s. 8d. to 5s. 4d.; Veal, 4s. 8d. to 5s. 6d.; Pork, 4s. 0d. to 4s. 10d.

October.—Beef, 4s. 4d. to 5s. 4d.; Mutton, 4s. 8d. to 5s. 4d.; Veal, 4s. 8d. to 5s. 6d.; Pork, 4s. 4d. to 5s. 0d.

EXCLUSIVE OF BULLION, &c., INTO AND FROM THE UNITED KINGDOM, FOR 1866-67.

In the Commercial Summary of this Almanack the Imports and Exports of each leading article of trade and manufacture, incident to our commercial occupations, have already been given, together with a total or summary of the same within certain periods therein specified. In the following tables the individual amounts, in respect to each country, are also afforded. According to the last annual return of the trade and navigation of the United Kingdom, the total Imports and Exports, &c., for the years stated, were as follows:—

Imports (1866) £295,254,274
" (1867) 275,183,137

The Exports for the same periods were:—
British Produce (1866) £188,917,536
" (1867).................. 180,961,923
Foreign and Colonial Produce (1866) 49,988,146
" (1867) 64,873,165

The total real value of the Imports and Exports of merchandise for the years specified, including British, Foreign, and Colonial Produce, were:—
1866 .... £534,195,956
1867 501,018,228

Showing a falling off of about 33 millions sterling, or about 6 per cent. But it must be borne in mind that although, apparently, there is a decrease in the value of both Imports and Exports, yet another item of great importance affects the result, generally, in every branch of trade; the price of the raw material fell largely in 1867. In cotton alone the depreciation of price equalled 50 per cent. (See remarks on the *Cotton trade* in the Commercial Summary.) Hence, relatively, our Exports, although nominally of less value in regard to price, exceeded, in 1867, with respect to quantity, those of 1866. Similar remarks apply to the question of Imports, for reasons of analogous, if not identical, characters.

In the returns, for which we are indebted for the following statistics, it is stated, that in the years specified below, the Imports of merchandize (excluding bullion and specie) were:—

From Foreign   1866.   1867.
Countries   £223,048,552   £214,448,592
From British
Possessions...   72,205,722   60,734,545
Giving the total already stated.

It here appears, that in all respects an apparent diminution occurs in 1867 to all the items of Imports and Exports, yet the total weight of each commodity was in excess of that of 1866.

In the following tables a detailed account is given of the Imports and Exports in regard to each country with which we have commercial relations. The *real* value of both total Imports and Exports is given. A considerable difference exists between the *real* and *computed* value, but the trade returns, followed statistically by the Government, depend on the tables here given.

TOTAL IMPORTS.

Foreign.	1866.	1867.
Russia	£19,624,680	£22,286,926
Sweden	4,001,856	4,756,503
Norway	1,611,359	1,721,362
Denmark Proper	2,167,920	2,511,456
Iceland, &c.	123,989	77,465
Danish West Indies......	107,993	184,830
Prussia..........................	6,866,751	7,383,619
Sclswg-Holstn; Lauenbg.	837,120	973,484
Carried forward ...£	35,341,668	39,895,645

	1866.	1867.
Brought forward ...... £	35,341,668	39,895,645
Hanover	311,557	559,434
Mecklenburg-Schwerin...	463,664	508,570
Oldenburgh; Kniphausen	32,664	66,618
Hanse Towns...................	10,576,831	9,415,188
Holland	11,768,913	10,822,328
Gold Coast	—	—
Java	8,152	13,773
Sumatra	—	—
Ind. Possns.	2	—
Curaçoa	25,942	22,533
Guiana..........................	62,815	79,201
Belgium	7,906,867	7,555,203
France	37,016,754	33,734,803
Algeria	48,405	33,357
Bourbon	5,082	—
Indian Possessions......	45,255	22,779
West Indies	3,852	4
Madagascar	4,130	—
Portugal Proper	2,517,828	2,324,541
Azores	368,571	327,551
Madeira	32,030	48,096
W. African Possns	71,308	136,999
Cape Verd Islands	41	6
East Africa	—	—
Macao	225,936	127,354
Spain	5,553,133	6,088,389
Canary Islands.............	393,639	521,746
Fernando Po	34,237	41,251
Philippines, &c.............	1,196,557	760,214
Cuba, &c......................	2,901,338	4,267,684
Italy	3,819,844	3,101,552
Papal Territory	5,491	5,162
Austrian Territories	1,369,831	1,203,660
Greece	673,963	885,793
Ionian I. (1st June, 1864).	205,635	360,890
Turkey..........................	5,276,447	4,051,547
Wallachia, &c.	441,928	525,857
Syria, &c.	137,908	150,841
Persian Gulf, &c.	28,053	34,928
Egypt (incl. Transit) ...	15,368,824	15,498,292
Tripoli	—	7,869
Tunis	—	6,325
Morocco	366,082	241,392
Western Africa	1,351,629	1,340,744
Eastern Africa	103,144	71,148
Madagascar,Nat. Territ'y.	3,276	—
Arabia (Muscat)	—	—
Persia	1	960
Borneo, &c....................	26,857	27,978
Siam.............................	14,490	—
Cochin China, Camboja	—	25,474
China, excl. of Hong Kong	10,620,452	9,213,049
Japan	273,745	317,799
Islands in the Pacific	62,321	26,535
Hayti	248,158	243,669
United States of America	46,854,518	41,045,272
Mexico	313,478	315,168
Central America	560,443	804,057
New Granada	1,542,664	983,511
Venezuela	202,036	85,943
Ecuador	120,889	107,424
Peru	3,022,017	3,701,362
Bolivia	173,855	140,043
Chili	2,943,242	4,417,568
Brazil	7,237,793	5,902,011
Uruguay	1,540,250	1,222,228
Argentine Confederation	1,073,013	911,851
Patagonia, &c................	—	—
Whale Fisheries,Northrn.	125,104	97,413
Total from For. Countries	223,084,552	214,448,592

BRITISH POSSESSIONS.	1866.	1867.
Heligoland	—	—
Channel Islands	£430,700	£404,083
Gibraltar	102,017	67,720
Malta and Gozo	115,638	84,471
Ionian I. (unt. Jun. 1, 1864)	—	—
Brit. Pos. on the Gambia	42,615	36,055
Sierra Leone	82,617	72,063
British Gold Coast	388,500	290,933
Ascension	3	6
St. Helena	13,247	97,397
South Africa, C. of G. Hope	2,536,270	2,584,574
Natal	183,053	156,711
Mauritius	1,330,218	889,812
Arabia; Aden	203	4
India: Bombay and Sinde	19,588,541	11,850,191
Madras	5,653,856	2,741,664
Bengal and Pegu	11,659,600	10,895,931
Straits Settlements	1,609,863	1,434,529
Ceylon	3,256,250	3,224,512
Hong Kong	282,273	183,373
Australia: West Australia	75,439	84,084
South Australia	1,274,007	1,665,870
Victoria	4,983,541	5,233,914
New South Wales	2,783,291	3,316,016
Queensland	341,362	459,275
Tasmania	400,980	406,430
New Zealand	1,564,648	1,717,882
British North America:		
British Columbia, &c.	66,794	63,681
Hudson's Bay Compny.	163,887	132,604
Newfoundland, &c.	443,898	522,621
Canada	4,402,922	4,373,299
New Brunswick	1,494,145	1,352,284
Prince Edward Island	151,037	177,672
Nova Scotia & C. Breton	144,880	145,351
Bermuda	43,480	9,489
British West India Isles:		
Bahamas & Turk's I.	109,229	99,145
Jamaica	1,229,410	1,134,340
Tortola & Virgin Gorda	20,211	16,693
St. Christopher	269,854	213,751
Nevis	39,982	30,966
Antigua	330,342	197,548
Montserrat	21,996	13,925
Dominica	62,234	73,446
St. Lucia	133,232	120,908
St. Vincent	231,262	248,980
Barbadoes	816,788	875,144
Grenada	149,985	173,767
Tobago	93,927	97,501
Trinidad	1,134,048	1,070,255
Brit. Guiana: Demerara	1,524,864	1,330,022
Berbice	164,950	171,544
British Honduras	239,795	180,610
Falkland Islands	23,838	10,659
Total from Brit. Posses.	72,205,722	60,734,545
Total from For. Countr.	223,084,552	214,448,592
Total from For. Countries and Brit. Possessions...	295,290,274	275,183,137

TOTAL EXPORTS.

FOREIGN.	1866.	1867.
Russia	6,915,576	7,250,701
Sweden	1,540,205	1,400,207
Norway	1,119,859	1,058,169
Denmark Proper	1,463,454	1,549,032
Iceland, &c.	11,145	13,928
Danish West Indies	765,524	594,270
Carried forward	£11,815,763	11,866,307

	1866.	1867.
Brought forward... £11,815,763	11,866,307
Prussia	3,432,682	5,377,545
Schles. Holst. & Lauenberg	148,231	119,349
Hanover	285,434	296,521
Mecklenburg-Schwerin	84,475	90,858
Oldenburg & Kniphausen	38,040	36,418
Hanse Towns	21,116,249	23,947,481
Holland	14,877,733	14,948,824
Java	1,729,695	1,348,780
Sumatra	578	445
Indian Possession	724	—
Curagoa	167,674	137,938
Guiana	41,892	30,539
Belgium	6,782,573	7,381,002
France	26,597,429	23,022,420
Algeria	15,743	27,626
Senegambia	11,045	345
India	—	2,074
West Indies	26,393	41,664
Guiana	760	409
Madagascar	12,743	2,734
Portugal Proper	2,369,600	2,119,875
Azores	137,190	114,525
Madeira	89,739	81,948
West Africa	57,297	10,949
Cape Verd Islands	35,311	32,225
East Africa	331	2,226
Indian Possessions		
Spain	3,143,057	2,085,706
Canary Islands	293,785	296,324
Fernando Po	14,500	19,219
Philippines, &c.	931,074	1,081,053
Spanish West Indies	2,413,368	2,388,997
Italy	6,905,810	5,879,372
Papal Territory	15,544	10,070
Austrian Territories	1,056,549	1,123,114
Greece	461,197	550,715
Ionian I. (1st June, 64)	480,142	465,126
Turkey	6,481,490	5,686,634
Wallachia and Moldavia	217,489	512,652
Syria and Palestine	1,569,557	1,150,804
El Hedjaz, &c.	23,932	55,312
Egypt	7,658,993	8,380,090
Tripoli	—	—
Tunis	77,488	70,866
Morocco	237,436	232,458
Western Africa	676,454	981,061
Eastern Africa, Nat. Sta.	56,673	35,491
Madagascar, Native Territory	1,628	585
Arabia (Muscat)	2,776	6,638
Persia	26,801	15,031
Siam	4,101	4,244
China (excl. Hong Kong)	5,208,474	5,109,613
Cochin China	940	612
Japan	1,559,750	1,694,000
Islands in the Pacific	139,764	20,811
Hayti	463,915	297,985
United Sates of America.	31,843,836	24,121,811
Mexico	1,332,504	890,434
Central America	165,166	253,003
New Granada	2,989,900	2,462,087
Venezuela	416,776	269,117
Ecuador	47,557	47,719
Peru	1,393,913	1,483,860
Bolivia	13,100	3,966
Chili	1,878,722	2,583,250
Brazil	7,358,141	5,822,918
Uruguay	1,419,683	1,495,692
States of the Arg. Confed.	2,880,787	2,909,856
Patagonia	—	—
Whale Fisheries, Northrn.	—	199
Total to Frgn. Countries £181,738,126	172,451,522

BRITISH POSSESSIONS.	1866.	1867.		1866.	1867.
Heligoland	£ 93	70	Brought forward £46,063,278		42,063,278
Channel Islands	638,229	604,318	Newfoundland, &c.	543,538	432,267
Gibraltar	1,219,742	781,929	Canada	4,446,332	4,245,552
Malta and Gozo	747,842	605,418	New Brunswick	843,931	701,022
Ionian I. until June 1, 1864	—	—	Prince Edward Island	203,550	132,240
British Poss., R. Gambia	75,947	107,095	Nova Scotia & Cape Br	1,448,313	1,093,431
Sierra Leone	239,287	254,987	Bermuda	46,260	51,607
British Gold Coast	301,486	362,342	British West India Isles:		
Ascension	10,478	6,209	Bahamas and Turk's Is	60,247	64,816
St. Helena	51,750	44,941	Jamaica	721,471	521,509
South Africa, C. of G. Hope	1,277,494	1,765,405	Tortola & Virgin Gorda	—	13,312
Natal	182,609	204,259	St. Christopher	95,691	102,014
Mauritius	583,403	384,938	Nevis	—	2,605
Arabia: Aden	65,735	80,591	Antigua	95,653	81,895
India: Bombay and Sinde	6,716,407	6,564,787	Montserrat	972	—
Madras	1,778,487	1,845,155	Dominica	23,317	19,344
Bengal and Pegu	12,176,425	14,452,453	St. Lucia	34,443	27,704
Straits Settlements	2,042,531	2,128,172	St. Vincent	58,590	48,800
Ceylon	1,126,704	805,368	Barbadoes	495,023	506,945
Hong Kong	2,469,159	2,561,791	Grenada	56,216	44,888
Australia: West Australia	123,659	88,359	Tobago	23,437	18,722
South Australia	1,542,452	969,441	Trinidad	462,490	384,499
Victoria	6,597,744	4,919,764	British Guiana: Demerara	706,382	616,528
New South Wales	3,165,937	2,216,119	Berbice	83,478	67,526
Queensland	561,693	311,477	British Honduras	155,630	154,687
Tasmania	261,840	228,923	Falkland Islands	21,628	8,355
New Zealand	2,367,454	1,623,596			
British North America:			Total to Brit. Possessions	57,167,556	53,383,566
British Columbia &c.	162,571	68,866	Total to Foreign Countries	181,738,126	172,451,522
Hudson's Bay Co.	53,896	56,525			
			Total to Foreign Countries		
Carried forward £46,063,278		42,063,278	and British Possessions	238,905,682	225,835,088

Chambers of Commerce.

ASSOCIATION OF CHAMBERS OF COMMERCE OF THE UNITED KINGDOM.—*Chairman of the Association*—S. S. Lloyd, Esq., Birmingham. *Deputy-Chairman*—C. M. Norwood, Esq., M.P. *Treasurer*—Darnton Lupton, Esq., Leeds. *Honorary Secretaries*—William Hirst, Esq., Leeds; Leonard Bruton, Esq., Bristol. *Agent in London*—James Hole, Esq., 29, Parliament Street.

Chambers with their Secretaries or Chairmen. Those only with a * prefixed are connected with the Association.

*Batley, M. S. Scholefield, Esq.
*Belfast, Samuel Vance, Esq.
*Birmingham, Henry J. Harding, Esq.
*Bradford, John Darlington, Esq.
*Bristol, Leonard Bruton, Esq.
*Cardiff, Alexander Dalziel, Esq.
Cork, Timothy Hegarty, Esq.
*Coventry, Henry I. Davis, Esq.
*Darlington, R. F. Laidlaw, Esq.
*Derby, William Chamberlain Watson, Esq.
*Dewsbury, J. Smith, Esq.
Dover, William Jacobs, Esq.
Dublin, Francis Codd, Esq.
*Dundee, Robert Sturrock, Esq.
Edinburgh, C. and Manufactures, James Greig, Esq.
*Exeter, F. Pollard, Esq. W. Cotton, Esq. (treas.)
*Falmouth,
Glasgow, James S. Fleming, Esq.
*Gloucester, P. J. W. Cooke, Esq.
*Goole, T. Clough, jun., Esq.
Greenock, Thomas King, Esq.
*Halifax, John Bailey Holroyde, Esq.
*Holmfirth, Samuel S. Booth, Esq.
*Huddersfield, Charles Mills, Esq.
*Hull, C. and Shipping, P. Bruce, Esq.
*Kendal, C. L. Braithwaite, Jun., Esq.
*Leeds, William Hirst, Esq.
Leith, Pillans Scarth, Esq., W.S.
Limerick, William Carroll, Esq.

Liverpool American, George James Duncan, Esq.
Liverpool, William Blood, Esq.
Llanelly, W. Roderick, Esq.
*Macclesfield, George William Clarke, Esq.
Manchester, Hugh Fleming, Esq.
*Middlesborough, James Morris, Esq.
*Newcastle and Gateshead, Robert Plummer, Esq.
*Northampton, M. P. Manfield, Esq.
North Shields and Tynemouth, Ralph Turnbull, Esq.
Norwich, C. S. Gilman, Esq.
Northwich, John Moore, Esq.
*Nottingham, Samuel Collinson, Esq.
*Plymouth, Thomas Jones Stevens, Esq.
*Rochdale, Charles J. Roberts, Esq.
*Runcorn, R. Falk, Esq.
*Sheffield, William Smith, Esq.
Shrewsbury,
*South of Scotland, T. Cathrae, Esq., & R. Stewart, Esq.
South Shields, Joseph M. Moore, Esq.
*Southampton, R. G. Bassett, Esq.
*Stockton-on-Tees, T. W. Hornsby, Esq.
*Stoke-upon-Trent, Matthew F. Blakiston, Esq.
Tynemouth, Ralph Turnbull, Esq.
*Wakefield, George Mander, Esq.
Waterford, George Gibson, Esq.
Wick, Alexander Wares, Esq.
*Wolverhampton, Edward John Gibbs, Esq.
Worcester, George Clarke, Esq.

Comparatively few years have elapsed since, in the "good old days" of coaching, a speed of 10 miles per hour was considered scarcely safe. One hundred years ago, from the state of the roads, the paucity of travellers, the danger of travelling, owing to highwaymen and many other causes, the time of transit from London to the North of England usually occupied the greater portion of three days. The genius of James Watt, however, has overcome all the impediments that existed in the old mode of travelling; the animate horse has been superseded by the inanimate steam-engine, and an average speed of 6 miles an hour has been, in many cases, transformed into one of 60. The highest rate of coach-speed never accomplished the journey between London and Glasgow in less than 50 hours, whilst at the present day the same is easily accomplished in less than 12 hours.

But not only has the speed of passenger traffic improved. Formerly the mode of transit for goods was either by road or canal. Within 30 years ago, bale goods from Manchester were not delivered in London earlier than on the fourth morning after their departure from the North. Coals, minerals, and other produce, now constantly delivered in a few hours from their sources of production, never reached London, except by a long sea-voyage, that might be reckoned in weeks. Two important and perishable products, milk and fish, could not be conveyed far by either canal or road, to the metropolis; now they are delivered daily from dairies and fishing ports 100 miles away, within two or three hours of their production or being caught. Perhaps one of the most striking instances, however, of the value of the railway system is to be found in the postal economy of this and other countries. A letter will reach the South of Spain, sent from London, in less time than was required 50 years ago for its transmission to London from Scotland. The produce of the most distant parts of the British kingdom, and even from Algeria in Africa, may be centralized in a few hours, or at most, in the latter case, days, in any town of the United Kingdom.

It is to the genius of George Stephenson that we are mainly indebted for the grand improvements, that with gas, the electric telegraph, and the discovery of photography, form an epoch in the history of the inventive genius of man. Before his time the idea of employing steam as an inland mode of communication was considered at once ludicrous and impossible. The first Railway Bill was passed in the year 1801, for the purpose of constructing an iron tramway between Wandsworth and Croydon; and it was intended that all using it should provide their own horses and carriages; differing, in fact, only from the ordinary roadway so far that iron was employed, to diminish friction, and consequently to allow of greater weight being drawn by the same horse-power. But the invention of the tramway does not date from this period, as it had been in use at least two centuries previously for facilitating the descent of coal trucks from the mine to the ship. In 1716, thin iron plates, nailed on to the wood-rails, were first employed. In 1767 some cast-iron rails were experimentally employed at the Colebrookdale Iron Works, and in 1791 Jessop laid down cast-iron-edge rails, with chairs, and on sleepers, at Loughborough in Leicestershire. The first edge-rail was laid down at the Penrhyn Slate Quarries in 1801.

This date brings us again to the Surrey iron railway, already named, which seems to have suggested the first idea of a railway for passenger traffic. In 1804 Trevithick laid the foundation of the locomotive system, by constructing a high-pressure traction engine for the Merthyr Tydvil Railway, subsequently improved upon by Blenkinsop and Brunton. In 1821 George Stephenson formed a colliery railway between Stockton and Darlington; this line, under Stephenson as engineer, was opened in 1825, and an engine constructed by him was employed; it drew 30 tons at the rate of 4 miles an hour. This line afforded the first for the conveyance of passengers by locomotive power.

Gradually the railway system, thus slowly progressing, took up the initiative of its present grandeur. In 1826, after an enormous battle against prejudice, local and personal interests, a bill for the construction of a line between Manchester and Liverpool was sanctioned by Parliament. Stephenson could scarcely have picked out a more trying scheme for the exercise of his abilities, nor yet one more promising in result. The moss land between the two towns was the greatest difficulty; Chatmoss is a swamp utterly destitute of solid basis, but this Stephenson overcame by laying a sub-stratum of fagots on which the line was constructed. The cuttings, tunnellings, viaducts, &c., all helped to hinder progress, but genius at last conquered, and the line at the present day remains a monument to the skill of the indefatigable colliery engineer, whose perseverance was only equalled by his abilities.

This railway was completed in 1829. In the following year a trial of four locomotives took place, of which the Rocket, constructed by Stephenson, gained the prize. It drew a gross total weight of 17 tons at an average speed of 14 miles per hour, with a maximum velocity of 29 miles. The engine weighed $4\frac{1}{4}$ and the tender $3\frac{1}{4}$ tons. Trevithick's engine had attained a speed of only 5 miles per hour. In 1831, consequent on improvements of the locomotive, Stephenson succeeded in drawing 90 tons on a level, at the rate of 20 miles an hour.

Consequent on the success of the Manchester and Liverpool line, Stephenson was appointed engineer to construct a line between London and Birmingham, now merged in the London and North-Western. In the construction of this railway still greater difficulties had to be overcome than in the Manchester and Liverpool line. The length was nearly four times as much, and the tunnelling at Watford, Kilsby, and other places almost overcame the energy of man. Under Brunel the Great Western Railway was constructed. Previously all the lines had been laid on what is commonly known as the "narrow gauge," which has an interval of 4ft. $8\frac{1}{2}$in. between each rail. Brunel proposed what is known as the "broad gauge," in which an interval of 7 feet exists between the rails. The "battle of the gauges" was fought for many years afterwards, and has perhaps, beyond any other cause, done the utmost injury to the shareholders of all the lines on which the two systems work. Singularly, in September, 1868, at the Ordinary

Half-yearly Meeting of the Great Western Railway, it was announced that the Directors intended, as far as possible, to substitute the narrow for the broad gauge on their lines, a plan already in part adopted by them on several branches. Brunel's bridges, steam vessels (as the Great Eastern), and railways, were gigantic blunders, and ruinous as the Thames Tunnel to the shareholders.

It will be unnecessary here to enumerate the numerous lines that sprung up in a few years. The Great Northern, Eastern Counties, South Western, South Eastern, Caledonian, &c., &c., form so many main lines from which branches by hundreds lead to the smaller towns of our country. The most singular feature of the railway system of the present day was the construction of the Metropolitan Underground Railway, that connects various parts of the Metropolis. The engineering difficulties that had to be met in its construction exceed those of any other line in the world. It, as a rule, runs beneath the most frequented roads of the Metropolis. Its success, however, has been enormous. During 1867-68, at least 25 million persons were conveyed by it. The principle is being extended to other large cities of the empire, and will not fail to confer similar benefits that the Londoner now enjoys.

On the Continent, in America, India, Australia, and generally throughout the civilized world, the railway system has spread. The Mont Cenis route, connecting France with Italy, may be cited as one of the most expensive and arduous undertakings that has yet been engaged in.

Generally, throughout Europe, the expense of land, labour, and materials, makes the cost of a railway very great, averaging, in some cases, upwards of £50,000 a mile; the Greenwich line cost £312,000 a mile, whilst for a few miles from some of the Great London termini, the cost per mile has been nearly £1,000,000 sterling. In America the abundance of timber, and the comparative want of value in respect to land, render the cost much less; hence in the United States the railway system has spread with astonishing vigour. The first railway there constructed was opened in 1827, and consisted of a line between some granite quarries and Boston. At the present day a line is in course of construction extending completely across the continent, from New York to San Francisco, and from 3,500 to 4,000 miles in length. A remarkable feature of American railways is the bridge over the St. Lawrence, constructed under the engineership of Robert Stephenson, who, associated with his father, has done more than any other man, for the extension of the railway system throughout the world.

The latest accurate statistics in regard to railways were furnished for the year 1867, in a return published in July, 1868, as printed by order of the House of Commons. From this the following particulars have been gleaned. *England and Wales:*—the total length of line opened on 31st December, 1867, was 10,037 miles. The total of passengers who travelled, 250,598,982. Of cattle, 2,310,368; of sheep, 7,171,412; and of pigs, 1,389,582 were conveyed. Coal and coke carried amounted to 43,936,443 tons. Other minerals, 12,891,296 tons; and of general merchandize, 40,278,991. The number of trains run was 5,224,846, making a total run of 122,063,941

miles. The total receipts from passengers were £13,534,281; from minerals, £6,481,638; from general merchandise, £11,105,440; making a total of receipts from all sources of £33,398,222. The total receipts from all sources in *Scotland* amounted to £4,209,158, on a length of lines open to the extent of 2,282 miles. The total length of mileage at work in *Ireland* was 1,928 miles; and the total receipts from all sources £1,872,619. In *England and Wales*, 6,980 locomotives were employed, worth £1,500 to £2,000 each; in *Scotland* 1,176 locomotives, and in *Ireland* 463. The entire length of lines open for the United Kingdom, at the end of 1867, was 14,247 miles, and the total passengers conveyed 287,688,113 The percentage of expenditure for all lines in the kingdom was exactly 50 per cent. of the total receipts, being just 1 per cent. more than in 1866. The entire authorized capital paid, or to be paid up, amounted to £642,853,408, of which the paid up capital was £391,870,328, which with debentures, &c., made up a total actual payment on account of capital equal to £502,262,887. The number percentage of passengers in respect to class in England was 10.81 first, 28.62 second, and 60.57 third class. The receipt percentage was 25.06 first, 32.91 second, and 38.44 third class, besides which were season-ticket holders amounting to 3.59 per cent.; the proportion of passenger receipts was 45.54, and of goods 54.46 per cent. The net receipts of all the railways in the United Kingdom afforded an average dividend on the paid up capital and loans of 3.91 per cent. The following give the totals of capital in 1867 for the lines named, including their various branches, &c., &c. *Great Eastern,* 728 miles, £29,564,938, no dividend paid. *Great Northern,* 571 miles, £22,350,000, with an average of 6 per cent. dividend. *Great Western,* 1,386 miles, £49,456,394, dividend small, varying from ⅝ to 5 per cent. *London and North Western,* 1,372 miles, 58,283,549, average dividend of 6 per cent. *London and South Western,* 503 miles, £17,822,389, average dividend 4½ per cent. *London, Brighton, and South Coast,* 350 miles, £18,471,000, with dividend of 2 per cent. *London, Chatham, and Dover,* 136 miles, £19,310,982, and no dividend. *Metropolitan,* 5 miles, £6,766,666, average dividend a little over 5 per cent., 7 per cent. being paid on £1,800,000. *Midland,* 942 miles, £35,539,003, with an average dividend of about 5 per cent. *North London,* 11 miles, £3,565,866, dividend 5¾ per cent. *South Eastern,* 346 miles, £21,214,974, dividend 3 per cent. In regard to accidents, the total of all persons killed in the United Kingdom was 209, and 795 injured, of whom only 17 passengers were killed and 8 injured by causes strictly within their own control, *i.e.* through their own carelessness; the total of passengers alone killed was 27, and of injured 750; the entire total given above including servants of companies, and others, besides passengers. The total of passengers' deaths is but 27 out of 287,688,113, the entire number who travelled on all the lines in the United Kingdom in 1867, or less than one in each 10,000,000. The entire number of accidents was 106, of which the greatest number, 41, occurred through collision of passenger and other trains; 16 accidents were caused by collision of passenger trains, and 17 by the whole or portion of such train running off the line. The total accidents involving loss or injury to life in respect of goods and mineral trains was only 11.

NOTHING is more uncertain than Human Life; for although we know that of 100,000 individuals alive at the age of three, a number will reach the ages of 50, 60, and 70, and that a few may live to be 80 or 90, yet no one knows which of the others will be cut off at 20, 30, or 40, or which will be removed between the latter years.

With this uncertainty before him, it behoves every man—every husband and father—to provide for those dependent upon him should he be removed; and this can only be accomplished by setting aside a portion of his income or earnings for the purpose. The families of those especially who are dependent upon professions or trades, or who have only a life-interest in an estate or office, cannot fail to be left in difficulties, and frequently in absolute distress, unless some provision be made.

Life Assurance offers facilities, to the provident man, above every other kind of investment as a means of providing for the maintenance of his widow and the education and bringing up of his children.

A man, aged 30, holding an appointment enabling him to put by £50 a year, all duly invested at compound interest at 5 per cent. would, in twenty years, have accumulated about £1,700. Few would be able to invest their money so advantageously, but to those who could, the results of twenty years' savings would be as stated. If, however, instead of living twenty years, death cut short his existence in five or ten, the amount put by would be very small.

By insuring his life and investing the same amount, £50, he would be able to secure about £2,250 to his representatives, even though he died within a week after making his first payment; or, by insuring so as to participate in the profits, and dying after 20 years, a still larger sum might be secured.

Besides providing for a family, there are many other purposes for which Life Assurance is available. One may be mentioned out of a hundred. When it is known that a tradesman's life is insured, his creditors will give him greater facilities for carrying on his business, knowing that even if he die before completing the business in which he is investing, their claims will be satisfied. Or another case: partners in a business may by this means secure themselves against the inconvenience of having the capital of a deceased partner suddenly withdrawn.

All classes are alike interested: the nobleman inheriting a rich but entailed inheritance, is thus enabled to provide for his younger children: the medical man, the barrister, the clergyman, the Government official, and mercantile clerk, may all, according to their several means, make provision for the loss of income which will be caused by their death.

It is only within the present century that the principles of Life Assurance have been understood or acted upon. Many of the objections and restrictions of the old companies were absolutely ridiculous and absurd, and tended to repel; but, as the system and its advantages become better known and appreciated by the masses—to find an uninsured man, even among agricultural labourers, will be an exceptional and rare occurrence.

Assurances may now be effected through the Post-office, for sums varying from £20 to £100. The charges are higher than in private offices.

The principles of Life Assurance are very simple; but to describe the mode upon which the offices conduct their business, and how they provide against losses, would occupy too much space.

Having determined to insure, it is necessary to select an office, and to make an application to be permitted to insure therein.

1. *How to Select an Office.*—This is by no means an easy question, although the offices are sufficiently numerous. Naturally, the insurer wishes to lay out his money to the best advantage, and to feel sure that his savings will be secure, and that the money will be paid without demur whenever the claim arises. Some offices offer the security of a wealthy proprietary—others, equally secure, have no proprietary, but are entirely mutual. Others again, quite secure, offer to insure on lower terms, and offer other inducements. Some are rigid in their terms, others are more accommodating. What the terms are for insurances effected at various ages may be seen in the following table, but the reader must not suppose that the highest charges are necessarily the dearest; on the contrary, some of the highest of all are in reality much cheaper than many lower ones. The would-be insurer must therefore judge for himself from the statements furnished by the offices. Attention should especially be given to the names and character of the Directors, and to the general standing of the office.

2. *How to Insure.*—Having selected an office, the insurer will have to fill up a printed form, stating his age, habits, state of health, and other particulars, and refer to some persons who have known him. If these inquiries prove satisfactory, he will be requested to see the medical officer, and if approved, he will be informed that on payment of a certain premium a policy will be granted.

. Insurers cannot be too careful in filling up their proposals. Any careless or unintentional mis-statement may invalidate the policy. Any *wilful* mis-statement or misrepresentation will certainly do so.

Should any person be rejected, there are other offices that make it a business to insure rejected, unhealthy, or diseased lives, but naturally at a high rate of premium.

ANNUAL PREMIUMS FOR LIFE ASSURANCES

In the following Offices, at the age of 22, 25, 30, 35, 40, 45, 50 and 55, to secure the payment of ONE HUNDRED POUNDS at death; the assured participating in the profits in all named except the Post Office.

OFFICES.	Age, 22.	Age, 25.	Age, 30	Age, 35	Age, 40.	Age, 45.	Age, 50.	Age, 55.	Established.
	£ s. d.	£ s. d.	£ s. d.	£ s. d.	£ s. d.	£ s. d.	£ s. d.	£ s. d.	
Albert	2 1 4	2 4 1	2 9 9	2 17 0	3 6 0	3 17 7	4 13 9	5 15 5	1838
Albion	1 19 10	2 3 3	2 9 6	2 16 8	3 5 11	3 16 9	4 11 11	5 15 14	1864

Offices.	Age, 22.			Age, 25.			Age, 30.			Age, 35.			Age, 40.			Age, 45.			Age, 50.			Age, 55.			Established
	£	s.	d.	£	s.	d.	£	s.	d.	£	s.	d.	£	s.	d.	£	s.	d.	£	s.	d.	£	s.	d.	
Alliance	1	18	11	2	2	6	2	9	2	2	16	8	3	6	6	3	17	8	4	14	2	5	19	11	1824
Amicable Mutual	1	14	6	1	17	1	2	2	3	2	8	6	2	16	5	3	6	10	4	11	11	5	1	6	1867
Atlas	2	1	2	2	4	3	2	10	2	2	17	5	3	6	3	3	17	4	4	11	1	5	8	8	1808
British Empire Mutual	1	19	4	2	2	4	2	8	3	2	15	4	3	4	2	3	15	7	4	11	1	5	13	7	1847
British Equitable	1	19	11	2	3	0	2	9	0	2	16	6	3	0	0	3	18	2	4	14	3	5	16	4	1854
British Mutual	1	17	9	2	0	11	2	6	11	2	13	7	3	2	5	3	12	8	4	6	3	5	6	1	1844
Briton, Medic.& General	2	0	4	2	3	10	2	10	1	2	17	6	3	6	9	3	16	2	4	10	10	5	14	8	1854
Caledonian	2	1	2	2	4	2	2	9	10	2	16	1	3	4	2	3	13	4	4	7	0	5	7	8	1805
Church of England	1	18	11	2	1	6	2	6	10	2	13	11	3	3	6	3	16	3	4	13	4	5	16	5	1840
City of Glasgow	1	19	0	2	2	3	2	8	5	2	15	5	3	4	6	3	14	10	4	9	10	5	12	9	1838
Clerical, Medical,& Gen.	1	19	3	2	2	6	2	8	9	2	15	9	3	5	0	3	15	6	4	10	9	5	13	9	1824
Clergy Mutual	1	17	0	2	0	2	2	6	4	2	13	0	3	2	2	3	12	4	4	7	4	5	10	4	1829
Commercial Union	2	0	7	2	3	8	2	9	5	2	15	9	3	4	2	3	13	10	4	7	8	5	9	2	1861
Crown	1	17	10	2	1	2	2	7	4	2	14	6	3	3	4	3	15	0	4	12	4	5	13	8	1825
Eagle	2	3	1	2	5	7	2	10	8	2	17	1	3	5	5	3	6	6	4	11	4	5	10	11	1807
Economic	1	16	3	1	19	0	2	4	3	2	10	11	2	19	9	3	11	9	4	7	6	5	4	8	1823
Edinburgh	1	19	1	2	2	0	2	7	7	2	14	6	3	3	2	3	14	2	4	9	0	5	9	1	1823
Emperor	2	0	3	2	3	4	2	9	3	2	16	6	3	5	7	3	17	2	4	13	0	5	16	0	1853
English	1	19	7	2	3	6	2	8	0	2	14	2	3	2	2	3	11	5	4	4	8	5	5	0	1867
English & Scottish Law	2	1	4	2	4	6	2	9	9	2	16	6	3	6	6	3	17	9	4	10	9	5	13	9	1839
Equity and Law	2	0	1	2	3	2	2	8	10	2	15	10	3	4	6	3	15	7	4	10	9	5	12	6	1844
Equitable Society	2	5	4	2	8	1	2	13	5	2	19	10	3	7	11	3	17	11	4	10	8	5	6	4	1762
European	2	0	3	2	2	9	2	8	1	2	15	2	3	3	9	3	15	0	4	10	7	5	11	9	1853
General	1	19	10	2	2	10	2	8	5	2	15	1	3	3	7	3	14	10	4	10	3	5	8	11	1837
Great Britain	2	3	4	2	6	0	2	11	4	2	18	4	3	7	10	4	0	7	4	17	8	6	0	8	1844
Gresham	2	1	2	2	4	0	2	9	7	2	16	7	3	5	10	3	18	3	4	14	7	5	16	5	1848
Guardian	2	2	8	2	5	4	2	10	7	2	17	0	3	5	0	3	14	11	4	8	0	5	4	8	1821
Hand-in-Hand	2	5	4	2	8	1	2	13	5	2	19	10	3	7	11	3	17	11	4	11	6	5	12	8	1696
Hercules	1	17	1	2	0	0	2	5	9	2	13	1	3	2	6	3	15	3	4	12	1	5	14	5	—
Imperial	2	2	5	2	5	0	2	10	3	2	16	8	3	4	11	3	15	10	4	10	2	5	8	11	1820
Imperial Guardian	2	0	11	2	4	0	2	9	11	2	17	3	3	6	7	3	18	7	4	14	2	5	16	4	1867
Imperial Union	2	0	5	2	3	2	2	8	5	2	15	8	3	4	6	3	15	4	4	11	9	5	11	5	1866
Lancashire	1	18	6	2	3	0	2	8	6	2	15	0	3	3	6	3	15	0	4	10	6	5	9	6	1852
Law Life	2	5	4	2	8	1	2	13	5	2	19	10	3	7	11	3	17	11	4	10	8	5	9	6	1823
Law Property	2	0	11	2	3	10	2	9	5	2	16	6	3	5	6	3	17	2	4	12	7	5	13	4	1850
Law Union	2	0	6	2	3	7	2	9	4	2	16	7	3	5	3	3	17	0	4	12	0	5	12	8	1854
Legal and General	2	2	1	2	5	1	2	10	9	2	17	7	3	5	11	3	16	7	4	10	9	5	11	0	1836
Life Assocn. of Scotland	2	0	6	2	3	10	2	10	0	2	17	0	3	5	2	3	17	2	4	13	4	5	13	4	1838
Lpool. & Lond. & Globe	2	0	11	2	3	10	2	9	5	2	16	5	3	5	5	3	17	2	4	12	7	5	13	4	1836
London and Lancashire	1	17	9	2	0	10	2	6	10	2	13	7	3	2	4	3	12	5	4	6	10	5	9	1	1862
London and Manchester	2	0	2	2	3	9	2	9	8	2	17	0	3	5	4	3	16	3	4	15	0	5	16	8	1866
Lond. & Provincial Law	2	0	10	2	4	0	2	9	10	2	16	5	3	4	10	3	15	9	4	10	2	5	8	8	1846
London and Southwark	1	19	9	2	3	0	2	9	4	2	16	5	3	5	8	3	16	0	4	12	2	5	16	0	1864
Lond. Assurance Corp.	2	2	0	2	5	0	2	10	8	2	17	0	3	5	1	3	15	10	4	10	7	5	8	11	1720
Lond. Life Association	2	10	9	2	13	6	2	19	3	3	7	0	3	17	0	4	9	9	5	7	6	6	9	6	1806
Manchester Provident	2	1	2	2	4	2	2	10	0	2	16	10	3	6	8	3	17	9	4	12	10	5	16	4	1866
Marine and General	2	1	2	2	4	3	2	10	2	2	17	5	3	6	3	3	17	4	4	11	1	5	8	8	1852
Metropolitan	2	1	3	2	4	0	2	9	9	2	17	5	3	6	4	3	18	11	4	12	0	5	9	1	1835
Midland Counties	2	3	0	2	4	10	2	9	11	2	16	2	3	4	8	3	15	0	4	9	6	5	7	11	1851
Mutual	2	1	8	2	4	7	2	10	2	2	17	5	3	7	6	3	17	11	4	12	7	5	14	4	1834
National Assurance Co.	2	1	2	2	3	3	2	10	2	2	17	5	3	6	3	3	17	4	4	11	1	5	10	4	1822
National Life Ass. Society	2	2	4	2	5	0	2	10	4	2	17	1	3	5	9	3	17	2	4	12	8	5	13	8	1830
National Provident	2	1	2	2	4	3	2	10	2	2	17	5	3	5	3	3	17	2	4	11	1	5	8	8	1835
National Widows	1	19	3	2	2	3	2	7	6	2	14	1	3	1	10	3	12	2	4	5	9	5	3	6	1867
North British	2	0	1	2	3	5	2	9	10	2	17	0	3	6	1	3	16	7	4	11	11	5	11	2	1809
Northern	1	18	8	2	1	11	2	8	0	2	14	11	3	3	11	3	14	3	4	7	4	5	7	3	1836
Norwich Union	2	1	3	2	3	8	2	8	10	2	14	10	3	2	0	3	11	0	4	6	0	5	5	3	1808
Patriotic	1	19	3	2	2	7	2	8	9	2	15	10	3	5	0	3	17	4	4	8	11	5	9	1	1824
Pelican	2	1	2	2	4	2	2	10	4	2	17	7	3	6	5	3	16	8	4	10	7	5	9	4	1797
Planet	2	0	2	2	3	0	2	8	5	2	15	6	3	4	5	3	15	4	4	12	11	5	14	7	1866

OFFICES.	Age, 22.			Age, 25.			Age, 30.			Age, 35.			Age, 40.			Age, 45.			Age, 50.			Age, 55.			Estab- lished
	£	s.	d.	£	s.	d.	£	s.	d.	£	s.	d.	£	s.	d.	£	s.	d.	£	s.	d.	£	s.	d.	
Post Office	1	18	0	2	0	10	2	6	7	2	13	8	3	2	9	3	14	5	4	9	10	5	10	0	1865
Protector	2	0	3	2	2	11	2	8	3	2	14	11	3	3	8	3	15	4	4	10	11	5	11	5	1853
Provident Clerks	1	17	7	2	0	1	2	6	4	2	13	5	3	2	8	3	16	1	4	12	2	5	17	4	1840
Provincial	2	2	8	2	5	4	2	10	7	2	17	0	3	5	0	3	14	11	4	8	0	5	4	8	1852
Provincial Union	2	1	2	2	4	9	2	10	8	2	18	0	3	6	4	3	17	8	4	16	0	5	17	8	1865
Provident	2	1	2	2	4	3	2	10	2	2	17	5	3	6	3	3	17	4	4	11	1	5	8	8	1806
Prudential	1	19	10	2	3	2	2	9	6	2	16	8	3	5	11	3	16	6	4	11	11	5	15	4	1848
Queen	1	17	5	2	0	4	2	6	1	2	13	6	3	3	0	3	14	9	4	9	6	5	10	6	1851
Reliance	1	19	7	2	2	11	2	9	4	2	16	9	3	5	10	3	18	0	4	14	2	5	13	8	1840
Royal	2	1	2	2	4	2	2	9	9	2	16	2	3	4	1	3	14	6	4	8	3	5	10	4	1845
Royal Exchange	2	2	10	2	5	11	2	11	7	2	18	2	3	6	3	3	17	0	4	11	3	5	8	6	1720
Royal Farmers	1	18	4	2	1	2	2	7	5	2	14	6	3	3	4	3	15	0	4	10	7	5	10	2	1840
Rock	2	5	4	2	8	1	2	13	5	2	19	10	3	7	11	3	17	11	4	10	8	5	6	4	1806
Sceptre	1	19	1	2	2	4	2	8	8	2	15	8	3	4	8	3	15	4	4	10	6	5	13	4	1864
Scottish Amicable	2	3	10	2	6	5	2	11	9	2	18	2	3	6	3	3	16	3	4	9	1	5	5	1	1826
Scottish Commercial	2	0	10	2	3	8	2	9	7	2	16	0	3	4	11	3	16	8	4	12	2	5	12	7	1865
Scottish Equitable	2	3	11	2	6	6	2	11	9	2	18	2	3	6	3	3	16	4	4	10	6	5	13	8	1831
Scottish Imperial	2	1	5	2	4	6	2	10	2	2	16	5	3	3	8	3	13	0	4	6	1	5	5	5	1866
Scottish National	1	19	6	2	2	8	2	9	0	2	15	10	3	4	6	3	14	0	4	8	6	5	9	6	1841
Scottish Provident	1	16	9	1	18	0	2	1	6	2	6	10	2	14	9	3	5	9	4	7	7	5	1	11	1837
Scottish Provincial	1	18	4	2	1	8	2	8	1	2	15	2	3	4	6	3	13	9	4	7	3	5	8	1	1825
Scottish Widows' Fund	2	3	11	2	6	6	2	11	9	2	18	9	3	6	3	3	16	4	4	10	7	5	13	8	1815
Scottish Union	2	0	9	2	4	3	2	9	11	2	16	9	3	5	0	3	15	1	4	7	9	5	9	3	1824
Sovereign	2	1	0	2	3	10	2	9	4	2	16	3	3	5	2	3	16	10	4	12	2	5	12	5	1845
Standard	2	2	9	2	5	4	2	10	7	2	16	11	3	4	11	3	14	9	4	8	6	5	6	11	1825
Star	1	19	3	2	2	7	2	8	9	2	15	11	3	4	11	3	15	5	4	10	6	5	13	7	1843
Sun	1	18	11	2	2	6	2	9	2	2	16	8	3	6	6	3	17	8	4	14	2	5	19	11	1810
Union	2	3	1	2	5	8	2	10	8	2	16	10	3	4	7	3	16	0	4	8	4	5	6	4	1714
United King. Temprce.	1	19	4	2	2	7	2	8	10	2	15	7	3	4	11	3	15	5	4	10	6	5	13	8	1840
Universal	2	0	5	2	3	3	2	8	10	2	14	11	3	3	0	3	12	2	4	5	6	5	5	10	1834
University	2	3	1	2	5	9	2	10	9	2	16	11	3	4	7	3	14	1	4	7	6	5	5	4	1825
Victoria	2	0	4	2	3	4	2	9	3	2	16	6	3	5	7	3	17	2	4	13	0	5	16	0	1860
West of England	2	2	9	2	5	8	2	11	3	2	17	11	3	6	1	3	16	2	4	9	1	5	5	6	1807
West. Counties & Lond.	1	18	6	2	1	9	2	7	11	2	14	9	3	3	9	3	14	0	4	8	9	5	11	5	1861
Westminster & General	1	19	3	2	2	7	2	8	10	2	15	10	3	5	0	3	15	5	4	10	6	5	13	8	1836
Yorkshire	2	0	3	2	3	7	2	9	7	2	16	3	3	5	0	3	14	10	4	9	1	5	10	10	1824

MARRIAGES.—In the year 1866, 187,776 marriages were solemnized, of which 146,040, or 78 per cent., were according to the rites of the Established Church; 8,911 Roman Catholics; 4,281 in Superintendent's offices; 63 Quakers; and 301 Jews. In 23 instances one or other of the parties had been divorced. 26,128 widowers, and 17,651 widows, were re-married. Of the widowers, 16,467 married spinsters, and 9,661 married widows; the remaining 7,990 widows married bachelors. 12,569 men, and 37,610 women, married under the age of 21. Of the 375,552 persons who married, 40,609 men, or 21 per cent., and 56,395, or 30 per cent., of women, signed the registers with marks.

LUNATICS: ENGLAND AND WALES.—In January, 1867, the number of persons in confinement in asylums of all kinds, were: males, 1,5731; females, 16,786; total, 31,917. The total number of admissions during the year was 10,488; discharged, 5,827; cured, 3,572; died, 3,365. On January 1, 1868, there were in confinement, 33,213, an increase of 1,296 on the year; and of the whole number in confinement, but 3,384 were deemed curable. The cost per head varied from 11s. 3¾d. per week in Norfolk, to £1 19s. 4¾d. at Manchester.

A YEAR'S WILLS.—In the year 1867, in which 471,102 persons died in England and Wales (probably half of them minors, and about half the others women), 37,497 probates of wills or grants of letters of administration were issued, 14,623 in London, and 22,874 in the English and Welsh provincial registries. The number is, of course, ever increasing. The increase in 1867 over 1866 was only 285, but 1867 was a year of lower mortality than 1866. The personal property of these 37,497 deceased persons was sworn under £92,302,570—viz., £53,111,975 in the cases disposed of in the London Court of Probate, or registry, and £38,190,595 in the cases in the country registries. In the year 1866 the property happened to be rather larger, reaching £93,180,794. The sums under which the property was sworn in 1867 were equal to £196 for every death in the year, reckoning the deaths of men, women, and children.

Probabilities of Life.

GOVERNMENT Annuities are based upon the following table calculated by Mr. Finlaison. It will be seen that of 100,000 boys alive at 3, but 94,417 will reach the age of 10, while of girls the number will be 94,551. At 50 the difference is much greater; of females there will then be 65,237 alive, and but 59,123 males. Nine females may reach the age of 100, but none of the other sex.

Age	Female.	Male.	Age	Female.	Male.	Age	Female.	Male.	Age	Female.	Male.	Age	Female.	Male.
3	100,000	100,000	23	86,549	84,787	43	70,860	65,194	63	53,170	42,049	83	15,287	8,575
4	98,900	98,750	24	85,803	83,583	44	70,045	64,314	64	51,958	40,556	84	13,547	7,183
5	97,852	97,723	25	85,058	82,396	45	69,233	63,440	65	50,675	39,014	85	11,971	5,868
6	96,972	96,873	26	84,318	81,242	46	68,430	62,571	66	49,322	37,426	86	10,516	4,658
7	96,206	96,166	27	83,576	80,183	47	67,629	61,733	67	47,887	35,708	87	9,148	3,538
8	95,561	95,541	28	82,832	79,160	48	66,831	60,887	68	45,374	33,951	88	7,849	2,564
9	95,016	94,968	29	82,085	78,155	49	66,036	60,023	69	43,831	32,162	89	6,586	1,771
10	94,551	94,417	30	81,331	77,163	50	65,237	59,123	70	42,209	30,338	90	5,362	1,170
11	94,135	93,888	31	80,583	76,191	51	64,454	58,171	71	40,462	28,474	91	4,182	729
12	93,739	93,372	32	79,825	75,231	52	63,668	57,118	72	38,629	26,603	92	3,080	449
13	93,327	92,877	33	79,059	74,283	53	62,872	55,993	73	36,717	24,757	93	2,132	260
14	92,879	92,385	34	78,276	73,355	54	62,061	54,789	74	34,705	22,967	94	1,390	140
15	92,387	91,877	35	77,478	72,446	55	61,223	53,512	75	32,623	21,266	95	847	70
16	91,749	91,335	36	76,649	71,547	56	60,348	52,171	76	30,538	19,569	96	488	29
17	91,061	90,705	37	75,814	70,646	57	59,437	50,773	77	28,370	18,013	97	247	11
18	90,332	89,979	38	74,980	69,742	58	58,486	49,331	78	26,120	16,443	98	106	3
19	89,573	89,142	39	74,148	68,829	59	57,492	47,871	79	23,833	14,832	99	37	0
20	88,803	88,200	40	73,317	67,907	60	56,458	46,397	80	21,554	13,223	100	9	..
21	88,048	87,174	41	72,496	66,990	61	55,408	44,935	81	19,308	11,630	101	0	..
22	87,300	85,999	42	71,677	66,086	62	54,316	43,493	82	17,206	10,059	..	..	..

EXPECTATION OF LIFE AT THE FOLLOWING AGES.

Age.	Male.	Female.	Age.	Male.	Female.	Age.	Male.	Female.	Age.	Male.	Female.	Age.	Male.	Female.
1	50·13	55·59	21	37·83	43·36	41	26·39	30·46	61	13·84	16·64	81	4·55	6·20
2	50·04	55·37	22	37·34	42·73	42	25·74	29·81	62	13·28	15·96	82	4·18	5·89
3	49·80	55·05	23	36·87	42·09	43	25·08	29·14	63	12·72	15·30	83	3·82	5·57
4	49·42	54·65	24	36·39	41·45	44	24·42	28·48	64	12·17	14·64	84	3·46	5·22
5	48·93	54·23	25	35·90	40·81	45	23·75	27·81	65	11·63	14·00	85	3·12	4·84
6	48·36	53·72	26	35·41	40·17	46	23·07	27·13	66	11·10	13·37	86	2·81	4·44
7	47·71	53·15	27	34·86	39·52	47	22·38	26·44	67	10·61	12·76	87	2·53	4·03
8	47·02	52·50	28	34·31	38·87	48	21·68	25·75	68	10·14	12·16	88	2·31	3·62
9	46·30	51·80	29	33·75	38·22	49	20·98	25·06	69	9·67	11·57	89	2·12	3·21
10	45·57	51·05	30	33·17	37·57	50	20·30	24·35	70	9·22	10·99	90	1·95	2·83
11	44·83	50·27	31	32·59	36·91	51	19·62	23·65	71	8·79	10·44	91	1·83	2·49
12	44·07	49·48	32	32·00	36·26	52	18·97	22·93	72	8·37	9·92	92	1·65	2·21
13	43·31	48·70	33	31·40	35·61	53	18·34	22·22	73	7·96	9·41	93	1·49	1·97
14	42·53	47·93	34	30·79	34·96	54	17·73	21·50	74	7·54	8·92	94	1·34	1·75
15	41·76	47·19	35	30·17	34·31	55	17·15	20·79	75	7·12	8·46	95	1·18	1·55
16	41·01	46·51	36	29·54	33·68	56	16·57	20·08	76	6·69	8·00	96	0·97	1·32
17	40·29	45·86	37	28·91	33·04	57	16·02	19·38	77	6·23	7·58	97	0·75	1·12
18	39·61	45·22	38	28·28	32·40	58	15·47	18·69	78	5·78	7·19	98	0·50	0·94
19	38·98	44·60	39	27·65	31·76	59	14·43	18·00	79	5·35	6·83	99	..	0·75
20	38·39	43·99	40	27·02	31·12	60	14·39	17·32	80	4·94	6·50	100	..	0·50

Calculated in years and hundredths.

If the Intestate die, leaving	His representatives take in the proportion following :—
Wife and child, or children	One-third to wife, rest to child or children : and if children are dead, then to the representatives (that is, their lineal descendants), except such child or children, not heirs-at-law, who had estate by settlement of intestate, or were advanced by him in his lifetime, equal to other shares.
Wife only	Half to wife, rest to next-of-kin in equal degree to intestate, or their legal representatives, or, if no next-of-kin, to the Crown.
No wife or child	All to next-of-kin and their legal representatives.
No wife, but child, children, or representatives of them, whether such child or children by one or more wives	All to him, her, or them.
Children by two wives	Equally to all.
If no child, children, or representatives of them	All to next-of-kin in equal degree to intestate.
Child and grandchild by deceased child	Half to child, half to grandchild, who takes by representation.
Husband	Whole to him.
Father, and brother or sister	Whole to father.
Mother, and brother or sister	Whole to them equally.
Wife, mother, brother, sisters, and nieces	Half to wife, residue to mother, brothers, sisters, and nieces.
Wife and father	Half to wife and half to father.
Wife, mother, nephews, and nieces	Two-fourths to wife, one-fourth to mother, and other fourth to nephews and nieces.
Wife, brothers or sisters, and mother	Half to wife, half to brothers or sisters, and mother.
Mother, but no wife, child, father, brother, sister, nephew, or niece	The whole to mother.
Wife and mother	Half to wife, half to mother.
Brother or sister of whole blood, and brother or sister of half blood	Equally to both.
Posthumous brother or sister, and mother	Equally to both.
Posthumous brother or sister, and brother or sister born in lifetime of father	Equally to both.
Father's father, and mother's mother	Equally to both.
Uncle or aunt's children, and brother's or sister's grand-children	Equally to all.
Grandmother, uncle, or aunt	All to grandmother.
Two aunts, nephew, and niece	Equally to all.
Uncle and deceased uncle's child	All to uncle.
Uncle by mother's side, and deceased uncle or aunt's child	All to uncle.
Nephew by brother, and nephew by half-sister	Equally *per capita.**
Brother or sister's nephew or nieces	Where nephews and nieces taking *per stirpes,* and not *per capita.*
Nephew by deceased brother, and nephews and nieces by deceased sister	Each in equal shares *per capita,* and not *per stirpes.*
Brother and grandfather	Whole to brother.
Brother's grandson, and brother or sister's daughter	To daughter.
Brother and two aunts	To brother.
Brother and wife	Half to brother, half to wife.
Mother and brother	Equally.
Wife, mother, and children of a deceased brother (or sister)	Half to wife, a fourth to mother, and a fourth *per stirpes* to deceased brother's or sister's children.
Wife, brother, or sister, and children of a deceased brother or sister	Half to wife, one-fourth to brother or sister *per capita,* one-fourth to deceased brother's or sister's children *per stirpes.*
Brother or sister, and children of a deceased brother or sister	Half to brother or sister *per capita,* half to children of deceased brother or sister *per stirpes.*
Grandfather and brother	All to brother.

* That is, taking individually and not by representation. Thus, if A die, leaving three brothers or sisters, they each take an equal part of his effects in his or her own right. But if either of them die, leaving children, his children would take his share *per stirpes,* that is, *through him,* and not in their own rights.

By the 19 & 20 Vict. all special *local* customs relating to intestates' estates are abolished.

ENGLAND.

LONDON.	Duty collected. Houses and Land.	Farm Stock insured.
Alliance	£39,358 0 11	£3,527,377
Atlas	22,567 16 7	1,394,435
Azienda Assicuratrice	119 19 7	nil.
British Nation	247 6 9	21,205
Church of England	3,182 18 2	148,298
Commercial Union	12,995 15 9	7,998,970
County	42,184 19 10	1,830
Emperor	623 9 4	91,099
European	3,147 14 7	471,803
General	12,114 9 7	215,042
Guardian	20,477 13 1	63,930
Hand-in-Hand	5,312 10 0	6,132
Hercules	1,037 13 9	nil.
Household	38 3 2	850,153
Imperial	34,594 2 1	160,220
Law	26,659 1 5	207,484
Law Union	7,315 15 1	506,102
London	20,859 3 8	121,454
London & Lancash.	11,187 12 7	3,700
London & Southwark	1,699 15 1	nil.
Netherlands	100 11 6	217,430
North British	19,776 1 11	4,510,041
Phoenix	75,344 1 7	nil.
Preserver	51 10 6	nil.
Royal Exchange	42,820 7 6	4,056,439
Royal Farmers	6,877 7 3	4,356,034
Sun	112,055 4 4	8,590,612
Union	16,718 2 1	259,721
Western	4,755 3 8	150,082
Westminster	18,178 9 0	298,264

COUNTRY.		
Birmingham. Alliance	£1,366 5 1	£9,425
Essex and Suffolk	4,077 19 10	1,585,763
Kent	9,052 8 7	1,145,805
Lancashire	21,959 11 10	1,146,213
Liverpool and Globe	88,995 2 6	4,497,470
Manchester	21,782 1 11	1,010,959
Midland Counties	2,884 3 2	1,277,759
Norwich Equitable	1,751 9 3	249,139
Norwich Union	46,999 6 0	10,457,395
Nottinghamshire	3,155 4 9	696,010
Oldham	14 0 10	nil.
Primitive Methodist	157 13 10	nil.
Provincial	6,677 10 7	1,754,328
Queen	13,558 4 5	166,736
Royal	63,869 11 0	2,352,485
Salop	2,528 11 5	669,041
Shropshire	1,245 16 10	375,917
West of England	28,558 6 3	1,450,198
Yorkshire	13,407 2 0	3,565,204
	£894,442 0 5	70,648,604

SCOTLAND.

	Duty collected. Houses and Land.	Farm Stock insured.
Scottish Union	£19,579 5 6	£1,754,008
North British & Merc.	21,304 7 1	1,940,006
Caledonian	9,407 0 9	983,927
Scottish National	4,637 18 0	637,697
Scottish	2,062 12 4	55,054
Scottish Commercial	3,491 15 8	53,685
Scottish Imperial	1,769 17 0	24,300
Northern Assurance	18,047 15 7	1,260,798
Scottish Provincial	6,935 14 9	803,979
Stewarton & Dunlop	1 11 0	25,196
	£87,637 17 8	7,544,650

IRELAND.

Alliance	£2,994 0 3	£113,714
Atlas	1,521 6 11	76,567
County	1,662 5 9	47,942
Etna	1,087 0 7	75,250
Imperial	1,324 1 10	80,543
Liverpool & London	3,703 10 0	116,663
North British & Merc.	1,261 17 9	48,013
National	3,593 2 2	57,085
Patriotic	2,944 2 6	85,553
Royal Exchange	2,020 19 10	82,025
Royal	5,386 13 5	249,387
Sun	4,067 7 10	122,644
West of England	2,430 5 4	132,241
By 26 other Offices	6,957 5 7	172,530
	£41,933 19 2	1,450,147

FIRE INSURANCE.

Common Insurances.—The charges are usually from 1s. 6d. to 2s. per cent. for insuring brick or stone buildings, with tiled or slated roofs, in which no hazardous goods are placed, or trade carried on—also household furniture and other ordinary contents.

Hazardous Insurances, 2s. 6d. to 3s. per cent. for insuring timber, and brick and timber, buildings with tiled or slated roofs, in which no hazardous goods are stored, and no trade is carried on—as also their contents.

Doubly Hazardous Insurances, 4s. 6d. to 7s. 6d. per cent.—Under this class are taken—timber, and brick and timber, buildings, containing hazardous goods, and the goods deposited therein Also china, glass, earthenware, pictures, and similar articles.

SUMMARY FOR THE YEAR 1867.

—	DUTY.	Allowance for Collection, at £4 per Cent.	£5 per Cent.	Farming Stock. Amount insured
	£ s. d.	£ s. d.	£ s. d.	£ s. d.
ENGLAND	894,442 0 5	8,955 13 2	33,504 17 3	70,648,604 0 0
SCOTLAND	87,637 17 8	... ...	4,381 17 2	7,544,650 0 0
IRELAND	41,932 19 2	... ...	2,039 6 11	1,450,147 0 0
£	1,024,012 17 3	8,955 13 2	39,926 1 4	79,643,401 0 0

The Lord Mayor, Aldermen, Common Council, & Officers of the City of London.

Lord Mayor.	Ward.	Residence.	Ald.	Mayor.	Sheriff.
Rt. Hon. Jas. Clarke Lawrence......	Walbrook	.... 90, Cannon Street............	1860	......	1862

Aldermen.

	Ward.	Residence.	Ald.	Mayor.	Sheriff.
Samuel Wilson, Esq.	Bridge Without	Roy. Lon. Militia, City Rd.			
Sir James Duke, Bart.	Farringd. Without	Laughton, Sussex	1831	1838	1833
Sir John Musgrove, Bart.	Broad Street	...... 32, Russell Square	1840	1848	1835
Thomas Challis, Esq.	Cripplegate	32, Wilson Street	1842	1850	1843
Thomas Sidney, Esq.	Billingsgate...........	71, Ludgate Hill	1843	1852	1846
Sir Francis Graham Moon, Bart.	Portsoken.	35, Portman Square	1844	1853	1844
David Salomons, Esq., M.P.	Cordwainer	26, Great Cumberland Pl.	1844	1854	1843
Thomas Quested Finnis, Esq.	Tower	79, Great Tower Street	1847	1855	1835
Sir Robert Walter Carden, Knt. ..	Dowgate	2, Royal Exchange Bldgs.	1848	1856	1848
John Carter, Esq.	Cornhill	61, Cornhill	1849	1857	1850
Sir William Anderson Rose, Knt.	Queenhithe	66, Upper Thames Street ..	1851	1859	1852
William Lawrence, Esq.	Bread Street	31, Bread Street............	1854	1862	1855
Warren Stormes Hale, Esq.	Coleman Street	West Heath, Hampstead...	1855	1863	1857
Sir Benj. Samuel Phillips, Knt....	Farringdon Within	40, Newgate Street	1856	1864	1858
Sir Thomas Gabriel, Bart.	Vintry	Commercial Road, Lambeth	1857	1865	1859
William Ferneley Allen, Esq. ...	Cheap	13, Waterloo Place............	1858	1866	1857

All the above have passed the Civic Chair.

	Ward.	Residence.	Ald.	Mayor.	Sheriff.
Thomas Dakin, Esq...................	Candlewick	3, Creechurch Lane	1861	......	1864
Robert Besley, Esq....................	Aldersgate	2, Fann St., Aldersgate St.	1861	......	1864
Sills John Gibbons, Esq.............	Castle Baynard	Calvert's Bdgs. Southwark	1862	......	1865
Sir Sydney Hedley Waterlow, Kt.	Langbourn	Carpenters' Hall, Lon. Wall	1863	......	1866
Andrew Lusk, Esq.....................	Aldgate	62, Fenchurch Street........	1863	......	1861
David Henry Stone, Esq.............	Bassishaw	80, Basinghall St. 13, Poultry	1864	......	1868
Wm. Jas. Richmond Cotton, Esq.	Lime Street....	47, St. Mary Axe...........	1866		
Joseph Causton, Esq.................	Bridge Within	47, Eastcheap	1867		
Thomas S. Owden, Esq..............	Bishopsgate	17, Devonshire Square	1868		

Sheriffs.—Alderman Cotton, 47, St. Mary Axe; C. W. C. Hutton, Esq.

Under Sheriffs.—Alexander Crossley, Esq., Robert Slee, Esq.,

COMMON COUNCIL.

Elected St. Thomas' Day, 1867.

Algar, Frederic, *Langbourn.*
Arnold, Joseph Gosling, *Bridge.*
Atkins, Samuel Elliott, Esq., *Deputy, Cornhill.*
Banister, John, Esq., *Deputy, Broad Street.*
Bauning, John Stephen, *Tower.*
Barber, Charles, *Portsoken.*
Barnes, William George, *Dowgate.*
Bedford, John Thomas, *Farringdon Without.*
Belville, Wm. John, *Vintry.*
Bengough, George Robert, *Farringdon Within.*
Bennett, John, F.R.A.S., *Cheap.*
Bishop, William, *Aldersgate Within.*
Blake, James Joseph, *Bridge Within.*
Blakesley, Benjamin, *Castle Baynard.*
Bonnewell, William Henry, *Farringdon Without.*
Bontems, John Francis, *Cheap.*
Bower, Benjamin, Esq., *Deputy, Billingsgate.*
Bowring, Henry, *Langbourn.*
Brass, William, *Cripplegate Within.*
Breffit, Edgar, *Dowgate.*
Burkitt, Edward, *Cripplegate Within.*
Burnell, Blomfield, Esq., *Deputy, Aldgate.*
Burrowes, Thomas, *Queenhithe.*
Butcher, J., Esq., *Deputy, Farringdon Without.*
Carritt, Frederick, *Bassishaw.*
Chaplin, Robert James, *Aldersgate Without.*
Christie, John Chris., Esq., *Deputy, Portsoken.*
Clark, William, *Coleman Street.*
Clements, William, *Cripplegate Within.*
Cockerell, George Joseph, *Castle Baynard.*
Cole, Alfred James, *Bread Street.*
Colls, Benjamin, *Coleman Street.*
Colman, Jeremiah, *Dowgate.*
Corke, J., *Cripplegate Without.*
Cotterell, Thomas, *Farringdon Without.*

Cotton, John Anderson, *Walbrook.*
Cox, Frederick, *Farringdon Within.*
Cox, Richard, *Broad Street.*
Cox, William, *Broad Street.*
Crispe, James, *Farringdon Within.*
Dadswell, Frederick, *Bishopsgate.*
Davis, John Charles, *Aldgate.*
Dearsley, Henry, *Billingsgate.*
Deiries, Moss, *Portsoken.*
De Jersey, Hen., Esq., *Deputy, Aldersgate Within.*
Elliott, John Hawkins, Esq., *Deputy, Candlewick.*
Ellis, John, *Langbourn.*
Ellis, John Whittaker, *Broad Street.*
Ellis, Richard, *Portsoken.*
Evans, John Charles, *Candlewick.*
Farlow, John King, *Candlewick.*
Farrar, Frederick, Esq., *Deputy, Castle Baynard.*
Figgins, James, *Farringdon Without.*
Finlay, John, *Langbourn.*
Fisher, George, *Lime Street.*
Foster, Thomas Willoughby, *Broad Street.*
Fowler, William Cave, *Aldersgate Without.*
Fricker, Thomas, *Langbourn.*
Frinneby, Frederick Richard, *Candlewick.*
Fry, Thos. Henry, Esq., *Deputy, Walbrook.*
Game, Charles Valentine, *Candlewick.*
Gibbins, Samuel, *Cheap.*
Gibbon, Henry, *Billingsgate.*
Glover, Frederick Kendal, *Farringdon Within.*
Gover, Henry, *Bridge.*
Gover, William Sutton, *Vintry.*
Gower, Jabez Samuel, *Cripplegate Without.*
Grimwade, Charles, *Cordwainer.*
Hadley, Simeon Charles, *Castle Baynard.*
Hammack, Henry Laurence, *Bishopsgate.*

Hale, John Hampton, *Castle Baynard.*
Harris, Henry, *Lime Street.*
Hart, Edward, *Coleman Street.*
Hartland, Thomas Pick, *Bridge.*
Hartridge, William, *Broad Street.*
Harvey, James, *Cripplegate Without.*
Hawtrey, Wm., Esq., *Deputy, Bread Street.*
Heath, Henry Hodsoll, *Tower.*
Heath, Samuel, *Bassishaw.*
Heeps, John Henry, *Bishopsgate.*
Heginbothom, Charles. *Tower.*
Hewett, William, *Candlewick.*
Hill, Henry, *Cordwainer.*
Homer, John James, *Cornhill.*
Hopgood, Metcalf, *Bishopsgate.*
Hoppe, Henry, *Cornhill.*
Howell, James, *Farringdon Without.*
Hudson, John, *Aldgate.*
Humphreys, Charles Oct., *Farringdon Within.*
Humphreys, Thomas Bennett, *Tower.*
Isaacs, Henry Aaron, *Aldgate.*
Israel, Henry Ash, *Portsoken.*
Jenkinson, William, *Coleman Street.*
Johnson, George Noah, *Bishopsgate.*
Johnson, Thomas, *Bridge Within.*
Jones, Hugh, *Cripplegate Within.*
Jones, Wm., Esq., *Deputy, Bishopsgate.*
Kebbel, Henry, *Queenhithe.*
Kelday, John, *Farringdon Within.*
Knight, Henry Edmund, *Cripplegate Within.*
Land, John, *Walbrook.*
Latimer, Fitz Henry, *Bishopsgate.*
Lawley, William, *Farringdon Without.*
Lindsey, Mark John, *Farringdon Within.*
Lintott, Thomas, *Walbrook.*
Lister, William, *Bassishaw.*
Locke, Anthony, Esq., *Deputy, Bassishaw.*
Longden, George Roger, *Castle Baynard.*
Lott, Thomas, Esq., F.S.A., *Deputy, Cordwainer.*
Lusher, James, *Farringdon Without.*
M'Cutchan, Ivie, *Bread Street.*
M'Dougall, Archibald, Esq., *Deputy, Queenhithe.*
M'George, Mungo, *Bread Street.*
Malcolm, John, Esq., *Deputy, Tower.*
Mason, George, Esq., *Deputy, Vintry.*
Maughan, Nicholas, *Bread Street.*
Maynard, Frederick, *Bread Street.*
Medwin, James, *Langbourn.*
Morey, Samuel Dance, *Cheap.*
Munday, Charles, *Farringdon Without.*
Murrell, Henry Edward, *Walbrook.*
Nind, Henry William, *Cripplegate Without.*
Northcott, William, *Billingsgate.*
Northway, John, *Tower.*
Obbard, Robert, Esq., *Dep., Farringdon Without.*
Orridge, Benjamin Brogden, F.G.S., *Cheap.*
Pallett, Robert, *Walbrook.*
Pantin, William, *Dowgate.*
Parker, John, Esq., *Deputy, Cripplegate Within.*
Parker, Thomas, F.S.A., *Castle Baynard.*
Paterson, John, *Aldersgate Within.*
Payne, William, *Farringdon Without.*
Pedler, George Stanbury, *Farringdon Without.*
Philipps, Richd. Nathaniel, *Farringdon Without.*
Philips, Thomas Rouse, *Cornhill.*
Pickering, John, *Cripplegate Without.*

Pill, Alfred, *Bread Street.*
Potter, Rowland Faulkner, *Farringdon Within.*
Read, Septimus, Esq., *Deputy, Cripplegate Witht.*
Reed, C., Esq., F.S.A., *Dep., Farringdon Within.*
Richards, Thomas Smallwood, *Bishopsgate.*
Richardson, John, *Bishopsgate.*
Ridley, Arthur Stone, *Bread Street.*
Rigby, Edward Robert, *Bishopsgate.*
Roberts, James, *Billingsgate.*
Robinson, Crescens, *Vintry.*
Rogers, Edward Dresser, *Aldgate.*
Rudkin, Thomas, *Farringdon Within.*
Saunders, J. E., F.L.S., F.G.S., *Coleman Street.*
Saunders, William Sedgwick, *Cordwainer.*
Sawbridge, Charles, *Cripplegate Within.*
Sewell, John, *Aldersgate Within.*
Shephard, Mark, *Vintry.*
Silverside, Giles, *Castle Baynard.*
Simpson, Thos. Bridge, Esq., *Dep., Lime Street.*
Sims, Davis, *Broad Street.*
Sims, George, *Aldersgate Without.*
Slowman, Ben, *Billingsgate.*
Smith, David, *Cripplegate Without.*
Smith, Edwin, *Tower.*
Snowden, Joseph, *Farringdon Within.*
Solomon, Henry, *Portsoken.*
Spiller, Edmund Pim, *Farringdon Without.*
Spilsbury, Benjamin, *Cripplegate Within.*
Staples, John, *Aldersgate Without.*
Stapleton, Robert, *Bishopsgate.*
Straker, Samuel, *Bishopsgate.*
Swainston, William Richard, *Coleman Street.*
Symonds, John, *Langbourn.*
Symonds, Thomas, *Lime Street.*
Taylor, Henry Lowman, *Cordwainer.*
Taylor, Robert, Sen., *Bridge.*
Taylor, Robert Parker, *Bridge.*
Tegg, Wm., Esq., F.G.S., *Deputy, Cheap.*
Terry, James, *Queenhithe.*
Teulon, William Hensman, *Aldgate.*
Thomas, John, *Bishopsgate.*
Thorp, Jonathan, *Cheap.*
Todd, Charles John, *Queenhithe.*
Truscott, Francis Wyatt, *Dowgate.*
Turner, Jesse, *Cripplegate Without.*
Turnley, Joseph, *Aldgate.*
Virtue, G., Esq., *Dep. Farngdn. Within (south side).*
Walker, John, *Queenhithe.*
Walter, George, *Farringdon Without.*
Warton, Charles, *Broad Street.*
Warwick, Robert Betson, *Vintry.*
Warwick, Robert Erlam, *Farringdon Within.*
Waterlow, Alfred James, *Cornhill.*
Waterlow, James, *Cornhill.*
Webber, Thomas, Esq., *Deputy, Langbourn.*
Webster, William, Esq., *Deputy, Coleman Street.*
Wheeler, William Sidney, *Farringdon Within.*
Whetham, Chas., Esq., *Deputy, Bridge Within.*
White, Thomas, Esq., *Deputy, Dowgate.*
Whiteside, Robert Butler, *Aldgate.*
Wilcox, Isaac, *Coleman Street.*
Wild, Henry Bowles, *Cheap.*
Wood, James, *Farringdon Without.*
Yoodley, Thomas, *Portsoken.*
Young, John, Jun., *Tower.*
Young, John Tonkin, *Billingsgate.*

OFFICERS.

Appointed by the Court of Aldermen.

	Elect.		Elect.
RECORDER.—Rt. Hon. Russell Gurney, Q.C.	1856	Cashier and Accountant.—Mr. William Ball...	1865
Steward of Southwark.—Mr. Serjt. Payne	1850	Clerk to the Sitting Justices.—Mr. G. Martin	1855
Clerk to the Lord Mayor.—Mr. G. C. Oke......	1865	Assistant.—Mr. Joseph Davie	1833
Assistant.—Mr. Thomas Holmes Gore	1865	Cashier and Accountant.—Mr. G. H. Griffin...	1848

Appointed by the Court of Common Council.

	Elect.
TOWN CLERK.—Frederick Woodthorpe, Esq.	1859
Common Serjeant.—T. Chambers, Esq., Q.C.	1857
Judge of the Sheriffs' Court.—Robert Malcolm Kerr, LL.D.	1859
Secondary.—George Wm. K. Potter, Esq.	1831
Comptroller.—Ferdinand Brand, Esq.	1854
Remembrancer.—William Corrie, Esq.	1864
Solicitor.—Thomas James Nelson, Esq.	1862
Coroner.—Mr. Serjeant Payne.	1829
Clerk of the Peace.—Edm. Jas. Read, Esq.	1865
Architect & Surveyor.—Horace Jones, Esq.	1864
High Bailiff of Southwark.—W. Gresham, Esq.	1859
Commissioner of Police.—Col. Jas. Fraser.	1863
Registrar of the Mayor's Court.—Woodthorpe Brandon, Esq.	1859
Sword Bearer.—Henry Wm. Sewell, Esq.	1860
Common Crier and Serjeant.—John Alexander Beddome, Esq.	1867
Clerk for Auditors.—W. Payne, Esq.	1854
Registrar Small Debts.—T. J. Nelson, Esq. pro tem.	
High Bailiff of ditto.—Mr. Abraham Brown	do.

	Elect.
Head Master City of London School.—Rev. E. A. Abbott, M.A.	1840
Second Master of ditto.—F. Cuthbertson, M.A.	1855
Head Master Freemen's Orphan Sch.—Marcus Tulloch Cormack, M.A.	1867
Prothonotary.—Ferdinand Brand, Esq.	1852
Keeper of Guildhall.—Mr. Henry Hadland	1868
Clerk and Collector of Coal Duties.—Mr. Wm. Mozart Russell	1837
Clerk and Registrar of Coal Market.—Mr. Jas. Renat Scott	1847
Marshal.—Mr. Frdk. Browne, Mansion Ho.	1852
Collector of City's Wine Dues.—Mr. S. Baylis	1847
Comptroller of City's Wine Dues.—Mr. H. Bezer	1847
Collector of Brokers' Rents.—Mr. J. Thornton	1861
Corn Shifter below Bridge.—Mr. Wm. Ruston	1827
Corn Shifter at Queenhithe. do.	1860
Fruit Meter and Shifter.—Mr. Isaac Mitchell	1861
Housekeeper at the Sessions House.—Mr. John Hoard	1846
Upper Beadle of Coal Market.—Mr. J. Stacy	1845

Elected by the Livery.

	Elect.
CHAMBERLAIN.—Benjamin Scott, Esq., F.R.A.S.	1858
Bridge Masters. { Mr. Thos. Plant Rose	1855
{ Mr. Edward Ledger	1855

Auditors of the City and Bridge House Accounts {		Elect.
	Mr. J. G. Dunn	1867
	Mr. J. Surman	1867
	Mr. W. H. Twentyman	1868
	Mr. Geo. Singer	1868

RECEIPTS AND EXPENDITURE for the Year ending 31st December, 1867.

Dr.	INCOME.	£
Rents and Quit-rents		124,379
Renewing Fines		4,689
Markets, viz.—		
Islington Cattle Market		32,329
Leadenhall		3,351
Newgate		5,983
Farringdon		1,260
Smithfield		270
Billingsgate		5,744
Duties, viz.—		
Metage of Corn		15,826
Groundage, &c. of Corn		353
Fruit Metage		2,295
Stamping Weights and Measures		130
Bequests		125
Brokers' Rents, Fines, and Fees		6,424
Mayor's Court Fees		5,729
Justiciary Fees		1,147
Interest on Government Securities		2,705
Interest on temporary Investments		4,417
On account of Prisons		4,418
„ Criminal Prosecutions		1,729
Southwark Bridge account		15,882
Holborn Valley Improvement account		1,890
Officers' surplus Fees and Profits		8,813
Casual, Sundry, and incidental Receipts		1,251
To Sale of Premises		2,787
To Sale of Securities		54,888
To Loan repaid		500
To Loans raised		316,000
Total		**£625,335**

Cr.	EXPENDITURE.	£
Expenses of Civil Government		40,315
Repairs and Improvement of Guildhall		1,948
Donations, Pensions, and Rewards		7,870
Educational expenses		7,288
Administration of Justice		7,984
Office of Coroner		1,378
Opening of Southwark Bridge, toll-free		5,605
Expenses in relation to the supply of Gas		5,704
Miscellaneous and incidental expenditure		10,907
City Library		1,067
Entertainment of the Sultan, and the Belgian Volunteers		26,701
Charges on Corporation Estates, viz.—		
Cost of Collection and Management		3,217
Rent-Charges, Rates, &c.		4,877
Charges on Markets, viz.—		
Metropolitan Cattle Market, Islington		49,034
Leadenhall		947
Newgate		891
Farringdon		1,182
Smithfield		625
Billingsgate		1,955
General Market charges and expenses		388
Return of Duties		122
Collection and Management of ditto		6,032
Charges on Brokers' Rents and Fines		415
Expenses of Magistracy		7,925
Police expenses (City's proportion)		17,030
Maintenance of Pauper Lunatic Asylum		392
Newgate Prison		5,030
Debtors' Prison		4,231
City Prison, Holloway		9,585
General Prison expenses		855
Balance overpaid 31st Dec., 1866		14,010
Construction, &c., of Metropolitan Meat and Poultry Market		79,360
Purchase of Property		2,386
Temporary Investments		162,371
Loans discharged		116,000
Balance in hand on 31st Dec., 1867		19,694
Total		**625,335**

LONDON CITY COMPANIES.

Company.	Hall.	Clerks.
Apothecaries	Water Lane	Robert Brotherton Upton, Esq.
Armourers and Braziers	81, Coleman Street	John Pontifex, Esq., 5, St. Andrew's Court.
Bakers	16, Harp Lane	Henley Grose Smith, Esq., 4, Warnford Ct.
Barbers	Monkwell Street	Henley Grose Smith, Esq., 4, Warnford Ct.
Blacksmiths	No Hall	William B. Garrett, Esq., 36, Great Tower St.
Bowyers	No Hall	Charles B. Arding, Esq., 23, Bedford Row.
Brewers	18, Addle Street	Charles Richard Vines, Esq.
Broderers (Embroiderers)	No Hall	Charles E. Freeman, Esq., 5, Budge Row.
Butchers	5½, Eastcheap	Joseph Daw, Esq., Sewers Office, Guildhall.
Carmen	No Hall or Livery	Alexander J. Baylis, Esq., Church Ct.Chmbs.
Carpenters	68, London Wall	Edward Basil Jupp, Esq., F.S.A.
Clockmakers	No Hall	Samuel Elliott Atkins, Esq., 6, Cowper's Ct.
Clothworkers	41, Mincing Lane	Owen Roberts, Esq., M.A.
Coach & Coach Har. Makers	Noble Street	George W. K. Potter, Esq., 20, Basinghall St.
Combmakers	No Hall	John James Kirkman Esq.
Cooks	No Hall	J. B. Towse, Esq., 24, Laurence Pountney La.
Coopers	Basinghall Street	John Boyer, Esq.
Cordwainers	7, Cannon Street	Henry Dunkin Francis, Esq., at the Hall.
Curriers	London Wall	Edward Burkitt, Esq.
Cutlers	6. Cloak Lane	James Beaumont, Esq., 23, Lincoln's InnFlds.
Distillers	No Hall	Thomas Browning, Esq., 13, Austin Friars.
Drapers	27, Throgmorton Street	William Henry Sawyer, Esq.
Dyers	10, Dowgate Hill	Henry Batt, Esq.
Fanmakers	No Hall	George Martin, Esq., Guildhall.
Farriers	No Hall	Sidney Smith, Esq., 1, Furnival's Inn.
Fellowship Porters	St. Mary-at-hill. No Livery	Griffith Thomas, Esq., Commercial Sl. Rms.
Feltmakers	No Hall	Alfred Peachey, Esq., 17, Salisbury Square.
Fishmongers	London Bridge	William Beckwith Towse, Esq.
Fletchers	No Hall	Charles Shepheard, Esq., 78, Coleman Street.
Founders	13, St. Swithin's lane	Algernon Wells, Esq.
Framework Knitters	No Hall	Robert Anderson, Esq., 2, Ingram Court.
Fruiterers	No Hall	O. C. T. Eagleton, Esq., 84, Newgate Street.
Gardeners	No Hall or Livery	Charles Shopheard, Esq., 78, Coleman Street.
Girdlers	39, Basinghall Street	John Clarke, Esq.,
Glaziers	No Hall	C. H. Lovell, Esq., 14, South Sq., Gray's Inn.
Glovers	No Hall	Frederick Richard Thomas, Esq., 3, Fen Ct.
Gold & Silver Wiredrawers	No Hall	C. Gammon, Esq., 9, Cloak Lane.
Goldsmiths	Foster Lane	Walter Prideaux, Esq.
Grocers	Grocers' Hall Court	William Ruck, Esq.
Gunmakers	No Hall	George Rutherford, Esq., 14, Gracechurch St.
Haberdashers	Gresham Street West	John Curtis, Esq.
Horners	No Hall	George Henderson, Esq., 22, Leadenhall St.
Innholders	6, College Street	Alexander Devas Druce, Esq., 10, Billiter Sq.
Ironmongers	117½, Fenchurch Street	S. Adams Beck, Esq.
Joiners	Joiners' Hall Buildings	Benj. Granger, Esq., 1, James St., Adelphi.
Leathersellers	St. Helen's Place	Charles Richard Vines, Esq.
Long Bow String Makers	No Hall or Livery	Charles Shepheard, Esq., 78, Coleman Street.
Loriners	No Hall	Thomas Davies Sewell, Esq., Guildhall.
Masons	Masons' Avenue	Frederick Gwatkin, Esq., 9, New Square.
Mercers	Ironmonger Lane	Henry Eugene Barnes, Esq
Merchant Taylors	30, Threadneedle Street	Samuel Fisher, Esq.
Musicians	No Hall	John Wood, Esq., 162, Aldersgate Street.
Needlemakers	No Hall	G. H. Cole, Esq., 1, Church Ct., Clement's La.
Painters	9, Little Trinity Lane	William Thompson, Esq.
Parish Clerks	24, Silver Street. No Livery	Joseph Wheeler, Esq.
Pattenmakers	No Hall	John Thornton, Esq., Guildhall.
Paviors	No Hall or Livery	R. Ellis, Esq., 2, America Square.
Pewterers	15, Lime Street	W. Dadley, Esq., 1, Anchor Ter., Southwark.
Plasterers	No Hall	Henry Mott, Esq., 22, Bedford Row.
Playing Cardmakers	No Hall	Joseph Daw, Esq., Sewers Office, Guildhall.
Plumbers	No Hall	J. B. Towse, Esq., 24, Laurence Pountney La.
Poulterers	No Hall	William Harry Sadgrove, Esq., 64, Mark La.
Saddlers	141, Cheapside	Charles Octavius Humphreys, Esq.
Salters	St. Swithin's Lane	David W. Martin, Esq.
Scriveners	No Hall	Park Nelson, Esq., 11, Essex Street, Strand.
Shipwrights	No Hall	John Young, Esq., 6, Frederick's Place.
Skinners	8, Dowgate Hill	Thomas Glover Kensit, Esq.
Spectaclemakers	Leadenhall Street	Thomas Davies Sewell, Esq., Guildhall.
Stationers	Stationers' Hall Court	Charles Rivington, Esq., 1, Fenchurch Bldgs.
Tallow Chandlers	5, Dowgate Hill	Edwin Bedford, Esq., 1, Staining Lane.
Tilers and Bricklayers	No Hall	Arthur Bird, Esq., 6, Bedford Row.
Tinplate	No Hall	Edward Burkitt, Esq., Curriers' Hall.

London City Companies—*continued.*

Company.	Hall.	Clerk.
Turners	No Hall	Charles I. Shirreff, Esq., 9, Fenchurch Street.
Upholders	No Hall	George Smith, Esq., 446, Camden Road.
Vintners	68½, Upper Thames Street	George Lomas, Esq.
Watermen and Lightermen	18, St. Mary-at-hill	Henry Humpherus, Esq.
Waxchandlers	Gresham Street West	Horatio Gregory, Esq.
Weavers	22, Basinghall Street	Alfred Carr, Esq.
Wheelwrights	No Hall	James Renat Scott, Esq., Coal Exchange.
Woolmen	No Hall	Charles Francis, Esq., 22, Austin Friars.

METROPOLITAN BOARD OF WORKS,

Office, Spring Gardens.—(Hours 9 to 4. Saturdays, 9 to 2.)

Chairman, Sir John Thwaites, £2,000.

Members of the Board.

Name.	Parish.	Residence.
Adams, B. H. Esq.	*St. Giles*	55, Torrington Square.
Beven, Thos. Esq.	*St. Matthew, Bethnal Gr.*	Stanley Villas, K. Edward's Rd., Hackney Rd.
Bidgood, Henry, Esq.	*St. James, Westminster*	7, Vigo Street, Regent Street.
Brooker, Jas., Esq.	*Plumstead, with Lewisham*	Brockley Park, Forest Hill.
Brushfield, Thomas, Esq.	*Whitechapel*	5, Church Street, Spitalfields.
Clark, W., Esq.	*St. George-in-the-East*	52, Wellclose Square.
Collinson, E., Esq.	*St. George, Southwark*	95, Blackman Street, Southwark.
Cook, E. R., Esq.	*Poplar*	Craven Cottage, Wellington Road, Bromley.
Dalton, W. H., Esq.	*St. Martin-in-the-Fields*	28, Cockspur Street.
Dixon, Benjamin, Esq.	*Limehouse*	3, Norway Place, Commercial Road East.
Elt, C. H., Esq.	*Islington*	1, Noel Street, Islington.
Evans, B., Esq.	*Newington, Surrey*	Acre House, Brixton.
Fowler, Francis, H., Esq.	*Lambeth*	The Lodge, Brixton Oval.
Freeman, Robert, Esq.	*Kensington*	12, Upper Phillimore Place, Kensington.
Gibbons, S. J., Alderman	*City of London*	Calvert's Buildings, Southwark Street.
Hall, John O., Esq.	*Holborn*	1, Brunswick Row, Queen Square.
Harris, Charles, Esq.	*St. Saviour, Southwark*	15, Fenchurch Street.
Healy, F., Esq.	*St. Pancras*	92, Regent's Park Road.
Hogg, Colonel	*St. George, Hanover Sq.*	26, Grosvenor Gardens.
Hows, W. A. H., Esq.	*St. Leonard, Shoreditch*	274, Kingsland Road.
Hudson, George, Esq.	*Woolwich*	Brewer Street, Woolwich.
Lammin, W. H., Esq.	*Fulham*	5, John Street, Adelphi.
LeBreton, P. H., Esq.	*Hampstead*	22, Thurlow Road, Hampstead.
Legg, Cyrus, Esq.	*Bermondsey*	Bermondsey Street.
Long, Jeremiah, Esq.	*St. Leonard, Shoreditch*	13, Park Street, Westminster.
Meaden, G. P., Esq.	*Wandsworth*	High Street, Clapham.
Moreland, Joseph, Esq.	*St. Luke, Middlesex*	7, Highbury New Park.
Newton, W., Esq.	*Mile End Old Town*	41, Stepney Green.
Nicholay, John Aug., Esq.	*St. Marylebone*	82, Oxford Street.
Phillips, John S., Esq.	*Strand*	5, Bishop's Court, Lincoln's Inn.
Richardson, G. B., Esq.	*Greenwich*	10, Stainton Pl., Shooter's Hill Rd., Blackheath.
Roche, C. M., Esq.	*Paddington*	98, Gloucester Terrace, Hyde Park.
Runtz, J., Esq.	*Hackney*	Lordship Road, Stoke Newington.
Saunders, J. E., Esq.	*City of London*	9, Finsbury Circus.
Savage, John, Esq.	*St. Mary, Islington*	54, Thornhill Square, Islington.
Shaw, A. N., Esq.	*St. Marylebone*	13, Poultry.
Taylor, H. Lowman, Esq.	*City of London*	10, Queen Street, Cheapside.
Taylor, Robert, Esq.	*Lambeth*	5, Dudley Villas, Clapham Road.
Taylor, Silas, Esq.	*St. Pancras*	Leighton House, Leighton Road, Kentish Town
Thompson, Edwd. J., Esq.	*Clerkenwell*	20, Douglas Road, Canonbury.
Tito, Wm., Esq., M.P.	*Chelsea*	42, Lowndes Square.
Turner, Thomas, Esq.	*Rotherhithe with St. Olave*	Treasurer's House, Guy's Hospital.
Westerton, Charles, Esq.	*St. George, Hanover Sq.*	27, St. George's Place, Hyde Park.
White, J. T., Esq.	*Westminster*	11, Parliament Street.

Clerk of the Board, John Pollard, Esq., £800.
Assistant Clerk, Edward Creasy, £700
Engineer, Joseph William Bazalgette, Esq., £2,200
Superintending Architect, George Vulliamy, Esq. £1,000.

Solicitor, William Wyke Smith, Esq., £1,250
Accountant, Edward Hughes, Esq., £600
Chief Officer, Fire Brigade, Capt. Eyre Massey Shaw, £750
Architect, Fire Brigade, Edward Creasy, (£200)

In addition to the Annual Report presented to Parliament, Mr. Tite, Colonel Sykes, and Mr. Sclater Booth, moved for additional papers; but notwithstanding these additions, the accounts put forward are of an exceedingly unsatisfactory and bewildering character, there being no fewer than eighteen different statements, some of them being for very large sums of money—the two which approach most nearly to balance-sheets are given below. The Board has contracted various lo ms, of which the amount outstanding, Jan. 1, 1868, was £6,552,366, while, according to another account, the sum was but £3,230,000. From 1st Jan., 1856, to 25th March, 1867, the Board had received £11,056,099 from all sources. It may be mentioned, that one of the separate accounts, that of the FIRE BRIGADE, is quite satisfactory, and a model which the accountant of the Board would do well to study; if the "General" and other accounts were drawn up in the same clear and distinct manner, the various Metropolis Vestries would be less dissatisfied with the proceedings of the Board.

NEW GENERAL ACCOUNT.

This, which ought to be the General Balance Sheet, is reduced to the merely subordinate position of being one of the eighteen different accounts.

Dr.	£	Cr.	£
Balance in hand, 26th March, 1866.........	14,004	PAYMENTS.	
RECEIPTS.		Sewerage and Drainage, £262,862—	
		Works, &c.	231,263
Assessments, &c.	171,461	Rent, Taxes, &c.	708
Sewerage and Drainage, £256,076—		Compensation for Damage...................	25
Loans from Bank of England	254,000	Loans, Annuities, &c.	23,039
Contributions, &c..............................	2,025	Incidentals	7,824
Incidentals	50	Metropolis Improvements, £159,318—	
Metropolis Improvements—		Purchase of Property........................	8,300
Transfer from Southwark and Westminster Account	25,000	Contributions to Works, &c................	14,071
		Transfer to Mortgage Debt Sinking Fund Account	6,000
Repayment of Tempor. Loans, £135,290—		Loans, &c.	30,947
Southwark and Westminster Communication Account, with Interest	10,290	Temporary Loans.............................	100,000
Thames Embankment, North	50,000	General Purposes, £75,775—	
Southern Embankment	50,000	Salaries, Wages, Office repairs and expenses, Rent, Taxes, Printing, Stationery, &c.	46,007
General Purposes, £26,908—		Compensation to late Officers	1,145
Fees under Metropolitan Building Act	115	Professional charges	3,769
Plans, &c., sold	34	Loans, &c.	9,853
Miscellaneous	89	Temporary Loan	15,000
Proportions of Establishment charges paid by Special Accounts	21,113	Sale of Gas Acts, £1,682—	
Interest on Cash Balances..................	5,555	Rents and Taxes for Testing Houses...	158
Sale of Gas Acts—		Salaries and Wages	1,114
Fees for testing Meters	1,076	Incidental	409
Cattle Diseases Prevention Acts—		Cattle Diseases Prevention Act—	
Proceeds of Sale of Carcases..............	240	Compensation for Cattle slaughtered, Inspectors' allowances, &c.	5,477
Repayments on account of Advances for the following Improvements—		Houseless Poor Act—	
Whitechapel	2,500	Reimbursement of expenses incurred by Parishes, Unions, &c...................	13,169
Holborn...	8,000	Advances on behalf of Special Accounts	22,306
		Balance in hand, 25th March, 1867 ...	74,964
Total	£615,557	Total £615,557	

GENERAL SUMMARY of Receipt and Expenditure for the Year ending 25th March, 1867.

Titles of Accounts.	Receipts in 1866-7.	Expenditure in 1866-7
Old General Account.............	48,220	52,593
New General Account	601,553	540,597
Covent Garden Approach ...	2,284	3,152
Southwark and Westminster	37,965	65,335
Victoria Park Approach	111	10
Finsbury Park	100	166
Southwark Park..................	20,599	3,045
Essex Reclamation..............	888	926
Fire Brigade......................	86,205	83,399
Whitechapel Improvement....	109,660	50,599
Holborn Improvement..........	61,401	20,862
Metropolis Main Drainage....	250,100	249,083
Main Drainage Rate Collect.	14,522	13,915
Thames Embankment, North	381,198	378,771
Southern Embankment	542,207	562,921
Mansion House Street	774,280	844,577
SINKING FUNDS:		
Mortgage Debts of the Board	21,000	...
Metropolis Main Drainage ...	195,811	220,086
Balance in hand	356,604	414,671
	£3,504,717	£3,504,717

METROPOLITAN GAS COMPANIES,

Capital and Dividends for 1867.

	Capital.	Dividend.
Chartered	839,965	55,641
City of London	456,340	30,100
Commercial	437,230	43,722
Equitable	300,000	30,054
Great Central	266,000	20,000
Imperial	1,966,442	136,001
Independent	222,500	16,312
London	755,569	49,456
Phœnix	925,414	69,187
Ratcliffe	117,000	10,000
South Metropolitan..	249,267	23,386
Surrey......................	257,460	19,940
Western	360,091	30,500
	£7,153,278	£534,299

EXHIBITIONS, PUBLIC BUILDINGS, MUSIC HALLS, THEATRES, AND OTHER PLACES AND OBJECTS OF INTEREST IN THE METROPOLIS AND SUBURBS.

THE following list comprises most of the Objects of Interest to persons visiting the Metropolis, also some of the suburban resorts frequented by Londoners, with the times of opening, prices of admission, and railway fares. But, as many of these vary occasionally, absolute accuracy is impossible. The daily papers, however, will generally, in their advertisement columns, supply the necessary particulars. Except where otherwise stated, "Open Daily" means every Week-day, and not Sundays.

EXHIBITIONS, &c.

ACADEMY, ROYAL, Trafalgar Square.—Exhibition of pictures by eminent painters, from 1st Monday in May to end of July, from 10 to 4. Admission, 1s. Evening, from 6 to 9, 6d.

ALEXANDRA PARK, Muswell Hill.—Not yet fully opened. 6 miles north of London. Railway fare, 6d., 8d., 1s., by Great Northern line.

ARCADES.—Lowther, 437, Strand; Burlington, 94, Piccadilly.

ART EXHIBITIONS.—Those not specially mentioned in the preceding or following lists are open at uncertain seasons. The usual period is between the beginning of May and the end of August.

BAZAARS.—Soho, 406, Oxford Street; London Crystal Palace, 9, Great Portland Street; Baker Street, 58, Baker Street, Oxford Street; Royal Bazaar, New Oxford Street; Pantechnicon, Motcomb Street, Belgrave Square, Free. The late Pantheon, Oxford Street, is now occupied as a wine-store.

CRYSTAL PALACE, Sydenham.—Access by several railways from London Bridge, Chatham and Dover Stations, Victoria Station, &c. Fare about 1s. Admission, 1s.; on Saturdays, 2s. 6d.

NATIONAL GALLERY, Trafalgar Square.—National collection of pictures, open Saturday, Monday, Tuesday, and Wednesday from 10 to 5 or 6. Closed entirely during October.

POLYTECHNIC INSTITUTION, 309, Regent Street. —Admission, 1s. Variety of entertainments, scientific, musical, and general. Open from 12 to 5 and 7 till 10 daily.

TUSSAUD'S WAXWORK, 58, Baker Street, Portman Square.—Open morning and night, from 11 to 10 p.m. in summer; in winter from 11 to dusk, and 7 to 10 p.m. Admission, 1s.

GARDENS.

BOTANICAL, Regent's Park.—Accessible by orders from Fellows only.

CREMORNE, near Chelsea.—Accessible by railway, omnibus, and boat, for 6d. Admission 1s.

HIGHBURY BARN and THEATRE.—Admission to both, 1s. Open daily throughout the year.

HORTICULTURAL, South Kensington.—Accessible by order from Fellows. At times, by payment at the gates. Free, August 26th, the birthday of Prince Albert.

KEW, BOTANICAL. — Accessible by railway, omnibus, and steam-boat, at a cost of 6d. Free. Open from 1 to dusk, week-days and Sundays.

NORTH WOOLWICH, north bank of the Thames. —Varied entertainments; fine esplanade. Access by rail and steam-boat, 4d. and 6d. Admission 6d. and 1s.

ROSHERVILLE, near Gravesend. — Access by railway and steam-boat, 1s. and 1s. 4d. Admission to all the attractions, 1s.

TEMPLE, on the north bank of the Thames, near Fleet Street, arrived at by passing through the Temple. Free.

ZOOLOGICAL GARDENS, Regent's Park.—Admission on Monday, 6d.; the rest of the week, 1s. On Sunday by an order from a Fellow.

MISCELLANEOUS.

BRIDGES.—London, Southwark, Blackfriars (rebuilding; notice the temporary wooden bridge), Waterloo, Westminster, Lambeth, Vauxhall, Battersea, Hammersmith (suspension), &c., &c.; and the various railway bridges over the Thames. There is a footway over the iron Railway Bridge at Hungerford; toll, ½d. The Thames Tunnel, from Rotherhithe to Wapping, is not now open to the public without an order from the East London Railway Company, by which it has been purchased.

COLLEGES.—Chiefly for external appearance, and not for inspection, are—University, Gower Street; King's, in the Strand, part of Somerset House; Gordon, Gordon Square; New College, St. John's Wood; Wesleyan, at Horseferry Road and Richmond; Gresham, in Gresham Street, City, where, during terms, lectures in Latin and English are delivered free, on law, music, physic, &c.; British and Foreign School Society's, Borough Road; Surgeons' (fine anatomical museum), Lincoln's Inn Fields; Heralds', Bennett's Hill, City, &c., &c.

HOSPITALS.—Guy's, Southwark; Bethlehem, Lambeth; St. Thomas, building on the Thames Embankment, Lambeth; St. Bartholomew's, West Smithfield; London, Whitechapel Road; Westminster, near the Abbey; Middlesex, Charles Street, Oxford Street; University College, Gower Street; St. Luke's (lunatic), Old Street, City Road; King's College, near Lincoln's Inn Fields; Small Pox, Highgate; Foundling, Great Guildford Street; Charing Cross, Agar Street, Strand; Royal Free, Gray's Inn Road; Consumption, Brompton; Christ's, see SCHOOLS; Chelsea (military); Greenwich (for seamen), Painted Hall free daily; special order required for other parts. The Royal Hospitals are: Chelsea, Greenwich, the Military Asylum, and Bethlehem. The Endowed Hospitals are: Bartholomew's, Guy's, St. Thomas's, and London.

PARKS.—St. James', near Charing Cross; the Green Park, adjacent to St. James'; Hyde Park (this should be visited from 3 to 5 during the season); Kensington Gardens; Victoria Park, at the East-end, near Hackney; Battersea Park; Regent's Park and Primrose Hill; all accessible from the centre of the metropolis at the cost of a 4d. ride by omnibus, railway, or steam-boat.

SCHOOLS, PUBLIC.—Westminster, near the Abbey; St. Paul's, near that Cathedral in the Churchyard; Charter House, near Aldersgate Street (but in course of removal); Christ's Hospital, or the Blue Coat School, in Newgate Street; Merchant Taylors', Suffolk Lane, Dowgate, near the Mansion House (removing to the Charter House); Mercers', College Hill; City of London, Milk Street, Cheapside, &c.

SOCIETIES.—See separate list.

THAMES EMBANKMENT.—A magnificent public promenade on the north and south sides of the Thames, between Lambeth, Westminster and Blackfriars. Open on the north shore from the Temple to Westminster Bridge.

MUSEUMS.

BRITISH, Bloomsbury.—Fine collection of objects of natural history, sculpture, &c., &c. Free. Monday, Wednesday and Friday, from 10 till dusk. To view Reading-room (open daily to readers), an order may be obtained in the great hall.

COLLEGE OF SURGEONS, Lincoln's Inn Fields.—Admission only by order of members of the College, every week-day from 10 till 4.

ECONOMIC GEOLOGY, Jermyn Street, Piccadilly.—Open every day free from 10 to 5, on Saturday from 10 to 10, but closed from the 10th of August to the 10th of September.

INDIA.—Formerly at Whitehall, but about to be transferred to the New India-office, Westminster.

KENSINGTON, SOUTH.—Collection of art treasures, manufactures, useful arts, patented inventions, pictures, &c., &c. Free Mondays, Tuesdays, and Saturdays, from 10 to 10; on other days from 10 to 4, 5, or 6, on payment of 6d. Patent museum always free.

SAULL'S MUSEUM OF GEOLOGY, 15, Aldersgate Street. Free at 11 a.m. on Thursdays.

SIR JOHN SOANE'S, Lincoln's Inn.—Contains many of Hogarth's pictures and other art treasures. Open on Wednesdays from February to August inclusive, and every Thursday and Friday in April, May, and June, from 10 till 4. Orders to be applied for, and will be sent by post.

SOCIETY OF ARTS MUSEUM, Adelphi.—Daily, free, except Wednesday, by order of a member.

UNITED SERVICE MUSEUM, Whitehall.—Admission daily, by order from a member.

MUSIC AND CONCERT HALLS, &c.

At all the music-halls the prices range from 6d. to 1s., with a varying extra charge for reserved seats. Those in the following list marked thus* being used for many purposes, it is impossible to give particulars as to prices of admission. The usual time of opening for music-halls is half-past 6, commencing at 7, and concluding about 11 P.M.

AGRICULTURAL HALL,* Upper Street, Islington. —Concerts, public meetings, horse-fairs, circus, &c.

ALHAMBRA, Leicester Square.—Music, ballet, refreshments, &c.

ARGYLL ROOMS, Windmill Street, Haymarket. —Music, dancing, &c.

CANTERBURY HALL, Lambeth Marsh.—Music, dancing, refreshments, &c.

DEACON'S, Sadler's Wells, near the theatre.

EAST LONDON, Limehouse.—Music, &c.

EGYPTIAN,* Piccadilly. — Various entertainments. Several rooms let to "entertainers."

EVANS', Covent Garden.—Part and glee singing, refreshments, &c.

EXETER HALL,* 372, Strand.—Used for public meetings of all kinds, concerts by choral societies, the Sacred Harmonic, &c. Chief place for the "May meetings."

FREEMASONS'* Great Queen Street.—Public meetings, dinners, &c.

GALLERY OF ILLUSTRATION, Waterloo Place, Regent Street.—Mr. and Mrs. German Reed.

HANOVER SQUARE ROOMS.*—Similar to Exeter Hall; but also used for public balls, bazaars, and fancy fairs.

ISLINGTON PHILHARMONIC, High Street, Islington.—Singing, refreshments, &c.

MACDONALD'S, 64, High Street, Hoxton.—Music, &c.

METROPOLITAN, Edgware Road.—Singing, &c.

MIDDLESEX, Drury Lane.—Singing, refreshments, &c.

NATIONAL ASSEMBLY ROOMS, 218, High Holborn. —Music, dancing, &c.

PAVILION, Tichborne Street, Haymarket.—Singing, &c.

POLYGRAPHIC HALL, King William Street, Strand.

PRINCESS'S CONCERT ROOM, at the rear of Princess's Theatre.—Occasional concerts, balls, &c.

RAGLAN, Theobald's Road.—Singing, refreshments, &c.

REGENT, Pimlico.—Music, comic entertainments, &c.

ROYAL CAMBRIDGE, Commercial Street, Shoreditch.—Music, &c.

SOUTH LONDON, London Road, near the Elephant and Castle.—Music, singing, &c.

ST. GEORGE'S HALL,* Langham Place.—Various entertainments.

ST. JAMES'S HALL,* Piccadilly and Regent Street.—Public meetings, concerts, various entertainments, &c.

WESTON'S, 242, High Holborn.—Music, singing, refreshments, &c.

WILLIS'S ROOMS,* King Street, St. James's. —High-class concerts, public meetings, balls, dinners, &c.

WILTON'S, Wellclose Square.—Music, singing, &c.

WINCHESTER, Southwark Bridge Road.—Music, &c.

PUBLIC AND PRIVATE BUILDINGS.

APSLEY HOUSE.—The residence of the Duke of Wellington, corner of Piccadilly and Hyde Park (may be viewed by permission).

BANK OF ENGLAND.—The business portion free. The private portions, as the safes, printing machinery, only by order of a governor.

BANKS.—*See separate list.*

BRIDGEWATER HOUSE, Cleveland Square.—The residence of the Earl of Ellesmere. Splendid gallery of paintings. Accessible free by order.

BUCKINGHAM PALACE, west end of St. James's Park. Admission by special order only, of the Lord Chamberlain, in the absence of Royalty.

CEMETERIES.—*Highgate, Kensal Green, Finchley, Nunhead, Abney Park, City of London,* and many others, all within access by a 6d. omnibus ride from the General Post-Office or St. Paul's, and by railway.

CLUB HOUSES.—Some of them, as the *Reform, Carlton, United Service,* &c., are elegant and large buildings. They are mostly situated in Pall Mall, St. James's Street, Regent Street, and adjacent neighbourhoods. Admission obtained through a member's order. The principal London clubs are:—*Alfred,* 23, Albemarle Street, 600 members; entrance fee, £30; annual subscription, £10. *Army and Navy,* corner of St. James's Square, Pall Mall, 1,450 members; entrance, £30; subscription, £6 11s. *Arthur's,* 69, St. James's Street, 600 members; entrance, £21;

subscription, £10 10s. *Athenæum*, Pall Mall, 1,200 members; entrance, £26 5s.; subscription, £6 6s. *Boodle's*, 28, St. James's Street. *Brooke's*, 60, St. James's Street, 575 members; entrance £9 9s.; subscription, £11 11s. *Carlton*, Pall Mall, 800 members, exclusive of peers and M.P.s; entrance, £15 15s.; subscription, £10 10s. *City of London*, 19, Old Broad Street; entrance, £26 5s.; subscription, £6 6s. *Conservative*, St. James's Street, 1,500 members; entrance, £28 5s.; subscription, £8 8s. *Erectheum*, corner of York Street, St. James's Square, 600 members; entrance, £21; subscription, £7 7s.; *Garrick*, Covent Garden, 300 members; entrance, £15 15s.; subscription, £6 6s. *Junior United Service*, Charles Street, 1,500 members; entrance, £30; subscription, £5 5s. *Military, Naval, and County Service*, Pall Mall, 1,500 members; entrance fees, £15, £21, and £30; subscription, £5 5s. *Oriental*, Hanover Square, 800 members; entrance, £21; subscription, £8. *Oxford and Cambridge*, Pall Mall, 1,170 members—585 from each university; entrance, £26 5s.; subscription, £6 6s. *Reform*, 105 Pall Mall, 1,400 members, exclusive of honorary, supplementary, and life members; entrance, £26 5s.; subscription, £10 10s. *Travellers'*, 106, Pall Mall, 700 members; entrance, £21; subscription, £10 10s. *Union*, Trafalgar Square, 1,000 members; entrance, £32 11s.; subscription, £6 6s. *United Service*, 116, Pall Mall, 1,500 members; entrance, £30; subscription, £6. *Windham*, 11, St. James's Square, 600 members; entrance, £27 6s.; subscription, £8.

CUSTOM HOUSE.—On the north bank of the Thames, east of London Bridge; long room free. Excellent view of the river from the terrace.

DOCKS.—*St. Katherine's, London, East and West India, Commercial, Victoria*, &c. All accessible by steamboat or railway at a cost of 4d. Wine-tasting orders may be obtained through the leading wine-merchants; otherwise, free.

GOVERNMENT OFFICES.—*War Office*, in Pall Mall; *Admiralty, Horse Guards, Treasury*, &c., also in Whitehall and Downing-street.

GUILDHALL, King Street, City.—Admission free. To the council chambers, &c. by a small fee. To the library by order.

HOUSES OF PARLIAMENT, near Westminster Bridge.—Admission free, by order of the Lord Chamberlain, obtained at a neighbouring office; also during the hearing of appeals in the House of Lords. Admission to the Strangers' Gallery during the sitting of the House, by member's order only.

INNS OF COURT.—The chief are the *Temple*, in Fleet Street; *Gray's Inn*, north of Holborn; *Lincoln's Inn*, between Chancery Lane and Lincoln's Inn Fields; and *New Inn*, Wych Street.

INSURANCE OFFICES.—*See separate list.*

KENSINGTON PALACE AND GARDENS. At the west of Hyde Park.

LAMBETH PALACE.—The official residence of the Archbishop of Canterbury, on the bank of the Thames, Lambeth.

LAW COURTS.—In Westminster Hall are the Courts of *Chancery, Queen's Bench, Common Pleas, Exchequer*, &c. In Lincoln's Inn, *Chancery* and *Vice-Chancery* courts. *Courts of Law and Equity* are also held at Guildhall in the City. *Bankruptcy* Court in Basinghall Street; *Central Criminal Court*, Old Bailey; *Middlesex Sessions*, Clerkenwell Green.

MANSION HOUSE, City.—The official residence of the Lord Mayor; the Egyptian Hall and ball-room are the chief attractions. Admission by order and a small fee.

MARKETS. — *Newgate* market, now superseded by the *New Dead Meat Market* in Smithfield; *Leadenhall* Market (Poultry), Leadenhall Street; *Billingsgate* (Fish), Thames Street; *Covent Garden* (Fruit); *King's Cross, Farringdon* and *Spitalfields* (Vegetables, meat), &c.; *Live Cattle Market and Abattoirs*, in Caledonian Road, Holloway.

MARLBOROUGH HOUSE.—The residence of the Prince of Wales at the east end of St. James's Palace.

MINT.—On Tower Hill, where the coinage of the kingdom is carried on. Admission only by special order of the Master.

MONUMENT.—Near London Bridge, at the end of King William Street. Fine views of the City, river, &c. Admission, 3d.

MONUMENT, DUKE OF YORK'S, St. James's Park.—View of park and west-end. Admission 6d.

MONUMENT, NELSON'S, Trafalgar Square.—Near which are several statues, &c.

NORTHUMBERLAND HOUSE, Charing Cross.—The town residence of the Duke of Northumberland.

POST OFFICE, St. Martin's-le-Grand. — Hall free. Should be visited a little before 6 P.M., when the business of letter-posting is greatest.

ROYAL EXCHANGE, Cornhill.—Free.

ST. JAMES' PALACE, in Pall Mall.—Drawing-rooms and *levées* held here during the season.

ST. PAUL'S CATHEDRAL, St. Paul's Churchyard.—The masterpiece of Sir Christopher Wren. Splendid architecture, whispering gallery, cross, and ball; monuments to celebrated men. Nave and transepts free; choir closed except during divine service. 6d. charged to whispering gallery; 1s. 6d. to the ball; 6d. to the clock, bell, library, and staircase, and 6d. to the crypt.

SOMERSET HOUSE, in the Strand.—Free. Now devoted to public offices.

STAFFORD HOUSE, at the corner joining St. James' and the Green Parks.

STATUES.—Equestrian statue of the Duke of Wellington, at the Arch opposite Apsley House, Piccadilly, and many others in the city and west-end.

TEMPLE.—South side of Fleet Street. The hall and church very interesting, as also the gardens. Church open during divine service to strangers, at other times by small fee.

TOWER.—Regalia, armouries, &c., &c. Admission by fee of 6d. to see the armouries, and the Beauchamp Tower; and 6d. to the jewel house.

WESTMINSTER HALL, adjacent to the Houses of Parliament.—Free. Doors on the west lead to the place of sitting of the Courts of Chancery, Queen's Bench, Common Pleas, and Exchequer. On the east side are entrances to the House of Commons. One of the largest and oldest buildings in the kingdom.

WESTMINSTER ABBEY, near the Houses of Parliament and Westminster Bridge.—Free to the chief parts of the building, and to other parts by fee of 6d. Contains many objects of interest, especially statues, &c., erected in honour of celebrated persons.

WHITEHALL, opposite Horse Guards.—Erected by Inigo Jones, intended for a banqueting house, now used as the Chapel Royal. King Charles I. was beheaded in front of it.

SUBURBAN RESORTS.

BROXBOURNE.—On the Eastern Counties Railway. Fine gardens, boating, fishing, amusements, &c. Scene of the Rye House Plot, close to it. Fare, by railway, 1s. and upwards.

DULWICH.—Access by railway and omnibus, fare 6d. Fine gallery of paintings at the College free each week-day.

ERITH.—By Gravesend boats or North Kent Railway. Garden, beautiful scenery, and many other attractions.

GRAVESEND.—30 miles from London by steamboat and railway ; fares 1s. to 1s. 6d. Windmill Hill, Springhead Gardens, Cobham Park, Tilbury Fort, fine views of the Thames (here a mile wide), shipping, sea-water bathing. Near are Rosherville Gardens.

GREENWICH.—The *Naval Hospital*, commonly known as *Greenwich Hospital*, the *Observatory*, *Blackheath*. Fare, 4d. from London Bridge, by boat or railway.

HAMPSTEAD HEATH.—Fine view of London. Access by railway and omnibus. Fare 6d.

HAMPTON COURT.—Built by Cardinal Wolsey. 13 miles from London ; 1s. railway fare. Gardens and splendid gallery of pictures open free daily (including Sundays), except Friday, from 10 till dusk.

HARROW.—Great public school. View from churchyard. Access by rail, 1s.

HIGHGATE HILL, CEMETERY, &c.—Fine views of London. Access by railway and omnibus. Fare 6d.

KENSAL GREEN, Harrow Road. — Extensive views, beautiful cemetery. Access by railway and omnibus. Fare 6d. and 8d.

LOUGHTON, BUCKHURST HILL, &c., on the Eastern Counties Railway. Fare 1s. — Beautiful scenery. A favourite resort for picnic parties, bean-feasts, &c. Situated on Epping Forest.

MOULSEY, near *Hampton Court.*—Fine view of the Thames, boating, and fishing.

RICHMOND.—The *Park* and adjacent villages, &c., as Twickenham, Sheen, Mortlake, Teddington, Thames Ditton, Pope's Villa, Earl of Dysart's house, boating, fishing, &c. &c. Access by railway, boat, and omnibus. Fare 1s.

WALTHAM ABBEY.—By Eastern Counties Railway. The Abbey, powder mills, fishing, boating, &c. Fare 1s.

WINDSOR.—22 miles from London. 1s. or 2s. railway fare, by South Western or Great Western Railways. Free in the absence of the Sovereign, by order obtained at Colnaghi's, Pall Mall East, London. Times mentioned on the tickets. Eton College is close by, also Datchet Meadows celebrated in connection with the *Magna Charta.*

WOOLWICH.—The *Arsenal, Repository, Dockyard, Barracks,* all free on Tuesdays and Fridays only. Orders required for inspection of the Arsenal. Access by railway and steamboat ; fares 4d., 6d., 8d., from London Bridge. For North Woolwich, *see* GARDENS.

THEATRES.

Except where otherwise stated, there is no half-price to the London theatres ; the doors are open generally at half-past six, the performances commencing at seven.

ADELPHI, Strand.—Orchestra stalls and boxes for six, 52s. 6d. ; first circle, 42s. ; amphitheatre, 31s. 6d. and 21s. ; orchestra (single), 6s. ; balcony, 5s. ; first tier, 3s. ; pit stalls, 2s. ; pit, 1s. 6d. ; amphitheatre, 1s. ; gallery, 6d.

ALEXANDRA, adjoining Highbury Barn Tavern. —Theatre open at 7.30 ; performances in the gardens at 5. Admission 1s., with higher prices to reserved seats.

ALFRED, New Church Street, Edgware Road.— Private boxes, 42s., 31s. 6d., 21s. ; orchestra stalls, 5s. ; dress circle, 3s. ; upper boxes and pit stalls, 2s. ; pit, 1s. ; gallery, 6d.

AMPHITHEATRE AND CIRCUS, Holborn.—Equestrian performances, tight-rope, &c. Open at 7 ; commence at half-past 7. Private boxes from 10s. 6d. upwards ; balcony, 4s. ; boxes, 3s. ; pit, 2s. ; gallery, 1s.

ASTLEY's, Westminster Bridge Road, Lambeth.—Orchestra stalls, 5s. ; private boxes, 21s. and upwards ; lower boxes, 3s. ; upper boxes, 1s. 6d. ; pit, 1s. ; gallery, 6d.

BRITANNIA, Hoxton.—Melodrama and farce. Stage boxes, 2s. ; boxes and stalls, 1s. ; pit, 6d. ; front gallery, 4d. ; back gallery, 3d.

CITY OF LONDON, Norton Folgate.

COVENT GARDEN.—Italian opera, &c. Open at 7, commence at 8. Stalls, 12s. 6d. ; grand circle 10s. 6d. ; reserved box seats (first tier) 7s. ; pit, 5s. ; amphitheatre stalls, 4s. and 5s. ; gallery 2s. ; private boxes, from one to five guineas.

DRURY LANE. — Drama, opera, &c. Private boxes from one to five guineas each. Stalls, 7s. ; dress circle, 5s. ; first circle, 4s. ; balcony, 3s. ; pit, 2s. ; lower gallery, 1s. ; upper gallery, 6d.

EAGLE, or GRECIAN, City Road.—Dramatic entertainments, concerts, &c. Boxes, 1s. ; pit, 6d. ; gallery, 4d. ; general admission, 1s.

EAST LONDON, OR EFFINGHAM, Whitechapel. —Melodrama, &c. Boxes, 1s. ; pit, 6d. ; gallery, 3d.

GAIETY, Strand (late the Strand Music Hall). — Drama, &c. Private boxes, 42s., 52s. 6d. ; stalls, 6s. ; dress circle, 4s. ; boxes, 2s. 6d. ; pit, 1s. 6d. ; gallery stalls, 1s. ; gallery, 6d.

GLOBE (The New). — Drama, &c. Private Boxes, 42s., 52s. 6d. ; stalls, 6s. ; dress circle, 4s. ; boxes, 2s. 6d. ; pit, 1s. 6d. ; gallery stalls, 1s. ; gallery, 6d.

HAYMARKET. — Private boxes, 31s. 6d., 42s. ; orchestra stalls, 7s. ; dress boxes, 5s. and 3s. ; upper boxes, 3s. and 2s. ; pit and amphitheatre, 2s. ; gallery, 1s. The lower prices are the second or half price, at 9 P.M.

HER MAJESTY's, Haymarket.—This theatre is in course of reconstruction, having been burnt in 1867.

HOLBORN.—Dramatic performances. Private boxes, 21s., 42s., 52s. 6d. ; stalls, 6s. ; dress circle, 4s. ; boxes, 3s. ; pit stalls, 2s. ; amphitheatre, 2s. ; pit, 1s. 6d. ; gallery, 6d.

LYCEUM, Wellington Street, Strand.—Various dramatic entertainments, ballets, &c. Private boxes, 42s., 63s. ; stalls, 6s. ; dress circle, 5s. ; upper boxes, 4s. ; pit, 2s. ; gallery, 1s.

OLYMPIC, Wych Street, Drury Lane.—Stalls, 6s. ; dress circle, 5s. ; amphitheatre stalls, 2s. ; pit, 2s. ; gallery, 1s.

PAVILION, Whitechapel. — Melodrama, opera, ballets, &c. Private boxes, 21s. ; dress circle, 1s. 6d. ; boxes, 1s. ; pit, 6d. ; gallery, 3d.

PRINCE OF WALES, Tottenham Street.—Stalls, 7s. ; dress circle, 5s. ; boxes, 3s. ; upper circle, 2s. 6d. ; pit, 1s. 6d.

PRINCESS'S, Oxford Street. — Private boxes, from 31s. 6d. to 52s. 6d. ; boxes, 4s. ; stalls, 6s. ; pit, 2s. ; gallery, 1s.

QUEEN'S, Long Acre, late St. Martin's Music Hall.—Dramatic entertainments. Private boxes, 31s. 6d., 42s., 52s. 6d. ; orchestra, 7s. ; balcony, 5s. ; upper circle, 3s. ; pit, 2s. ; amphitheatre, 1s. ; gallery, 6d.

ROYALTY, or SOHO, Dean Street, Soho.—Dramatic entertainments. Private boxes, 21s. to

42s.; stalls, 6s.; dress circle, 3s.; second circle, 2s.; pit, 1s.; gallery, 6d.

SADLER'S WELLS, Clerkenwell, near St. John Street Road.—Dramatic entertainments, concerts, &c. Private boxes, 11s. 6d., 21s., to 31s. 6d.; dress circle, 3s.; orchestra stalls, 2s.; pit stalls and upper boxes, 1s. 6d.; pit, 1s.; gallery, 6d.

ST. JAMES'S, King Street, St. James's.—Drama, opera, and occasionally French plays. Stalls, 5s.; boxes, 4s. and 3s.; pit, 2s.; gallery, 6d.

STANDARD, opposite Great Eastern Railway, Shoreditch.—Private boxes, from 10s. 6d. to 42s.; lower circle, 2s.; upper boxes, 1s. 6d.; balcony, 2s. 6d.; stalls, 1s.; pit, 6d.; gallery, 4d.

STRAND.—Various burlesque and dramatic entertainments. Open at six, commence at 7. Private boxes, 31s. 6d., and 42s.; stalls, 6s.; dress circle, 4s.; boxes, 3s.; pit, 1s. 6d.; gallery, 6d.

SURREY, Blackfriars Road.—Melodrama, farce, &c. Stalls, 3s.; dress circle, 2s.; upper boxes, 1s. 6d.; pit, 1s.; gallery, 6d.

VICTORIA, Waterloo Road.—Melodrama, farce, &c. Boxes and stalls, 1s.; pit, 6d.; gallery, 3d.

ST. GEORGE'S OPERA HOUSE, Langham Place,

Regent Street.—Dramatic entertainments, &c. Orchestra stalls, 4s.; stalls, 3s.; pit, 1s.; balcony, 2s.

BATHS AND BATHING-PLACES.—The *Serpentine*, in Hyde Park, the lakes in Victoria and Finsbury parks, all free till about 8 in the morning. All the following have to be paid for: *Lambeth Baths*, Westminster Road; *York Street Baths*, York Street, Westminster Road; *Peerless Pool*, near St. Luke's Hospital, City Road; *Great Smith Street*, near Westminster Abbey; *Endell Street*, Bloomsbury; *St. Marylebone Public Baths*, Marylebone Road, near Lisson Grove; *St. George's Public Baths*, 36, Davies Street, Mount Street, and Lower Belgrave Place, Pimlico; *Royal York Swimming Bath*, York Terrace, Regent's Park; *North London Baths*, Pentonville Hill; *Kensington*, 282, High Street; *East India Road*, Poplar; *Bermondsey*, Spa Road; *Metropolitan*, 23, Ashley Crescent, City Road; *City of London*, Milton Street.

BATHS AND WASHHOUSES.—Whitechapel, Endell Street Holborn, and Charing Cross.

Lords-Lieutenant of Counties.

ENGLAND.	
Bedford	Earl Cowper, K.G.
Berkshire	Earl of Abingdon.
Bucks.	Lord Carrington.
Cambridge	Earl of Hardwicke.
Cheshire	Marquis of Westminster, K.G.
Cornwall	Lord Vivian.
Cumberland	Earl of Lonsdale.
Derby	Duke of Devonshire, K.G.
Devon	Duke of Somerset, K.G.
Dorset	Earl of Shaftesbury, K.G.
Durham	Earl of Durham.
Essex	Lord Dacre.
Gloucester	Earl Ducie.
Hereford	Lord Bateman.
Hertford	Earl of Verulam.
Huntingdon	Earl of Sandwich.
Kent	Viscount Sydney, G.C.B.
Lancaster	Earl of Sefton.
Leicester	Duke of Rutland.
Lincoln	Earl Brownlow.
Middlesex	Duke of Wellington, K.G.
Monmouth	Duke of Beaufort, K.G.
Norfolk	Earl of Leicester.
Northampton	Lord Southampton.
Northumberland	Earl Grey, K.G.
Nottingham	Lord Belper.
Oxford	Duke of Marlborough.
Rutland	Earl of Gainsborough.
Shropshire	Viscount Hill.
Somerset	Earl of Cork and Orrery, K.G.
Southampton	Marquis of Winchester.
Stafford	Earl of Lichfield.
Suffolk	Earl of Stradbroke.
Surrey	Earl of Lovelace.
Sussex	Earl of Chichester,
Warwick	Lord Leigh.
Westmoreland	Henry Lowther, Esq.
Wiltshire	Marquis of Ailesbury.
Worcester	Lord Lyttelton.
York, E. Riding	Lord Wenlock.
" *W. Riding*	Earl Fitzwilliam, K.G.
" *N. Riding*	Earl of Zetland, K.T.
Tower Hamlets	Gn. Sir J. T. Burgoyne, Bt. G.C.B.
WALES.	
Anglesey	Marquis of Anglesey.

Brecon	Lord Tredegar.
Cardigan	E. L. Pryse, Esq.
Carmarthen	Earl of Cawdor.
Carnarvon	Lord Penrhyn.
Denbigh	R. M. Biddulph, Esq.
Flint	Sir S. R. Glynne, Bart.
Glamorgan	C. M. Talbot, Esq.
Haverfordwest	J. H. Scourfield, Esq.
Merioneth	Lord Mostyn.
Montgomery	Lord Sudeley.
Pembroke	Lord Kensington.
Radnor	Lord Ornathwaite.
SCOTLAND.	
Aberdeen	Earl of Kintore.
Argyll	Duke of Argyll, K.T.
Ayr	Marquis of Ailsa.
Banff	Earl of Fife, K.T.
Berwick	D. Robertson, Esq.
Bute	Lieut.-Col. F. D. C. Stuart.
Caithness	Earl of Caithness.
Clackmannan	Earl of Mansfield, K.T.
Cromarty	Duke of Sutherland, K.G.
Dumbarton	Sir James Colquhoun, Bart.
Dumfries	Earl of Dalkeith.
Edinburgh	Duke of Buccleugh, K.G.
Elgin, or Moray	Hon. Geo. S. Duff.
Fife	Sir Robert Anstruther, Bart.
Forfar	Earl of Dalhousie, K.T.
Haddington	Marquis of Tweeddale, K.T.
Inverness	Lord Lovat.
Kincardine	Sir James H. Burnett, Bart.
Kinross	Sir G. C. Montgomery, Bart.
Kircudbright	Earl of Selkirk.
Lanark	Lord Belhaven, K.T.
Linlithgow	Earl of Hopetown.
Nairn	William Brodie, Esq.
Orkney and Shetl.	Frederick Dundas, Esq.
Peebles	Earl of Wemyss.
Perth	Lord Kinnaird, K.T.
Renfrew	Earl of Glasgow.
Ross	Sir J. Matheson, Bt.
Roxburgh	Duke of Buccleugh.
Stirling	Duke of Montrose, K.T.
Sutherland	Duke of Sutherland, K.G.
Wigtown	Earl of Stair, K.T.

MEAT BROUGHT INTO LONDON FROM THE PROVINCES, BY RAILWAY, &c.

The present tendency of our meat supplies is to encourage the sending of slaughtered, rather than live animals to the Metropolis. For this there exist several reasons, but more especially that of the animal being killed and dressed when in the best condition, affords a more probable source of profit on its sale; the offal is now readily disposed of in most large towns for the purposes of manure, and many chemical manufactures. The following items state the quantity of fresh meat brought to London during the year 1867; the mode of carriage, and the distance on an average of transit, as stated, by a return to the House of Commons, in March 1868. By the Great Eastern Railway for eleven months, 11,081 tons—with an average per month of 1,007 tons, and an average of 70 miles of transit. By Great Northern Railway, 22,065½ tons—a monthly average of 2,005 tons, and an (unstated) average of, say 200 miles. By Great Western Railway, 5,959 tons nearly—with a monthly average of 541¾ tons, and an average distance of transit of 106 miles. By London and North-Western Railway, 16,102¼ tons—with a monthly average of nearly 1,454 tons, length of transit unstated, but including Scotland and portions of Ireland. By London and South-Western Railway, 4,573¼ tons—monthly average, 415½ tons, average of transit, 130 miles. By London, Brighton, and South Coast Railway, 329 tons—monthly average, 30 tons, and average transit of 60 miles. By London, Chatham, and Dover line, 88 tons nearly—or an average of 8 tons per month, transit 45 miles. By Midland Railway, *for the 12 months*, 4,340¾ tons—with a monthly average of 361¾ tons, and probable transit, on an average, of 150 miles. By South Eastern Railway for 11 months, 747¾ tons, monthly average 68 tons, and average of transit 70 miles.

AGRICULTURAL STATISTICS, GREAT BRITAIN.

	Wheat. Acres.	Barley. Acres.	Oats. Acres.
1866	3,350,394	2,237,329	2,759,923
1867	3,367,876	2,159,164	2,750,487
1868	3,646,260	2,149,201	2,753,240
1868 over	*278,384	†109,963	*2,753
1867 ...	or 8·2 pr ct.	or 4·9 pr ct.	or 0.1 pr ct.
1868 over	*295,866	†88,128	†6,683
1866 ...	or 8·8 pr ct.	or 4·0 pr ct.	or 0·3 pr ct.

Total Number of Live Stock, June 25.

1867	4,993,034	28,219,101	2,966,970
1868	5,416,159	30,685,980	2,303,857
1868 over	*423,120	*1,766,879	†663,122
1867 ...	or 8·5 pr ct.	or 6·1 pr ct.	or 22·3 pr ct.

The amount of land under potatoes in 1868 was 539,554 acres, against 492,217 in 1867 and 498,843 in 1866.

Increase (*) or Decrease (†).

The acreage under hops in 1868 was 64,488, against 64,284 in 1867 and 56,578 in 1866.

It is computed that the extra produce of wheat from the extended acreage under cultivation will be 1,200,000 quarters, which added to the extra yield per acre, will give a surplus wheat yield of 3,000,000 quarters for 1868 over the preceding year.

LIVE STOCK IMPORTED IN 1867.

Ports at which Imported.	Oxen and Bulls.	Cows and Calves.	Sheep and Lambs.	Swine and Hogs.	Agrgte. of all Kinds.
	No.	No.	No.	No.	No.
London	104,062	20,619	407,460	27,933	560,074
Cowes	404	—	173	71	648
Falmouth.....	3,455	257	2	—	3,714
Goole	23	98	79	400	600
Grimsby	17	13	36,135	673	36,838
Hartlepool ...	699	319	24,825	359	28,212
Harwich	393	2,432	12,764	6,649	22,238
Hull	6,279	10,589	9,416	3,867	30,141
Liverpool' ...	2,958	2	13,202	359	16,521
Middlesboro'	146	341	270	57	814
Newcastle ...	2,059	1,669	9,426	68	13,222
Newhaven ...	299	34	91	142	566
Penzance......	465	—	—	—	465
Plymouth ...	5,309	77	13	2	5,401
Poole	—	—	194	853	1,047
Portsmouth...	552	86	978	4,525	6,141
Shoreham ...	1,408	206	257	60	1,931
Southampton	4,348	177	2,848	1,877	9,250
Sunderland...	520	541	11,775	32	12,868
Leith	2,059	120	7,606	35	9,820
Glasgow	271	—	—	1	272
Grangemouth	—	—	2,140	—	2,140
Granton	248	31	2	—	281
Dublin	2,305	1	12	1	2,319
Other parts...	57	57	43	115	220
Total	138,336	39,612	539,716	48,079	765,743

OXFORD AND CAMBRIDGE BOAT RACE.

Yr.	Place of Rowing.	Winner	Time.	Won by
			m. s.	
1829	Henley 2m. 28.	Oxford	14 30	Many lngths.
1836	Westmin. to Put.	Camb.	36 0	1 minute.
1839	Westmin. to Put.	Camb.	31 0	1 min. 45 sec.
1840	Westmin. to Put.	Camb.	29 30	2–3ds length.
1841	Westmin. to Put.	Camb.	32 30	1 min. 48 sec.
1842	Westmin. to Put.	Oxford	30 45	13 sec.
1845	Putney to Mort.	Camb.	23 30	30 sec.
*1846	Mortlake to Put.	Camb.	21 55	Two lengths.
1849	Putney to Mort.	Camb.	22 0	Many lngths.
1849	Putney to Mort.	Oxford	Foul	Foul.
1852	Putney to Mort.	Oxford	21 36	27 sec.
1854	Putney to Mort.	Oxford	25 29	11 strokes.
1856	Mortlake to Put.	Camb.	25 50	Half length.
1857	Putney to Mort.	Oxford	22 50	35 sec.
1858	Putney to Mort.	Camb.	21 23	22 sec.
1859	Putney to Mort.	Oxford	24 30	Camb. sank.
1860	Putney to Mort.	Camb.	26 0	One length.
1861	Putney to Mort.	Oxford	23 27	48 sec.
1862	Putney to Mort.	Oxford	24 40	30 sec.
1863	Mortlake to Put.	Oxford	23 5	42 sec.
1864	Putney to Mort.	Oxford	21 48	23 sec.
1865	Putney to Mort.	Oxford	21 23	13 sec.
1866	Putney to Mort.	Oxford	25 48	15 sec.
1867	Putney to Mort.	Oxford	23 22	Half length.
1868	Putney to Mort.	Oxford	20 56	

* This year marked the introduction of the outrigger.

1867. **AUGUST.**

9. Accident at Bray Head, on the Dublin and Wicklow Railway, by the falling of a train over a cliff 40 feet high.

11. Great fire in Central Exchange Buildings, Newcastle-on-Tyne.

16. Explosion at the Faversham Powder Mills with loss of two lives.

19, 20. Remarkable thunder-storm in London. All the signal-bells of the telegraph stations rung violently during the night, and the wires were damaged. The storm was attended with a flood of rain, and extended over England and Scotland.

20. Ten excursionists drowned on the Humber, near Hull, through the upsetting of a boat.

— Explosion in a coal-mine at St. Helen's, Lancashire ; fourteen lives lost.

— First passage of a train over the Mont Cenis Railway, between France and Italy.

24. Horrible murder of a child, Fanny Adams, by Frederick Baker, at Alton, Hampshire.

SEPTEMBER.

6. Collision on the Thames between the Metis, a river steamer, and a steam collier, with loss of four lives.

9. Accident on the Midland Railway, by collision of two trains near New Mills, on the Peak Forest line, with loss of six lives, cattle, &c.

18. Fenian outrage at Manchester ; rescue of two prisoners, and murder of Sergeant Brett.

19. Severe earthquake at Canea. Millions of fish were driven into Canea Bay. Much damage done to the town.

OCTOBER.

5. Explosion of Boxer cartridges at Woolwich Arsenal ; twenty-four boys dreadfully burnt, and two instantaneously killed.

7. Early appearance of winter in London, most of the ponds, &c., being frozen. Snow and hail in the north.

9. Great fire in the Canongate, Edinburgh, with loss of five lives, through an explosion of fireworks.

21. Suspension of the Royal Bank of Liverpool.

23. Opening of the Queen's Theatre, Long Acre.

26. Grand banquet given at Paris to the Imperial Commissioners of the French Exposition, by the Commissioners of Foreign Governments.

27. Marriage of the King of Greece to the Grand Duchess Olga, at St. Petersburg.

29. Hurricane at St. Thomas's, in the West Indies ; loss of eighty vessels, and 1,000 lives.

NOVEMBER.

3. Closing of the French Exposition. The first detachment of British troops departed from Woolwich for Abyssinia in the first week of the month, having been preceded by the Bombay Contingent on the 7th ult.

4. Defeat of Garibaldi and his Italian Volunteers at Montana and Monte Rotondo, by Papal and French troops.

8. Explosion in a coal-mine at Rhondda Valley, South Wales, with loss of 170 lives.

13, 14. Remarkable fall of meteoric bodies, or "shooting stars."

18. Earthquake at St. Thomas's, West Indies.

23. Execution of three Fenians, Allen, Larkin, and Gould, at Manchester, for the murder of Sergeant Brett.

23. Serious bread-riots in Belfast, owing to high prices.

24. Fire at a farm-house at Middlewich, Cheshire ; seven lives lost.

26. Great fire at Pickford's goods' warehouses, Camden Town.

29. Destruction, by explosion, of the "Bubulina," a Greek war steamer, off Liverpool ; loss of upwards of twenty lives.

DECEMBER.

1. Fearful gales generally throughout the kingdom ; much damage to shipping, and many lives lost.

6. Destruction by fire of Her Majesty's Theatre, Haymarket, London.

7. Explosion at gunpowder works near Lake Windermere, with loss of several lives.

8. Monster funeral processions in many places for the Fenian murderers of Brett at Manchester.

13. Terrible explosion at the House of Detention, Clerkenwell, London, caused by Fenians intending to rescue Burke, confined in that prison. A whole street was laid in ruins, many lives were lost, and the surrounding neighbourhood greatly injured.

17. Remarkable explosion of nitro-glycerine at Newcastle-on-Tyne, with loss of four lives.

18. Terrible accident on the Lake Erie Railroad, U. S., through a train being thrown off the line by a defective rail ; forty-one persons burned to death, and many injured.

28. Explosion at the gunpowder mills, Faversham, with loss of eleven lives.

1868. **JANUARY.**

4. Slight shock of earthquake felt in the Vale of Parret, and other parts of Somerset.

4—11. General swearing-in of special constables throughout England, in consequence of the Fenian outrage at Clerkenwell.

4. Great eruption of Mount Vesuvius, with earthquakes, descent of lava, &c.

6. Arrival of the Duke of Edinburgh at Hobart Town.

7. Visit of the Prince of Wales to the patients (at St. Bartholomew's hospital) who were injured by the explosion (caused by Fenians) at Clerkenwell prison in December.

8. Sudden and mysterious disappearance of the Rev. B. Speke, causing great sensation throughout the country. He was discovered alive and well in Cornwall shortly afterwards.

9. Committal of Burke, Casey, and Shaw, to Warwick gaol for Fenianism, from the Bow Street police-office, London.

11. Wreck of the screw steamer, "Chicago," on a reef of rocks near Cork harbour ; all lives saved.

16. Landing of the remains of the Emperor Maximilian of Mexico, at Trieste.

17, 18. Severe gales on all coasts of the United Kingdom, with many wrecks and great loss of life.

18. Explosion of gunpowder at Newcastle-on-Tyne, with death of two men and injury to others.

— Attempted murder by Clancy, a Fenian, of two policemen, in Bedford Square.

18—25. Heavy gales throughout the Kingdom, with much loss of life and property at sea and on land. Loss of nineteen fishing vessels, and fifty-two lives near the Burry river on the Welsh coast.

19. Reports of the safety of Dr. Livingstone, the celebrated African traveller, reach Plymouth.

21. Great fire at the Royal Military College, Sandhurst.

24—31. Heavy rains and floods in the south of England.

26. Arrival of the advanced body of the Abyssinian expedition at Senafe.

28. Great fire at Chicago, U. S., with loss of property valued at three million dollars.

— Great landslip near Naples, by which several lives and houses were destroyed.

29. Explosion of a coal-mine at Iserholm, in Westphalia, with loss of 189 lives.

FEBRUARY.

1. A telegraphic message sent to San Francisco from London, and reply returned, through a distance, in all, of 14,000 miles, in two minutes.

— Loss of three lives at Bow through the falling of a chimney during a heavy gale.

1, 2. Tremendous gales throughout the kingdom.

8. Great damage on the banks of the Thames, through an unusually high tide.

11. Destruction of the Oxford Music Hall, Oxford Street, London, by fire.

18. Fire at the Charing Cross railway station.

19. Shocks of an earthquake at Alexandria.

20. Earthquake at Malta.

22. Great damage to the breakwater, Holyhead, during a heavy gale, by which most of the works in progress were destroyed.

22—29. Heavy gales on all the British coasts; with numerous wrecks and loss of life.

25. Resignation of the premiership by the Earl of Derby, and retirement into private life.

MARCH.

6. Serious religious and party riots at Rochdale.

8. Great storm at Liverpool.

12. Fearful hurricane at Mauritius, with destruction of sugar and other crops, many wrecks and loss of life.

— Attempted assassination of the Duke of Edinburgh by an Irishman named O'Farrell, at a picnic held at Clontarf, near Port Jackson, New South Wales. O'Farrell was tried on March 31st, found guilty, and executed April 21.

13. President Johnson was summoned to appear before the Senate Court of the United States under impeachment.

— Trial and conviction of Miles Weatherhill for the murder of Jane Smith, at Todmorden. The Rev. Mr. Plow was so ill-treated by Weatherhill as to cause his death on March 12.

19. Review of troops at Aldershot by the Queen.

20. Conviction of Captain Mackay at Cork, for treason-felony; sentence, twelve years' penal servitude.

28. Presentation to Mr. Brand, the late Liberal "whip," of a handsome testimonial by his party.

28 to April 4. Rioting at Charleroi, Belgium, by discontented miners, several lives lost.

Gift by Mr. Joseph Whitworth (of gun celebrity) of £100,000 to promote technical education.

During the month of March, 18,852 persons emigrated from Liverpool to the United States.

APRIL.

7. Great eruption of volcanoes in the Sandwich Islands.

7. Assassination of the Hon. D'Arcy M'Gee, an eminent member of the Canadian Parliament, and representative of Montreal West.

10. Great battle at Arogee, Abyssinia.

13. Taking of Magdala by storm, by Sir Robert Napier, and death by supposed suicide of King Theodore. The British and other captives had been previously given up by him.

— Grand Volunteer Review at Portsmouth.

15. Prince and Princess of Wales landed at Kingston, on a visit to Ireland.

— Assassination of James Howard Fetherstonhaugh, of Bracklyn Castle, on his road home from Dublin, aged 49.

20. Opening of the cause of Lyon *v.* Home, the spiritualist, for the recovery of £60,000, of which, it was alleged, he had defrauded Mrs. Lyon.

— Serious disturbances at Wigan through strike of colliers.

— Trial of Fenians connected with the Clerkenwell explosion in December.

21. Execution of O'Farrell for the attempted assassination of the Duke of Edinburgh.

27. Conviction and sentence to death of Barrett, for complicity in the Fenian outrage at Clerkenwell, in December, 1867. The two Desmonds, English, and Anne Justice, were acquitted.

30. Conviction of Burke and Shaw for treason-felony; the former being sentenced to fifteen, and Shaw to seven, years' penal servitude.

— Resolution passed by the House of Commons, tending to the disestablishment of the Irish Church.

The report of the Inspectors of Fisheries, issued early in this month, stated that during the year 1867 there were 33,321 boxes of salmon, weighing 1666 tons, delivered at Billingsgate market. Of these were—English and Welsh, 2405 boxes; Scotch, 23,006; Irish, 5411; the rest being from abroad.

MAY.

1. Murder of the Dover Priory station-master by Wells, a porter. The execution of the latter took place in the August following, and was the first private execution that occurred under the new Act.

2. Opening of the Thames Embankment between Lambeth and Westminster Bridges.

— Shocking attempt to murder an aged female in Great Tower Street, London.

4. Destruction of Greystoke Castle, near Ulleswater, long identified with the Howard (Norfolk) family.

6. Tremendous cyclone passed over Tennesse, ravaging the country through many miles.

7. Serious gas explosion at Berlin, attended with the loss of many lives and much property.

8, 9. Religious riots at Ashton-under-Lyne.

13. Laying the foundation-stone of the new St. Thomas' Hospital by the Queen.

19. Opening of the Leeds Art-Treasure Exhibition by the Prince of Wales.

20. Testimonial, value £1,000, presented to Dr. Richardson, in acknowledgment of his investigations into methods of rendering patients insensible of pain during surgical operations, &c.

26. Execution of Barrett at Newgate for his complicity in causing the Clerkenwell explosion in December, 1867.

29. Heavy thunderstorm in the metropolis and southern counties generally.

JUNE.

1. Opening of the Havre International Maritime Exhibition.

10. Assassination of Prince Michael of Servia.

—. Explosion of a nitro-glycerine factory at Stockholm, with loss of 15 lives and much property.

15. Opening of the Fell Railway over Mont Cénis for passenger traffic.

16–20. Triennial Handel Festival at the Crystal Palace.

20. Review of 27,000 volunteers by the Queen at Windsor.

26. Arrival of the Duke of Edinburgh at Portsmouth on his return from Australia.

27. Inauguration of the Cobden Statue at St. Pancras, London.

29. Rejection of Mr. Gladstone's Irish Church Suspensory Bill, by the House of Lords.

—. Terrible explosion of nitro-glycerine at Quenast, Belgium. Ten persons blown to atoms, and great loss of property.

JULY.

1. Public dinner at Willis's Rooms, London, to Cyrus Field, in acknowledgment of the services he had rendered to ocean telegraphy.

2. Vote of thanks by Parliament to the Abyssinian Army.

—. Arrival of Sir Robert Napier at Dover, on his return from Abyssinia.

6. Birth of a daughter to the Prince of Wales.

—. Discharge of Peto, Betts, and Crampton at the Bankruptcy Court, with liabilities of above £7,000,000.

8. Great *fête* at the Crystal Palace in honour of Sir Robert (now Lord) Napier for his successes in Abyssinia.

9. Settlement of a pension of £2,000 per annum on Sir Robert Napier, in consideration of his services in Abyssinia.

10. Cyclone at Barbadoes, with great damage to shipping, &c.

13. Visit of the Queen to the Duke of Edinburgh's ship, the *Galatea.*

14. Elevation of Sir Robert Napier to the peerage, in consideration of his services in Abyssinia.

15. Presentation of the Lancashire Famine Memorial Window to the Corporation of London.

18. And for some weeks after, many moors, forests, &c., on fire throughout England, arising, indirectly, from the intense heat.

20. Daring robbery of arms from a gunmaker's at Cork.

—. Discovery of the one hundredth planet of our system; and a new observation of Encke's comet—its thirteenth periodic return.

21. Unveiling of Lord Palmerston's memorial at Romsey.

— Presentation of the freedom of the City of London, with a sword, value 200 guineas, to Lord Napier.

23. Five persons drowned at Pontypool by the upsetting of a pleasure-boat.

25. Swarms of large gnats at Woolwich, arising from the intense heat (frequently 90° in the shade). These insects subsequently spread into the adjacent marshes and villages, attacking persons with all the effects of the tropical mosquito. Many deaths from sunstroke.

25. Explosion of gunpowder works at Black Beck, near Ulverston. Nine persons killed, and the whole of the premises destroyed.

— Death, by explosion of a new torpedo, of Lieutenant Meade, a son of Lord Clanwilliam, at Portsmouth; and also of one of his assistants named White.

26. Fires at Colyton and Collumpton, Devonshire, with destruction of 21 houses.

27. Fall of the hill Antelao, in the Tyrol, with loss of 11 lives and the destruction of a whole village.

28. Murder of two children by their father, Ezra Whitcook, a farmer, near Rochdale, Lancashire.

30. Opening of the north portion of the Thames Embankment, from Westminster to the Temple.

— Fearful accident at the Victoria Music Hall, Manchester, by a panic, caused through a false alarm of fire. Thirty persons crushed to death, and many others seriously injured.

31. Fire at the Jarrow Chemical Works, Gateshead, near Newcastle-on-Tyne, with estimated loss of £100,000.

July to August. Great drought throughout the whole of Europe, accompanied with fires on heaths, moors, corn-lands, &c., with general destruction of green crops.

AUGUST.

1. Seizure of a British schooner by the Spanish authorities at Carthagena, on the ground of alleged piracy.

5. A telegram from Valentia announced the breaking of the Atlantic Cable of 1866 at a distance of about 88 miles from Heart's Content, on the Newfoundland coast, a portion of the cable at which it was fractured in 1867.

10. Fire in King Street, Borough. Estimated loss, £30,000.

—. Great fire at Lisbon, with destruction of property valued at £100,000.

11. First private execution in the kingdom, at Maidstone, of Wells, a railway-porter, who killed the station-master at Dover.

13–16. Fearful earthquake in Peru and Ecuador. Immense loss of life and property; the former estimated at 50,000 persons, and the latter incalculable.

15. Opening of the railway between Suez and Ismailia by the Suez Canal.

16. Extraordinary motion of the sea in South California. A rise of 60 feet above, and a fall of the same extent below the usual level, being experienced. Doubtless related to the earthquake in Peru and Ecuador at that date.

17. Loss of five lives by the upsetting of a boat on Lough Rea, near Athlone.

18. Great thunderstorm in the West of England, 33 sheep killed by lightning near Tenbury.

—. Great solar eclipse, with complete obscuration of the sun, lasting six minutes; visible in India and adjacent countries. Interesting astronomical results were obtained.

—. Two distinct shocks of an earthquake at Gibraltar, attended with a strong easterly current in the Mediterranean. (See account of earthquake in South America, Aug. 13—16.)

19. Meeting of the British Association at Norwich.

—. Fire at Northumberland House, Charing Cross, the town residence of the Duke of Northumberland, with heavy loss of art treasures, &c. Amongst these was a Sèvres China vase, formerly belonging to Charles X. of France, and valued at £50,000, which was much injured.

20. Trial and conviction of Mackay, for the brutal murder of Mrs. Grossmith, in Spitalfields, on 8th May preceding.

20. Explosion of a boiler at the Mersey Steel and Iron Works, near Liverpool. Five persons killed.

— Horrible railway accident on the Chester and Holyhead line, near Abergele, through an express train running into a van containing petroleum, causing 34 deaths.

22. Great gale on the British coast, 100 lives being lost off the Mersey alone.

— Death of Count Louis de Cambacères on the Alps, near Chamouni, through falling over a tremendous precipice in descending from the upper part of the Glacier du Trient.

25. Great yacht race between the American schooner, the *Sappho*, and English yachts ; the *Cambria*, an English yacht, being the victor.

— Discovery of rich silver deposits on the Canadian side of Lake Superior.

— Great fire at St. Petersburg, with destruction of 100,000 bales of flax and 60,000 of hemp. Estimated loss stated to be 3¼ millions of roubles.

— Great fire at Prerari, a chief town of Moravia, with destruction of 150 houses.

— Burial of the remains of the victims of the railway collision and fire at Abergele, August 20, including 34 persons, of whom only one was properly identified at the inquest.

27. Opening of the tomb of William Rufus, in Winchester Cathedral. The skeleton was nearly perfect. Many interesting relics were discovered.

— Severe snowstorm and violent gale at Braemar; a remarkable circumstance, because the heat in the south of England was of a tropical character.

30. Immense and unusual fall of rain at Bombay, 12 inches being registered on this day by the rain gauge.

— Discovery, in New Zealand, of the richest gold-diggings in the world, an area of 150 ft. by 50 ft., being estimated to contain a value of one million sterling; average yield, 12 ounces of gold to a ton of rock.

— Accident on the Mont Cénis Railway, through the fall of an avalanche, 150 feet of the Fell line being swept away.

— Discovery of a rich gold country in the north of Cape Colony, near the Limpopo River, consisting of quartz veined with gold.

SEPTEMBER.

1. Official declaration of the United States Debt was fixed at 2,643,250,000 dollars, being an increase of nearly ten millions on the preceding month.

— Great fire in granaries and stores at Rotherhithe, estimated damage, £50,000.

3. Resignation by Garibaldi, through infirmity, of his seat in the Italian Parliament.

— Serious potato riot at Cork, in which 3,000 persons were engaged.

— Visit of the Hon. Reverdy Johnson, the newly accredited Minister of the United States, to Sheffield, being his first public appearance in England.

5. Cab-strike in London, owing to the demands of the cabmen to be admitted generally to railway stations, not being conceded by the directors of the metropolitan lines. It terminated with the defeat of the cabmen on the following Thursday.

— Burning of the steamer Atlanta whilst crossing the Atlantic Ocean. All hands saved.

5, 6. "No popery" riots in Manchester, owing

to the arrest of Murphy, an ultra-protestant lecturer.

6. Brutal murder of a man at Altrincham, by a gang of drunken Irish labourers.

8. Melancholy death by drowning of three out of four brothers, who were crossing Ulverstone Sands, Lancashire.

— First sheep and wool show in Ireland, held on the premises of the Royal Dublin Society; with distribution of £400 in money, besides 50 medal prizes.

— Opening of a new railway between Alexandria and Suez, *via* Azazieh, by which the overland journey will be reduced to ten hours, including stoppages.

— Private execution of Arthur Mackay, at Newgate, for the murder of Mrs. Grossmith, his mistress, of Norton Folgate. The first private execution in London, and the second in the United Kingdom.

9. Serious explosion of gas at the Bradford Theatre; also at Stratford with loss of one life.

12. Great festivities at Cardiff, in Wales, and Rothesay, in Bute, Scotland, in consequence of the coming of age of the Marquis of Bute. The property, which is said to be now worth £300,000 a year, is rapidly improving, and, in less than 20 years, will produce an income of half a million.

— Poisoning of a whole family at Drax, near Selby, through eating sour or putrid suet.

13. Great fire near Netley, Hampshire, with much destruction of farm produce.

14. Death of seven gunners at Malta, through an accidental explosion of a bomb-shell.

15. Destruction by fire of the *Nith*, a vessel on her voyage to Bombay, 30 miles south of Waterford Harbour.

16. Serious collision between an express and luggage train on the Chester and Holyhead Railway. One also at Tamworth.

— Potato riots at Cork, several persons severely injured.

— *et seq.* Great revolution in Spain, commencing with the fleet off Cadiz, and gradually spreading over the whole peninsula, attended with little bloodshed. Flight of Queen Isabella to France, and the formation of a form of Republican Government under Prim, Serrano, and others at Madrid.

— Fearful explosion of diamond oil near Newcastle-on-Tyne, causing five deaths, and injury to several persons.

17. Terrible explosion of a cartridge factory at Metz, in France. About 30 persons killed, and 80 severely injured.

— Severe shock of an earthquake felt at Constantinople. Little damage done.

18. Death of two miners at Newchapel, Staffordshire, through an accidental explosion of gunpowder in a coal mine.

— Examination of Byrne at Guildhall for supposed Fenianism, and possession of a large number of guns and other arms.

— Capture of an albacore, a tropical fish, weighing 5 cwt., and ten feet long, off Dawlish.

— Disgraceful disturbances in Lombard Street, City, owing to the denunciations of the banking interest by Father Ignatius (Rev. J. L. Lyne) whilst preaching.

19. Opening of the railway between Moscow and Kursk.

21. Great fire at a cotton mill at Middleton, near Manchester.

— Attempted murder and burglary in Westbourne Park, when Mrs. Russell, the inmate of the house, narrowly escaped with her life.

24 *et seq.* Second trial of Madame Rachael, the face enameller ("Beautiful for Ever"), for obtaining £1,400 under false pretences from Mrs. Borrodaile, ending in her conviction, and sentence of five years' penal servitude.

24. Two waterspouts seen at the mouth of St. George's Channel.

— Shock of an earthquake felt at Malta. No damage done.

25. Serious accident to a mail train between Dublin and Kingstown.

— Fall of a large pile of buildings used as a linseed store at Hull, with loss of nine lives.

— Heavy defalcations, amounting to about £10,000, by the borough accountant of Southport.

— Termination of a great shooting match in Belgium, the majority of prizes being won by British volunteers.

26 *et seq.* Great gales all round the coast, with much loss of life and numerous shipwrecks.

—. Great fire at the Cambrian Stores, Leicester Square, and narrow escape of ten persons.

— Two serious accidents at the new Midland Railway Station, King's Cross.

27. Sudden death from apoplexy of Count Walewski, the eminent French statesman.

— Disastrous wreck near Kimmeridge, with loss of all hands.

28. Explosion of a paraffin cask on the Cork and Queenstown Railway, with loss of two lives.

28. Foundering of the screw steamer *Florence* off the Nab Light, with loss of 26 lives.

— Fearful steam boiler explosion at the Moxley Iron Works near Bilston, with loss of 12 lives.

29. Accounts from Ecuador and Peru state that upwards of 50,000 lives were lost during the earthquakes of August 13 to 16, and 300,000 persons rendered homeless.

30. Singular discovery of a new eruptive disease, common throughout the country, affecting the feet, and due to the use of stockings dyed of yellow and red colours.

— Opening of the Twelfth Congress of the Social Science Association at Birmingham.

— Fearful explosion of fire-damp at Green Pit, near Ruabon, Wales, with loss of several lives, caused by carelessness.

— Conviction of Whelan for the assassination of Mr. D'Arcy McGee, at Montreal, Canada.

— Discharge of John Surratt, who had been long charged with complicity in the assassination of President Lincoln, U.S.

— Renewed Maori disturbances in New Zealand through the escape of 130 prisoners.

— Great floods in Bombay, with immense loss of life and property.

— Important discovery of coal seams at Old Barford, near Nottingham.

— Discovery of a silver bell, weighing 28 ounces, in a pool near Limerick, supposed to be one of the bells flung into the river during the old days of persecution.

Obituary, 1867-1868.

NAMES OF THE MOST EMINENT PERSONS WHO HAVE DIED BETWEEN 1ST AUGUST 1867, AND 30TH SEPTEMBER, 1868.

1867.   AUGUST.

7. Aldridge, Ira, Negro tragedian.

8. Isabella, Queen Dowager of the Two Sicilies, aged 51.

12. Mayo, fifth Earl of, aged 70.

16. Dunkellin, Lord, aged 40.

21. Northumberland, fifth Duke of, aged 89.

— Velpeau, D., one of the most eminent surgeons of France, aged 72.

25. Faraday, Michael, one of the most illustrious British philosophers. Was born in 1791; became assistant to Sir Humphry Davy and Dr. Brande in 1813, and acquired imperishable fame by his electrical discoveries, especially those of the laws of electro-chemistry, electromagnetism, magneto-electricity, and dia-magnetism, besides numerous contributions to chemical science. He was considered to be the most accomplished and accurate experimentalist of his day.

— Soulouque, Faustin, ex-Emperor of Hayti, aged 78.

31. Hope, Rear-Admiral Thomas, aged 57.

SEPTEMBER.

2. Parker, Vice-Admiral John, aged 62.

3. Howe, Elias, of Connecticut, inventor of the sewing machine.

17. Blackburne, Francis, Lord Chancellor of Ireland, aged 85.

— Bruce, Sir Frederick, British Minister to the United States of America; third son of the seventh Earl of Elgin, aged 53.

28. Turner, James Aspinall, an active liberal politician, manufacturer, &c., of Manchester, aged 70.

1867.   OCTOBER.

2. Troubridge, Colonel Sir Thomas, aged 52.

4. Jones, Avonia, a tragic actress.

5. Fould, Achille, a celebrated financial statesman of France, aged 67.

7. Kingsdown, Baron, Thomas Pemberton Leigh, an eminent English lawyer, aged 74.

17. Fitzhardinge, Baron Maurice Frederick Fitzhardinge Berkeley, aged 80.

18. Colchester, Baron, Charles Abbot, a British admiral, aged 69.

19. Lichfield, John L., Bishop of, aged 79.

24. Weiss, W. Hunter, vocalist, aged 48.

27. Wrottesley, Lord, a distinguished astronomer, aged 79.

31. Rosse, Earl of, an astronomer, celebrated for the construction of the largest telescope yet made, aged 67.

— South, Sir James, an astronomer, born in 1785; was one of the founders of the Royal Astronomical Society, and celebrated for the extent and accuracy of his observations, especially in reference to double stars, aged 82.

NOVEMBER.

5. O'Donnell, Marshal, Duke of Tetuan, of Spain, celebrated for his connection with the revolutions and politics of that country, aged 59.

8. Moray, John S., eleventh Earl of, aged 80.

21. Ogilvie, Sir John, author of "The Imperial Dictionary," &c.

24. Hamilton, Rev. James, D.D., long time minister of the Presbyterian Church, Regent-square, London, aged 53.

1867.   **DECEMBER.**

6. Lowther, Hon. Col. Henry Cecil, aged 77.

9. Dreyse, Herr Von, inventor of the needle-gun, aged 80.

12. Daubeny, Professor Charles, C.B., professor of chemistry, botany, &c., at Oxford, aged 72.

— Pacini, Signor, an eminent Italian singer, aged 71.

14. Carnwath, Thomas Henry, Earl of, aged 70.

16. Close, Colonel.

18. Clark-Kennedy, Colonel, aged 50.

21. Hogg, Colonel Gilbert, aged 52.

23. Clerk, Sir George, aged 80.

27. Harrington, Dowager Countess of, aged 69.

28. Mackie, James, M.P., aged 46.

— Marochetti, Baron. An eminent sculptor, aged 63. Many of his works grace the metropolis and other large cities in this country, one of the finest being that of Richard Cœur de Lion, erected near the Peers' entrance, Houses of Parliament.

29. Hannah, John, D.D., one of the most eminent Wesleyan ministers of his day, aged 75.

30. Macdougall, Patrick Campbell, professor of moral philosophy, Edinburgh, aged 61.

1868.   **JANUARY.**

4. Hauptmann, Moritz, a German composer, and part editor of the Works of Mendelssohn.

— Vœux, Sir Henry Des, aged 61.

5. Dickson, Vice-Admiral Sir Wm., aged 69.

6. Bridport, Samuel H., second Baron, aged 79.

9. Hopkins, Henry, D.D., Protestant Bishop of Vermont, U.S., aged 85.

10. Coquerel, A. L. Charles, pastor of the French Protestant Church, aged 72.

12. Miller, Sir Charles Hayes, aged 38.

17. Fowell, Rear-Admiral.

18. Ventry, Thomas Townsend Aremberg De Moleyns, Baron, aged 81.

19. Grier, Captain Robert, of fame in the Peninsular war, aged 75.

20. Brotherton, Sir Thomas, G.C.B., 1st Dragoon, Guards, aged 82.

22. Kean, Charles, the eminent actor, son of Edmund Kean. Was born January 18, 1811, at Waterford. He made his *debut* on the stage at Drury Lane, as Young Norval, Oct. 1, 1827. His connection with the Princess's Theatre, Oxford-street, lasted from 1850 to 1860, and, whilst eminently successful dramatically, proved the reverse as a money speculation. In 1863 he undertook a tour through America, Canada, Australia, &c., returning to the Princess's Theatre, London, in 1866. During this engagement he was seized with sudden illness, which terminated fatally.

23. Tyrconnel, Countess of, aged 67.

24. Davy, John, M.D., F.R.S., was brother of Sir Humphry Davy, the great chemist, and wrote, besides the life of his brother, many valuable scientific works, aged 77.

27. White, Lt.-Gen. Sir Michael, aged 77.

— Tully, J. H., orchestral conductor at Drury Lane, aged 53.

28. Head, Sir Edmund, aged 62.

30. Whitlock, Sir George Cornish, aged 70.

— Reade, Sir John Chandos, aged 82.

FEBRUARY.

2. Knatchbull, Sir Norton Joseph, aged 67.

5. Randall, Sarah, for forty years attached to the Royal Household of England, aged 77.

7. Torrington, Frances Harriet, Dowager Viscountess, aged 82.

1868.

7. Batty, William, formerly proprietor of Astley's Theatre, aged 67.

8. Burt, Dr. J. G. M., President of the Royal College of Physicians, Edinburgh.

— Brewster, Sir David, F.R.S., &c., at his seat near Melrose, N.B., aged 87. He was one of the most eminent philosophers of his day. He was best popularly known by his optical researches; but especially by the invention of the kaleidoscope and stereoscope. His researches and discoveries extended to every branch of experimental philosophy. He was the author and editor of many scientific works, periodicals, &c., one of the chief being the "Encyclopædia Britannica." He was one of the founders of the British Association, and, at the time of his death, Principal of the University of Edinburgh.

10. Whitehead, Captain Walter H., aged 72.

13. Loch, Admiral Francis Erskine, aged 79.

— Herepath, William, an eminent chemist, aged 72.

14. Churchill, Lady Spencer, aged 80.

15. Lemon, Sir Charles, aged 84.

19. Daly, Sir Dominick, Governor of South Australia, aged 70.

— Shee, Hon. Sir William, a justice of the Queen's Bench, and an eminent lawyer, advocate and judge, aged 63.

— Glasgow, Julia, Dowager Countess of, aged 71.

20. Baker, Dr. B. B., Director of the College at Corfu.

25. Gibson, Sir James Brown, K.C.B., formerly Director-general Medical Department of the Army, aged 63.

— Wensleydale, Baron James Parke, an eminent lawyer and judge, aged 86.

28. Anderson, Arthur, chairman of the Peninsular and Oriental Steam Company, aged 77.

29. Bavaria, Louis I., Charles Augustus, ex-King of, aged 88.

— Chrystie, Captain Thomas, a Trafalgar hero.

MARCH.

2. Webb, Colonel Robert Smith, aged 74.

— Bentinck, Baron von, Ambassador at London from Holland, aged 70.

— Byron, George Anson, seventh Baron, aged 78.

4. Rosebery, Archibald John Primrose, fourth Earl of, aged 85.

5. Macgregor, General John Alexander Paul.

— Kennedy, Lord William, aged 75.

— Hughes, Ball, an eminent sculptor, and pupil of Bailey, aged 62.

10. Neave, Sir Richard Digby, aged 75.

11. De Teissier, Baron James, aged 74.

— King, Major-General George, aged 56.

12. Fane, General Mildmay, aged 74.

— Plow, Rev. W., who died from injuries inflicted by Miles Weatherhill, at Todmorden.

15. Sawyer, Dr. William Collinson, Bishop of Grafton and Armadale, New South Wales, was drowned, aged 37.

17. Carington, Robert John, Baron, aged 72.

26. Kenah, General Sir Thomas, aged 89.

27. Cardigan, the Earl of, through an accidental fall from his horse. His name had long been identified with military and other matters, but more especially in connection with the celebrated charge in the Crimea, when the brigade of light cavalry that he commanded was almost entirely destroyed, aged 71.

28. Woodgate, Major John, a Peninsular hero, aged 80.

28. Jesse, Edward, an eminent naturalist, aged 87.

29. Badeley, Edward, a celebrated ecclesiastical lawyer.

— Hawkins, Miss Susan, a poetess of Border fame, aged 82.

— Anderson, Charles J., an African traveller.

APRIL.

7. Cottenham, Countess Caroline Elizabeth, relict of Lord Chancellor Cottenham, aged 65.

8. Wetherall, General Sir George Augustus, G.C.B., Governor of Sandhurst, aged 80.

— Harvey, Rear Admiral Thomas, aged 58.

— Mainwaring, Major-General Edmund Rowland, of the Indian Service, aged 61.

12. Copeland, William Taylor, senior alderman of the City of London, and long connected with a firm celebrated for the excellence of their ceramic ware, aged 78.

— Salisbury, James Brownlow William Gascoyne Cecil, second Marquis of, aged 77.

15. Abdy, Sir William, aged 89.

17. Reeve, Sir Thomas Newby, aged 70.

18. Simpson, Sir James, an eminent general. He took part in the Peninsular war, served in India, was chief at the staff in the Crimea in 1854, and subsequently there succeeded Lord Raglan as Commander-in-chief, aged 76.

20. Booth, Lieut-Col. William, aged 77.

21. Wood, Sir Francis, aged 34.

22. Betson, Lieut.-Gen. George John, aged 80.

23. Hampden, Rev. Renn Dickson, Bishop of Hereford, aged 75.

24. Scrimegeour, James S., Founder of the Union Bank of London, aged 73.

30. Auchmuty, General Sir Samuel Benjamin, a Peninsular hero, aged 86.

— Talbot, John Hyacinth, aged 79.

MAY.

1. Forbes, Walter, Baron, aged 69.

2. Carmichael, J. W., a marine artist, aged 69.

— Wenlock, Dowager Lady Caroline, aged 76.

— Calthorpe, Frederick Gough, fourth Baron, aged 78.

7. Fielding, Rev. Allen, grandson of the celebrated Fielding, aged 67.

8. Wilson, Colonel Sir John Morillyon, aged 80.

— Paty, General Sir George William, a Peninsular hero, aged 80.

9. Brougham and Vaux, Lord Henry, in his 90th year. His acquirements were of the most versatile order ; he having shone as a lawyer, philosopher, historian, contributor to periodical literature, political and social reformer, and, indeed, in almost every position that can be aspired to. With Birkbeck, he was the founder of Mechanics' Institutions, and generally identified himself with every educational cause. He was but once Lord Chancellor, having become distasteful to each of the leading political parties of the day. Few have done as much for law reform, social progress, and the extension of learning as did Henry Brougham. His death occurred during sleep, at Cannes, where he was buried.

10. Crawford, John, a distinguished Oriental scholar and ethnologist, aged 85.

12. Stopford, Vice-Admiral James John, aged 51.

15. Devereux, Rear-Admiral Walter Bourchier, aged 58.

16. Ogilvie, Inspector-General Dr. Alexander,

Royal Artillery, and an eminent military physician, aged 79.

18. Muskerry, Matthew Fitzmaurice Deane, third Baron, aged 73.

19. Guinness, Sir Benjamin Lee, the eminent brewer of Dublin, aged 71.

21. Dickson, Sir Colpoys, aged 61.

22. Halford, Sir Henry, son of the celebrated physician, whose name was Vaughan before taking that of Halford, aged 71.

27. Marsh, Sir Hen., second Baronet, aged 47.

28. Liddell, Sir John, M.D., F.R.S., honorary physician to the Queen, aged 74.

— Brudenell-Bruce, George John, aged 29.

— Narvacz, Marshal, Duke of Valentia and Marshal of Spain, aged 68, having been born in 1800. His name was long connected with the fortunes and misfortunes of his country, in which he played a distinguished part, and died in office.

— Burnet, John, an eminent engraver and writer on art, aged 83.

— Cormenin, Louis Marie de la Haye, Vicomte, an eminent French poet and politician, aged 80.

JUNE.

4. Baring, Hon. and Rev. Frederick, aged 60.

— Shrewsbury, John Chetwynd Talbot, eighteenth Earl of, aged 65.

— Chambers, Robert, once champion of the Thames and Tyne, aged 37.

10. Michael, Prince of Servia, through assassination.

11. Brooke, Sir James, Rajah of Sarawak, who rendered eminent service in the destruction of piracy in the Indian Seas, aged 65.

20. Claridge, Sir John Thomas, aged 75.

21. Dodgson, Charles, Archdeacon of Richmond, Yorkshire.

23. Lowther, Sir John Henry, aged 75.

29. Lillie, Sir John Scott, C.B., lieutenant-colonel, an eminent British officer, aged 78.

30. Spry, Sir Samuel Thomas, aged 64.

— Buchanan, James, formerly Minister to the British Court, and President of the United States in 1856.

— Vaughan, Rev. Robert, D.D., an eminent Independent minister, and writer on religious controversial subjects, aged 73.

— Matteucci, Signor Charles, a celebrated Italian senator, and equally so as a professor and man of science, especially in regard to electro-physiological researches.

JULY.

1. Thompson, Rev. Sir Henry, Prebendary of Chichester, aged 72.

6. Lover, Samuel, an eminent composer, writer, and vocalist. He was born in Dublin in 1797, and commenced life as an artist. He will be long remembered by his productions—" Molly Bawn," "The Emigrant's Farewell," "Kathleen Mavourneen," "Rory O'More," "The Four-leaved Shamrock," &c.

7. Lisle, George Lysaght, fourth Baron, aged 85.

13. Dunfermline, Ralph Abercromby, second Baron, aged 65.

— Kirwan, Antony Latouche, Dean of Limerick.

16. Bantry, Richard White, second Earl of, aged 68.

18. Coyne, Joseph Stirling, aged 65. Dramatist, and long connected with the Dramatic Society for the Relief of Decayed Artists.

21. Thomas, George, an eminent artist. He largely contributed as a sketcher to the *Illus-*

trated London News, and many of his paintings were highly admired, aged 44.

— Arbuthnot, General Sir Hugh, aged 85. He served under Sir John Moore, and was with him at Corunna; also under the Duke of Wellington.

— Seton, Sir Henry John, sixth Baronet, accidentally run over in St. James's Street, London, aged 72.

26. Cranworth, Sir Robert Monsey Rolfe, Baron, born December 18, 1790. He was twice Lord Chancellor, and previously Solicitor-General, Baron of the Exchequer, Vice-Chancellor, &c. An able judge, and noted for his endeavours in promoting law reform.

27. Walcott, Admiral John Edward, aged 78.

28. Wemyss, Lady Isabella, aged 68.

— Elliotson, John, M.D., F.R.S., born in 1785. One of the first medical men to adopt the stethoscope for the testing of lung-disease; but better known for his favouring mesmerism, and strong advocacy of phrenology.

— Sullivan, Robert, LL.D., promoter of national education in Ireland.

— Cattermole, George, painter in water colours, aged 68.

AUGUST.

1. Shannon, Richard Boyle, fourth Earl of, aged 59.

— Scott, General Alexander, aged 89.

2. Blakeney, Right Hon. Sir Edward, Field Marshal, Governor of Chelsea Hospital, &c., born in 1778. Served in the West Indies, Copenhagen, Peninsula, America, and at the capture of Paris in 1815.

3. Perthes, Boucher de Crèvecœur, founder of the science of archæo-geology, aged 80.

5. Lushington, Right Hon. Stephen Rumbold, aged 92.

6. Downshire, Arthur Wills Blundell Sandys Trumbull Windsor Hill, fourth Marquis of, an eminent patron of science, politician, &c., aged 56.

10. Cooke, John Douglas, Editor of the *Saturday Review.*

— Menken, Adah Isaacs, actress and equestrian, aged 27.

11. Crespigny, Sir Claude William Champion, aged 50.

— Pocock, Sir George Bartholomew, aged 89.

12. Goode, the Very Rev. William, D.D., Dean of Ripon, aged 68.

— Wymer, Sir George Petre, an Indian general of great eminence, aged 80.

13. Calder, Sir Henry Roddam, aged 78.

— Blachley, Lieut.-Gen., a Peninsular officer.

14. Higgins, Matthew James, better known as "Jacob Omnium," contributor to the *Times* and several periodicals, aged 53.

17. Abergavenny, Rev. W. N., Earl of, aged 76.

20. Peterborough, Right Rev. Dr. Francis Jeune, Lord Bishop of, aged 62.

— Farnham, Lord (aged 69) and Lady, killed or burned to death by the dreadful accident at Abergele, through the collision of the Irish mail-express with trucks containing petroleum. He was much noted for his historical and archæological researches.

23. Lumley, Hon. Lyulph Richard Granby William, aged 90.

24. Goulburn, Edward, sergeant-at-law, and judge of the Bankruptcy Court, aged 81.

—. Morner, Count Otto Von, an eminent Swedish politician, &c., aged 87.

—. Stevens, Thaddeus, an eminent American statesman.

25. Barton, William Henry, Deputy Master and Comptroller of the Mint, aged 66.

26. Farrant, Col. Francis, Chargé d'Affaires in Persia for the East India Company, aged 64.

28. Macintosh, General Alexander Fisher, a Peninsular hero, aged 73.

29. Calcott, Major George Berkeley, a Peninsular hero, aged 81.

— Walden, Charles Augustus Ellis, Baron Howard De, Baron Seaford, &c., a distinguished diplomatist. He had represented British interests in Sweden, Lisbon, and Belgium, being ambassador to that country at the time of his death, aged 68.

30. Smith, Dr. George, eminent as a scholar and preacher, amongst the Wesleyan body, aged 68.

SEPTEMBER.

3. Maclure, Robert, LL.D., Professor of Humanity in Aberdeen University, aged 60.

7. Tetuan, Duchess of, and relict of the Duke of Tetuan, of Spain.

5. Dabouchet, Jacques, one of the founders of the Paris Gas Company.

10. Hoste, Rear-Admiral, Sir William Legge George, aged 60.

15. Crossley, John, senior partner in the firm of Crossley and Sons, carpet factors, of Halifax.

16. Gard, Richard Sommers, Deputy Warden of the Stannaries.

18. Glentworth, Lady Annabella, Viscountess, aged 77.

— Majoribanks, Edward, the senior partner in the banking firm of Coutts and Co., aged 94.

24. Cumming, Rev. Joseph George, M.A., F.G.S., an eminent geologist and antiquarian, and author of several historical works on the Isle of Man.

— Milman, the Very Rev. Henry Hart, D.D., Dean of St. Paul's, celebrated as a poet and historian, was born in 1791, and educated at Eton and Oxford. A tragedy called "Fazio" was one of his early productions. He was ordained in 1816, and subsequently became known by the production of several poems, becoming, in 1821, Professor of Poetry at Oxford. His "History of the Jews," "History of Christianity," and many other literary productions, led to his preferment. He became Dean of St. Paul's in 1849.

27. Walewski, Florence Alexander, Joseph Colonna, Count de, an eminent French politician, diplomatist, writer, &c. He was a scion of a noble Polish family, and was born at the Castle Walewice, in Poland, May 4, 1810. He retired to France on the fall of the Polish cause, and commenced his diplomatic career in 1840 by a mission to Egypt. He was Ambassador to England in 1852, and filled other diplomatic appointments, becoming Minister of Foreign Affairs at Paris in 1855. His death occurred suddenly from an attack of apoplexy.

— Irving, Ebenezer, brother of Washington Irving, aged 93.

— Pfeiffer, Charlotte Birch, aged 68, a German dramatist and adapter.

— Paul, Sir John Dean, aged 66, formerly banker, in the firm of Paul, Strahan, and Bates, tried and convicted of fraud in 1855.

— Stevens, Major-General Thomas. He served upwards of sixty years in the navy (Royal Marines).

— Fulford, the Right Rev. Francis, D.D., Bishop of Montreal, and Metropolitan of Canada, aged 65.

The Parliamentary Session of 1868 will long be memorable in our national history for the remarkable political features it presented. During the later years of his life, Lord Palmerston had, with consummate tact, managed to hold in abeyance the two great questions of "Reform" and "Ireland"; and thus kept up a kind of *entente cordiale* between the contending parties in the House of Commons; but on his death, in 1865, the ancient feud was revived. Beside Liberals and Conservatives, a small party had arisen, headed by Mr. Bright, sufficiently numerous to influence a majority on either side of the House, as its members chose to vote. Lastly a fourth party appeared in the shape of the "Adullamites," that still further complicated affairs. It was owing to the influence which the last-named body exercised in the House of Commons, that the Liberal administration of Earl Russell and Mr. Gladstone gave way in 1866, and the reins of power passed to the hands of Earl Derby and his party.

Early in 1867 (Feb. 15) Mr. Disraeli laid on the table of the House a series of resolutions relating to Parliamentary Reform; on the 25th of that month he entered into full details of the scheme proposed. It will be unnecessary here to recapitulate such details, as, in a modified form, they have since been moulded into and passed as a Reform Bill for the three great divisions of the United Kingdom. At the commencement of March, 1867, Earl Derby had the unpleasant duty of announcing to the House of Lords that, owing to the measure of Reform his Government intended to propose, the Secretaries of War (General Peel), Colonies (Earl of Carnarvon), and India (Viscount Cranborne), had withdrawn from the Ministry. On the 18th of March Mr. Disraeli introduced the Bill for Amending the Representation of the People (England); when it was read a first time. On the Bill passing into Committee it had to undergo an amount of mutilation that materially altered its first features. On May 13, Mr. Disraeli introduced the Scotch Reform Bill, of which it need only be said that, with the Irish Reform Bill, its consideration and passing were delayed far into the session of 1868, of which full particulars are given hereafter. The Distribution of English Borough and County Seats long occupied the attention of the House, each party having to give way alternately, or to modify its propositions. On June 24, Earl Russell gave an intimation of the storm that was likely to arise, by praying for a Commission to Inquire into the Revenues of the Irish Church, the culmination of which will be found in 1868, in the three Resolutions carried by Mr. Gladstone for the Disestablishment of the Irish Church. On July 16 the English Reform Bill was read a first time in the House of Lords, and a second time on July 23; after a long debate, but without a division, passing into Committee on the 29th. On August 6 the Bill was read a third time and passed. The Lords Amendments on the Bill were considered by the Commons on August 8, and a Committee was appointed to discuss with the Lords points of difference, which were settled on August 12, the Bill receiving the Royal Assent on the 15th. Thus we may summarize the most important Parliamentary events of 1867—the passage of the English Reform Bill, leaving, for the ensuing session, the Scotch and Irish Reform Bills, bones

of contention between all parties in the House. How far such were taken advantage of will be seen in the following summary of the business of that Session. The Session of 1867 was prorogued on the 21st of August.

The period intervening between this and the succeeding Session was actively employed by both parties in furnishing topics of discussion for the approaching re-assembly of Parliament. In London and the Provinces the members attended numerous meetings, giving detailed explanations of their past, and pledges for their future, conduct.

The Houses of Parliament re-assembled in February (13th) with the usual formalities, much anxiety being felt, however, on the part of the Government, on account of the ill-health of the Earl of Derby. In the House of Commons on February 17, Earl Mayo gave notice of his intention to introduce an Irish Reform Bill on the 9th March, and the Lord Advocate asked leave to introduce a Bill to Amend the Representation of the People in Scotland, which was read a first time, the second reading being deferred to March 2. The chief debate of the week was on Wednesday, February 19, when Mr. Gladstone's Compulsory Church Rate Abolition Bill came on for second reading in the House of Commons. The bill was introduced to abolish the principle of compulsion, whilst provision was made for the protection of Churchwardens, who would be enabled to enforce the payment of liabilities incurred by them within the general scope of the law of contracts. After some discussion the second reading took place without a division. The Habeas Corpus Suspension (Ireland) Act Continuance, was the same night read a third time and passed. On Thursday, February 20, Mr. Gathorne Hardy brought in a Bill to provide for carrying out executions within a prison, instead of publicly; it was read a first time. Mr. T. Hughes obtained leave to bring in a Bill to Amend the Law in respect to Sunday Trading.

The business in the House of Lords was of minor importance during the first week of meeting. February 24, the Marquis of Clanricarde introduced a Bill to improve Land Tenure in Ireland, which was read a first time. The Habeas Corpus Suspension Act (Ireland) was read a second time, passing through committee on the following day. The business in the Commons was of a local character.

February 25 introduced one of the most remarkable occurrences of the Session. It has already been noticed that the Earl of Derby had suffered much from ill-health. On that day the Earl of Malmesbury in the House of Lords, and Lord Stanley in the Commons, announced that the noble earl had tendered his resignation as premier, which had been accepted by the Queen. The House of Lords was adjourned to Thursday so that the Irish Habeas Corpus Act might be passed, and the Commons adjourned to Friday, February 28, both in order to give time to effect fresh ministerial arrangements. A further adjournment was required, when it was announced that the premiership had been conferred on Mr. Disraeli. The business of the Session then commenced in earnest, and the following is a chronological summary of its chief points and results.

March 5.—LORDS. The new government under Mr. Disraeli's premiership presented itself before Parliament. Lord Cairns occupied the woolsack in the House of Lords. The Earl of Malmesbury, as leader of the Upper House made a few remarks, explaining generally that the future policy of the ministry would be that of the one to which it had succeeded. Earl Russell entered his protest against a government which openly professed one policy and followed another. The Duke of Marlborough indignantly inquired the meaning of the noble earl's observations, to which the latter replied by referring the Duke to a speech made recently by Mr. Disraeli at Edinburgh, in which that minister had stated he had been "educating his party" to receive a Reform Bill of a much lower rate of franchise than even the Liberals had offered, whilst he (Disraeli) had constantly professed an opposite intention, in practice, before the House, a course characterized by Lord Russell as a deception.

Commons. The new premier (Mr. Disraeli) had a hearty reception on rising to address the House. He commenced by deploring the retirement of the Earl of Derby into private life, and eulogized the eminent talents of that statesman. Referring to his own position, he relied on the full support of his colleagues. He stated that the future policy of the Government would be simply a continuation of that followed by the preceding Government, both at home and abroad. He regretted the necessity for continuing the suspension of the Habeas Corpus Act in Ireland, and deprecated any premature discussion of Irish affairs in general, promising that so far as laid in his power all should be done to promote public business, and he would give every facility to bringing forward motions by the Opposition Members of the House. Mr. Bouverie moved the adjournment of the House for the purpose of criticising the policy of the Conservatives, asking which of the many courses they had proposed was intended to be followed. This called forth a rebuke from Sir G. Bowyer, who claimed the highest indulgence for the new Premier.

March 6.—Commons. Mr. Shaw Lefevre brought the Alabama question before the House, saying that we should meet the United States in a liberal spirit. Lord Stanley, in reply, entered into a lengthened history of the matter, promising that whilst justice should be done to the sufferers, British interests and dignity could not be compromised by simply regarding it as a money question. Mr. Forster and Mr. Sandford followed. Mr. Gladstone expressed his obligation to Lord Stanley for his speech of thorough equity, and that he had not compromised the national honour by accepting a proposal of arbitration. Mr. Gladstone further promised the support of the Liberal party to the Government so long as they pursued their present policy in reference to the Alabama claims. Mr. Disraeli moved the second reading of the Corrupt Practices at Elections Bill. The Capital Punishment within Prisons Bill was read a second time. The Sale of Liquors on Sundays Bill (Ireland) was read a second time.

Lords. The Earl of Longford presented a petition from the son of General Shrapnel asking for a national reward for the invention of the celebrated shell of that name.

March 9.—Commons. The Scotch Reform Bill came on for a second reading, and was agreed to after some opposition on the part of certain Scotch members. The Home Secretary in answer to Mr. Lewis gave some explanation in reference to the Clerkenwell explosion of 13th Dec. 1867, stating that although warning had been

received by the police authorities of an intended rescue of Burke and others, it was not imagined that the attempt would have been made in the way it had been.

Lords. The Marquis Clanricarde moved for a copy of instructions given to the Irish Railway Commissioners, which was refused on the part of the Government by the Duke of Richmond. The Duke of Marlborough gave notice of a motion in reference to public elementary education.

March 11—Commons. The Church Rate question came before the House in reference to four bills that had been introduced. Mr. Hubbard moved the second reading of his bill for the "regulation" of Church Rates. The discussion of the clauses was taken up by Mr. Gladstone, Sir Stafford Northcote and other members, and the bill was eventually ordered to be reported and printed.

March 12—Commons. The adjourned debate on the condition of Ireland was resumed by Mr. Horsman, who stigmatized the policy of the Government as one of procrastination. Mr. Lowe deplored the peculiarity of Irish controversialists, considering that the cry of ill-treatment to Ireland was as absurd as it was unjust, entering into numerous particulars to prove his views. Mr. Mill taunted the Government with inconsistency, and attacked the Church establishment. The debate was wound up by Mr. Gathorne Hardy, who defended the Government policy.

Lords. The Marquis of Clanricarde's Tenure Bill was read a second time, and referred to a select committee.

March 13—Commons. Resumption of the debate on Ireland by Mr. Chichester Fortescue. Many Irish members took part. Mr. Bright urged the abolition of the Church of Ireland, and denied that such a measure would be revolutionary. Sir Stafford Northcote closed the debate for the night by a review of the different speeches, stating that the Government was prepared for inquiry, and promising a bill on the land question (Ireland).

Lords. Debate on the conduct of the Government in regard to the Reform Act commenced by the Duke of Argyll, who asked what measures the ministry proposed, to remedy the inconvenience occasioned by their uncertain course of procedure. Lord Chancellor Cairns replied, defending the Government. Earl Russell twitted the Conservatives on their utter want of a consistent policy. Earl Malmesbury in defending their policy urged that the Reform Bill of 1867 had been the result of a general compromise; that the Liberal party were equally liable to the charge of inconsistency, delay, &c., as his own side of the House. Earls Grey and Granville followed, the Earl of Devon closing the debate.

March 16—Lords. The Ecclesiastical Orders in Council Bill was read a third time and passed. The Bankruptcy Reform Bill was read a second time.

Commons. Irish debate resumed by Mr. Monsell, who took up the University, Land, and other questions. Mr. Butler-Johnstone, the Conservative member for Canterbury made a violent attack on the Ministry, considering their policy anything but statesman-like. Mr. Gregory urged the question of the stability of land tenure as of the highest importance to Ireland. Mr. Gladstone discussed each measure that the Government had introduced in regard to Education Church, Land, &c. &c. He showed the absolute necessity of religious equality in Ireland and urged on the House an emphatic declaration in reference to the Irish Church, to be followed by definite action on the subject. Mr. Disraeli replied in detail to preceding speakers, expressing his hope that a policy for Ireland would be found which should reconcile all differences and sorrows. Mr. Maguire's motion was at length withdrawn without a division, he having expressed himself sufficiently satisfied with the debate itself.

March 18.—COMMONS. Discussion on Mr. J. A. Smith's Bill for Regulating the Sale of Liquors on Sunday. It was read, after much criticism, a second time, and referred to a Select Committee for special inquiry.

March 19.— LORDS. Presentation, by the Bishop of London, of a petition from members of the Cambridge Senate against further relaxations of universities tests. The Archbishop of Canterbury promised an early report of the Ritual Commission.

COMMONS. Mr. White attacked the rating clauses of the Reform Act, and moved its amendment in respect of the compounding system. After some discussion, the motion was withdrawn. The Earl of Mayo brought in the Irish Reform Bill, explaining its general provisions. Mr. Gladstone regretted that the Bill was so limited, but reserved discussion on its merits. Mr. Lowe called attention to the proposed issue of a charter for a Roman Catholic University in Ireland, and the Earl of Mayo replied by stating that the matter was entirely in the hands of the House. The Naval and Military Estimates were brought on, but only a vote on account was obtained.

March 20.—LORDS. A Bill for the Regulation of Railways was, after some discussion, read a second time, on the motion of the Duke of Richmond.

COMMONS. Questions of Privilege; the Conflict of Allegiance of Emigrants, especially in reference to the United States; Postal Subsidies; Indian Local Matters; the Lambeth Workhouse Irregularities, &c., occupied the House. On the motion for going into a Committee of Supply, the number of dockyards now existing was discussed. The Government announced the intention of abolishing all "river" dockyards when the Chatham extensions were complete.

March 23.—COMMONS. On the resumption of the debate on the Irish Reform Bill, Mr. Gladstone moved three resolutions. The first declared that the Irish Church should cease to exist as an Establishment; the second, that new personal interests should not, for the present, be created by public patronage, and that the Ecclesiastical Commission should confine their inquiries to objects only of immediate necessity, or involving individual rights pending the decision of Parliament; and the third, that an Address be presented to Her Majesty, asking that, with a view to the purposes aforesaid, she would place at the disposal of Parliament her interest in all Church temporalities belonging to the dignitaries, &c., of the Irish Church. Mr. Gladstone entered into all particulars of the Irish Church, denouncing it as an anomaly and unnecessary, confirming his statements by statistics, history, &c. Lord Stanley moved an amendment, opposing Mr. Gladstone's resolutions, and defended the existence of the Irish Church, denouncing the resolutions as a mere electioneering cry. His amendment admitted the necessity of modification in regard to the temporalities,

but urged that any attempt at disestablishment or disendowment should be left for the decision of a new Parliament. The debate was continued by Viscount Cranborne, Mr. Laing, the Solicitor-General, and other members, and then adjourned.

LORDS. Committee on the Poor Relief Bill, which was referred to a Select Committee.

March 25.—COMMONS. Bill to Extend the Principle of the English Industrial Schools to Ireland. Referred to a committee. Second reading of the Tancred's Charity Bill lost.

March 26.—LORDS. Earl Stanhope moved for a Committee to Inquire into the Operation of the Ecclesiastical Titles Act, which, after some discussion, was assented to by the Earl of Malmesbury and the Committee appointed.

COMMONS. Army Estimates voted. Mr. Otway carried a motion, prohibiting the use of the cat (under the Mutiny Act) in time of peace.

March 27.— LORDS. Earl Russell asked for a report on the Neutrality Laws, expressing his dissatisfaction at Lord Stanley's offer to refer the Alabama claims to arbitration.

COMMONS. Motion in favour of the abolition of compulsory pilotage, by Mr. Candlish, opposed and withdrawn. Lord A. Hay called attention to the comparative merits of the British and native systems of government in India, preferring, in many instances, native rule. Sir S. F. Northcote admitted the wisdom of letting the natives govern themselves, but showed the advantages of British rule.

April 1.—COMMONS. The Chancellor of the Exchequer obtained leave to bring in a Bill for purchase, &c., by the Postmaster-General, of the electric telegraph lines in the United Kingdom. Mr. Hadfield moved the second reading of the Religious, &c., Building Sites Bill, which was read a second time. The House went into Committee on the Artisans and Labourers' Dwellings Bill.

April 2.—LORDS. Lord Stratheden drew attention to the affairs of Crete, asking for all correspondence. The Duke of Cambridge referred to the clause, introduced by the Lower House, in the Mutiny Bill, forbidding the use of the "cat" during time of peace, urging the inconvenience of such a proviso. Bill read a second time. Committee appointed to superintend the printing of petitions.

COMMONS. The debate on Mr. Gladstone's Irish Church resolutions was resumed by Mr. Roebuck, who supported them. Mr. Henley opposed them as a mere party question. General Peel followed on the same side. Mr. Lowe, on the simple question of the ratio between Protestants and Roman Catholics in Ireland, supported the resolutions. Mr. Osborne would vote for disestablishment, but did not desire the separation of Church and State. Sir S. Northcote supported the amendment, when the debate was adjourned to Friday.

April 3.—COMMONS. Before the resumption of the debate, Mr. Disraeli gave notice that he should move the adjournment of the House, at its rising, to Monday, April 20. After presentation of numerous petitions *pro* and *con.*, Mr. J. D. Coleridge resumed the debate in favour of Mr. Gladstone's resolutions, followed by Mr. Beresford Hope, Mr. Stansfeld, and other members. At length, in a crowded House, Mr. Disraeli rose to reply, stating the determination of the Government to stand or fall on the question of Lord Stanley's amendment, proposed on the part of the Cabinet. He believed the policy of Mr. Gladstone, if successful, would change the character of the country, deprive its people of some of their best privileges, and be dangerous to the tenure of the Crown. Mr. Gladstone replied at great length to all the arguments of previous speakers in opposition to his resolution. The House then divided, giving a majority of 60 against the amendment of Lord Stanley. Mr. Gladstone's motion was then put, when there appeared

Ayes 328
Noes 272

Majority for Mr. Gladstone's motion 56

The House adjourned at half-past three A.M., the discussion of the first resolution being fixed for Monday, April 27.

April 20.—COMMONS. The House reassembled after the Easter recess. Mr. Smollett criticized the conduct of the Indian Government in respect to certain Irrigation Companies, which was defended by Sir Stafford Northcote, on grounds of general policy. A motion, by Mr. Watkin, for an inquiry into the state of Ceylon, was negatived without a division. Progress was made in a Committee of Supply, objections being taken by Alderman Lusk and others, in reference to several items. The Boundary Bill was read a second time, and committed for April 30. The second reading of Mr. Hubbard's Church-rates Regulation Bill was deferred to 29th April.

April 22.—COMMONS. Mr. Monsell moved the second reading of the Burials (Ireland) Bill, which was subsequently read a second time. Mr. Hughes' Sunday Trading Bill, and that of Mr. McLaren referring to the Edinburgh Canongate Annuity Tax, were read a second time.

April 23.—LORDS. The murder of Mr. D'Arcy McGee in Canada was referred to by the Earl of Carnarvon. The Duke of Buckingham in reply read a despatch stating the circumstances of his assassination. The Compulsory Church Rates Abolition Bill, brought into the House of Commons by Mr. Gladstone, came on for its second reading this night in the Lords. The second reading was moved by Earl Russell, and was replied to by the Duke of Buckingham, who objected entirely to the voluntary system, and insisted on many modifications of the proposed measure. After a debate in which several bishops and noble lords joined, the discussion was adjourned to Friday, April 24, when Earl Russell agreed to the Bill being referred to a Select Committee. The Education Bill was read a second time in the House of Lords.

April 23.—COMMONS. The Chancellor of the Exchequer brought forward the Budget. Its chief features were the imposition of a Sixpenny Income Tax to cover the expenses of the Abyssinian war, the successful termination of which had been mentioned in the House during the week, and raising of the extra revenue to be in part anticipated by the issue of one million of Exchequer Bonds. After some discussion the motion of the Chancellor was agreed to, resolutions to be proceeded with on April 27. The House went into Committee on the Ecclesiastical Orders in Council Bill. Indian affairs briefly occupied the House.

April 24.—COMMONS. On a motion of Mr. Goldney to inquire into the expenses of Permanent Commissions, the Government, who opposed, was defeated by a majority of *one*. Mr. Monk

moved for the correspondence on the affairs of the Cretan insurrection.

April 27.—COMMONS. Debate resumed on Mr. Gladstone's resolutions in respect to the disestablishment of the Irish Church. The first resolution was discussed, the debate being begun by Mr. Watkin. After numerous speeches by members, including Mr. Horsman, the debate was closed for the night by Lord John Manners, who replied to Mr. Horsman on the part of the Government, when the House adjourned. Addresses of congratulation were voted to Her Majesty by both Houses, on the happy escape of the Duke of Edinburgh from an attempted assassination by O'Farrell, a Fenian, during the Prince's visit to New South Wales.

April 29.—COMMONS. Sir Colman O'Loghlen moved the second reading of his bill to repeal the power of the Crown of creating a new Irish peerage for every three that became extinct. Bill withdrawn. Mr. Wyld moved the second reading of the County Financial Boards Bill, select Committee appointed. Report of amendments of Artisans and Labourers' Dwellings bill; debate adjourned for a week. Second reading of the Church Rates Commutation Bill deferred. Railway and Joint Stock Company's Bill read a second time.

April 30.—COMMONS. Resumption of the debate on Mr. Gladstone's resolutions in reference to the Irish Church, begun by Sir Michael Beach against, and followed by Sir C. O'Loghlen in favour. Sir W. Heathcote felt little the effect of the result on the fate of a ministry constantly in a minority, but should vote against the resolutions. Mr. Baxter felt that the disestablishment of the Irish Church would strengthen the position of the Church of England. After speeches by several members Mr. Walpole rose, observing that the real question before the House at issue was the principle of religious establishments. Previous solemn compacts had been discussed with great levity, especially that of the Act of Union, in which the establishment of the Irish Church was a prominent feature. That compact had been repeatedly renewed. The supremacy of the Crown was involved in the question. In voting against the resolutions he considered that the way to realize the prosperity of Ireland was not to break down, but rather improve and sustain, existing institutions. Lord Elcho could not vote in favour of the resolutions. Mr. Gladstone rose and addressed the House at great length. He briefly recapitulated his reasons for the disestablishment of the Irish Church, declining to state his ideas as to the mode of appropriating its property. He denied that his resolutions were the offspring of coalition or conspiracy, and defended the apparent inconsistency of his present and former opinions on the ground of advance. It was the Conservative Government that was alone to be blamed for the introduction of the question of the Irish Church, because in connection with their policy they had proposed the establishment of a Roman Catholic university for Ireland. He did not expect that the settlement of the Irish Church question would be a panacea for all the evils of that country, but yet the question of the existence of an Irish Church was one of the highest importance in order to bring Ireland into the position of a strong part of the empire, instead of being, as at present, a danger and reproach. Mr. Disraeli then rose, stating that the Government objected to the disestablishment of the Irish Church as injurious to

Ireland. He denied that the Irish Church was an injustice. He considered that Mr. Gladstone's resolutions, if carried, would impair the influence of the Church of England. He believed that there was a party in the English Church of extreme opinions, who advocated the disunion of Church and State, with those whom he might call Romanists, and defended his remarks that Mr. Gladstone's policy was simply revolutionary. The Division then took place, when there appeared

For Mr. Gladstone's resolution	330
Against	265
Majority in favour	65

Mr. Disraeli then moved the adjournment of the House in order that the Government might consider its position. The House rose at three A. M. (Friday), and adjourned till Monday.

April 30.—LORDS. Compulsory Church Rates Abolition Bill referred to a Select Committee.

May 1.—LORDS. Lord Redesdale moved for some returns, and took the opportunity of lecturing the Government on the niggardly completion of the India and Foreign Offices. Several local bills passed.

May 4.—COMMONS. Mr. Disraeli entered into lengthened explanations of the course that would be adopted by the Government in face of the defeat on the preceding Friday. He entered into an account of the policy pursued by his cabinet since 1866. Defended remaining in office at the present juncture by quoting similar cases on the part of Liberal Governments that had been placed in like circumstances. Had advised Her Majesty to dissolve Parliament or receive their resignation. Her Majesty had declined the latter, but was prepared to dissolve Parliament so soon as the state of public business would permit, which Mr. Disraeli considered might be accomplished in the autumn of the year. Mr. Gladstone challenged the correctness of the doctrines and policy of the Government at the present issue. He denied, considering the great majority of the preceding Friday, that dissolution was a course open to the Government, no parallel of such a case existing. The Government had no chance of improving their position by an appeal to the country. He concluded by expressing himself generally satisfied with Mr. Disraeli's arrangement for the future conduct of business. Mr. Lowe briefly criticized the Premier's statements, followed by Mr. Newdegate and others. Mr. Bright thought the statement of the Prime Minister would astonish the country. He rapidly sketched the proceedings of the Session, and was convinced that Mr. Gladstone's policy would meet with the approval of the nation. He denied the right of Government to advise a dissolution, and considered that resignation was the only proper course. Mr. Disraeli replied briefly. He considered that a vote of want of confidence would have been a more straightforward course than that adopted by the Opposition, which he felt sure would have been met in favour of the Government. The consideration of the second and third of Mr. Gladstone's resolutions was deferred.

May 4.—LORDS. The Earl of Malmesbury briefly stated the course intended to be followed by the Government (as already described by Mr. Disraeli). Earl Grey demurred. The Lord Chancellor defended the course. After speeches from the Dukes of Somerset and Richmond and Lord

Feversham the debate closed. The Lord Chancellor withdrew his Bankruptcy Bill on account of the state of public business, and the House went into Committee on the Regulation of Railways Bill.

May 5.—COMMONS. Second reading of a Bill for the Assessment of Mines, and the Divorce and Matrimonial Causes Court Bill.

May 7.—COMMONS. Resumption of the debate on Mr. Gladstone's second and third resolutions, in reference to the Irish Church, which after a brief discussion were passed. The second reading of the Irish Reform Bill was moved by the Earl of Mayo. Mr. Chichester Fortescue moved several important amendments, but the Bill was read a second time.

May 8.—LORDS. Debate on the subject of a vote of £20,000 to Lady Darling, the wife of the late Governor of Victoria. After some discussion in opposition to the course taken by the British Government, defended by the Duke of Buckingham, the subject dropped.

COMMONS. The Army and Navy estimates accupied the attention of the House, as also on the following Monday. After long discussion the votes required by the Government were passed. Mr. Gathorne Hardy promised a general measure in reference to turnpike trusts.

May 11.—COMMONS. Lengthened debate on the Regium Donum and Maynooth questions, in consequence of Mr. Ayrton introducing a motion that when the Irish Church is disestablished the grant to Maynooth and the Regium Donum be discontinued too. After much discussion the motion was lost. Renewed motions on the same subject were proposed, the result being the passing of an amendment by Mr. Gladstone by which due regard should be had to personal interests in the withdrawal of such aids. Mr. Greene moved "That no part of the endowments of the Anglican Church be applied to the endowment of the institutions of other religious communities." This was lost, but an amendment (to the original resolution) by Mr. Whitbread to the effect that when the Irish Church was disestablished the grant to Maynooth and the Regium Donum should cease, was carried. An extraordinary scene followed the discussion, owing to the personality of the debate.

May 13.—COMMONS. Discussion on the Oxford and Cambridge Universities Bill at its second reading, opening both Universities to every subject, independent of religious tests. After long discussion the debate was adjourned. Debate on Mr. Ewart's Metric Weights and Measures Bill, which passed a second reading.

May 14.—COMMONS. Mr. Gladstone brought in his Suspensory Bill consequent on his resolutions for the disestablishment of the Irish Church. It was read a first time, the second reading being appointed for 22nd May. Lengthened discussion on the Boundary Bill in Committee. (May 17, a Select Committee was appointed to settle the boundaries of certain boroughs.) Supply votes taken, as also on the 15th. Long conversation on the site of the new Law Courts.

May 15.—LORDS. Discussion on the delay in laying the Report of the Ritual Commission before the House, in which Opposition and Ministerial members took part, the Government pleading delay of action in consequence of the recent votes in the Lower House.

COMMONS. Supply, and variety of business of minor importance.

May 18.—COMMONS. Discussion on the Scotch

Reform Bill, which resulted in the proposed extinguishment of ten small English boroughs; and that the condition of rate payment, as enforced the English Bill, should not be required in Scotland.

May 20.—COMMONS. Discussion on Sir C. O'Loghlen's Law of Libel Bill, which was committed and deferred for further discussion.

May 21.—COMMONS. Further explanation by Mr. Disraeli on the Ministerial crisis, especially in reference to the two defeats on May 18. The Committee on Election Petitions and Corrupt Practices at Elections Bill, resumed. After much discussion on the clauses as to appointing judges, &c., progress was reported. The Irish Church debate was resumed after a lengthened debate, in which the leading members on both sides took part. Mr. Gladstone's Bill passed its second reading on Friday, May 22.

Ayes.............................. 312
Noes............................. 258
                                  ___
                                   54

May 22.—LORDS. Lord Houghton presented a petition from the Newfoundland House of Assembly, complaining that the Earl of Carnarvon had prohibited the granting of mining grants on the "French shore," or about half the colony; a course defended by the Earl on the ground of precise treaties with the French on the subject. The Earl of Malmesbury gave notice that, on the following Friday (May 29), he should move a vote of thanks to Sir Robert Napier and his Abyssinian troops. A similar notice was given by Mr. Disraeli in the House of Commons.

COMMONS. Miscellaneous business of minor importance.

May 25.—Committee on the Scotch Reform Bill. Clause inserted, excluding all who have not paid, or were exempt from, poor-rates, on the ground of poverty, or have failed to pay rates by 20th July due on the 15th May preceding. Seven English boroughs to be disfranchised in place of ten, as resolved on May 18. Attention was called, by Mr. Maguire, to the "Murphy Riots" in Ashton-under-Lyne, Mr. G. Hardy, in reply, declining to issue a commission.

May 28.—COMMONS. Resumption of Committee on the Scotch Reform Bill, of which the greater portion was disposed of, the new clauses being postponed to a further day. Miscellaneous business transacted.

LORDS. Committee on the Poor Relief Bill, with alteration and addition of clauses.

May 29.—LORDS. Review of the Session, by Earl Russell, in respect to the existing state of political parties. Reply by the Earl of Malmesbury. Conversation on University Tests, with presentation of petitions against them.

COMMONS. Report on the Boundary Bill brought up; discussion, &c., as to the date of the dissolution of Parliament. Questions respecting the "Murphy" riots by Mr. Whalley, and conversation as to the site of the New Law Courts, Parliamentary Rules, &c. House adjourned for Whitsun holidays to 4th June.

June 4.—COMMONS. Personal explanations by Mr. Gladstone in reference to a letter he had written on the Irish Church question; and lively scene in the House. Conversation on the endowment of the Catholic Church in Ireland. Discussion on the grants for Education, Science, and Art Supply.

June 5.—COMMONS. Committee on the Established Church of Ireland Bill. After much discussion, with the addition of a clause, to the effect that every official appointed to Maynooth, should hold office after the passing of the Bill subject to the pleasure of parliament, the Bill passed through committee. The Thames Embankment and Municipal Corporations (Metropolis) Bills were brought on for second reading, which was prevented by a count-out.

June 8.—COMMONS. Committee on the Scotch Reform Bill resumed, new clauses added, and the Bill ordered to be reported. Committee on the Boundary Bill, the consideration of it being adjourned to June 11. Irish Reform Bill passed through Committee.

LORDS. Discussion on Public Schools on motion for papers by Earl Stanhope.

June 10.—COMMONS. Second reading of Married Women's Property Bill. Committee on Mr. Monsell's Burials (Ireland) Bill. Second reading of the Bill to Remove Political Disabilities of Revenue Officers deferred.

June 11.—LORDS. Committee on the Army Chaplains Bill, with lengthened discussion of certain clauses.

COMMONS. Committee on Boundary Bill, which passed. Report on amendments of the Scotch Reform Bill, received with additional amendments. Mr. G. Hardy introduced a bill to facilitate the dissolution of Parliament, which he thought might take place about 8th or 9th of December.

June 12.—COMMONS. Report on the amendments of the Established Church Ireland Bill received. Supply.

LORDS. Debate on the Bill for Amalgamating the Brighton, South Eastern, and South Coast Railways. Referred to a select committee.

June 15.—COMMONS. Discussion on the Government of India Act Amendment Bill. Miscellaneous business.

June 17.—COMMONS. Mr. Mill moved the second reading of the Municipal Corporations (Metropolis) Bill. The debate was adjourned.

June 18.—COMMONS. Resumption of Committee on the Irish Reform Bill. After several alterations an addition of clauses, and verbal amendments, it was ordered to be read a third time. Conversation on the batta, or extra-pay of the Abyssinian troops, the Marriage Law Commission, &c.

LORDS. Third reading of the Sale of Poisons and Pharmacy Bill. Report of Amendments on the Poor Relief Bill received. Discussion on the Religious, &c., Sites Bill.

June 19.—COMMONS. Scotch Reform Bill read a third time, and passed; followed by a count-out.

LORDS. Discussion on the New Law Courts, opened by the Marquis of Salisbury, bringing before the House the appointment of Mr. Street as architect in place of Mr. Barry, the Lord Chancellor defending the course adopted by the government.

June 22.—COMMONS. The Boundary Bill read a third time and passed, Mr. Monck complaining bitterly of the "count-out" on the preceding Friday.

June 24.—COMMONS. Withdrawal of Mr. Bruce's Elementary Education Bill.

June 25.—COMMONS. Personal explanation by Mr. Disraeli respecting a speech he had delivered at Merchant Taylors' Hall, in which he had assumed the highest possible credit for the policy of the Government. Committee on Corrupt Practices at Elections Bill. After discussion of clauses, progress was reported.

June 25-26.—LORDS. Great discussion on the second reading of the Suspensory (Irish Church) Bill, all the leading lay lords and bishops taking part, and raising arguments similar to those already epitomized as employed by the members of the Lower House. Earl Granville moved the second reading. The debate was adjourned till next day (Friday), when the proceedings were opened by the Earl of Carnarvon, and again adjourned to the following Monday.

June 26.—COMMONS. Debate on the second reading of the Metropolitan Cattle Market Bill, moved by Lord R. Montagu. Debate adjourned. Committee of Supply, Conversation on Indian Telegraphy, Publication of Reports, &c., &c.

June 29.—LORDS. Adjourned debate on the Suspensory Bill resumed, the Duke of Argyll opening in support; replied to by the Bishop of Oxford. Earl Russell spoke in favour of the Bill, and was replied to by the Lord Chancellor. Earl Granville followed, when a division took place.

For the second reading 97
Against 192

Majority 95

The bill was consequently lost.

July 1.—COMMONS. Debate on the second reading of the Oxford and Cambridge Universities Bill, which was read a second time.

July 2.—Vote of thanks, in both Houses of Parliament, to Sir Robert Napier, his officers, and troops engaged in the Abyssinian war.

COMMONS. Committee on the Election Bills, for expediting the process of registration. Vote of Army and Navy supplies.

July 2-3.—LORDS. Debate on the Boundary Bill. Owing to the strong feeling of the Opposition at the conclusion of Earl Russell's speech, most members on that side left the House in a body, as an indignant protest against want of faith shown by the Government. On the resumption of the debate on Friday (3rd), mutual explanations were given, and the Bill progressed.

July 3.—COMMONS. Adjourned debate on the Metropolitan Foreign Cattle Market Bill. Miscellaneous business.

LORDS.—Conversation on the Duke of Buckingham's despatch to Natal, respecting the consecration of a bishop in place of Bishop Colenso. Compulsory Church Rate Bill passed through Committee, after some amendments.

July 8.—COMMONS. Committee on the Promissory Oaths' Bill, and miscellaneous business.

July 9.—Both Houses voted an address congratulating Her Majesty on the recent *accouchement* of the Princess of Wales.

LORDS.—The Earl of Shaftesbury moved the second reading of the Uniformity of Public Worship Bill, but after much discussion, the Bill was lost. Committee on the Church Rates Abolition Bill. After a long debate, with amendments, the Bill passed.

COMMONS. Consideration of the Lords' amendments on the Reform Bills, which were assented to. Corrupt Practices at Elections Bill considered. Supply votes for army and navy.

July 10.—LORDS. Conversation on the report of the Commissioners on the Established Church (Ireland), the Windsor Volunteer Review, &c.

COMMONS. Discussion on religious education in Ireland; the abuses of the Consular Courts in Turkey and Egypt, &c.

July 13.—LORDS. Second reading of the Public Schools Bill.

COMMONS. Discussion on the Irish Registration Bill, which, with some alterations, was agreed to.

July 15.—COMMONS. Rejectment of the Investment of Trust Funds Supplemental Bill.

July 16.—LORDS. Duke of Richmond moved that the House should agree to the amendments made by the Commons in the Promissory Oaths Bill, which involved the consideration of the Coronation Oath, for a copy of which Lord Redesdale moved on Friday (17th). Amendments agreed to. Debate on the financial matters of the army and navy.

COMMONS. Discussion on the Metropolitan Cattle Bill deferred till Monday, when progress was reported. Discussion on the financial condition of the army and navy, continued on the following evening (Friday). Conversation on religious instruction in Ireland; Naturalisation and Expatriation, &c.

July 17.—COMMONS. Committee on Election Petitions and Corrupt Practices at Elections Bill. Some clauses disposed of, and progress reported. Committee on Poor Relief Bill; discussion on the appointment of workhouse chaplains, on the condition of Greenwich Hospital, &c.

July 18.—COMMONS. Second reading of the Appropriation Bill.

July 22.—COMMONS. Committee on the Election Petitions and Corrupt Practices Bill, the consideration of which, after some change, and addition of clauses, was adjourned. Oxford and Cambridge Test Bills withdrawn.

July 23.—LORDS. Committee on Public Schools Bill. After much discussion and alteration of many clauses, the report was received. The Bill passed on the following Monday, July 27. The Earl of Shaftesbury drew attention to a circular of the Russian Government, urging the disuse of explosive rifle balls in battle.

COMMONS. Discussion on the Metropolitan Cattle Bill. Considerable excitement in the House, which ended in the withdrawal of the Bill by the Government on the following day.

July 24.—COMMONS. Committee on the Regulation of Railways Bill, which, after a short debate, the addition of new clauses, &c., passed. Personal explanation on the part of Mr. Gladstone, in reference to the presence of a Mr. Finlen at a deputation he had received.

July 25.—COMMONS. Passing of the Election Petitions and Corrupt Practices at Elections Bill. This Bill was read a second time in the House of Lords on the following Monday. Consideration of the Compulsory Church Rates Abolition Bill, which were agreed to.

July 27.—COMMONS. Committee on Poor Relief Bill. Introduction of the Indian Budget by Sir Stafford Northcote. Numerous bills were withdrawn.

July 29.—COMMONS. Mr. Kinnaird called attention to a military order issued in Canada, forbidding volunteer officers preaching in their uniform, which Sir J. Pakington defended on the grounds of public policy.

July 30.—LORDS. The Duke of Marlborough moved an address to Her Majesty for a copy of a return showing the number of ecclesiastical parishes in England and Wales, the number of schools connected with the Church of England, and the daily attendance—all in 1866.

July 31.—COMMONS. Numerous notices were

given by members in respect to motions intended to be made in the ensuing session. Mr. Rearden rose, amidst the derision of the House, to move for leave to bring in a Bill, having, in effect, the repeal of the union between Great Britain and Ireland, the establishment of separate legislature, national debt, revenue, &c., &c., in that country, but was stopped by the appearance of "Black Rod" summoning Her Majesty's faithful Commons to the House of Lords, there to hear her Most Gracious Speech read by Commission. It embraced a brief epitome of the events of the Session, referring especially to the success of the Abyssinian Expedition, the improved condition of Ireland, the regulation of railways, purchase of telegraphic lines, and the improvement of civil and criminal procedure in Scotland. An intention of early dissolving Parliament was announced to "enable my people to reap the benefit of the extended representation which the wisdom of Parliament has provided for them."

The commission for proroguing Parliament was then read, and thus ended one of the most memorable Sessions that has been held since the passage of the Reform Bill of 1832.

A TABLE OF THE STATUTES
Passed in the Third Session of the Nineteenth Parliament of the United Kingdom of Great Britain and Ireland. 31 & 32 Vict.

1. An Act to apply the sum of two million pounds out of the Consolidated Fund for the service of the year ending the 31st March, 1868.
2. An Act to grant to Her Majesty an additional rate of Income Tax.
3. An Act to confirm a Provisional Order under "The Drainage and Improvement of Lands (Ireland) Act, 1863," and the Acts amending the same.
4. An Act to amend the Law relating to Sales of Reversions.
5. An Act for the amendment of "The Metropolitan Streets Act, 1867." Amendment of Section 6 of 30th and 31st Vict., cap. 134, Regulations as to Lamps, to be subject to approval of the Secretary of State.
6. An Act to forbid the Issue of Writs for Members for the Boroughs of Totnes, Reigate, Great Yarmouth, and Lancaster.
7. An Act to further continue the Act of the 29th Vict., c. 1, intituled "An Act to empower the Lord Lieutenant or other Chief Governors of Ireland to apprehend and detain for a limited time, such persons as he or they shall suspect of conspiring against Her Majesty's Person and Government."
8. An Act to provide for the acquisition of a site for a Museum in the east of London. Power to trustees to sell Land for purposes of London Museum, protection for interests omitted by mistake to be purchased, power to trustees to transfer lands, &c., to Department of Science and Arts.
9. An Act to regulate the disposal of extra receipts of Public Departments. Certain fees or casual receipts to be paid over to the Exchequer to the credit of the Consolidated Fund as the Commissioner of Her Majesty's Treasury may direct.
10. An Act to apply the sum of £362,398 19s. 9d. out of the Consolidated Fund to the service of the years ending 31st March, 1867 and 1868.
11. An Act to amend an Act to make further provision for the despatch of business in the Court of Appeal in Chancery.
12. An Act to facilitate the alteration of days upon which, and of places at which, Fairs are now held in Ireland.
13. An Act to apply the sum of six million pounds out of the Consolidated Fund to the service of the year ending 31st March, 1869.
14. An Act for punishing Mutiny and Desertion, and for the better payment of the Army and their quarters.
15. An Act for the regulation of Her Majesty's Royal Marine forces while on shore.
16. An Act to apply the sum of seventeen million pounds out of the Consolidated Fund to the service of the year ending 31st March, 1869.
17. An Act to further continue and appropriate the London Coal and Wine Duties. Continues duties and acts (24th & 25th Vict., cap. 42—26th and 27th Vict., cap. 46) for a further period of seven years. Coal duty of fourpence to be applied by Corporation of London for Improvements. Compensation or pensions to officers, in certain cases, to be regulated by 22nd & 23rd Vict., cap. 26. Compensations or pensions to be charged on duties. Duties to be applied in making free from toll the following Bridges on the Thames :—Kew, Kingston-upon-Thames, Hampton-Court, Walton-upon-Thames, and Staines ; and next Chingford Bridge and Tottenham Mills Bridge, upon the River Lea. Surplus to be applied as Parliament may direct.
18. An Act to give further time for making certain Railways.
19. An Act for declaring valid certain Orders of Her Majesty in Council relating to the Ecclesiastical Commissioners for England and to the Deans and Chapters of certain Churches.
20. An Act to enable persons in Ireland to establish Legitimacy and the validity of Marriages, and to be deemed natural-born subjects.
21. An Act to provide Compensation to Officers of certain discontinued Prisons.
22. An Act to amend the law relating to places for holding Petty Sessions and to Lock-up houses for the temporary confinement of persons taken into custody.
23. An Act to render valid Marriages solemnized in the Chapel of Frampton Mansel, Gloucester.
24. An Act to provide for carrying out of Capital Punishment within Prisons. Judgment of death to be carried into effect within walls of prison. Sheriff, chaplain, and surgeon, &c., to be present. Surgeon to certify death, and declaration to be signed by sheriff, &c. Coroner's inquest to be held within twenty-four hours after execution. Body to be buried within the prison walls ; or Secretaries of State, if satisfied on the representation of the visiting justices of of the prison that there is insufficient space, may appoint some fit place to be used accordingly. Term of not exceeding two years, with or without solitary confine-

ment, for signing false certificates. Certificates, &c., to be sent to Secretary of State, and exhibited on or near entrance to prison. Duties and powers may be vested in the under sheriff or other lawful deputy, with the authority of the sheriff. Duties of the gaoler, surgeon, and chaplain, may be vested in their deputies.

25. An Act to extend the Industrial Schools Act to Ireland.

26. An Act to enable certain guaranteed Indian Railway Companies to raise money on debenture stock.

27. An Act for raising the sum of £1,600,000 by Exchequer Bonds for the service of the year ending 31st March, 1869.

28. An Act to grant certain Duties of Customs and Income Tax.

29. An Act to amend the law relating to Medical Practitioners in the Colonies.

30. An Act to amend the Act of the 7th & 8th Victoria, chap. 44, relating to the formation of *quoad-sacra* Parishes in Scotland, and to repeal the Act of the 29th & 30th Vict., chap. 67.

31. An Act to amend an Act, 39th Geo. III., intituled "An Act for the better regulation of Stockbrokers."

32. An Act for annexing conditions to the appointment of persons to Offices in certain Schools.

33. An Act for the publication of Cotton Statistics. Forwarders of cotton to make monthly returns to the Board of Trade. Returns to be published. Penalty, not exceeding £20, if forwarder omit to comply with requirements.

34. An Act to alter some provisions in the existing Acts as to Registration of Writs in certain Registers in Scotland.

35. An Act to extend the provisions in "The Duchy of Cornwall Management Act, 1863," relating to permanent improvements.

36. An Act to make perpetual the Alkali Act, 1863.

37. An Act to amend the Law relating to Documentary Evidence in certain cases.

38. An Act for the appropriation of certain unclaimed shares of Prize Money in India.

39. An Act to give relief to Jurors who may refuse or be unwilling from alleged conscientious motives to be sworn in Civil or Criminal proceedings in Scotland.

40. An Act to amend the Law relating to Partition.

41. An Act to make provision in the case of Boroughs ceasing to return Members to serve in Parliament respecting Rights of Election which have been vested in persons entitled to vote for such members.

42. An Act to amend the Act 23rd & 24th Vict., c. 50, by abolishing the Rate imposed by the said Act on all occupiers of premises within the extended Municipal Boundaries of the City of Edinburgh.

43. An Act for extending the provisions of The Thames Embankment and Metropolis Improvement (Loans) Act, 1864, and for amending the powers of the Metropolitan Board of Works. London coal and wine duties, levied for any extended period, to be carried to improvement fund. Extension of guarantee by Treasury to raise further monies. Metropolitan Board to give their general fund as collateral security. Land may be charged as collateral security. Amount borrowed not to exceed one million eight hundred and fifty thousand pounds, in addition to sums authorized by Act of 1864. Fund to be applied in paying interest on securities, in paying other expenses incurred in respect of works authorized by the Embankment and Improvement Acts, and also in improving the metropolis in such a manner as may hereafter be enacted.

44. An Act for facilitating the acquisition and enjoyment of Sites for Buildings for Religious, Educational, Literary, Scientific, and certain charitable purposes. Grants of land for buildings for religious and certain other purposes to be exempt from 9th Geo. II., cap. 36, and sec. 2 of 24th and 25th Vict., cap. 9. Trustees may cause deeds to be enrolled in Chancery. Deeds or other instruments need not be acknowledged in order to enrolment.

45. An Act to carry into effect a Convention between Her Majesty and the Emperor of the French concerning the Fisheries in the seas adjoining the British Islands and France, and to amend the Laws relating to British Sea Fisheries.

46. An Act to settle and describe the limits of certain Boroughs and the Division of certain Counties in England and Wales, in so far as respects the Election of Members to serve in Parliament.

47. An Act to Amend "The Consecration of Churchyards Act, 1867."

48. An Act for the Amendment of the Representation of the people in Scotland. Every man entitled to be registered as a voter, and, when registered, to vote at elections for members of Parliament. Must be of full age; must have been an occupier or tenant for at least twelve calendar months; must have paid poor-rates. Lodger franchise for voters in burghs must be of full age; must have occupied, separately, for twelve months, unfurnished apartments of the value of £10. Ownership franchise for voters in counties. Occupation. For the City of Glasgow, no person to vote for more than two candidates. Electors employed for reward within six months of an election not to vote. New seats for the Universities of Glasgow and Edinburgh, and counties of Lanark, Ayr, and Aberdeen. Counties of Selkirk and Peebles to be united; and new district of burghs, to return one member. Certain counties to be divided, and each division to return a member. Registers of voters to be formed for new burghs and divisions of counties. Joint owners and joint occupants, if of the value of £5, entitled to vote, and husbands in right of their wives. Dwelling-houses to be specially entered in valuation rolls, and, in certain counties, to contain certain additional particulars. Provision for claims by persons improperly exempted from payment of poor-rates. Poor-rate to be demanded. Collector wilfully neglecting to do so, punishable. Payments for conveying voters for burghs to the poll illegal. Rooms to be hired for polling wherever they can be obtained. Franchise for universities. Expenses of valuation and registration of voters and remuneration of persons acting as assessor and town clerk, to be assessed on the burgh. Corrupt payment of rates to be punishable as bribery. Receipt of parochial relief to disqualify for counties as well as burghs. Members holding offices of profit from the Crown not to vacate their seats on acceptance of another office.

49. An Act to Amend the Representation of the people in Ireland. Franchises. Occupation in cities, towns, and boroughs. Lodger fran-

chise for voters in cities, towns, and boroughs. Registration of persons occupying lodgings. As to joint occupation in counties. Provisions as to premises occupied in succession in counties. No elector who has been employed for reward within six months of an election to be entitled to vote. Boundaries of parliamentary boroughs. Rooms for taking polls wherever they can be obtained. Members holding offices of profit from the Crown not to vacate their seat on acceptance of another seat. Payment of expenses of conveying voters in boroughs to the poll illegal. Returning officer, &c., acting as agent, guilty of misdemeanour. Notice of claim to vote in cities, &c., to be signed by claimant. Where value of premises in certain boroughs is not more than £4, the rate is to be made on the immediate lessors. In certain boroughs, occupiers of land, &c., where owners, now rated, shall be entitled to be registered. Collector-General of Rates to make lists of voters for the City of Dublin. Certain provisions of 13th and 14th Vic., cap. 69, to apply to Collector-General of Rates. Remuneration of Collector-General of Rates to be in the discretion of the Guardians of the Poor.

50. An Act to Amend the Acts for the administration of Prisons in Scotland.

51. An Act to Amend the Law relating to Fairs in England and Wales. Secretary of State to have power to alter days for holding fairs, on representation made to him. Notice of representation to be published in the *London Gazette*, and in three successive weeks in some newspaper in the county in which the fair is held. Owner of such fair to take such tolls and to enjoy such rights and privileges as he possessed previous to making such order.

52. An Act to Amend the Act for punishing idle and disorderly persons, and rogues and vagabonds, so far as relates to Gaming. Act may be cited as "The Vagrant Act Amendment Act, 1868." This and the Act passed in 5th Geo. IV., cap. 83, be construed as one Act. Persons gaming or betting in any public place, with any instrument, coin, or token, at any game of chance, to be deemed rogues and vagabonds, and may be convicted and punished. Act to take effect Oct. 1, 1868.

53. An Act to continue in force an Act 2nd Geo. II., cap. 19, for the better regulation of the Oyster Fishery in the River Medway.

54. An Act to render Judgments or Decrees obtained in certain Courts in England, Scotland, and Ireland respectively effectual in any other part of the United Kingdom.

55. An Act to provide for the Collection by means of Stamps of Fees, payable in the Courts of Law in Scotland, and in the Offices belonging thereto.

56. An Act to Amend the 25th & 26th Victoria, chap. 66, for the safe keeping of Petroleum. Act may be cited as "The Petroleum Act, 1868," and, so far as is consistent with the tenor thereof, read with 25th and 26th Vict., cap. 66. Petroleum shall include rock oil, Rangoon oil, Burmah oil, and any oil made from petroleum, coal, schist, shale, peat, or other bituminous substance, and any product giving off an inflammable vapour at a temperature of less than one hundred degrees of Fahrenheit's thermometer. Sec. 3 of 25th and 26th Vict., cap. 66 repealed. After 1st February, 1869, no petroleum, otherwise than for private use, to

be kept within fifty yards of a dwelling-house. Prohibition of sale for purpose of illumination. Inspector of Weights, &c., may test. Offences under "Petroleum Act, 1862 & 1868," may be tried as police offences by any magistrate. Mode of testing petroleum.

57. An Act to make provision for the appointment of Members of the Legislative Council of New Zealand, and to remove doubts in respect of past appointments.

58. An Act to Amend the Law of Registration, so far as relates to the year ending 1869.

59. An Act to Amend the Law relating to Reformatory Schools in Ireland.

60. An Act to make better provision for the management of the Curragh of Kildare.

61. An Act for removing Doubts as to the validity of certain Marriages between British subjects in China and elsewhere.

62. An Act to extend the provisions of "The Renewable Leasehold Conversion (Ireland) Act" to certain Leasehold Tenures in Ireland.

63. An Act to enable Commissioners appointed to inquire into the failure of the Bank of Bombay, to examine Witnesses in the United Kingdom.

64. An Act to improve the Registration of Writs relating to heritable property in Scotland.

65. An Act to Amend the Law relating to Voting Papers in Elections for Universities.

66. An Act to confirm certain Provisional Orders made under an Act, 15th Vict., to facilitate arrangements for the relief of Turnpike Trusts.

67. An Act to Amend the Law relating to the funds provided for defraying the expenses of the Metropolitan Police. May be cited as "The Police Rate Act, 1868." Annual sum for defraying expenses not to exceed ninepence in the pound. To Assistant-Commissioners, in addition to their salary, an allowance of not exceeding £300 may be given for house-rent. Provisions as to Metropolitan Police Acts, 3rd and 4th Wm. IV., cap. 81, and sec. 19, 20th and 21st Vic., cap. 64, repealed.

68. An Act to facilitate Liquidation in certain cases of Bankruptcy and Winding-up. May be cited as "The Liquidation Act, 1868." Act to have effect in case of bankruptcy, whether adjudication had been made before passing of Act or Deed of Arrangement, had been registered before the passing of this Act, and adjudication of bankruptcy supervenes before the completion of the liquidation under the deed. Power to prepare and file scheme. Provision in scheme as to secured creditors. Notice. Application for confirmation. Confirmation of scheme by court. Effect of scheme binding. Regard by court to wishes of creditors. Power for creditors to foreclose by notice. One of the chief amendments is that the creditors are to prove their debts when they execute the deed, and the value of the security held by a creditor is to be deducted in the amount for which he signs to make up the number of three-fourths necessary to make a deed. Full information as to debts and liabilities to be given, and notice inserted in the newspapers. Complete investigation will be afforded, and composition deeds will not be so easily effected as hitherto. General rules are to be framed to carry out the provisions of the Act.

69. An Act to assimilate the Law in Ireland to the Law in England as to Costs in Actions of

70. An Act to Amend "The Railways (Ireland) Act, 1851 and 1860," as to the trial of traverses.

71. An Act for conferring Admiralty Jurisdiction on the County Courts.

72. An Act to Amend the Law relating to Promissory Oaths. Form of oath of allegiance. Form of official oath. Form of judicial oath. Persons to take the oath of allegiance and official oath. Penalty on not taking required oath. Form of oath in this Act substituted for form in certain other Acts. Prohibition of oath of allegiance except in accordance with Act. The name of the sovereign for the time being to be used in the oath. Provision in favour of persons permitted to make affirmations. Regulations as to substitution of declarations for oaths. Penalty on not making declaration required by this Act.

73. An Act to Relieve certain Officers employed in the collection and Management of Her Majesty's Revenues from any legal Disability to Vote at the election of Members to serve in Parliament.

74. An Act to extend the powers of Poor Law Inspectors and Medical Inspectors in Ireland.

75. An Act to Amend the Law relating to Petit Juries in Ireland.

76. An Act to defray the charge of the pay, clothing, and contingent and other expenses of the Disembodied Militia; to grant allowances to Subaltern Officers, Adjutants, Paymasters, Quartermasters, Surgeons, Assistant Surgeons, and Surgeons' Mates of the Militia; and to authorize the employment of the non-commissioned officers.

77. An Act to Amend the Law relating to Appeals from the Court of Divorce and Matrimonial Causes in England.

78. An Act to Amend the Law relating to proceedings instituted by the Admiralty; and for other purposes connected therewith.

79. An Act to further Amend the Law relating to Railway Companies.

80. An Act to Amend the Contagious Diseases Act, 1866.

81. An Act to authorize loans of Public Money to the Portpatrick and the Belfast and County Down Railway Companies.

82. An Act to Abolish the power of levying the assessment "Rogue Money" in Scotland.

83. An Act to afford greater facilities for the ministrations of Army Chaplains. Prevents parochial clergymen from interfering with the ministrations of army chaplains in any parish.

84. An Act to Amend in several particulars the Law of Entail in Scotland.

85. An Act to apply a sum out of the Consolidated Fund, and to appropriate the supplies granted in this Session of Parliament.

86. An Act to enable Assignees of Marine Policies to sue thereon in their own names.

87. An Act to amend the Act 26th & 27th Vict., cap. 52, intituled "An Act to further extend and make compulsory the practice of Vaccination in Ireland."

88. An Act for transferring the Fee and other Funds of the Courts of Chancery and Exchequer in Ireland to the Consolidated Fund.

89. An Act to alter certain provisions in the Acts for the Commutation of Tithes, the Copyhold Acts, and the Acts for the Inclosure, Exchange, and Improvement of Land.

90. An Act to empower certain Public Departments to pay otherwise than to Executors or Administrators small sums due on account of pay or allowances to persons deceased.

91. An Act to settle an annuity [£2,000] upon Lieutenant-General Sir Robert Napier, G.C.B., G.C.S.I.. and the next surviving Heir Male of his body.

92. An Act to declare the powers of the General Assembly of New Zealand to abolish any province in that colony, or to withdraw from any such province any part of the territory.

93. An Act to remove Doubts respecting the operation of the New Zealand Company's Act.

94. An Act to authorize the further extension of the period for Repayment of Advances made under the Railway Companies Act, 1866.

95. An Act to Amend the Procedure in the Court of Justiciary and other Criminal Courts in Scotland.

96. An Act to Amend the Procedure in regard to Ecclesiastical Buildings and Glebes in Scotland.

97. An Act to make provision for the Audit of Accounts of Lunatic Asylums in Ireland.

98. An Act to make provision for the payment of Salaries to Clerks of the Peace and Clerks of the Crown in certain boroughs in Ireland.

99. An Act to continue certain Turnpike Acts in Great Britain, to repeal certain other Turnpike Acts, and to make further provision concerning Turnpike Roads.

100. An Act to Amend the Procedure in the Court of Session and the Judicial Arrangements in the Superior Courts of Scotland, and to make certain changes in the other Courts.

101. An Act to consolidate the Statutes relating to the Constitution and Completion of Titles to Heritable Property in Scotland, and to make certain changes in the Law of Scotland relating to Heritable Rights.

102. An Act to alter the qualifications of the Electors of places in Scotland under the "General Police and Improvement (Scotland) Act, 1862," or under the Act 13th & 14th Vict., chap. 33, and to amend the said Acts in certain other respects.

103. An Act to Amend the Law which regulates the burials of persons in Ireland not belonging to the Established Church.

104. An Act to Amend Bankruptcy Act, 1861.

105. An Act for enabling Her Majesty to accept a surrender, upon terms, of the Lands, Privileges, and Rights of "The Governor and Company of Adventurers of England trading into Hudson's Bay," and for admitting the same into the Dominion of Canada.

106. An Act for the prevention of the holding of unlawful Fairs within the limits of the Metropolitan Police District.

107. An Act to amend the Law relating to the Indorsing of Warrants in Scotland, Ireland and the Channel Islands.

108. An Act to Amend the Laws for the Election of the Magistrates and Councils of Royal and Parliamentary Burghs in Scotland.

109. An Act for the Abolition of compulsory Church Rates. Compulsory church rates abolished. Saving of rates called church rates, but applicable to secular purposes. Provision where money is due on security of such rates, may still be levied. Rates in the nature of church rates, made before the passing of this Act, may be collected and recovered as if Act not passed. Not to affect enactments in local acts, &c., where rates are made for purposes of tithes, customary payments or other property or charge upon property. Act not to affect vestries, &c. Trustees and others, under incapacity, may subscribe to voluntary

rate. Persons making default in paying rates, unable to inquire into or vote in respect of the expenditure of the monies arising from the church rates. Power to appoint church trustees.

110. An Act to enable Her Majesty's Postmaster General to acquire, work, and maintain Electric Telegraphs. Power to Postmaster-General to purchase undertakings of telegraph companies. Power to telegraph companies to sell. Acts, &c., of companies selling their undertakings to remain in force, and the powers thereof to be exercised by the Postmaster-General. Companies may require Postmaster-General to purchase their undertaking under certain circumstances. Provisions as to purchase. Postmaster-General to enter into certain contracts with certain railway companies. Application of sums received by Reuter's Telegraph Company, by virtue of agreement with Postmaster-General. Postmaster-General may acquire a right of way over the Bridgewater Canal, also over the Grand Junction Canal. Agreements confirmed by Act. Power to Postmaster-General to lease property, also to make regulations for conduct of business, and to fix charges. Power to enter into special agreements with proprietors of newspapers. Messages having priority to be specially marked. Payments to be made by means of stamps. Power to appoint offices for depositing messages. Punishment, not exceeding twelve calendar months, for disclosing or intercepting messages. Property in telegraph messages to be laid in Postmaster-General, Postmaster-General to pay rates, &c. Copies of regulations to be laid before Parliament. Provision as to payment of costs to railway and telegraph companies if objects of Act not carried out.

111. An Act to continue various expiring Laws.

112. An Act to Amend the Law of Registration in Ireland.

113. An Act to render valid Marriages solemnized in the Chapel of Blakedown, Worcester.

114. An Act to Amend the Law relating to the Ecclesiastical Commissioners for England.

115. An Act to Amend "The Sanitary Act, 1866."

116. An Act to Amend the Law relating to Larceny and Embezzlement.

117. An Act to Amend the District Church Tithes Act, 1865. and to secure uniformity of designation amongst Incumbents.

118. An Act to make further provision for the good government and extension of certain Public Schools in England.

119. An Act to Amend the Law relating to Railways. Railway companies are liable, during sea transit, as carriers, when required, to furnish particulars of charges for goods. After the 1st April, communication between the passengers and the company's servants to be provided under the following section:—"To maintain and keep in working order in every train which carries passengers, and travels more than twenty miles without stopping, such means of communication between the passengers and the company's servants, as the Board of Trade may approve." Penalty of £10 in each case of default. Penalty of £5 for making use of such communication without reasonable cause. Among the provisions is the following as to "Prize Fights":—Sec. 21. Any company letting for hire, or providing, a special train for conveying parties to be present at

any prize fight, to be liable to a penalty of not more than £500, or less than £200. One-half the penalty to be paid to the informer, and the other half to the treasurer of the county, in aid of the county rate, in which such prize fight shall be held, or attempted to be held. Service of the summons to be on the secretary of the company, or at his office, at least ten days before the day of hearing, and to be heard before, at least, two justices of the county.

120. An Act to relieve the Consolidated Fund from the charge of the salaries of future Bishops, Archdeacons, Ministers and other persons in the West Indies.

121. An Act to regulate the Sale of Poisons, and alter and amend the Pharmacy Act, 1852. From and after the 31st December, persons assuming the title of chymists and druggists, must be registered, unless they are pharmaceutical chymists. Certain articles mentioned in the schedule annexed to the Act are stated to be poisons, and other articles may be declared to be within the category. Chymists and druggists, within the meaning of the Act, to consist of all persons who, before its passing, had carried on, in Great Britain, the business of a chymist and druggist, in the keeping of open shop; and also of assistants and associates who, before the passing of the Act, were registered under the Pharmacy Act; and also all persons as may be registered under the present Act. For the protection of the public, it provides that any person of full age who can produce to the registrar of the Pharmaceutical Society, by the 31st December, a certificate that he has been, for not less than three years, actually engaged in the dispensing and compounding of prescriptions as an assistant to a pharmaceutical chymist, is, on passing such a modified examination as the Council of the Society may declare to be sufficient evidence of his skill, to be registered as a chymist under this Act. Those entitled to be registered at the passing of the Act are to be registered without the payment of a fee. The Council of the Pharmaceutical Society to make orders for regulating the register to be kept. Every registrar of deaths is required to give notice of the death of a chymist. Evidence of qualification of persons to be registered to be given to the registrar, and any appeal from his decision to be to the Council of the Pharmaceutical Society. An annual register to be kept. Restrictions as to the sale of poisons to be subject to penalties. Poisons to be labelled, and not to be sold to any person unknown, unless introduced by some person known to the chymist; and, before delivery, entry to be made in a book, and the signature of the purchaser attached, under a penalty of £5. Persons registered under the "Medical Act" are not be registered under this Act. Adulteration of Food Act to extend to medicines. From passing of Act, all powers vested in the Secretary of State by the Pharmacy Act are to rest in the Privy Council, and power is given to the Privy Council to erase the names of persons from the register.

122. An Act to make further Amendments in the Laws for the Relief of the Poor in England and Wales.

123. An Act to Amend the Law relating to Salmon Fisheries in Scotland.

124. An Act to Amend the Laws relating to the Inland Revenue.

125. An Act for Amending the Laws relating to Election Petitions, and providing more effectually for the prevention of Corrupt Practices at Parliamentary Elections.

126. An Act to enable Her Majesty the Queen to carry into effect a Convention made between Her Majesty and other Powers relative to a Loan for the completion of works for the improvement of the Navigation of the Danube.

127. An Act to prevent the removal of the Tower of the Church of Saint Mary Somerset, in the City of London.

128. An Act to extend the provisions of the Act 28th & 29th Vict., cap. 113, to persons who have held the office of Lord High Commissioner of the Ionian Islands.

129. An Act to Amend the Law relating to the Registration of British Possessions.

130. An Act to provide better Dwellings for Artizans and Labourers.

Law Cases Argued and Determined

In the year commencing at Michaelmas Term, 31 Vic., 1867.

LORD ROMILLY, MASTER ROLLS.—*In re The Blakeley Ordnance Co.*—Stocken's Case. Shares were forfeited for nonpayment of calls. Articles of Company declared that the forfeiture of shares should involve the extinction of all interest in, and claims and demands against the Company, in respect of the shares and all other rights incident to the shares; but that any member whose shares had been forfeited should be liable to pay the Company all calls owing on such shares at the time of forfeiture :—Held, that no interest was payable on calls owing in respect of the forfeited shares.

WOOD, V.C.—*In re Newton's Trusts.*—A testator, after bequeathing shares of his personal estate to each of his living brothers and sisters, their "heirs and assigns," bequeathed another share "to the heirs and assigns for ever of my late sister D.B. now deceased" :—Held, that under this bequest the next-of-kin of D.B. at her death, according to the Statutes of Distribution, were entitled.

WOOD, V.C.—*Walker v. Brewster.*—An injunction was granted to restrain a defendant from giving public fêtes for his own profit in his own ground, in the outskirts of a large town, where such fêtes, although in themselves properly conducted, brought together crowds of disorderly and noisy people to the annoyance and injury of the plaintiff, whose residence adjoined the defendant's grounds.

STUART, V.C.—*Wakeham v. Merrick.*—Where a sum of money is so bequeathed for payment of an annuity that the whole of the principal is dedicated to the annuity, the interest of the annuitant in the bequest is an absolute one; and he, or his representatives, will be entitled to be paid the whole of the sum.

MALINS, V.C.—*Burbridge v. Burbridge.*—Testator bequeathed "all his live and dead farming stock in and about the farm and farm buildings then occupied by him" :—Held, as against residuary legatees, that everything upon the farm belonging to the testator at the time of his death, including the animals, the unsold produce, and the growing crops, passed under the bequest.

WOOD, V.C.—*Penn v. Jack.*—A suit to restrain the defendants from infringing the plaintiff's patent. By the decree the defendants were ordered to pay to the plaintiff the damages which he had sustained :—Held, that the compensation to which the plaintiff was entitled was a sum calculated upon the basis to which the defendant had applied the invention, and that he was not entitled to any additional sum of money in respect of contracts which he had missed by reason of defendant's piracy.

MALINS, V.C.—*In re Overend, Gurney, and Co., Limited, ex parte Musgrave.*—Shares in Company were sold in the usual course of business on the Stock Exchange a few hours before the failure of the Company. The transfer was executed by the vendor, but not by the purchaser, and was never registered. Upon an application by the vendor to have the purchaser's name substituted for his own on the list of contributories in the winding-up of the Company:—Held, that the contract was binding as between the parties, but that upon the authority of Marino's case the Court had no jurisdiction, under the circumstances, to rectify the register. An analogous case (Grissell v. Bristowe) was similarly decided in December, 1868.

WOOD, V.C.—*Cook v. Forbes.*—In a suit between neighbouring manufacturers to restrain the defendant from carrying on his manufactory in such a way as to injure the plaintiff's property by the emission of noxious gases:—Held, that manufactory was lawful in itself, but required precaution to prevent the escape of injurious gases, would not be restrained from carrying on his manufactory, because occasionally, through the occurrence of accidents in the manufactory, the plaintiff was injured; but the Court would only interfere where the injury was grave or frequent.—Held also, that the plaintiff's rights to have his property protected from injury could not be enlarged by the fact that in manufactory a peculiar process of great delicacy was used.

MALINS, V.C.—*Miller v. Huddlestone.*—Testatrix having, under her husband's will, a power of appointment over £5,000, as part of his residuary estate, appointed the fund upon certain trusts, with a gift over, subject to a power of appointment given to her two nieces, to the extent of £1,000 each. One of the nieces exercised her power. The residuary estate proved insufficient to pay the full amount of £5,000 :—Held, that the appointee of the £1,000 had no claim to priority against those entitled to the residue of the fund, and that all must abate proportionately.

HOUSE OF LORDS.—*Routledge v. Low.*—An alien friend first publishing an original work of which he is author in England is entitled to copyright in such work under 5 & 6 Vic., c. 45, i. e., to the exclusive right of multiplying copies throughout the British dominions, provided that at the time of the publication he is residing, however temporarily, in any part of the British dominions. This is so, although temporary residence may be in a British Colony with an independent legislature, under the laws of which he would not be entitled to copyright.

QUEEN'S BENCH.—*Garnett and others, Appellants; Backhouse, Respondent.*—The appellants were the owners of a milldam on the river R., in connection with a mill, and were the occupiers of the bank on both sides of the river. The dam was above the mill, and consisted of stonework, with planks upon the top of it, and a baulk made of timber which could be raised at pleasure. By means of this dam the water was penned up to provide a supply for the mill, and while the baulk was down in its position, no salmon were able to jump over to pass up the river to the spawning beds. When the baulk was in that position, the water was sent down to the mill, so that the salmon could not pass up the stream to the dam. There were inequalities in the bed of the river below the dam, forming pools in which the salmon were left, when the water flowed away below the dam, and the appellants caught them at their own pleasure. The baulk was usually raised at nights, and during floods: —Held, that this dam was not a "fishing milldam," as it did not appear that it was intended to be used partly for the purpose of catching the fish, and therefore that the Commissioners of Fisheries had no jurisdiction under sec. 44 of the Act of 1865, to order it to be rendered incapable of catching fish.

COMMON PLEAS.—*Bennett* v. *Brumfitt.*—There is a sufficient signature within the 6 Vic., cap. 18, sec. 17, if the objector stamps on the notice of objection a fac-simile of his signature.

EXCHEQUER.—*Williams and another* v. *Rose.*—The protection of the certificate of Registration under sec. 198 of the Bankruptcy Act, 1861, does not extend to process in respect of debts accruing due after the date of registration of deed; and, therefore, a sheriff is liable in an action for an escape, if he discharge a debtor on the production of a certificate bearing date prior to the date of the judgment on which the debtor was arrested.

QUEEN'S BENCH.—*Glover* v. *London & South-Western Railway.*—A passenger by a railway carriage was ordered to leave it by the Company's servants under circumstances which did not justify them in what they were doing; and it appeared that upon leaving the carriage he left a pair of race-glasses upon the seat, which, as the train proceeded without him, he lost:—Held, that the loss of these glasses was not the natural result of the wrongful act, and that the plaintiff could not recover their value.

COMMON PLEAS.—*Parsons* v. *The Vestry of the Parish of St. Matthew, Bethnal Green.*—The common-law liability of a parish to repair its highways has not been transferred by the Metropolis Local Management Act, 1855 (18 & 19 Vic., c. 120) to the vestries constituted under that Act, and therefore no action lies against any such vestry at the suit of an individual who has sustained damage in consequence of a neglect to repair the common highway within the parish of such vestry.

EXCHEQUER.—*Ryder* v. *Wombwell.*—An infant bought on credit a pair of *solitaires*, composed of crystals adorned with diamonds, and a silver goblet for presentation to a friend, at whose house he had been staying:—Held, that *solitaires* are necessaries, and that the presentation goblet was not a necessary, according to the defendant's station and fortune.

QUEEN'S BENCH.—*Merioale, Appellant; The Trustees of the Exeter Turnpike Roads, Respondents.*—The duty of cleansing and keeping open ditches and watercourses for the keeping of turnpike roads dry, is cast, by sec. 113 of the 3 Geo. IV.,

c. 126 (the General Turnpike Act) not upon the occupants of adjoining lands, but upon the trustees themselves.

QUEEN'S BENCH.—*Lawrence, Appellant; King, Respondent.*—By sec. 25 of the Highway Act, 1864, if any horse, mare, or sheep is at any time found lying about the highway, the owner shall be liable to a penalty:—Held, that this liability may be incurred if sheep are allowed to lie about a highway, although they were under the control of a keeper at the time.

QUEEN'S BENCH.—*Greenslade* v. *Darby.*—Action brought by the plaintiff against the defendant for turning his sheep into a churchyard:—Held, that the right of property in the herbage was in the lay impropriator, and that inasmuch as he had not granted it to the plaintiff by endowment action was not maintainable.

EXCHEQUER.—*Ayles* v. *South Eastern Railway Company.*—In the absence of evidence to the contrary, trains running over a particular line of railway are to be presumed to be the property of, or at any rate under the control of, the Company to whom the line belongs, although other Companies may have running powers over the part of the line in question.

EXCHEQUER.—*Scott* v. *Stansfield; Slander.* No action is maintainable against a County Court Judge for words spoken by him in his judicial capacity while sitting in his court, even though the words be spoken falsely and maliciously and wholly irrelevant to the matter in issue before him.

LORD MAYOR'S COURT.—*Rhine* v. *Oppenheimer.* This was an action brought to recover £300 damages through the defendant representing a person to be safe in the way of trade, whereas he was not. Held that under 9 Geo. IV., cap. 4. a written reference must be given to uphold an action. Plaintiff accordingly non-suited.

MAGISTRATES' CASE.—*Ashby* v. *Harris: Burial Ground.* Burial Board under the Metropolitan Interments Acts, granted to A. R. right of making a private grave and the exclusive right of burial therein, to hold the same in perpetuity for the purpose of burial and erecting thereon a monument, the same to be kept in repair. A. R. buried her husband, erected a head-stone and surrounded the grave with a kerbstone. The board afterwards made a regulation that no person should be allowed to plant flowers, &c. on the graves, but that they themselves should do it at certain prices they fixed. Held that the board had no right to prevent A. R. from so planting the said grave.

IN THE COURT OF ARCHES.—*Daunt* v. *Crocker.*—The control of the church bells belongs to the incumbent; but to constitute an ecclesiastical offence, it is not sufficient to allege that the ringing complained of took place without his consent; it must be against his wishes, expressed either in a general or particular prohibition.

IN THE COURT OF ARCHES.—*Adlam* v. *Colthurst.*—The Court determined that the defendant had offended against the laws ecclesiastical by removing, without lawful authority, human bones from the churchyard of his parish to a field adjoining; issued a monition to him to replace such bones and the earth with them in the burial ground before a certain day. The defendant failed to comply with such monition, alleging that the field in which the bones and earth had been placed was no longer in his occupation or possession:—Held, that his conduct amounted to a contempt of Court.

CRIMINAL LAW.

The Queen v. *Keena*.—An indictment for embezzlement alleged the property embezzled to be money. The proof was that the prisoner had received a cheque, but no evidence was given that the cheque had ever been presented or cashed; nor did it appear that the maker had an account or balance at the bank:—Held, that in the absence of any proof that the cheque had been converted into money, the allegation in the indictment was not sustained, and a conviction upon such indictment must be quashed.

The Queen v. *Shepherd*.—Upon an indictment for cutting eight trees with intent to steal, whereby an amount of injury was done to them exceeding £5, framed upon the latter part of the 24 & 25 Vic., c. 96, s. 32, proof that the aggregate value of a number of trees cut at one time exceeded the amount of £5, will satisfy the indictment, though no one tree was worth £5.

The Queen v. *Dowey*.—An indictment charged the prisoner with obtaining money by falsely pretending that a five-pound bank note was of the value of £5. It appeared in evidence that the note was the note of a bank which had been made bankrupt forty years before, and had not re-opened, and the prisoner knew it. The bankruptcy proceedings were not produced, and there was no evidence as to what dividend, if any, had been paid:—Held, that the evidence was sufficient to justify the conviction of the prisoner.

Lyne, Appellant; Fennell, Respondent.—The bare use of the instruments and devices for catching salmon, enumerated in sec. 36 of the Salmon Fishery Act, 1865, is sufficient to render an unlicensed person using them liable to the penalty therein mentioned, without evidence that they were used for the purpose of taking salmon.

The Queen v. *Shaw*.—Held, that imbecility arising from natural causes, such as intemperance; or from natural decay of faculties, through old age; would constitute the patient affected thereby a person of unsound mind, within the section 8 & 9 Vic., c. 100.

COURT OF PROBATE AND DIVORCE, AND MATRIMONIAL CAUSES.

George v. *George*.—Alimony *pendente lite* refused to a wife who for some time before the institution of the suit had been, and still was, supporting herself in service.

In re the Goods of Martha Woods.—The deceased left in her will "one sovereign each to the executors and witnesses of my will for their trouble to see that everything is divided justly." No person was named as executor in the will; but opposite the names of the attesting witnesses, and beneath the signature of the deceased, were the words "witnesses and executors":—Held, that the deceased had failed to make a lawful appointment of executors.

Pitt v. *Pitt*.—A husband petitioning for a divorce must obtain leave to proceed without making a co-respondent, although the petition only charges adultery with a person unknown.

Yeatman v. *Yeatman*.—A husband who permanently puts an end to cohabitation with his wife against her consent, is guilty of desertion, although he may continue to support her. The words "desertion without cause," in sec. 25 of 20 and 21 Vic., c. 85, mean "desertion without reasonable cause," and are equivalent to "desertion without reasonable excuse."

Crabb v. *Crabb*.—Where the parties have separated under a deed of separation, such separation will not be converted into desertion merely because one of the parties does not fulfil all the terms of the bargain entered into with the other on parting.

Table of Income or Wages.

Per Year.	Per Month.	Per Week.	Per Day.	Per Year.	Per Month.	Per Week.	Per Day.	Per Year.	Per Month.	Per Week.	Per Day.
£ s.	s. d.	s. d.	s. d.	£ s.	£ s. d.	s. d.	s. d.	£ s.	£ s. d.	£ s. d.	£ s. d.
1 0	1 8	0 4½	0 0¾	8 8	0 14 0	3 2¾	0 5½	18 18	1 11 6	0 7 3¼	0 1 0½
1 10	2 6	0 7	0 1	8 10	0 14 2	3 3¼	0 5½	19 0	1 11 8	0 7 3¾	0 1 0½
2 0	3 4	0 9¼	0 1¼	9 0	0 15 0	3 5½	0 6	20 0	1 13 4	0 7 8¼	0 1 1¼
2 2	3 6	0 9¾	0 1½	9 9	0 15 9	3 7½	0 6¼	30 0	2 10 0	0 11 6½	0 1 7¾
2 10	4 2	0 11½	0 1¾	10 0	0 16 8	3 10¼	0 6½	40 0	3 6 8	0 15 4½	0 2 2¼
3 0	5 0	1 1¾	0 2	10 10	0 17 6	4 0½	0 7	50 0	4 3 4	0 19 2¾	0 2 9
3 3	5 3	1 2½	0 2	11 0	0 18 4	4 3¾	0 7¼	60 0	5 0 0	1 3 1	0 3 3½
3 10	5 10	1 4¼	0 2¼	11 11	0 19 3	4 5¼	0 7½	70 0	5 16 8	1 6 11	0 3 10
4 0	6 8	1 6½	0 2¾	12 0	1 0 0	4 7½	0 8	80 0	6 13 4	1 10 9¼	0 4 4½
4 4	7 0	1 7½	0 2¾	12 12	1 1 0	4 10¼	0 8¼	90 0	7 10 0	1 14 7½	0 4 11¼
4 10	7 6	1 8¾	0 3	13 0	1 1 8	5 0	0 8½	100 0	8 6 8	1 18 5½	0 5 5¾
5 0	8 4	1 11	0 3¼	13 13	1 2 9	5 3	0 9	200 0	16 13 4	3 16 11	0 10 11½
5 5	8 9	2 0¼	0 3½	14 0	1 3 4	5 4½	0 9¼	300 0	25 0 0	5 15 4½	0 16 5¼
5 10	9 2	2 1½	0 3½	14 14	1 4 6	5 7¾	0 9¾	400 0	33 6 8	7 13 10¼	1 1 11
6 0	10 0	2 3¾	0 4	15 0	1 5 0	5 9¼	0 9¾	500 0	41 13 4	9 12 3¾	1 7 4¾
6 6	10 6	2 5	0 4¼	15 15	1 6 3	6 0¾	0 10¼	600 0	50 0 0	11 10 9¼	1 12 10½
6 10	10 10	2 6	0 4¼	16 0	1 6 8	6 1¾	0 10½	700 0	58 6 8	13 9 2¾	1 18 4¼
7 0	11 8	2 8¼	0 4½	16 16	1 8 0	6 5½	0 11	800 0	66 13 4	15 7 8¼	2 3 10
7 7	12 3	2 10	0 4¾	17 0	1 8 4	6 6½	0 11¼	900 0	75 0 0	17 6 1¾	2 9 3¾
7 10	12 6	2 10½	0 5	17 17	1 9 9	6 10½	0 11¾	1000 0	83 6 8	19 4 7¼	2 14 9½
8 0	13 4	3 1	0 5¼	18 0	1 10 0	6 11	0 11¾				

By the above it may be seen at a glance what £1 to £1,000 a year is by the calendar month, week, or day. If the sum be guineas instead of pounds add one penny to each month, or one farthing to each week.

THE constant and rapid progress of Scientific Discovery and Invention, renders it impossible to give a complete summary of what has been recently effected. The following, however, affords an account of some of the most important or interesting results that have occurred during 1867-68, in most departments of scientific research, and its numerous applications to the Arts, Manufactures, &c.

CHEMISTRY.

ANALYSIS OF THE FIXED STARS.—One of the most remote possibilities that man could imagine is that of analysing the constitution of the fixed stars, the nearest of which is so far distant that although light travels at the rate of 190,000 miles per second, it would take nearly twenty years for it to arrive at the earth, supposing such a star was for a moment entirely eclipsed at its surface. Yet by means of the spectroscope, or spectrum analysis, Messrs. Miller and Huggins have detected in them the presence of the metals iron, sodium, magnesium, and other elementary bodies common to our earth.

DIALYSIS, GASES PERMEATING SOLIDS.—The diffusion of two gases with each other of any different specific gravity has long been known, this occurring even if they be separated by a diaphragm of plaster of Paris. It has recently been discovered, however, that hydrogen has the power of passing through iron, palladium, and even platinum : an astonishing fact that the lightest body in nature should be able to pass through the most solid. Allied to this is the method of *dialysis* invented by Dr. Graham. By separating a compound liquid, or one containing several substances in solution or suspension, from distilled water by means of a bladder, the soluble substances may speedily be removed into the latter. Even the gases, oxygen and nitrogen, composing the air, may be thus separated.

DISTILLING SEA-WATER.—The latest novelty for this object is the apparatus of Messrs. Chaplin, of Glasgow. In general principle it resembles the common still, as all such inventions must do, but by its peculiar arrangement cooking may also be carried on, and it is so constructed as to consume any kind of fuel: its advantages are convenience, rapidity, and economy.

DYNAMITE.—This is a new blasting powder, invented by M. Nobel. It consists of a mixture of nitro-glycerine with sand, &c. ; and whilst it has all the explosive power of the nitro-glycerine, it has none of its dangerous properties. Its blasting powers for quarry-work on the hardest rocks are enormous, whinstone being readily split into fragments by simply placing a little dynamite on the surface of the stone, and covering it with a little clay. On percussion and heat the material explodes, but by neither alone.

GELATINE AS A COVER FOR CORKS.—If gelatine be dissolved in glycerine by aid of heat, it affords a solution that, on being applied to pickle, wine, and other corked bottles, entirely excludes the air, far exceeding in efficacy sealing-wax.

FOOD.—According to Professor Frankland, the following articles of ordinary food have the relative power of sustaining respiration and circulation in the body of an average man during a period of twenty-four hours. In each instance the amount required is stated in ounces:—Cheshire cheese, 3; potatoes, 13½; flour of wheat, &c., 3½; bread, 6½; lean beef, 9¾; lean veal, 11½; lean boiled ham, nearly 8; fish, from 8½ to 16; white of egg, 23; milk, 21¼; cabbage,

32; butter and cocoa-nibs, about 2; cod-liver oil, 1¾; lump sugar, 4 ounces.

LIEBIG'S MEAT EXTRACT.—The high price of meat in this country, and its comparative want of value in South America and Australia, caused a large exportation of machinery from Glasgow in 1867, intended to extract the nutritive qualities of meat in those countries, after Liebig's process. The extract consists of only the most nutritive portions of the flesh, and as much of it as will lie on the point of a knife will afford as much real nitrogenous nutriment as is contained in a pint of the strongest beer. Several factories have been established to produce this extract, which is now largely imported into England.

LIQUID FUEL. — During the last two years numerous experiments have been made by Mr. Richardson, Captain Selwyn, Mr. Paul, and other practical men to render *dead oil*, a refuse of tar distillation, *petroleum*, and other inflammable oils of value as fuel in place of coal. The best mode of thus utilizing the former is to drive them by means of steam on to a layer of burning ashes or coke. Various patents have been taken out for the purpose, and it is stated that by proper management a steam boiler may be kept heated at a half or third of the expense of ordinary steam coal.

NITRO-GLYCERINE.—This material is produced by cautiously acting on glycerine, at a low temperature, with sulphuric and nitric acids. It is one of the most highly explosive and dangerous substances known, but is now largely employed for blasting in mines.

OXYGEN, NEW MODE OF PREPARING.—This gas, an essential constituent of air and water, is largely in demand for laboratory uses; but more especially for the oxy-hydrogen and oxy-calcium lights used to illuminate dissolving views, and for the oxy-hydrogen microscope. M. Mallet proposes the following cheap method on a large scale for producing the gas. Sub-chloride of copper, mixed with a little sand and slightly moistened, is to be placed in a retort, through which a current of air passes, with agitation of the mixture. The air converts the chloride into an oxy-chloride. By subsequently applying heat to the retort, the absorbed oxygen is given off, and may be collected in the usual way. The process may be evidently made continuous.

PARAFFIN.—This substance was discovered in 1830, but it was not till 1850 that, by the chemical knowledge of James Young, the oil was produced for burning purposes, and the solid paraffin as the material of the well-known "Gas Candles." At Mr. Young's works at Bathgate, near Edinburgh—the most extensive in the world—several thousand hands are employed. Boghead coal is the material from which the paraffin is distilled. Until 1866 the works above named alone existed in the Bathgate district; but in 1867 fresh discoveries of the coal having been made, the manufacture progressed throughout a length of country covering the coals for an extent of between twenty and thirty miles. The annual value of paraffin now produced in this country exceeds £10,000,000.

PARKESINE.—This substance, which is composed of vegetable fibre and oily matter, has been largely used as a floor-cloth, and has been applied as a covering for submarine cables. It resembles in its raw state ordinary vulcanized india-rubber. It readily takes colour painted on its surface, and is sufficiently plastic to be shaped by moulds. When hard, it is impervious to moisture, and, like gutta-percha, may be rolled into sheets, &c. Mixed with colouring matter, it can be made to imitate tortoiseshell, malachite, &c.

PHOTOGRAPHY, NEW APPLICATION OF. — By means of a kind of trumpet tube, having a thin membrane of india-rubber stretched over its larger orifice, the membrane being placed over the heart, the action of the heart and arteries can be photographed. Mercury is poured into the tube, and on the surface of the metal is a kind of eye, through which a ray of light enters, that acts on a sensitive plate moved by clockwork. The light passing through the "eye," acts on the sensitive plate, and registers the vibrating action of the heart or arteries.

SULPHIDE OF CARBON.—This liquid is applied for the purpose of extracting oil remaining in oilcake after pressure has done its utmost, and to remove the oil from soapsuds of silk-scouring factories. Being highly volatile, it is readily distilled off, leaving the fixed oil unchanged.

STARCH. — A great improvement has been made in the manufacture of starch. It depends on the slight difference of specific gravity between that article and its impurities. One part of crude starch (as from the potato, &c.), is mixed with two of water, and the mixture rotated in a copper drum. The pure starch, by centrifugal force, is driven to the outside of the drum, whence it is easily collected.

CHEMICAL MANUFACTURES IN ITALY. — There are few countries that possess greater mineral resources for the manufacture of chemicals than Italy, a fact due to the volcanic nature of the country, and its great production of semi-tropical fruits. The mineral products are chiefly sulphur, from which great quantities of sulphuric and, indirectly, nitric acid, are produced. Borax is obtained abundantly, and boracic acid from the Lagoons of Tuscany. Citric acid is contained in the juice of the lemon, which also affords its essential oil from the rind. Soda and potash are produced from burnt plants. Alum is a large natural product of a very pure kind, obtained by calcining alum-stone, dissolving in water, and subsequent crystallization. White lead is largely manufactured at Genoa and Leghorn. Cream of tartar is abundantly produced as a deposit from grape juice. Beside these articles, Italy produces corrosive sublimate, the carbonate and sulphate (Epsom salts) of magnesia, various salts of ammonia, the chloride and citrate of lime, &c., an amount of natural riches hitherto but slightly developed by the Italians.

ORIGIN OF ASPHALTE, PETROLEUM, AND OTHER MINERAL OILS.—A very interesting paper was read in August, before the United States National Assembly of Science at Massachusetts, on this question. It was pointed out that all rock oils may be divided into two classes, namely, those which contain paraffin, and afford asphalte by absorption of atmospheric oxygen, and consequent thickening; and those which contain no paraffin, and that produce paraffin by decomposition. The presence of nitrogen, to a greater or less extent, in all American oils, evidences that their origin has been from the decomposition of vegetable and animal substances; in proof of the latter, specimens have been collected showing the remains of bone cells, in which the petroleum existed. The absence of phosphorus and sulphur in all specimens, is accounted for on the ground of the solubility of the phosphates and sulphates formed during vegetable and animal decomposition in water. The theory thus promulgated very satisfactorily explains the formation of asphalte beds, as in Trinidad, where that substance and petroleum abound, and of that of rock oil under all circumstances.

EARTH-CLOSET SYSTEM.—One of the most important inventions of 1867-68, in a sanitary and social point of view, was that of the earth-closet system, invented by the Rev. H. Moule, and for the use of which in India the Government presented him with a gratuity of £500. Its merit consists simply in the fact, that dry earth containing alumina (clayey matter) will readily absorb and deodorise human excreta that fall upon it. A most excellent manure is simultaneously produced, equal in value to guano, because all the phosphates, ammonia, &c., are absorbed. In every respect indeed, scientifically and socially, the invention is of the utmost value.

BREAD.—The nutritive properties of bread depend on the starch and gluten it contains. Wheat starch, like all other kinds, affords heat to the body during digestion, whilst the gluten containing, as it does, nitrogen, repairs the loss of the tissues. Formerly the cells of the bread composed of gluten were formed by adding yeast or leaven, by the action of which, through fermentation and decomposition, carbonic acid is produced; this gas getting into the gluten *raises* the dough, that is, forms the cells. This plan, however, is at once wasteful, and frequently injurious, hence many others have been proposed by way of improvement; one is, that of producing the carbonic acid by mixing with the flour due proportions of carbonate of soda and hydrochloric acid, the products of which are common salt and carbonic acid gas. But the best method, and that by which the "Aerated Bread" is produced, is that of Dr. Dauglish. The carbonic acid is formed in a separate vessel, and then mixed, under high pressure, with water; this liquid is then mixed, also under pressure, with the flour, and the dough so formed, on being allowed to escape from the vessel, is light, porous, and makes pure, nutritious, and wholesome bread. Machinery only is employed in the process, hence it is perfectly cleanly.

LEAD TUBES OR PIPES.—Numerous serious and frequent fatal consequences have followed the use of lead pipes for conveying water into houses. By the invention of MM. Hamon and Lebreton-Brun, the danger is obviated. A tin tube is enclosed within the leaden one, and the two are drawn out by hydraulic power. The *inside* of the compound tube has therefore a tin in place of a leaden surface, and as tin is unacted on by air and water, all risk of poisoning is prevented.

WHITE GUTTA PERCHA.—The substance usually sold under this name is little better than a composition of three parts of white oxide of zinc, mixed with one of gutta percha, and is really valueless for all ordinary purposes. Pure white gutta percha may be prepared by digesting shreds of that material in methylated chloroform n which it dissolves; the solution is then to be filtered in close vessels. On the addition of spirits of wine to the liquid, the gutta percha is precipitated as a white bulky mass, which is easily converted into a solid by heat, and cooling.

EMBALMING.—The art of preserving human bodies by the process of embalming, was most successfully practised by the Egyptians, as the mummies now so abundantly found attest, the bodies having escaped putrefaction during a lapse of 3,000 years. Recent experiments by Professor Seely have produced interesting results. A human body was treated with carbolic acid (a product of coal tar), and after the lapse of 103 days not the least smell was perceived, whilst even the face retained its natural appearance. The asphalte or resin used by the Egyptians most probably owed its preservative power to the presence of carbolic acid.

MILK.—The results of an investigation by Dr. Lankester in regard to the quality of milk supplied in the west-end of London generally led to the conclusion that scarcely a drop of that liquid reaches the consumer as it leaves the cow. Out of fifteen specimens purchased at different shops, only two came up to within a degree or two of the standard quality of caseine and butter. In some cases the diminution was equal to 50 per cent., and in others it reached 80 per cent. below the natural product, as afforded in newly-drawn milk.

SODA LAKES OF MEXICO.—The usual mode of procuring soda for washing, bleaching, and other purposes in this country, is that of decomposing common salt by sulphuric acid, calcining the sulphate of soda thus produced with coal and saw-dust, and then dissolving out the soda with subsequent crystallization. The Lake Tecesco, a short distance from the City of Mexico, is situated on soil impregnated with a species of soda, and the lake itself consists of a concentrated solution of the carbonate and other salts of soda, including common salt. It is estimated, indeed, that its solid constituents equal 18 per cent. of the liquid. The mode of obtaining the soda is very simple. Mounds of the soil are bored with holes, into which bags are placed; into them the soda-earth soaks: the earth is then mixed with water, and the liquid dissolves out the soda, &c. By evaporation the soda is obtained, locally called *Tequesquite*, of which above four million pounds are produced annually, affording about one million and three-quarter pounds of the pure soda.

SILVERING GLASS.—The old method is that of laying on the clean surface of glass a sheet of tin-foil, rubbing this gently over with mercury and applying pressure; a coating of an amalgam of tin is thus formed, as seen in the ordinary looking-glass. By this plan only flat surfaces can be well silvered, but by the following, any surface, as a bottle, hollow globe, &c., may be readily silvered. A solution of 10 grains of pure nitrate of silver is made in an ounce of distilled water, and to this is added, drop by drop, liquor ammoniæ, until all precipitate is exactly redissolved. This should be kept in a glass stoppered bottle, *out of the light.* A second solution is to be made as follows:—Dissolve 10 grains of pure Rochelle salts in an ounce of distilled water, and filter the solution through white blotting-paper. To silver a glass, if a globe, &c., fill it with equal quantities of the two solutions, then let the sun's rays impinge on it, gently heating the outside. In about half-an-hour's time the silver will be com-

pletely reduced, affording a beautiful reflecting surface, applicable to ornamental, philosophical, and a great variety of other purposes.

ARTIFICIAL CAMPHOR.—Camphor, as is well known, is chiefly obtained from the wood of a species of laurel; it also exists in many other plants, even in this country. By mixing oil of turpentine with hydrochloric acid, in a vessel surrounded with ice, a solid artificial camphor may be obtained, having the smell of the ordinary article. This preparation has recently been put to several useful purposes in organic chemistry.

SEWAGE UTILISATION.—Nothing is of greater importance, in a sanitary point of view, than to get rid entirely of the sewage of towns. Hitherto this has been almost exclusively effected by running it into rivers. At Croydon, Rugby, Leicester, and near Edinburgh, however, by running the sewage on grass lands, the produce has been increased six to eight-fold. The year 1868 was particularly favourable for the trial of sewage. The great heat in July parched the whole country, so that scarcely a blade of grass was to be seen. At Barking and Tottenham, near London, several acres of meadow land were irrigated by sewage, to show experimentally its effects. Whilst the surrounding country presented a barren and brown appearance, the sewage-irrigated fields bore repeated luxuriant crops. The value of London sewage has been estimated at two-pence per liquid ton, and it has been proposed to utilize it both on the Essex and Kent shores of the Thames, and also in the reclamation of the Maplin Sands off the east coast of Essex, in the German Ocean.

NITRATE OF SILVER AND PHOTOGRAPHY.—The low price of this salt induces frequent adulteration, especially with saltpetre or nitrate of potash. M. Fritz Haugh recommends the following method of detecting the nitrate. Dissolve the suspected salt in distilled water, and add pure hydrochloric acid until all the silver is precipitated as chloride. Filter this off, and then evaporate the clear liquid left to dryness; the nitre not having been acted on by the hydrochloric acid, will be formed in a net-work of crystals, and, if weighed, will afford the amount of adulteration to which a previously known weight of the nitrate of silver had been subjected. The plan is simple, easy, and effective, and may be readily employed by the tyro in chemistry.

SNAKE POISON.—The chief element of snake-poisons is formic acid. By digesting this with chromic acid, readily obtained from bichromate of potass, by the addition of sulphuric acid, the result is the production of carbonic acid and water. Hence dilute chromic acid may be safely employed as an antidote to snake-poisons. It has been found that the poison infused by snake-bites may be successfully destroyed by applying carbolic acid to the wound. At the same time, ten drops of the acid, diluted with brandy and water, are to be administered at intervals until the stupor and drowsiness, usually following the bite of a snake, are removed. The plan has been extensively adopted in Australia.

WATER, COMPOSITION OF.—Hitherto, water has been universally considered as constituted of equal equivalents (one of each) of hydrogen and oxygen, a doctrine that lies at the basis of the present system of chemical science. But Mr. Wilde, in a communication to the *Philosophical Magazine,* of September, 1868, states that he has tried numerous experiments, which lead him to believe that water, instead of being composed of the two gases above named, is resolvable either wholly into oxygen or wholly into hydrogen, by the agency of electro-chemical action. The discovery, if accurate, will not fail to revolutionize almost every branch of experimental philosophy.

SOAP WASTED THROUGH HARD WATER.—The more lime-salts contained in water used for domestic purposes, the greater is the waste of all substances such as soap, tea, coffee, &c., used with it. After the great drought of July, 1868, it was found that in every 100,000 pounds of water supplied to London, there were from 19½ to 27 pounds of lime-salts, whilst the water supplied to Glasgow contained only a third of a pound, and that of Lancaster one-tenth of a pound. The loss in soap, &c., to the metropolis, is therefore immense compared to that in the two last-named cities.

ANCIENT SOUTH AMERICAN ALLOY.—A singular discovery was made in 1868, of a plate manufactured by the early inhabitants of South America, and ornamented with figures in relief. Its colour resembled copper. On analysis it was found to be composed of 35½ parts of gold, 12 of silver, and 52½ of copper. The specific gravity was 10·4, and its surface, when found, was coated with a green coat of sub-oxide and carbonate of copper; the alloy is one unheard of in modern metallurgy.

IRON PURIFICATION.—Mr. Bennett, of Pittsburgh, U.S., proposes to force carbonic acid, with atmospheric air, through molten iron to purify it from sulphur and phosphorus. He has adopted successfully a similar plan for removing the same impurities from copper, zinc, nickel, and other metals.

MORTAR, HARDENING OF, ARTIFICIALLY.—It is well known that newly-laid or made mortar gradually becomes hard, partly by absorption of the carbonic acid from the atmosphere, and in part by the union of the lime with the silica contained in the sand. By a process invented in Brunswick, the hardening of the lime is rapidly produced. The objects are placed in a tight chamber, where they are exposed to the action of carbonic acid for half an hour, by which time the lime portion is converted into a substance resembling marble (which is a carbonate of lime).

SULPHUR RECOVERED FROM ALKALI REFUSE.—The visitor to Glasgow and other alkali manufacturing towns will see scores of acres of ground covered to a depth of from 5 to 50 feet with the refuse derived from the manufacture of soda from common salt. Hitherto the sulphur contained in this was lost; by recent patents its recovery has been rendered easy. Each invention relies on the conversion of the sulphide of calcium, &c., into soluble compounds, by the action of air and moisture; on the removal of these compounds by the action of water; and, lastly, on the separation of the sulphur by the action of hydrochloric acid. If the plans be effectively carried out, the annual saving to this country would not be less than £300,000, equivalent to the cost of 50,000 tons of sulphur, for the supply of which we depend on Sicily.

AIR, IMPURITIES OF THE.—By means of the microscope, applied to the detection of air impurities, it has been discovered that a man inhales not less than 31½ millions of spores or organic germs in ten hours from impure air.

FUSING MINERALS.—Many of these are exceedingly refractory under the most powerful heat. If, however, a flux composed of a mixture of fluoride of sodium and sulphate of potash be employed, the fusion may be effected by even a single Bunsen's gas jet. Chrome iron ore, rutile, zircon, wolfram, and many other refractory minerals may thus be brought into rapid fusion.

ECONOMY OF WATER.—The intense heat of July and August, 1868, dried up most of the ponds ordinarily employed to water cattle. Were such stores of water protected by trees, a vast quantity of the liquid might be preserved in the hottest summer. In forty days an unprotected pond will lose by evaporation out of 14,000 gallons, about 9,000 gallons, which are sufficient to supply a flock of sheep for that period. Willows, which grow rapidly on the edges of streams, might thus be advantageously employed by the farmer to protect his standing stores of water.

CHARCOAL AS A WATER FILTER.—Dr. Frankland, F.R.S., was the first to show that animal charcoal will not only remove organic, but also many of the inorganic constituents of water. Mr. Skey, of New Zealand, proved in 1868, that even arsenic may thus be removed, showing still further the efficacy of animal charcoal for purifying water for drinking and other purposes.

THYMIC ACID AS A DISINFECTANT.—This acid, derived from oil of thyme, may be advantageously substituted for carbolic acid or creosote. It has no unpleasant smell, is powerfully antiseptic, and it is sufficient for disinfecting purposes to dissolve one part in 1,000 of water.

THE SPECTROSCOPE AND DETECTION OF BLOOD STAINS.—It has long been known that by means of the microscope the blood of different animals could be distinguished one from another, but when the blood stains were dry great difficulties occurred. By means of the spectroscope these have been overcome. By that instrument the presence of different metals in flame, even in the sun, may be detected by the bands or colours they form in the prismatic spectrum. Applying a modified form of the spectroscope, each chemical constituent of the bloodstain may be detected, and thus a valuable means of examination is afforded, especially in respect to the case of suspected murder.

SCHULTZE'S GUNPOWDER.—The chief characteristic of this powder is the use of saw-dust as the igniting material. The exploding temperature is 520° Fahr., and from this and other causes, whilst having great power, it has less danger than ordinary gunpowder.

PETROLEUM IN IRELAND.—It is stated that a Petroleum deposit was discovered in 1868, at Clones, in County Monaghan, Ireland, which promised to be as rich in oil as the famous wells of Pennsylvania in the United States, the production of which for some years past has been enormous.

ELECTRICITY.

ELECTRIC LIGHTHOUSES. — At Dungeness, on our southern coast, and on the opposite coast of France, are electro-lights that have been substituted in 1867-68 for the old oil-lamp. The light afforded is exceedingly intense, penetrates a fog, and in clear weather each spreads a cone of rays quite across the Channel, resembling in appearance the tail of a comet. Holmes' method is that employed at Dungeness, the electric force being obtained by the rotation of magnets opposite iron bars coated with wire, by which magneto-electricity is induced. Steam is the motive power applied.

POLICE AND THE TELEGRAPH.—The whole of the police and fire-engine stations of the chief portion of the metropolis have been put into mutual instantaneous connection by means of the electric telegraph. This has resulted in the utmost advantage, both in regard to the detection of criminals, and giving notice of fires in any part of London.

SPEED OF ELECTRIC TELEGRAPHY.—In January, 1868, a report of Mr. Gladstone's speech, containing 16,882 words, was transmitted from Liverpool to London in two hours and ten minutes; and on the following day another speech by that statesman was transmitted from Oldham to London with corresponding rapidity.

SUBMARINE TELEGRAPHIC SPEED.—On the 1st February, 1868, a message was transmitted from London to San Francisco and back, a distance of 14,000 miles, or nearly two-thirds of the circumference of the globe, in the short space of two minutes! Immediately afterwards, an eighty-word message was transmitted and repeated back between Heart's Content and San Francisco, little less than five minutes being occupied for the whole time of double transmission through a distance of 5,000 miles!

THE TOTAL LENGTH OF TELEGRAPHIC LINES amounts for the whole world to about 180,000 miles, of which the United States of America possess 52,957 miles; Germany, 28,347 miles; Russia, 22,992 miles; France, 18,964 miles; Great Britain and Ireland, 16,297; Turkey, 8,665; Italy, 8,216; Sweden, 3,507; Belgium, 1,089; Switzerland, 2,160; Canada, 5,050. Beside which are the two Atlantic cables, measuring 4,369 English, or 3,755 nautical miles, with other submarine cables of a length of 6,000 miles.

ELECTRICAL RAILWAY BREAK.—Amongst important inventions may be mentioned Achard's railway break. It is a combination of mechanical appliances put into action by electricity; its chief characteristic being an electro-magnet. This when excited forces collar discs on the wheels of the carriage. The break is of course under instantaneous management by the guard of the train, who, by simply letting on a current of electricity from either the voltaic battery or a magneto-electric machine, can at once set in action the break, or suspend its power.

MALTA AND ALEXANDRIA TELEGRAPH.—This line which has long been the *bête noire* of telegraphic engineers, and a source of enormous expense, was laid successfully direct between the two termini early in October, 1868. It is one of the most important of submarine cables yet laid, as it forms part of the great system of telegraphy between England and India, *viâ* Suez and the Red Sea.

ANGLO-DANISH TELEGRAPH.—After many discouragements, the line of telegraph between Sondervig in Denmark, and Newbiggin on the English coast, was successfully laid on September 11, 1868. The greatest depth at which the cable is sunk is 45 fathoms, but the average does not exceed from 25 to 30 fathoms. Its weight is 1,050 tons; the length between shores about 400 miles. The average sea-weight is 3 tons per mile, and the shore ends six tons.

THE INDO-EUROPEAN TELEGRAPH.—This scheme is intended to provide two almost entirely independent telegraphic lines to India, one by Persia, and the other by the Red Sea route. The necessary capital was subscribed for, and a large quantity of the material ready for operations in August, 1868.

ATLANTIC CABLE (FRENCH)—In 1861 a company was formed to lay and maintain a cable between France and the United States. The cable, in course of manufacture, is to be submerged from the Great Eastern in 1869. The route is from Brest across the Atlantic to the island of St. Pierre in the Gulf of St. Lawrence, and thence by an independent line to New York.

SUGAR BLEACHING BY ELECTRICITY.—Hitherto the decoloration of syrup in preparing loaf from brown sugar has universally been effected, on the large scale, by filtering the saccharine matter through layers of animal charcoal. Mr. Wilde's magneto-electric machine (already described in these notes) has been successfully applied in replacing the charcoal. A current of electricity from it is directed through the syrup, and consequently liberation of ozone results. The effect is a rapid bleaching of the liquor; and the importance of the invention has been recognized by sugar refiners to a large extent.

ELECTRICAL PIANO.—This instrument, like the electric organ, is actuated by a current of electricity. In the piano the hammers are supplied with electro-magnets, which press down the keys when the current passes over them. By adopting the arrangement of the Jacquard loom, that is, the use of perforated cards, each hole represents a note, and one key of the instrument. The card passes over a pair of rollers, and pins are so adjusted that they press through the holes of the cards. On so doing they touch other pins below, and thus convey the electric current to any desired and corresponding key on the piano. The key of course calls the hammer into motion, and a sound is produced by that note; thus, by one arrangement of the cards and wires, stretching to any number of pianos, they may all be made to play at the same moment an identical tune. By this ingenious contrivance a whole town might have music "laid on" by street wires, and the piano in each house called into action at the will of the inhabitant.

ORGAN PLAYED BY ELECTRICITY.—In August, 1868, an ingenious invention, by which the organ may be played by electricity, was publicly exhibited in London. In the ordinary way the player sits within the front of the organ, a position that renders it impossible for him to judge of the results of the sound, still less of the melodious blendings, and management of the swells, on which so much of the effects of the organ depends. By the electric method, the player and keys may be removed any distance from the instrument. The keys are connected with it by means of insulated wires, that convey electricity as the player presses each key, and act on electro-magnets, which open the pipe valves.

GALVANIZING IRON.—It is well known that iron exposed to atmospheric action soon corrodes, and at last is, metallically speaking, completely destroyed. Many methods have been proposed to arrest this destruction, but that of "Galvanizing" is most effective; it consists simply in coating the iron surface by a cover of zinc; the most recently improved method is as follows:—The iron is first freed from all oxide, &c., by immersion in a bath of sulphuric acid and water until perfectly clean. The sulphate of iron or copperas so formed is largely sold to the dyer. Zinc is melted in a large vessel, the upper edge of which is level with the floor of the workshop. The surface of the melted zinc is covered with sal ammoniac, which acts as a flux, the cleaned iron plate is then dipped into the melted zinc, which completely coats the surface and protects it from the action of air and moisture. Another and effective way has been patented by Messrs. Elkington, of Birmingham; it consists of depositing *pure* zinc or iron by electrical agency. The purity of the metal by this method renders its protecting effect much greater than that of the ordinary "galvanizing process."

EXCITING VOLTAIC BATTERIES.—These instruments, so largely used in telegraphy, electroplating, &c., are exceedingly troublesome in maintaining, owing to the rapid decomposition of the exciting liquids employed. M. Delaurier proposes the use of the following solution. It consists of 20 parts of the protosulphate of iron, 36 of water, 7 of sulphuric acid, and 1 of nitric acid. The action is powerful, no offensive gases are evolved, and the liquid is also economical in use.

ELONGATION OF METALLIC WIRES BY ELECTRICITY.—It is familiarly known that heat expands all metallic bodies, but it has only recently (1868) been demonstrated by M. Edland, that a current of electricity passed through metallic wires has a similar effect, although less in degree; a curious fact, proving the analogy of all the forces of nature.

ENGINEERING, &c.

BAKER'S ANTICRUSTATOR.—This instrument has for its object the removal of scale in steam-boilers. It consists of a "battery," or a brass casting, with sharp points of steel or platina. This is fixed in the boiler, so that it may be fully exposed to the current of steam that passes to the steam-chest; but insulated electrically from the boiler itself. The inventor ascribes its efficacy to the electricity that it collects or diffuses while in action.

GAS ENGINES. — Many attempts have been made to substitute a mixture of coal gas and air for steam as a motive power. The Lenoir, and Hugon gas-engines have been very successful, and during 1867-68 were largely adopted in establishments requiring but moderate power, as for working cranes, hoists, &c.

LOCOMOTIVES. — At the commencement of the year 1867 the seventeen chief railway companies of Great Britain and Ireland, owned in all 7,023 locomotive engines; of which 1,347 belonged to the London and North-Western Company.

MARINE ENGINEERING.—The method of water-propulsion, in place of the screw and paddle, was put to a real and effective test in H.M.S. Waterwitch, in 1867. Considering the difficulties that had to be encountered in carrying out what was practically a new principle of propulsion,—that of driving water against water,—the results were highly satisfactory: a speed of 10 knots per hour having been attained. The vessel could be almost instantaneously stopped and backed, and no danger can arise from injury to the propelling power, as in screw and paddle vessels.

RAILWAYS.—One of the greatest modern feats of railway enterprise is the construction of a railroad crossing the entire American continent, from New York to San Francisco. Its length will be 3,300 miles; greatest altitude above the sea-level, a little more than 7,000 feet; and of the total length, 700 miles will vary from that height to 1,000 feet above the sea-level. It is called the Pacific Railroad, and is being constructed by aid of grants, &c., from the Eastern or Atlantic States of the Union. When completed, the journey from New York to San Francisco will

only occupy five days. It is officially announced that the line will be open for traffic in the autumn of 1869.

RAILWAYS—EFFECT OF WIND ON TRAINS.—A difference of thirty per cent upon the resistance of a passenger train, results from a wind blowing at the rate of 27½ feet per second; retarding or accelerating the speed according as it is opposed to, or in the same direction as, that of the passage of the train.

RAILWAYS IN FRANCE.—The traffic receipts on the entire system of French railways, having a length of 9,738 miles, amounted, in 1867, to £26,259,763. The seven old main lines, having a length of 4,676 miles, produced £19,987,480, or an average amount of £4,274 per mile.

ROAD ROLLERS.—The irregular surface of a newly-made Macadamized road is notorious. In 1867, various forms of road-rollers, worked by steam, came into use, effecting in a few hours, the complete smoothing of the roadway, that formerly would have required weeks to perform.

SAILING IN THE AIR.—A meeting of the Aëronautical Society was held at the Crystal Palace, in 1868, at which numerous machines were exhibited that were said to be capable of air-flying, but the practical proof of their value remains to be tested. An ingenious invention is that of M. Kaufman, of Glasgow. It consists of two immense wings, moved by a steam-engine placed between them, and by which they are rapidly moved. The appearance of the machine is that of an enormous bat, but the success attending its use still leaves the ancient Dædalus unshorn of his laurels.

BREECH-LOADING SMALL ARMS.—The following table presents a view of the different systems upon which the armies of European States have been or are being (1868) provided with breech-loading rifles:

	Bore.	Ball.	Cartridge.	System.	Adopted.
	In.	Oz.			
England	0.577	1.097	Metallic	Enfield Snider	1866
France	0.432	0.880	Paper	Chassepôt	1866
France	0.699	1.584	Metallic	Converted	1867
Prussia	0.617	1.094	Paper	Needle-gun	1848
Austria	0.546	1.056	Metallic	Wantzel	1867
Italy	0.691	1.267	Paper {	Resembles Prussian }	1867
Belgium	0.432	0.880	Metallic	Albini	1867
Holland	0.495	...	Metallic	Snider	1867
Holland	0.699	...	Metallic	Snider	1867
Switzerland }	0.412	0.721	Metallic	{ Amsler Milbanck }	1866

RAILS ON COMMON ROADS.—In 1867 preliminary steps were undertaken to introduce the railway system of road-way on the ordinary roads of the metropolis. If a horse were employed on such a system, he could pull five or six times as much weight as on a Macadamized road, and with far less distress of body. The estimated cost of sleepers, rolling stock, &c., was £2,500 per mile. It was proposed, at suitable places, to employ steam power also. The fact of the ready-made roads being far more solid, firm, and substantial, than the best railroad way, is a prominent aid to the success of the scheme.

METROPOLITAN RAILWAY.—In the first half of 1868, 12,994,223 passengers were carried on this line, producing receipts equal to £128,474. The largest number that travelled on the line in one week was during Whitsuntide of that year, when 600,558 persons were conveyed. The largest daily traffic was on Whit-Monday, when 117,287 persons travelled on the line.

RAILWAY FRICTION.—By extended experiments conducted on some of the American railways in 1867, it was found that an ordinary goods waggon, on a level, indicated a friction of between six and seven pounds per ton.

RAILWAYS BENEATH THE THAMES.'—In 1868 active operations were in progress to convert the Thames Tunnel into a channel for the East London Railway, connecting the system of railways north and south of the Thames. It was also proposed to construct a tunnel and railway from the Tower to the opposite side of the river, at an estimated cost of £12,000, for the use of passengers only.

STEEL BOILERS.—Steam boilers for stationary and marine purposes are now often made of steel. In August, 1868, two large boilers were constructed, each ring of which was composed of a Bessemer steel plate, 26-ft. 6-in. long, and 3-ft. 6-in. wide. The thickness was 7-16ths of an inch, and they were intended to work at a pressure of 100 pounds per square inch. Smaller boilers, but a quarter of an inch thick, have been made, which were safely worked at a constant pressure of 75 pounds per square inch, showing an economy of weight of material compared with the best wrought iron, equal to 50 per cent. Steel ships' hulls, masts, spars, &c., give similar results.

METALS, MINING, &c.

ALUMINUM BRONZE.—An alloy of aluminum (the chief component of clay) and copper has come largely into use as a substitute for gold in cheap jewellery, &c. An alloy of one part of aluminum to nine of copper has been used in place of steel, in France, to receive the end of needles employed in punching the edges of postage stamps.

COAL IN AUSTRALIA.—New South Wales coal is now largely exported to India at an expense of half that sent from England, East India coal having been generally unsuited for marine and locomotive purposes. The consumption of Australian coal will doubtless be very large, and profitable to the Colony.

COAL MINE EXPLOSIONS.—A most ingenious invention was brought out in 1867, by Mr. Ansell, to indicate the probability of explosions from fire-damp or carburetted hydrogen. It depends on the law of diffusion of gases, which is adapted in such a way by the inventor, that when a dangerous admixture of air and gas occurs in the mine, the apparatus detects it, and points out the fact by an indicator. It would be equally applicable to the detection of gas-escapes in houses. The indicator is moved by a column of mercury in a U shaped tube, the metal being set in motion by the gas mixing with the air in the tube, through a stopping made at one end by plaster of Paris.

COAL WASHING MACHINERY.—In the smelting of iron it is of the utmost importance that the coke employed should be as free as possible from sulphur. In 1867-68, coal washing machines of various kinds were invented and adopted in this country for that purpose. By their use the iron

pyrites, the source of the sulphur, is removed, as well as clay-slate, and other impurities, from the coal, and great advantage arises from the adoption of the plan, which has been in general use for many years on the Continent, where coal is much more impure than our own.

CREUSOT IRON WORKS.—These, the greatest iron works in France, perhaps in the world, and owned by Messrs. Schneider & Co., produce annually 130,000 tons of pig iron, and 110,000 tons of wrought iron. The coal mines afford annually 250,000 tons, and the iron mines 300,000 tons of ore. The total population dependent on the works is about 24,000, of whom 9,500 are employed in them.

IRON PUDDLING.—One of the greatest improvements introduced into the manufacture of iron is the Wilson furnace, in which, by aid of a down-draught, the gas from slack-coal is mixed with air in the early operation of puddling. With one ton of such coal, 20 cwt. of blooms have been produced from 21½ cwt. of pig iron. In an economical and practical point of view, it is one of the most extraordinary inventions that has been brought out.

ROCK-BORING BY DIAMONDS.—The diamond is now largely used as a tool-end for boring hard rocks, and works economically, effectively, and is also indestructible. At first sight it would seem a costly method, but such is not the case, considering that a steel chisel was spoilt for every inch bored in a hard rock while forming the Mont Cenis Tunnel across the Alps, on the railway between France and Italy. The diamond is the hardest known body in nature; consequently nothing but a blow can injure it: direct wear of its surface being impossible, except by means of diamond powder.

ROCK TUNNELLING MACHINES were amongst the novelties of 1867, and they result in great saving of labour. One, patented by M. Berrens, as seen in the Paris Exposition, has been very successful. Another, patented by Captain Beaumont, will bore soft rock at the rate of 2ft. 3in. per hour, sandstone at the rate of 2ft. in an hour and a half, and granite at the rate of 10 inches per hour. Hydraulic and pneumatic engines for digging coal were also largely employed in 1867-68 in British and foreign mines, saving not only labour, but the lives of the miners.

STEEL AND THE MICROSCOPE.—The fracture of steel, that is, the appearance it presents when broken, is generally a test of its quality. In 1867, large numbers of microscopes were invented and constructed for the express purpose of examining the crystalline structure of the metal—another and highly important contribution of science to our manufacturing industry, that steel masters have found great advantage in adopting.

STEEL RAILS.—The use of Bessemer steel as a material for the rails of a railroad has been extensively adopted. One steel rail, experimented on at Camden Town, lasted longer than twenty iron rails, and still remained in excellent condition. The importance of this fact, in reference to economy and safety, cannot be rated too highly.

TESTING IRON BY MAGNETISM.—Mr. Saxby has invented a most ingenious method of testing the soundness of cast and wrought iron. For this purpose he employs the ordinary magnetic needle or compass, which indicates, by the difference in the amount of its oscillations, whether the iron be quite sound or have flaws.

MISCELLANEOUS.

PHENOMENA OF BALLOON ASCENTS.—In a communication addressed to the Academy of Sciences, a French *savant* gives an account of the phenomena he observed during a late scientific ascent in an air-balloon. As regards sound, he states that its intensity is propagated to a considerable height in the atmosphere. Thus he heard the whistle of a steam-engine at an altitude of 3,000 metres; the noise of a railway train passing, at 2,500 metres; the barking of dogs, at 1,800 metres; the report of a gun, the same; the cries of a large crowd, the crowing of cocks, and the noise of bells, at 1,600 metres; the sound of drums and the music of an orchestra, at 1,400 metres; the rumbling of carriages on a stone pavement, at 1,200 metres; the human voice, at 1,000 metres (five-eighths of a mile); the croaking of frogs, at 900 metres; and the chirping of a cricket, at 800 metres. It is not so in the case of a descending sound; for the voice of the aëronaut at an altitude of 100 metres cannot make itself heard distinctly. The clouds offer no impediment to an ascending sound. The average velocity per second in the latter case is about 340 metres. The quiet waters of a lake echo the sound best upwards. While the balloon moves in obedience to the current, its shadow sweeps either the earth or the clouds. It is generally black; but it sometimes happens that, falling on a darker spot than itself, it assumes rather a luminous appearance. In this case, examined through a telescope, it is found to consist of a dark central nucleus surrounded by numerous penumbræ. On the green trees of a forest it appears yellow. On the clouds, when they are white, and at the moment of issuing again into the pure sky with the sun shining, the air-balloon is minutely depicted with all its details, and of a greyish hue. When it has reached an altitude of 3,000 metres the sky appears dark and impenetrable, in proportion as there is a diminution of moisture. The light of the rising sun appears to penetrate through every terrestrial object, while that of the moon, which is always red, seems only to glide over them.

DESTRUCTION OF INSECTS.—Petroleum, paraffin, and other similar oils have been largely and successfully employed as a remedy against many insects, such as bugs, &c., that infest the household. A simple wash of the oil on the resorts of such vermin is only required.

DISEASE OF PARASITIC ORIGIN.—Dr. Richardson, of Cayuga Co., U.S., has shown that meat, if exposed to air and moisture, quickly generates an enormous quantity of parasitic creatures, that, entering the blood of man, produce and propagate disease. According to his investigation, a few drops of human blood so affected contain more than twenty times in number the whole population of man in the world.

RIFLES.—The long Enfield rifle consists of 53 parts, and passes in all through 740 processes of manufacture. Each process is carefully checked, so that uniformity in every respect may result. The accuracy of workmanship is such that any part will readily fit another, affording the greatest advantage in respect to military requirements.

GLASS FROM CRYOLITE.—By melting one part of cryolite with from two to four parts of silica, a glass is formed that not only receives a fine polish by the usual method, but is susceptible of being cast in a mould, and can be manufac-tured into a great variety of useful and ornamental articles.

FLOATING SEAWEED AS A MANURE.—It has long been known that the Sea of Sargasso, situated between the 17th and 18th degrees of north latitude, is loaded with floating seaweed. It has been proposed to utilize this as a manure. According to M. Leps, of the French Military Corps:— "The mass covers the surface of 20 degrees lat. and 15 degrees long., which at this distance from the equator, is equivalent to 1,300 kilos. in breadth, and 2,000 kilos. in height, and consequently gives a superficies of 260,000,000 of hectares, capable of supplying 2,600,000,000 tons of green marine manure. According to the quantities generally used in East Lothian, viz., fifteen quintaux to the acre, the European mass of the Sea of Sargasso might furnish manure to fertilize from 800,000,000 to 900,000,000 hectares. The efficaciousness of the *Varech* as a manure has been sufficiently proved, and wherever its use is possible, the crops are abundant, and the land rises in value." This seaweed is as equally fertilizing as any used on our coasts.

LIGHT.—The Magnesium.—A piece of magnesium wire having a diameter of 1-1000th of an inch, emits a light equal to that afforded by 74 candles made of stearine, and weighing five to the pound. The intensity of the magnesium light is equal to nearly 1-130th of that afforded by the sun on a bright November day.

VULCANIZED INDIA RUBBER.—By heating articles made of this substance with charcoal to a temperature of 150° Fahrenheit, the smell of sulphur may be entirely got rid of.

RAILWAY CARRIAGES.—The rate of human weight carried for a corresponding weight of carriage on railways, is out of all proportion to that of road carriages. An omnibus, weighing 1 ton, will carry 30 people weighing 37 cwt., whereas a first-class railway carriage, weighing 5 tons, only conveys 18 people (if full), weighing 22 cwt.

RAILWAY EXTENSION.—At the commencement of 1868 the total mileage of railways was 126,500 miles, of which 102,000 were in Europe.

THE NEEDLE GUN.—By means of two improvements, invented by H. H. Borst and Random, the efficiency of the Prussian needle was so increased as to permit of from fourteen to fifteen shots per minute. Two movements in loading were got rid of by these inventions, the hollow chamber between the charge was filled up, diminishing the escape of gas, and consequently increasing the force of the explosion on the ball.

GRANITE.—According to the celebrated French chemist Deville, granite contracts in passing from a melted to a solid state to an extent exceeding 10 per cent. of its melted bulk.

WATER EXPLOSION.—If water, from which every particle of air has been extracted, be heated above the boiling point, it will not give off much steam. But if any rough-surfaced body be dropped therein, the liquid will be instantly converted into steam, with enormous explosive force.

STEAM OMNIBUSES.—One of these was successfully tried in France in September, 1868; it easily carried 35 persons at the rate of 10 miles per hour.

SUSPENSION BRIDGE OVER THE FALLS OF NIAGARA.—In September, 1868, two of the cables forming part of the suspension bridge over the Falls were successfully fixed over the stream, and attached to anchorages.

PHOTOGRAPHY IN PRINTING INK.—This was

successfully accomplished, in 1868, by Mr. Sutton Hall, by an ingenious, but intricate process, and is applicable to the reproduction of patterns for almost any purpose.

FLOATING DOCK. — In September, 1868, an enormous floating dock, built at North Woolwich, on the Thames, was launched, intended for use at Bermuda, for docking naval vessels, and to which station it is to be towed in 1869. Its extreme length was 384 feet; breadth, 124 feet; breadth inside the dock, 124 feet; total depth, 75 feet 6 inches. It was constructed in the form of a double semi-cylindrical shell, and weighed 8,400 tons. It is to be raised or lowered for docking vessels by pumping in air or water respectively; for which purpose eight steam engines and pumps are provided. It is capable of docking the largest-sized war vessel.

ROAD STEAMERS. — A great improvement in traction engines has been effected by covering the tires with thick vulcanized india-rubber. This not only deadens the sound, but also diminishes the required amount of tractive power, owing to the elasticity of the material. Trials in September, 1868, at Leith, near Edinburgh, showed that a rough macadamized road or a level grass field might be, with equal ease, run over by such machines. The weight of the road steamer was between four and five tons, and yet the compression of the loose earth beneath the wheels was so small that a walking-stick could be pushed in the track with ease.

LOCOMOTIVE FUEL. — An interesting trial of petroleum, in place of coke or coal, was made in September, 1868, at Chalons, before the Emperor of the French. The locomotive which had been driving the royal train was replaced by another in which petroleum alone was used as fuel. The Emperor, with MM. Sauvage and St. Clair, occupied the tender. The experiment was a complete success, the distance from Chalons to Petit Mourmelon being traversed in a quarter of an hour less time than that required by the fastest usual express train.

COAL IN YORKSHIRE. — After continuous mining for five years, the Denerby Main Company succeeded in obtaining coal by reaching the Barnsley seam at a depth of half-a-mile from the surface of the ground. The seam is 9 feet thick, and of excellent quality. The result is highly interesting in a geological point of view, as it has upset the old theory that the carboniferous strata ends at the commencement of the magnesian formation. This seam underlies the latter.

WELSH COAL. — This kind of coal is now enormously used for steam purposes, and has been the foundation of the rent-roll of the present Marquis of Bute, stated to equal £300,000 per annum. The discovery of its value was accidental. Twenty years ago a quantity of it was sold to a Thames steamer for a trifle, it being considered useless as fuel; it was immediately discovered, however, that owing to its chemical character, it was of the highest value for supplying steam boilers for marine engines. The field extends from the Forest of Dean to Milford Haven.

STEAM GENERATED BY GAS. — One of the most recent improvements for the purpose is that patented by Mr. Jackson of London. The gas is mixed with air, and passes through a disc of wire gauze, where the mixture is ignited; the intensely hot air thus generated is made to pass through a multitude of tubes surrounded by water. In a 4-horse power boiler, occupying a diameter of 3 feet, a pressure of steam equal to 50 pounds per square inch can be generated from cold water in less than half an hour after the gas jets have been ignited. Until the engine is started, one or two of the gas jets is sufficient to keep up that pressure; after that, the whole of the jets are called into play, and the pressure maintained by simply regulating the supply of air and gas by means of an ordinary stop-cock; a wonderful reduction of labour compared with stoking with coal as fuel.

FISHING BY SCIENCE. — The whale fishery is proverbially dangerous, and, indeed, requires the hardiest seamen for its pursuit. An ingenious plan has been proposed for the destruction of the whale. The harpoon is fitted with two insulated conductors, connected by wires with a coil machine kept in the boat. On the harpoon being plunged into the whale's body, electric shocks of a powerful nature are sent until the animal is completely prostrated, and becomes an easy prey. Another plan proposed was that of firing an explosive shell into the body of the whale from a rifle, by which its vital parts would be destroyed.

MOON, EFFECTS OF THE, ON THE WEATHER. — From time immemorial it has been considered, popularly, that the changes of the moon affect the weather. Until very recently, however, all philosophers of the present day denied the possibility of such an influence. But in a paper read, early in 1868, before the Academy of Sciences, Paris, it was shown that the moon has an influence, due to its effect on the temperature of the earth. At new moon no heat is reflected to the earth by the moon, whereas, at full moon, we receive heat-rays. Consequently, the temperature of the atmosphere, &c., is affected, and necessarily an effect on the weather must follow.

FIRE ENGINES, STEAM-FLOATING. — Fire engines floating on the Thames have long been used; but formerly they required to be towed from their station to the site of the fire. In September, 1868, a new form of the engine was adopted and put into use by the Metropolitan Fire Brigade. The new machine is fitted with steam machinery, capable of propelling it at the rate of 12 miles an hour, and hence a great advantage will accrue in the readiness with which it may be moved from place to place in regard to waterside premises, dockyards, and warehouses generally.

COCHINEAL INSECTS IN ENGLAND. — One of the most interesting novelties introduced into England in 1868, in regard to Natural History, was that of the cochineal insect. A native of Central America, Mexico, and other climates, its natural food is the Cactus, well-known from the peculiarity of its structure and the rich red colour of its flowers. The cochineal, *Coccus cacti*, is extensively employed for dyeing silk and wool of various shades of red. The Zoological Society of London have, in their gardens, Regent's Park, numbers of these insects feeding on the Cactus, and at present they seem to thrive well.

FISH FARMS FOR SALMON PRODUCTION. — In New Jersey, U.S., an extensive establishment of this kind has been organized for the supply of eggs and young trout to rivers, &c., destitute of them. Advantage is taken of the spawning season, October, to collect the eggs of the female, deposited in the gravel of the stream. The eggs are then impregnated by hand with the milt of the male, and kept in suitable vessels until hatched. Fifteen grains of the milt are sufficient to impregnate 10,000 eggs; each of these is about the sixth of an inch in diameter, and weighs one grain. The fecundity of the fish is enormous; a trout of one pound weight will yield at least 1,000 eggs, and the proportion increases with the size of the fish. The average yield of young fish, however, does not exceed 25 per cent. of the eggs impregnated artificially.

AERIAL CRADLES FOR INFANTS.—Amongst the novel patents of 1868 was one granted to M. Achille B. Boyer, of Paris, for Improvements in the Construction of Cradles, suspended from a stand overhead. By means of simple mechanism the infant can be turned in any direction without removal from its warm covering, may be nursed by the mother, and otherwise attended to. Precisely similar methods are applicable to invalids' beds when motion is attended with pain. The plan is much more manageable than the waterbed of Dr. Arnott, hitherto almost exclusively used for the purpose.

SUBMARINE LAMP FOR DIVERS.—The Diving Bell has become one of the most important inventions of the day, on account of the numerous uses to which it is applied. In laying the foundations of piers, breakwaters, &c., beneath water at any state of the tide; for the examination of the state of a ship's bottom; the recovery of treasure from wrecks; it has rendered the highest service. But one hindrance to its utility is the small amount of light which penetrates the water. When it is remembered that an ordinary plate-glass window absorbs one-third of the rays of light that impinge on it, some idea may be gathered of the great loss of light occurring in a depth of 20 or 30 feet of dirty sea water. Many inventions have been brought out to remedy this evil. The electric and lime lights have been proposed, but the intense heat they generate breaks the glass enclosing them, and so destroys the lamp. Mr. Ward, of Port Glasgow, Scotland, has, by a recently patented invention, overcome the difficulty. He incloses an oil lamp within a cylindrical glass, from the top and bottom of which rises a tube reaching to the surface of the water. The hot air rising in one tube draws down cold air, to maintain the combustion of the wick, in the other, and so a flame may be kept up continuously. To prevent the fracture of the glass, he incloses the lamp in another glass cylinder; the intervening air prevents the breaking of either glass, by its non-conducting power, and hence the lamp may be completely depended on.

CAPTIVE BALLOONS.—This term is applied to balloons whose motion in the air is restrained to any particular place by means of a rope reaching to the ground, by which the position and height of the balloon can be regulated at pleasure. In the summer of 1868, the largest of its kind was exhibited near London; it had a cubic capacity of 300,000 feet, an ascensional power equal to 11 tons, from which, however, had to be deducted the weight of car and rope, the latter weighing about 4 tons. It was capable of carrying 30 people, with ballast. To render its ascending power as great as possible, pure hydrogen, obtained from water, in place of coal gas was used. The resistance or ascensive power of the balloon required a 200-horse power engine to overcome it and draw it down.

DEEP SEA DREDGING.—It was long, and indeed until recently, maintained, that at great depths the ocean is destitute of life. At the Annual Meeting of the United States National Assembly

of Science, however, this notion was shown to be erroneous, minute organisms having been brought up from a depth of nearly 300 fathoms. At still greater depths the remains of marine creatures of minute size, of the tertiary epoch, were abundant, especially *foraminifera*: these, in many parts of the Atlantic bed, form the covering of the *plateau*.

SAFETY COFFIN.—One of the most curious inventions of 1868, was that of a safety coffin, intended to obviate the results of premature burial, and invented by M. Vester, a German. The coffin was made larger than required by the size of the body; it had at the head a movable lid, communicating with the open air by means of a square trough from the bottom of the grave. The arrangement was such that a person might thus readily escape from the tomb. The inventor proposed to place refreshments in the coffin, as a prudent precaution against starvation!

LAMP GLASSES.—By an ingenious invention of Mr. Steane, of Barking, a great increase of transmitted light is effected in lamp globes or glasses. He constructs a globe of a double thickness of glass, having an intervening hollow space; this is filled with water, or other refracting liquid. The globe presents a convex form both inside and outside, and hence has the same effect on the transmitted light, in respect to surrounding objects, that a convex lens would have—as seen in the bull's-eye lantern.

GAS RETORTS.—In 1867-68, most of the old cast-iron retorts employed for distilling gas from coal were thrown aside, fire-clay retorts being substituted for them. Many advantages arise from the latter, but especially that of preventing the deposit of hard carbon from the coal. This substance resembles black-lead (an impure form of carbon) in most respects; its non-conducting power causes the rapid destruction of iron through the great heat required to permeate the carbon before the coal becomes sufficiently hot to give off gas; the carbon is a useless product, being scarcely combustible. A new method of charging and withdrawing gas retorts has been adopted by the Chartered Gas Company; it consists in employing steam machinery for the purpose. By an ingenious arrangement of scoops travelling on a platform, both operations are readily performed. The labour of the men is materially reduced, as is also the number required, whilst injury to health, caused by the old method, is obviated.

NEW PLANET.—One of the group of asteroids or minor members of our planetary system, was discovered by Dr. Peters, of the Hamilton Observatory, New York, in August, 1868. It has an apparent size equal to that of a star of the eleventh magnitude. It was first seen in the constellation *Pisces.* R.A., at 3 a.m., August 24, was 18° 0' 38", and 19° 0' 54" declination. Its motion was easterly. During the last 60 years, following the discovery of Juno, Pallas, Vesta, and Ceres, the number of asteroids, apparently fragments of a large planet, has been raised to about one hundred.

SKELETON LEAVES.—These beautiful objects, which show the solid structure of the leaves of plants, may be prepared as follows: Macerate a perfect leaf in water containing a little pearlash. The cellular tissues will gradually disappear, and what is left may be removed by a camel-hair brush. The brown colour may be removed by immersing the leaf in a weak solution of chloride of lime, and well washing in water; it should then be dried by pressure between blotting paper.

IMPROVEMENTS IN THE MANUFACTURE OF GAS.—In September, 1868, a patent, granted to Mr. Salmon, was fully specified. The invention has for its object the production of gas from spirit, oil, tar, or other matter of strong gas-generating power, to render the same useful for raising steam, warming, cooking, &c., and also for giving a much better light for illuminating purposes than that afforded by coal-gas. The materials are distilled in a close vessel heated by steam or other means. The gas is "scrubbed" by being passed through vessels filled with sponge, asbestos, or charcoal, and it is heated in other vessels, after being purified. The value of the patent consists chiefly in the use of matters hitherto refuse, but which may now be turned into economic use for all the purposes before named. The price of the gas is less than that of coal gas.

NEW FILTERING APPARATUS.—In nearly all chemical manufactures, in sugar refining, and many other processes, filtration is very essential, but hitherto the means have been frequently incomplete. A new mode of filtration was patented by Mr. Kirby, of London, in 1868. The invention consists of a combination of materials. A sheet of linen, calico, or other textile fabric is covered with a layer of paper pulp, such as that of which the common filtering paper of the chemist is made. Adhesion between the pulp and the fabric is obtained by subjecting the sheet to pressure under a hot roller. Water may thus be effectually filtered by mixing charcoal in powder with the pulp, and by using other substances suitable for such purpose, the complete filtration and purification of any kind of liquid may be obtained.

CARBOLIC ACID, A CURE FOR FOOT-ROT IN SHEEP.—Some very interesting experiments have been carried on at Victoria, Australia, in the use of carbolic acid for the above-named purpose. The acid should be mixed with some greasy substance, to make it adhere to the feet; and may be applied by means of a brush. For large flocks, troughs are filled with the mixture, and the sheep made to pass through it, by means of which the feet are effectually coated. The result is said to have been very successful.

VEGETATION IN CALIFORNIA.—In a paper read before the American National Academy of Sciences, in August, 1868, Professor Bryers stated that the bulk of the Californian forests consisted of pine, spruce, fir, and cedars, there being 50 species of conifers (fir) peculiar to the country. One of the largest of these trees has a circumference of 91 feet, is 260 feet high, and, judging from the number of rings in the trunk, it cannot be of a less age than about fourteen hundred years.

SEWAGE ON THE FARM.—At the meeting of the British Association at Norwich, in 1868, this important question came under discussion, which resulted in the appointment of Mr. Grantham to draw up annual reports, showing—1st. The special circumstances of each case, and the extent of district, population, &c. 2nd. The character of the sewage, and water supply adopted in the district, and the quantity of sewage at disposal. 3rd. The mode of disposing of the sewage, with description of the works and their cost. 4th. The result pecuniarily to the district, and to those who are selling or applying the

sewage to the land or otherwise in any form whatever.

DECAY OF STONE.—Mr. J. Spiller, of the Royal Arsenal, Woolwich, has invented a simple and effective method of preventing the decay of stone surfaces. It consists of washing them with a solution, in water, of superphosphate of lime. It has been extensively tried on several public buildings, exposed to the impure gases, smoke, &c., of towns.

FREEZING THE BRAIN.—Dr. Richardson discovered that by forcing a jet of ether on any portion of the exterior of the skull, the part of the brain immediately beneath ceases to act; all its power being suspended so long as a freezing temperature is maintained. The power entirely returns on the freezing influence being removed. The effect of freezing the fore part of the brain is to make an animal fall forward, while, by freezing the back of the brain, a reverse motion is produced.

PAPER FROM WOOD.—In the Paris Exposition of 1867, two machines were shown, by means of which wood of any kind could be converted into a material for making paper. The wood was rapidly ground down by means of a large rotating stone into a pulp. This was passed through a sieve to exclude the coarse particles. The pulp was then mixed with an equal quantity of that made from rags, and converted into paper by the ordinary machine. In America the process has been largely adopted.

PEARLS.—These when of large size are of great value, and have hitherto been chiefly supplied from the pearl fisheries of India. Within the last few years, our Scottish rivers have yielded many of great beauty from a species of mussel, indigenous to those streams. In 1867-68 pearls to a large amount in value were thus obtained, affording a highly profitable occupation for the inhabitants of some districts in Scotland. It is said that more than £10,000 worth have thus been taken within the last year or two.

SENSITIVENESS OF PLANTS.—An eminent French *savant* published surprising results in respect to this. He finds plants acted on by chloroform, electricity, and other agents affecting the nerves of animals. By means of a powerful electric shock, "sensitive plants" were made to close their leaves, and a strong shock killed one plant.

SINGING FLAMES.—In 1867, Dr. Tyndall, of Royal Institution, has published his discoveries on the effect that sound has on certain forms of flame. If the flame of a gas jet be just on the point of "roaring," it becomes sensitive to sound. It will vibrate, or dance in unison with the sounds of an anvil, pianoforte, or generally with all high notes of any musical instrument—the higher the notes the greater the effect. A flaring dip-candle may be employed for the same purpose.

STREET PAVEMENT.—A new mode of laying the roadway has been experimentally introduced into London. Blocks of granite 6 in. by 4 in. are laid down on an ordinary bed, and the interstices filled with small pebbles. Hot asphalte is then poured on, and the whole left to cool before traffic is resumed. By this method, not only do the blocks become more solidly fixed together, but all chance of water percolating between them is avoided; hence their position is very durable. The plan had been previously tried at Manchester.

STREET WATERING.—An invention for this purpose was introduced into Glasgow, in April, 1868 by Mr. Sim. On one side of the roadway, pipes were laid next the pavement, and connected with the water-main. The pipes were drilled with holes one-tenth of an inch in diameter. On turning the water on from the main, it squirted across the street, completely and speedily watering, and, if required, washing the roadway.

TUBE WELLS.—The method of obtaining water by inserting tubes in the earth, as practised during the Abyssinian Expedition of 1867-68, is by no means new, having been employed, in a modified form, for drawing brine from salt springs for fourteen years past in America. The plan is that of driving into the earth a pipe of small bore (pointed at the lower end and pierced with holes), by a kind of pile-driving process. Earth and sand first enter the pipe, followed by water, the pebbles exterior to the pointed end of the pipe in the earth acting as a kind of natural filter, excluding the entrance of more dirt after the first has been pumped out.

WATER SUPPLY AND CONSUMPTION. — The average of these in respect to the metropolis, for 1867, was 30½ gallons in all, per day, for each person, of which amount it is considered

that 25 gallons were consumed for domestic purposes by each inhabitant. The total daily supply averaged about 100,000,000 gallons.

WATER DEPOSITED BY RAIN.—One inch depth of rain falling on an acre of ground will amount in all to 226,225 gallons, or about 100 tons in weight.

CRYSTAL AND CELL FORMATION.—At the meeting of the British Association at Norwich in 1868, Dr. Tyndall showed that precisely the same forces and causes were operative in forming a mineral, vegetable and animal forms, a doctrine and fact that greatly simplifies the philosophical ideas of the nature of the three kingdoms.

CUTTING GLASS BY HOT AIR.—The use of hot air or gas has been largely adopted for cutting glass in place of the old methods. The hot air or gas issues from a pointed or flattened tube, and is driven directly upon the object to be cut. The latter is placed close to the tube, and revolves on its axis. By this means a narrow cylinder of heated glass is formed on the object, which, on being damped, causes the glass to divide at the desired part with extreme neatness. The plan is rapid, effectual, and far more certain than any other means yet adopted.

English Cathedrals, &c.,
THEIR AREA AND DIMENSIONS.

CHURCHES, &c.	Area. Feet.	Long. Feet.	Wide. Feet.
York Minster	63,800	486	106
St Paul's	59,700	460	9
Lincoln	55,530	463	80
Winchester	53,480	530	85
Ely	47,000	517	75
Durham	46,340	473	81
Westminster	46,000	505	75
Salisbury	43,515	450	88
Canterbury	43,215	514	72
Peterborough	41,090	426	73
Norwich	33,750	408	79
Worcester	33,100	387	70
Wells	32,140	388	69
Chester	31,680	350	74
St. Albans	31,140	425	65
Gloucester	30,600	408	83
Chichester	30,000	386	92
Exeter	29,600	383	72
Beverley	29,600	334	64
Lichfield	27,860	379	66
Hereford	26,850	325	74
Tewkesbury	26,000	317	71
Ripon	24,200	270	87
Rochester	23,300	310	68
Coventry	22,080	252	110
Manchester	18,340	215	112
Christ Church, Hants	18,300	303	60
St. Saviour's	18,200	272	61
Selby	17,800	283	59
Bath	16,600	215	72
Windsor	16,400	225	66
Redcliffe	15,500	230	56
Grantham	15,440	193	73
Carlisle	15,270	211	71
Ludlow	14,860	204	80
Bristol	14,200	171	72
Beverley	13,700	197	60
Leeds	13,140	160	35
Sherborne	13,110	200	60
Doncaster	12,600	169	65
Oxford	11,342	155	54
Wimborne	10,725	785	54

(Godwin's Archæologist's Handbook.)

Civil List Pensions.

Granted between June, 1867, and June, 1868.

MISS EMILY SOUTHWOOD SMITH, in consideration of the services of her father, Dr. Southwood Smith, in the cause of sanitary reform, £60.

MRS. ANNE WARNE ROBERTSON, in consideration of the services of her husband, the late Joseph Robertson, LL.D., in the illustration of the ancient history of Scotland, £100.

DAME LOUISA ELLIS, in consideration of the services of the late Sir Samuel Ellis, Lieut.-General in the Royal Marines, £60.

MRS. MARY MACONOCHIE, in recollection of the services of her husband, the late Captain Maconochie, R.N., in connection with the improvement of prison discipline, £60.

MRS. SARAH FARADAY (widow) and MISS JANE BARNARD (niece) of the late Professor Faraday, in consideration of the services rendered by him to chemical science, £150.

MISS CECILIA KITTO, MRS. FEROOZA QUENNELL, MISS HELEN RHODA KITTO, and MISS FRANCES EDITH TRACY KITTO, in consideration of the services of their father, the late J. Kitto, D.D., £100.

MISS ELIZA HINCKS, MISS ANNA FRANCES HINCKS, and MISS BIRTHIA HINCKS, in consideration of the services of their father, the late Edw. Hincks, D.D., as an oriental scholar, £100.

DAME KIRK BREWSTER, in consideration of the eminent services rendered to science by her late husband, Sir David Brewster, £200.

MR. JOHN CHARLES WARRINGTON LEECH and MISS ADA ROSE LEECH, in consideration of the attainments of their father, the late John Leech, as an artist, each £50.

MRS. MARGARET OLIPHANT WILSON OLIPHANT, in consideration of her contributions to literature, £100.

MISS MARIA SUSAN RYE, in consideration of her services to the public in promoting, by emigration and otherwise, the amelioration of the condition of working women, £70.

MR. GEORGE THOMAS DOO, F.R.S., in consideration of his attainments as a line engraver, £100.

BRITISH India, an extensive region of Asia between 8° 4′—36° N. lat. and 66° 44′—99° 30′ E. long., comprises an area of 1,004,616 square miles, with a population of 150,767,851. For administrative and political purposes, the British possessions in India have been distributed into the following principal divisions. Bengal Presidency, British Burmah, North-West Provinces, Punjab, Coorg, Hyderabad and Mysore, Oude, Central Provinces, Madras Presidency, Bombay Presidency, Sinde, all under British administration. There are also native states under British protection. The Governor-General in Council has under his direct administration the provinces of Oude, the Central provinces, British Burmah, and the territories of Coorg, Hyderabad, and Mysore. The Presidency of Bengal, the North-West Provinces, and the Punjab, have each a Lieutenant-Governor; and the Presidencies of Madras and Bombay, Sinde being included in Bombay, are each under a Governor, subject to the control of the Governor-General. The area of the Native States is supposed to be about 602,304 square miles, with a population of 48,366,348. The oldest history of India is entirely legendary—of the highest interest in an archæological point of view, but of little value as to the reality of the facts. The first certain record to be met with in ancient Hindoo history, is traceable to the year 300 B.C. Of its narration from the Mahommedan conquest in 1001, to Lord Canning's administration, commencing in 1856, and the final proclamation of the sovereignty of Q. Victoria, Nov. 1, 1858, the most important events to us commence with the grant by Q. Elizabeth, in 1600, of a charter to a number of London merchants, under the title of "The Governor and Company of Merchants trading to the East Indies." The charter, granted for fifteen years, was renewed from time to time with various modifications; but from its exclusive and prohibitive character, much difficulty and contention arose. In 1662, Charles II. gave the possessors permission "to make war and peace upon the native princes," a privilege of which they largely availed themselves for nearly 200 years. In 1698, the Crown granted another charter to a *new* East India Company, who offered a loan of £2,000,000 to the State. This naturally led to constant wranglings between the two Companies, which, in 1702, were united by Act of Parliament. A constitution (or laws for the government of the Company) was established and maintained until its final dissolution in August 1858. Properly speaking, the "Company" consisted only of merchants trading to and from India, which it not only monopolized, but extended the agency to China and other parts of the East. By degrees, avarice and ambition caused it to take part in the quarrels among the native princes, thus assuming an influence and authority at the native courts resulting in the acquisition of almost sovereign power over these vast regions. India thus became not only commercially profitable, but afforded the relations and friends of the directors opportunities of making vast fortunes by political (civil?) or military enterprises. The political affairs and progress of the Company, the great events, and their issues, which occurred in the intervals of 1773-1785 during the administration of Warren Hastings, the first Governor-General; 1786-1793, during the administration of Marquis Cornwallis; 1793-1798, of Sir John Shore; 1798-1805, of Marquis Wellesley; 1806-1813, of Lord Minto; 1813-1823, of the Marquis of Hastings; 1823-1835, of Lord Amherst and Lord William Bentinck; 1835-1842, of Lord Auckland; 1842-1844, of the Earl of Ellenborough; 1844-1848, of Lord Hardinge; 1848-1855, of the Marquis of Dalhousie; 1856-1862, of Viscount Canning; belong to the domain of history, and are too numerous and important to be comprised in this epitome. The events preceding the establishment or inauguration of a Governor-General must be briefly referred to. In 1745, 1761, great jealousy existed between the English and the French, who had established themselves in India. On the declaration of war between England and France, hostilities commenced in the Madras Presidency, which terminated at the peace of Aix-la-Chapelle in 1748. The struggle in the Carnatic, however, was long continued, under the pretext of supporting the claims of rival princes. Clive (originally a clerk in the Civil service at Madras), abandoning his pen for the sword, wherewith he carved for himself the first and most famous name in that great muster-roll of British soldiers and statesmen who have thrown such lustre on our occupation of India, laid the foundation of his country's supremacy in the East. His memorable defence of Arcot, and subsequent victories, broke the spell of French invincibility, and the concluding battle of Plassy, terminating in the overthrow of Surajah Dowlah, established the British rule. In 1760 he returned to England, but in 1764 was sent out to reform the mal-administration into which the country had lapsed after his departure. Having effected this, and purged the Indian government of oppression, extortion, and corruption, he returned finally to England in 1765;

having, in less than eighteen months, "restored perfect order and discipline in both the civil and military services, and brought back prosperity to the well-nigh ruined finances of the Company." The Indian revolt of 1857 eventuated in the cession, in 1858, of the Company's last charter of 1853, which would not otherwise have expired until 1873. It established a new era in the sovereignty of Victoria, now Empress of India and its dependencies. The seat of supreme government is Calcutta. The affairs of India are managed by a Secretary in Council for India, at the office in Downing Street, *vice* the India House, formerly in Leadenhall-street.

THE FINANCES OF INDIA.

Our East Indian possessions have long afforded one of the most difficult points of finance incident to the British Empire. The healths and lives of some of the most eminent financialists have been sacrificed in the attempt to reduce the question of revenue and expenditure to an equilibrium. In part, this problem has been solved; but it requires no great knowledge of money matters, geography, or social science, to perceive, that our East Indian administration has, with little exception, been a gross failure, and a disgrace to a country which boasts itself, statistically and otherwise, to be the leader of European nations in such respects.

A full account is given above of the topography and resources of our Indian possessions, extending from Ceylon to the Himalayas — a region, excepting Brazil, that may justly be considered as one of the richest that the world can produce. From the most refined delicacy of the tropical climate, to the productions of the north of Scotland, India may lay claim to universality; common sense therefore indicates, entirely apart from all political or other considerations, that such a country should not only be self-maintaining, but take a position that might command a first place of all the nations of the globe. But in respect to it, the old adage, that "while kings play, the people are ruined," unfortunately holds good. The system of our political government of India, especially characterized by change of policy, incident to a change of home government, is alone sufficient to account for a want of progress in every respect. Individuals, like nations, have their peculiarities, and whatever may seem for the moment advisable, must be adapted to the gradual changes required to develope what we consider a semi-barbarous state, to arrive at that which modern civilization supports on the conditions of safety, comfort, and social welfare. These remarks must be considered as simply prefatory to what will necessarily appear an unprejudiced account of the Finances of India. In our own islands, which, compared to the extent of our Indian possessions, are a mere spot on the face of the globe, it is rarely possible to present any accurate statistics for a period dating at least half to a whole year previous to their publication. The want of communication in India, and a variety of other causes, therefore entirely prevent anything like an accurate conclusion being drawn of the *financial present*.

According to the latest return, dated May, 1868, the gross revenue of India, for the year 1866-67, that is, from 1st May, 1866, to 31st March, 1867, was £42,122,433. This was constituted of the following items :—Land revenue, £19,136,449; tributes and contributions from Native states, £629,245; making the total of the land revenue, amounting to the sum of £19,765,694. Forests brought in

£311,340; akbaree (or excise), £2,119,789; income tax, £22,127; customs, £2,030,864; salt, £5,345,910; opium, £6,803,413; stamps, £1,803,777; the mint, £239,991; post-office, £496,439; telegraph (purely Indian), £197,355; ditto to and from England, £22,117; law and justice, £627,050; police, £188,169; marine, £228,543; education, £66,658; interest, £233,513; miscellaneous in India, £276,310; ditto in England, £67,871; army miscellaneous in India, £717,489; ditto in England, £10,879; public works, miscellaneous, £538,139. The net receipts for the year were £41,700,603, after deducting drawbacks, refunds, &c. The total charges against income were £7,215,697, leaving a net available income of £34,484,906.

The expenditure for the same year was made up of the following items :—Administration and cost of public departments, £1,271,284; law and justice, £2,397,788; police, £2,262,921; marine, £770,630; education, science, and art, £674,717; ecclesiastical, £144,360; medical, £261,801; stationery and printing, £301,764; political agencies and foreign services, £267,098; miscellaneous, £961,517; superannuations, &c., £766,472; civil, furlough, and absentee allowances, £79,305; army, £15,825,791; public works, (including £259,474 for supervision and cost of railways, and £111,681 loss of exchange on railway transactions), £5,396,599; interest on debt, £4,259,331; dividends to proprietors of East India Stock, £629,970; guaranteed interest on capital of railways and other public companies, deducting net traffic receipts, £731,049. Of this expenditure, £873,362 was incurred for stores, and £5,549,343 of other charges in England. Deducting the above expenditure from the net available income, it seems that on March 31, 1867, the excess of expenditure over income was £2,517,491, leaving, of course, a deficit to that amount against the exchequer.

On the 30th April, 1866, the aggregate balances of the treasurer of India amounted to £13,771,625, the debt incurred was £1,840,581 for loans, treasury notes, civil and other funds, sale proceeds of waste lands, local remittances, and there was a local Indian surplus of £4,918,160. On the payment side £1,902,865 of debt was discharged. Drafts in favour of London in respect to advances to public companies and miscellaneous payments £7,376,330. Balance of supplies between the presidencies, &c., on unadjusted accounts £194,117, leaving a balance of cash in hand in treasuries of £11,057,054 on 31st March 1867.

The following is a summary of the net receipts of each district, after deducting repayments. The sources of revenue in each are generally the same, although, of course, climate and other influencing circumstances modify them. Departments under the immediate control of the

Government of India, £1,686,48; the Oude territory, £1,212,746; Central Provinces, £1,040,723; British Burmah, £931,097; East and West Berar districts, £530,330; Eastern Settlements, £176,825; Government of Bengal, £13,498,400; North-Western provinces, £5,282,112; Punjab territories, £3,239,124; Presidency of Madras, £6,225,295; Presidency of Bombay, £7,767,597.

In the general balance, mention has already been made of a sum of £629,245 as "tribute and contributions from Native states," which is apportioned as follows. Various petty states, under immediate government control, £64,396; North-Western Provinces, £146,218; Punjab, £27,205; Madras, £315,108; Bombay and Sind, £76,318. The total charges for collection of the public income for each separate head was as follows: land revenue, £1,832,022; forest, £208,633; akbaree or excise, £234,225; income tax, £1,188; customs, £188,810; salt, £317,519; opium, £1,077,330; stamps, £80,226; mint, £131,146; post-office, £415,129; the electric telegraph, £286,086; making a total charge in India of the collection of revenues, including cost of salt and opium, of £4,772,314; certain allowances to district and village officers amount to £339,619. The charges on account of the administration of public departments are embraced under a great variety of separate heads; that of the general and political government amounts to £328,439, and includes salary of the Governor-general and members of the Council, £62,085; Governor-general's household, £16,364; Indian secretaries, £104,295; public offices, £32,562; board of examiners, £3,024; currency department, £51,207; allowance to the presidency bank for conducting the business of the treasury, £6,591; and tour charges of the Governor-general, £52,311; the latter being a large sum apparently, but really small considering the necessities and expenses of keeping Durbar, entertaining Eastern princes during the journey, &c. The expenses of the other departments, inclusive of similar charges for each were, Oude, £38,365; Central Provinces, £39,270; British Burmah, £28,083; East and West Berar, £8,219; Eastern Settlements, £12,496; Bengal, £143,350; North-western Provinces, £106,275; Punjab, £102,379; Madras, £117,419; Bombay and Sinde, £164,769; giving a total in India of £1,089,064 as the cost of administration. To these are to be added payments of home accounts in England of £182,220, making a grand total of the cost of administration and public departments of £1,271,284. The totals of other items of expenditure for law and justice, police, &c., &c., have already been given, and it is unnecessary to enter into minute details of each of the departments. The following items, however, are interesting:—The cost of suppression of Thuggee and Dacoity cost upwards of £12,000; in three districts, viz., Petty States, Oude and the Central Provinces, under the head of police. Under the head of education &c., £150,000 was devoted to museums, scientific institutions, and the general promotion of science. The salary, &c., of the Bishop and clergy figure at £9,565, under the head of ecclesiastical. The cost of printing and stationery is great, about £180,000 being expended in India, and £120,000 in England under those heads. Durbar presents, &c., amount to about £43,000 for the whole empire. Under the head of allowances, pensions, &c., the ex-king of Oude, Wazed Ally Shah, receives £110,000; Rajah Bahadoor, £17,875, conjointly with the widow of the late ruler: Mah-

ratta Choute, £10,811; Newab Nazim's personal allowance, £67,151; Her H. Manne Begum, £45,144; compensation in place of supply of salt to the French government, £51,970; the Rajah of Benares, £7,500; allowance to the relatives of the late Rajah of Tanjore, £41,968; stipend to the family of the late Newab of Masulipatam, £3,456; ditto to the family of Hyder Ally Khan and Tippoo Sultan, £4,011; Pagoda and Mosque allowances, £98,495; to which should also be added allowances to Zemindars, &c., £27,047; pensions to families of late Newab, the Carnatic dynasty, &c., £55,767; Azeem Jah Bahadoor, £12,700; family of the Newab of Kurnal, £10,718; ditto of the late Newab of Surat: Emandars of Bombay and Sinde, £386,109. The various allowances to the districts of the kind amount to £671,234, or about one-third of those for the rest of the empire. Amongst the miscellaneous charges, the following are interesting: Rewards for killing wild animals, £13,314; famine relief charges, (in Bengal only), £348,575; tea nurseries, endowed gardens, &c., £5,676; cotton experiments in Bombay and Sinde, £6,242; government stallions' charges, £1,207; purchase and keep of ditto, £1,313.

In respect to the cost of the army, the regimental allowance amounted to £3,612,018; commissariat, £1,429,635; army garrison and staff, £227,264; stud and various, charges £166,777; barracks, £193,214; medical, £201,936; ordnance, £195,802; sea transport, £154,772; education, £35,652. For the "Government of India," in Madras and Bombay similar charges amount to from one-third to half of the above sums. Under the head of non-effective services £558,634 is swallowed up by pensions for officers alone, independent of £16,500 allowed to "retired" officers, and pensions to widows and orphans about £16,500. The *non-effective service in England* costs the enormous sum of £1,048,845 in the shape of pensions, allowances, &c., &c. The head of public works includes too many details of roads, canals, railways, buildings, &c., &c., to allow of even a selection.

The Debt of India.—At the 31st March, 1867, the total debt charged to and due by the several Presidencies was £72,526,815; and the annual charge for interest, which varied from 3¾ to 10 per cent., amounted to £3,413,375. Out of this sum the registered debt for India and Bengal amounted to £67,999,839, bearing an annual charge for interest of £3,147,904. The whole of the remaining districts, &c., then were under debt to the extent of £2,471,252, at an annual charge of £164,182. The interest on 65 millions of the debt varied from 4 to 5 per cent., about one-half being charged at the rate of 4 per cent. The total amount of interest paid in India in the year 1866-67 was £2,919,548; but, including £33,490 for dividends on India 4 per cent. transfer loan, the grand total was £2,953,038. But besides the debt *in India*, there is also the *Home* debt, comprising East India bonds, debentures, India 4 and 5 per cent. Stocks, and East India Stock, the whole making an amount of £35,538,000, at an annual charge of £1,936,263. Of this sum about 27 millions is charged at the rate of 4 per cent., 2½ millions at 5 per cent., and 6 millions at 10½ per cent., the latter comprising the East India Stock.

The preceding figures give an account of Indian finance as it existed in the year 1866-67. The pound sterling is calculated at the rate of ten rupees at two shillings each.

For the year 1867-68 an estimate has been published of each of the details already entered into, and of which bare totals need only be here given. The gross revenues and receipts are estimated as follows:—

Estimated Heads of Revenue and Receipts for year ending 31st March, 1868.

In India.	Gross Receipts.
	£
Land revenue, including tributes and contributions from native States, forest, and Akbaree revenues, &c..	23,467,700
License tax	658,000
Customs	2,545,200
Salt	6,024,300
Opium	8,814,200
Stamps	2,393,900
Mint	237,300
Post-office	652,300
Telegraph (includes England, £26,916)	298,916
Law and justice	734,400
Police	261,700
Marine	259,200
Education	73,400
Interest	227,600
Miscellaneous (includes England, £61,452)	500,252
Army—Miscellaneous (includes England, £16,401)	735,401
Public works—Miscellaneous	479,500
	£48,363,269
Excess of expenditure over income, including public works extraordinary	1,106,077
	£49,469,346

On the other hand, the expenditure is estimated as follows:—

Estimated Expenditure for year ending 31st March, 1868.

	In India and England.
	£
Repayments, allowances, refunds, and drawbacks	341,700
Payments in realization of the revenue:	
Land revenue, &c.	2,467,700
License taxes	32,900
Customs	209,000
Salt	353,300
Opium	1,863,200
Stamps	118,323
Mint	171,346
Post-office	543,349
Telegraph	645,934
Allowances and assignments under Treaties and Engagements	2,082,379
Allowances to district and village officers, &c.	398,200
Total of the direct claims and demands upon the revenues, including charges of collection and cost of salt and opium	£9,227,331
Charges, including interest on debt and public works, ordinary	36,238,415
Guaranteed interest on the capital of railway and other companies, in India and in England, deducting nett traffic receipts	1,242,400
	£46,708,146

Brought forward	£46,708,146
Excess of income over expenditure, excluding public works extraordinary	1,655,123
General Total	£48,363,269
Public works extraordinary	£2,761,200
Total including above	£49,469,346

Of the above total the sum of £8,199,446 is a charge in England for stores and various other heads of expenditure.

From the preceding figures it will be perceived that the gross income for 1867-68 is estimated at about six millions greater than in 1866-67, whilst the expenditure is estimated at about five millions more, practically reducing the deficit of the former years to rather less than half. The resources of India render an expenditure of one million over income of small consideration; and the present financial condition of the country is both hopeful and encouraging.

Home Accounts.—In the preceding summary of the finances of India, frequent mention has been made of the home accounts—that is, such transactions relating to India as are carried on in England. The following is a brief summary of the most important items for 1866-67 to 31st March of the latter year. The total home receipts or income amounted to £19,231,382, including a balance of £2,818,780 at the beginning of the financial year; sale of stock, £1,731,898; borrowed on security of East India bonds, £1,000,000; miscellaneous, £109,867; remittance account, £294,030; army, £109,867; bills of exchange on India, £5,613,746; bullion from India, £882,302; Indian railways and other companies. £6,780,754. Under the head of expenditure the following are the most important items:—£90,000 paid off of 4 per cent. Indian debentures; £60,000 loan to Indian branch railway. Stamp stores, post-office, mint, &c., £51,513; telegraphic arrangements, £183,182; allowances to Duleep Sing, who also receives a pension from the Indian Government, and is now resident in England, £33,167; various charges on revenue for administration, &c., £699,666; superannuation, &c., £221,440; civil furlough and absentee allowance, £79,305; effective army cost, £2,336,563; non-effective ditto, £1,048,844; public works, £67,134; interest on debt contracted in England, £1,339,782; dividends to proprietors of East India Stock, £629,970; guaranteed interest on railways, £3,043,678; various payments on account of remittances, amounts paid, prize money, &c., £1,151,128; establishment and other charges, stores, &c., of Indian Public Companies, guaranteed by the Government, £3,973,328; making a total of expenditure of £15,132,603, and leaving a balance in favour of the home accounts of £4,098,779 to be carried to the debt of 1867-68.

The estimated accounts, including the balance for 1867-68, present a total income of £19,987,494, against which is an estimated expenditure of £17,154,485, leaving an estimated surplus of £2,833,009 to be carried to the debit of 1868-69, and diminishing the surplus of the preceding year by a million and a quarter sterling. Of this amount the Abyssinian expedition is charged with about one million, so that the difference is satisfactorily accounted for. Among the items charged in the current year is £11,513 for entertaining the Sultan at the India Office during his visit to England—a sum that would form a considerable amount in the annual income of a millionnaire. One important item deserves notice. Hitherto the whole of India has been dependent for its supply of quinine on Europe, but £489 has been expended on the introduction of the Cinchona plant into India, where it now flourishes exceedingly well, and promises to save a great annual expense formerly incurred in the purchase of quinine, which the plant produces. The army estimate for 1867-68 is fixed at £3,500,000, of which £2,363,130 is to be debited to effective service. The other items of expenditure do not materially differ from those already noticed in the budget for 1866-67, with the exception of an extraordinary charge, (but anticipated in the first estimate) by representatives of late Lord Clive, amounting to £23,079.

SECRETARY OF STATE FOR INDIA IN COUNCIL,

Charles Street, Westminster.

Secretary of State, The Rt. Hon. Sir Stafford Henry Northcote, Bart., C.B., M.P., £5,000.
Under-Secretaries of State, Herman Merivale, Esq., C.B., £1,500; Lord Clinton, £1,200.
Assistant Under-Secretary of State, James Cosmo Melvill, Esq., £2,000.

COUNCIL.

Sir Henry C. Montgomery, Bart. *(Vice-President);* Lieut.-Gen. Sir Robert J. H. Vivian, K.C.B.; Charles Mills, Esq.; Sir Jas. Weir Hogg, Bart.; Elliot Macnaghten, Esq.; Ross D. Mangles, Esq.; William J. Eastwick, Esq.; Henry T. Prinsep, Esq.; Sir Frederick Currie, Bart; Col. Sir Proby T. Cautley, K.C.B.; Wm. Urquhart Arbuthnot, Esq.; Sir T. Erskine Perry, Knt. Major-Gen. William Erskine Baker; Sir George Russell Clerk, K.S.I., K.C.B.; Sir Henry Bartle Edward Frere, G.C.S.I., K.C.B.; and Lieut.-Col. Sir H. C. Rawlinson, K.C.B.
Private Secretary to the Secretary of State, Walters Northcote, Esq., £300.
Assistant Private Secretary and Précis Writer, W. H. Benthall, Esq.
Assistant Précis Writer, H. Hill, Esq.
Priv. Sec. to Lord Clinton, W. N. Sturt, Esq., £150.
Priv. Sec. to Mr. Merivale, H. G. Walpole, Esq., £150.
Clerk of the Council, John Davison, Esq.
Secretary for Military Correspondence, Major-Gen. T. T. Pears, C.B.

SECRETARIES OF DEPARTMENTS.

Financial, Thomas L. Seccombe, Esq.
Judicial and Public, Sir H. L. Anderson, K.C.S.I.
Political and Secret, J. W. Kaye, Esq.
Public Works, Railway, and Electric Telegraph, W. T. Thornton, Esq.
Revenue, Francis W. Prideaux, Esq.

ASSISTANTS.

Financial, Hon. Frederic J. Hobart.
Military, J. P. Thom, Esq.
Political, J. R. Melville, Esq.
Public Works, Railway, and Electric Telegraph, E. P. A. Thompson, Esq.
Revenue, C. B. Phillimore, H. C. Pierson, C. A. J. Mason, A. Hobhouse, G.A.F. Shadwell, R. Dickinson, H. Waterfield, and C. R. Markham, Esqs.
Chief Clerk, M. Napier, Esq.
Director of Military Funds and Chairman of Consulting Committee, T. L. Seccombe, Esq.
Statistical Reporter, Searcher of Records, and Agent

to the Administrators-General of India, Marmaduke Hornidge, Esq.
Assistant, C. C. Prinsep, Esq.
Registrar and Superintendent of Copying Clerks, William A. Franks, Esq.
Dispatch Clerk, H. Herman, Esq.
Director-Gen. Store Department, Hon. G. C. Talbot.
Chief Clerk, H. O. G. Bedford, Esq.
Supervisor of Stamps & Coinage, G. M. Parsons, Esq.
Government Director of Inland Railway Companies, Juland Danvers, Esq.
Deputy, &c., Edmund P. A. Thompson, Esq.
Government Director of Madras Irrigation and Canal Company, Wm. T. Thornton, Esq.
Librarian, Fitz-Edward Hall, Esq., D.C.L.
Reporter on the Products of India and Keeper of the Museum (in London), J. Forbes Watson, M.D.
Inspector-General of Hospitals, Sir J. Ronald Martin, C.B., F.R.S.
Surgeon-Major, J. R. Miller, M.D.
Standing Counsel, William Forsyth, Q.C.
Solicitor, Henry S. Lawford, Esq.
Geographer, John Walker, Esq.
Surveyor of Shipping, Edward Ritherdon, Esq.
Keeper of Military Records, J. S. Bailey.

AUDITOR'S DEPARTMENT.

Auditor, Major-General J. Jameson.
Principal Transport Officer, Capt. J. B. Willoughby, R.N.

The business of the Overland Troop Service is under the superintendence of Capt. W. R. Mends, R.N., C.B., the Director of Transport Service at the Admiralty. *Resident Officer at Suez,* Com. A. W. Chitty.

The above form the chiefs of the Home Department of the Indian Government.

BENGAL PRESIDENCY,

One of the three British Presidencies in India, comprising three separate divisions—the Governor-General's domain (consisting of the Punjab, Oude, the Central Provinces, and British Burmah), the North-West Provinces, and Bengal Proper. These three provinces occupy an area equal to six times the size, and a population nearly five times the amount, of Great Britain. The plain of Bengal constitutes the basin of the Lower Ganges. Bengal Proper measures about 350 miles from east to west, by an average of about 300 miles from north to south, and covers an area of about 100,000 square miles. Calcutta, the Capital of the Presidency, and, indeed, of all British India, the chief commercial city of Asia, is situated on the left bank of the Hooghly, nearly 100 miles from its mouth, in lat. 22° 35′ N., and long. 88° 30′ E. The river adjacent to the city varies in breadth from a quarter to three-quarters of a mile, and affords an anchorage in five or six fathoms of water, suitable for vessels of the largest tonnage.

THE PROVINCE OF ASSAM contains 3,000 square miles, by far the greater part of which is available for cultivation. Its vegetable productions include the finest mangoes, bamboos, and treeferns; and the articles of commercial value which are known to exist in abundance, are caoutchouc, gums of various kinds, madder, cotton, teak, oil, seeds, timber, gold, and precious stones, iron, and coal; to these may be added silk and tea, both wild and cultivated. The chief interest, however, of Assam, arises from its probable future as a great source of tea, which, promises to be at once beneficial to the country and profitable to those employed in its cultivation.

CLIMATE OF INDIA.

January.—Thermometer ranges from 52° to 65° in the shade.

February.—Thermometer 58° to 75°, beginning of the month generally cool and comfortable to Europeans, but frequently disagreeable and unhealthy about middle.

March.—Thermometer 68° to 82°.

April.—Thermometer 80° to 90°.

May.—Thermometer 85° to 98°. The most trying month of the year, the heat most oppressive, and at times almost unbearable.

June.—Thermometer frequently rises to 99°, the weather exceedingly oppressive to the last degree, and many deaths arise from sunstroke; but the periodical rains usually set in about the 15th, and the air becomes cooler.

July.—Thermometer 80° to 90°, but there is generally much rain, and the weather then becomes cool and agreeable.

August.—Thermometer 80° to 90°. Rainy weather, with gales of wind.

September.—Thermometer 75° to 88°. Rain subsides, but winds continue.

October.—Thermometer 74° to 85°. Frequent rain till about 20th.

November.—Thermometer 68° to 75°. Pleasant weather; mornings and evenings cool.

December.—Thermometer 58° to 68°. To Europeans, this and the preceding are the pleasantest months in the year; the weather is generally cool and fine.

INDIA AND BENGAL GOVERNMENT.

The following gives an account of some of the chief particulars of the Government of India generally, located centrically at Calcutta, and also of the Government of Bengal Proper.

INDIA AND BENGAL GOVERNMENT.

The Governor-General and Viceroy, The Earl of Mayo, £25,000.

Extraordinary Member, Gen. Sir W. R. Mansfield, G.C.S.I., K.C.B., Commander-in-Chief, £8,000.

First Ordinary Member, G. N. Taylor, Esq., M.C.L., £8,000.

Second Ordinary Member, Maj.-Gen. Sir H. M. Durand, K.C.S.I., C.B., £8,000.

Third Ordinary Member, H. Turner Maine, Esq., £8,000.

Fourth Ordinary Member, J. Strachey, Esq., £8,000.

Fifth Ordinary Member, Sir R. Temple, K.C.S.I., £8,000.

Extraordinary Members, The Governors of the other Presidencies when the Council assembles within their territory.

Additional Members for Making Laws and Regulations, Marajah Meerza Vegearam Guzzeeputty Raj Munca Sultan Bahadoor; Rajah Sahib Dyal Bahadoor, K.C.S.I.; D. Cowie, Esq.; J. E. C. Brandeth, Esq.; M. J. M. S. Stewart, Esq.; J. Skinner, Esq.; J. Strachey, Esq.; Baboo Prosonno Coomar Tagore, C.S.I.; Kevajeh Abdool Ghani; F. R. Cockrell, Esq.; Rajah Sheoraj Sing, C.S.I.; H. Crooke, Esq.

SECRETARIES TO THE GOVERNMENT.

HOME.—*Secretary,* E. C. Bayley, £5,000; *Under-Secretary,* J. Geoghegan, £1,500.

FINANCE.—*Secretary,* E. H. Lushington, £5,000; *Under-Secretary,* G. A. M. Batten, £1,500.

FOREIGN.—*Secretary,* W. T. Seton-Karr, £5,000; *Under-Secretary,* J. W. S. Wyllie, £1,500.

MILITARY.—*Secretary,* Col. H. W. Norman, C.B., £4,200; *Deputy-Secretary,* Lt.-Col. H. K. Buru, £1,200.

PUBLIC WORKS.—*Secretary,* Lt.-Col. Dickens, £3,000; *Under-Secretary,* Capt. E. C. S. Williams, £960.

COUNCIL OF THE LIEUT.-GOVERNOR OF BENGAL FOR MAKING LAWS AND REGULATIONS.

President, W. Grey, Esq.

Members, V. H. Schalch; Baboo Degumber Mitta; A. T. T. Peterson; Baboo Ramanak Tagore Coomar Harendra Krishna Rai Bahadoor; H. T. Prinsep; S. S. Hogg; J. B. Smith; H. L. Dampier; H. Knowles; T. Acock; Baboo PearyChaud Mittra; T. H. Cowie.

GOVERNMENT OF BENGAL.

Lieutenant-Governor, W. Grey, Esq., £10,000.

Secretary, S. C. Bayley, £3,600.

Junior Secretary, H. L. Harrison, £1,800.

Under-Secretary, A. Mackenzie, £1,200.

NORTH WESTERN PROVINCES.

Lieutenant-Governor, Sir W. Mair, K.C.S.I., £11,300.

Secretary, R. Simpson.

Junior-Secretary, C. Robertson.

Under-Secretary, P. Henvey.

PUNJAB.

Lieut.-Governor, Sir D. F. McLeod, K.C.S.I., C.B.

Secretary, J. H. Thornton.

Military Secretary, Major S. Black.

Postmaster-General, Bengal, Maj. G. M. Battye. Of North West Provinces, C. R. Dore

BENGAL ECCLESIASTICAL DEPARTMENT.

Ld.-Bp. of Calcutta, Rt. Rev. R. Milman, D.D.

Archdeacon, Ven. J. H. Pratt, M.A.

Choplain to the Ld.-Bp. Rev. M. R. Burge, M.A.

Registrar and Secretary, W. H. Abbott.

Mint Master, Major H. Hyde, £3,600.

LAW DEPARTMENT.

Chief Justice, Hon. Sir Barnes Peacock, Kt.

Judges, G. Lock, Esq.; H. O. Bayley, Esq.; J. H. Norman, Esq.; F. B. Kemp, Esq.; L. S. Jackson, Esq.; J. B. Phear, Esq.; A. G. Macpherson, Esq.; E. Jackson, Esq; W. Markley, Esq.; F. A. B. Glover, Esq.; Duarkanath Mitta; C. T. Hobhouse, Esq.

LAW OFFICERS.

Advocate-General, T. H. Cowie, Esq.

Standing Counsel, J. Graham.

Solicitor, R. F. Stock.

Remembrancer, F. R. Cockerell, C.T.

VICE-ADMIRALTY COURT.

Commissary, The Chief Justice.

Registrar, R. Bellchambers.

Marshal, The Deputy-Sheriff.

HIGH COURT OF JUDICATURE OF NORTH-WEST PROVINCES.

Chief Justice, Hon. Sir Walter Morgan, Kt.

Judges, A. Ross, W. Roberts, J. B. Pearson, C. A. Turner, and R. Sparkie, Esqs.

Advocate-General, vacant.

Registrar, J. D. Sandford, B.A.

MEDICAL ESTABLISHMENT.

Inspectors-General of Hospitals, W. A. Green and J. Murray.

MADRAS PRESIDENCY,

Another of the three Presidencies of British India, named after the city which is its seat of Government; it lies between 8° 10′—20° 30′ N. lat., and 74° 50′—86° 40′ E. long.; and contains an area of about 170,351 square miles, with a population of 23,127,900. Its most valuable product is timber, chiefly used in ship-building With this the forests abound. Rice is largely cultivated, and sugar is produced in considerable quantities ; also cotton, indigo, and tobacco. Revenue in 1865 was £6,993,100. Expenditure, £6,230,200. Value of Exports, £10,182,273. The Government is vested in a Governor, assisted by a Council of five members, forming the Executive, and nine additional members (four of whom are non-official) for the purpose of making laws and regulations.

The following are the leading Officials of the Presidency :—

COUNCIL.

Governor, Right Hon. Lord Napier, K.T.
Members, Major-Gen. W. A. MacCleverty, Commander-in-Chief; Henry Dominic Phillips; Alexander John Arbuthnot.
Additional Members for making Laws and Regulations, John Bruce Norton (Advocate-General) ; Thomas Clarke ; R. S. Ellis, C.B. ; Alexander Forrester Brown; Wm. R. Arbuthnot; John C. Loch; Sharf-ool Omrah Bahadoor, K.C.S.I.; Gajalu Lutchmenasu Chetty, C.S.I.

SECRETARIES TO GOVERNMENT.

Political, &c., Secretary, A. J. Arbuthnot.
Deputy, C. G. Walker.
Revenue-Secretary, W. Hudleston.
Deputy Secretary, F. Brandt.
Military Secretary, Major-Gen. H. Marshall.
Dep. Secretary, Col. R. Hamilton.
Public Works Secretary, Col. C. A. Orr.
Deputy Secretary, Maj. J. H. M. S. Stewart.
Legislative Assist. Secretary, J. D. Mayne.

BOARD OF REVENUE.

Members, T. Clarke ; J. D. Sim ; G. S. Forbes.
Secretary, R. A. Dalyell.
Sub-Secretary, J. Grove.
Accountant-General, F. Lushington.
Deputy do., R. W. Lodwick.
Assistant, W. J. Raynor.
Postmaster-General, Lt.-Col. A. C. Pears.
Mint Master, Col. John Carpendale.
Assay Master, Surj.-Maj. G. J. Shaw, M.D.
Assistant, H. E. Hunter.

ECCLESIASTICAL DEPARTMENT.

Bishop of Madras, Right Rev. F. Gell, D.D.
Archdeacon, Ven. T. Dealtry, M.A.
Chaplain to Bishop, Rev. O. Dene, B.A.
Registrar, Rev. R. Murphy.

LAW DEPARTMENT.

Chief Justice, Hon. Sir C. H. Scotland, Kt.
Judges, Hon. Sir Adam Bittlestone ; Wm. Holloway ; Lewis Charles Innes ; C. C. George.

MEDICAL ESTABLISHMENT.

Inspector-General, W. Mackenzie, C.B., C.S.I.
Deputy Inspector-Gens. of Hospitals, J. G. Mayer; E. G. Balfour ; J. H. Orr ; J. A. Reynolds; R. H. Rennick ; J. M. Jackson.

BOMBAY PRESIDENCY,

Another of the three British Presidencies in India. Its area (including Sinde) is about 142,042 square miles, possessing a population of about 12,890,000 persons. The administration is vested in a Governor and three Councillors, subject to the control of the Governor-General of India in Council, and eight additional members, for making laws and regulations. It has the advantage over all the other Presidencies in respect to manufacturing industry, and boasts of the richest cotton-fields in India. The revenue from all sources for the year 1865 was £9,393,160.

The following are the leading Officials of the Presidency :—

Governor, Right Hon. Sir W. R. S. V. Fitzgerald.

COUNCIL.

Members, Lt.-Gen. Lord Napier, G.C.B., G.C.S.I.; B. H. Ellis ; S. Manfield, C.S.I.
Additional Members for making Laws and Regulations, L. H. Bayler (Advocate-General); Col. W. T. Marriott, C.S.I. ; George Foggo ; Shreeniwas Raogee Rao Saheb Punt Prutinidhi ; Minguldass Nuthoobhoy ; His Highness Meer Mahomed Khan Talpoor ; Trangee Musserwanjee Patel ; Alexander Brown.

SECRETARIES OF REVENUE, &c.

Chief, F. T. Chapman.
Under-Secretary, H. G. Jacomb.
Public Works, Col. M. K. Kenedy.
Under-Secretary, Lieut. T. F. Dowden.
Political, &c., Secretary, G. Gonne.
Under-Secretary, W. Wedderburn.
Military, &c., Sec., Col. W. F. Marriott, C.S.I.
Deputy-Secretary, Major J. A. M. Macdonald.
Secretary to Council for making Laws, &c., W. Wedderburn.
Commissioner of Customs, A. F. Bellasis.
Mint Master, Lt.-Col. J. A. Ballard, C.B.
Assay Master, Surgeon-Major, W. Collum.
Accountant-General, J. L. Lushington.
Postmaster-General, Surgeon-Major E. Impey.

ECCLESIASTICAL ESTABLISHMENT.

Bishop of Bombay, Rt. Rev. H. A. Douglas, D.D.
Retired do., Rt. Rev. J. Harding, D.D.
Archdeacon, Rev. C. H. Leigh.
Registrar, J. P. Bickersteth.

LAW DEPARTMENT.

Chief Justice, Hon. Sir Richard Couch.
Judges, Hon. Sir Joseph Arnould; H. Newton; M. R. Westrop; H. P. St. G. Tucker; A. B. Warden ; James Gibbs ; Sir Charles Sargent.

MEDICAL ESTABLISHMENT.

Inspector-General of Hospitals, F. T. Arnott.
Deputy Inspectors, A. Wright; T. Ward; W. Thom; S. M. Pelly.

Dates of some Events in the History of British India.

Sir Francis Drake's Expedition	1579	First Burmese War	1824
First Adventure from England	1591	Opening of Trade with India	1833
First Charter to London Company	1600	Afghan War	1838
Factories Established at Surat	1612	Cabul Massacre	1842
First English Ambassador (Sir T. Roe)	1615	Scinde Annexed	1843
Madras made a Presidency	1652	Sikh War, Battle of Aliwal	1846
Bombay Ceded to Charles II.	1662	The Punjab formally Annexed	1849
Calcutta Purchased	1698	First Indian Railway	1853
Clive takes Arcot	1751	Mutiny Commenced at Barrackpore	1857
Black-hole Atrocity, 20th June	1756	Cawnpore Surrendered to Nana Sahib	1857
Tippoo Saib Killed at Seringapatam	1799	East India Company Ceased to Govern, 1 Sept.	1858
Battle of Assaye, 23rd Sept.	1803	Lord Mayo appointed Governor-General	1868
Sepoy Mutiny at Vellore	1806		

ADEN,

A very important peninsula of Arabia, 118 miles from the entrance to the Red Sea, taken possession of by Great Britain in 1839, situate 12° 47′ N. lat., and 45° 9′ E. long., comprises an area of between 18 and 20 miles, and is doubtless of volcanic origin, consisting chiefly of a range of hills, which rise from 1,000 to 1,760 feet high. It enjoys almost perpetual sunshine, a cloudy day being very rare. It is a place of considerable note, resulting from its situation between Asia and Africa, resembling that of Gibraltar, between Europe and Africa. It is strongly fortified and well garrisoned. Its excellent port and abundant supply of water render it a valuable station *en route* from India to Europe. The population is estimated at 50,000. The annual imports and exports in transit amount to about £1,000,000.

Political Resident, Lieut.-Col. Sir Wm. L. Merewether, C.B., K.S.I., Bengal Staff Corps.

Officiating do., Lieut. Henry B. Abbott, 109 Foot.

Commanding the Troops, Col. Julius A. R. Raines, C.B., 95th Regiment.

Brigade Majors, Major E. L. Scott, 30th Bombay N.I., and Major H. Y. Beale, 12th Bombay, N.I.

Assistant Commissary-General, Capt. J. Clements, Bombay Staff Corps.

Ordnance Deputy Assistant Commissary, J. Osborne.

Examining Engineer, Capt. Harry Pym, R.E.

Dep. Inspect.-Gen. of Hospitals, Henry C. Foss.

Chaplain, Rev. Wm. Henry Cummins, M.A. (Bombay Establishment).

CEYLON,

An island in the Indian Ocean, to the southeast of the peninsula of Hindostan, is situated between 5° 55′—9° 51′ N. lat., and 79° 41′—81° 54′ E. long.; its area is about 24,700 square miles, or 15,808,000 acres. Its greatest length is from north to south, 266 miles; and greatest width 140 miles, from East to West. Many delusions as to its size appear to have existed in very early days: it was visited by the Greeks, Romans, and Venetians. In 1505 the Portuguese formed settlements on the west and south of the island, but were dispossessed in the next century by the Dutch. In 1795 the British took possession of the Dutch Settlements on the island, and annexed them to the Presidency of Madras; but six years after, in 1801, Ceylon was erected into a separate colony. In 1866 it contained a population of 2,088,122, of whom the most numerous were the Singhalese, descendants of those Colonists from the Valley of the Ganges who first settled in the island, B.C. 543.

Gross amount of Public Revenue in 1866	£962,874
Public Expenditure	917,670
Public Debt	450,000
Value of total Imports (including Bullion and Specie, £1,443,877) was	4,961,061
Total Imports from United Kingdom	1,390,687
Value of total Exports (including Bullion and Specie, £516,206)	3,586,454
Total Exports to United Kingdom	2,385,126

Total tonnage of vessels, exclusive of coasting trade (1,032,194 British, and 150,231 Foreign vessels), 1,182,425.

Principal Imports in 1866: Rice, 3,777,320 bushels; Coal and Coke, 65,671 tons; Fish, salted and dried, 70,190 cwt.; Grain (Paddy) 747,959.

Principal Exports: Areca Nuts, 94,584 cwt.; Cinnamon, 899,484 lbs.; Coffee (Plantation) 704,189 cwt.; Ditto (Native) 195,291 cwt.; Cotton manufactures, 3,441 packages, and 183,767 pieces; Cocoa-nut Oil, 83,801 cwt.; Spirits (Arrack), 137,359 gallons; Tobacco (unmanufactured), 25,143 cwt.

The Government is administered by a Governor, aided by an Executive Council of five members, and a Legislative Council of fifteen, including the Executive Council. Every measure and every question relative to the revenue of the island must be debated, must first receive the license of the Governor.

*†*Governor and Commander-in-Chief*, Sir Hercules G. R. Robinson, Colombo, £7,000.

Private Secretary, Henry C. Stewart, Esq., £300.

Aide-de-Camp, Capt. Hon. E. R. Bourke.

*†*Commander of the Forces*, Lt.-Gen. Studholme J. Hodgson.

*†*Colonial Secretary*, W. G. Gibson, Esq., £2,000.

*†*Prin. Assist. Do.*, F. B. Templer, Esq., £1,000.

Second Ditto, James Swan, Esq., £600.

*†*Treasurer*, George Vane, Esq., £1,500.

*†*Auditor-General*, R. J. Callander, Esq., £1,500.

Director of Public Instruction, J. S. Laurie, Esq.

Registrar-General, W. J. MacCarthy, Esq., £850.

Post-Master-General, H. Gillman, Esq., £800.

Inspector of Post Offices, H. Trotter, Esq., £500.

Sup. of Telegraph, W. H. St. Albin, Esq., £1,020.

Inspector of Prisons, Hon. J. T. Fitzmaurice, R.N.

†*Surveyor-Gen.*, Capt. A. B. Fyers, R.E., £1,200.

Assistant Surveyors, W. R. Noad, £750; J. Winzer, Esq., £650; G. A. Vetch, Esq., £600; J. J. Grinlington, Esq., £550; H. C. Parke, Esq., £500; J. E. Daveran, Esq., £450; J. O'Donnell, Esq., £400; T. S. Reynolds, Esq., £300.

Civil Engineer and Commissioner of Roads, W. E. Molesworth, Esq., £1,500, and £300 as *Director of Railways*.

Office Assistant, J. A. Caley, Esq., C.E., £750.

Com. of Pioneer Corps, Capt. J. Wilkinson, £600.

Architect, J. G. Smithers, Esq., £750.

Financial Assistant, R. Tatham, Esq., £750.

Provincial Assistant, Western Province, H. Byrne, Esq., C.E., £1,000.

Do. Central Province N. H. A. Evatt, Esq., £1,000.

Do. Southern Prov., J. F. Churchill, C.E., £800.

Do. Central Prov. N., A. Campbell, Esq., £800.

Do. North-West. Prov. A. C. Folkard, Esq., C.E., £600

Do. Nor. and East. Prov., J. D. Young, Esq., £600.

†*Customs, Principal Collector*, T. B. Stephen, Esq., £1,200.

Deputy Collector, W. D. Wright, Esq., £800.

Collector Southern Prov., W. Halliley, Esq., £700.

Do. Northern Do., H. S. Russell, Esq. (Gov. Agent).

Do. Eastern Do., H. E. O'Grady, Esq. (Gov. Agent).

Master Attendant, Colombo, J. Donnan, Esq., £600.

Do., Galle, D. W. Blyth, Esq., £600.

†*Government Agent, Western Province*, C. P. Layard, Esq., £1,500.

* *Executive Council;* † *Legislative Council.*

---

* In preparing the following accounts of the different Colonies and Possessions, the latest Government Returns have been consulted; in many instances the Sections have been revised by gentlemen officially connected with the Colonies: much information has been obtained from the "Colonial Office List," also from Local Directories, Gazetteers, and Almanacks.

Govt. Ag. N.W. Province, E. L. Mitford, Esq., £1,200.
Do. Southern Do., W. Morris, Esq., £1,400.
Do. Eastern Do., H. E. O'Grady, Esq., £1,200.
Do. Northern Do., H. S. Russell, Esq., £1,500.
†*Do. Central Do.*, P.W. Braybrooke, Esq., £1,300.
Temple Land Commissioners, P. W. Braybrooke (*ex officio*), and W. H. Wodehouse, Esq.

JUDICIAL ESTABLISHMENT.

Chief Justice, Sir E. S. Creasy, Knt., £2,500.
Senior Puisne Judge, C. Temple, Esq., £1,800.
Junior Do., C. H. Stewart, Esq., £1,800.
†Queen's Advocate, R. F. Morgan, Esq., £1,500;
Deputy Do., T. Berwick, Esq., £1000.
Deputy, Southern Circuit, C. E. Temple, Esq.
Registrar of SupremeCourt,W.J. Carver,Esq.,£600.

MIDLAND CIRCUIT.

District Judge of Colombo, G. Lawson, Esq., £1,200.
Commissioner of Requests and District Judge of Kandy, T. L. Gibson, Esq., £1,200.
District Judges, Commissioners of Requests, &c., J. W. W. Birch, Esq., £800; A. Y. Adams, Esq., £600; J. H. De Saram, Esq., £600; P. Templar, Esq., £600; F. C. Williaford, Esq., £600.
Police Magistrate, Colombo, D. E. De Saram, Esq., £600.

SOUTHERN CIRCUIT.

District Judges, Commissioners of Requests, and Police Magistrates, C. P. Walker, Esq., £1,200; C. H. De Saram, Esq., £800; G. W. Patterson, Esq., £600; H. Pole, Esq., £600; J. F. Dixon, Esq., £600; J. Parsons, Esq., £800 (also *Assistant Agent*); J. W. Gibson, Esq., £350.

NORTHERN CIRCUIT.

District Judge and Joint Commissioner of Requests at Jaffna, J. Morphew, Esq., £1,000.
District Judges, Commissioners of Requests, and Police Magistrates, A. H. Roozmalecocq, Esq., £800; L. Liesching, Esq., £800; W. C. Twynam, Esq., £800; *Assist. Gov. Ag.*, F. Jayetillike, Esq., £600; J. B. A. Bailey, Esq., £600; F. H. Campbell, Esq., £450; A. R. Dawson, Esq., £350; F. C. Fisher, Esq., £350; G. W. Templar, Esq., £350; R. Massie, Esq., £350; C. R. Curgenven, Esq., £600, (also *Assistant Government Agent*).

MEDICAL DEPARTMENT.

Principal Civil Medical Officer and Inspector of Hospitals, W. P. Charsley, Esq., M.D., £1,200, and consultation fees.
Colonial Surgeons, P. D. Anthonioz, Esq., M.D., and H. Dickman, Esq., £400 each.

POLICE.

Chief Superintendent,—vacant.
Acting Superintendent, G. W. R. Campbell, Esq., £1,200, and £288 allowances.

ECCLESIASTICAL ESTABLISHMENT.

Bishop of Colombo, Rt. Rev. Piers C. Claughton, D.D., £2,000, and £2 5s. per day travelling allowances.
Registrar of the Diocese, F. J. De Saram, Esq.
Archdeacon of Colombo, Rev. E. Mooyaart, M.A., also *Colonial Chaplain*.
Colonial Chaplains, Church of England, Ven. Archdeacon Mooyaart, £700; Revs. S. O. Glennie, £700; G. Schrader, £600; J. B. Bailey, £800; A. P. Lovekin, £700; W. F. Kelly, £200; S. W. Dias, £400; S. Nicholas, £300; S. Ondaatje, £250; E. C. La-Brooy, £300; A. Mendis, £125; C. Sennanayeke, £125. *Scotch Presbyterian*, Revs. J. K. Clarke, £450; J. Watts, £450; C. Murson, £450; A. Young, £450.

HONG KONG ("FRAGRANT STREAMS"),

An island situate off the south-eastern coast of China, at the mouth of the Canton river, between 22° 9' — 22° 1' N. lat. and 114° 5' — 114° 18' E. long. It is about 11 miles long and four wide, and comprises an area of 32 square miles, with a population, in 1866, of 115,098. It is separated from the mainland of China by a narrow strait (Ly-ee-moon Pass); the opposite peninsula, Kowloon, was ceded to Great Britain in 1861, and now forms part of Hong Kong. Hong Kong is one of those islands called by the Portuguese "Ladrones" or "Thieves," from the notorious habits of its old inhabitants. The colony, which is described as exceedingly beautiful, possessing one of the finest harbours in the world, surrounded by picturesque hills rising between 3,000 and 4,000 feet high, blending the wild scenery of Scotland with the beauty of Italy, was first ceded to Great Britain in January, 1841, which cession was confirmed by the Treaty of Nankin in 1842, and ratified in 1843. It is a military and naval station for the protection of our commerce; its excellent harbour affording convenient, safe, and commodious anchorage for our shipping. It is the centre of trade in many kinds of goods—chiefly opium, sugar, flour, oil, amber, cotton, ivory, betel, sandal wood, &c. As it is a free port, it is impossible to give a correct return of imports and exports. In itself, it has neither agriculture nor manufactures, and produces nothing either for export or consumption; indeed it is scarcely capable of affording sufficient provision for its inhabitants for a single day.

	£
In 1866 the gross amount of public revenue was	160,226
Public expenditure	196,009
Amount of public debt	15,625

The total tonnage of vessels, exclusive of coasting trade, was (1,047,447 British and 843,834 Foreign) 1,891,281.

The Government is administered by a Governor, aided by an Executive Council of four members, together with a Legislative Council of 9 members. There is a large police force in the colony, numbering 650 men, Chinese, Sikhs, and Europeans.

†Gov. and Com.-in-Chief, and Vice-Admiral, Sir R. G. MacDonnell, C.B., £5,000.
Private Secretary and A.-D.-C., Lieut. Francis Brinkley, R.A., £250.
Aide-de-Camp, Capt. J. T. B. Mayne.
†*Chief Justice*, Hon. John Smale, £2,500.
†Col. Sec. vacant, £1,500(C. Smith, Esq., acting).
Chief Clerk do. L. D'Almada e Castro, £500.
†*Judge of Summary Jurisdiction Court*,Henry John Ball, £1,500.
†Attorney-General, Hon. J. Pauncefote, £1,000.
†Colonial Treasurer, Hon. F. Forth, £1,000.
†Auditor-General, Hon. W. H. Rennie, £1,000.
Postmaster-General, F. W. Mitchell, £800.
Colonial Surgeon, J. Ivor Murray, M.D., £700.
Officer Commanding Troops, Major-Gen. Brinker.
Postmaster, Yokohama, J. Simpson, £500.
Master of the Mint, Thos. W. Kinder, Esq.,£1400.
Superint. of Bullion Office, C. L. Davies, Esq.,£800.
Assayer, C. Tookey, Esq., £800.
Superint. Coining Departmt.,F.M. Allen, Esq.,£800.
Do. Melting Departmt., F. A. Manning, Esq.,£800.
Bp. Victoria, Rt. Rev. C. R. Alford, D.D., £1,000.
Colonial Chaplain, Rev. W. R. Beach, £800.

---

* *Executive Council.*   † *Legislative do. ex officio.*

LABUAN,

A district of the Malayan Archipelago, is an island situated on the north-west coast of Borneo (from which it is about six miles distant), in 5° 14′ N. lat., and 115° 19′ E. long., comprising an area of 45 square miles, and possessing, in 1865, a population of 2,785 inhabitants. It was ceded to Great Britain in 1846, in consequence of the piracies of the Sultan of Borneo. It has a fine port, and there are no duties on exports or imports; the expense of its establishment being paid for chiefly out of the Imperial funds. The mines, which produce coal of good quality, and abundant in quantity, are leased to the Labuan Coal Company under certain stipulations; the quantity raised in 1865 was 11,830 tons. The gross amount of local revenue in 1866 was £7,370, and expenditure £6,960, the difference between revenue and expenditure being voted annually by the Imperial Parliament.

	£
Value of total Imports (including Bullion and Specie, £11,601)	109,135
Imports from United Kingdom	1,209
Value of total Exports in 1866, as far as they are complete	58,294
Total tonnage of vessels, exclusive of the coasting trade (34,327 British, 3,035 Foreign), 37,362.	

The trade of Labuan consists in distributing the products of the island and adjacent country—beeswax, camphor, hides, birds'-nests, and trepang—to Singapore, China, and other places in the same seas. Cotton goods and hardware are received from Singapore; pepper, sago, &c., from Borneo.

The government is vested in a Governor and Legislative Council.

Governor, Commander-in-Chief and Acting Consul-General in Borneo, J. Pope Hennessy, F.G.S., F.R.S.A., £800.
Private Secretary, B. A. Cody.
Clerk to Council, James A. St. John.
Bishop, vacant.
Secretary to Government and Auditor, J. G. Slade, £300.
**Treasurer and Police Magistrate,* H. Low, £500.
**Colonial Surgeon,* J. G. Treacher, £500.
Colonial Chaplain, Rev. J. Moreton, £350.
Superintendent of Convicts, James A. St. John.
**Harbourmaster and Portmaster,* C. C. de Crespigny, £300.

MAURITIUS; OR, ISLE OF FRANCE,

An island lying in the Indian Ocean, between 57° 17′–57° 46′ E. long. and S. lat. 19° 58′–20° 32′, comprising an area of 708 square miles, including the small dependencies of Seychelles or Mahé Islands, Rodrigues, &c., forming a group of 29 islands. The population at the last census (1861) was 310,050. The Mauritius was discovered by the Portuguese in 1507, who held possession thereof during the whole of that (16th) century. The Dutch were the first who made any settlement there in 1598, named the island Mauritius, in honour of their prince Maurice. In 1710 it was abandoned by them, and taken possession of by the French. During the last war with France it was a source of great mischief to our merchant vessels and Indiamen, from the facility with which sorties were made from it by French men-of-war and privateers. The British Government determined upon an expedition for its capture, which was effected by General Abercrombie

in 1810, and it has ever since remained a British possession. The surface of the island is in great part volcanic; its coast being fringed by extensive coral reefs, pierced here and there by the estuaries of small streams. Its principal towns are Port Louis, the capital (near which the celebrated Peter Botte mountain rears its head, sustaining on its apex a gigantic cone), and Grande Port. Port Louis comprises a spacious harbour, provided with an inner basin called the Fanfaron, wherein vessels can take refuge during the hurricanes which frequently occur here with fearful violence.

	£
Amount of Public Revenue, in 1866	639,577
Public Expenditure	700,048
Public Debt	1,000,000
Value of total Imports (including Bullion and Specie, £125,951)	2,227,093
Value of Imports from United Kingdom	499,100
Value of total Exports (including Bullion and Specie, £24,000)	2,525,805
Total Exports to United Kingdom	718,568
Total tonnage of vessels, exclusive of coasting trade (433,112 British, 175,044 Foreign), 608,156.	

The principal Imports in 1866 were:—Rice, 1,366,643 cwt.; Grain (except wheat), value of £141,208; Wheat, 118,128 bags; Cotton Manufactures, 5,084,583 yards plain, 5,504,179 yards coloured; Guano, 18,139 tons; Wine, valued at £104,278.

The principal Exports in 1866 were:—Rum, 475,048 gallons; Sugar, 2,480,385 quintals, valued at £2,277,035; Cotton Manufactures, plain, 1,455,308 yards.

The Government is administered by a Governor, aided by an Executive Council of three members, and a Legislative Council of 19 members; 8 official and 11 non-official, the latter chosen from the landed proprietors and principal merchants of the island.

*†*Governor and Commander-in-Chief,* Port Louis, Sir Henry Barkly, K.C.B., £7,000.
*†*Private Secretary,* Arthur Barkly, £300.
Aide-de-Camp, Captain Foll, £256.
Major-General on the Staff, General Milman, Commander of Forces.
Assistant Military Secretary, Colonel Milman.
Deputy Quartermaster-Gen., Lieut.-Col. P. Bayly.
Commanding Officer, R.A., Lt.-Col. Thring, £720.
Do. R. Eng., Col. Menzies.
Secretary to the Councils, C.M.DeJoux, £400 to £600.
*†*Colonial Secretary,* F. Bedingfield, £1,500.
†*Colonial Treasurer,* W. W. R. Kerr, £1,200.
†*Auditor-General,* E. Newton, £1,000.
†*Collector, Inter. Revenue,* E. B. Andrews, £1,000.
†*Collector of Customs,* H. Cooper, £1,000.
Colonial Postmaster, G. R. Saltwell, £625.
†*Protector of Immigrants,* H. N. D. Beyts, £1,000.
Chief Judge, Hon. C. F. Shand, £2,000.
First Puisne do., Hon. N. G. Bestel, £1,200.
Second ditto, Hon. G. B. Colin, £1,200.
Master of Supreme Court, V. Esnouf, £1,000.
Registrar do., F. Herchenroder, £900.
*†*Proctor and Advocate-General,* Hon. W. G. Dickson, £1,500.
*†*Substitute do.,* S. J. Douglas, £800.
Crown Solicitor, F. R. Bradford, £540.
Bishop, vacant.
Roman Catholic Bishop, M. Hankinson, D.D., £720.
Engineer (Railways), M. Connal, C.E., £750.
Locomotive Superintendent, W. Scott, £600.
Telegraph Superintendent, W. Eaton, £600.

---

* *Legislative Council.*

* *Executive Council.* † *Legislative do. ex officio.*

STRAITS SETTLEMENTS.

These Settlements, which comprise Singapore, Penang, and Malacca, were transferred from the control of the Indian Government to that of the Secretary of State for the Colonies in April, 1867, by an Order in Council, under the provisions of the Act 29-30 Vic. c. 115.

SINGAPORE is an island, situated off the southern extremity of the Malay peninsula, from which it is separated by a narrow strait about three-quarters of a mile in width; its length is about 27 miles, and its breadth 11 miles; and comprises an area of about 275 square miles. It was taken possession of by Sir Stamford Raffles in 1819. By virtue of a treaty it was first made subordinate to Bencoolen, in Sumatra, and in 1823 was placed under the Government of Bengal, but subsequently was incorporated with Penang and Malacca, under the Government of the Incorporated Settlement. The seat of Government is the town of Singapore, situate in lat. 1° 16′ N., and long. 103° 53′ E.

PENANG, or PRINCE OF WALES ISLAND, is an island about 14 miles long and 9 broad, situated off the west coast of the Malayan peninsula, at the entrance to the Straits of Malacca, ceded to the Government of India in 1786 by the Rajah of the neighbouring territory, Kedah. The climate is healthy and well adapted for the cultivation of spices, sugar-cane, and tapioca. The chief town is George Town, situate in 5° 24′ N. lat., and 100° 21′ E. long.

MALACCA, an extensive territory situated on the western coast of the peninsula between Singapore and Penang, comprises an area of about 1,000 square miles; it is one of the oldest European Settlements in the East, having been taken possession of by the Portuguese in 1511, and held by them till 1641, when the Dutch, after repeated attempts, succeeded in driving them out. It remained under the government of the Dutch until 1795, when it was taken possession of by the English, and held by them till 1818, when it was restored to the Dutch, and finally became a British possession, in pursuance of the Treaty with Holland, 17th March, 1824. In Malacca the Malays are the chief part of the population, the Chinese forming about one-sixth thereof. The Chinese Colonists include some of the most wealthy and intelligent of the merchants in the Straits, and are specially distinguished by the title of "Baba." The chief town is Malacca.

The sources from which the revenue is raised are alike in all the three Stations, consisting chiefly of a stamp duty, the exclusive privilege of preparing and retailing opium for smoking, the sale of spirits, and other exciseable commodities; land also bears its proportionate burden. The exports comprise—gutta percha, gambier, black pepper, india-rubber, buffalo horns, canes, sugar, rice, sago, tea, coffee, opium, &c.

The Straits Settlements in the aggregate comprise an area of 1095 square miles.

Gross amount of Public Revenue in 1866, including loan £144,366	£376,776
Gross Public Expenditure in 1866, including repayment of loan £142,288..	287,864
Value of total Imports	9,700,195
Imports from United Kingdom	2,026,425
Value of total Exports	9,924,088
Value of Exports to United Kingdom	1,248,829
Total tonnage of Vessels, including the Coasting trade, 1,897,279.	

The Government consists of a Governor, assisted by an Executive Council of 9 members, and a Legislative Council of 10 members, nominated by the Crown, including in each the Lieut.-Governors of the several settlements.

*†*Governor and Com.-in-Chief*, Col. Sir H. St. George Ord, C.B., R.E., £5,000.

Pri. Sec. & Clerk of Coun., H. F. Plow, Esq., £500.

Com. R. Eng., Capt. C. J. Moysey.

*†*Col. Sec.*, Lt.-Col. R. Macpherson, R.A., £1,800.

Chief Clerk, W. S. Leicester, Esq., £500.

*†*Treasurer, Commis. of Stamps, and Account.-Gen. of Supreme Court*, W. W. Williams, Esq., £1,000.

Chief Clerk, J. B. Leicester, Esq., £390.

Deputy Commissioner, G. Norris, Esq., £360.

*†*Auditor-General*, C. J. Irving, Esq., £1,000.

Chief Clerk, E. E. Isemonger, Esq., £500.

Surveyor-General, D. Quinton, Esq., £930.

†*Colonial Engineer and Controller of Convicts*, Hon. Major J. F. A. McNair, £1,400.

Deputy do., F. A. Sheppard, Esq., £760.

Assistant do., W. D. Baylis, Esq., £300.

Colonial Surgeon (Acting), J. Rose, Esq., £1,100.

Assist. do., &c. (do.), H. L. Randall, Esq., £600.

Colonial Chaplain, Rev. O. J. Waterhouse, £800.

Harbour Master and Registrar of Exports and Imports, &c., Lieut. Henry Burn, late I. N., £850.

Acting Postmaster-Gen., W. Cuppage, Esq., £500.

Commissioner of Police, S. Dunman, Esq., £1,150.

Do. Singapore, C. B. Waller, Esq., £500.

†*Chief Justice*, Sir P. B. Maxwell, Kt., £2,500.

Registrar, C. Baumgarten, Esq., £1,150.

Senior Clerk, G. W. Lecerf, Esq., £570.

*†*Attorney-General*, Thos. Braddell, Esq., £1,000.

Police Magistrates, J. D. Vaughan, Esq., and F. H. Gottlieb, Esq., acting, £850 each.

Judge of Court of Requests, vacant, £1,500.

Coms. do., F. H. Gottlieb and A. R. Ord, acting, £570 each.

PENANG.

Lt.-Gov., Georgetown, Hon. Lieut.-Col. A. E. H. Anson, £1,800.

Assist Treas. & Col. of Stamps, P. Jones, Esq., £570.

Assistant Engineer and Superintendent of Convicts, J. M. R. Magalhaens, £350.

Chaplain, Rev. J. Mackay, £800.

Assistant Surgeon (Acting) J. B. King, Esq., £1,000.

Harbour-Master and Registrar of Exports and Imports, &c., Lieut. H. Ellis, late I. N., £650.

Assistant Postmaster, A. E. Dodwell, Esq., £400.

Jud. of Sup. Court, Hon. Sir W. Hackett, Kt., £1,900.

Registrar, P. B. Maxwell, Esq., £1,050.

Senior Clerk, W. E. Maxwell, Esq., £570.

Solicitor-General, D. Logan, Esq., £500.

Police Magistrate, and Commissioner of Court of Requests, Hon. C. B. Plunket, £700.

Do. do., Province Wellesley, Lt. D. T. Hatchell, £700.

MALACCA.

*†*Lieut-Governor*, Hon. W. Cairns, £1500.

Assistant Treasurer, Collector of Stamps, and Assistant Postmaster, J. Doveree, Esq., £350.

Assistant Surveyor, vacant, £570.

Assistant Engineer and Superintendent of Convicts, C. A. Evans, Esq., £420.

Chaplain, Rev. G. F. Hose, £700.

Assist. Surg. (Acting), A. C. Maingay, Esq., £720.

Senior Clerk of Supreme Court, and Clerk of Court of Requests, W. Rodyk, Esq., £685.

Police Magist. and Com. of Court of Requests, Capt. A. R. Ord; Capt. F. L. Playfair *(Acting)* £700.

*   *Executive Council.*
†   *Official Members of Legislative Council.*

THIS vast territory, situated in North America, lies principally in a NE. and SW. direction, between 57° and 91° W. long., and 41° 30′ and 52° N. lat., and comprises a total area of 377,075 square miles. It consists of the several provinces of Ontario, Quebec, Nova Scotia, and New Brunswick, incorporated in one Dominion in the year 1867 (30 Vict. cap. 3). It is said to have been discovered by Sebastian Cabot in 1497. The French took possession of the country in 1525, and founded the first Settlement (Quebec) in 1608. In 1759 Quebec succumbed to the British forces under General Wolfe, and in 1763 the whole territory of Canada was ceded to Great Britain by the Treaty of Paris of that year. The Executive Government and authority is vested by the above Act in the Governor General, assisted by a Privy Council. The Legislative power is a Parliament, consisting of the Queen, an Upper House, styled the Senate, and a House of Commons. The Senate consists of 72 members, summoned thereto by the Governor-General—24 for Ontario, 24 for Quebec, and 24 for the Maritime Provinces of Nova Scotia and New Brunswick—to which may be added, by precept from the Crown, six additional members, two for each of the foregoing divisions. The House of Commons consists of 181 members, chosen every five years at longest; 82 being elected for Ontario, 65 for Quebec, 19 for Nova Scotia, and 15 for New Brunswick. The Act also provides for the future admission of the Colonies of Newfoundland, Prince Edward's Island, and British Columbia, or any of them, into the Union. Ottawa, on the river of that name, is the capital of the Canadian Union, and contains the legislative and government offices and buildings.

The timber trade, the original occupation of the people, is still the most valuable of its commerce, although fast yielding to that of agriculture; the timber and wood are principally supplied by the Valley of the Ottawa, the white or Weymouth pine being considered of most value. The value of the wood exported in 1866-67, was £2,789,729, of which that sent to Great Britain was worth £1,377,956: the quantity reserved for home consumption, as ship and house building, fuel, &c., will considerably more than double the above figures as to the total value of the wood supplied by the forests of Canada. The Fisheries of Ontario and Quebec, yielding in the total export of fish and oil, in 1866-67, £950,000, are deserving of notice as a branch of industry. The mineral resources of the country are scarcely yet developed: a great part, however, especially the shores of Lake Superior, is valuable for its mineral products, such as iron, zinc, lead, copper (a large supply of this mineral being found on the banks of Lake Huron, the export value of which, in 1866, amounted to £68,600), silver, gold, cobalt, &c., and sandstone, limestone, slate, and marbles of nearly every imaginable colour. An extraordinary export trade in mineral oil, "Petroleum," has been created. A large consumption also takes place in the Colony. During the last twenty years the agriculture of Canada has made vast progress, mostly in Ontario; the richest soil is found in connection with the Erie Peninsula. The annual average return for the whole Colony is 20 bushels per acre of wheat. The climate generally is the greatest obstruction to agriculture. Between the years 1841 and 1851 the agricultural productions of Canada increased 400 per cent.; in the latter year they were valued at £9,000,000, but in 1859 the wheat crop alone was estimated at 25,000,000 bushels, worth £4,500,000: the exports of farm produce are about equally divided between Great Britain and the States; Montreal, Toronto, and Quebec being the great centres of distribution. Kingston occupies a relation to the trade on the Lakes, similar to that of Quebec in regard to the sea; Toronto being second only to Kingston in its share of this large trade. Montreal commands a vast overland system of communication by canal and railway, both with Canada and the Eastern and Western States of the Union.

The following are some of the most interesting statistics in respect to the Dominion in 1866-67, the returns being made up to June 30, 1867.

Total value of Exports, including Bullion and Specie	£12,983,085
Value of Exports, including Bullion and Specie to the United Kingdom	4,008,370
Total value of Imports, including Bullion and Specie	16,806,157
Value of Imports from the United Kingdom, including Bullion and Specie	8,835,412
Gross amount of Public Revenue for the Four Provinces, in 1866	3,168,476
Gross amount of Public Expenditure for the Four Provinces in 1866	3,045,437
Gross amount of Public Debt for the Four Provinces in 1866	14,279,730

The principal Imports for the year 1866 were, coals and coke, 220,276 tons; Indian corn, 2,075,834 bushels; flour, 81,945 barrels; wheat, 2,011,416 bushels; cottons valued at £1,489,494; woollens valued at £1,492,122; silks, satins, &c., valued at £246,785; salt, 1,869,754 bushels; sugar (unrefined), 333,673 cwt.; molasses, 2,070,614 gallons; tallow, 2,069,754 lbs.; tea, 6,775,501 lbs.

The principal Exports were, barley and rye, 6,355,191 bushels; oats, 4,450,102 bushels; peas, 1,549,519 bushels; wheat, 2,339,588 bushels; flour, 855,558 barrels; white pine, 450,950 tons; red pine, 85,638 tons; horses, 27,811; cattle (horned) 146,641; sheep, 167,633; eggs, 1,811,100; butter, 93,293 cwt.; wool, 1,784,733 lbs.

Estimated population in 1868, 3,879,885.

The following afford particulars in reference to the Government, &c., of the country.

CIVIL ESTABLISHMENT.

Gov.-Gen. Rt. Hon., Sir John Young, Bt.,£10,000.
Governor's Secretary, Denis Godley, £750.
Prov. A.-D.-C., Col. Irvine, £500.
Mil. Sec., Lieut.-Col. Hon. R. Monck, £800.
A.-D.-C., Capt. W. L. Pemberton,

Privy Council.

President of Council,
Minister of Justice & Attorney-General, Hon. Sir J. A. MacDonald, K.C.B., D.C.L.
Min. of Militia, Hon. Sir G. E. Cartier, C.B., Bt.
Minister of Customs, Hon. S. L. Tilley, C.B.
Minister of Finance, Hon. Jno. Rose.
Min. of Pub. Works, Hon. W. McDougall, C.B.
Min. of Inland Rev., (vacant).
Sec. of State for the Prov., Hon. A. G. Archibald.
Min. of Marine & Fisheries, Hon. Ptr. Mitchell.
Postmaster-General, Hon. Alex. Campbell.
Minister of Agriculture, Hon. Jean C. Chapais.
Sec. of State of Canada, Superin.-Gen. of Indian Affrs., & Reg.-Gen., Hon. H. L. Langevin, C.B.
Receiver General, Hon. Edw. Kenny.

£1,250 each.

Clerk of Privy Council, Wm. H. Lee, £500.

Military.

Lt. Gen. Com. Forces B.N.A., Lt. Gen. Sir C. Ash Windham, K.C.B., Montreal.
Military Secretary, Lt. Col. Earle, £346.

A.-D.-C., Captain J. Hudson, Lt. R. C. Hare.
Maj.-Gen., J. J. Bissett, C.B.
A.D.C., Lieut. Fitz George.
Maj. of Brigade, Capt. C. Parsons.
Major-Gen. H. W. Stisted, C.B., Commander of Ontario and Toronto.
A.-D.-C., Capt. E. J. Fryer.
Maj. of Brigade, Capt. C. Parsons.
Comm. Off. Art., Lt.-Cl. G. L. Chandler, *Quebec.*
       Lt.-Cl. F. R. Glanville, *Kingston.*
       Col. F. G. Northall, *Montreal.*
       Col. R. P. Radcliffe, *Toronto.*
Comm. Off., Eng., Col. C. E. Ford, *Montreal.*
       Col. E. F. Bomchile, *Quebec.*
       Lt.-Col. Hassard, *Toronto.*
Dep.-Adj.-Gen., Col. J. E. Thackwell.
Assist.-Adj.-Gen. Lt. Col. W. Lyons.
Dep.-Q.-M.-G., Col. C. J. Wolseley.
Asst.-Q.-M.-G. Lt.-Col. Sir H. M. Havelock, C.B.
Adj.-Gen. of Militia, Col. Macdougall, £1,000.
Dep.-Adj.-Gen. of Prov. of Quebec,
      Ontario, Lt.-Col. W. Powell, £560.
Town Major, Quebec, Capt. J. Pope.
    ,,   ,, *Montreal*, Capt. P. Geraghty.
    ,,   ,, *Kingston*, Capt. E. Mackay,
Naval Storekeeper, D. Taylor, R.N., *Kingston.*

The Mercantile Marine, according to the returns of 1867, includes 5,822 vessels of all classes, representing an aggregate measurement of 776,343 tons; 983 vessels having a provincial, and 4,389 an imperial register. This fleet was manned by crews numbering in all 37,235 men; of whom 3,192 belonged to Ontario; 8,548 to Quebec; 6,027 to New Brunswick; and 19,288 to Nova Scotia. Of the whole number of craft, 3,974 were sea-going vessels; and 1,848 vessels were designed for lake or river navigation. No fewer than 2,136 vessels were under *five years of age*, representing a measurement of 417,647 tons. This included 222 paddle-steamers, and 114 screw-steamers, 9 of each being sea-going vessels: 164 ships, 397 barques, 117 brigs, 527 brigantines, 3,471 schooners, 61 sloops, 348 barges, 65 scows, 129 batteaux, 121 wood boats, and 77 vessels not rigged. Of the ships, barques, brigs, and brigantines—numbering in all 1,215 vessels—all except 37 were sea-going craft; while of the smaller vessels 1,760 were engaged in fishing.

The capital invested altogether in this mercantile fleet, was estimated to represent 23,583,062 dollars; but this is simply an approximation to the actual value of the shipping owned in the Dominion, and is, no doubt, an under estimate.

PROVINCES OF ONTARIO AND QUEBEC; OR, CANADA PROPER.

The area of these Provinces is 331,280 square miles, and the territory lies along both banks of the St. Lawrence, from its mouth till it reaches N. lat. 45°. It is an elevated country, but not traversed by any great mountain chain. Its chief rivers are the St. Lawrence and its tributary the Ottawa. Upper or Western Canada, now named the Province of Ontario, and Lower or Eastern, the Province of Quebec, are separated from each other by the river Ottawa. The inhabitants of Lower Canada, or Quebec, are chiefly of French descent, preserving their original language, religion, and customs; those of Ontario, or Upper Canada, are chiefly British.

The population of these two Provinces in 1866, was 3,090,000.

Gross amount of Public Revenue £2,640,183
Gross amount of Public Expenditure... 2,587,105

Gross amount of Public Debt £12,793,634
Total value of Imports 11,208,816
   ,,   ,, Exports 11,735,079
Total tonnage of vessels entered and cleared, exclusive of Coasting trade, 1,803,643.
Tonnage of British vessels, 1,603,135.
Tonnage of Foreign vessels, 200,508.

ONTARIO,

Formerly Upper Canada.—The government of this province is vested in a Lieut.-Governor, assisted by an Executive Council appointed by him. It sends its quota of 24 members to the Senate, and also 82 members, representing the 82 electoral districts into which the province is divided, to the Canadian Parliament. The principal cities are Toronto, the capital of the province, which has a population of 60,000; Hamilton, London, and Kingston.

Lieut.-Gov., Hon. W. P. Howland, C.B., £1,600.
A.D.C., Captain Fryer.

Executive Council :—
Attorney-General, Hon. J. S. Macdonald.
Secretary, Hon. M. C. Cameron.
Min. of Agricul. & Public Works, Hon. J. Carling.
Treasurer, Hon. E. B. Wood.
Comm. of Crown Lands, Hon. Stephen Richards.
Speaker of the Legis. Assem, Hon. John Stevenson.
Pres. of Court of Error, Hon. A. M'Lean, £1,250.
Chief Justice of Queen's Bench, Hon. W. H. Draper, C.B., £1,250.
Puisne Judges, do., Hon. J. H. Hagarty; Hon. J. C. Morrison, £800 each.
Clerk of Crown to do., L. Hayden.
Chief Justice of Common Pleas, Hon. W. B. Richards, £1,250.
Puisne Judges, do., Hon. Adam Wilson; Hon. John Wilson, £1,000 each.
Clerk of Crown to do., W. B. Jackson.
Chancellor, Hon. P. M. Vankoughnet, £1,250.
Vice-Chancellors, Hon. O. Mowat; Hon. J. G. Spragge, £800 each.
Master of Chancery, A. N. Buell.
Registrar of do., A. Grant.
Collector of Customs, Toronto, J. G. Smith.
   ,,   ,, *Kingston*, W. B. Simpson.
   ,,   ,, *Hamilton*, W. H. Kittson.
   ,,   ,, *Ottawa*, D. Graham.
Bishop of Toronto, A. N. Bethune, D.D., D.C.L., £1,250.
Dean of Toronto, Rev. H. J. Grassett, B.D.
Bishop of Huron, Benj. Cronyn, D.D., £600.
Bishop of Ontario, J. T. Lewis, D.D., £700.
Bishop of Rupert's Land, R. Machray, D.D., £700.

QUEBEC,

Formerly Lower Canada. — The government of this province is vested in a Lieut.-Governor and an Executive Council appointed by him. It sends 24 members to the Senate, and 65 representatives to the Canadian Parliament. The principal cities are Quebec, the capital of the province and the great seaport town of Canada: and Montreal, situate at the confluence of the Ottawa and the river St. Lawrence.

Lieut.-Governor, Sir N. F. Belleau, Kt., £1,600.
A.-D.-C., Lieut. A. Taschereau.

Executive Council :—
Premier, Hon. P. J. O. Chauveau.
Treasurer, Hon. C. Dunkin.
Attorney-General, Hon. G. Ouimet.
Solicitor-General, Hon. G. Irvine.
Comm. of Crown Lands, J. O. Beaubien.
Com. of Agriculture and Public Works, Hon. L. Archambeault.
Speak. of Legis. Coun., Hon. C. B. de Boucherville.

Chief Justice, Q. Bench, Hon. J. F. J. Duval, £1,250.
Puisne Judges, Queen's Bench, Hon. L. T. Drummond, W. Badgley, S. C. Monk, *Montreal*; R. E. Caron, *Quebec*, £1,000 each.
Assistant do., C. Mondelet, *Montreal.*
Chief Justice, Superior Court, Hon. W. C. Meredith, *Quebec.* £1,250.
Puisne Judges, Superior Court, Montreal, Hon. C. Mondelet, J. A. Berthelot, F. W. Torrance, R. Mackay, *Quebec,* Hon. A. Stuart, J. T. Taschereau, £1,000 each. *Three Rivers,* Hon. A. Polette, £800; *Sherbrooke,* Hon. E. Short, £1,000; *St. Jean,* Hon. F. Johnson, £800; *Sorel,* Hon. T. J. J. Loranger, £800; *St. Hyacinthe,* Hon. L. V. Sicotte, £800; *Aylmer,* Hon. A. La Fontaine, £800; *Montmagny,* Hon. J. N. Bossé, £800; *Kamouraska,* Hon. F. O. Gauthier, £800; *Saguenay,* Hon. De Roy, £700; *Gaspé,* Hon. P. Winter, £700; *N. Carlisle,* Hon. J. Maguire, £700.
Recorder, Montreal, J. P. Sexton.
　,, *Quebec,* J. Crémazie.
Judge of Sessions of Peace, Montreal, J. C. Coursol.
　,, *Quebec,* C. Doucet.
Judge of Vice-Adm. Ct., Hon. H. Black, C.B. £500.
Sheriff, Quebec, Hon. C. Alleyn, £600.
　,, *Montreal,* T. Bouthillier, £600.
Clerk of Appeal, J. U. Beaudry, £500.
Assist. do., L. W. Marchand, *Montreal;*
　Charles Drolet, *Quebec.*
Clerks of the Crown, Montreal, Dessaulles and Ermatinger.
Clerks of the Peace, do., Dessaulles & Ermatinger.
　,, *Quebec,* W. Duval.
Inspector of Registry Offices, G. Futvoye.
Coll. of Customs, Quebec, J. W. Dunscomb. £750.
　,, *Montreal,* A. M. Delisle, £750.
Harbour Master, Quebec, J. D. Armstrong.
　,, *Montreal,* J. Rudolf.
Bishop of Quebec, J. W. Williams, D.D., £400.
Bishop of Montreal, £1,000.
Chaplain to Forces, Rev. D. Robertson, M.A.

PROVINCE OF NEW BRUNSWICK.

Now incorporated with Canada, is the eastern division of the Continent of North America, and is situated between 45° 5'—48° 5' N. lat. and 63° 47'—67° 53' W. long., and comprises an area of 27,030 square miles; it is connected with Nova Scotia by a low isthmus. In the early part of the last century, New Brunswick belonged to the French, and was by them designated New France: it was first colonized by British subjects in 1761, and in 1783 by disbanded troops from New England. At the peace of 1763, New Brunswick, with the rest of Canada, was ceded by France to Great Britain, from which period to 1785 it was annexed to Nova Scotia, or Acadia, as it was termed by the French, when it was erected into a separate colony. It has subsequently been the subject of "boundary" disputes with the United States. In the year 1794 commissioners on both sides were appointed for a settlement thereof. Again, in 1835, at the Treaty of Ghent, the dispute was submitted to the arbitration of Leopold I., king of Belgium, whose decision was to be strictly binding; his award, however, was not concurred in by the United States, who refused the decision, and began to colonize the disputed territory. In 1839 the British Government again appointed commissioners with a view of settling the question, and again failed; thereupon Lord Ashburton was sent out from England with full powers to make a settlement, and after much negotiation, the present line,

which gives to Great Britain 893 square miles beyond the award of 1835, yields the navigation of the Upper St. John river to the United States. This treaty of settlement is styled "The Ashburton Treaty." The chief industrial pursuits rise from the produce of the forests and the fisheries, while the progress of agriculture increases annually, and the extensive mineral resources of the country receive more energetic attention. Coal is abundant, and is worked by a joint-stock company; antimony, copper, iron, manganese, and other valuable minerals are found in considerable quantites. Wheat, which produces 20 bushels, of 60 lbs. weight, to the acre, with Indian corn, barley, and oats are the principal cereals raised. The land, also, seems especially adapted for root-crops, an acre producing 6 tons of potatoes and 13 of turnips. The progress of the colony, compared with some others, has doubtless been slow; nevertheless, its commerce is gradually increasing. Fredericton, situate on the right bank of the St. John river, is the capital. St. John is the chief seaport.

	£
In 1866 the population was 295,000.	
Gross amount of Public Revenue	298,404
Gross amount of Public Expenditure...	281,188
Gross amount of Public Debt (1865) ...	1,249,174
Total value of Imports (1866)	2,083,499
Do. Imports from United Kingdom ...	843,109
Total value of Exports	1,327,855
Value of Exports to United Kingdom	620,715
Total tonnage of vessels entered and cleared, exclusive of Coasting trade: (British vessels, 1,287,600; Foreign vessels, 571,977)	1,859,577

New Brunswick forms one of the provinces of the Canadian Confederacy, the Provincial Government being administered by a Lieutenant-Governor, assisted by an Executive Council, and a Legislative Assembly elected by the people. It also sends its quota of members to the Senate, and representatives to the Canadian Parliament, as before mentioned.

GOVERNMENT.

Lieut.-Gov., Hon. S. Allen Wilmot, D.C.L., £3,000.
Private Secretary, George M. Campbell, A.M.
Aide-de-Camp, Lieut.-Col. J. Saunders.

EXECUTIVE COUNCIL.

President, Hon. E. B. Chandler.
Provincial Secretary, Hon. J. A. Beckwith, £600.
Attorney-General, Hon. A. R. Wetmore, £600.
Commis. of Board of Works, Hon. J. McAdam.
Surveyor-General, Hon. R. Sutton, £600.
Members without office, Hon. W. P. Flewelling and Hon. A. C. Desbrisay.
Clerk, F. A. H. Straton.
President of Legis. Council, Hon. J. S. Saunders.
Clerk of ditto, G. Botsford.
Chaplain of ditto, Rev. J. M. Brooke, D.D.
Speaker of House of Assembly, Hon. B. Botsford.
Clerk of ditto, C. P. Wetmore.
Chaplain of ditto, Rev. C. G. Coster, A.M.
Bishop of Fredericton, Rt. Rev. J. Medley, D.D., £1,000.
Chancellor, The Lieut.-Gov. for the time being.
Chancery Clerk, Hon. J. A. Beckwith.
Chief Justice, Hon. W. J. Ritchie.
Puisne Justices of Supreme Court, N. Parker, J. C. Allen, and J. W. Weldon.
Registrar and Clerk in Equity, W. Carman.
Clerk of the Pleas, W. Carman, £300.
Clerk of the Crown, W. H. Tuck, £200.
Circuit Clerk, Hon. J. S. Saunders.

Divorce Court, Hon. N. Parker, *Judge.*
        "   F. A. H. Straton, *Registrar.*
Judges of County Courts, Hon. J. G. Stevens, Hon. J. Steadman, J. W. Chandler, Hon. E. Williston, and Hon. Charles Watters.
Judge, Vice-Admiralty, Hon. R. L. Hazen.
Advocate-General, William Jack.
Registrar and Scribe, George Blatch.
Receiver-General, Hon. J. A. Beckwith.
Auditor-General, James S. Beek.
Post-office Inspector, Hon. J. McMillan.
Adjutant-General, Lieut.-Col. Maunsell.
Com. Troops, Col. F. P. Harding, C.B., 22nd Regt.
Com. Artillery, Capt. D. Moleyns.
Town Major, St. John's, Lieut. T. E. Jones (H. P. 4th Foot.)
Assist. Commissary.-Gen., — Monk, *St. John's.*
Deputy ditto, — Ewing, *Fredericton.*
Emigrant Officer, St. John's, R. Shives.

THE PROVINCE OF NOVA SCOTIA.

Also now incorporated with Canada, is a peninsula between 43°—47° N. lat. and 61°—67° W. long, and is connected with New Brunswick by a low fertile isthmus. It comprises an area of 15,670 square miles, or 9,984,000 acres, one-fifth part of which consists of lakes, rivers, and inlets of the sea, leaving rather more than 5,000,000 fit for tillage. Nova Scotia was discovered by John Cabot in 1497; it was colonized by the French, 1598, and taken by the English in 1627, and a grant made of it by James I. to Sir Wm. Alexander, who intended to colonize the whole country. James I. instituted the title of baronets there, with the professed object of encouraging the settlement therein; hence the title of "Nova Scotia" baronets. In 1632 it was restored to France, but again ceded to England in 1714 at the peace of Utrecht; after the peace of Aix-la-Chapelle in 1748, a settlement of disbanded troops was formed there by Lord Halifax, whose name the capital of the province now bears. The harbour of Halifax is not surpassed by any in the world. It is the principal naval station of North America, and the British Government have an extensive dockyard there. The comparatively small population consisted in 1861 of 330,000 inhabitants, one-fourth of whom were employed in agriculture. The capabilities of the soil and climate for agricultural operations have been much underrated; the average return of wheat per acre is 30 bushels, of other cereals from 40 to 50 bushels. 300 bushels of potatoes, and double that quantity of turnips, are produced, per acre, yet the science of farming appears to make little progress towards increasing or even maintaining the productive powers of the land. The dairy husbandry is further advanced than the arable. The forests are composed of similar trees to those of Canada and New Brunswick, the ash, beech, birch, maple, oak, pine, and spruce abounding. Coal and iron ore are plentiful in Nova Scotia; gold also has been discovered, the principal auriferous districts being Waverley, in Halifax County, Uniacke, Renfrew, and Oldham in Hants County, Sherbrooke and Wine Harbour in Enysboro County, all of which are now yielding fair returns. The principal fisheries are upon the Eastern coast. Here cod is obtained all the year round, often weighing 90lbs., also halibut, sometimes weighing 500 lbs. Salmon also are caught abundantly in the rivers and shores adjacent thereto. So abundant are mackerel, that one seine will take 300 barrels in a night—a barrel weighing 200 lbs.

There is probably no market so plentifully supplied with fish as Halifax: salmon, 6d. per lb.; delicately-flavoured whiting, 1d. each; trout, up to 4 lbs. each, 5s. a dozen; and small, 1s. a dozen. Lobster-catching is a common amusement in the harbour; the usual price is 1d., each, but sometimes 3d. is obtained. Game of all kinds is abundant.

Exports, imports, revenue, &c.—For the last 10 years there appears to have been a large increase in their value.

The following statistics of the gold-fields of Nova Scotia will be found interesting. The gross yield for the province from May, 1860, to 31st Dec., 1866, was in round numbers as follows:—From quartz only, 95,371 oz.; native gold, 2,587½ oz.; total, 97,958½ oz.; giving an approximate value of £381,832. Of the 13 districts, the yield of the three principal for the same period was as follows:—Waverley, from quartz only, 34,364½ oz.; Sherbrooke, 19,063¾ oz.; and native gold, 38 oz.; Wine Harbour, 13,402; the other districts varied from 9,000 oz. to 73 only. The estimated yield of the whole districts in 1867 was 27,000 oz.; the sustained total average yield per ton from the crushings of 90,850 tons of ore was 1 oz. 3 qrs.; the average earnings per man for the years 1865 and 1866 were £149. Upwards of 30 new companies were started in 1868 for mining purposes.

	£
The annual gross public revenue to September 30, 1865, was	341,771
,, public expenditure	279,364
,, public debt...	1,090,538
Total value of imports ...	2,876,202
Imports from United Kingdom	1,178,719
Total value of exports ...	1,608,619
Value of exports to United Kingdom	57,577

Total tonnage of vessels entered and cleared, exclusive of coasting trade.—British vessels, 1,618,462; Foreign vessels, 257,799, in all 1,876,261.

Nova Scotia also forms one of the provinces of the Canadian Confederacy, the provincial government being administered by a lieutenant-governor, aided by an executive council; it also furnishes its quota of members to the Senate, and representatives to the Canadian House of Commons, as previously specified.

Lieut.-Gov., Major-Gen. C. H. Doyle, C.B., £2,000.
Private Sec., Henry Moody, Esq., £400.
Executive Council.—Pres., Hon. W. Annand; *Attorney-Gen.,* Hon. M. J. Wilkins; *Provincial Sec.,* Hon. W. B. Vail; *Comm. of Works and Mines,* Hon. Robert Robertson *Without Office,* Hon. R. A. M'Heffy, Hon. E. P. Flynn, Hon. J. C. Troop, Hon. John Fergusson, Hon. J. Cochrane.
Provincial Aide-de-Camp, M. B. Daly.
Comm. of Forces, Major-Gen. C. H. Doyle.
Aide-de-Camp, Lieut. F. W. Cary.
Major of Brigade, Capt. W. Black.
Asst.-Q.-M.-Gen., Lt.-Col. G. E. Baynes.
Com. Off. R. A., Col. J. H. Francklyn, C.B.
Comm. Officer, R.E., Lieut.-Col. R. Burnaby.
Town Major, Col. A. F. Ansell, *Halifax.*
Chief Justice, Hon. Wm. Young, £800.
Judge in Equity, Hon. J. W. Johnstone, £800.
Puisne Judges, Hons. W. B. Bliss, £650; E. M. Dodd, W. F. Desbarres, L. M. Wilkins, £640 each.
Judge of Vice-Adm., Hon. W. Young, C.J.
Attorney-Gen., Hon. M. J. Wilkins, £320.
Clerk of Executive Council, Hon. W. B. Vail.
Pres. of Legis. Council, Alex. Keith.
Speaker of Assembly, J. J. Marshall.

Provincial Sec., Hon. W. B. Vail, £480.
Treasurer, Hon. W. Annand, £400.
Comm. of Public Works and Mines, Hon. Robert Robertson, £400.
Chairman, Railway Board, A. Longley.
Inspector of Post-office, Arthur Woodgate.
Reg. of Deeds, Halifax, W. H. Keating, £480.
Bishop, Hibbert Binney, D.D., £949.

Other American Possessions.

PRINCE EDWARD'S ISLAND.

This island is situated between 46°–47° N. lat., and 62°–64° W. long. Its area is 2,173 square miles, or about 1,380,000 acres. It was discovered by Sebastian Cabot in 1497, and first settled by the French, but was taken from them in 1758, and annexed to the Government of Nova Scotia in 1763, when it bore the name of St. John; but 5 years later, on a petition from its inhabitants, was constituted a separate colony, and its first governor, Walter Patterson, appointed in 1771. In 1800 it received its present title from Prince Edward, Duke of Kent, who took much interest therein. The island is divided into three Counties, King's, Queen's, and Prince's, each of which elects 10 representatives and 4 councillors. The land tenure has for many years been a source of agitation to this colony. At the close of the last century the whole island was parcelled out into 66 lots, and distributed amongst various persons, sundry impracticable conditions being attached to the various grants. For several years past the local government has, when opportunity offered, bought up the interests of these several proprietors, the estates so purchased being resold to the tenants, and the payment extended over a certain number of years. Its inhabitants, in 1866 consisting of a population of 90,000, were almost exclusively engaged in agriculture. The principal grain crop is oats, 1,440,500 bushels whereof were exported in 1866. Barley and wheat also are grown in smaller quantities. There is also a considerable export trade in horses, the island being well suited for rearing them. Its principal imports in 1866 were those of tea, 366,082 lbs.; of tobacco, 167,077 lbs.; and of molasses, 134,431 gallons. One-fifth of the whole revenue is spent in providing schools and teachers, insomuch that "there are almost more seminaries than roads to them."

Gross amount of public revenue in 1867 £52,017
" public expenditure 49,308
" public debt 86,313
Value of total imports 294,433
Value of imports from United Kingdom 125,737
Value of total exports 260,470
" to United Kingdom 104,258

Total tonnage of vessels entered and cleared, exclusive of coasting trade.—British vessels, 313,063; foreign vessels, 50,980 tons.

The government is vested in a Lieut.-Governor, nominated by the Crown, an Executive Council, consisting of nine members, appointed by the Lieut.-Governor, and forming a responsible Ministry; a Legislative Council of 13 members, and a House of Assembly of 30 members, both of which are elected by the people. The principal port is Charlottetown.

Lieut.-Gov., George Dundas, Esq., £1,500.
Pres. of Exec. Council, Hon. Joseph Hensley.
Pres. of Leg. Council, Hon. D. Montgomery, £50.
Speaker of Assembly, Hon. J. Wightman, £50.

Chief Justice, Hon. R. Hodgson, £400.
Master of the Rolls, Jas. H. Peters, £333.
Attorney-Gen., Hon. Jos. Hensley, £233.
Solicitor-Gen., Dennis Reddin, £133.
Colonial Sec., Hon. George Coles, £200.
Colonial Treasurer, Hon. J. Warburton, £200.
Comm. of Crown Lands, Hon. J. Aldous, £200.
Surveyor-General, Jos. Ball, £200.
Regis. and Keeper of Plans, J. A. Dingwell, £166.
Collector of Impost, William Clark, £200.
Clerk of Executive Council, Hon. George Coles.
Assistant do., Charles Des Brisay, £133.
Do., Legislative do., John Ball, £50.
Clerk of the Crown, Daniel Hodgson, £106.
Sheriffs, Hon. F. Longworth, R. Hunt, J. W. S. Macgowan.
Sec. to Board of Education, J. M'Neill, £50.
Visitors of Schools, W. Macphail, Robert Mackelow, John Macswain, *each* £100.
Chaplain for Leg. C., Rev. Dr. Jenkins.
Do. for H. Assembly, Rev. Thos. Duncan.
Con. Navigation Laws, Wm. Clarke.
Asst. Treasurer, J. Robins, £100.
Assistant Colonial Sec. and Road Correspondent, J. W. Morrison, £166.
Postmaster-Gen., Thomas Owen, £233.
Master of Normal School, H. Lawson, £133.

NEWFOUNDLAND,

This island is situated between 46° 30'–51° 39' N. lat. and 52° 15'–59° 60' W. long. on the north-east side of the gulf of St. Lawrence. Its area is 40,200 square miles, it was discovered by John Cabot in 1497, and as early as 1500 was frequented by the Portuguese, Spanish, and French for its fisheries. Sir Walter Raleigh and others attempted to colonize this island, but were unsuccessful. Sir George Calvert (Lord Baltimore) settled in the great peninsula in the south-east, and named it the *Province of Avalon*; the history of the island during the 17th and part of the 18th centuries is little more than a record of rivalries and feuds between the English and French fishermen, but by the treaty of Utrecht in 1713, ratified by that of Paris in 1763, the island was entirely ceded to England.

Labrador is an appendage to Newfoundland. The principal exports are codfish, cod and seal oils, and sealskin. The population consists of about 130,000 inhabitants.

	£
The gross amount of public revenue in 1866 including loan £18,644 was	150,290
The gross amount of public expenditure including portion of loan repaid £6,880, was	139,988
The gross amount of public debt was	202,018
Value of total imports	1,205,177
Value of imports from United Kingdom	531,198
Value of total exports	1,186,314
Value of exports to United Kingdom	327,867
Total tonnage of vessels entered and cleared exclusive of coasting trade (British 271,615, Foreign 24,361)	295,976

Principal imports, of which molasses 710,630 gallons, tea, 533,331 lbs. and flour 183,667 barrels, were imported in 1866.

Principal exports, of which codfish dry 716,690 quintals, cod oil 2,922 tuns, and sealskins 269,029 were exported in 1866.

In 1867 the total inward tonnage was 167,108, and outward, 146,172. There were exported 815,088 quintals of codfish, 4,923 tuns of seal oil, 3,497 cod oil, 378 refined cod liver oil, 399,041 seal skins, 60,474 barrels of herrings, and 2,472 tierces, and 1,867 barrels of salmon.

The Government is at present administered by a responsible Executive Council, also by a Legislative Council of 15 members, and a House of Assembly of 30 members, both of which are elected by the people.

Governor, Commander-in-Chief & Vice-Admiral, Anthony Musgrave, £2,000.
Private Sec., Anthony Musgrave, Jun., £200.
Speaker of Assembly, W. V. Whiteway, £200.
Colonial Sec., & Clerk of Executive Council, Hon. J. Bemister, £500.
Receiver-General, John Kent, £500.
Surveyor-General, J. Warren, £400.
Asst. Collector of Customs, J. Canning, £300.
Financial Sec., E. D. Shea, £300.
Chief Justice, Hon. H. W. Hoyles, £850.
Asst. Judge, Hon. B. Robinson, £650.
Second Assistant Judge, Hon. H. Hayward, £650.
Attorney-Gen., Hon. F. B. Carter, £500.
Sol. Gen., £200.
Chief Clerk, & Registrar, Supreme Court and Central Ct., M. W. Walbank, £350.
Chief Clerk & Registrar, Northern Circuit, L. W. Emerson, £200 and fees.
Registrar, Southern Circuit, H. T. B. Wood, *no salary but fees.*
Sheriff's Central District, J. V. Nugent, £300.
  ,,   *Northern*   ,,   G. C. Gaden, £300.
  ,,   *Southern*   ,,   J. Stephenson, £200.
Pres. of the Executive Council, L. O'Brien.
Bishop, Right Rev. Edw. Field, D.D., £1,200.
Asst. Bishop, Right Rev. John B. K. Kelly.
Judge of Admiralty Court, the Chief Justice for the time being.
Registrar   ,,   P. W. Carter, fees.
Marshal   ,,   Jas. Bayly, fees.
Garrison Chaplains, Rev. T. M. Wood, Rev. J. O'Donnell.
Postmaster-Gen., John Delaney, £300.
Commandant, Col. Fitz W. Walker.
Com. Officer, R. A., Major Strover.
Com. Officer, R. E., Capt. Phillpots.
Clerk of Peace, St. John's, R. R. Lilly.
Asst. War Storekeeper, J. Tunbridge.
Judge at Labrador, R. J. Pinsent, £200.
Collector of Customs, Labrador, T. Knight, £100, and 2½ per cent. on collection.

BRITISH COLUMBIA AND VANCOUVER'S ISLAND,

Which also include Queen Charlotte's and other adjacent islands, incorporated therewith by Act of Parliament in 1866, the youngest of the American colonies, are situated on the north-west coast of North America, in 49°-55° N. lat. and 115°-132° W. long., embracing an area of 220,000 square miles. Until 1858 British Columbia formed part of the territory over which the Hudson's Bay Company possessed the exclusive right of trading; but in that year large discoveries of gold were made in the rivers of the country, which attracted a vast immigration of gold-diggers from California, rendering it necessary for the British Government to take measures for the protection of life and property, and the maintenance of order; the Hudson's Bay Company's licence was revoked, and the country erected into a colony by an Act of Parliament 21 & 22 Vict. cap. 99. The colony, when first created, had no form of representative government; laws, in the shape of proclamations, were made by the Governor, submitted to the Queen, and laid before the Imperial Parliament for their sanc-

tion. In 1863, however, a Legislative Council was established by Order in Council. The population of the country is chiefly migratory, consisting of mining adventurers from California and all parts of the world, including a considerable number of Chinese. The settled white population may be estimated at from 12,000 to 16,000. Beside gold the country produces magnificent timber and good coal. The revenue is raised chiefly by means of Customs' duties. There is also a gold-diggers' licence of 20s. annually. Gold-quartz mining is also being prosecuted with considerable vigour and reasonable hopes of success. Agricultural operations have been greatly extended during the last three years, and have proved the quality of the land throughout the colony to be admirably adapted for the culture of cereals. Wheat, barley, oats, and other farm-produce of the colony may compare favourably with those raised in California, the climate being highly favourable to vegetation. The fur trade, also, is a noticeable feature, the skins exported being chiefly those of the mink, marten, sable, silver-fox, bear, beaver, sea and land otter, seal, deer, elk, and others of minor importance.

VANCOUVER'S ISLAND

Lies off the north-west coast of North America, between N. lat. 48° 20'—50°-55' and W. long. 123°-10'—128°-20', separated from the mainland by a channel, called in various parts by the name of Queen Charlotte's Sound, Johnstone Strait, and the Gulf of Georgia; its area has been roughly estimated at 13,000 square miles, the greater part of which is mountain and barren rock. It is supposed originally to have been part of the continent of North America. In 1792, Captain George Vancouver, R.N., entered the straits of Fuca, surveying and exploring as he proceeded; and having circumnavigated the land, determined its separate existence as an island. He named it Quadra, in compliment to Senor Quadra, the Spanish commandant at Nootka. This name has fallen into desuetude, and it is now only known as "Vancouver's" Island. The whole country is densely wooded; and except where the summits of the mountains (some of which rise to the height of 16,000 feet, affording no hold for plants) the soil is fertile and capable of successful cultivation. The first British settlement in Vancouver's Island was made at Nootka Sound, on the N.W. coast, in 1778, by some London merchants. Its possession was secured by treaty to Great Britain in 1846. Till 1849, the island was only occasionally resorted to by the servants of the Hudson's Bay and Puget Sound Companies, but in that year a lease was granted to the former company for 10 years, the British Government reserving to itself the right of resuming it at the expiration thereof on certain conditions. Accordingly, in 1859, it became a British colony, and in 1866 was united to British Columbia. The chief town of the island is Victoria, situated at its south-eastern extremity, possessing a flourishing population of 5,000 inhabitants.

	£
Gross amount of public revenue, 1866, British Columbia	90,586
Gross amount of public revenue, 1866, Vancouver's Island (including loan, £33,071)	88,894
Gross amount of public expenditure, 1866, British Columbia (including repayment of loan, £1,768)	95,651

Gross amount of public expenditure, 1866,
Vancouver's Island (including repayment of loan, £20,018)...................... 90,278
Public debt, British Columbia, 1866 293,078
  " " Vancouver's Island, 1866 ... 40,000
Total imports, British Columbia, 1866 298,149
Total imports, Vancouver's Island, 1865 594,297
Imports from U. K.—Brit. Columb., 1866 14,336
Imports from U. K.—Vancouver, 1865 ... 202,474
Value of total exports (exclusive of gold
  valued at £600,000), B. Columb., 1866.. 43,983
Value of total exports—Vancouver, 1865,
  (exclusive of gold—£426,193) 120,254
Value of total exports (including bullion
  and specie) to United Kingdom—British Columbia, 1866 10,495
Do., Vancouver's Island, 1865 26,804
Total tonnage of vessels entered and cleared
(exclusive of coasting trade)—British Columbia,
1866, 119,397. Vancouver's Island, 1865, 313,064.
Tonnage of British vessels entered and cleared:
—Foreign vessels, 1866, 25,382;—British Columbia, 1866, 94,015;—Vancouver's Island, 138,339.
Tonnage of British vessels entered and cleared:
—Foreign vessels, 1865, 174,725;—Vancouver's
Island, 1865, 138,339;—British Columbia, 25,382.

The government consists of a governor and
an executive council, together with a legislative council of 23 members, 5 of them being
the executive council, 9 being magistrates from
different parts of the country, and 9 unofficial
members selected by the votes of the inhabitants
of the several districts, Chinese and Indians
excepted. An * denotes such as are Members of
the Executive Council.

Gov. & Com.-in-Chief, Fred. Seymour, £4,000.
Private Sec., D. C. Maunsell, £350.
Colonial Sec., Arthur N. Birch, £800.
Chief Clerk to do., C. Good, £400.
Treasurer, Chas. W. Franks, £750.
Chief Clerk to do., J. Cooper, £400.
Attorney-Gen., H. P. P. Crease, £500.
Chief Com. of Lands & Works, J. Wm. Trutch, £800.
Assist. Surv. Gen., W. Moberly, £500.
Clerk, A. R. Howse, £300.
Clerk to do., T. Holmes, £300.
Coll. of Customs, W. D. Hamley, £650.
Chief Clerk to do., W. H. M'Crea, £360.
Chief Inspector of Police, C. Brew, £600.
Reg. Gen. of Deeds, A. T. Bushby, £500.
Postmaster-Gen., W. R. Spalding, £400.
Chief of Assay and Refinery, G. F. Claudet, £500.
Chief Melter, W. Hitchcock, £400.
Harbour Master, J. Cooper, £400.
Gold Com. & Police Magistrate, Kootenay, &c., P. O'Reilly, £800.
Assist. do., J. B. Gaggin, £500.
Do., J. C. Haynes, £500.
Chief Clerk, J. White, £450.
Assist. Gold Coms. & Police Magis., Yale & Lytton, E. H. Sanders, £500.
Do. Quesnelmouth, H. M. Ball, £500.
Do. Carribou, W. G. Cox, £700.
Do. Lilloett, Andrew C. Elliott, £500.
Judge of Sup. Ct., M. B. Begbie, £1,200.
Registrar, W. Pooley, £400.
Bp. of Columbia, Rt. Rev. Geo. Hills, D.D., £1,000.

RUPERT'S LAND; Hudson's Bay Company's
Territory.—The vast central region which constitutes three-fourths of British North America
was called "Hudson's Bay Company's territory," and is known by its lately revived title of
Rupert's Land, so named after Prince Rupert:
it is now merging into British America.

BRITISH GUIANA,

Includes the settlements of Demerara, Essequibo, and Berbice. This colony is a section of
the north-east portion of the South American
continent, extending from east to west about
200 miles, and comprising an area of about
76,000 square miles, lying between 8° 40′ N. and
0°·40′, and between the meridians of 57° and
61° W. Its precise boundaries being yet undetermined, it is impossible to compute its area
with exactness. This territory was first partially settled by the Dutch West India Company
in 1580, and was, from time to time, held by Holland, France, and England. Under the Dutch,
Demerara and Essequibo constituted one government and Berbice another, and this arrangement
continued also under the British government until
1831, when the three settlements were constituted
into one colony. It is uncertain whether Columbus ever landed here—nevertheless, the Spaniards
must have settled themselves in the neighbouring countries early in the 16th century. Towards
the close of the 18th century, the inhabitants
desired to place themselves under British sovereignty. This was effected in 1796, when the
colonies ceded to an expedition under Major-Gen. Whyte. At the peace of Amiens, in 1802,
they were restored to the "Batavian Republic,"
to be again surrendered to Great Britain in
1803, and finally confirmed at the peace of 1814.
In the colony of British Guiana the Roman
Dutch Civil Law is still in force in civil cases,
modified by Orders in Council and Local Ordinances, but the criminal law is administered in
the same manner as in Great Britain, yet without the intervention of a grand jury. There are
but two towns properly so called in the colony,
Georgetown and New Amsterdam. The cultivated portion of the colony is confined to the
sea coast, and to a short distance from the
rivers, Demerara and Berbice. Cotton and coffee
have nearly ceased to be cultivated, all the available resources of the country being concentrated
upon the production of sugar and rum. The
timber trade has also assumed a vastness little
dreamed of in bygone years.

The population—8th April, 1861 ...... £148,026
Gross public Revenue in 1866............ 304,817
Gross public Expenditure (including
  repayment of loan £27,140) ... 310,788
Public debt............................... 660,646
Value of Imports, 1866, (including
  £823,282 from the United Kingdom) 1,530,675
Value of Exports, 1866, (including
  £1,742,545 to United Kingdom)...... 2,170,967
The principal imports in 1866 consisted of
Rice, 18,041,256 lbs.; Flour, 80,262 barrels;
Fish (dried), 77,387 cwt.; and Spirits, 69,570
gallons. Principal exports: Molasses, 15,180
puncheons; Sugar, 91,861 hogsheads; Rum,
30,675 puncheons. Total tonnage (exclusive of
coasting trade), 336,983.

The government, which is essentially that of
centralization, consists of a Governor and a Court
of Policy of 12 Members, 6 Official and 6 Elective;
also a combined Court of Financial Representatives.

Governor and Commander-in-Chief, F. Hincks,
  C.B., £5,000.
Private Secretary, F. Hincks, Jun., £300.
Bishop, Rt. Rev. W. P. Austin. D.D., £2,000.
*Chief Justice and Judge of the Vice-Admiralty
  Court*, vacant.
Puisne Judges, Hon. R. C. Beete, and Hon. B. C.
  Norton, £1,500 each.

Government Secretary, Hn. J. R. Holligan, £1,500.
Assistant do., Edward Noel Walker, £600.
Attorney-Gen., Hon. J. L. Smith, £1,100.
Solicitor-Gen., W. H. Smith, £300.
Archdeacon, Demerara, Ven.H.H.Jones, M.A. £700.
Superin. of Penal Settlement, Capt. C. Kerr, £625.
Sheriff of Demerara and Police Magistrate,
  George Town, John Brumell, £1,000.
Do. Essequibo and Stipendiary Magistrate, W.
  Humphrys, £750.
Sheriff of Berbice and Stipendiary Magistrate, J.
  W. Swiney, £750.
Administrator-Gen., Henry Watson, £1,000.
Clerk of Supreme Court (Criminal), Clerk of the
  Inferior C. Court, and Registrar in Admiralty
  Court, J. S. Hitzler.
*Registrar do. do. Demerara, J. S. Hitzler, £833.
Senior Clerk, E. G. H. Dalton, £500.
Ten Stipendiary Magistrates, each £500.
Provost Marshal, Sir W. H. Holmes.
Receiver-Gen., W. R. Inglis, £1,000.
Auditor-Gen., W. B. Pollard, £1,000.
Colonial Book-keeper, G. Oudkirk, £700.
Comptroller of Import Duties, W. H. Ware, £1,000.
Supervisor of Aid Waiters, E. W. K. Crocker, £500.
Inspector of Schools, Rev. W. G. Austin, £650.
Harbour Master, N. T. Vesey, £500.
Surveyor of Crown Lands, Cathcart Chalmers,
  £100 and fees.
Inspector-Gen. of Police, N. Cox, £625.
Immigration Agent Gen., J. Crosby, £1,000.
Do. Agent (Chin.), T. Sampson.
Do. Agent (Calcutta), W. G. Jeffrey, £1,000.
Surgeon-Gen., E. A. Manget, M.D., £725.
Post Master, B. T. E. Dalton, £725.
Civil Engineer, W. B. Pollard, junr., £700.
Medical Inspector Dr. Shier, £1,000.
Rectors of Nine Parishes, each £500.
Incumbents of Two do., each £416 13s. 4d.
Scotch Church, Three Ministers, each £500.

BERBICE.

Sheriff, Jn. M'Swiney, £750.
Asst. Gov. Sec. and Rec. Gen., L. G. Tucker, £600.
Physician to Colonial Hospital, J. T. Hackett,
  M.D., £500.
Sub-Comp. of Customs, T. R. Gordon, £416.
Superintendent of Rivers and Creeks, Demerara,
  W. Des Vœux, £700.
Do. do. at Berbice, J. T. Vaughan, £600.
Do. do. at Essequibo, P. A. J. Grant, £500.
Harbour Master, Alex. Winter, fees.

HONDURAS, BRITISH.

British Honduras occupies a portion of the sea coast of the middle state of Central America of the same name. The boundaries of the British portion have never been exactly defined, but this is estimated to contain 13,500 square miles, embracing a small portion of the Mosquito territory, and a population, at the last census (1861), of 25,635. The country is generally mountainous, being traversed by the Cordilleras. The coast was discovered by Columbus in 1502, and its early settlement supposed to have been effected by adventurers attracted by the fine timber (mahogany and logwood) which grow on the banks of its

*Registrar's fees on an average of 8 years,
  £1076 5s. 8d.

rivers. In 1670 a treaty was entered into with Spain, acknowledging, in a measure, the territorial rights of Great Britain in the settlement, a treaty of which the settlers were not slow in taking advantage. Notwithstanding this and numerous subsequent treaties, it became the object of various hostile attacks by the Spaniards, jealous of the increasing numbers and boldness of the woodcutters, who were perpetually encroaching on their soil. In 1786, Great Britain obtained from Spain a specific grant of the settlement, under certain limitations as to the exercise of the rights of sovereignty and the cultivation of the soil; but the boundaries were very imperfectly defined. The territorial questions, which have since given rise to much discussion, have been those relating to the boundaries between Honduras, Guatemala, and the Republic of Mexico. In 1850, when the Clayton-Bulwer treaty was under discussion, it was particularly stipulated that the promise of Great Britain not to colonise or occupy Nicaragua, Costa Rica, and the Mosquito territory, or any part of Central America, did not apply to the settlement of British Honduras. Tobacco has been grown here with great success, and attention is being turned to the cultivation of the soil.

		£
Amount of Public Revenue in 1866......		27,334
Amount of Public Expenditure		31,094
Public Debt....................................		None
Value of total Imports (including		
£107,734) from Great Britain)		169,033
Value of total Exports (including		
£13,293, Bullion and Specie)		227,156
Value of Exports to Great Britain		169,013

Total tonnage of vessels, exclusive of coasting trade (25,620 British, 22,961 Foreign), 48,581.

Honduras abounds in mineral wealth—gold, silver, copper, iron, tin, platinum, limestone, marble, and coal. Besides valuable timber, the soil produces fruit trees, cotton, tobacco, sugar, coffee, indigo, potatoes, yams, plantains, bananas, &c.

The government is administered by a Lieut.-Governor (subordinate to the Governor of Jamaica), assisted by an Executive Council, appointed by the Crown, and a Legislative Assembly of eighteen elected and three nominated members. Belize—built on both sides of a river of that name—is the capital.

*Lieutenant-Governor, J. R. Longden, £1,800.
Private Secretary, Col. Hunt, R.M., £240.
*Colonial Secretary, Controller of Customs, Lieut.P.
  J. Hankin, R.N., £600.
Chief Justice, Hon. R. J. Corner, £1,000.
*Officer Commanding Troops, Lieut.-Col. Harley.
Fort Adjutant, Lieutenant Ferguson.
*Public Treasurer and Collector of Customs, Thos.
  Graham, £600.
Clerk to do., H. C. Usher, £200.
*Attorney-General, S. S. Plues, £500.
Speaker of Assembly, A. W. Cox, £100.
Clerk, J. Bristowe, £200.
Colonial Chaplain, Rev. R. Dowson, £600.
Incumbent, St. Mary's, Rev. A. Field, £300, and
  £200 as Garrison Chaplain.
Clerk of Courts and Keeper of Records, J. V.
  Leach, £600.
Assistant do., J. Liddle, £200.
Police Magistrate, S. Cockburn, £600.
*Immigration Agent, A. W. Cox, £200.

* *Executive Councillors ex officio.*

AUSTRAL-ASIA is a term etymologically equivalent to Southern Asia, but differing therefrom in its common acceptation.

Australia, the south-west division of Australasia, inasmuch as it is surrounded by water, would, according to the ordinary definition, be called an island; yet, from its vast magnitude, embracing an area of upwards of two millions and a half square miles, it is usually described as a continent. It is situated between the Pacific and Indian Oceans, at a distance of 2,500 miles to the south-east of Asia. This intervening space is occupied by the Eastern Archipelago and other groups of islands, the nearest of which is New Guinea. Australia comprises the several colonies of New South Wales, of which Sydney is the capital; Tasmania, of which Hobart Town is the capital; Western Australia, of which Perth is the capital; South Australia, of which Adelaide is the capital; Victoria, of which Melbourne is the capital; and Queensland, of which Brisbane is the capital. New Zealand consists of three islands, and is divided into nine provinces, with Auckland for its capital.

Australia, in the aggregate, contains an area of 2,582,070 square miles, with a rapidly increasing population, which in 1866 numbered 1,662,063.

	£		£
Gross amount of Public Revenue 1866	10,194,096	Value of total Exports (including	
Gross amount of Public Expenditure	10,140,296	£13,355,136 bullion and specie)	31,133,908
Public Debt	24,177,744	Value of Exports to United Kingdom,	13,555,881
Value of total Imports (including		Total tonnage of vessels, exclusive	
£3,736,694 bullion and specie)	36,030,708	of coasting trade (4,188,499 British,	
Value of Imports from Un. Kingdom	16,957,156	350,469 Foreign)	4,538,968

NEW SOUTH WALES.

The whole of the eastern part of Australia, now comprising the several colonies of New South Wales, Victoria, and Queensland, received the name of New South Wales from its first explorer, Captain James Cook, in 1770. The country is said to have been discovered by the Spaniards in 1609, and visited by several early navigators prior to its exploration by Captain Cook. The present colony of New South Wales took its origin in a penal settlement formed by the British Government when Capt. Arthur Phillip, R.N. its first Governor, arrived at Botany Bay in H.M.S. *Sirius*, in January, 1788, with six transports and three store ships, where they anchored, and subsequently proceeded to Port Jackson, which being more suitable than Botany Bay for the new settlement, the British ensign was for the first time hoisted on the shores of Sydney Cove, now the capital and sent of government, situated in 35° 52′ S. lat. and 151° 17′ E. long. It comprises an area of 323,437 square miles, and a population, in 1866, of 431,412. The great staple produce of this colony is wool, and of late years there has been an immense increase in its export. It also produces gold, silver, coal, iron, copper, cotton, and tobacco. Total number of arrivals in 1866 (including only 648 from the United Kingdom), 233,394. Total number of departures (including 1,024 to the United Kingdom), 14,080.

Chief productions of the colony in 1866, were

	£
Gold, 241,489 ozs., value	928,275
Coal obtained, 774,238 tons, value	324,049
Total Revenue, in 1866, derivable from Customs duties to the extent of nearly one-half, and land sales and rents, (including loan of £1,189,065) amounted to	3,253,179
Total Expenditure, 1866, (including Loan repaid, £1,024,527)	3,012,571
Public Debt	6,418,030
Value of Total Imports (including bullion and specie, £2,238,054)	8,867,071
Value of Imports from United Kingdom	3,352,768

	£
Value of total Exports (including bullion and specie, £3,350,164)	8,512,214
Exports, produce of Colony	2,539,723
Value of total Exports to United Kingdom	3,162,615

Total tonnage of vessels entered and cleared, exclusive of Coasting trade (£1,400,917 British, 113,818 Foreign), 1,514,735.

Principal Imports, in 1866: Beer and Ale, 1,650,460 gallons; Wine, 408,292 gallons. Spirits, Brandy, 264,530 gallons; Rum, 247,578 gallons; Gin, 103,655 gallons; Gold, 539,290 ozs. (value, £2,142,189;) Wheat, 1,093,081 bushels; Flour and Bread, 29,832 tons; Rice, 2,775 tons; Tea, 6,058,632 lbs.; Wool, 4,597,601; Boots and Shoes 11,378 packages; Linens, Drapery, &c., 24,037 packages, (value £1,056,751;) besides Hardware, Ironmongery, &c.

"Responsible government" was established by the Constitution Act, 18 & 19 Vict., c. 54, and is vested in a Governor appointed by the Crown, and an Executive Council of 7 members nominated by him; a Legislative Council, consisting of 27 members, together with a Legislative Assembly of 72 members elected thereto. Sydney possesses a University, with suffragan colleges annexed; also a Royal Mint.

Gov.-in-Chief, The Right Hon. the Earl of Belmore, £7,000.
Aide-de-Camp, Capt. H. M. Beresford. £173.

Executive Council.

Vice-President, Hon. J. Martin.
Colonial Sec., Hon. J. Docker, £2,000.
Colonial Treas., Hon. G. Eagar, £1,500.
Sec. for Lands, Hon. J. B. Wilson, £1,500.
Sec. for Public Works and Commiss. of Railways, Hon. J. Byrnes, £1,500.
Attorney-General, Hon. J. Martin, £1,500.
Solicitor-General, Hon. R. M. Isaacs, £1,000.
Clerk of Council, A. Budge, £500.

Legislative Council.

President, Hon. T. A. Murray, £1,200.
Chairman of Committee, Hon. G. Allen, £500.
Clerk of Council, R. O'Connor, £700.
Clerk Assistant, J. J. Calvert, £500.
Usher of Black Rod, H. J. Shadforth, £400.

Legislative Assembly.

Speaker, Hon. W. M. Arnold, £1,200.
Clerk of Assembly, C. Tompson, £800.
First Clerk Assistant, £600.
Parl. Librarian, W. M'Evilly, £400.
Under Secretary, H. Halloran, £800.
Chief Clerk, Wm. Goodman, £500.
Regist.-Gen., T. J. Jaques, £700.
Examiners of Titles, Lands Titles Office, G. K. Holden, Alex. Dick, £1,000 each.
Draftsman and Surveyor L. T. Off., R. M. Pearson, £500.
Commissioners of Lands Titles, R. Jones, A. W. Scott, fees.
Astronomer, G. R. Smalley, £600.
Government Printer and Inspector of Stamps, T. Richards, £600.
Supt. of Money Order Office, F. Hill, £500.
Under Sec. Finance and Trade, H. Lane, £800.
Collector of Customs, W. A. Duncan, £900.
Insp. of Distilleries and Sugar Refineries, H. Lumsdaine, £650.
Dep. Master Roy. Mint, Sydney, E. W. Ward.
Supt. of Bullion Office, Charles E. Louis, £850.
Do. Coining Department, J. Trickett, £730.
Practical Chemist, R. Hunt, £630.
Under Sec. Lands, M. Fitzpatrick, £800.
Surveyor-General, W. R. Davidson, £1,000.
Deputy do., F. S. Adams, £800.
Com. Crown Lands, A. O. Moriarty, £800.
Und. Sec. Pub. Works, John Rae, £600.
Engineer-in-Chief, J. Whitton, £1,500.
1st Assistant ditto, W. Mason, £700.
Colonial Architect, Jas. Barnet, £1,000.
Engineer-in-Chief for Harbours and River Navigation, E. O. Moriarty, £1,100.
Coal Fields and Mines, William Keene, £600.
Sup. Harbours, Lighthouses, and Pilots, F. Hixson, R.N., £650.
Auditor Gen., C. Rolleston, £900.
Chief Justice, Sir A. Stephen, C.B., £2,600.
Puisne Judges, J. F. Hargrave, A. Checke, P. Faucett, each £200.
Under Sec. Law Depart., W. E. Plunkett, £650.
Master in Equity, A. T. Holroyd, £1,000.
Prothonotary and Curator of Intestate Estates, D. B. Hutchinson, £700.
Chief Commiss. of Insolvents, G. H. Deffell, £1,000.
Crown Solicitor, J. Williams, £1,000.
Sheriff, H. McLean, £800.
Postmaster-General, A. A. Tighe, Esq., £1,500.
Secretary, S. A. Lambton, £600.

District Court Judges.

Metropolitan and Coast District, J. S. Dowling, G. B. Simpson, A. McFarland, each £1,000.
Western ditto, H. Cary, £1,000.
Northern ditto, C. Meymott, £1,000.
South-West ditto, H. R. Francis, £1,000.

Crown Prosecutors.

Sydney, E. Butler, £500.
Metropolitan, Wm. J. Foster, £500.
Southern ditto, W. R. Templeton, £500.
South-Western ditto, D. G. Forbes, £500.
Northern ditto, J. O'N. Brenan, £500.
Western ditto, J. Chambers, £500.
Clerk of the Peace, Cumberland and Coast, E. Rogers, £600.
Inspect.-Gen. of Police, J. McLerie, £912.
Secretary and Supt. to the Police, E. Fosbery, £500, and £95 for quarters.
Police Magis., Central Police Office, D. C. F. Scott, £600.
Clerk P. S., W. D. Meares, £500.
Water Police Magistrate, P. L. Cloete, £600.

Shipping Master, W. E. Shorter, £300.
Prof. of Classics and Logic, University of Sydney, C. Badham, D.D.
Prof of Maths., M. B. Bell, B.A., £325, fees, &c.
Prof. of Chemistry, J. Smith, M.D., £675, fees, &c.
Registrar, &c., Hugh Kennedy, £400, fees.
Agent for the Colony (resident in London), W. C. Mayne, £1,000.
Bishop of Sydney and Metropolitan, Fred. Barker, D.D. £2,000.
Bishop of Newcastle, Rt. Rev. W. Tyrrell, D.D., £500.
Bishop of Goulburn, Rt. Rev. M. Thomas, D.D.
Bishop of Grafton. Rt. Rev. James Francis Turner, D.D.   [£300.
Dean of Sydney, Very Rev. W. M. Cowper, M.A.,
Moderator of the Assembly of the Presbyterian Ch. of N.S.W., Rev. A. Thompson.
Warden St. Paul's Coll. (Ch. of E.), Rev. W. Scott, M.A., £500.
R. Cath. Archbishop, J. B. Polding, D.D., £800.
Rector St. John's R. Cath. Coll. Rev. J. Forrest, £500.
Accountant, J. Thompson, £600.
Commissioner of Railways, Hon. J. Byrnes.
Commisr. & Engineer for Roads, W. C. Bennett, £700.
Civil Enginr. Fitzroy Dry Dock, &c., G. K. Mann, £700.
Deputy Registrar of Titles, E. G. Ward, £600.
Inspector of Accounts, Auditor General's Department E. A. Rennie, £550.
Senior Clerk of Works, W. Coles, £600.
Chief Draughtsman, J. S. Adam, £600.
Railway do., J. W. Drewitt, £500.

Five District Surveyors, £500 each; six ditto, £400 each, and six ditto, £300 each.
Two Commissioners of Crown Lands, £500, and nine £450 each.
One Police Superintndt., £500; three do. £450 each.

NEW ZEALAND,

A colony in the South Pacific Ocean, consisting of three islands, called New Ulster, New Munster and New Leinster, or the Northern, Middle, and Southern or Stewart's Islands, and a number of islets scattered round the coasts. It is subdivided into nine provinces—Auckland, Wellington, New Plymouth, or Taranaki, Nelson, Otago, Canterbury, Hawke's Bay, Southland, and Marlborough. Each province is governed by a provincial council, and an elected superintendent. These islands lie between 34°—48° S. lat., and 166°—179° E. long. Portions of them were explored by Tasman, under the direction of the Dutch East India Company, in 1642, and visited at various times during the 18th century, and in 1777 by Captain Cook. The first settlement of Europeans was in 1814, but no colonization took place until 1839. In 1840, New Zealand was, by letters patent, erected into a separate colony, distinct from New South Wales. The whole group is upwards of 1,200 miles long, and 200 miles broad; its coast line extends over 1,000 leagues; the entire area of the colony is said to be 106,260 square miles, or 69,000,000 acres, of which two-thirds are fitted for agriculture and grazing. The north island is about 500 miles long, and 200 in greatest breadth, east to west, and contains about 32,000,000 acres. The middle, sometimes described as the south island, is 550 miles long, with an average breadth of 110 miles, and contains 45,000,000 acres. Stewart's Isle, said to be not only uninhabited, but uninhabitable, has a triangular shape, and comprises an area of about 1,000,000 acres. The whole white population of the colony in 1867 amounted to 220,092, viz., 133,102 males and 86,990 females. The native population is estimated at 38,540 in addition. The white population, consisting chiefly of emigrants from Great Britain, is scattered in small communities over the island, the wide intervals between these settlements being occupied chiefly by the natives (Maories), the bulk of whom inhabit the northern island. These are well armed, and skilful in the use of their rifles; and being, moreover, addicted to war, have given much trouble to the Government. In 1840, a treaty was concluded at Waitangi with the native chiefs, whereby the sovereignty of the islands was ceded to Great Britain, while the chiefs were guaranteed the possession of their lands, forests, &c., so long as they desired to retain them; the right of pre-emption, was, however, reserved to the Crown, if they wished to alienate any portion. Thus, New Zealand became a regular colony, and the seat of Government was fixed at Auckland. A year prior to this, an association, called the New Zealand Company, made a pretended purchase of tracts amounting to a third of the whole island, and for the ensuing 12 years the colonization of the island was conducted under its auspices, which proved so prejudicial to the prosperity of the country, that, after a long conflict with the Government, they, in 1852, resigned all their claims—never confirmed or acknowledged by the Government—on receiving £268,000 as a compensation for their outlay. The unscrupulous way in which the Company and others often took possession of lands to which the natives conceived themselves entitled, brought about, between 1843 and 1847, a series of perilous and bloody conflicts with those warlike tribes. They seemed afterwards to have laid aside their hostility, and began to compete with the white colonists in industry of every kind, as well as civilization generally; but in 1861 another outbreak took place, mostly confined to the Waikato river and the province of Taranaki, the head-quarters of the Maories. The rebellion, hitherto smothered for a time, has recently broken out afresh, and hostilities vigorously resumed.

The productions most peculiar to New Zealand are those of the Kauri pine, much valued for ship-building, from its lightness and elasticity (the resin of this tree forming one of its most valuable exports, Kauri gum, £70,572), and the native flax, considerable quantities of which are exported to the United Kingdom for the manufacture of ropes. The mineral riches of the colony promise abundant returns when they shall have been more fully explored. Gold has been found in many districts, the total quantity exported in 1866 being valued at £2,897,412. A rich iron ore, in the form of iron sand, has been found in Taranaki.

Auckland, situate in the north island, is the capital and seat of government, as well as an episcopal see. In 1866 the gross amount of public revenue was £1,978,711; the gross amount of public expenditure £3,293,250; public debt (including £1,917,675 for provincial Governments), £5,435,729. Value of total imports, £5,894,863. Value of imports from United Kingdom, £2,737,702. Value of total exports, £4,520,074 (including bullion and specie, £2,923,947). Value of total exports to United Kingdom, £1,713,062. Total tonnage of vessels entered and cleared, exclusive of coasting trade (597,539 British, 39,743 Foreign), 637,282. Principal imports, boots and shoes, value £228,163; cotton, woollen, silk,

&c., value £1,131,636; hardware, ironmongery, &c., value £402,665; ale and beer, 982,319 gallons, value £218,833; spirits, 633,200 gallons, value £231,864; sugar, 10,371 tons, value £362,303; tea, 1,773,582 lbs., value £195,349; tobacco, 1,311,273 lbs., value £102,429; wine, 309,267 gallons, value £118,797. Principal exports, gold and Kauri gum, already detailed; wool, 22,810,776 lbs., value £1,354,152.

The total quantity of land fenced, which in 1861 was 409,763 acres, and in 1864, 1,072,383 acres, had increased in 1867 to 3,455,535 acres; and the total quantity under crop, which, in 1861, was 226,219 acres, and in 1864, 382,655 acres, had increased in 1867 to 676,867 acres. The aggregate numbers of live-stock of all kinds (excepting poultry), which in 1858 were 1,728,093; in 1861, 3,038,557; and in 1864, 5,310,062, had increased in 1867 to 8,924,489. Taking sheep separately, the total number in the colony, which in 1858 was 1,523,324; in 1861, 2,761,383; and in 1864, 4,937,273, had increased in 1867 to 8,418,579.

The general Government consists of a Governor, aided by a Ministry, a Legislative Council, of 36 members, appointed by the Crown for life, and a House of Representatives, consisting of 76 members, elected for five years.

Governor and Commander-in-Chief, Sir George F. Bowen, G.C.M.G., £4,500.
Private Secretary, £300.
*Premier and Colonial Secretary, Hon. E. W. Stafford, £1,000.
*Colonial Treasurer, Hon. W. Fitzherbert, £1,000.
*Minister for Colonial Defence, Hon. T. M. Haultain, £1,000.
*Com. of Customs, Hon. J. C. Richmond, £1,000.
*Postmaster-General, Hon. John Hall, £1,000.
Speaker of Legislative Council, T. H. Bartley, £500.
Clerk of Legislative Council, L. Stowe, £350.
Speaker of House of Representatives, Sir D. Monro, £500. [bell, £500.
Clerk of House of Representatives, F. E. Campbell.
Under Secretary for Colonies, W. Gisborne, £600.
Chief Clerk, A. C. P. Macdonald, £350.
*Attorney-General, J. Prendergast, £1,000.
Assistant Law Officer, R. Hart, £600.
Secretary for Crown Lands and Registrar General of Lands, &c., A. Domett, £1,000.
Assistant Treasurer, J. Woodward, £600.
Accountant, C. T. Batkin, £600.
Secretary to General Post Office, G. E. Eliott, £600.
Inspector General Post Office, W. Gray, £500.
Under Secretary for Colonial Defence, J. Holt, £600.
Under Sec. for Native Affairs, W. Rolleston, £600.
Auditor of Public Accounts, C. Knight, M.D., £900.
Chief Justice, Sir G. A. Arney—on leave—£1,700.
Acting Chief Justice, J. S. Moore.
Puisne Judge, Wellington, A. J. Johnston, £1,500.
Do., Canterbury, H. B. Gresson, £1,500.
Do., Nelson and Westland, C.W. Richmond, £1,500.
Do., Otago, H. S. Chapman, £1,500.
District Judge, Auckland, T. Beckham, £800.
Do., Westland, E. Clarke, £900.
Do., Wellington, C. D. R. Ward, £900.
Do., Otago (Gold Fields), W. Gray, £1,000.
Bishop of New Zealand, Metrop.
Do. of Christchurch, Rt. Rev.H. J. C. Harper, D.D.
Do. of Wellington, Rt. Rev. C. J. Abraham, D.D.
Do. of Nelson, Rt. Rev. A. B. Suter, D.D.
Do. of Waiapu, Rt. Rev. W. Williams, D.C.L.
Do. of Dunedin, Rt. Rev. H. L. Jenner, D.D.

* These (with J. L. C. Richardson) form the Ministry.

PROVINCIAL GOVERNMENTS.
Superintendent, Auckland, J. Williamson.
Do., *Taranaki,* R. K. Richmond.
Do., *Wellington,* J. E. Featherston.
Do., *Nelson,* O. Curtis.
Do., *Canterbury,* W. S. Moorhouse.
Do., *Otago,* J. McAndrew.
Do., *Hawke's Bay,* D. Maclean.
Do., *Marlborough,* W. H. Eyes.
Do., *Southland,* J. P. Taylor.
Director of Geological Surveys, &c., J. Hector, M.D., F.R.S., £800.
Telegraph Engineer, Alfred Sheath, £600.
Marine Engineer, J. M. Balfour, C.E.

QUEENSLAND.

This, the most extensive Australian colony, situated in lat. 10° 30'—28° 30' S., and long. 141°—153° 30' E., comprises the whole north-eastern portion of the Australian Continent, and was formerly a part of New South Wales, but was separated therefrom, and erected into a distinct Colony, in December, 1859. Its eastern seaboard was discovered by Capt. Cook, who anchored in Moreton Bay in 1770 ; some years afterwards its coast was visited by Capt. Flinders ; but the first attempt to explore and settle any portion of the interior was made by Moxley, the Surveyor-General of New South Wales, who, in 1824, entered the River Brisbane, and selected the site of its future city of that name—now the capital of the colony and an episcopal see—on a spot about 20 miles from its mouth in Moreton Bay. The subsequent settlement of the country has followed the discoveries of a series of explorers. It possesses an area of 678,600 square miles (nearly double that of Canada), of which upwards of 500,000 are occupied by pastoral stations (i.e. equal to more than four times the area of the United Kingdom). It comprises "all and every the adjacent islands, their members, and appurtenances in the Pacific Ocean and in the Gulf of Carpentaria." Most of the productions of both temperate and tropical countries can be cultivated with success in Queensland. It is admirably adapted for the production of cotton (which is said to be indigenous here, and from the absence of severe frosts, perennial — its quality being affirmed by the judges at the International Exhibition to be "superior to cotton from any other part of the world" ; sugar and tobacco—also the growth of wool (the fleeces being of extreme fineness), which is as yet the staple production: gold, copper, coal, &c., have already been discovered in several districts ; timber also of fine quality, the Moreton Bay pine and the *Dammara robusta,* together with the cedar of Queensland, form valuable products for export. Onega Plains, a broad extent of country, situate in the rear of Port Denison, afford the richest pasturage—stock is reported to increase with such rapidity as to render statistics comparatively valueless. Col. Mundy asserts horses to be so numerous, that in many instances a squatter could mount a regiment of Cavalry at 24 hours' notice ; and only the best-bred animals are thought worth the trouble of breaking. Cattle and Sheep are plentiful, they are frequently condemned to the boiling-down process, and killed for the sake of their tallow and hides. But this necessity will quickly disappear with the increase of population, the amount of which in 1866 was, for this vast territory, only 96,172. The number of emigrants who left the United Kingdom for Queensland in 1865 amounted

to 12,551, of whom 1,469 were conveyed at the expense of the Colonial funds.

	£
Gross amount of Public Revenue in 1866 (including £102,699 raised by loans)	592,969
Gross amount of Public Expenditure	594,130
Public Debts	2,150,300
Value of total Imports (including £144,397 bullion and specie)	2,467,907
Value of Imports from United Kingdom	742,884
Value of total Exports (including £115,040 bullion and specie)	1,366,491
Value of total Exports to United Kingdom	£321,939

Total Tonnage of Vessels, exclusive of Coasting trade (386,516 British, 7,140 Foreign), 393,656.

Principal Imports—Beer and Ale, 645,680 gals. ; Wine, 93,371 gals. ; Spirits, 209,595 gals. (value £73,676) ; Flour and Bread, 14,727 tons ; Hardware and Ironmongery, value £134,042 ; Linen and Drapery, value £417,246 ; Sugar (unrefined), 3203 tons ; Tea, 855,459 lbs. ; Tobacco, 248,573 lbs. The principal Exports were—Wool, 14,346,239 lbs., value £987,659 ; Hides and Skins, value £35,170 ; Copper ore, value £33,918 ; Gold dust, value £85,561.

The Government is vested in a Governor, Executive Council, together with two houses of Parliament ; the Legislative Council, consisting of 20 Members nominated by the Governor, and a Legislative Assembly, consisting of 32 Members, which is elective.

Capt.-Gen., Gov.-in-Chief, and Vice-Adm., S. Wensley Blackall, £4,000 and allowances.
Private Secretary and A.-D.-C., Lt. Kerney, £300.

Executive Council.

The Governor.
Colonial Secretary, A. H. Palmer, £1,000.
Treasurer, R. R. Mackenzie, £1,000.
Post-Master General, T. L. M. Prior, £600.
Secretary for Lands, E. W. Lamb, £1,000.
Attorney-General, R. Pring, £1,000.
Clerk of Council, A. V. Drury, £400.

Officers of Legislative Council.
President, Hon. Col. M. C. O'Connell, £600.
Chairman of Comm., Hon. D. F. Roberts, £350.
Clerk, Hen. Johnson, £500.
Usher of the Black Rod, F. R. C. Master, £300.

Officers of Legislative Assembly.
Speaker, Hon. Gilbert Elliott, £600.
Chairman of Committees, C. Coxen, £350.
Clerk, L. A. Bernays, £500.
Do. Assistant, H. W. Radford, £300.
Parliam. Draftsman, J. Bramston, D.C.L., £500.
Parliamentary Librarian, R. Moffatt, £300.
Serjeant-at-Arms, E. B. Uhr, £300.

Judicial and Legal.
Chief Jus. Supreme Court, Hon. J. Cockle, £2,000.
Puisne Judge, do., Hon. A. J. P. Lutwyche, £2000.
Prothon. and Reg. do., J. R. Ball, £500.
Associates, J. Stockwell and W. K. Wright.

District Courts.
Judge (Metropolitan) E. Sheppard, £1,000.
Crown Prosecutor do., J. G. Jones, £500.
Judge (Northern) T. G. L. Innes, £1,000.
Crown Prosecutor do., W. H. A. Hirst, £500.
Judge (Western) C. W. Blakeney, £1,000.
Crown Prosecutor, do., J. K. Handy, £500.
Curators of Intestates' Estates, W. Pickering, and A. Raff.
Sheriff, A. E. Halloran, £600.
Crown Solicitor, R. Little, £400.

Auditor-General, H. Buckley, £700.
Collector of Customs, W. Thornton, £600.
Surveyor-General, A. C. Gregory, £700.
Deputy do., Major E. L. Burrowes, £500.
Colonial Architect, C. Tiffin, £600.
Eng. of Roads, R. Austin & F. J. Byerley, £600 each.
Engineer of Harbours, J. Brady, £600.
Registrar-General, F. O. Darvall, £600.
Deputy do., W. T. Blakeney, £400.
Health Officer,
Port Master, Lieut. Heath, R.N., £400. } £300.
Director of Botanical Gardens, W. Hill, £400.
Agent for Immigration, J. M'Donnell, £400.
Electric Telegraphs, W. J. Cracknell, £600.
Government Printer, W. Beale, £500.
Chief Com. Crown Lands, W. A. Tully, £600.
Under Colonial Secretary, A. W. Manning, £600.
Under Sec. for Public Lands, A. O. Herbert, £600.
Under Sec., Treasury, W. L. G. Drew, £690.
Commissioner of Police, D. T. Seymour, £600.
Eng. of Railways, A. Fitzgibbon and H. T. Plews.
Gold Comms, T. J. Griffin, C. J. Clarke. and G. W. Elliott.

Commissioner for Railways, A. O. Herbert.
Bishop of Brisbane, Rt. Rev. E. W. Tuffnell, D.D.
Archdeacon of do., Ven. B. Glennie, B.A.
Roman Catholic Bishop of do., J. Quinn, D.D.

SOUTH AUSTRALIA.

Recent legislation, by Royal Letters Patent, dated 6th July, 1863, has rendered this name a misnomer by extending the boundaries of the colony so as to include the entire centre of the Australian continent comprised between the Southern and Indian Oceans, and between 129th and 141st degrees of E. long. All the islands on the coast line are included in the territory of South Australia, extending about 1,600 miles, and comprising an area of 383,328 square miles, with a population of 169,153. It was first colonized, in 1836, by emigrants from Great Britain, sent out under the auspices of a company called the South Australian Colonization Company, who, in 1835, obtained a grant from the Imperial Government of the lands of this colony: the conditions were that the revenue arising from the sale of land—£1 per acre being the minimum price fixed—should be appropriated to the emigration of agricultural labourers; and the control of the company's affairs vested in a commissioner approved by the Colonial Secretary and a Governor of the colony appointed by the Crown. Captain Hindmarsh, R.N., was so appointed, and arrived in the colony on 26th December, 1836. The constitution of the colony was remodelled in 1856, and the present form of government substituted. It is essentially an agricultural and pastoral province, its breadstuffs and wool constituting nearly three-fourths of its exports. The lands purchased from the Crown, up to 1860, amounted to 2,104,000 acres, and those held upon lease for pastoral purposes occupied 27,000,000 acres in addition. The wheat and flour of South Australia are subjects of just pride to the settlers. The traveller may drive for many hundreds of miles amidst cornfields and vineyards cultivated by yeoman proprietors. The splendid samples of white wheat, which gained the first prize in the Great Exhibition, weighed 70 lbs. to the bushel; in fact, it has become the granary of the Eastern Settlements. After breadstuffs, the next most valuable production is wool, the average weight of the fleece being 3¼ lbs. This amounts to nearly one-third of the whole export. The vine culture is becoming a fast increasing and recognized branch of industry. Mining operations are pursued on a very extensive scale in the colony, the mineral wealth hitherto discovered consisting chiefly in copper, the Burra Burra Mine being the largest, and employing nearly 1,000 hands. South Australia possesses a large series of telegraphic lines, cheaply but substantially constructed. Adelaide, the chief city of the colony, and an Episcopal see, is situated on the eastern shores of St. Vincent's Gulf, about five miles from the sea shore.

In 1866, the gross amount of Public Revenue (including £25,405 loan) was...

	£
In 1866, the gross amount of Public Revenue (including £25,405 loan) was...	975,180
Gross amount of Public Expenditure (including repayment of loan £95,830)	1,084,709
Public Debt	775,600
Value of Total Imports (including £68,050 bullion and specie) was	2,835,142
Value of Imports from United Kingdom	1,880,273
Value of Total Exports (including £86,930 bullion and specie) was	2,858,737
Exports (produce of colony)	2,539,723
Value of Total Exports to United Kingdom was	1,155,866

Total tonnage of vessels, exclusive of coasting trade (323,339 British, 16,532 Foreign), 339,871. The principal Imports were: Malt Liquors, 431,161 gallons: Spirits, 75,730 gallons; Wine, 55,819 gallons; Tea, 833,073 lbs.; Tobacco, Manufactured, 323,257 lbs. ; Wool, 1,973,253 lbs.; Candles, 715,808 lbs.; Coals, Coke, &c., 82,830 tons; Drapery, value £847,101. The chief Exports were: Wool, 20,908,085 lbs., or 61,977 bales, value £1,064,487 ; Copper, 129,272 cwt., value £584,509; Corn and flour, 30,723 tons, value £502,595 ; Wheat, 46,756 quarters, value £126,601. The Government is administered by a Governor and an Executive Council of 5 Members, who constitute a responsible ministry, and are required to be Members of Parliament. The Parliament consists of a Legislative Council of 18 Members, and a House of Assembly of 36 Members, elected by ballot.

Capt.-Gen. and Gov.-in-Chief, Sir Jas. Fergusson, Bt., £4,000.
Aide-de-Camp, Major de N. Lucas, £500.
Com. of the Forces, Lieut.-Col. F. G. Hamley.
Chief Secretary, Hon. Henry Ayers, £1,300.
Attorney-Gen., Hon. R. B. Andrews, £1,000.
Treasurer, Hon. T. Reynolds, £900.
Chief Justice and Judge of Vice-Admiralty, Hon. R. D. Hanson, £1,500.
2nd Judge, B. Boothby, £1,300.
3rd do., Hon. E. C. Gwynne, £1,300.
Pres. of Leg. Council, Hon. John Morphett, £600.
Clerk of do., F. C. Singleton, £500.
Speaker of House of Assembly, Hon. G. S. Kingston, £600.
Clerk of do., G. W. de la P. Beresford, £500.
Com. of Crown Lands and Immigration, Hon. L. Glyde, £800.
Com. of Public Works, Hon. P. Santo, £800.
Surveyor-Gen., G. W. Goyder, £700.
Under Secretary, O. K. Richardson, £600.
Auditor-General, W. L. O'Halloran, £700.
Postmaster-Gen., J. W. Lewis, £700.
Coll. of Customs and Naval Offic., B. Douglas, £700.
Sheriff, W. R. Boothby, £500.
Master of Supreme Court and Reg. Vice-Admiralty Court, W. Hinde, £450.
Prothonotary and Reg., C. A. Wilson, £400.
Clerk of Arraigns, L. J. Pellham, £300.
Marshal, Vice-Admiralty Court, W. R. Boothby.

Crown Solicitor and Public Prosecutor, W. A. Wearing, Q.C., £600.
Commis. of Insolvency. H. E. Downer, £600.
Official Assignee, J. Cherry. £500.
Curator Intestate Estates, H. A. Wood.
Police Magistrate of Adelaide, S. Beddome, £500.
Registrar-Gen., W. B. T. Andrews, £700.
Deputy do., W. B. Carter, £500.
Reg. Gen. of Births, &c., J. F. Cleland, £400.
Com. of Police, Geo. Hamilton, £600.
Comp. of Convicts, F. W. Howell, £350.
Colonial Surgeon, R. W. Moore, £700.
Resident Medical Officer, Lunatic Asylum, J. Patterson, M.D., £500.
Immigration Agent, H. Duncan, M.D., £400.
Chief Inspector of Schools, W. Wyatt, £500.
Government Printer, W. C. Cox, £500.
Bishop of Adelaide, Rt. Rev. A. Short, D.D., £800.
Dean and Col. Chap., V. Rev. J. Farrell, M.A., £300.
Roman Cath. Bishop, Dr. L. B. Sheil.
Vicar-Gen., Very Rev. J. Smythe.
Observer and Superintendent of Telegraphs, Chas. Todd, £600.
Engineer and Architect, H. C. Mais, £750.
Sec. of Central Board of Main Roads, H. J. Andrews, £500.
Clerk of Executive Council, S. Deering.
Under Treasurer, E. W. Hitchin, £600.
Sec. to Commiss. of Crown Lands and Immigration, J. N. Blackmore, £500.
Sec. to Comm. of Public Works, W. S. M. Hutton, £500.
Assistant Auditor Gen., J. L. Haining, £450.
Asst. Sec., Chief Sec's. Office, and Govt. Statist, J. Boothby, £450.
Agent Gen. and Immigration Agent for South Australia, Francis S. Dutton, 37, Great George Street, Westminster, London.

TASMANIA, or VAN DIEMEN'S LAND,

Is an island in the South Pacific Ocean, off the southern extremity of Australia, from which it is separated by Bass's Straits. It lies between 41° 20′ – 43° 40′ S. lat., and 144° 40′ – 148° 20′ E. long., and contains an area of 26,215 square miles, or 16,778,000 acres of land, of which, on 31st March 1868, 281,383 were under cultivation. wheat 64,010, barley 6,860, oats 27,574, potatoes 10,768, hay 33,064: the culture of sugar-beet is receiving attention; also, that of hops, which is greatly increased. The Revenue from the land fund amounted in 1867 to £124,945. The population, on 1st January, was estimated at 98,455. This island was first discovered by Tasman. in Dec., 1642, and named by him "Van Diemen's" land in honour of his patron, the then governor of the Dutch possessions in India. It was subsequently partially explored by Capt. Cook. In 1803, Lieut. Bowen was despatched from Sydney with a few soldiers and convicts to form a penal settlement there, and finally fixed upon the spot where Hobart Town now stands. Until 1813 it became a place for transportation from Great Britian and New South Wales, of which colony it then was a dependency. In 1841 transportation to New South Wales having ceased, Tasmania, to which had been annexed Norfolk Island, became the only colony to which criminals from Great Britain were sent; but this ceased in 1853, when transportation to Tasmania was abolished. The climate is fine and salubrious, and well suited to European constitutions. The chief products of the colony are wool, which commands a high price in the English markets; the amount of last year's (1867) exports being £373,977. The butter and cheese of Tasmania are favourably known in the adjacent colonies, and largely exported to Victoria; the wheat ranks very high in the market for its superior nutritious quality, as proved by analysis; the yield per acre is large, and the sample heavy; one is mentioned from the banks of the Clyde, which weighed 70 lbs. to the bushel, and 50 bushels per acre are frequently obtained, although the average is but 20 bushels per acre, and this from ground which a Tasmanian farmer boasts of working without any dressing whatever!—the land in many instances being cropped with wheat and oats for several years without any application of manure, or any rest save an occasional summer fallow. On new land, however, it is said that 70 bushels of wheat, and 15 tons of potatoes per acre, are not an uncommon crop. The chief consumer of grain in this part of the world, is Victoria,—the corn market of Melbourne ruling the prices throughout the whole group of Australian colonies, New Zealand included. The woods of Tasmania are scarcely yet fully appreciated—the sources of supply are practically inexhaustible, abounding in the most beautiful cabinet woods and the largest-sized timbers, adapted for every variety of purpose. The myrtle is a tree of immense size, rising sometimes 200 feet high, and 24 feet in circumference; and the Huon pine, from its great durability and quality of resisting the attacks of insects, renders it valuable alike for furniture wood and for ship and house building. The pride, however, of Tasmanian timber-trees is the Blue Gum *(Eucalyptus globulus)*; it is found in abundance in the north, although that from the south is deemed the best, and hill-growth better than that of the valley; fine examples are found, varying from 300 to 350 feet high, and from 30 to 100 feet round the base. Its elasticity is greater than either the Moorung saul, Indian teak, or British oak. Of samples of oak, saul, and blue gum, 7 feet long and 2 inches square, the breaking weights were, 450, 881, and 1,031 lbs. respectively. The young trees are covered with a bluish-grey bloom, whence its name. The mineral kingdom is also well represented, but has not hitherto added much to the commercial produce of the colony. Copper exists in the north-east; also iron in many districts. Gold and auriferous quartz have been traced, the yield of the alluvial mines last year (1867) 144 oz., and 1,219 oz. were from 7,677 tons of quartz raised. Coal of a good quality, and in easily accessible positions, is very generally distributed over the island. The whale fishery also has been from early times an important occupation to the colonists, and is still successfully prosecuted. Tasmania is an episcopal see, Hobart Town is the chief city; it contains 27 places of worship, and a population of about 25,000 inhabitants. It has several handsome public buildings: the Government house, situate on the banks of the Derwent, in the Queen's Park, being one of the finest edifices in Australia.

Gross amount of Public Revenue, (including Loan £49,139), 1867	£272,953
Gross amount of Public Expenditure (including repayment of Loan, £18,900) 1867	255,552
Public Debt, 1867	1,018,900
Value of Total Imports, 1867	856,348
Value of Imports from United Kingdom, 1866	253,180

Value of total Exports, including £730 Bullion and Specie, (1867) £790,494
Value of total Exports to United Kingdom, (1866) 344,131

Number of vessels entered inwards 598, tonnage 97,390; vessels cleared outwards 631, tonnage 102,754.

The Constitution of Tasmania was settled by local Act (18 Vic., No. 17). By this Act the Legislative Council and House of Assembly are constituted "The Parliament of Van Diemen's Land." The former consists of 15 Members, elected for six years, and the latter of 30 Members, elected for five years. The Governor, who is appointed by the Crown, is aided by a Cabinet of responsible Ministers.*

Capt.-Gen.. Gov.-in-Chief, and Vice-Adm., Rt. Hon. George Ducane, £4,000, and £2,500 for Aide-de-camp, and other expenses.
Private Secretary, £350.
Chief Justice and Judge of Vice-Adm. Court, Sir V. Fleming, £1,500.
* *Colonial Secretary,* Hon. Sir Richard Dry, £700.
* *Colonial Treasurer,* Hon. T. D. Chapman, £700.
* *Attorney-General,* Hon. W. L. Dobson, £700.
Puisne Judge, Hon. Sir F. Smith, £1,200.
Pres. of Legis. Coun., Hon. W. E. Nairn, £200.
Speaker of House of Assem., Hon. R. Officer, £200.
Recorder of Titles, William Tarleton, £600.
Colonial Auditor, E. J. Manley, £600.
Bp. of Tasmania, Rt. Rev. C. H. Bromby, D.D., £800.
Bp. Rom. Cath. Ch., Daniel Murphy, D.D., £400.
Archdeacon of Hobart Town, R. R. Davies, M.A.
Do. Launceston, Ven. T. Reibey, M.A.
Surveyor-General and Commissioner of Crown Lands, J. E. Calder, £600.
Col. of Customs, Hobart Town, T. T. Watt, £500.
Do. Launceston, R. H. Willis, £500.
Clerk of Exec. and Legis. Coun. E. C. Nowell, £400.
Clerk of House of Assembly, H. M. Hull, £450.
Recorder, Launceston, J. Whitefoord, £500.
Comptroller-General, W. E. Nairn, £800.
Director of Public Works and Inspector of Telegraphs, W. R. Falconer, £500.
Registrar of Supreme and Vice-Admy. Courts and Curator of Intestate Estates, H. J. Buckland, £400.
Government Printer, J. Barnard, £500.
Assistant Colonial Secretary, B. T. Solly, £500.
Dep. Com. of Crown Lands, E. W. Boothman, £450.
Postmaster, Hobart Town, S. T. Hardinge, £450.
Inspector of Schools, T. Stephens, £400.
Geological Surveyor, C. Gould, £600.
Immigration Agent, B. T. Solly.

VICTORIA.

This territory was formerly a portion of New South Wales (known as the Port Phillip district), from which it was severed and erected into a separate colony by Act 13 and 14 Vict. c. 59, and although one of the youngest, and in point of area, the smallest of the Australian group, is already the most important in extent of commerce; indeed, it takes precedence of all other colonies, India alone excepted. It comprises the south-east corner of Australia at that part where its territory projects farthest into the southern latitudes; it lies between the 34th and 39th parallels of S. lat. and 141st and 150th meridians of E. long. Its extreme length from east to west is about 420 miles, its greatest breadth 250 miles, and its extent of coast line nearly 600 miles. From its position at the extreme south of the Australian continent it is often mistaken by English writers, and others not thoroughly acquainted with Australian geography, for an adjoining colony, topographically misnamed South Australia, Wilson's Promontory being the southernmost point in Victoria. The entire area comprises 86,831 square miles, or 55,571,840 acres, of which 530,000 were under cultivation in 1866. Its population is 653,902, the agricultural portion thereof being vastly outnumbered by the gold miners. From its geographical position it enjoys a climate far more genial to Europeans than any other colony within the continent of Australia. There are 276 miles of railway completed in Victoria, the total cost of which amounted to £9,850,359 7s. 1d., and the revenue arising therefrom in 1865. £717,162. Stage coaches also run to all parts of the colony, except those for which railway communication is available. There are 79 stations for electric telegraphs extending over 3,110 miles, producing a revenue of £35,000 in 1865. The chief sources of income until 1862 were the customs duties and sales of public lands, but a fresh source of revenue derivable from the railway system, amounting in 1865 to nearly £600,000, and from public works, has been recently added thereto. Prior to gold-mining, wool was the staple commodity of export from the colony. The colonial term of squatting has long since passed from its original semi-savage and outcast associations, and now represents an Australian rural aristocracy. The pastoral "stations" or "runs" heretofore parcelled out with a liberal hand to a small number, have become subdivided, and enclosed with good stout fencing. Agriculture, hitherto neglected, has within the last few years much improved, wheat and oats being the two cereals chiefly cultivated. Of the 530,000 acres under cultivation about 179,000 are wheat crops (the average yield being 19½ bushels per acre), and 102,000 oats (the average being 22 bushels per acre). The produce of the gold fields in 1866 was 1,480,597 oz., equivalent to £5,928,948.

Gross amount of public Revenue in 1866 £2,990,842
Gross amount of public Expenditure 2,629,568
Public Debt.................................... 8,844,855

About ⅞ths of this represents the railway system now completed; the remainder is the cost of water supply to Melbourne and other parts of the colony, and for town improvements (Melbourne and Geelong); the debt exists in the form of debentures terminable altogether in 1891.

Value of total imports in 1867 (including bullion and specie, £1,133,825)... 10,563,590
Value of imports from United Kingdom 7,846,828
Value of total exports in 1867, including £6,878,325 bullion and specie) 11,115,135
Total tonnage of vessels, exclusive of coasting trade in 1866 (1,182,452 British, and 143,268 Foreign) 1,325,721.

The principal Imports in 1866 were, Iron and steel, 28,852 tons. Sugar and molasses, 827,566 cwt. Spirits of all kinds, 1,303,020 gals. Wine, 645,004 gals. Tea, 7,049,703 lbs. Tobacco, cigars, and snuff, 4,149,764 lbs. Principal Exports in 1866 were, exclusive of gold and specie already enumerated, Tea, 1,527,537 lbs. Wool, 42,391,234 lbs. Value, £3,196,491.

Melbourne, the chief city and the seat of government, as also an episcopal see, is distinguished for its university, hospital, and other institutions, and contains 130,000 inhabitants.

The government is vested in a Governor appointed by the Crown, aided by an Executive Council or ministry consisting of 10 members, and a Parliament consisting of a Legislative Council of 30 members elected for 6 provinces, and a Legislative Assembly of 78 members for 49 districts.

Capt.-Gen. & Gov.-in-Chief, & Vice-Adm., Hon. Sir J. H. T. Manners-Sutton, K.C.B., £10,000.
Private Secretary, H. C. Manners-Sutton.
Aide-de-Camp, Lieutenant Rothwell, R.A.
Com. of Forces, Maj.-Gen. Sir Trevor Chute, K.C.B.
Com. R. Art., Col. C. H. Smith.
Clerk to Exc. Coun., Capt. J. H. Kay, R.N., £1,200.
Pres. of Legis. Coun., Sir J. F. Palmer, Kt., £1,000.
Clerk of Coun. and of Parl., G. W. Rusden, £1,000.
Speaker of Legis. Assem., Sir F. Murphy, £1,500
Clerk of Assembly, J. Barker, £1,000.
Librarian, Jas. Smith, £700.
Chief Secretary, Hon. J. McCulloch, £2,000.
Vice-Pres. of Land and Works, J. Higinbotham.
Under-Secretary, John Moore, J.P., £1,000.
Reg.-Gen.& Reg.Suprme.Ct., W.H.Archer,J.P.£900.
Chief Medical Officer, W. McCrae, M.B., £900.
Chief Commis. of Police, F. C. Standish, £900.
Police Magistrates, Melbourne, E. P. S. Sturt, £850. C. P. Hackett, £800.
Insp.-Gen. Penal Estab. W. I. N. Champ, £900.
Treas. (Finance), Hon. G. F. Verdon, 1,600, absent.
Under Treasurer, E. S. Symonds, £900.
Receiver and Paymaster, W. H. Hull, £625.
Commissioners of Audit, C. H. Symonds, Francis Jones, Alfred J. Agg, £1,000 each.
Com. of Crown Lands, Hon. J. M. Grant, £1,600.
Surveyor-General, C. W. Ligar, £1,000.
Assistant-Com. & Sec., C. Hodgkinson, C.E., £900.
Commissioner of Public Works, Hon. C. E. Jones.
Chief Clerk & Accountant, Alex. Galt, £600.
Director of Geol. Survey, A. R. C. Selwyn, £800.
Commis. of Customs, Hon. W. M. K. Vale, £1400.
Inspector-General, John Guthrie, £1,000.
Collector, Melbourne, J. Chatfield Tyler, £900.
Postmaster-General, Hon. G. V. Smith, £1,400.
Deputy-Postmaster-Gen., William Turner, £900.
Insp. of Postal Service, H. P. Bance, R.N., £620.
Superin. of Elec. Tel., S. W. McGowan, £850.
Minister of Mines, Hon. J. Sullivan, £1,400.
Secretary, R. B. Smyth, F.G.L.S., £750.
Commissioner of Railways, Hon. C.E. Jones, £1,000.
Engineer-in-Chief, Thomas Higinbotham, £1,200.

LOCAL STAFF.

Col.-Commandant, W. A. D. Anderson, £900.
Barrack-Master, C. H. Hall, £750.

ECCLESIASTICAL.

Bishop of Melbourne, Rt. Rev. C. Perry, D.D. £1,333.
Dean, Very Rev. H. B. Macartney, D.D.
Rom. Cath. Bishop, Right Rev. J. A. Gould, D.D.
Vicar-General, Very Rev. J. Fitzpatrick, D.D.

SUPREME COURT.

Chief Justice, Sir W. Forster Stowell, £2,500.
Judges, Sir R. Barry, E. E. Williams, Esq., Robert Molesworth, Esq., £2,000 each.
Attorney-General, Hon. G. P. Smith, £1,600.
Minister of Justice, Hon. T. Casey.
Secretary, A. W. Chomley, £600.
Crown Solicitor, H. F. Gurner, £1,000.
Prothonotary, J. A. Porter, £860.
Commissioner of Tithes, John Carter, £2,000.

WESTERN AUSTRALIA,

Formerly called the "Swan River Settlement," (from the River Swan, which joins the Indian Ocean, after watering a considerable district in the extreme south-west), is situated on the westward side of Australia, and includes all that portion of the island, from 129° E. long. to the Indian Ocean. Its extreme length, therefore, is, from north to south, 1,280 miles, and 800 from east to west. It embraces an area of 978,000 square miles. The occupied portion of the colony is about 600 miles from N. to S., and about 150 in average breadth, and had a population of 21,065 in the year 1866. It was first settled in 1829, and for many years made but little progress, notwithstanding the salubrity of the climate, which is equal to that of any part of the Australian continent. It is, however, now gaining ground. Western Australia is at present the only colony to which convicts from Great Britain are transported, and those only in limited numbers, but this will speedily cease. On the 31st of December, 1866, 1,784 convicts were in the hands of Government. Ticket-of-leave men earning their livelihood, 1,442. The Imperial convict expenditure in 1864 was £72,745; in 1865, £80,420; in 1866, £78,229. The cultivation of the land has been much retarded by the want of sufficient labour; bands of fertile soil, where sandalwood and other trees grow abundantly, and which are suitable for the culture of the vine, olive, and fig, occur in the middle districts. The produce of the vintage exceeds 25,000 gallons per annum. Good wheat-growing soils also exist over large areas in the northern division, and the produce is of good quality and yield. Magnetic iron ore, lead, copper, and zinc ore are found in large quantities; and there is a band of coal extending over 600 miles. The imports chiefly consist of sugar, tea, tobacco, spirits, beer, soap, ironmongery, and clothing of various kinds. The exports consist chiefly of wool, timber, copper ore—which is said to be exceedingly rich—and whale oil. Perth is the capital.

	£
In 1866 the gross amount of public Revenue was	89,383
The gross amount of public Expenditure	84,652
Public debt	none.
Value of total Imports (including £12,545 bullion and specie)	251,907
Value of Imports from United Kingdom	143,521
Value of total Exports	152,240
Value of total Exports to United Kingdom £103,732	
Total tonnage of Vessels exclusive of coasting trade (85,786 British, 27,950 Foreign)	113,736

The government is administered by a Governor appointed by the Crown, assisted by an Executive Council of six official members, also a Legislative Council, consisting of the same official and four non-official members, also appointed by the Crown, on the nomination of the Governor.

Governor and Commander-in-Chief, Sir B. C. C. Pine, £1,800.　[Hampton, £350.
Private Secretary and Clerk of Councils, G. B.
Commandant, Major R. H. Crumpton.
Chief Justice, A. P. Burt, £1,000.
Bishop of Perth, M. B. Hale, D.D.
Archdeacon, Ven. J. Brown, £300.
Colonial Secretary, Hon. F. P. Barlee, £800.
Surveyor-General, Hon. J. S. Roe, R.N., £500.
Comp.-Gen. of Convicts, Hon. H. Wakeford, £800.
Treas. & Col. of Rev., Hon. A. O'G. Lefroy, £550.
Attorney-General, Hon. G. F. Stone, £500.
Auditor-General, W. Knight, £450.
Postmaster-General, A. Helmich, £350.
Colonial Surgeon, J. Ferguson, £400.
Crown Solicitor, G. W. Leake, £250.

---

* These form the Ministry.

ANTIGUA,

The most important of the Leeward Islands, Caribbees, or Antilles, and the residence of the Governor-in-Chief of the British portion. It lies 17° 6′ N. lat., and in 61° 45′ W. long., and is about 54 miles in circumference, its area being about 183 square miles, equal to 117,120 acres, of which 60,000 are under cultivation. The population at the last census in 1861 was 37,125. Antigua was discovered by Columbus in 1493, who named it after a church in Seville, Sta. Maria la Antigua. It was first inhabited by a few English in 1632. Subsequently, in 1663, a grant of it was made by Charles II. to Lord Willoughby, who sent out a large number of colonists. After an interval of French occupation, it was declared a British possession by the treaty of Breda in 1666. The revenue of the colony—chiefly derived from taxes imposed by an Act of Parliament 1799—amounted, in 1866 (including a loan of £26,081), to £69,629, and its expenditure to £57,389, including repayment of loan, £1,019,—the public debt amounted to £47,655. The chief products consisted, in 1866, of sugar, 17,330 hogsheads, of molasses, 7,852 puncheons, of rum, 696 puncheons,—the value of total imports being £203,257, including £72,815 from Great Britain. The value of total exports, £291,861, including £277,386 to Great Britain. The total tonnage of vessels exclusive of coasting trade (55,079 British, 2,983 Foreign) was 58,062. The island is divided into eleven electoral districts, and the government is vested in a Governor (who is Governor and Commander-in-Chief of the Leeward Islands), aided by an Executive Council of 12 Members, and a Legislative Council of 24 Members, 12 of whom are nominated by the Crown, and 12 are elected by the several districts.

Government.

Governor and Commander-in-Chief, Col. Stephen J. Hill, C.B., £3,000.
Private Sec. and A. D. C., C. C. Lees, £300.
President of Legislative Council, Sir W. Byam, Kt.
Vice-President, Oliver Nugent.
Clerk of do., O. Humphrys, £180.
Chief Justice, Vice Chancellor, Judge of Vice-Adm. Court, Judge Advocate, &c., Sir Wm. Snagg, £1,000 and fees.
Attorney-Gen., Hon. R. W. Mara, L.L.D., £400.
Solicitor-General, J. R. Semper.
Treasurer and Comptroller of Customs, &c., H. Berkeley, £500.
Col. Secr. and Registrar of Births and Deaths, Hon. Edwin D. Baynes, £550; C. M. Eldridge, *Actg.*
Puisne Judge, Hon. Ch. H. Okey, £200.
Bishop, Rt. Rev. W. W. Jackson, D.D., £2,000.

BAHAMAS,

A chain of islands lying between 21° 42′—27° 34′ N. lat. and 72° 42′—79° 5′ W. long. The group consists of about twenty which are inhabited, and a vast congeries of about 3,000 islets and rocks, comprising an area of 3,021 square miles, and a population of about 40,000. The principal islands are New Providence (containing the capital, Nassau). St. Salvador, Harbour Island, Great Bahama, Long Island, Eleuthera, and Berry Islands. St. Salvador was the first land discovered by Columbus on his voyage in 1492. New Providence was settled by the English in 1629, and held by them till expelled by the Spaniards in 1641; who, however, made no attempt to settle there. It was again colonized by the English in 1657, but fell into the hands of the French and Spaniards in 1703, after which it became a rendezvous for pirates, who were eventually extirpated in 1718, and a regular colonial administration was established. In 1781 the Bahamas were surrendered to the Spaniards, but at the conclusion of the war were once more annexed, and finally confirmed to Great Britain by the Peace of Versailles in 1783. There are ten colonial custom-houses and ports of entry in the Bahamas, considerable quantities of salt, sponges, pine-apples, and oranges being exported, chiefly to England and the United States.

	£
Amount of Public Revenue in 1866	53,283
Public Expenditure	76,986
Total value of Imports (including £52,124 from Great Britain)	328,622
Value of total Exports (including £63,012 to Great Britain)	261,976
Total Tonnage of vessels entered and cleared, exclusive of Coasting trade: (79,636 British, and 42,314 Foreign)	121,950

The government is vested in a Governor, aided by an Executive Council of nine members, a Legislative Council of nine members, and a representative Assembly of 28 members.
Governor and Com.-in-Chief, John Scott, Esq., £3,000.
Pres. Legis. Council, Hon. W. H. Doyle.
Speaker of Assembly, Att.-Gen., and *Advocate-Gen.,* Hon. G. C. Anderson, £700.
Chief Justice, Chancellor, and Judge Vice-Admiralty Court, W. H. Doyle, £900 and fees.
Assist-Just. Gen. Court, Judge Co. Com. Pleas, and Comm. in Bankruptcy, Hon. C. F. Rothery, £650.
Colonial Sec. Lt. G. C. Strahan, R.A.
Receiver-Gen. and Treas., J.D. Dumaresque, £650 and fees.
Bp. of Nassau, Rt. Rev. A. R. P. Venables, D.D., £1,000.

BARBADOS,

The most windward of the Caribbee Islands, is situated in 13° 4′ N. lat. and 59° 37′ W. long. It is nearly 21 English miles long, and 14 in breadth, and comprises an area of 106,470 acres, or 166 square miles. The exact date of its discovery is not known; but its existence was first indicated in the charts of 1600. It is supposed to have been first visited by the Portuguese, who, from its rugged appearance and the number of bearded fig-trees they found therein, named the isle *Los Barbados.* It has been held successively by various owners, under grants from the Crown, but after the restoration of Charles II. the proprietary Government was dissolved, and the sovereignty of Barbados annexed to the British Crown. Population in 1861, 152,127. Bridgetown is the chief town and port. The island is almost encircled by coral reefs. It is divided into 11 parishes, each of which from an early date was presided over by a clergyman of the Church of England; and in 1824 episcopal jurisdiction was established here, as also for the Leeward Islands and British Guiana. Barbados possesses a college founded by General Codrington, a native of the island, who died 1710, and whose name it bears, and also a collegiate school attached thereto. An inland post-office was set on foot in 1852, since

---

* Executive Council *ex officio.*

amalgamated with the General Post Office. The principal products are Sugar 55,811 hds., Molasses 28,237 hhds., and Meat (salted), 1,859,507 lbs., were exported. The principal Imports are Rice, of which, in 1866, 4,250,922 lbs., Meat (salted), 2,667,000 lbs., Corn and Grain, 275,522 bushels, Butter 826,150 lbs., Flour and Wheat 82,675 barrels, were imported. The population is about 160,000.

Amount of Public Revenue in 1866......	£103,935
Amount of Public Expenditure (including repayment of loan, £6,000)..	95,838
Public Debt....................	3,541
Value of total Imports (including £379,725 from the United Kingdom),	988,082
Value of total Exports (including £817,980 to the United Kingdom) ...	1,246,844

Total tonnage of vessels, exclusive of Coasting trade (255,923 British and 60,398 Foreign), 316,321.

The local Government of Barbados consists of a Governor, who is also Governor-in-Chief of St. Vincent, Tobago, Grenada, and St. Lucia, an Executive Council of nine members (beside the Governor and the Lord-Bishop), a Legislative Council consisting of the same members, the Governor excepted, and a House of Assembly of 24 members, elected annually by franchise.

* *Gov. and Com.-in-Chief of Barbados and Windward Islands*, Rawson W. Rawson, £4,000.
Chief Justice, Sir R. B. Clarke, Knt., C.B., £2,000.
General Commanding Troops, Major-Gen. Ainslie.
†**President of Council*, Hon. Grant E. Thomas.
Speaker of Assembly, Hon. T. Gill.
Col. Sec. and Clerk of Council, A. F. Gore, £700., and fees, &c. £520.
†**Attorney-General*, Hon. J. Sealy, £500.
Solicitor-General, Hon. Charles Packer, £250.
†**Bishop*, Rt. Rev. Thomas Parry, D.D., £2,500.
Coadjutor Bp. and Archdeacon, Rt. Rev. H. H. Parry, £500.
Colonial Teasurer, J. S. Howell, £1,500.
Auditor-General, William B. Griffith, £700.
Comptroller of Customs, R. D. Fraser, £530.
Clerk of House of Assembly, S. Taylor, £400.
Superintendent Pub. Works (vacant), £500.
Harbour Master, E. G. Clawson, £575.
Insp. Gen. of Police, Capt. J. Clements, £480.
Provost-Marshal, Robert Reece.
Colonial Post Master, C. Tinling, £400.
Judges of the Assist. Court of Appeal, J. J. Tinling, J. H. King, and J. Prescod.
Chancellor of the Diocese, Hon. J. Sealy, fees.
Registrar, Admiralty, S. Husbands, fees.
Queen's Solicitor, Samuel Taylor, fees.
Principal of Codrington College, Rev. W. T. Webb, £500.

BERMUDAS.

The Bermudas, or Somers Islands, are a cluster of about 300 small islands (15 or 16 only of which are inhabited, the rest being of inconsiderable size), situated on the western side of the Atlantic Ocean in 32° 15′ N. lat., and 64° 51′ W. long., the largest, or Bermuda proper, containing about 20 square miles, on which Hamilton, the chief town, and present seat of government, is situated. These islands derive their name from Bermudez, a Spaniard, who sighted them in 1527, but they were first colonized by Admiral Sir George Somers, who was shipwrecked here in 1609, on his way to Virginia. The Virginia Company claimed them, and obtained a charter

of them from James I., in 1612. Subsequently a fresh charter was obtained for them by a new company called the Bermuda Company, which had purchased the territorial right, and introduced representative Government in 1620. It also compiled a body of ordinances for the colony.

During the civil war great numbers of emigrants from England were attracted hither by favourable reports of the climate and soil, but grave complaints were made by the inhabitants of the misgovernment of the colony, and the charter of the company was annulled by law at Westminster in 1684. Since then the Government has been appointed by the Crown, and laws for the colony enacted by a local legislature. The lands belonging to the company having thus become forfeited to the Crown, were, with the exception of some reserved for public use, granted in 1759 to purchasers on small quit-rents, extinguishable on the payment of a fixed sum of money. The nearest point of land is at Cape Hatteras, in North Carolina, 600 miles distant. Bermuda possesses a strongly-fortified Dockyard, where the North American squadron refits. A most remarkable Floating-Dock has just been constructed. The population in 1863 was 11,796. The gross amount of public revenue in 1866, including £1,000 loan, was £26,638; gross amount of public expenditure, £25,148; public debt, £1,500; value of total imports (including £38,305 from the United Kingdom) £192,123. Value of total exports (including £6,925 to the United Kingdom) £31,842. The total tonnage (83,534 British, and 15,080 Foreign vessels) was 98,614. The products of the island chiefly consist of potatoes and other esculent roots, bananas, oranges, peaches, and other fruits, and arrowroot of a very fine quality. The sea abounds with fish; a few whales and turtle are occasionally taken. The episcopal jurisdiction is annexed to the see of Newfoundland; there are nine parishes compressed into five livings.

The Government is vested in a Governor and privy council of 10 members, appointed by the Crown, who also act as a Legislative Council, and a representative House of Assembly consisting of 36 members.

*†*Governor and Commander-in-Chief*, Major-Gen. Sir F. E. Chapman, R.E., K.C.B., £2,746.
Private Sec., Lieut. J. Edwards Fleetwood, R.E.
Clerk of Council, J. E. Butterfield, £130.
Speaker, House of Assembly, Hon. G. S. Tucker.
Clerk of House of Assembly, W. H. Darrell, £170.
*†*Colonial Secretary*, M. G. Keon, £800.
Assistant Colonial Secretary, J. Tucker, £200.
*†*Chief Justice*, J. H. Darrell, £800, and fees.
*†*Assistant Judges*, N. T. Butterfield, and J. Wood.
Attorney-General and Advocate-General, S. B. Gray, £600 and fees.
Solicitor-General, Seth Harvey.
Provost Marshal, J. H. Trott, £250, and fees.
*†*Receiver-General*, T. A. Darrell, £450.

DOMINICA, or DOMINIQUE,

The loftiest of the Lesser Antilles, is an island situate in the centre of the Caribbean sea, between 15° 20′—15° 45′ N. lat. and 61° 13′ —61° 30′ W. long., about 29 miles long and 16 broad, comprising an area of 290 square miles, or 186,436 acres, a small portion only of which is cultivated, the major part being incapable of reclamation. It is of volcanic origin, very moun-

---

* Executive Council.　† Legislative do. *ex officio.*

tainous and picturesque. It was discovered by Christopher Columbus on his second voyage, on Sunday, 3rd December, 1493, hence its name. Several attempts having been made by the English to bring it into subjection, it was, by the treaty signed at Aix la Chapelle in 1748, stipulated between the English and the French that it should remain neutral, and, together with some other islands, be left in possession of the original inhabitants—the Caribs. In 1756, however, it became, by conquest, the property of the English. In 1771, the island was formed into a separate government, under the administration of Sir William Young, Bart., from which period to 1806, it became the object of repeated invasions by the French, who alternately held possession with the English. The population, at the last census, amounted to 25,065.

In 1866, the gross amount of Public Revenue (including of loan, £4,100)... £18,422

Gross amount of Public Expenditure (including repayment of loan, £1,246), £18,367

Public debt ... 9,620

Value of Total Imports (including 25,941 from United Kingdom) ... 62,188

Value of Total Exports (including £92,883 to United Kingdom) ... 106,452

Total tonnage of vessels, exclusive of coasting trade (12,714 British, 1,402 Foreign), 14,123. The principal productions are sugar, coffee, cocoa, cotton, tobacco, molasses, rum, copper ore, and cabinet woods. Roseau is the seat of government. The government is administered by a Lt.-Governor, aided by an Executive Council of 7 members and a Legislative Assembly consisting of 14 Members, 7 nominated by the Crown, and 7 elected by the people.

*Lt.-Govern., £1,300.

Private Secretary,

Chief Justice, and Judge of Vice-Admiralty Court, Hon. Sholto T. Pemberton, £600 and fees.

Assistant Justice, Hon. J. Garraway.

Colonial Secretary, Clerk of Council, &c., W. H. McCoy, £400 and fees £180.

Attorney-Gen., C. Lloyd, £200 and fees.

Treasurer, John Palmer, £380 and fees.

Stipendiary Magistrates, *W. Lynch, *H. Lloyd, £300, and £150 allowance each.

Police Magistrate, T. F. Lockhart, £300.

Roman Catholic Bishop, R. M. C. Poirier, D.D.

GRENADA,

An island of volcanic origin in the West Indies, said to be the most beautiful of the Caribbees, abounding in streams, mineral and other springs, is situate between the parallels of 12° 30'—11° 58' N. lat., and 61° 20'—61° 35' W. long. It is about 21 miles in length, and 12 in its greatest breadth, and contains an area of 133 square miles, and a population, in 1866, of 36,672, chiefly of African descent. The island was discovered by Columbus on his third voyage in 1498, and was named Ascension, at which time it was inhabited by the Caribs, who were subsequently exterminated by the French in 1650. Du Parquet, governor of Martinique, purchased Grenada from a French Company, and subsequently sold it for 30,000 crowns to the Comte de Carrillac. The governor appointed by the Comte exercised such tyranny that the most respectable settlers left the island: the Governor was eventually seized and executed by the colonists—"Lynched" after the

most approved fashion. In 1674 the island was annexed to the crown of France, and the proprietors received compensation for their claims; but in 1762 it surrendered to the English, and was formally ceded to Great Britain by the Treaty of Paris, 1763. In 1779 it was retaken by the French, and in 1783, by the Treaty of Versailles, finally restored to Great Britain.

	£
Gross amount of Public Revenue in 1866	21,140
Gross amount of Public Expenditure	21,204
Public Debt	9,000
Value of total Imports (including those from Great Britain, £5,215)	122,255
Value of total Exports (including those to Great Britain, £98,688)	113,237

Total tonnage, exclusive of coasting trade (26,482 British, 3,939 Foreign), 30,421.

The government consists of a Lieut.-Governor, Legislative Council, selected by the Crown, which is also the Executive, and a House of Assembly, of 26 members, elected by the people.

Lieut.-Governor, Major Robert M. Mundy, £1,300.

Private Secretary, H. Garraway.

Chief Justice, Vice-Chancellor, Judge of Vice-Admiralty Court, J. F. Gresham, £800.

Attorney-General, , £400.

Chaplain of Assembly, &c., Rev. J. A. Anton, £350.

Col. Sec. and Reg. Gen., Samuel Mitchell, £450.

Treas. and Compt. of N. Laws, W. Beveridge, £400.

Chief Treasury Clerk, T. Bell, £150.

Speaker of Assembly, W. Wells, M.D., £150.

Clerk of do., John Wells, £250.

JAMAICA,

Aboriginally Xaymaca, or Land of Wood and Water—an island situated in the Caribbean Sea, about 90 miles to the south of Cuba, within 17° 40'—18° 30' N. lat., and 76° 10'—78° 30' W. long. It is the largest, and one of the most valuable of the British West Indian Islands, being 140 miles in length, and 50 in extreme breadth, containing an area of 6,400 square miles, and a population, at the last census, of 441,255. It was discovered in May, 1494, by Columbus, who called it St. Jago. It was taken possession of by the Spaniards in 1509, and so great was the inhumanity of the conquerors, that 50 years after their occupation of the island, the native population is said to have entirely disappeared. In 1655, a British expedition, sent out by Oliver Cromwell, under Penn and Venables, attacked the island, which capitulated after a trifling resistance. After its capture, until the Restoration of Charles II., it remained under military jurisdiction. In 1670 it was ceded to Great Britain by the Treaty of Madrid. In 1807 the Slave Trade was partially abolished, at which time there were about 323,827 slaves. On the total abolition in 1833, Jamaica received £6,161,927 as her portion of the £20,000,000 granted by Parliament as compensation to the slave-owners. It is traversed from east to west by a heavily-timbered ridge, called the Blue Mountains, which rise to about 7,000 feet. From these mountains at least 70 streams descend to the north and south shores, but, with the exception of one (the Black River, and that only for small craft,) they are not navigable. Excellent harbours are everywhere to be found. After being for 200 years in the possession of Great Britain, its capabilities are still inadequately developed. The rebellion, of recent occurrence, resulting in such a fearful tragedy, does not come within our province to detail: the entire authority being *now* practically vested in the Governor, assisted by a Privy Council, consisting of six Members, and a Legislative Council, consisting of the Privy Council and six non-official Members, of whom three only are as yet appointed. Jamaica is an episcopal see. The seat of Government, is Kingston.

In 1866 the gross Revenue was............ £334,140
Gross amount of Expenditure (including repayment of Loan of £15,912)   404,078
Public Debt................................   757,317
Value of total Imports for Consumption (including £684,448 from U.K.)   1,030,796
Exports (including £971,080 to U.K.)   1,152,898
Total tonnage of Vessels, exclusive of Coasting trade (279,577 British; 51,940 Foreign.), 331,517.
Principal Imports, British goods, unenumerated (at the Port of Kingston only), value £276,878.
Fish, wet and dry, £86,657: Flour, £95,880.
Principal Exports: Coffee, 8,513,532 lbs., value £188,864; Ginger, 1,550,166 lbs.; Pimento, 4,866,239 lbs.; Rum, 1,769,716 gallons, value £235,929; Sugar, 600,837 cwt., value £557,441.
* *Captain-General and Commander-in-Chief*, Sir John P. Grant, K.C.B., £7,000.
Private Secretary, Alfred C. Plowden, £300.
A.-D.-C., Capt. W. O. Lanyon.
†* *Colonial Secretary,* Hon. H. T. Irving, £1,500.
†* *Finance. Do.,* Hon. E.E.Rushworth, D.C.L. £1,500.
†* *Director of Roads and Surveyor-General,* Col. J. R. Mann, R.E.
† *Colonial Architect and Deputy Do.,* G. B. Pennell.
†* *Collector of Customs,* Hon. W. G. Freeman, £800.
Auditor-General, Alex. Bravo, £750.
Inspector of Revenues, D. P. Trench, £800.
Island Secretary, Edward Jordan, C.B.
Immigration Agent, W. M. Anderson, £500.
Inspector of Schools, John Savage, £500.
Postmaster for Jamaica, A. J. Brymer, £600.
Commissioner of Stamps, E.P. Chapman, £300.
Reg.-Gen. Births and Deaths, J. J. Vidal.
Police Magistrate, H. J. Bicknell, £500.
Harbour Master, Capt. W. S. Cooper, R.N., fees.
Inspector-Gen. of Constabulary, Major J. H. Prenderville, £600, and £200 travelling expenses.

Judicial Department.
Chief Justice and Vice-Chancellor, Sir Bryan Edwards, £1,800.   [Ker, each £1,200.
Assistant Judges, Hon. E. Kemble, Hon. Alan
Encumbered Estates Court, Judges, Sir B. Edwards, J. F. Cargill, Alan Ker.
†* *Attorney-General,* Hon. Alex. Heslop, £740.
Advocate-General, Joseph S. Williams.
Crown Solicitor, A. W. Aikman.
Clerk of Supreme Court, W. T. March, £800.
Registrar in Chancery, Robert Russell, £600.
Pro. Marshal Gen., J. A. O'Sullivan.
Official Assignees, H. Hutchings, L. Hutchings, J. C. Hildslet.
Judge of Vice Admiralty Court, Sir B. Edwards.
Registrar of Do., E. B. Lynch.
Provost Marshal-General, J. A. Sullivan.
Bp. of Jamaica, Right Rev. A. G. Spencer, D.D., £1,400.   [£2,000.
Bp. of Kingston, Right Rev. R. Courtenay, D.D.,
Com. of the Forces, Maj.-Gen. L. S. O'Connor, C.B.

MONTSERRAT,

One of the Lesser Antilles, situated in 16° 45′ N. lat. and 62° W. long. It is about 12 miles in length, and 8 in breadth, comprising an area of

47 miles, and at the last census a population of 7,645; it is justly considered one of the most healthy of the Antilles, and its scenery is exceedingly beautiful. It was discovered by Columbus in 1493, and named by him after a mountain in Catalonia, which it is said greatly to resemble: it was colonized by the English in 1632; the French took it in 1664, and levied heavy imposts on its inhabitants; it was restored to the English in 1668, and again capitulated to the French in 1782; eventually the island came into possession of the English in 1783. About two-thirds of the island are mountainous and barren, the rest well cultivated: the chief products are sugar, rum, molasses; but cotton, tamarinds, and arrowroot are also exported.

In 1866, the gross amount of Public Revenue £5,325
Gross amount of Public Expenditure (including repayment of loan, £667   4,990
Public Debt................................   3,920
Value of total Imports (including £1,032 from United Kingdom)   18,685
Value of total Exports (including £12,866 to United Kingdom)...........   19,898
Total tonnage of vessels, exclusive of Coasting trade (11,573 British, 345 Foreign) 11,918.

Plymouth is the principal town. The government is vested in a President (subordinate to the Governor of the Leeward Islands), aided by an Executive and Legislative Council appointed by the Crown, and a Legislative Assembly consisting of 12 members, 8 elected and 4 appointed by the Crown.

President (Acting), W. R. Pyne.
Chief Justice, Sir William Snagg, £150.
Puisne Judge, Acting Police Magistrate, and Ex-Officio Coroner, E. B. Dyett, £250 and fees.
Queen's Counsel, John R. Semper, £131.
Colonial Sec. and Treas., J. Meade, £210 and fees.
Comptroller of Customs, J. Meade.
Provost-Marshal, R. H. Dyett, £120 and fees.
Colonial Surgeon, B. Johnson, £150.

St. CHRISTOPHERS (and ANGUILLA),

The former popularly called St. Kitts, is an island situate in lat. 17° 18′ N. and long.62° 48′ W. about 46 miles to the west of Antigua; it comprises an area of 68 square miles, its total length being 23 miles, and average breadth about five miles. The staple exports are sugar, rum, and molasses. St. Kitts, named by the natives "The Fertile Isle," was discovered by Columbus in 1493, and colonized by the English in 1623. In 1782, it was captured by the French, but restored the following year. The population in 1861, the time of the last census, was 24,440. St. Kitts, though united with Nevis and Anguilla for purposes of Government, has a Legislature of its own. Basseterre is the chief town.

In 1866, the Public Revenue amounted to   £24,505
The Public Expenditure.......................   24,926
Public Debt................................   none.
Value of Total Imports (including £94,902 from United Kingdom)   175,917
Value of Total Exports (including £139,172 to United Kingdom)...........   172,096

Total tonnage of vessels, exclusive of coasting trade (51,447 British, 13,027 Foreign), 64,474. The Government is administered by a Lieut.-Governor (subordinate to the Governor and Administrator-General at Antigua), aided by an Executive Council appointed by the Crown, and a Legislative Assembly consisting of a paid President ap-

* *Privy Council.* † *Legislative do. ex officio.*

pointed by the Governor, 3 ex-officio members, 6 nominated by the Crown and 10 elected by the people.

Lieut.-Governor, Capt. J. Geo. Mackenzie, R.N., £1,300 and fees.

Chief Justice, Judge of Vice-Admiralty Court and Judge of Court of Divorce, J. R. Semper, £600 and fees averaging £150, and £100 as Chief Justice of Anguilla.

Sec. to Government, Hon. E. Herbert, M.A., £400.

Auditor-Gen., Hon. R. Challenger, £300.

President of Legislative Assembly, Hon. J. S. Berridge, £150.

Clerk of Executive Council, W. Padmore, £100.

Do. of Legislative Council, T. P. Berridge, £100.

Treasurer, N. Hart, £500.

Police Magistrate, Attorney General, and Coroner for Basseterre District, Hon. F. S. Wigley, £600.

Colonial Secretary and Registrar, R. M. Rumsey, £136, and fees £145.

Registrar of Deeds and of Queen's Bench, R. M. Rumsey, fees £204.

Chairman of Board of Health, E. Herbert.

Serjeant-at-Arms and Provost Marshal, G. Wattley, £300, and fees £150.

Postmaster, J. S. Berridge, £150.

Surveyor of Roads and Superintendent of Public Works, J. Dickinson.

Police Magistrate, W. H. Davis, £300.

Inspector of Police, R. M. Wilson, £250.

Immigration Agent, W. Padmore, £250.

Superintendents of Hospitals and Gaol, J. H. Boon, M.D., £275.

Compt. of Revenue, George J. Evelyn, £350.

Principal of Grammar School and Inspector of Schools, H. M. Marshall, M.A., £400 and fees.

Archdeacon, Ven. G. M. Gibbs, M.A., £250.

NEVIS.

This island, which is but a single mountain, forms one of the group of the Lesser Antilles, and is situated in 17° 10' N. lat. and 62° 40' W. long. Its area is about 50 square miles, or 32,000 acres, of which 16,000 are fit for cultivation, and at the last census, in 1861, possessed a population of 9822. It was discovered in 1498 by Columbus, and colonized by the English in 1628. The soil is fertile, and the principal products are sugar, molasses, and rum. Cotton is largely cultivated. Charlestown, a seaport with a tolerable roadstead, is the seat of government. Its proximity to the Island of St. Kitts has rendered its union therewith for the purposes of Government both eligible and necessary. In 1866 there were 13 schools on the island attended by 2,100 scholars.

Amount of Public Revenue in 1866 ... 7,015
Gross amount of Public Expenditure (including repayment of loan, £1,862) 6,884
Public Debt 3,600
Value of Total Imports (including £8,579 from United Kingdom) 34,936
Value of Total Exports (including £27,845 to United Kingdom) 46,549

Total tonnage of vessels, exclusive of coasting trade (11,634 British, 5,638 Foreign), 17,272. The Government is vested in a Lieut.-Governor (St. Kitts), and an Executive Council, and also a Legislative Assembly of 10 members, 5 nominated by the Lieut.-Governor, and 5 elected, each of the 5 parishes returning one.

Lieut.-Governor, Capt. J. G. Mackenzie, R.N.

President, Walter Maynard, £500.

Colonial Secretary & Auditor, J. A. Iles, Esq., £300.

Treasurer, George Webbe, Esq., £291.

Comptroller, Nav. Laws Registrar of Shipg., G. Webbe.

Escheator & Casual Receiver, Geo. Weebe, fees.

Chief Justice, vacant, £250 and fees.

Judge, Court of Complaints, G. Webbe, £50 and fees.

Solicitor-Gen., Wm. Chambers, Q.C., £150.

Provost Marshal, B. C. Caines, £111 and fees.

Clerk of Crown, J. Maynard, fees.

Police Magistrate, Geo. W. Daniell, £150.

ANGUILLA, or LITTLE SNAKE,

Probably so called from its long and narrow figure, one of the Lesser Antilles. It is about 60 miles N.E. of St. Kitt's, 16 miles in length, and varies in breadth from 3 to 1¼ miles. containing an area of 35 square miles. Population 2,500, of whom 100 only are white. It forms part of the Government of St. Kitts, and sends one member to the Assembly. For local purposes, it is governed by a stipendiary magistrate, paid from the Imperial Treasury. This officer is assisted by a Vestry (of which he is chairman), constituted by Act of Parliament, composed of the rector and 11 elected members. The productions of the island are sugar, phosphate of lime, and salt, the revenue being chiefly derived from a duty on the latter. Cotton is also exciting attention, about 60 acres being under cultivation.

President, G. Alsbury, £500.

ST. LUCIA,

One of the windward divisions of the Caribbees, situate in 13° 50' N. lat., and 60° 58' W. long., at a distance of about 30 miles to the south-east of Martinique, and 21 to the north-east of St. Vincent. It is 42 miles in length, and 21 at its greatest breadth; it comprises an area of 250 square miles, and a population in 1866 of 29,519. Castries, the chief town of the island, is situated at the bottom of a deep bay, and contains about 900 houses and 3,500 inhabitants. At the period of its discovery, by Columbus, in 1502, it was inhabited by the Caribs, and so continued until taken possession of by the King of France in 1635. In 1639 the English formed their first settlement, but were all murdered in the following year by the Caribs. In 1642 the King of France, still claiming the right of sovereignty, ceded it to the French West India Company. No island has ever been the scene of such numerous hostilities and contentions for possession and conquest from the year 1662 to 1803, when it surrendered on capitulation to General Grinfield, since which period it has continued without interruption under British rule. It was the scene of Admiral Rodney's celebrated victory over the Count de Grasse in 1782, also of the sanguinary conflict under Sir Ralph Abercrombie, in May, 1796. Sir John Moore, the subsequent hero of Corunna, who distinguished himself in this campaign, was appointed Governor of the Island. St. Lucia has also undergone many changes in a legal and constitutional point of view, not the least important being the enactment of the "Saisee Reeth" ordinance, authorising the levy and sale of immovable property, but little dissimilar to the "Encumbered Estates Act." Much of the surface of the island is covered with hills, generally well wooded, and the coast abounds in secure, commodious, and defensible harbours. The principal exports are cocoa, sugar, molasses, and rum.

In 1866, the gross Revenue was £15,249
Gross amount of Public Expenditure .. 15,410

---

* Executive Council *ex officio.*

Public Debt...................................... £18,000
Value of total Imports (including
£31,715 from United Kingdom) 91,514
Value of total Exports (including
£98,789 to United Kingdom) 109,483
Total Tonnage (20,063 British, 2,857 Foreign),
22,920.

The Government consists of an Administrator (subordinate to the Governor-in-Chief of the Windward Islands), an Executive Council of 3 official and 2 non-official members, also a Legislative Council consisting of 5 official and 7 non-official members.

* *Administrator of the Government and Col. Sec.*, James Mayer Grant, £700.
Chief Justice, Hon. J. G. P. Athill, £700.
* *Attorney-General*, Hon. L. La Caxe, £400.
Solicitor-General, Hon. C. Mallet Paret.
* *Deputy-Registrar*, C. Delomel, £200.
Provost Marshal, C. Bennett, £400.
* *Colonial Treasurer*, Macnamara Dix, £400.
* *Aud. of Public Accounts*, T. Parker, £170.
Postmistress, Mrs. A. Richard, £100.
Chief Clerk, Gov. Off., J. H. Jennings, £180.
Govt. Printer, St. L. Coudrey, £150.
Stipendiary Magistrates, H. Busby, J. M. A. Aubert, C. R. Maclean, £300 each.
Chief Rev. Off., A. Dreuil, £260.
Harbour Master, Thomas Sugg, fees.
Town Clerk and Treasurer, R. Lartigue, £150.
Immigration Agent, F. M. Chadwick, £330.

ST. VINCENT,

An island belonging to the Windward group, about 21 miles south-west of St. Lucia, and 90 west of Barbados, situate in 13° 10′ N. lat., and 60° 57′ W. long.; it is 18 miles in length, and 11 in breadth, comprising an area of 131 square miles, and a population in 1861, of 31,755. Some of the Grenadines, a chain of small islands lying between Grenada and St. Vincent, are incorporated with the latter. It was discovered by Columbus in January, 1498, at which time, like many of the smaller islands, it was inhabited by the Caribs, who continued in undisputed possession till 1627, when Charles I. made a grant of it to the Earl of Carlisle, and subsequently in 1672 it was granted to Lord Willoughby. St. Vincent, like St. Lucia, has been subject to many alternations in possession, and vicissitudes of war, &c. In 1780 it was rendered memorable by the occurrence of the greatest hurricane of which there is any record in West India annals; it took place on the 10th October of that year, and extended its ravages chiefly to St. Vincent, Grenada, St. Lucia, and Martinique. The plantations were destroyed, the houses thrown down, and the loss of human life in the four islands has been computed at upwards of 20,000 souls. From 1783 to the period of the breaking out of the French Revolution St. Vincent appears to have enjoyed comparative prosperity and peace, but the Caribs and their allies (the French) again overran the island, burning the cane fields, plundering the houses, and murdering the English colonists. This state of things continued till the arrival of the " Zebra" sloop of war with succours from Martinique, then the British head-quarters. The contest was now carried on with alternations of good and ill-fortune, till the arrival of Sir Ralph Abercrombie with reinforcements in June, 1796. The same success which had attended the British arms at St. Lucia

* Legislative Council.

prevailed here also; after a series of conflicts the insurgents surrendered at discretion, and to the number of 5,080 were transported to the isle of Ruatan, in the Bay of Honduras on 11th March, 1797. The lands thus forfeited to the Crown were granted by Act of Parliament, 1804, to those residents who had been engaged in defence of the island. In 1809 Sir Chas. Brisbane was appointed governor, in which post he continued till his death in 1829: during his administration an impetus was given to agriculture and trade which soon raised the colony to an unexampled degree of prosperity. In 1846 a large number of Portuguese labourers, amounting to 2,400, immigrated hither, who have proved a valuable acquisition to the island. Kingston, the capital of St. Vincent, is situate at the bottom of an extensive bay, at the S.W. extremity of the island; it consists of three principal streets, each nearly a mile long, running parallel with the beach, and contains a population of about 5,000 souls. Various Orders in Council have at different times been promulgated for the government of the island, and in 1854 the " Encumbered Estates Act" was extended to St. Vincent.

The government under the Reconstruction Act of 1864, will be administered by a Lt.-Governor, Executive Council (not yet appointed), and a new Legislative Assembly.

The chief products are sugar, molasses, rum, arrowroot, and cotton. Its chief imports, linen, cotton, and woollen manufactures, flour, wheat, fish, &c.

In 1866 the gross Revenue was £21,240
The gross Expenditure (including
amount of loan repaid, £1421)......... 20,282
Public debt .... None
Value of total imports (including
£61,500 from United Kingdom) 158,158
Value of total exports (including
£183,580 to United Kingdom) 194,175
Total tonnage, 33,183 British.

Lieut.-Governor, George Berkeley, Esq., £1,300.
Private Secretary, W. G. Lardner.
Chief Justice & Vice-Chan., G. Trafford.
Colonial Secretary, E. D. Laborde, £400.
Auditor, E. H. Musson.
Clerk of Assembly, Jas. H. Brown, £166.
Attorney-General, J. C. Choppin, £400.
Treas. & Col. of Imports, H. Shaw, £750, and fees.
Provost-Marshal, Hen. H. Breen, £350 and fees.
Special Justice, R. Sutherland, £450.
Postmaster, G. Van Heijningen, £150.
Immigration Agent, J. H. Brown, £150.
Inspector-Gen. of Police, Major C. Creagh, £300.

TOBAGO,

The most southerly of the Windward group, 11° 9′ N. lat., and 60° 12′ W. long., about 70 miles to the south-east of Grenada, 18½ miles to the north-east of Trinidad, and 120 miles distant from Barbados; it is 32 miles long, and from 6 to 12 broad, and has an area of 97 square miles, and a population in 1861 of 15,410. The island was discovered by Columbus in 1498, and by him named " Assumption;" it was then occupied by the Caribs. The British flag was first planted here in 1580, and the sovereignty claimed by James I. in 1608. This, like the other West India Islands, has been subjected to the various alternations of possession and other vicissitudes of war and conquest; ultimately, in 1803, it was taken possession of by Commodore Hood and General Greenfield, and finally ceded in perpetuity to the British Crown.

Scarborough, the principal town, is on the south side of the island, and is situated on the south-western base of a hill 425 feet above the level of the sea, on which Fort King George now stands. Plymouth, another town opposite Scarborough, on the leeward shore, about 6 miles distant, is the landing-place for passengers from the Royal Mail Steam Company's vessels. Two-thirds of the island are still covered with primitive forests, comprising many varieties of hard wood and ornamental trees; the island produces sugar, molasses, rum—these being the principal exports —also cotton, indigo, and coffee; pimento grows wild.

The moneys in circulation are British coins, American eagles and dollars, doubloons, and colonial bank-notes. Weights and measures are the British imperial. In all cases not provided for by local enactments, the English statute law is in force.

Gross amount of public revenue in 1866	£9,815
Gross amount of public expenditure, (including loan of £613)	10,153
Public debt	1,534
Value of total imports (including 23,481 from United Kingdom)	57,645
Value of total exports (including £63,471 to United Kingdom)	69,872

Total tonnage of Vessels, 14,070 (British only).

The government consists of a Lieut.-Governor (subordinate to the Governor-in-chief of the Windward Islands at Barbados), assisted by a Privy Council of 7 members, a Legislative Council, also of 7 members, appointed by the Governor for life, and a Legislative Assembly of 16 members elected from the 7 parishes into which the island is divided.

Lieutenant-Governor, C. H. Kortright, £1.300.
Colonial Secretary, S. H. Hill, £200, and fees.
Speaker of Assembly, Robert Crooks.
Provost Marshal, C. I. Le Plastrier, £300 and fees.
Treasurer, C. A. Berkeley, £350.
Revenue Officer, J. Hamilton, £160.
Executive Committee, R. Gordon, C. F. Cadiz, A. Melville, £100 each.
Secretary of Executive Committee and Clerk of Privy Council, S. H. Hill, £100.
Clerk of Assembly, William Desvignes, £100.
Inspector-General of Police, R. Crooks, £250.
Stipendiary Justices, C. F. Cadiz, D. Yeates, S. F. Tizck, £200 each.

TRINIDAD,

The most southerly of the West India Islands, lying to the eastward of the continent of S. America, between 10° 3'—10° 50' N. lat., and 61°—62° 4' W. long.; its length is about 90 miles, and its breadth varying from 35 to 40. It is separated from the peninsula of Venezuela by the Gulf of Paria. It was discovered by Columbus in July, 1498, and thus named by him from the three mountain summits first perceived from the mast-head when discovered; but no permanent settlement was made there until 1588. In 1676 the French took possession of it, but soon after ceded it to Spain. In February, 1797, an expedition under the command of Admiral Harvey and Sir Ralph Abercrombie, consisting of 6,750 troops, was sent out to effect the reduction of Trinidad, which resulted in the surrender of the island, and Lieut.-Col. Picton (afterwards Gen. Sir Thomas Picton), was left as Governor in charge. In March, 1802, by a definitive treaty,

the full property and sovereignty of the island was ceded to His Britannic Majesty. It contains an area of about 1.754 square miles, with a population, in 1861, of 84.438. The chief town and port of entry, "Port of Spain," is one of the finest towns in the West Indies, having been rebuilt of stone after the destruction of the old (wooden) town by fire in 1808, and contains 18,080 inhabitants; the streets are long, wide, well paved, and shaded with trees. There is also a second town and port of entry, St. Francisco, 26 miles south from Port of Spain. A remarkable phenomenon exists here, that of a pitch lake, 99 acres in extent, near the village of La Brea. The soil of the island is rich and productive, its most important products being sugar, molasses, rum, coffee, cotton, arrowroot, &c., in addition to the cane, and various kinds of timber, and also the choicest of the West India fruits. The total extent of land under cultivation is about 70,000 acres. Coal is to be found in the district of Manzanilla. There is an island post-office, amalgamated with the General Post-office, and 21 post-offices throughout the island, There are nine established mail-routes, and four foot-routes for the transportation of mails, at a cost of £3.454 per annum, beside two local steam-boats for the conveyance of mails, police, and prisoners, at the contract cost of £4.500 per annum. Two general hospitals, a lunatic asylum, leper-house, house of refuge, &c., are maintained at the public expense.

Gross amount of Revenue in 1866	£226,218
Gross amount of Public Expenditure (including repayment of Loan, £18,581)	203,429
Public Debt	172,837
Value of total Imports (including £51,972 Bullion and Specie)	930,329
Value of total Imports from the United Kingdom	500,666
Value of total Exports (including £9,335 Bullion and Specie)	1,031,683
Value of total Exports to the United Kingdom	825,133

Total tonnage of Vessels (194,363 British; 86,941 Foreign), 281,304.

Principal Imports: Cottons, Linens, Woollens, value £166,481; Flour, 43,391 barrels, value £75,396; Hardware and Machinery, value £54,359; Meat, pickled and salted, 1,165,924 lbs., value £27,732; Rice, 8,843,162 lbs., value £68,931.

Principal Exports: Cocoa, 5,991,673 lbs., value £176,861; Molasses, 1,116,442 gallons, value £46,518; Rum, 89,984 gallons, value £8,998; Sugar, 91,150,000 lbs. : value £592,079.

The Government is vested in a Governor, an Executive Council, and a Legislative Council, all of whom are nominated by the Crown.

†Governor and Commander-in-Chief, Hon. A. H. Gordon, C.M.G., £3.500.
Private Secretary, A. J. L. Gordon, £300.
†Chief Justice and Judge of Vice-Admiralty Court, Hon. William George Knox, £1,500.
Commandant, Capt. Kelsall.
First Puisne Judge, Hon. H. T. Bowen, £1,000.
Second Do., Hon. H. Fitz Gerald, £1,000.
† Colonial Secretary, Hon. J. S. Bushe, £800.
†Attorney-General, Hon. C.W. Warner, C.B., £800.
†Solicitor-General, Hon. George Garcia, £200.
†Receiver-Gen. Hon. H. E. Bulwer, C.M.G., £800.

*Executive Council *ex officio.* † Legislative do. do.

†*Immigration Agent General,* Hon. H. Mitchell, M.D., £800.
Auditor-Gen. R. Russell, £600.
Marshal, Edward Murray, £360.
Regist.-Gen. H. A. Fitt, £500.
Assistant Receiver-General, E. J. Eagles, £500.
Sub Receiv.-Gen.(San Fernando), J. F. Knox, £500.
Postmaster-Gen., C. Chipchase, £350.
Regis. Sup. Ct., T. Warner, £600, C. Hobson.
Inspector of Schools, A. W. Anderson, £500.
Principal of Collegiate School, H. Deighton, £700.
Inspector of Police, H. G. Bushe, £500.
Super. of Prisons, D. Hart, £350.
Surveyor-General, L. H. Moorsom, C.E., £800.
Assistant, J. Meagher, £400.
Harbour Master, R. H. Stewart, £630.
Health Officer (Shipping) and Sanitary Insp., Vaccinator-Gen., &c., W.H. Stone, M.D., £395 16s. 8d.
Commissioner of Assessed Taxes, H. A. Fitt, £600.
Crown Solicitor, James Driggs, £300.
Roman Catholic Archbishop, Port of Spain, Most Rev. Dr. J. Gonin, £1,000.
Archdeacon, Ven. G. Cummins, M.A., £500.

THE VIRGIN ISLANDS.

A group of islands in the West Indies, partly belonging to Denmark, partly to Great Britain, forming a connecting link between the Greater and Lesser Antilles. They consist chiefly of a cluster of rocks. The largest in the group belonging to Great Britain is Tortola, situate in 18° 27′ N. lat., and 64° 40′ W. long. Such of the islands as are British became so in 1666. The most important in the Danish possession are St. Thomas, St. John, and Santa Croix. The area of the British possessions is 57 square miles, and the population in 1861 was 6,051. There is good pasturage for cows, sheep, and goats. A valuable mine of copper has been worked at Virgin Gorda, and gold, silver, and other minerals are said to have been found. Virgin Gorda Sound presents a magnificent and easily accessible harbour, entirely sheltered from hurricanes. A dangerous reef, however, stretches out from the island of Anegada, the wrecks upon which add considerably to the income of the inhabitants, who are said to obtain their livelihood chiefly by wrecking, as in the case of the *Paramatta.* In former times the Virgin Islands produced cotton in abundance, and recent experiments have further proved that they are capable, could the labour be found, of supplying England with no less than 20,000 bales annually. Recently (29th October, 1867) the islands were visited by a fearful hurricane, which was most destructive to life and property.

Gross amount of public Revenue in 1866...£1,994

* Executive Council.   † Legislative do. do.

Gross amount of Expenditure.................£1,964
Public debt ....None.
Value of total Imports 10,209
Value of total Exports 8,314
Total tonnage of vessels (British only) ... 8,085

The government is vested in a President (subordinate to the Governor-in-chief of the Leeward Islands at Antigua), an Executive Council, and a Legislative Council.

President Administering the Government, Sir C. A. H. Rumbold, Bart., £800.
Private Secretary, G. H. A. Porter.
Chief Justice, Hon. I. Farrington.
Puisne Judge, I. Farrington.
Colonial Secretary, Hon. G. H. A. Porter, £150.
Queen's Counsel, W. W. King and A. Berners.
Treasurer and Comptroller of Customs, Hon. I. Farrington, £150.
Provost Marshal, J. G. Gordon, £150.
Coroner, A. C. H. Smith, fees.
Colonial Chaplain, Rev. G. E. Yeo, £250.

TURK'S AND CAICOS (Cayos or Keys).

These Islands were formerly included among the Bahama group, from which they were separated in 1848; they lie between 21°—22° N. lat., and 71°—72° 30′ W. long. The population in 1861, was 4,372.

Gross amount of Public Revenue in
   1866 .... £16,335
Public Expenditure 14,276
Public Debt .... None.
Value of total Imports (including £9,535
   from United Kingdom.) 56,091
Value of total Exports (including £1493
   to United Kingdom) 54,310
Total Tonnage of Vessels (63,954 British;
50,504 Foreign) 114,458.

The Government is administered by a President (subordinate to the Governor of Jamaica), and a Council, composed of four Nominees, and four elected Members.

President of the Council of Government, Alexander W. Moir, £800.
Private Secretary, J. C. Bascome, £150.
Col. Sec. and Clerk of Councils, A. C. Lowe, £350.
Acting Do. Do., John C. Crisson.
Judge, Supreme Court, A. J. Duncombe, £450.
Queen's Advocate and Stipendiary Magistrate, F. Ellis, £487.
Assist. Pol. Magist., Caicos, St. G. D. Tucker, £150.
Comp. of Customs and Naval Laws, D. T. Smith.
Receiver-Gen. and Treasurer, D. T. Smith, £400.
Assistant Do. Salt Cay, S. S. Garland, £200.
Assistant Do. Do., Caicos, St. G. D. Tucker, £150.
Postmaster, G. Turk, and Aud., R. J. Darrell, £200.
Col.Surv. and Insp. Pub.Works, A. G.Wynns, £200.
Inspector of Public Schools, T. Ockendon, £200.

British Possessions in Africa.

CAPE COLONY.

The Cape of Good Hope, strictly speaking, is a small promontory near the S. W. extremity of the continent of Africa; but the extensive colony of that name is washed by the Atlantic and Indian Oceans on the west and south. It reaches in S. lat. from 28° 10′ to 34° 51′, and in E. long. from 16° 20′ to 28°, and contains an area of 200,610 square miles. British Kaffraria, formerly a separate government, was incorporated with Cape Colony in 1866. Capetown, the capital of the colony, and seat of Government, also an

Episcopal see, is built between Table Bay and Table Mountain, at the foot of the latter. In 1486, Bartholomew de Diaz, a Portuguese commander, discovered the Cape in the reign of John II. of Portugal. Vasco di Gama doubled it eleven years later, since which time it has been resorted to by European navigators of all nations, especially Portuguese, Dutch, and English. In 1620, two English East India commanders took possession of it in the name of Great Britain, but no settlement was formed. In 1652 it was colonized by the Dutch East India

Company, and remained in their hands till 1795, when the British Government took possession, but ceded it at the Peace of Amiens to its former possessors. It was again taken in 1806 by the English, to whom it was confirmed at the general peace in 1815, and has since continued a British colony. The settlers at the Cape are chiefly employed in the production of wool, wine, in the breeding of horses, sheep, and cattle, and the culture of wheat, barley, oats, &c. There is a railroad now complete between Cape Town and Wellington. The population in 1865 amounted to 566,158—Hottentot, 91,098; Kaffir 124,536; European, 204,859; other races, 145,655.

	£.
Gross amount of Public Revenue in 1866 (including Loan of £178,000)...	732,298
Gross amount of Public Expenditure (including Loan repaid £37,900)	691,733
Public Debt....................................	851,650
Value of total Imports (including Bullion and Specie £2,000)	1,942,281
Imports from the United Kingdom ...	1,280,529
Value of total Exports (including Bullion and Specie £8,821)	2,599,169
Exports to United Kingdom	2,087,663

Principal Imports in 1866: Apparel and Slops, £105,228; Beer and Ale, bottled, 95,970 gallons; do., in wood, 284,116 gallons; Cotton Manufactures, £325,551; Haberdashery and Millinery, £207,200; Rice, 100,402 cwt.; Sugar, 101,841 cwt.; Tea, 144,229 lbs.; Iron, bar and rod, 29,940 cwt.

Principal Exports: Wool, sheep's, 35,231,607 lbs. Sheepskins, 1,018,298; Goatskins, 678,364; Hides, ox and cow, 21,220; ivory, 40,969 lbs.; Wine, ordinary, 93,164 gal.; Ostrich feathers, 15,144 lbs. Total tonnage of vessels, exclusive of Coasting trade (399,338 British, 79,599 Foreign), 478,937.

The Government is vested in a Governor and Executive Council appointed by the Crown. There is a Legislative Council of 21 elected members, and a House of Assembly of 66 elected members.

The discovery of a rich gold country to the north of the Limpopo river, on the borders of the Transvaal Republic and Portuguese settlements, in 1868 has been fully confirmed. This new field of glistening quartz veined with gold has been named the "Victoria Diggings."

Gov. and Comm.-in-Chief, Sir P. E. Wodehouse, K.C.B., £6,500.
Private Sec. to do., George St. V. Cripps, £300.
Military Secretary, Capt. Taylor, R.A.
Clerk to Executive Council, J. C. Rivers, £500.
Clerk to Legislative Council, J. A. Fairbairn, £450.
Speaker, House of Assembly, Sir C. Brand, £1,000.
Clerk to do., J. Noble, £450.
Chief Justice and Judge of Vice-Adm. Court, Vacant, £2,000.
Master and Guardian of Orphans, J. Steuart, £800.
Registrar, Supreme Court, T. H. Bowles, £400.
High Sheriff, Percy Vigors, £600.
Colonial Secretary, Richard Southey, £1,500.
Chief Clerk, Colonial Office, L. Adamson, £450.
Treas. & Comp. of Revenue, J. C. Davidson, £1,000.
Attorney-General, W. D. Griffith, £1,200.
Clerk to do., J. B. Currey, £400.
Solicitor-General, S. Jacobs, £600.
Auditor-General, E. M. Cole, £800.
Collector of Customs, F. B. Pinney, £900.
Sub do. (Port Elizabeth), G. W. Browning, £750.
Surveyor-General, C. D. Bell, £800.
Inspector of Public Works, M. R. Robinson, £700.

Superintendent of Convicts, Charles Piers, £500.
Superintendent of Education, Langham Dale, LL.D., £600.
Astronomer Royal, Sir T. Maclear, F.R.S.
Commander of the Forces, Lieut.-General Sir R. P. Douglas, Bart. £1,000.
Bp. of Cape Town (Metrop.), Rt. Rev. R. Gray, D.D.
Bp. of Graham's Town, Rt. Rev. H. Cotterill, D.D.
Bishop of Orange River Free State, Rt. Rev. E. Twells, D.D.
Synod Dutch Reformed Church, Moderator, Rev. And. Murray, jun., £300.
R. C. Bishop, Most Rev. T. Grimley, D.D., £200.

COURTS UNDER SLAVE TRADE SUPPRESSION TREATIES.

British and Portuguese Mixed Commission :—
Commissioner and Arbitrator, E. L. Layard, £800.
H. F. M. Com., The Chevalier Alfred Duprat.
H. F. M. Arbitrator, E. A. de Carvalho.

SLAVE TRADE COMMISSIONERS.

Judge, £1,200, Capetown.
Arbitrator, E. L. Layard, £800.
Registrar, H. Mallet, £500, do.
Clerk, H. Bidwell, £300, do.

NATAL.

The colony of Natal derives its name from the fact of its discovery by the celebrated Portuguese navigator, Vasco di Gama, on Christmas-day, 1497; it lies on the south-east coast of Africa, about 800 miles from the Cape of Good Hope, between the 28th and 31st parallels of S. lat.; it comprises an area of 16,145 square miles, 10,500,000 acres, and has a seaboard of 170 miles. Its population, in 1866, was 193,103. The scenery in Natal is in parts picturesque in the extreme; it is well watered, no less than 23 distinct rivers run through into the Indian Ocean, but not one of them navigable. It has but one great harbour on its coast, D'Urban, or Port Natal, which is completely landlocked, but a bar prevents vessels above a certain tonnage from entering. From its discovery in 1497 until 1686, when a Dutch vessel was wrecked in the bay, little is known respecting it. In 1824, an officer of the Royal Marines (Lieut. Farewell), having the previous year visited it on an exploring voyage, endeavoured to colonize it. Meeting with no encouragement from the British Government in aid of his plans, he nevertheless induced some 20 enterprising individuals to join him. On their arrival, they met with Chuka, a powerful chief, who held despotic sway over various tribes. He sanctioned and promoted the formation of a settlement by this small band of Europeans, which was broken up at his death, 4 years later. The tribes thus amalgamated by Chuka have been since known under the title of Zulus. Towards the close of the year 1837 a large body of Dutch, boers from the Cape Colony taking offence at the restrictions placed on them by the British Government, migrated to Natal; many of them were treacherously murdered by Dirgaan, a Zulu chief, the murderer and successor of his brother Chuka. During the next two years the Zulus and Boers waged war with various success; but in 1839, the Dutch obtained a decisive victory. In consequence of these disturbances, the Governor of the Cape determined to take military possession of the district: after several severe collisions with the natives, attended with alternate success, the Dutch Boers eventually submitted to Colonel Cloete at Pieter-

* Executive Council.

maritzburg. In 1843 the district of Natal was, with the sanction of the Imperial Government, proclaimed a British colony by the Governor of the Cape; and in 1856 it was erected into a distinct and separate colony, free from the control of the Governor of the Cape. The coast region, extending about 25 miles inland, is highly fertile, and has a climate almost tropical, though perfectly healthy. Sugar, coffee, indigo, arrowroot, ginger, tobacco, and cotton, thrive amazingly, and the pine-apple ripens in the open air with very little cultivation; while the midland district is more adapted for cereals and usual European crops. Coal, copper ore, iron, and other minerals, are found in several places, and there is little doubt that when the great mountain range is properly explored, it will be found very rich in mineral wealth. Large forests of valuable timber abound in the kloofs of all the mountain-ranges, and many tracts along the coast are also well wooded. The large animals are gradually disappearing, although elephants are still occasionally met with in the dense bush of the coast region. Lions, leopards, wolves, and hyenas still hang on the outskirts of civilization. Municipal institutions have been granted to the principal towns; it forms the diocese of a bishop; education is receiving much attention, and schools are multiplying.

	£
In 1866 the gross amount of Public Revenue (including loan of £53,564)...	156,833
Gross amount of Public Expenditure (including loan repaid, £18,182).........	205,077
Public Debt	160,000
Value of total Imports (including £189,299 from United Kingdom)	263,305
Value of total Exports (including £128,093 to United Kingdom)	203,402
Total tonnage of Vessels (51,421 British, 348 Foreign), 51,769.	

Principal Imports — Apparel, &c., value £16,045; Ale and Beer, 101,236 gals.; Ironmongery, Machinery, Haberdashery, Cotton and Woollen Manufactures, &c. Principal Exports —Sugar, Wool (Sheep's), Cotton, Coffee, Hides, Feathers, Arrow-root, &c. The Government consists of a Lieut.-Governor, aided by an Executive Council and a Legislative Council, composed of 4 official and 12 elected members.

Lieut.-Governor, Robert William Keate, £2,500.
Private Secretary, R. H. Erskine, £150.
Chief Justice & Judge, V.-Adm. Court, W. Harding, £900.
1st Puisne Judge, H. L. Philipps, £800.
2nd Puisne Judge, H. Cope, £800.
Colonial Secretary, Hon. D. Erskine, £800.
Attorney-General, M. H. Gallwey, £700.
Senior Off. Com. Troops, Col. H. R. Browne.
Colonial Treasurer, John Ayliff, £600.
Secretary for Native Affairs, T. Shepstone, £700.
Auditor, J. P. Symons, £100.
Collector of Customs, G. Rutherford, £500.
Surveyor-Gen., P. C. Sutherland, £500.
Registrar of Deeds and Distributor of Stamps, F. S. Berning, £350.
Colonial Engineer, P. Paterson, £500.
Supt. Education, Dr. Mann, £400.
Port Captain, W. Bell, £350.
Postmaster-Gen., F. Becker, £350.
Clerk, Executive Council, R. H. Erskine, £50.
Clerk, Legislative Council, T. Foster, £250.
Chief Clerk, Colonial Office, T. G. Crowly, £300.
Clerk, Lieut.-Gov. Off., N. W. H. Bateman, £200.
Master of Supreme Court, J. Athorn, £300.

Registrar do., A. Mesham, £200.
Sheriff, A. Clarence, £250.
Capt. Mounted Police, A. B. Allison, £300.
Capt. Incp. V. Corps, L. J. Rolleston, £200.
Bishop, Right Rev. J. W. Colenso, D.D.
Roman Catholic Bishop, J. F. Allard, D.D.

WEST AFRICAN SETTLEMENTS.—SIERRA LEONE, GAMBIA, CAPE COAST CASTLE, AND LAGOS.

Sierra Leone (Mountain of the Lion) is the most considerable, as regards the number of European residents, of the British possessions on the West Coast of Africa, and also an episcopal see. The colony consists of a peninsula, terminating in Cape Sierra Leone, bounded on the north by a river of that name. It lies in 8° 30′ N. lat., and 13° 18′ W. long. This colony is 18 miles in length, by 12 in breadth, and comprises an area of 468 square miles, with a population, in 1866, of 41,806. It was ceded to Great Britain, in 1787, by the native chiefs. The climate is humid and unhealthy, the wet season—from May to November—being specially pestilential. Tropical fruits and plants grow luxuriantly in the more favourable regions, and coffee, sugar, and indigo have been introduced by the British. The exports consist chiefly of gold, palm oil, palm nuts, and ivory, but the most characteristic article of export is teak timber; it is much used in our dockyards, where it is called "African oak;" it is very heavy and close-grained, much more so than the true teak of the East Indies. The chief articles of import are cotton goods (nearly one-half the whole value), ready-made apparel, haberdashery, hardware, gunpowder, and rum. The taxation of the colony consists of an *ad valorem* duty of 4 per cent. upon all imports, except wines, spirits, and tobacco, on which specific rates are charged.

	£
Gross amount of public Revenue in 1866.	62,263
Gross amount of public Expenditure ...	60,539
Public debt	*nil.*
Value of total Imports (including £200,265 from United Kingdom)	251,212
Value of total Exports (including £774 bullion and specie)	259,719
Value of Exports to United Kingdom ...	73,874
Total tonnage of Vessels (74,841 British, 21,258 Foreign), ...	96,099

Freetown, in this colony, is the seat of the central government of the West African settlements. The Governor is aided by Executive and Legislative Councils, the latter consisting of four official and three non-official members.

*Governor and Commander-in-Chief, Sir A. E Kennedy, C.B., £3,500.
Chief Justice, H. J. Huggins, acting, £1,500.
*Colonial Secretary, George W. Nicol, £700.
*First Clerk do., and Clerk of Council, E.H. Beckles, £400.
Queen's Advocate, H. J. Huggins, £800.
*Collector of Customs, John Shaw, £600.
First Clerk do., J. F. Brown, £300.
Landing Surveyor, A. B. Hanson, £300.
Assistant Colonial Surgeon, R. Smith, £300, &c.
Treasurer, A. Pike, £600. [£350.
Cashier in Office do., and First Clerk, J. C. Salmon,
Registrar and Master of Superior Court, and Registrar Vice-Adm. Court, T. Marston, £400.
Registrar-General, A. Montagu, £300, &c.

* *Ex officio* members of both Executive and Legislative Councils.

Sheriff, John Meheux, £400.
Bishop, Rt. Rev. E. H. Beckles, D.D., £900.
Col. Chaplain, Rev. R. Hartshorn, M.A., £500.
Police Magistrate and Manager of Mountain Districts, Captain Alexander Bravo, 1st W.I. Regt., £500 and allowances.
Inspector-General of Police, Captain Bravo, acting, £400 and allowances, £91 5*s*.
Clerk of Police, Josh. Metzger, £200.

SLAVE TRADE COMMISSION.

Judge, £250 additional salary given to the Governor of Sierra Leone for discharging the duties of Judge.
Registrar, £1,000: £250 in consideration of increased duties devolving upon him.

BULAMA.

This island is a dependency of Sierra Leone, from which it is distant 350 miles, and was ceded to the British Government in 1792. It is situated at the entrance of the two large rivers Jeba and Rio Grande. Ground-nuts, beeswax, copal and gum are the principal exports. On the banks of the Rio Grande there are numerous mahogany trees. In 1862, the Imports were valued at £250,000; Exports, £239,720.

GOLD COAST

Is a name generally given to a portion of Upper Guinea, between 5°—4° 20' E. long., stretching along the Gulf of Guinea from the river Assini on the west, to the river Volti on the east. The settlement of the Gold Coast extends over a distance of 400 miles. In 1750, the African Company was constituted by Act of Parliament, with liberty to trade and form establishments on the west coast of Africa, between 20° N. and 20° S. lat. The forts and settlements constructed by and vested in this company under parliamentary grant were, in 1821, transferred to the Crown. The British territory has been defined by a Convention with the Dutch Government, which came into effect on the first day of the year 1868. It is an interesting fact, that these settlements, which were originally and pre-eminently occupied as slave factories at an early date, are now maintained as the most effectual check on the slave trade, and also as centres of commerce, carrying with it civilization and Christianity. The produce of the settlements of the Gold Coast is chiefly sent to Great Britain. Gold, one of the chief exports, is found in small grains, mixed with red loam, gravel, and sometimes in quartz. It is also fished up from the beds of streams, and is used as a currency by the natives, who even hoard it up in coffins and under the floors of their houses. Ivory and gum are also chief articles of export. The skins of the monkeys, who tenant the woods in thousands, form another important item of export to England. The southern coast is of all others the region of the oil-palm, where it grows in great profusion. Its fruit is borne in great bunches, and is somewhat like a huge yellow plum; the oil is extracted therefrom by beating, pressing, and boiling. The amount of population can scarcely be defined—it is described as a floating population, constantly coming and going—but estimated in 1860 as about 152,000 within a territory of 6,000 square miles.

Gross amount of Public Revenue, 1861...... £9,335
Since which no returns have been made.
Gross amount of Public Expenditure £9,195
Public Debt.. *nil.*

Value of Total Imports (including £119,170 from the United Kingdom)... 162,970
Value of Total Exports (including £85,368 bullion and specie) 145,918
Total Exports to United Kingdom 111,867
Total tonnage of vessels (24,814 British, 16,940 Foreign), 41,754. The Government, the seat of which is at Cape Coast Castle, is vested in an Administrator (subordinate to the Governor of the West African Settlements), assisted by a Legislative Council.

*Administrator, H. T. Ussher, £1,300.
Chief Magistrate and Judicial Assessor, Hon. W. A. Parker, £600.
Acting Private Sec., J. Grant-Elliott, £100.
Collector of Customs, vacant, £600.
Colonial Chaplain, Rev. R. Blake, £400.
Post-office Clerk, J. O. Ansah, £300.
Civil Comdt. (Accra), Lt. H. F. S. Bolton, £300.
Clerk of Councils, J. G. Elliott, acting, £100.
Clerk of Courts, T. Hutton, £150.
Interpreter to Courts, W. Thompson, £120.
Clerk to Administrator, A. J. Quansah, £50.

LAGOS (THE NIGER),

An island and port on the coast of Guinea, between the 1st and 10th parallels of E. long. and the south of the 10th parallel of N. lat. The permanent occupation of this territory being deemed absolutely necessary for the complete suppression of the slave trade in the Bight of Benin, and for the protection and development of the important trade (of which the town of Lagos was the seat) the treaty ceding the island to Her Majesty was, on the 6th August, 1861, signed by Docemo, the native chief, whereby Lagos and its dependencies, Badagry, &c., are now become British territory. Lead ore, indigo, and camwood, are abundant in the interior. Cotton grows wild, and is also cultivated, and will, doubtless, eventually be largely exported. The long-frequented road from Lagos to Rabba, a town on the Niger, distant 250 miles, has now a bi-weekly post,—an evidence of increasing civilization. The Government is vested in an Administrator (subordinate to the Governor of the West African Settlements), aided by a Legislative Council. All laws are subject to the approval of the Governor-General, who resides at Sierra Leone, and visits each settlement once a year. The population is about 6,500.

	£
In 1866, the Revenue amounted to	23,823
Expenditure	23,602
Imports	220,766
Exports	262,649

Administrator, Com. J. H. Glover, R.N., £1,500, &c.
Chief Clerk, W. Lewis, £350.
Coll. of Customs (Lagos), W. J. Maxwell, £500.
Do. (Badagry), J. Pilkington, £300.
Do. (Leckie), C. B. Macaulay, £100.
Do. (Palma), G. A. W. Wright, £145.
Chief Magistrate, Benj. Way, £800.
Stipendiary Magistrate, T. Mayne, £350.
Inspector of Houssa Police and District Magistrate, Lieut. Gerrard, £400.
Officer Com. Troops, Maj. Molesworth, 2 W. I. Rgt.

GAMBIA.

The settlement of Gambia occupies the banks of the river of the same name, as far up as Barraconda, but not continuously. It contains an area of 21 miles, with, in 1861, a population of 6939. The principal station, Bathurst, is on the

* Legislative Council.

island of St. Mary, at the mouth of the Gambia. The climate is notoriously unhealthy. The export trade, which at one time exhibited a considerable falling off (ascribed in some measure to the competition of the French, who now enjoy equal rights with the British throughout the coast) appears to have revived, and to be steadily increasing. It consists of wax, hides, ivory, gold-dust, rice, palm-oil, timber, and chiefly of ground-nuts. The Gambia River falls into the Atlantic Ocean by a large estuary, measuring, in some parts, nearly 27 miles across ; but contracts to little more than two miles between Barrapoint and Bathurst Town. This was one of the settlements at which the slave trade was extensively carried on.

	£
Gross amount of Public Revenue in 1866	19,080
Gross amount of Public Expenditure ...	17,682
Value of Total Imports (including £64,825 from United Kingdom)	108,189

	£
Value of Total Exports (including £19,201 to United Kingdom.............	158,370
Total tonnage of vessels (15,734 British, 39,673 Foreign)	55,416

The government is vested in an Administrator, subordinate to the Governor of the West African Settlements, assisted by a Legislative Council.
*Administrator, Rear-Adm. C. G. E. Patey, £1,300.
First Writer, R. G. M. Robertson, £300.
*Collector of Customs & Treas., G. H. Kneller, £700.
Chief Magistrate, D. P. Chalmers, £600.
*Colonial Chaplain, Rev. J. Robbin, £250.
Colonial Surgeon, W. H. Sherwood, M.D., £400.
Auditor, C. B. Primet, £200.
Clerk of Customs, C. F. Stubbs, £200.
Colonial Registrar, T. Johnson, fees.
Resident Manager of Combo, J. Smith, J.P., £80.
Resident Manager of Macarthys, B. Tanner, £300.

* Executive Council

British Possessions in the Southern Atlantic.

ASCENSION,

An isolated island in the South Atlantic, of volcanic origin, one peak rising to the height of 2870 feet, situated 7° 55' 55" S. lat. and 14° 25' 5" W. long. It is said to have been discovered by the Portuguese on Ascension Day, 1508, hence its name. Its area is about 35 square miles. It remained uninhabited till 1815, when the English took possession of it. It is in the charge of the Board of Admiralty, by whom a Naval Officer is appointed as Governor, whose rule is as absolute as if on board a man of war ; the population, chiefly Royal Marines, is about 500. The chief exports are turtle and birds' eggs. Among its indigenous productions are the tomato, castor oil plant, and pepper.

Government.
Officer in Charge, Captain A. Wilmshurst, H.M.S. "Flora," £1,000.
Naval Storekeeper, James Lewis, R.N.
Chaplain, R.N., Rev. J. Robinson.

FALKLAND ISLANDS.

These, the only considerable cluster in the South Atlantic, lie about 300 miles east north-east of the Straits of Magellan, stretching in S. lat. 51°—53° and W. long. 57°—62°. They consist of East Falkland (area, 3,000 miles), West Falkland (2,300 miles), and upwards of 100 small islands (islets, rocks, and sandbanks), with an area of about 1,200 miles, comprising in the aggregate 7,600 square miles, and a population, in 1866, of only 662. Mount Adam, the loftiest mountain in the colony, rises 2,315 feet above the level of the sea. The Falklands were discovered by Davis in 1592, and visited by Hawkins in 1594. After having successively belonged to France and Spain, they have since 1771 formed part of the British Empire. In 1820 the Republic of Buenos Ayres established a settlement in these islands, which was destroyed by the Americans in 1831. In 1833 they were taken possession of by the British Government for the protection of the whale fishery, and from that time to the present have so continued, being, as a whole, the most southernly-organized colonies of the British Empire. The climate is exceedingly healthy, and the inhabitants live to a great age. In winter the weather is less boisterous

than in the summer. Fruit and vegetables thrive exceedingly well, and are very abundant. Swans —white and black,—inland geese, wild duck, dotterel and teal, are very plentiful. Wild cattle, horses and pigs, are numerous. Sheep also are found to do well. The wool is of excellent quality, and realizes a high price in the London markets. The harbours swarm with fish during the summer months, and fine trout are found in the lakes and rivers of the interior. The exports consist of provisions, hides, horns, hoofs, bones, tallow, and wool. In 1866 the gross amount of public revenue was £9,024; the gross amount of public expenditure, £7,944 ; public debt, none. Value of total imports, £20,948. Value of total exports, £21,780 (these comprise the United Kingdom only.) Total tonnage of vessels, exclusive of coasting trade (47,983 British, 32,590 foreign), 80,573.

The government is vested in a Governor, aided by an Executive Council and Legislative Council, both appointed by the Crown.
Governor and Commander-in-Chief, Hon. W. C. F. Robinson, £1,000.
†Colonial Secretary, W. R. Pyne (on leave), £400.
†Acting Colonial Secretary, Henry Byng.
†Chief Magistrate, E. R. Griffiths, £525.
†Surveyor-General, Arthur Bailey, £400.
Colonial Chaplain, Rev. C. Bull, £400.

ST. HELENA,

Probably the best known of all the solitary islands in the world, is situated in the South Atlantic Ocean, 800 miles from the nearest land —Isle of Ascension—and 1,200 from the nearest point of the African Continent, in 15°30' S. lat. and 4° 46' W. long. ; it is 10¼ miles long and 6½ broad, and encloses an area of 47 square miles, with a population in 1861 of 6,860. St. Helena was discovered by the Portuguese navigator Juan de Nova Castella, on 21st May, 1501 (St. Helena's Day), and remained unknown to other European nations until 1588, when it was sighted by Capt. Cavendish on his return from his voyage round the world. It remained uninhabited until the Dutch became possessors of it ; in 1673 it was taken from the Dutch by Capt. Munden, of the English Navy, and soon afterwards the East India Company obtained a charter for its pos-

* Executive and Legislative Council, ex officio.   † Legislative Council, ex officio.

session, which they held from Charles II. until 1833 (with the exception of the period 1815 to 1821, that the British Government required it as a residence for Napoleon Bonaparte, who lingered here in hopeless captivity), when it was ceded by them to the British Government: it is frequented by ships on their homeward voyage from the East Indies for fresh provisions and water, which constitute in fact the chief trade of the island. There is one good inlet only on the north-west of the island—St. James' Bay, possessing a good harbour—where the chief town (James Town) is built.

	£
In 1866, the gross Revenue was	28,152
The gross Expenditure	26,109

Public debt	None.
Value of total Imports (including £63,656 from United Kingdom)	112,506
Value of total Exports (including £5,251 to United Kingdom)	11,653

Total tonnage of vessels, exclusive of Coasting trade (115,294 British, 23,088 Foreign), 138,382.

Gov., Vice-Adm. Sir Chas. Elliot, K.C.B. £2,000.

Col. Aide-de-Camp., Lt.-Col. Knipe.

Fort Adj., Lieut. Story, 99th Reg.

*Com. Detach. 99th Reg., Major Ely.

*Com. Officer, Col. Freeth, R.E.

Chief Justice & Judge of V. Adm. Ct., Wm. Robt. Phelps, £700.

Bishop, Right Rev. T. E. Welby, D.D., £550.

British Possessions in Europe.

MALTA,

Anciently Melita, an Island in the Mediterranean Sea, 56 miles from Sicily, about 17 miles in length and 9 in breadth, comprising with Gozo an area of 115 square miles. It possesses one of the finest harbours in the world, with such an even depth that the largest vessels may anchor alongside the very shore, forming an admirable station for a fleet. Of the islands Malta, Gozo, and Comino, we find mention at a very early date. The Phœnicians are said to have colonized it in the 16th century B.C. It was then possessed alternately by the Greeks, Carthaginians, and Romans. It is mentioned by St. Paul as the scene of his shipwreck,—tradition fixing the wreck on the north coast,—the locality being now called the "Port of St. Paul." The Saracens seized it in the 9th century, and the inhabitants have still a tinge of Moorish blood. Count Roger, of Sicily, conquered the island in 1092. In 1530 the Emperor Charles V. took possession of Malta, and granted it, with Gozo and Tripoli, in perpetual sovereignty to the Knights of the Order of St. John of Jerusalem, lately expelled by the Turks from their stronghold at Rhodes. The Knights, by degrees, raised the stupendous fortifications which render Malta so powerful, and otherwise spent their large income in beautifying the island. From the middle of the 16th century, Malta sustained many sieges; amongst the most remarkable was that of 1565, when 50,000 Turks perished. Though waging perpetual war with the Moslem, Malta remained in the possession of the Knights 200 years, until, in 1798, when overcome by treachery, and disorganized by internal quarrels, they surrendered their noble fortresses to the French. After a few months, however, the Maltese rose against their oppressors, and drove them to take refuge in the towns, where they blockaded them for two years. The French at length, reduced to extremities, surrendered the garrison of Valletta, and capitulated to the English auxiliaries, under General Pigot. Malta was taken possession of by Great Britain in 1800, and finally annexed thereto by the Treaty of Paris, 1814. There is an extensive arsenal and important dockyard, Malta being the head quarters of the Mediterranean fleet. The island is highly cultivated; its principal products are cotton and corn, (wheat, barley, beans). A large quantity of live stock, about 25,000 head, including 6,000 horned cattle, are also maintained on the island; the mules and asses of Malta are remarkable for their strength and beauty; the birds also are celebrated for their splendid plumage. The vegetable products, fruits, &c., comprise all that flourish in Italy; oranges, olives, figs, aloes, and many plants of a more tropical growth. Medina, the former capital of the island, known also as Civita Vecchia, is a handsome old town, and contains the ancient palace of the Grand Masters of St. John, the cathedral, and a college; its rival and successor is Valetta. The population of Malta in 1866 was as follows:—Maltese, 136,381; British residents, 1,418; Foreign, 1,253; total, 139,502, exclusive of the British troops and their families, amounting, in January, 1866, to 7,350.

	£
In 1866, the gross Revenue was	196,459
Gross amount of Public Expenditure...	185,449
Public Debt	206,628
Value of total Imports (including £26,809 from United Kingdom)	1,851,520
Value of total Exports (including £898,680 to United Kingdom)	1,324,496

Total tonnage of Vessels, exclusive of Coasting trade (253,210 Sailing Vessels only, British; 435,044 Sailing Vessels only, Foreign) 688,254 Steam Vessels, 1,681,060. Total, 2,369,314.

The Government is administered by a Governor, who is assisted by a Council consisting of 18 members, 10 official, and 8 elected. The Governor is President.

*Governor and Commander of the Troops, Lt.-Gen. Sir P. Grant, G.C.B., £5,000.

Mil. Sec., Capt. A. C. Grant, £300.

*Chief Sec., Sir V. Houlton, M.A., K.C.M.G., £1,000.

*Audit.-Gen., Richard Cornwall Legh, Esq., £600.

*Collector of Customs, G. B. Trapani, Esq., £500.

*Treasury Cashier, V. Borg, Esq., £350.

*Collector of Land Revenue, G. Villa, Esq., £500.

*Controller of Charit. Instit., F. N. Inglott, £400.

GIBRALTAR,

A rocky promontory, 3 miles in length, and ¾ of a mile in average breadth, and greatest elevation 1,439 feet, forming the southern extremity of Spain, and consisting of a strongly-fortified seaport town and fortress, is situated at the extremity of a low peninsula, which connects it on the north with Andalusia, in 36° 2′ N. lat., and 5° 15′ W. long. Five and a-half miles distant across the sea is the Spanish town of Algesiras, between which and Gibraltar lies the bay of Gibraltar, called also the Bay of Algesiras, which is about eight miles long by five broad, with a depth in the centre of upwards of 100 fathoms. The anchorage is not very good, and the bay much exposed, especially to the S.W

* Council of Government, ex officio.

winds, which do great damage to the shipping. Gibraltar has been known in history from a very early period. The Phœnician navigators called it *Alube*, which the Greeks corrupted into *Calpe*, its classical name. It derived its name from a Saracenic chieftain, Tarib ebn Zarca, who called it Gebel Tarif (the Hill of Tarif), of which Gibraltar is a corruption. For many years it was the object of various sieges between the Moors and Spaniards, by whom it was deemed impregnable, until in 1704 a combined Dutch and English force, under Sir George Rooke, after a vigorous bombardment, solved that problem; since which time it has remained continuously in possession of the British, notwithstanding the desperate efforts on the part of France and Spain to dislodge them. The most remarkable of these was the celebrated siege under General Elliot, and the glorious place it occupies in the British annals, commencing on the 21st of June, 1779, and concluding on the 13th of September, 1782, extending over three years, since which time the British possession of Gibraltar has been unmolested, and few events of any interest connected therewith have happened. Gibraltar being a seaport, is consequently the resort of Spanish smugglers, who drive a thriving trade by introducing contraband goods into Spain. The town of Gibraltar consists of three parallel streets, in which the Spanish and English architecture singularly intermingle. There are, nevertheless, some handsome structures. Gibraltar is an episcopal see. The law of England prevails, and Gibraltar is now under the control of the Secretary of State for the Colonies. Total population (including 6,638 military),22,100. Gross amount of public revenue, £34,744; public expenditure, £30,423; public debt, none. Imports and exports, no return since 1863. Total tonnage of vessels (1,587,260 British, 551,661 Foreign), 2,138,921.

Governor, Lt.-Gen. Sir R. Airey, G.C.B., £5,000.
Colonial Secretary and Inspector of Revenue, S. Freeling, Esq., £900.
Chief Clerk, W. Mitchell, Esq., £240.
Secretary to Board of Health, W. Mitchell, £50.
Collector of H, M. Revenues, S.H.O.Bryen,Esq.£600.
Inspector of Revenue, J. Bell, £320.
Inspector of Revenue, Allowances, £100.
Captain of Port, Captain A. Strode, £508. 7s. 6d.
*Lieut. of the Port,*Comdr.W.Wooldridge,R.N.£250.
Police Magistrate, Colonel R. S. Baynes, £500.
Colonial Engineer & Surveyor, W. Elliot,Esq.£500.
Chief Justice, Sir J. Cochrane, Knt., £1,000.
Master and Registrar of the Supreme Court, E. J. Baumgartner, Esq., £600.
Attorney-General, F. S. Flood, £800.
Bishop, Hon. & Rt. Rev. C. A. Harris, D.D., £1,200.

HELIGOLAND (HOLY LAND),

A small island in the North Sea, captured from Denmark in 1807, situate opposite to, and about 30 miles from, the mouth of the Elbe, in 7° 51′ E. long. and 54° 11′ N. lat. Area, inclusive of the adjacent island "Sandy," three-fourths of a square mile. The inhabitants—about 2,000 in number—hitherto supported themselves chiefly by fishing (the annual value of which averaged £5,000, consisting chiefly of oysters, lobsters, and haddocks), and by serving as pilots to the numerous strangers who visit this rising and fashionable bathing-place. The Heligolanders, however, are now beginning to turn their attention to building and letting lodg-

ings, on the proceeds of which they hope to live during the winter months. Steamboats run between Heligoland and Hamburg in summer only. Christianity was first preached here in the seventh century. The native inhabitants are divided into two classes, differing both in race and occupation, the one being fishers—Frisians—true to the habits, and descendants of the sea kings of old; the other, merchants, immigrants from Hamburg and other places on the mainland. Heligoland has become, within the last three years, a place of rendezvous for English fishing-smacks, as many as 70 or 80 being frequently at anchor in the roads in the summer months.

The government is vested in a Governor, appointed by the Crown, aided by an Executive Council, a form of government inaugurated by an Order in Council, 6th February, 1868.
Revenue in 1866 .... £3,106
Expenditure in 1866 3,300
Governor and Commander-in-Chief, Lieut.-Colonel Henry Fitzharding B. Maxse, £500.
* Government Secretary, H. Gatke, £120.
* Town Clerk, K. N. Michels.
Island Physician, Dr. Van Aschen.
Stipendiary Magistrate, W. Mains, Esq. R.N.

THE CHANNEL ISLANDS,

Though not colonial possessions, are, nevertheless, dependencies of the British Crown. Information respecting the early history of these islands appears to be furnished to us by their ancient Latin names—Guernsey, *Sarnia,* Jersey, *Cæsarea,* Alderney, *Riduna,* Sark, *Arica,* Herm, *Aruia*—hence it appears probable that the Channel Islands were known to the Romans. Mention is made in Cæsar's "Commentaries" of islands strongly resembling and presumably those in question; but their historical outline, laws, and customs, still observable at the present day, would be better compassed from the period of William the Conqueror, not the least portion of interest being their antiquities. They consist of a group of islands lying off the north-west coast of France, between Normandy and Britanny. They are from 120 (Guernsey) to 150 (Jersey) miles southward of Southampton, the nearest distance from the French coast being about 15 miles. They are the only portions of the Dukedom of Normandy, now belonging to the English Crown, to which they have been attached since the Conquest. The area of the whole is about 112 square miles, and the population in 1861 about 90,000. The climate is mild and suitable to invalids, the mean annual temperature ranging from 50° to 51°. The produce of the islands is principally agricultural; horticulture and floriculture pre-eminently flourish. The principal manure is sea-weed, gathered in vast quantities from the shores at certain seasons under strict regulations. Its annual value to Guernsey alone is estimated at £30,000. A large quantity is used in the manufacture of kelp and iodine. The land is held in small parcels, chiefly of 20 acres. The principal crops are potatoes, hay, turnips, mangold-wurtzel, and wheat, the yield of which averages 30 bushels to the acre. The Channel Islands are celebrated for their excellent breed of horned cattle, usually known as the "Alderneys," remarkable for their small size and symmetry, and for the quantity and quality of the milk which they yield.

---

* Council of Government, *ex officio.*   * Members of Executive Council.

The principal educational establishments are Victoria College in Jersey, and Elizabeth College in Guernsey, both having exhibitions at the University of Oxford and Cambridge attached thereto. The vernacular language of the islands is the old Norman French, but modern French is the language now used in the law courts of the islands. The church services are performed in French in the country parishes, but an English service takes place in most, if not in all, of the town churches. Though belonging to the British Crown, the islands have a certain independent status and action The principal officer in each island is the Lieut.-Governor —generally an officer in the British army, and supreme in all military matters,—having also certain civil and municipal duties to perform. The bailiff or judge is the first civil officer in each island, being appointed by the Crown generally for life. The jurats or magistrates are (in Jersey) 12 in number, and elected for life. The rectors of the different parishes have also a seat in all councils. Beside these officers, there are an attorney and solicitor-general, procureur-général, and avocat de la Reine, in each island, and a high sheriff, called in Jersey the *vicomte*, and in Guernsey the *prévôt*. The Royal Court in each island consists of the bailiff and jurats. The other members of the states or assemblies are, in Jersey, the constables of the 12 parishes, and 14 elected members called deputies. Until recently the Queen's writ had no force in the island, and the "Habeas Corpus Act" has only lately been admitted.

Guernsey and Dependencies.
Lieut.-Gov., Major-Gen. Charles R. Scott.

Guernsey.
Bailiff, Sir P. S. Carey.
Dean, Rev. W. Guille, M.A.
Militia, A.-D.-C. to the Queen, Col. Bell.
Government Secretary, Lieut.-Col. W. Bell.
Adjutant.-Gen. of Militia, Lieut.-Col. J. McCrea.
Comm. R.A., Lieut.-Col. R. K. Freeth.
Fort Major, Col. J. Miller.
Comm. R.E., Col. J. E. Freeth.
Staff Officer of Pens., Capt. J. E. Hervey.
Queen's Procureur, J. D. H. Utermarck.
Do. Controller, P. Jeremie.
Do. Receiver, W. Brock.
Do. Greffier, O. Carre.
Ordnance Storekeeper, &c., W. H. Jenny.

Jersey.
Lieut.-Governor and Commander-in-Chief, Major-Gen. Philip Melmoth Nelson Guy, C.B.
Secretary to Lieut.-Gov., W. H. Gardner.
Fort Major and Adjutant, Col. Jn. Fraser.
Staff Officer Pens., Capt. Harvey.
Comm. Officer, R.A., Hon. E. T. Gage, C.B.
Comm. Officer, R.E., Lt.-Col. E. C. A. Gordon.
Barrack Master, Capt. W. Fuller.
Deputy Storekeeper, S. Wright.
Customs Chief Officer, G. R. Radford.
Bailiff, John Hammond.
Dean, Very Rev. W. C. Le Breton, M.A.
Attorney-Gen., R. P. Marett.
Vicomte, John Le Couteur.
Queen's Advocate, G. H. Horman.
Receiver-Gen. Crown Revenues, P. J. Simon.

Alderney.
Judge, Thomas Clucas.
Queen's Procureur, T. N. Barbenson.

Queen's Greffier, W. T. Robilliard.
Queen's Receiver, John A. Gauvain.
Incumbent Garrison Chaplain, Rev. W. Ross.
Storekeeper, S. B. Maclean.

ISLE OF MAN (MONA).

An island of Great Britain, in the Irish Sea, in lat. 54° 3'—54° 25' N., and long. 4° 18'—4° 47' W., nearly equidistant from England, Scotland, and Ireland. It is about 30 miles long, and from 10 to 12 broad, containing an area of 180,000 acres, more than one-half of which are cultivated; at the southern extremity is a small island, or islet, called "The Calf of Man," containing 800 acres, the larger portion of which also is under cultivation, agriculture having made great progress in the last few years. The island possesses large tracts of the finest wheat land; about 20,000 quarters of wheat, and large numbers of fat cattle, are shipped to the English markets annually. The herring and cod fisheries afford employment to nearly 4,000 men and boys, the average annual produce of which exceeds £60,000; poultry of all kinds are numerous. The island is rich in minerals: copper, zinc, iron, and lead, nearly 3,000 tons of which are annually raised, some very rich in quality, containing as much as 108 ozs. of silver to the ton. There are also quarries of slate, stone, and black marble, which is extensively used for mantel-pieces. Myrtles, fuchsias, and other exotics, flourish throughout the year, The chief products are wheat, oats, potatoes, and flax. The population is about 53,000. The island, which possesses many objects of antiquarian interest, formerly belonged to the Dukes of Athol, who exercised sovereign power; but, in 1760 the sovereignty, and in 1826 the remaining privileges pertaining thereto, were purchased by the British Government. The island forms a separate bishopric, under the title of Sodor and Man; it contains four principal towns : Castletown, the capital and seat of Government, Douglas, Peel, and Ramsay. The Isle of Man has a Constitution and Government of its own, independent of the Imperial Parliament; it has its own laws, law officers, and courts of law. Its Legislative body is styled the Court of Tynwald, consisting of the Lieut.-Governor and Council, composed of the Bishop, two Deemsters or Judges, the Attorney-General, Archdeacon, Vicar-General and Water-Bailiff, and the House of Keys (24), who are the representatives of the people.

Lieut.-Governor, and Chancellor, Hen. B. Loch, C.B., £1,350, and fees.
Bishop, Hon. H. Powys, D.D., £1,500, and demesne lands.
Attorney-General, James Gell, £800.
First Deemster, W. L. Drinkwater, £800.
Second Deemster, J. C. Stephen, £800.
Clerk of the Rolls, M. H. Quayle, £900.
Receiver-General, Richard Quirk, £230.
Water Bailiff, Ridgway Harrison, £130.
Archdeacon, Ven. J. C. Moore, M.A., £700.
Vicar-General, R. Jebb, £400.
Clerk of Council, Secretary to Lieut.-Governor, and Treasurer of Island, J. T. Clucas.
Speaker of House of Keys, J. S. G. Taubman.
Secretary to do., Robert J. Moore.
Staff Captain commanding Troops and Pensioners, Major Dickson.

Foreign Countries with which this nation holds intercourse by means of Ambassadors or Consuls, giving the Name of the Sovereign or Ruler of each, with Statistics of the Size, Population, Products, and Commerce; distinguishing the Amount of Trade with this Country; Names of English Ambassadors and Consuls, with their Salaries, also of Foreign Ambassadors resident here.

ABYSSINIA,

Formerly a Kingdom, comprising the large tract of highlands in the East of Africa. Situate between 8° 30'—15° 40' N. lat., and 35°—42° E. long. It is divided into three States or Kingdoms, the Kingdom of Gondar, or Amhara, the Kingdom of Tigré, and the Kingdom of Shoa ; and is supposed to contain an area of 27,000 square miles, with a population of 4,500,000. There is no country in the world so productive of quadrupeds, tigers excepted. The land is very fertile, generally yielding two crops annually. Corn of different kinds abounds, also the tamarind, fig, and date. Coffee is indigenous. The imports are chiefly cotton, raw silk, metals, and leather. Exports, gold, ivory, muskhorns, slaves.

It has lately been the scene of one of England's greatest military exploits.

British Consul at Massowah, Capt. C. D. Cameron, F.R.G.S., £600. Allowance for expenses, £300.

ANHALT,

An independent Principality of Central Germany, surrounded by Prussian Saxony, situate in lat. 51° 40' N. and long. 12° 10' E., containing 869 square miles, and a population, according to the last census, of 197,050. The principal rivers are the Elbe and the Saale. Its forests are considerable. The manufactures are chiefly woollen, and a trade is carried on in earthen and metallic wares. The country is level and fertile, producing wheat, flax, rapeseed, hops, and tobacco. Wine, also, is produced on the Saale. The public income in 1868 amounted to £284,900, and the expenditure to £277,676 ; public debt, £325,231.

Reigning Prince, Leopold, Duke of Anhalt, born 1st October, 1794.

Minister Plenipotentiary, Lord A. W. F. S. Loftus, G.C.B. (Berlin).

Minister for Foreign Affairs and President of the Council, Dr. Sintonis.

ARGENTINE REPUBLIC,

Or the Provinces (14) of the Rio de la Plata, of which Buenos Ayres is the principal, extending between 22°—41° S. lat., and 57°—70° W. long. It is estimated to contain 1,100,000 square miles, with a population only of 1,171,800, or about one to a square mile. The country was discovered in 1517, and settled by the Spaniards in 1553. The productions are wool, hides, cotton, rice, sugar, indigo, and tobacco. Wheat and maize are cultivated principally in the south ; the other products are cocoa, cochineal, madder, cinchona bark, Paraguay tea, and various fruits. Agriculture generally is very backward. The mineral products are silver, coal, salt, alum, and sulphur. The manufactures are unimportant ; the Indians make ropes, fishing-nets, yarn, and other articles, from the fibre of the aloe; also saddle-cloths, blankets, and other fabrics, which they dye with much skill. In Cordova, morocco leather and turned articles are manufactured.

PRINCIPAL IMPORTS.

Woollen and Calico Tissues, value ...	£1,412,739
Haberdashery, &c.	873,895
Sugar, Rice, &c.	957,276

Wine and Gin	813,172
Coal, Iron, Wood	649,898

PRINCIPAL EXPORTS.

Wool	2,378,251
Hides (Ox and Cow)	958,266
Grease and Tallow	363,152
Sheep Skins and other animal products	241,698
Estimated amount of Revenue in 1865	1,659,014
" " in 1866	1,952,766
Estimated Expenditure in 1865	1,375,235
" in 1866	1,653,150
Estimated Public Debt in Oct., 1866 ...	6,496,742

Total number and tonnage of vessels entered and cleared at Buenos Ayres in 1866, 1867—514,951 tons, of which 252 vessels were British, and tonnage 76,511.

Total value of Imports, 1865	5,420,603
In 1866 from United Kingdom	2,844,306
Total value of Exports, 1865	4,399,355
In 1866 to United Kingdom	1,061,518

In 1865 there were 326 miles of railway completed throughout the Republic, and further extensions projected; some in course of construction; nearly the whole expense whereof has been guaranteed by the Government, and the capital subscribed for in England.

The capital of the Republic is Buenos Ayres, a city of about 140,000 inhabitants. Rosario, in Santa Fé, is a rising city, with about 16,000 inhabitants in 1864, and an export trade of about £540,000.

President, General Sarmiento.

Vice-President, Dr. Alsina.

Envoy Extraordinary and Minister Plenipotentiary in London, Senor Don Norberto de la Riestra, 1, George Street, Mansion House.

Secretary, Don Francisco A. Delgado.

Consul-General, Marmaduke B. Sampson, Esq., 1, George Street, Mansion House.

Buenos Ayres—Envoy Extraordinary and Minister Plenipotentiary, Hon. W. Stuart, £3,300.

Secretary of Legation, G. F. Gould, Esq., £500.

Second Secretary of Legation, Wilfred S. Blunt, Esq., £250.

Consul, Frank Parrish, Esq., £1,400.

Rosario—Consul, T. J. Hutchinson, Esq., £400.

AUSTRIA,

One of the largest States on the Continent of Europe, situate between 42°—51° N. lat., and 8°20' to 26° 20' E. long. It embraces an area of 227,334 English square miles, and a population (1867) of about 35,500,000, consisting of the following nationalities : viz., 8,782,000 Germans ; 6,521,400 Bohemians (Czechs), Moravians, and Slovacks ; 2,380,000 Poles ; 2,985,000 Ruthenians ; 1,203,600 Slovens; 5,400,800 Magyars ; 2,916,000 Croatians and Servians ; 2,884,000 Roumanians ; 1,121,000 Jews ; 589,100 Italians ; 152,800 Zingari ; 53,800 Bulgarians, Greeks, Armenians, &c., of whom 27,000,000 are Roman Catholics, 3,100,000 Greeks, 3,500,000 Protestants ; the remainder consist of Armenians, Mahomedans, Unitarians, and members of other creeds. The empire is divided into nineteen provinces, called also Crown lands (the Lombardo-Venetian territory having been ceded to Italy in 1859 and 1866).

German Monarchy. — Lower Austria, Upper Austria, Salzburg, Styria, Carinthia, Carniola, Coast Districts, Istria (Trieste), the Tyrol and Vorarberg, Bohemia, Moravia, Silesia, Galicia, Bukowina, Dalmatia.

Kingdom of Hungary.—Hungary, Croatia and Sclavonia, Transylvania, and the Military Frontier, also Woiwodina of Servia and the Banat of Temes.

The soil of Hungary produces yearly, on an average, 275,000,000 bushels of grain of all kinds; 20,300,000 bushels of potatoes, 2,000,000 tons of beetroot, and 240,000,000 gallons of wine, notwithstanding which agriculture has made but little progress; the vine cultivation being 504,776 acres, producing 4,200,000 hogsheads of wine, value £7,066,864. The number of sheep in Hungary is estimated at 12,000,000, and the yield of wool 333,838 cwt. Its mineral riches are very great, comprising gold, silver copper, iron, steel, quicksilver, lead, tin, zinc, also coal, valued, in 1866, at 35,975,004 florins. Austria is a wine-producing country, second only to France. Hungary supplies not only the largest quantity, but the finest quality. Austria possesses a large army, comprehending, even on a peace footing, 269,000 men and 42,000 horses, while its navy consists of 45 steamers, with 639 guns and 11,730-horse power, besides 20 sailing vessels with 145 guns.

	£
The estimated net Revenue for 1868 was	48,241,900
The estimated net Expenditure	50,438,530
Total amount of public debt, June, 1867	298,848,669
Expenditure for 1866	53,000,000

Number and tonnage of sailing and steam vessels belonging to Austria in 1865: vessels 9,491; tons, 332,592; crew, 33,548. Total number and tonnage of all vessels entered and cleared in 1865: vessels, 143,611; tons 6,405,664.

	£
Total value of Imports, 1865 (including Bullion and Specie, £2,097,030)	26,492,170
Total Value of Imports, in 1865, from United Kingdom	911,267
Exports (including Bullion and Specie, £1,959,090)	34,692,487
Exports to the United Kingdom, 1866	1,369,831
Value of Imports, 1866	24,516,800
Value of Exports, 1866	38,048,600

Principal articles of import:—Cotton (raw), cotton, woollen, and silk manufactures, precious metals and coin, sheep's wool, cotton and linen yarns. Principal exports:—Glass and glass wares, hardware, grain (wheat, spelt, &c.), leather, precious metals and coins, wood, sheep's wool, and woollen manufacturers. The commercial intercourse of Austria with the United Kingdom is comparatively small. Savings Bank.—In 1865 there were 526,620 depositors in the savings-banks throughout the empire, the deposits amounting to £11,888,567. The total length of railways open for traffic in the first half-year, 1867, was nearly 4,000 English miles. Cost of construction, £67,991,026. Receipts, £9,859,214; expenditure, £3,028,634; dividend, 9 per cent. Vienna is the capital.

Reigning Sovereign, Francis Joseph I., Emperor of Austria, King of Hungary and Bohemia, born 18th August, 1830, married April 24, 1854, Elizabeth, daughter of Maximilian Joseph, Duke of Bavaria.

Heir, Archduke Rudolph, Prince Imperial.

Minister of Foreign Affairs, Count Frederick Ferdinand von Beust.

Ambassador Extraordinary and Minister Plenipotentiary at London, Count Rudolf Apponyi, 18, Belgrave Square.

Councillor and First Secretary, Count Kalnoky.

Secretaries, Count Wolkenstein, and M. E. de Plener.

Consul-General, Sir Anthony N. Rothschild.

Director of the Consulate, Chevalier Ignatius de Schaeffer. Office, 29, St. Swithin's Lane.

Ambassador Extraordinary and Plenipotentiary at Vienna, Right Hon. Lord Bloomfield, G.C.B., £9,200.

Sec. of Embassy, E. R. Lytton, Esq., £1,000.

Military Attaché, Colonel H. H. Crealock.

2nd Secretaries, Hon. H. Wodehouse, £400; R. T. G. Kirkpatrick, £300; Arthur H. Seymour, Esq., £250.

3rd Secretaries, Edward H. C. Herbert, Esq., Hon. T. G. Grosvenor, £150 each.

Attaché, Edward G. Sartoris, Esq.

Chaplain, Rev. George L. Johnston, A.M., £300.

Vienna.—*Vice-Consul,* Sol. B. Werkersheim, Esq.

Ragusa and Cattaro.—*Consul,* Andrew A. Paton, Esq., £550.

Trieste.—*Consul,* Charles Lever, Esq., £100.

Fiume.—*Consul,* Charles T. Hill, Esq., £100.

BADEN, The Grand Duchy of.

A State of South Germany, situate at its southwestern extremity, in lat. 47°—49° N., and long. 7°—9° E.; it is divided into five districts or circles, viz.: Constance, Freiburg, Offenburg, Carlsruhe and Mannheim, and comprises an area of 3,838 square miles (English), 2,100 of which are under cultivation—wheat, oats, rye, barley, maize, potatoes, being the produce; and a population, in 1864, of 1,429,199 (including an army, in 1867, of 14,919 men and 38 guns), about two-thirds of whom are engaged in agriculture—the culture of fruit, chestnuts, walnuts, almonds, being an important branch, together with the vine, producing the average annual quantity of 14,000,000 gallons of wine; honey also is an important product. Its mineral products are alum, sulphur, silver, iron, copper, lead, and coal. There are 564 manufactories employing 64,800 hands; toys, trinkets, and tobacco, clocks, stuffs, and machinery being the chief, employing more than 9,000 hands, and producing annually £1,700,000. The principal exports are wine and timber. The Schwarzwald being one of the most remarkable pine forests In Germany, both as to its extent and loftiness of the trees, reaching there from 160 to 180 feet in height. Carlsruhe is the capital of the Duchy.

The Public Revenue, 1866, amounted to £1,424,542

Public Expenditure	1,624,577
Public Debt	9,256,728

Reigning Sovereign, Frederick I., Grand Duke of Baden, born 9th Sept., 1826, m. 20th Sept. 1856, Louise, daughter of William I., King of Prussia.

Heir Apparent, Fredk. William, b. 9th July, 1857.

Minister of State and Foreign Affairs, Rudolf von Freydorf.

Chargé, H. Simson, Esq., 16, Great St. Helen's.

Minister Pleny. and Envoy Extry. (Wurtemburg and Baden), George J. R. Gordon, Esq. (Stuttgardt), £2,300.

Chargé d'Affaires, Evan M. Baillie, Esq. (Carlsruhe), £500.

BARBARY,

Known to the ancients as Mauritania, Numidia, Libya, an extensive region in Northern Africa, situate between the Atlantic on the west, and the Mediterranean on the north and east, in lat, 25°—

37° N. and long. 10° W.—25° E. It is divided into three separate states called the "States of Barbary," viz., Morocco, Algiers, and Tripoli, which last includes those of Barca, Tunis, and Fez. The aggregate area is estimated at 820,000 square miles, with a population of about 13,200,000 inhabitants. Its coast line from east to west extends 2,600 miles. With the exception of Egypt, it is the most fertile country in Africa, producing an abundance of corn, wine, citrons, oranges, figs, almonds, olives, dates, and melons. The chief trade consists in fruits, in the horses called barbs, Morocco leather, ostrich feathers, indigo, wax, tin, and coral.

[For Morocco, see that head. For Algeria, see "France."]

TRIPOLI, a state and regency of the Ottoman Empire, on the northern coast of Africa, and the most easterly of the States of Barbary. Its area is roughly estimated at 200,000 square miles, and its population at 1,500,000, but this is uncertain. The coast line extends about 800 miles. The soil is fertile. All sorts of tropical fruits, grain, wine, madder, cotton, &c., are produced. As there are no rivers in the country, and rain seldom falls, vegetation is supported mainly by the copious dews which prevail here. The interior yields senna, dates, and galls. The carob and lotus are indigenous. The fruits, which are abundant and of exquisite flavour, consist chiefly of almonds, figs, apples, pears, plums, peaches, nectarines, grapes, and melons; whilst the vegetables are very fine, and similar to those of Europe. Rock-salt forms an important article of export. Cattle and sheep are reared in great numbers. Tripoli is also noted for its small but excellent breed of horses, and its strong and beautiful mules. The commerce of the country is carried on chiefly by caravans. The principal manufactures are carpets and cloaks, with other articles of clothing; besides these, Morocco leather, earthenware, sacking, and also potash. The military force of the country consists of a body of about 10,000 Turkish soldiers, whose duty it is to suppress insurrections; but who were formerly wont to vary it by creating them. The revenue is chiefly raised by tax or tribute; the natives (consisting for the most part of Libyan Berbers, Moors, and a few Arabs) pay to the Imperial Government by way of tribute a tenth of all the products of the soil; and there is, moreover, a special tax imposed on every olive and date tree, on every camel, on all horned cattle, on sheep and goats, and on Jewish residents. Principal articles of import, wheat, barley, oil, metals, British manufactures, wines and spirits. Principal articles of export: bullocks, ivory, wheat, barley, ostrich feathers, madder root, wool, &c. Total value of imports in 1866 (including £20,400 from United Kingdom), £67,450. Total value of exports (including £35,200 to the United Kingdom), £66,800. Number, tonnage and value of cargoes of British and Foreign vessels entered and cleared at the Port of Tripoli in 1866: 295 vessels entered, tonnage 17,987, value £67,450, of which 24 vessels, tonnage 4,006, value £15,950, were British; 192 vessels cleared, tonnage 17,537, value £66,800, of which 20 vessels, tonnage 3,300, value £17,600, were British. The government is vested in a Governor-general, who has the title, rank, and authority of a Pasha of the Ottoman Empire. He is appointed by the Sultan, and by him all the subordinate governors of the Tripolitan provinces, who bear the title of Beys, are appointed.

Gov.-Gen., Aali Riza, Pasha of Tripoli.
Tripoli, British Consul-Gen. at, F. R. Drummond Hay, Esq., £950.
Benguzi, Vice-Consul, Geo. Dennis, Esq., £500.
Governor of Tunis, Mohamed Sadik, Bey of Tunis.
Tunis, British Agent and Consul-Gen. at, Richard Wood, Esq., C.B., £1,600.
Vice-Consul, F. H. S. Werry, Esq., £450.
Susa, Vice-Consul, John Hy. Stevens, Esq., £300.

BAVARIA,

A Kingdom of Central Europe and principal State of Southern Germany; it is divided into two unequal parts, the eastern portion comprising eleven-twelfths of the whole, is situated between 47° 20'—50° 41' N. lat. and 9°—13° 48' E. long., the western part occupying the Rhine Palatinate, on the left bank of the Rhine. Bavaria is divided into eight circles, Upper Bavaria, Lower Bavaria, Palatinate, Upper Palatinate, Upper, Middle, and Lower Franconia, and Swabia, comprising an area of 29,637 square miles and a population, in 1867, of 4,824,421, of whom 3,176,333 are Roman Catholics, 1,233,804 Protestants, subdivided into Lutherans 906,386, Calvinists 2,431, Unitarians 325,077, Mennonites and Greek Catholics 5,560, and Jews 56,033, besides other denominations. The army (now being reorganzied) consists of 105,757 men, viz., 81,337 permanent, 24,420 reserve. The principal rivers are the Danube, Rhine, and the Maine. Its forests are extensive, covering nearly a third of the country, and consisting chiefly of pine and fir trees; the soil is highly productive, wheat, rye, oats, barley, being the chief products; buckwheat, maize, and rice are also grown, and tobacco is one of the staple products. The hop plant is most extensively cultivated, the average of land planted in 1867 being little short of 60,000 English acres, and the quantity of hops produced 286,785 English cwt., the yield having been extraordinarily great. Upper and Middle Franconia are styled the hop-gardens of Bavaria. The vine, as well as the hop plant, is freely cultivated; the *Steinwein* and *Bavarian beer* have obtained a world-wide celebrity. The chief minerals are salt (formerly a Government monopoly), coal, found throughout the kingdom, the produce of which in 1866 was 6,893,909 cwt., valued at £113,051; iron, copper, manganese, quicksilver, and cobalt are found in some places. The manufactures are for the most part unimportant and scarcely developed, consisting of linen (coarse), woollen and cotton goods, porcelain, jewellery, toys, clocks, mathematical and optical instruments, the latter being held in high repute; the brewing of beer is, however, the most important, and is carried to great perfection, there being nearly 6,000 taxed breweries, producing 100,000,000 gallons of beer annually, mainly consumed in the country. Nearly two-thirds of the revenue of the State are said to be derived from this source. The chief imports are sugar, coffee, woollens, silks, stuffs, drugs, hemp and flax; the chief exports are timber, grain, wine, hops, salt, beer, leather, glass, jewellery, &c.

	£
The total net Revenue for 1866 amounted to	5,878,605
The total Expenditure to	6,522,782
Total amount of Public Debt	2,969,267

The extent of combined railways is 1,624

English miles, with an invested capital of £19,987,016 ; the total receipts for the financial year 1866 were £2,328,482 ; and the total expenditure £1,164,102. Munich is the capital.

Reigning Sovereign, Louis (Ludwig), 2nd King of Bavaria and Count Palatine of the Rhine, born 25th August, 1845.

Heir Apparent, his brother, Prince Otho, born 27th April, 1848.

Minister of State and Foreign Affairs, Prince Clovis von Hohenlohe-Schillingsfürst.

Minister at London, Count Hompesch, 15, Half Moon Street.

Consul-General, R. Brandt, Esq., 3, Crosby Sq.

Envoy Extry. and Min. Pleny. at Munich, Sir F. H. Howard, K.C.B., £4,000.

Secretary of Legation, H. P. Fenton, Esq., £500.

Attaché, F. M. Sartous.

Attaché, Count Bray.

BELGIUM,

A Kingdom of central Europe, and one of the smallest of the European States, consisting of the southern portion of the former Kingdom of the Netherlands—in the time of the Romans forming part of *Gallia Belgica*—situate in lat. 49° 27' to 51° 30' N. and long. 2° 33' to 6° 5' E. It is divided into nine Provinces, viz. :- Antwerp, Brabant, West Flanders, East Flanders, Hainault, Liege, Limburg, Luxemburg, and Namur, comprising a total area of 11,267 square miles, and, in 1865, a population of 4,984,351, including an army of 100,000 men. The Roman Catholic is the prevailing religion, there being only about 12,000 Protestants and 1,500 Jews. The principal rivers are the Maas and the Scheldt, with the tributaries of the former, the Sambre, Ourthe, and Roer. There is no country in the world in which agriculture has attained so high a state of perfection, little more than one-eighth of the whole being uncultivated. Of 7,000,000 acres it is calculated that one-half is arable, one-fifth meadow and pasture, and one-fifth woods and forests ; the chief products are wheat, rye, barley, oats, flax, hemp, tobacco, potatoes, &c. In the campine or waste land, comprising about 500,000 acres, bees are successfully reared and are very productive. Belgium is rich in minerals, which, next to agriculture, constitute the chief source of national prosperity. These are copper, zinc, lead, iron, coal, the two latter abounding to a great extent : of iron, 1,018,231 tons were raised in 1865, valued at £393,180, and producing of the wrought material 898,992 tons, valued at £4,685,192, thus showing the value of labour ; and of coal, 11,840,603 tons, valued at £4,955,847, Belgium being the richest in this mineral of any known country except England. Flanders is noted for its breed of horses. The principal manufactures, which are also its chief exports, are carpets, linens, flax, woollen cloths, lace (made chiefly at Brussels, Malines (Mechlin), Louvain, and Bruges, and realizing enormous prices), cotton, hardware, and cutlery ; the great seats of metal manufactures—the ordnance foundries, steam-engines, &c., are Liége, Namur, Mons. The flax culture and preparation employs about 400,000 hands. The chief imports are Colonial produce and the raw material for woollen and cotton manufacture.

	£
The Public Revenue, in 1866, amounted to	6,563,580
Total Expenditure	6,343,170
Public Debt	25,070,221

Number and tonnage of all vessels entered and cleared, No. 8,970, 1,832,580 tons, of which 3,280 were British and the tonnage 822,282.

	£
Total real value of imports in 1865, exclusive of bullion & specie, including £30,256,813 for home consumption	54,597,735
Value of imports of home produce from the United Kingdom, 1866	2,872,386
Total real value of exports, exclusive of bullion and specie, in 1865, of which £24,066,052 was Belgian produce	48,171,946
Value of exports to the United Kingdom	7,906,849
Value of Bullion and Specie imported (including £1,050,465 from Great Britain)	2,161,804
Value of Bullion and Specie exported (including £117,535 to Great Britain)	952,615

The system of railways chiefly constructed, worked by, and under the control of the State, is very extensive, the total length, in 1866, being 1,419 English miles ; the total cost of construction £9,515,876 ; receipts from all sources £1,532,751 ; working expenditure £783,102 ; net revenue £749,649, being one of the chief sources of the State revenue. Brussels is the capital and seat of Government.

Reigning Sovereign, Leopold II., born 9th April, 1835, m., 22nd August, 1853, Marie, Archduchess of Austria.

Heir Apparent, Prince Leopold, Duke of Brabant, born 12th June, 1859.

Minister of Foreign Affairs, Charles Rogier.

Envoy Extray. and Minister Pleny. at London, Baron du Jardin, 78, Harley-street.

First Secretary, A. Van de Velde.

Counsellor of Legation, Barthol de Fosselaert.

Secretaries, M. O. Delepierre and Prince Alphonse de Chimai.

Consul, O. Delepierre, 60, Paternoster Row.

Vice do. Mr. J.G. Wich, 11, Bury Ct., St. Mary Axe.

Envoy Extry. and Min. Pleny. at Brussels, Lord John Saville Lumley, Esq., G.C.B., £4,000.

Secty. of Legation, Geo. Glynne Petre, Esq., £500.

Second Secty, Robert Percy Ffrench, Esq., £250.

Unpaid Vice-Consul, Thomas James Maltby, Esq.

Brit. Con. at Antwerp, Ed. A. Grattan, Esq., £500.

Ghent. (Vice Consul), Hayman Hye, Esq., £100.

Ostend, Edward T. Currey, Esq., £300.

BOLIVIA, REPUBLIC OF,

Formerly comprised in the Spanish Vice-Royalty of Columbia, under the name of the Peru, now deriving its name from the great liberator, Simon Bolivar ; it extends between lat. 12° 10' to 25° 30' S. and long. 58° to 70° 40' W., and occupies an area of 374,480 square miles. Its population is assumed to be about 2,000,000, the majority being aborigines. The mineral productions are very valuable ; the silver mines of Potosi, believed to be almost inexhaustible, while gold, partly dug and partly washed, is obtained on the eastern Cordillera of the Andes ; copper, lead, tin, salt, sulphur, are also known to exist. Its agricultural produce consists chiefly of rice, barley, oats, maize, cotton, cocoa, indigo, potatoes, the choicest fruits, cinchona bark, and medicinal herbs, &c., which are also its principal exports ; its chief imports being iron, hardware, and silks. The revenue is assumed to be about £360,000.

President. General Dalla Costa.

British Vice-Consul at La Paz, vacant.

British Consul General at Monte Video, acting.

Consul General in London, William Scholey, Esq., 5, Billiter-square.

BORNEO,

Next to Australia, the largest island in the world, discovered by the Portuguese in 1521, is situated in the Eastern Archipelago, extending from lat. 7° 4' N. to 4° 10' S., and from long. 108° 50' to 119° 20' E., about 800 miles in length and 700 in breadth, and containing an area of about 300,000 square miles, divided by the equatorial line into two portions, nearly equal in surface. The population, variously stated, is probably about 25,000,000, consisting chiefly of Malays, Dyaks, Papus or Negritos (the aboriginal inhabitants), Chinese, and Bugis, natives of the Celebes. It was divided into several districts, and governed by independent princes, who were perpetually waging war with each other. Several of the European powers have at various times endeavoured to establish Colonial settlements, but hitherto without success, until Sir James Brooke, a private English gentleman, landed on its coast in 1838 : his subsequent efforts to establish and extend the commercial relations of Great Britain with this part of the globe exhibit almost unexampled perseverance and enterprise, as exemplified in his vigorous government as Rajah of Sarawak, on the north-west coast, and also in the occupation of the small island of Labuan *(See British Colonies)* as a Colony and naval station. The British Government, however, recently refused, upon Sir James Brooke's retirement from Sarawak, to accept it, and annex it to the British Empire. Vegetation is extremely luxuriant; beside vast forests of iron-wood, teak, gutta percha, and ebony, the products of the vegetable kingdom consist of dye-woods, nutmegs, sago, camphor, cinnamon, citron, betel, pepper, ginger, rice, &c. The mineral kingdom includes gold, silver, diamonds (the principal diamond mines are those of Landak), iron, tin, and coal, the latter abundant. The principal imports are opium, tea, and a few manufactured goods ; the exports are carried on chiefly by the Malays, the Dutch, and the British.

Rajah of Sarawak, Charles Brooke, Esq.

Consul-Gen., Brunei, and Governor of Labuan, J. Pope Hennessy, Esq., £300.

Vice-Consul, Sarawak, John M. Elliot, Esq., £500.

BRAZIL,

The most extensive State of South America, discovered in 1500 by Pedro Alvarez Cabral, a Portuguese navigator, is bounded on the North by the Atlantic ocean, Guiana, and Venezuela ; on the West by Equador, Peru, Bolivia, Paraguay, and Argentina ; on the South by Argentina, and Uruguay ; and on the East by the Atlantic Ocean. This immense country extends between lat. 5° 10' to 33° 45' and 34° 32' ; extending between 2,414 miles from North to South, and 2,474 from West to East, containing an area of 2,253,000 square miles, and a population of 11,780,000, of whom 1,400,000 are slaves, and 5,000,000 Indians. It consists of 20 Provinces, 16 of which are along the coast, and 4 in the interior. It is unequalled for the number and extent of its rivers : the Amazon, the largest, though not the longest in the world; the Parana, Araguay, Paraguay, Uruguay, and others. Its forests are immense, abounding in the greatest variety of useful and beautiful woods, some possessing a peculiar fragrance, well adapted for dying, for cabinet work, or for ship-building ; among them are the cocoa-nut, mahogany, logwood, rosewood, Brazilwood, &c. Towards the interior the land rises, by gentle gradations, to the height of from 2,000 to 5,000 feet above the level of the sea, and in these regions European fruits and grain are reared in abundance, while the intermediate valleys are found extremely favourable for the raising of sugar, coffee, and all sorts of tropical produce. The forests afford a refuge to almost every species of quadruped, reptiles, and insects, while the birds are of wonderfu variety and beauty. Its agricultural produce is abundant ; maize, beans, cassava root, which is generally used as bread by all ranks, are very generally cultivated, as wheat, and other European cereals. The minerals are very considerable and valuable, comprising gold, silver, iron, diamonds, topazes and other precious stones, which are among the chief exports.

Estimated Revenue, 1868-9 .... £8,015,625
     ,,   1869-70 8,512,250
     ,,   Expenditure, 1868-9 7,714,000
     ,,   1869-70 7,963,425
Public Debt.................... 43,700,726
The value of Imports for 1866-67 ... 15,750,054
The value of Exports   ,, ... 17,555,250

Number and tonnage of all vessels entered and cleared in 1866, exclusive of coasting trade, 6,638 vessels—2,566,990 tons.

There are several principal towns, the chief of which also the seat of government, is Rio de Janeiro.

Reigning Sovereign, Pedro II., Emperor of Brazil, born 2nd Dec., 1825 ; married 4th Sept., 1843, Theresa, daughter of Francis I., King of the Two Sicilies.

Heir Apparent, The Imperial Princess Dona Izabel, *b.* 29 July, 1846 ; *m.* 15 Oct. 1864, to Gastor d'Orleans, Count d'Eu.

Minister of Foreign Affairs, Don J. M. da Silva Paranhos.

Envoy Extraordinary and Minister Plenipotentiary at London, Counsellor de Almeida Areas.

Secretary, Pereira d'Andrada.

Attachés, Chev. de Sonza Correa ; M. d'Aragas ; and F. de Carvalho Moreira ; Office of Legation, 9, Portman Square.

Liverpool, Consul-General at, Admiral John Pascoe Grenfell.

London, Vice-Consul at, Chevalier Luiz Augusto da Costa, 1, Gresham House.

Envoy Extraordinary and Minister Plenipotentiary, Rio de Janeiro, G. B. Mathew, Esq., C.B., £4,700.

Sec. of Legation, Hon. F. J. Pakenham, £700.

Second Secretary, R. G. Watson, Esq., £250.

Consul, G. M. S. Lennon Hunt, £1,800.

Bahia—Consul, John Morgan, Esq., £800.

Para—Consul, J. de Vismes Drummond Hay, C.B., *Maranhao,* £720.

Rio Grande de Sul—Consul, R. Callender, £950.

Santos—Consul, Capt. Richard F. Burton, £650.

BRUNSWICK,

A Duchy or State of Northern Germany, lying chiefly in lat. 51° 38'—52° 28' N., and long 9° 23' —11° 30', E., comprising an area of 1,526 English square miles, and a population in 1867 of 301,966, chiefly Saxon, nearly all of whom are Protestants, 4,000 being Roman Catholics, and 1,100 Jews. It is divided into six circles, for administrative purposes ; and is partly traversed by the Hartz mountains. The mineral products are gold, silver, lead, sulphur, alum, and salt in large quantities, besides marble, alabaster, gypsum. Its products include, besides the ordinary cereals, tobacco, hops, potatoes, and quantities of other leguminous plants. The pasture land is very extensive, great attention being devoted to the rearing of cattle and breeding of sheep, wool being an important article of commerce. The country is well timbered, and occupation afforded to a large number of people in cutting and preparing the timber. The chief manufactures are linen, woollen-cloth, stockings, metals, porcelain, paper, glass, &c. The total amount of revenue and expenditure for the financial period 1865-6, amounted alike to £766,200, and the public debt to £1,707,707. The Duke of Brunswick is one of the wealthiest of German Potentates, being in possession of immense private estates.

Reigning Sovereign, William I., Duke of Brunswick, born 25th April, 1806; succeeded to the Dukedom on the flight of his brother Duke Charles, who was declared by resolution of the Diet, 2nd December, 1830, "regierungsunfähig," or, "unfit to govern."

CENTRAL AMERICA,

Formerly composing one federal state, but now divided into five Republics and one Kingdom, that of Mosquito; it connects the two boundaries of North and South America, but its limits have not been exactly defined. Politically it consists of the Republics of Guatemala, San Salvador, Honduras, Nicaragua, and Costa Rica, occupying an area of about 250,000 square miles, with a population of about 2,300,000. From the year 1505, when it was conquered by Don Pedro Alvarade, the conqueror of Mexico, to 1823, it remained subject to Spain, but in that year it effected its independence.

GUATEMALA.—Situate in N. lat. from about 14° to 17° and in W. long. from 89° to 94°, comprising an area of 40,278 English square miles and a population of about 1,000,000. The chief exports are cotton, indigo (considered the finest), cigars, silver, cochineal, mahogany, and sarsaparilla.

	£
The total value of imports in 1856 amounted to	339,825
Total value of exports	336,068

President, Marshal de Camp Vincent Corna, *Guatemala.*
Envoy Extry. and Min. Pleny. at London, Don Juan de Francisco Martin.
Chargé d'Affaires at Guatemala (and for the several Republics), Edwin Corbett, Esq., £2000.
Unpaid Consul, George J. Hockmeyer, Esq.

SAN SALVADOR, the smallest, though in point of population the second, of the Central American Republics, contains an area of about 7,230 English square miles and a population, according to recent estimates, of 600,000. The principal agricultural products are indigo, coffee, cotton, tobacco, sugar, balsam (known as Balsam of Peru). Its mineral resources are not great, but rich veins of silver are found at Tabango, also iron mines near Santa Anna, these ores together form its principal exports, the total value of which in 1865 amounted to £423,904, and the imports to £442,680. San Salvador is the capital of the Republic.
President, Francis Duennas, *San Salvador.*
Minister Pleny. General Don Pedro Romulo Negrete, 2, Russell-square.
Attaché, Captain Don Francisco Carrera.
Consul, Edward Hall, Esq., £200, *Sonsonate.*

COSTA RICA, the most southern state of Central America, occupying the entire seabreadth from Nicaragua to New Granada, in N. lat. from 8° to 10° 40' and W. long. 83° to 85°, contains an area of 16,250 English square miles and a population of about 215,000 inhabitants.

It yields gold and silver, tobaco, sarsaparilla, indigo, sugar, cocoa and dye-woods; the staple product and export is coffee, of which, in 1865, 4,986 tons, value £323,709, were exported, beside hides, and cedar-wood. Recently, in consequence of the piratical exploits of the notorious filibuster, William Walker, Costa Rica suffered much commercially as well as politically. The total value of imports in 1867 amounted to £460,465, and the exports to £420,295. There is no national debt. San José is the capital.
President, Dr. J. M. Castro, *San José.*
Consul General in London, Edwin F. Hickman, Esq., 155, Fenchurch-street.
British Consul at San José, Allan Wallis, Esq., £200.

CHILI.

A republic of South America—of Spanish origin —lying wholly between the Andes and the shores of the Pacific, stretching coastwise from Bolivia to Patagonia, along lat. 25° 30' to 43° 20' S., and in long. 69° to 74° W., has an extreme length of 1,240 miles, and an average breadth of 120 miles; the great chain of the Andes runs along its east limit, rising from 13,000 to 14,000 feet above the level of the sea. It is subject to volcanic eruptions and earthquakes that have frequently resulted in great loss of life and property. Chili is divided into 13 provinces, which are again subdivided into 52 departments, the aggregate area of which has been officially stated at 139,335 square miles, and its population (1865) at 1,819,223. Vegetation and agriculture are extremely limited, and the implements of husbandry of the most primitive kind. Its mineral kingdom, however, is extremely rich. The mountains contain precious stones, as the agate, jasper, rock crystal, &c., and the rivers wash down rubies and sapphires. There are gold, silver, and copper mines, lead mixed with gold or silver, iron of the best quality and tin—almost all the copper contains a proportion of gold. The silver mines are found on the highest part of the Andes. The manufactures are earthen and copper wares, cordage, linens, soap, and brandy. The chief imports are cotton and woollen goods; hardware, principally from England; silks from France; linen from Germany, &c.; the chief exports being metals, wheat, flour, hides, and tallow. There are 336 miles of railway open for traffic, the total cost of which amounted to............ £427,215

The total revenue of the Republic chiefly from Customs and State monopolies) amounted in 1864 to ...	1,854,984
Total expenditure	1,614,073
Total amount of public debt in 1865	2,933,405
Total value of imports in 1866 (including bullion and specie, of which £1,852,436 was home produce of the United Kingdom)	4,171,293
Total value of exports (£5,336,102 domestic produce, and £2,943,112 exports to United Kingdom)	5,817,978

Number and tonnage of Foreign vessels entered and cleared in 1866:—Entered, 3,709, of which 1,496 were British; and tonnage, 1,414,612 tons, of which 935,820 tons were British. Cleared, 2919, of which 1415 were British; tonnage, 1,358,288 tons, of which 916,930 tons were British. The capital is Santiago, situated nearly in the heart of the country, and connected with Valparaiso, the principal port, by a railway of 90 miles in length, and also by telegraph communication.

President, Don José Joach. Joaquin Perez, *Santiago.*

Envoy Ext. and Minister Plenip. at London, Don Maximiniano Errazuariz.

Consul, Hen. Kendall, Esq., 1, Gt. Winchester St.

Santiago—Chargé d'Affaires and Consul-Gen., Wm. Taylour Thompson, Esq., £2,000.

Private Sec., George Smith, Esq., £250.

Constitution—Vice Consul, Ant. St. Cornish, Esq.

Coquimbo—Consul, Alexander Gollan, Esq., £300.

Caldera—Vice-Consul, John J. Murray, Esq., £250.

Huasco—Vice-Consul, A. L. Roberts, Esq., unpaid.

Valparaiso—Consul, Hen. W. Rouse, Esq., £1,450.

Talcahuano—Vice-Consul, R. Cunningham, Esq., £250.

CHINA.

The Chinese Empire is a vast territory in the south and east of Asia, comprehending five great divisions—viz., Mantchuria, Montgolia, Turkestan, Thibet, and China Proper; which last is divided into 18 provinces, including the two large islands of Formosa and Haenan. China Proper is included between 18°—40° N. lat., and 98°—124° E. long. Its coast line exceeds 2,500 miles, and its land frontier 4,400 miles, comprising an area of 1,297,999 square miles, and a population now estimated at 450,000,000. It possesses an army, according to recent reports, of only 600,000, and a navy of 1,900 ships, river and seagoing vessels, and 188,000 sailors. Various attempts had been made by Great Britain to open a trade with China, but unsuccessfully, till 1834, when the East India Company's monopoly ceased. As we are not about to give an account of the war resulting from the opium trade and other causes conducing to the opening of the commerce, suffice it to state that in 1842 five ports were opened to European trade, and subsequently in 1858, eight additional ports, the direct trade between Great Britain and China being now estimated at £10,000,000. Agriculture takes the lead of all other pursuits; every possible spot is now brought into cultivation, rice being the chief growth. Wheat, barley, and other European grain are raised also : but the most important of vegetable products is the tea-plant, the export value of which, to the United Kingdom alone amounted in 1866 to £10,443,488. Opium, camphor, tobacco, the white mulberry for the production of silk, are also among its chief vegetable products. Its principal mineral productions are copper, iron, tin, sulphur, coal, lapis lazuli, rock crystal, kaolin or porcelain earth, which, when worked up, has given the name of "china" to the beautiful and well-known ware. Its principal manufactures are porcelain-ware, silks, satins, cotton (nankeen), carvings in ivory, lacquered ware, filagree-work in gold and silver, &c. These, with silk and the products before enumerated, comprise the principal articles of export, and those chiefly to Great Britain.

	£
The total value of Imports in 1865 amounted to	47,700,904
Those from Great Britain and her colonies amounting to	18,282,994
Total value of Exports	34,721,817
Those to Great Britain amounting to	15,884,573

Total quantity of tea exported in 1865, 161,774,755 lbs.

Reigning Emperor, Tung-Chih, "Union in the cause of Law and Order," born 5th April, succeeded 22nd August, 1861.

Envoys Extraordinary and Ministers Plenipotentiary to the Treaty Powers, Hon. Anson Burlinghame, H.E. Chih-Kang, and H.E. Sun-Chia-Ku.

Interpreter, Windsor Lowder, Esq.

Pekin—Envoy Ext. and Min. Plen., and Chief Supt. of Trade, Sir Rutherford Alcock, K.C.B., £6,000.

Secretary, Chinese Sec. and Translator, T. F. Wade, Esq., C.B., £1,200.

2nd Secretary, Hugh Fraser, Esq., £500.

Do. do., Richard Conolly, Esq., £400.

Assist. Chinese Sec., J. McLeavy Brown, Esq., £600.

Do, and Accountant, John G. Murray, Esq., £500.

Surgeon, S. W. Bushell, Esq., £600.

Colonial Auditor, W. H. Rennie, Esq., £500, Hong-Kong.

Interpreters, Two 1st-class, £700 each ; five 2nd-class, £500 each ; four 3rd-class, £400 each.

Amoy—Consul, W. H. Pedder, Esq., £900.

Whampoa—Vice-Consul, H. F. Hance, Esq., £750.

Foochow—Consul, Chas. A. Sinclair, Esq., £1,000.

Kewkeang—Consul, Patrick J. Hughes, Esq., £900.

Ningpo—Consul, Wm. H. Fittock, Esq., £900.

Swatow—Consul, Geo. W. Caine, Esq., £800.

Taiwan—Consul, Robert Swinhoe, Esq., £800.

Tamsuy—Vice-Consul, Wm. Gregory, Esq., £600.

Tengchow—Vice-Consul, J. Markham, Esq., £750.

Tien-tsin—Consul, John Mongan, Esq., £900.

Taku—Vice-Consul, W. Hyde Lay, Esq., £500.

Canton—Consul, D. B. Robertson, C.B., £1,600.

Chin-Kiang—Consul, £900.

Hankow—Consul, W. H. Medhurst, Esq., £1,300.

New Chewng—Consul, T. T. Meadows, Esq., £1,300.

Shangai—Judge of Supreme Court for China and Japan, Sir Edmund Hornby, £3,500.

Deputy Judge, C. W. Goodwin, Esq., £1,100.

Consul, Charles A. Winchester, Esq., £1,500.

*Vice-Consul—*Thos. Adkins, Esq., £750.

COLOMBIA, UNITED STATES OF,

An extensive region in the Northern part of South America, comprising the several Republics of New Granada, Venezuela, and Ecuador.

NEW GRANADA, called also the New Kingdom of Granada, situate between the equator and 12° N. lat., and between 68° and 82° W. long. It is divided into 8 States, of which Panama is one. It occupies an entire area of 333,000 square miles, and possesses a population of about 2,800,000, of whom more than one-half are whites. It has been subjected to several revolutionary changes and civil wars. Its forests, which are very extensive, abound with all kinds of tropical vegetation. Among the trees are mahogany, cedar, fustic and other dye-woods, and medicinal plants. Its mineral productions are gold, silver, copper, iron, lead, coal, emeralds, pearls, &c. Its agricultural products consist of tobacco, coffee, cacao, plantains, wheat, and other cereals. Its manufactures, chiefly for home consumption, consist of woollen and cotton stuffs. The plains yield large quantities of hides and jerked beef. Total number, tonnage, and value of cargoes of vessels of all nations entered and cleared at the port of Panama in 1864 :—Vessels entered, 142; tonnage, 183,829; value, £12,886,858,. Vessels, British, 45; tonnage, 35,832; value, £3,224,973. Vessels cleared, 134; tonnage, 180,587; value, £5,707,713. Vessels, British, 43; tonnage, 34,529; value, £903,089. Bogota is the present capital.

President, General S. Gutierrez, Bogota.

Envoy Extraordinary and Minister Plenipotentiary at London, Senor Manuel M. Mosquera.

Bogota, Chargé d'Affaires and Consul-General, R. Bunch, Esq., C.B., £2,000.

Bogota, Vice-Consul, Charles O'Leary, Esq., £400.

Buenaventura, Vice-Consul, J.V. Cordova, unpaid.

Carthagena, Consul, Albany de Grenier Fonblanque, Esq., £800.

Sabanilla, Vice-Consul, Michael Constantine, Esq., £300.

Santa Martha, Vice-Consul, Frederick Stacey, Esq., £400.

Rio Hacha, Vice-Consul, unpaid.

Panama, Consul, C. A. Henderson, Esq., £1,200.

Chagres and Colon, Vice-Consul, Thomas C. Taylor, Esq., £400.

VENEZUELA, the most northerly of the Republics of South America, situate in lat. between 2°—12° North, and between 60°—73° W. lon. Within recent years it has been variously subdivided; it appears, however, that in 1866 it consisted of 21 provinces, comprising an area of 426,712 English square miles, and a population, according to the latest enumeration, of 1,594,433. Its great river is the Orinoco, which drains by far the greater part of it. For the most part the country is fertile; the lands in the mountainous district of the south-east, not exceeding 2,000 ft. in height, are distinguished by the name of *tierras calidas*, or the palm lands, upon which grow the sago palm, cocoa palm, and others, to a colossal size, yielding most valuable products; those between 2,000 and 7,000 are called the *tierras templadas*, or temperate lands, and those exceeding 7,000 are called *tierras frias*, or cold lands, mostly uninhabited. Among the forest trees are the mahogany, rosewood, satinwood, black and white ebony, and caoutchouc, fustic, and logwood. There are also forests or large tracts of the cinchona, or Peruvian bark tree. The cocoa, the finest in the world, coffee, sugar, indigo, and cotton, are extensively cultivated. Tobacco, also, is a profitable crop, and vegetables of all kinds abound. Agriculture is the chief pursuit, though only one-eighth of the whole area is under cultivation. The chief imports are manufactured goods, provisions, and wine. The chief exports are coffee, cocoa, cotton, sugar, tobacco, indigo, hides, tallow, dye woods and timber. Cattle, also, are a great source of wealth. Caracas, is the capital.

The executive is exercised by a President and Vice-President, there being also a Senate and House of Representatives.

President, Vacant.

Vice-President, do.

Consul-General at London, Francis Leander Davis, Esq., 35, King Street, Cheapside.

Caracas, Chargé d'Affaires and Consul-General, George Fagan, Esq., £1,200.

Maracaibo, Vice-Consul, E.T. Harrison, Esq. £200.

Bolivar, Vice-Consul, Lewis Joel, Esq., £300.

La Guayra, Vice-Consul, David Lobo, Esq., £300.

Maturin, Vice-Consul, James Schaeffer, unpaid.

Puerto Cabello, Vice-Consul, P. Murdock, unpaid.

ECUADOR, a republican state of South America and that portion of Colombia which lies on each side of the Equator, extending in lat. 1° 40' N. to 5° 50' S., and between 69° and 81° 20' W., measuring from North to South fully 500 miles, and from East to West nearly 850, presenting an area of about 300,000 English square miles, and with a population of about 1,100,000, mostly descendants of the Spaniards, aboriginal Indians, and Mestizoes. It was discovered by Pizarro in 1526, when it was comprised in the empire of the Incas. The giant chain of the Andes—the Chimborazo 21,400 feet, the Cotopaxi 18,880 feet, the Antisana 13,500 feet above the level of the sea, and others, rear their lofty heads. Ecuador is watered by the Amazon and its tributaries. There are extensive forests, and the cinchona bark tree is common.

Agriculture is considered to be in a backward state. Its products are cotton, sugar, coffee, cocoa, yams, tobacco, fruits, sarsaparilla, wheat and other cereals. Its minerals consist of gold, quicksilver, lead, iron, copper, and emeralds. Sulphur abounds near the Chimborazo. Its chief manufactures are woollen and cotton goods. The entire local and commercial relations of this state were deranged by an earthquake which occurred in August, 1868, destroying many cities, 30,000 lives, accompanied by an enormous loss of property. Ecuador is divided into 12 provinces. The total value of imports, at the port of Guayaquil in 1865, amounted to £635,000, and the total value of exports to £679,747. The total number, tonnage, and value of cargoes of all vessels entered and cleared at the port of Guayaquil in 1865, was 412, of which 110 were British; 114,794 tons, of which 8,968 were British. Value of cargoes, £1,314,747, of which £875,500 was British. Quito is the capital.

President, Dr. Xavier Espinosa, Quito.

Minister Plenipotentiary, Señor Antonio Florey, 3, Rue Blanche, Paris.

Quito, Chargé d'Affaires and Consul-General, Fred. Hamilton, Esq., £1,400.

Guayaquil, Vice-Consul, C. T. Smith, Esq., £200.

DENMARK,

A kingdom in the north of Europe, and the smallest of the Scandinavian kingdoms, is situated between 53° 23'—57° 45' N. lat. and 8° 5'—12° 45' E. lon. It is divided into—1. Denmark Proper, comprising the islands Seeland, Fünen, Laaland, &c., and the peninsula of Jutland. 2. The Faroe Isles, Greenland, and Iceland; and 3. Its colonies of Santa Cruz (St. Croix), St. Thomas, and St. John, in the West Indies. Denmark Proper comprises an area of 14,616 square miles, and a population (in 1864) of 1,717,802, nearly one-half of whom live exclusively by agriculture, and one-fourth by manufactures and trade. The common products are oats, barley, beans, peas, hops, hemp, potatoes, tobacco. Wheat is but partially cultivated. Its manufactures are, for the most part, for home consumption. The streams and shores abound in valuable fish, which form an essential branch of national industry. Its principal imports are manufactured goods (woollens, silks, cottons), iron, hardware, wine, fruit, tea, and colonial produce. Its chief exports are those of agricultural produce, butter, bacon and hams, flour, hides, skins, corn meal and oil-cake; horses and cattle, the latter principally to Great Britain, the value of which in 1866 amounted to £2,291,909 Oats and barley alone averaging 1,000,000

The public income for the year ending 31st March, 1868, amounted to 3,048,749

The public Expenditure 3,113,884

The estimated Revenue for 1869-70 is 2,443,015

,,   Expenditure for do.... 2,533,629

Public debt, 31st March, 1867, was 14,512,191

Total number and tonnage of all vessels entered and cleared at ports in Denmark, 1865 :—Vessels, 6,459; tons, 283,610 entered, of which 822 were, with a tonnage of 28,034 tons, Danish, and 5,637 vessels, with a tonnage of 255,676 tons, Foreign. Vessels cleared, 6,319; tons, 290,460, of which 869 vessels, with a tonnage of 2,788 tons, were Danish, and 5,450 vessels Foreign, with a tonnage of 262,572 tons. Vessels entered :—Danish, 282; tonnage, 28,034. Foreign, 5,637; tonnage, 25,576. Vessels cleared :—Danish, 869; tonnage,

2,788. Foreign, 5,450; tonnage, 262,572. Copenhagen is the capital.

A submarine cable was successfully laid in 1868 between the Danish and English coasts.

Reigning Sovereign, Christian IX. king of Denmark, born 8th April, 1818; married, 26th May, 1842, Louise, daughter of William, Landgrave of Hesse Cassel. Heir-apparent, Prince Frederic, born June 3rd, 1843. His eldest daughter, the Princess Alexandra, born 1st Dec., 1844, was married to H.R.H. Albert Edward, Prince of Wales, 10th March, 1863.

Minis. for For. Affs., Count Krag Juel Vind Frijs of Frijsenborg.

Envoy Ext. and Min. Plenip. at London, General J. de Bulow, 62, Wimpole Street.

Attaché, C. A. Goodf, Esq., 58, Oxford Terrace.

Secretary, L. J. de Koefoed.

Consul Gen., A. Westenholz, Esq., K.D., 42, Gt. Tower Street.

Copenhagen—Envoy Ext. and Min. Plenip., Sir C. Lennox Wyke, K.C.B., £4,000.

Secretary of Legation, Geo. Strachey, Esq., £500.

Second do., H. G. Macdonell, Esq., £250.

Attaché, Hon. H. G. Edwards.

Vice-Consul, A. de Capel Crowe, Esq., £150.

Elsinore—Consul, Bridges Taylor, Esq., £700.

Vice-Consul, W. R. Larlham, Esq., £150.

St. Croix—Consul, H. Norton Shaw, Esq., £650.

St. Thomas ,, Robt. Boyd Lamb, Esq., £400.

EGYPT.

A country in the north-east of Africa, extending from the Nile to the first cataract of the Nile (Syene), between 23° 50′—31° 35′ N. lat., and 25°—34° E. long. The country may be said to be the bed of the Nile, its only river (the sources of which, hitherto a matter of conjecture from the earliest ages, have lately been discovered by Capts. Speke and Grant, and others), extending about 3,500 miles, the last 1,500 of which, from its junction with the Atbara to its mouth, receives no tributary, the cultivated territory only extending to the limits of the inundation. It was formerly a province of the Turkish Empire, but became independent in 1811, and the government is now hereditary in the family of Mehemet Ali. For the history of Egypt, both past and present, as well as its antiquities, so replete with wonder and with awe, we must refer our readers to other sources. It is divided into Upper, Middle, and Lower Egypt, which last comprehends the Delta, and comprises an area estimated at 175,800 square miles, and a population of about 5,250,000 inhabitants, including Copts, Bedouin Arabs, Jews, Armenians, domiciled Europeans, Greeks, &c. The army, raised by conscription, amounts to about 30,000 men: the navy consists of 75 vessels of war. Its agricultural products consist of millet, maize, wheat, rice, melons, gourds, sugar, opium, tobacco, hemp, cotton, indigo, &c. It has no metals: but salt, nitre, marble, and red granite, of which the Pyramids are composed, are found. Its manufactures are confined chiefly to the potteries, which are extensive; cotton and woollen cloths are also made by the natives. It abounds in quadrupeds and reptiles.

The estimated revenue in 1864 was ...£4,250,000
The expenditure 3,575,000
The debt amounts to about 8,500,000
The value of Imports of home produce from the United Kingdom, in 1866, amounted to 7,540,504

The value of Exports to the United Kingdom, a large part of which pass merely in transit through Egypt, amounted to £15,368,824

Cairo is the principal city, and the railway now connects it with both Alexandria and Suez.

Reigning Sovereign, Ismail Pasha, G.C.B., Hereditary Viceroy, born 1830.

Alexandria, Agent and Consul-General at, Colonel E. Stanton, C.B., £2,550.

Consul, George E. Stanley, Esq., £1,800.

Vice-Consul, Henry H. Calvert, Esq., £300.

Legal Vice-Consul and Registrar, Philip Francis, Esq., £300.

Law Clerk, Frederick Arpa, Esq., LL.D., £350.

Cairo Consul, Thomas Fellowes Read, Esq., £600.

Suez Consul, George West, Esq., £200.

FIJI—FEEJEE ISLANDS,

A group of 225 islands in the South Pacific Ocean, 800 miles north of New Zealand, situated in 15° 30′—20° 30′ S. lat., and 177°—178° W. long., 80 of which are said to be inhabited, the total population being estimated at from 150,000 to 250,000. The principal are the Great Fiji and the Great Land. Vegetation is remarkably luxuriant, the chief productions being the bread-fruit tree, banana, plaintain, and cocoa; the sugar-cane, arrowroot, nutmeg, capsicum, tea plant, also flourish, and great care is bestowed on the culture of the yangona (kava), from which an intoxicating liquor is obtained. Cotton here grows wild. Agriculture, however, has been but little practised by the natives, consisting of several tribes who were more engaged in warfare (being fearful cannibals) than in cultivating the domestic arts. In 1861 the chiefs ceded the Island of Great Fiji to Great Britain, and it may therefore be considered, to all intents and purposes, a British possession. It is now making rapid progress in civilization and culture, flourishing plantations being established.

Consul at Ovalau, Leopold March, Esq., £300.

FRANCE.

The most westerly portion of Central Europe, extending from 42° 20′—51° 5′ N. lat., and from 8° 15′ E. long. to 4° 55′ W. long., bounded on the north by the Channel and Straits of Dover, which separate it from England. Its circumference is estimated at nearly 3,100 miles, and an area of 132,787,000 English acres, of which 85,000,000 are under culture (65 millions being arable, 10 millions grass and meadow lands, 5 millions vineyards, and 5 millions gardens and orchards). With Corsica and Savoy, it comprises 35 provinces, and is divided into 89 departments, including those of Corsica and Savoy. It possesses settlements and dependencies in Africa (including Algiers), Asia, and America. The principal rivers are the Seine, Loire, Garonne, and Rhone. The principal forests are those of Ardennes, Compiegne, Fontainebleau, and Orleans, consisting chiefly of oak, birch, pine, beech, elm, chestnut, and the cork tree in the south. Fruit trees abound, and are very productive, the principal being the olive, chestnut, walnut, almond, apple, pear, citron, fig, plum, &c. The vine is cultivated to a very great extent, as the wines of Bordeaux, Burgundy, Champagne, &c., will evidence. The chief agricultural products are wheat, barley, rye, maize, oats, potatoes, beetroot for the manufacture of sugar, hops, &c. Its mineral resources are great. Iron is found nearly all over the country. Copper, lead, silver, antimony, coal, also exist. The most important manufactures are those of watches, jewellery, cabinet work, carving, pottery, glass, chemicals, dyeing, paper-making, woollens, carpets, linen, silk, and lace. Its oyster fisheries are an important industrial feature. The population in 1866 amounted to 38,067,094, about 2,000,000 of whom are Protestants, and 160,000 Jews. The effective strength of the army, up to the 1st January, 1867, was 651,099, of whom 395,485 were in the regular army, and 255,614 in the army of reserve. The navy consisted of 340 steam vessels, with a total of 92,106 horse power, also 28 in course of construction, with a total of 12,670 horse power. These include 16 of the most powerful men-of-war, two of which carry 52 guns, 1,000-horse power each, one carrying 40 guns and 900-horse power, and 13 carrying each 36 guns and 900 horse-power each. The educational system is governmental, and is presided over by a Minister of Instruction, nearly one-half the expense being defrayed by the State, and the remainder by the departments; besides the naval and military schools and the Ecole Polytechnique, the State supports numerous colleges and schools for instruction in special branches of knowledge. As regards the "diffusion of knowledge," however, the press is under great censorial restrictions. The system of railways in France is very extensive, and, with the exception of about 200 miles, entirely in the hands of six great companies, forming an aggregate of 7,989 miles in operation, or working condition.

The principal Imports consist of cotton (raw), silk and floss silks, wool (raw), manufactures of silk, timber, coal and coke, coffee, hides and skins, woollen manufactures, grain, cattle, cotton manufactures.

Principal Exports, haberdashery, silk, woollen and cotton manufactures, apparel of all kinds, jewellery, silk (raw), skins, tanned, curried, &c., wine, metal wares and tools, sugar, spirits, &c.

	£
The revenue of 1867 amounted to	86,180,770
The expenditure	86,179,312
Estimated revenue, 1868	78,181,010
Estimated expenditure, 1868	78,178,685
Public debt	485,310,750

Total number and tonnage of merchant vessels, sailing and steam, belonging to France, 1865, 15,259 and 1,008,084 tons. Total number and tonnage of all vessels entered and cleared at the Ports of France, 1865 :—

Entered, 29,018, of which 14,551 were British. Tonnage, 4,986,930 tons, of which 2,046,834 were British. Cleared, 22,138, of which 10,853 were British—3,592,874 tons, 1,419,070 tons of which were British.

	£
Total value of Imports, 1865	141,096,000
Merchandise (Bullion and Specie)	26,376,348
Total value of Exports	163,460,000
Merchandise (Bullion and Specie)	20,257,146
Value of Imports of home produce from United Kingdom in 1866	11,696,016
Value of Exports to United Kingdom	37,016,576

Reigning Sovereign, Napoleon III., Charles Louis, born 20th April, 1808, elected Emperor 1st December, 1852; married Eugénie Marie de Montigo, second daughter of the Count de Montigo.

Heir Apparent, Napoleon Eugène Louis, Prince Imperial, born 16th March, 1856.

Minister for Foreign Affairs, Léonel Marquis de Moustier.

Ambassador Extraordinary and Minister Plenipotentiary, Prince de La Tour d'Auvergne, Albert Gate House, Hyde Park.

1st Secretary, M. le Vicomte de St. Ferriol.

2nd ditto,

3rd ditto, M. le Marquis de Caumont la Force.

Consul-General, Mons. Jules Fleury, 44, Queen's Gardens, Hyde Park.

Paris, Ambassador Extraordinary and Minister Plenipotentiary at, Right Hon. Lord Lyons, G.C.B., £10,000.

Secretary of Embassy, Hon. Julian H. C. Fane, £1,200.

2nd ditto, Ernest Clay Ker-Seymer, Esq., £400.

3rd ditto, Edward B. Malet, £400.

Military Attaché, H. S. Le Strange, Esq., £500.

Naval Attaché, H. E. H. Jerningham, Esq., £500.

Attaché, Registrar, and Consul, Falconer Atlee, Esq., £415.

Bayonne Consul, F. J. Graham, Esq., £550.

Bordeaux Consul, Thomas C. Hunt, Esq., £800.

Boulogne Consul, William Hamilton, Esq., £400.

Brest Consul, John D. Hay-Hill, Esq., £600.

Calais Consul, Capt. B. W. Hotham, £500.

Charente Consul, Hon. H. P. Vereker, £600.

Cherbourg Consul, Horatio Hammond, Esq., £500.

Corsica Consul, Edward Smallwood, Esq., £250.

Dunkirk Consul, Major N. Pringle, £500.

Havre Consul, F. Bernal, Esq., £900.

Caen Vice-Consul, C. G. G. Percival, Esq., £250.

Nantes Consul, Capt. R. C. Clipperton, £400.

Marseilles Consul, Edward W. Mark, Esq., £1,100.

Nice Consul, Adolphus La Croix, Esq., £300.

Algiers Consul-General, Lieut.-Col. R. L. Playfair, £935.

Algiers Vice-Consul, T. J. Elmore, Esq., £300.

Réunion Consul, Capt. W. F. Segrave, £1,150.

The colonies and foreign possessions of France in Africa are, Algeria, Senegal and its dependencies, the Islands of Bourbon (Réunion) and St. Marie in the Indian Ocean, Mayotte and its dependencies, portions of Madagascar, as also of the coast of Guinea. The total possessions in Africa cover an area of 95,700 square miles, with a population of 473,000 souls.

In America, the islands of Martinique and Guadaloupe; French Guiana, Cayenne, &c.; with St. Pierre and Miquelon near Newfoundland; forming together an area of 80,000 square miles, with a population of 301,500. In Asia, the Indian Settlements of Pondicherry, Mahé, &c., comprise altogether 10,800 square miles, with a population of 2,221,000. In the Pacific Ocean, two groups of the Marquesas and Tahiti, and New Caledonia, the whole forming an area of 9,560 square miles, with 84,000 inhabitants.

ALGERIA, the largest and most important of the French colonies in Africa, situated between 2° 10' W. long., and 8° 30' E. long.; the boundaries are not well defined, but are estimated to embrace an area of about 96,396,000 acres, of which 5,200,000 are under cultivation. Algeria is divided into three provinces, Algiers, Oran, Constantine; the population, consisting of several nationalities, French ;(about 122,000.) Spanish (58,000,) Italian, Maltese, German, Swiss, and other nations, is estimated at 218,000; also the Arabs are reckoned at about 2,652,000. Corn and other cereals are extensively cultivated, also the vine and the olive. Large forests of trees—the oak, cedar, pine, pistachio nut tree, &c., cover large tracts of the country, and furnish an abundant supply of timber and resin. The Oases of Sahara are noted for their dates. Cattle and sheep are reared in large quantities. The cultivation of the vine has made great progress of late years, especially in Algiers. In 1864, the vineyards of Algeria covered 87,000 acres, 50,000 of which were planted with black grapes, the remainder with white. The produce of the several provinces being as follows :—

ALGIERS,—10,500 acres ; 83,000 hectolitres, or 1,826,000 imperial gallons of wine ; and 8,500,000 lbs. of grapes for sale.

ORAN,—12,500 acres ; 20,000 hectolitres, or 440,000 imperial gallons of wine ; and 2,000,000 lbs. of grapes.

CONSTANTINE,—64,000 acres ; 30,000 hectolitres or 660,000 imperial gallons, and 4,100,000 lbs. of grapes.

The land was chiefly planted with the Burgundy, Alicante, and Grenache vines. The growth of cotton has recently been much and successfully encouraged. Nearly 8,000 acres have been sown, the produce of which amounted to 4,000,000 lbs. of raw cotton, the whole whereof has been exported to France, which also draws large quantities of agricultural produce, especially corn and cattle. Total official value of imports into Algeria in 1864, £5,458,352. Total official value of exports out of Algeria, £4,322,694. Value of imports of home produce from the United Kingdom into Algeria 1866, £15,636. Value of exports from Algeria into the United Kingdom, £48,405. The principal Imports consist of wheat, flour, potatoes, pulse, rice, sugar, fresh fruit, wine, seed, oil, timber, cotton manufactures, iron, soap, china, and stone ware. The principal Exports: wool, skins undressed, bones, hoofs and horns, rushes, fresh fruit, olive oil, cotton, tobacco, oxen, and sheep.

ISLE OF BOURBON (Réunion).—Principal Imports: woven fabrics of linen, silk, woollen, cotton, wrought metals, leather, ware, rice, grain, wine, wheat and wheatflour, wood, horses, mules, guano. Total value, £1,397,180. Principal Exports: sugar and syrup, rice, coffee, cloves. Total value, £949,363.

SENEGAL (St. Louis). — Principal Imports : woven fabrics of linen, cotton, tobacco (in leaf), wrought metals. Total value, £319,582.

Principal Exports: Arachide nuts, gums, various hides, skins, and cotton manufactures, brandy. Total value, £273,769.

SENEGAL (Gorée).—Principal Imports : woven fabrics of linen, cotton, yarns, arachide nuts, tobacco (in leaf). Total value, £297,484.

Principal Exports: Arachide nuts, hides, cotton manufactures, wax. Total value £266,645.

Total aggregate value of Imports, African colonies (Algeria excepted) £2,014,246 Total aggregate value of Exports, African colonies (Algeria excepted) £1,489,777 Principal articles of Import and Export from and to the American Colonies, with their total official value, in 1866 :

MARTINIQUE.—Principal Imports : linens, woollens, silk, and cotton goods; wheat, fluor, olive oil, codfish, leather wares, wrought metals, coals, &c. Total value, £1,083,911. Principal Exports : raw sugar, rum, cocoa, coffee, codfish, and wines. Total value, £733,796.

GUADALOUPE.—Principal Imports: woollen, linen, silk, cotton goods, olive oil, wheat-flour, wines, wrought metals, leather wares, codfish, &c. Value, £746,625. Principal Exports :

the same as Martinique, with the addition of annatto. Total value, £563,167,

GUIANA (French).—Principal Imports : woven fabrics of woollen and cotton, wheat and wheatflour, cattle and sheep, leather wares, wrought metals, and coal. Total value £391,353. Principal Exports : raw sugar, annatto, cloves, &c. Total value, £5,395.

ST. PIERRE AND MIQUELON. — Principal Imports : salt, for fisheries, wheatflour, and cottons. Total value £145,311. Principal Exports : codfish (wet and dry), and cod liver oil. Value, £305,533.

		£
Total value (American Colonies) Imports		2,367,270
„ „ Exports		1,607,891

FRENCH POSSESSIONS IN INDIA.—Principal Imports, 1866 : cottons, silks, wines of all kinds, rice, perfumery, &c. Total value £233,882. Principal Exports : rice, indigo, cotton, cotton manufactures, sesamum and, cocoa-nut oil, &c. Total value £831,166.

	£
Grand official Total of *all* French Colonial Possessions, Imports	10,073,750
Grand official Total of *all* French Colonial Possessions, Exports	8,251,528

Total aggregate number of *all* vessels, with tonnage of French vessels only, entered and cleared at the ports of several French Colonies (Algeria excepted), in 1864 : Vessels entered, 3,564; tonnage of French vessels only, 365,293. Vessels cleared, 3,533; tonnage of French vessels only, 376,860.

GERMANY,

The name given to that large portion of Central Europe, situate in lat. 44° 46'—54° 50' N., and in long. 6°—19° E. in which the German language and German race prevail. Its estimated area is 244,635 square miles, with a population, which is estimated at 38,000,000, belonging to north and south, with about 9,000,000 more belonging to Austria, in all 47,000,000 inhabitants. The following table gives the area and population of the various states of North and South Germany according to the census of 1861, with *rectification of territorial changes* made in consequence of the war in 1866 :—

Names of States.	Area in Eng. sq. miles.	Populatn.
1. Prussia	137,066	22,769,436
2. Saxony	6,777	2,225,249
3. Mecklenburg-Schwerin	4,834	548,449
4. Oldenburg	2,417	295,242
5. Brunswick	1,526	282,400
6. Saxe Weimar	1,421	273,259
7. Mecklenburg Strelitz	997	99,060
8. Saxe Meiningen	933	289,341
9. Anhalt	869	181,824
10. Saxe Coburg Gotha	816	159,431
11. Saxe Altenburg	509	137,883
12. Waldeck	466	58,604
13. Lippe Detmold	445	108,513
14. Schwartzburg Rudolstadt	340	71,913
15. Schwartzburg Sonderhausen	318	64,895
16. Reuss Schleiz	297	83,360
17. Schaumburg Lippe	212	30,774
18. Hamburg	148	229,941
19. Lubeck	127	87,518
20. Bremen	106	98,575
Total of North Germany	160,624	27,978,651

South Germany :		
1. Bavaria	29,347	4,657,367
2. Wurtemburg	7,675	1,720,708
3. Baden	5,851	1,369,291
4. Hesse Darmstadt	2,866	810,302
5. Reuss Greiz	148	42,130
6. Lichtenstein	64	7,150
South Germany	45,951	8,606,948
Total of the whole of Germany N. & S.	206,575	36,585,599

An account of the separate states will be found in their alphabetical order.

GREECE,

A maritime country and kingdom in the south-east of Europe, situate in lat. 36° 25'—39° 30' N., and long. 19° 36'—26° E., comprising an area of 19,950 square miles, including the Ionian Islands, and a population of 1,343,293 inhabitants. It consists of four divisions—Hellas—the Morea—the Cyclades—and the Ionian Islands. The forests are considerable, and consist mostly of pine, with a mixture of hard wood, including the oak, in the upper regions, and in the lower the chestnut and walnut are frequently met with. Vegetation is singularly rich and varied, but agriculture generally in a very backward state. The most important of the fruit trees are the olive, largely cultivated, the vine, orange, lemon, fig, almond, date, citron, pomegranate, and currant grape. The chief products are cotton, silk, wool, rice, tobacco, corn. The manufactures are few and unimportant, chiefly domestic; cotton, silk, and woollen stuffs, and dyeing in bright colours has been perpetuated. Its imports are cotton, and other manufactures, Colonial produce, and rum. Its exports consist of raw produce, cotton, currants, figs, and other fruit; tobacco, olive oil, honey, wax, gum, silk, and sponge. The Greeks are expert mariners.

Estimated Revenue in 1867	£1,153,295
Estimated Expenditure	1,005,673
The total Public Debt in 1868 amounted to	13,800,000
Value of total Imports in 1864	2,210,705
Value of total Exports	1,121,023
Value of Imports from United Kingdom, 1866	851,873
Value of Exports to United Kingdom	879,598

Total number and tonnage of all vessels (steam and sailing), cleared at the ports in Greece in 1864, 59,914 number, 3,440,050 tons, of which 493, with a tonnage of 211,240 tons were British.

Reigning Sovereign, George I., second son of the present King of Denmark, born 24th Dec., 1845, elected King of the Hellenes 18th (30th) March, 1863; married 27th Oct. 1867, to Olga, eldest daughter of the Grand Duke Constantine of Russia.

Minist. of For. Affairs, P. Delyanni.

Envoy Extra. and Minister Plenipoten., Sir Pierre Braïlas Arméni, 5, Lower Gore, Kensington.

Consul-General, M. Michael Spartali, 25, Old Broad Street.

Secretary. M. Lagiarides.

Athens—Envoy Extraordinary and Minister Plenipotentiary. Hon. Edw. Morris Erskine, £3800.

Sec. of Legation, Hon. G. J. W. Agar-Ellis, £500.

Second Secretary, William B. Smijth, Esq., £250.

Patras—Consul, Henry S. Ongley, Esq., £800.

Piræus—Consul, M. Merlin, £450.

Missolonghi—Vice-Consul, Jas. Black, Esq., £300.

Syra—Consul, St. Vincent Lloyd, Esq., £500.

Corfu—Consul-General, S. S. Saunders, Esq., C.M.G., £1,200.

Zante—Consul, Col. Hon. B. Wodehouse, C.M.G., £585.

Cephalonia—Consul, Sir C. Sebright, K.C.M.G., £500.

HANOVER,

Formerly a kingdom in North Germany, situate between 51° 18'—53° 22' N. lat., and 6° 43'—11° 35' E. long., formerly belonging to the Kings of Great Britain as hereditary successors of the Elector of Hanover, but upon the accession of Queen Victoria lapsed to the male heir next in succession, Ernest Augustus, Duke of Cumberland, whose son George V. succeeded thereto in 1851; the Prussian war of 1866, however, terminated in the conquest of Hanover, which now forms part of the dominions of Prussia. Hanover is divided into three separate districts, eastern, western, and southern, and again subdivided into 7 administrative divisions called Landdrosteien. The principal rivers are the Elbe, the Weser, the Leine (on which the capital, Hanover, is situated), the Aller, the Ems, the Vechte. The soil is generally of inferior quality and agriculture is backward, rye being the principal cereal grown, notwithstanding some improvements have been made during the last few years, the great subdivision of land and lack of capital being the main causes thereof. Its mineral resources are both rich and varied. Its industrial pursuits, beside mining and agriculture, consist chiefly in the rearing of cattle, the manufacture of tobacco, paper, hemp, thread, and linen, leather, and sugar refineries; the imports comprise English manufactured goods, colonial products, wine, spirits, and silk; the exports consist chiefly of mineral products, coarse linen and canvas, honey and wax, horses, cattle, wheat and rye, rape and linseed, oilcakes, hops, hams and sausages. For statistics, railways, &c., see Prussia. Hanover is the capital of the kingdom.

HANSE TOWNS,

Formerly known as the Free Cities, or Hanseatic Republics of Lubeck, Bremen, and Hamburg, situate in the North of Germany. *Hamburg* is located on the Elbe, 70 miles from its mouth. *Bremen*, a populous city on the Weser, 40 miles above its mouth, and next in commercial importance to Hamburg. *Lubeck*, on the Trave, 36 miles N.E. of Hamburg, has also extensive commerce. It was formerly an original member of the famous Hanseatic League, formed in 1241 for the protection of commerce.

HAMBURG possesses an area of 148 square miles, and a total population, in 1867, of 306,507. The revenue and expenditure, in 1866, amounted alike to £692,379

	£
The public debt, in 1865, amounted to	4,222,897
Total value of Imports at Hamburg, in 1867, amounted to	60,690,079
Total value of Imports of home produce from United Kingdom, 1867	19,176,852
Total value of Exports to United Kingdom	10,576,620

Total number and tonnage of all vessels entered and cleared at Hamburg, 1867, 5,055, 1,874,707 tons—of which 2,278 vessels and 1,170,336 tons were from United Kingdom; also with coals only from United Kingdom, 623,365 tons. Cleared, 5,071, 1,923,235 tons, of which 2,475 vessels and 1,230,699 tons were for United Kingdom. The mercantile navy of Hamburg consisted of 487 vessels of 239,865 tons, effective on 31st December, 1866.

BREMEN possesses an area of 73½ square miles, with a population, in 1865, of 104,006.

	£
The Revenue, in 1866, amounted to ...	309,832
Expenditure	360,503

The total value of Imports at the port of Bremen amounted, in 1866, to (including £2,893,404 from United Kingdom) 14,870,552

The total value of Exports (including £726,481 to United Kingdom) 13,388,219

Number and tonnage of vessels entered and cleared at the port of Bremen in 1866, 2,780, 747,570 tons, entered, of which 185, with a tonnage of 69,294 tons were from United Kingdom. Cleared 3,209, 768,264 tons, of which 175, with a tonnage of 64,260 tons, were for the United Kingdom.

LUBECK possesses an area of 109½ square miles, and a population, in 1867, of 49,183.

	£
The Revenue, in 1866, amounted to ...	105,750
Expenditure	111,250

Total value of Imports into Lubeck in 1866 (including £700,942 specie) 5,040,074

Number and tonnage of all vessels entered and cleared at the port of Lubeck in 1866, 1,829, 290,162 tons, of which 144, with a tonnage of 32,392 tons, were from Great Britain entered, and 1,840 vessels, with 292,566 tons, cleared, of which two only, with a tonnage of 648 tons, were for Great Britain.

Consul-General, James F. Wulff, Esq., 147, Fenchurch Street.

Hamburg—Minister Resident and Consul-General, John Ward, Esq., C.B., £2,000.

Consul, George Annesley, Esq., £300.

Bremen—Vice-Consul, Melchior Schwoon, unpaid.

Lubeck—Vice-Consul, W. L. H. Behncke, unpaid.

HAYTI,

Otherwise known as St. Domingo, (of which the Republic is the Western portion), after Cuba, is the largest of the West India Islands. It lies in N. lat. between 17° 37'—20°, and in W. long. between 68° 20'—74° 28'; it belongs to the group of the Greater Antilles, and contains an area, including the islands of Tortuga, Gonaive, &c., of 28,000 square miles, and a population of about 800,000. The mountains are richly and heavily timbered, and susceptible of cultivation nearly to their summits; it is probably the most fertile spot in the West Indies, whilst its excellent harbours, especially the Bay of Gonaive, offer considerable facilities to foreign trade. The principal productions are mahogany, logwood, honey, coffee, cotton, cocoa, these being the chief exports, also tobacco, wax, ginger and sugar. It contains mines of gold, silver, copper, tin, iron, though they are now unworked. Its commercial prosperity has been almost annihilated by repeated revolutions, alternating in despotism and anarchy. The area of the Republic of Hayti is 11,718 square miles, and the population about 560,000. Port-au-Prince, situate on the West coast, formerly the capital of the island of St. Domingo, and now of the Haytian Republic, is a place of some commercial importance.

The total value of Imports into Hayti in 1863, was £1,656,107, of which £503,630 pertained to Great Britain. Total value of Exports, £2,458,000. Number and tonnage of all vessels entered and cleared at the ports of Hayti in 1863, 850, tonnage, 158,286 tons, entered, of which 371 with a tonnage of 66,994 tons were British; and 832 vessels, with a tonnage of 152,897 tons, cleared, of which 354 with a tonnage of 63,133 tons were British.

President, General Salnave, elected 15th May, 1867, Port-au-Prince.

Minister Plenipotentiary, General Salomon, 8, Oxford Terrace, Hyde Park.

Attaché, E. Laroche.

Chargé d'Affaires and Consul-General at Port-au-Prince, Spencer St. John, Esq., £1,200.

Vice-Consul, Henry Byron, Esq., £500.

SAN DOMINGO, or the Spanish portion of the island, is the oldest settlement of European origin in America, having been founded in 1494, by Bartolomeo Columbus. San Domingo, the capital, is the oldest existing city in the Western or New World. Its trade is very limited, the harbour being unfit for large ships.

Vice-Consul, D. Leon, Esq., £200, San Domingo.

HESSE CASSEL, or ELECTORAL HESSE,

One of the central states in the west of Germany, situate in 50° 3'—to 51° 40' N. lat., and 8° 36'—10° 12' E. long., containing an area of 3,633 square miles, and a population in 1864 of 745,063, chiefly Protestants. The soil is very fertile and well adapted to agriculture. Cereals of all kinds yield good returns. There is abundance of fruit, and good wines are produced. Its minerals comprise copper, lead, cobalt, alum, large quantities of iron, coal, and salt, the last three of which are the property of the State. The mountain districts have many good mineral springs. Its manufactures are considerable, chiefly flannels, cotton and silk velvets, carpets, chemicals, wooden wares, guns, porcelain and jewellery. The exports consist chiefly of yarns, linen, iron and steel wares, wood, leather, grain, and mineral waters. There are nearly 1,000 miles of good public roads, beside 200 miles and upwards of railways, and its navigable rivers are numerous, affording great facilities for its internal and transit trade, both of which are considerable. The Electorate of Hesse now belongs to Prussia, which sees for statistics. Its annual revenue for the financial period 1864–6, amounted to £766,246; expenditure, 1864–6, £817,947; Public debt, £1,845,892.

HESSE DARMSTADT, or DUCAL HESSE,

A central state in the west of Germany and a Grand Duchy, situate between 49° 24'—51° 7' N. lat., and 7° 50'—9° 40' E. long., containing an area of 2,866 square miles, and a population in 1867 of 823,644, consisting of Lutherans, Roman Catholics, "United Evangelicals," or Unitarians, Reformed Calvinists, Jews, &c. It is traversed by the Rhine, the Maine, the Lahe, the Lahn, the Neckar, &c. The country is very fertile, and agriculture in a very flourishing condition, all cereals yielding abundantly, corn sufficiently so for exportation. Fruit also is abundant, and the vine highly cultivated, the southern districts being noted for the excellence of their wines, Niersteiner, Laubenheim, Liebfraumilch, Scharlachberger, &c. Its principal branches of industry besides agriculture, are wine-making, cotton, linen, and hempen manufactures, papier mâché goods, &c. Hesse Darmstadt has about 150 miles of railway traversing the duchy. Darmstadt is the capital.

Its annual Revenue for the financial period, 1866-8, amounted to .... £ 791,417
Expenditure for the same 781,080
Amount of Public Debt in 1865............. 228,916
Reigning Sovereign, Louis III., Grand Duke of Hesse Darmstadt, born June 9, 1806, married 26 Dec., 1833, Mathilde, daughter of Louis I., ex-King of Bavaria. She died 25 May, 1862.
Minister of Foreign Affairs, Baron Von Dalwigk.
Con. Gen., G. Worms, Esq., F.S.A., 1, Austin Friars.
Darmstadt, Secretary of Legation, Robert B. D. Morier, Esq., C. B., £650.
Consul, Theodor Kuchen, *unpaid*.

HOLSTEIN (SCHLESWIG-HOLSTEIN) AND LAUENBURG.

Holstein, a duchy of Northern Germany, incorporated with that of Schleswig in 1851, formerly belonging to Denmark, was a member of the Germanic Confederation, situated between 54° 26′ —53° 29′ N. lat., and 9°—11° E. long., possessing an area of 3,255 Eng. square miles, with a population of nearly 550,000. The principal rivers are the Elbe and the Eider, and the principal town, Altona. The products of the Duchy are for the most part wheat, barley, oats, potatoes, hemp, and flax. Its principal wealth consists in pastures, agriculture and rearing of cattle being the chief employment of the people. Its mineral products are lime and salt. Of Schleswig, comprising an area of 3,704 English square miles and a population of about 410,000, the principal products are barley, oats, and rye, with comparatively little wheat, hemp, or flax. Both S. and H. abound in turf, and the pasturage on which horses and horned cattle are bred is very good. The manufacture of woollen and linen goods, the rearing of cattle and ship-building are the principal branches of industry of Schleswig. Lauenburg, a duchy formerly belonging to the Crown of Denmark and a member of the Germanic Confederation, possesses an area of 455 square miles, and a population of about 50,000. For statistics, &c., see Prussia.

HONDURAS,

The middle State of Central America, stretching in N. lat. between 13° 10′ and 16°, and W. long. between 83° and 89° 45′, containing 42,000 English square miles, including a small portion of the Mosquito territory, and a population of about 360,000, mostly of aboriginal blood. The country is mountainous, being traversed by the Cordilleras. The soil produces valuable timber, mahogany, fruit-trees, cotton, sugar, tobacco, coffee, indigo, wheat, and other cereals. Its mineral wealth is great, consisting of gold, silver, copper, iron, tin, platinum, zinc, antimony, opal, amythests, coal, &c. The foreign trade is chiefly carried on with Great Britain, United States, and Spain. Comayagua is the capital.

President-Gen., Jose Maria Medina.
Minister Plenipotentiary at London, Don Carlos Gutierrez, Carlton Road, Tufnell Park.
Consul-General, Geo. B. Kerferd, Esq., 7, Tower Chambers, Liverpool.
Vice-Consul, George Wm. Wheatley, Esq., 156, Leadenhall Street.
Consular Agent at Omoa, John F. Debrot, Esq.
Consular Agent at Truxillo, Wm. Melhado, Esq.

ITALY,

A peninsula in the South of Europe, consisting of a considerable stretch of mainland, beside several islands, situate between lat. 36° 35′ —47° N., and long. 6° 35′—18° 35′ E. It is divided into 68 provinces, including Piedmont and the Lombardo-Venetian States, lately ceded (1866) to Italy, as also the Island of Sardinia, and comprises an area of 98,154 square miles, with a population of 24,223,458. Its coast line is estimated at about 2,000 miles, having the several bays and gulfs of Gaeta, Naples, Genoa, Salerno, &c. It possesses the volcanic mountains of Vesuvius, Etna, and Stromboli. The chief rivers are the Po, with its numerous tributaries, the Tiber, the Adige, and the Arno. Its mineral and thermal springs are innumerable, possessing many sanative and curative properties. Agriculture is said to be in a very backward condition; nevertheless, the annual yield of cereal crops is considerable, sufficing not only for home consumption, but also for exportation. Its wines are numerous; but, with the exception of "Lachryma Christi," Vino Dásti, and Marsala, are very inferior and unfit for export. The finest olives and olive oil are furnished by Florence, Lucca, and Naples. The railway system is making rapid progress throughout the peninsula; the most important line is that of Mont Cenis, connecting this country with France, already partially in operation. The mails between Great Britain and India will shortly be transferred to this line. In Lombardy the cultivation of the mulberry tree and rearing of the silkworm form the principal occupation of the people, upwards of 17,000,000 trees being required to supply food for the worms. The annual revenue produced by the silk exported from the Lombardo-Venetian provinces is estimated at about £500,000. Cotton, also, is grown extensively, and subsequently manufactured in the native looms. Fruits abound, and are of exquisite flavour, such as grapes, oranges, lemons, almonds, figs, dates, melons, pistachio nuts, all of which are largely exported. The supply of sea and fresh-water fish is considerable, sardines and anchovies being largely exported. Towards the north, quarries of very beautiful marble (Carrara) exist. The Imports chiefly consist of sugar, coffee, and other colonial produce, muslins, calicoes, linens, woollens, hardware, and dye-stuffs. The chief Exports, raw silk, rice, fish, fruit, sulphur, marble, velvet, mosaics, &c. The manufactures are woollen, linen, and cotton goods, lace, straw hats, leather, pottery, and glass. Chemicals are largely manufactured, as also paper, the number of paper mills being 536, and the quantity of paper made 210,213 quintals, or 412,918 cwt., and the consumption of rags 367,034 quintals, or 710,959 cwt. In 1864 the army consisted of 196,100 men, and the navy of 106 vessels of war, with 1,468 guns.

The Revenue in 1866 amounted to ...£31,762,766
The Expenditure to 36,444,652
The Total Amount of Public Debt in 1865 was................................. 211,503,298
The Interest thereon...................... 10,340,915
Total Value of Imports for 1865 (of which £38,666,947 was entered for home consumption) 40,954,562
Total Exports (of which £22,331,423 was that of domestic produce) 24,525,471
Value of Imports of home produce from the United Kingdom to Italy in 1866 5,821,530

Value of Exports to the United
   Kingdom £3,820,744
  Number and tonnage of all vessels entered
and cleared at ports in Italy, inclusive of coasting trade, 1865, 19,701 vessels, 3,256,110 tons entered, 19,581 vessels, 3,272,354 tons cleared; 2,827
British vessels, with a tonnage of 675,615 tons,
entered, and 2,076 British vessels, with a tonnage of 402,411 tons, cleared. Florence is now
the capital of Italy and the seat of government.
The religion of the country is essentially Roman
Catholic. There are thirteen universities in
Italy, including those in the Roman States.

Reigning Sovereign, Victor Emmanuel II., King of
  Italy, born 14th March, 1820, married April
  12th, 1842, the Archduchess Adelaide of Austria.
Heir Apparent, Prince Humbert, born 14th
  March, 1844.
Minister of Foreign Affairs, Gen. Menabrea.
Envoy Extra. and Minister Plenipoten.,

Charge d'Affaires, Count Maffei, 28, Davies Street.
Attachés, Chev. Cotta, Chev. G. Vigoni, and M.
  Paterno.
Consul-General, Baron Heath, F.R.S., F.S.A., &c.
Vice-Consul, Robt. A. Heath, Esq., Consulate
  Office, 31, Old Jewry, E.C.
Florence.—Envoy Extra. and Minister Plenipoten.,
  Sir A. B. Paget, K.C.B., £5,600.
Secretary of Legation, Edw. Herries, Esq., £950.
Second Secretary, Hon. F. R. Plunkett, £350.
      ,,   A. H. Mounsey, Esq., £250.
Brindisi, Consul, Henry Grant, Esq., £400.
Cagliari (Sardinia), Consul, Edward H. Walker,
  Esq., £350.
Genoa, Cons, Montagu Yeates Brown, Esq., £850.
Leghorn, Consul, Alex. McBean, Esq., £350.
Ancona, Vice-Consul, Gustavus Gaggiotti, £215.
Naples, Consul-General, Edw. Walter Bonham,
  Esq., C.B., £1,200.
Gallipoli, Vice-Consul, Hen. Stevens, Esq., £100.
Palermo (Sicily), Cons., Jn. Goodwin, Esq., £450.
Messina, Vice-Consul, Jos. Richards, Esq., £150.
Turin (Piedmont), Con., D. E. Colnaghi, Esq., £650.
Venice, Consul-Gen., Wm. Perry, Esq., £500.
Vice-Consul, Edw. Valentine, Esq., £800.
Spezzia, Vice-Consul, Edw. Valentine, Esq., £250.

JAPAN,

An extensive empire consisting of several large
islands, the principal of which are Niphon,
Japan Proper, or the Japanese Mainland—
Sikok—Kiu-sui, and Yesso, the latter being an
adjunct—situated at the eastern extremity of
Asia, in the N. Pacific Ocean, between 31°—
45° 30′ N. lat. and 129°–150 E. long.; and subdivided into provinces, departments, and districts. It comprises an area estimated at
166,500 square miles, and a population of
35,000,000, governed by upwards of 200 princes
called Daimios, each of whom is absolute lord
in his own territories, the majority possess an
army sufficient to protect their country when
threatened. This combined Federal army amounts
to 370,000 infantry, and 40,000 cavalry, to which
must be added the Imperial army kept up by
the Tycoon or Sovereign, which amounts to
80,000 infantry, cavalry, &c. The country in
general is fertile, indented with magnificent
harbours, the soil productive, rich in mineral
wealth, and teeming with every variety of agricultural produce. It is rich in mineral products;
the gold mines of Matsumai have long been
celebrated. Silver, copper (the chief mineral),

iron, sulphur abound; also agates, cornelians,
jaspers, &c. It possesses an abundant supply
of coal. Among the most remarkable of its
vegetable productions is the varnish-tree, with
the juice of which the natives lacquer or "japan"
their furniture, &c. The camphor tree, the
paper mulberry, the vegetable wax-tree, the
chestnut, oak, pine, beech, elm, maple, cypress,
&c., are also noteworthy; the evergreen oak and
the maple being the finest of all Japanese trees.
Bamboos, palms, bananas, &c., also flourish.
The tobacco plant, tea-shrub, potato-rice,
wheat, and other cereals are all cultivated,
agriculture, upon which the Japanese bestow
great care and thoroughly understand, being
their chief occupation; in fact, nothing can exceed their agricultural industry. The floral
kingdom is rich, beautiful, and varied. Its
fruits, which are abundant, consist chiefly of the
winter pear of very large size, oranges, lemons,
peaches, apricots, plums, figs, and nuts of all
kinds. The chief manufactures, &c., are those
of silk and cotton—lacquering or "japanning"—
porcelain, in which they are said to excel the
Chinese, lithochrome printing, drawing, engraving, &c. The chief imports consist of sugar,
coffee, spices, lead, tin, and iron ware; and
from Europe, of printed cottons, cambrics,
shirtings, ginghams, flannels, and window-glass.
The chief exports are copper, camphor, tea, silk,
lacquered ware, painted paper, &c. The internal
trade of Japan is very extensive, and rigid regulations are in force to protect and encourage
home industry. Foreign commerce is far from
being encouraged, notwithstanding the various
treaties with several European states, under or by
which the ports of Nagasaki, Kanagawa, and
Hakodadi were thrown open. The value of imports
from Great Britain in 1866 amounted to
£1,447,070, and of exports to Great Britain,
£273,745. Jeddo or Yeddo is the capital. The
government of Japan appears to be that of a
federal oligarchy, the nominal head of the State
being the "Mikado" or spiritual sovereign,
whose authority, extending over all matters
connected with religion and education, is subordinate to the temporal sovereign or "Tycoon,"
while neither appear to have any general authority over the whole state, this being actually
divided with the feudal princes or Daimios.

Present Tycoon of Japan, Shotsulashi Chiunagon,
  born 1835, succeeded to the throne in August,
  1867, Yeddo.
Heir Presumptive, his brother, Prince Mimbou-
  tayon, born 1851, educated in France. The
  Mikado residing at Miako.
Minist. of For. Affairs, Kousje-Yamato-no-Kami.
*Yeddo, Envoy Extraordinary Min. Plen. and Consul
  General*, Sir Harry S. Parkes, K.C.B., £4,000.
Sec. of Legation, Francis O. Adams, Esq., £800.

LIBERIA,

An independent negro republic of West Africa,
on the Grain coast of Upper Guinea, situate
between 4° 50′—7° N. lat. and 6° 50′—12° 30′ W.
long., comprising an area of 60,000 miles, with
upwards of 500 miles of coast line, and possesses
a population of about 600,000, one-fourth of whom
are free blacks, and about 5,000 have acquired
the English language. It was established as a
republic in 1847. The Liberians have built and
manned coast traders, and have a number of
vessels engaged in commerce with Great Britain
Germany and the United States—the principal
exports are coffee, sugar, palm oil, camphor,

indigo, ivory, gold dust, &c. products of the soil.
—the exports and imports are not distinguished
per se, but incorporated with those of Guinea.
in the English Blue-book. Constitution and
government similar to that of the United States;
the language is English.
President, J. S. Payne.
Vice-President, James W. Priest.
*Consul-General,*G. Ralston,Esq.15,LanghamPl.W.
*Vice-Consul,*E.Fox,Esq. 5, Newman'sCt. Cornhill.

MADAGASCAR,

An island of the Indian Ocean situated to the
north-east of the African continent in lat. 11° 57′
—25° 38′ S., and long. 43°—51° E., extending over
an area larger than the British Isles, and containing a population of upwards of 5,000,000. It
is 1,030 miles in length, and 360 at its greatest
breadth, containing an area estimated at 225,000
square miles. The early history of this island
is involved in mystery. The French, in the 17th
century, made an attempt to settle in the country,
but found its climate unhealthy. In the year 1816
diplomatic and commercial relations were entered
into between Great Britain and Radama, King
of the Hovas, whose influence and authority extended over a great part of Madagascar. The
soil is in general fertile, with rich pasturage and
magnificent forests abounding in valuable trees
and medicinal plants; the other products being
rice, sugar, silk, cotton, indigo, cocoa nuts,
bananas, potatoes, indigo, pepper, &c. The
mineral products are gold, silver, copper, lead,
iron (which is abundant), and coal. The principal manufactures are jewellery, chains, neck-
laces, carpets, cotton, &c. An active import and
export trade is carried on in native produce—
linen, ribbons, glass, &c. Tananarivo, "The
City of a Thousand Towns," is the capital and
seat of Government.
Reigning Sovereign, Ranavolo II., received as
Queen, 1st April, 1868.
British Consul at Tananarivo, T. Conolly Pakenham, Esq. £950.
Tamatare, Vice-Consul at, J. E. Creceaux, unpaid.

MECKLENBURG-SCHWERIN.

A grand duchy or state of Northern Germany,
situate in 53° 40′ N. lat., and 12° E. long., comprising an area of about 5,100 English square
miles, with a population of 553,884. The country,
though generally flat, is extensively covered with
wood; the soil is of good quality, and adapted to
the growth of corn and rearing of cattle, which
constitute the principal native industry; there is
considerable commerce through the two ports of
Rostock and Wismar. There were in 1862, 413
vessels, with a tonnage of 97,966 tons, belonging
to these ports. The exports of M. Schwerin consist
chiefly of agricultural produce, the annual value
of which averages £1,146,000. The value of imports of home produce from the United Kingdom
into M. Schwerin amounted in 1865 to £51,252,and
the exports from M. Schwerin to the United Kingdom £324,564. The annual receipts of the duchy
(according to the Almanach de Gotha, 1865)
amounted to £65,217, and the expenditure
was equivalent. The total amount of debt
£1,326,591, but no official budget is ever published. Schwerin is the capital of the duchy.
Reigning Sovereign, Frederick Francis II., Grand
Duke of Mecklenburg-Schwerin, b. Feb. 28,
1823, m. 3 Nov. 1849 to Princess Augusta of
Reuss Schleiz, who died March 3, 1862; 2ndly,
May 12, 1864, to Princess Anna, daughter of
Louis II., late Grand Duke of Hesse Darm-

stadt, who died April 15, 1865; 3rdly, July 4,
1868, to Princess Marie of Schwartzburg
Rudoldstadt.
Heir Apparent, Prince Fred. Fran., b. Mar.19, 1851.
Chief Min. of State, Jaspar J. B. W. Von Oertzen.
Consul General, Siegerich Christopher Kreeft,
Esq., 124, Fenchurch Street, E.C.
Min.Plen.,&c., LordAug. W. F. S. Loftus, G.C.B.,
Berlin.
Consul-General, John Ward, Esq., C.B., *Hamburg.*
Vice-Consul, Rostock, Chas. Schultze, Esq., *unpd.*

MECKLENBURG-STRELITZ,

A grand duchy and state of Northern Germany,
situated in lat. 53° 25′ N., and long. 13° 25′ E.,
comprising an area of nearly 1,000 square miles,
and a population of about 100,000 according to
the last census, since which time emigration has
draughted off upwards of 8,000. The duchy is
divided into two portions, Stargard, or duchy of
Strelitz, and the principality of Ratzeburg. The
country is flat and generally similar in character
to M. Schwerin. The principal products are
corn, exported chiefly to Great Britain, cattle
and sheep, hides, wool, tobacco, butter, cheese,
and fruits. Very nearly one-half of the country
belongs to the Grand Duke. No official budget
is ever published, the whole of the public revenue
being appropriated to the civil list of the Grand
Duke. New Strelitz is the capital of the Duchy.
Reigning Sovereign, Frederick William I., Grand
Duke of Mecklenburg-Strelitz, b. Oct. 17,
1819, m. June 28, 1843, Augusta, daughter of
H.R.H. Adolphus Frederick, late Duke of
Cambridge.
Heir Apparent, Prince Adolphus Frederick, born
July 22, 1848.
Minister of State, Baron de Hammerstein.
Min Plen., &c., Lord Aug. W. F. S. Loftus, G.C.B.
Consul General, John Ward, Esq., C.B.

MEXICO, REPUBLIC OF,

A vast extent of country constituting the south-
west extremity of North America, founded by
Spain, situated between 16°—32° N. lat. and 95°
—115 W. long., comprising one of the richest
and most varied zones in the world. It is divided
into 22 states, 6 territories, and 1 federal district,
that of Mexico, making in all 29 political
divisions—comprehending an area of 846,615
square miles, and a population of about 8,218,000
—consisting, to the extent of more than one-half,
of Indians, who speak the Aztec or old Mexican
language, Mestigos or Mixed races numbering
1,500,000, and 40,000 Europeans, among which the
Spaniards predominate. The Spanish Creoles,
or "whites," born in America of European
extraction, form the aristocracy of the country.
It possesses several excellent harbours, Vera Cruz
and Tampico being the principal ports. The
soil, which is generally fertile, produces bananas,
pine apples, oranges, peaches, apricots, manioc,
grapes, olives, and all the fruits, cereals, and
vegetables of Central and Southern Europe.
The medicinal plants are also very numerous,
sarsaparilla, jalap (from Jalapa), ipecacuanha,
copaiba, dragon's blood, vanilla, the agave or
Mexican aloe, and various spices; the mahogany, rosewood, ebony, and India-rubber trees
also abound. The products of its mines, which
rank among the richest in the world, comprise
not only the precious metals—silver being long
the great staple of Mexican exports, the annual
average produce of which is valued at £3,000,000
—but iron, copper, lead, tin, quicksilver, alum,
and many kinds of precious stones. Its

manufactures are unimportant, consisting of all kinds of cabinet works, pianofortes, the working of gold and silver plate; with tissues of cotton, wool and silk, &c. The chief imports are bale goods, including woollens, cottons, linen, and silks. The chief exports are gold and silver in coin, bullion, and plate, the drugs before enumerated, sugar, flour, and indigo.

	£
The estimated Revenue for 1866 amounted to	3,300,000
Estimated Expenditure to	5,900,000
Value of Imports of home produce from the United Kingdom in 1865 amounted to	1,898,056
Value of exports to the United Kingdom	3,216,924

There is a line of railway from Vera Cruz to the city of Mexico, 300 miles in extent, now forming, called the "National Mexican."

From the conquest of the country in 1521 to 1821, the date of the declaration of independence from Spain, Mexico formed one of the four great vice-royalties of Spanish America, since which time, with one late melancholy exception, it has been governed by a president, elected for four years, and a congress consisting of a house of representatives and senate. Mexico is the chief city and seat of government.

President of the Republic, Benito Juarez.

Consul General in London, Don Carlos Pedro Schaeffer, 4 Adams Court. E.C.

Mission and Consulate withdrawn 21st Dec. 1867.

MOROCCO, EMPIRE OF,

One of the Barbary States, situate in the N.W. of Africa, between 28° and 36° N. lat. and 2° 15′ — 11° 40′ W. long. The empire is divided into four territories: Fez, Morocco, Suse, and Tafilet, which are again subdivided into 33 districts, each under the superintendence of a "Caid," but the semi-independent tribes are ruled by their own chiefs, and scarcely acknowledge the authority of the Sultan. M. contains in the aggregate 250,000 square miles, with a population of about 8,500,000 inhabitants, the majority of whom are Moors. The Jews, however, are very numerous, especially in the cities. Among the chief products of the country are wheat, barley, rice, maize, and sugar; among fruits the figs, almonds, pomegranate, lemon, orange, and date are common, while cotton, tobacco, hemp, &c., are largely produced both for home use and for export. Morocco is said to be rich in mineral treasures: antimony, iron, copper, lead, tin, the three last in considerable quantities. Gold and silver also are found. Wool is very plentiful. Goats afford another very valuable commodity, their skins supplying that leather which, under the name of "Morocco," is so distinguished for its pliancy, softness, and beauty. In the production of this last and the brilliancy of its colours they excel. Tangier and Mogador are the chief ports. The principal exports are wool, carpets, saddlery, hides, leather, grain, cattle, and sheep; and the imports, cotton, linen, and muslin goods, tea, coffee, sugar, hardware, &c. Morocco is the capital.

Sultan, Sidi Mohammed, succeeded 1859.

Tangier, Consul-General and Minister Resident at, Sir John Hay Drummond Hay, K.C.B., £2,000.

Consul, Horace Phillips White, Esq., £450.

MUSCAT,

The most powerful of the Arab States, situate in 23° 40′ N. lat. and 58° 45′ E. long. The whole territory, consisting of Muscat Proper and the islands Ormuz and Kishm, on the Persian Gulf, and several islands—Zanzibar and others—on the east coast of Africa, extends to about 176,000 square miles, with a population of 2,500,000. The standing army consists of 30,000 men, and the navy of 87 vessels, with 730 guns, the merchant vessels at least, 2,000, comprising 37,000 tons. The value of its annual imports is estimated at £1,000,000, and its revenue at £900,000. Its exports consist of dates, raisins, wheat, drugs, coffee, pearls (from the Persian Gulf), ivory, tortoise-shell, skins, hides, wax, &c. The capital is Muscat, which has a very good harbour, and is a most important centre of trade, where the productions of Europe, Africa, and the East are exchanged.

Imaum, or Sovereign.

Muscat, Consul and Political Agent at, Lieut.-Col. H. F. Disbrowe.

Zanzibar, Consul and Political Agent at, St. Adrian Churchill, C.B.

ZANZIBAR, OR ZANQUEBAR, is situate on the east coast of Africa, between 2° N. lat., and 39° 30′ E. long., extending upwards of 1,000 miles, having no ascertained limit. The Island of Zanzibar, by far the richest and most important of the Sultan's (Imaun of Muscat) dominions, is distant from the coast about 30 or 40 miles, and is about 45 miles in length, varying from 15 to 30 in breadth, comprising an area of about 400,000 acres, with a soil of more than ordinary fertility, covered with woods and plantations of perpetual verdure. The principal products are cloves, rice, sugar, cane, manioc, millet, cocoa-nuts, and fruits, especially oranges, of the finest quality. The population of the island is estimated at 250,000. The chief people are Arab landed proprietors possessing large plantations, and numerous slaves; beside these, are the free blacks, and slaves from Madagascar, &c., and about 6,000 natives of India, through whose hands nearly all the foreign trade passes. Zanzibar, the chief town, is extensive, with a population of 50,000. The trade is very considerable. In 1863 the Imports (upon which a duty of 5 per cent. only is levied), consisting of cotton goods, beads, arms, brass wire, &c., amounted to £544,903; and the Exports, consisting of gum, copal, cloves, ivory, cocoa-nut, oil, seeds, &c., amounted to £467,053.

Vice-Consul, John Kirk, M.D.

NAVIGATORS' AND FRIENDLY, OR TONGA, ISLANDS.

The former consist of a group of nine islands, chiefly of volcanic origin, in the South Pacific Ocean, to the north of the latter, in lat. 13° 30′—14° 30′ S., and long. 168°—173° W. The area of the group is estimated at 2,650 square miles, with a population of 56,000. Its forests include the bread-fruit, cocoa-nut, banana, palm, orange and lemon trees, pine-apples, yams; coffee, nutmeg, wild sugar-cane and other important plants grow luxuriantly. Trade is chiefly carried on with Sydney. The government is vested in the hereditary chiefs.

THE FRIENDLY OR TONGA ISLES, a group of, at least, 150 islands or islets, situated in the South Pacific, only 30 of which are inhabited, the greater part being mere rocks or shoals, stretching in S. lat. from 18° to 23°, and in W. long. from 172° to 176°. Discovered by Tasman in 1643, but received their name (Friendly) from Captain Cook. The vegetable products and flora are the same as those of Navigators' Islands and the Fiji group generally. The principal, or Tonga, islands, contain a population of about 25,000. Cocoa-nut oil is the only important export.

Consul at Samoa (Navigators' Islands), John Chauner Williams, Esq., £450.

KINGDOM OF THE NETHERLANDS, (USUALLY CALLED HOLLAND).

A kingdom of W. C. Europe, situate in lat. 50° 46'—53° 34' N., and long. 3° 24'—7° 12' E., consisting of 11 provinces, including part of the Duchy of Limburg (and Grand Duchy of Luxemburg), and containing a total area of 12,685 square miles, with a population, including Luxemburg, of 3,795,932, the majority belong to the Dutch Reformed Church; the remainder are Roman Catholics, Lutherans, Jews, &c. The land is generally flat and low, intersected by numerous canals and connecting rivers; in fact, a network of water-courses. The principal rivers are the Rhine, the Maese, and the Scheldt. Railways, to the extent of 659 miles, have been constructed. The chief products of the country are potatoes, rye, barley, oats, wheat, buckwheat, chicory, madder, clover, flax, hemp, tobacco. Horticulture is generally pursued, its tulips and other bulbous plants being celebrated everywhere. The principal manufactures are ships, bricks, linen, rich damasks, cotton, woollen, and silk fabrics. Schiedam and Rotterdam are celebrated for "Geneva" distilleries; Amsterdam for its diamond-cutting trade, about 10,000 hands being employed thereat, and dependent thereon. Its chief exports consist of refined sugar, flax, cheese, butter, cattle, sheep, madder, geneva, &c. The Royal navy consisted, on July 1, 1867, of 56 men-of-war steamers, with 606 guns, and 68 sailing men-of-war, with 647 guns, and an army of 1,744 officers and 55,760 men. There are several dependencies belonging to the Netherlands in the East and West Indies and on the west coast of Africa, the principal of which are Java and Madura, comprising together an area of 683,776 square miles, and a population of 20,094,957.

	£
The Netherlands revenue, in 1866, amounted to	8,953,648
The expenditure to	9,080,042
Public Debt in 1868	81,003,032
The Budget of 1867 amounted to	8,264,666
Total value of Imports in 1865, including transit	46,007,066
Total value of Imports, including transit	37,434,801
Total value of Exports, including transit	36,582,594

of which £28,340,609 was that of Dutch produce.

Total number and tonnage of all vessels entered and cleared at all Netherlands' ports in 1867 :— 8,609 vessels, tonnage 2,039,310 tons entered, of which 1,012,942 tons were British, and 8,788 vessels with tonnage 2,121,992 tons cleared, of which 1,055,351 tons were British. The Dutch Navy, on the 31 December, 1867, consisted of 2,159 ships, with 540,164 tons. Amsterdam is the capital; the Hague being the residence of the Court.

Reigning Sovereign, William III., King of the Netherlands, &c., born 19th February, 1817, married 18th June, 1839, SophiaMatilda, second daugh. of William I., late K. of Würtemberg.

Heir Apparent, William, Prince of Orange, born 4th September, 1840.

Minister for Foreign Affairs, T. M. van Roest van Limburg.

Minister in England,

Counsellor and 1st Secretary, Mons. Denis Everwijn, 15, Sloane Street.

Priv. Sec. and Consul-General, J. W. May, Esq., 20½. Great St. Helen's.

The Hague, Envoy Extraordinary and Minister Plenipotentiary at, Vice-Admiral Hon. E. A. J. Harris, C.B., £4,000.

Secretary of Legation, J. H. Burnley, Esq., £500.

2nd Secretary, Hon. T. J. H. Thurlow, £250.

Amsterdam, Consul, J. G. C. L. Newnham, Esq., £750.

Rotterdam. Consul, Sir R. F. Turing, Bart., £400.

Batavia (Java), Consul, James McLachlan, Esq., £200.

Curaçao, David a Jesurun, unpaid.

Surinam, Consul, Duncan C. Monro, Esq., £150.

NICARAGUA,

A republic of Central America, situate between 10° 45'—15° N. lat. and 83° 20'—87° 30' W. long., containing an area of about 57,000 English square miles, including a large portion, geographically, of the Mosquito territory. Estimated population, 400,000, of whom about 40,000 are whites, 10,000 negroes, the rest Indians and other races. The country is in many districts densely wooded, the most valuable trees being mahogany, Brazil-wood, Nicaragua-wood, cedar, and logwood. The pastures are splendid, and support vast quantities of cattle. The chief products are the sugar-cane, cacao, cotton, indigo, tobacco, with nearly all the fruits and edibles of the tropics—plantains, bananas, bread-fruit, arrowroot, citrons, oranges, limes, lemons, pine apples, guavas, &c., the chief exports being medicinal herbs, as ipecacuanha, aloes, sarsaparilla, ginger, gum acacia, &c. The northern part is rich in minerals, producing gold, silver, copper, iron, and lead; but they are not now, as formerly under the Spaniards, efficiently worked, the incessant political distractions materially injuring the prosperity of the country, which has been the arena of frequent revolutions, subsequent even to the great revolution of 1821. No return is made of its imports and exports. Managua is said to be the seat of government, but St. Leon is the largest town.

President, Fernando Guzman, St. Leon.

Consul-General at London, James L. Hart, Esq., 3, St. Helen's Place.

Consul at Nicaragua, James Green, Esq., £750, Grey Town.

Vice-Consul, George Paton, Esq., unpaid.

OLDENBURG,

One of the minor states of North Germany, and a Grand Duchy, situate in 53° 8' N. lat. and 8° 18' E. long., comprising an area of 2,394 English square miles, and a population in 1867 of 314,416, more than two-thirds of whom are Lutherans, one-fourth Catholics, 1,600 Jews, the remainder Evangelicals and other sects. It is divided into three distinct and widely separated territories: Oldenburg Proper, Lübeck (a principality distinct from the Hanse Town of the same name), and Birkinfeld. Of Oldenburg Proper, agriculture and the rearing of cattle constitute the chief sources of wealth. It has no manufactures, with the exception of some linen and stocking looms and a few tobacco works; but there are numerous distilleries, breweries, and tan yards throughout the duchy. The exports are horses, cattle, hides, linen, thread, and rags, chiefly to Holland and the Hanseatic cities. The total revenue in 1866 amounted to £332.965, and the expenditure to £323.565. The amount of public debt in 1865 was £621,585. Though favourably situated for maritime commerce, its trade is chiefly confined to that of a coasting trade, carried on in small vessels of from 20 to 40 tons. The total number and tonnage of *all* vessels entered and cleared at ports in Oldenburg in 1865 was as follows: 2,132 vessels and 206,508 tons entered, of which 488 vessels and 99,410 tons belonged to Great Britain. 1,996 vessels and 207.360 tons cleared, of which 519 vessels and 112,286 tons belonged to Great Britain. The principality of Birkinfeld, lying on the south-west of the Rhine, contains an area of 192 square miles, and a population of about 34,500. Its soil is not very productive, save in the more sheltered valleys, where it yields wheat, flax, hemp, and oil seeds. It is well wooded, and its mineral products are of some importance, as iron, copper, lead, coal, and building stone. Oldenburg is the capital of the duchy.

Reigning Prince, Peter L., Grand Duke, born 8th July, 1827, married 10th of February, 1852, Elizabeth, daughter of Prince Joseph, of Saxe Altenburg.

Heir Apparent, Prince Frederic Augustus, born 16th November, 1852.

Chief Minister, Baron Peter F. L. van Rössing.

Consul-General, Chevalier Ewing Pye de Colquhoun, G.C.O.N.

Oldenburg, Consul-General, John Ward, Esq., B.C., resident at Hamburg.

ORANGE RIVER (FREE STATE),

A Republic of Dutch Boers, who, after retiring from Natal, when declared a British Colony, established themselves in the country lying between the two great branches of the Orange River. It forms a connecting link between the Cape Colony, the Transvaal Republic, and Natal, and comprises an area of 50,000 square miles, with a population of about 30,000, two-thirds of whom are white, and the remainder coloured. The Free State is divided into five districts; Bloem-Fontein, with its capital of the same name, being the chief.

President,

Bishop, in connection with the Church of England, Right Rev. Edward Twells, D.D.

Consul-General in England, M. P. G. Van der Byl.

THE PAPAL STATES; or, STATES OF THE CHURCH,

A comparatively small territory in Central Italy. Previous to 1859 it consisted of twenty districts, comprising an area of 17,218 English square miles, and a population of 3,124,688 inhabitants, but is now reduced to five "legations" or districts,—Rome and the Comarca, Cività Vecchia, Viterbo, Veiletri, and Frosinine, possessing an area of 4,891 square miles, and about 700,000 inhabitants. The Papal army consists of about 16,000. Independent of fever and ague, which are most essentially products both of climate and the soil, especially the Pontine Marshes and Comacchio; its other products are wheat, maize, hemp, tobacco, wine, and oil. These, with a few manufactured goods, consisting of silks, woollens, and leather, form its chief exports. The principal river is the Tiber. Notwithstanding the Papal States possess an excel-

lent port (Civita Vecchia), its international trade is very small, the imports consisting chiefly of iron and coal. The value of imports from United Kingdom in 1866 amounted to £14,853, and exports to United Kingdom to £5,491. There are four lines of railway in the Papal States, extending altogether 84 miles (English). Rome is the capital and seat of government.

Sovereign Pontiff, Pius IX., born 13th May, 1792, elected 16th June, 1846.

Minister of State and Foreign Affairs, Cardinal Giacomo Antonelli.

Rome, Secretary Employed on Special Service, Odo W. L. Russell, Esq., £1,000.

Consul, Joseph Severn, Esq.

PARAGUAY,

An independent Republic of South America, situate between 17°—27° S. lat., and 54°—58° W. long. Its total area is variously estimated at from 75,000 to 85,000 square miles, five-sixths of which are encompassed by the rivers Parana and Paraguay, and contains a population of 1,400,000. It was discovered by Sebastian Cabot in 1526, was ruled as an independent state for nearly two centuries by the Jesuit missionaries, and is now divided into 25 departments, in the central of which Asuncion, the capital, is situated. Nearly one-half of the country, which consists of forests and pasturage lands, is national property. Many of the national estates have been let out in small tenements at low rents, with a view to their cultivation, the chief crops being maize, rice, coffee, cocoa, indigo, manioc, tobacco, sugar-cane, and cotton. The natural productions are very varied, but do not include the precious metals and other minerals common to South America. Much valuable timber is found in its forests. Among its principal trees are several species of dyewood, and many yielding juices, as the caoutchouc or India rubber, and the valuable shrub called "Maté," or Paraguay tea plant—one of its principal articles of commerce; medicinal plants also are very numerous. There are but few manufactures, sugar, rum, cotton, woollen cloths, and leather, being almost its only industrial productions. The commerce of the country is, for the most part, in the hands of the government, who hold a monopoly thereof. The government speedily raised an effective force of 60,000 men, with field-pieces and battery guns amounting in all to 400. The imports in 1863 were 885,841 piastres, and the vessels entered and cleared amounted to 412, with a tonnage of 16.650 tons. There is but little direct commercial intercourse with the United Kingdom, but the spirit of the former exclusive system is being broken up.

President of Paraguay, Don Francisco Solano Lopez, born 1827.

Secretary for Foreign Affairs,

Consul-General in London, Benjamin Bucke Greene, Esq., 15, Philpot Lane, E.C.

PERSIA,

Called by the natives Iran, is the most extensive, opulent, and powerful native kingdom of Western Asia, situated between 26°—40° N. lat. and 44°—61° E. long., extending 700 miles from north to south, and 900 miles from east to west, and comprising an area of 648,000 square miles, with a population of 11,000,000. It is divided into 13 districts, and has scarcely a river that can be termed navigable, though some of them extend several hundred miles in length, and possess great volume of water. Some of its immense valleys abound with the rarest and most valuable vegetable productions; those chiefly cultivated are wheat, of the very finest quality, barley, and other cereals, cotton in profusion, sugar, rice, tobacco. The vine flourishes in several districts, the wines of Shiraz being celebrated. The mulberry tree is largely cultivated, silk being one of the most important products of the kingdom. Its minerals are very unimportant, with the exception of salt; copper, lead, antimony, sulphur, naphtha, &c., are found, also turquoises and some other precious stones. The most important manufacture is that of silk, of the richest and most gorgeous kind. The Persians excel in their dyes, also in brocade and embroidery. Arms, carpets, shawls, felts, cotton and woollen fabrics are among the manufactures. The Persian government has no debt, and its royal treasury contains immense wealth in gold and other valuables, viz. :—Gold coin to the amount of £1,500,000; gold furniture and plate, £500,000; the crown jewels, valued at £2,000,000. The estimated revenue for the year 1868-9 amounts to £1,965,000, and the expenditure to £1,700,000. The army consists of 105,500 men. The value of the imports average £2,500,000, and the exports £15,000,000, but they have diminished during the last three years by nearly £1,000,000, owing to the failure of the silk crop in Ghilan. The commerce of Persia is extensive, and chiefly carried on with Russia by the Caspian, and with British India by way of the Persian Gulf. Teheran is the capital.

Sovereign, Shah Nasser ed De..., born 1829.
Chargé d'Affaires, General Hadji Mohsin Khan.
1st Secretary, Col. Mohamed Aga, 6, Kensington Gardens Terrace.
Teheran, *Envoy Extraordinary and Minister Plenipotentiary at*, Charles Alison, Esq., C.B., £5,000.
Secretary of Legation, R.F. Thomson, Esq., £750.
Oriental Secretary, W. J. Dickson, Esq., £600.
2nd Secretary, Augustus St. Mounsey, £400.
Resht, Consul at, Wm. George Abbott, Esq., £800.
Tabreez—Consul-General, Keith Edward Abbott, Esq., £820.

PERU,

An important maritime Republic of South America, about 1,200 miles in length, situate in lat. 3° 20'—21° 30' S. and in long. 68°—81° 20' W. Its general outline somewhat resembles a triangle, and its area is estimated at about 503,000 English square miles, with a population consisting of Creoles, Mulattos, Quarteroons, Cholos, and Indians, of 2,865,000. There is, however, a wide and unexplored expanse of country on the east side of the Andes, the possession of which is still in dispute between Peru and Brazil. This territory the "Amazones" is capable of supporting 30 millions more inhabitants. The "Chincha Islands," three in number, about 12 miles off the coast in 13°—14° S. lat., are famous as the source from whence Europe has been supplied with Peruvian guano, two hundred convicts being employed on the north island, embracing an area of 202 acres covered with guano, in cutting and loading the ships therewith, while the guano on the middle island, to the extent of 140 acres, has been chiefly worked by the Chinese, the quantity of guano exported in 1866 being 351,674 tons, of which 74,851 were for Great Britain. It is calculated that the deposits on these and the Lobos Islands contain about 16,000,000 tons of the estimated value (at

£13 per ton) of £208,000,000 sterling. The island of San Lorenzo forms the harbour of Callao. Peru is divided into three regions. *The Coast* or *Low Peru* is a sandy desert, lying between the Western Cordillera and the sea. In this region rain is unknown, but this is compensated, in a great measure, by the abundant dews which fall at night. *The Sierra* or *High Peru*, situated between the two Cordilleras, consists of mountains and barren rocks, interspersed with fertile and cultivated valleys, rich in tropical productions, the cliffs and sides of which, almost to Alpine altitude, are covered with verbenas, lupins, salvias, fuchsias, calceolarias, heliotrope, &c. The mountain slopes are covered with waving crops of wheat, barley, and other cereals; also potatoes; higher up the llama, vicuna, and alpaca find pasturage. The mountain chains consist of the Knot of Kuzco and Knot of Pasco. The former comprises six minor mountain-chains, and possesses an area thrice as large as that of Switzerland. The latter, or Knot of Pasco, contains the table-land of Bombon, 12,300 feet above the level of the sea, as well as other table lands at a height of 14,000 feet, being the highest of the Andes or Eastern Cordillera, where perpetual snow-clad winter reigns. The *Montana*, forming two-thirds of the entire area of the country, consists of vast, impenetrable forests and alluvial plains of inexhaustible fertility, and rich in all tropical productions, yet is almost altogether unproductive to man, being inhabited only by a few scattered tribes of wild Indians—murderous, untameable savages—repudiating the slightest approximation to civilization. The forests consist of huge trees, remarkable for their beauty and the value of their gums. Among the products in spontaneous abundance are the cinchona or Peruvian bark, caoutchouc, gum copal, indigo, vanilla, copaiba, sarsaparilla, ipecacuanha, &c.; and on its western fringe, where a few settlements still exist, tobacco, sugar, cotton, coffee, and cocoa are very successfully cultivated. The ancient history and civilization of Peru does not come within our province. The vegetable productions embrace those of the temperate as of the tropical climes. All European cereals and vegetables are cultivated with perfect success. Fruits of the most delicious flavour in every variety abound. The llama and alpaca wool are largely exported to Great Britain, notwithstanding which almost all the woollen fabrics used by the Peruvians as clothing are manufactured in England. Its mountainous districts abound in mineral wealth—gold and silver ore—in which pure silver is embedded, copper, lead, quicksilver, iron, tin, &c., emeralds, precious stones, and nitrate of soda, also borax, of which the supply appears to be inexhaustible.

The principal imports are European goods, live stock, provisions, tallow, Paraguay tea, cordage, &c.; the exports, gold, silver, wine, guano, sugar, Peruvian bark, pimento, wool, &c. Lima 120,000 inhabitants, is the capital of Peru.

Annual Revenue for 1867 amounted to	£2,689,083
Expenditure to	3,105,421
The amount of Public Debt or Liabilities (the whole of which are secured by the Guano deposits)	21,691,752
Total Value of Exports (including bullion and specie) in 1865 amounted to	6,245,491
The Value of Imports of Home Produce from the United Kingdom in 1866 amounted to	1,354,697
Exports to the United Kingdom	3,016,907

President of the Republic, Colonel José Balta.
Foreign Minister, José Barrenechea.
Envoy Extra. and Minister Plenipot., vacant.
Secretary of Legation, Don Juan Jara Almonte.
Consul in London, Don Manuel de la Quintana, 21, Gower Street.
Lima, British Chargé d'Affaires and Consul at, Gen. Hon. Wm. Geo. Stafford Jerningham, £2,000.
Callao, Consul, C. A. Henderson, Esq., £1,450.
Vice do., Douglas C. Hastings, Esq., £200.
Islay, Consul, £500.
Arica, Vice-Con., G. Hodges Nugent, Esq., £300.

PORTUGAL,

The most westerly kingdom of Europe, and a part of the great Spanish Peninsula, lies in 36° 55′—42° 8′ N. lat. and 6° 15′—9° 30′ W. long., being 338 miles in length from N. to S., and averaging about 100 in breadth from E. to W. Continental Portugal contains an area of 34,840 English square miles; but possesses, with its insular appendages, the Azores and Madeira, an area of 36,310 English square miles, with an aggregate population of 4,323,993. Portugal is divided into six provinces : Minho (containing the district of Oporto), Tras os Montes, Beira, Estremadura (containing the district of Lisbon), Alemtejo, and Algarve. Its colonial possessions are numerous in Africa and Asia and the Indian Archipelago, containing an area of 526,041 square miles, and a population of 3,687,228. The principal rivers of continental Portugal are the Tagus, the Douro, the Minho, and the Guadiana. The chief products are wheat, barley, oats, maize, flax, hemp, and the vine in elevated tracts ; in the low lands, rice, olives, oranges, lemons, citrons, figs, and almonds. There are extensive forests of oak, chestnuts, sea-pine, and cork. Cattle are numerous. Oxen are employed as beasts of draught, mules and donkeys as those of burden. Agriculture is much neglected, notwithstanding the richness of the soil ; the cultivation of the vine and the olive being almost the sole branches of industry ; the rich red wine, known to us as "Port," being shipped from Oporto. Its mineral products are important, being chiefly manganese, antimony, lead, copper, iron, marble, slate, coal, and salt, which last from its hardness is in demand. Its manufactures consist of gloves, silk, woollen, linen, and cotton fabrics ; metal and earthenware goods, tobacco, cigars, &c. Wine, however, is the chief industrial product of the country. In the year 1863, since which time we have no returns ; the quantity shipped from Oporto consisted of 34,905 pipes, of which 30,044 were imported into Great Britain. At the present time the average annual import approximates £100,000 in value. The exports consist almost entirely of wine, fruits, oil, and cork and salt. The imports are chiefly manufactured goods : hardware, linen, hats, shoes, stockings, &c.; corn and flour.

		£
Annual Revenue for 1866-7		3,596,659
Expenditure		4,748,964
The Public Debt in 1867 amounted to		47,330,000
The Interest whereon is		1,441,000

The Value of Imports of Home Produce from the United Kingdom to Portugal in 1866 was 1,992,902
And of Exports to the United Kingdom 2,517,828
Number of all vessels entered and cleared at the port of Lisbon in 1864: 1,322 vessels, of which 463 with a tonnage of 125,795 tons were British, entered ; 1,335 vessels, of which 457 with a tonnage of 124,532 tons were British, cleared. Number of all vessels entered and cleared at Oporto in 1864 : 983 vessels, of which 216 with a tonnage of 50,958 tons, were British, entered ; 938 vessels, of which 177 with a tonnage of 58,291 tons, were British, cleared. There are about 600 miles of railway now open for traffic, principally in the environs of Oporto, Lisbon, Santarem, and Vigo, the country being otherwise nearly without roads; the total want of canals rendering the internal traffic of the country almost impracticable, and presenting a barrier to its material prosperity. The army consists of about 31,000, and the navy of 36 ships—many in bad condition and scarcely seaworthy, with 364 guns, manned by about 3,000 sailors. The colonial army amounts to about 24,000 troops. Lisbon is the capital, and the seat of government.

THE AZORES, a group of nine islands in the Atlantic Ocean belonging to Portugal, from which they are distant 800 miles, ranging between 36° 55′ — 39° 44′ N. lat. and 25° 10′ — 31° 16′ W. long. The area of the group is estimated at 1,134 square miles, with an aggregate population of 251,894, being an average of 450 to the square mile, indicative of the salubrity of the islands. The exports are oranges, wine, brandy, grain, provisions, and coarse linen ; and the imports, woollens, cotton, hardware, iron, glass, cordage, pitch, tar, timber, rum, coffee, sugar, and tea. The want of a good harbour is a great drawback. The mountains range from 1,860 to 7,600 feet high. The principal island is St. Michael's.

MADEIRA, an island in the N. Atlantic Ocean, on the N.W. coast of Africa, in lat. 32° 43′ N. and long. 17° W., belonging to Portugal, and distant 620 miles from Lisbon. It contains, with Porto Santo and Las Desertas, the other islands forming the group, 336 square miles, and a population of 111,764. It consists altogether of lofty mountains, reaching the altitude of 6,000 feet, on the declivities of which the productions of the island, date-palm, plantain, sugar-cane, pomegranate, fig, coffee, &c., are raised. Vines form the chief object of cultivation ; but wheat, barley, oats, coffee, and arrowroot are raised to some extent. In the city of Funchal (the principal town), the most opulent portion of the inhabitants consist of British merchants and invalids. The imports are chiefly woollen, linen, and cotton manufactured goods, iron, flour, earthenware, &c. The exports consist chiefly of wine (more than two-thirds of the whole exports), sugar, oranges, lemons, wickerwork, hides, &c. The trade is chiefly with Great Britain. The value of imports in 1866 amounted to £243,156, and of exports, £82,799.

Reigning Sovereign, Dom Luis 1st, King of Portugal, *b.* 31st October, 1838, *m.* 6 October, 1862, Mary Pia, daughter of King Victor Emmanuel of Italy.
Heir Apparent, Carlos, Prince Royal, *b.* 28th September, 1863.
Minister in London, Count Saradio, 12, Gloucester Place, Portman Square.
Consul General, Senhor Francisco Van Zeller, 8, St. Mary Axe, E.C.
Lisbon, Envoy Extry. and Min. Plenry. at, Hon. Sir C. Augs. Murray, K.C.B., £4,400.
Secretary of Legation, Hon. E.R.Lytton, £500.
Second Secretary, J. P. Harris, Esq., £250.
Lisbon, Consul, George Brackenbury, Esq., £900.

Cape Verd Islands, Consul, T. Miller, Esq., £400.
Loanda, Consul and Slave Trade Commissioner,
 Watson Vredenburg, Esq., £1,000.
Madeira, Consul, Geo. H. Hayward, Esq., £300.
Oporto, Consul, O. J. H. Crawford, Esq., £600.
Azores, (St. Michael's), Samuel Vines, Esq., £400.

PRUSSIA,

An extensive kingdom of Central Europe, comprising the larger portion of Germany, situate in lat. 49° 7'—55° 52' N., and long. 5° 50'—22° 50' E. Prior to the war of 1866 it was divided into ten provinces, with an area and population as under (according to the Almanach de Gotha, 1865):

	Area in sq. miles.	Population.
1. Prussia Proper	24,739 ...	2,866,866
2. Posen	11,260 ...	1,485,550
3. Pomerania	12,111 ...	1,389,739
4. Silesia	15,577 ...	3,390,695
5. Brandenburg	15,417 ...	2,467,759
6. Saxony	9,573 ...	1,976,417
7. Westphalia	7,727 ...	9,718,065
8. Rhenish Prussia	10,230 ...	3,215,786
9. District of Hohenzollern	444 ...	64,675
10. ,, Jade	5 ...	250

The troops quartered beyond the Prussian boundary numbered 14,720, giving for the whole of Prussia at this period a population of 18,491,220, with an area of 107,183 square miles. Since the war of 1866 the kingdom of Hanover, electorate of Hesse, duchy of Nassau, principality of Hesse Homburg, republic of Frankfort-on-the-Main, and the duchy of Schleswig-Holstein, and Lauenburg, with detached portions of Bavaria and of Hesse Darmstadt, have been incorporated with Prussia, giving an additional area of 22,309 square miles, and a total population of 24,042,730. Prussia possesses a large number of navigable rivers in close proximity with each other, viz., the Niemen, the Pregel, the Vistula, the Oder, the Elbe, the Weser, the Rhine, and numerous tributaries, the Moselle, Lahn, &c. The Baltic forms a number of gulfs and bays. Its principal mountains are the Hartz, the Brocken, and the Reisengeberge, the latter reaching an altitude of 5,000 feet. The forests are extensive, occupying an area of nearly 10,000,000 acres, chiefly consisting of fir. Its minerals consist of iron, copper, lead, alum, nitre, zinc, cobalt, sulphur, nickel, arsenic, baryta, also amber, agate, jasper, onyx, &c., and, in a small degree, silver. Salt from the brine springs of Pr. Saxony is abundant, also coal. All metals, salt, precious stones, and amber belong to the Crown. Agriculture and the rearing of cattle constitute the principal sources of employment and wealth of the rural population of the entire monarchy. Wheat, rye, oats, barley, pease, millet, rape-seed, maize, linseed, flax, hemp, tobacco, hops, &c., are extensively cultivated and largely exported. The western division is noted for its excellent fruits and vegetables, and the Rhenish provinces stand pre-eminent for their wines. Prussia has upwards of 100 mineral springs, possessing various properties and virtues. Its manufactures consist chiefly of linens, for which Silesia, Pr. Saxony, and Westphalia have long been noted. The cotton works are very extensive, chiefly carried on by steam; there being 3,300 machines in operation in Rhenish Prussia, and many more in other parts, independent of the hand looms, of which, in 1863, 264,135 were in operation. Beside these there are numerous manufactories of silk, woollen, mixed cotton and linen fabrics, including shawls, carpets, &c.; woollens are made, more or less, in almost every town and large village. Next in importance are leather, earthenware, glass, paper, tobacco, and working in metals. Brewing is a business of great importance. The principal imports comprise coffee, tea, sugar, cotton, and other produce of the colonies, wines, silk, fruit, manufactured goods, tin, furs, dye-stuffs. The principal exports comprise linens, woollens, hardware, corn, wool, timber, pitch, linseed, tobacco, mineral waters; to these may be added horses, horned cattle, hams, salt meat, &c., and from the Rhenish provinces, wine.

THE ZOLLVEREIN was a Customs League between the North German Confederation and the South German States. It was first commenced by Prussia in the year 1828, with some of the Minor States, and was gradually enlarged by the entrance into it of nearly all the other German States, together with the Kingdoms of Bavaria, Wurtemburg, and Saxony. This League not being of a permanent nature, came to an end during the political disturbance of 1865-66, and, so far as the South German States were concerned, was only kept up by temporary agreements, which are now replaced by the present Treaty, concluded on 1st November, 1867.

There are six celebrated universities in Prussia, and the whole of the educational establishments are, more or less, under the immediate control of the "Minister of Public Instruction and Ecclesiastical Affairs," assisted by an Under-Secretary of State. The Royal Family belong to the Reformed or Calvinistic faith; but the majority of the population consists of Protestants, who number about 14,500,000; of Roman Catholics, about 8,000,000; of Mennonites and other Christian sects, about 18,000; and of Jews, 260,000.

The army, in 1866, consisted of 609,699, on war footing (208,576 on peace footing), with a reserve of 104,414 men. The navy, according to the returns, 1867, consisted of 3 screw steamers, 9 frigates, 8 gun boats, 1st class; 15 do., 2nd class, 1 yacht, and 3 corvettes, with a total of 7,020-horse power, and 224 guns; also of 3 sailing frigates, 3 brigs, 3 schooners, and 50 gun boats, mounting 315 guns. In 1867 the Prussian navy was manned by 2,190 seamen and boys, officered by 1 admiral, 1 rear do., 19 captains, 146 commanders and lieutenants, 40 of whom were in reserve; independent of these were 12 companies of marines, artillery, and infantry, numbering 1,200 men. Of Prussian railways, 6 belong to the State, 7 others are under Government control, being partly constructed by the State, and the rest, about two-thirds of the whole, belong to private companies; the total length of them extends to 3,925 miles of single, and 1,289 miles of double lines, constructed at a cost of £6,694,224. Total receipts in 1864, £8,987,509. Average receipts per English mile, £2,200. Cost per cent. upon gross revenue 49·16. Net revenue per English mile, £1,164. To these must now be added the plexus of railways in the kingdom of Hanover, which consists of 550 English miles, constructed at an expense of £7,580,901. Gross receipts in 1863, £838,085, Total expenses, £418,331. Net revenue, £419,754.

	£
Estimated amount of public Revenue of Old Provinces of Kingdom, 1867	25,339,480
Estimated amount of public Revenue of Hanover, Schleswig Holstein, &c.	6,348,387
Total	31,687,867

Estimated amount of public Expenditure of the Old Provinces of the Kingdom, 1867 25,339,480

Estimated amount of public Expenditure of Hanover, Schleswig-Holstein, &c. 6,348,387

Total amount of public Debt, 1866 42,123,064

Total value of Imports (Dantzic and Stettin), 1866 7,973,735

Total Value of Exports (Dantzic and Stettin), 1866 5,268,467

Value of Imports of home produce from the United Kingdom to Prussia, including £174,884 to Hanover in 1866 1,975,296

Value of Exports from Prussia, including £311,557 from Hanover to the United Kingdom in 1866 7,178,220

Total number and tonnage of all vessels entered and cleared at the Ports in Prussia, in 1865 :— 10,427 vessels, 852,089 tons, entered, of which 3,196 vessels, with a tonnage of 450,174 tons, belonged to Great Britain; 10,368 vessels, 847,537 tons, cleared, of which 2,949 vessels, with a tonnage of 403,434 tons belonged to Great Britain. Berlin is the capital of the Prussian Dominions.

Reigning Sovereign, William, King of Prussia, &c., K.G.; born 22nd March, 1797; married 11th June, 1829, Augusta, daughter of Charles Frederick, Grand Duke of Saxe Weimar.

Heir Apparent, Crown Prince Fred. William, born 18th October, 1831; married 25th January, 1858, Victoria, Princess Royal of Great Britain.

Minister for Foreign Affairs and Premier, Count Otto von Bismarck Schönhausen.

Ambassador Extraordinary and Plenipotentiary Count Bernstorff, 9 Carlton House Terrace.

Coun. and 1st Sec. of Embassy, Herr M. F. de Kette.

Secretaries of Embassy, M.M. de Schmidthals and Count Galen.

Consul-General, M. de Twardowski, *ad. int.,* 106, Fenchurch Street.

Berlin—Ambassador Extraordinary and Minister Plenipotentiary, Lord Augustus W. F. S. Loftus, G.C.B., £8,000.

Sec. of Embassy, Hon. Lionel S. S. West, £900.

Second Secretaries, Geo. H. Wyndham, Esq., £350. R. T. J. Kirkpatrick and Percy Mitford, Esqrs., £250 each.

Military Attaché, Col. C.P. B. Walker, C.B., £500.

Consul General, Victor de Magnus, unpaid.

Dantzic—Consul, William A. White, Esq., £650.

Frankfort—Consul, Theod. Kuchen, Esq., unpaid.

Königsberg—Consul, Wm. J. Herstlet, Esq., £600.

Memel—Vice Consul, William Ward, Esq., £300.

Stettin and Swinemunde—Consul, Joseph A. Blackwell, Esq., £600.

Do.—Consular Agent, John A. Bauman, Esq.

RUSSIA,

An Empire comprising one-seventh of the territorial surface of the globe, and extending over a large portion of its northern regions. In addition to Russia in Europe, situate between lat. 40° 20′ — 70° N., and 18° 60°— 45′ E. long, and embracing more than half of that continent, it comprehends one-third of Asia, and, until lately, included also a large section of North America. The empire comprises: Russia in Europe, Siberia (northern Asiatic provinces), Caucasia (South Asiatic provinces), Finland and Poland, and a new province called Russian Turkestan. It contains an area of 7,770,882 square miles,

with a population of 76,497,168. The established religion of the empire is the Russo-Greek Church, officially called the Orthodox Catholic Faith. The majority of Poles, calculated at 2,750,000, are Roman Catholics; there are also 2,000,000 Lutherans, 2,750,000 Mahometans, 1,250,000 Jews, 20,000 Armenians, besides other denominations. The empire is divided into several governments, viz: the Northern Provinces, Great Russia, Baltic Provinces, White Russia, Lithuania, Little Russia, New Russia, Wolga and Caspian Provinces, Oural Provinces, Siberia, Transcaucasia, Finland and Poland. The principal rivers are the Volga, Oural, Dnieper, Dneister, Don, Dwina, Duna, Neva. The Volga is the largest in Europe, and navigable almost to its source.

The nominal strength of the Russian army is 1,135,975 on the war footing, and 812,096 on the peace footing; to these must be added 129,000 Cossacks on military service. The navy consists of two great divisions, the Baltic fleet and that of the Black Sea; comprising 258 steamers, and 36 sailing vessels; the Black Sea fleet number 43, the Caspian 32, and the Pacific 33; the remainder being stationed chiefly at Cronstadt or Sweaborg. The social scale, or grade of society, is very distinctly marked in Russia, each state having, as it were, its privileges clearly defined.

Russia is eminently an agricultural country, the soil being extremely fertile, though only a small portion (275,000,000 acres,) is under cultivation. The chief cereals raised are wheat, barley, oats, buckwheat, millet, and specially rye, the staple food of the inhabitants. Hemp and flax are extensively cultivated, and of late years, potatoes, and tobacco. Gardening is an important branch of industry. The forests and woodlands are very extensive, occupying an area of 486,000,000 acres. Oak, lime, maple, and ash trees predominate. Timber is the chief article of internal commerce. The Ural mountains, which contain nearly all the mineral riches of the country, are the principal seat of mining and metallic industry; producing gold, silver (from the Altai mines), platinum, copper, iron of very superior quality, rock-salt, marble, and kaolin or china-clay. An immense bed of coal, apparently inexhaustible, has lately been discovered near Kharkoff, in the basin of the Donet, and now being worked, capable of supplying Russia with 25,000,000 cwt. annually.

Independent of its metallurgical factories, 15,460 in number, and employing 465,000 hands, it possesses many extensive handicraft manufacturing establishments, for weaving, tanning, fur-dressing, &c. Linen is chiefly manufactured by hand-looms; the chief manufacture being spinning and weaving flax and hemp. Woollen and worsted stuffs, fine cloths and mixed fabrics, are also produced. Silk spinning and weaving are carried on in the factories at Moscow, which is renowned for its brocades, and gold and silver embroideries.

The chief imports are sugar, coffee, tea, and other colonial produce. Woollens, cotton, and cotton cloths, silk, dye-stuffs, wine, fruits, machinery, &c. The chief exports are grain, wooden wares, hides and skins raw and dressed, flax, hemp, tallow, wool (sheeps'), linseed, and hemp seed.

Russia has a large railway system. The state railways already opened extend to upwards of 900 miles, while others, the Orel-Vitebsk, &c.,

aro in course of construction. Those belonging to private companies exceed 2,200 miles.

	£
Total estimated amount of Revenue, 1867	70,276,277
Total estimated amount of Expenditure, 1867	70,276,277
Amount of Public Debt, 1866	274,544,770
Total value of Imports, 1866	32,503,932
" " into Asiatic Russia, 1866	2,460,213
Total value of Exports, 1866	35,293,810
" " from Asiatic Russia, 1866	2,523,015

Total number and tonnage of all vessels entered and cleared at ports in Russia in 1865 : 11,648 vessels, of which 2,644 were British, and 2,396,372 tons, of which 767,372 were British, entered; and 11,839 vessels, of which 3,858 were British, and 2,390,370 tons, of which 1,163,410 were British, cleared.

The two principal cities aro St. Petersburg and Moscow. The former is the capital and seat of government.

Reigning Sovereign, Alexander II., Emperor and Autocrat of All the Russias, of Moscow, Kiew, Vladimir, Novgorod, Czar of Cazan, Czar of Astrakan, Czar of Poland, Czar of Siberia, Czar of the Tauric Chersonese, Czar of Georgia; Lord of Pleskow, and Grand Duke of Smolensk, Lithuania, Volhynia, Podolia, and Finland; Duke of Esthonia, Livonia, Courland, and Semigalle, Samogitia, Bialostock, Carelia, Twer, Ingoria, Perm, Viatka, Bulgaria, &c.; Lord and Grand Duke of Lower Novgorod, Tchernigow, Riazan, Polotsk, Rostow, Yaroslaw, Beloorsersk, Oudor, Obdor, Condia, Vitebsk, and Mstislaw; Ruler of all the Northern country, Lord of Iberia, Cartalinia, Cabardia, and the province of Armenia; Hereditary Prince and Sovereign of the Princes of Circassia and other Montagnard Princes: Successor of Norway, Duke of Schleswig-Holstein, Stormarn, Dithmarsen, and Oldenburg, &c.; born, 29 April, 1818; married, 28 April, 1841, Maria, daughter of the Grand Duke Louis II., of Hesse Darmstadt.

Heir Apparent, Grand Duke Alexander; born, 10 March, 1845.

Minister of Foreign Affairs, Prince Alexander Michael Gortchakoff.

Consul-General,

Ambas. Extraordinary and Minister Plenipotentiary, Baron de Brunnow, Chesham Ho., Belgrave Sq.

Counsellor, M. de Sebouroff.

First Secretary, Count Koskull.

Second Secretary, Mr. Capniste.

Consul-General, Alexander de Berg, Esq., 32, Gt. Winchester Street, E.C.

Vice-Consul, Frederick Knapp, Esq.

St.Petersburg, Ambassador Extraordinary and Minister Plenipotentiary at, Rt. Hon. Sir Andrew Buchanan, G.C.B. £9000.

Secretary of Embassy, H. Rumbold, Esq., £1,050.

Second Secretary, V. A.W. Drummond, Esq. £400.

Military Attaché, Col. R. Blane, C.B.

Consul and Translator, Thos. Michell, Esq., £800.

Archangel, Charles Renny, Esq., £300.

Berdiansk (Sea of Azof,) J. Zohrab, Esq. £500.

Helsingfors (Finland,) W. Campbell, Esq. £400.

Kertch (Crimea,) Peter Barrow, Esq. £500.

Theodosia, Vice-Consul, E. B. B. Barker, Esq. £400.

Moscow, Consul, Frederick Roberts, Esq.

Odessa, Consul-General,

Nicolaïeff, Vice-Consul, G. A. Stevens, Esq. £500.

Riga, Consul, James Grignon, Esq. £850.

Poti, Vice-Consul, Robert Wilkinson, Esq. £400.

Taganrog (Sea of Azof,) Consul, J. P. Carruthers, Esq. £400.

Warsaw, Consul-General, Lt.-Col. C. E. Mansfield. £1373,

Soukoum Kale, £600.

SANDWICH ISLANDS,

A rich, beautiful, and interesting chain of islands, situate in the North Pacific Ocean, forming the kingdom of Hawaii (formerly Owyhee), running from south-east to north-west in lat. 19°—22° N. and long. 155°—161° W., discovered by Captains Cook and King in 1778. They consist of 13 islands, 8 of which are inhabited. All are very mountainous, and appear to be chiefly of volcanic origin; they occupy a united area of about 6,000 square miles, with a population of about 67,000 inhabitants. Hawaii, the largest of the group, contains two mountains, Mouna Kea and Mouna Loa, each rising 14,000 feet. The inhabitants appear to be of the same race as those of New Zealand, the Society and Friendly Isles, and the Marquesas. The islands produce fine pasturage in abundance, and large herds are reared to supply the whalers and merchant vessels. Wheat is raised in the uplands, and in the valleys coffee, sugar, cotton, arrowroot, cocoa, breadfruit, and various European and West Indian fruits. The imports are chiefly manufactured goods, while the exports consist of oil, sperm and whale, sugar, coffee, rice, pulse, hides, corn, &c. The islands are well situated for trade, being in the route between America and China, and constant communication is maintained with San Francisco. A treaty of commerce, navigation, and friendship between Her Majesty Queen Victoria and the King of the Sandwich Islands was signed at Honolulu in 1851. Honolulu, in the island of Oahu, is the capital and principal port. Total value of imports in 1867, £391,482. Total value of exports, £335,932. Total number and tonnage of vessels entered at the ports in the Sandwich Islands in 1867,134; of which 31 were British; and 67,268 tons, of which 16,620 were British.

Reigning Sovereign, Kamehama V., born 11th December, 1830.

Minister for Foreign Affairs, M. de Varigney.

Consul-Gen., Manley Hopkins, Esq., 4, Royal Exchange Buildings, E.C.

British Commissioner and Consul-Gen. at Oahu, Major J. H. Wodehouse, £1,500.

SAXONY,

A kingdom of North Germany, the second in importance and population of the minor German States, situate between 50° 10'—51° 25' N. lat., and 11° 55'—15° E. long., comprising an area of 6,777 English square miles, with a population of 2,343,994, nine-tenths of whom are Lutherans, and about 50,000 Roman Catholics, the Reformed Church, Jews, &c., being, even in the aggregate, a very small minority. More than one-half of the whole surface is arable, which has always been in a high state of cultivation; its agricultural products consist of the usual cereals and leguminous plants, with rape, buckwheat, hops, flax, and fruits of all kinds suited to the climate. The forests supply timber of excellent quality. and in such abundance as to render them a great source of industry and wealth. The minerals are another great source of wealth, the ores being both rich and abundant. Most of the mines belong to the Crown, and consist of silver, tin, bismuth, cobalt, iron, zinc, lead, nickel, arsenic, &c., beside coal, marble, porcelain earth, and various gems, as topaz, chrysolite, amethyst, carnelian, garnets, &c. Manufacturing industry has been greatly developed, and in some branches carried to a high degree of perfection, employing about three-fifths of the population; the linen manufacture employs more than 16,000 looms, but cotton spinning and weaving are in a measure superseding it. Broadcloth, merinoes, silks, mixed silk and woollen goods, thread, muslin-de-laines, laces, and embroideries, maintain a high reputation. Saxon pottery and porcelain, "the Dresden china," have long been famous; all these form its chief exports. The great fairs of Leipsic are the chief medium of commerce. The imports are chiefly corn, wine, salt, cotton, silk, flax, hemp, wool, coffee, tea, &c. Saxony is a limited and hereditary monarchy; it has several principal towns, as Dresden, Leipsic, the great book-mart, &c., Freiburg, Meissen, the seat of the potteries, and Chemnitz the Manchester of Saxony; Dresden is, however, the chief city, and the seat of Government.

Total amount of Revenue in 1866........£1,663,740
Total amount of Expenditure 2,048,847
Amount of Public Debt 9,912,049

The railways of Saxony, extending 252 miles, and constructed at an expense of £6,398,550, are, for the greater part, State property, and yield a very considerable revenue.

Reigning Sovereign, John I., King of Saxony; born 12th Dec., 1801; married 21st Nov., 1822, Amelia, daughter of Maximilian I., King of Bavaria.

Heir Apparent, Albert, Duke of Saxony, born 23rd April, 1828.

Minister for Foreign Affairs, Baron Richard von Friesen.

Consul at Liverpool, Charles Stoess, Esq.

Dresden—Chargé d'Affaires, Joseph Hume Burnby, Esq., £700.

Leipsic—Consul-General, J. A. Crowe, Esq., £750.

SAXE COBURG-GOTHA,

One of the larger of the minor German States, situated in about 51° N. lat. and 10° 44' E. long, comprising together an area of 816 English square miles (i.e., not quite so large as Leicestershire), and a population, at the last census, of 164,527, the majority of whom are Protestants. Agriculture is the principal occupation of the people, considerable quantities of corn and flax being raised, also potatoes and other leguminous plants. Its mineral wealth includes iron, cobalt, manganese, and coal (chiefly in Gotha), also marble, porcelain earth, millstones, and salt. Manufactures are of little importance, and chiefly confined to the production of pitch, tar, potash. The breeding of horses, cattle, and sheep is successfully conducted. The Crown and State revenues are kept separate, the amount of the former, in 1865, was £83,925, and the expenditure, £57,851; while revenue and expenditure of the latter were alike £90,975. Gotha is the capital of the Duchy.

Reigning Prince, Ernest II., Duke of Saxe Coburg, born June 21, 1818, married May 3, 1842, Alexandrine, daughter of Leopold, late Grand Duke of Baden.

Heir Presumptive, H.R.H. Alfred, Duke of Edinburgh, K.G., 2nd son of Queen Victoria, born 6th August, 1844.

Minister of State, Baron von Seebach.
Coburg, Chargé d'Affaires at, Charles T. Barnard, Esq., £850.

SIAM,

An extensive kingdom of Eastern Asia, situated in the heart of the peninsula between India and China, in lat. 4°—22° N. and long. 96°—102° E., bounded by the Gulf of Siam and the Malay Peninsula. It is about 1,100 miles in length and 350 in breadth. Its area is estimated at about 250,000 square miles, and its male population at about 5,000,000, of whom 2,000,000 are Siamese, 1,150,000 Chinese, 1,500,000 Malays and Laos. The country generally consists of mountains, swamps, and jungles. The great river Menam, or Meinam Bangkok, traverses the centre of the country, and inundates the valley through which it runs. The surface of country within the direct influence of these inundations, which generally commence in June and end in November, is estimated at 12,000 square miles; yet, properly speaking, the actual valley of Meinam embraces an area of 22,000 square miles, and forms a tract of country which for fertility cannot be exceeded by any other portion of the globe. There are several ports along its coast line, two (Paknam and Paklat), are defended by forts, Meeklong (a beautiful city with floating bazaars, fine pagodas and gardens) and others. A system of agriculture has, within the last few years, been introduced, and the quantity of agricultural produce exported greatly increased. The soil is very rich, requiring but little outlay of labour and capital to insure abundant harvests. The chief products are rice (the staple food of the inhabitants), sugar, guava, mango, dauries, coffee, cocoanuts, tobacco, sago, and gums. There is not a region in the world where the fruits are more varied or more delicious. Teak, sandal, rosewood, and the Aquila or "Eagle tree," renowned for its perfume, and used at all religious ceremonies, are the chief woodland products. Its minerals consist of gold, silver in combination with other metals; copper, iron, lead, and tin are abundant, and extensively worked by the Chinese. Precious stones are found in great number and variety. The principal manufactures are vases, urns, and other vessels, in the making of which gold is embossed upon silver, gold beating, iron founding, and manufactures of fine cloth, glass wares, and pottery. Export duties are levied upon all goods which leave the country. The chief exports are silk, piece goods, scarlet cloth, opium, hardware, cutlery, arms, sweetmeats, with numerous other products. In 1864, 879 vessels of all nations (including 281 British) of 330,184 tons (225,980 British) entered and cleared at the port of Bangkok. The imports amounted to £1,167,697; the exports amounted to £1,317,922. The principal articles were, rice 125,507 tons, sugar 83,000 cwt., and large quantities of hides, horns, gums, &c. Bangkok, a city of more than 400,000 inhabitants, is the capital of Siam, and comprises three divisions, the town itself, the floating town, and the royal palace, this arrangement being necessary on account of the annual inundations of the River Meinam, to which the city is exposed. There are no regular streets, and each house has a small boat or canoe ready for use. The government is an absolute and hereditary monarchy, and there are two kings. The first is the actual monarch; the second receives about one-third of the revenue, and acts more in the capacity of a prime minister. The supreme king, Somdetch, who died October 1, 1868, was a practical astronomer, could both speak and write English, and had been a careful student of our National writers.

First King,
Second King,
Bangkok, Cons. at, Thos. Geo. Knox, Esq., £1,200.
Interpreter, Harry Alabaster, Esq., £500.
First Assistant, W. H. Newman, Esq., £400.
Second Do., H. G. Kennedy, Esq., £350.

"SOCIETY ISLANDS," OR "TAHITI,"

Form a portion of the French colonial possessions. Tahiti, the principal island, called "The Gem of the Pacific," is about 110 miles in circumference, and contains a population of about 9,000. The chief products are the bread-fruit, cocoa-nut, plantains, the youte or cloth-plant, besides a variety of others. The exports consist of pearls, pearl shell, cocoa-nut oil, sugar, and arrowroot. The chief town is Papiete, with a safe harbour, a p tent slip for vessels of 400 tons, and careening quays.

Number and tonnage of all vessels entered and cleared at the port of Papiete, in 1864 :—

Entered, 101 ; tonnage, 10,342 ; value of cargo, £87,791 ; of which 13, with a tonnage of 1,948 tons, cargo valued at £17,670, were British.

Cleared, 105 ; tonnage, 11,019 ; value of cargo, £53,599, of which 13, with a tonnage of 1,948 tons, and cargo valued at £9,985, were British.

Consul, George Charles Miller, Esq., £600.

SPAIN,

A kingdom situated in the south-west of Europe, between 36°—43° 45' N. lat. and 3° 20'—9° 20' W. long., bounded on the south by the Mediterranean and Atlantic, on the west by the Atlantic and Portugal, and on the north by the Bay of Biscay and France, from which it is separated by the Pyrenees, and occupying the larger portion of the great Iberian peninsula. Its greatest length is about 560 miles, and average breadth 380 ; its coast line extends 1,317 miles, 712 formed by the Mediterranean, and 605 by the Atlantic. It was formerly divided into 14 provinces (now sub-divided into 49), called the Ancient Provinces, still best understood, viz. :—New Castile, La Mancha, Old Castile, Leon, Asturias, Galicia, Estramadura, Andalusia, Murcia, Valencia, Navarre, Arragon, Catalonia, Basque Provinces, with the Canary and Balearic Isles (Majorca, Minorca, &c.), comprising an area of 193,508 English square miles, and a population, in 1864, of 16,287,675. To these must be added its several colonies in America—Cuba, Porto Rico, part of Virgin Islands, and St. Domingo, comprising an area of 70,466 square miles and a population of 2,070,000 : the Philippine Islands in Asia and Oceania, 53,299 square miles, with a population of 2,900,000 : the African possessions in the Gulf of Guinea, Fernando Po, Tetuan, &c., 1,435 square miles, with a population of about 30,000 ; making a grand total of 318,708 square miles in area, with a population of 21,286,675 inhabitants. Spain proper contains a series of mountain ranges, the Pyrenees, the Cantabrian Mountains, the Sierra Guadarrama, S. Morena, S. Nevada, the highest peak of which reaches 11,660 feet, Montes de Toledo, &c. The principal rivers permeating the country are the Douro, the Tagus, the Guadiana, the Guadalquiver, the Ebro, and the Minho. The country alternating with hill

and dale, is plentifully watered by streams abounding with fish, the meadows yielding rich pasturage ; the soil, generally fertile, is artificially irrigated, and well adapted to agriculture and the cultivation of heat-loving fruits, as olives, oranges, lemons, almonds, pomegranates and dates. The agricultural products comprise wheat, barley, maize, oats, rice, hemp and flax, both of the best quality. In Grenada, cotton, coffee, sugar, and cocoa are raised. The vines are cultivated in every province ; in the south-west, near Xeres, the well-known Sherry and Tent are made ; in the south-east the Malaga and Alicant. "Corn and wine and oil" abound ; the quantity of wine produced in 1862, was 134,612,000 gallons, of which 28,573,336 gallons were exported, and realized the sum of £3,219,947; 83,600 converted into brandy, and 105,202,724 gallons consumed within the country. The quantity of wheat exported in 1861 amounted to 120,012,200 bushels ; of olive oil, 2,492,688 gallons, realizing £813,813, but the quantity of oil produced is about 5,000,000 gallons annually. The manufacturing industry is rapidly advancing. The imports of coal amounted in 1862 to 5,634,027 cwt, independent of 7,000,000 extracted from native mines. The cotton manufactures have been advancing with great rapidity, the import of cotton having gradually increased from 233,898 cwt. to 798,229 cwt. in three years. Cottons, silk, silk twist, the working of esparto grass into mats, baskets, shoes, &c., afford further branches of industry. The manufactures of tobacco, arms, and gunpowder are carried on by the Government. The principal articles imported are gold and silver, bullion, specie, &c., sugar, yarn, woollen fabrics, silk, raw cotton, iron, machinery, railway materials, coals, dried fish, cocoa and hides. The principal exports, wine, silk, metals, dried fruit, flour, green fruits, olive oil, wool, grain, vegetables, cork, seeds, salt ; the trade is almost confined to France and Great Britain. The pilchard, anchovy, and tunny fisheries are valuable. The national church of Spain is the Roman Catholic, and the entire population, with the exception of about 60,000, adhere to it. The army was permanently reduced in 1866 to 85,000 men in time of peace. The navy consists of 35 sailing vessels, mounting 641 guns, and 78 war steamers with 556 guns and 6,810 horse-power, and manned by 1,121 officers, 12,986 sailors, and 7,980 marines. Madrid is the capital and seat of government.

	£
Total estimated Revenue, 1867	26,845,408
" Expenditure, 1867	26,369,293
Public Debt	163,977,472
Value of total Imports (including £3,927,615 bullion and specie)	19,898,671
Value of total Exports (including £1,944,668 bullion and specie)	14,128,515

Total number, tonnage and value of cargoes of all vessels entered and cleared at ports in Spain and the Balearic Islands in 1864 :—Vessels entered, 10,487 ; tonnage, 1,681,312 ; total value, £19,898,671. Vessels cleared, 8,565 ; tonnage, 1,455,038 ; total value, £14,128,515. Length of railways open for traffic in 1864, 2,524 English miles ; the total amount of capital raised for their construction was £51,304,725, the entire revenue derived from which amounted to £2,985,916. The whole of the railways belong to private companies ; but nearly all have obtained guarantees or "subventions" from the Government, which pay 6 per cent.

Regal Government, at present in abeyance. During the interregnum, the management of the State is conducted by a Junta or provisional government.

Envoy Extraordinary and Minister Plenipotentiary, ... Mansfield Street.
First Secretary of Legation, Don Gorgoino Petano.
Second Ditto, Don Luis del Arco.
Attachés, Don José Delavat and Marquis de Sof-raga.
Consul-General, Don Urbano Montejo, 5, Jeffreys Square.

CUBA, the largest of the West India Islands, belonging to Spain, situate between 19° 50'—23° 10' N. lat. and 74° 10'—85° W. long., measuring 750 miles in length, with an average breadth of 50 or 60 miles, has an area of 48,489 square miles, with a population of 1,359,238, of whom 764,750 are whites, 225,938 free blacks, 368,550 slaves. The country is generally mountainous, but great fertility exists in the valleys, and in many parts the sides of the mountains are covered with dense forests. The chief products, which for the most part comprise its exports, are ginger, long pepper, and all spices; aloes, mastic, cassia, manioc, maize, cocoa, bananas, wax, honey, rum, potatoes, and yams. Tobacco grows to great perfection; also the sugar-cane, coffee, cotton, and indigo. The chief imports are cod-fish, flour, rice, jerked beef, olive-oil, &c. The mineral products consist of iron, copper (which abounds in the copper mountains), coal, and limestone. In addition to Havana, the capital and chief port, it has several large towns which communicate with each other by railway. Number and tonnage of all vessels entered and cleared at the port of Havana in 1855:—Vessels entered 1,543, of which 400 were British; tonnage, 429,385, of which 124,208 was British. Vessels cleared, 1,400, of which 366 were British; tonnage, 387,328, of which 113,772 was British.

PORTO RICO, one of the Spanish West India Islands, lying between 17° 55'—18° 30' N. lat. and 65° 40'—67° 10' W. long., comprising an area of 3,969 square miles, with a population in 1864 of 615,574, of whom 323,032 are whites, 249,900 free blacks, and 42,642 slaves. The island is remarkably fertile, and beautifully diversified with woods, hills, and valleys. It produces all the different fruits which are common in the West Indies, sugar, tobacco of the finest quality, and cotton remarkable for its length of fibre, tenacity and whiteness. Cattle and sheep are extensively reared. There were in the island in 1864 553 sugar estates, 335 distilleries, 57 cattle estates, 54 tobacco, and 53 coffee plantations, and 10 tanneries. Its imports, the value of which in 1865 amounted to £2,230,119, consist of cotton, woollen, linen, silk, and embroidered goods; metals, hardware, provisions, as ale, porter, wine, fruits, &c. Its exports, the value of which in 1865 amounted to £1,026,413, consist chiefly of sugar, molasses, coffee, tobacco, cotton, rum, hides, and cattle. San Juan (commonly called Porto Rico) is the chief port and capital of the island. Number, tonnage and value of cargoes of all vessels entered and cleared at the ports of San Juan and Ponce, 1864: Vessels entered, 806, of which 201 were British; tonnage, 102,400, of which 32,744 was British. Value, £1,254,578, of which £209,345 was British. Vessels cleared, 801, of which 200 were British; tonnage, 101,962, of which 31,623 was British. Value, £461,695, of

which £198,250 was British. A series of railways is being constructed throughout the island.

PHILIPPINE ISLANDS, a group of islands in the Asiatic Archipelago, to the N. of Borneo and the Celebes, in 5° 30'—19° 40' N. lat. and 117° 15'—126° 5' E. long., three-fourths of which belong to Spain, comprising an area of 52,647 square miles, with a population of 2,679,500. Immense forests spread over the islands, clothing the mountains to their summits with ebony, iron-wood, cedar, sapan-wood, gum-trees, &c. There is a great variety of fruit trees, including the orange, citron, breadfruit, mango, cocoa-nut, guava, tamarind, &c., other important products of the vegetable kingdom being the banana, plantain, pine-apple, sugar-cane, cotton, tobacco, indigo, coffee, cocoa, cinnamon, vanilla, &c., with rice, wheat, maize, and various other cereals. Gold is found in river beds and detrital deposits, and is used as a medium of exchange. In Mindanao, iron is plentiful, copper, quicksilver, sulphur in unlimited quantity, and saltpetre. There are also fine coal beds. The manufactures consist of government Manilla cigars, cigar-cases, beautiful mats in different colours, and hats from fibres, earthenware, &c.; and domestic weaving, such as fabrics of silk, cotton, abaca or Manilla hemp, and very fine shawls and handkerchiefs from the fibre of pine-apple-leaves (these are called "piñas," and often sell for two ounces of gold each), is pursued by the females. The principal imports are cotton, woollen, and silk goods, agricultural implements, watches, jewellery, &c. The chief exports are sugar, tobacco, cigars, indigo, abaca (of which 25,000 tons are annually exported), coffee, rice, dyewoods, hides, gold-dust, and bees-wax. Total value of imports in 1864, £2,679,052. Total value of exports, £2,296,178. Manilla is the capital of the Spanish possessions, of which alone we have treated.

Madrid, Envoy Extra. and Min. Plenipot. at, Sir J. T. Fiennes Crampton, Bart., K.C.B., £5,500.
Secretary of Legation and Minis. Plenip. at, £700.
Second Secretary, John Walsham, Esq., £350.
Alicante, Consul at, Col. Benj. Barrie, £400.
Barcelona, Consul at, James Hannay, Esq., £800.
Bilbao, Consul at, Horace Young, Esq., £550.
Cadiz, Cons. at, Alex. Graham Dunlop, Esq., £800.
Carthagena, Consul at, E. J. Turner, Esq., £400.
Corunna (Galicia), Consul at, F. Glennie, Esq., £650.
Fernando Po (W. Coast Africa), Consul at, Chas. Livingstone, Esq., £700.
Havana (Cuba), Consul-Gen. and Commiss. Judge at, W. W. F. Synge, Esq., £1,800.
Trinidad de Cuba, Vice-Consul at, Charles T. Bidwell, £300.
Malaga (Andalusia), Consul at, W. Penrose Mark, Esq., £400.
Manilla (Philippine Isles), Consul at, George T. Ricketts. Esq., £1,150.
Vice do., W. Graham Kerr, Esq., £300.
Sual, Vice-Consul at, José de Bosch, £400.
Iloilo, Vice-Cons. at, Nicholas Loney, Esq., £400.
Palma (Balearic Isles), Consul at, James R. Graham, Esq., £300.
Porto Rico, Consul at, H. A. Cowper, Esq., £850.
Seville (Andalusia), Consul at, Manuel J. Williams, Esq., £300.
Teneriffe (Canary Isles), Henry Colley Grattan, Esq., £550.

SWEDEN AND NORWAY (SCANDINAVIA.)

The kingdoms of Sweden and Norway, now united under one sovereign, embrace between them the entire north-western peninsula of Europe, usually called Scandinavia, situate between lat. 55° 22'—71° 12' N., and long. 4° 50'—31° 15' E., bounded by the Gulf of Bothnia, the Atlantic, and partly by the Baltic. The KINGDOM OF SWEDEN is divided into 25 Governments or Län, and comprises an area of 168,042 square miles, with a population of 4,200,000, who, with the exception of (in 1862) 381 Roman Catholics, 1,208 Jews, and probably about 14 Mormons, are all Protestants, the great bulk of whom are generally well educated. Four-fifths of the population are devoted to agriculture, though but very few are owners of the land they are cultivating. The coast line, deeply indented with bays and fjords or firths, is about 1,400 miles in extent. The country, for the most part mountainous, may be divided into three separate districts—the northern and central are mining, the southern is agricultural. The lakes are exceedingly numerous, nearly one-eighth of the country being covered by them; Lake Wener occupying an area of 2,120 square miles. Lake Wetter, and Lake Maeler, being the principal. The climate is favourable to the growth of grain. The principal articles of cultivation are, in addition to the various cereals, potatoes, hemp, flax, tobacco, hops, which are generally grown in sufficient quantities for home consumption. The forests are very extensive, covering a fourth part of the surface of the country, and consisting of pine, beech, fir; these are of great importance, as supplying not only pitch and tar, but also, in the absence of coal, the chief fuel. The mineral products are extremely rich; copper in abundance, iron of superior quality, that known as the Dannemora iron being converted into the finest steel; gold and silver in small proportions; lead, nickel, zinc, cobalt, alum, sulphur, porphyry, marble, and some coal of very inferior quality. Mining forms an important branch of industry, about 25,000 persons being engaged in the iron trade. The manufactures, employing about 100,000 persons, are confined chiefly to those of domestic use, consisting of woollens, cottons, linens, paper, sugar, tobacco. Tanning is carried on to some extent, also shipbuilding. The chief articles of import are coffee, coals, sugar, rice, tobacco, and other ordinary Colonial produce, window glass, yarn, wool, cotton, hides, salt, spirits, manure, and machinery. The chief articles of export are cattle, wheat, rye, oats, iron, timber, copper, cobalt, alum, hemp, homespun linen, leather, furs, paper, tobacco, pitch, tar, &c.

The annual Revenue of Sweden, in

1868, amounted to	£2,025,626
Annual Expenditure	2,305,173
Total amount of Public Debt	3,600,000
Total value of Imports 1865 (including £36,443 Bullion and Specie)	5,831,277
Total value of Exports (including £507 Bullion and Specie)	6,004,777
Value of Imports of home produce from the U. Kingdom into Sweden, 1865	1,700,000
Value of Exports from Sweden to the United Kingdom	3,000,000

Total number and tonnage of Swedish vessels belonging to Sweden in 1865: vessels 3,155; tonnage, 292,334 tons. Total number and tonnage of all vessels entered and cleared, with cargoes, at ports in Sweden, 1865: vessels entered, 4,946 with a tonnage of 636,194 tons; vessels cleared, 9,458, with a tonnage of 1,535,772.

Sweden possesses one colony in the West Indies, the Island of St. Bartholomew, which is distant about 30 miles from St. Christopher (or St. Kitt's), the area of which is about 35 square miles, with a population of about 2,800. It produces sugar, tobacco, cotton, and cocoa.

The army of Sweden consists of four distinct classes of troops: the national militia, numbering 33,450 rank and file; the conscription troops numbering 95,300; the enlisted troops (to which belong the royal guards, hussars, and artillery), numbering 8,700; militia of Gothland numbering about 8,000. The coast is protected by several fortresses, each having small garrisons. The navy, in 1866, consisted of 2 screw steamers, 350-horse power, and 72 guns each; 3 screw frigates of 250-horse power, and 10 guns; 8 corvettes, containing 6 guns each, 6 of which are iron clad; 125 gun boats, from 60 to 70-horse power; and a turret ship, after the American model, and others are building. The navy, when fully manned, comprises 34,578 sailors, marines, &c

There are 432 miles of railway opened in Sweden, the construction of which cost £42,907 per mile; the total receipts whereof in 1865 amounted to £248,880; the working expenses, £148,736; leaving a net revenue of £100,144.

NORWAY,

A conjoint kingdom and sovereignty with Sweden, is about 1,100 miles in length, and its greatest width 250. It comprises an area of 121,779 square miles, and a population of 1,701,478. It is divided into 18 provinces or amts; the coast line is extensive, and deeply indented with fjords. The surface of the country is uneven, comprising a succession of mountains and valleys. A large extent of the mountain districts produces only lichens, mosses, and hardy berry-yielding plants; the Scotch fir, spruce, and birch cover extensive tracts, and constitute the chief wealth of the country, the value of which in some years exceeds £1,000,000; the hardier fruits, as strawberries, cherries, raspberries, &c., are abundant, and very good. Agriculture, though pursued with some vigour of late, is still unable to furnish sufficient produce for home consumption; hence it has been necessary to import considerable quantities of corn and potatoes. Flax and hemp are raised in some parts of the country; in others, barley and oats. Next in importance to the timber trade are the fisheries, which give employment to about 16,000 men, from January to April, the duration of the cod fishery, off the Loffoden Islands; the number of boats engaged therein, including 300 larger vessels, being about 2,600. The quantity of fish taken often exceeds 16,000,000, realizing an average value of £375,000. In some years the herring fishery on the south-west coast is even more remunerative, from 500,000 to 600,000 tons of fish being not unfrequently caught; hence the collective fisheries may be estimated to produce an annual return of £1,050,000. In Finmarken the reindeer forms the only wealth and source of subsistence of the inhabitants. The mineral products are similar to those of Sweden. Shipbuilding, in all its branches, is almost the only industrial art that is extensively and actively prosecuted, and in the long winter the Norwegians employ their compulsory leisure in weaving, spinning, and making articles of clothing, and the domestic implements required in their households. The imports consist chiefly of the necessary articles of consumption, as corn, salt, fresh and salted meat, butter, oil, wine, tobacco, hemp, flax, sailcloth, and manufactured goods of all descriptions. The chief exports consist mainly of timber, salmon, lobsters, minerals, furs, feathers, down, and Wenham Lake (so called) ice. The navy consists of 150 vessels of war, with 500 guns, and 4,000 men, exclusive of the naval reserve. The regular army consists of 12,000 troops.

Total amount of Revenue, 1866 ....£1,073,250
Expenditure 1,073,250
Public Debt.................................... 1,854,157

Number of merchant vessels belonging to Norway in 1866, 5,407; tonnage, 705,898. Total number and tonnage of all vessels entered and cleared at ports in Norway, 1866 : — Vessels entered, 12,457, of which 537 were British; tonnage, 1,349,394, of which 55,790 were British. Vessels cleared, 12,271, of which 547 were British; tonnage, 1,296,160, of which 55,384 were British.

The principal seats of trade are Christiana, Drammen, Bergen, Stavanger, and Trondhjem. Stockholm is the capital of Sweden, and seat of Government of the United Kingdoms; Christiana is the chief city and capital of Norway.

Reigning Sovereign, Charles XV., King of Sweden and Norway, born 3rd May, 1826; married 19th June, 1850, Louise, eldest daughter of Prince Frederick of the Netherlands.
Min. of Foreign Affairs, Count C. Wachtmeister.
Envoy Extraordinary and Minister Plenipotentiary, Baron Hochschild, 2, Gt. Cumberland Street.
Secretary of Legation, Count de le Gardie.
Consul-General, Charles Tottie, Esq., 2, Alderman's Walk, New Broad Street.
Stockholm—Envoy Extraordinary, and Minister Plenipo., Hon. G. S. S. Jerningham £3,400.
Secretary of Legation, Hon. Nassau Jocelyn, £500.
Second Secretary, W. G. Sandford, Esq., £250.
Consul, Gerald R. Perry, Esq., £550.
Gottenburg, Consul, C. F. Engström, Esq., £400.
Christiana (Norway) Consul-General, John R. Crowe, Esq., C.B., £900.

SWITZERLAND, (THE REPUBLIC).

The Helvetia of the Romans, a country of Central Europe, situated between 45° 50'—47° 50' N. lat., and 5° 58' — 10° 30' E. long. It is divided into 25 Cantons, and comprises a total area of 15,991 English square miles, with a population of 2,510,494, who are nearly divided between Roman Catholics and Protestants ; the number of other sects and Jews being about 5,000 each. It is the most mountainous country in Europe, having the Alps, averaging from 5,000 to nearly 16,000 feet in height, not only along the whole of its southern and eastern frontiers, but throughout the chief part of its interior. Mont Cervin, Mont Rosa, the Jungfrau, Mont Blanc, Mont St. Gothard, Great St. Bernard, are the chief, besides others less familiarly known. Of the valleys, the most remarkable is that of the Rhone. Rich cornfields and luxuriant pastures, extend along the base of many of these mountains. The rivers are numerous but rapid, consequently, for the most part, unnavigable; as the Rhone, Rhine, Ticino, Reuss, the Aar, &c., with their tributaries. The lakes are equally numerous and beautiful, as well as of great depth; the principal are those of Geneva, Leman, Constance, Neufchatel, Lucerne, Thun,

Zurich, &c. Agriculture is followed chiefly in the valleys, where wheat, oats, maize, barley, flax, hemp, and tobacco are produced. The fruits consist of grapes, peaches, prunes, cherries, walnuts, and chestnuts. The pastoral districts produce cheese, butter, tallow, and hides, which form the chief articles of export. The mountain pastures form full two-fifths of the whole available surface and supply the chief occupations of the people, herdsmen and shepherds. It is estimated that there are upwards of 1,000,000 horned cattle, one-fourth of which consist of milch cows, the produce of the dairy being valued at £1,500,000 annually. Sheep are of an inferior breed, and their wool coarse ; goats are numerous and fine. In Vaud and Neufchatel the vine is successfully cultivated, and in the Thurgau, and on the shores of Lake Constance, there are extensive orchards, where cider and kirschwasser (a species of cherry brandy) are prepared, the latter being a liquor largely consumed in Switzerland, and much prized elsewhere. The rivers and lakes abound with fine fish, more especially trout.

The forests cover about one-sixth of the whole surface, and, where the houses, or chalets, are chiefly built of wood, and coal is not procurable for fuel, wood-cutting becomes an important branch of industry. The mineral kingdom furnishes silver, copper, iron, lead. Marble, porphyry, alabaster, and sulphur, are occasionally found in the mountains ; also rock-salt. The principal salt-springs are at Bex, in the valley of the Rhone ; beside these, there are many mineral springs.

The manufactures consist chiefly of linen, lace, thread, woollens, and cottons; clocks and watches have long been the staple products of Geneva and Nenfchatel ; while leather, silks, gloves, porcelain, pottery, tobacco and snuff, cheese, sugar, &c., are made Beside its two universities (Basle and Geneva,) it has several colleges and schools of high repute. The principal articles of import are corn and pulse flour, wine, sugar, molasses, salt, raw cotton, coal and coke, iron raw and in plates, railway carriages, &c. The principal exports are woods of all kinds, rough, sawn, and cut, charcoal, cheese, raw cotton, cotton-yarn and twist, cotton cloths and stuffs, &c.

The military establishment consists of four classes : the Federal army, numbering 87,730 men ; the army of reserve, 49,765; the landwehr or militia, 65,359; the landsturm or army of defence, 150,000; making a total of 352,854 troops.

Total estimated amount of Revenue, £
1866 767,000
Total estimated amount of Expenditure 776,600
Total official value of Imports, 1865...... 210,440
 „   „   „   280,358

The government is vested in a parliament, consisting of two chambers, a state council of 44 members, and a federal council of 128 members ; both chambers united are called the Federal Assembly. The President and Vice-President are the chief magistrates of the republic ; the former has a salary of £400 per annum, the other £340. Both are annually elected.

President of Federal Council, Dr. J. Dubs, *Zurich.*
Vice-President Ditto Emile Welti, *Argovia.*
President of Federal Assembly, S. Kaiser, *Soleure.*
Vice President Ditto E. Borel, *Neufchatel.*
Agent and Consul-General, London, John Rapp, Esq., 21, Old Broad Street.

Berne, *Envoy Extraordinary and Minister Plenipotentiary, at*, Alfred G. G. Bonar, Esq. £2800.
Secretary of Legation, R. P. French, Esq. £400.
Geneva, *Consul at*, A. Mackenzie, Esq. Unpaid.

TURKEY (THE OTTOMAN EMPIRE),

Comprehending all the countries under the authority of the Sultan—Turkey in Europe, Turkey in Asia, Roumania (Wallachia and Moldavia), comprising altogether 1,857,690, with a population of 37,930,000, consisting of several races, viz., Turks, Greeks, Armenians, Jews, Sclaves, Roumains, and Albanians (in Europe alone), Tartars, Arabs, Druses, Kurds, Turcomans, Tsiganes; and various religions, as Mussulman, Greeks, Armenians, Roman Catholics, Jews, &c. Turkey in Europe and Turkey in Asia are designated "Turkey Proper."

TURKEY IN EUROPE, the smaller of the two divisions of Turkey Proper, is bounded by the Austrian and Russian dominions, and situated in 39°—48° 20′ N. latitude and 15° 40′ —30° E. longitude, containing an area of 207,438 square miles, and, including the Principalities, a population of 17,030,000. It is subdivided into nine provinces: Roumelia, Thessaly, Albania, Herzegovinia, Montenegro, Bosnia, Croatia, Bulgaria, Servia, with Moldavia and Wallachia. The soil is for the most part fertile, but owing to the oppressive system of taxation, long in force, little progress has been made in agriculture. The cultivated products are maize, rice, cotton, rye, barley, millet; the natural products are the pine, beech, oak, lime, and ash, with the apple, pear, cherry, and apricot in the basin of the Danube; the palm, maple, sycamore, walnut, chestnut, carob, box, myrtle, laurel, &c., south of the Balkan; large forests of pine and fir in the north-west; the olive, orange, citron, vine, peach, plum, and others in Albania; and abundance of roses in the valley of the Maritza. The mineral products are iron in abundance, lead ore blended with silver, copper, sulphur, salt, alum, but no coal. Its manufactures are unimportant and almost entirely domestic, such as woollen and cotton stuffs, shawls, leather, firearms; with dyeing and printing works. Constantinople is the capital of Turkey in Europe, as also of the Empire and has a population variously estimated at from 960,000 to 1,100,000.

TURKEY IN ASIA, the larger of the two divisions, is situated in lat. 30°—42° N., and long. 26°—48° E., and comprises an area of 660,870 square miles, with a population of 16,050,000 inhabitants. It is divided into several districts —Anatolia or Asia Minor, Armenia, Kurdistan, Mesopotamia, and Syria, including Palestine.

The military force of Turkey is divided into— 1st, the regular active army, called "Nizam;" 2nd, the reserve, or "Redif;" 3rd, the contingents of auxiliaries, consisting of the tributary provinces of Wallachia, &c.; 4th, the irregular troops, numbering altogether 459,360 troops, on a peace footing. The navy, which has been entirely remodelled within the last ten years, consists of about 60 vessels, manned by 34,000 sailors, and 4,000 marines.

	£
Total estimated amount of the public Revenue of the Turkish Empire, 1865	14,589,855
Total estimated amount of Expenditure	14,425,525
Public debt	69,142,270
Annual charge thereon	4,807,342

Value of Imports and Exports to and from the various ports in Turkey:—

	Imports.	Exports.
Smyrna (1865)	£2,271,221	£4,046,338
Rhodes (1866)	1,295,218	185,582
Aleppo (1866)	1,276,486	538,772
Salonica (1865)	732,975	1,193,311
Scio (1864)	225,073	164,264
Mytilene (1864)	121,949	187,392
Cyprus (1866)	158,711	290,323
Scala Nuova (1864)	44,900	167,400

Number and tonnage of all vessels entered and cleared at the several ports of Turkey, 1865:—

CONSTANTINOPLE. — Entered 21,122 vessels, tonnage 3,741,706; cleared 20,741 vessels, tonnage 3,743,623.

SMYRNA. — Entered 1,543 vessels, tonnage 496,601, value £2,271,221; cleared 1,532 vessels, tonnage 494,770, value £4,046,338; of which 174 vessels, tonnage 115,713, value £1,053,924, entered; and 181 vessels, tonnage 116,862, value £2,320,652, cleared, were British.

RHODES.—Entered and cleared, 752 vessels, tonnage 265,073.

SCIO.—Entered 1,788 vessels, tonnage 206,487, value £255,073; cleared 1,724 vessels, tonnage 198,495, value £164,264.

MYTILENE.—Entered 1,624 vessels, tonnage 156,450, value £121,950; cleared 1,689 vessels, tonnage 159,303, value £187,392.

SALONICA. — Entered 746 vessels, tonnage 173,335; cleared 750 vessels, tonnage 174,807.

CYPRUS.—Entered 728 vessels, tonnage 170,252, value £159,103; cleared 723, tonnage 170,799, value £291,361.

Reigning Sovereign, Abdul Aziz, Sultan of Turkey, born 9th February, 1830.

Minister for Foreign Affairs, His Highness Fuad Pasha.

Ambassador Extraordinary and Plenipotentiary, Musurus Pasha, 1, Bryanstone Square.

First Secretary, Stephen Musurus Bey.

Seed. Secs., Ashmed Tia Bey & Paul Musurus Bey.

Chancellor, Henry Trewby, Esq.

Consul General, M. Paul Gadban, Ethelburga House, 71, Bishopsgate Street Within.

Constantinople—*Ambassador Extraordinary and Plenipotentiary*, Hon. Henry G. Elliott, £8,000.

Secretary of Embassy, H. P. T. Barron, Esq. £900.

Oriental Secretary of Legation, Thomas Fiott Hughes, Esq., £600.

Second Secretary, Lionel Moore, Esq., £400.

Consul General and Judge of Supreme Court, Levant, Sir Philip Francis, £1,500.

Vice-Consul, Law Secretary, and Registrar, James Lane, Esq., £450.

Aleppo—*Consul*, James Henry Skene, Esq., £700.

Bagdad—*Cons. Gen.*, Col. Sir A. B. Kemball, C.B.

Belgrade (Servia)—*Consul General*, I. A. Longworth, Esq., C.B., £1,300.

Beyrout (Syria)—*Consul General*, George J. Eldridge, Esq., £1,250.

Bosnia—*Consul*, W. R. Holmes, Esq., £900.

Bucharest (Wallachia)—*Agent and Consul General*, John Green, Esq., C.B., £1,500.

Crete—*Consul*, Charles H. Dickson, Esq. £620.

Damascus—*Consul*, Edward Thos. Rogers, Esq., £850.

Dardanelles—*Consul*, £450.

Erzeroum (Kurdistan)—*Consul*, John G. Taylor, Esq., £900.

Galatz—*Consul*, G. Bourchier Ward, Esq., £900.

Janina (Yanina), Albania—*Consul*, Major Robert Stuart, £1,050.

Jassy—*Consul*, A. B. St. Clair, Esq., £600.

Jerusalem—Cons., Noel Temple Moore, Esq., £950.

Monastir—Consul, Chas. John Calvert, Esq., £800.

Adrianople—Vice-Cons., Jno. E. Blunt, Esq., £500.

Roustchouk—Consul, Sir R. A. O. Dalyell, Bart., £850.

Salonica—Consul, Richard Wilkinson, Esq., £600.

Scutari—Consul, Richard Reade, Esq., £700.

Smyrna—Consul, R. W. Cumberbatch, Esq., £900.

Trebizonde—Consul, W. Gifford Palgrave, Esq., £650.

ROUMANIA (Wallachia, Moldavia, and Bessarabian Provinces).

WALLACHIA, a province in the north-east of European Turkey, and the larger of the two Danubian Principalities, comprises an area of 27,500 English square miles, containing 36 towns, 3,325 villages, with a population of 2,400,920. Bucharest is the capital. The soil is amongst the richest in Europe, and but for the ravages of the locust and the fearful summer droughts, would be also the most productive. The climate is extreme—summer heats and winter colds are intense. The agricultural produce consists of corn, maize, millet, beans, and pease. Vines and fruits of various kinds are abundant, but its chief wealth consists in the pastures, which feed numerous herds of cattle and sheep. Excellent wool is exported. The forests are very extensive. The imports are chiefly the manufactured goods of Western Europe, and the exports wool, lambs' skins, hides, feathers, maize, tar, tallow, honey, salt in block, and cattle. The military force amounts 25,000 men.

MOLDAVIA, the lesser of the two Danubian principalities, situated in the N.E. extremity of European Turkey, comprises, with the new Bessarabian provinces, an area of 18,482 English square miles, containing 36 towns, of which Jassy is the chief, and 2,016 villages, with a population of 1,463,927 inhabitants. The soil, like that of Wallachia, is fertile in the extreme, but possesses also the like drawbacks, together with great lack of cultivation; nevertheless it produces large quantities of grain, fruit, and wine. The forests are of great extent and importance, but the riches of the country consist mainly in its cattle, sheep, and horses, of which immense numbers are reared on its far-stretching pastures. Owing to the multitude of lime trees, bees are extensively reared. Minerals and precious metals are said to be abundant. Trade, the great centre of which is at Galatz, is almost exclusively in the hands of Jews, Armenians, and Greeks, who have settled there. The imports and exports are similar to those of Wallachia. Moldavia has no manufactures except some for home consumption. The military force amounts to 18,000 men. The estimated revenue for the Principality of Roumania in 1866, was £1,988,752; expenditure, £2,191,846; public debt, £2,926,002.

Total value of imports and exports of Moldo-Wallachia in 1865:—Imports, £2,572,409; exports, £4,526,138; value of imports of home produce from United Kingdom 1866, £185,598; value of exports to United Kingdom, £441,628.

Quantities of produce of principal articles exported in 1865:—Wheat 1,376,667 qrs., rye 118,186 qrs., maize 901,969 qrs., barley 365,313 qrs., oats 13,100 qrs., millet 26,043 qrs., flour 105,335 cwt., tallow 4,677 cwt., planks 390,784, staves 333,313.

Total number and tonnage of all vessels cleared from the mouth of the Danube, 1865:—

2,676 vessels, of which 213 were British, and 442,229 tons, of which 64,155 were British.

Hospodar, or Prince of Roumania, Charles, second son of the late Prince Charles of Hohenzollern-Sigmaringen, born 20 April, 1839, elected 10 May, 1866, confirmed 11 July, 1866.

UNITED STATES OF AMERICA,

A Federal Republic consisting of 36 partially independent States, (6 Eastern or New England, 4 Middle, 11 Southern, and 15 Western) and 9 organized Territories, occupies the central portion of North America from lat. 24° 30'—49° N., and long. 66° 50'—124° 30' W. The area is variously estimated at from 2,800,000 to 3,000,000 English square miles, or, 1,921,288,233 acres. This supposed area, however, is exclusive of the vast district known as "Russian America" or Alaska, lately purchased of the Russian Government. Only one-fourth of the country is to any great extent in a state of civilization. The population at the last census, in 1860, consisted of 26,975,575 white, 488,005 free coloured, and 3,953,760 slave inhabitants, making a total of 51,445,089; since which period, to the end of 1866, according to a careful enumeration by the Bureau of Statistics, the population has advanced to 34,505,882, being an increase that has occurred chiefly in the Western States, the Southern States having been greatly depopulated by the late civil war.

Though occupying the central portion of a continent, more than two-thirds of the frontiers are shores of lakes and oceans with numerous bays and sounds, rivers and lakes; the coast-line, inclusive of these bays, &c., is estimated at about 33,000 miles. The principal bays are the Chesapeake, Delaware, and Massachusetts. The principal rivers are the Mississippi and the Missouri, which traverse the country from their sources in the highlands of Minnesota, till they fall into the Gulf of Mexico, a distance of 4500 miles; the Hudson, Delaware, Potomac, Connecticut, Merrimac, Susquehanna, and others emptying themselves into the Atlantic, or its bays and sounds; the Alabama, Colorado, Rio Grande, Tombigbee, and others, which, together with the Mississippi, empty themselves into the Gulf of Mexico; the Oregon, Sacramento, San Joaquim, and others emptying themselves into the Pacific. Beside these are many small rivers emptying into the great lakes, and finding their outlet through the St. Lawrence; with others which empty into the salt-lakes of Utah. The principal lakes, (beside those divided with British America), are, Lake Michigan, the Great Salt Lake, Lake Champlain, Pyramid Lake, and many smaller lakes in Maine, New York, Minnesota, &c. The water-slopes have been estimated as follows: the Pacific slope 766,000 square miles; the Atlantic, lake and gulf slope, east and west of the Mississippi, 955,000 square miles; the Mississippi valley, drained by the Mississippi and its tributaries, 1,218,000 square miles. The chief mountains are those comprising the great chain of the Alleghanies, extending 900 miles in length, from near the mouth of the St. Lawrence to the confines of Georgia, and are nearly 200 miles in breadth; and the Rocky Mountains, which rise to an elevation of 9,000 feet. The soil is of every variety, from the sterile deserts of the great Western plains and Utah, to the inexhaustible fertility of the Mississippi valley, to the east of which, save in Illinois and Indiana vast forests of valuable timber exist, as beech, birch, maple, oak, pine, spruce, elm, ash, walnut; and to the South, live oak, water-oak, magnolia, palmetto, tulip-tree, cypress, &c. The mineral kingdom produces in great abundance, copper, iron, coal, lime, salt; as also lead, which, in Missouri, appears inexhaustible; there are also rich lead mines in Illinois and Wisconsin. In California, beside silver, iron, copper and lead, gold is found in great abundance; quicksilver is found in Kentucky, also coal, the supply of which is said to be equal to any country in the world; the coal formation extending on the western side of the mountains from Lake Ontario to the river Tombigbee, a distance of 800 miles. Nitre, more than sufficient for the whole States, is found in Kentucky, Tennessee, and Virginia. The salt-springs are so numerous and copious in their produce as to appear almost inexhaustible. In a country so extensive there must, of necessity, be a considerable diversity of agriculture, which holds the first place in the national industry. Wheat is cultivated from one extremity of the Union to the other. Maize, or Indian corn which is indigenous to America, is cultivated to the greatest advantage in the middle and Western States. Tobacco is cultivated in Maryland, and continued throughout the Southern States, also partially in the Western. Cotton and rice are the great staples of all the Southern States, and the leading exports of the Union. The sugar-cane grows in low and warm situations. Oats, rye, and barley are raised in all the Northern and in the upper districts of the Southern States. Hay, hops, potatoes, hemp, flax, silk, madder, and indigo, are also abundantly produced. The climate is generally favourable to the production of fruits, which abound throughout the whole extent of the territories. In the Northern States, apples, pears, cherries, peaches, currants, gooseberries, plums, &c., are afforded in great abundance. Towards the South the fruits which flourish best are pears, pomegranates and water-melons, which grow to an enormous size, and are probably superior to any in the world. The other fruits are figs, apricots, nectarines, olives, almonds, oranges, lemons, limes, and citrons, which abound in the Southern States. In the pine barrens, grapes grow to a large size, and are of excellent flavour. The vine grows spontaneously in most of the Southern and Western States. Hops also are raised in the middle and Western States; the mulberry tree grows spontaneously. In 1860 there were 409,849,633 acres occupied as farms, the average size of which (nearly all held by their cultivators in fee simple) was 199 acres; in New England, 96 acres; in the Southern States, 320 acres. The cultivated land was estimated at 163,261,389 acres; of which 33,000,000 were occupied with hay and pasturage, 31,000,000 with maize or Indian corn, 11,000,000 with wheat, 7,500,000 with oats, 5,000,000 with cotton, 1,200,000 with rye, 1,000,000 with peas and beans, 1,000,000 ordinary potatoes, 750,000 with sweet potatoes, 690,000 with buckwheat, 400,000 with tobacco, 400,000 with sugar cane, 300,000 with barley, 175,000 with rice, 110,000 with hemp, 100,000 with flax, 500,000 as orchards, 500,000 as gardens, 250,000 as vineyards, and 1,000,000 with miscellaneous crops. There were of plantations of cotton, producing 5 bales and upwards, 74,031; of rice, producing 20,000 lbs., 551; of tobacco, producing 3,000 lbs. and upwards, 15,745. The quantities of the chief agricultural productions of 1865 were, Indian corn, 704,427,000 bushels; wheat, 148,553,000; rye, 19,543,000; barley, 11,391,000; oats, 225,000,000; buckwheat, 18,000,000; potatoes,

101,000,000; hay, 23,538,740 tons; tobacco, 183,317,000 lbs. Seeds distributed gratis by the Department of the Interior—763,231 packages. In 1865, 557,212 acres of the public land (the aggregate of which is estimated at 1,400,524,033 acres) were sold by the Government Land Office, for the most part at the ordinary price of 1¼ dollar per acre. Vast quantities of land impoverished, exhausted, and abandoned, have, by improved systems of agriculture under Government assistance, been reclaimed, and are again productive.

The chief imports are coffee, cotton, raw and manufactured linens, lead, rice, silk, soda, sugar, tea, tobacco, wool and woollen materials, gold and silver coin and bullion. The principal exports—and those chiefly to the United Kingdom—are whale and spermaceti oil, beef, tallow, hides, hams and bacon, butter, cheese, pork, wheat, flour, Indian corn, meal, cotton, rye, tobacco, in leaf and manufactured, hops, candles, tea, and sugar.

At the commencement of 1861, prior to the desolating war, the United States army consisted of 14,000 regular troops. The total number called into the field by the Federal side from 1861 till the end of the war in 1865 amounted to 2,653,062, or nearly one-fourth of the entire population of the Northern States. The Southern, or Confederate States, had in the field during the greater part of the war 400,000, three-fourths of whom, it is estimated, they lost from disease and wounds; the residue were entirely disbanded in April, 1865. Of the Northern army there remained 210,000 on the pay-rolls on 1st August, 1865. Since 1st December, 1867, the number of troops in the regular army consisted of 1,570 officers and 47,820 men, while the nominal strength of the militia force of the United States consisted of 50,110 officers and 2,225,870 men. The naval force of the United States consists of 75 Monitors, 40 screw and paddle, and 112 sailing vessels, carrying in all 4,443 guns, the most remarkable of which are the Colorado, screw frigate, 3,425 tons; Brooklyn, a screw corvette, 2,200 tons; Powhattan, paddle-corvette, 2,400 tons; New Ironsides, iron-clad frigate, 3,486 tons; Roanoke, 3 turrets, 3,435 tons; Dictator, 1 turret, 3,033 tons. The navy, as at present organized, contains 2,048 officers of all ranks (one admiral, one vice do., and 27 rear-admirals), and 13,600 men. The United States possess 8 dockyards, viz., Portsmouth, Charlestown, Brooklyn, Philadelphia, Norfolk, Washington, Pensacola, and Mare Island. The manufactures being protected by high duties on foreign importations, have had a rapid development, those of cotton, woollen, and mixed fabrics, leather in boots and shoes, steam engines and machinery, railway and other carriages, oil cloth, paper, agricultural instruments, india-rubber goods, &c., being the principal. It is estimated that there are 920 manufacturies for the production of cotton fabrics, 2,000 for the production of woollen, and of mixed cotton and woollen fabrics. The plexus of railways throughout the United States consists of 60,000 miles, constructed at a cost of £1,264,336,000, belonging to 511 separate companies.

	£
Estimated Revenue to 30th June, 1868	81,160,000
Estimated Expenditure to 30th June, 1868	76,000,000

Amount of Public Debt on 1st September, 1868, 2,643,256,285 dols. or £550,678,392

Principal ports of United States: New York, Boston, Charleston, Philadelphia, Baltimore, Buffalo Creek, Oswego, San Francisco, and Detroit.

Total registered and enrolled tonnage of the commercial navy of the United States in 1866, 4,310,778 tons. Total tonnage of *all* vessels entered and cleared at ports of the United States in 1865: entered, 2,943,661 American, 3,216,967 Foreign; total, 6,160,628. Cleared, 3,025,134 American, 3,595,123 Foreign; total, 6,620,257. Total number of *all* vessels entered and cleared at ports in the United States 1865: vessels entered, 22,741, of which 793 were British, and 17,279 belonged to British possessions. Vessels cleared, 23,433, of which 802 were British, and 17,718 belonged to British possessions. In 1866, 13,580 British vessels entered with tonnage of 2,793,072 tons. In 1866, 13,936 British vessels cleared with tonnage of 3,096,790 tons. The following are statistics of:

	£
Value of Imports of Merchandize in 1866	89,023,166
Bullion and Specie	2,151,907
Total	91,175,073
Total Value of Imports from Great Britain up to 30th June, 1866, including Bullion and Specie	27,620,898
Total Value of Exports to Great Britain, including Bullion and Specie	40,743,460
Value of Exports of Merchandize 1866	99,553,646
Bullion and Specie	17,925,848
Total	117,479,494

Value of Exports 1867, 834,350,653 dols. or 173,823,952¾
Value of Exports 1858, 352,339,669 dols., or 73,404,097¾
In 1866 the amount of cotton exported was 650,572,829 lbs., value 281,385,223 dols., or 58,621,921½

The value of British produce and manufactures exported to the United States, including California, in 1867, was £21,825,703, against £28,499,514 in 1866, and £15,344,392 in 1863; in the five years 1863-67 the increase was £6,481,311. The value of the principal articles of British produce exported in each of the years 1863 and 1867 respectively was as follows:—Woollens, £3,439,199 and £3,590,681; iron, £2,107,427 and £3,298,289; cotton, £2,155,035 and £3,166,603; linens, £1,282,010 and £2,918,530; tin, £831,779 and £1,477,450; apparel and haberdashery, £800,902 and £972,245; soda, £356,574 and £801,746; hardware and cutlery, £349,447 and 719,269; earthenware and porcelain, £356,329 and 711,349; machinery, £50,037 and £336,484. The value of foreign and colonial produce and manufacture exported to the United States, including California, last year was £2,296,108, against £4,352,393 in 1863. This large decrease in the five years of £2,056,285, is chiefly owing to a falling off in the exports of cotton, wool, and hemp. The value of these exports in each of the years 1863 and 1867 was—raw cotton, £1,391,749 and £16,319; wool, £1,049,919 and £210,293; hemp, £74,441 and £14,311. The value of the imports from the United States, including California, to the United Kingdom was £19,572,033 in 1863 and £41,045,272 in 1867, showing the large increase in the five years of £21,473,239. The value of some of the principal articles exported in each of the years

1863 and 1867 was as follows:—raw cotton, £644,138 and £25,721,079; corn, £7,433,491 and £6,723,963; cheese, £925,007 and 1,470,017; tobacco, unmanufactured, £1,536,145 and £1,079,005; bacon and hams, £2,411,771 and £727,627; lard, 996,675 and £586,324; oilseed cake, £258,013 and £473,602; petroleum, £658,632 and £364,675; tallow, £526,559 and £321,095; rosin, £3,506 and £254,762; oil, £324,207 and £567,749; skins and furs, £201,691 and £231,637. The total amount of the cotton crop in 1867-8 was 2,581,000 bales, and the export 1,656,000 bales, of which 1,229,000 was destined for Great Britain.

Coinage in 1866: Gold, value, 37,429,430 dols.; silver, value, 1,596,646 dols.; copper, value, 646,570 dols. Total value, 39,672,647 dols.

Acreage cultivated in 1867: 58,709,376 acres; value of produce, 1,504,543,690 dollars, or £313,446,602.

Immigrants landing in New York 1865, 195,075, of whom 70,338 were from Ireland, 27,144 from England, 3,961 from Scotland, and 505 from Wales.

The government of the United States is, by the constitution of 1787, entrusted to three separate authorities: the executive, the legislative, and the judicial; the executive being vested in a President, who is elected by the popular vote of all the states, for four years, but eligible for re-election. There is also a Vice-President who is *ex-officio* President of the Senate; and in case the President should die or resign before the expiration of his term of office, assumes the presidency for the remainder of the term. The capital and seat of government is Washington.

President, Andrew Johnson, who succeeded, after the assassination of Abraham Lincoln, in 1865.

President for 1869, Gen. Ulysses S. Grant.
Vice-President for 1869, Schuyler Colfax.
Secretary of State, till March, 1869, W. H. Seward.
Envoy Extra. and Minister Plen., Hon. Reverdy Johnson, 4, Upper Portland Place.
Sec. of Legation, Benj. Moran, Esq., 20, Norfolk Terrace, Westbourne Grove.
Despatch Agent, B. F. Stevens—Offices, 147, Great Portland Street. [Sq.
Consul in London, Freeman H. Morse, 33, Princes
Vice-Consul, Joshua Nunn, 1, Dunster Court, Mincing Lane.
Consul in Liverpool, Thomas H. Dudley.
Washington, Envoy Extra. and Minister Plen. at, Edward Thornton, Esq., C.B., £5,600.
Sec. of Legation, Francis C. Ford, Esq., £700.
Baltimore, Cons. at, H. T. A. Rainals, Esq., £950.
Boston, Consul at, Francis Lousada, Esq., £200.
Buffalo, Cons. at, Henry W. Hemans, Esq., £400.
Charleston, Consul at, Henry P. Walker, Esq., £950.
Chicago, Consul at, John E. Wilkins, Esq., £400.
Galveston, Consul at, Arthur T. Lynn, Esq., £300.
Mobile, Consul at, F. J. Cridland, Esq., £700.
New Orleans, Cons. at, Denis Donahoe, Esq., £700.
New York, Consul at, and Judge, Mixed Court, E. M. Archibald, Esq., C.B., £2,600.
Arbitrator, W. Dudley Ryder, Esq., £800.
Philadelphia, Consul at, C. E. K., Kortright, Esq., £950.
Portland, Consul at, H. J. Murray, Esq., £650.
San Francisco, Consul at, Wm. Lane Brooker, Esq., £1,600.
Savannah, Consul at, Wm. Tasker Smith, Esq., £500.

URUGUAY,

A republic in South America, situate in lat. 30°—35° S., and long. 53° 30'—58° 22' W., containing an area of about 75,000 square miles, and a population of upwards of 250,000. Agriculture is ceasing to be in the backward state it was until very recently. Small quantities of rice, peas, beans, flax, hemp, cotton; wheat, and other cereals are raised; but the wealth of the country is derived from its pasturage, which supports large herds of horned cattle, horses, and sheep, the wool of which is of a superior quality. The principal river is the Uruguay and its affluents, of which the Rio Negro is the chief. The imports consist of woollen goods, household furniture of all kinds, agricultural implements, timber, &c., the chief exports being salted and jerked beef, hides, horn, hair, and tallow to the value of £2,000,000 in the aggregate. The number and tonnage of British vessels entered and cleared at the port of Monte Video (the capital), in 1866, was 257 vessels, tonnage 160,154 entered; 323 vessels, 139,843 tons, cleared. *President*, General Lorenzo Battle.

Consul General at London, Edward Bernard Neill, Esq., 2, Cannon Row, Westminster.

Monte Video, Consul-General and Chargé d'Affaires at, Wm. Garrow Lettsom, Esq., £1,695.

Vice-Consul, Major J. St. John Munro, £500.

WURTEMBURG,

A kingdom of South Germany, situate between 47° 30'—49° 35' N. lat., and 8° 15'—10° 30' E. long., occupying an area of 7,675 English square miles, and having a population, in 1867, of 1,778,479 inhabitants. It possesses rich pastures, cultivated fields, orchards, gardens, and hills covered with vines; the forest, grain, and pasture land, being nearly equally distributed throughout. Wheat, oats, barley, hemp, hops, rye, potatoes, (which form the principal food of one-fourth of the population), beans, maize, turnips, being the principal agricultural products. The extent of land under cultivation in 1864 was 1,812,845 acres (English).

The value of farm produce in 1864 was £11,857,673, and that of the vineyards, £375,029, while the garden and orchard produce, consisting of peaches, apricots, grapes, apples, pears, cherries, damsons, walnuts, &c., was estimated at £350,000. The quantity of wine produced in 1866, was 4,825,600 imperial gallons, value £344,727. The peat lands are extensive, and yield annually £45,000. The minerals, consisting chiefly of cobalt, bismuth, silver, copper, malachite, iron, granite, limestone, ironstone, fireclay, &c., abound in the neighbourhood of the Black Forest; mineral springs are numerous throughout the kingdom. The principal rivers are the Danube and the Neckar. The manufactures generally are linen, woollen, cotton, and silk fabrics, wool and cotton spinning, carpets, porcelain, leather, tobacco, iron and steel goods, cabinet-work, &c. There are many oil mills, breweries, and brandy distilleries.

The principal exports are grain, cattle, wood, salt, oil, leather, woollen, cotton, and linen fabrics, beer, wine, &c. The army on a peace footing consists of 10,581 men, with a war establishment of 26,838. Several railroads, belonging to the State, extending 378 miles, traverse the country; a sum of £5,500,000 has already been sunk in them; and in 1868, a debt of £3,721,000 was incurred for their extension.

Estimated Public Revenue, 1867-70: £

	£
Total for the 3 years	5,304,613
Expenditure for 1867	1,869,260
Total amount of Public Debt, 1868	7,033,911

No return of the value of Imports and Exports. Stuttgardt, containing a population of 69,084, is the capital.

Reigning Sovereign, Charles, King of Würtemburg, born March 6, 1823; married 13th July, 1846, the Grand Duchess Olga of Russia. [Broad-st.

Consul in London, S. Cahlmann, Esq., 28, New *Stuttgardt—Envoy Extraordinary and Minister Plenipotentiary*, G. J. R. Gordon, Esq., £2,300.

Secretary of Legation, E. M. Baillie, Esq., £400.

Foreign Monies and their English Equivalents.

Country.	Chief Coin.	Eng. Value. s. d.	Country.	Chief Coin.	Eng. Value. s. d.
Austria	Florin	1 11	Norway	Rix Dollar	4 6
Belgium	Franc	0 9½	Persia	Tomaun	10 0
Brazil	Milreis	2 3	Portugal	Milrei (about)	4 7
Bremen	Thaler or Dollar	3 3½	Prussia	Thaler or Dol. (abt.)	2 11
Buenos Ayres (Argentine Rep). }	Dollar	3 6	Do.	Groschen	0 1⅛
Canada	Dollar	4 2	Roman States	Lira	0 9½
China	Tael	6 6	Do.	Scudo	4 2
Do.	Dollar (varies)	4 6	Russia	Rouble	3 2
Cuba	Dollar	4 2	Spain	Real Vellon (about)	0 2½
Denmark	Rigsbank Dollar	2 3	Do.	Escudo	2 0
Egypt	Piastre	0 2½	Sweden	Rixdollar	1 1¼
France	Franc	0 9½	Switzerland	Franc	0 9½
Germany } or Zollverein. }	Thaler / Florin	3 0 / 1 8	Turkey	Piastre (nearly)	0 2¼
Greece	Drachma	0 8½	United States of America }	Dollar	4 2
Hamburg	Mark Current	1 3	Uruguay	Dollar	3 6
Do.	Mark Banco	1 6	West Indies, British }	Dollar	4 2
Holland	Florin	1 8			
India	Rupee, nearly	2 0			
Italy	Lira	0 9½			
Japan	Ichibu	1 4½			
Java	Florin	1 8			
Mexico, Chili, Peru }	Dollar (about)	4 2			

In this, as in all British Colonial Possessions, English money is current of each denomination. In the preceding table the equivalent values are given as near as possible, but generally foreign monies are not exactly commensurate with English, as the course of exchange continually varies, affecting consequently the relative values.

The French metrical system is based upon the length of the fourth part of a terrestrial meridian. The ten-millionth part of this arc was chosen as the unit of measures of length, and was called *metre*. The cube of the tenth part of the metre was adopted as the unit of measures of capacity, and denominated *litre*. The weight of distilled water at its greatest density which the litre is capable of containing was called *kilogramme*, of which the thousandth part, under the name *gramme*, was adopted as the unit of weight. The multiples of these measures proceeding in decimal progression are distinguished by the employment of the prefixes *deca, hecto, kilo,* and *myria*, from the Greek, and the subdivisions by *deci, centi,* and *milli,* from the Latin.

MEASURES OF LENGTH.

EQUAL TO	Inches.	Feet.	Yards.	Fathoms.	Miles.
Millimètre	0·03937	0·003281	0·0010936	0·0005468	0·0000006
Centimètre	0·39371	0·032809	0·0109363	0·0054682	0·0000062
Décimètre	3·93708	0·328090	0·1093633	0·0546816	0·0000621
Mètre	39·37079	3·280989	1·0936331	0·5468165	0·0006214
Décamètre	393·70790	32·808992	10·9363306	5·4681653	0·0062138
Hectomètre	3937·07900	328·089917	109·3633056	54·6816528	0·0621382
Kilomètre	39370·79000	3280·899167	1093·6330556	546·8165278	0·6213824
Myriamètre	393707·90000	32808·991667	10936·3305556	5468·1652778	6·2138242

Inch = 2·539954 Centimètres.—Foot = 3·0479449 Décimètres.—Yard = 0·9143835 Metre.

SQUARE, OR MEASURES OF SURFACE.

EQUAL TO	Sq. Feet.	Sq. Yards.	Sq. Perches.	Sq. Roods.	Sq. Acres.
Centiare, or square mètre	10·764299	1·196033	0·0395383	0·0009885	0·0002471
Are or 100 square mètres	1076·429934	119·603326	3·9538290	0·0988457	0·0247114
Hectare or 10,000 sq. mètres	107642·993419	11960·332602	395·3828959	9·8845724	2·4711431

Square Inch = 6·4513659 Square Centimètres.—Square Foot = 9·2899683 Square Décimètres.—Square Mètre or Centiare.—Acre = 0·40467102 Hectare.

CUBIC, OR MEASURES OF CAPACITY.

EQUAL TO	Cubic Inches.	Cubic Feet.	Pints.	Gallons	Bushels
Millilitre, or cubic centimetre	0·06103	0·000035	0·00176	0·0002201	0·0000275
Centilitre, or 10 cubic centimètres	0·61027	0·000353	0·01761	0·0022010	0·0002751
Décilitre, or 100 cubic centimétres	6·10271	0·003532	0·17608	0·0220097	0·0027512
Litre, or cubic décimètre	61·02705	0·035317	1·76077	0·2200967	0·0275121
Centistère	610·27052	0·353166	17·60773	2·2009668	0·2751208
Hectolitre, or décistère	6102·70515	3·531658	176·07734	22·0096677	2·7512085
Stère, or cubic mètre	61027·05152	35·316581	1760·77344	220·0966767	27·5120846
Décastère	610270·51519	353·165807	17607·73414	2200·9667675	275·1208459

Cubic Inch = 16·386176 Cubic Centimètres.—Cubic Foot = 28·315312 Cubic Décimètres.

MEASURES OF WEIGHT.

EQUAL TO	Grains.	Troy Ounces.	Avoirdupois lbs.	Cwt. = 112 lbs.	Tons = 20 cwts.
Milligramme	0·01543	0·000032	0·0000022	0·0000000	0·0000000
Centigramme	0·15432	0·000322	0·0000220	0·0000002	0·0000000
Décigramme	1·54323	0·003215	0·0002205	0·0000020	0·0000001
Gramme	15·43235	0·032151	0·0022046	0·0000197	0·0000010
Décagramme	154·32349	0·321507	0·0220462	0·0001968	0·0000098
Hectogramme	1543·23488	3·215073	0·2204621	0·0019684	0·0000984
Kilogramme	15432·34880	32·150727	2·2046213	0·0196841	0·0009842
Myriagramme	154323·48800	321·507267	22·0462126	0·1958412	0·0098421

Grain = 0·064799 Gramme.—Troy ounce = 31·103496 Grammes.—lb. Avoirdupois = 0·453592 Kilogrammes.—Cwt. = 50·802377 Kilogrammes.

THE SYSTÈME USUELLE.

This system is an adaptation of the above for local and other purposes; its chief divisions are as follows:—

WEIGHTS USED BY BUTCHERS, GROCERS, AND RETAIL DEALERS.

Avoirdupois.	Grammes.	lbs.	ozs.	dr.	Avoirdupois.	Grammes.	lbs.	ozs.	dr.
Livre usuelle (½ Kilo)	500 = 1	1	10½		Once	31.5 = 0	1	1¾
„ half	250 = 0	8	13⅜		„ half	15.6 = 0	0	8⅞
„ quarter	125 = 0	4	6½		„ quarter	7.8 = 0	0	4½
„ eighth	62.5 = 0	2	3¼		Gros	3.9 = 0	0	2¼

MEASURE OF LENGTH USED BY DRAPERS, &c.

	ft.	in.	parts.			ft.	in.	parts.
Toise	= 6	6	9		Aune eighth	= 0	5	10⅞
Pied (foot)	= 1	1	1½		„ sixteenth	= 0	2	11⅜
Pouce (inch)	= 0	1	1⅛		„ one-third	= 1	3	9
Aune (yard)	= 3	11	3		„ one-sixth	= 0	7	10½
„ half	= 1	11	7½		„ one-twelfth	= 0	3	11¼
„ quarter	= 0	11	9¾					

MEASURE OF CAPACITY.

Boisseau ... ·125 litres = 2·837 English gallons. | Litron ... 1·074 Paris pinte = 2½ English pint.

MEASURES OF LENGTH.

	Inches.	Feet.	Yards.	Poles.	Chains.	Furlgs.
Foot	12					
Yard	36	3				
Pole or perch	198	16½	5½			
Chain	792	66	22	4		
Furlong	7,920	660	220	40	10	
Mile	63,360	5,280	1,760	320	80	8

PARTICULAR MEASURES OF LENGTH.

12 lines 1 inch.
3 barleycorns 1 inch.
3 inches 1 palm.
4 inches 1 hand.
A cubit 18 inches.
A pace, military, 2 ft. 6 in.
A pace, geometrical, 5 feet.
A fathom 6 feet.
A cable's length 240 yards.
A degree 69⅓ miles, or 60 nautical miles.
A league 3 miles.

SQUARE OR SURFACE MEASURE.

	Inches.	Feet.	Yards.	Poles.	Chains.	Roods.
Square foot	144	1				
Square yard	1,296	9	1			
Rod, pole, or perch	39,204	272¼	30¼	1		
Square chain	627,624	4,356	484	16	1	
Rood	1,568,160	10,890	1,210	40	2½	1
Acre	6,272,640	43,560	4,840	160	10	4

A square mile contains 640 acres, 2,560 roods, 6,400 chains, 102,400 rods, poles, or perches, or 3,097,000 square yards.

OLD APOTHECARIES' WEIGHT.

				Troy
20 Grains		1 Scruple ℈	=	20 grs.
3 Scruples	=	1 Drachm ʒ	=	60 ,,
8 Drachms	=	1 Ounce ℥	=	480 ,,
12 Ounces	=	1 Pound ℔	=	5760 ,,

Apothecaries compounded by this weight, but bought and sold their drugs by avoirdupois.

NEW APOTHECARIES' WEIGHT.

Ounce .... = 437½ grs.
Pound, 16 ozs. .... = 7,000 ,,
Same as Avoirdupois.

FLUID MEASURE.

			Marked
60 Minims ♏	=	1 Fluid Drachm	fʒ
8 Drachms	=	1 Ounce	f℥
20 Ounces	=	1 Pint	O
8 Pints	=	1 Gallon	gal.

PARTICULAR WEIGHTS.

A Firkin of Butter	=	56 lbs.
A Firkin of Soap	=	64 ,,
A Barrel of Raisins	=	112 ,,
A Barrel of Soap	=	256 ,,
A Fodder of Lead, London & Hull	=	19½ cwt.
,, ,, Derby	=	22½ ,,
,, ,, Newcastle	=	21½ ,,

MEASURES OF TIME.

60 Seconds	=	1 Minute.
60 Minutes	=	1 Hour.
24 Hours	=	1 Day.
7 Days	=	1 Week.
28 Days	=	1 Lunar Month.
28, 29, 30, or 31 Days	=	1 Calendar Month.
12 Calendar Months	=	1 Year.
365 Days	=	1 Common Year.
366 Days	=	1 Leap Year.

ANGULAR MEASURE.

60 Seconds	=	1 Minute.
60 Minutes	=	1 Degree.
30 Degrees	=	1 Sign.
90 Degrees	=	1 Quadrant.
4 Quadrants, or 360°	=	1 Circumference, or Great Circle.

CUBIC OR SOLID MEASURE.

1728 Cubic Inches	=	1 Cubic Foot.
27 Cubic Feet	=	1 Cubic Yard.
40 Do. of Rough or 50 Do. of Hewn Timber	=	1 Ton or Load.
42 Cubic Feet of Timber	=	1 Shipping Ton.
108 Cubic Feet	=	1 Stack of Wood.
128 Cubic Feet	=	1 Cord of Wood.
40 Cubic Feet	=	1 Ton Shipping.

LIQUID MEASURE.

	Gals.	Qrts.	Pts.
Gill	...	...	¼
Four Gills	...	...	1
Quart	...	...	2
Gallon	...	...	8
Firkin or Quarter Barrel	9	36	72
Kilderkin or Half Barrel	18	72	144
Barrel	36	144	288
Hogshead of Ale	54	216	432
Hogshead of Wine	63	252	504
Puncheon	84	336	672
Butt of Ale	108	432	864
Pipe or 2 Hogsheads	126	504	1008
Tun or 2 Pipes	252	1008	2016

Practically the only measures in use are gallons and quarts, the others are merely nominal; *e.g.*, the hogshead of 54 gallons, *old measure*, contains but 52 gallons, 1 quart, 1 pint, and 3.55 gills imperial measure—and of wine six nominal quarts go to the gallon.

DRY OR CORN MEASURE.

4 Quarts	=	1 Gallon.
2 Gallons	=	1 Peck.
4 Pecks	=	1 Bushel.
3 Bushels	=	1 Sack.
12 Sacks	=	1 Chaldron.
8 Bushels	=	1 Quarter.
5 Quarters	=	1 Load.

MEASURES OF WEIGHT.—AVOIRDUPOIS.

27⅓ Grains	=	1 Dram	=	27⅓	Grains
16 Drams	=	1 Ounce	=	437½	Grains
16 Ounces	=	1 Pound	=	7000	Grains
8 Pounds	=	1 Stone of Butcher's Meat.			
14 Pounds	=	1 Ordinary Stone.			
28 Pounds	=	1 Quarter (qr.).			
4 Quarters	=	1 Hundredweight (cwt.).			
20 Cwt.	=	1 Ton.			

This weight is used in almost all commercial transactions and common dealings.

HAY AND STRAW.

Truss of Straw, 36lbs.
Truss of Old Hay, 56lbs. (after 1st September).
Truss of New Hay, 60lbs.
Load, 36 Trusses = Straw, 11cwt. 2qrs. 8lb.; Old Hay, 18 cwt.; New Hay, 19 cwt. 1 qr. 4 lb.

WOOL.

			cwt.	qr.	lb.
7 Pounds	=	1 Clove	0	0	7
2 Cloves	=	1 Stone	0	0	14
2 Stones	=	1 Tod	0	1	0
6½ Tods	=	1 Wey	1	2	14
12 Sacks	=	1 Last	39	0	0

Silk is frequently weighed by the "Great pound," of 24 ozs.

TROY WEIGHT.

3⅙ Grains	=	1 Carat		
24 Grains	=	1 Pennyweight		
20 Pennyweights	=	1 Ounce	=	480 grs.
12 Ounces	=	1 Pound	=	5760 ,,

Laws relating to Hackney Carriages.

The following abstract of the various Laws relating to Hackney Carriages has been drawn up for the guidance of drivers and of the public by Sir Richard Mayne, Chief Commissioner of Police for the Metropolitan district :—

Fares are according to distance or time, *at the option of the hirer, expressed at the commencement of the hiring*; if not otherwise expressed, the fare to be paid according to distance.

No driver is compellable to hire his carriage for a fare according to time, at any time after eight o'clock in the evening, and before six o'clock in the morning.

An agreement to pay more than legal fare is not binding, any sum paid beyond the fare may be recovered back.

Driver not to charge more than the sum agreed on for driving a distance, although such distance be exceeded by the driver.

If the driver agree beforehand to take any sum less than the proper fare, the penalty for exacting or demanding more than the sum agreed upon is 40s.

Driver may demand a reasonable sum as a deposit, from persons hiring and requiring him to wait, over and above the fare to which driver is entitled for driving thither. If driver refuse to wait, or go away before expiration of time for which deposit shall be sufficient compensation, or if driver shall refuse to account for such deposit, the penalty is 40s.

Hirer refusing to pay the fare, or for any damage and compensation for loss of time, may be committed to prison.

The number of persons to be carried shall be distinctly marked on such carriage, and the driver shall, if required by the hirer, carry by such carriage the number of persons marked thereon, or any less number.

FARES BY DISTANCE.

WITHIN A RADIUS OF FOUR MILES FROM CHARING CROSS.

If hired when standing on a stand, for any distance not exceeding a mile, 1s.

Above the number of three persons carried, sixpence extra for each person.

For any distance exceeding a mile, for every mile, and for any part of a mile not completed, at the rate of 6d.

When not standing on a stand, for each mile and for any part of a mile not completed, at the rate of 6d.

Above the number of two persons carried, sixpence extra for each person for the whole hiring.

Two children under the age of ten to be counted as one adult person.

One shilling for every mile, or part of a mile, beyond four miles (radius) from Charing Cross, if carriage discharged beyond such four miles.

No driver shall demand or receive any sum by way of Back Fare, for the return of the carriage from the place at which discharged.

When the driver shall be required by the hirer to stop for fifteen minutes, or for any longer time, the driver may demand and receive a further sum (above the fare to which he shall be entitled, calculated according to distance), of sixpence for every fifteen minutes completed, that he shall have been so stopped.

FARES BY TIME.

One hour, or any part of an hour, 2s.

For every fifteen minutes, or less, beyond one hour, 6d.

Each person above two, the whole hiring, 6d. extra.

No driver shall demand or receive any sum by way of Back Fare, for the return of the carriage from the place at which discharged.

If the driver is required to drive more than four miles an hour, for every mile or part of a mile above four miles, 6d. extra.

Two children, under the age of ten years, to be counted as one adult person.

LUGGAGE.

A reasonable quantity of luggage is to be carried in or upon the carriage without any additional charge, except :—

When more than two persons are carried inside any hackney carriage, with more luggage than can be carried inside the carriage, a sum of 2d. for every package carried outside the carriage, is to be paid.

GENERAL REGULATIONS, MISCONDUCT, &c.

Hackney carriage standing in the street, unless actually hired, to be deemed plying for hire; and the driver obliged to go with any person desirous of hiring such carriage: should he refuse, the driver must produce evidence of having been actually hired at the time.

The driver is to drive at a reasonable and proper speed, not less than six miles an hour, unless in cases of unavoidable delay, or when required by the hirer to drive slower.

The driver shall (unless he have a reasonable excuse, to be allowed by the Justice before whom the matter shall be brought in question) drive to any place within the Metropolitan Police District, or City of London, to which he may be required by the hirer, not exceeding six miles from the place where hired.

The driver shall (unless he have a reasonable excuse, as above stated) drive for any time not exceeding one hour from the time when hired.

The proprietor of every hackney carriage shall keep distinctly painted, both on the inside and outside of such carriage, a table of fares, which may be legally demanded, and the driver shall have with him at all times, when plying for hire, the Authorized Book of Fares, and produce the same when required.

In case of any dispute between the hirer and driver, the hirer may require the driver to drive to the nearest Metropolitan Police Court or Justice Room, when the complaint may be determined by the Sitting Magistrate without summons; or if no Police Court or Justice Room be open at the time, then to the nearest Police Station, where the complaint shall be entered, and tried by the Magistrate at his next sitting.

Every driver of a hackney carriage shall, when hired, deliver to the hirer a card, on which shall be printed the number of the Stamp Office plate on such carriage, or such other words or figures as the Commissioner of Police may direct.

Penalty of 40s., or one month's imprisonment, for each offence against any of the above provisions.

All property left in any hackney carriage shall be deposited by the driver at the nearest Police Station within twenty-four hours, if not sooner claimed by the owner; such property to be returned to the person who shall prove to the satisfaction of the Commissioner of Police that the same belonged to him, on payment of all expenses incurred, and of such reasonable sum to the driver as the Commissioner shall award.

Driver not wearing his metal ticket conspicuously on his breast at all times during his employment, or refusing to produce such ticket for inspection, or refusing to permit any person to note the writing thereon, or wearing ticket with writing not distinctly legible, to forfeit 40s.

Every person using or wearing a ticket without having a licence in force relating to such ticket, or wearing a ticket resembling the tickets issued by the Commissioner of Police, to forfeit 5l.; such ticket may be seized by any constable or person employed for the purpose by the Commissioner of Police.

Driver allowing another person to act as driver in his place, also any person acting as driver without consent of proprietor of the carriage, to forfeit 40s.

Person acting unlawfully as driver may be taken into custody by a constable, and charged before a magistrate.

If driver permit or suffer any person to ride or be carried in, upon, or about such carriage, without express consent of person hiring the same, penalty, 20s.

Driver guilty of wanton or furious driving, or causing hurt or damage by carelessness or wilful misbehaviour; or drunk during his employment, or making use of insulting or abusive language or gesture, or any misbehaviour, to forfeit 3l., or to be imprisoned for two months with or without hard labour at discretion of Justice; and in case of such hurt or damage, Justice may order compensation, not exceeding 10l., to be paid by the proprietor, and recovered by him from the driver by whose default such sum shall have been paid.

If driver of hackney carriage shall stand or ply for hire, or suffer same to stand across any street or common passage, or alley; or shall feed the horses in any street, road, or common passage, save only with corn out of a bag, or with hay which he shall hold or deliver with his hand; or if driver shall refuse to give way, if he conveniently can, to any other carriage, or shall obstruct or hinder the driver of any other hackney carriage in taking up or setting down any person: or shall wrongfully, in a forcible or clandestine manner, take away the fare from any other proprietor or driver; penalty, 20s.

Every driver of a hackney carriage who shall ply for hire elsewhere than at some standing or place appointed for that purpose, or who by loitering or by any wilful misbehaviour shall cause obstruction in or upon any public street, road, or place, shall for every such offence forfeit the sum of 20s.

Driver of hackney carriage leaving same unattended in any street or road, or at any place of public resort or entertainment, whether hired or not; penalty, 40s.; and constable, &c. may drive such carriage to a place of safety.

Every driver is bound to have for reference the authorized book or Table of Fares, this will enable any person to tell the fullest amount he can be called upon to pay to any part of the metropolis.—To the places named the exact fares are stated—to any place not mentioned the fare can easily be calculated by referring to the nearest place for which the fare is given; thus the fare to any part of the City cannot be above sixpence more than that given to the Bank, and then only when the Bank has to be passed from the place of hiring.

EXCISE LICENCES AND DUTIES.

	£	s.	d.
Appraisers	2	0	0
Auctioneers	10	0	0
Brewers brewing for sale a quantity of beer, not exceeding 20 barrels	0	12	6
" exc. 20 and not exc. 50 bar...	1	7	6
" exceeding 50 barrels	2	0	0
" exc. 100 and not exc. 1,000—for every 50 barrels	0	15	0
" exc. 1,000 and not exc. 50,000 for every 50 bar. over 1000	0	14	0
" exc. 50,000—for every 50 barrels over 50,000	0	12	6
Beginners (and a surcharge)	0	12	6
*Brewers using sugar	1	0	0
*Brewers selling beer by retail, not to be drunk on the premises	5	10	3

Brewers of spruce or black beer for sale, if brewed on premises where no other kind of beer is brewed, and brewed without hops or other bitter, or yeast or other fermenting matter, and of a specific gravity of not less than 1·180 deg.; if the quantity brewed within the year ending 10th Oct. before taking out the licence do not exc. 20 bar.

	£	s.	d.
(not exc. 20 bar.)	0	10	6
Exc. 20 and not ex. 50 bar.	1	1	0
50 " 100	1	11	6
100 " 1,000	2	2	0
1,000 " 2,000	3	3	0
2,000 " 5,000	7	17	6
5,000 " 7,500	11	16	3
7,500 " 10,000	15	15	0
10,000 " 20,000	31	10	0
20,000 " 30,000	47	5	0
30,000 " 40,000	63	0	0
40,000	78	15	0
*Beer retailers (publicans) rated under £20 per ann.	1	2	0½
At £20 or upwards	3	6	1¾
If spirit licence not also taken out	3	6	1¾
*Retailers of beer, cider, and perry, to be drunk on the premises	3	6	1¾
Not to be drunk on the premises	1	2	0½
Occasional licence, for every day, not exceeding 3 days at one time	0	1	0
*Retailers of cider and perry	1	2	0½
" table-beer	0	5	0
Licensed victuallers' occasional licence, not exc. 6 days, for each day	0	2	6
*Cards (Playing), sellers of (if makers)	1	0	0
if not makers	0	2	6
*Chicory, or other vegetable, applicable to the uses of chicory or coffee, per cwt.	1	4	3
*Coffee, tea, cocoa, chocolate, or pepper dealers	0	11	6½
In house rated to relief of poor at less than £8 per ann.	0	2	6
*Dealers in gold and silver plate:—			
Above 2 oz. gold, or 30 oz. silver	5	15	0
Under 2 oz. and above 2 dwts. gold; under 30 oz. and above 5 dwts. silver.	2	6	0
*Refiners of gold or silver	5	15	0
Dogs of any kind	0	5	0

This tax may be paid at any Money Order Office.

	£	s.	d.
Game licences, if taken out after 5th April and before 1st Nov., to expire on 5th April following	3	0	0
If taken out after 5th April, to expire on 31st October	2	0	0
If taken out after 1st November to expire on 5th April next	2	0	0
Gamekeepers	2	0	0
Hackney carriages, London, per week (If not used on Sundays, 1s. less.)	0	7	0
Hawkers and pedlars:—Travelling on foot, without any horse or otherbeast	2	0	0
Travelling or trading with a horse or other beast	4	0	0
If with more than 1 horse or beast, for each such horse or beast	4	0	0
House agents, not being licensed appraisers or auctioneers, &c.	2	0	0
Income tax 6d. in the pound; if income less than £200, 6d. per pound on a proportion of the same	0	0	6
Malt, from barley ....bush.	0	2	7
and 5 per cent.			
From beer or bigg ....bush.	0	2	0
and 5 per cent.			
*Maltsters, making not exc. 50 qrs.	0	7	10½
" " 100 "	0	15	9
" " 150 "	1	3	7½
" " 200 "	1	11	6
" " 250 "	1	19	4½
" " 300 "	2	7	3
" " 350 "	2	15	1½
" " 400 "	3	3	0
" " 450 "	3	10	10½
" " 500 "	3	18	9
" " 550 "	4	6	7½
exceeding 550 "	4	14	6
Beginners (and a surcharge)	0	7	10½
Not exceeding 5 qrs.	0	2	7½
*Malt roasters	20	0	0
*Dealers in roasted malt	10	0	0
Medicines (Patent) dealers, &c.:—			
In London and Edinburgh	2	0	0
In any other city, burgh, or town corporate	0	10	0
Elsewhere	0	5	0
*Paper or Pasteboard makers	4	4	0
*Passage vessels, or packet boats, on board which liquors and tobacco are sold	1	1	0
*Pawnbrokers, London	15	0	0
* elsewhere	7	10	0
*Postmasters keeping 1 horse or 1 carriage	5	0	0
Not exceeding 3 horses or 2 carr.	10	0	0
" 4 " 3 "	15	0	0
" 5 " 4 "	20	0	0
" 6 " 5 "	25	0	0
" 8 " 6 "	30	0	0
" 12 " 9 "	40	0	0
" 16 " 10 "	50	0	0
" 20 " 15 "	60	0	0
Exceeding 15 "	70	0	0
Exceeding 20 horses, then for every additional number of 10 horses, and for any additional number less than 10, over and above 20, or any other multiple of 10 horses, the further additional duty of	10	0	0
Property tax, see *Income Tax.*			
Race-horses, for each horse	4	0	10
Railways, per £100 on Passenger traf.	5	0	0
*Soap makers	4	4	0
Spirits, home made, proof ....gall.	0	10	0
* " distillers or rectifiers	10	10	0
* " dealers not retailers	10	10	0
* " retailers whose premises are rated under £10 per annum,	2	4	1

Licenses marked thus are * alone transferable.

	£	s.	d.
Spirit retailers whose premises are rated at £10 and under £20 per an.	4	8	2¼
20 ,, 25	6	12	3½
25 ,, 30	7	14	4
30 ,, 40	8	16	4¾
40 ,, 50	9	18	5¼
50 or upwards	11	0	6
*Spirits (Methylated) makers of	0	10	0
,, ,, retailers of	0	10	0
*Stage carriages—original licence	3	3	0
,, supplementary do.	0	1	0
If licensed only to carry not more than eight persons and the driver—original licence	0	10	0
supplementary do.	0	0	6
Occasional licences for one day only—one-horse	0	5	0
two-horse	0	5	0
drawn by more than two horses	0	10	0

For every day (not to exceed six) after the first, a further duty of one-half the above rates.

	£	s.	d.
*Still makers	0	10	6
*Stills—Chemists keeping or using	0	10	0
Sugar, Home-made—			
Refined (Great Britain)......cwt.	0	12	0
White-clayed ,, ,,	0	11	8
Yellow Muscovado ,, ,,	0	10	6
Brown do. ,, ,,	0	9	7
Not equal to Brown do. ,,	0	8	6
Molasses do. ,,	0	3	6
Sugar used by brewers ,,	0	3	6
*Sweets, dealers in	5	5	0
,, retailers of	1	2	0½
Tea, per lb.	0	0	6

*Tobacco and Snuff manufacturers :—
If quantity of tobacco and snuff work weighed for manufacture within year

	£	s.	d.
ending 5th July do not exc. 20,000 lbs.	5	5	0
Exc. 20,000lbs. and not exc. 40,000	10	10	0
40,000 ,, 60,000	15	15	0
60,000 ,, 80,000	21	0	0
80,000 ,, 100,000	26	5	0
100,000	31	10	0

Beginners to pay £5 5s., and, within 10 days after 5th July following, to pay the difference between that sum and the licence duty chargeable at the above rates for the quantity manufactured up to said 5th July.

	£	s.	d.
*Tobacco and snuff, dealers in	0	5	3
Occasional licences, per day	0	0	4
*Vinegar makers	5	5	0
*Wine dealers (or grocers selling wine not to be consumed on the premises) not licensed to retail spirits and beer, if rent under £50	2	2	0
Above £50	5	5	0
*Wine to sell in refreshment houses, to be consumed on the premises, if of annual rent below £50	3	3	0
Above £50	5	5	0

STAMP DUTIES.

	£	s.	d.
ADMISSION to the degree of a barrister-at-law	50	0	0
As an attorney or proctor, or as writer to the signet	25	0	0
As a member of any Inn of Chancery in England	3	0	0
AGREEMENT, or memorandum of agreement, under hand only, the matter thereof amounting in value to £5 or upwards	0	0	6
Amounting to 2,160 words, for every 1,080 words above the first	0	0	6

	£	s.	d.
Or lease for less than a year of a furnished house, the rent exceeding £25	0	2	6
Agreement or memorandum for letting a dwelling-house or tenement, or any part thereof, for any period less than a year, at a rent payable weekly or monthly, and not exceeding the rate of 3s. 6d. per week	0	0	1
ANNUITY, release, or re-conveyance, or re-purchase of, under provision in original grant	1	15	0
With progressive duty of	0	10	0
APPOINTMENT—in writing, not being a deed or will	1	15	0
Of a new trustee, where the property is subject to one and the same settlement, if one of such deeds or instruments bear a 35s. stamp, the others or other thereof, the same duty as a duplicate or counterpart.			
Of a chaplain	2	0	0
Of a gamekeeper	1	15	0
Of a commissioner in Chancery	1	0	0
APPRAISEMENT or VALUATION of any estate or effects, or of any interest therein, or of dilapidations, repairs, materials, or artificers' work, where the amount of the appraisement or valuation shall not exceed £5	0	0	3
Exceeding £5, and not exc. £10	0	0	6
,, 10 ,, 20	0	1	0
,, 20 ,, 30	0	1	6
,, 30 ,, 40	0	2	0
,, 40 ,, 50	0	2	6
,, 50 ,, 100	0	5	0
,, 100 ,, 200	0	10	0
,, 200 ,, 500	0	15	0
,, 500	1	0	0
APPRENTICESHIP INDENTURES :—If the premium be under £30	1	0	0
£30 and under £50	2	0	0
50 ,, 100	3	0	0
100 ,, 200	6	0	0
200 ,, 300	12	0	0
300 ,, 400	20	0	0
400 ,, 500	25	0	0
500 ,, 600	30	0	0
600 ,, 800	40	0	0
800 ,, 1,000	50	0	0
1,000 or upwards	60	0	0
If no premium	0	2	6
ARTICLES of association, and memorandum of association of a joint-stock company	1	15	0
Of clerkship to attorney, solicitor, or proctor	80	0	0
ASSIGNMENT for benefit of creditors	1	15	0
AWARD—in England or Ireland, and award or decreet arbitral in Scotland, where the amount or value of the matter in dispute shall not exc. £5	0	0	3
Exceeding £5 and not exc. £10	0	0	6
,, 10 ,, 20	0	1	0
,, 20 ,, 30	0	1	6
,, 30 ,, 40	0	2	0
,, 40 ,, 50	0	2	6
,, 50 ,, 100	0	5	0
,, 100 ,, 200	0	10	0
,, 200 ,, 500	0	15	0
,, 500 ,, 750	1	0	0
,, 750 ,, 1,000	1	5	0
,, 1,000, and also in all other cases not above provided for	1	15	0

BANKRUPTCY :—
London Court, or to a County Court,

	£	s.	d.
by traders whose debts do not exceed £300	1	0	0
Every order of discharge	1	0	0
Every registration of trust deeds	0	10	0
Every summons of "judgment debtor, or debtor"	0	2	6
Every admission of such debtor	0	2	6
Every deposition of good defence	0	2	6
Every bond with sureties	0	5	0
Every search for petition or other proceeding	0	1	0
Every application for any meeting	0	5	0
Every allocatur for costs, &c., not ex. £5	0	1	6
Exceeding £5 and not ex. £10	0	2	6
,, 10 ,, 20	0	5	0
,, 20 ,, 30	0	7	6
,, 30 ,, 50	0	10	0
,, 50 ,, 100	0	15	0
,, 100 ,, 150	1	0	0
,, 150 ,, 200	1	10	0
,, 200 ,, 300	2	0	0
,, 300 ,, 500	3	0	0
,, 500 and upwards	5	0	0

BARGAIN AND SALE.—To be enrolled—of any estate of freehold in England and Ireland, on any other occasion than a mortgage or sale — £5 0 0

CERTIFICATE—to be taken out yearly by every attorney, solicitor, proctor, writer to the signet, notary public, and sworn clerk, residing within 10 miles of the G. P. Office, London; or either in the city or shire of Edinburgh, or in the city of Dublin, or within 3 miles thereof, if admitted for 3 years past — 9 0 0

If less — 4 10 0

If residing elsewhere, and admitted for 3 years — 6 0 0

If less — 3 0 0

By a conveyancer, special pleader, or draughtsman, residing within 10 miles of the G. P. Office; or in Dublin, or within 3 miles thereof — 9 0 0

If residing elsewhere — 6 0 0

By 28 & 29 Vict., c. 96, s. 6, the duty on certificates taken out by conveyancers and special pleaders within the first three years of their practice is reduced one-half.

CERTIFICATE.—Of scrip — 0 0 1

For registry of designs — 5 0 0

COMPOSITION DEEDS between debtor and creditor — 1 15 0

Also a duty of 5s. on every £100, or fraction of £100, of the sworn or certified value of the estate or effects comprised in, or to be collected or distributed under such deed, with limit of such duty to £200.

CONTRACT NOTE, relating to the sale or purchase of any stocks or shares to the amount of £5, or upwards — 0 0 1

CONVEYANCE—where the purchase or consideration money expressed in or upon the principal or only deed, instrument, or writing of conveyance shall not exceed £5 — 0 0 6

Exceeding £5 and under £10	0	1	0
,, 10 ,, 15	0	1	6
,, 15 ,, 20	0	2	0
,, 20 ,, 25	0	2	6
,, 25 ,, 50	0	5	0
,, 50 ,, 75	0	7	6
,, 75 ,, 100	0	10	0
,, 100 ,, 125	0	12	6
,, 125 ,, 150	0	15	0

	£	s.	d.
Exceeding £150 and under £175	0	17	6
,, 175 ,, 200	1	0	0
,, 200 ,, 225	1	2	6
,, 225 ,, 250	1	5	0
,, 250 ,, 275	1	7	6
,, 275 ,, 300	1	10	0

And where the purchase or consideration money shall exceed £300, then for every £50, and also for any fractional part of £50 — 0 5 0

Of any kind not otherwise charged — 1 15 0

COPYHOLD AND CUSTOMARY ESTATE:—

Admittance out of court, or the memorandum thereof — 0 2 6

Exceeding 2,160 words, for every additional entire 1,080 words — 0 2 6

Surrender or Admittance in court, or the memorandum thereof, the yearly value exceeding 20s. — 1 0 0

Not exceeding 20s. — 0 5 0

Copy of Court Roll of several surrenders, admittances, and other acts for perfecting a Common Recovery of such estates, the yearly value exceeding 20s. ... (5 times £1, or) — 5 0 0

Not exceeding 20s. (5 times 5s., or) — 1 5 0

Voluntary Grant, or the memorandum thereof, out of court—or copy of court roll thereof made in court—with or without admittance, the clear yearly value exceeding 20s. ... (twice 20s., or) — 2 0 0

Not exceeding 20s. ... (twice 5s., or) — 0 10 0

Progressive Duty. See that title.

Licence to demise, or memorandum thereof, if granted out of court, and the copy of court roll of any such licence, if granted in court, the clear yearly value of the estate therein expressed not exceeding £75, the same duty as on a lease at a yearly rent equal to such value.

In all other cases — 0 10 0

COST-BOOK.—Mines.

Any written request or authority to the purser or officer of a mining company, conducted on the cost-book system, to register any transfer of shares in such mine; or any notice of such transfer — 0 0 6

DONATION or PRESENTATION, by whomsoever made, of or to any ecclesiastical benefice, dignity, or promotion. Where the net yearly value of any such benefice, dignity, promotion, or perpetual curacy shall exceed £50, and not exceed £100 — 1 0 0

Exceeding £100 and not exc. £150	2	0	0
,, 150 ,, 200	3	0	0
,, 200 ,, 250	4	0	0
,, 250 ,, 300	5	0	0

And where such value shall exceed 300 — 7 0 0

Also (where such value shall exceed £300), for every £100 thereof over and above the first £200, a further duty of — 5 0 0

Also, to any benefice in Scotland — 2 0 0

LICENCE—to use a patent, for a money consideration — 1 15 0

Auctioneers — 10 0 0

Bankers — 30 0 0

Pawnbrokers, residing in metropolis — 15 0 0

,, ,, elsewhere — 7 10 0

For Hawkers of goods, wares, and merchandise, and his beast of burden, each — 4 0 0

2. When having only one beast of bur-

	£ s. d.
den, being ass, mule, or a horse not exc. 13 hands, for not above 6 months	2 0 0
Exc. 6 months and not exc. 1 year ...	4 0 0
3. When travelling on foot only, for 6 months	1 0 0
Do. do. for 1 year	2 0 0
Letter of Licence from creditors to a debtor	1 15 0
Licences, Annual—Attorneys, conveyancers, proctors, and notaries, London, Edinburgh, and Dublin	9 0 0
Elsewhere (half only, for the first 3 yrs.)	6 0 0
Bankers	30 0 0
MEMORIAL—For registering an annuity, deed, &c.—and progressive duty, each	1 0 0
Other deeds, for every skin or sheet...	0 2 6

PROBATES OF WILLS, and Letters of Administration:—

With a Will annexed.			Without a Will
Exc. £	and under £	£	£
100	200...	2	3
„ 200	„ 300...	5	8
„ 300	„ 450...	8	11
„ 450	„ 600...	11	15
„ 600	„ 800...	15	22
„ 800	„ 1,000...	22	30
„ 1,000	„ 1,500...	30	45
„ 1,500	„ 2,000...	40	60
„ 2,000	„ 3,000...	50	75
„ 3,000	„ 4,000...	60	90
„ 4,000	„ 5,000...	80	100
„ 5,000	„ 6,000...	100	150
„ 6,000	„ 7,000...	120	180
„ 7,000	„ 8,000...	140	200
„ 8,000	„ 9,000...	160	240
„ 9,000	„ 10,000...	180	270
„ 10,000	„ 12,000...	200	300
„ 12,000	„ 14,000...	220	330
„ 14,000	„ 16,000...	250	375
„ 16,000	„ 18,000...	280	420
„ 18,000	„ 20,000...	300	465
„ 20,000	„ 25,000...	350	525
„ 25,000	„ 30,000...	400	600
„ 30,000	„ 35,000...	450	675
„ 35,000	„ 40,000...	525	785
„ 40,000	„ 45,000...	600	900
„ 45,000	„ 50,000...	675	1,000
„ 50,000	„ 60,000...	750	1,125
„ 60,000	„ 70,000...	900	1,350
„ 70,000	„ 80,000...	1,050	1,575
„ 80,000	„ 90,000...	1,200	1,800
„ 90,000	„ 100,000...	1,350	2,025
„ 100,000	„ 120,000...	1,500	2,250
„ 120,000	„ 140,000...	1,800	2,700
„ 140,000	„ 160,000...	2,000	3,150
„ 160,000	„ 180,000...	2,400	3,600
„ 180,000	„ 200,000...	2,750	4,050
„ 200,000	„ 250,000...	3,000	4,500
„ 250,000	„ 300,000...	3,750	5,625
„ 300,000	„ 350,000...	4,500	6,750
„ 350,000	„ 400,000...	5,250	7,875
„ 400,000	„ 500,000...	6,000	9,000
„ 500,000	„ 600,000...	7,500	11,250
„ 600,000	„ 700,000...	9,000	13,500
„ 700,000	„ 800,000...	10,500	15,750
„ 800,000	„ 900,000...	12,000	18,000
„ 900,000	„ 1,000,000...	13,500	20,250
Above 1,000,000, for every 100,000 & any fractional part of 100,000...		1,500	2,250

PROGRESSIVE DUTY—On any deed or instrument chargeable with duty (unless specially charged or exempted), containing, with any schedule, &c., indorsed or annexed, 2,160 words, or upwards, and the *ad valorem* not exceeding 10s. a stamp equal to such *ad val.* duty.

	£ s. d.
Exceeding 10s. and 2,160 words, then for every entire quantity of 1,080 above the first	0 10 0
In every other case not specially charged	0 10 0

WARRANT OF ATTORNEY—To confess a judgment given as a security for payment of money, or for transfer of shares or stock, the same duty as on a bond.

	£ s. d.
For payment of money already secured by another deed or instrument charged with *ad val.* duty exceed. 5s.	0 5 0
For securing any sum exceeding £100, executed by a person in actual custody under arrest	0 5 0
Not otherwise charged	1 15 0
WRIT OF ERROR	1 0 0

BILLS OF EXCHANGE AND PROMISSORY NOTES.
Inland Bill of Exchange, or Promissory Note,—

		£ s. d.
Not exceeding £5		0 0 1
Exc. £5	and not exc. £10	0 0 2
„ 10	„ 25	0 0 3
„ 25	„ 50	0 0 6
„ 50	„ 75	0 0 9
„ 75	„ 100	0 1 0
„ 100	„ 200	0 2 0
„ 200	„ 300	0 3 0
„ 300	„ 400	0 4 0
„ 400	„ 500	0 5 0
„ 500	„ 750	0 7 6
„ 750	„ 1,000	0 10 0
„ 1,000	„ 1,500	0 15 0
„ 1,500	„ 2,000	1 0 0
„ 2,000	„ 3,000	1 10 0
„ 3,000	„ 4,000	2 0 0
„ 4,000, for every £1,000 or part of £1,000 thereby made payable		0 10 0

Foreign Bill of Exchange, or Promissory Note, drawn in, but payable out of, the United Kingdom, if drawn singly or otherwise than in a set of three or more, the same duty as Inland Bills.

If drawn in sets of three or more, for every bill of each set, where the sum payable thereby shall not exceed £25 ... 0 0 1

		£ s. d.
Exc. £25	and not exc. £50	0 0 2
„ 50	„ 75	0 0 3
„ 75	„ 100	0 0 8
„ 100	„ 200	0 0 8
„ 200	„ 300	0 1 0
„ 300	„ 400	0 1 4
„ 400	„ 500	0 1 8
„ 500	„ 750	0 2 6
„ 750	„ 1,000	0 3 4
„ 1,000	„ 1,500	0 5 0
„ 1,500	„ 2,000	0 6 8
„ 2,000	„ 3,000	0 10 0
„ 3,000	„ 4,000	0 13 4
„ 4,000, for every £1,000 or part of £1,000 thereby made payable		0 3 4

Foreign Bill of Exchange, or Promissory Note made, or purporting to be made out of the United Kingdom, but payable within the United Kingdom, the same duty as on an Inland Bill of the same amount, not exceeding £500 (adhesive stamp to be used).

Drawn out of, and payable out of the United Kingdom, but negotiated in the United Kingdom, the same duty as on Foreign Bills drawn in and payable out of the United Kingdom, not exceeding £500 (adhesive stamp).

Foreign Bill of Exchange for the payment of

money exceeding £500, drawn out of the United Kingdom, and payable, or endorsed, or negotiated within the United Kingdom,

	£	s.	d.
For every £100, and part of £100 of the money thereby made payable (adhesive stamp)	0	1	0

Bill of Exchange payable on demand, and endorsed out of the United Kingdom, shall be deemed a Foreign Bill of Exchange, and be charged with *ad val.* duty, as on an Inland Bill of Exchange.

	£	s.	d.
BILL OF LADING	0	0	6

BILLS OF SALE—absolute, same duty as on a Conveyance; conditional, as on a Mortgage.

BOND, MORTGAGE, or WARRANT OF ATTORNEY, given as a security for the payment of any definite and certain sum:

	£	s.	d.
Not exceeding £50	0	1	3
Above £50 and not above £100	0	2	6
,, 100 ,, 150	0	3	9
,, 150 ,, 200	0	5	0
,, 200 ,, 250	0	6	3
,, 250 ,, 300	0	7	6
Above £300, then for every £100 or fractional part thereof	0	2	6

and progressive duty on words.

	£	s.	d.
Any other warrant of attorney	1	15	0

Bond collateral with a mortgage:—

Where the sum secured shall not exceed £800, the same duty as on a mortgage for the like amount.

	£	s.	d.
Where the sum shall exceed £800	1	0	0

Bond, Transfer or assignment of; for every sum of £100 or fractional part

	£	s.	d.
of £100	0	0	6
CERTIFIED COPY or extract of or from any register of births, baptisms, marriages, deaths, or burials	0	0	1
CHARTER-PARTY	0	0	6
COMMISSION to any officer in the Army or Royal Marines	1	10	0

COPY, attested, of any deed, agreement, &c.—

Where made for use of any party to such deed, &c., or taking any interest immediately under such deed, &c., the same duty as for the original instrument.

Where made for use of any person not being a party to such deed, &c., or taking any interest immediately under same

	£	s.	d.
	0	1	0
And for every entire quantity of 700 words after the first 700	0	1	0

DEBENTURE or Certificate entitling any person to receive any drawback, &c., where the drawback or bounty shall

	£	s.	d.
not exceed £10	0	1	0
Exceeding £10, and not exc. £50	0	2	6
Exceeding £50	0	5	0
Certificate preliminary to the foregoing	0	4	0

DECLARATION of any use or trust, concerning any property by writing, not a deed or will, nor otherwise

	£	s.	d.
charged	1	15	0
DEED not specifically charged, nor expressly exempted	1	15	0

DELIVERY ORDER of goods of the value of 40s. or upwards, lying in any dock, wharf, or warehouse, such order being signed by the owner of the goods, on the sale of the property

	£	s.	d.
(to be paid by the person requiring it)	0	0	1
DOCK WARRANT	0	0	1
DRAFT, or Order, or Letter of Credit, for the payment of any sum of money, whether to the bearer or order, on demand, or to have credit given for sum mentioned therein	0	0	1

DUPLICATE or Counterpart of Deed of any description, chargeable with stamp duty, under any Act, where such duty (exclusive of progressive duty) shall not amount to 5s., the same duty as on original, including progressive duty, if any.

	£	s.	d.
Where same (exclusive as aforesaid) amounts to 5s. or upwards	0	5	0

Where, in the latter case, any such deed contains 2,160 words, then for every 1,080 words above the first, a

	£	s.	d.
further duty of	0	2	6

ECCLESIASTICAL LICENCES:—

	£	s.	d.
For marriage, if special	5	0	0
For non-residence of clergyman	1	0	0

To hold the office of lecturer, &c., or for licensing a building for the performance of divine service, or for authorizing any matter relating to a consecrated building or ground,

	£	s.	d.
(save where expressly exempted)	0	10	0
Licence not otherwise charged	2	0	0

EXCHANGE, DEED OF—If only a sum under £300 be paid for equality of

	£	s.	d.
exchange	1	15	0

But if £300 or upwards be paid, the same *ad val.* duty as on a conveyance on the sale of lands, &c.

	£	s.	d.
GAMEKEEPER, appointment of a	1	15	0

GRANT or LETTERS PATENT of any honour or dignity, viz.:—Duke, £350; Marquis, £300; Earl, £250; Viscount, £200; Baron, £150; Precedence, £100; Baronet, £100; Archbishop, £100; Bishop, £100; any other honour or dignity, £30.

	£	s.	d.
Grant or licence by sign manual to take a surname pursuant to will or settlement	50	0	0
Similar grant on voluntary application	10	0	0
Grant of Arms or armorial bearings only	10	0	0

INSURANCE POLICIES—FIRE: Policy of

	£	s.	d.
Insurance	0	0	1

Besides 1s. 6d. per cent. per annum.

INSURANCE POLICIES—LIFE: For any

	£	s.	d.
sum not exceeding £25	0	0	3
Exceeding £25 and not above £500, for every £50 and any fractional part of £50	0	0	6
Exceeding £500 and not exceeding £1,000, for every £100 and any fractional part of £100	0	1	0
Exceeding £1,000, for every £1,000 and any fractional part of £1,000	1	10	0

Accidental Death, or Personal Injury, or Insurance from Loss or Damage upon Property of any kind, except from fire, when the premium shall

	£	s.	d.
not exceed 2s. 6d.	0	0	1
Exceeding 2s. 6d. and not exceeding 5s.	0	0	3
Exceeding 5s., and for every 5s. or fractional part of 5s.	0	0	3

Sea—Upon any voyage whatever, for every full sum of £100, and for any fractional part of £100, thereby in-

	£	s.	d.
sured	0	0	3

For every policy for Time, for every £100, and any fractional part of £100 thereby insured, for any time not

	£	s.	d.
exceeding six months	0	0	3
Exceeding 6, and not exc. 12 months	0	0	6

JUDGMENTS:—For and upon every assignment of any judgment

	£	s.	d.
	1	15	0

	£	s.	d.
LEASES:—Lease or Tack of any lands, tenements, &c. at a yearly rent, without any sum of money by way of fine or premium, where the yearly rent shall not exceed £5	0	0	6
Exceeding £5 and not exc. £10	0	1	0
,, 10 ,, 15	0	1	6
,, 15 ,, 20	0	2	0
,, 20 ,, 25	0	2	6
,, 25 ,, 50	0	5	0
,, 50 ,, 75	0	7	6
,, 75 ,, 100	0	10	0
,, 100, then for every £50, and for every fractional part of £50	0	5	0

Lease, with a premium or fine, pays *ad valorem* conveyance duty on the amount thereof, in addition to the duty on the rent.

Agreement for a lease for any term not exceeding 7 years, or containing the terms on which such lands, &c., are let, held, or occupied, the same duty as on a lease.

	£	s.	d.
Lease or tack of any furnished dwelling house, for any term or period of time less than a year, or any agreement, minute, or memorandum of agreement, containing the terms and conditions on which any such house is let, occupied, or held, for any such term or period of time, where the rent for such term or period shall exceed £25	0	2	6
Progressive duty, if 2,160 words, for each 1,080 words	0	2	6

LEGACY and SUCCESSION DUTY:—

Lineal issue or lineal ancestor of the predecessor ... £1 per cent.

Brothers and sisters of the predecessor and their descendants ... £3 per cent.

Brothers and sisters of the father and mother of the predecessor, and their descendants ... £5 per cent.

Brothers and sisters of a grandfather or grandmother of the predecessor, and their descendants ... £6 per cent.

Any other person ... £10 per cent.

Legacy to husband or wife exempt.

	£	s.	d.
LETTER OF ALLOTMENT of any share of any Company, or of any loan	0	0	1
LETTERS OF ATTORNEY, &c., made by a petty officer, seaman, or marine, for receiving prize-money or wages	0	1	0
For the sale, transfer, or receipt of any of the government funds exceeding £20, or dividends exceeding £10 per annum	1	0	0
Not exceeding in value £20; or for receipt of money, &c., not exceeding £20, or any periodical payment not exceeding £10	0	5	0
Proxy to vote at any specified meeting of a joint-stock company	0	0	1
For receipt of dividends or interest of any of the Government stocks or funds, or of the stocks, funds, or shares of any joint-stock or other company, if for receipt of one payment only	0	1	0
If for continuous receipt	0	5	0
For receipt of any sum not over £20	0	5	0
Letter of license from creditors	1	15	0
Letter, or power of attorney of any other kind	1	10	0
MORTGAGE.—Transfer or Assignment of, for every £100, or fractional part thereof	0	0	6
Mortgage, release or reconveyance of, where the sum secured shall not exceed £1,400, the same duty as on a mortgage.			
In any other case	1	15	0
NEWSPAPERS—Sheet not exceed. 2,295 square inches, exclusive of margin	0	0	1
Supplement not exceeding 1,148 sq.in.	0	0	0½
For any two such supplements	0	0	1
PASSPORT	0	0	6
PATENT for Inventions (Letters):—			
On petition for grant of letters patent	5	0	0
On certificate of record of notice to proceed	5	0	0
On warrant of law officer for letters patent	5	0	0
On the scaling of letters patent	5	0	0
On specification	5	0	0
On the letters patent, or a duplicate thereof, before the expiration of the 3rd year	50	0	0
On the letters patent, or a duplicate thereof, before the expiration of the 7th year	100	0	0
On certificate of record of notice of objection	2	0	0
On certificate of every search and inspection	0	1	0
On certificate of entry of assignment or licence	0	5	0
On certificate of assignment or licence	0	5	0
On application for disclaimer	5	0	0
On caveat against disclaimer	2	0	0
On office copies of documents, for every 90 words	0	0	2
PROTESTS—Where the stamp duty on the bill or note does not exceed 1s., the same duty as on the bill or note.			
Protest of any other bill or note, and protest of any other kind, and other notarial act whatsoever	0	1	0
PROXY (or Power of Attorney) to vote at any one meeting of shareholders of or in any joint-stock company, or other company or society whose shares are transferable, or to vote at any one meeting of proprietors or contributors to funds of any institution for education or charity	0	0	1
RECEIPT or DISCHARGE for money, or the acknowledgment by post of the safe arrival of securities of money, amounting to £2 or upwards	0	0	1
SCRIP CERTIFICATE—For and upon any scrip certificate entitling any person to become proprietor of any share in any company	0	0	1
SETTLEMENTS.—Any deed, whether voluntary or upon any consideration, other than a *bona fide* pecuniary consideration, whereby any definite sum or sums of money, or share in any of the Government Banks of England or Ireland, East India, or any other company or corporation, shall be settled upon or for the benefit of any person or persons, if the value of such shares or stocks shall not exceed £100	0	5	0
Exceeding £100, then for every £100, or part	0	5	0
TRANSFER OF SHARES in Companies	1	10	0
VOTING PAPER	0	0	1

ASSESSED TAXES.

	£	s.	d.
ARMORIAL BEARINGS.—For any person chargeable with the duty for any carriage at the rate of £3 10s.	2	12	9
Not being so chargeable	0	13	2
CARRIAGES.—For every carriage with four wheels, drawn by two or more horses or mules	3	10	0
Drawn by one horse or mule only	2	0	0
For every carriage with four wheels, each of less diameter than 30 inches, drawn by 2 or more horses or mules not exceeding 13 hands in height ...	1	15	0
Drawn by 1 such horse or mule only	1	0	0
For every carriage with less than four wheels, drawn by 2 or more horses or mules	2	0	0
Drawn by 1 horse or mule only	0	15	0
Drawn by 1 pony or mule only, not exceeding 13 hands	0	10	0

When kept and used solely for the purpose of being let for hire without horses, one-half of the above-mentioned duties respectively.

	£	s.	d.
Carriages used by common carriers, principally for the carriage of goods, but occasionally for the conveyance of passengers, when such carriages have 4 wheels...............................	2	6	8
When less than 4 wheels	1	6	8
HAIR POWDER.—For every person who shall use hair powder	1	3	6
HORSES.—For every horse or mule exceeding the height of 13 hands, used for riding, or drawing a carriage chargeable with duty	1	1	0

Note.—One horse used by a farmer for riding or drawing a carriage ....

	£	s.	d.
For every other horse or mule exceeding 13 hands in height	0	10	6
For every horse or mule used by a common carrier in drawing any carriage chargeable with the duty of £2 6s. 8d., or £1 6s. 8d.	0	10	6
For every pony or mule not exceeding 13 hands, used for the purpose of riding, or drawing any carriage chargeable with duty	0	10	6
And for every such pony or mule kept for any other purpose	0	5	3

	£	s.	d.
One horse used by a farmer for riding, or drawing a carriage	0	10	6
One horse used by any rector, vicar, or curate, doing duty in his church or chapel; by any minister of any religious sect or persuasion, being the regularly ordained or officiating minister, and not following any secular occupation, except that of a schoolmaster; by any person practising as a physician, surgeon, or apothecary; being duly qualified so to practise, for riding or drawing a carriage, *provided 1 horse only be kept*	0	10	6
One horse used by a bailiff, shepherd, or herdsman, for riding, &c.............	0	10	6
HORSE DEALERS' DUTY.—Every person exercising the business of a horse dealer within London, Westminster, and Liberties; the Parishes of St. Mary-le-bone and St. Pancras, in Middlesex; the Weekly Bills of Mortality; and the Boro' of Southwark...	27	10	0
Every person exercising the business of a horse dealer elsewhere	13	15	0
HOUSE DUTY.—On each inhabited dwelling-house of the annual value of £20 or upwards, occupied as a farm-house by a tenant or farm-servant, or in which articles are exposed for sale, a duty of 6d. per pound; all others......	0	0	9
MALE SERVANTS.—For every servant of the age of 18 or upwards	1	1	0
Under that age	0	10	6

[These duties are payable for every maitre d'hôtel, house steward, valet de chambre, butler, cook, house porter, footman, coachman, groom, stable helper, gardener, gamekeeper, huntsman, or by whatever name male servants, really acting in any such capacity, shall be called; as also for every male person employed in any of the above capacities, and not being a servant to his employer, if the employer shall be chargeable to the duty on one servant or carriage, or for more than one horse; and for servants employed as waiters, or in any of the before-mentioned capacities in taverns, &c., and for coachmen, &c., let on job.]

	£	s.	d.
Under-gardeners and under game-keepers .... each	0	10	6

A TABLE OF THE NUMBER OF DAYS FROM ANY DAY IN ONE YEAR TO THE SAME IN ANY OTHER.

	Jan.	Feb.	Mar.	Apr.	May.	June	July.	Aug.	Sept.	Oct.	Nov.	Dec.
January	365	31	59	90	120	151	181	212	243	273	304	334
February...............	334	365	28	59	89	120	150	181	212	242	273	303
March	306	337	365	31	61	92	122	153	184	214	245	275
April	275	306	334	365	30	61	91	122	153	183	214	244
May	245	276	304	335	365	31	61	92	123	153	184	214
June	214	245	273	304	334	365	30	61	92	122	153	183
July	184	215	243	274	304	335	365	31	62	92	123	153
August	153	184	212	243	273	304	334	365	31	61	92	122
September	122	153	181	212	242	273	303	334	365	30	61	91
October.................	92	123	151	182	212	243	273	304	235	365	31	61
November	61	92	120	151	181	212	242	273	304	334	365	30
December	31	62	90	121	151	182	212	243	274	304	335	365

EXAMPLE.—To find the number of days from the 10th May to the 10th October following. Find May in the first column, and then in a line with that under October, is 153 days. If from the 10th May to the 25th October it would be 15 days more, or 168 days; but if from the 10th May to the 1st October, it would be 10 days less, or 143 days. In leap-year, when the last day of February is included between the two dates, there will be one day more than by the table.

THE British Postal system is perhaps the most completely organized, and certainly the most extensive of any civilized nation. The introduction of the penny rate and the employment of stamps have chiefly tended to produce the perfection of the whole service. It would be impossible to give the full details of the subject, but the following have been selected as of most general use.

INLAND LETTERS sent to or from any part of the United Kingdom are charged as follows:

		Not exceeding in weight ½ oz.	...	1d.
		,, 1 oz.	...	2d.
		,, 1½ oz.	...	3d.

And so on in the proportion of one penny for each half ounce. If the postage be not paid in advance, a *double postage* will be demanded on delivery; and if the prepaid postage be insufficient, *double the amount of the deficiency* will be charged.

NEWSPAPERS AND PERIODICALS.—While letters are forbidden to be sent otherwise than by post, newspapers and periodicals may be forwarded in any way. If the latter have an impressed stamp, the paper must be so folded that the stamp shall appear on the outside, otherwise the paper will be liable to postage. All stamped papers, &c., must be posted within 15 days of the printed date of issue. If the publication be addressed to a person residing within the free delivery of the place where it is posted, it becomes liable to a postage of 1d., which must be prepaid by affixing a stamp. Thus, to forward a stamped paper within the three-mile circle of London, a penny stamp, *besides the impressed stamp*, is required. The latter, however, will still be of avail for the country post. Any infringement of these rules will cause the publication to be charged as an unpaid book-packet, with double book-postage.

BOOK-POST.— Under this title any printed matter may be forwarded. No packet must exceed two feet in length or one foot in width; any of greater size will be refused.

Both ends of the packet must be open. If this be not observed, or it contain anything that can be construed into the nature of a "letter," the entire packet will be charged "unpaid" letter postage, *i.e.*, at the rate of 2d. for each half ounce in weight. It is therefore important that no writing should be on any part of the packet, except that of the address. This regulation, however, does not affect manuscripts of any kind, provided that they do not have the nature of a letter in their character or object.

The rate for all parts of the United Kingdom is 1d. for each quarter of a pound or portion thereof. The postage must be prepaid by affixing stamps. If it be not sufficiently paid, the packet is sent, but charged on delivery with the deficiency, together with an additional rate. If a packet be sent unpaid it will be charged with a double book-postage on delivery. String may be employed to make the packet secure, but it must not be so tied as to prevent the examination of the packet at its two ends. In cases of suspicion, the packet will be cut open for examination at the office. For similar reasons a packet must contain nothing sealed up so as to prevent ready examination.

For convenience sake, the delivery of a "book-post" or newspaper may be delayed for a period not exceeding twenty-four hours, as in case of press of business through heavy mails of letters.

PARLIAMENTARY PROCEEDINGS may be sent with or without covers, open at the ends, for a postage of one penny for each quarter of a pound. The words "Parliamentary Proceedings" must be written or printed outside the packet. Pre-payment is optional. As a book-post "Proceedings" may be sent to the colonies. This regulation refers to the Colonial Book-post also, but the rates in this case are higher than the inland rate.

PATTERN AND SAMPLE POST.—The extension of the book-post system for the transmission of patterns and samples has been productive of great advantage to commercial men, facilitating as it essentially does the transaction of all kinds of business between parties at a distance apart, and to a considerable extent diminishing expense by saving that of a regular traveller. The following are the most important rules in regard to the pattern and sample post.

The postage is charged at the rate of 2d. per quarter of a pound and any portion thereof. The limit of weight is 24 ounces, and any packet sent above that weight will be sent to the Returned Letter Branch. Postage must be prepaid in affixed stamps.

There must be no writing nor printing on the packet or cover, or the packet will be treated as an unpaid letter. Exception, however, is made in respect to the address of sender and receiver, trade marks, numbers, and prices of the articles. There must be no enclosure other than the samples. Any particulars as to price, &c., must be written or printed on labels attached to the samples, and not on loose pieces of paper. If the latter are found in the packet they will be removed and charged separately as letters, with an additional fee of one penny. The packet must be open at both ends; but seeds, &c., may be enclosed in boxes or bags, fastened in such a manner as to be readily opened for examination, or in transparent bags. Infringement of this rule will cause the packet to be charged as a letter. If the postage be not prepaid, it will be charged double on delivery. If the payment by stamps affixed be deficient, that deficiency will be charged, together with an additional rate of twopence. Packets may be delayed 24 hours, as has been stated in regard to book-postage.

All articles in the least degree likely to be dangerous, through any cause of injury, are forbidden to be posted. A packet containing such articles will be stopped, and notice given to the sender, who may obtain it on personal application, by payment of a fine equal to the amount of postage it is liable to as a packet of patterns. Patterns and samples may be sent abroad *to certain colonies and foreign stations;* generally the conditions are the same, except as regards the rate of postage. The weight is not limited to 24 ounces. Packets sent to Portugal, Madeira, the Azores, Cape de Verde, France, Turkey, Syria or Egypt, by French post, must not exceed 18 inches long, wide, or deep; to any other places the limits are 24 inches long, and 12 inches in breadth or depth. Pattern Packets sent *viâ* Belgium or Austria to Continental addresses, must not exceed 8 ounces in weight, and the weight of a packet to Portugal, Madeira, the Azores, and Cape de Verde, is limited to 1 pound. No samples of intrinsic value can be sent to foreign countries, except the United States, and transparent bags for the conveyance of seeds, &c., can only be employed for transmission to the United States, Holland and its possessions, Belgium, Denmark, Portugal and its possessions, and Austria, *viâ* France.

POSTAGE STAMPS.—These may be obtained of any postmaster, together with Stamped Envelopes. Sub-postmasters are only required to keep penny labels in stock, but they must procure, when asked, others of a higher value. The postage stamps at present issued are for 1*d.*, 2*d.*, 3*d.*, 4*d.*, 6*d.*, 9*d.*, 10*d.*, 1*s.*, 2*s.*, and 5*s.* All letters, &c., for inland transmission must be prepaid in stamps; those for the colonies and foreign parts may be paid for either in money or stamps. The stamps should be fixed on the right hand top corner of the letter, book or pattern post. Licences to sell stamps may be procured free of expense by any respectable person on application to the officer of Inland Revenue, Somerset House, London, or in the provinces to the stamp distributor of the district. All postmasters may, but are not compelled to, purchase stamps at a discount of 2½ per cent. from the nominal value, but not less than two stamps; that is, no separate stamp will be purchased. A charge of ½*d.* is made for stamps of any value less than 1*s.* 8*d.*, and so on, in proportion for any higher value.

REGISTRATION OF LETTERS.—The object of registration is to make delivery of the letter more secure, but confers no liability on the Post-office to recompense the sender in case of loss. The system holds a check on the letter-carriers, because, in the event of letters, &c., being wrongly delivered, it is easy to trace them, and the cause of non-delivery at the proper address. The fee for registration is *fourpence* for a letter, newspaper, book or other packet, to any place within the United Kingdom or the colonies. The registration and postage fee must be prepaid, if inland, by stamps, but if for abroad either by money or stamps. If letters enclosing coin are *sent unregistered* they will be *charged on delivery with a double fee, viz., eightpence*, and may, on press of business, be delayed in delivery. On registration, the postmaster will give a receipt for the letter, &c. A letter, if dropped into the box without having been presented at the office and marked "registered" will be charged with double fee, that is eightpence, although sufficient stamps for registration had been affixed in the first instance. Parliamentary notices may be registered. A list should be furnished at the time of registration, for the use of the office, and a duplicate, to be retained by the sender. The postmaster will sign and stamp each separate list, so as to ensure their correctness, and also as a protection to the sender in respect to the requirements of the law. Notices relating to votes for Members of Parliament, poll books, jury summonses, &c., may also be forwarded under the registration system, within certain conditions.

MONEY ORDERS.—This system has been at last extended to almost every town and village in the United Kingdom, and also to the Colonies. It affords, if proper precautions be taken, an almost complete safety for the transmission of money, and, practically, any amount may be thus sent, although the highest amount granted in one order is limited to £10. The following is the commission charged:

A sum not exceeding £2	3*d.*
Above £2 and not exceeding £5	6*d.*
„ £5 „ „ £7	9*d.*
„ £7 „ „ £10	1*s.*

The christian and surname of both sender and intended receiver, with the address of each, must be given. Forms of application, ready for filling up, may be had at the money order offices. On obtaining the order, care should be taken to name the office at which it is to be made payable, otherwise the order will only be cashed at the *Head Office* of the town, district, &c. To enable the receiver to send a receipt for an order, the sender may obtain one payable ten days after date, fixing on it a receipt stamp; this affords still greater security for the transmission of money. Post-office orders may be paid into a banker's hands as cash; the name of the receiving bank should be written across the order, and the receipt signed at the same time by the intended receiver. No receipt stamp is required for an ordinary money order on payment. Payment of an order should be applied for before the end of the second calendar month after issue, as regards inland orders; in respect to the colonies, before the expiration of six months. If the order have lapsed, the applicant can be furnished with instructions as to the course he must follow to obtain payment. If the order be not paid within twelve calendar months of the date of issue, all claim to the money is forfeited. The payment of an order, otherwise than to the person entitled to it, confers no obligation on the part of the Post-office to make the loss good. To prevent risk of loss, in regard to money orders, the sender should not sign his name in the letter enclosing it, but simply his initials. He may avail himself of the ten day order, already named; make the order payable through a bank; or send the order in a letter separate from that by which he advises its transmission; a rule being not to pay an order unless the receiver can furnish the name and address of the sender. A list of all money order offices in the Kingdom, the colonies, or in foreign countries, will be found in the British Postal Guide, issued monthly, or the requisite information may be obtained of any postmaster. The charge of colonial commission varies from three to four times that charged on inland orders.

POST-OFFICE SAVINGS' BANKS. — A money order office is generally also a *Post-Office Savings' Bank.* Full information, in a printed form, may be obtained by intended depositors of any such office. It can only be here briefly noticed that deposits of any amount not less than a shilling, not including pence, and not more than £30 in one year, are received on deposit. The hours of business are generally those of the money-order office of the place; but on Saturdays the time is usually much extended beyond that of other days in the week. Interest is allowed at the rate of 2½ per cent. (or sixpence in the pound) per annum, that is at the rate of one halfpenny per pound per month. There are numerous regulations to be observed, which cannot here be detailed. It will be sufficient to add that the great object of the Post-Office Savings' Banks is to give absolute safety to the depositor, to encourage saving habits, and to give every facility for carrying out such objects. Deposits already made in other savings' banks may be easily transferred to the Post-Office. Neither conditions of age nor sex are imposed on any one desirous of becoming a depositor, and strict secrecy is maintained in respect to the name of the depositor, the amount due to him, &c., &c.

GOVERNMENT INSURANCES AND ANNUITIES.— The Post-Office undertakes both these branches of insurance, but the limits of this Almanack forbid any details being given. But, as in the case of the savings' banks, the Government offers every facility for the purpose of life insurance, &c., that may be adopted by any person. The limits of the amount assured range between £20 and £100, and payments may be made fortnightly, monthly, quarterly, annually, or by a single lump sum at the time of insurance. All particulars can be obtained at a head post office, although only certain of them are opened for the purpose of insurance, &c.

By a recent return to the Houses of Parliament, it appears that at the end of the year 1867 there was a balance due to depositors in the Post-Office Savings Banks of £9,749,929. The total amount received from depositors during the year was £21,567,035, and the total repaid, £11,817,106. The number of transactions was:—deposits, 7,013,748; withdrawals, 2,106,642; new accounts, 1,380,750; closed accounts, 529,754; remaining-open accounts, 850,996. The total cost of the Post-Office Savings Banks, from their first establishment to the end of 1867, has been £268,531; the total number of transactions, including deposits and withdrawals, 9,120,390; the average cost of each transaction, 7·066d., or a trifle over the original estimate of 7d; the total value of securities in which the savings have been invested amounted to £9,687,004, exclusive of a sum of £150,105, for dividends, &c., not received at the end of 1867.

There are numerous miscellaneous rules, &c., in connection with the business of the postal system that cannot here be detailed, but the daily experience of all sending or receiving letters will be sufficient to guard them against any contingency of loss, &c., provided ordinary precautions are observed. Any required information on such minor points will be readily supplied by the postmasters.

LONDON DISTRICT OFFICES.—For the convenience of delivery, &c., the Metropolis is divided into districts. The capital letters following each are abbreviations of the names of each district, and *should be marked at the bottom of the address on the right-hand corner of the letter, packet, &c.* This will not only save labour at the Post-Office, but facilitate early delivery. The following are the names, &c., of each district :—Northern, N.; North-Eastern, N.E.; North-Western, N.W.; South-Eastern, S.E.; South-Western, S.W.; Eastern, E.; East-Central, E.C.; Western, W.; Western-Central, W.C. It may be briefly stated that the N. includes Islington, Holloway, &c.; the N.E., Kingsland, Stoke Newington, Hackney, &c.; the N.W., Highgate, Hampstead, Kentish Town, Camden Town, &c.; the S.E., Southwark, Peckham, Greenwich, Rotherhithe, &c.; the S.W., Lambeth, Wandsworth, Battersea, &c.; the E., Whitechapel, Mile End, Bow, Stratford, &c.; the E.C., the City and portions of Clerkenwell; the W., all the West-End beyond Oxford Street, Tottenham Court Road, &c., and the W.C., such portions as are embraced between E.C., N.W., and W., the Thames forming the southern boundary of the West-Central district. The deliveries and despatches vary in number, according to the distance from the head office in St. Martin's-le-Grand, or the sub-head office of each district, and the times of each are denoted in the windows of each office. The latest time for posting inland letters for evening mails is 6 p.m. at the chief office, and from half-past 4 to half-past 5 at the sub-offices, pillar-posts, &c. Registration should be effected not later than half-an-hour before closing of the boxes. "Late fees," beyond that of the ordinary postage, paid by stamps, are allowed in certain cases, and at the head offices till 6½ p.m., and on payment of an extra fourpence for registered letters. For

sample postage, the extra charge varies from one penny upwards at offices near the central one. Letters for the morning mails may be posted at periods varying from 3 a.m. to 5 a.m. at the *pillar boxes.* At the receiving-houses, none are taken in after 9 p.m. on the preceding evening. Strangers should carefully bear in mind that there is neither collection nor delivery in London on Sunday at any receiving house, but letters for the country morning mails may be dropped into the *street pillar-boxes* for transmission on the following morning. Letters addressed to persons at the "Post-Office," London, are only delivered at the head office in St. Martin's-le-Grand. If not claimed within two months from abroad; within one month, if inland; or within a fortnight, if posted in town, they are sent to the Returned Letter Office. Letter receivers at the sub-offices are not required to take charge of letters so addressed, but may do so at their option, and may charge a fee. Re-directed letters are liable to fresh postage. Imperfectly addressed letters, those refused, or addressed to persons who cannot be found, are sent to the Returned Letter Office, St. Martin's-le-Grand, whence, after varying periods, they are, if possible, returned to the writers.

COLONIAL AND FOREIGN POSTAGE.—The great number of Colonial and Foreign Postal Nations prevents the possibility of more than an abstract of the list being given in this Almanack. Ample information, on every point, will be obtained on consulting the "Monthly British Postal Guide." In certain cases the prepayment of postage is optional, in others it is compulsory. At some stations the registration system is incomplete, and at others none whatever exists. Generally speaking, when the dates of making up the mails occur on Sundays (in London), letters should be posted on the preceding evening; exceptions, however, occur in this respect, the mail being occasionally delayed until the following day (Monday). The following affords some of the most important particulars in relation to letters posted either to the Colonies or abroad. Where "daily" is expressed, Sundays are excepted. The letters M. E. refer to morning and evening.

NEWSPAPERS, &c., FOR THE COLONIES AND FOREIGN PARTS.—The rates charged for postage greatly vary, not only in respect to distance, but also on account of the different means of transit. Generally all newspapers are limited, if registered, to a weight not exceeding four ounces, the postage rate of which is given in the second column of the following table. The weight allowed for books, &c., is also limited. Packets of patterns are almost universally confined, if sent to any place in continental Europe, to a weight *not exceeding eight ounces.* No bookpacket or packet of patterns can be forwarded to India if exceeding five pounds in weight, nor if above three pounds to New South Wales and Queensland. Water colour drawings are not allowed to be sent in a book-packet to France or Algeria. Packets of patterns to Spain are charged letter postage, namely, sixpence for each quarter of an ounce. Portugal limits the weight of a book parcel to one pound. In the second column of the following list registered papers are named separately, but at the option of the sender they may be forwarded as a book-packet. With these additional particulars the tables will furnish all necessary information. Newspapers, &c., must always be prepaid, and that with stamps only.

FOREIGN AND COLONIAL BOOK, &c., POSTAGE.

	Registered Newspapers, &c.	Newsprs., Books, and Pats. 2 oz. to 4 oz.	Ev. addl 4 oz.		Registered Newspapers, &c.	Newsprs., Books, and Pats. 2 oz. to 4 oz.	Ev. addl 4 oz.
		s. d.	s. d.			s. d.	s. d.
Alexandr. vià Marseilles	2d. not ex. 4 oz.	0 4	0 4	Lubeck	2d. not ex. 4 oz.	0 4	0 4
„ S'hampton	1d.	0 3	3	Do.	Do.	0 3	3
„ French Pkt.	2d. not ex. 4 oz.	0 4	0 4	Madeira	3d.	0 4	4
Antigua	1d.	0 3	0 3	Malta, by France	3d. not ex. 4 oz.	0 4	4
Ascension	1d.	0 3	0 3	„ Southampton	1d.	0 3	3
Australia(S.) S'hampton	1d.	0 4	0 4	Mauritius	3d. not ex. 4 oz.	0 6	0 6
„ Marseilles	3d.	0 6	0 6	Mexico	1d.	0 3	3
Austria	2d. not ex. 4 oz.	0 4	0 4	Natal	1d.	0 3	3
Azores	3d.	0 4	0 4	Newfoundland	1d.	0 3	3
Bahamas	1d.	0 3	0 3	N. S. Wales, S'hampton	1d.	0 4	4
Barbadoes	1d.	0 3	0 3	„ Marseilles	3d.	0 6	0 6
Belgium	1d. not ex. 4 oz.	0 3	0 3	New Zealand, Panama	2d. not ex. 4 oz.	0 4	4
Bermuda	1d.	0 3	0 3	„ S'hampton	1d.	0 4	4
Brazil	1d.	0 3	0 3	„ Marseilles	3d.	0 6	0 6
„ French Packet	2d. not ex. 4 oz.	0 4	0 4	Norway	2d. to 5d. 4 oz.	0 6	0 6
Bremen	2d. not ex. 4 oz.	0 4	0 4	Papal States	1d. per 4 oz.	0 3	3
British Columbia	Do.	0 4	0 4	Portugal	3d. not ex. 4 oz.	0 4	4
Cairo, vià Marseilles	2d. not ex. 4 oz.	0 4	0 4	„ vià S'hampton	2d. not ex. 4 oz.	0 3	3
„ Southampton	1d.	0 3	0 3	Queensland, S'hampton	1d.	0 4	4
Constanple. vià France	3d. not ex. 4 oz.	0 5	0 5	„ Marseilles	3d.	0 6	0 6
„ Marseilles	2d. not ex. 4 oz.	0 4	0 4	St. Helena	1d.	0 3	3
Demerara	1d.	0 3	0 3	Saxony	2d. not ex. 4 oz.	0 4	4
Egypt, vià Marseilles	2d. not ex. 4 oz.	Let. rate		Shanghai, vià Marseilles	3d.	0 6	0 6
„ Southampton	1d.	Do.		„ Southampton	2d.	0 4	4
France	1d. not ex. 4 oz.	0 3	3	Sierra Leone	1d.	0 3	3
Gibraltar vià S'hampton	1d.	0 3	3	Spain	4 oz. 2d.	0 4	4
Gold Coast	1d.	0 3	3	Suez, vià Marseilles	2d. not ex. 4 oz.	0 4	4
Greece by French Packet	1d. not ex. 4 oz.	0 3	3	„ Southampton	1d.	0 3	3
„ Belgium	Do.	0 3	3	Sweden	2d. to 4d. 4 oz.	0 5	5
Hamburg	2d. not ex. 4 oz.	0 4	4	Switzerland	2d. not ex. 4 oz.	0 4	4
Hesse	Do.	0 4	4	Tasmania, Southampton	1d.	0 4	4
Holland	1d.	0 4	4	„ Marseilles	3d.	0 6	0 6
Hong Kong, Marseilles	3d.	0 6	0 6	Turkey	2d. not ex. 4 oz.	0 4	4
„ Southampton	2d.	0 4	4	United States	Do.	0 3	3
India, vià Marseilles	3d. not ex. 4 oz.	0 6	0 6	Vancouver's Island	2d. 4 oz.	0 4	4
„ Southampton	2d. not ex. 4 oz.	0 4	4	Victoria (Aus.) S'hamptn	1d.	0 4	4
Italy	2d. not ex. 4 oz.	0 4	4	„ Marseilles	3d.	0 6	0 6
Jamaica, Southampton	1d.	0 3	0 3	West Indies, British	1d.	0 3	3
Japan, Marseilles	3d.	0 6	6	W. Australia, S'hampton	1d.	0 4	4
Labuan	3d.	0 6	0 6	„ Marseilles	3d.	0 6	0 6

DATES AND RATES OF FOREIGN AND COLONIAL LETTER POSTAGE, &c.

MAILS, when made up (in London).	COUNTRIES, &c. (e) denotes that prepayment is compulsory, it being in all other cases voluntary; (a) that an *additional charge* is made on delivery; (in) that the registration is *incomplete*, not extending beyond port of arrival; and (none) that *no registration* can be effected.	RATE					
		Not exceeding ¼ oz.	Above ¼ oz. and not exceeding ½ oz.	Above ½ oz. and not exceeding ¾ oz.	Above ¾ oz. and not exceeding 1 oz.	Registration Fee.	Charge beyond ordinary Rate on Letters not wholly prepaid
		s. d.	s. d.	s. d.	s. d.	s. d.	
E., 9th and 23rd each month }	AFRICA (British)	0 6	0 6	1 0	1 0		...
E., every Friday	„ (Foreign)	eao 0 6	0 6	1 0	1 0	in 4	...
M., every Saturday	Aden, vià Marseilles	1 1	1 1	2 2	2 2	0 4	9d. each.
E., every Friday	„ vià Southampton	0 9	0 9	1 6	1 6	0 4	9d. each.
M., every Saturday	Alexandria	0 9	0 9	1 6	1 6	0 4	9d. each.
M., 1st, 8th, 16th, and 24th each month.	„ vià Southampton	0 6	0 6	1 0	1 0	0 4	3d. per ½ oz.
	„ vià Belgium	0 9	0 9	1 6	1 6	0 4	2d. per ½ oz.
M., 2nd, 9th, 17th, and 25th each month.	„ vià France	0 8	1 2	1 10	2 4	0 4	2d. per ½ oz.
M., 2nd and 17th ea. mo.	Antigua	1 0	1 0	2 0	2 0	0 4	1s. each.

DATES AND RATES OF FOREIGN AND COLONIAL LETTER POSTAGE, &c.—*continued.*

Mails, when made up (in London).	Countries, &c. (*c*) denotes that prepayment is *compulsory*, it being in all other cases voluntary; (*a*) that an *additional charge* is made on delivery; (*in*) that the registration is *incomplete*, not extending beyond port of arrival; and (*none*) that *no registration* can be effected.	Rate. Not exceeding ¼ oz.		Above ¼ oz. and not exceeding ½ oz.		Above ½ oz. and not exceeding ¾ oz.		Above ¾ oz. and not exceeding 1 oz.		Registration Fee.		Charge beyond ordinary Rate on Letters not wholly prepaid.
		s.	*d.*	*s.*	*d.*	*s.*	*d.*	*s.*	*d.*	*s.*	*d.*	
M., 9th each month ...	Argentine Confed	*ca* 1	0	1	0	2	0	2	0	*in*	4	...
E., 23, and M. 24 ea. mo.	,, by French Pkt.	*ca* 0	8	1	4	2	0	2	8	*none*		...
Information may be obtained at any P. Office.	Australia South. via Sthptn	*c* 0	6	0	6	1	0	1	0	0	4	6*d*. each.
	Australia South. via Marseilles	*c* 0	10	0	10	1	8	1	8	0	4	6*d*. each.
M. 2nd each month ...	Australia South. via Panama	*ca* 0	6	0	6	1	0	1	0	0	4	6*d*. each.
M. and E., daily	Austria, viâ France	0	6	1	0	1	6	2	0	0	4	2*d*. per ¼ oz.
M. and E., daily	,, viâ Belgium	0	6	0	6	1	0	1	0	0	4	,, ½ oz.
M. and E., daily	,, viâ Italy	0	8	1	4	2	0	2	8	0	9	...
M. and E., daily	Azores, viâ France	0	6	1	0	1	6	2	0	0	4	2*d*. per ¼ oz.
M., 9th each month ...	,, viâ Southampton	0	6	0	6	1	0	1	0	0	4	2*d*. per ½ oz.
M. and E., daily	Baden, viâ France	0	6	1	0	1	6	2	0	6*d*. ¼ oz		...
M. and E., daily	,, viâ Belgium	0	6	0	6	1	0	1	0	0	4	2*d*. per ½ oz.
Varying dates	Bahamas	1	0	1	0	2	0	2	0	0	4	1*s*. each.
M., 2nd and 17th ea. mo.	Barbadoes	1	0	1	0	2	0	2	0	0	4	1*s*. each.
M. and E., daily	Bavaria, viâ France	0	6	1	0	1	6	2	0	6*d*. ½ oz		...
M. and E., daily	,, viâ Belgium	0	6	0	6	1	0	1	0	0	4	2*d*. per ½ oz.
M. and E., daily	Belgium direct	0	3	0	3	0	6	0	6	0	4	3*d*. each.
M. and E., daily	,, viâ France	0	4	0	4	0	8	0	8	0	4	,,
M., 2nd and 17th ea. mo.	Berbice	1	0	1	0	2	0	2	0	0	4	1*s*. each.
Varying dates	Bermuda, viâ Halifax	1	0	1	0	2	0	2	0	0	4	,,
M., Tues. E. Wed. & Sat.	,, viâ New York	0	7	0	7	1	2	1	2	0	4	6*d*. each.
Varying dates	,, via St. Thomas	1	0	1	0	2	0	2	0	0	4	1*s*. each.
M., 9th each month ...	Brazil, viâ Southampton }	*ca* 1	0	1	0	2	0	2	0	*in*	4	...
E., 19th each month ...	,, viâ Liverpool }											
E., 23, & M., 24 ea. mo.	,, by French Packet	0	9	1	6	2	3	3	0	9*d*. ¼ oz		...
M. and E.	Bremen, viâ Belgium	0	6	0	6	1	0	1	0	0	4	2*d*. per ½ oz.
M., ev. Tues., & E., ev. Wed. and Sat.	British Columbia	1	0	1	0	2	0	2	0	0	4	...
M. and E.	Brunswick, viâ Belgium	0	6	0	6	1	0	1	0	0	4	2*d*. per ½ oz.
M. and E.	,, viâ France	0	8	1	4	2	0	2	8	8*d*. ¼ oz		...
E., every Friday	Cairo, viâ Marseilles	0	6	1	0	1	6	2	0	0	4	3*d*. per ¼ oz.
M., every Saturday ...	,, viâ Southampton	0	6	0	6	1	0	1	0	0	4	6*d*. each.
M., 1st, 8th, 16th, and 24th each month.	,, viâ Belgium	0	11	0	11	1	10	1	10	0	4	2*d*. per ½ oz.
	,, viâ France	0	11	1	10	2	9	3	8	0	9	2*d*. per ¼ oz.
	California. See U. States.											
M., Tu., E., Wed. & Sat.	Canada, viâ U. States	0	7	0	7	1	2	1	2	0	4	6*d*. each.
E., every Thursday ...	,, by Packet	0	6	0	6	1	0	1	0	0	4	,,
E., 23rd each month ...	Cape Coast Castle	0	6	0	6	1	0	1	0	0	4	,,
E., 9th and 24th ea. mo.	Cape of Good Hope	1	0	1	0	2	0	2	0	0	4	1*s*. each.
E., ev. alternate Friday	Ceylon, viâ Marseilles	1	1	1	1	2	2	2	2	0	4	9*d*. each.
M., ev. alternate Sat....	,, viâ Southampton	0	9	0	9	1	6	1	6	0	4	,,
E., 17th, M., 18th ea. mo.	,, by French Packet	1	1	1	1	2	2	2	2	0	4	,,
E., ev. alternate Friday	China, not Hongkong, viâ Mseilles	1	4	1	4	2	8	2	8	0	4	1*s*. each.
M., ev. alternate Sat....	,, viâ Southampton	1	0	1	0	2	0	2	0	0	4	,,
E., 17th, M., 18th ea. m...	,, by French Packet	*ca* 1	4	1	4	2	8	2	8	0	4	...
M. and E., daily	Coburg, by Belgium	0	6	0	6	1	0	1	0	0	4	2*d*. ½ oz.
M. and E., daily	,, by France	0	6	1	0	1	6	2	0	6*d*. ¼ oz		...
E., Tues. & Fri., & M., Wed. & Sat. (in sumr.)	Constantinople, viâ France }	0	8	1	2	1	10	2	4	0	4	2*d*. per ¼ oz.
E., ev. Mon., and M., ev. Tues. (in winter).	,, ,, ,, }											
E., ev. Th., & M., ev. Fri.	,, viâ Marseilles ...	0	6	1	0	1	6	2	0	0	4	3*d*. per ¼ oz.
M., 2nd and 17th ea. mo.	Cuba, by W. India Packet	*ca* 1	0	1	0	2	0	2	0	*in*	4	...
M., ev. Tues. & E., ev. Wed. & Sat.	,, viâ U. States	*ca* 1	0	1	0	2	0	2	0	*in*	4	...
M., 2nd & 17th ea. mo.	Demerara, viâ Southampton	1	0	1	0	2	0	2	0	0	4	1*s*. each.
E., 6th, M., 7th ea. mo.	,, F. Packet	1	0	1	0	2	0	2	0	0	4	,,
M. and E., daily	Denmark, viâ Belgium	0	4	0	4	0	8	0	8	0	4	2*d*. per ½ oz.
M. and E., daily	,, viâ France	0	9	1	6	2	3	3	0	9*d*. ¼ oz		...
M., 2nd & 17th ea. mo.	Dominica	1	0	1	0	2	0	2	0	0	4	1*s*. each.
E., every Friday	Egypt, viâ Marseilles	*ca* 0	6	1	0	1	6	2	0	*in*	4	...
M., every Saturday ...	,, viâ Southampton	*ca* 0	6	0	6	1	0	1	0	*in*	4	...

DATES AND RATES OF FOREIGN AND COLONIAL LETTER POSTAGE, &c.—*continued.*

Mails, when made up (in London).	Countries, &c. (*c*) denotes that prepayment is *compulsory*, it being in all other cases voluntary; (*a*) that an *additional charge* is made on delivery; (*in*) that the registration is *incomplete*, not extending beyond port of arrival; and (*none*) that *no registration* can be effected.	Rate. Not exceeding ¼ oz.	Above ¼ oz. and not exceeding ½ oz.	Above ½ oz. and not exceeding ¾ oz.	Above ¾ oz. and not exceeding 1 oz.	Registration Fee.	Charge beyond ordinary Rate on Letters not wholly prepaid.
		s. d.	*s. d.*	*s. d.*	*s. d.*	*s. d.*	
M., 1st, 8th, 16th, and 24th monthly.	{ Egypt, viâ Belgium	*ca* 0 9	0 9	1 6	1 6	*none*	...
	{ „ viâ France, &c.	*ca* 0 8	1 2	1 10	2 4	*none*	...
M. and E., daily	France and Algeria	0 4	0 8	1 0	1 4	4*d.* ½ oz	4*d.* per ½ oz.
M. and E., daily	Frankfort	0 6	0 6	1 0	1 0	0 4	2*d.* per ½ oz.
M., every Saturday	Gibraltar	0 6	0 6	1 0	1 0	0 4	6*d.* each.
E., ev. Th., & M., ev. Fri.	Greece	0 8	1 4	2 0	2 8	8*d.* ½ oz	...
E., Tues. and Friday	„ viâ Belgium	0 10	0 10	1 8	1 8	0 4	2*d.* per ½ oz.
M., every Wednesday	„ viâ Italy	0 8	1 4	2 0	2 8	0 4	...
M., 17th each month	Grey Town	*ca* 1 0	1 0	2 0	2 0	*in* 4	...
M., 2nd & 17th ea. mo.	„ viâ Panama	*ca* 2 0	2 0	4 0	4 0	*in* 4	...
M. and E.	Hamburg, viâ Belgium	0 6	0 6	1 0	1 0	0 4	2*d.* per ½ oz.
M. and E.	Hanover, viâ Belgium	0 6	0 6	1 0	1 0	0 4	„
M. and E.	Heligoland, viâ Hamburg	0 8	0 8	1 4	1 4	0 4	„
M. and E.	Hesse, viâ Belgium	0 6	0 6	1 0	1 0	0 4	„
M. and E.	„ viâ France	0 6	1 0	1 6	2 0	6*d.* ½ oz	...
M. and E.	Holland, viâ Belgium	0 3	0 3	0 6	0 6	0 4	3*d.* each.
M. and E.	„ viâ France	0 6	1 0	1 6	2 0	6*d.* ½ oz	2*d.* per ½ oz.
E., 1st Sat. in ea. mo.	Honduras (British)	1 0	1 0	2 0	2 0	0 4	1*s.* each.
M., 2nd & 17th ea. mo.	„ (Foreign)	*ca* 2 0	2 0	4 0	4 0	*in* 4	...
E., ev. alternate Friday	Hongkong, viâ Marseilles	1 4	1 4	2 8	2 8	0 4	1*s.* each.
M., every alternate Sat.	„ viâ Southampton	1 0	1 0	2 0	2 0	0 4	„
E., 17, & M., 18 ea. mo.	„ by French Packet	1 4	1 4	2 8	2 8	0 4	„
E. every Friday	India, via Marseilles	1 1	1 1	2 2	2 2	0 4	9*d.* each.
M., every Saturday	„ viâ Southampton	0 9	0 9	1 6	1 6	0 4	„
E., 17, & M., 18 ea. mo.	„ by French Packet	1 1	1 1	2 2	2 2	0 4	„
E., ev. Mon. & Tues., & M., ev. Tues. & Wed.	Ionian Islands, viâ Italy	0 8	1 4	2 0	2 8	0 4	...
M. & E., daily	Italy (not Papal States)	0 6	1 0	1 6	2 0	0 4	6*d.* each
M., ev. Fri., & 7, 8, 17, 18, 27, & 28 to Messina; M. 7, 17, & 27 to Palermo.	„ by French Packet	0 6	1 0	1 6	2 0	0 4	„
M. and E.	„ viâ Belgium	0 11	0 11	1 10	1 10	0 4	2*d.* per ½ oz.
M., 2nd & 17th ea. mo.	Jamaica, viâ Southampton	1 0	1 0	2 0	2 0	0 4	1*s.* each.
E., 14, & M., 15 ea. mo.	„ by French Packet	1 0	1 0	2 0	2 0	0 4	„
See China Mail {	Japan, viâ Marseilles	1 4	1 4	2 8	2 8	0 4	„
	„ viâ Southampton	1 0	1 0	2 0	2 0	0 4	„
E., 17, & M., 18 ea. mo.	„ by French Packet	*ca* 1 4	1 4	2 8	2 8	0 4	„
	Labuan (see China)	1 4	1 4	2 8	2 8	0 4	„
M. and E., daily	Lubeck, viâ Belgium	0 6	0 6	1 0	1 0	0 4	2*d.* per ½ oz.
M. and E., daily	„ viâ France	0 6	1 0	1 6	2 0	6*d.* ½ oz	...
E., 9th & 23rd ea. mo.	Madeira, direct }	0 6	0 6	1 0	1 0	0 4	2*d.* per ½ oz.
M., 9th each month	„ viâ Lisbon }						
	Malta, viâ France	0 6	1 0	1 6	2 0	0 4	6*d.* each.
E., 7th, & M., 8th ea. mo.	Mauritius	0 10	0 10	1 8	1 8	0 4	„
M., 2nd each month	Mexico, viâ Southampton	*ca* 1 0	1 0	2 0	2 0	*in* 4	...
E., 14, & M., 15 ea. mo.	„ by F. Packet	*ca* 1 0	1 0	2 0	2 0	*none*	...
M. ev. Tu., E. Wed. Sat.	„ viâ New York	*ca* 1 0	1 0	2 0	2 0	*in* 4	...
E., 24th each month	Natal	1 0	1 0	2 0	2 0	0 4	1*s.* each.
E. Alternate Saturdays	New Brunswick, viâ Halifax	0 6	0 6	1 0	1 0	0 4	6*d.* each.
M., ev. Tu., E., ev. Wed.	„ viâ U. States	0 7	0 7	1 2	1 2	0 4	„
E. Alternate Saturday	Newfoundland	0 6	0 6	1 0	1 0	0 4	„
Information obtained at any Post Office. }	N. S. Wales, viâ Southampton	*c* 0 6	0 6	1 0	1 0	0 4	„
	„ viâ Marseilles	*c* 0 10	0 10	1 8	1 8	0 4	„
M., 2nd each month	„ viâ Panama	*c* 0 6	0 6	1 0	1 0	0 4	„
M., 2nd each month	N. Zealand, viâ Panama	*c* 0 6	0 6	1 0	1 0	0 4	„
Information obtained at any Post Office. }	„ viâ Southampton	*c* 0 6	0 6	1 0	1 0	0 4	„
	„ viâ Marseilles	*c* 0 10	0 10	1 8	1 8	0 4	„
M., 2nd and 17th ea. mo.	Nicaragua, viâ Panama	*ca* 2 0	2 0	4 0	4 0	*in* 4	...
M. and E.	Norway, viâ Denmark	0 8	0 8	1 4	1 4	0 4	2*d.* per ½ oz.
M. and E.	„ viâ Sweden	0 11	0 11	1 10	1 10	0 4	„
M. and E.	„ viâ France	1 2	2 4	3 6	4 8	1 2¼ oz.	...
E., ev. alt. Sat.	Nova Scotia, viâ Halifax	0 6	0 6	1 0	1 0	0 4	6*d.* each.

DATES AND RATES OF FOREIGN AND COLONIAL LETTER POSTAGE, &c.—*concluded.*

MAILS, when made up (in London).	COUNTRIES, &c. (*c*) denotes that prepayment is *compulsory*, it being in all other cases voluntary; (*a*) that an *additional charge* is made on delivery; (*in*) that the registration is *incomplete*, not extending beyond port of arrival; and (*none*) that *no registration* can be effected.	RATE. Not exceeding ¼ oz.	Above ¼ oz. and not exceeding ½ oz.	Above ½ oz. and not exceeding ¾ oz.	Above ¾ oz. and not exceeding 1 oz.	Registration Fee.	Charge beyond ordinary Rate on Letters not wholly prepaid.
		s. d.	*s. d.*	*s. d.*	*s. d.*	*s. d.*	
M., ev. Tu., E., ev. Wed. & every alternate Sat.	Nova Scotia, viâ United States ...	0 7	0 7	1 2	1 2	0 4	6*d.* each.
	Oregon. See U. States.						
M., 2nd & 17th ea. mo.	Panama, viâ Southampton	*ca*1 0	1 0	2 0	2 0	*in* 4	...
E., 6th, & M. 7th ea. mo.	„ French Packet	*ca*1 0	1 0	2 0	2 0	*none*	...
M., ev. Tues., & E., ev. Wed. & Sat.	„ viâ New York.........	*ca*1 0	1 0	2 0	2 0	*in* 4	...
E., ev. Tues. and Sat...	Papal States, French Packet	0 6	1 0	1 6	2 0	6*d.* ¼ oz	...
M. and E.	„ viâ Belgium	0 11	0 11	1 10	1 10	0 4	2*d.* per ½ oz.
M., 2nd & 17th ea. mo.	Peru, viâ Southampton............ }	*ca*2 0	2 0	4 0	4 0	*in* 4	
E., 6th, & M., 7th ea. mo.	„ by French Packet .... }						...
M. & E..........................	Poland, viâ Belgium	0 9	0 9	1 6	1 6	0 4	3*d.* per ½ oz.
M. & E..........................	„ viâ France.....................	1 2	2 4	3 6	4 8	1 2	...
M. & E..........................	Portugal, viâ France	0 6	1 0	1 6	2 0	0 4	2*d.* per ¼ oz.
M., 9th each month ...	„ viâ Southampton.........	0 6	0 6	1 0	1 0	0 4	2*d.* per ½ oz.
E., 23, & M., 24 ea. mo.	„ by F. Packet	0 6	1 0	1 6	2 0	0 4	2*d.* per ¼ oz.
M. and E., daily	Prussia, viâ Belgium	0 6	0 6	1 0	1 0	0 4	2*d.* per ½ oz.
M. and E., daily	„ Rhenish.....................	0 6	1 0	1 6	2 0	6*d.* ¼ oz	...
	other parts.....................	0 8	1 4	2 0	2 8	8*d.* ¼ oz	...
Information obtained at any Post Office. }	Queensland, viâ Southampton ...	*c*0 6	0 6	1 0	1 0	0 4	6*d.* each.
	„ viâ Marseilles	*c*0 10	0 10	1 8	1 8	0 4	„
M., 2nd each month ...	„ viâ Panama	*c*1 4	1 4	2 8	2 8	0 4	...
	Rome, &c. See Papal States.						
M. and E., daily	Russia, viâ Belgium	0 9	0 9	1 6	1 6	0 4	3*d.* per ½ oz.
M. and E., daily	„ viâ France	1 2	2 4	3 6	4 8	1 2*	...
E., 9th each month......	St. Helena	1 0	1 0	2 0	2 0	0 4	1*s.* each.
M. and E., daily	Saxony, viâ Belgium	0 6	0 6	1 0	1 0	0 4	2*d.* per ½ oz.
M. and E., daily	„ viâ France.....................	0 8	1 4	2 0	2 8	8*d.* ¼ oz	...
E., ev. alternate Friday	Shanghai, viâ Marseilles,...........	1 4	1 4	2 8	2 8	0 4	1*s.* each.
M., ev. alternate Sat....	„ viâ Southampton	1 0	1 0	2 0	2 0	0 4	„
E., 17, & M. 18, ea. mo.	„ by French Packet	1 4	1 4	2 8	2 8	1 4†	...
E., 9th & 23rd ea. mo...	Sierra Leone	0 6	0 6	1 0	1 0	0 4	6*d.* each.
E., ev. alternate Friday	Singapore, viâ Marseilles............	1 4	1 4	2 8	2 8	0 4	1*s.* each.
M., ev. alternate Sat...	„ viâ Southampton......	1 0	1 0	2 0	2 0	0 4	„
E., 17, & M., 18 ea. mo.	„ by F. Packet	1 4	1 4	2 8	2 8	0 4	„
M. and E. daily	Spain, viâ France........................	0 6	1 0	1 6	2 0	0 4	Double deficient postge.
E., every Friday.........	Suez, viâ Marseilles	0 6	1 0	1 6	2 0	0 4	3*d.* per ¼ oz.
M., every Saturday ...	„ viâ Southampton...............	0 6	0 6	1 0	1 0	0 4	6*d.* each.
M. and E., daily	Sweden, viâ Denmark	0 6	0 6	1 0	1 0	0 4	2*d.* per ½ oz.
M. and E., daily	„ viâ Stralsund	0 9	0 9	1 6	1 6	0 4	„
M. and E., daily	„ viâ France.....................	1 2	2 4	3 6	4 8	1 2*	...
M. and E., daily	Switzerland, viâ France	0 5	0 10	1 3	1 8	5*d.* ¼ oz	1*d.* per ½ oz.
Information obtained at any Post Office. }	Tasmania, viâ Southampton	*c*0 6	0 6	1 0	1 0	0 4	...
	„ viâ Marseilles.	*c*0 10	0 10	1 8	1 8	0 4	...
M., 2nd each month ...	„ viâ Panama	*ca*0 6	0 6	1 0	1 0	0 4	...
E., every Thursday ...	Turkey..	*ca*0 6	1 0	1 6	2 0	*none*	3*d.* per ¼ oz.
M., ev. Tues., & E., ev. Wed. & Sat.	United States..............................	0 6	0 6	1 0	1 0	0 4	...
M., ev. Tues., & E., ev. Wed. & Sat.	Vancouver's Island	1 0	1 0	2 0	2 0	0 4	...
Information obtained at any Post Office. }	Victoria (Aus.), viâ Southampton	*c*0 6	0 6	1 0	1 0	0 4	6*d.* each.
	„ viâ Marseilles ...	*c*0 10	0 10	1 8	1 8	0 4	„
M., 2nd of each month	„ viâ Panama	*ca*0 6	0 6	1 0	1 0	0 4	„
M., 2nd & 17th ea. mo.	W. C. of S. America.....................	*ca*2 0	2 0	4 0	4 0	*in* 4	...
M., 2nd & 17th ea. mo.	West Indies (British)	1 0	1 0	2 0	2 0	0 4	1*s.* each.
Information obtained at any Post Office. }	West. Australia, viâ Southampton	*c*0 6	0 6	1 0	1 0	0 4	6*d.* each.
	„ viâ Marseilles ...	*c*0 10	0 10	1 8	1 8	0 4	„

* ¼ oz. † ½ oz.

INDEX.

NOTE.—The Editor takes this opportunity of thanking those gentlemen who kindly corrected the portions submitted to them; but for this assistance it would have been impossible to offer so complete a work to the Public.

As far as practicable the latest Parliamentary papers have been made use of in the compilation of this Almanack; but in some instances the papers for the preceding year, as being more complete and reliable, have been preferred.

Fractional monies have generally been omitted in details, although included in totals; hence apparent discrepancies.

Difficulties incidental to a new publication of this magnitude, have interfered with the proper arrangement of some articles, and the observance of due proportion in others: it is also to be feared that some errors may have crept in, such as that on page 41, where, from the accidental substitution of a figure instead of o, a quantity of rain such as has not been seen since the time of Noah is said to have fallen on a perfectly dry day.